Teacher's Wraparound Edition

Skills for Personal & Family Living

Frances Baynor Parnell
Educational Consultant and Author
Wilmington, North Carolina

Teaching strategies written by the following:

Karen Arentsen
Downers Grove, IL

Geraldean Bayles, CFCS
Homewood-Flossmoor High School
Flossmoor, IL

Teresa L. Dec
Calumet City, IL

Jo Ann Macander, CFCS
Thornridge High School
Dolton, IL

Claudia McGuire
Eisenhower High School
Blue Island, IL

Publisher
The Goodheart-Willcox Company, Inc.
Tinley Park, Illinois

Copyright 2004

by

The Goodheart-Willcox Company, Inc.

Previous edition copyright 2001

All rights reserved. No part of this book may be reproduced, stored in a retrieval system, or transmitted in any form or by any means, electronic, mechanical, photocopying, recording, or otherwise, without the prior written permission of The Goodheart-Willcox Company, Inc. Manufactured in the United States of America.

International Standard Book Number 1-59070-101-1
1 2 3 4 5 6 7 8 9 10   04   09 08 07 06 05 04 03

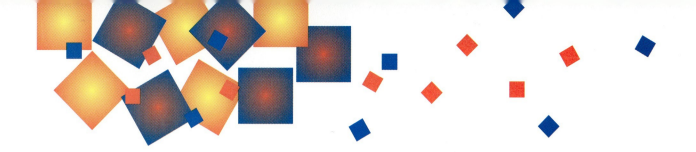

Teacher's Wraparound Edition
Contents

Features of the Student Edition T4
Features of the Teacher's Wraparound Edition T6
Features of the Teacher's Resource Portfolio and CD T8
Other *Skills for Personal and Family Living* Teaching Resources T10
Strategies for Successful Teaching T12
   Helping Your Students Develop Critical Thinking Skills T12
   Problem-Solving and Decision-Making Skills T13
   Using Cooperative Learning T13
   Helping Students Recognize and Value Diversity T13
Assessment Techniques T14
   Performance Assessment T14
   Portfolios T15
Teaching the Learner with Special Needs T15
Using Other Resources T18
National Standards for Family and Consumer Sciences Education T23
Correlation of National Standards with *Skills for Personal and Family Living* T24
Scope and Sequence Chart T25

Skills for Personal & Family Living

This comprehensive family and consumer sciences text has had a complete makeover! Review these pages to see what we've done! Key features of the *Student Edition*:

- **Chapter opening photos** will interest students in reading the chapter.
- **Full-color illustrations,** referenced within the text, help students associate visual images with written material.
- **Logical organization,** colorful headings, and readable typeface facilitate reading comprehension.

Careers related to the chapter material are listed from entry-level jobs to those requiring a college degree, raising student awareness of career options.

Objectives make students aware of the skills they are building as they read the topic.

New terms appear in boldface where they are defined.

Topics break down the chapter content, allowing you the flexibility to assign specific topics as needed.

Topic Terms lists new vocabulary in order of appearance, enhancing student recognition of important concepts.

Features of the Teacher's Wraparound Edition

A variety of teaching elements appear in the margins of each page of the Teacher's Wraparound Edition to guide you in reviewing and reinforcing the chapter content.

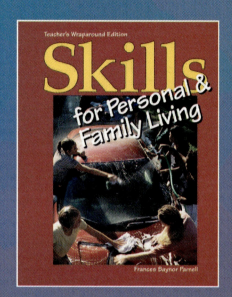

Chapter Outlines—Provide you with a quick overview of the main points covered in each topic in the chapter.

Introductory Activities—Stimulate students' interest in the chapter content, motivating students to want to read.

Vocabulary—Reinforcement activities, such as defining, using in sentences, using glossary, or comparing.

Reflect—More personal than discussion questions; often ask the student to apply content to their own lives.

Resource—Related material from the *Student Activity Guide* or *Teacher's Resources*.

Activity—Activities that reteach and reinforce chapter concepts.

Family Enrichment Activities—These at-home activities encourage students to apply what they learn to their family life.

Enrich— More involved and challenging activities for students. Includes role-playing, research topics, and field trips.

Note—Additional information to expand content or spark student interest. Includes statistics, facts, historical notes, and notes to the teacher.

Across the Curriculum—Ideas are given for relating the chapter content to other curriculum areas, such as math, science, language arts, and social studies.

Example—Use to illustrate an important point in chapter material.

Discuss—Questions to reteach or reinforce learning.

Citizenship and Service—These activities relate or apply chapter information to the community and encourage students' concern and involvement as citizens.

Career Preparation Activities—These activities help students relate chapter learning to careers.

Putting Technology to Use—Ways to incorporate the use of technology, particularly the Internet and computer software programs, are provided.

Problem-Solving Practice—Activities are provided to help students develop critical-thinking, decision-making, and problem-solving skills.

Answers to the *Check It Out!* review questions appear below the questions in each topic.

FCCLA Activities—Individual or group projects encourage student participation in FCCLA and reinforce classroom learning.

Features of the Teacher's Resource Portfolio

Everything you need for teaching a chapter in *Skills for Personal and Family Living* is conveniently grouped together in an easy-to-use binder! The content of the portfolio is also available now on CD!

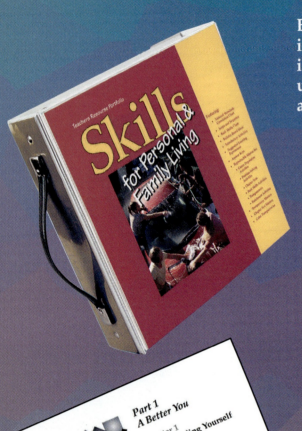

Teaching Materials are listed by chapter and by topic to assist in planning daily lessons.

Activities to **Reteach, Reinforce, Enrich, and Extend Concepts** are described. These include diverse experiences—debates, field trips, speakers, etc. Many activities promote critical thinking, problem solving, and decision-making skills.

Bulletin Board ideas are described and illustrated for each chapter.

Student Learning Experiences described for each major concept make it easy for you to plan stimulating lessons.

Reproducible Masters and ready-to-use **Color Transparencies** are provided for all chapters in the text.

Answer Keys provided for text review questions, chapter tests, and activities in the *Student Activity Guide*.

National Standards Correlation Chart indicates where topics related to the National Standards for Family and Consumer Sciences Education are covered in the text.

Basic Skills Chart identifies activities in the text and supplements that encourage the development of verbal, reading, writing, math, science, and analytical skills.

A reproducible **Chapter Test** is provided for each chapter.

Other *Skills for Personal and Family Living* Teaching Resources

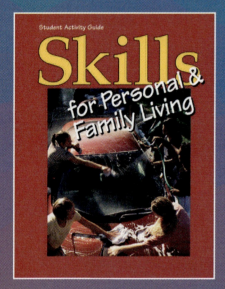

Use these additional resources to reteach, reinforce, enrich, and assess student learning!

The Student Activity Guide
Includes numerous activities to help students review and apply chapter concepts.

Many activities require students to use the higher order thinking skills of analysis, synthesis, and evaluation.

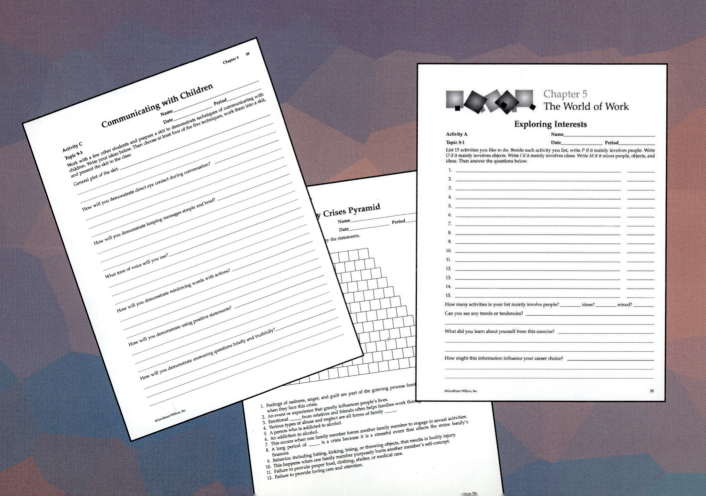

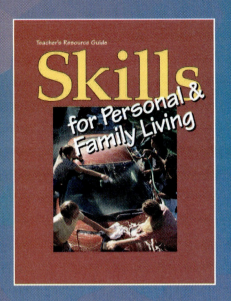

The Teacher's Resource Guide

Contains all of the items included in the *Teacher's Resource Portfolio* except for the color transparencies.

Some teachers like to keep a copy of the *Teacher's Portfolio* at school!

Teacher's Resource CD with GW Test Creation Software

This exciting ancillary puts all the contents of the *Teacher's Resource Portfolio* plus the new, easier-to-use *GW Test Creation Software* all on one CD-ROM! Everything you'll need for planning lessons and creating tests is only a few keystrokes away. Print off just what you need. Quick and convenient access too all the resources in the portfolio.

Features of the *GW Test Creation Software*:
- New program features guide you step-by-step through the creation of a formatted test!
- 25 percent more questions in addition to those found on the printed tests.
- Create customized tests using any chapters or chapter questions; alter questions; add your own questions to the database.
- Questions in a variety of formats: true/false, multiple choice, matching, and essay.
- Available in Windows/Macintosh.

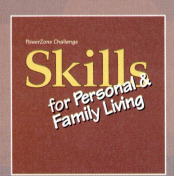

PowerZone Challenge CD

Students can review text content using our new out-of-this world game! The futuristic-looking graphics will hold students' interest, while question content reinforces students' learning experience!

Features of the *PowerZone Challenge CD*:
- "Quiz-bowl" format of challenging questions.
- 3-D graphics, sound effects, and voice-overs.
- Multiple choice content questions and matching vocabulary questions for each chapter.
- Adjustable play-period clock.
- Up to four students or teams can play at a time.

Introduction

Skills for Personal and Family Living is a comprehensive text designed to help students meet the challenges of their daily lives with confidence. Students will learn basic information and practical skills related to such topics as interpersonal and family relationships, career preparation, life management, healthy living, foods and nutrition, clothing, and housing.

Strategies for Successful Teaching

You can make the *Skills for Personal and Family Living* subject matter exciting and relevant for your students by using a variety of teaching strategies. Many suggestions for planning classroom activities are given in the various teaching supplements that accompany this text. As you plan your lessons, you might also want to keep the following points in mind.

Helping Your Students Develop Critical Thinking Skills

As today's students leave their classrooms behind, they will face a world of complexity and change. They are likely to work in several career areas and hold many different jobs. Providing young people with a base of knowledge consisting only of facts, principles, and procedures will be doing them a disservice. They must, in addition, be prepared to solve complex problems, make difficult decisions, and assess ethical implications. In other words, students must be able to use critical thinking skills. These skills are often referred to as the higher order thinking skills. Benjamin Bloom listed these as

- analysis—breaking down material into its component parts so that its organizational structure may be understood;
- synthesis—putting parts together to form a new whole; and
- evaluation—judging the value of material for a given purpose.

In a broader perspective, students must be able to use reflective thinking in order to decide what to believe and do. According to Robert Ennis, students should be able to

- define and clarify problems, issues, conclusions, reasons, and assumptions;
- judge the credibility, relevance, and consistency of information; and
- infer or solve problems and draw reasonable conclusions.

Students have the right to be taught how to think critically—it cannot be an option. To think critically, one must have knowledge. However, critical thinking goes beyond memorizing or recalling information. Critical thinking cannot occur in a vacuum; it requires individuals to apply what they know about the subject matter. It requires students to use their common sense and experience. It may also involve controversy.

Critical thinking also requires *creative thinking* to construct all the reasonable alternatives, consequences, influencing factors, and supporting arguments. Unusual ideas are valued and perspectives outside the obvious are sought.

Finally, the teaching of critical thinking does not require exotic and highly unusual classroom approaches. Complex thought processes can be incorporated in the most ordinary and basic activities, even reading, writing, and listening, if these activities are carefully planned and skillfully executed.

Help your students develop their analytical and judgmental skills and to go beyond what they see on the surface. Rather than allowing students to blindly accept what they read or hear, encourage them to examine ideas in ways that show respect for others' opinions and different perspectives. Encourage students to think about points raised by others. Ask them to evaluate how new ideas relate to their attitudes about various subjects.

Debate is an excellent way to explore opposite sides of an issue. You may want to divide the class into two groups, each to take an opposing side of the issue. You can also ask students to work in smaller groups and explore opposing sides of different issues. Each group can select students from the group to present the points for their side.

Problem-Solving and Decision-Making Skills

An important aspect in the development of critical thinking skills is learning how to solve problems and make decisions. This is such an important skill for students to have in today's world that it is explained fully in Chapter 1 of *Skills for Personal and Family Living*. Some very important decisions lie ahead for your students, particularly those related to their future education and career choices. The steps in the decision-making process are outlined in this chapter.

In addition, every chapter of the text has an accompanying problem-solving practice activity for you to use with your students. These reproducible masters can be found in the *Teacher's Resource Guide*, *Teacher's Resource Portfolio*, and the *Teacher's Resource CD*. The activities are designed to help your students develop critical thinking, decision-making, and problem-solving skills.

Simulation games and role-plays allow students to practice solving problems and making decisions under nonthreatening circumstances. Role-playing allows students to examine others' feelings as well as their own. It can help them learn effective ways to react or cope when confronted with similar situations in real life.

Using Cooperative Learning

Because of the new emphasis on teamwork in the workplace, the use of cooperative learning groups in your classroom will give students an opportunity to practice teamwork skills. During cooperative learning, students learn interpersonal and small-group skills that will allow them to function as part of a team. These skills include leadership, decision making, trust building, communication, and conflict management.

When planning for cooperative learning, you will have a particular goal or task in mind. You will first specify the objectives for the lesson. Small groups of learners are matched for the purpose of completing the task or goal, and each person in the group is assigned a role. The success of the group is measured not only in terms of outcome, but in terms of the successful performance of each member in his or her role.

In cooperative learning groups, students learn to work together toward a group goal. Each member is dependent on others for the outcome. This interdependence is a basic component of any cooperative learning group. Students understand one person cannot succeed unless everyone succeeds. The value of each group member is affirmed as learners work toward their goal.

The success of the group depends on individual performance. Groups should be mixed in terms of abilities and talents so there are opportunities for the students to learn from one another. Also, as groups work together over time, the roles should be rotated so everyone has an opportunity to practice and develop different skills.

You will also need to monitor the effectiveness of the groups, intervening as necessary to provide task assistance or to help with interpersonal and group skills. Finally, evaluate students' achievement, and help them discuss how well they collaborated with each other.

Helping Students Recognize and Value Diversity

Your students will be entering a rapidly changing workplace—not only in the area of technology, but also in the diverse nature of its workforce. Years ago, the workforce was dominated by white males, but 85 percent of the new entrants into the workforce at the start of this century will be women, minorities, and immigrants. The workforce is also aging. Over half of the workforce will be people between the ages of 35 and 54. Because of these changes, young workers will need to be able to interact effectively with those who are different from themselves.

The appreciation and understanding of diversity is an ongoing process. The earlier and more frequently young people are exposed to diversity, the better able they will be to bridge cultural differences. If your students are exposed to different cultures within your classroom, they can begin the process of understanding cultural differences. This is the best preparation for success in a diverse society. In addition, teachers have found the following strategies to be helpful:

- Actively promote a spirit of openness, consideration, respect, and tolerance in your classroom.
- Use a variety of teaching styles and assessment strategies.
- Use cooperative learning activities whenever possible. Make sure group roles are rotated so everyone has leadership opportunities.
- When grouping students, make sure the composition of each group is as diverse as possible with regard to gender, race, and nationality. If the groups present information to the class, make sure all members have a speaking part. (Sometimes females and minorities do not do the speaking.)
- Make sure one group's opinions are not over-represented during class discussions. Seek opinions of under-represented persons/groups if necessary.
- If a student makes a sexist, racist, or other comment that is likely to be offensive, ask the student to rephrase the comment in a manner that will not offend other members of the class. Remind students that offensive statements and behavior are inappropriate in the workplace as well as the classroom.
- If a difficult classroom situation arises based on a diversity issue, ask for a time out and have everyone write down their thoughts and opinions about the incident. This allows everyone to cool down and allows you to plan a response.
- Arrange for guest speakers who represent diversity in gender, race, and ethnicity even though the topic does not relate to diversity.
- Have students change seats from time to time throughout the course, having them sit next to people they do not know well.
- Several times during the course, have students do anonymous evaluations of the class, asking them if there are any problems with which you are unaware.

Assessment Techniques

Various forms of assessment need to be used with students in order to evaluate their achievement. Written tests have traditionally been used to evaluate performance. This method of evaluation is good to use when assessing knowledge and comprehension. Other methods of assessment are preferable for measuring the achievement of the higher-level skills of application, analysis, synthesis, and evaluation.

Included in the *Skills for Personal and Family Living Teacher's Resource Guide* and the *Teacher's Resource Portfolio* are objective tests for each chapter in the text. The *Check It Out!* sections in the text can be used to evaluate students' recall of key concepts. The activities suggested in *Try It Out!* and the questions given in *Think About It!* will provide opportunities for you to assess your students' abilities to use critical thinking, problem solving, and application.

Performance Assessment

When you assign students some of the projects described in the text, a different form of assessing mastery or achievement is required. One method that teachers have successfully used is a rubric. A **rubric** consists of a set of criteria that includes specific descriptors or standards that can be used to arrive at performance scores for students. A point value is given for each set of descriptors, leading to a range of possible points to be assigned, usually from 1 to 5. The criteria can also be weighted. This method of assessment reduces the guesswork involved in grading, leading to fair and consistent scoring. The standards clearly indicate to students the various levels of mastery of a task. Students are even able to assess their own achievement based on the criteria.

When using rubrics, students should see the criteria at the beginning of the assignment. Then they can focus their effort on what needs to be done to reach a certain level of performance or quality of project. They have a clear understanding of your expectations of achievement.

Though you will want to design many of your own rubrics, several generic ones are included in the front section of the *Skills for Personal and Family Living Teacher's Resource Guide, Teacher's Resource Portfolio,* and *Teacher's Resource CD.* These are designed to assess the following:
- *Individual Participation*
- *Individual Reports*
- *Group Participation*

These rubrics allow you to assess a student's performance and arrive at a performance score. Students can see what levels they have surpassed and what levels they can still strive to reach.

Portfolios

Another type of performance assessment that is frequently used by teachers today is the portfolio. A **portfolio** consists of a selection of materials that students choose to document their performance over a period of time. Students select their best work samples to showcase their achievement. These items might provide evidence of employability skills as well as academic skills. Some of the items students might include in portfolios are
- work samples (including photographs, videotapes, assessments, etc.) that show mastery of specific skills
- writing samples that show communication skills
- a resume
- letters of recommendation that document specific career-related skills
- certificates of completion
- awards and recognition

The portfolio is assembled at the culmination of a course to provide evidence of learning. A self-assessment summary report should be included that explains what has been accomplished, what has been learned, what strengths the student has gained, and any areas that need improvement. Portfolios may be presented to the class by the students. The items in the portfolio can also be discussed with the teacher in light of educational goals and outcomes. Portfolios should remain the property of students when they leave the course. They may be used for interviews with potential employers.

Portfolio assessment is only one of several evaluation methods teachers can use, but it is a powerful tool for both students and teachers. It encourages self-reflection and self-assessment of a more global nature. Traditional evaluation methods of tests, quizzes, and papers have their place in measuring the achievement of some course objectives, but other assessment tools should also be used to fairly assess the achievement of all desired outcomes.

Teaching the Learner with Special Needs

The students in your classroom will represent a wide range of ability levels and needs. Special needs students in your classes will require unique teaching strategies. The chart on the next page provides descriptions of several of the types of special needs students you may find in your classes, followed by some strategies and techniques to keep in mind as you work with these students. You will be asked to meet the needs of all of your students in the same classroom setting. It is a challenge to adapt daily lessons to meet the demands of all your students.

	Learning Disabled*	Mentally Disabled*	Behaviorally Emotionally Disabled*
Description	Students with learning disabilities (LD) have neurological disorders that interfere with their ability to store, process, or produce information, creating a "gap" between ability and performance. These students are generally of average or above-average intelligence. Examples of learning disabilities or distractibility, spatial problems, and reading comprehension problems.	The mentally disabled student has subaverage general intellectual functioning that exists with deficits in adaptive behavior. These students are slower than others their age in using memory effectively, associating and classifying information, reasoning, and making judgments.	These students exhibit undesirable behaviors or emotions that may, over time, adversely affect educational performance. Their inability to learn cannot be explained by intellectual, social, or health factors. They may be inattentive, withdrawn, timid, restless, defiant, impatient, unhappy, fearful, unreflective, lack initiative, have negative feelings and actions, and blame others.
Teaching Strategies	• Assist students in getting organized. • Give short oral directions. • Use drill exercises. • Give prompt cues during student performance. • Let students with poor writing skills use a computer. • Break assignments into small segments and assign only one segment at a time. • Demonstrate skills and have students model them. • Give prompt feedback. • Use continuous assessment to mark students' daily progress. • Prepare materials at varying levels of ability. • Shorten the number of items on exercises, tests, and quizzes. • Provide more hands-on activities.	• Use concrete examples to introduce concepts. • Make learning activities consistent. • Use repetition and drills spread over time. • Provide work folders for daily assignments. • Use behavior management techniques, such as behavior modification, in the area of adaptive behavior. • Encourage students to function independently. • Give students extra time to both ask and answer questions while giving hints to answers. • Avoid doing much walking around while talking to MD students as this is distracting for them. • Give simple directions and read them over with students. • Use objective test items and hands-on activities because students generally have poor writing skills and difficulty with sentence structure and spelling.	• Call students' names or ask them questions when you see their attention wandering. • Call on students randomly rather than in a predictable sequence. • Move around the room frequently. • Improve students' self-esteem by giving them tasks they can perform well, increasing the number of successful achievement experiences. • Decrease the length of time for each activity. • Use hands-on activities instead of using words and abstract symbols. • Decrease the size of the group so each student can actively participate. • Make verbal instructions clear, short, and to the point.

*We appreciate the assistance of Dr. Debra O. Parker, North Carolina Central University, with this section.

Academically Gifted	Limited English Proficiency	Physical Disabilities
Academically gifted students are capable of high performance as a result of general intellectual ability, specific academic aptitude, and/or creative or productive thinking. Such students have a vast fund of general knowledge and high levels of vocabulary, memory, abstract word knowledge, and abstract reasoning.	These students have a limited proficiency in the English language. English is generally their second language. Such students may be academically quite capable, but they lack the language skills needed to reason and comprehend abstract concepts.	Includes individuals who are orthopedically impaired, visually impaired, speech-impaired, deaf, hard-of-hearing, hearing-impaired, and health-impaired (cystic fibrosis, epilepsy). Strategies will depend on the specific disability.
<ul><li>Provide ample opportunities for creative behavior.</li><li>Make assignments that call for original work, independent learning, critical thinking, problem solving, and experimentation.</li><li>Show appreciation for creative efforts.</li><li>Respect unusual questions, ideas, and solutions these students provide.</li><li>Encourage students to test their ideas.</li><li>Provide opportunities and give credit for self-initiated learning.</li><li>Avoid overly detailed supervision and too much reliance on prescribed curricula.</li><li>Allow time for reflection.</li><li>Resist immediate and constant evaluation. This causes students to be afraid to use their creativity.</li><li>Avoid comparisons with other students, which applies subtle pressure to conform.</li></ul>	<ul><li>Use a slow, but natural rate of speech; speak clearly; use shorter sentences; repeat concepts in several ways.</li><li>Act out questions using gestures with hands, arms, and the whole body. Use demonstrations and pantomime. Ask questions that can be answered by a physical movement such as pointing, nodding, or manipulation of materials.</li><li>When possible, use pictures, photos, and charts.</li><li>Write key terms on the chalkboard. As they are used, point to them.</li><li>Corrections should be limited and appropriate. Do not correct grammar or usage errors in front of the class, causing embarrassment.</li><li>Give honest praise and positive feedback through your voice tones and visual articulation whenever possible.</li><li>Encourage students to use language to communicate, allowing them to use their native language to ask/answer questions when they are unable to do so in English.</li><li>Integrate students' cultural background into class discussions.</li><li>Use cooperative learning where students have opportunities to practice expressing ideas without risking language errors in front of the entire class.</li></ul>	<ul><li>For visually and hearing-impaired students, seat them near the front of the classroom. Speak clearly and say out loud what you are writing on the chalkboard.</li><li>In lab settings, in order to reduce the risk of injury, ask students about any conditions that could affect their ability to learn or perform.</li><li>Rearrange lab equipment or the classroom and make modifications as needed to accommodate any special need.</li><li>Investigate assistive technology devices that can improve students' functional capabilities.</li><li>Discuss solutions or modifications with the student who has experience with overcoming his or her disability and may have suggestions you may not have considered.</li><li>Let the student know when classroom modifications are being made and allow him or her to test them out before class.</li><li>Ask advice from special education teachers, the school nurse, or physical therapist.</li><li>Plan field trips that can include all students.</li></ul>

Using Other Resources

Student learning in your class can be reinforced and expanded by exposing your students to a variety of viewpoints. Information may be obtained through various government offices and trade and professional organizations. Local sources of information might include cooperative extension offices, state departments of labor, and employment agencies.

The following is a list of various trade and professional organizations, government resources, and companies that may be able to provide you with resources for use in your classroom. Names, addresses, phone numbers, and Web site addresses are included. Please note that these addresses may have changed since publication of this resource book.

*Trade and Professional Organizations**

American Association of Family and
  Consumer Sciences (AAFCS)
  1555 King St.
  Alexandria, VA 22314
  (703) 706-4600
  www.aafcs.org

American Association for Vocational
  Instructional Materials
  735 Gaines School Rd.
  Athens, GA 30605

American Bankers Association
  1120 Connecticut Ave., NW
  Washington, DC 20036 (202) 663-5000

American Bar Association
  750 North Lake Shore Dr.
  Chicago, IL 60611
  (312) 988-5000

American Council of Life Insurance
  1001 Pennsylvania Ave., NW
  Suite 500 South
  Washington, DC 20004
  (202) 624-2000

American Council on Consumer Interests
  240 Stanley Hall
  University of Missouri
  Columbia, MO 65211-0001
  (573) 882-3817

American Dietetic Association
  216 W. Jackson Blvd.
  Chicago, IL 60606-6995
  (800) 366-1655
  www.eatright.org

American Educational Research
  Association (AERA)
  1230 17th St., NW
  Washington, DC 20036

American Medical Association
  515 N. State St.
  Chicago, IL 60610
  (312) 464-5000
  www.ama-assn.org

American Savings Education Council
  www.asec.org

American Stock Exchange, Inc.
  86 Trinity Place
  New York, NY 10006
  (212) 306-1000

Association for Career and Technical
  Education
  1410 King St.
  Alexandria, VA 22314

Automotive Consumer Action Program
  8400 West Park Dr.
  McLean, VA 22102
  (703) 821-7144

Center for Science in the Public Interest (CSPI)
  1875 Connecticut Ave., NW, Suite 300
  Washington, DC 20009
  (202) 332-9110

Chamber of Commerce of the United
  States of America
  1615 H St., NW
  Washington, DC 20062

Concord Coalition
  Citizens for America's Future
  1019 19th St., NW, Suite 810
  Washington, DC 20036
  (202) 467-6222

Consumer Federation of America
  1424 16th St., NW, Suite 604
  Washington, DC 20036
  (202) 387-6121

Consumers Union
www.consumerreports.org

Crafted with Pride in the USA Council, Inc.
1045 Avenue of the Americas
New York, NY 10018
(212) 819-4397

Credit Union National Association, Inc.
PO Box 431
Madison, WI 53701
(608) 231-4000

Food and Agricultural Organization of the United Nations
www.fao.org

Insurance Information Institute
110 William St.
New York, NY 10038
(212) 669-9200

Mayo Health Oasis
www.mayo.ivi.com

National Academy of Sciences
www.nas.edu

National Center for Educational Statistics
nces.ed.gov

National Center for Health Statistics
www.cdc.gov/nchswww/default.htm

National Center for Injury Prevention & Control
www.cdc.gov/ncipc

National Center for Research in Vocational Education (NCRVE)
www.vocserve.berkeley.edu

National Consumer Law Center
18 Tremont St., Suite 400
Boston, MA 02108
(617) 523-8010

National Consumers League
1701 K St., NW, Suite 1201
Washington, DC 20006
(202) 835-3323
www.natlconsumersleague.org

National Council of Better Business Bureaus
4200 Wilson Blvd., Suite 800
Arlington, VA 22203-1838
(703) 276-0100

National Council on Economics Education
1140 Avenue of the Americas, Second Floor
New York, NY 10036
(212) 730-7007

National Foundation for Consumer Credit, Inc.
8611 Second Ave., Suite 100
Silver Spring, MD 20910
(301) 589-5600

National Fraud Information Center
Consumer Fraud Hot Line
(800) 876-7060

National Institute for Consumer Education
www.emich.edu/public/coe/nice

National Institute on Aging
www.nih.gov/hia

National Institutes of Health
www.nih.gov/od/odp.whi

National Insurance Consumer Helpline
(800) 942-4242

National Safety Council
1121 Spring Lake Dr.
Itasca, IL 60143-3201
(630) 285-1121

National Taxpayers' Union
108 N. Alfred St.
Alexandria, VA 22314
www.ntu.org

Public Voice for Food and Health Policy
1101 14th St., NW, Suite 710
Washington, DC 20005
(202) 371-1840

World Agricultural Outlook Board
Public Information Office
(202) 720-5447

World Health Organization
www.who.ch

Government Resources*

Sources of General Information

The Consumer Information Center (CIC) publishes the free *Consumer Information Catalog*, which lists more than 200 free and low-cost government booklets on a wide variety of consumer topics. Copies of the catalog can be obtained by using the Web address of *www.pueblo.gsa.gov*, writing to *Consumer Information Catalog*, Pueblo, CO 81009, or calling (719) 948-4000.

The Federal Information Center (FIC), which is administered by the General Services Administration (GSA), can help you find information about United States government agencies, services, and programs. The FIC can also tell you which office to contact for help with problems. You can contact the FIC online or by calling (800) 688-9889.

Specific Federal Agencies

Centers for Disease Control and
    Prevention (CDC)
    Public Inquiries—(404) 639-3534
    www.cdc.gov

Consumer Education for Teens
    www.wa.gov/ago/youth

Office of Consumer Affairs
    Department of Commerce
    14th & Constitution Ave., NW
    Washington, DC 20230
    (202) 482-5001

Office of Public Affairs
    Department of Education
    400 Maryland Ave., SW
    Washington, DC 20202
    (800) 872-5327

Office of Consumer and Public Liaison
    Department of Energy
    Washington, DC 20585
    (202) 586-5373
    www.eren.doe.gov

National Health Information Center
    Department of Health and Human Services
    PO Box 1133
    Washington, DC 20013-1133
    (800) 336-4797

Office of Fair Housing and Equal Opportunity
    Department of Housing and Urban Development
    451 7th St., SW, Room 5100
    Washington, DC 20410
    (202) 708-4252

Office of the Secretary
    Department of the Interior
    1849 C St., NW
    Washington, DC 20240
    (202) 208-3100

Coordinator of Consumer Affairs
    Department of Labor
    200 Constitution Ave., NW
    Washington, DC 20210
    (202) 693-4650

Bureau of the Public Debt
    Public Affairs Officer
    Office of the Commissioner
    Department of the Treasury
    999 E St., NW, Room 553
    Washington, DC 20239-0001
    (202) 691-3502

Public Information Center
    (PM-211B)
    Environmental Protection Agency
    Washington, DC 20007
    (202) 342-3338

Consumer Assistance Branch
    Federal Communications Commission
    1919 M St., NW, Room 254
    Washington, DC 20554
    (202) 418-0200

Office of Consumer Affairs
    Federal Deposit Insurance Corporation
    550 17th St., NW
    Washington, DC 20429
    (800) 934-3342

Federal Trade Commission (FTC)
CRC-240
Washington, DC 20580
www.ftc.gov

Food and Nutrition Information Center of the National Agricultural Library
www.nalusda.gov/fnic

Consumer Affairs and Information
Food and Drug Administration (FDA)
Department of Health and Human Services
5600 Fishers Lane, Room 16-63
Rockville, MD 20857
(301) 443-3170
www.fda.gov

Internal Revenue Service
1111 Constitution Ave., NW
Washington, DC 20224
(800) 829-1040
www.irs.ustreas.gov

Securities and Exchange Commission
Office of Filings, Information, and Consumer Services
450 5th St., NW
(Mail Stop 2-6)
Washington, DC 20549
(202) 942-7040

Small Business Administration
www.sba.gov

Social Security Administration
www.ssa.gov

Product Safety Hotline
U.S. Consumer Product Safety Commission
1111 18th St., NW
Washington, DC 20207
(800) 638-2772
www.cpsc.gov

USDA Food and Consumer Services
Consumer Affairs
(703) 305-2281

USDA Information
(202) 720-2791

U.S. Government Printing Office
Publications Office
(202) 512-1800

U.S. House of Representatives
www.house.gov

Consumer Advocate
U.S. Postal Service
475 Lenfant Plaza, SW
Washington, DC 20260-6720
(202) 268-2284

U.S. Senate
www.senate.gov

*Other Resources**

The following is a list of various companies, associations, and groups that may serve as resources for additional teaching materials. Most provide videos and/or computer software. Many provide printed materials. Contact these organizations for their latest catalogs.

AAVIM
220 Smithonia Rd.
Winterville, GA 30683
(800) 228-4689
(software, videos, and publications)

AGC Educational Media
1560 Sherman Ave., Suite 100
Evanston, IL 60201
(800) 323-9084
FAX: (708) 328-6706

Bergwall Productions, Inc.
540 Baltimore Pk.
PO Box 2400
Chadds Ford, PA 19317

Cambridge Educational
PO Box 2153
Charleston, WV 25328-2153
(800) 468-4227
(videos, software, CD-ROM, printed materials)

Concept Media
2493 Dubridge Ave.
Irvine, CA 92606
(800) 233-7078

Creative Educational Video
PO Box 65265
Lubbock, TX 79464-5265
(800) 922-9965

Distinctive Home Video Productions
391 El Portal Rd.
San Mateo, CA 94402
(415) 344-7756

Durrin Productions
1748 Kaorama Rd., NW
Washington, DC 20009
(800) 536-6843

Films for the Humanities and Sciences
PO Box 2053
Princeton, NJ 08543
(800) 257-5126

The Health Connection
55 W. Oak Ridge Dr.
Hagerstown, MD 21740
(800) 548-8700
(pamphlets, books, teaching aids, posters, and audiovisual aids)

Human Relations Media Video (HRM)
175 Tompkins Ave.
Pleasantville, NY 10570
(800) 431-2050
(videos for guidance, health, and conflict resolution)

Internet Fraud Watch
(800) 876-7060
www.fraud.org

Mail Order Action Line
1120 Avenue of the Americas
New York, NY 10036
(212) 768-7277

Meridian Education Corp.
236 E. Front St.
Bloomington, IL 61701
(800) 727-5507
(videos/multimedia)

NIMCO, Inc.
PO Box 9102, Highway 81 North
Calhoun, KY 42327
(800) 962-6662
(textbooks, videos, and slides)

RMI Media Productions
2807 West 47th St.
Shawnee Mission, KS 66205
(800) 821-5480
(educational videos)

Teaching Aids, Inc.
PO Box 1798
Costa Mesa, CA 92628-0798

Teen-Aid
723 E. Jackson
Spokane, WA 99207-2647
(509) 482-2868
FAX: (509) 482-7994
(videos, teaching modules, lesson plans, pamphlets, overheads, and posters)

Career and Technical Student Organization Web Sites

Business Professionals of America (BPA)
www.bpa.org

DECA—An Association of Marketing Students
www.deca.org

Family, Career and Community Leaders of America (FCCLA)
www.fcclainc.org

Future Business Leaders of America–Phi Beta Lambda
www.fbla-pbl.org

Health Occupations Students of America (HOSA)
www.hosa.org

National FFA Organization
www.ffa.org

SkillsUSA–VICA
www.skillsusa.org

Technology Student Association (TSA)
www.tsawww.org

*Note: The addresses, phone numbers, FAX numbers, and Web site addresses listed may have changed since the publication of this *Teacher's Wraparound Edition.*

Correlation of National Standards with *Skills for Personal and Family Living*

In 1998, the National Standards for Family and Consumer Sciences Education were finalized. This comprehensive guide provides family and consumer sciences educators with a structure for identifying what learners should be able to do. This structure is based on knowledge and skills needed for work life and family life, as well as family and consumer sciences careers. The National Standards Components include 16 areas of study, each with a comprehensive standard that describes the overall content of the area. Each comprehensive standard is then broken down into content standards that describe what is expected of the learner. Competencies further define the knowledge, skills, and practices of the content standards and provide the basis for measurement criteria.

By studying the text *Skills for Personal and Family Living*, students will be introduced to many of the competencies included in the National Standards. To help you see where these standards are covered, a *Correlation of National Standards with Skills for Personal and Family Living* has been included in the *Teacher's Resource Guide* and *Teacher's Resource Portfolio*. If you want to make sure you prepare students to meet the National Standards for Family and Consumer Sciences Education, this chart should be of interest to you.

Scope and Sequence Chart

A *Scope and Sequence Chart*, located at the end of this introduction, identifies the major concepts presented in each chapter of the text. This special resource is provided to help you select for study those topics that meet your curriculum needs.

Goodheart-Willcox Welcomes Your Comments

We welcome your comments or suggestions regarding *Skills for Personal and Family Living* and its ancillaries as we are continually striving to publish better educational materials. Please send any comments you may have to:

Editorial Department
Goodheart-Willcox Publishers
18604 West Creek Drive
Tinley Park, IL 60477-6243
Phone: 1-800-323-0440

or to send a memo to the editor, visit our Web site at
www.goodheartwillcox.com

Correlation of National Standards with *Skills for Personal and Family Living*

In planning your program, you may want to refer to the correlation chart below. This chart correlates the Family and Consumer Sciences Education National Standards with the content of *Skills for Personal and Family Living*. It lists the 16 comprehensive standards in the left column, followed by the Topics in *Skills for Personal and Family Living* that contain content related to each standard in the right column. Because this is an introductory comprehensive text for family and consumer sciences, additional courses will need to be taken by students in order to achieve all of the specific competencies contained in any one comprehensive standard.

Comprehensive Standard	Topics with Related Content
CAREER, COMMUNITY AND FAMILY CONNECTIONS 1.0 Integrate multiple life roles and responsibilities in family, work, and community settings.	Topics 3-2, 4-3, 5-1, 5-3, 6-3, 7-2, 10-1, 10-2, 18-3
CONSUMER AND FAMILY RESOURCES 2.0 Evaluate management practices related to the human, economic, and environmental resources.	Topics 10-1, 10-3, 10-4, 10-5, 10-6, 11-1, 11-2, 11-3, 11-4, 11-5, 12-5, 13-2, 15-2, 15-3, 19-1, 19-3, 19-4, 23-1, 23-2, 23-3, 25-3
CONSUMER SERVICES 3.0 Integrate knowledge, skills, and practices required for careers in consumer services.	Topics 5-1, 5-2, 5-3, 10-3, 10-4, 10-6, 11-1, 11-3, 11-4, 11-5
EARLY CHILDHOOD, EDUCATION, AND SERVICES 4.0 Integrate knowledge, skills, and practices required for careers in early childhood education and services.	Topics 5-1, 5-2, 5-3, 9-1, 9-7
FACILITIES MANAGEMENT AND MAINTENANCE 5.0 Integrate knowledge, skills, and practices required for careers in facilities management and maintenance.	Topics 5-1, 5-2, 5-3, 13-1, 13-2, 19-5, 25-1, 25-2, 25-3
FAMILY 6.0 Evaluate the significance of family and its impact on the well being of individuals and society.	Topics 6-1, 6-2, 6-3, 7-1, 7-2
FAMILY AND COMMUNITY SERVICES 7.0 Integrate knowledge, skills, and practices required for careers in family and community services.	Topics 2-3, 2-4, 3-3, 5-1, 5-2, 5-3, 6-3, 7-3, 8-1, 9-1, 9-6, 9-7
FOOD PRODUCTION AND SERVICES 8.0 Integrate knowledge, skills, and practices required for careers in food production and services.	Topics 5-1, 5-2, 5-3, 15-1, 16-1, 16-2, 16-4, 17-1, 17-2, 17-3, 17-4
FOOD SCIENCE, DIETETICS, AND NUTRITION 9.0 Integrate knowledge, skills, and practices required for careers in food science, dietetics, and nutrition.	Topics 5-1, 5-2, 5-3, 14-1, 14-2, 14-3, 14-4, 15-1, 15-4, 16-1, 16-2
HOSPITALITY, TOURISM, AND RECREATION 10.0 Integrate knowledge, skills, and practices required for careers in hospitality, tourism, and recreation.	Topics 5-1, 5-2, 5-3, 18-1, 18-2, 18-3
HOUSING, INTERIORS, AND FURNISHINGS 11.0 Integrate knowledge, skills, and practices required for careers in housing, interiors, and furnishings.	Topics 5-1, 5-2, 5-3, 23-1, 23-2, 23-3, 24-1, 24-2, 24-3
HUMAN DEVELOPMENT 12.0 Analyze factors that impact human growth and development.	Topics 1-2, 1-3, 1-4, 8-2, 9-2, 9-3, 9-4, 9-5, 9-6, 12-1, 12-2, 12-3, 12-4, 14-3, 14-4
INTERPERSONAL RELATIONSHIPS 13.0 Demonstrate respectful and caring relationships in the family, workplace, and community.	Topics 1-1, 2-1, 2-2, 2-3, 2-4, 3-1, 3-2, 3-3, 4-1, 4-2, 5-3, 7-1, 7-3
NUTRITION AND WELLNESS 14.0 Demonstrate nutrition and wellness practices that enhance individual and family well being.	Topics 9-2, 12-1, 14-1, 14-2, 14-3, 14-4, 15-1, 15-2, 15-3, 15-4, 16-1, 16-2, 16-3, 16-4, 17-1, 17-2, 17-3, 17-4
PARENTING 15.0 Evaluate the impact of parenting roles and responsibilities on strengthening the well being of individuals and families.	Topics 6-1, 6-2, 6-3, 8-1, 9-2, 9-3, 9-4, 9-5, 9-6, 9-7
TEXTILES AND APPAREL 16.0 Integrate knowledge, skills, and practices required for careers in textiles and apparel.	Topics 5-1, 5-2, 5-3, 9-2, 19-2, 19-5, 20-1, 20-2, 20-3, 20-4, 21-1, 21-2, 21-3, 22-1, 22-2, 22-3, 22-4

Scope and Sequence

In planning your program, you may want to use the Scope and Sequence Chart below. This chart identifies the major concepts presented in each chapter of the text. Refer to the chart to select for study those topics that meet your curriculum needs. Bold numbers indicate chapters in which concepts are found.

Part One A Better You

Personal Development
1: Understanding yourself; your heredity; your environment; your self-concept; character development; your growth and development; growing chronologically, physically, emotionally, intellectually, and socially; developmental tasks of teens; personal priorities, goals, and standards; roadblocks in development; tactics that aid personal development; solving problems and making decisions
5: Your interests; aptitudes, and abilities

Interpersonal Relationships
1: Adopting personal behavior standards; behavioral self-controls; building supportive relationships; growing socially; developmental tasks of teens
2: Understanding relationships; developing positive relationships; types of relationships; benefits of positive relationships; qualities needed for positive relationships; developing friendships; dating; love; responsible relationships; negative relationships; ending a negative relationship; negative peer pressure; the marriage relationship; learning to love; facts that influence marital success; the engagement period; making marriage work
3: Communication skills; verbal communication; nonverbal communication; communication in relationships; barriers to open communication; importance of communication in relationships; communication in the workplace; conflict resolution; types of conflicts; causes of conflict; reactions to conflict; constructive methods of handling conflict
4: Being a team member; effective leadership; to be involved in your community
5: Succeeding on the job

Communication and Leadership
1: Building supportive relationships
2: Developing positive relationships; qualities needed for positive relationships; developing friendships; dealing with sexual pressures; ending a negative relationship; factors that influence marital success; the engagement period; making marriage work
3: Communication skills; verbal communication; nonverbal communication; technology and communication; importance of communication in relationships; barriers to open communication; communication in the workplace; conflict resolution; causes of conflict; reactions to conflict; constructive methods for handling conflict; violence: a destructive method of handling conflict
4: Leadership and citizenship skills; leaders and followers; being a team member; opportunities of leadership; effective leadership; organizations that work; youth and professional organizations; getting organized; choosing effective programs and activities; your rights and responsibilities as a citizen; to be informed; to vote; to obey the law; to pay taxes; to protect the environment; to be involved in your community
5: The job interview; entrepreneurship; succeeding on the job; qualities of successful employees

Health, Safety, and the Environment
1: Your environment; influences on behavior; human needs; high-risk behavior
2: Facing sexual decisions; rape
4: To protect the environment

Life Management Skills

1: Personal behavior standards; human needs; personal priorities, goals, and standards; management skills

3: Communication skills; verbal communication; nonverbal communication; technology and communication; conflict resolution; constructive methods for handling conflict

4: Leadership and citizenship skills; your rights and responsibilities as a citizen; to be informed; to vote; to obey the laws; to pay taxes; to protect the environment; to be involved in your community

5: The world of work; career planning; know your interests, aptitudes, and abilities; learn about careers; your education choices; other factors affecting your career choice; making a career decision; finding a job; applying for a job; the job interview; creating your own job; succeeding on the job; qualities of successful employees; technology in the workplace; work schedules and income; understanding your paycheck

Family Living

1: Your cultural heritage; human needs; building supportive relationships

2: Understanding relationships; developing positive relationships; types of relationships; the marriage relationship; learning to love; factors that influence marital success; the engagement period; making marriage work

3: The communication process; verbal communication; nonverbal communication; barriers to open communication; when negative feelings occur; conflict resolution; causes of conflict; reactions to conflict; constructive methods for handling conflict

Parenting and Child Development

2: Types of relationships; developing positive relationships

3: The communication process

Part Two Today's Families

Interpersonal Relationships
6: Roles of family members; functions of the family; family structures vary; family structures change; divorce; remarriage

7: Building functional families; making and keeping families strong; the relationship of work and family life; handling family crises

Communication and Leadership
6: Societal influences; world events

7: Making and keeping families strong; managing multiple roles; family challenges

Health, Safety, and the Environment
7: Crises; family violence; substance abuse; serious illness or accidents

Life Management Skills
7: Making and keeping families strong; balancing family and work; the relationship of family and work; managing multiple roles; the role of the employer; skills for coping with crises

Family Living
6: What is a family?; roles of family members; functions of the family; single living; family structures vary; factors influencing families; family structures change; family life cycle; divorce; remarriage

7: Family challenges; building functional families; making and keeping families strong; fulfilling family rights and responsibilities; balancing family and work; the relationship of work and family life; the role of the employer; managing multiple roles; handling family crises; family violence

Parenting and Child Development
6: What is a family?; roles of family members; functions of the family; family structures; family life cycle; divorce; remarriage.

7: Balancing family and work; the relationship of work and family life; managing multiple roles; finding child care; family violence

Part Three   Caring for Children

Interpersonal Relationships
8: Deciding about parenting; the challenges of parenting; deciding whether to have children
9: Being a responsible caregiver; meeting children's social and emotional needs; teaching independence and responsibility; providing guidance; communicating with children; role of play in social-emotional development; helping children overcome fears; meeting children's intellectual needs; role of play in intellectual development; emotional and social development

Communication and Leadership
9: The role of society in protecting children's rights; providing guidance; communicating with children;

Health, Safety, and the Environment
8: Children of teen parents; family planning; infertility; pregnancy; prenatal development; heredity; medical care during pregnancy;
9: Health of caregivers; meeting children's physical needs; role of play in physical development; creating a healthy and safe environment; helping children overcome fears; first aid; early brain development; physical growth; children with special needs; selecting quality child care

Family Living
8: Deciding about parenting; the goal of parenting; challenges of parenting; teen parenting; deciding whether to have children; family planning; adoption
9: Meeting children's physical needs; meeting children's social and emotional needs; meeting children's intellectual needs; the first year; children from one to five

Parenting and Child Development
9: Being a responsible caregiver; the role of society in protecting children's rights; meeting children's physical needs; serving food; choosing clothes; the role of play in physical development; creating a healthy and safe environment; meeting children's social and emotional needs; teaching independence and responsibility; providing guidance; communicating with children; the role of play in social-emotional development; helping children overcome fears; meeting children's intellectual needs; the role of play in intellectual development; enrichment activities for children; selecting toys; the first year; newborn babies; care of newborns; infants; children from one to five; toddlers; preschoolers; children with special needs; child care options; types of child care; selecting quality child care

Textiles and Clothing
9: Choosing clothing for children

Food and Nutrition
9: Serving foods to children

Part Four Managing in Today's World

Interpersonal Relationships
10: The management process; identify and prioritize your goals; recognize your personal priorities and standards; determine your resources; form a plan; implement the plan; balancing personal, family, work, and leisure time

Communication and Leadership
10: The management process; identify and prioritize your goals; recognize your personal priorities and standards; determine your resources; form a plan; implement the plan; evaluate the results
11: Consumer decisions; the impact of technology on consumers; consumer protection laws; consumer rights and responsibilities

Health, Safety, and the Environment
10: Health insurance
11: The role of advertising; consumer protection against deceptive advertising; consumers and the law; consumer protection laws; consumer rights and responsibilities

Life Management Skills
10: Learning to manage; the management process; identify and prioritize your goals; recognize your personal priorities and standards; determine your resources; form a plan; implement the plan; evaluate the results; managing your time; reasons to plan time; steps in time management; managing time wisely; energy and task management; managing your money; the basics of budgeting; reducing flexible expenses; budgeting with a computer; using financial services; choosing a financial institution; using a checking account; saving for the future; why save?; factors in deciding how to save; savings accounts; decisions about securities; planning an estate; meeting insurance needs; insurance basics; life insurance; health insurance; automobile insurance; housing-related insurance; filing a claim
11: Consumer decisions; making shopping decisions; deciding where to shop; deciding when to buy; deciding what to buy; managing technology; evaluating advertisements; using consumer credit; applying for credit; shopping for credit; using credit wisely

Family Living
10: Learning to manage; managing your time; managing your money; the basics of budgeting; reducing flexible expenses; budgeting with a computer; using financial services; using a checking account; saving for the future; why save?; factors in deciding how to save; meeting insurance needs
11: Consumer decisions; making shopping decisions; deciding when to buy; deciding what to buy; using consumer credit; applying for credit, shopping for credit; using credit wisely

Part Five   Healthy Living

Interpersonal Relationships
12: Maintaining a healthy mental state; stress and your health; depression; when people need help; health risks; sexually transmitted diseases; decisions that affect your health

Health, Safety, and the Environment
12: Your physical fitness; the importance of good health; being physically active; the importance of sleep; the importance of leisure activities; good grooming; caring for your skin, teeth, hair, hands, and feet; your mental health; stress; depression; when people need help; health risks; tobacco; alcohol; other drugs; sexually transmitted diseases; decisions that affect your health; medical services; selecting a physician; emergency medical services
13: Personal safety and security; preventing accidents in the home and on the road; providing for security; emergency procedures; a healthful environment; factors affecting the environment; pollution; how you can help
14: Healthful eating; nutrients; recommended nutrient intakes; Food Guide Pyramid; Dietary Guidelines for Americans; nutritional needs change; balancing calories and energy needs; meeting energy needs; controlling your weight; eating disorders

Life Management Skills
12: Your physical fitness; grooming; your mental health; health risks; when you need medical services
13: Personal safety and security; preventing accidents; a healthy environment; how you can help

Family Living
12: Health risks; when you need medical services; selecting a physician; emergency medical services
13: Preventing accidents in the home; providing for security
14: Nutrients; recommended nutrient intakes; Food Guide Pyramid; Dietary Guidelines for Americans; nutritional needs change; needs of children and teens; needs of adults; needs of people who are ill; balancing calories and energy needs; meeting energy needs; eating disorders

Parenting and Child Development
14: Healthful eating; recommended nutrient intakes; Food Guide Pyramid; Dietary Guidelines for Americans; nutritional needs change; needs of children and teens; balancing calories and energy needs; controlling your weight; eating disorders

Food and Nutrition
12: The importance of good health
14: Nutrients at work for you; carbohydrates; proteins; fats; minerals; vitamins; water; recommended nutrient intakes; Food Guide Pyramid; Dietary Guidelines for Americans; nutritional needs change; needs of pregnant women and infants; needs of children and teens; needs of athletes; needs of adults; needs of people who are ill; balancing calories and energy needs; meeting energy needs; controlling your weight; eating disorders

Housing, Interiors, and Home Maintenance
13: A safe home and environment; personal safety and security in your home

Part Six   Planning and Preparing Meals

Health, Safety, and the Environment
15: Meal management; planning for nutrition; buying information; storing foods
16: Before you cook; safety and sanitation; cooking smart
18: Dining out; types of restaurants; making healthful food choices

Life Management Skills
15: Meal management; planning meals; shopping for food; storing foods
18: Making dining enjoyable; hosting a meal; manners when dining; ordering from a restaurant menu; restaurant etiquette; paying the check

Family Living
15: Planning meals; shopping for food; cultural and societal influences; when you are the meal manager
18: Serving food; making dining enjoyable; hosting a meal; manners when dining

Food and Nutrition
15: Meal management; planning meals; planning for nutrition; variety in meals; when you are the meal manager; shopping for food; preparing a shopping list; deciding where to shop; deciding how much food to buy; recognizing quality in foods; buying information; unit pricing; open dating; food labeling; Nutrition Facts Panel; storing foods properly; technology in food packaging
16: Before you cook; know your equipment; major appliances; portable appliances; kitchen utensils; safety and sanitation; make it safe; keep it sanitary; using a recipe; understanding how to use recipes; learning cooking methods; cooking smart
17: Buying, storing, and preparing foods; meat, poultry, fish, and alternates; storing meat, poultry, fish, and alternates; preparing meat, poultry, fish, and alternates; buying fruits and vegetables; storing fruits and vegetables; preparing fruits and vegetables; buying cereal products; storing cereal products; preparing cereal products; cakes and cookies; milk and milk products; buying dairy products; storing dairy products; preparing dairy products
18: Serving food and dining out

Skills for Personal and Family Living

Part Seven Meeting Your Clothing Needs

Health, Safety, and the Environment
19: Choosing and caring for clothes; physical needs for clothes; reading labels and hangtags; caring for clothes; laundering steps; energy conservation in clothing care
20: Safety with sewing tools
22: Recycling clothes

Life Management Skills
19: Choosing and caring for clothes; planning your wardrobe; shopping for clothes; shopping guidelines; judging quality; reading labels and hangtags; caring for clothes

Textiles and Clothing
19: Choosing clothes that meet your needs; factors that influence clothing decisions; choosing clothes for specific occasions; choosing clothes that look good on you; color; the other design elements; consider the principles of design; planning your wardrobe; factors to consider in wardrobe planning; extending your wardrobe; shopping for clothes; shopping guidelines; understanding fashion terms; judging quality; reading labels and hangtags; caring for clothes; daily clothing care; laundering steps; prepare clothes for laundering; understand laundry products; drying clothes; ironing and pressing; dry cleaning; packing and storing clothes
20: Preparing to sew; selecting fabrics; fibers; yarns; fabric construction; fabric finishes; dyeing fabrics; printing fabrics; selecting patterns; take your measurements; determine your figure type and size; deciding on a pattern; the pattern envelope; selecting fabric and notions; choosing a fabric; how much fabric is needed; choosing notions; sewing equipment; small equipment; the sewing machine; the serger; safety with sewing tools
21: The first steps before sewing; begin with the pattern; the pattern guide sheet; altering your pattern; prepare the fabric; preshrinking and pressing; check the grain; the pattern layout; pinning; cutting the fabric; marking the fabric
22: Sewing techniques; stitching techniques; darts; seams; tucks, pleats, and gathers; interfacing; facings; waist treatments; sleeves; pockets; zippers; fasteners; hems; sewing knit fabrics; extending the life of clothes; repairing clothes; altering clothes; restyling clothes; recycling clothes

Part Eight A Place to Call Home

Health, Safety, and the Environment
23: Choosing a place to live; meeting your housing needs; physical needs; social needs; psychological needs
24: Furnishing your home
25: Keep it clean; plan ahead for easy cleaning; maintaining the home; conserving energy in the home; energy sources; outlook for the future; you can conserve energy

Life Management Skills
23: Meeting your housing needs; housing alternatives; renting or buying housing
24: Furnishing your home; arranging furniture

Family Living
23: Choosing a place to live; meeting your housing needs; physical needs; social needs; psychological needs; housing alternatives; multifamily dwellings; trends in housing; renting or buying housing
24: Decorating your home; furnishing your home

Housing, interiors, and Home Maintenance
23: Meeting your housing needs; physical needs; social needs; psychological needs; housing alternatives; single-family houses; multifamily dwellings; trends in housing; renting or buying housing; choosing housing
24: Elements of design; principles of design; goals of design; decorating your home; floor coverings; wall treatments; windows and window treatments; lighting; furnishing your home; choosing furniture; arranging furniture; using accessories
25: Caring for your home; cleaning supplies and equipment; make a cleaning schedule; maintaining the home; who should make repairs; plumbing repairs; using carpentry tools; electrical problems; conserving energy in the home; energy sources; outlook for the future; you can help conserve energy

Skills for Personal & Family Living

Frances Baynor Parnell
Educational Consultant and Author
Wilmington, North Carolina

Contributor for Sewing Chapters
Joyce Honeycutt Wooten
Burgaw, North Carolina

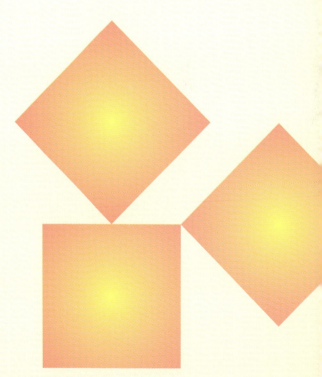

Publisher
The Goodheart-Willcox Company, Inc.
Tinley Park, Illinois

Copyright 2004

by

The Goodheart-Willcox Company, Inc.

Previous editions copyright 2001, 1997, 1994, 1988, 1984, 1981

All rights reserved. No part of this book may be reproduced, stored in a retrieval system, or transmitted in any form or by any means, electronic, mechanical, photocopying, recording, or otherwise, without the prior written permission of The Goodheart-Willcox Company, Inc. Manufactured in the United States of America.

Library of Congress Catalog Card Number 2002029969

International Standard Book Number 1-59070-100-3
1 2 3 4 5 6 7 8 9 10   04   09 08 07 06 05 04 03

Library of Congress Cataloging-in-Publication Data
Parnell, Frances Baynor.
    Skills for personal and family living / by Frances Baynor Parnell; contributor for sewing chapters, Joyce Honeycutt Wooten.
    p. cm.
    Includes index.
    ISBN 1-59070-100-3
    1. Home economics. 2. Life skills. I. Wooten, Joyce Honeycutt. II. Title.
TX167 .P38 2004
640--dc21   2002029969

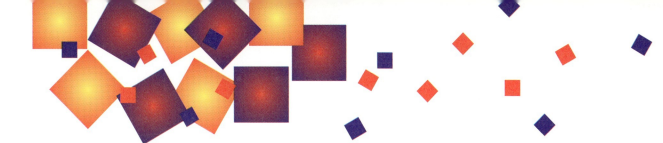

Introduction

Skills for Personal and Family Living is a comprehensive text designed to help you meet the challenges of daily life with confidence. It will help you develop a range of skills related to interpersonal and family relationships, getting and keeping a job, management, healthy living, foods and nutrition, clothing, and housing.

Each chapter in the text is divided into several topics. Topics begin with a set of objectives and a list of vocabulary terms to help prepare you for reading. At the end of each topic, a few questions are given to help you review important concepts. Further review of important information is provided at the end of each chapter.

Each chapter concludes with a feature article that focuses on a different issue of concern to teens in today's society based on a nationwide survey of teens. Reading these features will help prepare you to make important decisions in your life.

Another feature, which appears at the end of each part of the book, is called "Career Times." These features describe career opportunities in the various fields of family and consumer sciences. Descriptions of the rewards and demands of the career field, personal qualities needed for success, and preparation requirements are just a few of the types of information you will read about in the "Career Times."

About the Author

Frances Baynor Parnell was a secondary family and consumer sciences teacher for 32 years and served as department chair. She is currently co-owner of Comfort Zone Partners, an educational consulting firm. She is also president of Natural and Family Resources, Inc., which provides opportunities to be involved in cultures around the world. She has conducted research and completed a project on work and family skills to supplement family and consumer sciences education programs in North Carolina. In addition to writing this text and its supplements, Frances coauthored the book *Guarding Your Own Mental Health in a Fast-Paced World*. She has written numerous articles for professional publications. She has conducted many workshops and given frequent presentations. She has also contributed her expertise and leadership to a number of professional and civic organizations, which have earned state and national recognition in areas of environmental concerns.

During her years of teaching, Frances has received such awards as the North Carolina Home Economics Teacher of the Year, the Outstanding Educator Award (from East Carolina University, where she received her B.S. and M.S. degrees), and the Frances Hutchinson Teacher of the Year Award.

Contents in Brief

Part One — A Better You
Chapter 1 Understanding Yourself 15
Chapter 2 Understanding Relationships 47
Chapter 3 Communication Skills 79
Chapter 4 Leadership and Citizenship Skills 106
Chapter 5 The World of Work 130

Part Two — Today's Families
Chapter 6 Understanding Families 165
Chapter 7 Family Challenges 183

Part Three — Caring for Children
Chapter 8 Preparing for Children 209
Chapter 9 Meeting Children's Needs 225

Part Four — Managing in Today's World
Chapter 10 Learning to Manage 275
Chapter 11 Consumer Decisions 315

Part Five — Healthy Living
Chapter 12 Your Health and Fitness 355
Chapter 13 A Safe Home and Environment 383
Chapter 14 Healthful Eating 404

Part Six — Planning and Preparing Meals
Chapter 15 Meal Management 437
Chapter 16 Before You Cook 457
Chapter 17 Buying, Storing, and Preparing Foods ... 486
Chapter 18 Serving Food and Dining Out 513

Part Seven — Meeting Your Clothing Needs
Chapter 19 Choosing and Caring for Clothes 531
Chapter 20 Preparing to Sew 565
Chapter 21 The First Steps Before Sewing 593
Chapter 22 Sewing Techniques 607

Part Eight — A Place to Call Home
Chapter 23 Choosing a Place to Live 635
Chapter 24 Applying Design in Your Home 650
Chapter 25 Caring for Your Home 674

Contents

Part One   A Better You

Chapter 1
Understanding Yourself 15
Topic 1-1   All About You 16
- Your Heredity 16
- Your Environment 16
- Your Cultural Heritage 17
- Your Personality 18
- Your Self-Concept 20

Topic 1-2   Your Growth and Development 23
- Growing Chronologically 23
- Growing Physically 23
- Growing Emotionally 23
- Growing Intellectually 24
- Growing Socially 24
- The Developmental Tasks of Teens 25

Topic 1-3   Influences on Behavior 27
- Human Needs 27
- Personal Priorities, Goals, and Standards 29

Topic 1-4   Strategies for Personal Development 35
- What Contributes to Quality of Life? 35
- What Roadblocks Might Lie Ahead? 36
- What Tactics Can Aid Personal Development? 37

Teens Are Talking About…Socially Responsible Behavior When Hosting Parties 44

Chapter 2
Understanding Relationships 47
Topic 2-1   Developing Positive Relationships 48
- Types of Relationships 48
- Benefits of Positive Relationships 50
- Qualities Needed for Positive Relationships 50

Topic 2-2   Developing Friendships 52
- Friendships 52
- Dating 55
- What Is Love? 57
- Responsible Relationships 57

Topic 2-3   Negative Relationships 60
- What Is a Negative Relationship? 60
- Ending a Negative Relationship 60
- Negative Peer Pressure 61
- Sexual Harassment 62
- Rape 63

Topic 2-4   The Marriage Relationship 64
- Learning to Love 65
- Factors That Influence Marital Success 66
- The Engagement Period 71
- Making Marriage Work 73

Teens Are Concerned About…Intimate Relationships 75

Chapter 3
Communication Skills — 79
Topic 3-1 The Communication Process — 80
- Verbal Communication — 80
- Nonverbal Communication — 84
- Technology and Communication — 87

Topic 3-2 Communication in Relationships — 90
- The Importance of Communication in Relationships — 90
- Barriers to Open Communication — 91
- When Negative Feelings Occur — 93
- Communication in the Workplace — 94

Topic 3-3 Conflict Resolution — 95
- Types of Conflicts — 95
- Causes of Conflict — 96
- Reactions to Conflict — 97
- Constructive Methods for Handling Conflict — 98
- Violence: A Destructive Method of Handling Conflict — 101

Teens Are Talking About…Facing Peer Pressure — 103

Chapter 4
Leadership and Citizenship Skills — 106
Topic 4-1 Leaders and Followers — 107
- Being a Team Member — 107
- Opportunities for Leadership — 108
- Effective Leadership — 110

Topic 4-2 Organizations That Work! — 113
- Youth and Professional Organizations — 113
- Getting Organized — 114
- Choosing Effective Programs and Activities — 117

Topic 4-3 Your Rights and Responsibilities as a Citizen — 120
- To Be Informed — 120
- To Vote — 121
- To Obey the Law — 121
- To Pay Taxes — 123
- To Protect the Environment — 124
- To Be Involved in Your Community — 125

Teens Are Experiencing…Leadership — 127

Chapter 5
The World of Work — 130
Topic 5-1 Career Planning — 131
- Understanding Career Planning — 131
- Know Your Interests, Aptitudes, and Abilities — 132
- Learn About Careers — 133
- Your Education Choices — 135
- Other Factors Affecting Your Career Choice — 138
- Making a Career Decision — 139

Topic 5-2 Finding a Job — 142
- Finding Job Openings — 142
- Applying for a Job — 143
- The Job Interview — 146
- Creating Your Own Job — 148

Topic 5-3 Succeeding on the Job — 151
- Qualities of Successful Employees — 151
- Technology in the Workplace — 154
- Work Schedules and Income — 155
- Understanding Your Paycheck — 156

Teens Are Concerned About… Finding Jobs — 158

CAREER TIMES: Career Information— The Key to Unlocking a Successful Job Search — 162

Part Two   Today's Families

Chapter 6
Understanding Families — 165
Topic 6-1 What Is a Family? — 166
- Roles of Family Members — 166
- Functions of the Family — 166
- Single Living — 168

Contents

Topic 6-2 Family Structures Vary 170
   Family Structures 170
   Factors Influencing Families 172
Topic 6-3 Family Structures Change 176
   Family Life Cycle 176
   Divorce 177
   Remarriage 179
Teens Are Talking About…Divorce in Their Families 180

Chapter 7
Family Challenges 183
Topic 7-1 Building Functional Families 184
   Making and Keeping Families Strong 184
   Fulfilling Family Rights and Responsibilities 187
Topic 7-2 Balancing Family and Work 189
   The Relationship of Work and Family Life 189
   Managing Multiple Roles 191
   The Role of the Employer 192
Topic 7-3 Handling Family Crises 195
   What Is a Crisis? 195
   Skills for Coping with Crises 196
   Types of Crises 198
Teens Are Concerned About…Relationships with Their Parents 202
CAREER TIMES: Homing in on Family and Community Services Careers 206

Part Three Caring for Children

Chapter 8
Preparing for Children 209
Topic 8-1 Deciding About Parenting 210
   The Goal of Parenting 210
   The Challenges of Parenting 211
   Teen Parenting 212
   Deciding Whether to Have Children 214
   Family Planning 215
   Infertility 216
   Adoption 216

Topic 8-2 Pregnancy 217
   Prenatal Development 218
   Heredity 219
   Medical Care During Pregnancy 220
Teens Are Experiencing…Early Parenthood 223

Chapter 9
Meeting Children's Needs 225
Topic 9-1 Being a Responsible Caregiver 226
   Who Are the Caregivers? 226
   Characteristics of Responsible Caregivers 227
   Responsibilities of Caregivers 230
   Resources for Caregivers 231
   The Role of Society in Protecting Children's Rights 232
Topic 9-2 Meeting Children's Physical Needs 233
   Serving Food 233
   Choosing Clothes 234
   The Role of Play in Physical Development 236
   Creating a Healthy and Safe Environment 237
Topic 9-3 Meeting Children's Social and Emotional Needs 240
   Helping Children Develop Independence and Responsibility 241

Providing Guidance 242
The Role of Play in Social-Emotional Development 246
Helping Children Overcome Fears 247
Topic 9-4   Meeting Children's Intellectual Needs 248
The Role of Play in Intellectual Development 248
Enrichment Activities for Children 249
Selecting Toys 251
Topic 9-5   The First Year 253
Newborn Babies 253
Infants 254
Topic 9-6   Children from One to Five 257
Toddlers 257
Preschoolers 258
Children with Special Needs 260
Topic 9-7   Child Care Options 261
Types of Child Care 261
Selecting Quality Child Care 264

Teens Are Concerned About…
Child Abuse and Neglect 267

CAREER TIMES: The ABCs of Careers in Early Childhood Education and Services 272

Part Four   Managing in Today's World

Chapter 10
Learning to Manage 275

Topic 10-1   The Management Process 276
Identify and Prioritize Your Goals 276
Recognize Your Personal Priorities and Standards 277
Determine Your Resources 277
Form a Plan 279
Implement the Plan 280
Evaluate the Results 280
Topic 10-2   Managing Your Time 281
Why Plan Your Time? 281
Steps in Time Management 282
Managing Time Wisely 284
Energy and Task Management 285
Topic 10-3   Managing Your Money 286
The Basics of Budgeting 286
Reducing Flexible Expenses 289
Budgeting with a Computer 290
Topic 10-4   Using Financial Services 291
Choosing a Financial Institution 292
Using a Checking Account 294
Topic 10-5   Saving for the Future 299
Why Save? 299
Factors in Deciding How to Save 300
Savings Accounts 301
Decisions About Securities 301
Planning an Estate 303
Topic 10-6   Meeting Insurance Needs 304
Insurance Basics 304
Life Insurance 305
Health Insurance 306
Automobile Insurance 308
Housing-Related Insurance 310

Teens Are Talking About…Money Management 312

Chapter 11
Consumer Decisions 315

Topic 11-1   Making Shopping Decisions 316
Deciding Where to Shop 316
Deciding When to Buy 319
Deciding What to Buy 320
Topic 11-2   The Impact of Technology on Consumers 323

Technology Options Available	323
Managing Technology	326

Topic 11-3 The Role of Advertising 330

How Advertising Affects Consumer Spending	331
Types of Advertising	331
Evaluating Advertisements	332
Consumer Protection Against Deceptive Advertising	333

Topic 11-4 Using Consumer Credit 334

What Is Credit?	334
Types of Credit	335
Applying for Credit	336
Why Credit Costs	338
Shopping for Credit	338
Credit Contracts	339
Using Credit Wisely	340

Topic 11-5 Consumers and the Law 342

Consumer Protection Laws	342
Consumer Rights and Responsibilities	343

Teens Are Experiencing…The Impact of Advertising 349

CAREER TIMES: Cashing in on Consumer Services Careers 352

Part Five Healthy Living

Chapter 12
Your Health and Fitness 355

Topic 12-1 Your Physical Fitness 356

The Importance of Good Health	356
Being Physically Active	357
The Importance of Leisure Activities	358
The Importance of Sleep	358

Topic 12-2 Good Grooming 360

Caring for Your Skin	360
Caring for Your Teeth	362
Caring for Your Hair	363
Caring for Your Hands and Feet	364

Topic 12-3 Your Mental Health 365

Maintaining a Healthy Mental State	365
Stress and Your Health	366
Depression	367
When People Need Help	370

Topic 12-4 Health Risks 371

Tobacco	371
Alcohol	372
Other Drugs	373
Sexually Transmitted Diseases	373
Decisions That Affect Your Health	374

Topic 12-5 When You Need Medical Services 375

Selecting a Physician	375
Emergency Medical Services	377

Teens Are Concerned About…Sexually Transmitted Diseases 379

Chapter 13
A Safe Home and Environment 383

Topic 13-1 Personal Safety and Security 384

Preventing Accidents in the Home	384
Preventing Accidents on the Road	387
Providing for Security	389
Emergency Procedures	392

Topic 13-2 A Healthful Environment 394

A Healthful Environment	394
Factors Affecting the Environment	394
Pollution	395
How You Can Help	399

Teens Are Experiencing…Security Problems 402

Chapter 14
Healthful Eating — 404

Topic 14-1   Nutrients at Work for You — 405
- Carbohydrates — 405
- Proteins — 406
- Fats — 407
- Minerals — 407
- Vitamins — 409
- Water — 412
- Recommended Nutrient Intakes — 414

Topic 14-2   Making Daily Food Choices — 415
- The Food Guide Pyramid — 415
- The Dietary Guidelines for Americans — 418

Topic 14-3   Nutritional Needs Change — 420
- Needs of Pregnant Women and Infants — 421
- Needs of Children and Teens — 422
- Needs of Adults — 424

Topic 14-4   Balancing Calories and Energy Needs — 425
- Meeting Energy Needs — 425
- Controlling Your Weight — 426
- Eating Disorders — 429

Teens Are Concerned About…Healthful Eating and Weight Management — 430

CAREER TIMES: Taking a Bite out of Food, Science, Dietetics, and Nutrition Careers — 434

Part Six   Planning and Preparing Meals

Chapter 15
Meal Management — 437

Topic 15-1   Planning Meals — 438
- Planning for Nutrition — 438
- Variety in Meals — 441
- When You Are the Meal Manager — 442

Topic 15-2   Shopping for Food — 445
- Preparing a Shopping List — 445
- Deciding Where to Shop — 445
- Deciding How Much Food to Buy — 446
- Recognizing Quality in Foods — 447

Topic 15-3   Buying Information — 448
- Unit Pricing — 448
- Food Labeling — 449
- Other Sources of Information — 452

Topic 15-4   Storing Foods — 452
- Properly Storing Foods — 452
- Technology in Food Packaging — 453

Teens Are Experiencing…Shopping for Food — 455

Chapter 16
Before You Cook — 457

Topic 16-1   Know Your Equipment — 458
- Major Appliances — 458
- Portable Appliances — 462
- Kitchen Utensils — 463

Topic 16-2   Safety and Sanitation — 467
- Make It Safe — 467
- Keep It Sanitary — 468

Topic 16-3   Using a Recipe — 472
- Understanding How to Use Recipes — 472
- Learning Cooking Methods — 476

Topic 16-4   Cooking Smart — 479
- At Home — 480
- At School — 481

Teens Are Experiencing…Meal Management Challenges — 483

Chapter 17
Buying, Storing, and Preparing Foods — 486

Topic 17-1 Meat, Poultry, Fish, and Alternates — 487
- Buying Meat, Poultry, Fish, and Alternates — 487
- Storing Meat, Poultry, Fish, and Alternates — 491
- Preparing Meat, Poultry, Fish, and Alternates — 492

Topic 17-2 Fruits and Vegetables — 495
- Buying Fruits and Vegetables — 495
- Storing Fruits and Vegetables — 496
- Preparing Fruits and Vegetables — 498

Topic 17-3 Cereal Products — 500
- Buying Cereal Products — 501
- Storing Cereal Products — 502
- Preparing Cereal Products — 503
- Cakes and Cookies — 505

Topic 17-4 Milk and Milk Products — 507
- Buying Dairy Products — 508
- Storing Dairy Products — 509
- Preparing Dairy Products — 510

Teens Are Concerned About...The Taste of Foods — 511

Chapter 18
Serving Food and Dining Out — 513

Topic 18-1 Serving Food — 514
- Family Mealtime — 514
- Types of Meal Service — 515
- Tableware — 516
- Table Accessories — 516
- Setting the Table — 517

Topic 18-2 Making Dining Enjoyable — 519
- Hosting a Meal — 519
- Manners When Dining — 519

Topic 18-3 Dining Out — 521
- Types of Restaurants — 521
- Ordering from a Restaurant Menu — 523
- Making Healthful Food Choices — 523
- Restaurant Etiquette — 524
- Paying the Check — 525

Teens Are Experiencing...Work in Fast-Food Restaurants — 526

CAREER TIMES: Culinary Arts and Hospitality Careers Take the Cake — 528

Part Seven Meeting Your Clothing Needs

Chapter 19
Choosing and Caring for Clothes — 531

Topic 19-1 Choosing Clothes That Meet Your Needs — 532
- Factors That Influence Clothing Decisions — 532
- Choosing Clothes for Specific Occasions — 535

Topic 19-2 Choosing Clothes That Look Good on You — 536
- Color — 537
- The Other Design Elements — 540
- Consider the Principles of Design — 542

Topic 19-3 Planning Your Wardrobe — 543
- Factors to Consider in Wardrobe Planning — 543
- Extending Your Wardrobe — 544

Topic 19-4 Shopping for Clothes — 546
- Shopping Guidelines — 546
- Understanding Fashion Terms — 547
- Judging Quality — 548

Reading Labels and Hangtags	549
Consider the Cost	550
Topic 19-5 Caring for Clothes	**551**
Daily Clothing Care	551
Laundering Steps	552
Drying Clothes	557
Ironing and Pressing	558
Dry Cleaning	558
Energy Conservation in Clothing Care	559
Packing and Storing Clothes	560

Teens Are Talking About...The Status of Clothes — 562

Chapter 20
Preparing to Sew — 565

Topic 20-1 Understanding Fabrics	**566**
Fibers	566
Yarns	571
Fabric Construction	571
Fabric Finishes	574
Dyeing Fabrics	574
Printing Fabrics	575
Topic 20-2 Selecting Patterns	**576**
Take Your Measurements	576
Determine Your Figure Type and Size	577
Deciding on a Pattern	577
The Pattern Envelope	579
Topic 20-3 Selecting Fabric and Notions	**580**
Choosing a Fabric	580
How Much Fabric Is Needed?	582
Choosing Notions	582
Topic 20-4 Sewing Equipment	**583**
Small Equipment	583
The Sewing Machine	586
The Serger	587
Safety with Sewing Tools	588

Teens Are Concerned About...The Fashion Appeal of Sewing Patterns — 590

Chapter 21
The First Steps Before Sewing — 593

Topic 21-1 Begin with the Pattern	**594**
The Pattern Guide Sheet	594
Topic 21-2 Prepare the Fabric	**598**
Preshrinking and Pressing	598
Check the Grain	598
Topic 21-3 Pattern Layout, Cutting, and Marking	**600**
The Pattern Layout	600
Pinning	602
Cutting the Fabric	602
Marking the Fabric	603

Teens Are Concerned About...The Value of Sewing Skills — 605

Chapter 22
Sewing Techniques — 607

Topic 22-1 Stitching Techniques, Darts, and Seams	**608**
Stitching Techniques	608
Darts, Tucks, Pleats, and Gathers	609
Seams	611
Topic 22-2 Supporting Fabrics	**613**
Interfacing	613
Facings	614
Topic 22-3 Construction Techniques	**616**
Waist Treatments	616
Sleeves	617
Pockets	618
Zippers	618
Fasteners	619
Hems	620
Sewing Knit Fabrics	622
Topic 22-4 Extending the Life of Clothes	**624**
Repairing Clothes	624
Altering Clothes	625
Restyling Clothes	625
Recycling Clothes	626

Teens Are Concerned About...Clothing Styles — 628

CAREER TIMES: Sewing Up Careers in Textiles and Apparel Design — 632

Part Eight A Place to Call Home

Chapter 23
Choosing a Place to Live — 635

Topic 23-1 Meeting Your Housing Needs	**636**
Physical Needs	636
Social Needs	636
Psychological Needs	636

Contents

Topic 23-2 Housing Alternatives	**638**
Single-Family Houses	638
Multifamily Dwellings	639
Trends in Housing	640
Topic 23-3 Renting or Buying Housing	**641**
Choosing Housing	641
Renting Housing	642
Buying Housing	645
Teens Are Talking About…Moving Away from Home	*647*

Chapter 24
Applying Design in Your Home — 650

Topic 24-1 The Elements and Principles of Design	**651**
The Elements of Design	651
The Principles of Design	655
The Goals of Design	658
Topic 24-2 Decorating Your Home	**659**
Floor Coverings	659
Wall Treatments	660
Windows and Window Treatments	661
Lighting	661
Topic 24-3 Furnishing Your Home	**664**
Choosing Furniture	664
Organizing Living Space	667
Using Accessories	669
Teens Are Concerned About…Decorating on a Budget	*670*

Chapter 25
Caring for Your Home — 674

Topic 25-1 Keep It Clean!	**675**
Why Clean?	675
Cleaning Products and Equipment	676
Making a Cleaning Schedule	679
Plan Ahead for Easy Cleaning	681
Topic 25-2 Maintaining the Home	**683**
Household Repairs	683
Plumbing Repairs	685
Using Carpentry Tools	688
Electrical Problems	689
Topic 25-3 Conserving Energy in the Home	**692**
Energy Sources	692
Outlook for the Future	694
You Can Help Conserve Energy	694
Teens Are Talking About…Conserving Energy and Natural Resources	*700*
CAREER TIMES: Opening the Door to Careers in Housing, Interiors, and Furnishings	702
Appendix	704
Acknowledgments	709
Photo Credits	710
Glossary	712
Index	729

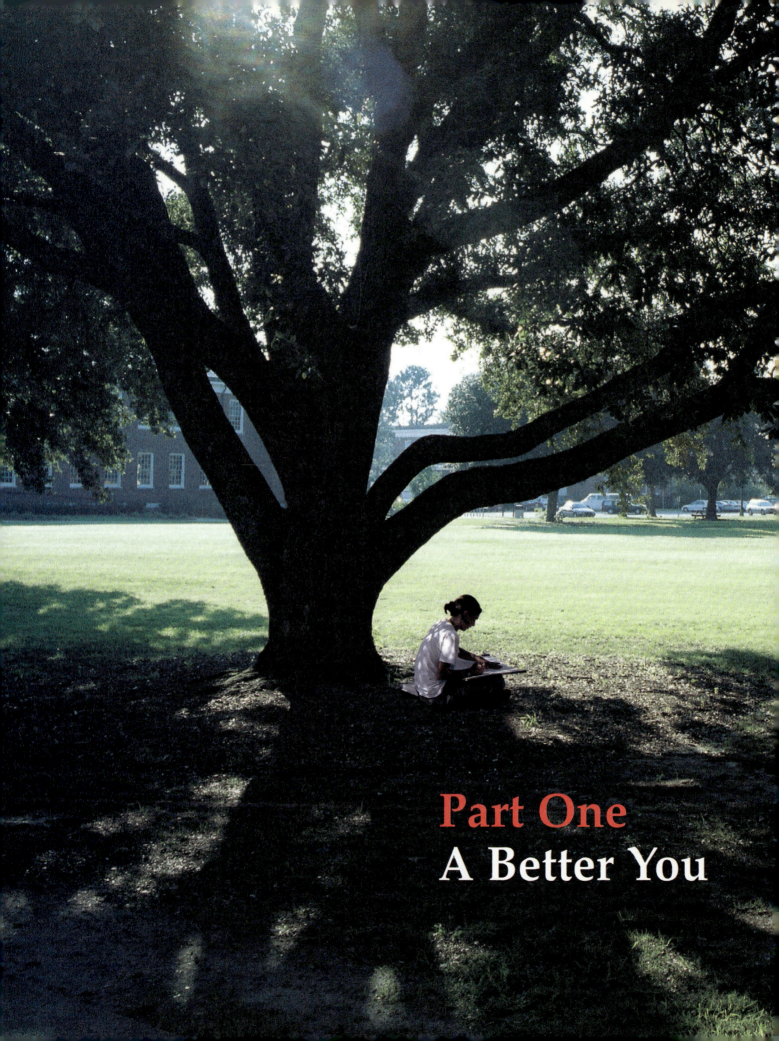

Part One
A Better You

Chapter 1
Understanding Yourself

Careers

These careers relate to the topics in this chapter:

- summer camp counselor
- teacher's aide
- caseworker assistant
- family and consumer sciences teacher

As you study the chapter, see if you can think of others.

Topics

1-1 All About You
1-2 Your Growth and Development
1-3 Influences on Behavior
1-4 Strategies for Personal Development

Introductory Activities

1. If this is the start of a school year or semester, ask students to discuss any goals they may have for the coming year/semester. Ask students to define *goals*. Mention they will be learning more about goal setting in this chapter.
2. Ask students how they make important decisions—do they make them quickly or think them through? What factors do they consider? Have they ever made decisions they regretted?

Topic 1-1
All About You

I. Your Heredity
   A. Inherited Traits
II. Your Environment
III. Your Cultural Heritage
   A. Race and Ethnic Groups in the United States
IV. Your Personality
   A. Character Development
      1. Character Traits
V. Your Self-Concept
   A. Positive and Negative Self-Concept
   B. Improving Your Self-Concept
      1. Be Realistic About Your Expectations of Yourself
      2. Develop Your Talents and Abilities
      3. Look for Positive Relationships with Others
      4. Spend Time Doing Activities You Enjoy
      5. Develop a Sense of Humor
   C. Your Self-Esteem

Topic 1-2
Your Growth and Development

I. Growing Chronologically
II. Growing Physically
   A. Physical Changes
III. Growing Emotionally
   A. Emotional Changes
IV. Growing Intellectually
V. Growing Socially
   A. Social Changes
VI. The Developmental Tasks of Teens
      1. Accept Physique and Use the Body Effectively
      2. Establish Emotional Independence from Parents and Other Adults
      3. Achieve New and More Mature Relations with Age-Mates
      4. Adopt Socially Approved Masculine or Feminine Adult Roles
      5. Select and Prepare for an Occupation
      6. Develop a Personal Attitude Toward Marriage and Family Living
      7. Adopt Personal Behavior Standards
      8. Accept and Adopt Socially Responsible Behavior

Topic 1-3
Influences on Behavior

I. Human Needs
   A. Physical Needs
   B. Safety and Security Needs
   C. Love and Acceptance Needs
   D. Esteem Needs
   E. Self-Actualization
   F. Comparing Needs and Wants
      1. The Relationship of Needs and Wants
II. Personal Priorities, Goals, and Standards
   A. Personal Priorities
      1. Factors Affecting Your Personal Priorities
      2. Personal Priority Conflicts
      3. Personal Priority Judgments
   B. Goals
      1. Short-Term and Long-Term Goals
      2. Visionary Goals
      3. Steps in Setting and Achieving Goals
      4. Meeting Your Goals
   C. Standards
      1. Standards, Personal Priorities, and Goals

Topic 1-4
Strategies for Personal Development

I. What Contributes to Quality of Life?
II. What Roadblocks Might Lie Ahead?
III. What Tactics Can Aid Personal Development?
   A. Learn Management Skills
   B. Learn to Solve Problems and Make Decisions
      1. Making Routine Decisions
      2. Steps in Decision Making
   C. Avoid High-Risk Behavior
   D. Influences on Your Behavior and Decisions
   E. Build Supportive Relationships

Topic 1-1
All About You

Objectives
After studying this topic, you will be able to
- identify the five factors that help make you a unique person.
- describe how personality develops.
- list ways to improve self-concept.
- relate self-esteem to a positive self-concept.

Topic Terms
heredity
environment
cultural heritage
ethnic group
personality
character
empathy
self-concept
self-esteem

1-1 Heredity causes both similarities and differences in people. How does your heredity influence you?

You are a unique person. From the moment you were conceived, you have been unique. No other person is exactly like you—you look, think, and act differently from anyone else. This makes you quite special. Like you, all other people are unique. They, too, are special in that they look, think, and act differently from everyone else.

Part of learning about yourself is understanding the different factors that make you a unique person. These include your heredity, environment, cultural heritage, personality, and self-concept.

Your Heredity

All people are influenced by their heredity. **Heredity** is the sum of all traits passed on through genes from parents to children. Heredity causes people to be alike in many ways. Almost everyone is born with two arms, two legs, two eyes, two ears, a nose, and a mouth. Heredity also causes people to be different. Some are tall; others are short. Some have black hair; others have blond hair. Some have great intellectual potential; others have limited intellectual potential. See 1-1.

Inherited Traits

To begin understanding yourself, you need to know that you were born with certain *inherited traits*. Your skin, hair, and eye color are inherited traits, as are your facial features, body build, and height. Mental and physical abilities are also inherited. You have little, if any, control over your inherited traits. However, these traits greatly influence the way you look, think, and act.

Knowing your hereditary background can help you in other ways. You may be able to adapt your lifestyle to help you emphasize some traits and play down others. For instance, you can study harder if you want to develop your mental abilities. If you inherited dry hair, you can select hair care products that will make your hair more manageable.

Your Environment

Your inherited traits are influenced by your environment. Your **environment** is made up of everything that surrounds you. As an infant, you had little control over your environment. As you are growing older, you are gaining more control. In the future, you will probably be able to choose the environment in which you will live.

 Across the Curriculum

Biology. Discuss the science of genetics and inherited traits in depth.

Resource:
Understanding Others While Celebrating Differences, reproducible master, TR

Vocabulary:
Compare *heredity* and *environment*.

Discuss:
In what ways do you look like your parents?

Resource:
Inherited Traits, Activity A, SAG

Resource:
The Science of Heredity, reproducible master, TR

You have two different types of environments: psychological and physical. Both types strongly influence your personal development.

Your *psychological environment* is composed of attitudes expressed by people around you. It includes the feelings and beliefs of your family members, teachers, classmates, and friends. These people influence the attitudes you have. You partially control your psychological environment through your choice of friends.

Your *physical environment* is composed of objects around you. One main factor in your physical environment is the place where you live, 1-2. If you were raised on a farm, you had different childhood experiences from someone who was raised in a city. You had little control of your physical environment as a young child. As you grow older, you have more options. You can choose to live in a rural area, a small town, a suburb, or a large city.

Your environments—both psychological and physical—influence the way you look, think, and act. As you learn more about your environments, you can understand yourself better.

1-2 Everyone is influenced by environment. Your physical environment may include a neighborhood park.

Your Cultural Heritage

Most people are strongly influenced by their cultural heritage. It helps to make everyone unique. Part of learning about yourself is understanding how your own cultural heritage makes you unique. Understanding cultural differences between you and others is equally important.

Your **cultural heritage** is made up of learned behaviors, beliefs, and languages that are passed from generation to generation. Your family helps you learn about the culture of your society. Their guidelines and beliefs become part of your heritage. The foods you eat, the holidays you celebrate, and the traditions you observe are part of your culture. Through all these cultural experiences, you learn appropriate behavior for your culture.

Race and Ethnic Groups in the United States

The cultural heritage of people in the United States has been shaped by Native Americans and immigrants who have settled in this country. As a result, all Americans are part of an ethnic group. An **ethnic group** is a group of people who share common racial and/or cultural characteristics such as national origin, language, religion, and traditions. These characteristics make them a distinct part of the society.

Diverse customs, beliefs, languages, and races have evolved as people from many lands have immigrated to the United States. Today, many different ethnic groups exist in this country. Some of the major groups include the following:

- *Native Americans*—These people are descended from the original North Americans.
- *European Americans*—These people immigrated from European countries including Spain, England, Germany, France, and Holland.
- *Asian Americans*—These people immigrated from China, Japan, Korea, the Philippine Islands, and Indonesia.

Note:
Developmental psychologists have long debated whether heredity or environment has a greater influence in shaping people's lives. Identical twins are often involved in studies on this issue because they have the same set of inherited traits.

Reflect:
What foods and holiday traditions enjoyed by your family reflect your cultural heritage?

Enrich:
Research the immigration history of one of the ethnic groups listed. When did people from the nations mentioned begin coming to the United States? In what region(s) did they primarily settle?

Family Enrichment Activity
Have students ask their parents about their cultural heritage. Have them write a paper describing their cultural heritage in the following categories: food, holidays, traditions and customs, religion.

> **Enrich:**
> Hold a debate on the following topic: Can the United States still be considered a "melting pot" of cultures?

> **Activity:**
> Divide a sheet of paper into two columns. Label one column *positive* and the other *negative*. Brainstorm a list of personality traits and place them in the appropriate columns.

- *African Americans*—These people are descendants of black racial groups of Africa.
- *Hispanics*—These people immigrated from Mexico, Puerto Rico, Cuba, Central and South America, and other Spanish cultures.

Ethnic groups are important as they help to maintain a culturally healthy society. This is because a blending of all these groups' cultures makes American culture truly unique. Understanding this may help you appreciate your own cultural heritage. It also may help you appreciate others as they model their cultural heritages, 1-3.

Your Personality

Your personality results from a special blending of your heredity, environment, and cultural heritage, 1-4. **Personality** is the total of all the behavioral qualities and traits that make up an individual. It includes the way you feel, the way you think, the way you speak, the way you dress, and the way you relate to others. Your personality is a combination of all the traits that make you unique. These traits develop over a period of time.

Your personality is made up of many different traits. *Traits* are qualities that make you different from other people. Some of these traits are considered more desirable than others. Are you cheerful, cooperative, or easy-going? These are examples of desirable personality traits.

1-4 The way you interact with your friends is a part of your personality that makes you unique.

1-3 Cultural diversity among people helps to maintain a healthy society.

>
> **Citizenship and Service**
> This activity is designed to encourage appreciation of the cultural heritage of the people of the United States. Have each student interview a person of an ethnic group different from the one(s) to which the student belongs. Ask the class to prepare a list of questions they might ask during their interviews. Then ask students to share information they learned about the ethnic groups. How does a better understanding of different cultures help them be better citizens?

On the other hand, being lazy, moody, or grumpy are less desirable traits. How would you describe yourself?

Character Development

Some parts of your personality are described as *character traits*. **Character** refers to inner traits, such as conscience, moral strength, and social attitudes. It is the inner you—that force that guides your conduct and behavior toward acceptable standards of right and wrong.

Character development, like other personality traits, begins in childhood. Children are taught that certain behaviors are acceptable while others are not acceptable, 1-5. For example, young children may be told not to hit others. They learn to conform because an inner control tells them not to do so. As character continues to grow, children develop acceptable standards of behavior that they use voluntarily. They can then face new situations and know right from wrong. This happens even when no one is there to guide their behavior.

Character Traits

Common character traits include caring, fairness, respect, trustworthiness, responsibility, and citizenship. *Caring* is a trait that describes people who are kind to others. Caring people are friendly to everyone, not just their close friends. They are helpful and respond quickly to the needs of others. Caring people have empathy. **Empathy** means they understand how others feel even when their own personal feelings may differ. They also show sympathy. They know to give a caring hug when others are hurting.

Fairness is the ability to be honest and impartial—to act in an objective, unbiased way. Those who are fair show no prejudice toward others' opinions, ideas, or ways of doing things. All people are treated impartially.

Respect means to hold in high regard. Every individual deserves the respect of others and should be treated with courtesy. You may not agree with someone on a particular issue, but you can respect his or her right to see the issue differently. You still remain friends. You admire others for standing up for what they believe, and you respect them for it. Respect for personal property means caring for it. If it is borrowed, it is returned in the condition it was received. Respect for authority means obeying the rules and laws established for the well-being of all. Acting with consideration and even admiration toward people, laws, and property describes a respectful person.

Trustworthiness means you can be relied upon. For instance, if a friend tells you a secret, you do not tell anyone else. Your friend trusts you. Trustworthy people can be relied upon to keep their promises. Trustworthiness is important in building strong relationships. Employees are expected to be trustworthy. They can be trusted to do their jobs to the best of their abilities.

Responsibility means being accountable for your actions and obligations. Whether you like your responsibilities or not, you

Example:
Children may be taught that sharing is acceptable while lying and stealing are not acceptable.

Resource:
Character Traits, Activity B, SAG

1-5 As children interact with parents and other adults, they develop acceptable standards of behavior.

Putting Technology to Use
Have students use the Internet to research academic articles on character development.

Resource:
A Look at Your Positives, Activity C, SAG

Discuss:
What kinds of situations do you think might cause a teen to develop a negative self-concept?

are accountable for them. That means you can be counted upon to complete your assigned tasks. There are many duties or obligations that you are responsible for at home, at school, and at work. These may include taking care of your belongings and performing work assigned to you. Responsibility for your actions means you accept the consequences for what you do, good or bad. Responsibility and trustworthiness are traits that work together. If you take care of your responsibilities, you are a trustworthy person.

Citizenship (as a character trait) refers to the quality of a person's response to membership in a community. Citizenship is usually conferred upon you at birth. You become a citizen of the country and state in which you are born. You are also a citizen of the community in which you live. Loyalty to country and community is expected of its citizens. When you complain yet fail to do your part, you show disloyalty. If services or facilities are not as you would like, you have a duty to make them better. You can work to make needed changes. This is the mark of good citizenship at any level of government.

Your Self-Concept

At an early age you began developing your own self-concept. Your **self-concept** is your view of yourself. This view was largely influenced by people around you and the way you interpreted their behaviors toward you.

Positive and Negative Self-Concept

When people showed approval of you and the things you did, you received a positive message such as, "Hey, I'm all right. People like what I do." Positive feelings like these helped you develop a *positive self-concept*, 1-6.

If you have a positive self-concept, you will see yourself as a lovable and worthwhile person. You will expect most people to accept you. Chances are they will receive you and want you for a friend.

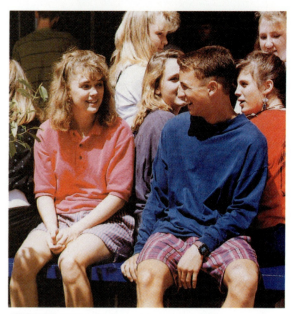

1-6 Friends who accept you for who you are help you develop a positive self-concept.

When people showed disapproval, you received a negative warning. You may have felt a sense of personal rejection. You may have thought, "Hey, I don't think they like me, because they don't seem to like what I do." Many messages such as these would tend to promote a *negative self-concept*. Every person receives some positive and some negative messages. However, it lies within the individual to measure his or her own self-worth.

If you have a negative self-concept, you will feel uncertain. You may not see yourself as lovable or worthwhile. You will hesitate to reach out to others in fear of possible rejection. You may feel a little uncomfortable about yourself. You may even make others feel uncomfortable when they are with you.

Improving Your Self-Concept

Because your self-concept continues to be formed throughout your life, having a positive self-concept is important. Liking yourself and feeling good about yourself allows your personality to grow and develop even more.

If you would like to feel better about yourself, you can learn to improve your

Across the Curriculum

Social studies. Explain how people born in other countries can become naturalized citizens of the U.S. Have students discuss how the character trait of citizenship is affected by this process.

self-concept. Doing so can help you deal with negative feelings and make desired changes. As you learn more about yourself and learn to accept yourself, you will gain more self-confidence. You will have the confidence to try new activities and accept any challenges you face. As a result, your self-concept will become more positive. There are several steps you can take to start improving your image of yourself.

Be Realistic About Your Expectations of Yourself

This is one way to improve your self-concept. Remember that no one is perfect. Know that you will do some things well. Know, also, that you may not do some things as well as other people. In other words, look for balance in your life. Know that some times in your life will be great, while other times will be fair. Feel good about yourself whenever you do something, whether or not you are the best at doing it.

Don't be afraid of failure. Failure can be beneficial if it forces you take a fresh look at yourself. Think about what went wrong. Find a way to make a comeback. With that comeback you experience a sense of freedom that allows you to take new risks. You may find untapped inner resources as you redirect your plans for your life.

Develop Your Talents and Abilities

Another way to improve your self-concept is to work to develop your talents and abilities, 1-7. If you are a member of Family, Career, and Community Leaders of America, take on a special project that will give you an opportunity to develop a new skill. Who knows—you might be the top salesperson in the fund-raiser. Maybe you will help others fight hunger by collecting double the number of canned products for the local food bank.

Look for Positive Relationships with Others

All people need positive reinforcement to develop a healthy self-concept. While people determine their own self-worth, they weigh the attitudes expressed toward them by others. Living in a negative psychological environment and maintaining a positive outlook is difficult. Therefore, surrounding yourself with some positive people who support you is important.

1-7 You can improve your self-esteem by getting involved in an activity you do well. If you know you are a good runner, go out for track and become even better.

Reflect: What are some talents and abilities you could develop to help improve your self-concept?

Reflect: Who are some of the people that support you emotionally and help you develop a positive self-concept?

Spend Time Doing Activities You Enjoy

All people need to spend time alone to think about their lives, their hopes, and their dreams. Learn to enjoy being alone and doing activities that only you might enjoy. Maybe you like reading poetry or playing the piano. These activities will help you relax and give you pleasure. You may enjoy running. Many people find exercise a way to help them relieve tension and see things more clearly.

 Putting Technology to Use
Ask students to give a presentation on activities they enjoy. Students should use presentation software and include digital pictures or scans to illustrate their topics.

Discuss:
How would you describe someone with a good sense of humor?

Reflect:
How does your self-esteem affect your relationships with your peers?

Develop a Sense of Humor

Most importantly, develop a sense of humor. Learn to laugh at yourself. Don't become embarrassed. A sense of humor adds a soft touch to otherwise hurtful situations. It can take the sting out of cutting remarks and sarcasm. It can help you be comfortable in touchy situations. Finally, it can help others feel comfortable with you.

Your Self-Esteem

Self-esteem is the sense of worth you attach to yourself—it's a word used to describe a positive self-concept. Taking pride in yourself and your accomplishments shows self-esteem.

Your self-esteem is an important part of you. It is a personal statement you make to yourself that describes your self-worth. You are a worthy person. If you feel you are a worthwhile person, it will show in your relationships with others. If you accept yourself you are more likely to accept others. Those who lack self-esteem think little of themselves. Therefore they don't think others will like them. Sometimes in an attempt to make friends, they give in to negative peer pressure. They may get involved in behaviors that are not in their best interest.

An important fringe benefit of self-esteem is that you are likely to demonstrate more responsible behavior. You have the strength to make your own decisions. Knowing that you are not dependent upon others for your sense of worth, you can use your best judgment. You are less likely to be influenced by negative peer pressure. Your demonstration of responsible behavior makes you a better person, and it also makes you a positive example for others, 1-8.

Having self-esteem does not mean that everything you do will be successful. However, it does help you to maintain a realistic view of your successes and failures. You will be more likely to try harder to reach your goals and fulfill your responsibilities if you have self-esteem.

1-8 People with strong self-esteem often choose careers where they can help others.

Check It Out!
1. Explain how heredity causes people to be alike and to be different.
2. Your _____ environment is composed of attitudes expressed by people around you. Your _____ environment is composed of objects around you.
3. How does your cultural heritage help to make you unique?
4. What three factors blend together to form a person's personality?
5. Describe a person with a positive self-concept.
6. Explain the relationship between self-esteem and self-concept.

Check It Out! (Answers)
1. People are born with similar physical characteristics—eyes, nose, mouth, two arms, two legs—that make them alike. People are born with a combination of physical and mental hereditary characteristics, such as height, hair color, eye color, skin color, and intellectual potential that make them different from others.
2. psychological, physical
3. Through your family, you learn about the culture of your society. You also learn about family guidelines and beliefs; this becomes part of your heritage. The combination of these experiences makes you unique.
4. your heredity, environment, and cultural heritage
5. (Student response.)
6. The sense of worth you attach to yourself—pride in yourself and your accomplishments—describes a positive self-concept.

Topic 1-2
Your Growth and Development

Objectives
After studying this topic, you will be able to
- identify different types of growth.
- list developmental tasks of teens.

Topic Terms
maturity
chronological growth
physical growth
puberty
adolescence
hormones
emotional growth
intellectual growth
social growth
peers
developmental tasks

If growth and development can be summarized in one word during the teen years, that word would be *change*. The change that occurs between childhood and adulthood is frequently described as **maturity.** Changes that occur will be chronological, physical, emotional, intellectual, and social. As you mature, your physical, personal, and behavioral characteristics will become more adult.

Growing Chronologically

Chronological growth refers to a person's age. This is the only type of growth that takes place at the same rate for all people. Each birthday automatically adds another year to your age. Chronological maturity is often used for legal purposes. People have to prove their age to obtain a driver's license, vote in government elections, or enlist for military service.

Growing Physically

Physical growth refers to the changes in your body stature. Your physical growth is influenced by heredity and health habits. The way you choose to eat, exercise, and care for your body will influence your physical development.

An important stage of physical growth is called **puberty.** In this stage of development, an individual becomes capable of sexual reproduction. This stage lasts two to three years and is characterized by rapid growth—the fastest rate of growth since infancy. Puberty ends when sexual reproduction becomes possible, but growth continues. Puberty generally begins between the ages of nine and eleven for girls. It begins between the ages of eleven and thirteen for boys.

Adolescence is a term used to describe that period from puberty until growth ceases and adulthood is reached. This period usually lasts until young women are 15 to 17 years of age. Adolescence usually lasts until young men are 17 to 20 years of age.

Physical Changes

Physical changes that take place during adolescence are caused, in part, by hormones. **Hormones** are chemical substances in the body that trigger certain types of physical growth. The most noticeable changes are a sudden growth spurt and the development of adult characteristics. Visible signs of sexual development appear. Members of both sexes experience an increase in their muscle tissue that results in a weight gain. Skeletal development causes increased height and wider shoulders among males.

Other physical changes among males include the enlargement of the genitals, the appearance of pubic hair, and a deepening of the voice. Facial and underarm hair appear later.

Females increase in height. They also have an increase in fat, or *adipose tissue*. Breasts enlarge, and pubic and underarm hair appears. The menstrual cycle begins shortly after these physical changes occur.

Growing Emotionally

Emotional growth refers to development in the range of feelings and the ability to express these feelings. The hormones that

---

Vocabulary:
From this vocabulary list of new terms, ask students if they can identify the types of growth that will be discussed. Can they think of examples of each type of growth?

Vocabulary:
Ask students to explain the relationship between the terms *puberty* and *adolescence*. (Answer: Puberty marks the beginning of adolescence.)

Reflect:
Think of some of the ways you have grown physically in the past two years.

Across the Curriculum
Health. Discuss the physical changes that occur during adolescence.

Discuss:
Do you agree that *sensitive* is a good word to describe teens' emotions?

Discuss:
What are some environmental factors that stimulate your thinking?

stimulate changes in physical development during puberty and adolescence stimulate changes in the emotional state as well.

Emotional Changes

It is common during adolescence to have significant emotional swings. Perhaps you will feel moody—up one minute, but down the next. You may find yourself desperately wanting independence from your family. A little later, however, you long for the security that your family offers. There are times you will want to express your own identity. You may want trendy clothes or a new haircut. At other times you will want to be just like everyone else, 1-9. You may feel you are on an emotional roller coaster.

Sensitive is a key word to describe teens' emotions. Adolescents crave acceptance and are sensitive to criticism. They are sensitive about their personal appearance and want to know they are attractive to others. Sometimes they are critical of themselves. Their self-concept may be weak at times, like the young man who was feeling down when he said, "I'm a real loser." A caring friend pointed out some of the young man's strengths. After reflecting on this, the young man replied, "Yes, I do some things really well, but some I don't do well at all. Actually, I must be pretty balanced."

Growing Intellectually

Intellectual growth means developing the ability to reason and form complex thought patterns. It is influenced by your heredity, environment, and desire to learn. When your environment offers learning experiences, you are stimulated to think and look for new solutions to problems.

During adolescence, you experience a sudden increase in your ability to think about your world. When you were younger, you needed to see concrete examples for any problem to be solved. Now you can understand more abstract concepts.

If you have a desire to learn, intellectual growth will occur throughout your life. Many elderly people are still enthusiastic about learning new things. If your environment lacks stimulation, or if you lack the desire to learn, your intellectual growth will be impaired.

Growing Socially

Social growth means developing the ability to get along with other people. You begin this process in early childhood as you learn to take turns and share. Through years of playing and working together, people learn to get along with others. They also learn that different people like different activities, 1-10.

Social Changes

Growing socially is sometimes complex in the teen years. As you mature in other ways, your relationships with adults change. You no longer wish to be treated as a child by parents, teachers, and other adults. You want more control over your social situations; you want to spend more time with your peers. **Peers** are other people who are your age.

1-9 The desire to be like your peers but still have your own identity is a natural part of growing up.

Across the Curriculum
Psychology. Discuss how environment influences intellectual growth.

1-10 How well do you get along with others? A socially mature person has good times with others and enjoys life.

With added control comes added responsibilities. You must learn to interact with adults on a more mature level while showing respect for their wisdom and authority. You must learn to interact with your peers in ways that foster your positive development and theirs.

The Developmental Tasks of Teens

During your teenage years, you will be challenged to meet your personal needs and handle new expectations placed on you by society. Robert Havighurst, an educator and behavioral scientist, has described what he calls **developmental tasks**. These are tasks or skills society has come to expect of people at various ages. Success in these tasks leads to contentment and success in the developmental tasks that will come later in life. Some of Havighurst's developmental tasks for the teen years are described below.

Accept Physique and Use the Body Effectively

You face many physical changes during adolescence. Understanding these changes and becoming comfortable with their results is an important developmental task. In addition, managing your health becomes your responsibility instead of that of your parents. This involves caring for your body daily. You should also see health care professionals when necessary.

Establish Emotional Independence from Parents and Other Adults

To become emotionally independent from your parents and other adults is another task. As a child, you were strongly dependent upon your parents. During the teen years, you struggle between your desire for dependence and your need to be independent. As you learn to analyze your alternatives, you will make more decisions independently. You will become less emotionally dependent on your parents.

Achieve New and More Mature Relations with Age-Mates

Peer interaction reaches a peak of importance during the early and middle teen years. The degree to which you are able to make friends and be a part of a peer group is important for overall social and psychological development.

Adopt Socially Approved Masculine or Feminine Adult Roles

With increased physical and sexual maturity, you need to incorporate into your personal identity a set of attitudes about what it means to be male or female. You establish a sense of masculinity or femininity. You must also adopt a set of standards concerning your sexual behavior.

Select and Prepare for an Occupation

This task is to establish career goals. When you analyze your aptitudes, abilities, and interests, you will get some clues regarding careers in which you might be successful. You can begin preparing for a career while you are in high school. Choosing courses and electives that will prepare you for a career that interests you is one step to take. A part-time job or volunteer work in a related field may assist you in making a career choice, too. See 1-11.

Develop a Personal Attitude Toward Marriage and Family Living

As you mature, it is natural to think about your future—including marriage and children. Many adults choose to marry and start their own family. Others prefer a single lifestyle. Some married couples

Discuss:
Think of a TV program involving teens. How do the adolescents show respect for authority? How do they show they are taking responsibility?

Discuss:
What are some decisions you feel teenagers should make without their parents' advice?

Activity:
Ask students to list what they think are the sex roles of men and women today. Then ask them to write down what they think their grandparents would have written. Share and compare the lists.

Enrich:
Go to the guidance center and take an aptitude test.

Putting Technology to Use
Have students use word processing software to create a chart with two columns. In one column, students should list the developmental tasks of teens. In the other column, students should list ways they feel they have met or will meet the goals of these tasks.

> **Reflect:**
> Think of the last socially responsible and socially irresponsible behaviors you demonstrated in public.
>
> **Resource:**
> *The Developmental Tasks of Teens,* transparency master, TR
>
> **Resource:**
> *Havighurst's Developmental Tasks,* Activity D, SAG
>
> **Resource:**
> *Personal Behavior Standards,* reproducible master, TR

1-11 Are you interested in finding out more about retail careers? A part-time job in a department store would provide valuable experience.

1-12 One way to show responsible behavior is to perform to the best of your ability in school.

choose not to have children. During the teen years, you will begin to consider these options. The opinions and attitudes you begin forming now will become the basis for choices you make as an adult.

Adopt Personal Behavior Standards

During the teen years, you assess the morals and standards you have been taught by your parents and other significant people in your life. From what you have learned about right and wrong, you adopt your own set of personal standards to guide your behavior. Most young people model their behaviors after those of socially responsible people.

Accept and Adopt Socially Responsible Behavior

Risk taking is common among early adolescents. As you move toward maturity and adopt personal standards of behavior, you also develop behavioral self-controls. You learn to control your impulses. When you demonstrate responsible behavior and show good judgment, people will accept you as a young adult, 1-12.

> **Check It Out!**
> 1. Name the type of growth that refers to changes in body stature.
> 2. Explain the difference between emotional growth and intellectual growth.
> 3. _____ growth is how you relate to other people.
> 4. List the developmental tasks of the teenage years as described by Robert Havighurst.

> **Check It Out! (Answers)**
> 1. physical growth
> 2. Emotional growth is the way you express your feelings, while intellectual growth is the ability to reason and form complex thought patterns.
> 3. Social
> 4. The developmental tasks of teens: accept physique and use the body effectively; establish emotional independence from parents and other adults; achieve new and more mature relations with age-mates; adopt socially approved masculine or feminine adult roles; select and prepare for an occupation; develop an attitude toward marriage and family living; adopt personal behavior standards; accept and adopt socially responsible behavior

Topic 1-3
Influences on Behavior

Objectives
After studying this topic, you will be able to
- describe how the five levels of human needs influence behavior.
- relate how wants differ from needs.
- explain how personal priorities, goals, and standards are interrelated.

Topic Terms
needs
self-actualization
wants
personal priorities
goals
short-term goals
long-term goals
visionary goals
standards

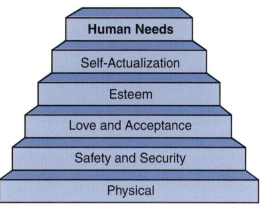

1-13 In Maslow's ranking of human needs, physical needs have first priority.

All humans share certain needs. These needs cause people to behave as they do. Most behaviors are attempts to satisfy a need or to remove something that is not needed. In an effort to satisfy needs, you will establish personal priorities, goals, and standards for your life.

Human Needs

Needs are basic items that are required for living. All people have the same basic needs. These needs must be met for proper growth and development.

Abraham Maslow, a famous psychologist, identified five levels of human needs. He then ranked these needs in order of priority. As you read chart 1-13, notice that more needs are related to the psychological environment than to the physical environment. Observe, however, that physical needs are more urgent. They must be fulfilled before the psychological needs can be considered.

Physical Needs

Physical needs include food, water, clothing, and shelter. These items are necessary for good health, for comfort, and to sustain life. People fulfill their physical needs in different ways. Some people are vegetarians. Others enjoy meals that include meat. Some people like to make their clothes. Others enjoy shopping at exclusive clothing boutiques. Some people live in simple cabins in the woods. Others live in high-rise apartment buildings. Regardless of how these needs are met, they must be at least partially satisfied before going on to other needs.

Safety and Security Needs

People need to feel free from danger, risk, or injury in their surroundings. People need to feel safe in their own homes. In addition, they need to feel safe from financial disaster or hurting remarks by others.

Knowing what to expect in the future helps people fulfill their needs for security. No one can know exactly what will occur in the future. However, people need to have some idea of what to expect. This helps them plan activities and behaviors. They can establish daily routines to add to their sense of security.

Love and Acceptance Needs

People need to feel loved by other people. Everyone needs to know the warmth of human affection. They need to feel that their presence is important to other people. No one should expect to be loved by every person he or she meets. However, everyone does need to be accepted, supported, praised, and loved by others.

Vocabulary:
Ask students to use each of the terms in the list in a sentence. Collect the sentences. Return them to the students after they have read the topic and have them revise any sentences where they used the terms incorrectly.

Resource:
Maslow's Hierarchy of Human Needs, color transparency CT-1, TR

Resource:
Human Needs, transparency master, TR

Resource:
Human Needs as Defined by Maslow, Activity E, SAG

Example:
An example of a safety need is to live in a home without fear of abuse from any family members.

Across the Curriculum
Economics. Discuss the economies of developing countries as opposed to industrialized nations. Ask students how this relates to Maslow's hierarchy of needs.

Discuss:
What are some ways to show children they are loved and accepted?

Activity:
Ask each student to make a list of at least ten things he or she does well.

Vocabulary:
Ask each student to write a definition of *self-actualization* using his or her own words.

The basis for loving relationships begins during childhood. If parents and caregivers show love and support, most children will feel accepted and loved, 1-14. Children experiment with a variety of behaviors. Those that bring desired responses are repeated as the children seek attention. Behaviors that bring negative responses are not repeated. In this trial-and-error method, children learn positive behavior patterns. As children grow, they continue to learn ways of getting along with people and gaining acceptance and love.

Esteem Needs

As individuals grow satisfied with the way their needs for physical comfort, safety, and love are being met, they begin to need esteem. People seek respect and admiration. They need both self-esteem and the esteem of others.

One way to achieve esteem is to have pride in what you do, 1-15. Everyone can do something well. Your talents may not

1-15 Doing the best job possible on a research report can help you establish your self-esteem.

be the same as those of your parents, brothers and sisters, or best friends. You may have to try several different activities before you find your true talents. However, if you search, you will find them. Focus on your strengths. Once you have found your talents and have developed them, you will be able to like yourself and have pride in yourself. You will have a sense of importance and confidence. You will be able to fulfill your need for self-esteem. At the same time, you will be well on your way to achieving the esteem of others.

Self-Actualization

Self-actualization is the highest level in Maslow's ranking of human needs. To reach this level, all other needs must be at least partially satisfied.

Those who reach the level of **self-actualization** have the need to develop to their full potential. They know what is important to them. They have set goals for themselves, and they have reached many of them. Now they may strive for goals outside of themselves, such as a quest for beauty, truth, or justice. They seek self-fulfillment by expressing their true selves. They are accepting of their own weaknesses and those of others. They are in tune with reality.

1-14 Children need to feel secure in their family relationships. Parents who provide praise, support, and encouragement help their child develop a healthy personality.

Across the Curriculum
Psychology. Discuss how important esteem is in an individual's development.

Topic 1-3 Influences on Behavior

To understand yourself, you need to recognize your present level of need. Which needs have you fulfilled? How have you fulfilled them? Think of some of your experiences during the past few years. Try to see how your needs have influenced your behavior.

As you try to understand other people, remember that needs influence behavior. People's behaviors differ according to the level of need they are trying to fulfill.

Comparing Needs and Wants

Do you know the difference between needs and wants? Sometimes the meaning of these words is confusing. However, each one has a distinct meaning. Understanding the relationship between both terms is important as both affect your behavior.

As described above, everyone has the same basic needs. However, people have different wants. **Wants** are those things people desire, but don't need. They are not necessary for survival. They may bring satisfaction, but life will go on without them. Sometimes people want something they don't really need. The latest computer game or an expensive piece of jewelry might be an example.

The Relationship of Needs and Wants

There is a relationship between wants and needs that affects your behavior. For example, you need food in the morning before you begin your schoolwork. You may want to eat at home, or you may want to eat in the cafeteria after you arrive at school. Either way your need has been satisfied, but you chose the way you wanted to satisfy it.

Wants for some people may even be needs for others. For example, in most families an adult needs to work to provide a family income. Such an income is used to provide for the family's needs and perhaps some of the items the family wants. A teen in that same family may want to work too, but for different reasons. The teen's basic needs, however, would be met whether or not he or she earned an income. The adult who works to supply family needs may want to work outdoors—in a construction trade perhaps. Another adult who works to meet certain needs may want to work indoors drafting house plans.

As you define your needs and wants, you may recognize the necessity to meet the basic needs of dependent family members. You may have to sacrifice some wants to be able to do this. Good management techniques will enable you to balance needs and wants. This allows the family to satisfy its needs and have some resources left to help satisfy some wants, 1-16.

1-16 Would you be satisfying a want or a need by renting a video?

Personal Priorities, Goals, and Standards

People satisfy their needs in different ways. If this were not so, everyone would eat the same kind of food and live in the same kind of houses. Instead, life is full of variety. Each person is unique with his or her style of living. Each person's decisions and behaviors are different from those of anyone else. Three factors that contribute to the differences between people are their personal priorities, goals, and standards.

Discuss:
Ask students for some examples of how their wants and needs have influenced their behavior in the past.

Activity:
List five of your needs and five of your wants. Write an explanation of the relationship between your needs and wants. Then develop a plan to achieve some of these.

Putting Technology to Use
Have students make lists of items they want or need. Then have students use charting software to make a chart showing what percentage of the items are wants and what percentage are needs. Have students discuss the results illustrated by their charts.

Reflect:
How have your personal priorities changed in the past three years?

Discuss:
How do you think your personal priorities would change if you won a million dollars?

Personal Priorities

Personal priorities are the beliefs, feelings, and experiences you consider to be important and desirable. Honesty, friendship, freedom, happiness, popularity, health, education, beauty, or status may be personal priorities you consider important. The combination of personal priorities you have and the importance you give each one makes you unique. Your personal priorities become a part of your personality.

Your personal priorities affect your behavior. Consciously or unconsciously, they guide the decisions you make every day. If education is important to you, you might choose to spend an evening studying rather than watching TV. If adventure is something you value, you probably would choose an exciting hobby, 1-17.

Your personal priorities were not given to you at birth; they have developed over time. All the experiences you have had throughout your life have contributed to your set of personal priorities. Your future experiences will also affect your personal priorities. Some personal priorities will become more important to you. Others will become less important. Your set of personal priorities will never be final. They will change just as you change.

1-17 Ballooning is a sport for people who value adventure and excitement.

Factors Affecting Your Personal Priorities

Many factors influence the development of your personal priorities. One important factor is your relationships with other people. Your first basic personal priorities were learned from the people who took care of you as a young child—your parents, other family members, babysitters, and preschool teachers. You may not have always understood the words they were saying. However, you could recognize the love, warmth, honesty, and other personal traits they demonstrated. Children imitate people they admire.

As you grew older, you probably began to adopt the personal priorities of other children who were your friends. As you made new friends, they may have encouraged you to change some of your personal priorities. (This is why parents are often concerned about their children's friends.) A similar pattern probably will occur throughout your life. The people you meet, especially your peers and friends, will continue to influence what you consider to be important.

Your experiences, along with your education and knowledge, also affect your personal priorities. Something can't be important to you if you don't know anything about it. Once you have experienced or studied something, you can then decide if it will become a part of your personal priorities.

Needs are another factor that influence personal priorities. If you had not eaten for three days, you would put a high priority on food. You likely would trade two tickets to the best rock concert of the summer for a good dinner. Someone who has just moved from a rural area to a city may have the need to feel secure. That person may place a high priority on home security measures. Friendship and love may be important to someone who has just lost a close friend. In all these examples, people's needs influenced their personal priorities.

Your personal priorities are also influenced by your religious beliefs and morals. The presence or absence of religious

Across the Curriculum
English. Have students write a paper about people they think have influenced their personal priorities the most.

teachings and experiences can affect your choice of personal priorities. These, in turn, affect your concepts of right and wrong and of good and bad.

Personal priorities are affected by the family life cycle. When a couple first marries, material possessions may be important to them. They may want a house, furnishings, a car, and other possessions. If they have children, their personal priorities are likely to change, 1-18. Being financially secure and having nearby playgrounds, friends, and schools for their children may take on new importance. When their children have grown and left home, their personal priorities will change again. Convenience, nearness to family members and friends, and leisure activities may become more important.

1-18 A family with children may prefer to live in a neighborhood with many children and nearby parks.

Personal Priorities Conflicts

People are constantly faced with conflicts in their personal priorities. These conflicts can create many frustrations. For instance, someone whose personal priorities include both honesty and friendship may be torn when choosing between telling the truth and saving a friendship.

Personal priorities can have an impact on your interests. For instance, if you think education is more important than sports, you may choose to join the math club instead of the volleyball team.

Personal priority conflicts often arise in families. For example, a family's personal priorities might include job success, prestige, and close friendships. A job promotion may create a conflict among these. The promotion would be a mark of success and would add to the family's prestige. However, it would mean moving to another state and leaving good friends. The family must decide which personal priorities are more important to them. This will determine whether or not the job promotion is accepted.

Personal Priority Judgments

When you make a *personal priority judgment*, you assign a level of importance to a certain item or action. You may think a flower is pretty, a song is good, a cake tastes terrible, or a person is mean. When you make personal priority judgments, you should remember that you are a unique person with a unique set of personal priorities. Your particular personal priorities cause you to behave in a certain way. They influence the choices you make. They affect your reactions to ideas and objects.

Before you criticize other people for making judgments that differ from yours, stop and think. How well do you know those people? Do you know what is important to them? Do you know what prompts them to make their decisions?

Personal priorities vary from person to person. Try to keep an open mind about the personal personal priorities of each individual. If you do, you will be able to understand and get along with other people better.

Goals

Although they guide behavior, people may not always be aware of their personal priorities. Goals are more specific. **Goals** are the aims people consciously try to reach. When you reach one of your goals, you attain something you wanted and considered important. Your efforts are regarded with satisfaction.

Resource:
Personal Priorities Inventory, Activity F, SAG

Reflect:
Think of some other ways personal priorities create conflict in a person's life.

Discuss:
What makes other people's judgments different from yours?

Across the Curriculum
Social studies. Review how the U.S. jury system works and why U.S. citizens are entitled to trial by jury.

Activity:
Have students brainstorm a list of ways they could attain the goal of becoming an astronaut.

Reflect:
What are your short-term goals for today? Will any of these help you reach any long-term goals you might have?

Discuss:
Name some long-term goals teens may have.

People set goals that reflect their personal priorities. Perhaps one of your personal priorities is physical fitness. You might set a goal of jogging one mile each day. Perhaps you value knowledge. You might set a goal of earning a degree from a nearby college.

Your goals help to make you unique. Even when you have the same personal priorities as someone else, your goals may differ. For instance, everyone values food to some degree. The goals people set for obtaining food differ widely. One person may set a goal of eating dinner out at least once a week. Another person may set a goal of eating only natural and homemade foods. Someone else may set a goal of staying on a certain diet—vegetarian, weight loss, or weight gain. Although food is a personal priority for all, goals concerning food differ.

Some goals involve only yourself. Some involve your family and friends. Some involve groups, 1-19. Some even involve people and organizations you don't know yet. For instance, you may want to get married, but you may not have found the right person. You may want to work in the sales department of a large company, but you may not know at which company.

1-19 Through teamwork, group members can accomplish many goals they might not achieve alone.

Short-Term and Long-Term Goals

You may have several goals at the same time. Some are **short-term goals**. You can reach these goals in an hour, a day, or even a week. Others are **long-term goals**. You may need several months or even several years to reach these goals.

Suppose you want to be the best high jumper in your state. This would be a long-term goal. As a freshman, you could join the track team. During the next four years, you could try to reach many short-term goals. You could work to get in good shape. You could set a goal of jumping a little higher each week. You could try winning the high jump events at track meets. Finally, you might be ready to reach your long-term goal. Perhaps you could win first place in the high jump event at the state track meet. You would be considered the best high jumper in the state!

Visionary Goals

You may have a few goals that you don't really expect to achieve. These can be called **visionary goals**, 1-20. Though you know you probably won't reach these goals, they are worthwhile. They can inspire you to do more than you thought you were capable of doing. They may also add some interesting experiences to your life.

Suppose you had a visionary goal of winning an Olympic gold medal for high jumping. You may never be able to reach such a goal. However, imagining yourself jumping over the high jump bar at the Olympics could give you a mental edge over your opponents. It could help you win a local meet. The effort you put into reaching this visionary goal could yield interesting experiences. You might get the chance to talk to and work out with other prospective members of the Olympic team. You may even have the chance to compete in the Olympic games and win!

Steps in Setting and Achieving Goals

Have you thought about your goals? What careers interest you? What do you want from life? Setting goals is an important part of achievement. Goals give you a

Across the Curriculum

English. Have students write a research report. Students should choose as their topic a historical figure who must have had visionary goals. Students should also include ways this person worked to achieve his or her goals.

Topic 1-3   Influences on Behavior

1-20 A visionary goal of becoming a band director may inspire you to join your high school band.

sense of direction. They add motivation to keep you moving forward.

The first step in setting and achieving goals is to make a list of what you want out of life. Be as honest with yourself as possible as you make your list. Be sure to include both short- and long-term goals. You may want to set some visionary goals for yourself, too. Just remember to keep them in their proper perspective. Don't feel disappointed if your visionary goals are never achieved.

The second step is to consider your personal priorities. Determine which ideals and objects are the most important. Make a list of these personal priorities. How will they influence the goals you have listed? You will not want to give up what you consider important to achieve your goals. For instance, suppose owning a new car was one of your goals. You could ask your parents to give you the money you need. However, if you value independence and personal achievement, you would find another way to reach your goal.

The third step is to list ways you could achieve your goals. Give yourself several options. Life continuously changes. You change, and the people around you change. Likewise, the situations and problems you face change. Having a few alternate plans is always a good idea.

Although you need to include options in your list, you should keep the list realistic. You should not count on luck to help you achieve your goals. You might win a huge sweepstakes, but your chances are not very good. You probably will have to find another way to achieve your goals.

The fourth step is to make some definite plans. Goals will not be reached unless specific steps are taken. Try to group some short-term goals with related long-term goals. Perhaps achieving some short-term goals will lead you closer to the achievement of your long-term goals. On the other hand, you may find you have to sacrifice some goals to achieve others. For instance, you may have to give up some free evenings to take courses at a nearby school. You may have to give up a summer vacation to earn money for a new car. You may have to delay marriage until you have become established in a career.

The final step in setting and achieving goals is to establish deadlines and rewards. Deadlines, or time goals, help you direct your efforts. They state what needs to be done first, what should be done next, and what can wait. A final deadline or time goal can help you work efficiently to get a job done.

Meeting Your Goals

When you meet a deadline, you deserve a reward. You can challenge yourself more fully when you know your efforts are worthwhile. Unpleasant tasks need special rewards. You can promise yourself a weekend vacation, a free afternoon, or a new shirt. The size of the reward is not as important as feeling good about completing the task and achieving the goal.

The key to success in setting and achieving goals is knowing yourself and what you want to accomplish. Unfortunately, some people do not know what they really want in life. They simply try a variety of activities. By keeping their options open, many find what is right for them. You can save yourself a great deal of time and frustration by trying to know yourself. You can do this by thinking about your personal priorities, your goals, and the methods you use to achieve your goals.

Discuss:
Name a sports figure. What sacrifices do you think he or she made to attain the goal of becoming a professional athlete?

Activity:
Make a list of some long-term goals you would like to achieve. Think about what you want out of life as you make your list. Then, beside each goal, identify the personal priorities that have influenced your choice of long-term goals.

Reflect:
How would you choose to reward yourself for achieving one of your goals?

Putting Technology to Use
Have students do an Internet search for the words *achieving goals*. Have students tell how many matches were returned for their search and give a few examples of Web sites suggested. Ask students why they think so many people write about how to establish and achieve goals.

Discuss:
How are standards related to personal priorities? to goals?

Resource:
Personal Priorities, Goals, and Standards, reproducible master, TR

Standards

Standards are accepted levels of achievement. There are many different kinds of standards. People have standards for their appearance and how well they do certain skills. They have standards for the quality of their possessions, too. Different people have different standards. For instance, one student might have a standard to answer every test question correctly. Another student might have a standard to simply get a passing grade. See 1-21.

Standards, Personal Priorities, and Goals

People's standards are related to their personal priorities and goals. Their standards will be high for the items they value and the goals they want to achieve. For instance, a person considers cleanliness a personal priority. That person will probably have high standards related to the upkeep of the house.

Like personal priorities and goals, people acquire their standards through personal contacts and their experiences. Therefore, people from the same culture, and especially the same family, often have similar standards.

Knowing your own standards and what you expect from life can help you understand yourself more fully. In a similar way, you can have a better understanding of other people if you notice what standards they apply to their own lives.

Check It Out!
1. List the five levels of human needs according to Maslow. Give one example of each need.
2. Give an example to show how personal priorities influence the decisions that a person makes.
3. List five factors that influence the development of a person's personal priorities.
4. Give an example of a short-term goal, a long-term goal, and a visionary goal.
5. Describe how standards are related to personal priorities and goals.

1-21 These students have set high standards for academic performance. Maintaining this standard takes careful preparation.

Check It Out! (Answers)
1. physical needs, safety and security needs, love and acceptance needs, esteem needs, and self-actualization (Examples are student response.)
2. (Student response.)
3. (List five:) relationships with other people; your experiences, including education and knowledge; your needs; your religious beliefs and morals; and the family life cycle
4. (Student response.)
5. People's standards will be high for the items they value and the goals they want to achieve.

Topic 1-4
Strategies for Personal Development

Objectives
After studying this topic, you will be able to
- summarize factors that contribute to a quality life.
- identify roadblocks to personal development.
- explain the importance of management skills.
- outline the steps in the decision-making process.
- explain the consequences of risk-taking behavior.
- relate the importance of significant others.

Topic Terms
management   emulation
decision   decision-making process

Quality of life is a phrase used to describe many factors that work together to foster personal well-being. How would you describe a good life? What do you want out of life? What is most important to you and your family? These are questions you might ask yourself in forming your view of a quality life.

What Contributes to Quality of Life?

The following are some of the factors people mention when describing a quality of life:

- **Good health.** Your health and the health of the other members of your family is very important. Remember the last time you were ill. Did you tell yourself "if I can just get better, everything will be okay"? People often don't realize how important their health is until they lose it.

- *Environmental factors.* Clean air and water, a safe neighborhood, and access to recreational facilities are just some of the environmental factors that can impact the quality of your life.

- *Emotional closeness.* To feel you are loved and to feel love for others is often a factor in describing a quality life. Without this emotional tie to at least one other person, life may not be as satisfying as it could be. People who feel loved are usually happier, more enthusiastic, healthier, less prone to illness, and generally live longer.

- *Social ties.* Having friends and feeling a part of a community is often included in describing a quality of life. Those who feel isolated and alone are usually less likely to be satisfied with their lives.

- *Educational opportunities.* Your educational options impact your quality of life. Everyone has the right to a good education in a safe school environment. Qualified teachers and up-to-date classroom materials allow you to reach any educational goals you set for yourself. A variety of educational opportunities are available after high school. If you choose to pursue these, they can greatly impact the quality of your life in the years to come.

- ***Satisfying work***. Wages bring buying power and some of the essentials of a quality life, such as nutritious food and health care. A work environment that is free of hazards to your physical and emotional health is also important. Being a productive member of a work group can give you personal satisfaction, 1-22.

You cannot always change the circumstances under which you live. However, you can look for ways you can change your life to bring it closer to the quality you desire. A positive attitude helps. Those who think of their glass as half full will enjoy a better quality of life than those who feel their glass is half empty.

Vocabulary:
How do you think the term *decision* will be related to the term *decision-making process*?

Discuss:
How do you feel your friends contribute to the quality of your life?

Reflect:
Imagine you are an adult who has won the lottery. Do you quit your job? Why or why not?

Across the Curriculum

Social studies. Have students research an environmental problem that affected quality of life for a community. How were people affected? What was done to correct the environmental problem?

Enrich:
Have students bring in a newspaper article about an occurrence involving violence. How did the violence affect families of the victims? the community? the country?

Resource:
Overcoming Roadblocks, Activity G, SAG

1-22 Having a job you enjoy and that brings satisfaction is often an important part of a quality life.

What Roadblocks Might Lie Ahead?

As you strive to achieve the quality of life you desire, there will be roadblocks along the way. These roadblocks may interfere with the quality of your life. This may be a temporary setback that can be overcome with hard work. Some people will be challenged to do so, whereas others may give up altogether.

Some roadblocks may be permanent obstacles. If such a roadblock occurs, you must find a way to cope with the situation. No matter what the obstacle, you can find a way to bring quality and meaning to your life.

The roadblocks typically encountered are usually the opposite of those factors that make for a quality life. For example, poor health can present special challenges. If you or someone close to you is injured or develops a major health problem, it will significantly impact your life. You may be challenged in new ways to live a normal life.

The abuse of alcohol or other drugs can be a roadblock. Such abuse can interfere with personal relationships, educational goals, and employability. Drug addictions, which lead to physical dependence on a drug, can seriously interfere with people's lives. Other types of addictions can also occur, such as addictions to gambling. These can be as difficult to overcome and as destructive of people's lives as physical addictions.

Emotional closeness may be difficult to attain if you lack self-esteem. If you have not learned to love yourself, it may be difficult for you to love someone else. Your challenge will be to find ways to improve your self-esteem in order to overcome this roadblock. Emotional dependencies can also leave people feeling unable to control their destinies. These feelings of inadequacy can lead to severe depression.

Stress in the workplace can be a debilitating factor for some people. Such stress can be caused by work that is too demanding, keeping people away from family and friends. Working extremely long hours and spending days and even weeks away from home can make it difficult to have a normal family life. A threatening psychological environment or sexual harassment can also create an intolerable work situation. Other work situations that can create roadblocks are low-paying jobs that make it difficult to meet living expenses. The stress of living from paycheck to paycheck can impact many aspects of a person's life. The prospect of unemployment is also a possibility.

Violence or the threat of violence is another potential roadblock. Anyone who lives in fear for his or her health and safety cannot live a satisfying life. Violence can occur on the street or within the home. It can be gang violence or violence within the family, such as spouse or child abuse. Just the threat of violence can create an intolerable situation. Those who live with such threats cannot move forward with their lives until the threats to their safety are removed.

Across the Curriculum
Health. Discuss the effects stress can have on a person's health.

These are just some of the potential roadblocks that you may be facing now, or may face in the years ahead. Others may also lie in your path as you move toward adulthood.

What Tactics Can Aid Personal Development?

Learning some tactics that can aid in your personal development may be helpful to you in overcoming these roadblocks, should any occur. You will always have problems to solve. Some are small; some are large. One of the keys to solving your problems lies in making wise decisions. Learning to make decisions is a skill that will help you in your personal development.

Making decisions is also a part of managing your life. You are the manager in charge of your life. That means you have important decisions to make every day that will help you reach your goals and avoid the roadblocks. Avoiding risks along the way will also help you, as will building relationships with people.

Learn Management Skills

The way you manage your daily life will greatly influence the quality of your life. You are the manager of your life. That means you are responsible for making the choices and decisions that will move you toward your goals. **Management** is defined as wisely using means to achieve goals. By the decisions you make on a daily basis, you move closer to your goals. You move toward something you want to achieve—something that is important to you.

Management is such an important skill that it is discussed at length in Chapter 10. There you will learn about the management process. You will learn how to identify your goals and plan steps to reach your goals. If you are a good manager, you will be more likely to achieve the quality of life you desire. Management skills will help you solve problems and make decisions.

Learn to Solve Problems and Make Decisions

A **decision** is a conscious or unconscious response to a problem or an issue. Whenever you make up your mind about what you will do or say, you are making a decision. Some decisions are made without thinking; they just happen. Some decisions are actively made after much thought. Either way, your personal priorities, goals, standards, needs, and wants will affect the decisions you make.

Making Routine Decisions

Some decisions seem simple. These routine decisions are made often, without much thought. For instance, most teens have homework to do. To get it done, they set aside some time each day. Doing homework becomes a habit. They do it without thinking about the pros and cons. There are other ways to make routine decisions as well.

Impulsive decisions are made on the spot. You see something; you want it; you get it, 1-23. Perhaps you are in the supermarket. A product promoter is serving

1-23 People often buy items they see on an impulse.

Resource:
How You Make Routine Decisions, reproducible master, TR

Reflect:
What are some impulsive decisions you have made in the past week?

Across the Curriculum

Consumer education. Discuss the concept of *impulse buying* with students in your discussion of impulsive decisions. Ask students if they've ever been sorry about a purchase they made impulsively.

Resource:
The Decision-Making Process, transparency master, TR

Discuss:
Name some other important decisions where using the decision-making process might be helpful.

bite-size portions of a new brand of pizza to shoppers. It looks good, so you pick up a portion and pop it into your mouth. You never asked yourself "should I taste this?" You just tasted it impulsively.

Habit causes you to make many daily decisions without even thinking about them. You get up in the morning and automatically brush your teeth because it is a habit. You never pause to list the pros and cons, because you know it's a healthy thing to do.

Emulation is a regular source of decisions for teens. **Emulation** means you do what most other people around you are doing. What do you wear to school? Students usually dress like other students. If your school has an official uniform, you get up in the morning and put it on. If your school has an "unofficial uniform" such as jeans, sweatshirts, and athletic shoes, you probably emulate that dress code.

Creativity is the motivator for some decisions. You just want to do something different. For instance, when Sara's family decided to spend more time together, she suggested an old-fashioned marshmallow roast. "We wanted to do something together, and eating our dessert outside offered a change," Sara explained.

Default is the act of not making a decision. For example, you could not decide whether to go to the movies or go to the dance. You ended up doing neither. You stayed home. By not deciding between the two options you had considered, you ended up making a decision by default.

Steps in Decision Making

Some decisions are more complex. Deciding whether or not to get a part-time job, making a career choice, or buying a car are examples. These will need to be made more carefully as many of these decisions tend to have long-lasting effects. When you have important decisions to make, the decision-making process can help you make the decisions that are best for you. The **decision-making process** is a set of logical steps to follow when making complex decisions.

1. ***Define the problem or the decision to be made.*** Be sure that you recognize the real problem and its importance to your life.
2. ***Establish your goals.*** Review your long-term goals and what you want out of life. Review the short-term goals you have set for yourself, too. Then establish new, additional goals related to the problem.
3. ***Prioritize your goals.*** List your goals in order of importance, placing the goals you want to accomplish most first on your list. Direct most of your efforts toward your major goals. Your less important goals can be put on a waiting list.
4. ***Look for resources.*** Make a list of everything available to you that will help you reach your goals.
5. ***Identify alternatives.*** Make a list of all the pros and cons of each alternative. Try to keep an open mind as you do this. Avoid letting any personal prejudices become stumbling blocks to progress. A good way to test alternatives is to ask yourself these questions:
   - Would I want to keep this decision a secret from others?
   - Will this decision hurt anyone (including myself) either emotionally or physically?
   - Can this decision have a negative influence on my goals?

   Answering yes to any of these questions means caution. You may want to reconsider the decision and choose another alternative.
6. ***Make a decision.*** If you have been guided by your most objective thinking, you will probably be happy with the decision you make. Decision making often involves taking risks. You may make some errors and create some conflicts. However, if you follow these steps, most of your decisions should produce good results.
7. ***Carry out the decision.*** After thinking through and making your decision, take action to carry it out. This can be a difficult step, but it is important. You must make the effort to follow through.

Putting Technology to Use
Have students form small groups and plan skits showing how students emulate each other. Have groups videotape their skits and show them to the class.

Topic 1-4 Strategies for Personal Development

8. *Evaluate the results of your decision.* Once a decision is made and action is taken, the result cannot be changed. This is part of learning to take responsibility for your decisions by accepting the consequences. You can, however, benefit from past experience by using it to help you make a future decision. To do this, you need to evaluate your decision. That means looking back on your decision and judging its success. Did your decision solve your problem? Did the decision help you reach your desired goal? Are you satisfied with the results? Try to see what did or did not work. In evaluating your decisions, you learn from your mistakes as well as from your successes, 1-24.

1-24 This bulletin board reminds students to evaluate results on a daily basis.

As you can see, the decision-making process can be applied to all kinds of decisions and problems. You can use it for important decisions you make every day. The steps can also be applied to more complex decisions such as those involving your education, your career, parenthood, or major purchases. These major decisions can impact your family, friends, society as a whole, and your future. The example in 1-25 shows how you can use this step-by-step approach.

Avoid High-Risk Behavior

Risks involve uncertainty, and they often have an element of danger. There may even be the possibility of harm or loss. Risk-taking behaviors are common among teens. It is a normal part of their desire for independence. Some teens get a natural high from taking risks. They feel alert, excited, and alive. Others like to take risks to prove they can stretch the limits and succeed.

Not all risks are bad. There is a positive side to risk-taking. The kicker on the football team took a risk when the coach asked him to attempt an impossible field goal. He made it! Shawn risked being turned down when he invited someone new to the fall dance. The acceptance was enthusiastic.

Many risks, however, are quite serious due to their consequences. They can result in physical or mental harm to a person, cause injury or death, and even affect the lives of innocent people. These consequences are severe. Young people should carefully analyze the risks they take and consider the possible outcomes. Some risks, such as having sex, using illegal drugs, drinking alcohol, smoking cigarettes, and driving while intoxicated, can have lifetime consequences. Some risks can endanger the health and well-being of others. No one has the right to take risks that might cause harm to others.

Some teens think they are immune to danger, but no one really is. Consider any risk seriously. Then, if you choose to proceed, plan ahead to reduce the gravest consequences. For instance, if you want to raft a dangerous river, train for it and go with a team of rafters who are also well trained. Before you take off, secure your helmet and life vest, know how to avoid falling off, and know how to get back on if you do.

Choose your risks wisely and think through all possible outcomes. Riding in a car is a routine risk, but doing so without fastening your seat belt raises the risk factor. Riding with someone who has been drinking raises the risk level even higher. Going to a party can be great fun. Using

Activity:
Use the steps in the decision-making process to make the following decision. You have been invited to a graduation party on a night you are scheduled to work at your part-time job. What would your decision be? Write down the thought process you would use to make this decision.

Discuss:
Evaluate the possible consequences of the decision you made concerning work versus the graduation party.

Resource:
Making a Decision, Activity H, SAG

FCCLA Activity
Have your chapter discuss the similarities and differences between the eight steps of the decision-making process presented in the text with the Planning Process developed by FCCLA. Have chapter members use both methods with an upcoming decision the group will be making. Compare the results and discuss which process worked best.

Discuss:
Do you think this problem is realistic for teens?

Discuss:
Can you think of any other resources this person might be able to use?

Using the Decision-Making Process

1. **Define the problem or the decision to be made.**
   Imagine that your problem is not spending enough time with your family. Sometimes you hardly feel you know them.

2. **Establish your goals.**
   You would like to spend at least one hour with your family each day. However, you have many other important goals and activities.

3. **List your goals in order of importance.**
   This is difficult when everything you do seems important. Before you try to prioritize your goals, try to think of reasons why you are not already reaching them. Why are you not already spending time with your family? You have a 7:30 class each morning so you get up earlier than other family members. Your regular school day ends at 3:30. You go to the elementary school to tutor children in after-school care and get home at 5:00. You go to your room and take a thirty-minute nap. You then spend thirty minutes doing your assigned chores. Dinner is not served at your house until 7:00 or later, so you eat with your friends at a fast-food restaurant. You work from 7:00 to 9:00, go home, do your homework, and take a shower. You try to be in bed by 11:15 each night.

   You conclude that your busy schedule keeps you from spending time with your family. Your main goal will be to find a way to reorganize your daily schedule to free one hour of your time.

4. **Look for resources.**
   This problem involves family interactions, so family members are the most important resources. They will help you carry out your decision.

5. **Study the alternatives.**
   - You could drop your 7:30 driver's education class, but you must take this class before you can get a driver's license.
   - You could end your volunteer activity at the elementary school.
   - You could stop taking your 5:00 nap and spend 30 minutes with your older brother. However, your parents are still at work. You also find the nap relaxing; you feel you need that after a busy day.
   - You agreed to accept the chores as part of your family duty.
   - You could prepare dinner and eat at home, but your parents don't come home until 6:00. This means you would eat alone and not with the family.
   - You could stop working in the evening, but this is your only source of spending money.
   - You must shower at night so the bathroom will be available to others in the morning.
   - You must do your homework.
   - Staying up later is impossible. Besides, everyone else goes to bed at 10:30.

6. **Make a decision.**
   You realize you must work through this with your family since it involves them. Change must involve them if it is to be successful.

   You decide to renegotiate your cleaning chores with your mother. Changing chores could free you at 5:30 to prepare dinner for the whole family. You will plan to have dinner ready at 6:00 when your parents get home from work. The whole family can eat together from 6:00 to 6:45. You can then go to work. Your brother already cleans the kitchen after dinner so that will not change his schedule. Your mother can then assume your cleaning chores since you will be preparing dinner. She will do your chores after dinner or before she goes to work in the morning. The whole family eats together and talks about the day's activities.

1-25 The decision-making process is a helpful tool that can be used to resolve important issues.

(Continued)

Putting Technology to Use
Have students think of a decision they faced recently. Ask them to make a list of any technological devices that served as resources and influenced the decision. (Examples include pagers, cell phones, computers, and video cameras.)

Topic 1-4 Strategies for Personal Development 41

> 7. **Carry out the decision.**
> You begin planning menus that you can prepare in 30 minutes. Your mother helps you prepare some foods on the weekend that can be frozen and used during the week. This also gives you more time to spend with your mother. You become the chef for the evening meals and the family eats together.
>
> 8. **Evaluate the results of your decision.**
> Immediate results were achieved by changing the usual cleaning chores to meal preparation. The family likes the change, also. The original goal of having an hour together had to be altered a little. Forty-five minutes seems the best you can do right now. Everything is working well with one exception. Incoming telephone calls interrupt dinner. Each family member decided to tell his or her friends that the family observes "family time" between 6:00 and 6:45. Friends must call at other hours or leave a message on the phone answering machine.

1-25 (Continued)

Discuss:
Do you agree with the decision that was made in Figure 1-25? Would you have chosen a different solution?

Discuss:
Why do some people choose risky behavior even when they know the consequences will be negative?

Reflect:
What do you think are the greatest influences on your decisions and behaviors?

drugs while you are there increases the risk factor. The use of illegal drugs can lead to serious health consequences and even death. There is also the risk of possible arrest for possession of drugs. When people are under the influence of drugs or alcohol, they are also less able to make good decisions involving their behavior. None of these consequences can lead to positive outcomes concerning the quality of your life.

Influences on Your Behavior and Decisions

As you use the decision-making process to help guide your choices and behavior, you already know that you will need to review your options and resources. You will probably consider your family's wishes and expectations for you, too. However, there are other influences on your decisions that may not always occur to you. This includes your family's culture and the traditions with which you have grown up. In addition, you will be influenced by the diverse cultures of the people around you.

Your peers and the expectations of society as a whole are important influences on your behavior. You may find yourself behaving in ways that you think other people will find appropriate. In some cases, demographics may influence you. *Demographics* refers to the character of a population, such as expansion, age, or income. For instance, the growing population of older adults may inspire you to choose a career in health care.

Economics will be an important factor in your decision making. The economic condition of your local area, the country, and the world can influence how you manage your personal finances and spend your money. You will learn in later chapters about managing your income and spending.

Just as you are influenced by other factors, your decisions and behavior influence others. Your family can be affected by minor decisions such as what you want for dinner and major decisions such as where you choose to live as an adult. You can be influenced by your friends, but your behavior, both positive and negative, can also set an example for them.

Some of your actions can affect society, too. For instance, choosing not to drink and drive keeps others safe. Choosing a meaningful career means you will accept a responsible role in society.

The decisions you make today will affect your future as an adult—including your future family. For example, maybe you want to feel secure about your job and finances before you start a family of your own. Beginning to think now about a career you will enjoy and managing your current spending will help prepare you for a comfortable lifestyle as an adult.

Problem-Solving Practice
Learning to Use the Decision-Making Process, reproducible master, TR. After students have become familiar with the steps involved in making decisions, have them work in small groups to apply the process to a typical problem or decision teens may face. For this activity, students are to create their own hypothetical problem.

Reflect:
In what ways do your family members act as your support group?

Discuss:
Have you ever had a relationship where you felt you were more supportive to the other person than he or she was to you? How did the relationship make you feel?

Build Supportive Relationships

You will come in contact with many people throughout your life. Some of these people will be very close to you. They are the people who will love you, encourage you, support you, and make you feel worthwhile. These are likely to be your parents, your close friends, and may eventually include a marriage partner. Even in the workplace, you may find a mentor who will help you along in your career.

The relationships you share with these people have a great effect on the quality of your life. You are healthier, both physically and mentally, when you have these significant relationships in your life. Your happiness and success in life are closely related to your ability to form meaningful relationships with others.

1-26 Having a parent who will support you when problems arise is important to your overall well-being.

The significant people in your life will support you in times of stress, 1-26. They will help you solve problems and find direction. Supportive relationships go both ways. That means both people in the relationship meet needs and contribute to the personal development of the other. Relationships involve sharing feelings, experiences, problems, interests, and activities. People share and work toward common goals. They respect each other. They also trust each other, knowing that each is honest and reliable. Openness is also important to any relationship. Sharing thoughts, opinions, and feelings is key to a successful relationship.

Unfortunately, some people lack this supportive network of people. They are unable to form meaningful and positive relationships with others. What happens when people lack these relationships? Self-esteem suffers. They feel unworthy of anyone's love. They may attempt to fill this void in various ways. For instance, a young woman may feel if she gets pregnant and has a baby, she will have someone to love her. She thinks her baby will always be there for her. This is the wrong reason for having a baby. She is choosing to have a baby for selfish reasons and is not considering the welfare of her child. Some young people join gangs to fill their need to be a part of a group. Once they are in the gang, they get trapped into participating in unhealthy or illegal activities that may include violence. Many times it is difficult to get out of a gang safely.

As you can see, it is important to surround yourself with people who will support you in a positive manner. Some young people feel they are lacking such a support group. If you feel this way, try to connect with some caring adults. If not your parents, there are other adults who can help you. An older sibling, a grandparent, a favorite teacher, your clergy, a neighbor, or your employer are all possible candidates. Close friends should also be an important part of your support group, 1-27.

Career Preparation Activity

Influences on Career Decisions and Career Success, reproducible master, TR. After studying this chapter, have students complete this activity to relate what they have learned about personality traits, personal priorities, and goals to career decisions and success in the working world.

Topic 1-4   Strategies for Personal Development

1-27 For many young people, close friends can provide support in both good times and bad.

To enlarge your circle of supportive relationships, be the first to smile and say hello to new acquaintances. You may get a few negative responses, but most people are waiting for someone to make the first move. It only takes a few words to initiate a relationship, but it can also be accomplished through deeds. When you perform an act of kindness—expecting nothing in return—it may lead to a long-lasting friendship. You will learn more about positive relationships in the next chapter.

Check It Out! (Answers)
1. (List three. Student response.)
2. (List three. Student response.)
3. You are responsible for the choices and decisions that will move you toward your goals.
4. define the problem, establish your goals, list your goals in order of importance, look for resources, study the alternatives, make a decision, carry out the decision, evaluate the results of the decision
5. (Examples are student response.)
6. (Give three. Student response.)

Check It Out!
1. List three factors that can contribute to a quality life, and give an example of each.
2. Identify three roadblocks to personal development.
3. Explain what it means to be the manager of your life.
4. List the eight steps in the decision-making process.
5. Give an example of a positive risk and an example of a risk that can have negative consequences. Explain your answers.
6. Give three characteristics of a supportive relationship.

Discuss:

Have your class divide into small groups to debate the points made in the article. Ask them to decide if they agree or disagree with the following viewpoints stated in the article:
- It is better not to host a party than to assume the responsibility.
- The host should keep guests under control.
- If teens host parties, they must accept the responsibilities involved.

Discuss:

Have the groups respond to the tips for responsibly hosting parties that are listed in the feature. Do they agree or disagree with these suggestions? Then have them add their own suggestions to the list. Discuss the possible consequences if some of these tips are not followed.

TEENS ARE TALKING ABOUT...

Socially Responsible Behavior When Hosting Parties

How can teens show socially responsible behavior when hosting parties? When responding to this question, the discussion group had mixed reactions. Some group members thought it was better not to host a party than to assume the responsibility. Others felt a party would be fun for the host's friends, but the host would have to keep the guests under control. The group did agree on one point—if teens do host parties, they must accept the responsibilities involved. "Careful planning and parental involvement is needed to keep parties under control," they concluded. The group offered teens these tips for responsibly hosting parties.

- Plan your guest list ahead of time. Invite people who get along well together. Invite an equal number of boys and girls so that each person will have someone with whom to dance.

- Designate one area of the house for the party. Rearrange the furniture, if necessary, and remove any items from the room that could be damaged by guests. Inform guests that they must stay in the designated area during the party.

- To keep a party fun and entertaining, provide some refreshments and music. Have plenty of snacks and nonalcoholic beverages. Good music will put everyone in a good mood. Plan a special activity for guests (like swimming, games, or outdoor sports) when they need a break from dancing.

- During the party, make sure that all of your friends get attention—everyone wants to have a good time. No person wants to feel left out.

- Parents should be on call when you are hosting a party in case uninvited people appear. Uninvited people who are not your friends may cause trouble. They have no responsibility to you as a host and can be difficult to handle. If this should occur, parents need to be around as authority figures to offer needed help.

- Keep in mind that you are responsible for your guests' safety, too. Don't let guests get out of control. Adult supervision helps greatly; parties are less likely to get out of control when guests know that adults are near. If a guest arrives intoxicated, plan for a designated driver to take him or her home. Finally, be sure to end the party at a reasonable hour.

- As a host, you also must remember that you are responsible for your parent's home and property. Invite people who can be depended upon to act responsibly. Keep guests in the designated areas of your home and yard. After the party, take responsibility for cleaning and putting the house back in order.

Chapter Review

Summary

Learning all about you means looking at yourself and your present stage of development. You are growing toward adulthood, so you are in a state of change. Your heredity, environment, cultural heritage, personality, and self-concept are factors that help make you a unique—and special—person.

All teens grow and develop at different rates physically, emotionally, intellectually, and socially. Part of this growth involves handling developmental tasks to become an active member of society.

As a unique person, you have needs, personal priorities, goals, and standards. Each one affects your behavior. The way you meet your needs, the personal priorities you adopt, and the goals and standards you set for yourself will have a great effect on your life.

An important part of personal development is deciding what makes a quality of life for you. You also need to be aware of possible roadblocks that may lie ahead. Developing tactics that can aid your personal development will help you along the way. Begin by learning some management skills. You can also learn how to solve problems and make decisions. Some decisions are routine, while others are more complex. Using the decision-making process is a skill you can use to help make the best decisions for you. In addition, you need to be aware of certain high-risk behaviors that can have negative consequences. It is best to avoid these risks. Finally, building supportive relationships can have a positive effect on the quality of your life.

Think About It!

1. Summarize some ways you are influenced by each of the following: (a) heredity, (b) environment, (c) cultural heritage, (d) personality, and (e) self-concept.
2. What advice would you give to a friend who makes this statement: "I really feel down! I'm the shortest one in gym class, my grades aren't that great, and I don't feel like I fit in. I don't know what to do!" Base your response on the five areas of growth and development.
3. List the developmental tasks of teens in their order of importance to you. Which task has had the greatest effect on your personality development?
4. Imagine visiting a developing country where people have never had enough food. Juan, a thin-looking teenager, is your host. He greets you and prepares to help you settle into your room. Using Maslow's five levels of needs, predict the order in which he will do the following (first, second, third, and so on): (a) show you the wedding necklace he has crafted for his future bride; (b) get the snake out of your bed; (c) introduce you to his friends; (d) take you to lunch; and (e) take you to a nearby stream to wash your clothes. On what factors did you base your predictions? Did you predict that he would use the order that you would most prefer? Why might he respond differently from the way you would?
5. Why is it important to understand how needs, personal priorities, goals, and standards are interrelated?
6. List some "quality of life" factors that are important to you. Be prepared to explain why you selected each factor.
7. Discuss the relationship between problem solving and decision making.

Activity:
Return the sentences the students wrote using the terms for Topic 1-3 on page 27. Have them correct any sentences where they used the terms incorrectly.

Note:
Point out that decisions begin with problems. It is important to first identify the problem. Sometimes this is the hardest step. What really is the problem? Once the problem has been identified, the decision-making process can begin. Sometimes the decision-making process is called the *problem-solving process*.

Enrich:
In *Try It Out!* Activity #2, some students may wish to make a display using more than pictures, such as actual items that represent their cultural heritage. If possible, arrange for the students to place the items in a school display case.

Resource:
PowerZone CD Challenge. Have students play the chapter review game to reinforce text content.

How can you benefit by using the decision-making process?

8. Forecast an important decision that you must make in the near future. For example, you might decide where to work or go to college after high school. How would you use the eight steps in the decision-making process to reach your decision?
9. Do you feel that advances in technology influence your decisions and behavior? Explain why or why not.
10. Why is it important to have a support group of significant others in your life?
11. Describe someone you know whose career involves the use of some specific skills presented in this chapter.

Try It Out!

1. Select a character from a movie, book, or TV program. Explain how this character has been influenced by his or her psychological and physical environments.
2. Use magazine pictures to make a class bulletin board depicting cultural heritage. Choose an appropriate caption for the bulletin board.
3. Trace around your hand on a sheet of paper. Within the lines, write at least 10 words or phrases that describe you. Ask a friend to review the words you wrote to determine whether they tend to reflect a positive or negative self-concept. Determine how you can convert the negatives to positives.
4. Describe what you would consider the ideal person—someone who is at the peak in all five types of growth. Compare your ideas with those of your classmates. How do your ideas differ from their ideas?
5. List all the activities you did yesterday. Then list Maslow's five levels of human needs. Match your activities with the needs you were trying to fulfill—either consciously or subconsciously.
6. Describe how people might show they have the following personal priorities: beauty, love, religion, security, adventure.
7. Work in small groups to list some common presonal priority conflicts teens have to resolve. Perform skits to show possible solutions to the conflicts.
8. Write a biographical sketch of an imaginary person. Set a long-term goal for this person. Then set several short-term goals to help the person reach his or her long-term goal. Finally, list the resources the person could use to reach the goals.
9. Choose a real or imaginary problem. Write a paper explaining how you could use the decision-making process to solve the problem.
10. Choose a song, story, book, or movie that illustrates a supportive relationship. Write a paper describing the relationship and the role the relationship played in each person's development.

Chapter 2
Understanding Relationships

Careers

These careers relate to the topics in this chapter:

- peer counselor
- social caseworker's aide
- youth director
- school counselor

As you study the chapter, see if you can think of others.

Topics

2-1 Developing Positive Relationships
2-2 Developing Friendships
2-3 Negative Relationships
2-4 The Marriage Relationship

Introductory Activities

1. As you take attendance, have each student say the first name of someone he or she respects and trusts. Ask students to identify how they are related to the people they have named.
2. Ask students how they would describe a positive relationship and a negative relationship. As you study the chapter, draw parallels between their responses and text material.
3. Collect a series of cartoons related to dating and marriage. Reproduce them on a transparency. Discuss the meaning of each. Encourage class members to agree or disagree with the situations depicted.

Topic 2-1
Developing Positive Relationships

I. Types of Relationships
  A. Parents
  B. Siblings
  C. Peers
  D. Romantic Relationships
  E. Work Relationships
II. Benefits of Positive Relationships
III. Qualities Needed for Positive Relationships
  A. Mutual Respect
  B. Trust
  C. Openness
  D. Reliability

Topic 2-2
Developing Friendships

I. Friendships
  A. Types of Friends
  B. Meeting New People
  C. Forming Friendships
  D. How to Make Friends
II. Dating
  A. Group Dating
  B. Random Dating
  C. Steady Dating
III. What Is Love?
  A. Is It Love or Infatuation?
IV. Responsible Relationships
  A. Facing Sexual Decisions
  B. Dealing with Sexual Pressures
  C. Showing Affection in Other Ways

Topic 2-3
Negative Relationships

I. What Is a Negative Relationship?
II. Ending a Negative Relationship
  A. Recovering from a Negative Relationship
III. Negative Peer Pressure
  A. Managing Negative Peer Pressure
IV. Sexual Harassment
V. Rape
  A. Date and Acquaintance Rape

Topic 2-4
The Marriage Relationship

I. Learning to Love
  A. Types of Love
II. Factors That Influence Marital Success
  A. Family Background
    1. Family Lifestyle
    2. Family Relationships
    3. Family Customs
  B. Personal Priorities, Goals, and Standards
    1. Personal Priorities
    2. Goals
    3. Standards
  C. Emotional Maturity
  D. Age for Marriage
    1. Teenage Marriages
  E. Social Activities
  F. Parental Approval
  G. Attitude Toward Marriage
III. The Engagement Period
  A. Examining the Relationship
    1. Discussing Important Issues
  B. Wedding Plans
  C. Plans for a Future Home
  D. Length of Engagement
  E. Ending an Engagement
IV. Making Marriage Work
  A. Early Marital Adjustments
  B. Nurturing a Marriage

Topic 2-1
Developing Positive Relationships

Objectives
After studying this topic, you will be able to
- discuss five types of relationships.
- list four benefits of positive relationships.
- describe how to develop four key elements that form the basis of positive relationships.

Topic Terms
sibling
networking
mutual respect

2-1 Spending time with friends helps people become more aware of the needs of others during the teen years.

Vocabulary: Have you heard of the term *networking*? In what context? (Answer: The business world.) How do you think this term will fit into the theme of this topic?

Reflect: What personal relationship comes to your mind as a positive relationship in your life? Is it a relationship with a parent, best friend, sibling, or someone else?

Example: Examples of parental dominance include setting limits on children's behavior, requiring children to go to bed at designated times, and seeing that children eat the necessary foods for good health.

Discuss: What might happen to a child when the parents do not allow the child to take on more responsibility? What might happen when the parents give the child too much responsibility?

You will be involved in many different relationships throughout your life. Most of them will be positive relationships. Positive relationships are those that are healthy and satisfying for you and the people with whom you relate.

Positive relationships do not happen automatically. You have to work to develop them. In order to build positive relationships, you must feel true concern for other people. This sense of concern increases during adolescence. During the teen years, people become less self-centered and more aware of the needs of others. See 2-1.

Types of Relationships

Learning to get along with others begins at an early age. Most people learn to develop positive relationships at home with their parents and siblings. Later, they expand their relationships to include peers, romantic partners, coworkers, and others. Learning about these different types of relationships can help you form successful bonds with others.

Parents

Infants form their first relationships with their parents. Infants are totally dependent upon their parents and other caregivers to supply all of their needs. These needs include the physical needs of food and clothing, as well as emotional and social needs. Children need to feel secure and loved. Because of this need, they tend to behave in ways that will assure their parents' love. As they grow older, they become more and more capable of supplying some of these needs themselves.

In early adolescence, children begin to demonstrate a measure of independence. Parents are still responsible for their children. However, the weight of responsibility begins to shift away from parent toward the child.

This change in the parent-child relationship often causes conflict between parents and children. Parents may relinquish too much or too little control. Children may want too much or too little responsibility. Communication is needed to maintain a positive relationship between parents and their children during this period.

Relationship patterns established between parents and teens are often followed by teens in their later relationships. Studies show that young people who get along well with their parents tend to relate well to their own children. Girls who form good relationships with their fathers have

Family Enrichment Activity

Have students ask one of their parents to share a pleasant memory about one of his or her parents. Then ask students to discuss the following question with their parents: How do you feel your relationship with your parents has affected the way you relate to me?

good relationships with their future husbands. Boys who get along well with their mothers interact well with their future wives. Families who build positive relationships tend to produce future families who also build positive relationships.

Siblings

Young children also begin building relationships with their siblings at an early age. **Siblings** are brothers and sisters. Siblings relate to one another on more equal terms. This type of interaction often leads to competition. Sometimes jealousies emerge as siblings compete with one another.

Building positive relationships with siblings prepares children to build positive relationships with their peers. Learning to handle jealousy and competition with siblings helps children know how to handle these situations with friends. See 2-2.

2-2 Sibling relationships prepare children to interact with peers.

Peers

Relationships with peers become very important during the teen years. These positive relationships form a support system for teens. Having friends reassures teens that other people are facing the same changes and decisions they are.

You cannot choose your family members, but you can choose your friends. You are likely to choose friends with whom you can build positive relationships. Most people tend to choose friends who have characteristics similar to their own. Perhaps you look for friends who are dependable, honest, sincere, thoughtful, and willing to help others.

You must have realistic expectations of others if you want to build positive relationships with them. Do not expect your peers to be perfect or to fit your exact mold. You must learn to accept your friends as they are. You may not always like what your friends do. You may not always agree with their opinions. However, they have rights just as you do. You grow by being exposed to their different attitudes and beliefs.

Not all of your peers will be your friends. You will not have enough in common with some of your peers to build friendships. However, even acquaintances can become an important part of your relationship network.

Romantic Relationships

During the later teen and adult years, romantic relationships become important to many people. Romantic relationships are positive because caring for someone and knowing he or she cares for you adds meaning to life. Sharing the joys and sorrows of daily experiences helps couples grow closer. Partners encourage each other to develop to their full potential as human beings.

Some romantic relationships lead to marriage. Marriage relationships grow and change as the people in them grow and change. To keep marriage relationships positive, couples need to work to keep lines of communication open. Each partner must

Discuss:
If you have siblings, what are some ways they taught you to build positive relationships with others? How can only children learn to establish relationships with others?

Activity:
Write down the characteristics of some of your friends. Do you see yourself as possessing these same characteristics?

Reflect:
Think ways in which you have grown by being exposed to opinions and beliefs of your peers.

Resource:
Types of Relationships, Activity A, SAG

FCCLA Activity
Have students working on the Interpersonal Communications STAR Event evaluate how strong communication would impact positive relationships with parents and siblings.

> **Discuss:**
> What are some other ways you can develop positive relationships with others?
>
> **Activity:**
> Write a paper about the benefits received from a positive relationship. The relationship can be one from a TV show, a movie, or one you have experienced.
>
> **Resource:**
> Benefits of Positive Relationships, reproducible master, TR
>
> **Reflect:**
> Think of a networking group at your school. How can this group help people form positive relationships?
>
> **Resource:**
> Networking for a Job, color transparency CT-2, TR

make his or her needs known. Each partner must also strive to meet the needs of his or her spouse.

Work Relationships

People form less intimate relationships with their coworkers. Coworkers can enjoy working together even if they do not have much in common outside of work. They can enjoy job-related successes together. See 2-3.

Positive work relationships are based on respect for the feelings of others. A good attitude will help you relate to those with whom you work. Accept your fair share of responsibilities. Do not expect others to do your work for you. On the other hand, do not assume that you can get along without your coworkers. Most jobs are a team effort. If you show consideration to coworkers, they will be likely to cooperate with you.

Benefits of Positive Relationships

Positive relationships produce many benefits. Research has shown that relationships can affect a person's physical and emotional well-being. People who maintain positive relationships have fewer physical illnesses. They are also less prone to diseases and tend to live longer. Their emotional well-being is enhanced because they know people care about them. They can share their problems with these people and thereby reduce the stress of daily living.

Positive relationships also provide social benefits. You are more likely to go places and get involved in activities when someone can join you. Your present relationships can serve as bridges to future relationships. Your social circle will expand as you meet new people.

Economic well-being can be a benefit of positive work relationships. People who relate well on the job are likely to enjoy their work. This will encourage them to stay on the job. They will increase their chances of being promoted and getting more pay raises.

2-3 Relationships with coworkers center around shared job experiences.

Networking is another benefit of positive relationships. **Networking** means forming an interconnected group whose members work together to help one another. Some networks are social. The people involved help one another make social contacts. This type of network might help a new student feel welcome in school.

Other networks are business related. Participants try to help each other succeed in the world of work. Members of the network may help one another find jobs, learn new skills, or get promotions. These relationships can impact career success.

Qualities Needed for Positive Relationships

As you read earlier, positive relationships do not happen automatically. Both people involved must work to develop four key qualities that form the basis for positive relationships. These qualities are mutual respect, trust, openness, and reliability.

Mutual Respect

Mutual respect means each person regards the other with honor and esteem. People in positive relationships do not

Citizenship and Service
Discuss with students how positive relationships can result in networking in the community. Ask students to list people in the community with whom they have or can develop positive relationships. Then ask them to explain the benefits that might come from networking with these people. For instance, a positive relationship with a park director might make it easier to reserve the park for a group activity.

expect each other to agree on everything. Neither person tries to force an opinion or idea on the other. They respect each other's right to differ. They respect each other for who they are.

Building mutual respect between teens and adults is sometimes a challenge. Some teens feel threatened by the experience and maturity of adults. They think adults judge them unfairly. On the other hand, adults fear that teens believe adults are not in touch with current youth culture.

Teens and adults both need to feel they are valued by one another. Teens can benefit by seeking wisdom from adults. Likewise, adults can be inspired by the enthusiasm of youth. Such worthwhile exchanges can help teens and adults build mutual respect and develop positive relationships, 2-4.

Trust

Trusting people means having confidence in them. In a positive relationship, you must trust the other person. However, you must also prove that you are trustworthy. You must be careful not to betray the confidence that is vested in you. You must be able to keep secrets. You must not laugh at friends who share serious concerns with you. You must not encourage others to participate in activities that are not in their best interests.

Trust in a relationship can be fragile. If you give advice that backfires, you may not be trusted in the future. When advice is sought, it may be better to help friends view situations from several different perspectives. Allow them to analyze the possible alternatives and choose their own plan of action.

Openness

Openness in a relationship refers to an atmosphere in which people feel free to share their thoughts and feelings. You must create this atmosphere for people with whom you relate. You must make them feel comfortable about opening up to you.

You must also be willing to open up to others. No one can second-guess what you think or feel. People cannot meet your needs unless you tell them what your needs are. See 2-5.

Reliability

People in positive relationships must be reliable. If you say you will do something, people must be able to count on you to do it. If you say you will be somewhere, people must be able to depend on you to be there.

Discuss:
What are additional ways teens can benefit from their relationships with adults? What are additional ways adults can benefit from their relationships with teens?

Reflect:
How do you know when you can trust another person? Has your trust ever been betrayed? How did that make you feel?

Activity:
Write a response to the following statement: I shouldn't have to tell you how I feel. If you love me, you should know how I feel!

Resource:
The Keys to Positive Relationships, reproducible master, TR

2-4 Teens and adults both benefit from spending time together.

2-5 Being able to communicate openly helps people build positive relationships.

Putting Technology to Use
Have students use a drawing program to illustrate how developing positive relationships is a two-way effort. For instance, mutual respect can be illustrated with a cycle graph. Building trust could be illustrated with building blocks.

Discuss:
How do mutual respect, trust, openness, and reliability help to form positive relationships?

Vocabulary:
Dating will be discussed in Topic 2-2. What do you think are the differences between group dating, random dating, and steady dating?

Reflect:
Do you remember your first friend? Who was it? Are you still friends?

Reliability goes beyond keeping your word. It also refers to routine patterns of behavior. For instance, perhaps people can rely on you to take a leadership role in a group. Maybe they can count on you to remain calm, even in frantic situations. Reliability helps people know what to expect from others in relationships.

Check It Out!
1. True or false. Relationships between parents and teens can affect teens' future relationships.
2. Forming an interconnected group whose members work together to help one another is known as _____.
3. What are the four key qualities that form the basis for positive relationships?

Check It Out! (Answers)
1. true
2. networking
3. mutual respect, trust, openness, reliability

Topic 2-2
Developing Friendships

Objectives
After studying this topic, you will be able to
- name three types of friends.
- describe factors that lead people to form friendships.
- explain three types of dating.
- explain the difference between love and infatuation.
- analyze factors involved in a responsible relationship.

Topic Terms
multicultural society   steady dating
group dating   infatuation
random dating   abstinence

Friends make successes more exciting and failures less painful. They are an important influence in your life.

Friendships

Friends are people who know, like, and trust each other. They are people who spend time together, sharing thoughts and feelings. Friends complement one another's positive traits. They also care enough to tactfully point out habits and attitudes that may need to be changed.

Friendship is the bond that forms between friends. This bond is built through a process of give and take as two people learn to appreciate each other. The best friendships develop between people who share experiences, interests, and personal priorities.

Types of Friends

The type of friendship two people share is determined by the strength of the bond between them. An *acquaintance* is someone you know, but who is not a close friend. You know your acquaintances by name, but you probably do not spend much social time with them.

You may think of many of your friends as *good friends*. These are people with whom you share common interests. You talk, have fun, and enjoy social activities together, 2-6. Acquaintances may become good friends if you spend time with them.

One or two of your good friends might become your *best friends*. These are the friends with whom you share your deepest thoughts and feelings. They are the ones you ask for advice when you have a problem. Best friends often share a common background and lifestyle.

Meeting New People

The first step in making friends is meeting people. You might admire a certain person in your school. However, you can't be friends unless you can first meet the person. Do not overlook opportunities to meet people of different ages, cultures, and ethnic backgrounds.

Most of the people you meet will be close to you in age. These are the people you meet in your classes, at club meetings, and at parties. However, you may have the opportunity to meet people of different ages, too. Don't exclude older or younger people from your friendships. You can enjoy talking with older people and learning from their life experiences. Sometimes adults can provide other viewpoints that you had not considered. Even younger friends can be important to you. They may make you feel important when they seek out your advice.

Most of the people you meet are likely to live close to you. For instance, if you live in Utah, you will meet more people from Utah than from Texas, Maine, or France. Likewise, you will meet more people from your neighborhood than from the other side of town. If you do meet people from other neighborhoods, states, or countries, take advantage of the opportunity.

We live in a **multicultural society**. That means there are people from many different cultures living in the same communities. Be open to forming friendships with people from different backgrounds. Through these friendships, you can learn about other

Discuss:
What is the difference between an acquaintance and a friend?

Enrich:
Write a one-page paper describing your best friend. What makes this friend special to you?

Discuss:
Where do you meet friends besides at school? Where do adults meet friends?

2-6 People enjoy sharing time with their good friends.

Career Preparation Activity

Exploring Careers in Relationships, reproducible master, TR. Students are to select an occupation that interests them and involves working with people. Possible occupations include social worker, school counselor, and youth director. Students are to use either O*NET (online.onetcenter.org) or the *Occupational Outlook Handbook* to find out more about the occupations they choose.

Reflect:
Do you and your friends have similar personalities? Why do you think this is the case?

Activity:
Make a list of interests you and your best friend have in common. Then explain how these interests help determine the activities you plan together.

cultures, including different religions, beliefs, and customs. You can learn about likenesses and differences. As you do so, you will probably discover there are more likenesses than differences. Differences are more likely to be limited to dress, food habits, and social traditions. You may not agree with all you learn, but be open to this wider view of the world. You will probably see that most cultural groups have much in common.

Forming Friendships

You don't form friendships with everyone you meet. Friendships are more likely to form between people who have similar personalities, common interests, and like personal priorities.

You are likely to form a friendship with someone who has a personality similar to yours. If you are quiet, you will probably prefer being with someone else who is quiet. If you are outgoing, you will probably enjoy being with someone who is outgoing. When people think and act alike, they usually enjoy being together.

Friendships are also likely to develop between people who have common interests. Friends generally share the same interests. You can meet new people with similar interests while doing those things you enjoy, 2-7. For example, you might take your pet for a walk and meet another pet owner. If you volunteer with a group that is working on a project that interests you, you will meet others with similar interests.

You will probably form friendships with those who share your outlook on life. They will think about issues in the same way as you. Your personal priorities are likely to be similar, as are your goals.

You want to develop friendships with those who have personal priorities similar to yours because your friends influence your behavior. You want to do things together, so you need to be with a friend who has behavior standards similar to yours. If you go to a party, will your friend act in the same manner as you? Peer influence is at its greatest during the teen years. Be alert to the influence your friends have on you. Do these influences help you grow

2-7 These two students met through their common interest in video production.

Putting Technology to Use
Use greeting card software to create a card for a friend.

to your fullest potential? Friends should not drag each other down. Friendships should be mutually beneficial.

How to Make Friends

Have you ever gone to an event where you did not know anyone? You were probably nervous and even a bit scared. However, this is the best way to meet new people. If you are afraid to go up to someone you do not know and start a conversation, you need to make yourself approachable. People are more likely to approach you when you are alone than when you are in a group. Those who hesitate to break in on a group conversation have no barriers when you are by yourself.

No one wants to be rejected or made to feel silly if they do make an effort to talk to you. They need to feel they will be received warmly. Strangers are more likely to strike up a conversation with you if you

- show you are interested in them
- focus on what they are saying
- ask questions
- provide feedback to keep the conversation moving
- are open-minded

Remember, you don't have to wait for someone to speak to you. You can make that important first move. What do you have to lose?

Dating

The factors that attract people to friends also attract them to dating partners. Spending time with dating partners can teach people lessons that help them prepare for marriage.

While people are dating and having fun, they are also learning about themselves. Through dating, people learn how to give and take in personal relationships. They become aware of why these relationships are important to them. They learn to recognize the impact their words and actions can have on the lives of other people.

Dating helps people learn about members of the opposite sex. Dating shows a man that all women are not like his mother and his sisters. It shows a woman that all men are not like her father and her brothers.

Group Dating

First dating experiences for young people often take the form of **group dating**. This is when a number of people of both sexes go out together. Each member of the group has fun without feeling especially close to any one person. Each person is free to get to know all the members of the group. Teens today may refer to group dating as "hanging out."

Group dating is an easy way to begin dating. Young people can interact with members of the opposite sex without pressure. For instance, with a whole group to carry on conversations, no one feels on the spot to keep talking. After learning to feel comfortable in a group, most people become ready to date as couples.

Random Dating

Random dating, also called casual dating, allows people to date more than one person at a time. See 2-8. For instance, suppose Terry takes Sara to a dance on Friday night. Sara not only socializes with

2-8 Random dating partners can have fun without becoming seriously involved.

Discuss:
Have you ever been rejected by someone you were trying to make friends with? How did you feel the next time you tried to meet new people?

Resource:
Dating Attitudes, Activity B, SAG

Discuss:
What are some advantages and disadvantages of group dating and random dating?

Problem-Solving Practice

Relationship Riddle, reproducible master, TR. Students are to read a case study that presents a problem in a relationship. Then they are to work in small groups to answer questions, applying the decision-making process to the problem.

> **Discuss:**
> How do you know when you are ready to begin a steady relationship?

> **Discuss:**
> Sometimes steady dating relationships are difficult to end. Why does this happen? What advice can you give for easing out of a steady relationship?

> **Resource:**
> *Developing Relationships,* Activity C, SAG

> **Resource:**
> *Dating Tips,* transparency master, TR

Terry, she also meets and interacts with his friends. Terry may go with Maria to a picnic on Saturday. Here he meets and interacts with Maria's friends. If Terry continues random dating, he will have the chance to socialize with many different people. If Sara and Maria continue random dating, they too will meet more new people. This in no way reduces the fun or the value of the social experiences they share with Terry.

In casual dating, everyone grows socially, and no one feels disloyal or jealous. The dating objectives are fun and entertainment. Everyone is learning about getting along with other people, but no one is falling in love.

Steady Dating

Through random dating, two people may meet and find that they like each other very much. They may agree to date only each other. This is called **steady dating**, but may be referred to as "going out." If someone is said to be going out with another person, they are probably in a steady dating relationship.

Steady dating provides several types of security. For instance, you know that someone likes you and cares about you. You know that someone understands you and enjoys being with you. You can relax and be yourself without fear of rejection.

Another type of security is not having to worry about spending the evening with someone you do not know. When you date someone for the first time, you take some risks. The person may have a different idea of fun than you have. You may spend the evening watching a baseball game when you really wanted to go to a movie. The person may cause trouble between you and your parents by keeping you out too late. When you date someone steadily, there are fewer chances for problems. You have a good idea of what to expect from your date.

Some teens may feel that steady dating gives them the security of having a date when they "need" one. They won't have to go to dances or parties alone. However, this is not a good reason to date. First, you may lead your dating partner to believe you care for him or her more than you really do. Second, going places by yourself can build your self-esteem. You may even meet new people who recognize and admire your confidence!

Although steady dating provides some security, it does not guarantee perfect peace and unity. Conflict occurs in any relationship. When a conflict occurs in random dating, the couple may just stop seeing each other. The commitment involved in steady dating encourages the couple to resolve their conflicts. By learning to handle conflicts in a positive manner, the couple's relationship can continue.

Sometimes even steady dating partners cannot resolve their conflicts. This is normal. When this happens, partners may decide to end their relationship—perhaps willingly, perhaps not so willingly. Either way, former partners must adjust to the change. They also need to seek new interests. See 2-9.

2-9 Calling friends and focusing on other interests can help a person adjust to the change after the end of a steady relationship.

Across the Curriculum
English. Discuss famous couples in literature. Have students choose one story or novel involving a "dating" couple and write a paper exploring their relationship. Is the relationship portrayed realistically, or is it romanticized?

Topic 2-2   Developing Friendships   57

What Is Love?

Suppose you have met and been attracted to someone. You have dated each other for a long time. You like each other very much. Now you are wondering if you are in love with each other. How can you be sure?

Unfortunately, a person's affection cannot be measured by any objective standards. It has no height, weight, or volume. A person's affection cannot be compared against a standard definition of love, either.

The word *love* has many different meanings. It can mean the way you feel when your brother mows the lawn for you. It can mean the way you feel when your friend lets you borrow a new sweater. It can mean the way you feel when you are going steady with someone.

Love involves caring more about your mate than yourself. You want your mate to be happy. You look for ways to express your affection. You may send flowers. You may cook a special dinner. You may just give your mate an unexpected hug and say, "I love you."

Is It Love or Infatuation?

Infatuation is often confused with love. **Infatuation** is an intense feeling of admiration. Although both of these emotions are directed toward another person, they differ in many ways.

You can be infatuated with someone you have never met, such as a political leader or a famous singer. You can also be infatuated with a fantasized image of someone you know. For instance, you may know the star of your school's wrestling team. You could build a fantasized image around him. You could view him as an ideal blend of good looks, strength, and courage.

Infatuation in a relationship is often short-lived. It may begin quickly and focus on just one trait, such as a person's appearance or special skill. It may end just as quickly if one person becomes impatient, bored, or dissatisfied with the relationship.

People may fall into infatuation, but they rarely fall into love. People are more likely to grow into love slowly as they learn more about each other. The focus of love is on the other person as a whole. When you love someone, you know the person well. You have a realistic view of the person's strengths and weaknesses. Since time and care are needed to build a love relationship, people are likely to try to make it last longer.

Perhaps the surest sign of infatuation is that it is self-centered. A person is concerned about his or her own feelings and desires. Love, on the other hand, is unselfish. A person in love thinks about the other person first. The other person's wants, needs, and feelings are most important, 2-10.

2-10 A couple who is in love focuses on meeting each other's needs.

Responsible Relationships

Steady dating usually means that two people spend a great deal of time together, often alone. As they do so, they may develop feelings of love for each other.

Enrich:
Write a poem entitled *Love is a...* Use the poem to express your definition of love.

Reflect:
How do you feel when someone says "I love you"?

Discuss:
How do you know when you are really in love and not just infatuated with someone?

Resource:
Dating Relationships, reproducible master, TR

Across the Curriculum
English. Review some of the most famous love poems. Ask students why there have been so many different definitions and comparisons for the concept of love.

Reflect:
How can you avoid a situation where you are pressured to have sex?

Activity:
Have students research the symptoms of STDs such as gonorrhea, syphilis, chlamydia, and herpes.

Discuss:
Do you think signing a contract is really effective in helping teens choose abstinence? Why or why not?

When this happens, it is only natural that the two will want to express their affection in some way. Certain hormones become active during the teen years, and the body changes, too. Sexual urges may become strong, especially between two people who are attracted to each other. In some relationships, there may be pressure for sexual relations.

It is normal to experience sexual desires, but it is important to think through how you feel about having a sexual relationship. You need to think about this in case you find yourself in a situation where you are being pressured to have sex. If you know where you stand, you will be able to make a decision quickly, if necessary. You should also have a plan of action that will help you out of any difficult situation.

Some teens are pressured into a sexual relationship they are not ready for. They may feel pressure from their date or even pressure from their friends. They may feel they are being left out if they do not give in to sexual pressures. Messages from the media—movies, television, and music—seem to imply that "everyone is doing it," even though this is not the case.

If young people give in to these pressures, they may experience many emotions. They may feel shame and experience feelings of guilt. They may feel used rather than loved. Their self-esteem may suffer if they have compromised their personal priorities, standards, and morals.

In addition to emotional consequences, there are physical consequences. Sexually transmitted diseases (STDs) can sometimes occur as a result of sexual activity. Some STDs are life threatening. Another possible consequence is pregnancy. A pregnancy can alter the future of both partners. Anyone involved in a sexual relationship must be aware of these possible consequences.

Facing Sexual Decisions

Every day you make decisions. Some are important decisions; others are not. If you decide to skip lunch, the decision will impact you for about six hours—if you don't skip lunch regularly. Deciding to have a sexual relationship can affect the rest of your life. If you make a careless choice, your life and your health may be jeopardized.

Self-esteem impacts almost all the decisions you make. If you feel good about yourself, you trust yourself to make good decisions. Having self-esteem can help you make important decisions that are right for you. If you always need the approval of others, you may tend to let others make decisions for you. If you lack self-esteem, you may let them pressure you into doing what they want you to do. If you think you lack self-esteem, plan now to make changes in your life. You need to be able to make decisions for yourself and stick to them.

Sexual **abstinence** is a choice to refrain from sexual intercourse until marriage. There are many reasons young people are choosing abstinence. Many chooseabstinence for moral reasons, believing that sexual relations belong only in marriage. Abstinence fits with their personal priorities and standards and frees them from guilt. Others choose abstinence for reasons of health and safety. They recognize that sexually transmitted diseases and infertility can result. They do not want to risk their health nor their chances of having children later on. Many teens see abstinence as a matter of personal integrity and an expression of self-esteem. They have control of their lives. They have goals they want to reach. They don't want to risk a pregnancy until they are ready for this responsibility.

Because teens are aware of the negative impact that sexual activity can have on their lives, there is a growing movement for sexual abstinence. Contracts are even available. Teens sign declarations stating they will abstain from sexual activity until marriage. This movement, plus other educational programs, are making a difference. The rate of teenage pregnancies is starting to decline.

Putting Technology to Use
Have students do an Internet search for current information on STDs, including statistics, prevention, and treatment.

Dealing with Sexual Pressures

When you make the decision not to have sex, you need to be prepared to follow through with your decision. Others must respect your decision. Make sure your date knows what your limits are. Talk about how you both feel. Knowing your limits can help you both stop before you go too far.

Practice saying no. You can just say, "No." It's your right. You do not need to give any explanations or reasons, but you need to be firm. Other suggestions for what to say are given in 2-11. If you know what you will say and do, it will be easier for you.

Avoid situations that may be difficult to handle. Do not spend time alone together in either of your homes when no one else is there. Go out with other couples or groups. Also stay away from parties where alcohol and drugs are available. Their use can cloud judgment.

Showing Affection in Other Ways

How do you let your partner know that you really care for him or her without having sex? There are as many ways as there are people. Talk about your lives, your hopes, and your dreams. Be there to listen when he or she is going through a difficult time. Write love letters and poems that point out the unique traits you like in your partner. Draw cartoons that depict your partner in some special way. Play a special song just for the two of you. Go dancing or go for long walks, holding hands. Plan a picnic for two. Put a note in his or her locker or tuck it in a pocket. Make special greeting cards. Add some hugs and kisses. Be creative! There are many ways to say "You are truly special to me."

Ways to Say No to Sexual Activity

"I'm not ready for sex."

"If you love me, you won't pressure me."

"You mean a lot to me, and I want to keep it that way."

"I don't want to lose respect for you."

"I respect myself too much."

"I believe in waiting for marriage."

"I'm more comfortable in a group of our friends. We're spending too much time alone."

2-11 If someone is pressuring you to have sex, use one of these ways to say no.

Check It Out!
1. Name and describe three types of friends.
2. List two ways dating helps people prepare for marriage.
3. True or false. Infatuation is based on reality, not fantasy.
4. State three reasons why young people are choosing sexual abstinence.

Check It Out! (Answers)
1. An acquaintance is someone you know, but who is not a close friend. A good friend is someone with whom you share common interests. A best friend is someone with whom you share your deepest thoughts and feelings.
2. Dating helps people learn about themselves. Dating helps people learn about members of the opposite sex. (Students may justify other responses.)
3. false
4. (List three:) moral reasons, reasons of health and safety, as a matter of personal integrity and an expression of self-esteem

---

Enrich:
Have students check out the National Campaign to Prevent Teen Pregnancy at their Web site, www.teenpregnancy.org. The site contains statistics, resources, and tips for teens and parents.

Reflect:
Think of someone you know who is in a negative relationship.

Activity:
List additional characteristics that make a relationship negative.

Discuss:
Suggest positive ways of ending a negative relationship.

Reflect:
Why do you think it is often hard to end emotionally abusive relationships?

Topic 2-3
Negative Relationships

Objectives
After studying this topic, you will be able to
- describe a negative relationship.
- explain how to end and recover from a negative relationship.
- explain how a code of behavior can help you manage negative peer pressure.
- give examples of sexual harassment.
- explain what rape is and how to avoid being a rape victim.

Topic Terms
peer pressure
sexual harassment
rape
acquaintance rape
date rape

So far in this chapter, you have read about positive relationships, including friendships and dating relationships. Unfortunately, not all relationships are positive. Learning how to identify and end negative relationships can help you protect your social and emotional health.

What Is a Negative Relationship?

A *negative relationship* is one that is neither healthy, satisfying, nor successful for one or both of the people involved. A negative relationship goes beyond simply being annoyed with another person or being tired of the relationship. A negative relationship threatens a person's physical and/or emotional well-being.

Negative relationships often involve some level of abuse. This abuse can range from name-calling and put-downs to physical violence. Verbally humiliating someone can cause emotional scars. The person may begin to feel unworthy, or even deserving of the abuse. He or she may lose self-esteem. Physical violence can result in cuts and bruises, broken bones, or even death. To avoid these destructive forces, negative relationships must be ended.

Ending a Negative Relationship

You may think that anyone who is in a negative relationship would want to end the relationship immediately. A person can detach himself or herself from a peer or coworker who is causing a negative relationship. However, ending a relationship with a parent, sibling, or dating partner can be much more difficult.

Some people find it hard to end even the most harmful relationships. A child may feel trapped by financial dependence on his or her parents. A wife may fear further abuse from her husband. Dating partners may be ashamed to turn to family or friends for help.

The first step in ending a physically abusive relationship is to get away from the abuser. Children and youth may need help with this step. Teachers, doctors, police officers, and religious leaders can guide young people to sources of assistance.

A plan should be formed to get away from an abuser in advance to avoid panic in a moment of crisis. Some clothes and a few personal items might be left with a friend. Money, keys, and important papers should be safely stored. These items can then be retrieved quickly if an emergency escape becomes necessary. Following an abusive incident, a police report should be filed as soon as possible. Any needed medical care should be obtained. Victims can then move into a shelter. There they will be able to get counseling and legal advice.

Emotionally abusive relationships are not life threatening. However, they must still be ended to preserve the well-being of the people involved. Again, getting away from the abuser is the first step. This gives the abused person a chance to regain some of his or her self-esteem. It gives the abuser a chance to face his or her use of negative relationship patterns.

Not all negative relationships must end unhappily. Relationship patterns that lead to negative relationships can be

Across the Curriculum
Psychology. Discuss why many people stay in abusive relationships.

Topic 2-3 Negative Relationships

stopped. Counseling can help people change negative patterns of interaction.

Recovering from a Negative Relationship

Recovering from a negative relationship takes time. Spending some of this time alone can help begin the recovery process. People can use time alone to think about what may have led to the negative relationship patterns. They can consider how these patterns might be avoided in future relationships. See 2-12.

Taking time to look back on the relationship may be helpful. However, this time should not drag on too long. People recovering from negative relationships need to get on with their lives. Pushing themselves to get involved in group activities will help them avoid spending too much time alone.

Not all of a person's relationships will be negative. His or her positive relationships may become more important during the recovery period. The support of family and friends can provide comfort during this time of healing.

2-12 Spending some time alone can give a person the chance to reflect on the causes of a negative relationship.

Some negative relationships leave lasting scars. Some people find it hard to build new relationships. Their self-esteem has been damaged. Counseling may be needed to help these people regain a sense of self-worth. Only after learning to love themselves will these people be able to love and trust others again.

Negative Peer Pressure

Negative relationships are sometimes the result of negative peer pressure. **Peer pressure** is the influence a person's peers have on him or her. Peer pressure is positive when it is used to encourage someone to adopt acceptable behavior. For instance, someone might use positive peer pressure to prompt a friend to study for a test. See 2-13. Peer pressure is negative when it is used to urge someone to adopt unethical behavior. For instance, someone might use negative peer pressure to persuade a friend to shoplift.

Managing Negative Peer Pressure

Managing negative peer pressure is a skill all people need to develop. The first step to managing negative peer pressure is to identify when it is being used. Some teens have trouble with this step. This is because these teens have not decided what types of behavior they think are unethical. In other words, they don't know what activities they consider to be right and wrong.

Developing a code for your behavior will give you a defense against negative peer pressure. You won't have to make quick decisions about whether or not something is right for you. You will simply follow your code.

Your code will be based on your personal priorities. It will define what unethical behavior means for you. For instance, you may decide it is okay to tease people about things they say. However, you might decide it is wrong to tease people about their appearance or their skills. Therefore, if your friends start booing a basketball player for missing a

Enrich:
Make a list of agencies in your community that can help people deal with negative relationships.

Discuss:
What are some examples of negative peer pressure that occurs among teens?

Reflect:
Think of the last time you applied peer pressure to another person. Was it negative or positive?

Discuss:
You are in a store with some friends and suddenly realize they have stolen a compact disc. Do you feel this is unethical? What would you do?

Putting Technology to Use

Have students make use of word processing software to make pamphlets on ways to manage negative peer pressure. Make copies of the pamphlets and pass them out to the rest of the student body.

Activity:
Talk to your parents or teachers about their codes of behavior. Discuss with them ways they avoid breaking their codes when they are pressured by their peers.

Resource:
Code of Behavior, Activity D, SAG

Resource:
My Code of Ethics, reproducible master, TR

2-13 Positive peer pressure might be used to encourage students to show support for their school teams.

shot, you won't feel pressured to join them. Booing goes against your code of not teasing people about their skills.

Parents and other trusted adults can help you form a code of behavior that is right for you. Talking to these adults can also help reassure you when your code is tested, 2-14.

You will probably adapt your behavior code and beliefs from time to time. However, it is best not to do so when you are under pressure. Try to choose friends who will not urge you to act irresponsibly. Also, learn to avoid situations that might pressure you to break your code of behavior. When you run into unexpected pressure, try using your sense of humor. You can jokingly resist peer pressure without sounding afraid or unsure.

Sexual Harassment

A very difficult negative relationship is one that involves sexual harassment. **Sexual harassment** is defined as unwanted or unwelcome sexual advances, requests for sexual favors, or other verbal or physical sexual conduct. Sexual harassment can be a leering stare. Comments with sexual overtones are considered sexual harassment. Body contact, such as brushing too close to another person or deliberately touching someone in a sexual manner, are other examples of harassment. Sometimes demands are made for sexual favors with the promise of certain benefits if the person complies. This, too, is sexual harassment. All types of sexual harassment are illegal.

You probably hear more about sexual harassment in the workplace, but it can

2-14 Talking to an adult can help reassure a teen about his or her code of behavior.

Across the Curriculum
Social studies. Have students study the laws pertaining to sexual harassment cases in the last ten years.

happen anywhere, between people of all ages. It can happen at school, at home, and at social functions.

Being a victim of sexual harassment can be very frightening. Some victims feel ashamed and think they somehow are responsible. They may also try to ignore it, hoping it will stop on its own. Sometimes people are unsure whether or not sexual harassment is actually happening. To help you recognize behaviors that are often considered sexual harassment, review the list in 2-15.

If you think you are a victim of sexual harassment, speak up. Tell the harasser that you resent the behavior, and you will take action if it continues. The person may not realize that you feel sexually harassed. If you do not say anything, the person may think you welcome the behavior. If you say something, it might stop.

If the harassment does not stop, talk to a person in charge. At home, you can tell a parent; at school, you should speak to a counselor. If sexual harassment occurs at work, speak to your supervisor. If your supervisor is the harasser, talk to the person designated by your employer to handle sexual harassment complaints. The important thing is to speak up. Do not allow the harassment to continue. You have the right to expect others to respect you as a person.

Rape

Rape is one of the most serious types of personal attacks. **Rape** is the crime of forcing another person to submit to sexual relations. During recent years, rape has increased rapidly. Young people under the age of 18, especially women, are often the victims. The majority of rapes occur at night. Many occur in the victim's home, at or near a friend's home, or on the street. Persons who rape strangers are more interested in gaining power over their victims than in satisfying themselves sexually. The victim may be in danger of being killed by the attacker.

Date and Acquaintance Rape

Rape committed by someone the victim knows is far more common than rape by a stranger. In over half of all reported cases involving teens, the rapist was someone the victim knew. **Acquaintance rape** occurs between people who know each other. This may be a friend, someone at school, a coworker, or someone the victim just met. **Date rape** is the rape of a dating partner. In most cases of date or acquaintance rape, victims thought they could trust their attackers because they knew them.

When a person says no, yet is forced to have sex, it is rape. What the victim chooses to do to get through the rape encounter does not change the charge. Even if the victim used poor judgment, it is still rape. Rape is illegal; poor judgment is not.

How can you prevent acquaintance or date rape from happening? Take extra precautions to avoid situations where you could be attacked. Learn to recognize situations that could get out of control. If someone tries to take advantage of you, or if the person's actions make you uncomfortable, be prepared to leave. Learn to say no. Let the other person know you mean what you say.

Discuss:
What is the difference between joking with friends and sexual harassment?

Discuss:
Some young grade school students have been suspended for teasing other students. Do you agree or disagree with those who say "Boys will be boys"? At what age should children be taught that teasing can be considered sexual harassment?

Note:
Emphasize the fact that although society usually thinks of sexual harassment victims as being women, men are also often victimized.

Identifying Sexual Harassment

Behaviors that are often considered sexual harassment include unwanted and unwelcome

- sexual language
- sexual name-calling
- pressure to engage in sexual activity
- personal questions about someone's sexual behaviors
- sexist or sexual remarks about a person's clothing, body, or sexual activities
- demands for sexual favors
- staring at, touching, or grabbing a person in a sexual manner

2-15 Any of these behaviors can be considered sexual harassment if they are unwanted and unwelcome.

Putting Technology to Use
Have students look up *rape prevention* on the Internet. Have them compile a list of rape prevention tips from information on Web sites.

Discuss:
What are the reasons many rape incidents are not reported?

Enrich:
Research local social services agencies that provide rape counseling.

Resource:
Understanding Relationships, reproducible master, TR

Vocabulary:
Try to write a one-sentence definition of each type of love listed in *Topic Terms* for Topic 2-4. Check to see if your definitions are correct as you read the topic.

Rape can be an extremely traumatic experience for the victim, with serious long-term effects. Many victims are afraid to report rape by strangers and are even less likely to report date rapes. They may be afraid of getting into trouble with their parents, or may blame themselves for the incident.

Reporting incidents, however, is important for preventing other rapes. Medical care and counseling are needed to help victims recover from the experience. *Rape crisis centers* are community agencies that provide for victims' needs. They can arrange for medical help, as well as counseling. Counseling provides emotional support that helps victims regain their self-esteem and trust in others.

Check It Out!
1. True or false. Being angry with a dating partner is an example of a negative relationship.
2. Give three reasons why some people find it difficult to end negative relationships.
3. What is the first step to managing negative peer pressure?
4. Give three examples of sexual harassment.
5. True or false. Rape is usually committed by a stranger.

Check It Out! (Answers)
1. false
2. (List three:) They may feel trapped by financial dependence. They may fear further abuse. They may be ashamed to turn to family or friends for help.
3. identifying when negative peer pressure is being used
4. (List three. Student response.)
5. false

Topic 2-4
The Marriage Relationship

Objectives
After studying this topic, you will be able to
- identify four different types of love in a marriage relationship.
- describe factors that influence mate selection and marital success.
- explain the importance of the engagement period and the process of adjusting to married life.

Topic Terms
altruistic love
companionate love
romantic love
sexual love

Marriage can be the closest and most satisfying relationship between two people. Loving someone and being loved in return can make life more meaningful and enjoyable.

In marriage, you can share the experiences of daily life with someone you love. You can laugh together and cry together. You can share your thoughts and feelings. You are encouraged to do your best and to be your best—to develop your full potential as a human being. You, in turn, encourage your mate to develop to his or her full potential.

Getting married does not magically end all problems. Getting married does not guarantee you love, happiness, and security forever. Marriage is a growing, changing relationship. It has to grow and change because people grow and change. The challenge of marriage is to grow closer together rather than farther apart. If a couple meets this challenge, the marriage will be strong and healthy. If the couple does not meet this challenge, the marriage may end in divorce.

Marriage is a part of most people's lives. They prepare for marriage by dating. They learn to love, and they choose a mate.

Topic 2-4 The Marriage Relationship

They announce their engagement and plan their wedding. Then they work together to build a successful marriage.

Learning to Love

In American culture, dating serves many important functions. It helps people learn more about interpersonal relationships. Besides encouraging positive peer relationships, it helps people evaluate the personality traits they like or dislike in others. People learn to recognize the give-and-take involved in getting along with members of the opposite sex. The entire dating experience helps people prepare for marriage and be more successful marriage partners.

After dating for a while, two people may decide they are in love. They may wonder if they really love each other enough to spend the rest of their lives together. The surest sign of love is that it's unselfish. If you are in love, you think about the other person first, not about your own feelings and desires. The other person's wants and needs are most important. You enjoy making the other person happy and find special ways to express your affection.

Sharing is an important part of the kind of love that leads to marriage. When you are in love, you and your mate enjoy spending time together, 2-16. You find that activities are more fun and chores are less boring when you share them.

Communicating is one way of sharing. By communicating, you and your mate can share each other's thoughts and feelings. When one is happy, the other can share in that happiness. When one is upset, sad, or confused, the other can help by listening with empathy.

Good communication helps you and your mate know each other better. By staying in touch with each other's thoughts, you and your mate can grow closer and closer together. Without good communication, each of you may become involved in your own thoughts and plans. You and your mate may drift apart. Eventually, you may find that you have little in common.

2-16 Activities are more fun when you share them with someone you love.

Types of Love

Learning to love helps people prepare for marriage. Recognizing the four types of love found in most marriages is also important. Altruistic love, companionate love, romantic love, and sexual love mix together in a marriage relationship.

Altruistic love is based on the concern a person has for the well-being of another. A person enjoys helping and providing for a mate.

Companionate love is a feeling of deep friendship. This is the feeling shared by couples who are friends and companions as well as spouses. These couples have mutual respect and affection for their mates. They have similar interests and goals. This is the most common type of love in the daily lives of most married couples, 2-17.

Romantic love usually reaches a peak during engagement or early marriage. It is a very emotional type of love. Two people

Reflect:
Think of one important perspective you have learned about personal relationships from dating.

Discuss:
Do you feel it's important to share everything with your spouse?

Activity:
Rank the four types of love in the order of their importance in a marriage with number one being the most important. Write an explanation for your ranking.

Across the Curriculum
Social studies. Discuss how marriages took place in the past or how marriage rituals differ in other cultures.

2-17 Companionate love is the most common type of love in married life. Spouses share friendship as well as love.

idealize each other and are devoted to each other. They enjoy being together. They ignore the rest of the world and create their own little world of peace and happiness.

When romantic love continues throughout a marriage, it adds strength and depth to the marriage relationship. However, romantic love seldom lasts. One reason may be that the everyday contact between mates forces them to see each other realistically. Their idealized visions fade when they see each other scrubbing floors, folding laundry, and mowing lawns.

Sexual love is the fourth type of love found in marriage. It is an extension of the intimacy and communication of the relationship. It helps marriage partners confirm their love and need for each other.

Factors That Influence Marital Success

Many factors will help determine whether or not your future marriage succeeds. Having several positive factors is not a guarantee that your marriage will be happy. Having several negative factors does not necessarily mean that you will have a bad marriage. However, a couple who have several positive factors working for them have a better chance to make their marriage last. The following factors are known to influence marital success.

Family Background

Similar family backgrounds can strengthen a marriage relationship. At first, you may think that your family is not that important. After all, your mate should be interested in you, not your family. However, your family background has left lasting marks on you.

Family Lifestyle

Where you have grown up affects you in many ways. People from different regions of the United States have slightly different lifestyles. They dress differently, they talk differently, and they eat different foods. They have different occupations. People from large cities, suburbs, small towns, and farms have slightly different lifestyles, too. They may have different views on subjects such as privacy, recreation, and politics.

Family Relationships

Another aspect of your family background is the relationships within your family, 2-18. How do you get along with your siblings? Have you learned to compromise? If you are female, have you learned something about men from your

2-18 Relationships among members of your present family may influence the relationships that will form within your future family.

Putting Technology to Use

Have students use word processing software to create a survey form. Ask students to survey married couples to determine how important family background is in the success of their marriage. Discuss in class what questions to include on the survey. Have students compare their results.

brothers? If you are male, have you learned something about women from your sisters? The lessons you learn from your siblings will help you adjust to living with your mate.

The relationship you have with your parents may form the pattern for your future relationship with your own children. Do you have a good relationship with your parents? Can you talk with them? Can you settle conflicts in positive ways? Have you proven to them that you are responsible? Do they trust and respect you?

The relationship between your parents may affect your relationship with your mate. Do your parents communicate well? Do they show affection to each other often? How do they settle conflicts? Do they compromise, or does one parent always win? People learn from their parents and often imitate them. If your parents have a good relationship, you have the advantage of seeing how a good relationship works. If your parents do not have a good relationship, you aren't doomed. You can learn from their mistakes and make your marriage a good one.

Family Customs

Family customs are another part of your family background. How do you celebrate birthdays and holidays? What kinds of vacations do you take? Who handles the money matters in your family? Who does the cooking and cleaning? Who is in charge of disciplining the children? You may take your family customs for granted now. However, they will affect the customs you follow when you establish your own family.

Personal Priorities, Goals, and Standards

To live in peace and harmony, marriage partners need to have similar personal priorities, goals, and standards. You have to know a person well before you begin to learn about his or her goals, standards, and personal priorities. This is why the time you spend dating someone is so important.

Personal Priorities

A person's personal priorities affect many day-to-day matters. Someone who considers career success important may put extra time and energy into college classes and part-time jobs. Someone who feels close family ties are important may be involved in many family activities. Someone who values physical fitness may spend time and money playing golf, tennis, and basketball. The list could go on and on. People invest effort, time, money, and other resources in the activities that are important to them, 2-19.

Reflect:
Make a list of positive lessons you have learned from your siblings and parents that will help you form relationship patterns in your future family.

Discuss:
In TV shows, are married couples depicted as sharing personal priorities, goals, and standards? Name some fictional couples that seem to have realistic marriages. What qualities make their relationship realistic?

2-19 A couple who share personal priorities, goals, and standards for family unity have a better chance for a successful marriage.

Across the Curriculum

English. Have students write a paper describing some of their family customs, such as holiday celebrations, money matters, and disciplining children. Ask them to indicate whether they would like to include these customs in their future families. How might differences in customs affect a marriage?

Discuss:
Do you agree or disagree with the following statement? In order to have a successful marriage, a couple must have the same personal priorities and goals.

Reflect:
What standards do you hold that could cause conflict in a relationship?

Vocabulary:
Write a definition for *emotional maturity*.

Activity:
Think of an emotionally mature person you know. What characteristics make him or her emotionally mature?

Goals

Closely related to personal priorities are goals. The goal of a person who thinks career success is important may be to become a company president. The goals of a person who values close family ties may be to get married and have children. The goal of someone who has a personal priority of physical fitness may be to win a basketball tournament.

Standards

Couples should share similar standards. Standards can affect daily routines. For instance, some people have high standards for cleanliness. They may expect everyone to help keep the home clean and neat. Some people have high standards for personal appearance. They may spend great amounts of time shopping for just the right clothes. They also may devote large amounts of time getting dressed every morning. Other people have high standards for promptness. They are always on time, and they expect others to be on time, too.

Following rules is another kind of standard. Some people never break a rule or law. They never park in spaces reserved for people with disabilities. They never cheat on their income tax. Other people don't mind bending rules, as long as they don't hurt anyone and they don't get caught.

As time passes, personal priorities, goals, and standards become more and more important in a relationship. Unless these goals and standards are shared, resentment may grow. One spouse may resent all the time the other spouse spends at work. One spouse may resent all the money the other spouse spends for clothes. One spouse may become irritated when the other one continually bends rules. A marriage has a better chance for success when the partners have similar personal priorities, goals, and standards.

Emotional Maturity

Another factor relating to marital success is emotional maturity. The more emotionally mature couples are, the

2-20 As individuals mature, they are usually better prepared to build a successful marriage.

better their chances are for successful marriages, 2-20.

Emotionally mature persons are in control of their own lives. They make their own decisions. They accept responsibility for the consequences of their decisions. They recognize their own needs, personal priorities, and goals. They have enough self-discipline to sacrifice short-term goals in order to achieve long-term goals.

Emotionally mature people have their share of frustrations, failures, and disappointments, too. They accept these problems as part of life. They bounce back quickly from their problems and move on.

Because emotionally mature people have their own lives under control, they can be more understanding of others. They recognize other people's needs and personal priorities in addition to their own. They can offer emotional support to their mate so the mate can fulfill needs and meet goals, too.

Emotionally mature individuals deal with reality rather than fantasy. They do not expect people to be perfect. They know

Across the Curriculum

Psychology. Explore the concept of emotional maturity and its impact on marriage.

that everyone has both strengths and weaknesses. They are willing to share, cooperate, and compromise to get along with others. They do not ignore or run away from problems. When a conflict arises in marriage, an emotionally mature couple deals with it. They talk about it and resolve it in a way that satisfies both of them.

Age for Marriage

Age is an important factor in marital success. It is often a sign of emotional maturity. The younger couples are when they marry, the less likely they are to have successful marriages. Because marriage requires maturity, older couples usually have greater chances of success in their marriages.

Teenage Marriages

A couple without emotional maturity will have trouble building and maintaining a strong, healthy relationship. Many teen couples lack this emotional maturity. As a result, few teens are able to handle the pressures and responsibilities of marriage.

Financial demands are another reason for the failure of teenage marriages. Money can be an especially important issue to teenage couples. Neither spouse may have received enough education or training to get a good job. If both spouses remain unskilled, their financial pressures will grow. If one works while the other goes to school, their financial situation will gradually improve. However, the mate without the education may resent working so hard for the education of the other. At the same time, the mate with the education may begin to feel superior to the uneducated mate. The emotional pressures may destroy their marriage.

Emotional maturity grows with age. This is why emotionally mature people are usually better prepared for married life. They have had more time to handle responsibilities and to become independent. They have had more chances to interact with people and are more likely to choose compatible mates. They have had time to receive education or training. They may have even had time to establish careers.

Social Activities

Having fun is an important part of married life. You don't have to do everything together, but you should have some common interests. You might enjoy going to concerts, playing cards, riding bikes, or watching sports.

A healthy social life includes activities with other people, too. Both you and your mate will bring some friends into the marriage. These friendships are important and should be continued. After you are married, your friends and your mate's friends may socialize with both of you. In addition, you will make some new friends together. Developing these mutual friendships is one of the adjustments you will need to make early in marriage.

Parental Approval

Parental approval is a positive factor in a marriage. Studies show that most successful marriages have the consent of all parents.

Why is parental approval important? It shows that the parents realize their child is mature enough to be married. It shows they are willing to entrust their child's well-being to the care of the future mate. It also shows they are supportive of the relationship.

Why do parents sometimes disapprove? Parents want their children to live happy lives. They may recognize some weak traits in the person their child wants to marry. They feel that in time, the child will recognize the weak traits, too. Disapproval is often their way of saying you should wait a while and learn a little more about this person before you commit yourself to marriage.

Parents want to see their children plan and achieve goals, 2-21. Consider Nikiah's case, for instance. Nikiah's parents wanted her to reach her educational goals. Nikiah had taken high school courses that would prepare her for a career in nursing. After graduation, she planned to attend nursing school. Shortly before high school graduation, Nikiah announced she wanted to marry rather than attend nursing school.

> **Discuss:**
> Do you think teenagers should marry? Why or why not?
>
> **Discuss:**
> Do you agree it is important to continue to see your old friends after you are married? Can this sometimes become a problem?
>
> **Reflect:**
> Would you marry someone your parents did not approve of? Should children listen to their parents' advice about marriage?

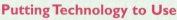

Putting Technology to Use

Have students search the Internet for current statistics on teen marriages. What percentage of these marriages succeed?

Discuss:
Do you agree that parental approval might influence whether a couple will stay together when serious conflicts arise?

Enrich:
Invite a marriage counselor to class to speak about factors that influence marital success.

2-21 Most parents want their children to achieve educational goals.

Her parents protested. They thought that she would later regret not having gone to nursing school. After several discussions, Nikiah compromised with her parents. She went to nursing school and continued to date the young man she wanted to marry. Their wedding took place shortly after her graduation from nursing school. Both sets of parents approved of the marriage and were happy for the young couple. Later, both Nikiah and her husband had successful careers in addition to their happy marriage. They were glad they had waited.

In any marriage, the spouses will have many adjustments to make. They will have many conflicts to settle and many compromises to make. If the parents do not approve of the marriage, the spouses have less incentive to settle their differences. They may give up easily. They may think, *Our parents said this marriage would be a mistake, and it is. We might as well give up.*

On the other hand, spouses seem to compromise more readily if their parents approve of their marriage. They may think, *Our parents thought this marriage would work. We don't want to disappoint them by giving up so easily. What's wrong with our marriage? What can we do to make it better?* This positive viewpoint can save a marriage that might otherwise fail.

Attitude Toward Marriage

The attitude spouses have about marriage plays a major role in their marital success. Too often, people think that marriage means living happily ever after. However, all marriages have conflicts and challenges. Since people have different personality traits, marriage means bringing two different people together. Each has likes and dislikes, good moods and bad moods, strengths and weaknesses. In marriage, the process of give-and-take is a part of daily life.

People with positive attitudes see marriage as a long-term goal. They have more realistic expectations about marriage. They are content to build and strengthen their relationship over a number of years. They find satisfaction in small successes. They expect their marriage to last, 2-22.

Others have less positive attitudes toward marriage. They may see marriage as a short-term goal. They seem to expect their marriage to be a temporary relationship that may end someday.

People tend to find what they seek in a relationship. A couple who seek a long-lasting relationship tend to find ways to

2-22 If a couple expect their marriage to last, they are likely to work at strengthening their relationship and developing common interests.

Putting Technology to Use

Have students review the factors contributing to marital success discussed on pages 66-70. Have students use graphing software to make a graph showing the rankings of the factors according to importance in their opinions. Have students share their graphs and discuss their reasons for rankings.

make their marriage last. A couple who seek a temporary relationship will find reasons to end their marriage.

The Engagement Period

The engagement period helps couples prepare for marriage. It marks the end of dating and the start of a couple's plan for married life.

In American society, the engagement period has several functions. It is a time for a couple to examine their relationship. It is a time for them to establish good relationships with their future in-laws. They will also make plans for their wedding and future home.

Examining the Relationship

The engagement period gives a couple the chance to take a closer look at their relationship. To do this, the couple must be able to communicate openly with each other. They need to share ideas, feelings, opinions, and facts that will influence their marriage. This gives them a chance to test their ability to discuss even controversial topics. It also gives them a chance to test their ability to respect differing points of view. A couple who can openly communicate (talk and listen to each other with interest and respect) have a head start on a good marriage.

Discussing Important Issues

Chart 2-23 lists some important issues that engaged couples need to discuss. Every couple could add other issues of importance to them. Through leisurely discussions of each issue, the two persons will learn a great deal about each other. They will undoubtedly have some differences. They will have to determine the importance of their differences. They will have to decide if and how their differences can be overcome. They will have to evaluate the strength of their love. Even love cannot make differences and conflicts between two people disappear. However, love can make the differences seem smaller and easier to overcome. When two people in love work together to settle their differences, their relationship grows even stronger.

Issues to Discuss During Engagement

Your attitudes toward marriage
Your readiness, as a couple, for married life
Your expectations—
  of your husband or wife
  of your first year of marriage
  of your fifth, tenth, twentieth, and
    fortieth years of marriage
Educational goals
Career goals
Family goals—
  having or not having children
  establishing family customs
  relationships with in-laws
Friendships—
  old and new
  individual and shared
Social activities
Differences in—
  age
  where you were raised and where you live
    now
  nationality
  race
  religion
  social class
Marriage roles—
  sharing responsibility
  resolving conflicts
  sharing household chores
  caring for and disciplining children
Financial matters—
  present financial status
  financial goals
  what your monthly budget will be
  how financial decisions will be made
  who will handle the money
Where you will live
What transportation you will need

2-23 Open communication about important issues helps a couple prepare for marriage.

On the other hand, honest discussions of important issues may warn the couple they have problems. They may have too many minor differences. They may have a few major differences they cannot resolve. If they have serious conflicts during

Discuss:
How long should the engagement period last in order to accomplish its functions?

Activity:
Form small groups. Have each group make a list of important issues to discuss before marriage. Then have them rank the issues in the order of their importance. For each issue, discuss the importance of agreement between the future husband and wife.

Resource:
Are You Ready for Marriage? reproducible master, TR

Putting Technology to Use
Have each student interview a married couple. Students should create a questionnaire in word processing software using the issues listed in Figure 2-23. Have students ask the couples if they considered all these points before marrying, and if their opinions differed on any points.

Discuss:
What could a person do to win the respect and approval of future in-laws?

Enrich:
Write a one-page paper describing the type of wedding you would like. What would you do if you and your future spouse have something completely different in mind?

Enrich:
Divide the class into small groups. Have each group look in the local newspaper and determine the cost of an average apartment. Also have them look at furniture ads and estimate the cost to furnish an apartment. Determine the total cost of furnishing the apartment and paying rent for one year.

engagement, they can't expect the situation to change after their wedding. A wise couple will give their relationship an honest test before they accept the commitment of marriage.

When an engagement is announced, the future in-laws begin to look at the couple differently. In-laws can have a major role in determining the success or failure of a marriage. Taking time to win their respect and approval can pay rich dividends during marriage. Establishing good relationships with in-laws is another function of the engagement period.

Wedding Plans

Another function of the engagement period is planning the wedding, 2-24. A wedding is a social event. It gives people a chance to celebrate the start of a couple's new life together. A wedding can also give a couple a good start for their life as husband and wife. The wedding should be planned around the couple's desires. The parents' desires should also be considered. As the wedding is being planned, the couple and their future in-laws have the chance to strengthen their relationships.

Many different factors affect wedding plans. The region of the country in which the couple lives is one factor. A couple's

2-24 Careful planning during the engagement can make the wedding more enjoyable for everyone.

age, religious beliefs, family culture, and family customs are other factors. Some couples prefer simple weddings while others want more elaborate weddings. A traditional ceremonial wedding is chosen by many couples, while others prefer a simple civil wedding ceremony.

Plans for a Future Home

The engagement period gives a couple time to make arrangements for their future home. They will have to find a house, condominium, or apartment. Their choice will depend on where they work, as well as their financial situation.

Besides finding a home in a convenient location, they will have to furnish it. Most couples start by combining the furniture they already have. Many also buy used furniture or borrow from families and friends. If they can afford it, some purchase new pieces.

No one way of finding and furnishing a home is better than any other way. What is important is that the couple discuss options and share in making the decisions. Then these first challenges of sharing a home can be fun and exciting.

Length of Engagement

How long should an engagement last? The answer is relative. Couples who have known each other for a long time before becoming engaged may have a shorter engagement period. Studies show that the most successful marriages are between people who have known each other five years or more. A high degree of success is also experienced by those who have known each other two to four years. Those who have known each other less than six months have a significant decline in marital success.

Ending an Engagement

While an engagement is considered a preparation for marriage, not all engagements end in marriage. Many couples who approach engagement seriously find that they are not ready to commit themselves to marriage. They may find their differences

Family Enrichment Activity

Encourage students to talk with their parents about the parents' engagement period, wedding ceremony, and marriage. Students should ask their parents to evaluate both positive and negative aspects of these events. Students should also ask parents to help them set some goals for these events in their lives.

are too great to resolve. For a couple in this situation, a broken engagement is better than a broken marriage.

Making Marriage Work

People continually grow and change. It makes sense that a marriage relationship would continually grow and change, too. The most obvious changes occur early in marriage. Throughout a marriage relationship, the greatest challenge for most couples is to grow closer together, not farther apart.

Early Marital Adjustments

Whenever two people start a new life together, adjustments have to be made. Since no two people are alike, this is to be expected. Most newlyweds will be faced with several adjustments as they adapt to their new lifestyle. Their success in making these adjustments will affect the quality of their relationship.

Adjusting to a new home is one change for newlyweds. If they had been living with their parents, their new dwelling may seem small. Their furnishings may seem simple and sparse. The couple will have to adjust to housing they can afford. With a good attitude, the couple can enjoy the challenge of gradually improving their home.

Newlyweds have to adjust to some new daily living habits and routines, 2-25. Morning and evening schedules will have to be adjusted to fit the couple's needs. Meal patterns will have to be adjusted according to food preferences, cooking skills, and time schedules. Plans will have to be made so that household chores such as doing laundry, dusting, and mowing the lawn are done. Good communication and cooperation will help the couple make these adjustments easily.

Social activities tend to change and become less expensive. Married people tend to set many long-range goals. These goals may include further education, home ownership, and parenthood. Such goals require financial commitments. To meet their long-range goals, a couple may spend less money for recreation.

2-25 Sharing household duties helps this couple build a closer relationship.

Relationships with family members and friends may change, too. A spouse usually receives top priority in marriage. Wise parents, other family members, and friends realize this is an important adjustment for newlyweds. This does not mean that others are forgotten. Since newlyweds tend to spend more time together, they have less time for family and friends.

Nurturing a Marriage

Subtle changes occur continuously in marriage. As people grow older, they face new challenges and accept new responsibilities. Some of their interests and attitudes change. Good communication helps marriage partners keep in touch with each other's changing personality. Then they can change together. Their relationship can become closer and stronger.

Reflect:
Do you know someone who wanted to break an engagement but did not? Are they happily married?

Discuss:
What are some common marital adjustments that may need to be made in the early stages of marriage?

Resource:
Adjusting to Married Life, reproducible master, TR

FCCLA Activity

Encourage students working on the Interpersonal Communications STAR Event to develop a project designed to achieve one of the following goals:
- help engaged couples discuss important issues before marriage
- strengthen communication between people and their in-laws

> **Discuss:**
> Do you know a couple that seems to have a "perfect" marriage? How do they handle disagreements?
>
> **Reflect:**
> Think of an older couple you know that has been married a long time, such as grandparents. Do you think of their marriage as "romantic"? What factors help their marriage succeed today?

Two people can grow closer together in marriage, but they cannot achieve perfection. No person is perfect. No marriage is perfect. A couple should not expect to feel total love for each other all the time. They should not be disappointed if love seems to fade and then reappear. Sometimes a couple's love will have periods of growth; other times it will level out. If they have a strong relationship and keep communication lines open, their love will return.

Just as love has its ups and downs, so does happiness. Trying to maintain constant happiness can drain a marriage relationship. Married people should stay in tune with each other's feelings, supporting each other through these ups and downs. They may find happiness together in special occasions, such as anniversaries and holidays. They may also find happiness in simple acts of kindness and thoughtfulness. Sometimes one spouse may feel unhappy or upset. This is a normal part of most relationships. By offering love and understanding during these times, a couple can work through these feelings.

Any marriage will have good times and bad times. A successful marriage is one in which both partners want success and are willing to work for it. They focus on their love for each other and the good times they share. They make an effort to communicate their thoughts and feelings to each other. When problems or differences arise, they work together to resolve them.

> **Check It Out!**
> 1. The kind of love that is based on the concern a person has for the well-being of another is __ __ love.
> 2. Name three factors that influence a person's choice of a marriage partner.
> 3. True or false. The relationships among members of a person's family may influence the relationships that will form within his or her future family.
> 4. Name two reasons for the high rate of failure in teenage marriages.
> 5. List three functions of the engagement period.
> 6. True or false. In a successful marriage relationship, a couple continually grows and changes.

> **Check It Out! (Answers)**
> 1. altruistic
> 2. (List three:) family background; personal priorities, goals, and standards; emotional maturity; age; social activities; parental approval; personal attitude toward marriage
> 3. true
> 4. emotional immaturity and financial problems
> 5. (List three:) examine the relationship, establish good relationships with in-laws, make wedding plans, find a home
> 6. true

TEENS ARE CONCERNED ABOUT...

Intimate Relationships

Lila R. Montambo, an experienced educator, shares teens' concerns about this important societal issue. Besides researching the topic, she conducts seminars on intimacy for various groups. Montambo has a master's degree in nursing and a Ph.D. in psychology. She has 24 years of experience in nursing education and cardiology.

Q: *Many teens question how they will know when they are ready for an intimate relationship. How would you advise them on this issue?*

A: First, let's define intimate relationships. An intimate relationship is a series of interactions between people that produce intense feelings of security and self-worth.

Studies have shown intimate relationships are made up of 15 components. I believe all are important to intimacy. Many people form sexual relationships before intimacy has time to grow and develop. They should be aware that sex is only one of the 15 components of an intimate relationship.

I would ask teens to examine relationships they have already experienced to help them recognize the feelings that result from true intimacy. To do this, I would have them think about each of the components of intimacy listed below. Then they would identify a person with whom they have shared each of the components. The person may be of the same sex as themselves, the opposite sex, younger, or older.

Think of a person

- you can meet at a high level of understanding. When you are together, you can talk about anything or everything. This is *intellectual intimacy*.
- who makes you feel good. You feel at peace with this person. Just being in his or her presence is like getting a warm pat on the back. This is *emotional intimacy*.
- you would seek out at a party because you are proud to be seen with this person. You know he or she will not betray you with a cold shoulder. This is *social intimacy*.
- with whom you can have fun. Being with this person is fun, even when you are not doing anything. This is *recreational intimacy*.
- with whom you are not afraid to disagree. You know you can work out any problems you may have. This is *conflict-resolution intimacy*.
- you like to hug. You would even kiss this person if he or she were the right sex or age for your kissing standards. This is *affection*—a mark of intimacy.
- you want to be near. You feel a sense of contentment with him or her. When problems occur, you want to stay and work them out. This component is known as *cohesion*.
- with whom you feel a sense of belonging. You are neither too good for each other nor too bad. You feel just right. You can be yourself without any false pretenses. This is *identity*.
- who enjoys the same kinds of activities you enjoy. You can shop together without boredom because you enjoy browsing in similar shops. You can even share living environments because you like similar thermostat settings. This shows *compatibility*.
- who lets you be you. You feel like an independent human being. This person allows you space to grow without making you feel guilty or threatened. This shows *autonomy*.

Note:
The way this feature is handled will depend on the age and maturity of your students and the community in which you live. It is recommended that you not have a classroom discussion concerning this feature unless you feel comfortable discussing intimate relationships with your students.

Discuss:
How would you define intimate relationships? Do you agree with Ms. Montambo's definition?

Discuss:
- Do you agree that trust underlies each of the components of an intimate relationship?
- How is intimacy related to self-worth and self-esteem?
- How can the physical act of having sex cause guilt, hurt, jealousy, and other painful emotions? Do you agree that having a sexual relationship with one person can affect many other people?
- Ms. Montambo states, "Sexual intimacy may make you lose the ability to become truly intimate." What is your reaction to this statement?
- Do you agree with Ms. Montambo when she states "a stronger intimacy has more of the components"?

- who lets you say what you want to say. You feel that you can express anything and still be accepted. When you talk to this person, he or she does not use either body language or words to put you down. You can even enjoy periods of silence together without feeling uncomfortable because you are not talking. This is *expressiveness*.
- to whom you can tell a secret knowing he or she will not tell. You can talk with this person about issues important to you and your well-being. This is *self-disclosure*.
- who understands the way you feel and supports you when you are feeling up or down. This is *empathy*.
- who feels the same way about you that you feel about him or her. You feel that you are traveling on a two-way street—together. This is *mutuality*.
- you do not fear this person in any way. You know he or she is on your side. You can count on him or her to say what you need to hear, not what you want to hear. You truly believe this person has your best interest at heart. He or she will never hurt you. This is *trust*.

All relationships are built on a measure of trust. If you review all the components of intimacy named above, you will recognize that trust underlies each one.

This has been a long answer, but teens—and all people—need to understand the real meaning of intimacy. Chances are they identified many different people as they considered the different components of intimacy. People are intimate with many different people—all ages and both sexes. People need this intimacy to form a strong sense of self-worth and develop self-esteem.

A truly intimate relationship would only exist between perfect people. Since no one is perfect, people must look for a realistic measure of intimacy. One way to evaluate the strength of intimacy is to recognize that a stronger intimacy has more of the components. The fewer the components, the weaker the intimacy. Intimacy is a two-way passage. A person should be capable of both giving and receiving intimacy.

People are ready for intimacy when they know themselves and their true needs (not wants and desires). The needs of teens change every day. Teens need to recognize that sex is only one component of intimacy. They need to intellectually control their hormones, or they may become sexually intimate at the risk of other areas of development.

Q: *How would having sex affect the teens involved?*

A: Unless other components of intimacy are present, sex is a physical act that will not meet the other needs of individuals. Guilt, hurt, jealousy, and other painful emotions are by-products of the physical act of sex without the other components.

Q: *Who else might be affected by a teen's decision to have a sexual relationship?*

A: The partner is certainly affected. He or she will carry guilt for any negative feelings that occur. Consider also the possibility of a pregnancy and the impact it would have on the baby. Those who love you are also affected. They empathize with your feelings and your pain. Actually, everyone within your realm of family, friends, coworkers and all of society is affected. When you are hurt, your personality changes. A personality change affects everyone around you.

Q: *How does having sex affect relationships between dating partners?*

A: If you were on an intimacy ship, it would capsize if the other components were not present to balance the sex act. Sex without trust, for example, would be devastating. It would be an excruciatingly painful hurt. The sex urge is so strong—like the desire to eat—that it tends to preempt other things of great importance. When dating partners become involved in sex, they tend to allow sexual intimacy to take precedence over other components of intimacy. When sexual intimacy becomes the focus, growth in other areas of intimacy takes a backseat in the relationship. Sexual intimacy may make you lose the ability to become truly intimate.

Q: *Do you have any other thoughts about intimate relationships you would like to share with teens?*

A: Be aware of the true meaning of intimacy. Don't confuse intimacy with sex. Sex may be nothing more than a physical act. Sex may also be an expression of those deep and abiding feelings of true intimacy and trust. True intimacy binds and personalizes a relationship that sustains two partners throughout life.

Chapter Review

Summary

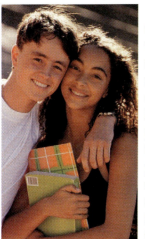

Building positive relationships with parents, siblings, peers, romantic partners, and coworkers will help you throughout your life. These relationships will bring you physical, emotional, social, and economic benefits. Mutual respect, trust, openness, and reliability will help you build relationships that are positive.

Many of your positive relationships will be with acquaintances, good friends, best friends, and dating partners. You will be attracted to these people partly because you meet each other's complementary needs. Through group dating and random dating, you will find partners with whom you want to have steady relationships. As you learn the difference between love and infatuation and learn how to have a responsible relationship, you will build more mature, lasting relationships.

Unfortunately, many people experience negative relationships. If you recognize that a relationship is damaging for you or the other person involved, it should be ended. Some negative relationships are the result of negative peer pressure. Forming a code for your behavior will help you manage this peer pressure. You should know how to recognize sexual harassment and how to avoid being a victim of either sexual harassment or rape.

Marriage can be the closest and most satisfying relationship between a couple. However, it takes prior preparation and continual effort to maintain this relationship.

Several factors influence marital success including having similar family backgrounds, personal priorities, goals, and standards. Sharing social activities, having emotional maturity, and having parental approval also help marriages succeed. The engagement period is a time to examine relationships, establish positive in-law relations, and plan for the wedding.

Think About It!

1. Evaluate the relationships between you and your parents, siblings, peers, romantic partners, or coworkers. Give five suggestions for improving relationships with the group you choose.
2. Which of the benefits of positive relationships do you consider to be most important? Explain your answer.
3. Explain how you can develop each of the four key elements that form the basis for positive relationships.
4. Evaluate the importance of acquaintances, good friends, and best friends in your social life. Describe how you would be affected if your best friends moved away.
5. Identify three complementary needs that you and a friend or dating partner meet for each other.
6. Which type of dating do you think most helps people to mature socially? Explain your answer.
7. Describe a situation in which you were infatuated with someone. How were you able to identify your feelings as infatuation rather than love?
8. What are some possible consequences of continuing a negative relationship?
9. What would you say to a best friend who was hesitant to end a negative relationship?
10. Give two examples of negative peer pressure faced by students in your school.

Activity: Have students debate the subject of peer pressure—the good and the bad. How can peer pressure be beneficial for teens? How can peer pressure be detrimental for teens?

Reflect: Do you hope to marry someday? Has what you have learned in this chapter encouraged you or discouraged you?

Activity: You might divide the class into small groups and assign one of the relationships in *Think About It!* #1 to each group. Have each group prepare a list of suggestions for improving relationships in their category. Share lists with the rest of the class.

Note:
Students may be reluctant to share with you information regarding their personal lives. However, in writing, students will reflect about their relationships and perhaps come to a better understanding of their true feelings. Therefore, tell students they do not have to sign their names to their papers if they do not want to do so.

Enrich:
Have students send their fictitious letters from *Try It Out!* #5 to actual advice columnists who write for magazines or newspapers. When a response is received, compare the advice given by students with the advice given by a professional advice columnist.

Note:
You might want to ask that some of the descriptions in *Try It Out!* #7 be performed as role-plays.

Resource:
PowerZone CD Challenge. Have students play the chapter review game to reinforce text content.

11. What factors do you think have the most influence on a person's choice of marriage partner?
12. List ten issues you think are especially important for a couple to discuss during engagement. Explain your responses.
13. What steps can newlyweds take to make their marriage adjustments easier?
14. Name a career that is of interest to you. Tell how the skills taught in this chapter could help you become successful in that field of employment.

Try It Out!

1. Write a short essay describing your most significant positive relationship. Explain how you have benefited from this relationship and what elements helped you build it and keep it strong.
2. Select two couples from movies, TV shows, or books that have complementary needs. Discuss how their complementary needs affect their relationship.
3. Create a bulletin board display of pictures and cartoons related to random and steady dating.
4. Research the characteristics of infatuation and love. Design a poster to illustrate your findings.
5. Write a fictitious letter to an advice columnist. Ask for advice on how to end a negative relationship, recover from a negative relationship, or manage negative peer pressure. Exchange letters with a classmate. Write a response to the letter you receive using information you learned in this chapter.
6. Assign two sets of personal priorities, two goals, and two standards to an imaginary engaged couple. Write a short story describing how the personal priorities, goals, and standards of these two people would affect their relationship.
7. Describe a typical day for an imaginary couple in the first week of their marriage (after the honeymoon). Then describe a typical day after six months, after three years, and after ten years of marriage. Show how the couple has grown and changed.

Chapter 3
Communication Skills

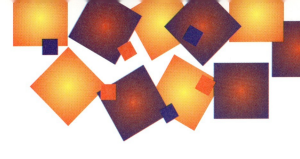

Careers

These careers relate to the topics in this chapter:
- reading tutor
- youth services worker
- consumer services representative
- editor

As you study this chapter, see if you can think of others.

Topics

3-1 The Communication Process
3-2 Communciation in Relationships
3-3 Conflict Resolution

Introductory Activities

1. Ask students to define *communication*. Discuss the following questions: Why is communication important? Which is more important to good communication—speaking or listening? What is the difference between hearing and listening?
2. Ask students why they should be aware of their own communication skills. Why should they be aware of the communication skills of others?
3. Have your students sit in a circle and play the "gossip game." Whisper a short message into one student's ear. Have students whisper the message from one to another saying what they heard. When the last student has received the message, ask that student to repeat the message out loud. Discuss why the message changed and how communication could be improved.

Topic 3-1
The Communication Process
I. Verbal Communication
   A. Listening
      1. Barriers to Good Listening
      2. Become an Active Listener
   B. Speaking
      1. Developing Speaking Skills
      2. How to Start a Conversation
II. Nonverbal Communication
   A. Your Appearance
   B. Your Actions
   C. Body Language
      1. Forms of Body Language
   D. Personal Space
III. Technology and Communication
   A. Cellular Phones
   B. Pagers
   C. Voice Mail
   D. Computers

Topic 3-2
Communication in Relationships
I. The Importance of Communication in Relationships
   A. Communicating Positive Feelings
II. Barriers to Open Communication
   A. Stereotypes
   B. Prejudices
   C. Coded Messages
   D. Gender Differences
III. When Negative Feelings Occur
   A. Handling Negative Feelings
IV. Communication in the Workplace

Topic 3-3
Conflict Resolution
I. Types of Conflicts
II. Causes of Conflict
III. Reactions to Conflict
   A. Negative Reactions
   B. Positive Reactions
IV. Constructive Methods for Handling Conflict
   A. Use "I" Messages
   B. Decide Who Owns the Problem
   C. Learn to Negotiate and Compromise
   D. Use the Conflict Resolution Process
   E. Mediation
      1. Peer Mediation
V. Violence: A Destructive Method of Handling Conflict

Chapter 3 Communication Skills

Vocabulary:
What do you think are forms of verbal communication? What are forms of nonverbal communication?

Resource:
Journal Entry, reproducible master, TR

Reflect:
Think of a recent verbal exchange you had with a teacher. Evaluate the communication that took place between you. How could you have improved that communication?

Activity:
Sit quietly in a room full of noise. Clear your mind of other thoughts and write down everything you hear. Which of these sounds might you have missed if you had not been concentrating on listening?

Topic 3-1
The Communication Process

Objectives
After studying this topic, you will be able to
- improve your listening and speaking skills.
- begin and develop conversations more easily.
- use several forms of nonverbal communication to communicate more effectively.
- describe the use of several types of electronic communication.

Topic Terms
communication
verbal communication
nonverbal communication
active listener
feedback
passive listener
reflection
manners
body language
personal space
technology
Internet
e-mail
World Wide Web
online

To develop good relationships with other people, you have to be able to communicate. **Communication** is the process of conveying information in such a way that the message is received and understood. Through communication, you can share ideas, opinions, and facts with others. In close relationships, you can also discuss and share your problems and feelings.

Good communication is a skill you will use throughout your life. It is based upon a mutual effort between people to understand one another. Speakers must try to make their messages relevant to the listeners. At the same time, listeners must open their minds to the messages being sent.

All forms of communication—speaking, listening, reading, and writing—can be grouped into two different categories. The first is **verbal communication**, which involves the use of words. **Nonverbal communication** is the second category; this involves sending messages without words. In this topic, you will learn more about these two forms of communication.

Verbal Communication
Communication skills are just like word processing skills or baseball skills. You can learn them, practice them, and improve them. The first steps in improving your verbal communication skills are learning to listen and to speak well.

Listening
Listening plays an important role in communication. A spoken message is worthless unless someone hears it and listens to it. Hearing and listening, however, have two different meanings. You hear many sounds all day long. Radios, electric shavers, kitchen appliances, cars, and airplanes are just a few examples. If you really listened to all these sounds, you would not have time to think about anything else. Instead, you have developed the habit of ignoring unimportant sounds. This is usually a good and helpful habit. If you aren't careful, however, you may find yourself slipping into this habit more often than you should. You may be ignoring spoken messages that people are trying to send to you.

Barriers to Good Listening
Recognizing what gets in the way of good listening can help you learn to overcome these barriers. The habit of ignoring sounds is just one barrier to good listening.

Forgetting all or part of the message is a common communication barrier. Even if you listen to what is being said, there is a chance for a communication failure. Studies show that people remember as little as 25 percent of the information they

Across the Curriculum
English. Work with students on writing business letters. Have students critique one another's letters on clear verbal communication.

receive through listening. People remember more when they see, read, or verbally repeat the message they hear. Listening by itself does not always ensure good communication.

Another barrier to good listening is not understanding the message being sent. The message a person sends to you may not be the same message you receive. The speaker may pronounce words differently if he or she is from a different part of the country. People from the South pronounce some words differently from people in the Midwest. The speaker may use slang expressions or words that are unfamiliar to you. You may think the speaker is joking when he or she is serious. Even the tone of voice can change the meaning of what is said. These are just a few of the factors that can interfere with good listening.

Become an Active Listener

Listening is important to good communication because you listen more often than you speak. With practice, you can develop good listening skills.

A good listener is an **active listener**. This means the listener gives the speaker some form of feedback. **Feedback** lets the speaker know the message is getting through to the listener and how it is being received. The feedback can be a nod, a smile, or even a comment that lets the speaker know the message is received.

A **passive listener** may hear the spoken words, but not the meaning of the words. A passive listener does not respond to the speaker in any way. The speaker doesn't know if the message is being received or not. Have you ever spoken to someone who didn't seem to really be listening to you?

By using active listening, you improve the entire communication process. The following are some tips to help you:

- *Ask questions to clarify the message*. This shows you are not only hearing what the speaker is saying, but processing it. You are trying to understand the speaker and preparing to act on the message. Speakers should try to present information clearly. Listeners have the responsibility of seeking clarification if the information is confusing. Receiving the right message is a two-way process. As you listen, ask for added details. Ask the speaker to go over any points you have not clearly understood.
- *Pay attention*. Focus your attention on the speaker. Use eye contact. Do not let your mind race ahead of what is being said. Avoid daydreaming or letting your mind wander to other topics. See 3-1.
- *Be interested*. You will listen better if you have a sincere desire to know what the other person is saying and feeling. With genuine interest in the speaker, it becomes easier to focus attention on him or her.
- *Be patient*. Give the speaker time to present his or her message. Do not interrupt and take over the speaking role.
- *Keep the speaker in mind*. Expect the information to come from the speaker's background of experiences or point of view. To listen, you have to

3-1 A good listener shows sincere interest in what the speaker is saying.

Activity:
Read a poem to yourself. How much of it can you remember? Read another poem and then listen to someone recite it. Which poem can you remember better?

Reflect:
Think of the last time you daydreamed in class. How much of that lesson could you remember as you left the class? How much did you remember the next day?

Activity:
Ask students to make a special effort to stop, breathe deeply, and listen for the remainder of the day. Discuss what they experienced the next day in class.

Putting Technology to Use
Have students use drawing software to illustrate the cycle of communication. Make sure they include speakers, listeners, and feedback.

Enrich:
Practice using the tips for good listening the next time you hear a lecture. See if you are able to understand and recall more of what the speaker said using these tips.

Activity:
List words teens use that may have different meanings for adults. What communication problems might result from the use of these terms?

Discuss:
What is meant by *constructive criticism*? How can you criticize a person's bad habits without hurting his or her feelings? Is it sometimes more difficult to criticize other people than to receive criticism yourself?

put aside your previous thoughts and biases for the moment. Concentrate on the person who is speaking to you.

- *Stay focused.* Some people are too busy thinking about what they will say in response to a speaker. As a result, they fail to listen to what is said. When someone is speaking, listen. When the person stops, you can collect your thoughts and then respond. The speaker will respect you for listening, thinking about what was said, and making a thoughtful response.

- *Use reflection.* When you use **reflection**, you repeat in your own words what you think was said. The speaker sees in a "mirror" the message that was sent, but in words reflected back by the listener. The receiver might say, "If I understand you correctly, you are saying…" With reflection, the speaker can easily see if a message was misinterpreted.

- *Listen to the speaker's tone of voice.* Sometimes the way something is said is just as important as what is said. For instance, a comment like, "You look sad," might be judged as sarcastic, critical, or sympathetic, depending on how it was stated.

Speaking

Speaking is the most widely used form of verbal communication. Speaking and listening are equally important in the two-way communication process.

You spend much of your day speaking with others. The way you speak affects your life in many ways. It affects your relationships with your family members and your friends. It affects your daily interactions with teachers, classmates, coworkers, and employers, 3-2. Speaking clearly will help you express your thoughts, feelings, and ideas to others.

Have you noticed that some people have better speaking skills than others? You could listen to them for hours and not lose interest. With practice, you too can develop your speaking skills.

3-2 Good communication skills are important in both personal and business relationships.

Developing Speaking Skills

How good are your speaking skills? Do you send clear messages when you speak to others? Do others interpret your messages correctly? The way you speak affects the impressions people form of you. If your skills need improvement, try using some of these techniques:

- *Keep the listener in mind.* Use words the listener will understand. This is especially important if the listener has a different cultural or educational background from you or if the listener is a child. To communicate clearly, you need to be aware of the meanings others may attach to the words you use.

- *Keep messages short and simple.* Use simple language and proper grammar. Explain your message clearly. Leave no room for confusion and you are more likely to be understood.

- *Be considerate of others' feelings.* Think before you speak. Avoid making comments that may hurt someone. If criticism is needed, try to make it constructive. Try to suggest ways to improve or change a behavior that is bothering you. Sometimes praise works better than criticism. Praise what you do like, and that action will probably be repeated. Ignore what you do not like, and that action will probably be stopped.

- *Be open and honest.* This is especially true when you are talking to your close friends, 3-3. Don't expect them to

Across the Curriculum

Speech. Have students prepare speeches during study of this topic. Ask the students to also give their prepared speeches and have classmates critique them on the criteria listed in "Developing Speaking Skills."

3-3 Open and honest communication is especially important among friends.

How to Start a Conversation

Another way to develop your speaking skills is to practice starting a conversation. Good conversation skills are useful in many situations. For instance, you notice an interesting-looking person standing alone at a party. You would like to talk to the person, but you don't know what to say. Does this situation sound familiar? To be prepared, have a few conversation openers in mind, such as the following:

- *Ask questions.* Questions work in almost any situation, 3-4. When you use questions to start conversations, ask questions that require more than a yes or no answer. Examples are, "What do you think about…?" "How do you feel about…?" "What do you think would happen if…?" Ask the person a key question about himself or herself. Ask about his or her work, hobbies, or family. Almost everyone has a good personal story to tell. Most people enjoy talking about themselves.
- *Make a sincere compliment.* Another good conversation starter is to compliment the person about something—appearance, clothing, possessions, or accomplishments. Compliments make people feel good about themselves. When they feel good, they are likely to relax and begin talking.

read your mind. They can't. If you want them to know what you want or how you feel, you will have to tell them.

- *Respect the listener.* Good rapport between a speaker and a listener aids good communication. Good rapport is built upon respect and sincerity. Talking down to a person or showing disrespect will cut off communication lines.
- *Be positive.* People enjoy listening to someone who has a positive outlook on life. On the other hand, people become bored listening to someone who complains all the time. Using a pleasant tone of voice and maintaining eye contact are ways of conveying a positive attitude. This encourages others to listen and respond positively to the speaker.
- *Check to see whether your message is being received accurately.* Questions such as "What do you think?" or "How do you feel about this?" will draw your listener into a speaking role. He or she will then reflect on what you have said and give you some feedback. This will tell you if your message has been understood. You will know if you should go back and explain something again or go ahead with new information.

Concentrate on one communication skill at a time. Listening and speaking skills improve with practice.

3-4 Asking a question that requires an explanation is a good conversation starter.

Resource:
Listening and Speaking, Activity A, SAG

Discuss:
What are some poor conversation openers you have heard or used yourself?

Activity:
Watch a TV talk show. Write down some of the ways the host or hostess encourages good discussions. Note the types of questions that are asked.

Resource:
Conversation Openers, reproducible master, TR

Activity:
Turn to the people on either side of you and give them compliments that could start conversations.

Family Enrichment Activity
Encourage students to talk to a family member about a topic of mutual interest. Instruct them to practice good listening skills during their conversations.

Resource:
The Art of Conversation, Activity B, SAG

Activity:
Form a small group. Start talking about a topic. After every minute, change the topic of conversation. What effect did the frequent change of subject have on the conversation?

Discuss:
How important is a person's appearance when you meet someone for the first time?

Reflect:
Think of a situation when you were with someone who used poor manners. How did you feel?

■ *Mention something you have in common with the other person.* If you know the person, mention a subject you know the person thinks is interesting. Discussions of current events, movies, books, and sports events can keep a conversation going.

If you and the person to whom you are talking both know some of the same people, you can talk about them. However, this type of conversation can be risky. Be sure to say only positive things. Don't begin by criticizing someone who may be this person's neighbor, cousin, or best friend!

■ *Discuss one topic.* A personal conversation is more likely to be successful if you explore just one key point of common interest. Look for an interesting depth in that topic rather than trying to cover many topics. A constant change of subjects may drive the other person away.

Practice will help you feel more comfortable talking with people. Try not to be shy. Chances are the person you want to meet would like to meet you, too. Try not to be afraid of saying the wrong words. Just relax and be yourself. Concentrate on enjoying the conversation and the other person's company.

Nonverbal Communication

People communicate in many ways other than the spoken or written word. Communication that does not involve words is called nonverbal communication. The way a person looks, dresses, acts, and reacts are forms of nonverbal expression.

Your Appearance

Does your appearance send the message you want it to send? When people meet you, what is their first impression? People form their impressions of you based on the way you look. Often these judgments are made quickly. Before you say anything, your appearance is sending a message to them. Are you communicating a positive message about yourself?

Good grooming is one way to send a positive message. Clean, neatly styled hair, trimmed nails, and a clean body help create an attractive appearance. It shows you care about yourself and the way you look.

The clothes you wear communicate a message about you, too. They are clues to your lifestyle and personality. They tell others where you plan to go, what you plan to do, and how you feel about yourself. Neat, clean clothes that fit well help create a positive image. Studies show people generally respond more favorably to those who are well groomed and well dressed.

Your Actions

The actions you take can send messages to others. For instance, **manners** are rules to follow for proper conduct. Using good manners sends the message that you want others to feel comfortable. In most cases, having good manners is as simple as being kind to others and using common sense.

Other actions will send the message that you care about people's feelings. Using the words *please,* *thank you,* and *excuse me* shows courtesy and respect to others. Sending a note of thanks or a card to cheer someone up reflects thoughtfulness, 3-5. Giving a gift on a special occasion tells people you are considerate. Using a pleasant tone of voice lets others know you want them to feel at ease.

Body Language

When you nod your head, shake your fist, or point your finger, you are communicating without words. With **body language**, you are using body movements, such as facial expressions, gestures, and posture, to send messages to others.

Although you are not using words, your messages can be crystal clear. The expression on your face can convey your mood before you even begin to talk. See 3-6. When you walk into the kitchen and find that someone has prepared your favorite dinner, a kiss and a hug can help you say

Problem-Solving Practice
A New Student at School, reproducible master, TR. Students are to read a case study about a new student with whom they are having trouble communicating. They are to answer questions to suggest ways to open up the lines of communication.

3-5 A card can help you communicate your feelings of concern for another.

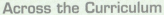

3-6 This young woman's facial expression gives a nonverbal clue to her mood.

a multicultural society, it is important to be aware of possible differences in body language. In some cultures, the way a message is delivered is more important than the actual content of the message.

While some specific body language varies among cultures, in some ways body language is a worldwide language. A person from any culture is likely to understand your gestures meaning yes, no, come, stop, up, and down.

Forms of Body Language

You may not always be aware of the body language messages you are sending. Some of your expressions or gestures may be habits. Others are spontaneous reactions to what is happening around you.

Posture is one form of body language. An erect posture tells others that all is well. A slumped posture can suggest fatigue, boredom, illness, and other negative or painful messages. The sound of footsteps is a clue to the posture and mood of a person yet unseen. Some footsteps sound happy and energetic. Others sound bored or tired.

Arms help to convey messages, too. Extending your arms toward a person is a sign of approval. It's like saying, "I like you," or "Come nearer." Folding your arms creates a barrier and may even suggest disapproval. It is like saying, "I will stay in my place, and I hope you will stay in yours."

Hands aid communication in many ways. Some people are said to "talk with their hands." This means they use hand gestures to make their spoken messages clearer. Hands reaching out toward others suggest acceptance and approval. Hands in pockets suggest a lack of interest. Hands on hips seem to give a defensive message. Raising hands is a form of body language used in classrooms. Hand motions are often used to say hello or goodbye. Some hand motions say, "Speak softly." Other hand motions cause an entire band to begin playing loudly.

A *handshake* is a way of communicating in business and social situations. Handshakes can be cold and uninterested, or they can be warm and friendly. Some handshakes

thank you. With a smile and a shake of your head, you can let someone know that you agree. With a wink, you can say, "I like you."

People from different cultures have developed certain body language that is unique to their culture. Because we live in

> **Reflect:**
> Think of the last gift you gave to another person. What kind of body language did the receiver use to show his or her appreciation?
>
> **Discuss:**
> Describe your posture at this very moment. What message are you sending to others about yourself?
>
> **Activity:**
> Try talking with your hands at your sides. Then hold a conversation while using hand gestures. Which way made the conversation easier for you?

Across the Curriculum
Business. Discuss the importance of a firm handshake in the business world.

Activity:
Shake three different people's hands in class. What different messages did you receive? Describe how each handshake differed.

Reflect:
Think of the last time you had a conversation with someone who didn't make eye contact with you. How did you feel?

Resource:
Body Language, Activity C, SAG

are limp and lifeless. Others are forceful and crushing. A firm, friendly handshake is usually best. It communicates a positive image of the person.

Nodding is a positive form of body language. It is a sign of approval. It says, "I like what I see and hear," or "I am aware of your presence." It is used most often to encourage repetition of the approved behavior. Be aware, however, that in some cultures nodding merely means I'm listening. It does not necessarily mean agreement with what is being said.

Facial expressions send interesting messages, 3-7. A person can look interested, bored, happy, sad, excited, tired, pleased, angry, smart, silly, confused, worried, or thoughtful. That same person can glance, glare, stare, frown, snarl, or smile at you.

Facial expressions can help clarify other body language messages. For instance, a clenched fist accompanied by a frown suggests anger. In contrast, a clenched fist accompanied by a smile suggests approval.

Some facial expressions are made without thinking. Other expressions are made with a specific purpose in mind. The intended message is quite clear, 3-8.

People from this country tend to greet people with smiles on their faces. Even if they are greeting strangers, they will usually smile. This is not generally the case among other cultural groups. Europeans, Asians, Arabs, Africans, and South

3-7 Facial expressions can communicate a variety of emotions.

3-8 This young man is using body language to signal his excitement.

Americans are more formal in their greetings. They may use titles and last names when meeting others. Americans may mistake this formality for rudeness and unfriendliness, but this is not the case. The mainstream U.S. culture is more informal than many other cultures.

Eye contact is a clue to what a person is thinking. A good example can be seen in classrooms. Students usually avoid eye contact with a teacher when they have not prepared their lessons. Instead of looking at the teacher, unprepared students try to look busy so the teacher won't call on them. During a class discussion, students who don't know a particular answer are likely to look away until another student answers. Then they will turn their attention back to the discussion. Students who know the answers are likely to look directly at the teacher.

In some cultures, people are taught to never make eye contact with someone who is in authority. Again, being aware of possible cultural differences is important.

When you communicate with others, keep body language in mind. You will be able to pick up clues about other people that

Across the Curriculum
Social studies. Discuss the meanings of body language of different cultures.

will help you interpret their messages. You can also use body language to make your spoken words clearer and more effective.

Personal Space

Your **personal space** is the area around you. When others enter this space, your reaction is a form of nonverbal communication. The way you allow people to use your personal space depends upon the way you feel about these people. You may enjoy the closeness of a hug from a special person, or a whisper in your ear from another. A quick handshake may be as close as you wish to be with others. When a person enters your personal space you feel either comfortable or uncomfortable. Your behaviors reveal the way you feel.

Have you ever hugged family members or friends you hadn't seen for a while? You knew they didn't feel you were invading their space. Conversely, have you ever touched a person who quickly withdrew from you? This reaction said you were getting too close for their comfort.

The place or situation you are in also affects the use of your personal space. For example, when your date puts an arm around you, you may respond by snuggling a little closer. You may like the warmth of the touch. If he or she tries the same hug at school, you may respond by withdrawing. Perhaps you feel this behavior is inappropriate in public. You may also respond positively to a friendly hug, but negatively to a forceful hug.

Most Americans like to stay about an arm's length from each other when they speak. This is not the case in other cultures. Greeks, Mexicans, South Americans, Indians, Pakistanis, and Arabs, for example, like to be closer. This closeness makes some Americans feel uncomfortable. An awareness of this cultural difference can help you avoid any misinterpretation of another's actions.

Technology and Communication

Technology, the use of scientific knowledge for practical purposes, has led to many new ways for people to communicate with each other. No longer do you have to wait a week or more to receive a written response for a letter you sent. You can send a message around the world in an instant. It is possible to receive a reply equally fast.

These new communication devices are popular because they are time-savers for those who use them properly. On the other hand, their prevalence in people's lives can make them time-wasters as well. They are having a significant impact on people's lives, both at home and at work. Though most people see many benefits to these new methods of communication, others see some drawbacks. The following are some popular electronic devices used for communication.

Cellular Phones

Cellular telephones provide two-way voice communication without the direct wire connections required of standard telephones. Voice transmissions are sent by radio waves to towers and switching centers that relay the messages to their destinations. You must buy cell phone services from a provider and pay a monthly fee for the service. Unfortunately, these costs can be high.

The portability and small size of cell phones have made them very popular. They can be carried easily in a pocket, briefcase, or backpack and used practically anywhere. This allows instant communication from wherever you are, which is particularly beneficial in emergency situations. Cell phones are also being paired with global positioning devices to provide emergency assistance and information to travelers.

Pagers

Pagers are one-way battery-powered communication devices. Pagers allow a person to be contacted at any time. Some pagers receive only numbers, such as the phone number of the caller. Others receive numbers and letters allowing a written message to be received. Some can receive short voice messages. The newest pagers

> **Reflect:**
> When was the last time someone entered your personal space? How did you feel? What did you say or do?
>
> **Resource:**
> *Communication*, reproducible master, TR
>
> **Discuss:**
> What are some pros and cons of cellular phones and pagers?

Citizenship and Service

Visiting with Older Adults, reproducible master, TR. Students will visit a retirement center or nursing home and talk with one of the residents. Students are to note the verbal and nonverbal communication skills they use, as well as those used by the older adult.

> **Activity:**
> Have students research the current prices of pagers and cellular phones.
>
> **Discuss:**
> Should there be a law to prohibit talking on cellular phones while driving? Why or why not?
>
> **Discuss:**
> Ask how many students have special phone features such as voice mail, caller ID, or call waiting. How are these features helpful in communication?

allow some two-way communication. All allow immediate communication from sender to receiver.

Family members may use pagers to stay in touch with each other. A parent can be paged at work if a child needs to speak to the parent. The parent can then call home or wherever the child is. Children are also sometimes given pagers so parents can reach them with messages to call.

Pagers can be used by people who have disabilities or health problems, or by elderly people who live alone. A special portable transmitter can provide a direct connection with emergency assistance. See 3-9. School-age children who are home alone, people with physical problems, and potential crime victims find these safety devices a comfort to have and use, if needed.

The use of both pagers and cell phones can be disturbing to other people if used in public places. Though popular with students, many schools ban their use. If you use either of these devices, have consideration for the people around you when at school or in a public place. Beepers should be turned to vibration mode and cell phones should be turned off when ringing will disturb others. Conversations on cell phones should not take place where other people can hear them. It is inconsiderate of people to talk on their cell phones in movie theaters or restaurants. Other people are trying to watch the movie or are having their own conversations. They should not have to listen to yours.

Voice Mail

Voice mail is received by a telephone answering machine. If no one answers the phone, the caller leaves a recorded message for the recipient to listen to later. The message can be played back on the answering machine or it can be accessed from another telephone. Voice mail is common in offices today, but more and more families are using it at home as well.

Answering machines have several advantages. Family members can eat meals together undisturbed and allow their voice mail to record messages. Family members who need to communicate with other family members can also leave messages on answering machines. For example, if parents are at work, children can leave messages about where they will be and when.

When leaving a voice mail message, there are certain courtesies you should follow. Be sure to

- speak clearly and distinctly.
- give your name and telephone number.
- keep your message brief (30 seconds is ideal), but explain the reason for your call.
- minimize the need for a call back if possible. For instance, if a meeting date has changed, give the date for the postponed meeting.
- give the date and time.
- let the person know the best time to reach you.

3-9 People who wish to live independently, but want to know they can reach help in an emergency, can wear special pagers.

Putting Technology to Use
Have students call their own voice mail or answering machine and practice leaving concise messages.

Computers

The **Internet** is an international network of computers that are joined together. It is available to anyone who has a computer, a modem, and an Internet service provider. The Internet is a popular source of information and entertainment. It also allows instant communication to anywhere in the world through e-mail. **E-mail** stands for electronic mail, which is a message delivered to your computer from another. E-mail allows you to communicate with anyone who has an e-mail address whether they are near or far.

E-mail is an important method of communication in the workplace. It often replaces in-house office memos or written correspondence to customers or clients. If e-mail is used as a form of communication at work, see 3-10 for some points to keep in mind.

Extended family members who live distances apart have found e-mail to be an excellent way to stay in touch with each other. Grandparents can e-mail their grandchildren in their homes or college dorm rooms. Parents can e-mail important messages to their school-age children at home or spouses in other workplaces.

The **World Wide Web** is a part of the Internet that carries messages containing pictures, color, and sound. It contains large collections of documents accessible at sites called *Web sites*. Web sites (named Web because of the World Wide Web) can be used to find all kinds of information. These sites are maintained by educational institutions, companies, organizations, government agencies, and even by individuals. When you access the Internet, you are **online**. You can locate information needed for research assignments without leaving your home. Online resources also allow you to access current news, weather, the stock exchange, government documents, or your own bank account. An amusement park that you are considering for a visit may have a Web site that provides information to help you make plans. Online shopping is another possibility for the Internet user. From your computer, you can purchase almost anything from grocery items to airline tickets.

Though access to the Internet can lead you to vast amounts of information, there are some precautions. The Internet is not owned or controlled by any one organization. Anyone can place any type of information on the Internet, whether accurate or not. Therefore, if you are using it for research, you should focus on using reliable sources. Check the accuracy of information provided by unfamiliar sources. The government currently does not regulate the Internet, and little information is censored. Children can accidentally wander into sites that are meant for adults only.

E-Mail Etiquette

- Grammar, spelling, and punctuation must be accurate, as in any written form of communication.
- Use a single-subject line so the receiver can easily decide the importance of the message.
- Begin with a friendly and appropriate greeting. Use a first name only if you know the person.
- Do not yell (using all upper-case letters is considered YELLING). It is not appropriate in business reports or letters.
- Avoid using emoticons in business communications. *Emoticons* are keyboard characters that are typed in configurations to indicate body language, such as :-) for a smile. Use them in personal e-mail messages only.
- Do not use e-mail to deliver extremely sensitive information. A face-to-face message or telephone conversation is better to prevent misunderstandings.
- Be aware that e-mail is not secure. If using e-mail at work, your employer can read your mail.

3-10 If you use e-mail to communicate at work, follow these guidelines.

Activity:
Have students make a list of all the emoticons they use in their e-mails and their meanings.

Discuss:
Should information on the Internet be censored or government-controlled?

Resource:
Communicating Through Technology, Activity D, SAG

Putting Technology to Use
Have students find a Web site that offers a lot of information, is colorful, and has features that are easy to use. Ask students to print off the home page and discuss what they like best about the site.

Vocabulary:
Write definitions for *stereotypes* and *prejudice* in your own words. See if your definitions are correct as you read this topic.

Discuss:
Are there risks to communicating openly?

Check It Out!
1. Name two barriers to good listening skills.
2. True or false. People are more likely to remember a message they hear if they do not repeat it verbally.
3. Briefly describe five techniques for improving speaking skills.
4. List four suggestions for starting a conversation.
5. Explain how nonverbal communication is related to your appearance.
6. Identify five forms of body language. Give an example for each form.
7. List three electronic means of communication. Give an example of how each can be used to benefit communication.

Check It Out! (Answers)
1. forgetting all or part of a message; not understanding the message being sent
2. false
3. (Describe five:) keep the listener in mind, keep messages short and simple, be considerate of others' feelings, be open and honest, respect the listener, be positive, check to see if your message is being received accurately
4. ask questions, make a sincere compliment, discuss something you have in common with the other person, discuss one topic
5. People quickly form first impressions based on the way you look. Good grooming sends a positive message that shows you care about yourself and the way you look.
6. (Identify five:) posture, arm and hand gestures, handshake, nodding, facial expressions, eye contact (Examples are student response.)
7. (List three. Student response.)

Topic 3-2
Communication in Relationships

Objectives
After studying this topic, you will be able to
- state the importance of open communication in relationships.
- list ways to communicate positive feelings.
- describe barriers to communication.
- suggest methods for handling negative feelings.
- give tips for communicating in the workplace.

Topic Terms
open communication
stereotypes
prejudices
coded messages
role expectations
diverse

People often speak of **open communication**. This means a free flow of ideas, opinions, and facts among the people involved. They may not agree on everything, but they respect one another's point of view. They can have intelligent discussions about views that differ from their own. All ideas are treated with interest, curiosity, and respect.

Clearly communicating your thoughts and feelings is part of open communication. In this topic, you will learn more about skills you can use to develop open communication in your relationships. These include communicating positive feelings, overcoming barriers, and handling negative feelings.

The Importance of Communication in Relationships

Open communication has many benefits, especially in personal relationships. It allows people to learn more about themselves and other people. It helps people express their feelings to their friends and family. Using it helps strengthen relationships. Overall, it can lead to richer, more satisfying relationships. See 3-11.

Communicating Positive Feelings

Each person is responsible for his or her own happiness. Do you want to be happy? If so, you must work toward that goal. Thinking positively about most situations in life will help you be happy. Your positive attitude encourages open communication.

3-11 Open communication allows people to express their ideas and feelings freely.

Good feelings are contagious. If you are a positive person and communicate this to others, they will feel happier, too. See 3-12. The following list suggests ways to communicate positive feelings. Decide which suggestions would be most helpful to you.

- Whenever you meet someone, be the first one to say hello.
- Offer praise and compliments when they are deserved.
- Defend people who are the object of harmful gossip.
- Smile and look happy. Show your positive personality traits.
- Look others in the eye when you talk to them, and speak clearly.
- Show concern for others by asking them about matters that are important to them.

Barriers to Open Communication

Communicating with others is not always easy. Many barriers stand in the way of open communication. A few of the barriers are physical in nature, such as speech and hearing disabilities. However, most barriers to open communication are social or psychological. Understanding

Discuss:
Do you agree or disagree with this statement: Each person is responsible for his or her own happiness.

Reflect:
How do you communicate positive feelings to others?

3-12 People who communicate their positive feelings enrich the lives of others.

Putting Technology to Use
Have students use a drawing program, clipart, and a color printer to create a bulletin board showing barriers to communications.

Discuss:
What stereotypes must teens overcome that interfere with open communication?

Reflect:
How have you shown prejudice toward another person? How do you think that prejudice developed?

Discuss:
Give some examples of coded messages that teens use with their peers.

these differences can help you avoid them. Some of the most common ones are described on the following pages.

Stereotypes

One barrier to open communication is stereotyping. A person who **stereotypes** others has a set belief that all members of a group will behave in the same ways.

Stereotypes put labels on groups of people. These labels may be based on a group's age, sex, race, or religion. For instance, some people may believe that all young men should participate in sports or all elderly people are forgetful.

Because every person is different, neither of the above statements can be true for all people within these groups. If you pay attention to stereotypes like these instead of accepting individual differences, you may misinterpret messages. To be a good listener, you must have an open mind. You must ignore stereotypes and give people the chance to communicate as individuals.

Prejudices

Another barrier to open communication results from prejudices. **Prejudices** are opinions that people form without complete knowledge. They are usually based on a lack of facts and a lack of understanding. People with prejudices do not accept that others' beliefs can be different from theirs. Prejudices might include negative attitudes toward religions, races, cultures, nationalities, socio-economic groups, cities, geographic regions, or foods.

Many prejudices lead to negative behaviors such as name-calling. Prejudiced people may choose to avoid certain groups or individuals. They usually do not seek understanding or new meanings. They have already made up their minds. It's as if they are saying, I already know about that, or I already know about your kind. These actions set up barriers and prevent good communication from taking place.

Here is an example of a young man who had a prejudice toward certain foods. When the young man took his date out to dinner, she ordered roast lamb. She soon realized he was embarrassed to be seen with a date who ate lamb. He did not eat meat and thought of it as unwholesome. He also felt prejudice toward her because she ate a food that he didn't consider acceptable. Because of his prejudice, the couple never dated again. Such a prejudice toward people and objects—in this case food—hampers good communication.

Some prejudices come in the form of love. For example, parents are naturally proud of their children. They may think their son or daughter is the best looking, most talented, and most personable individual. This may be true, but such an attitude is usually padded with a little pride and prejudice. Loving people is important. However, maintaining an ability to be rational about all people and objects is important, too.

Coded Messages

When people try to communicate without saying what they really mean, they are using **coded messages**. Listeners are forced to make assumptions as they decode the speakers' messages. Although coded messages hinder good communication, some people continue to use them. See 3-13.

One tricky statement to decode is, "Give me your honest opinion." Some people may really want your opinion. Others say this when they really mean, "Tell me I am right. Support me in what I have done." You must decode the message according to the situation. Your clues may be the person's tone of voice and facial expression.

Another example of coding is when a young man asks a young woman, "What are you doing Saturday?" His message is a coded one. He doesn't really want to know what she is planning to do. This is his way of saying, "Will you be free on Saturday? I would like to see you then." He hopes the girl will recognize the coded message and interpret it correctly. However, she may respond with another coded message. Then he must decode her message. Does she have time to see him on Saturday? Is

Across the Curriculum
Sociology. Discuss how stereotypes and prejudices are formed about different groups of people.

Topic 3-2 Communication in Relationships

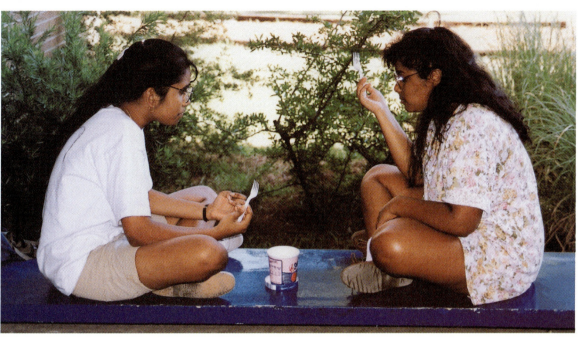

3-13 Good friends know their friendship depends on open communication. They avoid using coded messages to express their thoughts and feelings.

she too busy to see him or doesn't she want to see him? As you can see, communicating with coded messages is risky.

Teasing is a type of coded message. The way a person teases is the key to decoding the real meaning of the message. Teasing is a means of getting someone's attention. It's usually a way of saying "I like you." Teasing can almost always be decoded as a type of compliment. However, some forms of teasing and joking can cause problems in personal relationships. Some people say harsh things in a joking manner when they really mean what they are saying. They don't have the nerve to say it otherwise. This type of joke is cruel and can easily hurt someone's feelings.

Gender Differences

Sometimes, differences between males and females create some barriers to communication. These barriers may be related to role expectations. **Role expectations** are patterns of socially expected behavior. That is, people learn to behave the way they think society expects them to behave. They also expect certain role behaviors from others.

Certain roles are associated with being male or female. For males, some of these roles include brother, son, boyfriend, husband, and father. Female roles include sister, daughter, girlfriend, wife, and mother. Both men and women also have expectations as to how the opposite sex should fulfill their roles. For instance, some husbands may expect their wives to cook and do household chores. A girlfriend may expect her boyfriend to pay for every date.

Role expectations can create confusion. This is because people don't always agree on the behavior for certain roles. Today, some of the barriers created by gender differences are diminishing. As society's view of male and female roles continues to change, people's views of role expectations will change, too.

When Negative Feelings Occur

Every person has negative feelings at times. When you hold back negative feelings, they may become stronger and more frustrating. You need to know how to vent your emotions. Even negative feelings can be communicated in a useful, constructive way.

> **Resource:**
> *Communicating in Code,* Activity E, SAG
>
> **Enrich:**
> Talk to an administrator, teacher, or counselor at your school. Ask about role expectations of students while they are at school.
>
> **Activity:**
> Have the males in class write their role expectations of females. Have the females in class write their role expectations of males. Ask volunteers to share their lists with the class, and note areas of agreement and disagreement concerning sex roles.

 FCCLA Activity
Have students working on the Focus on Children STAR Event visit a child care center and observe the way teachers communicate with the children. Students should also notice the way children communicate with one another. Ask students to write recommendations for eliminating any communication barriers they observe.

Reflect:
How do you feel about the guidelines for handling negative feelings? Which ones work best for you?

Resource:
Communication in a Dating Relationship, reproducible master, TR

Discuss:
Why is it important to avoid gossiping in the workplace? How is this even more important than avoiding gossip at school?

Handling Negative Feelings

There are many ways you can resolve negative feelings. You must first wish to communicate effectively and be willing to take the first steps to resolving these feelings. As you read the following suggestions, think about yourself. Which of these guidelines would be most helpful for you?

- Discuss your negative feelings with the person whose behavior is bothering you. Don't complain to others until you have spoken with that person. People who are not involved in a problem usually can't do anything about it.
- Keep a simple issue simple. Don't add other issues to it, building it up until it becomes a major problem.
- Do not reopen old issues that have already been settled.
- Discuss the problem without making nasty comments and accusations that would hurt the other person.
- Recognize your own faults and accept them. Don't blame them on others.
- Try to be pleasant rather than grouchy.
- Help people see that you like them, even though you don't like their behavior.
- Say what must be said and stop. Don't continue talking about one issue and repeating yourself.
- Try to end on a positive note. Make a positive comment about the person or the situation.

Communication in the Workplace

The communication skills you have learned to use in your personal life can help you communicate at work. The circumstances differ, however. You have known your family and close friends for a long time, and you have learned how to communicate with them. When you begin a job, you will meet many new people. In today's world, the workforce is likely to be very **diverse** (differing from one another). Workers differ by age, ethnicity, and gender. Increasing numbers of workers have disabilities. Due to the diverse nature of the workforce, communication can be more challenging.

The goals of communication at work are to pass along information and to build effective work relationships. Different styles of communicating and different interpretations of communications can interfere with attaining both of these goals. People from different backgrounds may define problems differently. They bring their personal goals, priorities, and standards to their jobs. When diverse people form team-based work groups, disagreements may occur. It is important to remember that every person is different. That does not mean they are difficult. By thinking of someone as just different, you become less judgmental. You can be more open to their opinions and ideas.

Many of the effective communication techniques that you use in other settings can also be used on the job. In addition, the following points can be helpful:

- Keep conversations unrelated to work to a minimum. These prevent you and other employees from doing your work. Your personal life should be kept private. Workplace gossip should be avoided. Professionalism is expected of employees.
- Show courtesy to customers and clients, 3-14. Do not keep them waiting while you finish a conversation with a fellow employee.
- Use good listening skills. Listen carefully when directions are given. Ask questions to prevent any misunderstandings.
- Use standard English at work, not slang. For example, say *yes* rather than *yeah*.
- Avoid telling jokes at work. Because of the diverse nature of the workforce, some people may be offended by an innocent joke.
- If misunderstandings occur, discuss them with the person involved. It is possible to respectfully disagree.

Career Preparation Activity

Communicating for a Living, reproducible master, TR. Students are to interview someone who works in a field requiring communication skills, such as teaching, public relations, marketing, writing, or personnel. They are to share interview responses in class and indicate whether they would be interested in working in this field.

Topic 3-3
Conflict Resolution

3-14 When communicating with customers, their needs always come first.

Objectives
After studying this topic, you will be able to
- identify some types and causes of conflict.
- explain possible negative and positive reactions to conflict.
- describe constructive and destructive methods of conflict resolution.
- list the steps in the conflict resolution process.
- explain the use of mediation.

Topic Terms
conflict
scapegoating
negotiation
compromise
conflict resolution process
mediation
peer mediators

Vocabulary: Have you ever heard anyone referred to as a *scapegoat*? What was the situation in which the term was used?

Reflect: Think about how you resolved your last conflict. How did you feel when the conflict was resolved? How could you have resolved the conflict in a better way?

Each person has a unique way of viewing and reacting to every situation. When people live and work closely, as they do in families, friendships, and on the job, conflicts are bound to arise. A **conflict** is a struggle between two people or groups who have opposing views. The ability to resolve a conflict is an important skill in good communication.

Types of Conflicts

There are all types of conflicts. Some are small, such as a disagreement between two people over a trivial matter, 3-15. You and a friend may disagree over where to go after school. Disagreements can grow into larger conflicts if the two people are not willing to reach an agreement peacefully.

Conflicts can also occur within families—between husbands and wives, parents and children, or among siblings. Again, the conflicts can be small and easily resolved. They can also be over important issues. Maybe you and your parents disagree about how late you should be able to stay

Check It Out!
1. True or false. In open communication, people know each other so well that they agree about everything.
2. Give five examples of ways to communicate positive feelings.
3. A communication barrier based on opinions that people form without complete knowledge is known as _____.
4. Identify five ways to communicate negative feelings.
5. What makes communication in today's workplace challenging?

Check It Out! (Answers)
1. false
2. (Examples are student response.)
3. prejudice
4. (Identify five:) Discuss your feelings with the person whose behavior is bothering you; keep a simple issue simple; don't bring up issues that have been settled in the past; avoid making comments that could hurt the other person; recognize and accept your own faults; try to be pleasant, not grouchy; show people you like them, even though you don't approve of their behavior; say what must be said and stop; try to end the discussion on a positive note.
5. diversity in age, ethnicity, and gender

Activity:
Bring in several copies of a daily newspaper. In small groups, have students find articles reporting on conflicts. Have them state the conflict and try to determine the basic cause of the conflict.

Reflect:
Think of a conflict you had recently with a friend or family member. Was the cause a result of miscommunication? a personality conflict?

Discuss:
Do you agree or disagree with the statement that conflicts occur more often between parents and their children during the teen years? Explain your answer.

Resource:
Neither Right nor Wrong—Just Different, reproducible master, TR

3-15 Even good friends can have conflicts because they are together so much of the time. What's important is to choose a method of resolving the conflict that is fair to all.

out on weekend nights. Bringing up an issue that is causing a conflict is a good way to begin to deal with the problem. Listening to each other's views and talking about them can usually lead to good solutions.

Conflicts are not confined to interpersonal relationships. They can occur between larger groups—even entire nations. Throughout the world, there are nations that are at war with other nations. These, too, are conflicts, but on a much larger scale. Many times the conflicts between nations are based on some of the same differences that cause conflicts between individuals. Differences in religious beliefs and practices are often at the core of many national conflicts. Disagreements over government policies also lead to major conflicts.

Causes of Conflict

Causes of conflict can be trivial or significant. It is important to take an objective look at the conflict and try to determine the cause. Knowing why the conflict occurred will likely help in resolving it.

Many conflicts occur because of poor communication. Have you ever made arrangements to meet some friends, and they never showed up? You may have been really angry until you found out they never received your message, or they misunderstood where you were to meet. Many times a failure to communicate can be more serious. Has anyone ever said to you, "If you had told me, this all could have been avoided"? If a parent or your boss said this to you, you may have been in real trouble!

Some conflicts result from specific situations. For instance, perhaps you and your friend both like the same boy. He starts paying more attention to you than to your friend. She starts acting weird, complaining about everything. She never used to be like that. Suddenly, you're arguing all the time, and then you have a really big fight. The situation has led to a conflict between the two of you.

If people have very different personalities, they could be on a collision course. For instance, consider this couple. She is neat and organized, likes to be on time, and always seems to be in control. He is completely disorganized, can never find anything, and is always running late. These two people could be very happy together, each benefiting from the other's strengths. On the other hand, they could be miserable together. Their very different personalities could lead to some major conflicts.

Conflicts often occur between parents and their children during the teenage years. The role of parents is to guide their children as they grow toward adulthood. Parents are responsible for their well-being until they are adults. The role of teens is to develop independence. They are anxious to be able to make decisions for themselves. Finding a happy medium between these opposing roles is often difficult. Parents and children often pull in opposite directions. Conflicts frequently occur during these tumultuous years.

Differences in personal priorities can lead to conflicts, as you learned in Chapter 1. Your personal priorities are important to you. If someone else does not have the same personal priorities as you, conflicts can arise. The degree of conflict depends on the importance of the personal priority to you. For instance, your parents may think

Across the Curriculum

History. Have students study the causes of different wars. Could these conflicts have been avoided? Were any caused by a failure in communication?

Topic 3-3 Conflict Resolution

good grades are most important, while you think your performance on the volleyball team is most important. You want to spend time practicing when they want you to study more. This difference in personal priorities can lead to disagreements. A friend may value having a good time, while you may value getting into a good college. This could lead to disagreements about how you spend your free time together.

Some conflicts can be traced to cultural differences. For example, the American culture encourages quick decision making. This is not characteristic of all cultures. A quick decision is not admired among the Japanese, for example. The American culture is one where people are always busy and active. People from many other cultures do not believe in this active lifestyle. They prefer a more relaxed pace. The concept of time also varies among cultures. Americans follow daily schedules timed to the minute. They expect punctuality, 3-16. Other cultures place more emphasis on relationships than on schedules. Being late is not a problem for them. These are just a few examples of cultural differences that can lead to conflict if people are unaware of them.

Reactions to Conflict

Conflict is normal. There will always be disagreements between people. It is how people react or respond to these disagreements that determines whether they ignite into major conflicts or just go away. Negative reactions can escalate conflicts and lead to hostility and personal attacks. Some even end in violence. Positive reactions can lead to solutions that both parties can accept. Many actually lead to personal growth.

Negative Reactions

Avoidance is a common reaction to conflict. Some people just walk away. This might be a good response if a person is concerned that an argument could escalate into violence. A cooling-down period might be good for everyone involved. In most cases, however, avoidance simply puts off resolution. It does not solve the problem. Instead, resentment builds up as the person tries to suppress hurt feelings. If this continues over a period of time, it can lead to an explosion of emotions when the person finally reaches a breaking point.

Reflect:
Has a difference in values ever caused a conflict between you and a friend or your parents?

Discuss:
Have you ever experienced any of these negative reactions to a conflict? Was the conflict resolved?

Enrich:
Have students research additional examples of cultural differences that could lead to conflict.

3-16 Many Americans become frustrated if they cannot keep to their planned schedules.

Across the Curriculum
Social studies. Discuss lifestyle differences in cultures, such as the example of daily schedules given above.

Discuss:
Many personal injury lawsuits are really the result of personal negligence, but the injured person is trying to make money off of the injury. Who might be the scapegoat in such cases?

Reflect:
Think about the last verbal argument you had with someone. How did it make you feel?

Discuss:
Do you agree or disagree with the statement that violence portrayed in the media leads to more violent behavior in society?

Discuss:
Give some examples of "I" messages.

Some people attempt to resolve conflicts by blaming others. This is called **scapegoating**. The person blamed for the problem is the scapegoat. Everyone else is freed of the responsibility for the problem because they can blame this other person. This is not a resolution because no one tries to solve the conflict. The conflict goes on with both parties feeling it is "not my problem."

Some responses to conflict include arguing, becoming angry, and name-calling. When one person becomes angry and begins yelling, the other person is likely to become angry as well. Verbal attacks fly back and forth. People say hurtful things they often regret later. They feel belittled when their self-esteem is under attack. It is sometimes hard to forgive people when such outbreaks occur. An atmosphere of hostility prevails.

The most destructive reaction to conflict is violence. If tempers flare out of control, shoving, hitting, or pushing can result. Some people first experience hitting as children. They think this is an acceptable form of reaction because their parents hit them. They also see more violence portrayed in the media—on television and in movies. As they become older, they may use this same form of behavior. A physical reaction to conflict is never the answer. It can lead to child abuse, spouse abuse, or elder abuse. It can also lead to violence outside the home.

Positive Reactions

There are ways people can react to conflict that will help the situation. First, you can learn to control your emotions. Lashing out in anger usually solves nothing. You can also ask the other person to remain calm. Both people need to stop, take a deep breath, and quiet their emotions.

It is also important to listen. Instead of shouting, stop and listen to what each person is saying. Focus on the real problem as you exchange views. Don't bring up other issues. Focus on the current conflict. Try to remain neutral. Do not jump to a judgment before everyone has his or her say. Then you are ready to find a real solution to the conflict.

Learning to react positively when a conflict occurs is an important life skill that can lead to personal growth. It is a sign of maturity when you can control your emotions, listen to other viewpoints, and avoid jumping to conclusions. These skills will help you in your personal relationships as well as in work situations. Teamwork is stressed in today's workplace. You might someday be working closely with other employees in a work setting. Because conflicts will arise, reacting positively can lead to constructive resolution of these conflicts. An employer will recognize and appreciate your ability to handle conflict in a mature manner.

Constructive Methods for Handling Conflict

To resolve a conflict, each person has to assume responsibility for his or her feelings. The emotions you feel may be caused by others, but they belong to you. If you wish to lessen stress that occurs in conflict, you must be willing to resolve the conflict. Try these techniques for starters.

Use "I" Messages

Use "I" messages instead of "you" messages. This means you take ownership for your feelings. You state what you feel or think instead of criticizing the other person. Say "*I* think you are ignoring me" rather than "*You* are ignoring me". You might further say, "When I think you are ignoring me, I feel hurt. I don't like being ignored." As you express your feelings, you are taking credit for them.

"You" messages, on the other hand, come across as accusations. "You are ignoring me" places blame on the other person and may aggravate the situation. When taking ownership and saying "I think" or "I feel" you avoid accusing the other person of negative behaviors.

Family Enrichment Activity
Have students describe two problems that may occur in families and write "I" messages that will help them resolve the conflicts.

Learn to send "I" messages. For example, "When you tell so-called funny stories about me to my professional friends, I am embarrassed." Can you see in this example that you are assuming responsibility for your feelings of embarrassment? A "you" message sounds like an accusation. "You embarrass me when you tell your so-called funny stories about me to my professional friends." The "you" message places the blame on the other person.

Decide Who Owns the Problem

Whose problem is it? When a problem exists between two people, both own the problem. Even when one person creates the problem, he or she makes it a problem for the other. State your point of view in a way that will not create an argument. Seek feedback to determine how the other person is receiving your message. To avoid misunderstandings, use clarifying messages periodically, 3-17. Try comments such as: "If I am hearing you correctly, you are saying that..." or "I think I heard you say..."

3-17 When resolving a conflict with another person, state your point of view calmly and clearly. Then ask for feedback.

Learn to Negotiate and Compromise

An important method for resolving conflicts is negotiation. **Negotiation** means communicating with others in order to reach a mutually satisfying agreement. Such an agreement usually involves a compromise. In a **compromise**, both parties agree to give up something. Each person gives up something of importance to obtain something else that also has importance.

Negotiation and compromise must be considered carefully. Some issues may be so important to you that you will be unwilling to negotiate and compromise. For example, you may not wish to compromise your moral views or spiritual views. For this reason, you will not enter into a negotiation that would require you to make a compromise. What is important is that you negotiate and compromise when it is appropriate.

The purpose of negotiation and compromise is to remove conflict. Four methods are commonly used.

- *You win/I lose*. The person who wins is happy with this compromise. The person achieved what he or she wanted. However, you may feel the person took advantage of you. You may feel like a loser. You are likely to be unhappy about your loss. The conflict is likely to resurface at a future time. A power struggle is likely to persist.
- *I win/you lose*. This is the opposite of the above situation. You feel happy because you achieved what you wanted. However, the person who loses may not be happy about being the loser. This conflict is likely to resurface. One person had to compromise too much.
- *I lose/you lose*. Negotiations apparently became very difficult this time. Both you and the other person are losers. So many compromises were made that neither person's wishes were met. No one is happy.
- *I win/you win*. This is the ideal way to resolve conflicts. Both parties were able to talk through the situation. You were able to negotiate in such a way that

Discuss:
How do parents teach very young children to compromise? Can you give an example?

Reflect:
Can you think of an issue you would not be willing to compromise on?

Resource:
Resolving Conflicts, Activity F, SAG

Across the Curriculum

History. Cover examples of negotiation and compromise between nations. Discuss the individuals representing all parties and their qualifications as negotiators.

> **Reflect:**
> Think of a conflict you can't resolve. Can you think of a new way to work toward a resolution?
>
> **Resource:**
> *Conflict Resolution,* reproducible master, TR
>
> **Discuss:**
> In divorce proceedings, who acts as the mediator?

each achieved what he or she wanted. Neither person forced his or her ideas on the other. Both parties probably made compromises. Neither was forced to compromise anything that was cherished. Those items that were lost were not highly valued, so there were no losers. Both are now happy winners.

You must recognize that some conflicts cannot be resolved. There are people who create conflicts and refuse to resolve them. Some people make unfair demands upon others. If this happens, you may have to give up your responsibility toward resolution. You may have to recognize that the problem is not yours and leave it with the person who owns it.

In these situations, relations between the people involved will suffer. Perhaps the relationship is already weak. Remember that relationships are between at least two people. Sometimes every person has to be willing to stand alone. When efforts toward negotiation and compromise don't work, you can still feel you tried your best. In spite of the outcome, you have gained some experience from having tried to resolve the issue.

Use the Conflict Resolution Process

In some instances, a more formal process may be needed to resolve the conflict. The **conflict resolution process** is a step-by-step form of communication that allows conflicts to be worked out in a positive manner. The process should be used as soon as possible after a conflict occurs. This prevents anger and tension from building. It should also take place in private with only the individuals or parties involved present. Everyone needs to remain calm and be willing to listen to each other. These are the steps to follow.

1. *State the problem.* All participants must have the opportunity to tell their view of what is causing the problem. Each person must listen carefully and stay focused on the main issue. All must agree on exactly what the problem is.
2. *List possible solutions.* The next step is to suggest all potential solutions. Think of as many solutions as possible even if some seem unworkable. An idea can sometimes spark a better solution. Everyone should be able to speak freely and without criticism.
3. *Evaluate each possible solution.* Take a closer look at the best possible solutions. Which ones do both parties like? Which ones seem to solve the problem? Use negotiation skills until a compromise solution can be reached.
4. *Pick the best solution.* Finally, both parties must agree to the best solution. It won't be a solution unless everyone is in agreement.
5. *Carry out the solution.* A plan should be made to carry out the solution. State what each party will do and when they will do it. Keep it simple. Also, decide what actions the parties will take if a conflict occurs again.
6. *Evaluate the results.* The process does not end until the solution has been put into action and the results are evaluated. If a conflict is still occurring, the process needs to begin again.

Following these steps, where everyone involved is allowed to speak freely, should lead to satisfactory solutions. More serious and escalating conflicts can be avoided.

Mediation

Some efforts to resolve conflicts between parties just do not work without outside help. Mediation may be needed. In **mediation,** a third person is called upon to help reconcile differences between the conflicting parties. This person is called a *mediator.* Through mediation, an attempt is made to settle the dispute and find a peaceful solution to the conflict, 3-18. The opposing parties talk to each other with the help of the mediator. Mediators can assist in school, work, and even international disputes. They are often included in the conflict resolution process.

A mediator is sometimes needed to settle family disputes. Family members live under the same roof, share meals and

Putting Technology to Use

Have students work in small groups to describe a situation involving conflict. Then have them describe how the same conflict could be resolved using each of the methods of negotiation and compromise. Students should use charting software to create charts showing the methods and corresponding resolutions. Ask them to share examples with the class.

Topic 3-3 Conflict Resolution

3-18 Sometimes a teacher acts as a mediator to resolve conflicts between students.

Example:
Sisters Marisa and Janet share a room. Marisa is mad at Janet because she throws her stuff all over the room while Marisa puts her things away. Who might mediate this conflict if the girls can't resolve it themselves?

Resource:
Mediators Can Help, Activity G, SAG

Activity:
Have students check the local phone book to find out what local resources are available to help victims of domestic violence. Share with the class.

living space, work together, and play together. Conflicts are bound to occur. The conflict resolution process can be used by family members to resolve their conflicts. The two family members can talk about the problem and find a solution acceptable to both. Sometimes mediation may be needed. Who becomes the mediator? Anyone who is not emotionally tied to the issue can become the neutral third party. When mom and daughter have a strong difference of opinion, dad or son might be the mediator who helps bring about a win/win solution.

Peer Mediation

Many schools use **peer mediators**. These are students who are trained in the conflict resolution process. They listen and act in an unbiased manner to help fellow students settle their differences. Peer mediators are selected for their leadership skills, emotional maturity, and interest in helping others. They are often preferred as mediators because students feel more comfortable with a peer. They may feel another student can understand their problems better than an adult. Hopefully, solutions can be found. When conflicts cannot be resolved, the parties involved may have to agree to disagree, but in a peaceful manner. This necessitates respect for all concerned.

Violence: A Destructive Method of Handling Conflict

You have learned of constructive ways to deal with conflict. Is there such a thing as a destructive method of dealing with conflict? If a conflict is settled, how can it be destructive? The answer is if an act of violence is used. If physical force is used against another person or group that harms them to the point where they are completely subdued and afraid to speak up, then a destructive method of handling conflict has been used. The conflict is ended only because one person or party has been injured or even killed by another person or group.

Gangs often use this form of conflict resolution. It also happens within some families. It may take the form of spouse abuse, child abuse, or elder abuse. If conflicts arise, one family member may attempt to completely dominate another family member. Physical force is often

Putting Technology to Use
Have students visit the Web site for the organization Teens Against Gang Violence at www.tagv.org.

Enrich:
Have students research the Internet to find out exactly how much taxpayers pay per year on criminals in prisons.

used, but emotional abuse can be equally devastating. Suicide also falls into this category. A person may feel there is no way out and attempt suicide.

Remember that violence does not solve a conflict. Violence is costly to society in terms of tax dollars spent on criminals in prisons. It is also costly to people in terms of lowered self-worth and lost dignity in addition to physical pain and suffering.

Always strive for positive resolutions of conflicts where differences are settled peacefully and friendships and families are kept intact. Conflict resolution skills will benefit you throughout your life as they foster relationships, increase job productivity, and prevent violence.

Check It Out!

1. State three possible causes of conflict.
2. Give an example of a negative reaction to conflict and an example of a positive reaction to conflict.
3. Why are "I" messages more successful than "you" messages in resolving conflicts?
4. Name the most ideal negotiation and compromise method.
5. List the steps in the conflict resolution process.
6. Why is mediation sometimes needed to resolve conflicts?

Check It Out! (answers)

1. (State three:) poor communication, specific situations, different personalities, parent/children roles, differences in personal priorities, cultural differences
2. (Student response.)
3. "I" messages help you take credit for your feelings as you express them. "You" messages sound like accusations.
4. I win/you win method
5. State the problem. List possible solutions. Evaluate each possible solution. Pick the best solution. Carry out the solution. Evaluate the results.
6. Some efforts to resolve conflicts do not work without outside help. A mediator is a neutral third party who listens to both sides in an unbiased manner.

TEENS ARE TALKING ABOUT...

Facing Peer Pressure

Peer pressure is something that every teen must face in one way or another. Different teens are affected by peer pressure in different ways. In a group discussion, Nicole, Thomas, Rob, LeAnne, Ryan, Rique, and Anne talked about peer pressure.

Group members agreed that peer pressure is a big problem. Lying, cheating, stealing, using drugs, drinking alcohol, and having sex were all mentioned as high-pressure issues.

Rique seemed to feel that most peer pressure does not come from close friends. He said, "Most friends will not pressure you into doing something you don't want to do. Friends care about your emotional and physical stability. People you do not know well are a different story. They may not care about your feelings or your value of life."

Although one member expressed the opinion that peer pressure is more serious than most people believe, Nicole disagreed. She believes that there is not as much peer pressure as most people say. As an example, she said if a teen wants to drink, alcohol is always available. If a teen doesn't want to drink, however, no one is going to put on pressure.

One student pointed out that the term *peer pressure* is often used as a scapegoat. Some teens do what they want to do. Then they claim that peer pressure was the cause of their actions. Group members agreed that teens need to remember that they are responsible for their own behavior.

Group members mentioned a number of negative effects that can result from giving in to peer pressure. LeAnne feels that giving in to pressure can cause teens to lose self-esteem and begin forming bad habits. She says that giving in may also cause teens to lose friends who resist such pressure. Thomas thinks that peer pressure keeps people from pursuing some of their goals. Ryan believes peer pressure causes teens to disobey their parents and their teachers. Rob pointed out the positive value of peer pressure. He said teens can be pressured into giving up bad habits.

The group indicated that some teens give in to peer pressure because they do not want peers to think they are afraid. Others give in to be popular.

The teens were asked how they cope with peer pressure. Many said they find it helpful to talk about their feelings. Talking with the person causing the pressure was suggested as a way to directly deal with the problem. Group members said they may also consult with parents, friends, or counselors.

The group had some advice for other teens who face peer pressure. Rique recommends avoiding situations where pressure might occur. He also suggested questioning peer relationships. "If your friend tries talking you into something you don't want, ask yourself if this person is really a friend," he advises.

Another group member stated that teens should expect that they will face pressure. Teens need to anticipate what they will do in advance so they will not have to react under pressure.

LeAnne feels if teens are careful about the friends they choose, they are a lot less likely to experience negative peer pressure.

The group agreed that teens need to get to know themselves and be willing to take a stand for what they know is right. Standing strong is tough, but it is worth it.

Discuss:
- Do you agree with Rique that most peer pressure does not come from close friends?
- Is peer pressure a big problem for teens, or do you agree with Nicole when she says there is not as much peer pressure as people say?
- Have you seen peer pressure used as a scapegoat? Can you cite some instances?
- In what ways did the teens interviewed deal with peer pressure? (List these on the chalkboard and have students give their views as to the possible effectiveness of each in dealing with peer pressure.)

> **Note:**
> Studies have shown that in an eight-hour day,
> - we spend about four hours in listening activity
> - we hear for about two hours
> - we actually listen for an hour
> - we understand thirty minutes of that hour
> - we believe only fifteen minutes' worth of what we listen to
> - we remember just under eight minutes' worth

> **Note:**
> Success in any career depends on good communication skills. Though reading and writing are essential, it is through listening and speaking that people interact most frequently. For most people, formal education in communication has been directed at those skills that are used least in the workplace: reading and writing. Surveys show most Americans have had about 12 years of formal training in writing and 6 to 8 years in reading. They have had only one or two years in speech-related courses and virtually no formal training in listening.

Chapter Review

Summary

Developing your ability to communicate well will help you throughout your life. To do this, you will want to improve your verbal communication skills. This involves speaking and listening. As a speaker, you need to send clear messages. As a listener, you want to receive and understand messages.

Nonverbal communication is an important part of the communication process, also. As you talk with people, you will become aware of the many messages you receive through nonverbal communication. Your appearance, your manners, and your body language are just a few of the ways you convey messages without words.

Technology has led to new forms of communication. These include cellular phones, pagers, voice mail, and computers. With these new forms of communication come new rules regarding appropriate use of these mediums.

Open communication is important in personal relationships. Sharing positive feelings with others encourages open communication. Recognizing common communication barriers such as stereotypes, prejudices, coded messages, and gender differences helps people overcome them.

Negative feelings can occur in relationships. Learning to handle these feelings in a positive way is another important communication skill. Because of the diversity of today's workplace, communication in the workplace is especially important.

No matter how well people communicate, conflicts are still going to occur. There are many types and causes of conflicts, just as there are negative and positive reactions to them. Conflicts can best be resolved through negotiation and compromise. The conflict resolution process can also be used to resolve conflict. Mediation by a neutral third party is sometimes necessary. Violence is a destructive method of conflict resolution.

Think About It!

1. Why do you think good communication is easiest when people know one another and have similar backgrounds?
2. How would you rate your verbal communication skills at school and at home? Based on your rating, what steps would you take to improve your listening and speaking skills?
3. Choose conversation openers that you think would help you begin and develop a conversation with each of the following:
   A. A soccer player.
   B. A child in a pet store.
   C. A teacher whose class you enjoy.
   D. Parents of your dating partner.
4. In your opinion, is it fair to judge people on the basis of nonverbal communication? Explain your answer.
5. Apply the concept of open communication to an employee/employer relationship. When will open communication help this relationship? When will it hinder the relationship?
6. Summarize the benefits of communicating positive feelings. How do you communicate positive feelings to others?
7. Select and rank any five barriers to communication listed in this chapter. Use the number one as the most frequently observed barrier. Use the number five as the least frequently observed barrier.

8. Imagine that someone is very angry with you. Suggest ways that you would want that person to handle his or her negative feelings.
9. What in your opinion is the least desirable way to resolve a conflict?
10. In what careers would good communication skills be especially helpful? Explain your answer.

Try It Out!

1. Try to improve your listening and speaking skills by having a conversation with another person about any topic. When one partner speaks, the other listens. Neither person may respond to any statement without first summarizing what the partner has said. Incorrect summaries must be clarified before the conversation continues.
2. The same words can be used to convey different meanings by changing the tone of voice. Ask classmates to say one statement three different ways to convey three different meanings. Examples are: "I like the new youth director." "That's a nice looking outfit you're wearing."
3. Ask classmates to demonstrate desirable skills in communicating the following messages. Discuss each message after it is delivered. Tell why you think the speaker chose a certain phrase, speaking style, or tone of voice.
    A. Describe your favorite meal to your best friend.
    B. Describe your favorite meal to your grandparent.
    C. Ask a restaurant waiter to recook a hamburger that is too rare.
    D. Ask a salesclerk to recheck a sales slip that you think is wrong.
    E. Communicate with a 4-year-old who wants to eat cookies just before dinner.
    F. Role-play a situation in which a talkative young man is dating a quiet young woman.
4. Work in a small group to develop a list of communication barriers. Exchange lists with another group. As a team, discuss some ways to overcome barriers.
5. Brainstorm as a class and suggest as many stereotypes as you can. Discuss how such stereotypes could limit your ability to communicate with others.
6. Select a possible conflict between two students who are working together on a class project. Demonstrate the four methods used to negotiate and compromise.
7. Role-play the use of the conflict resolution process. Describe a hypothetical situation that might occur in your school where the conflict resolution process could be used. Have classmates take roles as the two groups in conflict. If your school has peer mediators, ask one of them to participate in the role-play.

Enrich:
Go to the library and find several references on communication to help in developing the list of communication barriers for *Try It Out!* #4.

Resource:
PowerZone Challenge CD. Have students play the chapter review game to reinforce text content.

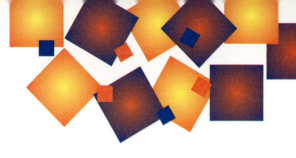

Chapter 4
Leadership and Citizenship Skills

Careers

These careers relate to the topics in this chapter:
- restaurant crew leader
- community affairs director
- personnel manager
- city supervisor

As you study this chapter, see if you can think of others.

Topics

4-1 Leaders and Followers
4-2 Organizations That Work!
4-3 Your Rights and Responsibilities as a Citizen

Introductory Activities

1. *Leaders and Followers,* reproducible master, TR. Use this activity to encourage your students to begin thinking about leadership skills. They are asked to read statements concerning leaders and followers and indicate whether they agree or disagree with each one. Discuss the statements in class.
2. Ask students to identify some social concern groups, such as AARP, NOW, SADD, and NAACP. Ask how leadership has played a role in the effectiveness of these groups in lobbying for policy changes.
3. Ask students to think of leadership efforts that failed because there was a lack of followers.

Topic 4-1
Leaders and Followers
I. Being a Team Member
  A. Qualities of Effective Team Members
II. Opportunities for Leadership
  A. Types of Leadership
  B. Leadership in Action
III. Effective Leadership
  A. Set an Example
  B. Motivate Followers
  C. Guide Planning
  D. Use Tact
  E. Give Recognition
  F. Promote Cultural Diversity

Topic 4-2
Organizations That Work!
I. Youth and Professional Organizations
II. Getting Organized
  A. Electing Officers
  B. Holding a Meeting
III. Choosing Effective Programs and Activities
  A. Stay Within the Limits
  B. Publicize
  C. Evaluate Your Accomplishments

Topic 4-3
Your Rights and Responsibilities as a Citizen
I. To Be Informed
II. To Vote
  A. Registering to Vote
III. To Obey the Law
  A. Public Laws
    1. Criminal Laws
  B. Civil Laws
  C. The Court System
    1. Small Claims Court
IV. To Pay Taxes
  A. Types of Taxes
V. To Protect the Environment
VI. To Be Involved in Your Community

Topic 4-1
Leaders and Followers

Objectives
After studying this topic, you will be able to
- explain the roles of leaders and followers.
- demonstrate the qualities of effective team members.
- identify three types of leadership.
- describe five functions performed by group leaders.

Topic Terms
team	democratic
leader	laissez-faire
follower	motivation
diversity	brainstorming
autocratic leadership	tact

Throughout life, you will be a member of several groups. Your family is a group. Your classes are groups. You may also be involved with clubs, bands, scouts, sports teams, and choral groups. See 4-1.

4-1 Group involvement is an important part of life for many people.

Each member of a group can affect the success of group activities. Learning how to work with others will allow you to contribute to a group's effectiveness. In the process, you will develop positive relationships with your peers. Participating in group activities will also promote your social and emotional development.

Being a Team Member

A **team** is a group of people organized around a common goal. Every good team has leaders and followers. No team can exist with just one or the other. When team leaders and followers work toward the group's goal, they are practicing good teamwork.

A **leader** is a person who influences the behavior of others. Leaders take charge and help group members set and achieve group goals. Good leaders inspire the trust of their followers and respond to their teammates as friends. They involve all group members in planning, conducting, and evaluating group activities.

No person is a leader in all situations. A leader in the drama club may be a follower in the band. An athletic leader may be a follower on the yearbook staff. A business leader may be a follower in a social setting. You will be needed to lead in some cases and follow in others.

A **follower** is a person who supports a group by helping put goals into action. The best plans of any group will not yield results without the support of dedicated followers. Followers are needed to supply time, talents, energy, and other resources to achieve team goals. Followers take direction, but also help leaders determine the best course of action. Most people develop team skills by first assuming a follower role. They grow into leadership positions gradually as they develop self-esteem.

For a team to function effectively, leaders and followers must show a spirit of give and take. Followers must be willing to take a leadership role when their expertise is needed to achieve the team's goal. Likewise, leaders must recognize that

Vocabulary:
What do you think might be the differences between an autocratic leader and a democratic leader?

Discuss:
What kinds of groups may teens join at your school? Make a list of clubs for teens at your school or in your community.

Reflect:
How have you contributed to a group as a follower?

Putting Technology to Use
Have students use presentation software to give a presentation on a group to which they belong or have belonged.

Discuss:
Think of a championship professional sports team. Who are the team's leaders? How well do team members work together?

Reflect:
Have you ever tried to have a conversation with someone who speaks a different language? How hard was it to communicate? How effective would a working relationship with this person be?

Activity:
Have students take turns leading the class discussion. Ask students how this was an opportunity for leadership.

sometimes a follower is better suited to temporarily take charge. When team members work well together, they do what needs to be done, no matter what titles they have.

Both leaders and followers are needed to build strong teams at school, in the community, and in the workplace. Teams are especially important in the workplace. Consequently, employers try to hire individuals who have good teamwork skills.

Qualities of Effective Team Members

Team members put the interests of the team first and always emphasize "we" instead of "me." They keep open minds and come to meetings willing to discuss all ideas. They expect others to have different ideas and opinions. They do not become offended when their ideas are criticized. They use humor whenever appropriate, but never in a way that offends someone. They do their share of work, complete assignments on time, and keep a positive attitude. Effective team members try to do what is best for the team.

Members of teams that operate effectively pay close attention when others speak. Sometimes ideas expressed by teammates of different cultural backgrounds do not immediately make sense. People of every culture have unique beliefs, values, customs, traditions, and religious practices that are often reflected in their views. Sometimes a language barrier exists, making it difficult for them to express ideas clearly. When communicating with individuals of other cultures, extra patience and understanding is needed by everyone.

You will encounter people from other cultural backgrounds throughout life. This influence is the result of a multicultural society. Sometimes the term **diversity** is used to refer to the condition of a team whose members represent many different cultures. Diversity presents opportunities to share cultural traditions and customs. When everyone's culture is respected, individuals feel free to express opinions and views. The team benefits from the open, honest discussions. Often more and better ideas result.

On the other hand, diversity can create team conflict unless there is an effort to understand other cultures and a strong commitment to cooperation. Some additional ways to demonstrate team commitment are listed in 4-2.

Qualities of Committed Team Members

- Smile and use a pleasant tone of voice.
- Remain quiet until you have the floor.
- Think highly of every team member—including yourself.
- Make an effort to bring out members who may be shy.
- Seek clarification when something is not clear.
- Be willing to compromise on issues that can be handled effectively in several different ways.
- Celebrate your team's successes and the ability of members to work well together.

4-2 These personal qualities are signs that members are committed to their group.

Opportunities for Leadership

Leaders are people who step up and take charge of a situation. They are needed at all levels of human organization. Countries, states, cities, businesses, schools, and clubs all need leaders. Your skills as a leader may be used in a number of ways, both now and in the future.

Right now, you may be needed to lead class discussions, club meetings, or athletic rallies. You may know a student who has personal problems and needs your encouragement to seek counseling. You may serve on a team headed by a weak leader and have some ideas for motivating the group.

If you become a parent later in life, you will be a leader to your children. You may serve a leadership role in your community and possibly run for an elective office. No doubt you will join community and social

Across the Curriculum
English. Have students write essays on the U.S. president's leadership abilities.

groups devoted to your interests and possibly hold leadership positions.

In the workplace, you will have many opportunities to lead. Unlike the past, when supervisors told workers what to do, today's workplace uses a teamwork approach. Employees are expected to work well as teammates and share the leadership role as assignments dictate. Group members must possess the teamwork skills of creative thinking, decision making, and conflict resolution. A leader must know how to organize and manage the team's resources. Participation in school clubs and organizations, discussed in Section 4-2, will help prepare you for leadership.

Types of Leadership

There are three basic types of leadership. The first type, **autocratic leadership,** demands the cooperation of others. The autocratic leader has full control of the group and makes all the decisions for the group.

Autocratic leadership stresses meeting goals. It demands that team members perform as directed to reach goals. Autocratic leaders may seem harsh at times. However, their followers receive the satisfaction of knowing they have done more than they thought they could do. Some people would never try unless, in a kind but firm manner, a good leader says, "Do it."

Democratic leadership stresses the needs and wishes of individuals. The group discusses matters of policy. Members are encouraged to participate in decision making by voting. See 4-3.

In a democratic group, members have the power to select a leader to act in their best interest. They trust the leader to make good decisions for the group. If the leader fails to consider the group's wishes, however, the members have the power to choose a new leader.

The third type of leadership is called **laissez-faire.** Laissez-faire leaders play down their roles in groups. They are on hand only to serve as resources.

Laissez-faire leadership allows true freedom. Members may do whatever they

4-3 In the democratic style of leadership, decisions are discussed by all group members.

want to do. The group is not pressured to move forward on a schedule. An active group may fail to reach goals due to a lack of organization. In the end, members may feel that little has been accomplished in spite of their individual efforts.

All three types of leadership have good points. Autocratic leadership may be needed to help some people become productive and meet fixed deadlines. Democratic leadership takes advantage of members' ideas and provides the organizational structure to accomplish goals. Laissez-faire leadership fosters individual creativity, even though it may result in a low degree of productivity. See 4-4.

The secret to involving all members is to know how and when to use all three types of leadership. You must vary your leadership style to fit the people in the group as well as the situation. Take care not to become a bossy autocrat. Do not get carried away with the laissez-faire style, or your group may not accomplish anything. Democratic leadership usually works best, but you cannot expect it to work in every situation.

Discuss:
Have you been in a group where there has been laissez-faire leadership? What was it like?

Enrich:
Form several small groups. Have each group role-play a situation that shows the different types of leadership styles.

Across the Curriculum

Social studies. Have students research a country with an autocratic type of leadership. Students should write a paper comparing and contrasting that leadership to the democratic leadership of the U.S.

Activity:
Write about a situation that shows a leader using one, two, or all three types of leadership.

Resource:
What Type of Leader Are You? Activity A, SAG

4-4 Laissez-faire leadership works well in situations where group members need to use their creativity.

Leadership in Action

The following example shows how all three types of leadership can be used to achieve a single goal.

Consider the case of a school club leader who asks the members for suggestions to improve the student lounge. The overwhelming majority of members express a need to replace the worn, outdated draperies. (These actions are democratic. The opinions of all members were sought.)

The club members know they must first get approval to make any changes. They also know they must find ways to raise funds to pay for replacing the draperies. The club leader may ask a small task force to research the group's options and present ideas to the total membership. The leader may also ask a member to get the permission needed to replace the draperies. (Both of these actions are autocratic because the leader alone made the decisions.)

Once the membership hears and discusses the alternatives, the group usually votes. (This is democratic. However, if the leader makes the final decision without taking a vote, the action is still considered democratic because the leader got suggestions from the members.)

When working with those members who will actually replace the draperies, the leader may use a different approach. The leader may suggest they get prices for ready-made and custom-made draperies. They can compare these prices with the cost of the materials needed to make the draperies themselves. (Note, the leader neither tells them what to do nor consults with them. The leader only suggests. Some very creative ideas may result from this laissez-faire approach. Group members may need to meet several times to discuss the possibilities. However, the decision is theirs to make.)

All three types of leadership were used in this example. A leader's success is often based on knowing how and when to use each type.

Effective Leadership

Leaders perform a number of functions in a group. They must set a good example, motivate followers, and guide group planning. Leaders also need to use tact and give recognition to those who deserve it.

Set an Example

When you are the leader of a group, you need to set an example for the other members. Although you have extra responsibilities as leader, you also have the responsibility of doing your share of the work. If you fail to participate, you set a poor example for your followers. They may see no reason to help with projects if you are not helping, too. Also, they may lose respect for you and begin to resent you. See 4-5.

On the other hand, you should not try to do all the work by yourself. If you are a good leader, you will get other people involved. Try to place all members on one or more active committees. Give others the chance to participate and have the satisfaction of being useful and needed. Involving more people will allow more work to be done and more goals to be achieved.

Putting Technology to Use
Have students videotape meetings of different school organizations. View the videos in class and discuss how the group leaders set examples for the other team members.

Topic 4-1 Leaders and Followers

4-5 Leaders as well as followers must participate in group efforts.

> **Vocabulary:**
> What is the difference between intrinsic and extrinsic motivation? Can you give an example of each type?
>
> **Discuss:**
> What methods have you seen used to effectively motivate group members?

Another way you can set an example is by cooperating with everyone. Some large groups tend to divide into little groups of friends. You, too, may feel more comfortable working with your friends. However, you must remember that you are leading the entire group. You must go outside your usual circle of friends to include everyone. Your example will encourage others to work together for the good of the group.

Motivate Followers

As a leader, you may need to motivate followers to get involved in group projects. **Motivation** is a force that gives people a reason to take action.

Some people have *intrinsic motivation*. Their motivation comes from within themselves. They set many goals for themselves and willingly work to achieve those goals. Group members who are intrinsically motivated show enthusiasm. They never need to be prodded. Instead, they always look for ways to help.

Other people need *extrinsic motivation*. This motivation comes from a person's environment. Leaders can provide followers with extrinsic motivation by helping them notice their environment. A choir director may say the choral group sounds better when members are smiling. A scoutmaster may comment that the flowers in the city park need weeding. Such suggestions from leaders can motivate followers to take action. See 4-6.

Some followers are very willing to help but have no idea what needs to be done. Watch for these individuals, and

4-6 This choir director uses extrinsic motivation to encourage his group to prepare well for a concert.

 Putting Technology to Use
Have students search the Internet for Web sites that give tips in motivating groups.

Enrich: Form a small group to practice the brainstorming technique. Brainstorm ways your school can raise money for more computers.

Activity: Write a list of do's and don'ts for being a tactful leader.

Resource: *Leaders Involve Others*, reproducible master, TR

recommend tasks to them so they can enjoy being productive team members. Without positive direction, these people often get lost in confusion.

What about those who refuse to get involved? If you know their reasons, you may be able to motivate them. For instance, some people may not think they are capable of doing a job. You could help these people find tasks that better match their skills. This will allow them to develop more self-confidence.

Some people may refuse to get involved because they are too busy. They may have numerous other commitments. You might motivate these people to take on small tasks. This will allow them to participate without devoting a large amount of time. These people can take on larger tasks when their schedules are less hectic.

Guide Planning

Being involved in the planning motivates group members to participate. With careful planning, a group can successfully handle several projects and activities. Your role as leader is to guide the planning. Be sure the group thinks through a plan and is able to carry it out. Summarize thoughts frequently to ensure that all members understand the same meaning.

During a planning session, a leader can encourage a group to express ideas by brainstorming. **Brainstorming** is a group problem-solving method in which individuals offer all ideas that come to mind. It is a technique that requires rapid thinking and a constant expression of ideas. Some of the ideas will be really wild, but that does not matter. The goal is to develop many ideas, not a few well-planned thoughts. No one is allowed to criticize any ideas, so members offer them without fear of embarrassment. Later, the group decides which ideas to pursue, sometimes combining two or more brainstorming thoughts. The ideas that motivate the most members will be put into action.

Brainstorming has two benefits. First, the group is likely to find answers to its problems or challenges. Secondly, the opportunity to offer suggestions promotes member participation and motivation.

Use Tact

Successful leaders need to have tact. **Tact** is knowledge of what to do or say to avoid offending others. If being tactful is not one of your strong qualities, work on developing it. Tact will help you work with others without hurting them or making them angry.

Getting group members to do their share of tasks often requires tact. Most people like being *asked* to do something rather than being *told* what to do. Some leaders are afraid that if they ask followers to do something, the followers will refuse. Therefore, they just tell the followers what to do, even though this approach often causes friction. Eventually group members may not cooperate willingly.

Tact is necessary whenever you deal with people. Being kind and considerate is always appreciated. A smile with a pleasant tone of voice is important in all situations. This is true whether you are a leader or a follower.

Give Recognition

Leaders also need to give followers the recognition they deserve. Your encouragement can help bring out the best in others. When their efforts enable the group to reach a goal, give them the credit. See 4-7.

4-7 Giving awards is one way a leader can recognize the efforts of individual group members.

Career Preparation Activity

Leadership in a Career, reproducible master, TR. Each student is to identify a job title he or she would like to have someday. After interviewing someone in that position or conducting library research, students are to answer questions about how various leadership skills could be used in the position.

One way leaders can give recognition is with a sincere "thank you." People need to know their personal efforts are important and truly appreciated. The leader should take the time to congratulate the person in front of the group so everyone knows that individual efforts are noticed and valued.

Promote Cultural Diversity

One of the responsibilities of a group's leader is to promote cultural diversity. The acceptance of other cultures begins with an understanding of them. Therefore, a leader might encourage group discussion about cultural differences. The leader also might plan cultural activities, asking group members of differing backgrounds to plan the events. This will help bring down barriers in the group, enabling group members to work together better.

Check It Out!
1. True or false. A strong leader always performs as a leader, never as a follower.
2. Suggest five qualities of effective team members.
3. List and describe the three basic types of leadership.
4. A force that gives people a reason to take action is _____.

Check It Out! (Answers)
1. false
2. (Suggest five:) put team interests first, keep open minds, expect others to have different opinions, are not offended when their ideas are criticized, use appropriate humor, do their share of work, complete assignments on time, keep a positive attitude, pay close attention when others speak (Student response may include Chart 4-2.)
3. Autocratic leadership involves a leader who has full control of the group and makes all the decisions for the group. Democratic leadership stresses the needs and wishes of individuals, and members are encouraged to participate in decision making by voting. Laissez-faire leadership allows members to do whatever they want to do, and leaders are on hand only to serve as resources.
4. motivation

Topic 4-2
Organizations That Work!

Objectives
After studying this topic, you will be able to
- name three youth organizations and three professional organizations and tell the purpose of each.
- explain how a group's constitution and bylaws act as guidelines for electing officers and holding meetings.
- demonstrate how a group can use the planning process to establish a goal around which programs and activities can be organized.

Topic Terms
constitution
bylaws
parliamentary procedure

What makes an organization successful? Its purpose is a key factor. A group's purpose is its reason for existing. A group sets goals to help achieve its purpose.

Youth and Professional Organizations

One purpose of most youth organizations is to help prepare young people for their adult roles in society. Perhaps you are a member of such a group. Most schools offer a range of organizations that encourage student participation. Chart 4-8 describes several popular youth organizations.

As an adult, you may become involved in an organization that enhances your profession. The purpose of these organizations is to promote the career areas in which their members work. Professional organizations may achieve this purpose by funding research, offering scholarships, and sponsoring meetings to keep members updated. Chart 4-9 lists a number of

---

Discuss: What are some other ways leaders can give recognition to group members?

Resource: *Leading a Group,* Activity B, SAG

Resource: *How Do I Rate as a Leader?* reproducible master, TR

Vocabulary: Have you heard of the term *parliamentary procedure*? Have you ever used parliamentary procedure?

Reflect:
What are the purposes of one of the groups or organizations to which you belong? Are these contained in some written form?

Enrich:
Interview a member of one of the groups listed in Figure 4-8. Find out the purposes of the organization, leadership style practiced, and activities in which the group is involved. Indicate whether you would like to be a member of this group.

Activity:
Review the constitution of one of the organizations from your school. Are all the listed items included in that constitution?

Discuss:
Name some bylaws you have seen included for organizations to which you belong.

Youth Organizations

Business Professionals of America (BPA)	Promotes skills and aptitudes needed by a world-class business workforce.
DECA—An Association of Marketing Students	Helps students learn about marketing, merchandising, management, and related subjects.
Future Business Leaders of America (FBLA)	Assists students in choosing business occupations and helps them become competent, successful business leaders.
Family, Career, and Community Leaders of America (FCCLA)	Encourages personal growth, leadership development, family and community involvement, and preparation for the multiple adult roles of family member, wage earner, and community leader. It is the only student organization with the family as its central focus.
Health Occupations Students of America (HOSA)	Helps members build their physical, mental, and social well-being while developing into competent leaders and health care workers.
National FFA Organization	Teaches leadership, character development, sportsmanship, cooperation, service, improved agriculture, and citizenship to students studying agriculture.
Technology Student Association (TSA)	Develops the leadership and personal abilities of students as they prepare for their roles in a technological society.
Skills USA—VICA	Helps students develop leadership and teamwork skills and prepares them to enter trade, industrial, technical, and health careers.

4-8 These career and technical student organizations help prepare teen members for future work roles.

professional organizations related to the field of family and consumer sciences. Many of these have chapters that students can join to get an inside view of the profession.

Getting Organized

Organization is another factor that contributes to a group's success. Members know what to expect when a group follows set guidelines for electing officers and holding meetings. These guidelines are stated by the group's constitution and bylaws.

Many groups are local chapters of national organizations. All the chapters share the same purpose as the national organization. They also follow the same basic constitution and bylaws.

The **constitution** is a set of laws that govern an organization. In its simplest form, a constitution usually includes the following:

- name and purpose of the group
- membership requirements
- the group's officers, their duties, and the method of election
- basic meeting requirements, such as the number of people that must be present before a meeting can be held
- procedures for changing the constitution

Many groups also have bylaws that accompany the constitution. The **bylaws** are a set of specific rules that expand the constitution by giving more information. For instance, bylaws list the names and functions of committees. They state the order of business and any other information that is needed to make the constitution clear. The rules stated in the bylaws are more likely to need changing from time to time.

Putting Technology to Use
Have students check out the Web sites for each of the organizations listed in Figure 4-8.

Family and Consumer Sciences Professional Organizations

American Dietetics Association (ADA)	Serves dietitians who work in hospitals, schools, colleges, universities, business institutions, and industry.
American Association of Family and Consumer Sciences (AAFCS)	Serves individuals working in all areas of family and consumer sciences to help individuals and families develop living skills and adjust to limited resources and a changing environment.
American Society of Interior Designers (ASID)	Serves interior designers interested in establishing a professional code of ethics and an educational standard for all designers.
Association for Career and Technical Education (ACTE), Family and Consumer Sciences Division	Serves career-focused family and consumer science educators.
Consumer Science Business Professionals (CSBP)	Serves business professionals who integrate consumer trends and perspectives into business solutions.
Family and Consumer Sciences Education Association (FCSEA)	Serves supervisors and teachers of family and consumer sciences.
International Association of Clothing Designers (IACD)	Serves designers of apparel for a variety of markets.
National Association for the Education of Young Children (NAEYC)	Serves administrators and teachers in schools for very young children.
National Extension Association of Family and Consumer Sciences (NEAFCS)	Serves employees of the Cooperative Extension Service interested in opportunities to improve their skills as family and consumer science educators.
National Restaurant Association (NRA)	Serves those involved in one of the many aspects of the foodservice industry.
Society of Consumer Affairs Professionals (SOCAP)	Serves those in industry responsible for creating and maintaining maximum customer satisfaction and loyalty.

4-9 These professional organizations promote the careers of members working in various areas related to family and consumer sciences.

> **Enrich:** Invite a guest speaker to come to class who is a member of one of the professional organizations listed in Figure 4-9. Have the speaker tell about the organization and explain the role professional memberships play in a person's career.
>
> **Discuss:** How is the candidate nominating process for a group similar to the nominating process for a public office in the U.S.?
>
> **Reflect:** What are some other common standing committees? Which committees might you serve on?

Electing Officers

Your group's constitution and bylaws will state the officers to elect and their duties. Knowing the duties expected of various offices will help you nominate people qualified to handle the jobs if elected. See 4-10.

Different groups nominate candidates for offices in different ways. Some groups simply accept nominations from the members during a business meeting. Other groups have interested persons submit requests to run for offices. Many groups have a nominating committee that prepares a list of candidates to present to the full membership. In every case, members vote to determine the winners.

In addition to officers, most groups need to elect or appoint chairpersons for the *standing*, or permanent, committees. Membership, publicity, and fund-raising committees are examples of standing committees. Your group's method for selecting chairpersons will be described in

Across the Curriculum
Ask the heads of other departments to speak about professional organizations related to their subject matter.

Discuss:
What types of ad hoc committees have you served on? Did the experience prompt you to join other committees after the task had been completed? Why or why not?

Resource:
Using Parliamentary Procedure, reproducible master, TR

Resource:
Tips for Productive Meetings, color transparency CT-3, TR

Enrich:
Attend a school board or town council meeting and observe parliamentary procedure in action. Report on how the use of parliamentary procedure enabled business to be conducted quickly and democratically.

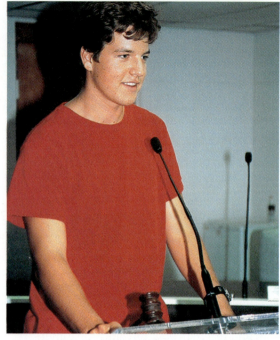

4-10 A group's constitution will describe the duties of the group's president and other officers.

Before a group can take action, members must vote. Before the vote, a motion must be made. A *motion* is a suggestion to take action. One group member makes a motion and another member seconds it. To *second* a motion means to show support for it.

After a motion has been made and seconded, group members have an opportunity to discuss the motion. Under parliamentary procedure, the discussion must focus on the topic of the motion. Only one person can speak at a time. All members must be given an equal opportunity to state their opinions. During the discussion, a member may move to *amend,* or change, the motion. When the discussion is over, a vote is taken. The group must follow the decision of the *majority,* 4-11. Usually a majority equals half the total number of members present plus one.

your bylaws. Some groups elect all committee chairpersons. In other groups, the president or a committee appoints chairpersons.

Chairpersons are also needed for ad hoc committees. An *ad hoc committee* is one that is appointed to perform a specific task. When that task is completed, the committee dissolves. A committee to plan this year's homecoming float is an example of an ad hoc committee.

Holding a Meeting

Most groups follow guidelines to help them conduct meetings in an orderly fashion. The guidelines most often used by groups are called **parliamentary procedure.**

Using parliamentary procedure, a meeting usually begins with a call to order. Then the minutes of the last meeting are read. The *minutes* are an official record of what took place at the meeting. The minutes are followed by reports from standing and ad hoc committees. Any unfinished business from the previous meeting is discussed next. Finally, the group discusses any new items of business.

4-11 Group decisions are reached by a majority vote.

FCCLA Activity
Have your chapter prepare for the Parliamentary Procedure STAR Event by following parliamentary law while running business meetings throughout the year.

Choosing Effective Programs and Activities

Some people join organizations because they need outlets for their energy and ideas. Unfortunately, it seems there are never enough of these people. According to research, about 10 percent of the members in a typical group do most of the work. About 80 percent tag along and enjoy belonging to the group. The other 10 percent criticize and complain about what is being done.

As a leader, your job is to be sure to keep the interest of the active members and involve the others more. If you succeed, your group will be doing better than most. As you work toward this goal, try not to let the criticism of a few members squelch your enthusiasm.

The key to keeping members involved is planning good activities. The activities of a group should be planned around one main goal for the year. The goal should relate to the personal needs and priorities of group members. It should make a difference in the lives of the members. Having one main goal provides a standard for measuring the group's progress throughout the year. It also creates a focus that builds interest.

A good way to involve members in establishing a group goal is through the planning process. See 4-12. This process is similar to the decision-making process you

Group Planning Process

Identify Concerns

Discuss concerns related to a problem that bothers your group, such as:
- If youth in your community are littering, why?
- What does littering have to do with your group?
- How are littered areas currently being cleaned?
- What is currently being done to reduce the littering problem?
- What effects does littering have on the community as a whole?

Set Your Goal

Narrow down your concerns. Decide what you can realistically do and set a goal, such as:
- Design materials to help other youth make intelligent decisions about littering.
- Develop a campaign to promote the understanding of the need for a clean environment.
- Volunteer in civic cleanup programs.

Form a Plan

Decide the *who, what, when, where,* and *how* of your project:
- Consider how to finance your project, who to reach, how to reach them, what resources to develop, and how to publicize your project.

Act

Put your plan into action:
- Make a workable timetable to keep track of your progress. Revise it if and when necessary.

Follow Up

Evaluate:
- Evaluate your efforts as you work on your project. Learn from your mistakes as well as from your successes. Make changes when necessary.

4-12 The steps of this planning process can help any group plan a project. An example is shown for studying the problem of littering.

Putting Technology to Use
Have students working in small groups follow the steps of the planning process and write a plan to get your school involved with recycling paper. Have students use word processing or publishing software to create a newsletter promoting the plan.

> **Discuss:**
> Think of a problem that was resolved by a group to which you belong. Was either the planning process or decision-making process used? If not, how was the problem handled? Did the method work successfully? Would either of these methods have worked better?
>
> **Resource:**
> *Selecting Programs and Activities,* transparency master, TR
>
> **Discuss:**
> What limits does the school place on clubs affiliated with the school?

read about in Chapter 1. It was developed by the Family, Career, and Community Leaders of America and is widely used by their chapters. However, the planning process will work equally well with any group. It is not a foolproof formula for a successful project. Rather, it is a process designed to get your group started. You may need to rearrange, revise, or repeat the steps to make the process work for you.

A group's goal can be represented in every program and activity. For instance, your group's goal might be to improve communications. Programs could be built around ways to communicate with people. Emphasis could be placed not only on verbal communication, but also on body language, music, and poetry. A fundraising project might be selling note cards or stationery. A related activity could be becoming pen pals with people of other cultures. You might sponsor a fashion show that features clothes that communicate. You could communicate food customs by preparing international dishes. Going on a picnic with preschoolers might help you improve your communication with children. Although the activities are varied, they all relate to communication. Questions that guide the selection of programs and activities appear in 4-13.

Stay Within the Limits

All groups have to operate within limits. You have limited amounts of time and money to spend on activities. You have a limited number of members who can participate. In order to have a successful group, you must avoid planning projects that are beyond your resources.

Certain school rules often limit what a group can and cannot do. When planning programs and activities, it is important for your group to follow these rules. You should not do anything that jeopardizes your group's relationship with others. You want to keep on good terms with other groups in your school. You need to preserve the respect of school officials. You also need to maintain the support of the community.

Selecting Programs and Activities

Is this program or activity consistent with the overall purposes of the group?

Will it help us attain our goals?

In what ways will members benefit?

In what ways will others benefit?

Will the program or activity be enjoyable?

Can it be completed within a reasonable length of time?

Will it provide opportunities for members to grow as individuals?

Will all people who wish to work on this program or activity be permitted to do so?

Will it be so difficult that members will become discouraged?

Will this program or activity provide a break from the usual routine?

4-13 Asking these questions can help group members select worthwhile programs and activities for their organization.

If you have concerns about whether or not your group is operating within the rules, investigate before proceeding. Sometimes the limits can be stretched a bit to accommodate special situations. However, it is best to get approval in advance. Your group is likely to suffer negative consequences if it tries stretching the limits without permission.

There may be times when your group cannot do something you want it to do. Accept the facts. Part of learning about group participation is learning to cope with disappointments.

Publicize

You need to let people know about your group's exciting programs and activities. Your group should have a publicity committee to help get the word out. Publicizing your group's plans can also attract new members to the group. Publicity can help build support for your group in the community, too.

Family Enrichment Activity
Encourage students to plan and hold family council meetings. Meetings should be kept brief and simple, with the focus being on one main topic of discussion. Topics might include distributing household tasks fairly among family members or planning a family recreation activity. Summarize the meeting and plan for similar meetings on a regular basis.

You may want to announce upcoming events in your school and local newspapers. If you plan something very newsworthy, you might want to contact local radio and TV stations. The yearbook is another important place to publicize school groups. If your group is part of a national organization, you might submit stories for their state and national publications. Once you start, you will find many interesting ways to publicize your group. See 4-14.

At the beginning of the year, get the names of contact people at newspaper offices and media stations. Ask these people to describe the types of information they want to receive. This will help you know how to prepare material and where to send it when events are happening.

Be sure your announcements include all the information needed to enable people to participate. Tell who sponsors the event. Describe the plans and state when and where the event takes place.

Pictures make news articles more interesting. When possible, include a large black-and-white glossy photo with your story. Be sure to identify the people in the photo. This type of publicity does more than attract the attention of people outside the group. It also increases the pride group members feel for their organization.

Evaluate Your Accomplishments

Make a point of evaluating your group's programs and activities. Check to see how much your group has accomplished toward achieving your goal. Groups that do not take time to do this miss one of the real satisfactions of work. You may be surprised at all you have done.

Evaluating your accomplishments can help you improve in the future. As you think back, try to remember some activities that sounded great but did not work. Discuss why those activities failed. Discuss how your group can prevent similar failures in the future.

Did you have some projects that were not as great as they could have been? Was more careful planning needed? Did you have too few resources? Were some committees too busy? Were some committees bored? Asking these questions will help you determine how the group can have more success with future projects. See 4-15.

Enrich:
Make a poster to advertise a comedy show your club will host as a fund-raiser.

Enrich:
Contact a newspaper editor to speak to the class about public relations for clubs and organizations.

Activity:
List as many ideas as you can think of for a group or club to use in publicizing an upcoming event.

Resource:
Choosing and Evaluating Group Activities, Activity C, SAG

4-14 A display is an effective way to publicize past projects and attract interest in the group.

4-15 One way to evaluate the success of a charity fundraiser is to count the number of participants and amount of contributions raised.

Citizenship and Service
Have students research seat belt and child restraint laws in your state. Ask them to develop posters to explain these requirements to parents. Obtain permission to display students' posters in local malls and other public places.

Vocabulary:
What do you think might be the difference between a direct tax and an indirect tax?

Reflect:
How do you contribute to your community as a responsible citizen?

Check It Out!
1. What is the purpose of most youth organizations?
2. List five types of information an effective constitution should include.
3. What is the key to keeping members involved in a group?

Check It Out! (Answers)
1. to help prepare young people for their adult roles in society
2. the name and purpose of the group; membership requirements; the offices to be filled, their duties, and the method of election; basic meeting requirements; procedures for changing the constitution
3. planning good activities around one main goal that relates to personal needs and priorities

Topic 4-3
Your Rights and Responsibilities as a Citizen

Objectives
After studying this topic, you will be able to
- explain the importance of being an informed citizen and exercising your right to vote.
- summarize the role of the court system in interpreting public and civil laws.
- describe several types of taxes.
- list conservation measures you can take to help protect the environment.
- consider why community involvement is important to individuals, especially teens.

Topic Terms
public law	progressive tax
misdemeanor	direct tax
felonies	indirect tax
civil law	volunteers

School groups are not the only place where you have the opportunity to be a leader. You can also be a leader in your community in your role as a citizen.

You are a citizen of your city or town, your state, and your country. As a citizen, you have certain rights and responsibilities. You have a right to enjoy the freedoms that are protected by federal laws. You have the responsibilities of becoming informed, voting, obeying laws, paying taxes, and protecting the environment. Fulfilling your responsibilities will help you protect your rights and the rights of others.

To Be Informed

You have a right to information about the world around you. You have a responsibility to use that information to be an informed citizen.

Topic 4-3   Your Rights and Responsibilities as a Citizen

Laws and government policy affect how you live. You need to be aware of how new and revised laws and policies might affect your rights and the rights of others. For instance, a change in the education policy could affect the schools you attend. Factors in the economy can limit your ability to find a job and purchase goods and services. New environmental standards will affect the air you breathe and the water you drink. International events can alter your sense of security.

As an informed citizen, you can work to resist negative conditions and make positive changes. When you are knowledgeable, you can speak to other citizens about issues that concern you. You can write to your political leaders to express your views. By being informed, you can take steps to defend your rights. See 4-16.

To Vote

Voting is both a right and a responsibility. It is a privilege to be able to help choose your government leaders. People in many nations do not have that freedom. It is your duty to cast your ballot on election days. If you do not vote, you will be letting other people choose your leaders for you.

Many people do not exercise their right to vote. A lack of information keeps them from knowing the candidates and their views. You can avoid this problem by reading newspapers and watching the news on TV. Find out what the issues are. Make a point of learning how candidates stand on the issues. You will then be able to determine which candidate's views are most like yours. This will help you know how to cast your vote.

Registering to Vote

If you are 18 years old and a United States citizen, you may register to vote. Registering puts your name on a list, showing that you are allowed to vote in a certain place.

You are responsible for registering to vote. Even if you are eligible to vote, you will not be able to do so unless you register. In most states, you must register about 30 days before an election in order to vote. Once you have registered, however, you will not need to register again unless you move. You can find out where to register in your area by contacting your local government offices.

To Obey the Law

Although people sometimes complain about laws, life would be chaos without them. You have a right to the benefits that laws provide. You have a responsibility to obey laws that govern your behavior. For instance, you have a legal right to a public education. However, you also have a legal responsibility to attend school until you reach a certain age.

Public Laws

Two main categories of laws govern people in the United States. These are public laws and civil laws. **Public laws** govern the relationship between people and their government.

4-16 Citizens can stay informed of their rights and responsibilities by researching laws and government policy in a library or on the Internet.

Activity:
Read a local newspaper. Find out what changes are taking place in your community and write a paper telling how they will affect your life.

Activity:
Invite a local politician or political candidate to address your class. Make a list of questions to ask the speaker.

Resource:
Make Yourself Heard, reproducible master, TR

Enrich:
Obtain a sample of a voter registration card. Review the questions that are asked. Why are each of these questions included on the voter registration form?

 Problem-Solving Practice
Decision Making and Lawmaking, reproducible master, TR. Students are to select a recent piece of state or local legislation. Then they are to suggest how lawmakers might have used the decision-making process while debating the legislation.

> **Reflect:**
> When was the last time you were with someone who was speeding in a car? Did you know speeding is a minor criminal offense punishable by law?

> **Enrich:**
> Visit a courthouse in your community where civil suits are being heard.

> **Resource:**
> *The Law of the Land,* Activity D, SAG

Criminal Laws

Criminal laws are a type of public law. They protect citizens from acts that are considered wrong or unfair. Traffic violations and kidnapping are examples of such crimes. In criminal law, the government is always the *prosecution,* or accuser. The person being charged with the crime is called the *defendant.*

Criminal cases involve two kinds of crimes—misdemeanors and felonies. **Misdemeanors** are minor criminal offenses. Speeding, disorderly conduct, and petty theft are misdemeanors, 4-17. The punishment for such crimes may be a fine or short jail sentence.

Serious crimes are called **felonies.** Rape, robbery, murder, and arson are felonies. The punishment for most felonies is a long prison sentence. In some states, the most serious felonies may be punishable by death.

Civil Laws

The other main category of laws is **civil law**. This area of law deals with disputes between private citizens. Divorce suits and contract disagreements are examples of cases involving civil laws. In civil law, the person making the complaint is the *plaintiff*. The other party is known as the *defendant*.

Every person has the right to protection by both civil and criminal law. Every person has the responsibility to obey the law. When people obey the law, they protect each other without the need for court action. Because people do not always act responsibly and follow the law, the court system stands ready to hear cases and make rulings that uphold the law.

The Court System

The U.S. Constitution and the constitutions of the various states established the court system. This system gives courts the power to review and settle disagreements about civil laws. It also gives them the power to try and punish people for disobeying criminal laws.

There are two separate court systems in the United States. *Federal courts* primarily hear cases dealing with federal law. *State courts* hear most criminal and civil cases involving people within a state.

There are several different types of courts in both the state and federal court systems. The nature of a case determines the type of court that hears it. See 4-18.

Cases are first heard in *trial courts.* A judge or a jury may decide trial cases.

People who disagree with verdicts reached in trial courts can take their cases to an *appellate court.* A panel of judges who reach a decision by majority vote hears appeals. The judges look for legal errors that might have occurred during the previous trial. If they find such errors, they have the power to reverse the previous verdict.

Small Claims Court

Minor disputes over small amounts of money may be settled in small claims court. These courts are rather informal. Plaintiffs and defendants present their cases directly to a judge. Lawyers are not necessary and court fees are low. This makes small claims court an affordable option for most people.

4-17 In some states, driving a car without wearing a safety belt is a misdemeanor.

Across the Curriculum
Social studies. Discuss court systems of other nations that influenced the formation of the U.S. court system.

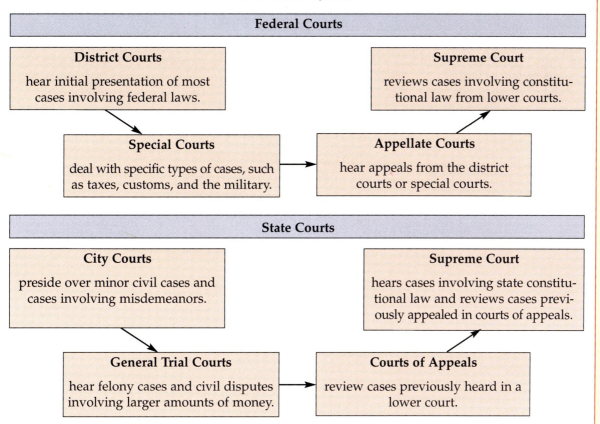

4-18 Each level of the state and federal court systems handles different kinds of cases.

To Pay Taxes

Like laws, people often complain about taxes. Also like laws, taxes are needed to create the type of society to which U.S. citizens have grown accustomed. Federal, state, and local governments collect taxes. Tax dollars are used to pay for national defense, postal services, health inspection services, and police and fire protection. Roads, parks, and schools are also funded by taxes, 4-19.

As a citizen, you have a right to the services provided by tax dollars. You also have a responsibility to pay taxes. Monitoring the fairness of tax laws is both a right and a responsibility.

Types of Taxes

A number of different taxes are collected to generate money for government services, 4-20. These taxes can be classified in different ways. Some taxes are **progressive taxes.** In other words, as the item being taxed increases, the rate of tax increases. For instance, income tax is a progressive tax. The more you earn, the higher is the percentage of tax you pay.

Direct taxes are those charged directly to the people who are to pay them. Sales tax is an example of a direct tax. **Indirect taxes** are included in the price of taxed items. Excise tax is an example of an indirect tax. To get an idea of how these taxes affect citizens, suppose gasoline and antifreeze both cost $1.50 a gallon. Excise tax of 20 cents a gallon is *included* in the price of the gasoline. However, sales tax of 6 percent is *added* onto the price of the antifreeze. Therefore, you will have to pay $1.50 for a gallon of gasoline. A gallon of the antifreeze, on the other hand, will cost you $1.59.

Putting Technology to Use
Have students use spreadsheet software to make a list of all the purchases they make in a week. Have them place the price of the items in one column, the amount of tax in another, and the totals in a third. Have them add the columns to see how much tax they have paid and how much their totals are as compared with the base costs of the items.

Reflect:
Do you feel you are getting your money's worth from the government for the taxes you pay?

Reflect:
As a responsible citizen, what are you doing to protect the environment?

4-19 Parks are just one of many public facilities that are funded by tax dollars.

Types of Taxes

Income tax	Provides the greatest source of government income. The tax is deducted from a worker's paycheck. Income tax is also collected on sources of income, such as investment dividends and interest.
Social Security tax	Is paid jointly by employers and employees. The employee's portion is deducted from each paycheck. This tax provides income to those no longer working because they reach retirement age or become disabled. It also provides survivor's benefits to a worker's dependents.
Sales tax	Is collected by some state and local governments. It is added to the cost of many goods and services when purchases are made.
Excise tax	Is included in the price of specific items and services. Gasoline and cigarettes are among the items on which excise taxes are paid.
Property tax	Is levied by state and local governments on real estate and personal property, such as cars, boats, and jewelry. It is paid by property owners, but is included as part of the rent charged on leased properties.

4-20 Different types of taxes pay for a wide range of government services.

To Protect the Environment

You are not just a citizen of a city, state, and nation. You are also a citizen of the world. As such, you have a right to live in a clean, healthy environment. You also have a responsibility to help keep your environment clean and healthy.

Protecting the environment means doing your part to help keep the air and water supply clean. It also means conserving the land and its resources. See 4-21.

Measures you can take to protect the environment include using environmentally safe products. Choose nontoxic cleaning agents and biodegradable detergents. Use rechargeable batteries. Avoid personal care products that are tested on animals.

Waste from product packaging takes up a lot of space in landfills. You can lessen the environmental impact of packaging by following the slogan *reduce, reuse, recycle.* Reduce the amount of packaging material you bring home by choosing products with minimal packaging. For instance, select unpackaged fruits and vegetables instead of produce sold on foam trays wrapped in plastic. Reuse empty product containers whenever possible. Plastic tubs are great for storing office and sewing supplies, and

Putting Technology to Use
Have students review the charts showing the breakdown of federal tax dollars for the last 40 years at the Tax Foundation's Web site, www.taxfoundation.org/taxdollar.html. How has the use of Americans' tax dollars changed?

4-21 FCCLA members pick up trash around their school and in other areas of their community.

glass bottles can be refilled with other liquids. Recycle as many product containers as possible. Glass, metal, paperboard, and many plastics can be recycled into other materials.

Conservation measures at home can help save electricity, gas, and water. You can preserve limited natural resources by turning off lights, television, and other power-operated items not being used. When no one is home, adjust your heat and air conditioner settings accordingly. Take short showers to save water. Be aware of how much water is running needlessly when brushing teeth and shaving. Make sure the dishwasher is full before running it. Always adjust the clothes washer's water level to each load. Walk, ride a bicycle, use public transportation, or carpool to reduce the use of gasoline. Always try to take the most direct route when driving.

To Be Involved in Your Community

Taxes provide most of the public services needed, but never stretch far enough to cover everything. This is why volunteers are welcomed in many government and nonprofit agencies. **Volunteers** are people who provide valuable services by offering their time, talents, and energy free of charge.

People who become involved in their communities take pride in them. They enjoy knowing they make a positive contribution. Such contributions can make the community more beautiful, such as freshly painted park benches, litter-free sidewalks, and holiday decorations. Volunteering also makes a noticeable difference in people's lives. Examples include making food baskets for the needy and helping people learn to read.

Most communities have a roster of volunteer opportunities available. However, you might see a specific need and simply inform the people in charge that you want to fill it. Think about your interests and abilities in deciding where you want to devote your efforts. That will lead you to find a volunteer opportunity that matches your enthusiasm.

Volunteering can benefit you in more ways than you imagine. You learn more about your community and your neighbors. You meet new friends and receive the personal satisfaction of seeing that your help really matters. You also perfect your skills and can also gain new skills.

Volunteering can help you determine your career interests. By gaining firsthand experience in related areas, you can better decide which direction in life appeals most to you. For example, if your interests include working with children and oil painting, you could seek a job that includes both. Some possible jobs that merge these interests are likely found in community recreation programs and local child care centers. If your interests change, you can always shift to other types of volunteer work to explore new areas.

Your volunteer experience will be a valuable asset when you try to obtain your first job. See 4-22. First-time job seekers who have no previous job experience to report can always list their volunteer work. Such work is just as important to employers as job experience gained in a paid position. Also, some of the people you help by volunteering may keep you informed of job openings in your field of interest. They

Resource:
Protecting the Environment, Activity E, SAG

Discuss:
Name some places in your community where you might volunteer.

Reflect:
Think of a career in which you are interested. What type of volunteer work might you do in relation to that career area?

Across the Curriculum
Social studies. Discuss ways citizens can fulfill roles as leaders and followers in the community.

Discuss:
Why is it important for people to realize the benefits of volunteering?

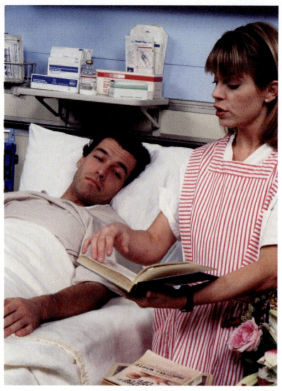

4-22 In addition to the job skills learned while volunteering, you also develop important interpersonal skills by working with the general public and cooperating with coworkers.

can vouch for your ability to do a good job to a potential employer you may want to impress. They may even offer you a full-time job when you leave school.

Later, when you meet the age requirement, you may wish to serve on a local committee or run for an elective office. Most of the big issues affecting a community are resolved in the political arena. The many different roles of public service are important, and dedicated people are always needed to fill them.

Check It Out!

1. What requirements must a person meet to register to vote in the United States?
2. Minor criminal offenses are called _____. Serious crimes are called _____.
3. List five services provided by tax dollars.
4. What steps can citizens take to lessen the environmental impact of waste from product packaging?
5. State three results of volunteering that can help teens get a full-time job in the future.

Check It Out! (Answers)

1. being at least 18 years old and a United States citizen
2. misdemeanors, felonies
3. (List five:) national defense, postal services, health care, police protection, fire protection, roads, parks, schools
4. *Reduce* the amount of packaging material brought into the home by choosing products with minimal packaging. *Reuse* empty product containers. *Recycle* as many product containers as possible.
5. (State three:) perfect skills, develop new skills, determine career interests, gain first-hand job experience, meet people who can offer them a job or help them get one

TEENS ARE EXPERIENCING...

Leadership

George Jackson, a high school senior, is getting lots of leadership experience. He is currently serving as a district president of a state student council association. He is also the cochair and only student member of a subcommittee for a county health commission.

George's simple but successful style of governing is based on the following four keys to leadership:

1. Envision—Know the goals you wish to accomplish.
2. Energize—Get people excited about the goals.
3. Empower—Give people the information, skills, materials, and encouragement to accomplish the goals.
4. Model—Demonstrate that goals are important by your own actions.

George uses his leadership style to encourage group members to participate in projects that don't interest them. He always tries to make certain everyone knows how important his or her contribution is to the achievement of the goal. "I want people to know that group goals cannot be accomplished without them," he says.

George also thinks praise motivates group members. "People need to know they are appreciated," he says. "I make a point of thanking them publicly for a job well done."

George was asked how he handles conflict between group members. "I like to talk things out and find a compromise," he says. "I try to avoid a vote where you have winners and losers. As a leader, I don't want to lose the skills of a single person because he or she lost the vote."

"I hate to tell people they aren't doing a good job," George continues. "However, you cannot let two or three people in a group make 100 people miserable. If efforts to resolve conflict fail, you might have to ask people to leave the group."

When asked if he sometimes finds it necessary to take charge of a group, George nodded.

"Sometimes a leader has to step in and take charge in order to accomplish what is necessary. However, if the leader steps in too often, the organization will fall apart. People know you will take charge and they wait for you to do it. A good leader has to also be a good follower."

George gives a few important tips to remember. "Don't let your ego get in the way. Use humor to generate action. Know when to push forward; know when to back off. Don't fight for your idea." He adds, "Scare tactics don't work either. Ask people; don't tell. Request; don't order."

George also emphasized the importance of communication skills. "The ability to communicate is important to leadership," he says. "Know how to write. Know how to put words into letters." He admits that writing is one of his weaknesses, for he is visually impaired. He overcomes this weakness by typing all of his correspondence. He feels this is necessary because he thinks poor handwriting diminishes a person's image as a leader.

When asked to summarize his strategies for being an effective leader, George again emphasized the four keys to leadership. "They adapt to any situation," he says. Using these keys can help the leader of any organization.

Discuss:
Have students reread the section "Effective Leadership" on pages 110-113. Then use the following discussion questions:
- How do George's four keys to leadership correspond to the leadership functions described in Topic 4-1?
- Do you think George is implementing the five functions described in the topic?
- What examples from the feature article indicate to you that George is following the advice given in the text?
- How have you seen conflict handled in group situations?
- Do you agree with George that a leader may have to ask people to leave if efforts to resolve conflict fail?
- Were you surprised to learn that George is visually impaired? How might this disability have impacted his leadership roles?

Note:
Students might be interested in knowing how federal tax dollars are spent. The following is the breakdown:

22% Social security
22% Health and medical
18% National defense
15% Income security
9% Net interest on the national debt
4% Education and social services
3% Veterans benefits and services
4% Transportation
2% Energy and environment
3% Other

Note:
Leadership skills are important in any work situation according to the authors of *Workplace Basics*. One of the seven skills employers want in their employees is organizational effectiveness and leadership.

Chapter Review

Summary

Both leaders and followers are needed to create teams. An effective team is the result of committed members who put team goals first. Diversity among team members is viewed as a positive factor, instead of a negative influence that divides the team. Through teamwork, members can develop leadership skills.

Leaders are likely to use a combination of autocratic, democratic, and laissez-faire leadership styles. Leaders are expected to set an example to motivate group members. They need to use tact and give recognition as they guide group planning, too.

As a teen, you may belong to one or more youth organizations. You may join a professional organization when you enter the workplace. These and all organizations need to follow some guidelines in order to be effective. Groups need to elect officers who will hold meetings and plan worthwhile programs and activities. Group events need to be publicized to generate interest and evaluated to improve future planning.

Leadership skills used in youth and professional groups are also used by citizens in the community. As a citizen, you have a responsibility to be informed, to vote, and to obey laws. You also have a responsibility to pay taxes and protect the environment. Performing these tasks will help you protect your personal and legal rights.

Volunteering allows you to give back to your community. It can also help you gain experience and friendships that will be beneficial in getting a job in the future.

Think About It!

1. Describe an instance when you filled the role of a follower. How did you act in that role? Then describe an instance when you filled the role of a leader. How did you act in that role?
2. What type of leadership would you recommend in each of the following situations? Explain your choices.
    A. Organizing the planting of a vegetable garden with a group of young 4-H members who have no prior gardening experience.
    B. Planning a fundraiser for a church youth group.
    C. Serving as a campaign manager for a friend who is running for a seat on the student council.
    D. Teaching a new play to a football team.
3. Imagine you are the captain of the volleyball team that is selling candy to raise money. As an effective leader, explain how you might set an example, motivate followers, guide planning, use tact, and give recognition for this project.
4. Imagine that your Family, Career, and Community Leaders of America chapter has a concern about traffic along Main Street where young children walk to school. Use the planning process described in Figure 4-12 to form a plan that addresses this concern.
5. What rights do you value most as a citizen? What responsibilities can you fulfill to help protect those rights?
6. Write a brief reaction to this statement: taxes should be abolished.
7. Why should protecting the environment be a global effort rather than a local effort?

8. In what ways can leadership skills be helpful to homemakers? In what other careers do you see leadership skills being particularly helpful?

Try It Out!

1. Read a biography or an autobiography of a famous leader. Share the story with your classmates. Work together to identify the leadership style he or she used most often. Also list the leadership skills the leader used to involve his or her followers.
2. Present a brief skit to the class to illustrate a good leadership skill.
3. Make a list of extrinsic motivators you think would be most effective for people in your age group.
4. Work in a small group to investigate the rules of parliamentary procedure. Role-play the proper use of parliamentary procedure for discussing an issue and taking a vote at a meeting.
5. Contact the office of a local newspaper or radio station. Find out what format an announcement for a school club event should follow. Prepare an announcement in the proper format, making sure you include all necessary information. Exchange your announcement with a classmate for critiquing.
6. Design a poster encouraging citizens to fulfill one of their responsibilities.
7. Complete each of the following sentences:
   A. I will know and exercise my rights and responsibilities as a citizen because...
   B. I will be an informed citizen because...
   C. I will be a voting citizen because...
   D. I will be a law-abiding citizen because...
   E. I will be a tax-paying citizen because...
   F. I will protect the environment because...
   G. I will become a volunteer because...
   H. I will run for elective office someday because...

Note:
Have students study *Robert's Rules of Order* or some other reference on parliamentary procedure. Assign a student to report on each of the following: the order of business; make a main motion; second a main motion; amend a motion; table a motion; read and approve the minutes; the treasurer's report; give a committee report; define new business and unfinished business; adjourn a meeting.

Note:
Have a member of the school newspaper staff visit your class and explain the format they prefer for announcements of school events.

Resource:
PowerZone Challenge CD. Have students play the chapter review game to reinforce text content.

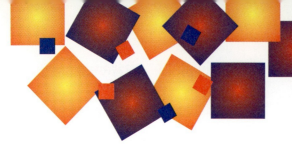

Chapter 5
The World of Work

Careers

These careers relate to the topics in this chapter:
- human resources assistant
- personnel assistant
- career counselor
- training director

As you study this chapter, see if you can think of others.

Topics

5-1 Career Planning
5-2 Finding a Job
5-3 Succeeding on the Job

Introductory Activities
1. Have students complete and discuss the following sentences:
   - The most important thing to look for in a job is…
   - I would like a job that…
   - Skills I have that will help me get a job are…
   - Getting a job will be…
   - Job interviews…
   - A good career is one that…
   - Twenty years from now I will be working as…
   - Most people work…
   - My first day at work…

Topic 5-1
Career Planning
I. Understanding Career Planning
II. Know Your Interests, Aptitudes, and Abilities
   A. Your Interests
   B. Your Aptitudes
   C. Your Abilities
III. Learn About Careers
   A. Career Information Resources
      1. Talk with People
      2. Use Library Resources
   B. Exploring Careers in Family and Consumer Sciences
      1. Using Your Family and Consumer Sciences Skills
IV. Your Education Choices
   A. Sources of Education
      1. Career Preparation During High School
      2. Career Preparation After High School
V. Other Factors Affecting Your Career Choice
   A. Your Lifestyle
   B. Potential Income
   C. Working Conditions
VI. Making a Career Decision
   A. Making a Career Plan
   B. Creating a Career Ladder

Topic 5-2
Finding a Job
I. Finding Job Openings
   A. People
   B. School
   C. Want Ads
   D. The Internet
   E. Employment Agencies
      1. State and Federal Employment Services
      2. Private Employment Agencies
   F. Direct Contact
II. Applying for a Job
   A. Sending a Letter of Application and Resume
   B. Applying by Telephone
   C. Filling Out a Job Application
III. The Job Interview
   A. Be Prepared
   B. Look Your Best
   C. Show Confidence
   D. Have a Positive Attitude
   E. Sending a Follow-Up Letter
IV. Creating Your Own Job
   A. Entrepreneurship: Pros and Cons
   B. Getting Started

Topic 5-3
Succeeding on the Job
I. Qualities of Successful Employees
   A. Positive Attitude
   B. Dependability
   C. Honesty
   D. Ethics
   E. Cooperation
   F. Job Readiness Skills
   G. Good Appearance
      1. Becoming a Professional
II. Technology in the Workplace
III. Work Schedules and Income
   A. Part-Time and Full-Time Jobs
   B. Earning an Income
IV. Understanding Your Paycheck
   A. Paychecks and Paycheck Deductions
   B. Taxes and Other Deductions
      1. Income Taxes
      2. Social Security Taxes
      3. Other Deductions

Topic 5-1
Career Planning

Objectives
After studying this topic, you will be able to:
- explain how your interests, aptitudes, and abilities relate to your career choices.
- identify resources used for career planning.
- determine factors to consider in making career decisions.

Topic Terms
job	cooperative education
career	apprenticeship
interests	Tech prep
aptitude	internship
abilities	mentor
job shadowing	career plan

Are you ready for the world of work? Have you thought about what type of career you want to pursue after you graduate? Do you know what types of jobs can help you reach your career goal? Now is the time to begin thinking more seriously about your career options.

How will you match yourself with the career that is right for you? In this topic, you will take a closer look at all the factors affecting your career choice so you can make a wiser decision. Your career choice will require careful thought and planning. After all, it will have long-term effects on your future lifestyle.

How do you get started in planning a career? You begin by evaluating yourself. What interests you? What do you do well? Then you gather career information through different sources and explore the options that interest you. When you are ready to narrow down your career options, use the decision-making process to make the best choice for you.

Understanding Career Planning

As you begin your career planning, you will hear the terms *job* and *career*. Do you know the difference between them? The meanings are easily confused. Understanding the difference is important.

If you work now, your **job** is whatever you do to earn a living. Your job consists of many tasks—all the duties you perform while you work. Perhaps you wait on customers, take inventory, and operate a cash register. Other people who have the same type of job would do similar tasks. See 5-1.

A career is a much broader concept than a job. Your **career** will be a series of jobs you hold over a period of years, often in the same or a related field. Through career planning, each job you have will help you prepare for your career goal. During your career, you may change jobs several times. As your career progresses, you may be promoted to higher-level positions and your responsibilities may increase. Career-focused planning in high school will help you gain insights into the skills and education needed for the career of your choice. You will then know what courses will best correlate with your career plans.

5-1 Anyone who rings up merchandise must be able to work the cash register.

Vocabulary: Do you think there is a difference between a job and a career? What do you think is the difference between an aptitude and an ability?

Discuss: Discuss the difference between a job and a career. Do you agree there is a difference between these two terms?

Across the Curriculum
English. Have students choose a career they would like to learn more about. Have them spend some time researching this career and write a paper summarizing their findings.

Resource:
Exploring Interests,
Activity A, SAG

Discuss:
What other careers can you think of that involve working with people? objects and tools? ideas?

Reflect:
Have you ever taken an aptitude test? If so, what did it tell you about your aptitudes?

Know Your Interests, Aptitudes, and Abilities

Start your career planning by getting to know yourself better. Evaluate your interests, aptitudes, and abilities. This will help you make a more satisfying career choice.

Your Interests

The first step in career planning is to identify your interests. Your **interests** are all the activities you like to do. What do you most enjoy doing? How do you spend your free time? What hobbies do you like? What subjects most interest you in school? Your answers to these questions are important. These preferences, which are based in part on your personal priorities, will affect your career choice. See 5-2. Once you recognize what brings you satisfaction, you can look at jobs that would provide the same type of satisfaction.

You can learn more about your interests by taking an *activities preference inventory*. Most school guidance departments can give this type of test to students. The test is designed to help you determine if you prefer working with people, objects, or ideas. Most jobs fit into one of these areas.

The inventory is like a multiple-choice test. You are given several choices and must select the one choice that most appeals to you. After completing the test, you are given a key to score yourself. The results will give you some ideas about your main interests relating to people, objects, or ideas.

If the inventory shows you enjoy working with people, you might like a career in sales, social work, teaching, or nursing. If you enjoy working with objects and tools, you might enjoy constructing buildings, sewing, or operating office or laboratory equipment. If you enjoy planning or evaluating projects more than actually doing them, you enjoy working with ideas. Then, a career in research, marketing, or publishing might be best for you.

Although you should look for a career that deals with your main interests—people, objects, or ideas—many jobs involve all three areas. For instance, sales associates work mostly with people, but they must have objects to sell and ideas about how to sell them.

Your Aptitudes

You need to have more than an interest in a career to be successful in it. You also need an aptitude for it. **Aptitude** is your natural talent and your potential for learning. When you have an aptitude for a certain skill, you can learn the skill easily and perform it well.

Aptitudes are often related to job success, 5-3. If you have a natural talent for writing, you would have a good chance for success in a journalism career. If you have an aptitude for working with numbers, perhaps you could become a successful accountant. On the other hand, if you do not have an aptitude for music, a singing career might not be your best choice.

Aptitudes are often tested in schools. The guidance counselor can discuss your test scores if you want to know more about your aptitudes. Keep in mind, however, the results will not give you definite answers to your career questions. They will not tell you that you will be a success in one field and a failure in another. Rather, the results will indicate your strong areas. That information will give you an idea of the kinds of careers in which you have the best chances for success.

5-2 People who prefer working with children would probably not be happy working with computers.

Across the Curriculum
Guidance. Discuss aptitude tests. Make tests available for anyone who wishes to take them.

5-3   A person with a musical aptitude may quickly learn to play an instrument.

Your Abilities

Although you have certain natural aptitudes, you must develop your abilities. **Abilities** are your powers to perform. They are your skills in doing tasks. You develop your abilities through training and practicing. See 5-4. Abilities may be mental or physical. For example, you may have the ability to easily solve complex math problems or to be a gymnast.

Developing an ability to perform a task is easier if you have an interest and an aptitude. However, a strong interest and hard work can help to overcome low aptitudes.

Interests, aptitudes, and abilities are interrelated. When considered together, they help indicate several possible career choices that would suit you well. Ideally, you will select a career that addresses your interests and uses your aptitudes and abilities.

Learn About Careers

When you have a better understanding of yourself, you can begin considering careers that interest you. If you wonder how to find the career that is best for you, the answer may be found through

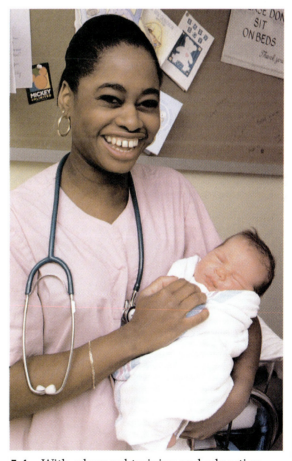

5-4   With advanced training and education, you could develop the abilities needed for a health-related career.

Discuss:
Which of your abilities have you developed through training and practice?

Reflect:
Can you think of a time when your strong interest and hard work helped you overcome a lack of ability?

 Putting Technology to Use
Have students use drawing software to create Venn diagrams illustrating the relationship between interests, aptitudes, and abilities in choosing careers.

research. Taking advantage of the many resources available will help you make the choice that is right for you.

Career Information Resources

Many school and community resources are available to help you learn more about careers. Talking with people and gathering information at the library are two ways to get started.

Talk with People

People are valuable sources of career information. Begin with yourself. Have you had a job? If so, did you like it? What did you most like about the job? What did you dislike? Would you like a career that is somehow related to that job?

Your friends, relatives, neighbors, and other people in the working world are good resources. Ask them about their jobs. This will help you learn about different jobs. Ask how they chose their careers. What are the good and the bad points of their jobs? As you talk with others, consider which types of jobs you might enjoy.

Talking with a school guidance counselor about your interests, aptitudes, abilities, and career goals may be helpful, 5-5. The counselor can answer your questions about career opportunities. He or she can tell you about the education and experience needed for various careers. The counselor can suggest several schools that offer programs in your area of interest. Most counselors have files of career information from various schools. They may even set up meetings for you with recruiters from various schools.

Use Library Resources

Most libraries are rich sources of career information. Look in both school and public libraries. A good place to begin your research is the computer subject index or the card catalog. Look under *careers*, *jobs*, or *vocations* for general information. If you are interested in a certain field, such as nursing or electronics, look under that topic.

Another library resource is the *Readers' Guide to Periodical Literature*, which indexes magazine articles. It lists the articles that appear in major magazines by subject, such as *employment* or *careers*. Each reference gives the title of the article, the name and date of the magazine, and the page number. The advantage of magazine articles is they have current information.

Check the reference section for career information guides. These guides help people explore career options and identify occupations of interest. One commonly used guide is the *Occupational Outlook Handbook*, published by the U.S. Department of Labor (DOL). It gives information about occupations, training requirements, expected earnings, work conditions, and future job prospects.

The DOL provides the latest information on today's occupations through an online database called the O*Net. This valuable information can be accessed at online.onetcenter.org. The O*Net describes the occupations and the training and education requirements for each.

Exploring Careers in Family and Consumer Sciences

Exploring different career options now will help you make a future career choice. Have you thought about using the skills you have gained in this course in your

5-5 School guidance counselors often assist students in making career decisions.

Discuss: Ask students to describe people they know who seem to enjoy their work. Discuss why these people find satisfaction with their jobs.

Enrich: Invite a career counselor to come to class to talk about various career opportunities and sources of career information available in the guidance office.

Note: Many libraries have computers available for researching periodicals, making the use of the *Readers' Guide* unnecessary. If your school or community library has these available, you may want to have a librarian explain their use to your class.

Resource: *Careers in Family and Consumer Sciences*, color transparency CT-4, TR

Across the Curriculum
English. Have students select and research one of the career areas of family and consumer sciences. Have them research careers in this area and prepare a report for the class. Discuss what information they should include in their reports.

career? If so, you may want to take a closer look at family and consumer sciences.

The field of family and consumer sciences is devoted to improving the quality of individual and family life. Careers in this field are often divided into six smaller groups according to subject matter. They are as follows:
- child development and family relations
- foods, nutrition, and hospitality
- money management and consumerism
- textiles and clothing
- housing and interior design
- education and communication

The chart in 5-6 shows careers in family and consumer sciences at three different levels. The course you are taking now will help prepare you for an entry-level position, such as a caseworker's aide. One to two more years of training and education would prepare you for an intermediate-level position. A food service assistant or home health aide are examples. A four-year college degree is required for many professional positions, such as a teacher.

As the chart shows, you can choose careers within one career area, or *cluster* (group of related jobs). Suppose careers in textiles and clothing interest you. There are many choices. You could operate a sewing machine to tailor garments or make new clothes in your home. You could be a salesperson in a clothing store or a fashion buyer for a chain of stores. You could be a clothing and textiles teacher, fashion editor, apparel designer, or textile scientist.

Using Your Family and Consumer Sciences Skills

You will be able to use your skills in family and consumer sciences in whatever career you choose. If, however, you choose a career in this field, many of the same skills overlap into the six subject areas. For example, an extension specialist who teaches nutrition would have career skills in education as well as foods and nutrition.

Even if you choose a career outside family and consumer sciences, you can use the skills you learn in this course both in your career and at home. For example, business careers related to marketing food products require knowledge of foods, business practices, and consumer trends. You may not want a career in food service or family services, but you will still need the abilities to cook for yourself and care for your own family.

Your Education Choices

As you learn more about various careers, you should consider the type and amount of education and training needed. How much education will you need to achieve your career goal? Is specialized training required? Finding the answers to these questions is the next step in the career planning process.

Today's workplace is a complex and competitive environment. It is wise to develop knowledge and skills that can be applied to several jobs since the job market keeps changing. New technologies are creating new jobs while making some traditional jobs *obsolete* (out-of-date). A good education offers a person many more job advantages, such as more interesting work with higher wages. Most jobs require extra training and education after high school.

Sources of Education

In Chapter 4, you learned that volunteering in your community could prepare you for the workplace. Holding a part-time job provides work experience, too. In addition to these job-learning opportunities, there are several other ways to learn about jobs firsthand.

Career Preparation During High School

Often students begin exploring career options through **job shadowing** programs. These give students knowledge of a particular career area through a one-day visit to a job. The student accompanies an experienced person to work and observes that person's activities. Teens are sometimes given opportunities to shadow parents for a day to develop a deeper understanding of their

Resource:
Gathering Career Information, reproducible master, TR

Note:
Technology is changing the world of work very rapidly. People typically change jobs, and even careers, many times during their working years. Students may not realize their formal educational training will likely not end with high school or college.

Discuss:
Can you think of some jobs that have become obsolete as the result of new technology?

Citizenship and Service
Have the class plan and carry out volunteer activities related to family and consumer science career cluster skills. For instance, volunteering to sort garments for a clothing collection agency would relate to the fashion and apparel cluster. Offering child care for low-income families would relate to the child development cluster.

Enrich: Choose a job or career from the chart. Research that career and write a report.

Discuss: Are any of you employed in any of these entry-level positions? Had you thought of these jobs as beginning steps on your career ladder?

Careers in Family and Consumer Sciences

	Child Development	Family Relations	Foods, Nutrition, and Hospitality
Entry-Level Positions	Babysitter Parent's helper Nursery school aide Child care center aide Playground assistant Camp counselor's aide	Homemaker's aide Caseworker's aide Senior citizens' center aide Camp counselor	Busperson Dishwasher Cook's helper Short-order cook Stock clerk Restaurant server Host Caterer's helper
Positions that Require More Training	Playground director Teacher's aide School food service worker Scout leader Recreational leader	Help-line counselor Counseling paraprofessional Senior citizens' center staff worker Youth services worker Homemaker services director	Dietitian's helper Food service manager Restaurant manager Food purchaser Sanitation supervisor Quality control supervisor Pastry and dessert chef Chef or chief cook Baker Restaurant owner Demonstrator
Positions that Require a College Degree	Nursery school teacher Designer of children's clothing, furniture, or toys Writer of children's books, stories, or games Child care center or nursery school administrator Child welfare worker	Social worker Crisis center counselor Family budget counselor Family/marriage therapist School counselor Family health counselor	Dietitian Executive chef Sales manager Marketing executive Advertising manager Caterer Editor or writer Food technologist Nutritionist Product developer Food stylist

5-6 You can obtain the skills needed for an entry-level position in a family and consumer sciences careers while still in high school. With additional training and education, you can advance to higher-level positions.

work responsibilities. Job shadowing can help teens improve their employability skills.

Some high school programs provide students with actual job experience in their respective fields of interest. These are called *work-based learning programs.* The programs combine classroom instruction with on-the-job experience.

There are several different types of work-based learning programs, but they share many qualities. For example, the student spends several hours per week both in the classroom and at a specified work site. Students receive school credits for their work experience. Usually they receive pay, too, but not always. The student's on-the-job training is carefully supervised. The program coordinator, usually one of your teachers, makes sure all key parties support the student's training agreement. Key parties include the school, employer, student, and the student's parents (or guardians). Work-based learning programs include the following:

- **Cooperative education,** frequently called a co-op program, prepares students for an occupation immediately after high school through a paid job experience.

Career Preparation Activity
Exploring Family and Consumer Science Careers, reproducible master, TR. Each student is to identify a family and consumer sciences career group that interests him or her, plan a career ladder within that group, and identify education sources for climbing the ladder.

Careers in Family and Consumer Sciences

Money Management and Consumerism	Fashion and Apparel	Housing and Interior Design	Education and Communications
Consumer affairs aide Consumer survey assistant Office worker Consumer product tester assistant	Stock clerk Salesclerk Cashier Alterationist's assistant Laundry attendant Display assistant Clothing repair specialist Fabric salesperson	Upholsterer's helper Designer's aide Home lighting aide Home furnishings salesperson	Babysitter Nursery school assistant Youth counselor
Consumer service representative Consumer product specialist assistant Credit bureau research clerk Loan officer assistant Bank teller Collection agent	Sewing machine operator Presser/finisher Buyer Fashion photographer Fashion writer Store manager Dry cleaner Alterationist Tailor/reweaver	Drapery/slipcover maker Designer's assistant Upholstery and carpet cleaner Appliance/furnishings salesperson Home lighting designer Real estate agent	Teacher's aide 4-H leader
Retail credit manager Money investment adviser Consumer survey specialist Consumer affairs director Loan officer Consumer product specialist Consumer money management director Financial planner	Fashion designer Textile designer Marketing specialist Market researcher Display artist Researcher or tester Clothing consultant Merchandise manager	Textile designer Kitchen designer Home furnishings adviser Home furnishings editor Home furnishings buyer Interior designer Merchandising specialist Home service director Public housing consultant Home planning specialist	High school family and consumer science teacher Family and consumer science professor Curriculum specialist County extension agent Adult educator

Discuss: How are internships different from jobs?

Reflect: Have you made any decisions about what to do after high school? What are some of your options?

- **Apprenticeship** programs provide training for a skilled trade. Apprenticeships usually require a legal agreement that you will work for the employer for a designated length of time in exchange for the instruction.
- **Tech prep,** or the technical preparation education program, often combines two years of high school courses with two years of postsecondary education. This program of study prepares students for a wide range of technical careers.
- An **internship** offers paid or unpaid work experience to learn about a job or industry. An internship is usually a more advanced program of study.

At the job site, a supervisor is responsible for the student's performance. The supervisor may appoint an employee to train the student or may choose to do the training alone. A person who knows how to do the job and teaches the student to do it well is called a **mentor.** This person often answers the student's day-to-day questions.

Career Preparation After High School

Sometimes high school graduates obtain job experience by joining the military. Others may gain job experience by volunteering for the Peace Corps or a similar organization. Usually, though, graduates go on to schools of higher education to prepare for their careers.

Putting Technology to Use
Have students use the Internet to research tech prep and apprenticeship programs in an area of interest to them.

Enrich:
Visit your local community college. Pick up information about courses and degree programs they offer, or talk to a counselor.

Discuss:
Ask students what role they think a job should play in a person's life.

Reflect:
Think about your goals and personal priorities, which you identified in a previous chapter. How will they influence your desired lifestyle? your career choice?

- *Professional schools* offer training in a specialized field, such as becoming a chef, fashion designer, or computer technician. Schooling consists of classroom training and hands-on experience. You receive a certificate or diploma at the end of the course. You may be required to pass a test to receive a license to work in the profession.
- *Community colleges* offer skills training or comprehensive programs. At the end of the two-year programs, students usually receive a certificate or associate degree. Community colleges offer many areas of study, which often reflect the job needs of the area. Graduates include medical and legal secretaries, child care workers, hairdressers, practical nurses, and hotel managers. See 5-7. Some students transfer to a university for additional education.
- Most *college* or *university programs* are designed for four years of study. They give students a broad background of general knowledge and extensive instruction in a specific subject. Bachelor's degrees are given in many categories. Examples are interior design, textiles and clothing, food and nutrition, counseling, journalism, computer technology, advertising, and education.

Some companies offer on-the-job training to employees. Sometimes this training helps new employees learn the unique work methods and philosophy of their employer. At other times, on-the-job training prepares employees to handle more challenging jobs. However, when individuals are hired by a company, they already possess the skills they need for an entry-level job in their field.

Your education will be a major factor in determining your job choices. You need to choose the right type of education for the career you want.

Other Factors Affecting Your Career Choice

When making any career decision, you will consider many factors. First, you consider your interests, aptitudes, and abilities. Then, you consider the educational requirements and training needed. Finally, you will consider other important factors, such as your lifestyle, potential income, and working conditions.

Your Lifestyle

How will your career affect the way you live? In matching yourself to the right career, think about your desired lifestyle, 5-8. What personal priorities and goals are important to you? In addition to liking your job, consider the impact it will make on your future life. Where do you want to live? Some jobs may be easier to get in a large city or certain parts of the country. Do you plan to marry and have a family? If so, consider the working hours that will be required for some careers. If you value time with your family, would nighttime or long working hours interfere with your family life? Your friendships and how you spend your leisure time will also be affected.

5-7 Students in community college programs can learn skills related to specific career areas, such as data processing and office administration.

Putting Technology to Use
Have each student make a database of professional schools, community colleges, or universities in which the student is interested.

Topic 5-1   Career Planning

5-8 If you are considering a career in retail sales, you may have to work longer hours. How will this affect your lifestyle?

Potential Income

Income is another factor to consider in your career choice. How much income do you want to earn? What income can you expect to earn in your chosen career? This will affect how much money you will have available to spend. Will it provide for personal and family needs? What is the income potential of this career?

Be cautious about making high income your top goal. Many people who achieve top-paying jobs do not find the satisfaction they expected. Their ties to their family, friends, and community often bring greater personal rewards. Obtaining a good income is a very worthwhile goal, but not if it replaces important goals in other areas of your life.

Working Conditions

Besides working hours, it is important to consider working conditions in your career choice. Are there certain environmental conditions to which you would object? For instance, would it bother you to work in noisy, dusty conditions? Would you prefer to work in a quiet office setting? Do you want the same type of responsibilities every day or a variety of tasks? Do you like a great deal of independence or constant team interaction? Every job has certain desirable and undesirable conditions. Your choice should be the most satisfying for you.

Consider the effect your career could have on your physical and mental health. Some careers are very stressful while others are not. Some people work well under intense pressure while other individuals do not. If stress reduces the quality of your productivity at work, it will probably affect your lifestyle as well.

Making a Career Decision

Choosing a career can be one of the hardest decisions to make. However, making a decision now will give you a head start on career planning. You can use the decision-making process to evaluate your career choices and make a wise decision. (Take a few minutes to review the steps outlined in Chapter 1.) As a result, you will have a better idea of where you want to direct your life. You can start setting your career goals now and working toward them.

Throughout your working life, you will consider different jobs and even different careers. This is very common today. It is rare for a person to stay in the same job for a lifetime. By using the decision-making process, you can consider new opportunities as they arise and the career direction that is best for you at that time.

Look at Beth's career changes. During high school, she worked as a salesclerk in a clothing store. She liked fashion and decided to study fashion design in an area college. She used her knowledge to create fashion displays for the store's merchandise. Her abilities in displaying fashions became useful when a local drama group needed help developing costumes for their play. As a hobby, Beth helped design the costumes for that play and several others. Soon she realized she wanted to know more about historical costume design. She

Discuss:
How important will potential income be to your career choice? Would it be at the top of the list or farther down?

Activity:
Make a list of your preferred working conditions. Make another list of conditions you would not want to work under at a job.

Reflect:
Why is it a trend today to change jobs instead of staying in one company your whole life? How is this different from 30 years ago?

Putting Technology to Use
Have students research OSHA regulations for working conditions at www.osha.gov.

Activity:
Create an alternate career plan for Beth assuming her primary interest is salesmanship.

Resource:
Influences on Career Choices, Activity B, SAG

Discuss:
How is finding a fulfilling career more difficult if you don't have a career plan?

went back to school for an advanced degree in clothing and textiles, with a specialization in historical clothing. After graduation, she took a job at her state's capitol building. She is now responsible for displaying and preserving her state's historical clothing collection.

Beth's love of clothing fashion was the motivating force behind her career decisions. If her primary interest were salesmanship instead of fashion, her career would have taken a different course. It is easier to look back on a person's life and observe a common theme rather than identify what lies ahead. However, by making plans now, you can direct your life along the path you want. When new opportunities or interests arise, you can then adjust your plans.

Making a Career Plan

As you explore your interests, aptitudes, and abilities, look for career options that seem to fit you. Once you decide what type of career you want to pursue, begin identifying what it will take to achieve that goal. A list of steps to follow to achieve a career goal is called a **career plan.** You would take a step every few years of your life, identifying the following for each step:

■ job experience
■ education and training
■ extracurricular and volunteer activities

The chart in 5-9 shows a career plan for a person wanting to become a kindergarten teacher. It represents one of many different career plans that could be developed to reach that same goal.

Every student can begin preparing for his or her career now by making a career plan. This is also the time to take the first step. Mapping a career plan on paper helps a person develop a course of action and stick to it.

A well-developed career plan can eliminate some of the frustration of planning a career because you always know where you want to go and what you need to do

Career Plan for Kindergarten Teacher

	Job Experience	Education and Training	Extracurricular and Volunteer Activities
During Junior High School	Babysitter	Choose topics related to early childhood education for extra credit or when subjects are optional.	Play with and help guide younger children in the family as well as the neighborhood.
During High School	Playground assistant	Take a college preparatory program.	Teach neighborhood youngsters to read better and enjoy team sports.
During College	Part-time nursery school aide	Obtain a bachelor's degree in elementary education with an emphasis in early childhood education. Also obtain a teacher's certificate.	Help direct activities at a summer camp.
After College	Kindergarten teacher	Consider obtaining an advanced degree (to become a teacher of kindergarten teachers).	Help develop preschool and after-school programs for young children.

5-9   A career plan is a guide to the career-related goals you want to accomplish in the foreseeable future.

Putting Technology to Use
Have students use charting software to create career plans for themselves like the one in Figure 5-9.

Topic 5-1 Career Planning

next. As with any other goal setting, you make a plan, implement it, and evaluate your progress along the way. You may want to adjust your plan as your interests or goals change.

Creating a Career Ladder

You can see how one job in a career field often leads to another. A career ladder illustrates this concept. The career ladder shown in 5-10 is for careers in child development. A student considering a career as a kindergarten teacher could also use it.

The bottom rung of the ladder shows jobs requiring little or no experience. Traveling up the ladder leads to related jobs of increasingly greater responsibility. You will notice that these jobs require more education and experience. The top of the ladder shows jobs that require education beyond a bachelor's degree—either a master's degree or a doctorate.

As you make your career decisions, try to consider the overall picture. Try to make choices that will give you the greatest satisfaction. In doing so, you create the quality of life you desire. The decision-making process is a skill you can always use to manage your life and make better career decisions.

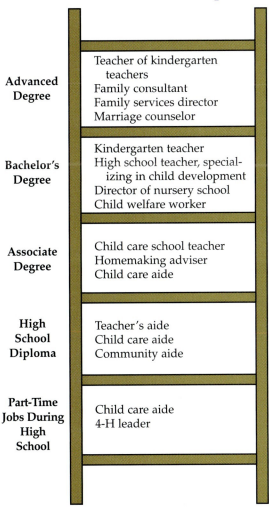

5-10 This career ladder in child development shows how a person can advance from job to job.

Check It Out!

1. Explain how a person's interests, aptitudes, and abilities affect his or her job satisfaction.
2. List five sources of career information.
3. Name the six subject matter areas in the field of family and consumer sciences.
4. True or false. Most students receive a bachelor's degree after two years of study at a community college.
5. Besides interests, aptitudes, and abilities, name three other factors to consider in making a career decision.

Check It Out! (Answers)

1. (Student response.)
2. (List five:) yourself, friends, relatives, people in the working world, school guidance counselor, library resources, *Readers' Guide to Periodical Literature, Occupational Outlook Handbook,* Internet sources such as O*Net
3. child development and family relations, foods and nutrition, money management and consumerism, textiles and clothing, housing and interior design, education and communication
4. false
5. your lifestyle, potential income, and working conditions (Students may justify other responses.)

Activity:
Have each student draw a ladder on a sheet of paper and label the five steps as shown in Fig. 5-10. Ask each student to choose a career and then try to list jobs in this career at each of the five levels.

Resource:
Climbing the Career Ladder, transparency master, TR

Vocabulary:
Do you know what an entrepreneur is? Do you know any entrepreneurs?

Enrich:
Investigate any job placement services offered by your school and report to the class how to use these services.

Activity:
Bring the classified section of a newspaper to school. Look at the types of jobs that are in demand. Note the abbreviations used in the ads. Do you know what they mean?

Topic 5-2
Finding a Job

Objectives
After studying this topic, you will be able to
- describe sources used to find job openings.
- complete a job application form neatly and accurately.
- prepare for a successful job interview.
- list the advantages and disadvantages of being an entrepreneur.

Topic Terms
personal fact sheet
references
resume
entrepreneur

Once you have a career plan in mind, your next step is to find a job that fits it. Perhaps you would like to hold a part-time job while in high school. This can help you gain valuable skills and experience while you explore your career choice. Having a job provides some income and helps you learn job responsibilities and communication skills.

Finding a job takes work. You must make the effort to find job openings that fit your qualifications—do not wait for an employer to come to you! Next, you need to apply for positions that interest you. Finally, you must interview with an employer. If you receive a job offer, you must then decide whether or not to accept it.

Finding Job Openings

The first step in getting a job is finding job openings. How do you find an employer who is looking for a worker with your qualifications? Job openings can be found through a variety of sources. Some of the most common sources are listed here.

People

If you want a job, let people know. Tell everyone you know—your friends, parents, relatives, and neighbors. Someone may have seen a help-wanted sign. Someone else may have heard about a new business that is looking for employees. Another person may know about a job opening where he or she works. Many personnel directors say the best information about a company's plans comes from current employees.

School

Your school can be another source of job leads. Some schools have job placement programs. If your school does not have one, contact a person who could help you. This could be a counselor, teacher, or the person in charge of community relations. These are the people that employers would probably call about job openings. If the key people in your school know you want a job, they can tell employers about you.

Want Ads

To get an idea of the job market in your area, look at the want ads in local newspapers. These ads are located in the classified section of the newspaper. They give brief descriptions of all kinds of jobs, 5-11. If you see an ad that interests you, respond right away. Job openings listed in want ads are often filled shortly after the ads appear.

The Internet

The Internet is one of the easiest places to find job openings all over the country. Companies may post jobs on their own Web sites. Newspapers usually have a Web site that includes the same want ads they print. In addition, many Web sites are devoted exclusively to job openings. These sites may even offer tips on interviewing and preparing your resume.

Employment Agencies

Going to an employment agency is a more formal approach to job hunting. State and federal agencies provide free employment services to jobseekers. Private agencies may charge a fee for their services.

State and Federal Employment Services

Check the telephone book for the location of your nearest state employment

Putting Technology to Use
Have students look online for want ads. Have them make a list of Web sites where job listings are posted.

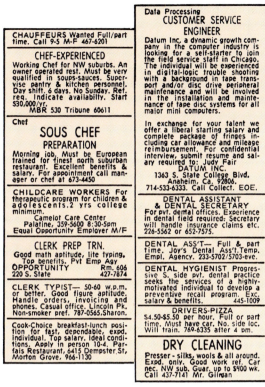

5-11 Reading the want ads in your local newspaper is one way of finding job leads.

service office. Counselors there can review your education and experience. They can talk with you about job requirements and help you set realistic career goals. Placements are made for all kinds of jobs.

The Civil Service Commission is a federal agency. It hires the people who work for the United States government. Civil service jobs are available throughout the country. They are available in almost any line of work. To get a civil service job, you may be required to pass an exam. You must meet certain education and experience requirements. The requirements vary for different types of jobs. The placement services of the Civil Service Commission are free.

Military recruitment offices can be considered a type of employment agency. They offer jobs and careers. They also offer educational benefits and options for education that could lead to other careers.

Private Employment Agencies

Another option to consider is a private employment agency. These charge the employer or the job seeker a fee for their services. Most agencies are specialized. Some may handle just one type of job, such as office jobs. If an agency offers you a position, use caution. Read any contract that is offered to you carefully. Do not sign it until you understand all the terms of the agreement.

Direct Contact

If you want to work for a certain company, try a direct approach. Contact the head of the company or the personnel director. Write a letter, make a phone call, or visit the company in person. Sometimes a combination of methods works best. For instance, you may write a letter and follow it with a personal visit. The company and the situation will determine how you apply for work.

Applying for a Job

Before you apply for any job, you need to gather and organize some personal information about yourself. Write down this information neatly on a sheet of paper. Then you can take it with you whenever you fill out a job application. Your **personal fact sheet** should include your Social Security number, education, work experiences, skills, honors and activities, hobbies, and interests. Also list at least three **references**. These are people who know you well and can vouch for your good work. A teacher, club adviser, former employer, or family friend—all are good choices. Ask in advance for permission to use their names.

When you find a job opening that interests you, you must apply for it. Depending on the type of position, this may be done by sending a letter of application and resume, using the telephone, or applying in person.

Sending a Letter of Application and Resume

For many jobs, you will need to write a *letter of application* to the person in charge

Enrich: Invite someone from the Civil Service Commission to speak to the class about civil service jobs.

Enrich: Role-play making a phone call or a personal visit to a company to check on job openings.

Resource: *Sources of Job Openings*, reproducible master, TR

Discuss: What are the advantages of having a personal fact sheet with you when applying for a job?

Putting Technology to Use
Ask students to use word processing software to create personal fact sheets for themselves. Have them save the files to be updated when necessary.

Resource:
Personal Fact Sheet, Activity C, SAG

Enrich:
Write a letter of application for a job. Exchange your letter with one from a classmate. Critique each other's letter.

of hiring. In it, be as brief and concise as possible. Begin by expressing your interest in the job. Then briefly describe your qualifications for the job opening. Finally, request an appointment to discuss your qualifications in person. Most good letters of application contain no more than three paragraphs.

Be sure to send a resume with your letter of application, 5-12. A **resume** is a brief

---

Terry C. Pinkham
204 Quail Run Road
Oak Park, TN 30241
(321) 555-4567
tpinkham@provider.com

Employment Objective	Day camp counselor
Education 2002-present	Oak Park High School, Oak Park, TN
Work Experience 2002-2003	Babysitter for two school-age children
Summer 2003	Volunteered in church nursery with school-age children
Honors and Activities	Member of Family, Career and Community Leaders of America for two years
	Member of Spirit Club for three years
	Member of Student Council during junior year
	Member of choir for three years
	Member of National Honor Society for one year
	Student of the Week, Oak Park Center for Youth

References available upon request.

5-12 A resume is a brief overview of your qualifications for employment.

Across the Curriculum

English. Work with students on writing appropriate business letters. Stress the importance of proofreading letters for appropriate grammar and punctuation.

account of your education, work experience, and other qualifications for employment. The information from your personal fact sheet can help you prepare your resume. Your resume should be neatly typed, well organized, and easy to read. A good resume sparks the employer's interest in you. It should get the employer interested in asking you for an interview. As a teen you may have no job experience to report. If so, focus on your volunteer activities as well as your interests and abilities.

Your list of references should be typed on a page separate from your resume. At the bottom of your resume, state: "References are available on request." When you are successful in obtaining an interview, be prepared to list your references at that time.

Applying by Telephone

When calling an employer, state your name and the position that interests you. Have ready your list of questions to ask about the position. Take notes during your conversation. Being polite and courteous will help you make a good impression. If you are interested in the job, ask for an interview. Be sure to set up the date, time, and location for the interview with the employer.

Filling Out a Job Application

When you apply in person for a job, you will be asked to fill out an application form. Completing an application form neatly and accurately is important, 5-13. If you do not fill it out correctly, you may not be considered for the job.

In some cases, you may be interested in working for a company that has no current job openings. Some companies accept applications even if they do not have openings. When an opening does occur, they look through the applications and pick out the best.

When you are asked by an employer to complete an application form, keep the following tips in mind:
- Read through the entire application before you write anything on it. Be sure you know the correct information

5-13 It is a good idea to practice completing job applications before you apply for the job you want.

to write for each of the questions. You do not want to give the same responses for two or three different questions.
- Look for specific directions on how to fill out the form such as *write, print,* or *use black ink.* Follow the directions carefully. Be as neat as possible.
- Refer to your personal fact sheet or resume as you complete an application form. It should include most of the information you need.
- Never leave a question unanswered. The reader may think you were careless and overlooked it. If a question does not apply to you, write "does not apply" or draw a line through the space.
- Give complete and accurate information. If you have no full-time work experience, mention part-time jobs like baby-sitting and volunteer work you have done. If you are asked for information you do not know, get the answer from your personal fact sheet.
- Carry a pocket-size dictionary with you so you can check your spelling.

Activity:
Ask one of your parents to bring home a job application from his or her place of employment. Fill out the application form and note any sections you could not complete.

Resource:
Filling Out a Job Application, transparency master, TR

Resource:
Employment Application, reproducible master, TR

Putting Technology to Use
Have students create a resume using word processing or resume-creating software. Have them save the files to be updated when necessary.

Activity:
Make a list of do's and don'ts for successful job interviews. Begin with the ideas presented in this chapter and then add your own.

Discuss:
What are some additional questions employers are likely to ask during a job interview?

Note:
Employers often form their opinion about a job applicant within the first few minutes of a job interview. This is why a person's appearance is so important when applying for a job.

- Be prepared to give the name, title, address, and phone numbers of people for whom you have worked, either for pay or for volunteer work. Provide the same information about your references.

The Job Interview

When you visit a company to complete an application form, it is a good idea to be prepared for an interview. The employer might want to interview you right away. If you get this chance, you will want to take advantage of it. In other cases, the employer may look over your application first and contact you later. He or she may call you at home to set up an appointment for another day.

Be Prepared

How can you prepare for an interview? Do some research related to the company, 5-14. Learn about the products it sells or the services it offers. Talk to people who work there or know others who work there. Find out all you can about the job opening. Review your own qualifications for the job.

Be ready to answer questions the employer may ask: "What do you know about our company?" "What kind of work are you seeking?" "Why do you want to work for us?" "Why do you think you are right for the job?" When an interviewer sees that you have researched the company, he or she learns two important facts about you. One is you really want the job. The other is you are willing to put extra effort into something that is important to you.

Look Your Best

First impressions are important when you meet someone. This is just as true for employers as for new friends or dates. You will want to look your best for an interview.

Good looks begin with good grooming. Your hair should be clean and neatly styled. If you wear makeup, keep it to a minimum. Jewelry, too, should be kept to a minimum. Your hands should be clean, and your fingernails should be trimmed neatly.

Clothes are a major part of your appearance. Again, cleanliness and neatness are key. Clothes should also be appropriate for the occasion. If you are applying for a job in a bookstore, dress the same way you would dress to work in the store, but slightly better. If you are applying for a job as an auto mechanic, you can wear casual clothes, but they should be clean and neat.

Looking your best shows self-respect. You may have one idea of how to look your best and the interviewer may have another. Avoid dressing in a way that may invite criticism. Body piercings, tattoos, extreme hairstyles, and very tight or skimpy clothing may prevent you from getting the job you want.

Show Confidence

How you act is an important factor in any interview. You can show your self-confidence right away by coming to the interview alone. If family or friends come with you, it may appear that you cannot handle responsibilities on your own.

Arrive at least five minutes early for your appointment. Tell the secretary or person in charge your name and the name of the person you are meeting. Then wait patiently to be welcomed into the interviewer's office.

5-14 Prepare yourself for a job interview by researching the company's background.

Putting Technology to Use
Have students role-play interviews with one student as the employer and one student as the applicant. Videotape the interviews so students can see areas in which they need to improve before interviewing for jobs.

Greet the interviewer with a firm handshake. When you are offered a seat, sit in a comfortable position, but do not slump. Use good posture and look alert. Never chew gum or smoke.

An interview is your chance to "sell" yourself. Speak positively about yourself and your experiences. Be prepared to discuss your work experiences, abilities, interests, and career goals. If you believe you can do the job and you want the chance to try, say so. See 5-15.

Have a Positive Attitude

Your attitude tells the interviewer as much about you as your words do. Try to express a positive, "can do" attitude. Act interested in what the interviewer is saying. Be enthusiastic about the job. You do not have to overdo these emotions. If you really want the job, you will be able to express your feelings naturally. Trying too hard will make you look insincere, pushy, or desperate.

You can answer some interview questions with a *yes* or *no* answer. Other questions will require more complete answers. Speak slowly and clearly, using good grammar. Be completely honest. It is never to your advantage to lie.

As the interview continues, you will have a chance to ask questions. You may want to ask about specific job duties, the hours you will work, and possibilities for advancement. If the job is offered and you are interested, you may then ask about pay, vacation time, and other benefits.

The interviewer should bring up the topic of pay. If the job is available at a specific pay rate, your decision should be easy to make. Either you will accept or reject the rate. By rejecting a fixed rate, you reject the job. However, if the pay level is flexible and the job appeals to you, you should say "salary is negotiable." This means you are willing to discuss pay after all the benefits and other features of the job are discussed.

Do not feel obliged during the interview to declare the specific pay you expect. You will want to consider all that you learned about company benefits and weigh them accordingly. If the interviewer presses you to declare a salary level, state a range that is not excessive. For example, you may say, "Somewhere between (state two amounts), but I am flexible." You will not want to make the mistake of quoting a pay so high that the interviewer eliminates you from consideration.

At the end of an interview, you should thank the interviewer for considering you for the job. Do not be disappointed if you are not offered the job right away. In most cases, other people will be interviewed, too. You may even be asked to come in for a second interview. If this is the case, expect your desired salary to be discussed. A final choice may not be made for several days or even longer.

Before you leave, be sure to ask the interviewer when a final decision will be made. The interviewer may promise to

5-15 Showing confidence during a job interview makes a good impression on the interviewer. Be prepared to tell the interviewer how your skills relate to the job.

Discuss:
How can you show confidence when you are at an interview? What might show that you lack self-confidence?

Activity:
Form a small group. Discuss the best way to answer questions typically asked at a job interview.

Discuss:
What are some additional questions you might want to ask during a job interview? What questions should you not ask?

Resource:
Interviewing with Intelligence, Activity D, SAG

Across the Curriculum
Business. Have the teacher discuss important tips to remember when interviewing.

Resource:
Interview Follow-Up Letter, Activity E, SAG

Discuss:
Do you agree or disagree with the following statement? "I didn't get the job. It was a waste of my time to go."

Reflect:
Which qualities do you possess that could help you succeed as an entrepreneur?

contact you on a certain date to let you know if you will be hired. You also can ask the interviewer if you may call him or her in a few days. In either case, sending a follow-up letter after the interview is a good idea.

Sending a Follow-Up Letter

Sending a follow-up letter after every interview is a matter of courtesy. It is a way to thank the interviewer as well as remind him or her of your interest in the job.

A *follow-up letter* is a brief letter written in business form. See 5-16. It thanks the interviewer for taking the time to talk with you about the job opening. More importantly, it reminds the interviewer of your interest in the job. If you remember an important point you wish you had mentioned during the interview, you may add that to the letter.

If the interviewer does not contact you as promised, follow up with a telephone call. When you make the call, be brief. Just say something like, "Good afternoon, Mr. Smith. This is Roberta Jones calling. I filled out an application and had an interview with you on (state the date). I am still interested in the position and wonder if you have made your decision." Whatever the interviewer's response, be as pleasant and positive in your manner as you were during the interview.

Do not be discouraged if you do not receive a job offer right away. Looking for a job takes time and patience. Learn from the experience. You may interview with several employers before you find the best job for you. In the meantime, keep looking for jobs and going to interviews. Follow up on each one. Eventually, you will get a job.

Creating Your Own Job

Another option to finding a job is creating your own job. Many people fulfill their career goals by creating their own jobs rather than working for other people. They are called entrepreneurs. **Entrepreneurs** start and manage their own businesses. They also assume all risks and responsibilities. For many people, entrepreneurship is a rewarding and satisfying experience.

Entrepreneurship: Pros and Cons

Being an entrepreneur has both advantages and disadvantages. One main advantage is that you are your own boss. You make your own decisions, rules, and business policies. You can be as creative as you want to be in trying out new ideas. You create your own work schedule. If you manage your business well, you have the potential to make as much money as you want.

Being an entrepreneur has some disadvantages as well. Managing a business is a big responsibility that takes hard work and dedication. Until the business develops a good reputation, entrepreneurs must work during many evenings and weekends without taking vacations. Often no profit is made in the first year. Most entrepreneurs live off their savings until their businesses start to make money. If you make a wrong

---

204 Quail Run Road
Oak Park, Tennessee 30241
June 3, 2004

Mr. C.L. Stone, Personnel Manager
Camp McGhee
106 S. Main Street
Oak Park, Tennessee 30241

Dear Mr. Stone:

Thank you so much for taking time to interview me yesterday.

I am excited about the possibility of working as a camp counselor during the summer. My interview made me more certain that this would be a good place for me.

I eagerly await your decision and look forward to hearing from you

Sincerely yours,

Terry C. Pinkham

Terry C. Pinkham

5-16 Sending a follow-up letter after a job interview is a courtesy the interviewer will appreciate.

FCCLA Activity
Encourage chapter members to go through the steps of applying for a job as they participate in the Job Interview STAR Event.

decision, you cannot blame anyone else. Financial problems and poor management decisions are two common reasons why small businesses fail.

Getting Started

If you think you have what it takes to succeed as an entrepreneur, you can start right now. Make a list of all your interests and skills. Your business should be something you enjoy doing. Next, survey your market. Make a list of all the people you know who might pay for the products you make or the services you deliver. Consider the start-up costs and how much work you can handle. Then check to make sure you have the equipment and space needed to get started. Decide how much you will charge for your product or service. Estimate the profits you expect after paying business expenses. Finally, find ways to promote your business. See 5-17.

There are a number of ways to use interests and skills to start a business. The following cases show how two people successfully created their own businesses.

Karen, a high school student, needed to earn some money to attend the annual meeting of the Family, Career, and Community Leaders of America. She did not have a job, except occasional babysitting. Since she knew how to decorate cakes and plan parties, she decided to start a temporary business. To publicize it, she prepared leaflets and placed them in the teachers' mailboxes at school. She listed party refreshments she could make. She also offered to make cookies, cakes, pies, and other baked goods.

Karen's business grew quickly. She baked and decorated many birthday cakes. She also catered several birthday parties and an anniversary reception. The end result was worth the effort. She earned enough money to attend the meeting. When she returned from the convention, her local newspaper wrote a feature story about her. This attracted more people to her business. As a result, she decided to continue catering on a part-time basis.

While in college earning a forestry degree, Rashon started an outdoor service business to support himself. He enjoyed being able to study and work at the same time. He also liked being financially independent. When he was too busy, he hired other college students to help him.

By the time he graduated, Rashon knew what career he wanted. His college education had given him a solid business background. He liked being his own boss and he was willing to work hard for long

Activity:
Complete the following sentence: "I (would/would not) like to be an entrepreneur because…" Write a one-page paper explaining your response.

Resource:
Where Do Entrepreneurs Get Their Ideas? Activity F, SAG

5-17 These enterprising teens decided to use their skills to become entrepreneurs. They find entrepreneurship a challenging and rewarding experience.

 Putting Technology to Use
Have students look online for Web sites of people who have started their own online businesses. What types of services are available? Do students think online businesses have a good chance of being successful? Why or why not?

Activity: Form a small group. Brainstorm a list of entrepreneurship ideas for teens. Share with the class.

Reflect: Based on your interests, aptitudes, and abilities, what job might you create for yourself?

hours. His wide variety of outdoor services included surveying land, building speed bumps in parking lots, and painting lines to mark parking spaces. He enjoyed the challenge of learning new tasks. Also, he was willing to approach people and offer his services. He decided to become a full-time entrepreneur.

Few people combine their interests, aptitudes, and abilities into a truly customized job. However, the above examples show it can be done. People who acquire the needed skills and work hard can achieve their goals.

Are you interested in creating your own job? Sometimes the hardest part is deciding what to do. You must study your interests, aptitudes, and abilities to make a good decision. The suggestions in 5-18 may spark your imagination. The examples listed in the chart show only a few of the many ways you can earn money on your own.

Once you decide what you want to do, you must also make sure there is a demand for your business. For instance, a children's party service would not be profitable in a neighborhood where there are no children. Another part of starting a business is setting appropriate fees. They should be high enough to cover expenses and deliver a profit. At the same time, they should be low enough to attract clients. In creating your own job, you must use the same good judgment needed in setting any other goal.

Be an Entrepreneur

Gift Shopping Service
Do not have time to shop for those special gifts? Local teen will do your shopping for you! Gift wrapping and mail service also available. Hourly fee charged. 555-1212

Vacation Service
Going out of town? Let me take care of those routine household tasks. I can collect mail, care for pets, water plants, and do yard work—all for one low fee. Call for more details. 655-9881

Letter Addressing Service
Talented teen with neat handwriting. Will address wedding invitations, party invitations, and holiday greeting cards. Call for a free sample of my work. 656-6200

Baking Service
If you do not have time to prepare the homemade baked goods you like to eat, call me. I will bake and deliver your favorite breads and desserts. 555-3754

Fruit Basket Service
A thoughtful way to welcome houseguests or show a friend you care! Personalized fresh fruit baskets arranged and delivered for you. Local delivery to hospitals, hotels, or your home. Call for more details. 555-1492

Lawn and Garden Care
One time or all-the-time yard care. Grass mowing, weeding, edging, planting, raking, or clean-up. Free estimates. 565-0321

Birthday Party Catering Service
Celebrate your child's birthday with no hassles! For one set fee, I arrange a party for up to 15 children. The fee covers your expenses, including the cost of the cake, punch, cups, napkins, favors, and entertainment. A variety of party themes available. 565-2387

5-18 Have you ever thought about becoming an entrepreneur? If so, one of these ideas might appeal to you.

Check It Out!

1. List five sources a job seeker might use for finding job openings.
2. Name three ways to apply for a job.
3. True or false. If a question on an application form does not apply to the applicant, the applicant should leave it blank.
4. List five points job applicants should keep in mind about their behavior during an interview.
5. Explain the purpose of writing a follow-up letter after an interview. What points should the letter include?
6. List two advantages and two disadvantages of becoming an entrepreneur.

Check It Out! (Answers)

1. (List five:) friends, parents, relatives, neighbors, school job placement program, school counselor, vocational teacher, want ads, the Internet, state employment agency, federal employment agency, private employment agency, direct contact with an employer
2. sending a letter of application and resume, applying by telephone, or filling out a job application in person
3. false
4. (Student response. See pages 146-148 in the text.)
5. A follow-up letter is sent as a courtesy to thank the interviewer for his or her time and to remind the interviewer of your interest in the job. It should also include any important points you may not have covered during the interview.
6. (List two for each.) Advantages: being your own boss, making your own business decisions, trying out new ideas, creating your own work schedule, earning a high income Disadvantages: being responsible for all decisions, working long hours, suffering financial problems or poor management, living off savings until a profit is made

Topic 5-3
Succeeding on the Job

Objectives
After studying this topic, you will be able to
- identify the qualities and skills needed for job success.
- discuss work schedules and compensation.
- describe the deductions taken from an employee's paycheck.
- distinguish between gross income and net income.

Topic Terms
work ethic
telecommuting
hourly wage
salary
fringe benefits
gross income
net income

Vocabulary: Do you know the difference between gross income and net income?

Discuss: What qualities would you look for in an employee if you were the boss?

What qualities are needed for job success? The same personal qualities that help you get a job can also help you keep it. Most employers look for certain qualities when they hire employees. They want employees who have skills to get the job done and work well with others. Most successful employees share many of these same qualities. As you read this topic, think about the personal qualities you have now. Developing these qualities will increase your chances of being a successful employee, too.

Qualities of Successful Employees

Several qualities are key factors in job success. Having a positive attitude, being dependable, being honest, and getting along well with others will contribute to your becoming a successful employee.

Positive Attitude

Your attitude plays a big role in your success on the job, 5-19. It shows how you think and feel about other people and situations. A positive attitude will help you learn your job duties, work with others, and get ahead in your career.

If you have a positive attitude, you always try to do the best job possible. You accept your fair share of the responsibility without complaining. You accept criticism

5-19 People who have positive attitudes are willing to tackle any job task.

Across the Curriculum

Math. Include math problems on hourly wages, gross income, net income, and taxes.

Reflect:
Think of someone you know who has a positive attitude. Would you like working with this person? Why?

Discuss:
Why does an employer want an employee who is dependable? honest?

Discuss:
Do you think most workers today have a strong work ethic? Has this changed any in recent decades? Is a work ethic as important today as it was in the past?

Discuss:
Some employees avoid asking questions of their supervisors. Is this good or bad?

as a means of improving your job performance. You are willing to try new tasks. If you enjoy your work, you are more likely to do a better job. This makes you a more valuable employee.

A positive attitude helps you get along with others, too. People enjoy working with someone who is friendly and cheerful most of the time. Being courteous and showing respect for others are positive qualities to have.

Dependability

If you are dependable, your employer can count on you to be reliable and responsible. You get your work done and do not expect others to do it for you. You have a good attendance record and start work on time every day.

Honesty

Another personal quality of a good employee is being honest. Employers want employees they can trust. That means telling the truth, keeping any promises you make, and dealing with people fairly.

Being honest also means putting forth your best effort on the job. You do the job you are assigned and do not waste time. Employers expect you to give an honest day's work for an honest day's pay.

Ethics

A **work ethic** is a standard of conduct for successful job performance. Your concepts of fairness, right and wrong, and good and bad affect your work ethic.

A strong work ethic will help you achieve personal satisfaction, 5-20. Successful employees work not only for the company but also for personal satisfaction. Chances are that your boss will not compliment you daily for your work. Consequently, you need to develop personal feelings of satisfaction from the work you do. You need to set high standards for your work and take pride in meeting them. In turn, personal satisfaction will make your work seem more important and more enjoyable.

5-20 Successful employees develop feelings of personal satisfaction from doing their work well.

Cooperation

An ability to work well with all people is important for job success. This means you can work with people of all ages, of both genders, and of different backgrounds. You show respect and courtesy to your boss, your coworkers, and customers.

Part of getting along with others is working as a team member. To show others you want to be cooperative, you accept your share of the work. You make an effort to contribute to the group's goal. Each group member should feel free to make worthwhile contributions. Combining the special traits and skills of each person allows the group to achieve the best results.

Good working relationships are based on respect for others' feelings. Follow directions carefully. Ask questions when you do not understand how to do a task. Do not expect your coworkers to do your work for you. On the other hand, never assume that you can get along without your coworkers. If you willingly cooperate with them, they will cooperate with you.

Across the Curriculum

Business. Discuss the importance of work ethics in the business world. How would companies be affected if none of their employees followed a standard of conduct?

Topic 5-3 Succeeding on the Job

Being friendly, respectful, and enthusiastic will help you become part of a team.

Job Readiness Skills

What skills are required of people who enter the workforce? What do they need to know to perform well on the job?

These questions were examined by the U. S. Department of Labor. The group that handled the study was the Secretary's Commission on Achieving Necessary Skills (SCANS), also called the SCANS commission. It identified five skills needed to become an effective employee in today's workplace. These skills, called SCANS competencies, include competence with

- resources
- interpersonal skills
- information
- technology
- systems

The SCANS commission also identified three foundation elements workers need before they can use the competencies well. These include basic skills, thinking skills, and important personal qualities. Considered together, they are known as *workplace know-how*. They are also called *job readiness skills*. See 5-21.

The skills people need for success in the workplace cannot be developed separately. Each builds upon and supports another. You can develop job readiness skills at school and through part-time jobs, but there are other ways. Extracurricular activities, community involvement, volunteer activities, and projects at home can help prepare a student's job readiness.

Good Appearance

Whether fair or not, others judge you by your appearance, either consciously or subconsciously. What you wear to work reflects how you feel about your work. Try to look your best every day because neatness shows respect for yourself and others.

Most employers enforce dress codes that list clothing styles and items inappropriate for the workplace. They know the importance of clothing to maintaining a businesslike atmosphere. Customers, too, expect business people to dress appropriately. They do not want to be served by workers who appear sloppy or dressed for some other occasion. Customers often take their business elsewhere if a company does not maintain businesslike surroundings.

Workplace Know-How

For effective, on-the-job performance, workers need the five competencies and three-part foundation of skills and personal qualities listed below.

SCANS Competencies

Workers with job readiness skills know how to use

- **resources**—They know how to allocate time, money, materials, space, and workers.
- **interpersonal skills**—They work well on teams, teach others, serve customers, lead, negotiate, and interact well with people from culturally diverse backgrounds.
- **information**—They know how to acquire and evaluate data, organize and maintain files, interpret and communicate, and use computers to process information.
- **systems**—They understand social, organizational, and technological systems. They can monitor and correct performance. They can design or improve systems.
- **technology**—They can select appropriate equipment and tools, apply technology to specific tasks, maintain equipment, and troubleshoot equipment problems.

The Foundation

Developing scans competencies requires

- **basic skills**—reading, writing, arithmetic, mathematics, speaking, and listening.
- **thinking skills**—the ability to learn, reason, think creatively, make decisions, and solve problems.
- **personal qualities**—individual responsibility, self-esteem, sociability, self-management, and integrity.

5-21 Employees are expected to have these skills and abilities.

Reflect:
When was the last time you worked as a team member to accomplish a project? Did cooperation among group members help the group achieve their goal? Did any group members not cooperate?

Discuss:
What types of skills do you think employers are looking for when they hire an employee? Do you have most of these skills? If not, how can you acquire them?

Putting Technology to Use

Have students investigate the SCANS Web site at  wdr.doleta.gov/scans.

Resource:
Qualities of Successful Employees, reproducible master, TR

Discuss:
How have you learned to operate new computerized equipment? Do you think this is more difficult for employees?

Becoming a Professional

When you display all the positive qualities discussed, you are on the road to becoming a professional. A professional is an employee who keeps a courteous, conscientious, and businesslike manner. When companies hire new employees, they look for people who fit this description. They want to maintain a good public image and seek employees who share their concern.

Becoming a professional is not a goal reserved for certain careers. Any employee can, no matter what his or her job is. A professional is easy to spot. See 5-22. It is the person who demonstrates the following qualities:

- smiles and greets everyone pleasantly
- remembers and uses correct names and titles
- treats everyone with respect
- keeps a calm disposition
- avoids talking negatively about coworkers and customers
- wears conservative clothing from head to toe
- chooses a becoming and conservative hairstyle
- avoids excessive use of perfume and cologne
- limits jewelry and makeup
- practices good hygiene
- uses proper etiquette

Professionals uphold the standards of the company and set positive goals for themselves. They avoid doing anything that disrupts the work environment. They focus on doing their jobs well and helping the company succeed.

Technology in the Workplace

Advances in technology have changed many aspects of our lives. Computer technology is used in every industry to make time-consuming and demanding tasks quicker and easier. As technology continues to change our world, people must adjust to new roles and responsibilities.

All jobs are affected by innovative technology. In factories, computerized robots perform the most dangerous and monotonous jobs efficiently. Sales teams receive records of purchases as soon as they are made anywhere in the company and can readily determine future inventory needs. In offices, people can use e-mail, facsimile (FAX) machines, and video conferencing to stay in touch with coworkers and clients. See 5-23. People can also use these devices to work out of their homes. This is called **telecommuting.**

With every technological device comes a need for specialists who can operate and service it. In some businesses, new job positions are created to fulfill these needs. In other cases, job roles are expanded to include new duties. Job expansion also creates a need for more education. People must have the knowledge and training necessary to operate new equipment.

5-22 A well-groomed appearance and a pleasant smile are two clues that this person is a professional.

Putting Technology to Use
Have students choose one computerized tool, such as a FAX machine, e-mail, or scanner, and write instructions for operating it. Have students write the instructions as though they are for someone unfamiliar with any computer tools or terms. (Students will probably need to operate the tool themselves while breaking steps down into detailed instructions.)

Topic 5-3   Succeeding on the Job

5-23 Desktop video conferencing allows people to work together even though separated by long distances.

Repetitive body motions can cause this work hazard over extended periods. Also, telecommuters who have limited opportunities for personal interaction sometimes feel isolation and loneliness.

Technology impacts every aspect of the workplace. It promotes greater speed, efficiency, and accuracy in the workplace. However, competence with technology is just one of five skills that effective workers are expected to have. Employees with workplace know-how also need competence with resources, interpersonal skills, information, and systems.

Work Schedules and Income

You have just read about what your employer expects from you on the job. In return for your services, you will receive compensation (a paycheck). Your work schedule and pay will depend on the type of job you have and number of hours you work.

Part-Time and Full-Time Jobs

There are some basic differences between part-time and full-time jobs. Part-time work involves less than 40 hours per week. Many part-time jobs, however, offer less than 20 hours of work per week. Part-time employment offers a flexible work schedule and shorter work hours. Some people need this type of work schedule to meet their lifestyle needs and wants. Students often work part-time during evenings or weekends while going to school. However, part-time work usually offers lower wages and fewer benefits. For some, the hours may be inconvenient. In some families, for instance, one spouse may have to work on weekends, which may interfere with family activities.

At some point in their careers, many people change from part-time to full-time work. People who work 40 or more hours per week are considered *full-time employees*. Full-time employment offers less flexible work schedules and longer working hours. However, it also offers more income and benefits.

There is great demand for people who excel in the use of today's technologies. Competition among employers for these skills increases the salary employees can command. The salary for a position will also increase as the education and duty requirements for the position increase.

Instead of being apprehensive about learning how to use new tools in their jobs, employees are advised to expect and welcome change. The latest innovations in technology soon become obsolete. Workers must stay flexible enough to adopt new procedures and work methods. As devices are developed to perform tasks more accurately, some jobs are eliminated. Thus, people can no longer prepare for one career or know what new technologies will affect their jobs in the future. Lifetime learning is essential for those who plan to hold wage-earning jobs during all of their productive years.

Occasionally technological changes bring some negative results. Physical ailments such as carpal tunnel syndrome increase with the growth of technology.

Discuss:
Is it fair to expect older employees to learn how to use new technology? Why or why not?

Activity:
List the advantages and disadvantages of part-time versus full-time work.

Family Enrichment Activities
Have students interview their parents about their work responsibilities. Ask students to share information about their parents' work schedules and tasks in class. Have them keep this information in mind as they develop a list of ways they can assist parents at home. Encourage students to try some of the suggestions listed in an effort to lighten parents' dual-role responsibilities.

Discuss:
Do you think it's better to be paid an hourly wage or a salary?

Note:
If you work for an employer who pays you in cash, you still must pay taxes to the government and file a tax return.

Resource:
Paycheck Deductions, transparency master, TR

Resource:
Your Paycheck Stub, Activity G, SAG

Earning an Income

Employees who are paid a set amount of money for each hour they work earn an **hourly wage.** Many part-time and full-time employees earn an hourly wage, 5-24. If they work more than 40 hours per week, they are usually paid overtime. *Overtime pay* is usually one and one-half times the employee's hourly wage. For instance, an employee who earns $6.50 per hour would receive $9.75 per hour of overtime pay.

In certain types of jobs, employees earn a salary. A **salary** is a set amount of money paid for a certain period of time. For instance, teachers sign a contract to do a specific job for a certain salary amount. To fulfill their contract, they spend time in and out of the classroom. Some full-time employees earn an annual salary, with the amount divided into equal payments during the period. If salaried employees in professional positions work more than 40 hours a week, however, they do not receive overtime pay.

Many full-time workers receive financial extras called **fringe benefits.** These benefits are provided by the employer in addition to the worker's regular paycheck. What types of fringe benefits can you expect when you work full-time? This depends on the company where you work. However, many companies offer the following benefits: health and life insurance, paid vacation time, paid sick days, savings plans, and retirement plans.

5-24 Many teens who work part-time earn an hourly wage.

Understanding Your Paycheck

One of the benefits of part-time or full-time employment is earning an income. When you receive your first paycheck, you may be surprised. The amount you were promised when you were hired will be different from the amount you receive in your paycheck. Why do you not get to keep all the money you earned? A part of your earnings are deducted from each paycheck by your employer for taxes and other benefits. An important part of understanding your paycheck is knowing what comes out of your paycheck and where it goes.

Paychecks and Paycheck Deductions

The paycheck stub attached to your paycheck provides important information about your earnings and deductions. The total amount of money you earn *before* deductions is your **gross income.** The actual amount of your paycheck *after* deductions is your **net income,** sometimes called your *take-home pay.* Though payroll deductions vary for individuals, about two-thirds of a person's wages remain after deductions are made. The paycheck stub in 5-25 shows an example of earnings and common deductions.

Taxes and Other Deductions

Your paycheck stub lists the various deductions your employer subtracts from your gross pay. The following list includes some of the most common paycheck deductions:

- federal and state income taxes
- Social Security taxes
- health and life insurance
- savings and retirement plans
- union dues
- charitable contributions

Income Taxes

Your employer deducts federal and state income taxes from your paycheck. This tax money is the government's main source of income. The government uses the tax money to provide services, programs,

Problem-Solving Practice
Occupation Obstacles, reproducible master, TR. Students are to use the decision-making process to solve a problem presented in a case study.

Topic 5-3   Succeeding on the Job

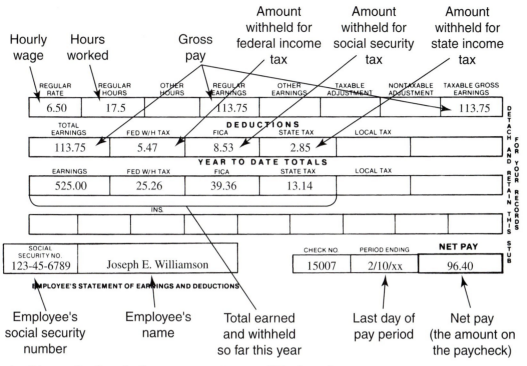

5-25 As this paycheck stub shows, your net pay will be less than your gross pay.

Note:
The federal income tax is a progressive tax, taking a larger percentage of high incomes than low incomes. The range may be from 15% for the lowest income levels to 39.6% for the highest income levels. The government changes this rate from time to time.

Enrich:
Go to the library and research the history of social security. Prepare a report for the class.

and facilities to all citizens. The amount of tax taken out of your paycheck is based on how much you earn. The more you earn, the higher the rate of taxes you will have to pay.

Social Security Taxes

Another deduction is made for Social Security taxes. This amount may be listed under the letters FICA (Federal Insurance Contributions Act) on your paycheck stub. The federal government administers the Social Security program. It provides retirement, disability, and survivor benefits to eligible working citizens. As with federal income tax, your contribution is a percentage of your earnings. Whatever you pay, your employer pays a matching amount for you.

Other Deductions

The taxes already described are mandatory—you must pay them. Other deductions from your paycheck are made with your permission. Health insurance and life insurance may be available to you through your employer. Premiums may be deducted from your paycheck, or your employer may pay the insurance premiums at no cost to you.

Many other possible payroll deductions exist. Deductions may be made for benefits such as a retirement plan or a credit union savings plan. If you join a union, your employer will deduct your union dues. Any contributions you make toward raising funds for a company-endorsed charity may also be deducted by your employer.

Check It Out!
1. List three qualities needed for job success. State some examples of each quality.
2. Name two advantages of each: a part-time and a full-time work schedule.
3. Name two forms of income that an employee may earn.
4. Give three examples of fringe benefits.
5. Explain the difference between gross income and net income.

2. Advantages of part-time work include a flexible schedule and shorter work hours. Advantages of full-time work include higher income and better benefits. (Students may justify other responses.)
3. hourly wage and salary
4. (List three:) health insurance, life insurance, paid vacation time, paid sick days, savings plans, retirement plans
5. Gross income is the total amount of money an employee earns before deductions. Net income is the amount of money left after all deductions from the gross amount.

Check It Out! (Answers)
1. (List three:) positive attitude, dependability, honesty, work ethic, cooperation, workplace know-how or job readiness skills, good appearance (Examples are student response.)

TEENS ARE CONCERNED ABOUT...

Finding Jobs

Discuss:
- How many of you are developing computer skills? What jobs can you think of that currently require the use of computers? What jobs are likely to require computers in the future that do not do so today?
- Think of a job for which teens might apply. How should a young person dress for an interview for this job?
- How difficult do you think it is for teens to conform to employers' standards?
- How important is it to get to work on time? Do you know anyone who has lost a job for failing to meet this basic job requirement?
- How many service jobs can you name? Do any of these interest you? How important is it for a young person to look at career fields with good growth potential?

Debbie Davis Snyder and Sonja D. Robinson have developed a model program for teens under the Job Training Partnership Act (J.T.P.A.). The goal of their program is to give students a vision of what they can do with their lives through step-by-step guidance.

As J.T.P.A. counselors, both take special pride in helping students recognize their full potential. Their roles are to identify students who have one or more barriers to employment. To qualify for the program, students must be 14-21 years-old and at risk for dropping out of school. The counselors' main goals are to help these students find and keep jobs and stay in school. Snyder and Robinson also work with employers, families, the community, and various agencies to ensure each student's success.

Experienced professionals with advanced degrees in counseling, they have 25 years of experience in counseling teens. In addition to receiving professional recognition for their program, they have conducted numerous school workshops to share their programs' successes.

Q: *What job skills should teens be acquiring?*

A: Teens can acquire a variety of job skills while they are in high school. The skills they learn now will help them get jobs and keep jobs. Here are some of the most important skills teens need to develop.

- Be patient and willing to take time to learn job skills. Some students are so eager to work, they do not take time to prepare for the working world.
- Learn computer skills. Many of today's and tomorrow's jobs will require using a computer. For instance, accountants must be able to use spreadsheet programs. Research is mainly done through the Internet.
- Practice interview skills and know how to dress for an interview. Some styles are great for school, but may not be appropriate for going to an interview.
- Learn business-world skills. It's fine for a teen to be an individual and display his or her own identity. However, in the workplace, a teen will need to conform to the employer's standards.
- Practice work-retention skills. Getting a job is a small percentage of the task. Keeping it requires more effort. Develop and demonstrate a positive attitude toward work, the employer, and other employees. Practice being dependable. Other employees need to know they can count on teen workers. Be punctual as well. Teens need to get to work on time and have their work done on time. They need to be an energetic part of the team.

Q: *What career fields will provide the greatest opportunities for teens in the near future?*

A: Service careers will be the most employable careers of the future. Services may range from health care such as physical therapy to cleaning or automotive repair. As the population continues to grow, more human services will be needed. As a result, more workers will be needed to provide these services.

Q: *What tips would you offer a teen to help him or her find a first job?*

A: Finding a job is hard work. It takes patience, persistence, and some advance preparation. The reward is you will

Feature-Related Activity

If students are not familiar with your state laws, you may want to ask them to investigate the state and federal laws that apply to them and share their findings with the class.

find the job that's right for you. The following tips may be helpful to any teen looking for that first job:

- Plan to spend as much time looking for a job as you will spend working once you get the job. For example, if you hope to work twenty hours each week, be prepared to spend twenty hours finding that job. Do not get discouraged if you do not get job offers immediately.
- Have realistic expectations when looking for a job. Chances are you will have to start with entry-level positions. Do not expect to start as a secretary. You will have to work your way up to that job.
- Go alone when applying for a job. When several students appear together, employers assume they have difficulty functioning independently. Also, the employer usually has only one job to offer.
- It never hurts to overdress a little for an interview. This shows employers that you respect their position and care enough to look your best.
- Watch your appearance, especially your hair. Wear it in a neat, manageable style. Trendy hairstyles may be a deterrent to finding a job. Many employers—especially those in food service—will have specific requirements for hair management. Also, every workplace has its image. You must be willing to adapt to the image and standards of your workplace. It is not the responsibility of the employer to adapt to your standards.
- Be persistent. Keep in contact with prospective employers so they will remember you, your name, and your face. Many employers think those who try hard to get a job will work hard once employed. Personal contacts with employers are usually more effective than telephone contacts.
- Know and practice good manners. For example, after an initial contact or an interview with an employer, ask, "May I drop by to see you periodically about this job?"
- Watch your mannerisms. During an interview, do not pick your fingers nervously, chew gum, or drink soda. These habits are distracting.
- Know the child labor laws in your state and be prepared to follow them. Certain limits are set on teens' working hours as well as the types of jobs they can perform. A work permit is required for 14- and 15-year-olds. Teens from ages 16 to 18 also may have limitations on working hours. By law, teens under age 18 can't operate hazardous equipment (machinery with movable parts). To protect your rights, do not apply for jobs for which you do not qualify.
- If you do not find just the job you want, be willing to take another job offer. This will help you get experience and a good recommendation. You will be able to change jobs later.
- Before you accept a job offer, make sure you have transportation to and from the job.
- Learn from your job hunting experiences. Know that you will learn something new each time you apply for a job. Always ask yourself, "What should I do differently next time?" "How can I improve my approach?"
- Seek as many job opportunities as possible. Go for two or three jobs with hopes that you will receive one offer. If you look at only one opportunity at a time, you may take a long time to find a job.

Q: *What additional advice would you offer teens to encourage their success in the working world?*

A: If you are willing to prepare yourself, you will find doors are always open to you. There will always be a way to get where you want to go.

You can succeed in the working world if you are willing to work to achieve it. You must be willing to search out and use the resources that are available to you. If you need further education to improve your skills, use the resources available in high school. Once you reach that first job goal, you will have other goals in mind to keep you moving. Find out about the resources available to you after high school, also.

Know where you want to go and be willing to take one step at a time. This is how successful people operate. No one starts out to be president of the company. People grow into those positions. Know also that failure is an inherent part of success. Do not let failure deter you for long. Remember that Alexander Graham Bell was not trying to invent the telephone. The telephone grew out of one of his failures.

Discuss:
- If you now work, how long did it take you to land this job? Do you agree that people should plan to spend as much time looking for a job as they will spend working once they get the job?
- Do you know anyone who went with a friend to apply for a job? Did the person get the job? Do you agree or disagree with this advice?

> **Note:**
> For *Try It Out!* #1, bring to class a variety of career information resources for students to use in preparing their career profiles, or arrange for the class to meet in the school library.

Chapter Review

Summary

Learning more about yourself—your interests, aptitudes, and abilities—is the first step in matching yourself to the right career. Many resources are available for gathering career information. As you get closer to making a career decision, you may want to explore careers in family and consumer sciences. In setting your career goals, consider the training you will need. Making a career decision now will help you get started in reaching your goals.

Use resources such as people, agencies, and want ads to find job openings. Applying for job openings may involve sending a resume, calling the employer, or applying in person. A job interview is your chance to make a favorable impression on the interviewer. After the interview, sending a follow-up letter is important. Another option in job hunting is to create your own job by becoming an entrepreneur.

Once you have a job, you will want to be successful at it. A positive attitude, dependability, honesty, and an ability to work with others will help ensure your success. Your work schedule and income will vary depending on whether you work part-time or full-time. In return for your hard work, you receive a paycheck. Understanding what comes out of your paycheck is also important for job success.

Think About It!

1. Why is evaluating your current interests, aptitudes, and abilities an important part of career planning?
2. How could family and consumer science skills be used in your career?
3. Briefly summarize the factors you think will affect your career choices.
4. What are the advantages of using the decision-making process to make a career decision?
5. What preparation(s) for finding a job do you think will be most important for you? Why?
6. What recommendations would you make to a friend who is thinking of starting a business?
7. If you were an employer, what three qualities would you most want in an employee? Explain your answer.

Try It Out!

1. Choose a career that interests you and write a career profile. Include the following information in your profile: nature of the work, places of employment, training and qualifications needed, advancement opportunities, typical salaries, and social and psychological factors related to this career choice.
2. Make a list of five careers that interest you. Then show how you would use the decision-making process to reach a career decision.
3. Collect several different job application forms. Complete one of them.

4. Role-play several different job interviews. As a class, evaluate each interview situation.
5. Write a follow-up letter to the interviewer in one of the role-play interviews described in the previous activity.
6. Brainstorm a list of possible jobs you could have as a teen entrepreneur.
7. Create a bulletin board showing how paycheck deductions are used to fund government programs and facilities.

Enrich:
Have each student choose one of his or her ideas from *Try It Out!* #6 and develop a plan to start an entrepreneurship.

Resource:
PowerZone Challenge CD. Have students play the chapter review game to reinforce text content.

LEADING GUIDE TO THE WORLD OF WORK
CAREER TIMES
VOLUME 1, NUMBER 1

Career Information—The Key to Unlocking a Successful Job Search

Job opportunities may come knocking at the doors of some individuals. However, most people must go out and seek jobs for which they are suited. Many potential employees have found the key to a successful job search is gathering needed information.

Employment Opportunities

One of the first pieces of information any would-be worker needs is an overview of employment opportunities in a given career field. Job searchers need to find out what workers do in the field. People who are looking for jobs also need to know who might hire them.

A good place to go for this information is the *Occupational Outlook Handbook*. This resource is on the shelves of most public libraries. For those who are connected to the Internet, there is also an online version. This handbook provides information about many occupations. Readers can find out about education and training requirements, chances for advancement, and earnings potential for the careers of their choice.

Entrepreneurial Opportunities

Many workers want to find out about entrepreneurial, or self-employment, opportunities that are open to them. These people may seek the challenge of owning and operating a business and making it a success. Perhaps they simply desire the freedom of setting their own hours.

Opportunities exist for entrepreneurs in nearly every career field. Those who want to be self-employed need to study their market. They must identify a need for a product or service. Then they must find a way to meet that need.

Starting a business can be costly. Before assuming the financial risks of entrepreneurship, it is worthwhile to gain experience working for someone else.

Rewards and Demands of Careers

Every job has rewards. Likewise, every job places demands on workers. When searching for a job, it is valuable to investigate these advantages and challenges. Weighing the benefits against the burdens can help a worker decide whether a position will meet his or her goals.

Preparation Requirements

People who will be entering the world of work need to know how to prepare for their chosen careers. Each field offers positions at three basic levels. Entry-level jobs require the least amount of training. Many jobs at this level require no more than a high school diploma. Mid-level jobs usually take a two-year degree or some other specialized training. Community colleges offer programs to prepare workers for mid-level jobs. Professional-level jobs usually call for a four-year degree. Some positions at this level are open only to those who have advanced degrees. Colleges and universities can train people for careers at this level.

Young workers need to gather information about the world of work to make choices about their future careers.

Jobs at the three levels form a career ladder. Workers often begin at the bottom of the ladder in positions that require little training. As they gain experience, workers move up the ladder to jobs that involve more responsibilities and offer higher wages.

Personal Qualities Needed for Success

Certain qualities are needed for success in any job. For instance, all workers profit from basic skills such as reading, writing, and math. Being able to communicate and get along with people are other skills needed by every member of the workforce. However, each career field also requires employees to have some specific personal traits. For instance, workers in the child care field will not get far without patience. Those wishing to work in the area of fashion design must have creativity. Talking with employers and employees in a given career is a good way to find out what personal qualities are desirable.

Some people with disabilities may be concerned about finding job openings suited to their special needs. State offices of vocational rehabilitation or departments of labor offer services to help meet unique work-related needs. School counselors should be able to help students with disabilities make contact with these state-supported services.

Future Trends

The world is changing, and the workplace is changing, too. Young workers especially need to be aware of forces that might affect their jobs in the future. They need to seek answers to two key questions: Will advances in technology create new opportunities for me in the future? Will changes in technology make my job unnecessary in the future? Answers to these questions should be factored into the career choices people make.

Career Interests and Abilities

Many people, especially teens, wonder how to decide if they really want to go into a given career area. One way they can find out is to assess their interests and abilities. Enrolling in related courses in high school will help teens see how much interest they have in a certain field. Shadowing someone who works in the field can provide a lot of insight to the daily tasks involved in a specific job. Part-time or volunteer work in a related program can also help people find out about the work environment.

A good education forms a solid foundation for any career field a person might choose.

Part Two
Today's Families

Chapter 6
Understanding Families

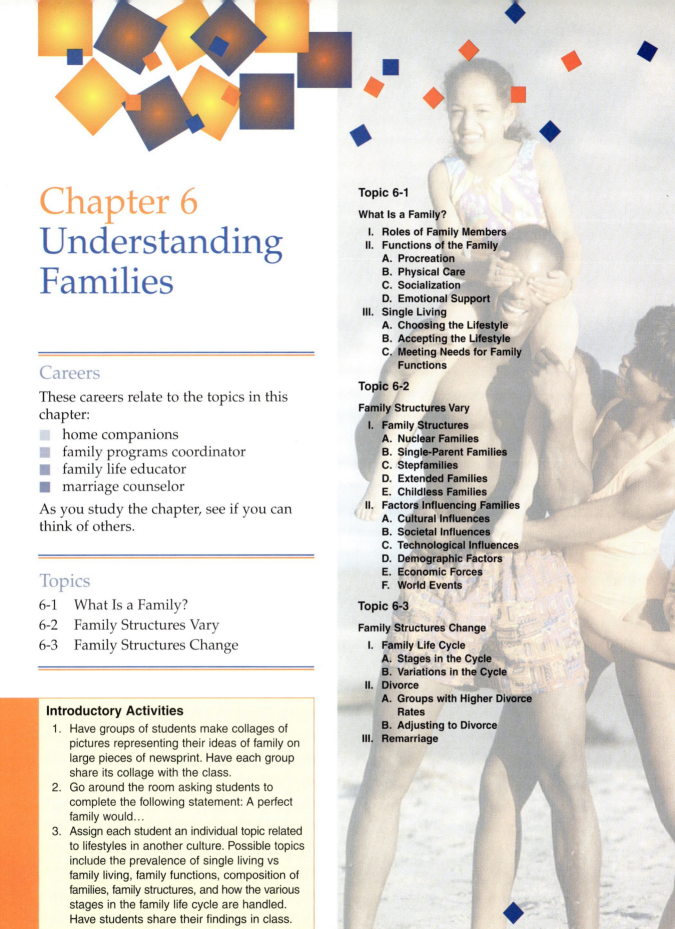

Careers

These careers relate to the topics in this chapter:
- home companions
- family programs coordinator
- family life educator
- marriage counselor

As you study the chapter, see if you can think of others.

Topics

6-1 What Is a Family?
6-2 Family Structures Vary
6-3 Family Structures Change

Introductory Activities

1. Have groups of students make collages of pictures representing their ideas of family on large pieces of newsprint. Have each group share its collage with the class.
2. Go around the room asking students to complete the following statement: A perfect family would…
3. Assign each student an individual topic related to lifestyles in another culture. Possible topics include the prevalence of single living vs family living, family functions, composition of families, family structures, and how the various stages in the family life cycle are handled. Have students share their findings in class.

Topic 6-1

What Is a Family?
I. Roles of Family Members
II. Functions of the Family
   A. Procreation
   B. Physical Care
   C. Socialization
   D. Emotional Support
III. Single Living
   A. Choosing the Lifestyle
   B. Accepting the Lifestyle
   C. Meeting Needs for Family Functions

Topic 6-2

Family Structures Vary
I. Family Structures
   A. Nuclear Families
   B. Single-Parent Families
   C. Stepfamilies
   D. Extended Families
   E. Childless Families
II. Factors Influencing Families
   A. Cultural Influences
   B. Societal Influences
   C. Technological Influences
   D. Demographic Factors
   E. Economic Forces
   F. World Events

Topic 6-3

Family Structures Change
I. Family Life Cycle
   A. Stages in the Cycle
   B. Variations in the Cycle
II. Divorce
   A. Groups with Higher Divorce Rates
   B. Adjusting to Divorce
III. Remarriage

Vocabulary:
Define the term *family* in your own words.

Reflect:
What skills have you learned from your family that will help you throughout your adult life?

Resource:
Family Roles, Activity A, SAG

Activity:
Write a short paper describing your role as a family member.

Resource:
Thinking About Family Roles, reproducible master, TR

Topic 6-1
What Is a Family?

Objectives
After studying this topic, you will be able to
- describe roles of family members.
- name functions the family unit performs for individuals and society.
- analyze how people with a single lifestyle meet their needs for the functions provided by families.

Topic Terms
family
procreation
socialization

The family unit forms the foundation of society. Most people are raised in family settings. In these settings, they learn skills and share experiences that will shape the rest of their lives. See 6-1.

The term **family** can be defined in a number of ways. One common definition is: two or more people related by blood, marriage, or adoption. This definition emphasizes the structure of the family unit.

Other definitions emphasize the roles, responsibilities, rights, and relationships of family members. For example, a family can be described as two or more persons committed to one another over time who share resources, responsibility for decisions, personal priorities, and goals.

What makes the family such an important unit? To answer this question, you must take a closer look at the roles family members fulfill. You must also consider the functions families provide for individuals and society.

Roles of Family Members

Each member of a family has special roles to play. Such roles include parent, child, spouse, sibling, and income provider. The behaviors expected of people in these roles vary from family to family.

Many of your family roles were inherited when you were born. At birth, your sex determined your role as son or daughter, brother or sister, and niece or nephew.

Some of your family roles are assigned to you. You are expected to fulfill certain responsibilities as a result of assigned roles. For instance, if you are an older sibling, you may have to fill the role of caregiver to younger siblings. You might have the responsibility of watching them from time to time.

Some roles are chosen. If you have talent in the kitchen, you might choose the role of family cook. If you enjoy being outdoors, you may take on the responsibility of caring for the lawn.

Functions of the Family

Through their various roles and responsibilities, family members form an interactive unit. This unit provides for the physical, mental, emotional, social, and spiritual well-being of its members. It also provides a number of functions for society. Culture, society, and technology are strong influences on the family. Besides these, demographic factors, economic forces, and world events can also affect the family.

6-1 Skills children learn in a family setting are often used throughout their adult lives.

Family Enrichment Activity
Encourage students to plan a sharing time with their family members. Each member is invited to bring photos or objects that remind him or her of a favorite family memory. Family members should pass around the items they bring to the sharing time as they relate their memories.

Procreation

One of the basic functions of the family is **procreation,** or the bearing of children. Most people are born into a family environment. Parents have children to express their love for each other. They desire the experience of raising children and watching them grow into unique adults. They want their children to carry on the heritage and traditions of their family line. See 6-2.

The function of procreation assures the continuation of society. As children are born into families, the population is maintained. As the children become adults, they join the workforce to produce goods and services. They spend dollars to stimulate the economy. They have children of their own who will follow the same cycle.

Physical Care

When parents supply their children with food, clothing, and shelter, they are providing the function of physical care. This function also includes providing medical care and creating a safe and healthy environment.

Society helps families with the function of physical care. If parents cannot afford food, shelter, or medical care, public assistance and charitable programs try to meet those needs. If families face unsafe situations, police and fire departments can assist them.

Society is not set up to provide complete physical care for all people. Therefore, families serve a vital function by satisfying some of these needs themselves.

Socialization

Another important function of families is the **socialization** of children. This means teaching children to conform to social standards. As parents socialize their children, they act as authority figures in the home. In this role, they establish reasonable rules of conduct. Parents set limits that protect their children and teach them appropriate behavior.

Teaching children about their heritage is part of socialization. Children need to learn about their cultural background. Parents can share family traditions with children and help the children develop pride in their ancestral roots.

Education is also part of the socialization process. Parents provide infants and young children with general guidance and moral education. They act as role models to provide career and vocational training. Parents are also responsible for enrolling their children in formal education programs. As children get older, therefore, schools and other agencies assume part of the responsibility for socialization.

Emotional Support

Perhaps the most critical function of families in today's society is the emotional support of family members. No other social unit can replace the family for providing children with love and nurturing. Parents form a bond with their infant children. As children grow, parents are there to comfort children when they are sad. They can reassure children when they have doubts. They can forgive children when they make mistakes. See 6-3.

6-2 Parents choose to have children to fulfill their desire to share their love and help shape the life of another human being.

> **Discuss:**
> Do you agree that procreation is one of the basic functions of the family? Why or why not?
>
> **Discuss:**
> Do you consider withholding physical care of a child by a parent child abuse? Who would you go to if you knew a child was being denied basic physical care by his or her parents? What would you do?
>
> **Enrich:**
> Make a poster of socialization skills you feel parents should teach their children.

FCCLA Activity

Encourage students who are working on the Family Ties unit of the Power of One program to set goals for increasing their role in providing some of the functions of the family for family members. After carrying out a plan of action to achieve those goals, ask students to write a two-page report explaining how this project has made a difference in their own lives.

Discuss:
How important is the function of emotional support in single-parent families?

Resource:
Teenagers and Family Functions, reproducible master, TR

Enrich:
Survey adults who live a single lifestyle. What do they like about being single? What do they dislike about being single?

6-3 Helping children feel secure in a new setting is one way parents provide emotional support.

Children are not the only family members who require support. Parents rely on their children to let them know they are loved and appreciated. Parents also count on support from each other. Parents need to make their marriage a priority. Partner-centered marriages provide stability in the home and create a secure atmosphere for all. Children as well as parents benefit from a family that is led by a strong partnership.

Single Living

Not all people live in families. Many adults are single. They may live alone or with roommates. These adults must find other resources to meet their needs for functions provided by the family.

Choosing the Lifestyle

People choose a single lifestyle for different reasons. Some single people want time to explore their own interests. Some people want to travel before they settle down. Some people want a single lifestyle while they finish their education or establish careers.

Some see a single lifestyle as a temporary one. Others want to remain single permanently. They may choose this lifestyle because they value their privacy and enjoy being alone. These people like to relax in peace and quiet. They prefer the personal freedom offered by a single lifestyle. They would rather be alone with their thoughts than feel obligated to interact with another person.

People who are committed to their careers or to civic, social, or religious activities may also choose a single lifestyle. Such people devote all of their attention, time, and energy to their special interests. They do not have enough time for the types of relationships involved in marriage or parenting.

Putting Technology to Use
Have students use the Internet to research statistics on single adults. What percentage of the population stays single today as compared to 50 years ago? a hundred years ago? Why do students think this is the case?

Accepting the Lifestyle

A single lifestyle is not always chosen. Widowed people are forced to accept a single lifestyle when their mates die. Likewise, people must make a transition to a single lifestyle when a divorce occurs.

Some people who would like to be married must accept a single lifestyle. Some of these people never find the right person to be a marriage partner. Some had a painful relationship in the past and are afraid to develop a new relationship. Some become involved in caring for aging parents and do not have time to meet potential partners. Others travel so much with their careers that they are never in one place long enough to develop a relationship, 6-4.

Meeting Needs for Family Functions

Regardless of the reasons for their lifestyle, single people need the functions provided by families. They must find other means of meeting these needs.

Adult single people must work to earn a living and provide for their own physical care. They pay for their own housing. They buy their own food and clothing. They rely on physicians when they get sick. They turn to public agencies, such as police and fire departments, for help with their needs for safety.

Many single people have a strong network of friends. These friends serve as a source of emotional support. They provide love and encouragement when family members are not available.

Some single people live with roommates. Roommates help share the expenses of food, housing, and other physical needs. They provide one another with a sense of security. They also help meet emotional needs by providing companionship.

Although people in a single lifestyle do not live with family members, they often maintain close relationships with them. Visits, letters, e-mail, and phone calls provide the family contact many single people require.

Check It Out!
1. What are the three ways family members get their various roles?
2. What are the four main functions of the family?
3. List four reasons people choose a single lifestyle.

Check It Out! (Answers)
1. Family roles are inherited, assigned, or chosen.
2. procreation, physical care, socialization, emotional support
3. (List four:) to explore personal interests, to travel, to finish an education, to establish a career, to enjoy personal freedom, to devote time and energy to a special interest

---

Discuss:
How can single people meet their needs for family functions provided by families?

Resource:
Which Lifestyle Is for Me? reproducible master, TR

6-4 Some people who are highly involved with their careers do not have time to establish relationships with potential marriage partners.

Vocabulary:
What do you think is meant by the term *family structure*?

Activity:
Write a one-page paper describing a typical family.

Reflect:
List ten families you know. How many of these are nuclear families?

Topic 6-2
Family Structures Vary

Objectives
After studying this topic, you will be able to
- describe characteristics of various family structures.
- name six factors that can influence family responsibilities.

Topic Terms
family structure
nuclear family
single-parent family
stepfamily
extended family
childless family
media
demographics

How would you describe a typical American family? Your answer to this question is likely to differ from the answers given by your classmates. This is because there is no "typical" American family. Some families have two parents and some families have one parent. Some families have stepparents and stepchildren. Some families have grandparents, aunts, uncles, and cousins. Some families have children and some families do not.

Family Structures

Family structure refers to the makeup of a family group. It is based on the relationships of the members in the family. Each of the five basic structures is able to provide the main family functions for its members.

Nuclear Families

A **nuclear family** is a family group that consists of a man and woman and their children, 6-5. This structure gives children the comfort and security of family ties with both parents. It gives them a solid base for the development of human relationships. The nuclear family also gives children a view of adult roles modeled by their parents.

In nuclear families, husbands and wives usually seek their chief companionship and emotional support from each other. Children receive attention, love, encouragement, and guidance from their parents. Close family interaction in this structure can promote a feeling of togetherness. It can help family members build strong, healthy relationships.

6-5 The nuclear family structure can provide an excellent environment for rearing children.

Citizenship and Service
Arrange for students to volunteer time to a family service organization in your community. Possible organizations might include Big Brothers, Big Sisters, Habitat for Humanity, homeless shelters, and food banks.

Topic 6-2 Family Structures Vary

Single-Parent Families

In the **single-parent family** structure, one adult lives with one or more children. The adult may be widowed, separated, divorced, or never married. The single parent must provide the functions of a family without the aid of a spouse.

The lack of adult role models is a concern in many single-parent families. Children learn gender-appropriate behavior from adults. A little boy living with his single mother misses opportunities to learn male role behavior from his father. Likewise, a little girl living with her single father misses opportunities to learn female role behavior from her mother.

Organizations designed to help fill the vacant adult roles in single-parent families exist in many communities. Big Brothers and Big Sisters are organizations with this purpose. The Big Brothers organization matches adult men with young boys who lack male influence in their homes. The Big Sisters organization operates in the same way to match adult women with young girls. The adults help to provide friendship and guidance to young people.

The parents in single-parent families often miss the companionship of other adults. They can find support and understanding in organizations like Parents Without Partners (PWP). Local chapters of this international organization sponsor many social and educational activities. These events help group members adjust to their roles as single parents. Some activities include children to allow them to interact with adults of the sex opposite that of their own parents.

Cooperation is the key to success in single-parent families. Each member should be aware of the needs and concerns of other members. When one family member has a problem, another member may be able to understand and offer help. See 6-6.

Stepfamilies

When a single parent marries, a **stepfamily** is formed. The husband, the wife, or both spouses have children from other marriages. Thus, the stepfamily structure includes the roles of stepparents and stepchildren.

6-6 A single-parent family structure can encourage a high degree of sharing and a strong commitment between family members.

The members of a stepfamily must be flexible enough to adjust to a new lifestyle. In most cases, at least some of the family members were previously part of a nuclear family. They may have faced the crisis of death or divorce. They have adjusted to a single-parent family structure. Making the adjustment to a stepfamily may be stressful for them. To cushion this adjustment, each family member must try to be understanding and cooperative.

A stepfamily is usually a new experience for everyone involved. Each person brings his or her hopes and doubts into the family. New relationships form. Besides adjusting to each other, husbands and wives must adjust to each other's children. The children must adjust to a new parent as well as new brothers and sisters.

Without cooperation, the adjustment to a stepfamily could be difficult. Even with cooperation, there may be some problems at first. If everyone in the family keeps trying, however, the result could be a strong, healthy family unit. The new combination of interests, skills, and other resources could make the stepfamily lively and exciting.

Note: The fastest growing family structure between 1980 and 1990 was the single-parent family headed by a man.

Discuss: What are the advantages and disadvantages of single-parent families?

Discuss: What are some adjustments that may need to be made when living in a stepfamily?

Activity: Have students role-play a stepfamily eating breakfast together. Follow-up with a discussion of advantages and disadvantages of living in a stepfamily.

Career Preparation Activity

Career Challenges Faced by Single Parents, reproducible master, TR. Students are to interview the head of a single-parent family about the effects of his or her family structure on his or her career.

> **Discuss:**
> Why might a couple choose to remain childless?

> **Note:**
> In 1990, according to the U.S. Census Bureau, only about one household in three contained a child under age 18.

> **Resource:**
> *Analyzing Family Structures and Lifestyles,* Activity B, SAG

> **Resource:**
> *Exploring Family Structures,* reproducible master, TR

Extended Families

In an **extended family** structure, other relatives live with parents and their children. Grandparents, aunts, uncles, and/or cousins might be part of an extended family. This family structure is less common today than in the past.

An extended family takes care of its own members. Aging parents receive care from their children rather than from nursing homes. Grandparents and other adults care for the children. Children gain general knowledge and learn specific skills from the adults.

In most extended families, members offer each other economic support. The family can take advantage of each member's knowledge, skills, time, and energy. One person may be interested in gardening and cooking. Someone else may enjoy sewing clothes for the family. Other members might be talented in home or car maintenance or in handling financial affairs. By combining the resources of all the family members, the household can be run economically.

Childless Families

A fifth family structure is the **childless family**. A childless family is a couple without children. Some childless couples are not able to have children and prefer not to adopt. Other couples choose not to have children. In the past, relatives and society might have criticized this decision. Today, this has become an acceptable option. See 6-7.

People who do not have children of their own may choose to interact with children in other settings. They might spend time with nieces or nephews. They might also do volunteer work with children in their community.

Factors Influencing Families

Families are affected by outside forces, both good and bad. Parents try to take advantage of the positive influences to enhance the family's well-being. They also try, to the extent possible, to shield family members from negative influences.

6-7 Childless couples may prefer to concentrate on goals other than raising children.

Cultural Influences

Perhaps the strongest influence in shaping family structure is the cultural heritage of the individuals involved. Culture shapes a person's expectations for the different roles of various family members. The U.S. population includes people from cultures throughout the world. Therefore, newlyweds may have different expectations for their new life together if they come from different cultural backgrounds.

Respect for the extended family is a strong influence among people of many cultures, including Hispanic Americans, African Americans, and Asian Americans. Newlyweds may be expected to live with the husband's parents. If the newlyweds form their own home, they may learn that family members will soon be joining them. The visits may range from short-term stays of cousins, aunts, or uncles to long-term living arrangements with the parents. Traditional Chinese parents take great pride in depending totally on their children. The parents view this as a sign of successful

Problem-Solving Practice

Caring for Grandma, reproducible master, TR. Students are to work in small groups and use the decision-making process to help solve the problem described in a case study.

parenting. The benefits of the extended family include help with housekeeping and child care tasks. While the son or daughter raised in an extended family may feel comfortable with this living arrangement, his or her spouse may not.

The cultures that value extended families are also likely to emphasize family interests over the individual's. This may be expressed by the family deciding what career their son or daughter eventually pursues. The parents may regard these decisions as theirs to make since they will rely on the children's earning power in their old age. A family-arranged marriage is another sign of a family that emphasizes family interests over the individual's. See 6-8.

Societal Influences

Through the socialization process, parents teach children the do's and don'ts of society. The family interprets the standards of society to help children understand what behaviors are expected of them. By learning these important lessons through teaching and training, children understand how the standards apply to their lives. With parental love and support, children then grow into productive members of society.

In a democratic society, free expression is allowed and encouraged. Sometimes the ideas and personal priorities expressed are not consistent with what children learn from their families. Peers, for example, can strongly influence individuals to join group activities, for good or bad.

Advertising and other forms of media can also influence individuals to behave contrary to their training. **Media** are channels of mass communication, such as magazines, television, radio, and the Internet. These influences can convey beliefs, priorities, and standards of conduct contrary to a family's view of what is right and proper.

When negative influences from society begin to make an impact, parents are challenged to work harder in the role of socializing their children.

Technological Influences

Many of the time- and energy-saving tools and appliances used in homes are the result of technology. These devices help families manage their lives and provide physical care to their children.

Telecommuting, discussed in Chapter 5, is also possible as a result of technology. Telecommuting allows parents to earn income while staying home. When parents work from their homes, they can tailor their schedules to include both roles of parent and income producer. As a result, they mesh the responsibilities of being a parent with those of being an employee, 6-9.

One of the most important benefits of new technology is the ability to communicate easily with others. By linking to the Internet, family members living apart can stay in touch through e-mail. With special equipment, they can share family photos and custom-made soundtracks, such as thank-you messages or birthday greetings. The latest technology in home computers can even

6-8 Couples contemplating marriage would benefit from meeting each other's families to experience their customs and personal priorities firsthand.

Discuss: How does your cultural background influence your family's structure?

Enrich: Have students hold a debate on the good and bad effects of the media on family values.

Discuss: How many out-of-town relatives do you keep in touch with using the Internet?

Across the Curriculum

Social studies. Discuss the emphasis on family in different cultures.

Reflect:
Do you think the Internet helps keep family members separated by distance closer than the telephone or letters? Why?

Discuss:
How many people do you know over the age of 60? 70? 80?

Activity:
Ask students to make a list of the pros and cons of living in an extended family.

6-9 Mothers of young children especially value telecommuting careers.

send live-action pictures and sound anywhere. Broadcasts of holiday celebrations and family events help family members throughout the world share common experiences. Communication technology increases the ability of families to provide emotional support to distant members.

Demographic Factors

Many demographic factors indicate that families are changing. **Demographics** are statistical qualities of the human population. By checking demographics, many trends can be observed.

A major trend affecting the family is the high percentage of women working away from home. Historically, the man was the breadwinner while the woman tended to the home and family. Today the majority of mothers hold jobs outside the home. If fathers are also away at work, some outside help is needed to care for young children. Extended families are very helpful in this situation. With one or more other adults living with the family, someone is always present to care for the children. Without this help, parents often share—with a babysitter, child care worker, or teacher—their responsibilities for providing physical care and socialization to children.

Another trend that impacts families is the growing senior citizen population due to increasing lifespan. When seniors are healthy, they can lead independent lives. When their health begins to fail, their lifestyles must change, too. Seniors with physical or mental disabilities must be watched closely so they do not fall prey to accidents or safety hazards. As seniors move in with their middle age "children" to watch over them, extended families are created, 6-10. Many middle-age adults have the double responsibility of raising children and providing care to aging parents.

Another important demographic trend is the high mobility of the U.S. population. Compared to past generations, when moving once or twice was common, today's families move five or more times. Often they move so parents have better job opportunities. The move may benefit the family financially, but it can negatively impact members emotionally. Left behind are cousins, aunts, uncles, and grandparents that provided emotional support. Often they provided physical support, too, especially in helping with child care. In these situations, parents must fill the void created by moving away from beloved family members.

6-10 When an aging parent decides to live with his or her child's family, an extended family is formed.

Putting Technology to Use
Have students use the Internet to find statistics on the percentage of women working away from home. Have them find statistics from the last 50 years, then use graphing software to make a graph illustrating the trend.

Economic Forces

Economic forces have much to do with a family's well-being. The absence of good jobs causes some families to leave familiar surroundings, seeking opportunities elsewhere. Left behind is the family support system that helped in times of need.

If one salary does not satisfy family needs, one parent must work multiple jobs or both parents must earn incomes. In these cases, parents are often faced with finding alternatives for handling part of their child care responsibilities. When older children are present, more household and child care responsibilities are usually assigned to them.

World Events

Family development is influenced not only by events within the country, but also by world situations. People of the world are no longer isolated from each other. New communication systems make worldwide information readily available. Therefore, events that occur in one country become common knowledge around the world within minutes.

Social and political unrest in one area of the world can influence countries on the other side of the globe. Family members can be separated when there is a need to send military troops abroad. Natural disasters such as floods or earthquakes can devastate whole cities. After such events, families from distant countries may donate money, clothing, and food to assist the victims. Many U.S. citizens travel to other countries to administer health care, make home repairs, rebuild public facilities, and even help rebuild neighborhoods.

The family is no longer an independent economic unit, 6-11. Families depend on global markets to satisfy needs for many products. For example, consider what happens when a war interferes with shipments of petroleum from oil-producing countries. Less fuel is available to drive cars and heat homes, causing prices to skyrocket. Families have no choice but to pay the higher prices. Often they must alter their lifestyles and postpone unnecessary purchases, too. Higher fuel costs eventually increase the prices of all goods and services, affecting everyone's pocketbook. This, in turn, influences the general economy. When the public has less spending power, companies respond by producing less and, thus, cutting jobs. Events in other parts of the world can have long-term effects on families in your area.

6-11 A high price on in-season produce usually indicates bad weather in the areas where the produce was grown.

Check It Out!
1. A married couple with children describes the _____ family structure.
2. Name three organizations that can help fill the gaps in single-parent families.
3. List six factors that can affect the responsibilities of family members.

Check It Out! (Answers)
1. nuclear
2. Big Brothers, Big Sisters, Parents Without Partners (Students may justify other responses.)
3. cultural influences, societal influences, technological influences, demographic factors, economic forces, world events

Discuss: Child care can be expensive. Should both parents work if most of one's salary will be used to pay child care costs?

Enrich: Have students research a past natural disaster. Ask them to write a report on how the disaster affected families in the area.

Resource:
Family Life Cycle, transparency master, TR

Activity:
Make a list of occurrences that can cause the family to move into a new stage of the family life cycle.

Topic 6-3
Family Structures Change

Objectives

After studying this topic, you will be able to
- list the six stages of the family life cycle.
- determine the consequences of divorce.
- explain why second marriages are more likely to be successful for people whose first marriages ended in divorce.

Topic Term

family life cycle

Family structures do not always remain the same. They may change as new members are added to a family or as present members leave. For instance, a nuclear family may become an extended family or a single-parent family. Some of these changes occur as a result of the natural passage of time.

Family Life Cycle

While family structures vary, each structure includes basic stages of growth and development called the **family life cycle**. See 6-12. Studying this cycle can help people prepare for the challenges that may exist in their own families.

Stages in the Cycle

The family life cycle contains six main stages and a number of substages. The first main stage is known as the *beginning stage*. Families in this stage consist of a husband and wife. While in this stage, couples make adjustments to marriage and form foundations for their future families. There may be many money pressures as couples try to establish a new home. There may be time pressures, too, as spouses try to build careers, finish a higher education, or perhaps do both.

During the years when a family is growing, it is in the *childbearing stage*. This stage includes the birth of the first child through the birth of the last child. This is a very busy period since attention to the child is full-time. If a parent cannot stay home with the child, arrangements must be made so the child receives quality care.

Family Life Cycle

Beginning Stage	Childbearing Stage	Parenting Stage	Launching Stage	Mid-Years Stage	Aging Stage
• Married couple without children	• Couple from birth of first child through birth of last child	• Couple with child(ren)	• Couple with child(ren) leaving home	• Couple with independent child(ren) living away from home	• Couple during retirement until death of both spouses

6-12 Family life follows a series of stages as couples age and children come and go.

Putting Technology to Use
Have students use drawing software, a digital camera, or a scanner to create a poster of their family. Have students indicate at the bottom of the poster which stage(s) of the family life cycle their family is currently experiencing.

Whether a career couple hires outside help or one spouse stays home full-time, there is considerable money pressure.

The family continues to grow in the *parenting stage*. Parents provide for the children, while the children pursue their individual interests and school activities. This tends to be the most expensive stage of the family life cycle. Food and clothing costs increase as children grow. Having enough space for everyone to live comfortably may require modeling the family home or moving to a larger one. School activities and sports often involve extra fees. Saving money for the children's college educations occurs during this period. Also, tension between the spouses can develop if there is no plan for handling the many housekeeping and child care duties.

The *launching stage* is when children begin to leave home and become independent of their parents. They may leave for college and continue after graduation in their chosen careers. Some may find jobs and move to their own housing; others marry and start their own families.

The launching stage is followed by the *mid-years stage* when all children have left and the couple is again independent. During this period, couples enter their peak earning years. They can spend more of their income on themselves instead of the children. They may do so by upgrading their homes or taking more frequent vacations. They may also become grandparents in this stage.

The final stage of the family life cycle is the *aging stage*. This stage begins at the time of retirement and continues until both spouses die. During this stage, one spouse may live alone after the death of the other. When the spouses are financially secure and enjoying good health, it is a very rewarding period. Time can be devoted to lifelong interests at whatever pace is comfortable. When problems begin to surface over finances and/or health, life can become unpleasant. Tensions may develop with other family members who try to offer assistance.

Variations in the Cycle

Families are unique and do not always fit a given mold. Many families have overlaps in the stages and substages of the life cycle. For example, a family may include a baby, school-age children, and teenagers all at one time. A family may launch an older child while a preschooler is still at home.

Sometimes many years separate the stages of a family's life cycle. For example, a couple may have a teenager before their second child is born. This family experiences the qualities of both the childbearing and parenting stages.

As individuals progress through the stages of the family life cycle, they are faced with different roles and responsibilities. Roles change as family members grow older. For example, in the beginning stage, a man has the role of husband and provider. In the childbearing family stage, he takes on the additional role of father, 6-13. In the aging stage, he no longer has the role of provider and may have to accept the role of widower.

Divorce

Changes in family structure are not always the result of time passage. A change from a nuclear family to a single-parent

6-13 A man takes on a new family role with new responsibilities when he becomes a father.

Discuss: What adjustments must men and women make as they move from the beginning stage to the aging stage?

Resource: *Family Life Cycle,* Activity C, SAG

Note: Forecasters say that 6 percent of today's children will live with a single parent at some time before they reach age 18.

Across the Curriculum
Sociology. Discuss how the family unit has remained a constant in the evolution of the human race.

Discuss:
Why do you think these groups have a higher divorce rate?

Enrich:
Invite a family counselor to talk to the class about the adjustments family members must make when a couple seeks a divorce.

Resource:
Divorce, reproducible master, TR

family is often the result of divorce.

Divorce is common in today's society. Many couples decide they have problems and differences that cannot be resolved. They believe they would be happier living apart, so they get a divorce.

Groups with Higher Divorce Rates

Divorce rates are high among people of all ages, economic levels, and religions. However, certain groups of people are more likely to divorce than others.

Teen marriages have a high divorce rate. This is especially true of teen marriages in which the bride is pregnant. Many of these couples are not ready to handle the responsibilities of marriage and parenthood.

Marriages in which spouses have a low level of education also have a high divorce rate. Lack of education often prevents people from getting good jobs that pay higher wages. Living on very little money is difficult. It becomes more difficult when expenses increase because children arrive. This adds stress to a couple's marriage relationship.

Marriages in which spouses have mixed or no religious ties are another group of marriages with a high divorce rate. On the other hand, spouses who share strong religious beliefs are more likely to have stable marriages.

Adjusting to Divorce

Divorce creates many changes for many people. The two former spouses have to break their emotional ties to each other. They have to go through the legal process of ending their marriage. They have to set up two separate households. This means changing their budgets and usually leading simpler, less costly lifestyles.

Divorced persons have to learn to think of themselves as individuals again. They have to adjust to independence. They have to learn to make decisions by themselves and lead their own lives. See 6-14.

Divorce affects not only the couple, but also the people they know. Friends, neighbors, and colleagues of the couple may choose sides and become either "his" or "her" friends. Some people who have a

6-14 Divorced persons must adjust to establishing a home without the former spouse.

Across the Curriculum

English. Have students do a research report on divorce. Students may want to choose topics such as the high divorce rate, the process of divorcing, or adjusting to a divorce. Students should use current resources and include a bibliography in their reports.

negative view of divorce may not want to remain friendly with either member of the divorce. Other people may remain supportive and help the divorced persons make new social contacts.

Children of a divorced couple face many changes, too. They have to adjust to living with one parent and visiting the other parent. They may have to move to a new home. They may have to go to a new school and meet new friends. In addition, they have to adjust to the changes in their parents' social lives.

Remarriage

Remarriage is another event that causes family structures to change. Many single-parent families become stepfamilies when divorced people remarry.

Second marriages are usually more successful than first marriages. One reason is that spouses are older and usually more mature. They are more willing to invest the time and energy needed to make their marriages work. They have learned from their mistakes. They have a better idea of the kind of person they want for a marriage partner. They also have more realistic views of what they can and cannot expect of a spouse and of a marriage.

Second marriages have just as many challenges as first marriages have. When children from previous marriages are involved, second marriages may have even more challenges. Cooperation and communication can help spouses successfully handle these challenges. Spouses in second marriages may be more willing to cooperate with each other. They may try harder to keep communication lines open. This helps them keep in touch with each other's thoughts and feelings. Communication also prevents minor problems from growing and becoming major problems. With good cooperation and communication, any marriage can be successful. See 6-15.

6-15 Communicating and spending time together can help a couple build a successful marriage.

Check It Out!

1. What are the six stages of the family life cycle?
2. True or false. When a couple divorces, their friends, neighbors, and colleagues are affected.
3. What are two reasons that second marriages are more likely to be successful for people whose first marriages ended in divorce?

Check It Out! (Answers)

1. beginning stage, childbearing stage, parenting stage, launching stage, mid-year stage, aging stage
2. true
3. (List two:) are older and more mature; are more willing to invest the time and energy needed to make their marriages work; have learned from their mistakes; have a better idea of the kind of person they want for a marriage partner; have more realistic views of what they can and cannot expect of a spouse and marriage

Resource:
Changing Lifestyles, Activity D, SAG

Resource:
The Impact of Divorce, reproducible master, TR

Discuss:
React to the following statement: With good communication and cooperation, any marriage can be successful.

TEENS ARE TALKING ABOUT...
Divorce in Their Families

Discuss:
- How can the divorce of a teen's parents affect a person physically? What examples are given in the feature?
- What emotional changes might a teen encounter when parents divorce? What examples are given in the feature? What other emotional changes might occur?
- Tiffany stated that she learned many lessons because of her parents' divorce. What were these? What positive lessons did Jim learn?
- What should a teen do if divorcing parents ask the teen to take sides in the dispute? to spy on the other parent? to tell what the teen has heard the other parent say?

About half of all marriages in the United States end in divorce. Children as well as spouses are affected by divorce. In a group discussion, Ty, Luke, Jim, Tanya, Leroy, and Tiffany talked about how teens are affected when their parents divorce.

Ty said he didn't like to think his parents could get a divorce, but he knew it could happen. He also said he would be pretty sad if it did.

The group was asked how a divorce would affect teens physically. Jim said his parents' divorce created a lot of confusion. He explained that, although he moved to a new town with his mom, he really wanted to live with his father. This issue created quite a battle.

The group was asked about the emotional effects divorce might have on teens. Luke said, "Stress isn't unusual in teens when their parents are splitting up. Stress may make it hard to concentrate on schoolwork, athletics, and other important things. Stress sometimes causes teens to turn to drugs.

"Teens are often competitive in school and at home," Luke continued. "A divorce may change competition into fighting."

Tanya reinforced Luke's response. She said, "Teens will be depressed about the divorce. Their grades may drop. They may snap at their friends, get into trouble with their teachers, and fight with family members." Tanya also thinks children may try to make their parents feel guilty about getting a divorce.

Leroy explained that he came through his parents' divorce feeling less stress than many teens: "My mom said, 'Whatever happens between your father and me is not your fault. Parents have problems, too. A divorce is because of something that happened to them.'"

Coping with changes created by divorce was addressed. Tiffany said, "Believe it or not, I learned innumerable lessons because of my parents' divorce. I learned to cherish the time I had with both of them. I gained a sense of independence by learning how to take care of myself. I have gained knowledge about relationships. Love can be shared between many people and can be shown in many ways. I love my parents equally, no matter what."

The group was asked what advice they would give to teens whose parents were getting divorced. Jim said he would tell them that a divorce is not as bad as it sounds. "Divorce has good points as well as bad points," he stated.

"At first, it may seem like a divorce is all bad. Parents may fight continuously, and you may feel like you have to take sides. You are drawn into their conflict and sometimes asked to spy or tell what you heard."

Jim went on to explain that, on the good side, divorce helps teens mature quickly. It can also allow them to avoid an abusive parent. He concluded by saying, "Accepting your parents' divorce gets easier as you get older."

Leroy advised, "It's not your fault that your parents got the divorce. You will probably be better off if they are apart because they need space to grow."

Tiffany added, "Going through a divorce may be difficult, but good things can come of it."

Feature-Related Activity
Divide the class into small groups. Ask each group to develop a list of "Survival Skills" for teens whose parents are divorcing. The groups might also discuss how divorce can be prevented—what couples can do to keep their marriages alive and well.

Chapter Review

Summary

The family is the most important social unit in cultures throughout the world. Each person fulfills various inherited and assigned roles as a family member. The family provides the functions of procreation, physical care, socialization, and emotional support for its members.

Families take the form of different family structures. A nuclear family includes a husband, wife, and their children. A single-parent family has one parent and one or more children. A stepfamily contains stepparents and stepchildren. An extended family includes one or more relatives outside the nuclear family, such as an aunt or a grandmother. A childless family consists of a couple without children. Single people do not live in any of these family structures. They must meet their needs for the functions provided by a family in other ways.

Various outside forces may affect the roles and responsibilities of family members. Culture, society, and technology are strong influences. Some demographic factors that affect families include more women working outside the home, the longer lives of elderly family members, and more families moving more often. Economic forces and world events can also affect families.

Throughout their lives, the structures of families change. Some of these changes occur as a family goes through the stages of the family life cycle. Other changes in family structure are the result of divorce or remarriage.

Think About It!

1. What are three ways family members might demonstrate commitment to one another?
2. Describe your family roles and the roles of two of your family members.
3. Which of the functions provided by families do you think is most important? Explain your answer.
4. How do people with a single lifestyle meet their needs for each of the functions provided by families?
5. Which of the family structures discussed in this chapter do you feel is best equipped to provide the functions of the family? Explain your answer.
6. Which of the factors that influence families most affects yours? Explain.
7. If you were going to choose a family-related career, which one would you choose? Why?
8. Which stage in the family life cycle do you think would be the most exciting stage for parents? Explain your answer.
9. List two consequences a divorce would have for each of the following: a husband, a wife, and children.
10. If your first marriage ended in divorce, what would you do to help avoid divorce in your second marriage?

Try It Out!

1. Using your library resources, prepare a bibliography of books and magazine articles that classmates can use for further research about families.
2. Write a story about a family in the year 2030. Describe how roles of family members and functions provided by the family might change in the future.

Activity:
Have students draw their future family life cycles. Have them predict and indicate at what age (or if) they will enter each of the stages.

> **Note:**
> You might ask students to also bring in cartoons to add to the bulletin board. Ask them to identify the stages of the family life cycle depicted in the cartoons.
>
> **Resource:**
> *PowerZone Challenge CD.* Have students play the chapter review game to reinforce text content.

3. As a class, prepare a series of posters, each portraying a different family structure.
4. Role-play a scene or two depicting the advantages and disadvantages of single living.
5. Prepare a bulletin board using magazine pictures or family photos contributed by class members. Write clever captions to identify the various stages of the family life cycle represented.
6. Research the current statistics on divorce and remarriage. Share your findings in an oral report.
7. Look in the yellow pages of the telephone directory to find family and marriage counseling services available in your area.

Chapter 7
Family Challenges

Careers

These careers relate to the topics in this chapter:
- community service worker
- companion for the homebound
- child welfare research assistant
- family crisis counselor

Topics

7-1 Building Functional Families
7-2 Balancing Family and Work
7-3 Handling Family Crises

INTRODUCTORY ACTIVITIES

1. Read students a recent newspaper article about a specific challenge or crisis affecting a family in your area. Ask students if they think this challenge or crisis is typical of many families and, if so, why they think families are commonly faced with such problems. If they don't think this challenge or crisis is typical, ask them why they think this particular family was affected.
2. Ask students what they think are the most common problems facing families today and the reasons behind the problems.
3. Guest speaker: Invite a family counselor to speak to your class about what he or she considers to be the greatest challenges facing families today.

Topic 7-1
Building Functional Families

I. Making and Keeping Families Strong
   A. Communicate Effectively
   B. Solve Problems
   C. Get Help When Needed
   D. Spend Time Together
   E. Show Appreciation
   F. Show Respect
   G. Understand Each Other
II. Fulfilling Family Rights and Responsibilities
   A. Sharing Personal Priorities and Goals
   B. Sharing Responsibility for Decisions
   C. Sharing Resources
   D. Sharing a Lasting Commitment

Topic 7-2
Balancing Family and Work

I. The Relationship of Work and Family Life
   A. The Effects of Work on Family Life
   B. The Effects of Family Life on Work
II. Managing Multiple Roles
   A. Set Priorities
   B. Make Choices
   C. Find Child Care
III. The Role of the Employer
   A. Flexible Work Arrangements
   B. Employee Benefits That Help Families

Topic 7-3
Handling Family Crises

I. What Is a Crisis?
   A. Characteristics of Crises
II. Skills for Coping with Crises
III. Types of Crises
   A. Unemployment
   B. Family Violence
      1. Types of Family Violence
      2. Why Family Violence Occurs
      3. Where to Get Help
   C. Substance Abuse
      1. Where to Get Help
   D. Serious Illness or Accidents
   E. Death

Vocabulary:
Compare the term *functional* with *dysfunctional*. Discuss what the prefix *dys* means.

Note:
All families go through periods of crisis. This does not necessarily mean they are dysfunctional.

Topic 7-1
Building Functional Families

Objectives
After studying this topic, you will be able to
- describe characteristics of functional families.
- list techniques family members can use to build a functional family.
- explain how functional families fulfill their family rights and responsibilities.

Topic Terms
functional family
dysfunctional family
codependency

In today's complex world, people face the challenge of keeping the family unit strong. This challenge is not always easy to achieve. However, many families face the challenge by making family life a top priority. Family members know and accept the responsibility they have for each other. They are committed to working together and making special sacrifices to help each other.

Making and Keeping Families Strong

A strong, healthy family is also called a **functional family**. A functional family provides a positive environment. Each family member is encouraged to grow and to reach his or her fullest potential, 7-1. A functional family tries to stay balanced. The family works together to meet the needs of each member. In turn, each family member carries out his or her roles and responsibilities. Together, the family works to keep their unit strong, healthy, and happy.

Functional families have certain qualities in common. They communicate effectively. When problems arise, they try to solve them. Spending time together is important to them. Family members appreciate and support each other. Each member tries to understand the roles of other family members. Above all, they value family life.

Functional families also realize they are not perfect. Their lives don't always run smoothly. However, they have a sense

7-1 Functional families provide for the physical, social, emotional, and spiritual needs of their members. They put the family first.

FCCLA Activity
Suggest that chapter members who are working on the Interpersonal Communications STAR Event might consider developing a community project designed to build more functional families through strengthened family communication. For example, they might plan a family communications workshop to be offered through an adult education program in your community.

of purpose. They work hard to overcome obstacles and stay strong. They feel the rewards are worth the effort they put into the relationship.

Have you thought about what you can do to strengthen your family and help keep it that way? Some helpful techniques you and your family can use to achieve this goal are described below.

Communicate Effectively

Functional families communicate effectively. They talk about problems, express their needs and feelings, and listen to each other. They respect others' opinions, even if those opinions differ from their own. When they disagree, they use open communication to solve the problem. This helps them develop a sense of trust. Good communication promotes growth for all family members.

You can find ways to communicate more effectively with your family. Make a point to talk with other family members. Listen carefully to make sure you understand the other person's viewpoint. Plan to have mealtimes together to talk about daily events, or set up a regular family meeting. When schedules are hard to coordinate, notes, e-mail messages, and telephone calls can be a pleasant surprise. This method may also help your family stay in touch with members who are away from home. Communicate positive feelings by planning special events the family can enjoy together. Communicate your understanding of others' feelings. Sincere words like "I love you" accompanied by a hug or a kiss can lift spirits or mend broken feelings.

Solve Problems

Functional families try to resolve problems and conflicts in positive ways. When all family members tackle problems together, they develop a feeling of joint ownership. Jointly owned problems are usually easier to solve. There are more people to identify possible solutions.

Get Help When Needed

Functional families admit they have as many problems as less-healthy, or dysfunctional families. A **dysfunctional family** provides a negative environment that discourages the growth and development of family members. The difference between a functional family and dysfunctional family is the way they look at problems and solve them. For example, some dysfunctional families try too hard to help their members. They may assume responsibility for family members who have serious problems by covering for them. This is called **codependency.** A pattern of unhealthy behaviors is used by family members to cover up the problem. This adversely affects the emotional health of everyone in the family and does not help the family member who has the problem.

Functional families look for positive outcomes in all types of situations—even problem situations. They deal with the problems instead of being destroyed by them. When they cannot solve a problem themselves, they seek outside help.

When your family faces what you consider a real problem, try using the problem-solving process. Openly discuss the problem; don't let it build up inside. State your feelings using I-messages. Avoid name-calling or blaming someone else for your problem. Try for an I win/you win situation by compromising or negotiating for a satisfactory solution. If a serious problem arises that cannot be resolved within the family, suggest seeking help outside the family.

Spend Time Together

Functional families spend time together whenever possible. They bring a sense of play and humor into their leisure time. Family interactions are balanced, so all members feel involved. Some families go to the movies, work on hobbies together, or have a family game night. What is most important is they do something together as a family. See 7-2.

You can find ways to spend time with your family, too. Look for special activities

Resource:
Functional/Dysfunctional Families, Activity A, SAG

Discuss:
How can you use the ideas and techniques discussed in Chapter 3 to improve family communication?

Enrich:
Brainstorm ideas families might use to keep in touch with members who are away from home.

Enrich:
Invite the school psychologist or another psychologist to speak to the class on family communication.

Family Enrichment Activity
Discuss with students the importance that spending time together holds for members of functional families. Encourage students to plan a special activity that will allow them to spend some quality time with their family members.

Discuss:
"The family that plays together stays together."

Enrich:
Brainstorm inexpensive activities families might enjoy together.

Reflect:
How have you shown appreciation to other members of your family?

Resource:
Giving a Gift of Appreciation, reproducible master, TR

7-2 Many families enjoy spending time together by taking an annual vacation trip.

7-3 Helping with raking the leaves is one way to show appreciation.

you and your family can share together, like biking, jogging, or preparing evening meals. Help plan a family vacation or outing. Share family celebrations like birthdays and anniversaries. Celebrate religious and patriotic holidays together. Start a new family tradition that will help create happy memories, such as visiting a museum or planting trees. Plan ahead with your family so everyone can get involved.

Show Appreciation

Functional families find ways to show appreciation. This form of emotional support encourages a secure and loving environment. Showing appreciation through words or actions contributes to each member's well-being and self-esteem, 7-3.

You can show family members appreciation in your everyday actions. Offer to help out without being asked. Thank others when they help you. Give sincere compliments about a job well done or when someone looks nice. Create your own special event for a family member. Let others know they are special in your life by the things you say and do.

Show Respect

No two members of a family are exactly alike. To keep families strong, members need to show respect for each other. This can be done in a number of ways. They can respect each other's ideas and opinions, recognizing not everyone will agree on every matter. Listening to what everyone has to say, no matter how old they are, is important. Each individual will have likes and dislikes. These, too, should be respected.

Family members can respect each other's privacy, as well as their personal belongings. Asking if you can borrow an item that belongs to a brother or sister rather than taking the item without a word shows respect. Showing respect for older members of the family is important in most cultures. When you show respect for family members they feel valued and loved.

 Putting Technology to Use
Have students use greeting card or drawing software to make an appreciation card for a family member.

Respect is an important part of emotional support and leads to feelings of trust.

Understand Each Other

Functional families try to understand the changing roles of each family member. They recognize family tensions may increase during the period of adolescence. The adolescent is learning independence, while parents are beginning to give up some controls. It is a period of uncertainty and adjustment for both adolescents and parents. Both parties must try harder to understand and accept the changes that occur during this period. All must make an extra effort to show respect for each other and to trust one another.

Understanding your changing role may help you understand your parent's point of view. Your parents are watching you grow from a child to an adult. During this time, you and your parents won't always agree. Being patient and understanding may be helpful. Try speaking and acting in ways that help make this transition smoother for both sides. You may find some of the tips listed in 7-4 to be helpful, too.

Fulfilling Family Rights and Responsibilities

In most families, family rights and responsibilities are closely linked. For each right a family member has, a responsibility comes with it. Functional families are committed to fulfilling these rights and responsibilities. They do so by sharing personal priorities and goals, responsibility for decisions, resources, and a commitment to each other.

Sharing Personal Priorities and Goals

Family members have a right to expect support and guidance as they establish personal priorities and goals. Family members also have a responsibility to provide this support and guidance for one another.

Functional families share what is important to them both directly and indirectly.

Strengthening Parent-Teen Relationships

- Conduct family meetings so everyone will have opportunities to bring up issues for discussion.
- Recognize potential problems and be willing to talk about them.
- Encourage open discussion by listening and trying to understand the other's point-of-view.
- Communicate honestly and truthfully.
- Respect each other.
- Negotiate fairly.
- Communicate without manipulating each other. For example, avoid trying to get your own point across by making others feel guilty.
- Use a normal tone of voice.
- Maintain self-control. When tempers flare, communications close.
- Try to read and respond to nonverbal communication.
- Seek clarification when you do not understand.
- Learn to laugh and cry together.
- Always remember—in good times and bad—that you are a family.

7-4   It's not always easy for parents and teens to relate well to each other. For those who can, however, the rewards are worth the efforts. Here are some tips that can help parents and teens strengthen their relationships.

Parents directly teach their children *morals*—a sense of what is right or wrong. Children also learn what is important to their parents indirectly by watching what goes on around them. When family members live with certain personal priorities, these become important to all members. As a result, family members share many personal priorities even if they are not actually discussed. See 7-5.

Functional families help members develop personal priorities by being supportive. When a family member says, "I think…" or "I believe…" others listen with respect and understanding. As a

Reflect:
Has there been a time when you haven't been understanding of a parent's point of view? Did this misunderstanding lead to a conflict?

Discuss:
"Do as I say, not as I do."

Resource:
Teenagers in Functional Families, transparency master, TR

Putting Technology to Use
Have students role-play typical parent/teen conflicts. Videotape the role-plays for later discussion. Use Chart 7-4 to discuss the simulated conflicts.

Reflect:
Do your family members encourage you to share your goals with them? How does this contribute to your family relationships?

Activity:
In small groups, discuss resources teens can contribute to help families function better.

7-5 Families who share personal priorities and goals create a positive environment that keeps the family strong.

family, they are able to discuss issues openly. Open discussions also help family members develop good communication skills, self-respect, self-confidence, and self-esteem.

When family members share what they feel is important, they are likely to share goals, too. Families set goals that reflect their personal priorities. These goals give direction to their lives. When they share certain goals, it's easier for family members to work together with enthusiasm. Each person may try a little harder if the family is planning a vacation or saving for a new house.

Functional families encourage people to share goals. Family members can offer each other companionship as they work toward their goals. They can also celebrate together when their goals are reached.

Sharing Responsibility for Decisions

Family members have a right to learn and to practice decision-making skills within the warm and supportive setting of the family unit. They also have a responsibility to provide input for family decisions that need to be made. Together, members of functional families can discuss ideas and explore alternatives. They can make wise decisions that are best for the entire family.

Sharing Resources

Functional families work together for the well-being of all members. Each member has a responsibility to contribute the special resources he or she has to offer. Each member also has a right to share in the resources contributed by others. Family members enjoy a sense of fulfillment in giving and receiving.

The time, energy, interest, knowledge, and skills contributed by family members have economic value. When family members exchange these resources, they also help each other grow emotionally, intellectually, and socially. They all become better people. They help ensure economic security for their members.

Functional families use their resources for home management. They establish realistic expectations and set priorities. Preparing work schedules and assigning responsibilities to all family members helps to establish a balanced workload. Working together to manage the home gives members a sense of belonging. It also teaches job skills that will be useful when family members become wage earners.

Across the Curriculum

Social studies. Discuss similarities between family members who share responsibilities for making family decisions and members of congress who share responsibilities for making national decisions.

Sharing a Lasting Commitment

Sharing commitment to one another is a right and a responsibility of family members. In functional families, a lasting commitment is the tie that binds family members. Commitment is an expression of love. It provides individualized attention to the needs of each person. This lasting commitment adds to a person's sense of security. At the end of a hard day, a worker needs to know that emotional support can be found at home. After surgery, a patient needs to know that family members will help make the recovery easier. People need to know they are not alone—their family will always be there for them.

The commitment among family members provides opportunities for giving, as well as receiving. Cooking a special meal or mowing the lawn without being asked are thoughtful gestures that make everyone feel good. Just being there to listen is important also.

Check It Out!
1. Identify five qualities functional families have in common.
2. Explain the difference between a functional family and a dysfunctional family.
3. Explain how functional families fulfill their family rights and responsibilities.

Check It Out! (Answers)
1. (Identify five:) communicate effectively, solve problems, get help when needed, spend time together, show appreciation, show respect, understand each other
2. A functional family provides a positive environment that encourages growth and development. A dysfunctional family provides a negative environment that discourages growth and development.
3. Functional families fulfill their rights and responsibilities by sharing personal priorities and goals, sharing responsibilities for decision making, sharing resources, and sharing a lasting commitment to one another.

Topic 7-2
Balancing Family and Work

Objectives
After studying this topic, you will be able to
- explain the relationship between work and family.
- recognize ways working families can manage multiple roles.
- identify ways employers can help dual-career families manage work and family roles.

Topic Terms
dual-career families
multiple roles
priorities
job sharing
flextime
flexible workweeks
tailored paychecks

Families face challenges every day. One of the biggest challenges they face today is balancing the roles and responsibilities of work and family life. Not only do working parents provide economic support for family members, they must also fulfill their parental roles. Work should be an enjoyable part of a well-rounded life. Work rewards and responsibilities should be balanced with those of personal and family life.

As employers face changing trends in the economy, they are trying to support harmony between work and family life. Family-oriented employers are adapting new programs and benefits to meet the needs of working parents. By allowing more choices, employers are helping working parents balance their work and family responsibilities.

The Relationship of Work and Family Life

The relationship between work and family life is complex. Each affects the other in both positive and negative ways.

Resource:
What Family Living Means, reproducible master, TR

Vocabulary:
Compose a short paragraph using Topic 7-2 terms.

Activity:
List ten careers you feel would be especially satisfying to you.

> **Resource:**
> *Family Life and Work*, transparency master, TR

> **Discuss:**
> Are there other negative effects of work on family life?

> **Resource:**
> *Balancing Family and Work*, Activity B, SAG

Work affects the quality of family life; in turn, the quality of family life affects work performance.

The Effects of Work on Family Life

Work has both positive and negative effects on family life. Many workers find satisfaction in developing their professional roles as well as contributing to the family's income. Job satisfaction is one positive effect that carries over to family life. People who find jobs for which they are well-suited receive more satisfaction from working. This helps them focus more positively on family responsibilities when they are at home. Work satisfaction gives them more confidence in managing everyday tasks and problems.

Parents who enjoy their work can convey this attitude to their children. They can encourage children to perform work tasks at home and praise them for well-done jobs. This helps children develop positive attitudes about work. Positive attitudes and skills family members learn at home can be carried over into the workplace.

Work can have a positive effect on family relationships. Managing work and family time effectively becomes a shared effort among family members. Family relationships are often strengthened if members strive to be more supportive of each other in meeting responsibilities. Children often become more self-reliant and independent when both parents work. Sharing household tasks may improve relationships among family members, especially fathers and children, 7-6.

Work can have negative effects on a worker's personal and family life, too. Time management and role overload are two common challenges faced by families with working members. Workers' job demands may leave them little time for themselves, family members, socializing, recreation, and household chores. Job demands may leave them too busy or too tired to devote enough time to family responsibilities.

Trying to fulfill too many roles can lead to role overload. Role overload can cause physical and emotional strain, which can lead to fatigue and irritability. Households with two working parents, single parents, and mothers with young children often experience the most difficulty with role overload, 7-7. These households

7-6 This father and daughter are working together to complete family chores.

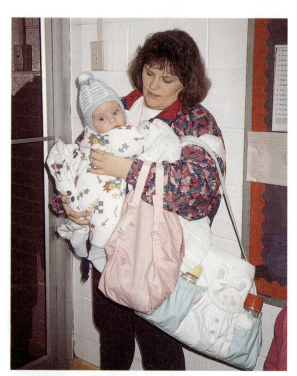

7-7 Because a working mother with young children has many responsibilities to fulfill, she is more likely to experience role overload.

Career Preparation Activity

Scheduling Work and Family Time, reproducible master, TR. Students are to read a case study about a teenager with a busy schedule. Then they are to plan a weekly schedule for the character in the case study to help her balance her family time and work.

have fewer family members with time available to handle child care, household, and job tasks.

When both spouses work outside the home, meeting family needs becomes even more challenging. Families in which both spouses are employed are called **dual-career families**. Spouses in these families must try to balance their work and marriage roles. If they have children, they also must manage their parenting roles. Dual-career families often need to make special efforts to keep communication open. Since family members may be away from home often, they must make the most of their time together.

The Effects of Family Life on Work

Just as work affects family life, family life affects work in positive and negative ways. Strong family relationships have a positive effect on work performance. A supportive family gives workers added energy to meet job demands.

Some aspects of family life can have negative effects on work performance. Having overly demanding family responsibilities is one example. Responsibilities such as caring for small children, elderly family members, or family members with disabilities place added role strain on workers. Work performance may suffer as the worker may be more tired, absent more often, and more focused on family matters.

Managing Multiple Roles

People who combine family roles with their career roles have **multiple roles**. Balancing multiple roles is not easy since work roles often conflict with family roles. Fulfilling each of these roles places demands on all family members. Careful planning is needed for these families to meet their responsibilities. Managing family resources, such as time and energy, also becomes important.

Working parents face many decisions about how to manage their responsibilities at home and at work. Good managerial skills and relationship skills are the keys to balancing their busy lives. Setting priorities and making choices about household tasks, child care, and family schedules can help them make wiser decisions.

Set Priorities

To manage multiple roles, families have to learn to manage their time. This means the family must set priorities and then make choices accordingly. **Priorities** are important tasks ranked in order of importance. To set priorities, they must decide which tasks are most important to the family and then rank them in order of importance. Successful families need priorities to help them keep their focus and complete tasks. They must ask: "What is of greatest importance to this family?" The answers will vary for different families. Decisions will be based on many factors, including family responsibilities. Some families may decide spending more time together is important. Others may choose to focus on meeting other basic needs. See 7-8.

In making career-related decisions, parents must consider their children's needs, their own personal needs, and their career needs. Will their jobs provide enough financial resources? Will a job change interfere with the time they can spend with their children? Can they take on new job responsibilities and still devote quality time to family members?

Make Choices

Setting priorities is bound to create some priority conflicts that will need to be resolved. For instance, working late at the office might help a parent get a promotion and earn more money. However, this would mean spending less time with the children. This creates a conflict between the priorities of money and family interaction. Family members will have to pull together to make a choice.

Basic relationship skills help families work through situations when choices need to be made. Support, open communication, negotiation, and compromise help

Discuss:
For those of you from dual-career families, what do you see as the advantages and disadvantages of having both parents employed?

Note:
Ask each student to interview at least one dual-career couple and summarize their comments.

Resource:
Roles, Goals, and Priorities, reproducible master, TR

Activity:
Place on the chalkboard the following heading: "If my family had more time together, we might…" Have each student use colored chalk to complete the sentence.

Putting Technology to Use
Have students use drawing software, a scanner, and clipart to create a bulletin board entitled *The Many Hats We Wear*. Each hat should represent a role children and parents might assume in the family.

Reflect:
What responsibilities do you assume in your home? Are there additional tasks you are capable of performing?

Activity:
Working in small groups, discuss and record methods of simplifying meal preparation. (Good nutrition should not be jeopardized.) Also list ways housekeeping tasks can be simplified.

Discuss:
Should employers provide programs to help workers balance work and family responsibilities? How might employers benefit? What are the disadvantages to employers?

7-8 Many families value their time together. Table games are a fun way to spend time together.

families make choices and keep responsibilities in balance. Family members can support one another to avoid feelings of guilt or resentment about work responsibilities. Single parents may look to close friends and relatives for extra support. All family members may have to accept responsibility for household tasks such as laundry, cleaning, and cooking. Parents may sometimes need to adjust work responsibilities so they can spend more time with the family. They might have to make choices about working less overtime, changing to a part-time job, or working from home.

Working families must realize they can't have it all. That is, in balancing family and work, they must have realistic expectations. They must be prepared to face potential problems. There are trade-offs between family life and work. Combining both is not always easy. Family time will have to be carefully planned. Housekeeping standards may have to be lowered. Some family activities may have to be missed. Job and career advancement may be slower.

Find Child Care

Working parents may need to make child care arrangements for their children. They must choose child care arrangements that best fit their needs and their children's needs. Some of the options available are discussed later in Topic 9-7.

The Role of the Employer

In today's economy, employers are finding it more beneficial to help employees balance work and family roles. One way they do this is by offering flexible work arrangements that help employees handle family responsibilities. Offering family-related employee benefits is another option many are taking.

Such programs and benefits help both businesses and employees. Businesses are looking for new ways to increase productivity and cut costs. Hiring and training new, less-skilled workers can be costly for them. Not only do employers want to keep skilled employees, they want to increase employee morale. If employees are

Across the Curriculum
History. Discuss how families balanced family life with work in the past. Include discussions on poor working conditions, child labor, and the evolution of unions in the United States.

satisfied with their jobs, they are often more productive and committed to their employer.

Flexible Work Arrangements

Employers are more willing to accommodate working parents by offering flexible work options. Such options provide more opportunities for working parents to be available to their children and other family members as needed.

Telecommuting is one option. In this type of arrangement, an employee works from an office set up at home, 7-9. The employee is connected to the office by electronic technology—a computer, modem, and telephone. Advances in technology, including fiber optics and satellites, have made this option possible. Companies are finding telecommuting makes good business sense. Work-at-home employees tend to work more hours, have better morale, and take fewer sick days.

Job sharing is another option growing in popularity. In **job sharing**, two people divide the work responsibilities of one job. Each person works on a part-time basis rather than full-time. This enables working mothers to remain in the workforce and still spend time with their children.

7-9 For employees seeking a flexible work schedule, telecommuting is a popular choice. In this arrangement, a computer in the home is linked with the company's main computer.

Flextime plans mean employees can set their own work schedule within certain terms. Some may choose to start later in the day to avoid heavy morning and evening traffic. Parents with school-age children can benefit from this plan, too. One parent can start work earlier and arrive home by the end of the school day. The other parent can start work later and be home to see the children off to school in the morning.

Core hours are observed by companies that allow flextime. The total workday may run from 7:00 A.M. through 7:00 P.M. All employees must be on hand during core hours. Core hours may be from 10:00 to 11:30 A.M. and from 1:30 to 3:30 P.M. Employees are free to schedule the remaining hours to their convenience. This plan allows flexibility for parents to arrange their work schedules around their children. Medical appointments, school visits, and even parent volunteer hours at school can be easily arranged around core hours.

Flexible workweeks are in use at some companies. Some employees are now moving to four-day, 40-hour workweeks. They work a 10-hour workday rather than a traditional eight-hour workday.

Employee Benefits That Help Families

Employee benefits provided by the employer are known as fringe benefits. Fringe benefits are regarded as hidden pay. Life and health insurance, profit-sharing plans, and paid vacations are traditional fringe benefits offered by employers. On-site child care and parent education seminars are popular, family-oriented fringe benefits. See 7-10. Some companies provide college scholarships for children of their employees. Fringe benefits may even include family discounts for club memberships or amusement park tickets.

Tailored paychecks allow employees to plan benefits that meet their own wants and needs. A married employee or parent might need and want different benefits from those wanted by a single employee. The stage in the family life cycle also affects the type of benefits chosen.

> **Discuss:**
> What are the advantages and disadvantages of each of the flexible work arrangements?
>
> **Activity:**
> Have students ask their parents if flexible work arrangements are available where they work. If so, find out how employees feel about these work options.
>
> **Reflect:**
> In your family, which flexible schedule would fit your needs?

 Putting Technology to Use
Have students use the Internet to research statistics on the percentage of companies that offer job sharing, flextime, and flexible workweeks.

Activity:
Form small groups. Compile a more complete list of possible employee benefits the McRaes and the Moengas would find beneficial.

7-10 Some employers offer child care assistance or on-site child care facilities as a benefit for their employees.

Check It Out!
1. Describe one effect of work on family life.
2. When both parents are employed outside the home, the family is called a _____-_____ family.
3. List four flexible work options offered by some employers that help employees balance work and family.

Check It Out! (Answers)
1. (Student response.)
2. dual-career
3. (List four:) telecommuting, job sharing, flextime, core hours, flexible workweeks

For example, the McRaes are a young, career-oriented couple with young children. They need cash to meet living expenses. They also need income protection for a spouse and children in the event of disability or death. A tailored paycheck plan would allow the McRaes to receive more cash and more income protection. These benefits are needed by their young and dependent family.

The Moengas have different needs as they approach retirement. At ages 55, they are eager to build their retirement income. Their children are living independently. A tailored paycheck would allow the parents to receive less cash and to contribute a larger sum to a retirement program.

Topic 7-3
Handling Family Crises

Objectives
After studying this topic, you will be able to
- describe the types of events that can lead to a crisis.
- describe skills and resources for handling family crises.
- summarize the effects of various types of crises on families.

Topic Terms
crisis
support system
physical neglect
emotional neglect
physical abuse
emotional abuse
sexual abuse
substance abuse
addiction
drug abuse
alcoholism
alcoholic
enabler
support group

As you have read, a family's life is filled with challenges. Some of these challenges are fairly routine and easily managed. Others are much more serious, affecting the whole family system.

Facing difficult challenges is not easy. However, difficult challenges can occur at any time in your life. That's why learning about these challenges and the changes that can result is important. This can help you prepare for and manage these events in your own life. Knowing what resources are available to help you deal with these challenges is also worthwhile.

What Is a Crisis?

At some point in their lives, most people face some type of crisis. A **crisis** is an event or experience that greatly influences people's lives. These events cause people to make difficult changes in their lifestyles. The greatest challenge of a crisis is knowing how to handle these changes.

A crisis affects families in different ways. That is, a crisis to one family may not be a crisis to another. How the family views the situation and adjusts to it determines the impact it will have. For example, an unexpected baby may be a crisis in one family, but a welcome addition for another. Moving to a new home may be an adventure for one family, but an extremely stressful adjustment for another. Loss of a job may mean a temporary loss of income for one family, but the stepping stone to a better job for another.

Characteristics of Crises

What types of events can lead to a family crisis? Crisis-producing events have certain traits that make it difficult for families to adjust to change. Four of these traits are described below.

- *A devastating event that causes a great loss for the entire family.* Property loss from a fire, a tornado, or an earthquake is an example. An automobile accident resulting in the disability or death of a family member or friend would be another example, 7-11.
- *A stressful event that affects the entire family.* For example, moving and adjusting to a new home would be stressful for the entire family. A long period of unemployment would have serious effects on all family members.
- *An event that requires major adjustments by family members.* A major change in the family structure, such as separation, divorce, or remarriage would affect the way a family functions.
- *An event that occurs suddenly or unexpectedly.* A sudden loss of income, sudden illness, or the death of a loved one can be difficult for family members to face.

Sometimes a crisis is not triggered by a single event. It may be caused by a series of stressful events that build up over a period of time. The family may not realize a crisis is building until it actually happens. For instance, the combination of ending a

Vocabulary:
Distinguish between emotional neglect and emotional abuse.

Activity:
Working in small groups, have students list and describe types of family crises.

Resource:
Put the Pieces Back Together, color transparency CT-5, TR

Across the Curriculum
Health. Have students research and write a report on the effects of substance abuse on the body.

> **Reflect:**
> Recall times when you have acted in an unusual manner because of stress build-up.
>
> **Resource:**
> *Skills for Coping with Crises*, transparency master, TR
>
> **Discuss:**
> How can you plan to handle a crisis before it happens? Is this the same as preventing a crisis?

7-11 A serious accident can be the devastating event that causes a family crisis.

relationship, moving to a new home, and starting a new job could lead to a crisis.

How does a crisis event affect the family? The entire family system is affected. This is because the whole family's ability to function normally is changed. Family members are unable to carry out their roles and responsibilities. They need to use coping skills to adjust to the changes that have taken place. These skills help return balance to their lives as quickly as possible.

Skills for Coping with Crises

Why do some families seem to cope well during a crisis, while others let it destroy their lives? Functional families face a variety of crisis situations; they cope well because they communicate and cooperate. They have the confidence to meet any challenge. They deal with a crisis in three ways. First, they join together as a family to face the crisis head-on. Second, they focus on a positive aspect of a problem situation. They react positively and try to make the best of the situation. Third, they make use of their support system.

A **support system** is a network of people and organizations family members can turn to during a crisis. The primary support comes from relatives, friends, neighbors, teachers, and coworkers. These are individuals a family can contact in an emergency. For instance, a neighbor might look after a child on a moment's notice if the parents are suddenly called away. A support system also includes public and private agencies that help families. These agencies may provide health care, child care, financial aid, or legal assistance. Professionals at these organizations are trained to provide assistance to families during a crisis.

Dysfunctional families are unable to deal with crises in healthy ways. Many are poor problem solvers. They become locked into one way of responding to family problems. Anger, violence, and alcohol abuse are common responses. Some of these responses create new crisis situations. Dysfunctional families often depend on other people to rescue them from crises.

A crisis event cannot be ignored—it requires some type of response. A family who uses coping skills learns to handle these challenges. Learning how to handle change and unexpected events when they occur is the key to surviving any crisis. Families can use various resources to help them pull through difficult situations. One resource is developing effective coping skills. A number of techniques may be helpful.

- ■ *Plan how to handle a crisis before it happens.* To be prepared for change, families need to anticipate how to handle crises. As a family, they can plan how they would handle certain crisis situations. This helps the family in two ways. First, they can plan strategies that might help when the unexpected happens. Second, it prompts them to do as much as possible to prevent the problems from occurring.

Putting Technology to Use

Have students use drawing software to make a chart showing the organization of their support systems. Students should indicate themselves in the middle of the chart with primary support close around them. Other means of support can be placed farther away from the student.

- *Have clearly defined family goals.* This technique helps the family remain focused when emergencies arise. For example, the Browns have four family goals. They are to communicate openly, respect and support each other, deal fairly with problems, and get the best education possible. A major job transfer will not impact on this family heavily; they can meet these goals in many different settings. However, having a child flunk out of college might be a major upset for them, since they value education. How would they handle this crisis? They would discuss it, respect and support the child, and perhaps encourage the child to find other educational opportunities. The Brown's family goals helped them solve their problem in a sensible way.
- *Maintain family unity.* In a crisis situation, family members need to band together, get involved, and help out. Families that are supportive of each other have stronger emotional ties. They are better able to survive difficult times. Once they begin working together to solve a problem, they are likely to stay unified.
- *Build on previous successes.* Families should use whatever techniques worked best for them in the past to help them through a crisis. For instance, if relatives or friends offered emotional support in the past, families should seek their help again. See 7-12.
- *Maintain feelings of affection.* Feelings of affection among family members are especially important during difficult times. Although each family has its own way of expressing affection, an extra effort by each member can be helpful.
- *Place family needs before personal needs.* During a crisis, some family members may want to put their personal plans on hold. This is especially important if those plans would place additional stress on the family. For instance, a family member might delay moving out or buying a car until the crisis has passed.

Reflect:
What are your family's goals?

Enrich:
Set up a display table in the classroom to exhibit children's books on coping with crises. Ask students to bring books to supplement the available library books.

Discuss:
Is it easy to put the needs of your family before your own needs? Give examples of instances when this might be important.

7-12 Emotional support from friends can help teens work through a crisis.

Putting Technology to Use
Have students use word processing software to make pamphlets about coping with family crises. Have students pass the pamphlets out to the rest of the school.

> **Enrich:**
> Many movies portray family crises. Select a suitable current release and discuss the causes, effects, supports, and solutions.
>
> **Activity:**
> Collect or design bumper stickers with abuse or neglect messages.
>
> **Note:**
> Husbands can also be victims of abuse.

- *Find ways to get help with family responsibilities.* Working together to share decision making and other family responsibilities is important. However, if extra help is needed, let others who have offered to help do so. Call on people in your support system.
- *Seek help for problems.* Some problems cannot be resolved within the family or seem too large to handle. In these cases, a family should not be afraid to seek outside help. Families also should know many resources are available to help them. Knowing what help is available, where to find it, and how to ask for it are important coping skills.

Where can a family seek help? Friends, relatives, and neighbors can provide emotional support or emergency assistance. Professional help can be found through local community services and government agencies. It is important to develop a support system of groups and individuals to whom you can turn for help.

Types of Crises

All families face different types of crises. Some of these—family violence, substance abuse, and death—are more difficult to face and manage than others. Learning more about each type can help families cope if one occurs.

Unemployment

A family's financial situation can change suddenly if a main provider becomes unemployed. This can happen for a number of reasons, many of which the individual has little control over. For example, a company may have to downsize and eliminate jobs if the economy declines. Sometimes, a serious health problem can force an individual into unemployment. Whatever the reason, unemployment drastically changes the income level of the family, and that can lead to a crisis. If a new job cannot be found right away, bills may not be paid. The family may find it harder to buy essentials such as food.

While a new job is sought, communication and cooperation among family members can help. With communication, the family can decide which wants and needs they can forego. The unemployed person could provide services that the family might otherwise hire others to do, such as child care, laundry, or lawn care. Teens might find part-time jobs. Families who band together and support each other can usually find ways to work through the crisis.

Family Violence

In some dysfunctional families, poor family relationships can lead to violence within the family. A family member may resort to violence as a way of expressing anger or resolving conflicts. Unfortunately, this behavior often becomes a pattern that is repeated over and over again.

Types of Family Violence

Family violence may take several different forms. One form of family violence is *neglect*. Neglect is a less violent, but serious form of abuse. It threatens the physical and mental well-being of family members. Neglect occurs when the needs of family members are not met. Not providing proper food, clothing, shelter, medical care, and parental supervision are forms of **physical neglect**.

Another form of neglect is emotional neglect. **Emotional neglect** is the failure to provide loving care and attention. A neglected family member who receives no signs of affection may grow to feel unloved and unlovable.

Abuse is the most damaging form of family violence. There are different forms of abuse. **Physical abuse** happens when one family member physically injures another family member. Abusive behavior includes hitting, kicking, biting, or throwing objects. This form of abuse often causes serious injury, or sometimes death.

Emotional abuse happens when one family member purposely damages another member's self-concept. It destroys the abused person's self-esteem and makes the person feel worthless. This happens when

Across the Curriculum
Health. Have students research instances where children who were neglected emotionally developed physical health problems. What is the link between mental/emotional health and physical health?

the abuser constantly yells, teases, or insults the abused. It can also occur in parent-child relationships when parents have unrealistic expectations of a child. They expect the child to perform tasks that the child cannot do. Then they blame and punish the child for failing.

Sexual abuse in families occurs when one family member forces another family member to engage in sexual activities. One type of sexual abuse is *incest*. This is sexual activity between people who are closely related, such as between a father and a daughter.

Acts of physical violence within a family can occur among all family members. Children and wives are the most frequent victims. Children may be physically or emotionally abused by one or both parents. Husbands may batter wives causing serious physical injuries. Sometimes children are the abusers rather than the victims. Adolescent children may assault their parents when something they want is withheld from them. Siblings may attack each other to settle an issue.

Why Family Violence Occurs

Why does family violence happen? The reasons vary. Abusive family members often have low self-esteem. They may feel unloved by other family members. Some adults may have been abused as children, so they have not learned to express their emotions properly. The abuser cannot deal with his or her emotions through acceptable behavior, so he or she becomes aggressive.

In families where physical violence is common behavior, the children may adopt the same type of behavior. Unemployment, financial problems, marital problems, job pressures, substance abuse, or illness are also contributing factors.

Where to Get Help

With help, neglect and abuse can be prevented. Various programs, facilities, and support groups are available to help families break out of the cycle of family violence.

Many types of programs are available in local communities. Community service organizations are listed in the Yellow Pages of local phone books. Look under the heading "Social Service Organizations." Information about individual and group counseling services is also available from local mental health associations. Government programs and services are listed under the local county name in the phone book. Emergency shelters are located across the country for providing temporary housing to abused women and their children.

Parents Anonymous is a self-help group that helps abusive parents and abused children. Most cities have chapters of this national organization.

If you know parents who are experiencing a great deal of stress, you can help. First, offer your friendship. Individuals who abuse or neglect their children often feel unloved themselves. Another way to help is to offer to babysit for them. Urge them to get out of the house—to go places and to do things.

There may be times when you must protect abused children. This may mean reporting the abuse and neglect of parents to a social service agency. Most agencies have special counselors to help parents and their children when cases are reported. Reporting is the key to such service. Counselors cannot help a family unless the situation is brought to their attention by a report.

Substance Abuse

One of the most serious crises affecting families involves substance abuse. **Substance abuse** is the use of illegal drugs or the misuse of legal drugs such as alcohol. The misuse of a substance, such as alcohol, can lead to physical and psychological addiction. An **addiction** is a dependence of the body on a continuing supply of the drug. After an addiction has developed, taking the drug away will cause agonizing withdrawal symptoms. When one family member becomes addicted, the entire family is affected.

Drug abuse is the use of a legal or illegal drug for a purpose other than its intended use. Illegal drugs include heroin,

Resource:
Family Crises Pyramid, Activity C, SAG

Activity:
Compose one-minute public service announcements that inform listeners about available social services.

Resource:
Curbing Emotional Abuse, reproducible master, TR

Citizenship and Service
Ask students to identify services available to families in your community. Have them compile their findings into a directory. Make directories available through the chamber of commerce and/or real estate agencies for new families moving into the community.

> **Enrich:**
> Have students debate the difference between someone who wants to help an addict and an enabler.
>
> **Discuss:**
> Why must the user be able to admit he or she needs help before anyone can provide help?
>
> **Activity:**
> Have students look up support groups such as AA on the Internet.

cocaine, and marijuana. Legal drugs, such as over-the-counter medications and prescriptions, can be abused as well.

An addiction to alcohol is called **alcoholism**. Like diabetes or cancer, alcoholism is a type of disease. A person who suffers from this disease is an **alcoholic**.

People become addicted to alcohol and other drugs for many different reasons. In response to the drug or alcohol, some may feel more relaxed. Some use it to deal with or overcome problems, such as job-related stress or family problems. However, addiction can trigger other stressful problems, such as losing a job. This added stress can cause the addict to drink or abuse drugs even more, which may lead to another more serious crisis.

Substance abuse seriously affects all family members. The spouse and children of an addict may have a hard time accepting the problem. They may blame themselves for the problem. As a result, they may avoid seeking help because they are too ashamed or embarrassed. A spouse may deny his or her mate is an alcoholic or drug user. Younger children may not understand an alcoholic parent's behavior. Teens may try to hide the problem from others, or avoid spending time at home. Because of their problems at home, children's schoolwork may suffer, 7-13.

Codependency often occurs in families of addicts as family members try to find ways to survive the crisis. A family member may become an **enabler**—someone who unknowingly acts in ways that contribute to an addict's drug use. The enabler wants to help the alcoholic or drug addict with his or her problem. In so doing, they make the problem worse by denying that a problem exists. Enablers cover up for the behavior of the addict, allowing the addict's behavior to manipulate their own. They may lie for the addict or give excuses for the addict's actions. They unknowingly perpetuate the addiction.

To help an alcoholic or drug addict, family members should seek assistance from outside sources. Learning about the

7-13 Because of problems they are experiencing at home, some teens may find it hard to concentrate on schoolwork.

disease, talking about it, and learning coping skills can help family members handle the crisis. They may need professional help to identify any codependency behaviors.

Overcoming alcoholism or drug addiction is not easy, but it can be done. However, the user must make the decision to stop. They must first admit they have a problem and need help before anyone can help them. During the recovery period, an alcoholic or drug addict needs strong family support combined with professional help to overcome the illness.

Where to Get Help

Professional help is available from many local sources. Treatment and prevention services are available through community hospitals and health centers, family service agencies, and the National Council on Alcoholism (NCA). For more information, look in the Yellow Pages of the phone book under "Alcoholism Information and

Problem-Solving Practice
Helping Family Members Deal with Loss, reproducible master, TR. Using given examples, students are to use the problem-solving process to determine how a family might help family members deal with loss.

Treatment" or "Drug Abuse Information and Treatment."

Alcoholics Anonymous (AA) is a nationwide support group for alcoholics. *Narcotics Anonymous (NA)* is a support group for drug addicts who want to recover from their addiction. A **support group** is a group of people who share a similar problem or concern. The goal of AA and NA is to help alcoholics and drug addicts help themselves to recovery. Help for family and friends of alcoholics is available through *Al-Anon*. Teen children of alcoholic parents can seek support by joining *Alateen. Nar-Anon* is for family members and friends of drug addicts.

By seeking out a support group, people find other individuals who are experiencing a similar crisis. Members of the support group come together to discuss common concerns, problems, and issues. People benefit from support groups by learning they are not the only ones with certain problems. They are able to talk with others who truly understand their situations. They share helpful information and resources while they listen and learn from each other.

Serious Illness or Accidents

A serious illness or accident can be a crisis for a family. The emotional drain of watching a loved one suffer or the anxiety felt when awaiting the outcome of an operation can be stressful for family members. Even the physical care of the patient at home can take a huge toll on the care provider—both physically and emotionally. The high costs of medical care can be a significant drain on a family especially if the income provider is the one who is sick or injured.

Support groups may be a source of strength for the family during this type of crisis. Learning more about a certain illness from other people who have had family members with this illness can be very beneficial. Spiritual ties help some families. The support of friends and relatives becomes even more important.

Death

Death is another crisis that all families face. Although death is as much a part of the family life cycle as birth, dealing with the loss can be difficult. However, families must learn to accept death as a reality of life.

When a loved one dies, family members often experience a variety of emotions. Feelings of sadness, anger, and guilt are common. Such feelings are normal responses to a loss and are part of the grieving process. They may feel sadness because they miss the person. Some may feel angry that the person died and left them behind. Others may feel guilty about unfinished business, such as owing an apology or saying "I love you."

Accepting the reality of the loss can be hard. However, acceptance is an important part of adjusting to the loss. Then family members can take action to handle those feelings and get on with their lives. Although time will help ease the pain, family members can take other steps to work through their grief. They can

- accept the support of friends, relatives, and other people around them.
- talk about their feelings of sadness. They should not be ashamed to cry if they feel sad.
- recall the happy memories they shared with the deceased person with other family members and friends.

Check It Out!
1. List four traits of crisis events.
2. List eight coping skills that can help families survive a crisis.
3. Explain how alcoholism affects all family members.
4. List three steps family members can take to work through grief.

Enrich: Ask a speaker from Alcoholics Anonymous or Al-Anon to address the class. Students should prepare questions in advance to ask the speaker.

Activity: Review a book about coping with death. Would this book be helpful to a person coping with such a loss?

Check It Out! (Answers)
1. (List four:) a devastating event that causes a great loss for the entire family; a stressful event that affects the entire family; an event that requires major adjustments by family members; an event that occurs suddenly or unexpectedly.
2. (List eight:) Plan how to handle the crisis before it happens; have clearly defined family goals; maintain family unity; build on previous successes; maintain feelings of affection; place family needs before personal needs; find ways to get help with family responsibilities; seek help for problems.
3. (Student response.)
4. (List three:) accept the support of others, talk about their feelings of sadness, and recall the happy memories shared with the person

Activity:
Before students read this feature, ask them to write their answers to some of the questions posed to Dr. Baldwin. Then have them compare their answers to his when they read the feature. You might ask them the following questions from the interview:
- What problems are commonly seen in relationships between parents and teens?
- What are the most common causes of teen-parent problems?
- How can parents and teens resolve problems that occur?

Discuss:
Ask students to react to the following statement from the feature that indicates how self-esteem is often linked to possessions: "You are only as good as the possessions you own." What kinds of problems does this belief cause for some teens and their parents?

TEENS ARE CONCERNED ABOUT...

Relationships with Their Parents

Professionals, such as Bruce A. Baldwin, Ph.D., are trying to help teens with this issue. Baldwin combines two areas of expertise in responding to teens' concerns about relationships with their parents. Having raised two teenagers, he believes he knows his audience. As a practicing psychologist, he believes he knows his subject matter.

A well-known speaker and author, Baldwin is also nationally known for his seminars. He travels extensively throughout the United States promoting those qualities he considers important to family life. He has written three books relating to family-life issues.

Q: *What problems are commonly seen in relationships between parents and teens?*

A: There are two kinds of problems. First, there are basic separation issues. Teens are growing up and striving to be independent. Parents must adjust to this stage of development. Second, there are contemporary issues—drugs, sex, and the age in which we live. As teens strive for independence, they will try things—experiment. This is difficult for parents because the consequences can be disastrous. For example, experimentation with sex can result in pregnancies or sexually transmitted diseases—including AIDS. This frightens parents. The problem is magnified because parents are busier and have less time for parenting.

Q: *What are the most common causes of teen-parent problems?*

A: Less time for parents to be parents. For many parents, the economy necessitates two careers. Working parents have less time for their children and for themselves. Single parents are further challenged by trying to perform the role of two parents.

Television—through advertising—also instills certain expectations in today's teens. Because they see a product on TV, they expect to have it. Both teens and adults experience problems when self-esteem is linked to possessions. The message is: "You are only as good as the possessions you own." This attitude forces a lot of spending. People get into trouble trying to keep up with this superficial standard they establish for themselves.

There is also a breakdown in the community. Communities are larger. People may not even know each other. Social institutions—such as schools, churches, and even police departments—are larger now. They cannot help as they did in previous times. The officer on the beat may not personally know teens and their parents anymore. In the past, kids might have received a verbal reprimand because the officer knew them. The officer might have taken them back home because the parents were known. Without this level of recognition, teens today may be arrested for offenses that might have merited a severe scolding in earlier times.

These days, parents don't communicate much with other parents. It is especially difficult in metropolitan areas. As a father, I admit that I was quick to call parents of my teens' friends when I suspected something was going on. However, that doesn't happen much anymore. It takes extra effort and time to communicate within families, and we just don't take time to communicate with others.

Q: *How can parents and teens resolve problems that occur?*

A: That depends upon the kind of problems. Parents have to change the way they relate to teens versus the way they related when the children were younger. If there are serious problems, parents may have to take an active role, step in, and mandate better behavior. For example, drug use is a serious problem that requires a strong parental stand.

Preferably, parents and teens could sit down and talk about the problem together. Parents need to help teens understand the situation, recognize choices available, and choose an acceptable option. Parents need to shift into the role of a resource person as much as possible. Teens learn more as they make choices and assume responsibility for the choices they make. Sometimes they make mistakes, but teens learn from mistakes. If the consequences of a mistake are serious, however, parents may still need to impose solutions (which teens may not like).

Q: *Do you have any specific messages you would like to share with teens and parents?*

A: I have several messages I would like to share with teens and parents:

- Many teens feel insecure. They need consistent positive feedback and support. It is easy for a parent to become critical. A wise parent sees what a teenager needs. Perceptive parents can see through their teenager's facade and give that young person what is needed. Teens fight limits, but they need limits. Good discipline is also important. Parents need to set limits so everyone knows what is and what is not acceptable. Teens fight hugs, but they need hugs. Wise parents set limits and give hugs anyway.
- Parents need to be reminded that teens are delightful. The teen years are important years—precious years that are important in many ways. They end too soon and need to be enjoyed while they last.
- It is really important for families to be families. Keep family life as a priority. Family members may be home, but they aren't together. They don't eat together or talk together. Home base is disappearing—this has a long-term and destructive effect on teens later in life.

Q: *If teens and parents would like to improve the quality of their family life, what advice would you offer to them?*

A: My advice to teens is to:

- Communicate and plan time to be with your family. Tell parents what you would like. Say, "This is what I need." Say, "I need positive feedback," or "We need to go fishing or go to school games together."

To parents, I would say:

- You may need to lower your standards. Don't expect perfection from your teenager. Adolescents are in a state of transition and still learning. They are not children any longer, but they are not yet adults, either.
- Finally, remember that a family's standard of living does not equate to quality of life. Material possessions beyond basic needs will never replace the quality of family life that is forfeited to acquire them. Person-to-person communication is a far more important message than that sent by a certain brand name product. Time spent with the family is more important than time spent watching another family on TV. That means turning the TV off and turning the family on.

> **Discuss:**
> Have students discuss the impact television has had on family relationships, such as the effects of advertising on the desire for possessions and the time spent watching TV rather than communicating with each other.

> **Discuss:**
> Ask students to agree or disagree with the following: "Teens fight limits, but they need limits…Teens fight hugs, but they need hugs. Wise parents set limits and give hugs anyway."

Chapter Review

Summary

Making and keeping the family strong and healthy is a challenge faced by all families. Functional families don't just happen—family members must work together to achieve this goal. They are committed to communicating with each other, solving problems, showing appreciation, understanding each other, and sharing with each other.

Families face many different types of challenges. Balancing work and family roles and responsibilities is a continuing challenge, especially for dual-career families and single parents. For these families, good management and relationship skills are the keys to balancing their busy lives. To accommodate working parents' needs, more employers are offering flexible work schedules and employee benefits.

Of all the challenges families face, crises are the most difficult. The key to surviving a crisis is learning coping skills. Coping skills help families handle the changes a crisis causes. However, some types of crises, such as family violence, substance abuse, and death, are much more difficult to handle. Knowing how to cope and where to get help can help families work through these situations.

Think About It!

1. Do you think it's important for families to build strong, healthy relationships? Explain why or why not.
2. Evaluate how your parents balance their work and family roles. What types of problems do they encounter in trying to balance these roles? Why do you think it's important for them to balance these roles? What steps can you take to help them manage family responsibilities?
3. Functional families tend to cope better with crisis situations. Why do you think these families cope better with crises than others? What steps can a family take to prepare for a crisis?
4. Think of a crisis situation you have experienced in your family. How did you cope with the situation? How did other family members handle the situation? If the same crisis happened again, how would you handle it?
5. Suppose a friend confides in you that he or she suspects the children he or she babysits are being abused. What advice would you give to your friend about this situation?

Try It Out!

1. Review the qualities of functional families in Topic 7-1. For each quality, suggest one activity teens could do at home to help strengthen their families. Then develop a poster based on your suggestions titled: "Ways to Strengthen Your Family."
2. Contact the personnel departments of several businesses in your local area. Determine what policies or programs these employers are offering to help workers balance work and family responsibilities. Which employee

---

Activity: Have students interview their parents about *Think About It!* #2 and write papers summarizing their comments.

Note: For *Think About It!* #4, if students cannot recall crises in their families, have them read newspaper or magazine articles describing crises events other families have had to deal with. Have them write papers answering these questions from the information provided in the articles.

Resource: *PowerZone Challenge CD.* Have students play the chapter review game to reinforce text content.

benefits are most popular? As a class, evaluate whether or not employers are meeting the needs of families in your area. What other types of family benefits do you think would be helpful for them to offer employees?

3. Survey several dual-career families to determine how they manage their work and family responsibilities. Summarize your results in a report to the class.

4. Research a family crisis that you have heard or read about recently. Write a report about your findings. Include information about possible causes, the effect on family members, coping skills, and where to get help.

5. As a class, develop a list of resources that are available in your community to help families with crises. Use your local phone book to compile the list of social service agencies, organizations, and services available. Develop a master list that can be made available to students in your school.

6. Invite a panel of professionals from various social service agencies to discuss their careers. What type of education and training is needed in this career area? What do they consider most satisfying about their careers? What do they consider least satisfying about their careers?

7. Interview a social services counselor to determine how that agency provides help for families in crisis.

8. Research resources available on the Internet that can help families during a crisis. Prepare a report to share with the class.

CAREER TIMES

LEADING GUIDE TO THE WORLD OF WORK

VOLUME 1, NUMBER 2

Homing in on Family and Community Services Careers

People in family and community services help improve the welfare of the community. They work to create a better quality of life for individuals and families.

Employment Opportunities

People in the family and community service field may work for health care or social service agencies. Some people in this field work for schools, businesses, or government agencies. These professionals may have a broad knowledge of family and community services. However, many workers focus on an area such as family studies or youth services.

Entrepreneurial Opportunities

People with a desire to be self-employed in this area have a number of options. For instance, many counselors are in private practice. Some work with individuals in certain age groups, such as teens or older adults. Others counsel couples or families. A lobbyist for family and community issues is another worker in this field who may be self-employed.

Rewards and Demands of Family and Community Services Careers

People who work in family and community services find it rewarding to touch the lives of others in positive ways. These workers enjoy seeing members of healthy families work toward common goals. The workers also feel fulfilled when they help troubled people find ways to deal with their problems.

Some jobs in family and community services can emotionally drain the workers who do them. For instance, many workers find it stressful to work with clients who are in physical or emotional pain. Workers may have to put in long hours and work evenings to meet the needs of their clients. This type of schedule can place a strain on a worker's personal life.

Preparation Requirements

People can start preparing for family and community services careers when they are in high school. The type of training needed depends on the kind of work a person wants to do. Preparation also depends on the needs of the people a worker will serve. Taking classes to prepare for college is a good start.

Some workers in the family and community services field specialize in assisting older adults.

Courses in business and psychology may also prove helpful. Taking part in the school's chapter of Family, Career and Community Leaders of America (FCCLA) can help build leadership skills.

Entry-Level Jobs

Most entry-level jobs in family and community services require little formal training. For instance, a child care aide or a camp counselor is likely to receive on-the-job training. Workers in entry-level jobs may also attend some training workshops.

Mid-Level Jobs

People working in mid-level careers need some training beyond high school. Someone working as a home companion may have been trained in a vocational school. A caseworker's aide might be expected to have a two-year degree. An associate's degree in human services technology would prepare a worker for a job at this level.

Professional-Level Jobs

Family and community services jobs at the professional level require at least a four-year degree. A family and consumer sciences teacher has at least an undergraduate degree. An extension agent and a director of social services will also have four-year degrees. A counselor, such as a substance abuse counselor, has an advanced degree. Degrees for jobs at this level might be in such programs as social work, youth services, and family studies.

Personal Qualities Needed for Success

An ability to understand human nature will help people succeed in this career area. Workers need a true concern for people and their problems. Counselors and social workers must be able to communicate with and relate to clients. These professionals must respect the need to keep all client records confidential. Those in leadership roles need skill in guiding people and managing resources. All workers in this field will benefit from a desire to be life-long learners. Being able to use good judgment and be objective and flexible will also help workers succeed in this field.

Future Trends

The number of jobs in the field of family and community services is expected to increase. Some jobs will be in the area of research. The impact of technology on the family and the effect of television violence on children are current topics of study. Services for older adults will be in greater demand as the population ages. A larger number of immigrants will increase the need for workers who can speak more than one language. Employment counselors will be in demand to help people who are looking for jobs. In many of these careers, the pay will remain low for the level of responsibility.

Career Interests, Abilities, and You

You need to assess your skills, interests, and abilities. This will help you find out if a career in family and community services is for you. Taking a family and consumer sciences course in family relations might help you decide. Shadowing an extension agent or a social worker will give you an idea of what the job involves. Volunteer work can also help you assess your interest in helping others. Offer your services to the Salvation Army or the Red Cross. Work with these organizations can tell you much about your career interests.

Career Ladder for Family and Community Services
Advanced Degree
Alcohol and drug abuse counselor
Family therapist
Social welfare administrator
Bachelor's Degree
Extension agent
Rehabilitation counselor
Social worker
Associate's Degree
Coordinator of volunteer services
Counseling paraprofessional
Lobbyist
High School Diploma
Caseworker's aide
Geriatric aide
Pre-High School Diploma
Volunteer in family- and community-related agencies

A social worker may serve as an advocate for people with disabilities.

Part Three
Caring for Children

Chapter 8
Preparing for Children

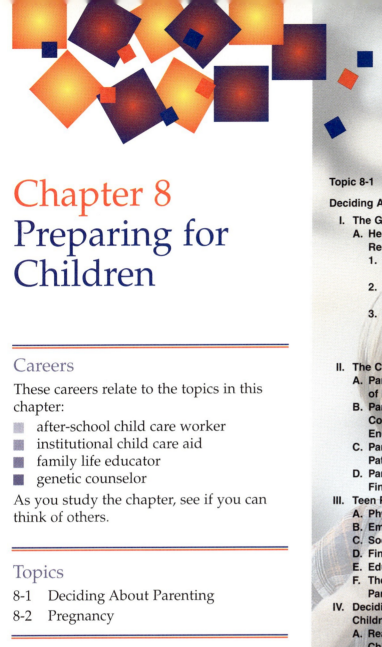

Careers

These careers relate to the topics in this chapter:

- after-school child care worker
- institutional child care aid
- family life educator
- genetic counselor

As you study the chapter, see if you can think of others.

Topics

8-1 Deciding About Parenting
8-2 Pregnancy

Introductory Activities

1. Collect a series of cartoons related to parenting. Reproduce them on a transparency. Discuss the meaning of each and encourage class members to agree or disagree with the situations depicted.
2. Read students a list of typical parenting activities, such as changing diapers, driving kids to meetings, and attending school plays. Ask students to indicate which activities they would consider pleasures and which they would consider drudgery. Tabulate and compare results of class members for discussion.

Topic 8-1
Deciding About Parenting

I. The Goal of Parenting
   A. Helping Children Grow Up Responsibly
      1. Teaching Personal Priorities and Standards
      2. Letting Children Learn Through New Experiences
      3. Recognizing the Importance of Other People in Children's Lives
II. The Challenges of Parenting
   A. Parenting Is an Expression of Love
   B. Parenting Involves Commitments of Time and Energy
   C. Parenting Requires Patience
   D. Parenting Involves a Major Financial Commitment
III. Teen Parenting
   A. Physical Risks
   B. Emotional Challenges
   C. Social Challenges
   D. Financial Challenges
   E. Education and Career
   F. The Children of Teen Parents
IV. Deciding Whether to Have Children
   A. Reasons for Having Children
   B. Reasons for Not Having Children
   C. Other Factors Affecting Parenthood Decisions
V. Family Planning
VI. Infertility
VII. Adoption
   A. Agency Adoptions
   B. Independent Adoptions

Topic 8-2
Pregnancy

I. Prenatal Development
   A. The Germinal Period
   B. The Embryonic Period
   C. The Fetal Period
II. Heredity
   A. Congenital Disabilities
      1. Age of the Mother
   B. Genetic Counseling
   C. Prenatal Testing
III. Medical Care During Pregnancy
   A. Signs of Pregnancy
   B. Seeing a Physician
   C. Guidelines for Good Health

Discuss:
Do you agree that couples should try to learn more about children before becoming parents, or do most people already know enough?

Activity:
Make a list of resources available to couples to help them learn more about children.

Discuss:
What might happen to a child who grows up in a family where the parents do not have firmly established personal priorities and standards?

Resource:
Teaching Children Personal Priorities, reproducible master, TR

Topic 8-1
Deciding About Parenting

Objectives
After studying this topic, you will be able to
- state the goal of parenthood.
- describe the challenges of parenthood.
- recognize the challenges faced by teen parents.
- analyze the factors that influence parenthood decisions.
- explain the types of adoption.

Topic Terms
parenting
infertility
adoption
agency adoption
independent adoption
closed adoption
open adoption

Parenting is the name given to the process of raising a child. It includes all of the love, care, and guidance given by parents in this process. Parenting begins with the birth or adoption of a child and lasts a lifetime. Even if the marriage breaks apart, parents are still the parents of their child.

Before committing themselves to parenting, people should have a full understanding of the demands and rewards of this important role. Any goal started without knowledge and planning has little chance for success. Likewise, people who begin parenting without knowledge and planning may fall short of their parenting goals.

The Goal of Parenting

The primary goal of parenting is to help children grow and become mature, independent individuals who can make their own decisions and accept responsibility for their actions. In simpler words, it might be stated in this way: The goal of parenting is to help children grow up responsibly.

There is no step-by-step recipe you can follow to reach this goal of parenting. Each child is unique, and each situation is unique. The best way to prepare yourself for parenthood is to learn as much as possible about children. The more knowledge you have, the better able you will be to handle any situation that occurs.

Helping Children Grow Up Responsibly

Helping children grow up responsibly is not always easy. One of the most important—and most difficult—tasks for parents is to teach their children personal priorities and standards. Another difficult task is to allow children to learn through new experiences. Parents also need to help their children learn to interact with other people.

Teaching Personal Priorities and Standards

To teach children how to evaluate the importance of something, parents first must have firmly established personal priorities and standards of their own. They must be living a lifestyle that reflects their beliefs. Then their children will be able to follow their examples and adopt similar personal priorities and standards. See 8-1.

Letting Children Learn Through New Experiences

Parents have a strong urge to cushion the path for their children. They should realize, however, that their help may actually hinder their children's development. Whenever possible, a child who demands, "Let me do it myself," should be allowed to try. The child may not do the job perfectly, but perfection is not always necessary. Having the child learn to do it may be more important than having it done perfectly.

Recognizing the Importance of Other People in Children's Lives

This is an important factor in helping children grow up responsibly. Babies are happy to be completely dependent on their parents. As children mature, however, they want and need to meet many different people. Parents with a healthy attitude about their children recognize this as a

Putting Technology to Use
To introduce the topic of parenting, ask your students to use charting software to make a three-column chart. In the first column, ask them to list some of the joys of parenting. In the second column, ask them to list the responsibilities parenting brings. In the third column, have them list some of the challenges parents face. Have students share and compare their lists in class.

8-1 These children are learning the importance of family mealtimes shared together.

positive mark of growth. Parents with a less healthy attitude may feel jealous about the loss of their children's attention.

The Challenges of Parenting

Being a parent involves commitments of love, time, energy, patience, and money. Most people gladly accept these commitments in order to have the rewards of parenthood, 8-2. They look forward to rocking a baby to sleep and to watching their children play. They want to take pride in the accomplishments of their children. When the children reach adulthood, their parents look forward to the companionship they will all share.

Parenting Is an Expression of Love

For many couples, having a child is a way of fulfilling the deep love they have for one another. After the child is born,

8-2 Both father and mother play important roles in the development of their children.

Putting Technology to Use

Have students interview parents about what they consider to be challenges of parenthood. In class, brainstorm questions students might ask and have students use word processing software to create an interview planning sheet.

Resource:
The Challenges of Parenthood, transparency master, TR

> **Reflect:**
> Have you ever taken care of a baby that kept crying? How did you feel? Imagine taking care of a crying baby for an entire day and night.
>
> **Enrich:**
> Research the cost of raising a child from birth to the age of 18.
>
> **Enrich:**
> Invite teen parents to class to talk about the rewards and challenges of teen parenting.

creating an atmosphere of love and acceptance is important to the child's emotional development. Parents need to show their love and affection to one another and to their child. A climate of love in the home lays the foundation for self-esteem and trust.

Parenting Involves Commitments of Time and Energy

Babies have to be fed, bathed, and clothed. Their cries have to be answered, even in the middle of the night. Sometimes the tasks involved in caring for a child seem endless, and parents become discouraged. One young parent said, "All my life, I wanted my own little baby. I needed to love and take care of someone, but I didn't have a realistic view of parenthood. I thought only about the good points. Now I sometimes feel guilty. I get so tired that I honestly cannot enjoy caring for my baby as I always thought I would."

Parenting Requires Patience

One frustration of parenthood is the hundreds of questions that children ask. One young couple decided to take their child to a playground. They expected to relax and talk while their child played. Instead of going off to play, the child sat at their feet and began asking questions. Some of the questions seemed silly to the parents. In cases like this, however, parents must remind themselves that this type of behavior is normal for young children. They must try to avoid becoming impatient.

Parenting Involves a Major Financial Commitment

The costs of having and rearing a child are increasing. The costs for clothing, furniture, and toys the child will need add up quickly. As children grow, their financial needs increase. Housing, food, transportation, medical care, and recreation become major expenses, 8-3. Education costs can be great if private schools are chosen, or if the child wishes to pursue a college degree.

8-3 For parents, expenses for instruments and lessons for their children must be considered.

An additional financial consideration is the loss of one spouse's income. This can happen if one of the parents gives up a job to stay home and care for the child. If both parents continue to work, child care will be an expense. It is important for couples to consider how they will meet these financial commitments.

Teen Parenting

Parenting in the teen years presents many challenges for young couples. Few teenage parents are aware of the time, energy, and money required to rear a child. Many are not prepared to face the physical, emotional, social, and financial challenges of parenthood.

Physical Risks

Teenage mothers face several health risks during pregnancy. A lack of medical care or poor nutrition during pregnancy

Across the Curriculum
Health. Discuss the health risks involved in teenage pregnancy.

puts both mother and child at risk. Pregnancy-related illnesses and complications are also more common for teen mothers. Because their own bodies may still be developing, they have higher risks of having premature, low-birthweight babies. The infant death rate is also higher for teen mothers than for mothers in their twenties. As research shows, a mother's age does make a difference in pregnancy. The best childbearing years for women are from ages 20 through 32.

Emotional Challenges

Teen parenthood will affect the young parents emotionally. Many teenage marriages occur because the young woman becomes pregnant. Because of emotional and financial pressures, these marriages have a fairly high divorce rate. The addition of a child adds even more pressures. Young couples, who are still growing up themselves, are often unable to deal with all the pressures they face.

Teen parents must cope with sudden changes in their roles from adolescents to parents. This often causes more emotional stress. They are faced with the challenge of growing up overnight to assume adult roles as parents. Their own parent-child roles are often conflicting. They are parents to their babies while they remain children of their own parents.

One teen mother said it this way. "The baby is mine when she needs care. No one babysits so I can go out on weekends. I have to stay home and do that. When decisions that affect the welfare of my baby must be made, my mother makes them. I need her help very much, but I do feel resentful when she acts like my baby is really her baby."

Social Challenges

The arrival of a baby greatly hinders teen parents' social life. Working and child-care responsibilities mean they are less likely to experience a normal social life with friends their age. Their opportunities to socialize with their friends are limited. They see their friends have more freedom and fewer responsibilities. This sometimes creates feelings of frustration and even anger.

Financial Challenges

Teen parents face many financial difficulties as they enter the adult world. Many lack stable financial resources, such as secure jobs. In trying to meet expenses, they are more likely to drop out of school and have low-paying jobs. Many also lack the skills and training needed to advance in their jobs.

Although some teenage parents choose to marry, a large percent do not. This usually means the father is separated from his child and may not offer any financial support. If the mother chooses to raise the baby, she assumes most of the responsibility for the baby's daily care. Many young mothers drop out of school to care for their babies. With little formal education, most do not find jobs to support themselves and their children. They cannot afford child-care services either. Many resort to federal aid programs for financial support.

Many states have laws requiring fathers to support their children. In these states, teenage fathers are responsible for paying child support. Many are likely to drop out of school in an effort to earn the money for payments. With little formal education, their chances of finding employment to support themselves and pay child support are not good.

Education and Career

While some teen parents, who have strong support at home, are able to finish their high school education, many drop out of school. Without a high school diploma, they find it difficult to obtain good-paying jobs. They will also be unable to further their education beyond high school. Without at least a high school education, the young parents will find it hard to achieve their career goals. This may severely limit their lifetime earning potential. Not only do teen parents suffer the economic consequences, but their children suffer also.

Reflect:
Do you think you are ready for marriage and children right now? How would your lifestyle change if you were to become a parent?

Discuss:
Do you feel states should require unmarried teen fathers to support their children? How many of them do you think take on that responsibility voluntarily?

Resource:
Teen Parenting: Risks and Challenges, Activity A, SAG

Problem-Solving Practice
Education for Teen Parents, reproducible master, TR. Students are to read a case study about teen parents. Then they are to work individually or in small groups and use the decision-making process to decide how the teen parents might meet their educational goals.

Resource:
The Question of Parenthood, color transparency CT-6, TR

Reflect:
Do you hope to have children some day?

Discuss:
Do you think a couple is being selfish if they choose not to have children?

The Children of Teen Parents

Teens are still developing physically, intellectually, emotionally, and socially. They are usually not yet financially independent either. Because of such factors, their children are subject to more risks than children born to older parents.

- *Physical Risks.* A young mother may not be aware of certain prenatal behaviors that could put her unborn child at risk. For example, taking certain nonprescription medications may harm a fetus. A poor diet can result in an underdeveloped or low-birthweight baby. Smoking cigarettes can lead to a premature birth. Excessive alcohol consumption can cause *fetal alcohol syndrome,* a condition that includes physical and mental disabilities.
- *Intellectual Risks.* The first two years of life are critical because the child is building the mental foundation that will dictate behavior through adulthood. Young parents may lack the time to adequately nurture the development of their child, especially if they must work, attend school, and also care for their child.
- *Emotional Risks.* Recent research has shown that emotional development is the foundation of intelligence. Even newborns have emotional needs. They are best met through such activities as rocking, touching, soothing, talking, and singing. Young parents may again be unable to spend this quality time with their babies.
- *Social Risks.* Studies show that children born to teen parents are more likely to become parents themselves when they are teenagers.
- *Financial Risks.* Because teen parents may lack education and job skills, their children have a greater chance of living in poverty.

Deciding Whether to Have Children

One of the most important decisions a couple will make together is whether to have children. Although this decision is a personal one, parenthood should also be a joint decision made by husband and wife together. Many personal factors need to be considered, including reasons for having or not having children. To make a wise decision, each partner needs a clear understanding of each other's feelings and goals as they relate to parenthood.

Reasons for Having Children

Why do so many people choose to have children? For many parents, bringing a child into the world is an expression of love. Sharing the joys and responsibilities of rearing a child brings many couples closer together. The desire to have a family lifestyle is another reason for having children. Many people want to enrich their lives and share their experiences with children. They don't want to miss the special experiences of life that children make possible, 8-4. Fulfilling role expectations is also a reason for having children. People who have grown up in a stable family setting know that someday they will be parents, too.

Reasons for Not Having Children

Most couples choose to have children. However, after careful evaluation of their feelings, others choose not to become parents. Personal freedom, career concerns, medical problems, financial concerns, and fears are reasons people often give for not having children. Some couples may prefer the freedom of a childless lifestyle. The demands of a career may make others unwilling to take time to rear a child. Others may have physical traits or hereditary diseases they do not wish a child to inherit. The expense of rearing a child may

Career Preparation Activity

Matching Work to Personal and Family Goals, reproducible master, TR. Students are to consider their educational and career goals in relation to their goals for marriage, a future home, and children.

Topic 8-1   Deciding About Parenting   215

8-4   Sharing experiences with his child fulfills the life of this parent.

decide to remain childless. Couples who decide they are ready to have children begin the process of family planning. See 8-5.

Family Planning

The process of family planning involves making specific decisions about having children. Couples need to decide when to begin their family, how many children they want, and when to have other children. These decisions are influenced by religious views, physical health risks, financial concerns, career goals, and personal desires. Couples who plan their families are usually better prepared to meet the demands of parenthood, as well as their children's needs.

deter some. An unhappy childhood or fear of rearing a child may influence other couples' decisions.

Other Factors Affecting Parenthood Decisions

Couples making a decision about parenthood will consider many personal factors. Each factor can affect their final decision. One factor they should discuss is the short- and long-term goals they have set for their life together. How will children fit into these goals? Another factor a couple needs to evaluate is their own relationship. Is it strong and growing? Are they secure in their roles as husband and wife? Would a child enrich their relationship? Are they both ready to accept the roles of father and mother?

Besides determining if they want to have children, couples also need to decide if they are ready to have children. They should not feel obligated to have children just to satisfy their friends and relatives. They also should not feel selfish if they

Discuss:
If a couple's relationship is not strong and growing, how will having a child affect it?

Resource:
Pros and Cons of Parenting, Activity B, SAG

8-5   Couples who want children and are prepared to handle the responsibilities should be encouraged to have children.

FCCLA Activity
Encourage students working on the Interpersonal Communications STAR Event to develop a project designed to encourage married couples to consider all the factors involved in becoming parents before deciding to have children.

> **Enrich:**
> Research the options available for infertile couples who wish to have children. Prepare a report for the class.

> **Enrich:**
> Research the process of adopting a child either through an agency or independently. Prepare a report for the class.

> **Reflect:**
> How would you feel about adopting an older child? a child with a physical disability? a child with emotional problems?

Infertility

Many couples plan for a baby and find that conception does not occur. **Infertility** is the condition of being unable to conceive. In these cases, a couple may choose to seek medical help. Advances in human reproduction technology have improved many couples' chances of having a baby.

Adoption

Some couples who want to become parents adopt a child. **Adoption** is the legal process through which a child's legal guardianship is transferred from the birthparents to adoptive parents.

Reasons for adopting children vary. Some couples are unable to have children of their own for physical reasons. Others prefer adoption to pregnancy for medical reasons. There may be some genetic problems in their hereditary backgrounds. Single adults often desire to fulfill their parenthood goals through adoption.

When a couple decides to adopt a child, they have different options available. They may choose an **agency adoption** and contact a state or private adoption agency to make an adoption plan. They could also arrange for an **independent adoption** through a lawyer. In this type of adoption, they do not work with a licensed adoption agency but arrange for a private adoption.

The couple must also decide whether to have a closed or open adoption. A **closed adoption** allows for no contact between the birthparents and the adoptive family. There is no ongoing relationship between the child and his or her birthparents. In an **open adoption**, the birthparents maintain some ongoing contact with the child. Open adoptions are more common today than in the past. The welfare of the child is the major concern of any adoption.

Agency Adoptions

When an adoption agency receives a request for an adoptive child, a thorough study of the prospective parents is made. The study usually includes at least three interviews. The agency interviewer tries to determine the motivations, maturity, sensitivity, and responsibility of the prospective parents. The couple are also required to undergo physical examinations. The agency must know that the parents are in good health.

An adoption agency carefully selects a family for each child. The agency handles all of the arrangements. Most agencies try to match a child's physical traits and background to those of the prospective parents.

Because there are fewer babies available for adoption, the process may take several years. Waiting lists are often long, especially for babies.

Some agencies handle adoptions of babies from foreign countries. This is an option some couples choose. However, it can be expensive if the couple has to travel to the foreign country to pick up the baby. Usually this type of adoption is faster, and the requirements are less rigid for the adoptive parents.

Even though it is difficult to adopt a baby, many other children are waiting to be adopted. Many of these children are older, or have physical or emotional problems. These children need good homes with loving parents, too. Children who have disabilities are just as capable of loving and being loved as other children.

Independent Adoptions

In most states, arrangements can also be made for an independent adoption. Birthparents sometimes ask their doctor if he or she knows someone who wants to adopt their baby. They may also contact a lawyer who specializes in adoptions. In any independent adoption, it is important that both the birthparents and the adoptive couple have legal assistance.

In both agency and independent adoptions, final adoption papers are not issued until a child has lived with adoptive parents for a stated period of time. This time period varies from state to state. During this time, a state caseworker will visit the home. The caseworker will

Across the Curriculum

Health. Discuss reasons some couples experience infertility. Also discuss environmental factors such as drugs and alcohol that can cause congenital disabilities.

determine whether or not the adoption is in the best interests of the child. This is for the welfare of the child and the parents. Once the adoption is final, the family is bound together legally. They can then concentrate on strengthening their emotional ties.

Check It Out!
1. State the primary goal of parenthood.
2. Name two typical challenges faced by teen parents.
3. List three reasons why many people choose to have children.
4. Identify two personal factors affecting a couple's decision about parenthood.
5. Birthparents who want to remain in contact with their baby may select _____ adoption.

Check It Out! (Answers)
1. to help children grow up responsibly
2. (List two:) possible physical health risks for mother and child during pregnancy, coping with role changes, dealing with financial pressures, coping with changes in their social lives
3. (List three:) an expression of love, to have a family lifestyle, to share the experiences their children will have, to fulfill role expectations
4. (Identify two. Student response. See pages 214-215 in the text.)
5. open

Topic 8-2
Pregnancy

Objectives
After studying this topic, you will be able to
- briefly describe the three stages of prenatal development.
- explain how human traits are inherited from parents.
- list at least five guidelines for good health during pregnancy.

Topic Terms
conception
sperm
ovum
zygote
prenatal development
embryo
placenta
umbilical cord
fetus
genes
chromosomes
congenital disability
genetic counseling
ultrasound
amniocentesis
obstetrician

Resource:
The Role of Expectant Parents, reproducible master, TR

Enrich:
Talk to an unwed mother who did not have the support of a husband during her pregnancy. How did she cope? Where did she get her support?

Having a baby is a family affair. The father and mother can share in the happiness and excitement of the pregnancy period. Together, they can prepare for the baby's arrival. Once the baby is born, they will share both the responsibilities and the rewards of parenthood.

The mother must carry the physical burdens of pregnancy, labor, and delivery. These burdens can be lightened, however, by the emotional support of the father. He can encourage the mother to eat properly and to get enough rest. He can also take part in her exercise program. This type of support helps not only the mother, but makes the father feel involved in the pregnancy, too. See 8-6.

A pregnancy changes the relationship between marriage partners. Married life will continue to change once the new baby arrives. Couples can prepare by learning about some of the adjustments that may need to be made. This can help make pregnancy and parenting happy experiences.

Note:
The entire prenatal development period takes approximately 40 weeks.

Enrich:
Invite a gynecologist to speak to the class about prenatal development.

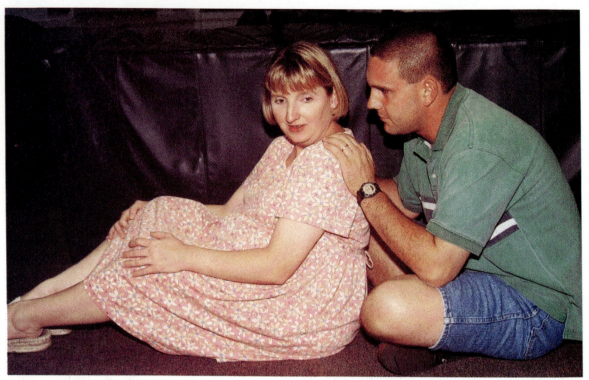

8-6 An expectant father can help support his pregnant wife as together they prepare for the birth of their child.

Prenatal Development

Conception is the beginning of pregnancy. It occurs when a **sperm**, or male reproductive cell from the father, unites with an **ovum**, or female reproductive cell from the mother. This union forms a single-celled organism called a **zygote**.

Prenatal development is the growth of a baby in the mother's womb from conception until birth. This period marks the most rapid growth rate of the entire lifetime.

The Germinal Period

Prenatal development occurs in three stages. The first stage, which lasts about two weeks, is called the *germinal period*. During this time, the zygote divides into two cells. Those two cells divide into four cells, and those four cells divide into eight. Cell division continues throughout the pregnancy and beyond until a person reaches adulthood. As the cells divide, they begin to form specialized tissues, such as bone tissue and muscle tissue.

The Embryonic Period

The second stage of development begins when the zygote attaches itself to the wall of the mother's uterus. This stage is known as the *embryonic period* and the zygote is now called an **embryo**. During this stage, the placenta is formed.

The **placenta** is an organ that takes care of both nourishment and excretion for the unborn child. It is connected to the embryo by the **umbilical cord**. This cord carries nutrients and oxygen from the mother to the embryo. It also carries wastes from the embryo back to the mother.

The embryonic stage lasts until the eighth week after conception. During these weeks, almost all of the baby's organs will be formed.

The Fetal Period

The third stage of prenatal development is called the *fetal period*. The embryo is now called a **fetus.** This stage lasts until the baby is born. During this time, the organs that were formed during the second stage continue to develop and begin to function.

Across the Curriculum
Biology. Discuss genetics as well as the stages of prenatal development in greater depth.

Heredity

During the stages of prenatal development, expectant parents are apt to wonder what their new baby will be like. Will it be a boy or a girl? Will it have brown eyes or blue? Will it grow tall? What color hair will it have? The answers to these questions are mapped out by a child's heredity.

Many human traits are inherited from parents. The traits each person inherits are determined by their genes. **Genes** are the basic units of heredity, 8-7.

Genes are carried on thread-like structures called **chromosomes**. Each human cell, except the reproductive cells, has 46 chromosomes. The reproductive cells each have 23 chromosomes. When a sperm and ovum unite, the zygote formed has 46 chromosomes—23 from the mother and 23 from the father. As the zygote divides, each cell formed will have 23 pairs of chromosomes, or a total of 46 chromosomes. One chromosome from each pair originated from the father. The other chromosome originated from the mother.

Each chromosome contains many genes. Genes occur in pairs. Like chromosome pairs, in each gene pair, one gene originates from the father and one originates from the mother. Each inherited trait is controlled by at least one pair of genes. Some traits are controlled by several pairs of genes. The genes from the mother work with the genes from the father to determine the appearance of each trait in the child.

Congenital Disabilities

Most babies are born strong and healthy. A small percent of babies, however, have **congenital disabilities**, which are disabilities that exist from birth. Such disabilities may be either physical or mental. Some congenital disabilities do not appear until months or years after a baby is born.

Some congenital disabilities are caused by heredity. Such disabilities result when one or both parents pass one or more faulty genes to their child. If the trait controlled by a faulty gene pair develops abnormally, the child may exhibit a disability. Cystic fibrosis and muscular dystrophy are inherited congenital disabilities.

Not all congenital disabilities are caused by heredity. Some are caused by the environment surrounding the fetus during pregnancy. For instance, if the mother becomes infected with rubella (German measles) during pregnancy, certain congenital disabilities can appear in her baby. Drugs, alcohol, and nicotine from cigarettes are other environmental substances that can cause congenital disabilities, 8-8. This is why pregnant women should avoid drinking, smoking, and taking drugs.

Age of the Mother

Research shows that a mother's age is related to the rate of incidence of some congenital disabilities and other infant health problems. Ages 20 through 32 are considered the best childbearing years. Teenage mothers have a higher incidence of premature delivery, low-birthweight

Reflect: What traits have you inherited from your parents?

Note: It is the father's chromosome that determines the sex of the baby. An X chromosome produces a girl. A Y chromosome produces a boy.

Reflect: Ask your parents if they know of any congenital disabilities that run in your family.

Discuss: What environmental factors can cause congenital disabilities?

8-7 The traits a child inherits from his or her parents are determined by genes at the time of conception.

Putting Technology to Use
Have students use the Internet to research current information on one congenital disability. Have them prepare a report to present to the class.

Enrich:
Research and explain the role of genetic counseling regarding congenital disabilities.

Reflect:
Amniocentesis can determine the sex of a baby before birth. Would you want to know your baby's sex before birth?

Resource:
A Healthy Pregnancy, Activity C, SAG

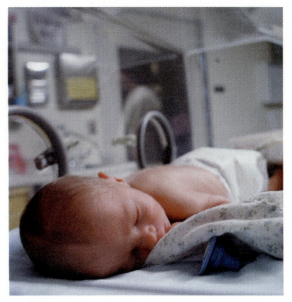

8-8   Most pregnant women avoid drugs, alcohol, and nicotine in order to have healthy babies.

babies, and infant mortality. Mothers over the age of 35 also have increased risks. For instance, they are more likely to have a child with Down syndrome. This disorder may affect both the physical and mental development of a child.

Genetic Counseling

Some couples choose to have genetic counseling before they decide to have a child. **Genetic counseling** is used to predict the likelihood that a couple will have a child with an inherited congenital disability. A genetic counselor will review a couple's medical histories and run lab tests. The counselor will then interpret gathered information based on knowledge of heredity and congenital disabilities. Counselors explain the nature of any possible disability and the probability of its occurrence. They also explain what having a child with the disability would mean to everyone concerned. Couples must make their own decisions, but they can make better decisions when they know the facts.

There are two main reasons for having genetic counseling. One reason is that a prospective parent may know that his or her family members carry genes for an inherited disability. The other reason is that the prospective parents may have already given birth to a disabled child. Such couples may want to know their chances of giving birth to a nondisabled child.

Prenatal Testing

Tests are often given to pregnant women to evaluate the health of their babies. A test commonly given to check the development of the fetus is the **ultrasound**. The test is given by passing an ultrasonic probe over the abdomen of a pregnant woman. This enables the fetus to be observed on a monitor or as a photograph. Through this process, the child's sex, position, and stage of development can be studied. Ultrasound can also detect some congenital disabilities, 8-9.

Another prenatal test that is often given, especially to older mothers, is **amniocentesis**. This test involves inserting a needle in the mother's abdomen. A small amount of the fluid surrounding the fetus is withdrawn. This amniotic fluid contains fetal cells that can be grown in a laboratory and examined. This test allows irregular chromosomes that cause some hereditary disabilities to be identified.

Medical Care During Pregnancy

A woman's health practices affect not only herself, but her unborn child as well. During pregnancy, one health practice that is important to both mother and baby is getting proper medical care.

Signs of Pregnancy

Missing a regular menstrual period is usually a woman's first sign of pregnancy. (This is not always a valid sign. Menstruation may be delayed for other reasons, too.) In addition, her breasts may feel fuller and more tender. Some women have morning sickness in the early months. However, all pregnancies are unique. Thus, all pregnant women will not necessarily have the same symptoms.

Putting Technology to Use
Bring in photographs taken during ultrasounds. Try to get photos of fetuses in different stages of development. Have students point out the head, body, arms, and legs of the fetus in each photo and describe how the differences in development stages are apparent.

Topic 8-2 Pregnancy

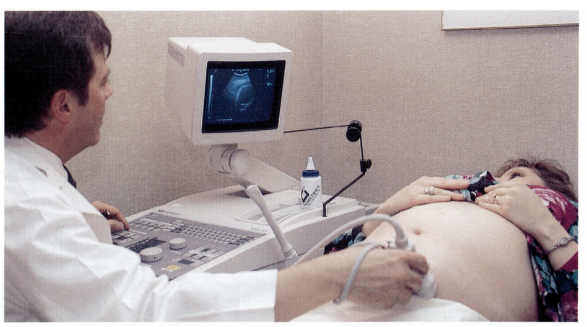

8-9 The ultrasound test is commonly given to a pregnant woman to check the position and development of her baby.

Discuss:
Why is it especially important for a pregnant teen to see a doctor as soon as she suspects she's pregnant?

Resource:
What Will You Give Your Baby? transparency master, TR

Seeing a Physician

A woman should see a physician as soon as she suspects pregnancy. Some women visit a family physician. Others prefer an **obstetrician**, who is a specialist in the care of pregnant women.

Early prenatal care improves a woman's chances of delivering a healthy baby. In addition to health care, a physician can be a source of support. He or she can answer a woman's questions and ease her concerns.

Both expectant parents may wish to visit the physician together. Then both can hear what is said about the pregnancy. They can learn together what to expect.

Guidelines for Good Health

The health habits formed by a young girl can affect her pregnancy in later years. For instance, a girl who has good eating habits can more easily make adjustments for her nutrient needs during pregnancy. Good health habits should be developed at a young age and maintained throughout life.

Following the guidelines below is especially important during pregnancy. A pregnant woman should

- follow the advice of her physician.
- eat a balanced diet every day. The physician will advise her of any special dietary needs and supplements.
- exercise moderately. Walking is usually good. Again, the physician may suggest special activities and exercises.
- keep an eye on her weight. The physician will tell a woman how much weight she should gain during her pregnancy. See 8-10.
- get enough sleep—seven or eight hours each night. She should allow time for rest during the day, too.
- avoid smoking and smokeless tobacco products.
- avoid alcohol.
- avoid taking any medication, even aspirin. Everything the mother takes into her body reaches the fetus she is

Citizenship and Service
Have students design posters featuring the guidelines for good health for a pregnant woman. Distribute the posters to hospitals and clinics in the community.

Resource:
Pregnancy Terms,
Activity D, SAG

Resource:
What Makes a Healthy Pregnancy?
Activity E, SAG

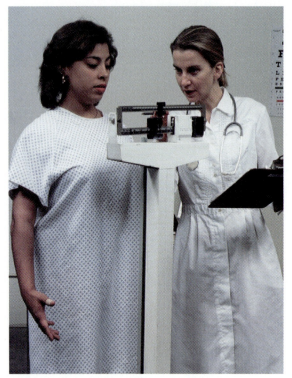

8-10 A physician monitors a woman's weight gain throughout her pregnancy

Check It Out!
1. A _____ is formed when a sperm and ovum unite.
2. True or false. Although congenital disabilities exist from birth, some do not appear until months or years after a baby is born.
3. List five guidelines for good health during pregnancy.

Check It Out! (Answers)
1. zygote
2. true
3. (Student response. See pages 221-222 in the text.)

carrying. Medication may affect the tiny fetus differently than it affects the mother. A physician who knows of the pregnancy may prescribe any needed medication.

■ inform her dentists and physicians of her pregnancy before an X ray is taken. X rays can damage the baby's developing cells and cause congenital disabilities. Ways to protect the fetus from the X rays can be used.

■ do everything possible to avoid viral diseases. Some viral diseases, such as rubella (German measles), can cause congenital disabilities and stillbirths.

TEENS ARE EXPERIENCING...

Early Parenthood

LaCresu, age 17 and a high school senior, is a teenage parent. She knew her monthly period was late. Then when she went for her annual physical, the doctor confirmed that she was seven weeks pregnant.

LaCresu started receiving regular prenatal care by the time she was three months pregnant. Her doctor advised her to stay away from junk food and use the Food Guide Pyramid as a daily food guide. She was given a prenatal dietary supplement to insure adequate vitamins and minerals during her pregnancy. Exercise was also recommended. She was told to walk 15 to 20 minutes a day. As for weight gain, she was told to keep it gradual—no more than a pound a week.

When interviewed about her pregnancy, LaCresu was asked if there was anything she couldn't do while pregnant. She said in addition to avoiding junk food, she was advised to avoid strenuous exercises. She was also told, "No smoking, no drugs, and no alcohol."

During pregnancy, LaCresu noted changes in her eating habits, saying she had to force down food. "My social life seemed different, too," she said. "Everyone just hovered over me asking questions."

LaCresu was asked if she had any health problems and discomforts during pregnancy. She said she had lots of headaches, but she was able to sleep them off. She also had abdominal pains, backaches, and leg cramps.

The baby was born one month prematurely. Prepared childbirth classes helped LaCresu handle this unexpected turn of events. "Knowing the breathing routines and concentrating made it easier for me," she remarked. "My mom was my coach."

Another surprise came after the baby was born. "I thought I would know how to take care of my daughter," LaCresu said. "Actually, I didn't know anything. I didn't know how to feed or hold her. I was afraid she would break." LaCresu explained that the nurse helped her learn how to care for her daughter when she was in the hospital.

When LaCresu came home from the hospital, her mother and grandmother helped her care for the baby. "At first, my daughter awoke about three times each night," she said. "If Mom did not get there first, I was there. We would feed her and change her diaper."

LaCresu commented on how demanding her new role as a mother has been. "During pregnancy, I didn't ever think about the baby coming. Then she came and I had to grow up suddenly. One day I felt like a teenager. The next day I felt like an adult. That was scary.

Without my mother and my grandmother, I don't know how I would have handled it."

LaCresu was asked about her baby's father. She said, "Her father comes to see her, but he doesn't seem to see her needs. It seems like he considers her to be my responsibility."

LaCresu is planning for the future. She has someone who can watch her baby during the day so she can return to high school. She wants to graduate and go to college. "I want to be a nurse," she says, "but I have a lot of expenses now. I will need to work a year or two and save some money before I can start college."

Discuss:
- Which of the "Guidelines for Good Health" listed on pages 221-222 did LaCresu follow during her pregnancy?
- Why is prenatal health care so important for a teenage mother?
- LaCresu noted some changes in her social life during her pregnancy. What were these? What other social changes might a teen encounter during a pregnancy?
- How can pregnant teens prepare themselves for parenthood? What can they do to prepare for parenthood before they become pregnant?
- How do you think LaCresu could have managed caring for her baby if her mother and grandmother were not there to help her? How would this affect her plans to graduate and go to college?
- The baby's father sees the baby, but not the baby's needs. Do you think this is typical? What, if anything, can or should LaCresu do to encourage his involvement in raising the baby?

Chapter Review

Summary

Examining attitudes toward parenthood is important. Like marriage, parenting involves many goals and challenges. Parenthood challenges are likely to be magnified among teen parents. Many personal factors affect a couple's decision about whether or not to have children. Some couples fulfill their parenthood goals by adopting a child.

Even before a child is born, parents must create a healthy atmosphere for a baby. During pregnancy, a developing child starts out as a zygote before becoming an embryo and then a fetus. Babies inherit numerous traits from their parents. Genetic counseling and prenatal testing can help parents determine whether a child will inherit a congenital disability. Pregnant women need to receive proper medical care and follow guidelines for good health to protect their developing babies.

Think About It!

1. Describe the responsibilities of parents to their children.
2. Discuss the pros and cons of teen parenting.
3. Why do you think deciding about parenthood may be more difficult than deciding about other major lifestyle factors, such as careers?
4. How does an agency adoption differ from an independent adoption? How does a closed adoption differ from an open adoption?
5. Choose four guidelines for good health during pregnancy. What would be the possible consequences of ignoring each of the guidelines you chose?

Try It Out!

1. List several factors people should consider before they become parents. Compare your list with those of your classmates.
2. Write a character sketch of an imaginary couple who should not have children. Share your ideas with your classmates.
3. Create a booklet for prospective parents entitled "The Challenges of Parenthood." Find pictures to illustrate the booklet and write descriptive captions under each picture.
4. Interview parents and childless couples. Based on your findings, discuss
   - the advantages and disadvantages of having children
   - the reasons for not wanting children
   - the best age for becoming parents
   - the consequences of unwanted pregnancies
5. Invite a speaker from a local adoption agency or an adoptive parent to discuss what a couple can expect when they apply for adoption.
6. Make a model or draw a diagram to illustrate how human traits are inherited from parents.

Resource:
PowerZone Challenge CD. Have students play the chapter review game to reinforce text content.

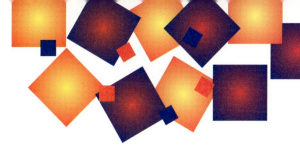

Chapter 9
Meeting Children's Needs

Careers

These careers relate to the topics in this chapter:
- infant care assistant or babysitter
- nanny
- Head Start teacher
- social worker

Topics

- 9-1 Being a Responsible Caregiver
- 9-2 Meeting Children's Physical Needs
- 9-3 Meeting Children's Social and Emotional Needs
- 9-4 Meeting Children's Intellectual Needs
- 9-5 The First Year
- 9-6 Children from One to Five
- 9-7 Child Care Options

Introductory Activities

1. Have students sit in a circle and play "I remember…" Ask students to recall events from their early childhoods they would like to share with the group. After all students who wish to share have had an opportunity to do so, relate the stories to the topics to be studied in the chapter.
2. Ask volunteers to share experiences they have had while babysitting or caring for younger brothers and sisters. What are some of the pleasant experiences they have had with children? What are some of the problems they have had in caring for young children? Can they relate any humorous events?

Topic 9-1
Being a Responsible Caregiver
I. Who Are the Caregivers?
II. Characteristics of Responsible Caregivers
   A. Personal Qualities
   B. Personal Skills
   C. Knowledge and Experience
   D. Good Health
III. Responsibilities of Caregivers
IV. Resources for Caregivers
V. The Role of Society in Protecting Children's Rights

Topic 9-2
Meeting Children's Physical Needs
I. Serving Food
   A. Mealtime Psychology
   B. Involving Children in Meal Preparation
   C. Snacks
II. Choosing Clothes
   A. Fit
   B. Fabric and Construction
   C. Self-Help Features
   D. Size of Wardrobe
III. The Role of Play in Physical Development
IV. Creating a Healthy and Safe Environment
   A. Health Care
   B. Safety
   C. First Aid in Emergencies

Topic 9-3
Meeting Children's Social and Emotional Needs
I. Helping Children Develop Independence and Responsibility
II. Providing Guidance
   A. Communicating with Children
   B. Developmentally Appropriate Guidance
   C. Guidance Techniques
      1. Using Consequences
   D. Parenting Styles
III. The Role of Play in Social-Emotional Development
IV. Helping Children Overcome Fears

Topic 9-4
Meeting Children's Intellectual Needs
I. The Role of Play in Intellectual Development
II. Enrichment Activities for Children
   A. Books
   B. Stories
   C. Art Activities
   D. Music Activities
   E. Watching TV and Videotapes
III. Selecting Toys
   A. Age Appropriateness
   B. Safety

Topic 9-5
The First Year
I. Newborn Babies
   A. Characteristics of Newborns
   B. Care of Newborns
      1. Feeding
      2. Sleep
      3. Bathing
      4. Clothes
      5. Diapers
II. Infants
   A. Early Brain Development
   B. Physical Growth of Infants
   C. Emotional and Social Growth of Infants
   D. Intellectual Growth of Infants

Topic 9-6
Children from One to Five
I. Toddlers
   A. Physical Growth of Toddlers
      1. Toilet Learning
   B. Emotional and Social Growth of Toddlers
   C. Intellectual Growth of Toddlers
II. Preschoolers
   A. Physical Growth of Preschoolers
   B. Emotional and Social Growth of Preschoolers
   C. Intellectual Growth of Preschoolers
III. Children with Special Needs
   A. Inclusion

Topic 9-7
Child Care Options
I. Types of Child Care
   A. Child Care in the Parent's Home
   B. Child Care in the Caregiver's Home
   C. Child Care Cooperatives
   D. School or University-Sponsored Child Care Programs
   E. Church or Social Group Programs
   F. Government-Sponsored Child Care Programs
   G. Employer-Sponsored Child Care Services
   H. Privately Owned or Franchised Child Care Centers
II. Selecting Quality Child Care
   A. Comfortable, Homelike Setting
   B. Age-Appropriate Programs
   C. Adequate Adult Supervision
   D. Consistent, Quality Care Provided by Caregivers
   E. Other Factors

Topic 9-1
Being a Responsible Caregiver

Reflect:
Are you a child's caregiver? What are your roles as a caregiver?

Reflect:
Write down the names of all the caregivers you had throughout your childhood. Are there any you remember as your favorites with some special memories of times you shared?

Discuss:
Have you taken on the role of caregiver for someone? What were your responsibilities?

Discuss:
Are grandparents today more or less likely to provide care for their grandchildren? Explain your answer.

Objectives
After studying this topic, you will be able to
- name possible caregivers for children.
- list characteristics of a responsible caregiver.
- describe the responsibilities of caregivers.
- identify helpful resources for caregivers.

Topic Terms
caregiver
chat room
hot line
foster care

9-1 Many different people will provide for a child's care through the growing years.

A **caregiver** is a person who provides care for someone else. A caregiver may be responsible for an elderly person, a disabled person, or a young child. In this chapter, you will learn about caregivers who provide care for young children.

A child may have many different caregivers, including parents, grandparents, babysitters, and teachers, 9-1. You, too, may be a child's caregiver. You may have younger brothers and sisters. You may babysit for children in your neighborhood. You may even choose a career that involves working with children.

Some caregivers see their chief role in child care as a physical one. Providing food, clothes, and shelter is indeed important. However, caregivers also serve as role models. Children learn to behave by the examples set for them by their caregivers. Children are dependent upon their caregivers to help them grow socially, emotionally, and intellectually as well as physically.

Who Are the Caregivers?

Many people may fill the role of caregiver for a child. The primary caregivers are the parents. They have the main responsibility for providing for their child's needs. There are times, however, when they cannot be with their child. Then other caregivers fulfill this important role.

Many of a child's caregivers are related to the child, such as siblings, grandparents, aunts, uncles, and other relatives. Older brothers and sisters may occasionally be left in charge of their younger siblings. After-school care is often provided by older siblings. Grandparents, if they live near their grandchildren, may have an important role in their grandchildren's lives, 9-2. They may care for the child for a short time on an as-needed basis, or for a

Putting Technology to Use
Have students search the Internet for Web sites on caregivers. What tips are given to make caregiving tasks easier?

Characteristics of Responsible Caregivers

Every person is not equally qualified to be a caregiver. Some people are uniquely talented in the care of children, while others may have some skills to learn. Where do you fit in the picture? The characteristics of responsible caregivers fall into four categories: personal qualities, personal skills, knowledge and experience, and health.

Personal Qualities

A person who is responsible for the care of children should have certain personal qualities. Responsible caregivers

- *enjoy children*. They find each child to be unique and fascinating. They feel energized in the presence of children. Good caregivers have a sense of humor and have fun with children. People who enjoy children find them easy to love.
- *are patient*. They do not count the times a child asks "Why?" They can read the same books aloud, tell favorite stories, and play the same game again and again. They know that children learn at different rates. They can patiently wait for children to learn to do things for themselves, like tie their shoelaces. See 9-3.
- *are flexible*. Children can be unpredictable. Caregivers must be prepared for anything and be willing to adapt to changing circumstances.
- *are alert to children's needs*. Children must be supervised at all times. Caregivers are always watchful to foresee and prevent problems that may occur. In the event that a child's safety is endangered, they are there to immediately offer aid and comfort. Emotional and social needs are also met promptly.
- *exercise self-control*. Caregivers should exhibit a calm and gentle demeanor. Caring for children can be stressful and tiring at times. Good caregivers know when to take a personal "time out" and calm themselves

9-2 This grandfather is happy to fix his granddaughter's bike.

longer, more regular period of time. In the case of a single parent, the grandchild and his or her parent may even live with them. They may provide much of the child's care if the parent must finish school or work.

Other caregivers may be employed by the family to care for the child in their absence. These include babysitters, child-care providers, and preschool teachers. Babysitters generally provide care in the child's own home for a few hours at a time. Sometimes children are dropped off at a sitter's home. Many more children today are spending a portion of each day in a child-care center or preschool. Here professional child-care workers become the caregivers.

Guardians and foster parents may be responsible for a child's care. These individuals are legally required to care for a child if the parents are unable to do so.

Sometimes the role of caregiver is more informal. For example, a caring neighbor may invite a child to go on an outing to give the parents some much-needed free time together. The neighbor becomes a caregiver for the time they are out.

Enrich:
Investigate the legal requirements in your state for becoming foster parents. Share your findings with the class.

Resource:
Wanted: Child Caregiver, transparency master, TR

Discuss:
Do you think it is possible to be a good caregiver if a person lacks any of the personal qualities listed?

Career Preparation Activity

Caregiving as a Career, reproducible master, TR. Students are to interview a caregiver. After recording the interviewee's responses to the questions on the handout, students are to evaluate their feelings about caregiving as a career.

Discuss:
Imagine a child care center without routines and rules. What might it be like?

Activity:
Have students work in pairs. Ask each student to make a list of ten negative statements that tell children what not to do. Have the students exchange their lists and rewrite each negative statement as a positive statement that tells children what to do.

Resource:
Child Caregiver Interview, Activity A, SAG

9-3 Caregivers must be patient and allow children to learn skills for themselves.

down. Sometimes caregivers need to "count to ten" to keep their emotions under control.

- *are consistent.* A responsible caregiver establishes routines and rules that are followed regularly. This prevents children from becoming confused. Bedtime, mealtimes, and other daily activities become rituals. This means they are conducted in the same manner each time. Children learn to depend on these routines. For instance, if children follow a certain bedtime routine night after night, they are more likely to go to bed without a problem. Rules also must be enforced consistently. This gives children a sense of security. If not, children learn that rules are meaningless and can be ignored.
- *set good examples.* Children like to imitate the behavior of adults because it makes them feel grown up. They especially imitate those whom they admire. They learn what to do—right or wrong—from watching others. Good caregivers know this and are careful to set good examples.

Personal Skills

Certain personal skills are needed to give care to young children. The skills needed by responsible caregivers include communication skills, judgment skills, and management skills.

Caregivers must be able to communicate with both children and adults. When communicating with children, they need to speak clearly and use words the children can understand. Using simple language is important. Young children have limited vocabularies. Also using positive statements will help children know what is expected of them. In other words, they tell children what to do rather than what not to do. For example, instead of saying "Do not run," they say "Please walk."

Caregivers may also need to communicate with other adults. Babysitters and child-care professionals need to be able to communicate with the child's parents or guardians about the care and needs of the child. They also may need to communicate with other caregivers if they are in a group child-care facility.

Judgment skills are important for caregivers to have. Every day child caregivers are required to make decisions on how to handle situations involving the children in their care. For example, they must help children deal with conflicts. All children have differences from time to time. The caregiver must know how and when to get involved. Sometimes children can be allowed to work through conflicts on their own. At other times, a decision must be made quickly to avoid a dangerous situation.

Conflicts between adults and children are bound to occur as children enter their toddler years. Again, judgment skills are needed. Caregivers are expected to use mature judgment in handling these disagreements. They need to know effective guidance techniques and how to use them. To foresee and prevent is the best way to avoid problems. Making sure children have a healthy, safe environment is another preventive measure. If children

Across the Curriculum
Sociology. Discuss the personal qualities of people who tend to be caregivers vs people who tend to require care.

have ample age-appropriate toys and materials to explore, it is less likely that problems will arise.

Certain management skills can benefit caregivers. It helps to plan ahead. There may be moments when everything seems to happen at once. A responsible caregiver should try to foresee possible needs and prepare for them. For instance, having a good supply of diapers on hand shows good planning. Having activities planned to keep children actively involved shows planning, 9-4. Knowing where the first aid supplies are kept and making sure all supplies are available shows good planning. Then when unexpected events happen, the caregiver is ready.

A responsible caregiver also knows how to manage time well. Caregivers can organize their time, set priorities, and distinguish between important and urgent matters. There is always more that could be done. If caregivers are to be ready for their responsibilities, they will need to make choices that make good use of their time. They will need to use basic time management skills. You will learn more about time management in Chapter 10.

Knowledge and Experience

Some knowledge about child growth and development is important for caregivers no matter what their role. All child caregivers need to know what children are like. Knowledge is basic to knowing what to expect of children at different ages—their needs, abilities, and interests. This understanding helps caregivers plan appropriate activities to meet their developmental needs. It helps them understand children's behavior and how to respond. For instance, if caregivers know children start becoming afraid of leaving their parents at about eight months, they can plan ways to help children through this stage.

The more experience caregivers have in being with children, the more they will learn about caring for them. New parents who have not been around babies are always very nervous when they become

Discuss: Do you "plan ahead" when you babysit? Give some examples.

Activity: Look under the "Skills and Characteristics" columns in the *Developmental Charts* in the Appendix. For some of the characteristics listed, explain how a lack of knowledge of this skill or characteristic could affect the guidance provided by a caregiver.

Reflect: Think about the first time you babysat a child. If you are now an experienced babysitter, compare how you felt then with how you feel now. Are you less nervous and more sure of yourself now?

9-4 Quality caregivers plan a variety of activities to keep children actively involved.

Across the Curriculum

English. Write a paper completing one of the following statements: I would like to be a caregiver because...I would not like to be a caregiver because...I would make a good caregiver because...I would not make a good caregiver because...

> **Activity:**
> Have students ask their parents to compare how they felt with their first baby to how they felt when they had subsequent children. Did they become more comfortable in their parenting role?
>
> **Activity:**
> Have students investigate ways new parents can learn about child development and parenting. What resources are available in your community? Report to the class and compare findings.
>
> **Discuss:**
> How does a caregiver teach a child right from wrong?

parents for the first time. They are afraid at first to even hold their babies for fear they might harm them. Newborns seem so fragile. Soon parents become quite comfortable with their babies. After the second or third child, they are experienced caregivers and feel much more comfortable in their role as parents.

This is true for all caregivers. Experience is often the best teacher. The more caregivers are around children, the more they learn about how to care for them. They become more comfortable in their presence. When you babysit a child for the first time, you probably feel nervous. After a while, you feel much more at ease as you get to know the child. You know more of what to expect from the child and how best to guide him or her.

New caregivers can learn about children by reading books on child development. Many child care classes are also available. This is another way to learn about children. Your school probably offers a child development or parenting class that you could take. Classes are also available for adults. These classes may be offered at your local community college.

Professional child care workers must meet state licensing requirements in order to work with young children. A few positions require little training or experience. Most child care jobs, however, require a person to have additional education beyond high school. A two-year associate's degree in child development or a related area is often a minimum requirement. In order for a child care facility to be licensed by the state, the child care workers must meet these educational requirements. Licensing requirements vary from state to state.

Good Health

Health is an important factor for caregivers. Much energy is expended physically, mentally, and emotionally during a day spent with children. The physical movement involved is almost continuous. Staying mentally alert to a child's ongoing needs gives little time to relax. The responsibility of helping each child develop to his or her fullest potential can be challenging. A lot of energy is expended. Good health is vital in order for caregivers to function to the best of their ability in this caregiving role.

Responsibilities of Caregivers

Parents and other caregivers have tremendous responsibilities in their roles as caregivers. It is not an easy task. Anyone taking on this role must be ready to fulfill some very important jobs. They are responsible for meeting children's many needs, including the following:

- ■ *Physical needs.* A child's physical needs must be met. These include providing the child's food, clothing, shelter, and medical care. Caregivers are responsible for the health and safety of the children in their care.

- ■ *Social needs.* A child must learn to interact with other children and adults. Children need to learn valuable lessons in sharing, communicating, and compromising, 9-5. Children also need to develop character. They have to learn to behave in ways that are acceptable to society. Children are not born knowing right from wrong.

9-5 Caregivers are responsible for helping children develop the social skills of sharing and communicating.

Across the Curriculum

Social studies. Have students research state licensing requirements for child care centers. How recent are these regulations? How do they protect the children? the caregivers?

Caregivers have the responsibility of guiding children in ways that will promote their moral development.

- *Emotional needs.* Children need to feel loved no matter what they do. They also need to learn how to express their emotions in acceptable ways. This sometimes requires caregivers to set limits. Through love and guidance, parents and other caregivers help children grow toward independence.
- *Intellectual needs.* Caregivers must provide children with opportunities that will help them grow and learn. They can help children develop their language and thinking skills by providing them with suitable learning opportunities.

Resources for Caregivers

How can you learn to be a responsible caregiver? Don't assume knowing how to care for a child is intuitive. Be prepared to learn as much as you can using the many resources available to you. As stated above, there are many classes you can take to learn about children, but there are other resources as well. Some can be used to gain general information about child care. Others may be called on in special situations.

You might begin by checking your local library for books and magazines you think will be helpful. In addition, if you have access to a computer you can go online and check out various Web sites for information. You must be very cautious, however, in selecting Web sites. Some you can count on for reliable information; others you cannot.

There are also many chat rooms where you can communicate with several people on the same topic. A **chat room** provides a forum for a number of people to "chat" over the Internet at the same time. For instance, you could pose a child-rearing question you might have. Other people then offer their opinions. These are not expert opinions, however. These are just ideas of people who may have had a similar problem and found a solution that worked for them. Sometimes these ideas will provide an answer to a simple question you might have as a caregiver.

Get acquainted with the various public and private agencies available in your community. There are services for child care and parent education, and even recreation. Most will also have educational literature to distribute. Many of these agencies provide services for families in times of need. Some agencies can diagnose and treat health problems. Others offer financial advice and assistance. Look in the Yellow Pages or Blue Pages of your local phone directory to find the names and locations of the various agencies in your community. City, county, and state government agencies will be listed. These agencies can also refer you to volunteer organizations and support groups that provide various types of assistance.

In emergency situations, you might want to call a hot line. A **hot line** is a number people can call for information or other assistance with a specific problem. Many hot lines operate 24 hours a day. Persons familiar with the particular crisis will answer the phone, offer guidance, and refer callers to local services. If an emergency occurs with a child in your care, you may need to call 911 for medical assistance, 9-6.

A support group might also be a resource for a caregiver. A support group is a group of people who share a similar problem or concern. Members join together regularly to discuss the concern they have in common. The group might be led by a professional counselor who has special knowledge of the problem.

There are many kinds of support groups. Many are organized to provide support for people who have a family member who has a certain illness. Others are organized for parents dealing with certain problems. For example, *Share* is a support group for parents who have lost a newborn through miscarriage, stillbirth, or infant death. *Child Find* is for parents trying to find missing children. Support groups meeting

> **Activity:**
> Have students ask new parents they know what resources the parents found to be helpful for providing child care advice. What books and magazines do they read for advice?
>
> **Activity:**
> As a class, develop a list of five questions concerning child care. Then ask each student to visit a Web site or chat room that provides child care information to see if they can find the answers to these questions. Report back to the class. Rank the online resources in the order of most authoritative to the least authoritative.
>
> **Resource:**
> *What Would You Say?* reproducible master, TR
>
> **Activity:**
> Look in your local phone directory and list the names and locations of the agencies in your community that provide various types of assistance for caregivers.

FCCLA Activity

Suggest that chapter members who are working on the Focus on Children STAR Event might consider compiling an activity booklet for caregivers. Booklets could include suggestions or directions for books, fingerplays, games, and recipes for doughs, paste, and finger paints. Chapter members can plan a parent-child get-together to demonstrate selected activities from the booklet.

Discuss:
What is meant by the statement "It takes a village to raise a child"?

Discuss:
What are some of the child labor laws that have been enacted to protect children in the workplace?

9-6 A child in your care may need to be taken to a health clinic if there are signs of serious illness.

in your local community are often listed in the phone book. Medical professionals can also refer you to support groups.

The Role of Society in Protecting Children's Rights

Children are a precious resource. They are our hope for the future. Parents and other adults care for them while they are young. Children are easily hurt because they are physically weaker than adults and cannot reason as adults. It is society's responsibility to protect them.

In the United States, parents have the rights of guardianship and determine their children's upbringing. They are responsible for their physical care and their financial support. They provide moral teachings, provide for their education, and make health care choices. If the parents do not provide for these needs of their children, the state can act on the child's behalf and provide protection. This might mean the state would require foster care in extreme situations. **Foster care** is care provided for a child who needs a home temporarily. Children may be placed in foster homes because they have been abandoned, abused, or neglected by their parents. In other situations, children's parents may be temporarily unable to care for them and ask the state for help.

Laws are also passed to protect children's rights. School attendance, for example, is required by law up to a certain age. There are child labor laws that protect children from unsafe working conditions or jobs that interfere with their education. States also provide child welfare services. These services offer food and assistance to families who are unable to make provisions on their own.

All caregivers are responsible for the well-being of the children in their care. It is society's responsibility to make sure all children receive that care. If the parents cannot provide that care, other adults will. Legislative policies are made to protect children as they grow to adulthood.

Check It Out!
1. Name four types of caregivers for children.
2. List five characteristics of a responsible caregiver.
3. Describe the four main responsibilities of caregivers.
4. State four helpful resources for caregivers.

Check It Out! (Answers)
1. (Name four:) parents, grandparents, babysitters, teachers, siblings, aunts, uncles, other relatives, friends
2. (List five:) enjoy children, are patient, are flexible, are alert to children's needs, exercise self-control, are consistent, set good examples
3. to provide for children's physical needs, social needs, emotional needs, and intellectual needs
4. (State four. Student response. See page 231.)

Topic 9-2
Meeting Children's Physical Needs

Objectives
After studying this topic, you will be able to
- describe how a child's likes can be used to encourage good eating habits.
- explain factors to consider when selecting clothes for children.
- identify benefits children gain from physical activity.
- list guidelines to help parents maintain a healthy and safe environment.

Topic Terms
self-help features
active-physical play
manipulative-constructive play
immunizations
communicable diseases
first aid

9-7 Healthy snacks help meet a child's nutrient needs.

Vocabulary: What do you think a self-help feature might be?

Discuss: How else can parents help children develop independence and responsibility?

Discuss: Do you feel it's a good idea to force children to eat foods they don't like? Why or why not?

Resource: *Mealtime Psychology*, reproducible master, TR

A child's basic physical needs must be met before other needs can be satisfied. Parents have a responsibility to provide for their children's physical needs. They must supply adequate food, clothing, shelter, and medical care. Parents must also teach children how to eat, dress, and care for their bodies. This will help children develop independence and assume responsibility for their own physical care.

Serving Food

Food is one of a child's primary physical needs. Parents need to provide nutritious meals for their children. However, children have small stomach capacities. Therefore, they may not be able to eat all the foods they need at meals. Thus, snacks become an important part of a child's food plan each day, 9-7.

Mealtime Psychology

Children sometimes need to be persuaded to eat foods that are good for them. Parents can use a bit of mealtime psychology to accomplish this goal.

Parents should try to avoid making an issue over food habits. When a fuss is made over behavior—even bad behavior—children enjoy the attention. Children will repeat the behavior to get more attention. Children eat best when parents praise their good habits and ignore undesirable ones.

Some children do not like to drink milk. However, their developing bodies need the calcium and phosphorus found in milk. Parents can serve milk-rich foods to make up for a lack of milk in the diet. Ice cream, custard, cream soups, and cheese are alternatives to milk that are popular with children.

Putting Technology to Use
Have students check out information on the Food Guide Pyramid for Young Children at www.usda.gov.

Reflect:
What were your favorite meals as a child? Were they brightly colored, child-size, or prepared especially for you?

Discuss:
Why do you think children are more likely to eat foods they help prepare?

Resource:
Children's Meals and Snacks, Activity B, SAG

Discuss:
Would you like to wear only clothes someone else had chosen for you? Why or why not?

Children like small servings of food. Many children are discouraged from eating by the sight of a large plate of food. Providing children with small portions allows them to ask for second helpings when they enjoy a food.

Children like bright colors. Foods like bright yellow peaches or bright green broccoli often appeal to them. Children are also likely to enjoy eating from a table set with brightly colored plates and glasses. They may even prefer one special plate and always want to be served from it.

Children like foods prepared especially for them. Parents may try making a smaller biscuit or a mini pizza for a child. They can draw a funny face on a hamburger with mustard and ketchup. Syrup can be used to write a child's name on a pancake. Children will find such foods more fun to eat.

Involving Children in Meal Preparation

Children like to choose their own food. Adults can encourage small children to eat by allowing them to help with the menu plan. They can provide children with a variety of healthy food options. For instance, parents might ask children whether they would rather have carrot sticks or celery sticks. They could offer bananas or apples. Then the children can choose which foods they want to eat.

Children are more likely to eat foods they help to prepare. Children can spread peanut butter on crackers. They can prepare vegetables for a raw salad. They can beat eggs that are to be scrambled. These tasks teach children food preparation skills as well as encouraging them to eat.

Snacks

Snacks supplement the foods children eat at meals. To avoid interfering with meals, snacks should not be given near mealtimes. Snacks should be served at least an hour before meals are to be served. Snacks should be nutritious and help meet the body's requirements for a balanced diet. See 9-8.

Healthy Snacks
Fruit juices
Fresh fruits
Raisins
Toast
Strips of turkey or lowfat ham
Frozen yogurt
Pudding
Pretzels
Popcorn
Cheese cubes
Carrot and celery sticks
Crackers with peanut butter
Peanuts
Sunflower seeds
Unsweetened dry breakfast cereal

9-8 A variety of foods that appeal to children can be served as nutritious snacks.

Children like snacks that can be eaten with their fingers. Many ready-to-eat breakfast cereals make good finger foods. Raisins, orange sections, and crackers are also good choices to offer.

Choosing Clothes

Clothes are another basic physical need for children. However, clothes provide more than just physical protection. Clothes can help children develop decision-making skills. As with foods, children like to choose the clothes they wear. Parents can offer two options and allow children to select the outfit they wish to wear.

Clothes can also help stimulate intellectual development. Children can be asked to identify the colors of their clothes. They can name items pictured in fabric prints, too.

Parents need to provide children with clothes that are warm and comfortable. They must consider the fit, fabric, and construction of the garments they select for their children. They also need to look for features that will make it easy for children

Across the Curriculum

Math. Have students use catalogs and newspaper sale ads to select clothes for a child to wear for one week. Make sure they include sleepwear, shoes, and outerwear. Students should cut out the outfits and mount on paper with the price of each outfit listed. Have them add up the total cost and ask if they are surprised at what it costs to clothe a child.

to dress themselves. Following a few guidelines can help parents select clothes that their children will enjoy wearing.

Fit

Parents need to think about how a garment fits a child. Children grow very rapidly. Keeping up with their changing sizes can be expensive. However, parents should resist the temptation to buy large clothes in the hopes that children will be able to wear them longer. Instead, parents should try to buy clothes that fit, but also allow a little extra room for growth. See 9-9.

A child's clothes must fit properly to allow for comfort and safety. Children need clothes that allow freedom of movement as they play. Clothes that are too tight can bind and restrict them. Clothes that are too loose may cause children to trip and fall.

Children's clothes are often sized according to the age of the child most likely to wear them. Since children grow at different rates, however, this is not always a valid guide. The best way to check for correct fit is to allow children to try on garments. When this is not possible, clothing can be chosen by a child's measurements. A child's height, weight, chest, and waist should be considered when evaluating fit.

Fabric and Construction

Parents should consider the fabrics used to make garments when choosing clothes for their children. Children prefer soft fabrics that feel good against their skin. Knits are quite popular because they give with the child's movement. Play clothes made of absorbent fibers help to absorb perspiration. Firm weaves and close knits help clothes resist the wear and tear children put on them.

Parents also need to look at the construction of children's clothing. Garments need to be sturdy enough to withstand hard use and frequent laundering. Double-stitched seams, well-made buttonholes, and securely attached fasteners are signs of durable construction.

Self-Help Features

Children can be encouraged to gain independence by being allowed to dress themselves. In fact, most children insist on dressing themselves by the age of three.

When selecting clothes for children, parents can look for self-help features. **Self-help features** are clothing design details that make clothes easier for children to put on and take off. They include elasticized waistbands and large neck and arm openings, 9-10. Large buttons or snaps that are easier for little fingers to manipulate are self-help features, too.

Size of Wardrobe

Parents may wonder how many clothes a child should have. This depends on many factors. The climate, the availability of laundry facilities, and the family's personal priorities affect the size of a child's wardrobe.

9-9 Shoulder straps can be adjusted to extend the wear of garments as children grow.

> **Note:**
> Some families cannot afford to buy new clothes when children wear out or outgrow their clothes. You might discuss with the class what options these families could consider.
>
> **Activity:**
> Bring in samples of children's clothes and have students compare the quality of the fabric and construction of each item. Make a list of construction details to look for in a durable garment.
>
> **Resource:**
> *I Can Dress Myself*, transparency master, TR

Putting Technology to Use
Have students find a Web site that features children's clothing. Have them print out a page to use for class discussion. Ask students to point out the self-help features in the clothes as well as fabric and construction. Ask if children would find these clothes appealing and why.

Discuss:
Under what circumstances might a young child lack opportunities for developing large muscle skills?

Discuss:
Name some toys and games that help children develop small-muscle skills.

Activity:
Form small groups. Have each group make up a game children would enjoy. Have them demonstrate the game to the class.

9-10 An elasticized waistband and stretchable neck and arm openings are self-help features that make this outfit easy for a child to put on.

Because children grow rapidly, new clothes must be purchased often. If children have large wardrobes, they may not get much use out of each garment. Many parents prefer to buy a few sturdy garments that can be washed and worn repeatedly. Children can get full use out of such garments before outgrowing them.

The Role of Play in Physical Development

Meeting children's physical needs includes providing them with opportunities to play. Both active-physical play and manipulative-constructive play are important to physical development.

Active-physical play helps children develop their large-muscle skills. They use their large muscles for movements like walking, running, hopping, jumping, and skipping. Movement helps them gain an understanding of space and the position of the body in space. They learn to understand concepts such as *front, back, side, up, down, high, low, through,* and *between*. Children learn to react quickly. They also gain more control over their body movements. As children get older, this control allows them to master more refined physical skills, such as skiing, skating, and dancing.

Manipulative-constructive play helps children develop small-muscle skills. The small muscles are those that control the wrists, hands, thumbs, fingers, and ankles. As smaller, finer muscles develop, you will see children picking up blocks with their fingers. As their skills develop, they begin to stack the blocks. By manipulating objects, children learn about the world around them.

Small-muscle development encourages eye-hand coordination. For instance, children learn to pick up shaped objects and drop them into containers with matching shapes for openings. Other small-muscle tasks include writing, drawing, stacking, stringing beads, and fitting puzzles and building pieces together. Caregivers need to provide children with play materials that will help them develop these small-muscle skills.

Physical skills improve as a child grows and develops. For example, an infant will crawl after a rolling ball. A preschooler might run after a ball. An older, more surefooted child might kick a ball. Each child has demonstrated a higher level of physical development.

Games and play activities can be chosen to help build physical skills. Children enjoy walking, running, jumping, balancing, and swinging their arms. They like to throw, catch, roll, and bounce balls. Riding tricycles and playing with outdoor equipment are also fun physical activities, 9-11. The appendix suggests other appropriate play activities to introduce at various stages of a child's skill development.

Social, emotional, intellectual, and physical development are all interrelated. Therefore, activities that stimulate physical growth will stimulate growth in other areas as well.

Across the Curriculum

Health. Reinforce the value of physical activity throughout life. How will participation in physical play activities help children set life habits?

Topic 9-2 Meeting Children's Physical Needs

9-11 Physical activity, such as using a walkabout, helps children develop large muscle skills.

Creating a Healthy and Safe Environment

Physical needs include the need for proper health care and a safe environment. Failure to meet these needs can result in illnesses, accidents, or even death.

Health Care

Parents have a responsibility to protect their children's health. Providing nutritious food, adequate clothing, and a warm home will help keep children healthy. However, children are still likely to become ill from time to time. When this happens, parents have a duty to see that their children receive proper medical care. Children should be taught not to fear doctors, dentists, and other health professionals who might provide this care. See 9-12.

Children can be taught to be responsible for their own health. Parents can teach children proper eating and sleeping habits and dressing skills. Parents can also set a positive example by practicing good health care themselves.

The following guidelines will help parents establish a healthy routine for their children:

- Maintain a clean environment.
- Teach children the importance of body cleanliness.
- Take children for regular medical checkups.
- Keep children's immunizations up to date. **Immunizations** are injections or drops given to a person to provide immunity from a certain disease.
- Keep children away from people who have **communicable diseases.** These are illnesses that can be passed on to other people, such as colds and sore throats. Also, discourage habits that might spread communicable diseases, such as sharing drinking cups.
- Have a knowledge of common childhood illnesses and diseases. Be familiar with their symptoms and how to treat them.
- Treat wounds, bites, and stings promptly.
- Avoid foodborne illnesses by carefully selecting, preparing, and storing foods.

9-12 Children can handle an unexpected hospital stay better if they have been taught not to fear doctors.

Discuss:
Do you know children who fear doctors and dentists? How did their fear develop?

Enrich:
Invite a pediatrician to speak to the class about caring for children's health.

Activity:
Have students research the impact of communicable diseases on society in the past. For example, are measles usually seen as life-threatening today? How is this different from 100 years ago?

Putting Technology to Use
Have students use word processing software to make posters listing ways to avoid communicable diseases. Hang the posters throughout the school.

Discuss:
Can you think of any additional guidelines to add to the list on this page?

Note:
In many states it is the law that all infants and children be secured in a car seat. Inform students of the legal requirements in your state.

Discuss:
Name some products used to help protect children from dangers in the home.

Safety

Caregivers have two responsibilities regarding children's safety. They must make the environment as safe as possible for children. Also, they must teach children to recognize and avoid safety hazards.

Parents need to look for safety hazards from a child's low vantage point. They should look for possible hazards to a child who is learning to sit, creep, stand, or walk. Parents must remove all items that could be dangerous to young children. They must teach older children to avoid dangerous items and to stay out of harmful areas.

The following guidelines will help parents maintain a safe environment for their children:

- Supervise children at all times. Their mobility, desire for independence, and curiosity prompts them to explore items that could be hazardous.
- Teach safe use of toys and play equipment.
- Avoid giving children toys that are sharp or fragile or that have small pieces that can be swallowed.
- Place gates at the top and bottom of stairs to prevent falls.
- Keep sharp and breakable objects out of the reach of children.
- Keep hot water, hot food, and other hot objects out of children's reach to prevent burns.
- Keep medicines and cleaning agents in a locked cabinet. Do not remove product labels.
- Place fencing around swimming pools, garden ponds, and other bodies of water to prevent accidental drownings. Supervise children constantly when they play near water.
- Provide safe, sturdy places for children to climb. Watch children closely when climbing is allowed.
- Keep plastic bags and large sheets of plastic away from children to prevent suffocation.
- Protect children from electrical hazards. Unused outlets should be capped with a safety device or covered with electrical tape. Keep appliance cords out of a child's path to prevent tripping. Do not allow cords to hang where children could grab them. If an appliance has a retractable cord, leave only the length that is needed outstretched. Use electrical appliances near the back of the counter where children will find it hard to reach them.
- Check fire extinguishers regularly and know how to use them.
- Plan and practice evacuation procedures for the home in case of fire.
- Secure children in a car seat for even short distances. The middle of the back seat is the safest spot for the car seat. Older children should always use safety belts. See 9-13.

9-13 Car seats help protect children while traveling.

Putting Technology to Use
Have students use word processing software to create a pamphlet informing parents about children's safety.

First Aid in Emergencies

No matter what you do as a caregiver to prevent injuries to children, accidents are bound to happen. If so, you need to know what to do. **First aid** is emergency care or treatment given to people right after an accident. It relieves pain and prevents further injury. Caregivers need to know basic first aid procedures so they can treat minor injuries promptly. The following are some basic first aid techniques:

- *Small cuts and abrasions:* Wash area with soap and water. Apply mild antiseptic and bandage.
- *Deep cuts or puncture wounds:* Place a clean cloth or bandage over the wound. Press the wound with the palm of your hand to stop the bleeding. Then get medical help.
- *Minor burns:* Place the burned area in cool water for a few minutes until the pain subsides. Do not apply ointment.
- *Severe burns:* Have the child lie down. Do not put anything on the burn or try to remove any material stuck to the skin. Get medical help right away.
- *Broken bones:* If you think the child has a broken bone, get medical help. Do not move the child.
- *Splinters:* Wash the area with soap and water. Using a pair of tweezers, remove the splinter at the same angle it entered the skin. Cover with a bandage.
- *Insect stings:* If the child is stung by a wasp, bee, hornet, or yellow jacket, watch for an allergic reaction. A rash or swelling is a mild reaction. If the child is weak and collapses and has abdominal cramping, get prompt medical help.
- *Electric shock:* Do not touch the child with your bare hands until the electrical connection is broken or you, too, will be shocked. Either turn off the electricity or use a wooden stick, a cloth, or a rope to pull the child away from the source. If the child is not breathing, give *cardiopulmonary resuscitation (CPR)* if you are certified to do this. This technique includes rescue breathing and forcing the victim's heart to pump blood. Get medical help immediately.
- *Choking:* If a child cannot speak or breathe, he or she may be choking on something. Another sign is bluish lips and fingernails. You should immediately perform an abdominal thrust (Heimlich maneuver). The steps in this procedure are outlined in 9-14.

Have the phone number for the poison control center posted near the phone. If a child swallows a substance that could be poisonous, you will need to call this number immediately. Be prepared to tell the staff member what the child swallowed. Then follow his or her directions.

Performing the Abdominal Thrust (Heimlich maneuver)

Infants and Toddlers

1. Place the child over your arm or thigh so the child's head is down. The child's abdomen should be against your arm or thigh. Support the head and neck with one hand.
2. Strike the child sharply with the heel of your hand three or four times between the shoulder blades until the object is dislodged.

Older Children

1. Pick the child up from the rear around the waist, or kneel over the child.
2. Place fist of one hand above navel, but well below rib cage. Cover fist with other hand. For a very small child, use two fingers from each hand.
3. Pull upward with both hands quickly, but gently three to four times. Use less force for smaller children.
4. Repeat if necessary to dislodge the object from the windpipe.
5. Watch breathing and check pulse. Be prepared to give mouth-to-mouth breathing.

9-14 Knowing when and how to perform an abdominal thrust is important when a child is in your care.

Enrich: Bring in a first aid kit. Discuss with students when each of the supplies should be used.

Activity: Have students make a list of community phone numbers to use in an emergency.

Note: A choking victim should still consult a doctor after the abdominal thrust has been performed. An injury may have occurred during the procedure.

Across the Curriculum

Health. Have a health professional demonstrate the appropriate way to perform the abdominal thrust and CPR.

Vocabulary:
What do you think of when you hear the word *guidance*? (Note: Some students may think guidance means discipline and/or punishment.)

Discuss:
How does children's social interaction with peers differ from interaction with family?

If serious illness or injury occurs, seek professional help immediately. You may need to call for an ambulance. For some emergencies, you may want to take the child to a hospital emergency room or clinic for treatment. The severity of the injury will determine which action you should take.

Check It Out!

1. True or false. Parents should repeatedly scold children who refuse to eat foods that are good for them.
2. List four factors to consider when selecting clothes for children.
3. Explain the difference between active-physical play and manipulative-constructive play.
4. List five health and five safety guidelines parents should follow to protect their children.

Check It Out! (Answers)

1. false
2. fit, fabric, construction, and features that make it easy for children to dress themselves
3. Active-physical play helps children develop their large-muscle skills. Manipulative-constructive play helps them develop their small-muscle skills.
4. (Student response. List five of each. See pages 237-240 in the text.)

Topic 9-3
Meeting Children's Social and Emotional Needs

Objectives
After studying this topic, you will be able to
- explain how to help children develop independence and responsibility.
- summarize techniques for communicating with children.
- give suggestions for guiding children's behavior.
- describe the role of play in social-emotional development.
- describe ways to help children overcome their fears.

Topic Terms
guidance
developmentally appropriate practices
modeling
positive reinforcement
redirecting
prompting
consequences
time out

The social and emotional development of children is an important part of their overall development. *Social development* is the process of learning to relate to other people. Very early in life, children begin to interact with their parents and siblings. As they get older, they interact more with people outside their family, including caregivers, teachers, playmates, and school friends. As they interact with others, they learn to cooperate, to share, and to follow directions. They develop their communication skills. Children become friendly and confident as they spend time with other people.

Emotional development refers to feelings and emotions and the way children express their emotions. Children show such emotions as love, fear, happiness, and frustration from a very early age. As they get older, they learn to control some of their emotions. Learning to express anger and frustration in acceptable ways shows emotional growth. For example, preschoolers might cry if they are unable to have the toys they want. Older children understand and accept explanations of why they can't have the things they want. Though disappointed, they control their emotions and are much less likely to cry.

As children interact with parents, siblings, and others, they experience and express many emotions. They feel love from their parents, and they respond in a similar manner. They develop a sense of trust.

All children need to feel loved for emotional growth to occur. Without this feeling of love, other aspects of development will be adversely affected. Recent studies have shown that emotional development lays the foundation for intelligence. At each stage of development, emotions lead the way, and learning facts and skills follow.

Helping Children Develop Independence and Responsibility

A child's social needs include learning skills that will help him or her become an independent person. Children also need to learn to accept responsibility for their actions as they begin to interact with others. Caregivers can use a number of techniques to help children develop independence and responsibility.

Young children want to become independent. This is evidenced by two-year-olds who insist, "I can do it myself." Caregivers can help children build independence by giving help only when children need it. Caregivers often perform chores for children, even though the children could do the chores themselves. In many cases, a better approach would be to wait for the children while they do the chores. Then the caregiver can praise the children for their efforts. Children want the praise and approval of their caregivers.

Decision-making skills are needed for independent living. Caregivers can help children learn these skills by allowing them to make as many choices as possible. The choices don't have to be major ones. For instance, children can help choose the foods they eat, the clothes they wear, and the activities they do. See 9-15. By being involved in the decision-making process, they gain self-confidence.

Children can help make many decisions every day. However, you should offer a choice only when you plan to abide by the decision. It is unfair to ask children to make decisions and then disagree with their choices. This harms children's self-concepts. It leads them to believe that you don't care what they think. It makes them feel their decisions are invalid.

One way to avoid this situation is to offer a child two equally acceptable alternatives. For instance, don't ask a child what he or she wants to eat for dinner. The child might say, "Candy," which you are unlikely to consider a worthwhile entree. Instead, ask if the child would rather have turkey or ham. This allows the child to choose between two nutritious options.

Another way caregivers can help children build independence is by allowing them to solve their own problems when possible. When given a chance, many children are able to find satisfactory solutions.

9-15 Children learn decision-making skills when they are allowed to choose their own toys.

> **Discuss:** In what ways do parents hinder children from becoming independent?
>
> **Discuss:** What decisions can young children be allowed to make? What decisions should they not be allowed to make? How old must they be to make these decisions?
>
> **Resource:** *Giving Children Choices*, reproducible master, TR

Across the Curriculum

Psychology. Ask students how they can tell if a child is trying to manipulate a caregiver by crying, temper tantrums, and hitting. What are the best ways of handling this behavior?

Reflect:
Can you think of a situation in which your parents let you work out a disagreement between another sibling and yourself? What did you learn from that experience?

Vocabulary:
What is the difference between intrinsic and extrinsic guidance? Give examples of each.

Enrich:
Visit a child care center and observe how the teachers communicate with the children.

A father told of his children who quarreled about who would sit in the front seat of the car. He decided to let them try to work it out. After much fussing, they came to a decision. One child would always sit in the front seat when they were leaving home. The other child would always sit in the front seat for return trips. The children's own solution worked out very well.

A goal of child care is helping children prepare to become responsible adults. An important part of being responsible is accepting the consequences of decisions. Children need to learn that they will have to live with the results of their decisions—good or bad.

Suppose a child was given a choice of an apple or a banana for snack time, and the child chose the apple. After taking a few bites, the child said, "I don't want this apple. May I have a banana instead?" One good way for a caregiver to handle the situation would be to say, "You don't have to finish the apple now. I will put it away, and you can eat it later. However, you cannot have a banana. You chose an apple for this snack time. When it is snack time again, you may have a banana." This shows the child that he or she must accept the consequences of the decision that was made.

Another way children develop responsibility is by being encouraged to care for their own belongings. This can be done by providing storage within their reach. Low closet rods and dresser drawers help children to keep their clothes in place. Easy-to-reach shelves allow children to store their own toys, 9-16.

Providing Guidance

Meeting children's social and emotional needs includes helping them learn behavior that others will find acceptable. Children need guidance to help them handle life's experiences. **Guidance** includes everything caregivers do and say to promote socially acceptable behavior.

Factors in a child's environment that guide his or her behavior are called

9-16 Accessible storage helps children develop responsibility as they learn to care for their own belongings.

extrinsic guidance. This is the type of guidance caregivers provide. A caregiver's goal is to encourage children to begin guiding their own behavior. When children adopt a socially acceptable behavior pattern, they are practicing *intrinsic guidance*. Intrinsic guidance is also known as *self-control* or *self-discipline*.

Communicating with Children

Caregivers communicate with children in order to guide them. Children can be guided by both verbal and nonverbal messages. The following techniques can help make communication with children more effective:

- *Maintain eye contact during conversations.* Eye contact makes listening easier for a child. It also helps you, the speaker. By looking into a child's eyes, you can usually tell when the child understands. You may need to kneel down to a child's level in order to do this.
- *Keep messages simple and brief.* When talking with a young child, use small words and short sentences. Give children only one or two simple instructions at a time. Children become confused when too many difficult words are used or too many directions are given at one time.

Putting Technology to Use
Have students use the Internet to research recent articles on guidance. Do the authors of the articles seem to agree with one another's advice? How do they differ?

- **Speak in a relaxed voice.** Use a calm, quiet, relaxed tone of voice with children. They are more likely to listen to this type of voice. Then when you must raise your voice in an emergency, they will be more likely to pay attention to you.
- **Reinforce words with actions when necessary.** Remember that actions speak loudly. For instance, suppose Tommy is busy playing when you call him to dinner. He ignores your call. You may need to go to him, take him by the hand and say, "Let's eat now." By walking the child to the table, your message is made clear.
- **Use positive statements.** Emphasize what children should do rather than what they should not do, 9-17. For instance, suppose two children were throwing sand in the sandbox. You could say, "Don't throw the sand." Since throwing was fun, however, the children are likely to begin throwing something else. A more effective approach might be to say, "Instead of throwing the sand, try using it to build a sand castle." Another positive approach might be, "I see you want to throw something. Here is a ball. See if you can throw it instead." Children are easy to distract—especially if the tone of your voice makes your idea sound like fun.
- **Answer children's questions briefly and truthfully.** No matter what children ask, a simple answer is likely to satisfy their curiosity. Answer any question in a manner appropriate for the child's level of understanding.

Developmentally Appropriate Guidance

Caregivers need to use different guidance techniques for children of different ages. A technique that is effective with four-year-olds may not work with toddlers. **Developmentally appropriate practices** are those that are suited to the developmental characteristics and needs of the individual child.

By the time children reach the toddler stage, they are old enough to understand simple words. Caregivers can use brief statements, such as "Pet the bunny gently." Toddlers should be able to follow such simple directions.

Caregivers need patience when they are with toddlers. Children of this age have a very short attention span. Caregivers may need to repeat a suggestion many times before a toddler adopts the desired behavior.

Resource:
Communicating with Children, Activity C, SAG

Activity:
Have students work in pairs with one student making a negative statement and the other student changing it to a positive statement.

Discuss:
Why do you think toddlers have a short attention span?

Using Positive Statements

Negative	Positive
"Don't spill your milk."	"Hold your glass steady."
"Don't talk with your mouth full."	"Wait until you have swallowed your food before you begin talking."
"Don't put your feet on the chair."	"Keep your feet on the floor."
"Don't yell."	"Please talk softly."
"Don't push and shove."	"Keep your hands by your side."
"Don't interrupt when others are talking."	"Wait for your turn to talk."
"Don't throw blocks."	"Keep the blocks on the table, please."
"Don't pull the kitten's tail."	"Pet the kitten gently."
"Don't leave the toys on the floor."	"Put the toys on the shelf."
"Don't get paint on your clothes."	"Put on a smock."

9-17 Positive statements clearly tell children what they should do.

Across the Curriculum

Speech. How are the suggestions for speaking to children similar to recommendations for any other type of communication? How do they compare to recommendations for giving a good speech?

Resource:
The Role of Guidance, Activity D, SAG

Discuss:
Many people continue to use physical punishment when disciplining their children. What reasons might they give for doing so? Are these reasons valid?

By the age of four, children are beginning to be able to reason. Briefly explaining why a certain behavior is or is not appropriate will help children use acceptable behaviors.

Guidance Techniques

Caregivers can use a number of techniques to guide children's behavior. Caregivers must first act as positive role models. Children learn by imitating others. Whenever you speak, you are **modeling** behavior. At an early age, children are aware of the actions of the adults around them, 9-18. They copy the behavior of the adults they see every day. If you want their behavior to be positive, you must model that behavior yourself and set a good example.

Children need to have limits set for them. These may be called rules. They are made to keep children safe. For example, a young child may be allowed to play only in the fenced back yard away from the street. This is a limit set to protect the child. Limits should be reasonable and appropriate for the child's age. An older child may be allowed to play anywhere within the caregiver's view. With permission, an older child may even play at another child's home.

If rules are made, they must be consistently enforced. If not, the child becomes confused. Using the above example, a young child may play in the front yard one day instead of the back yard. If the rule is not enforced, the child will play in the front yard on other days. The child broke the rule and nothing happened. When limits are consistent, children are more likely to respect them. When they are not consistent, children will ignore them.

Children's behavior can often be molded by rewarding positive behavior. This is called **positive reinforcement.** Caregivers should try to reward good behavior with attention and praise. Undesirable behavior should be ignored if possible. Gestures as well as words can be used to guide behavior. A smile, a nod, or a gentle hug will reinforce positive actions.

Even babies realize that if an action brings a desired response, repeating the action will bring a repeated response. For instance, a baby sitting in a high chair may throw a spoon on the floor. If you give the spoon back to the baby, he or she may throw it on the floor again. If you give the spoon back a second time, the baby is likely to think you are playing a game. The baby is too young to understand if you say, "Keep your spoon on the tray." The best way to handle this situation is to simply stop giving the spoon back to the baby.

Another guidance technique is **redirecting,** or focusing the child's attention on something else. For instance, suppose a child wants a toy another child has. Offering the child a different toy is a way of turning his or her attention in a different direction. The key to redirecting is providing an appealing substitute.

Caregivers can use a technique called **prompting.** Questions can prompt children to exhibit desired behavior. A caregiver might ask "Where does the ball belong?" A

9-18 Children are eager to receive attention from caregivers and are likely to model their behavior.

Across the Curriculum

Social studies. Discuss "guidance techniques" directed at whole nations, such as Wilson's Fourteen Points following WWI or the no-fly zone in Iraq. Have students discuss whether these methods are examples of positive reinforcement.

child may respond by putting the ball on the proper shelf. Asking "What are you supposed to do when you are finished painting?" may encourage children to wash their hands.

Caregivers need to give children time to make a transition from one activity to another. Play is important to children, and they do not like to be suddenly interrupted. If possible, a warning should be given five or ten minutes before a change of activities. This gives children time to finish what they are doing.

Children tire of activities quickly due to their short attention spans. A caregiver may need to provide new activities for children to encourage positive behavior, 9-19.

Positive reinforcement should be used as much as possible to guide children's behavior. When misbehavior occurs, however, consequences may become part of the guidance process.

Using Consequences

Consequences are results that follow an action or behavior. When using consequences, the negative results of the child's own actions influence future behaviors. If a child's health or safety is at risk, a caregiver must step in at once. However, if a child's well-being is not at risk, consequences can act as a deterrent to inappropriate behavior. For instance, playing with food is inappropriate behavior at the dinner table. Suppose a child plays with his or her food until it becomes cold. He or she then asks to have the food reheated in the microwave oven. The request is not honored. The child learns that the consequence for not eating promptly is to eat cold food.

Caregivers can set up consequences that relate to misbehaviors. These are called *logical consequences.* For instance, a child who throws blocks may not be allowed to play with the blocks for a period of time. Once consequences are imposed, they must be enforced. Otherwise, children will not learn from the consequences of their behavior.

Another logical consequence might be a time out. A **time out** involves moving a child away from others for a short period of time. It should be used only when a child's disruptive behavior cannot be ignored. The child needs time to calm down and gain self-control. A time out is not appropriate for children younger than the age of four. Younger children are not able to understand their behavior can have negative consequences. The time out should be limited to three minutes.

A caregiver should be careful never to threaten to withdraw love. A child needs to feel loved regardless of his or her behavior. Love should not be used as a reward that has to be earned by a child. It should be given freely.

> **Activity:**
> Make a list of ten questions you can use to prompt children into exhibiting desirable behavior.
>
> **Discuss:**
> What are the advantages and disadvantages of using logical consequences as a deterrent to inappropriate behavior?
>
> **Reflect:**
> What is your opinion of using a time out for punishment? What would you do if the child would not stay in the time out area?

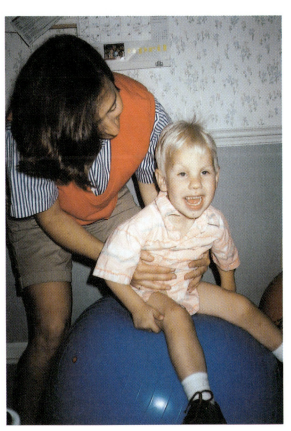

9-19 Providing children with interesting activities reduces behavior problems.

Across the Curriculum

Sociology. Discuss criminals who are repeat offenders. Why doesn't the concept of consequences act as a deterrent to their behavior?

> **Reflect:**
> Will you use the same type of parenting style with your children as your parents practice in your home? Why or why not?
>
> **Resource:**
> *Parenting Styles,* reproducible master, TR
>
> **Discuss:**
> Why is it important for games to be age-appropriate?

Parenting Styles

Parents tend to develop a parenting style they use to guide their children's behavior. Parenting styles can be grouped into three categories:

- *Authoritarian parents* tend to rule single-handedly. They maintain control and expect conformity. The children are not encouraged to negotiate or present different views.
- *Permissive parents* allow children to set their own rules. Children are allowed to make most of their decisions. Without boundaries, these children may feel insecure. They sometimes fear the natural consequences of decisions they are not prepared to make.
- *Democratic parents* allow freedom within structure. Rules are established and explained. Children are allowed to ask questions and present their views. Children feel secure because they know what to do and why they are doing it.

The Role of Play in Social-Emotional Development

Though extrinsic guidance is important in helping children develop socially and emotionally, children also learn through their play. As children play, they interact with the world of people and objects. As they do so, they develop socially and emotionally. For instance, a game that babies enjoy playing is peek-a-boo. They will play this game with their caregivers. It helps them develop a sense of trust. The face of the caregiver reappears after it disappears. This is an important learning for infants.

Caregivers can promote social-emotional development by initiating play activities appropriate for the age of the child. Peek-a-boo games with infants can be followed with games such as pat-a-cake. Still later, the game might be rhyming words. The actual game is not as important as the social interactions and the trust that forms between caregiver and child.

As children get older, they play more with other children, 9-20. This group play

9-20 A group of neighborhood children may work together to set up a lemonade stand.

Putting Technology to Use
Have students look up the term *parenting styles* on the Internet. Have them browse through some of the Web sites returned as matches. Discuss in class the range of information offered on the Internet on the topic of parenting. Do students think most of these sites provide useful information? Why or why not?

promotes skills such as cooperation, sharing, and property rights. Playing with others helps children learn to give and receive. Self-esteem develops when there is a balance between giving and receiving. The goal is to help children learn to make and maintain relationships where they also develop healthy self-concepts.

Helping Children Overcome Fears

Children between the ages of two and six are quite likely to develop a number of fears. Meeting children's emotional needs involves helping them handle their fears.

A caregiver needs to respect a child's fears. A caregiver can try to find out the reason for a child's feelings. This may suggest ideas for helping the child overcome his or her fright. For instance, a boy had a fear of swimming. His parents asked why he was afraid. The boy said he wouldn't be able to breathe if his head went under the water. The parents used this information to gradually introduce the boy to shallow water. Soon the boy felt safe enough to get his head wet.

A caregiver can encourage a child to overcome a fear. However, the caregiver should avoid forcing the child into a situation that he or she finds frightening. Children will try new experiences when they feel ready. Forcing them only prolongs their apprehension.

The majority of children's fears are fears of unfamiliar objects and situations. As children gain experience with something, they typically lose their fear of it. Caregivers need to clearly explain new circumstances before children have a chance to become fearful. For example, children are often afraid of doctors. A caregiver can use a toy medical kit to show a child tools similar to those used by doctors. This will help the child feel more relaxed when he or she sees these tools in a doctor's office.

A caregiver may be able to distract a child's attention away from his or her fears. A two-year-old cried when riding over a bridge on the route to her home. Her caregiver asked her why she was afraid of the bridge. The child said, "It goes hmmm." The caregiver said, "Since the bridge hums to us, maybe we can hum to it next time." They rehearsed their humming sound several times. On the next trip, the child looked forward to humming so much that she did not cry. Through distraction, the child's attention was diverted from her fear of the bridge to humming.

Check It Out!

1. Describe three ways caregivers can help children develop independence.
2. Everything caregivers do and say to promote socially acceptable behavior is called _____.
3. Describe three guidance techniques you can use to guide children's behavior.
4. True or false. Most fears among children are caused by bad experiences they have had.

Check It Out! (Answers)

1. (Student response. Describe three. See pages 241-242 in the text.)
2. guidance
3. (Describe three. See pages 244-245 in the text.)
4. false

Discuss:
How would you help a child overcome fear of the dark?

Discuss:
Do you agree that "the majority of children's fears are fears of unfamiliar objects and situations"? Why or why not?

Vocabulary:
Define *multicultural*.

Discuss:
Why is play so important in a child's development? Do you think of play as children's "work"?

Reflect:
When you engaged in imitative-imaginative play as a child, what person or object did you most like to pretend to be? Why?

Topic 9-4
Meeting Children's Intellectual Needs

Objectives
After studying this topic, you will be able to
- explain the role of play in intellectual development.
- describe various enrichment activities that stimulate children intellectually.
- list guidelines for selecting toys for children.

Topic Term
imitative-imaginative play
dramatic play
socio-dramatic play
multicultural book

As children grow, they develop intellectually. They gain the ability to reason and use complex thought processes. They also learn how to use their imaginations and think creatively.

Caregivers need to provide children with stimulating activities. However, they should be careful not to challenge children to do too many difficult tasks. Children need to value themselves and feel good about what they do. This helps them develop self-esteem.

The latest research shows that it is more important for children to be confident, curious, motivated, and persistent as they enter school than to be able to recite numbers, letters, and colors. Intellectual development will occur when there is a positive social-emotional foundation.

The Role of Play in Intellectual Development

Children learn through their play activities. They experiment to see how things work. They use their imaginations and try new ideas. Play allows children to experience different sights, sounds, textures, smells, and tastes. Children are introduced to their environment and objects in their environment. They learn to use these resources. Through play they learn number concepts such as more and less and large and small. Puzzles and nesting toys help them see size and shape relationships. Many activities encourage creative thinking. Some activities can also be chosen to help children build reasoning skills. All of these activities lead to learning, but without any pressure to succeed.

Children play in many ways. In active-physical play, children use their large muscles as they run, hop, jump, and skip. They use their small muscles as they play with toys, such as puzzles, beads, and blocks.

In **imitative-imaginative play,** children use their imaginations as they pretend to be other people or objects. This form of play begins at about two years of age. At this age, children are capable of having an object stand for something else. For instance, a cardboard box might represent a car or a plane. By three or four years of age, children begin **dramatic play**. This form of play involves role playing. A child imitates another person or acts out a situation, but does so alone. See 9-21. **Socio-dramatic play** involves several children imitating others and acting out situations together. They

9-21 This child is playing the role of a television announcer.

Putting Technology to Use
Have students visit a child care center and videotape children at play. View the videos in class to identify in which types of play children are engaging.

Topic 9-4   Meeting Children's Intellectual Needs

mimic such adult roles as mommy, daddy, doctor, or astronaut. They make decisions and learn problem-solving skills. Language concepts also develop as they generate plots and story lines. Creativity and imagination are fostered.

Enrichment Activities for Children

Not all activities provide the same types of intellectual stimulation. Books, stories, music activities, art activities, and toys all give children different learning experiences. Offering children a variety of activities gives them the opportunity to use a range of skills.

Books

Reading to children is one of the best ways to help them learn language skills. Children build their vocabularies as they associate pictures with words in a book. They practice communication skills by talking about stories. They develop reasoning skills when they answer questions about a story.

Children develop an interest in books at an early age. The content of books should be chosen with a child's age in mind, 9-22. Very young children enjoy books about objects that are familiar to them. Animal stories are favorites. Children like to identify the animals pictured and make animal noises.

Books can expose children to a wide range of ideas. Look for books that show both men and women in various careers. This will allow children to explore nontraditional work roles. Also select **multicultural books**. These are stories that involve characters from a variety of racial and ethnic groups. Such books can help children develop positive attitudes about sex roles and other cultures.

Children should be permitted to handle their own books. Books for small children should be sturdy. Heavy cardboard and fabric pages are easy to turn and will not tear easily. When reading books with paper pages, teach children to turn pages carefully.

9-22   Children enjoy books from a very early age.

Repair torn pages with clear tape so children will not be tempted to tear them more.

Stories

Stories can provide intellectual stimulation by encouraging children to use their imaginations. Children might be motivated to memorize stories and repeat them. They can use dramatic skills by acting out a story as it is told. Children may also develop creativity by illustrating a story with art.

Caregivers can show regard for children by preparing stories that meet the children's interests. Good storytellers put a lot of action into stories. They change the tone of their voices to fit the moods of the story. They use their hands to create sounds as needed.

Stories can be chosen to create a desired setting. Exciting stories are best before playtime. Happy, peaceful stories are best before bedtime.

Some stories are old favorites that have been told to children for generations. Others are created on the spot. On a rainy day, a storyteller may make up a tale about the rain. On a sunny day, a story about the sun can be created. In the spring, a story about flowers and how they grow would

Resource:
Teaching Through Play, Activity E, SAG

Activity:
Have students select various children's books and evaluate them for vocabulary, interest, pictures, sex roles, and cultural awareness.

Resource:
Books for Children, reproducible master, TR

Enrich:
Have students work in pairs and develop a story. Have them present the story to the class.

 Citizenship and Service
Arrange for students to give a presentation on "Teaching Children to Live in a Multicultural Society" at your public library. Have students make a display of multicultural books from the children's section of the library. Have them prepare a discussion of the various aspects of diverse cultures that are illustrated in the books. Invite people from different ethnic groups in your community to participate in the presentation. Ask them to share examples of children's stories, art, and music that are typical of their heritage.

Reflect:
Do you have some artwork you created as a child? Bring it in and share it with the class. Do you recall how people reacted to your artwork?

Discuss:
Can you recall some of your favorite children's songs? Why were these your favorites? (Note: Students may mention songs that had actions with them.)

Resource:
Songs for Children, reproducible master, TR

Resource:
Planning Around a Theme, reproducible master, TR

be appealing. Young children like stories about themselves. A recap of their day's activities can become a story.

Art Activities

Art activities teach children about colors, lines, and shapes. They also provide children with an opportunity to develop creativity.

Children are not always able to verbalize their thoughts and feelings. Art materials can help children express emotions when they do not have words to say what they mean.

Children should use a variety of art materials. Modeling clay is a favorite medium for artistic expression. Crayons and paints are also popular, 9-23.

Caregivers can give children some basic guidelines about how art materials should be used. For instance, they might require children to wear smocks when working with these materials. They may show children how to avoid dripping paint or how to make different shapes with clay. However, adults should not control art activities too carefully. They should not tell children what to make or how to make it. Children should be given freedom to be creative.

9-23 Painting gives children a chance to express their creativity.

Caregivers should not criticize children's artwork. They should also avoid trying to guess what children have made. A child's confidence can be shaken when a caregiver incorrectly identifies something the child has made. A wise alternative would be to say, "This is interesting. Tell me about it." The child may explain what a sculpture or drawing represents. The child might also tell what he or she was thinking as the object was being created.

Music Activities

Music introduces children to a number of concepts. Children develop an awareness of rhythm as they play with instruments. They gain an understanding of pitch and can identify high and low notes. They learn about rhymes as they sing the words of songs.

Music has appeal to children of all ages. Even babies seem to find soft music relaxing and soothing. They like musical toys. They wave their arms and kick their legs in response to the sound of music.

Children like songs they understand. Sometimes they will enjoy singing with a caregiver. At other times, they will want to perform alone. Children especially like action songs so they can use their bodies. Caregivers shouldn't worry if they cannot sing well. Children will still enjoy the rhythm of music.

Musical instruments also provide fun learning experiences for children. Children love to participate in rhythm bands. They can take turns beating drums, shaking tambourines, or ringing triangles. Children also enjoy making rhythm sounds with sandpaper blocks, rhythm sticks, finger cymbals, shakers, and bells.

Music, like stories and books, can help to create a desired mood. Exciting music can help awaken a sleepy child in the morning. Soft, quiet music can help an excited child relax at bedtime.

Watching TV and Videotapes

Some people think watching TV and videos is a negative activity for children. However, these mediums have several

Across the Curriculum

English and art. Write and illustrate a children's storybook that focuses on children around the world. Share the book with classmates and friends.

positive traits. They give children a chance to slow down after an active day of play. Many TV shows and videotapes are educational, too. They teach children such basic concepts as numbers and letters. They present examples of accepted social behavior, like sharing and telling the truth. They also inform children about current issues, such as the environment.

Caregivers should resist the temptation to use the television as a babysitter. Whenever possible, caregivers should watch programs with children. They can ask children questions about programs to stimulate the children's thinking.

Caregivers should be actively involved in helping children select appropriate programs. Children need to be able to understand the programs and videos they watch. Those that will confuse or upset them are not recommended.

Programs must be selected according to the maturity of children. Shows that are frightening or contain adult subject matter should be avoided. Children cannot always separate fiction from reality. Watching scary videos and TV shows may cause children to have nightmares. They may fear the frightening events they have seen will happen to them. The easiest way to prevent such fears is to control which shows children watch.

Selecting Toys

Toys are tools to help children grow physically, emotionally, socially, and intellectually. They should be chosen to stimulate—but not overstimulate—a child's total development.

Age Appropriateness

Caregivers should select toys that are appropriate for a child's age. Age is a clue to a child's skill level. For instance, one-year-old children do not have the strength or coordination needed to ride a tricycle. However, most one-year-olds are able to walk. Therefore, a pull toy is a good choice for a one-year-old. The child can play with the toy while walking. The tricycle would be a better choice for an older child who has developed more muscle skill, 9-24.

Toy manufacturers often state on the label the age of the child for whom the toy was designed. Look for these age suggestions on labels as you consider the purchase of toys. The need for a lot of adult assistance is a sign that a toy is too complicated. Wait and purchase such a toy when the child is able to handle it with less supervision.

The interests of a child should also be considered when selecting toys. Some children prefer quiet activities, such as puzzles. Many children enjoy role-playing. For this group, housekeeping toys and occupational toys, such as tool chests, might be good choices. Active children like climbing toys and wheel toys. As children get older, many begin to enjoy scientific toys.

Safety

Safety is another key consideration when choosing toys for children. Avoid the following:
- toys with small parts that can be swallowed
- sharp points that can poke

9-24 This boy is proud that he is able to ride this car and make it "go."

Discuss:
What are some children's shows and movies you have recently watched? Which ones were the most appropriate for children to see?

Activity:
Make a list of programs and movies you feel are inappropriate for children to watch because they contain frightening scenes.

Resource:
Stimulating Science Activities, reproducible master, TR

Resource:
Age-Appropriate Toys, color transparency CT-7, TR

Putting Technology to Use
Ask students to research currently popular children's toys. Ask students to evaluate the toys on age appropriateness and safety. Have students use presentation software to share their findings with the class.

Resource:
Shopping for Toys, Activity F, SAG

- rough or sharp edges that can cut
- long cords or strings (for infants and young children)
- flammable materials
- nonwashable dolls and stuffed toys
- toxic paints
- poorly made toys that can easily fall apart

Children are disappointed when toys break. Broken toys are also hazardous. Therefore, look for durable, well-made toys. See 9-25.

Caregivers should check the instructions that accompany toys. They can demonstrate the safe use of toys to children.

All toys are hazardous when they are left on floors, stairways, and driveways. Children should be taught responsibility for their own belongings. Caregivers can insist that children keep all toys stored when not in use. Providing adequate and safe storage space will help children with this task.

Check It Out!

1. Explain the difference between dramatic play and socio-dramatic play.
2. What are three concepts children can learn through music activities?
3. List three guidelines to follow when selecting toys for children.

Check It Out! (Answers)

1. Dramatic play involves role playing. A child imitates another person or acts out a situation, but does so alone. Socio-dramatic play involves several children imitating others and acting out situations together.
2. rhythm, pitch, rhyme
3. (List three. Student response. See pages 251-252 in the text.)

9-25 The softness of these foam blocks makes them safe toys for young children.

Topic 9-5
The First Year

Objectives
After studying this topic, you will be able to
- describe the characteristics and basic needs of newborns.
- summarize the physical, emotional, social, and intellectual development of infants.

Topic Terms
pediatrician
newborn
sudden infant death syndrome (SIDS)
infant

The first year of life is an exciting time for babies and their parents. Babies have changing needs as they grow and develop. Parents can create a nurturing environment to help meet those needs.

Parents will have many questions as they observe the development of their babies. A **pediatrician** is a doctor specializing in the care and development of children. He or she can be a vital source of information for parents when problems arise.

Newborn Babies

For the first month of life, a baby is called a **newborn**. Having a newborn in their home will be a big adjustment for parents and other family members. Parents must be prepared to care for this new little person.

Characteristics of Newborns

Newborns look different from older babies. The average newborn weighs about 7½ pounds and is about 20 to 21 inches long. The newborn's skin may appear red and wrinkled. The head may be misshapen. The chin recedes, the nose is flattened, and the ears are pressed against the head. (Some of these characteristics are less apparent on babies delivered by cesarean section.) The eyebrows and eyelashes may be barely visible. Some newborns are nearly bald.

Newborns have large heads compared to their bodies. They often have bowed legs and bulging abdomens. Newborns also have very short necks, sloping shoulders, and narrow chests.

Care of Newborns

Newborns have relatively simple needs. They need to eat and sleep. They need to be kept clean, warm, and dry. Above all, they need to be loved, 9-26.

Feeding

Babies are not able to digest solid foods until they are four to six months old. Therefore, parents must choose breast milk or formula to provide all the nutrients their newborn needs. Newborns need to be fed six to eight times a day. They generally wake up once or twice during the night to be fed.

Sleep

Newborns sleep about 18 to 20 hours a day. They tend to sleep about four to five hours at a time. Then they awaken for an

9-26 Newborns' needs are very basic, but their main need is for love and affection from all family members.

Vocabulary: Do you know what a pediatrician is?

Resource: *Picture a Newborn*, transparency master, TR

Enrich: Invite the mother of a newborn to speak to the class about the adjustments family members must make when a new baby arrives.

Note: Whole milk is not recommended until the baby is 6 months old. Newborns need about 2 to 2 ½ oz. of breast milk or formula per pound of body weight in a 24-hour period.

Across the Curriculum
Health. Discuss why most experts say breast milk is more healthful for babies than formula.

Note:
Newborns adjust to regular household sounds, so it isn't necessary to whisper or tiptoe while they are sleeping.

Resource:
Development of Infants, Activity G, SAG

Discuss:
Have you ever bathed a baby? What is most difficult about bathing a baby?

hour or so to be changed and fed before going back to sleep.

Babies need a firm, flat mattress for support and posture development. The mattress should fit inside the crib very snugly. There should be no way for children to get their heads caught between the crib and the edge of the mattress.

Sudden infant death syndrome (SIDS) is a concern of parents. SIDS is the sudden death of an apparently healthy baby during sleep. Although the cause is still unknown, several factors may be involved. As a precautionary measure, caregivers should place babies on their backs rather than their stomachs when placing them in the crib to sleep. This practice has reduced the rate of SIDS significantly. Also keep stuffed toys, pillows, and soft bedding out of the crib to prevent suffocation in bedding.

Bathing

For the first few weeks after birth, babies should be given sponge baths several times a week. Once a baby's navel has healed, he or she may be given tub baths. The baby's eyes, ears, nose, and face are cleaned first. Then the baby is carefully lowered into a small tub containing a few inches of warm water. The baby's body should be gently washed with a mild soap. Caregivers should be sure to clean the diaper area and the folds of the baby's skin. After a thorough rinsing, the baby is lifted out of the tub and gently patted dry with a soft towel, 9-27. Baby oil or lotion may be applied to moisten a baby's tender skin.

Clothes

Clothing for newborns should be made of soft, flame-retardant fabrics. Garments should be loose fitting and easy to put on and take off. Clothing should be appropriate for the existing temperature. Infants can quickly become too hot or too cold. Use sweaters and blankets as needed.

Diapers

Diapers are a basic clothing need of babies for two or more years. Parents may choose cloth or disposable diapers.

9-27 Wrapping an infant in a soft towel will give him or her a feeling of security after a bath.

Newborns need to be changed about 10 times a day. Changing diapers promptly and thoroughly cleansing the diaper area will help prevent diaper rash.

Infants

Babies up to 12 months old are called **infants**. During these months, babies change in many ways. When watching for signs of development, parents need to remember that each child is an individual. The signs of growth mentioned here are averages. Each child will develop at his or her own rate.

Early Brain Development

Scientists have recently discovered that experiences soon after birth affect much of the brain's development. The first two years of life are critical in determining how the circuits of the brain are wired. How the brain grows is dependent upon emotional interaction, and that involves

Putting Technology to Use
Have students check out the Web site for the American Sudden Infant Death Syndrome Institute at www.sids.org.

the parents and other caregivers. Babies whose parents and caregivers talk and read to them and play simple games with them have enhanced intellectual, physical, and emotional development.

The first few years of a baby's life are the most important ones for brain development. Some abilities are acquired more easily during certain time-sensitive periods. These are sometimes referred to as "windows of opportunity." Time taken to interact with the baby then will have lifelong positive effects. Time lost can be difficult to make up later.

If physical and emotional needs are met in a predictable, responsive way in the first years of life, the foundation is set for healthy emotional development. Emotional health is necessary for the development of intelligence.

Physical Growth of Infants

In their first year of life, infants will triple in weight. They will grow to 1½ times their length at birth. Their large and small muscle skills develop at an amazing rate. Parents can notice changes almost daily.

Infants progress from reflex actions to controlled muscle movement. Newborns are not able to hold up their heads. For this reason, their heads must be carefully supported when they are being held. By six months, infants can roll over. At seven months, many babies are beginning to crawl. (Once infants reach this stage, increased supervision will be needed to protect them from hazards.) Eight-month-old babies can sit alone for a period of time. By 10 months, infants may be able to stand up by themselves. Many children are able to start walking by their first birthdays.

Emotional and Social Growth of Infants

Emotionally and socially, infants, like all people, need love and attention from others. From birth, infants respond to human contact and a warm, loving environment.

Infants begin to show emotions at a very young age. Two-month-olds can show when they are distressed, excited, or happy. By five months, the range of emotions has expanded to include fear, disgust, and anger. Eight-month-old infants often demonstrate fear of strangers and may seek the comfort of parents in a stranger's presence. By the time infants are 10 months old, they begin to cry less frequently. At one year, babies begin to develop their own identities. They are also able to recognize emotions expressed by others.

Socially, newborns can recognize a parent's voice. As they grow older, infants respond to familiar faces. They also begin to show sensitivity around strangers. By five or six months, infants start to enjoy playing games like peek-a-boo. At nine months, they begin to show interest in play activities of others. At 12 months, infants socialize by practicing communication skills with adults.

Intellectual Growth of Infants

Newborns receive information and show intellectual development through their senses. They follow moving objects with their eyes and listen attentively to sounds with their ears, 9-28. By two months, infants are able to discriminate between different

9-28 Babies' visual world begins with black and white. The sharp contrast is easier to perceive and provides needed visual stimulation.

Activity:
Look through current magazines and find pictures of newborns and infants. Explain how you can tell their approximate age.

Discuss:
How can parents know what their infants are feeling when infants can't express their feelings in words?

Across the Curriculum

Biology. Have students read current journal articles on early brain development. What affects early brain development? How can caregivers contribute to development?

Activity:
Make a list of small objects that should be kept away from infants because they could choke on them.

Reflect:
Recall a mother you have seen talking to her infant. What kind of a message do you think the baby was receiving from the mother's tone of voice?

Resource:
The First Year, reproducible master, TR

voices. They also show preference for people over objects. At three months of age, infants begin to show signs of memory. As infants grow older, they remain alert for increasingly longer spans of time. By six months, infants show improved eye-hand coordination. At eight months, infants understand simple concepts, such as *in* and *out.* Ten-month-old infants will search for hidden objects. By their first birthdays, many children can put nesting toys together correctly. They may also show a preference for one hand over the other.

Toys provide infants with intellectual stimulation. Babies like toys that appeal to the senses. Bright colors, varied textures, and interesting sounds attract their attention. Since infants tend to put objects in their mouths, toys need to be kept clean. Children should not be allowed to play with small objects that could be swallowed.

Language development is a sign of intellectual growth. Newborns cry to express their needs. By three months, infants make vowel sounds, like *ooh* and *ah.* Consonant sounds begin to appear in the fourth month. Five-month-olds understand their own names. Infants begin to recognize some words at eight months. At nine months, infants may say *mama* and *dada.* They can also follow simple directions. By the end of the first year, most infants have a vocabulary of several words. They begin to use language to express themselves.

Speaking to infants will have a great impact on their language development. Newborns do not understand words, so the content of your message is unimportant. However, speaking to them allows them to enjoy human contact and helps them become familiar with specific voices, 9-29. Newborns can perceive a parent's mood. Therefore, parents should speak in pleasant tones that reflect an interest in and love for the child.

The content of messages becomes increasingly important as infants grow older. Infants begin to understand the words being spoken to them at about eight months. They begin to repeat the words they hear

9-29 Speaking to and interacting with infants is important to their intellectual growth.

by 11 or 12 months. Parents have a responsibility to use messages that provide guidance with love. They must also teach children to use appropriate terms.

Check It Out!
1. Describe three characteristics of newborns.
2. About how many hours will an average newborn sleep each day?
3. Explain briefly what has been learned about early brain development.
4. How much will a baby's weight and length increase in the first year of life?
5. Give three examples of intellectual growth of infants.

Check It Out! (Answers)
1. (Describe three. Student response. See page 253 in the text.)
2. Newborns sleep about 18 to 20 hours a day.
3. (Student response.)
4. In their first year of life, infants will triple in weight. They will grow to 1½ times their length at birth.
5. (List three. Student response. See pages 255-256 in the text.)

Topic 9-6
Children from One to Five

Objectives
After studying this topic, you will be able to
- give examples of physical, emotional, social, and intellectual characteristics of toddlers and preschoolers.
- describe types of special needs children might have and how to meet those needs.

Topic Terms
toddler
preschooler
children with special needs
physical disability
mental disability
learning disability
emotional disorder
gifted or talented
inclusion

9-30 Caregivers should expect different behaviors from children of different ages.

Vocabulary: What do you think is the age difference between a toddler and a preschooler?

Resource: *Signs of Growth*, Activity H, SAG

Discuss: What are some other ways children can develop their large and small muscle skills?

Caregivers need an understanding of what they might expect from children within a given age range, 9-30. Knowing about patterns of growth and behavior is helpful. Caregivers should also remember that all individuals are unique. Sometimes a toddler will behave as a five-year-old. At other times, the same toddler may behave as an infant. Caregivers must always maintain a flexible attitude as they work with individual children.

Children have much to learn about themselves, other people, and the world. Children do not need to be pushed to learn. They absorb much of what they need to know from their environments. Thus, a rich environment offers rich learning experiences. (See Appendix.)

Toddlers
One- and two-year-old children are called **toddlers**. This term comes from the unsteady way children move, or toddle, when they begin to walk. As children gain mobility, they have more opportunities to develop mentally and socially.

Physical Growth of Toddlers
During the toddler years, parents will see steady improvements in their child's large muscle skills. As leg muscles develop, toddlers become able to run, jump, kick, and climb as well as walk. Strengthening arm muscles enable 18-month-old toddlers to throw a ball and 36-month-old toddlers to catch one.

Small muscle skills also improve as children grow. They become able to fill and empty containers, turn knobs, and build block towers. They like to scribble, paint, play with modeling clay, and string beads. By the time a toddler is 30 months old, he or she can turn the pages of a book.

Toilet Learning
One important physical skill most children master toward the end of the toddler years is toilet learning. As children learn to control their muscles, toilet learning will

Across the Curriculum
Health. Have students research neuromuscular diseases such as muscular dystrophy and Lou Gehrig's disease. How are toddlers' muscle skills affected by these diseases?

Note:
In order for toilet learning to be successful, the sphincter muscles, which control elimination, must mature. This does not happen until about 18 months of age.

Enrich:
Go to a shopping mall or grocery store and observe toddlers with their parents. What kinds of struggles do you see going on? Is this typical toddler behavior?

Discuss:
What techniques can parents use to encourage language skills in their toddlers?

Resource:
Toddler Talk, reproducible master, TR

come naturally. Children should not be pushed to learn how to use the toilet. At some point, children will begin showing signs of awareness of their bowel movements. At this time, caregivers can begin offering the "potty" about every two hours. This helps a child stay dry. The child may have frequent bathroom accidents, but caregivers should not show disappointment. It's best to praise desired behaviors and to let undesired ones pass with minimum attention. Success in toilet learning, like other successes, will come in time.

Emotional and Social Growth of Toddlers

A toddler's emotions are difficult to predict. Many toddlers have strong reactions and react differently at different times. Their expanding range of emotions includes pride, affection, stubbornness, jealousy, and sympathy. Toddlers are quite self-centered and are often demanding, possessive, aggressive, and insecure. They seek approval and are easily hurt by criticism.

You may have heard older toddlers called the "terrible twos." Behaviors displayed at this age may be caused by insecurity. Perhaps their growing knowledge of the world makes two-year-olds suddenly feel small. To cope with this new feeling, they try to act big. They become very independent and do everything loudly. They frequently respond by saying no, even when they plan to do what is asked. Wise adults learn to phrase conversations so children are not given a chance to say no as a response.

Young toddlers enjoy *solitary play*, 9-31. They like to play beside other children rather than with them. They prefer the company of family members to the company of others. Two-year-olds can be expected to be socially aggressive. They do not like to share and have not learned to say please. Instead, they snatch the toys they want.

Intellectual Growth of Toddlers

Intellectually, toddlers have an increasing attention span. They begin to show signs of memory. They are able to

9-31 Young toddlers enjoy playing by themselves.

identify shapes and familiar objects. Toddlers enjoy imitating others, and by 20 months of age, they begin to enjoy imaginative play. Concepts learned during the toddler years include the differences between *one* and *many* and between *before* and *after*. Toddlers display active curiosity. They use thought processes to solve simple problems, and they enjoy putting puzzles together.

Toddlers show rapid increases in their language skills. They understand more words than they can say. Between the ages of one and three, however, toddlers' vocabularies will grow from three or four words to over 500 words. Two-year-olds use language to show their understanding of simple concepts. They begin to speak in two- and three-word sentences.

Preschoolers

Three-, four-, and five-year-old children are called **preschoolers**. During the preschool years, children become increasingly independent as they acquire new skills.

Physical Growth of Preschoolers

Physically, preschoolers do not gain weight and height as fast as younger children. However, large muscle skills

Across the Curriculum

Speech. Have students research speaking problems such as stuttering or lisping. How do such conditions originate? What corrective actions can be taken if a child begins to show signs of such problems?

continue to become more refined as children grow. Preschoolers have better balance and coordination. Large muscle skills expand to include hopping, skipping, dancing, and jumping rope. Preschoolers have improved accuracy in throwing and catching. They are able to use tricycles and other pedal toys. They enjoy playing on playground equipment, such as swings, slides, and jungle gyms. They can also dress themselves with greater ease.

Improved small muscle skills allow preschoolers to unbutton buttons and pull up large zippers. By age four or five, they can also lace their shoes and may be able to tie knots. They can brush their teeth and feed themselves with spoons and forks. Preschoolers can draw shapes and cut on lines with scissors. They can put puzzle pieces together and turn pages in a book, too.

Emotional and Social Growth of Preschoolers

Three-year-olds are generally cooperative and like to perform simple chores. Being a helper seems special at age three. Four-year-olds tend to be emotionally unpredictable. Four-year-olds are friendly one minute and quarrelsome the next. They like being independent and resist pressures placed on them by demonstrating stubbornness and temper. Five-year-olds generally try to please, so this is a pleasant age. They tend to be more patient and generous and less combative. They express their feelings through language rather than emotional outbursts.

Preschoolers are proud of their parents. They seek comfort, approval, and emotional support from parents. However, friends are important to preschoolers, too, 9-32. Preschoolers make friends easily and begin to seek status among their peers. They play cooperatively with their friends.

To encourage social growth, preschoolers should be given opportunities to practice sharing. They need to learn to assume responsibilities and develop dependability.

9-32 Preschoolers enjoy playing with other children their age.

Intellectual Growth of Preschoolers

Throughout the preschool years, attention span and concentration skills continue to improve. By age five, many children are eager to go to school. Intellectual growth at this age is shown by a child's ability to plan in advance. A five-year-old can tell you what he or she is going to draw before drawing it.

Preschoolers ask many questions to learn about their environments. Caregivers must show an interest in children and give honest, but simple, answers.

Caregivers can show an interest in preschoolers' intellectual growth by asking questions as well as answering them. Which is larger? Which is smaller? Which is taller? Which is shorter? Which is near? Which is far? What color is this? Which one is blue? Questions such as these are often called *reading readiness* exercises. They help prepare children for reading lessons that will come later.

Preschoolers learn how to count and begin to understand number concepts. Their vocabularies expand to over 2000 words. They enjoy listening to rhymes and stories. They also enjoy games and puzzles that allow them to use their word and number skills.

With their larger vocabularies, preschoolers begin to speak in complete sentences. Their grammar reflects that

Enrich:
Design a teaching device that can be used to teach preschoolers one of these small muscle skills.

Discuss:
How can parents encourage social growth in their preschoolers?

Enrich:
Have students observe a preschool teacher. Identify methods used to encourage intellectual growth of preschoolers.

Resource:
Preschool Play, reproducible master, TR

Family Enrichment Activity
Encourage students to watch a cartoon and a sitcom on television with their family members. Suggest that a family discussion follow concerning the suitability of the programs for preschool children.

> **Reflect:**
> Have you ever had a relationship with someone who has a physical or mental disability? As a family member or friend, what special challenges do *you* encounter?
>
> **Enrich:**
> Invite a special needs teacher to talk to the class about teaching children with learning disabilities.
>
> **Discuss:**
> What special needs do gifted children and children with disabilities have in common? How are their needs different?

used by people around them. Therefore, caregivers have a responsibility to use correct grammar since they are serving as role models for children.

Children with Special Needs

All children have needs. Some have greater needs than others. Children with disabilities and gifted and talented children are often called **children with special needs.** These children may need more or different care than average children, including extra support, instruction, or guidance.

Some special needs are described below:

- A **physical disability** limits a person's body or its functions. Limitations include either leg or arm movements or both. Physical disabilities also include vision, hearing, or speech impairments.
- A **mental disability** limits the way a person's brain functions. The child's intellectual abilities, when compared with the average, are a year or more delayed. These children have a limited learning capacity. Learning takes place slowly. Mental disabilities range from mild to severe.
- A **learning disability** is a limitation in the way a person's brain sorts and uses certain types of information. It does not affect overall brain function. *Dyslexia*, for example, impairs the ability to read. The dyslexic person sees certain letters and numbers either backwards or inverted. Learning disabilities may also affect math skills. Many learning disabilities can be treated. Others can be overcome with training in ways that compensate for the disability.
- An **emotional disorder** limits the way a person functions emotionally and socially. An emotional disorder may cause a child to be too insecure or fearful to play with other children. On the other hand, the child may be too aggressive. Emotional disorders are often marked by extremes of behavior, and can limit a child's ability to concentrate. Unfortunately, these disorders do not go away on their own. They require a diagnosis by a health care professional.
- A **gifted or talented** child shows outstanding ability in either a general sense or in a specific ability. A gifted child may have above average intelligence overall or excel in a specific academic area. A talented child may possess extraordinary skill in an area such as art, music, or athletics.

Children with special needs require the same basic care as other children. They need love and support. They need encouragement to develop their skills and overcome their weaknesses. They may also need some extra attention in certain areas. For instance, a child with a mental disability may need directions to be given one step at a time. This child may also need to have directions repeated more often. However, caregivers should resist the urge to do a child's tasks for him or her. The child needs to do as much as possible on his or her own, 9-33. This will help the child develop independence and a strong self-concept.

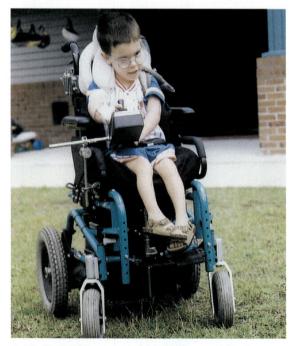

9-33 Providing ways for children with physical disabilities to do things on their own helps their self-esteem.

Problem-Solving Practice
Preparing for a Parenting Challenge, reproducible master, TR. Students are to use the decision-making process to help solve the problem described in a case study.

Inclusion

There was a time when educators thought it was best to teach special needs children with others who had similar needs. There were separate classes for the gifted and for those with specific disabilities. Today, most children with special needs are placed in classes with nondisabled children for at least a part of each day. This practice is called **inclusion**—the placing of students of varying abilities in the same class. It is believed that all children benefit from being together.

Including all children in the same classrooms helps them all experience and value diversity. Nondisabled children learn valuable lessons in understanding, caring, and compassion. Children with disabilities benefit from the acceptance and assistance of their nondisabled peers. Special needs children learn valuable social skills that prepare them for society at large.

Children with special needs create unique challenges for their caregivers. They even create hardships at times. Caregivers must treat each child according to his or her needs. Professionals can assist caregivers in meeting the unique needs of a special child. Every child deserves an opportunity to be the best person he or she is capable of being.

Check It Out!

1. List four small muscle skills that develop during the toddler years.
2. By age three, how many words does the average toddler have in his or her vocabulary?
3. True or false. Five-year-olds tend to express their feelings through emotional outbursts.
4. Explain the difference between a mental disability and a learning disability.
5. What is inclusion?

Topic 9-7
Child Care Options

Objectives
After studying this topic, you will be able to
- identify child care options.
- list factors parents should consider when choosing a child care facility.

Topic Terms
nanny child care cooperatives

Vocabulary: Discuss the many duties performed by Mary Poppins.

Resource: *Types of Child Care*, transparency master, TR

Resource: *Child Care*, Activity I, SAG

Many child care experts feel the ideal environment for child rearing is in the home with at least one parent present. However, this arrangement is not always possible, especially in dual-career or single-parent families. The numbers of women entering the work force are increasing every year. With this increase comes a rapidly growing demand by parents for quality child care. There are several options available to parents for child care. Considering each option carefully and then choosing the one that best meets their needs is important.

Types of Child Care

Many types of child care options are available to parents. Once parents identify the options available, they should evaluate the pros and cons of each one. This will help them make the best choice for their child's needs.

Child Care in the Parent's Home

This is the most desirable and convenient type of child care. In this option, the caregiver comes to the parent's home. Often the caregiver is a relative, grandparent, or close friend. Whomever the parents select, the caregiver should be a warm, loving person who interacts well with children, 9-34. This person should have similar viewpoints as the parents about child rearing.

Check It Out! (Answers)
1. (List four:) fill and empty containers, turn knobs, build block towers, scribble, paint, play with modeling clay, string beads, turn the pages of a book
2. 500
3. false
4. A mental disability limits the way a person's brain functions, delaying a child's intellectual abilities. A learning disability is a limitation in the way a person's brain sorts and uses certain types of information.
5. the placing of students of varying abilities in the same class

Note:
Child care in the parent's home is the most frequently used form of substitute child care. Discuss why this might be.

Discuss:
Would you ever consider becoming a nanny? Why or why not?

Discuss:
What are the pros and cons of child care cooperatives?

9-34 Parents want a caregiver who will interact with their child as they would.

Many parents prefer this option, especially for their infants and toddlers. Children feel more secure in a familiar setting where they receive individualized attention. They receive more consistent care. Their physical, social, emotional, and intellectual needs can be met more easily.

Some families obtain the services of a nanny. A **nanny** is a trained caregiver who provides quality care for children in the parent's home. Live-in nannies receive room and board, plus a salary for their services. Although this type of care is expensive, it is consistent. Some nannies also do household chores, which lightens the parents' workload when they are home. This allows the parents more time to spend with their child when they are home.

Child Care in the Caregiver's Home

This has been the most common type of child care in the United States. Most parents like having their young children in a family-type setting. This encourages children to develop a close relationship with the caregiver. Other benefits include less structure that allows time for play and relaxation. The hours are usually more flexible and the care costs less. Children are less likely to be over-stimulated by the activities of a large group of children. Most states require these homes to be licensed, but this is difficult to enforce.

Child Care Cooperatives

Child care cooperatives are formed by groups of parents who share in the care of the children. These programs allow parents more control over the child care program. They formulate policy, establish the budget, determine the instructional program, and provide care for the children. Parents also hire teachers or other personnel who may be needed. Cooperatives are often formed so parents can take turns caring for children. They pay for the care of their children by working in the center. Instead of paying a fee for child care, many volunteer for a certain number of hours.

Across the Curriculum
Social studies. Have students research the state and local regulations for child care in a caregiver's home. Discuss the regulations in class. What is the reasoning for these regulations?

School or University-Sponsored Child Care Programs

Some parents enroll their children in a school or university-sponsored program where student teachers are being trained in child care. These programs offer high quality in both staff and curriculum, 9-35. Availability is limited to university towns or school systems that provide the caregiver training.

Church or Social Group Programs

Child care programs sponsored by church or social groups usually cost less because the sponsor helps fund the costs. For example, church-sponsored child care would likely be based in one of the church buildings. Eliminating the cost of providing a facility cuts the operating expense greatly. The staff for these programs are not only responsible to the parents, but also to the sponsor. These are usually high-quality programs.

Government-Sponsored Child Care Programs

Programs such as Head Start are sponsored by the government. These programs are offered to lower-income working families who may need low-cost child care. Again, the sponsor underwrites the expense of operating the facility. However, the program must meet strict guidelines to be licensed. Fees charged for participation are very low or nonexistent.

Employer-Sponsored Child Care Services

Businesses are becoming more involved in helping working parents meet child care needs. These programs are increasing as their records show that employees are more dependable when child care is provided for their children. Companies who provide child care have less turnover and less absenteeism among workers.

> **Discuss:** Head Start programs welcome volunteer assistance from children's parents. Why is this a positive idea?
>
> **Enrich:** Research local employers to see if child care facilities are provided. If no facilities are available, ask if other benefits are offered to employees who have young children.

9-35 College child care programs offer quality care for children and excellent training for future child care workers.

Putting Technology to Use
Have students create a Web site that explains each type of child care discussed in the chapter. Students may list the names of community child care programs on the site after receiving permission from the programs.

> **Resource:**
> *Evaluating Child Care*, reproducible master, TR
>
> **Activity:**
> Check the state licensing requirements for adult-child ratios in child care facilities. Discuss the importance of not exceeding these numbers.
>
> **Note:**
> It is important that children like their caregivers. Parents should not resent this bond.

Employers sponsor different types of child care facilities. On-site child care facilities are located on the company grounds, so parents are close at hand if their children need them. Some facilities are off-site, near the workplace. Others are existing child care facilities contracted by the company for their employees. In each of these options, employers may pay all or part of the child care costs.

Privately Owned or Franchised Child Care Centers

These child care facilities are profit-motivated. Privately owned child care centers are operated as any other business except they provide child care. Most franchised child care centers started as privately owned centers. Entrepreneurs saw an opportunity to meet a need, so they created a larger group of centers. These chains try to offer uniform facilities, equipment, and programs. Similar services are often provided in all centers under the franchise. If parents like the franchise in New York, for instance, they can expect the same services in Oklahoma.

Selecting Quality Child Care

Putting time and effort into choosing quality child care is important for parents. They need to consider their needs, as well as their children's needs. They realize that their children's development will be affected by the child care environment and the caregivers. The health and safety of their children is a concern as well. Knowing what to look for in a quality program and knowing the right questions to ask are the keys to successful child care experiences, 9-36.

When deciding among the child care options, parents need to consider many factors. The four major factors include the setting, programs, adult-child ratios, and caregivers.

Comfortable, Homelike Setting

The physical setting of the room should be comfortable and appeal to children. Furnishings should be child-sized and the decor cheerful and bright in color. A homelike and flexible setting is needed to provide for active play, quiet play, group play, and independent activities.

Age-Appropriate Programs

Although programs differ in content and approach, children should be in programs appropriate for their stage of development. Infants and toddlers have some unique needs. Programs for these children should not be scaled-down versions of programs designed for preschoolers. Activities for younger children should help them to trust the adults who care for them. Programs for older children should offer a variety of learning experiences.

Adequate Adult Supervision

Because children need personalized care, the adult-child ratio should be considered. Many states outline requirements regarding the adult-child ratio for licensed facilities. In most cases, one adult is considered appropriate for three infants, four toddlers, or eight preschoolers.

Consistent, Quality Care Provided by Caregivers

The quality of care given by child care workers is important. They should be well trained and experienced for their work with children. They should enjoy interacting with young children and be friendly and affectionate toward them. Each child should feel appreciated and be given encouragement and praise. See 9-37.

Caregivers should understand that building trust and self-confidence is important in the early years. They should provide opportunities for children to experiment and to be creative. Children should be urged to ask questions, investigate, make decisions, and assume responsibilities. Guidance should be firm, fair, and consistent with the child's needs.

The quality of care can be observed by visiting a child care facility. High quality facilities should be busy, happy places.

Citizenship and Service

Have students identify needs of child care centers, particularly nonprofit ones. Identify projects students might do to improve facilities or assist as volunteers. Projects might include planting trees, painting playground equipment, reading stories to children, and assisting with physical care.

Topic 9-7 Child Care Options 265

Selecting Quality Child Care

The Facility
- Does the care facility meet state, county, and city licensing requirements? Is it checked regularly by authorities to see that certain standards are maintained?
- Does the care facility have a good reputation?
- Is the care facility in a convenient location?
- What is the cost for each child?
- Are alternative schedules available to meet various needs for hours per day and days per week?

The Setting
- Does the setting have a warm, homelike atmosphere?
- Are the rooms and play areas designed and decorated with children in mind?
- Is the care facility equipped with a variety of safe play equipment and arranged with safety in mind?
- What precautions are taken to prevent children from wandering away and to prevent strangers from entering the premises?
- Are the restrooms clean, easy for children to use, and in good repair?
- Do the children have a comfortable and quiet place for naps?
- Is there an isolated place for an ill child?
- Is good emergency care available for the children if the need arises?
- Is the food nutritious, well prepared, and suited to the age of the children?

The Programs
- Are the children grouped according to age? Are suitable activities planned for each age group?
- Are children allowed to choose some of their own activities? Are they allowed time for quiet individual play as well as active group play?
- Is each child respected as an individual?
- Are the needs of the parents recognized by the caregivers?

The Adult-Child Ratio
- What is the adult-child ratio?
- Are all areas of the care facility supervised at all times?
- If a child needs individual attention at times, would this be available?

The Caregivers
- Are the caregivers well trained and experienced?
- Are interactions between caregivers and children pleasant?
- Do the caregivers encourage the physical, intellectual, emotional, and social development of the children?
- Do the caregivers attend promptly to children's needs?
- Are the caregivers calm, gentle, and fair to the children? Do they have a good sense of humor?
- Do the caregivers use guidance techniques without the use of harsh punishment?
- Do the children seem happy?

Enrich: Arrange to visit a child care facility in your area. Using the chart on this page, evaluate this facility.

Resource: *Child Care Checklist*, Activity J, SAG

9-36 Parents should carefully evaluate each of these factors before selecting a child care program.

Children should be seen learning and playing under the supervision of friendly, alert adults.

Other Factors

The location of the care facility and the fees charged for care are other factors parents may also consider. These two items are important. However, they must not be weighed too heavily against the goals of parenting. Parents want to be sure that their children will grow and learn. They want to provide their children with a safe, healthy setting. When parents are working, they also want their children to receive warm, loving care.

Putting Technology to Use
Have students create pamphlets advertising a local child care facility. Have them include positive points about the center based on the questions in Chart 9-36. (Pamphlets should not be distributed without the permission of the center.)

9-37 Child care workers should demonstrate a positive attitude toward their work. They should enjoy interacting with children, as well as encourage each child's development.

Check It Out!

1. True or false. Many people think the ideal environment for child rearing is in the home with at least one parent present.
2. List eight child care options.
3. List four factors parents should consider when choosing a child care facility.

Check It Out! (Answers)

1. true
2. (List eight:) care in the parent's home, care in the caregiver's home, child care cooperatives, school-sponsored programs, university-sponsored programs, church group programs, social group programs, government-sponsored programs, employer-sponsored services, privately owned centers, franchised centers
3. (List four:) setting, programs, adult-child ratio, caregivers, location, fees

TEENS ARE CONCERNED ABOUT...

Child Abuse and Neglect

Over two million cases of child abuse and neglect are reported each year in the United States. Sadly, many more cases are not reported. Experts estimate that for every neglect or abuse case reported in a community, two more are known and not reported.

Karen J. Farestad, Ph.D, has been working on behalf of vulnerable children and families for more than 15 years. She is Associate Director of the Children's Division of the American Humane Association (AHA). For over 100 years, the AHA has been involved in protecting the well-being of children.

Q: *Why do parents abuse their children?*

A: Most parents, even those who abuse their children, want to be good parents. Abuse happens in every income and age group, in every racial group, and to children of both sexes. Researchers can't predict with certainty which parent will become abusive or neglectful. However, we know that abuse is associated with the following factors:

- Extreme stress, such as loss of a job or housing.
- Extreme isolation, as when someone who is stressed has no one else to share the burdens they are experiencing.
- Unrealistic expectations for children, such as expecting children to be toilet trained before they are physically ready.
- A lack of understanding of effective discipline methods that do not involve physical or emotional punishment.
- A lack of basic resources for food, shelter, or clothing that prevent a parent from providing basic necessities for their child.
- Experienced abuse as a child.
- Abuse alcohol or drugs when children are under their care.

Any of the above factors, or a combination of factors, can contribute to the children being abused or neglected.

Q: *Studies have shown that child abusers were often abused as children. How can this cycle be broken?*

A: Some teens who have been victims of abuse are concerned that they, too, will abuse their children. They are concerned that they will not be able to control it. This is not true. Many, many victims of abuse have overcome this experience and have been successful parents of happy children. However, if you have been a victim of abuse, or if you are now a victim of abuse, you need to know that

- abuse is wrong
- you are not to blame for this abuse
- you need to talk to someone about your abuse
- you can get help to stop the abuse and to stop the emotional hurt caused by the abuse you have suffered

Abuse can pass from generation to generation under certain circumstances. It happens when parents who have been victims of abuse don't learn new ways to parent. It happens when their old anger and pain boils over, and they misdirect that anger and pain to their own child. One young woman was sexually and physically abused by her older male cousin. In turn, she abused her younger male cousin. She told her therapist she did this because she was "mad at boys for hurting her" and she wanted to "hurt back." With the help of her therapy, she understood that she was only passing her pain on to someone else.

Q: *How can teens recognize signs of child abuse when caring for children?*

A: All forms of abuse are very harmful to children, but the symptoms of abuse vary. In the case of physical abuse, children may have frequent or unusual bruises in various stages of healing. Cigarette burns, or unexplained fractures or cuts are other physical symptoms. Children who have been the victims of abuse may exhibit self-destructive behavior. They may be excessively withdrawn, depressed, or aggressive. Children who have been the victims of sexual abuse may show the above

Discuss:
- Both abused children and abused adults often feel they are to blame. Why do you think this is so?
- What would you do if you suspected a child you babysit is being abused?

Discuss:
- You must be fairly certain a child is being abused before you contact an agency. What might happen if it was determined that a child you reported was not being abused?
- What can you do to help a family that shows signs of stress?

Activity:
Look in the phone book and find the phone numbers of county and state agencies that should be contacted if child abuse is suspected.

---

signs, too. They may also exhibit inappropriate sex play or premature understanding of sex. If a child tells you that he or she has been abused, take that report seriously.

Significant changes in a child's behavior should always be discussed with the parent who is responsible for the child's care. In addition, discussing any concerns you have with your own parent or another trusted adult may be helpful. These adults can help you evaluate the situation, particularly if a child has told you that he or she is being abused.

Q: *What should teens do if they suspect child abuse when caring for children?*

A: Every community has a public service agency that is responsible for professionally evaluating situations involving child abuse. This agency determines whether or not a child has been abused and if the family needs help. This agency is usually called "Child Protective Services." It is listed in the phone book under the Social Services Department or Public Welfare Department of your county or state government.

Some people mistakenly believe it is their responsibility to decide if a child has been abused. This is not true. It is a citizen's responsibility to help report suspected abuse to the public agency. It is that agency's responsibility to assess the situation and make a determination. Sometimes teenagers feel able to handle this reporting responsibility. Other times they need the help of a trusted adult to make such a report.

The real solution to child abuse is for the whole community to get involved in helping families in stress before abuse occurs. As a teenager, you can help with this problem. Sometimes people feel overwhelmed when they learn that over one million children are abused each year, and think "I can't possibly help." This is not true. Child abuse is solved one child at a time.

Oftentimes we see signs of stress in a family to whom we are close. You may notice a parent speaking or acting in ways that show he or she is stressed out. If you are a babysitter, you might be able to help by offering to babysit or to fix dinner. Encourage the parents to get out of the house for a short time. All parents of young children experience stress in their lives. Some stresses are worse than others—during a divorce, or when someone loses his or her job. Even holidays, when children are excited and expectations become high, are extremely stressful.

The responsibility to save a million children from child abuse is more than any of us can bear. However, if each of us were to help one child and one family, we really could solve this problem. If you know of a friend, a child you babysit, or a family in your neighborhood who needs a hand, lend it. That much you can do.

Feature-Related Activity

Have students look for newspaper articles about child abuse cases to bring to class. As they read the articles, have them identify possible factors, such as those listed in the feature, that may have contributed to the potential for abuse.

Chapter Review

Summary

Many people may fill the role of caregiver for a child. The primary caregivers are the parents. Responsible caregivers have certain personal qualities, skills, knowledge, and experience. The responsibilities of caregivers include meeting children's physical, social, emotional, and intellectual needs.

Parents must make sure that children's physical needs are met. They need to offer children a variety of nutritious and appealing foods for meals and snacks. They must consider the fit, features, fabric, and construction of the clothes they select for their children. Parents need to encourage their children to be physically active. They also need to create a healthy and safe environment for their children.

Parents must meet children's social and emotional needs as well as their physical needs. They need to communicate with their children and teach them independence and responsibility. They need to provide guidance to direct their children's behavior. Parents also need to help their children learn to overcome fears.

Parents must not overlook their children's intellectual needs. They can stimulate children's intellectual development by reading to them and telling them stories. Art and music activities can be intellectually stimulating. When choosing toys that promote intellectual growth, parents must consider age appropriateness and safety.

Parents must quickly learn how to care for their newborns during the first year of life. Then as infants grow physically, emotionally, socially, and intellectually, parents will enjoy watching for signs of development.

Although growth is fastest in the first year, children from ages one to five continue to develop with amazing speed. Parents must provide an atmosphere that will foster growth in all areas. Parents will also have to address any special needs that their children might have.

Many types of child care options are available for families. In selecting quality child care, parents must consider several factors. Selecting the option that best meets their needs and their child's needs is important.

Think About It!

1. Rank the characteristics of responsible caregivers from the most important to the least important in your view. What did you choose as the most important characteristic and the least important characteristic?
2. How would you encourage children who are fussy eaters to eat foods that are good for them?
3. What types of games and play activities would you use to help children develop physically?
4. Describe some problems you have had when working with small children. How might good guidance techniques have simplified the situations?
5. What techniques do you think would be most effective for guiding a child's behavior? Explain your answer.
6. What types of activities would you prefer to use to stimulate a child intellectually? Explain your answer.
7. What do you think would be the greatest challenge of caring for a newborn?

Reflect: Do you hope to have children someday? Has what you have learned in this chapter encouraged you or discouraged you?

Reflect: After reading this chapter, do you now have a better idea of what it takes to meet children's needs? Do you think you will make a good parent?

Resource: *PowerZone Challenge CD.* Have students play the chapter review game to reinforce text content.

8. What would you expect if you were babysitting a toddler? What would you expect if you were babysitting a preschooler?
9. If you were a working parent, how would you select child care for your children? What factors would you consider in making your selection?

Try It Out!

1. Many parents and caregivers today use the Internet as a source for child care information. Visit several Web sites for parents and caregivers. Set up a check sheet for evaluating the Web site. Which would you rate the highest for accuracy, objectivity, currency, and coverage?
2. Develop a checklist of factors that would help you select clothes for children.
3. Plan some activities designed to teach children independence and responsibility. Invite some children to class or volunteer to work in a preschool program and conduct the activities. Write a report about the results.
4. Write a story about a child. In the story, describe factors in the child's environment that provide extrinsic guidance. Also describe a situation in which the child practices intrinsic guidance.
5. In a small group, discuss fears that you had as a young child. Talk about what you think motivated the fears. Describe the role older individuals played as you overcame them.
6. Observe a children's story hour at your local library. Give a brief oral report describing how the librarians stimulate interest as they read.
7. Visit a toy department and compile a list of five toys that would be appropriate for preschoolers. Briefly describe how each toy will foster the development of a child.
8. Investigate how to feed, bathe, clothe, or diaper a newborn. Use a doll to give a demonstration to the class.
9. Investigate programs in your school district that are available to assist children with special needs. Find out if any of these programs are designed for preschool children. Report your findings in class.
10. Pretend you are a working parent who needs to select child care. Visit both an in-home service and a child care facility in your local area. Develop a checklist to evaluate the caregivers, programs, and services each provides. Then list the pros and cons of each facility. Based on your comparison, which type of child care would you choose for your child? Explain your answer.

Children learn a lot about their world by exploring on their own.

CAREER TIMES
LEADING GUIDE TO THE WORLD OF WORK

VOLUME 1, NUMBER 3

The ABCs of Careers in Early Childhood Education and Services

People in careers in early childhood education and services help meet the needs of young children. Those employed in this area work with children up to five or six years of age. Some workers provide only physical care and emotional comfort. Others teach children, helping to meet their mental and social needs.

Employment Opportunities

This field includes the full range of workers in child care centers, from teachers to cooks. It also includes people who develop materials for children, such as toys and books.

Preschool teachers and their assistants work in public or private centers. Teachers help children learn basic physical, mental, emotional, and social skills. Teacher's assistants help teachers with tasks such as record keeping, preparing instructional materials, and setting up learning centers. The services provided by teacher's assistants allow teachers more time for teaching.

Managers set the objectives and standards for child care centers. These professionals supervise the staff and make sure the center meets state regulations. Managers are also in charge of budgeting, marketing, hiring, and other administrative functions. In larger child care centers, a manager may have an assistant.

Some child care workers work mostly with infants. These employees feed, diaper, comfort, and play with babies. Other workers attend to the basic needs of older children by involving them in activities that stimulate development.

Family child care providers are self-employed. They care for children in their homes and may do all the tasks described above. Nannies may also perform a variety of tasks for children. However, nannies live in the homes of the children for whom they care.

Entrepreneurial Opportunities

Child care workers who want to be self-employed and have a sense of business management have a number of options. These entrepreneurs may provide family child care in their homes. They may also care for children in the parent's home. Entrepreneurs can choose to run child care centers or early childhood education centers. The goal in a child care center is to supervise children and keep them safe while they play. The focus in early childhood education centers is on providing preschool learning experiences. Running a cleaning, catering, or transportation service for a child care center is another option for an entrepreneur.

Rewards and Demands of Careers in Early Childhood Education and Services

Children have unique ways of rewarding those who care for them and help them feel secure. Child care workers often receive smiles, hugs, and words of affection from the children in their care. People who work with children are also rewarded by the knowledge that they

From aides to administrators, positions in a child care center fall at all levels of the career ladder.

are making a difference in young lives. Child care workers see their reflection through the children with whom they work. This may help the workers improve their communication skills, experience learning, and fine-tune their personal skills.

Working with children can place a demand on patience and physical stamina. Each child is unique and makes different demands on a caregiver. Attending to each child's interests and problems requires a great deal of standing, walking, bending, stooping, and lifting. Providing fair but firm discipline and being on the alert to foresee and prevent problems can also be demanding. Child care workers often face stressful conditions, low pay, and few benefits. Employee turnover in this occupation is high. Those who stay are frequently asked to help train new employees.

Preparation Requirements

Educational requirements for child care careers vary from state to state. Some states require training such as health and first aid, fire safety, and child abuse detection and prevention. Future workers in this field need to check the job requirements in their states.

High school students wishing to work with young children would be wise to take at least one child-related course. Those who want to become teachers should take college preparatory courses.

Entry-Level Jobs

A minimum amount of education is required for entry-level jobs. For instance, an elementary school teacher's aide needs only a high school diploma.

Mid-Level Jobs

People in mid-level careers often learn needed skills through a two-year program or some specialized training. A recreation director or a nanny would likely receive this type of training.

Professional-Level Jobs

As a rule, a person working at the professional level has at least a four-year degree. A university professor who trains child care teachers would be likely to have a doctorate. Elementary, kindergarten, and preschool teachers are among the professionals who work in this area. Managers of child care centers work at this level, too.

Personal Qualities Needed for Success

People who work with children are role models and should set a good example. Workers in this field should be prepared to share love and demonstrate caring. They need a healthy sense of humor. They should understand child growth and development. Good health, physical stamina, and emotional stability are essential.

Those who teach or provide daily care must be flexible in planning activities. This requires creativity, resourcefulness, and organization. Child care workers need to be full of new ideas. They should have an interest in art, music, dancing, singing, and crafts. These activities all help stimulate learning and encourage social interaction among children.

Young children tend to be noisy and impulsive. Therefore, patience is a necessary quality for working with children. Child care workers also need a positive attitude that expects the unexpected.

Future Trends

The large percentage of mothers in the workforce has created a great demand for child care services. There is currently a shortage of child care workers in the United States. Shortages are expected to continue as long as the wages for workers in this field remain low.

Career Interests, Abilities, and You

To find out if working with young children interests you, consider taking a child development course in high school. Volunteer and part-time work experiences can also help you see if this field suits you. You might baby-sit or work at a day camp. You could also tutor elementary school children in reading or volunteer to work with children in an after-school program. Talk with others who have chosen a child-related career. Ask them about their duties and experiences. This will help you see if you have the skills, interests, and traits essential for this important career.

Career Ladder for Early Childhood Education and Services

Advanced Degree
Child psychologist
Children's librarian
Pediatrician

Bachelor's Degree
Child care administrator
Preschool teacher
Toy designer

Associate's Degree
After-school program coordinator
Math or language tutor
Recreational director

High School Diploma
Bus driver
Recreation aide
Teacher's assistant

Pre-High School Diploma
Babysitter
Child care center aide
Day camp counselor

Part Four
Managing in Today's World

Chapter 10
Learning to Manage

Careers

These careers relate to the topics in this chapter:
- credit counselor
- account manager
- financial planner
- family economics specialist

As you study the chapter, see if you can think of others.

Topics

10-1 The Management Process
10-2 Managing Your Time
10-3 Managing Your Money
10-4 Using Financial Services
10-5 Saving for the Future
10-6 Meeting Insurance Needs

Introductory Activities

1. Introduce the concept of management to students by telling them *management* means using what you have to get what you want. Explain that things people have are called *resources*. Explain that things people want are called *goals*. The term *goals* was introduced in Chapter 1. Ask if students recall how personal priorities are related to goals. Explain that these terms will be used again in this chapter as they study money management.
2. Ask what kinds of problems students have concerning money—besides not having enough! Relate the problems students identify to the topics that will be covered in this chapter.

Topic 10-1
The Management Process
I. Identify and Prioritize Your Goals
II. Recognize Your Personal Priorities and Standards
III. Determine Your Resources
   A. Nonhuman and Human Resources
   B. Resource Limitations
   C. Flexibility of Resources
      1. Substituting Resources
      2. Combining Resources
      3. Exchanging Resources
IV. Form a Plan
V. Implement the Plan
VI. Evaluate the Results

Topic 10-2
Managing Your Time
I. Why Plan Your Time?
   A. Short-Term Goals Are Met
   B. Long-Term Goals Are Met
   C. Visionary Goals Are Addressed
II. Steps in Time Management
   A. Planning
      1. Get Organized
      2. Consider Goals and Personal Priorities
      3. Make To-Do Lists
      4. Create a Weekly Plan
   B. Implementing the Plan
   C. Evaluating the Plan
III. Managing Time Wisely
   A. Using Time Management Aids
   B. Using Time Management Strategies
IV. Energy and Task Management
   A. Balancing Personal, Family, Work, and Leisure Time

Topic 10-3
Managing Your Money
I. The Basics of Budgeting
   A. Establish Financial Goals
   B. Determine Sources of Income
   C. Estimate Expenses
   D. Compare Income and Expenses
   E. Write the Budget and Keep Records
   F. Evaluate the Budget
II. Reducing Flexible Expenses
   A. Food
   B. Clothing
   C. Transportation
   D. Recreation
   E. Other Expenses
   F. Future Expenses
III. Budgeting with a Computer

Topic 10-4
Using Financial Services
I. Choosing a Financial Institution
   A. Financial Services
      1. Savings Accounts
      2. Checking Accounts
      3. Debit Cards
      4. Automated Teller Machines (ATMs)
      5. Loans
      6. Certified and Cashier's Checks
      7. Traveler's Checks
      8. Safe-Deposit Boxes
      9. Other Financial Services
   B. Types of Institutions
II. Using a Checking Account
   A. Types of Accounts
   B. Opening an Account and Making a Deposit
   C. Writing a Check
   D. Endorsing a Check
   E. Balancing Your Checkbook

Topic 10-5
Saving for the Future
I. Why Save?
II. Factors in Deciding How to Save
III. Savings Accounts
   A. Regular Savings Accounts
   B. Certificates of Deposit
IV. Decisions About Securities
   A. Why Invest in Securities?
   B. Stocks
   C. Bonds
   D. Mutual Funds
V. Planning an Estate

Topic 10-6
Meeting Insurance Needs
I. Insurance Basics
II. Life Insurance
   A. Term Insurance
   B. Whole Life Insurance
   C. Universal Life Insurance
III. Health Insurance
   A. Types of Health Coverage
      1. Workers' Compensation
   B. Health Maintenance Organizations
   C. Preferred Provider Organizations
IV. Automobile Insurance
   A. Types of Auto Coverage
   B. Automobile Insurance Premiums
V. Housing-Related Insurance
   A. Filing a Claim

Vocabulary:
What do you think might be the difference between a human resource and a nonhuman resource?

Reflect:
How many of you find yourselves so busy that you forget to do your homework or show up late for an appointment? Learning about the management process and practicing it will help you take better control of your life.

Reflect:
Think of a goal you would like to reach or a problem you would like to solve.

Topic 10-1
The Management Process

Objectives
After studying this topic, you will be able to
- explain the management process.
- identify your resources, recognize their limits, and apply techniques to make the most of them.

Topic Terms
management
resource
management process
nonhuman resource
human resource

You live in a busy world. You have to keep track of responsibilities, assignments, and deadlines. Keeping all these details straight is not always easy. Learning some management skills can help you maintain control of your life.

Management can be defined as wisely using means to achieve goals. The means used are called resources. **Resources** may be time, objects, services, or abilities.

Management involves following a series of steps called the **management process.** You begin the process by identifying your goals. Then you must recognize your personal priorities and standards and determine what resources you have available. You must form a plan and put it into action. The final step of the management process is to evaluate the results. This process will help you use your resources efficiently to solve problems, make decisions, and meet goals, 10-1.

The management process can be used by families and other groups as well as by individuals. It helps all members know what goals have been set and what plans are to be followed. Otherwise, group resources may not be used efficiently and group goals might not be met. For instance, in one family, all members needed to know that cleaning the house on Saturday was a family goal. Then

The Management Process
1. Identify your goals.
2. Recognize your personal priorities and standards.
3. Determine your resources.
4. Form a plan.
5. Implement the plan.
6. Evaluate the results.

10-1 Using the management process helps people wisely use their resources.

members would not plan to meet other goals, such as seeing a movie with friends. When cleaning started, the plan outlining each person's responsibilities needed to be followed. This prevented such problems as having two people dust the furniture at different times during the day.

Identify and Prioritize Your Goals

You need to know where you are going in order to decide the best way to get there. The first step in the management process is to clearly identify your goals and rank them in priority order. The most important goal is *number one,* the second is *number two,* and so on. This will help you make decisions in line with your goals as you progress through the other steps.

The management process can be used to solve problems. Finding a solution to a problem is actually a goal. Suppose your car is in the repair shop, and you cannot drive to the game on Friday night. Your problem is that your car is not available. However, focusing on your problem will not make your car available any faster. Your goal is to find another way to get to the game. Focusing on your goal can spur you into action by getting the management process started.

Groups may find it harder to get through this first step than individuals. Since each member may have different personal priorities and standards, setting goals may not always be easy. Some members may have to compromise on the goals they want to set.

FCCLA Activity
Encourage members working on the Financial Fitness program to develop a project applying concepts from this chapter. Suggested projects include: assembling this information into a resource booklet for teens seeking new sources of income; interviewing students about how they spend money for a school newspaper article; comparison shopping for a major purchase to make the most of financial resources.

Recognize Your Personal Priorities and Standards

You tend to take actions that support your personal priorities and maintain your standards. Therefore, you need to recognize the personal priorities and standards that relate to your problem. They will affect the way you choose to reach your goal. For instance, if you think health and exercise are important, you might consider walking to the game. If you value convenience, you are more likely to ask a friend to pick you up. Suppose you have a high standard for promptness. You may not want to ride with a friend who cannot get to the stadium in time for the kickoff.

Determine Your Resources

The types and amounts of resources people have vary. The third step in the management process is to assess your resources. This will help you determine which to use to reach your goal.

Nonhuman and Human Resources

Resources can be classified as nonhuman or human. See 10-2. **Nonhuman resources** are not physically or mentally part of a person. They include time, money, possessions, and community resources. *Community resources* are parks, schools, libraries, and other facilities that are shared by many people. Kitchen equipment and food supplies are nonhuman resources that could help you reach a goal of satisfying hunger. Public transportation is a nonhuman resource that could help you reach your goal of getting to the game.

Human resources come from within people. They include skills, knowledge, talents, energy, and people themselves. Athletic skill is a human resource that helps ballplayers achieve the goal of winning a game. Teachers are human resources that help students reach the goal of getting an education. Energy needed to walk is a human resource you could use to get to the game.

People do not always recognize the value of their human resources. These resources can often be used in place of nonhuman resources. For instance, sewing skills can be used instead of money to make clothes rather than buy them. Although fabric and sewing items cost money, they cost a lot less than a finished garment. Also, cooking skills can be used to prepare food at home instead of spending considerably more money to eat out.

Many times, human resources need to be used with nonhuman resources to reach goals. For instance, skill in operating a computer is a human resource. However, it must be coupled with the nonhuman resource of a computer in order to be useful. With this blend of resources, countless goals can be reached. You could write reports and calculate math problems to reach goals at school. You could type letters and send electronic mail to reach communication goals. You could access information to achieve research goals.

Time is a special resource. All people have the same amount of time, 24 hours a day, but use it differently. Because the use of time is unique to every person, this resource will be given individual treatment in Topic 10-2.

Resources

Human	Nonhuman
abilities	appliances
communication	car
creativity	clothing
dedication	fire and police
enthusiasm	protection
flexibility	food
interests	housing
knowledge	libraries
optimism	money
people	parks
skills	schools
talents	time

10-2 Both human and nonhuman resources can be used to meet goals.

> **Reflect:**
> Identify personal priorities and standards that relate to your goal.
>
> **Activity:**
> Brainstorm a list of nonhuman resources available in your community.
>
> **Reflect:**
> What resources do you possess that could help you reach your goal?

Across the Curriculum

Social studies. Have students think of developing countries. What types of human resources do the people of these countries possess? What nonhuman resources do they lack? How does this lack of nonhuman resources influence the development of the countries?

> **Discuss:**
> What is the difference between an expendable resource and an expandable resource?
>
> **Activity:**
> Make a list of expandable resources people may possess.
>
> **Activity:**
> Form a small group. Make a list of resources. Then make a list of substitutes that could be used in place of those resources.

Resource Limitations

All people have a variety of resources. However, they have limited amounts of each resource. No one has an endless amount of money, time, energy, or any other resource.

The limits on resources will be different at different points in your life. For instance, the longer you work, the greater your income is likely to be. This means you will have more money available when you are older than you do now. On the other hand, as you get older, you are likely to have less energy than you do now.

In addition to being limited, many resources are expendable. In other words, they can be used up. For instance, a piece of paper is an expendable resource. It can be used to reach the goal of sending a letter. The piece of paper cannot be used again to reach a future goal of writing a report. See 10-3.

Not all expended resources are gone forever. Some can be renewed. For instance, taking a nap or eating a snack can restore your energy.

Some resources are actually expandable. Solving problems, making decisions, and using skills, for example, tend to improve with use. In fact, they may weaken when not used.

10-3 Food is an expendable resource. It can be used only once to meet the goal of satisfying hunger.

Knowing which resources are limited and which can be renewed or expanded can help you plan. You need to think about how future goals might be affected before deciding to use resources for present goals. You do not want to deplete a resource now if you will need it in the future. In your goal of getting to the game, taking public transportation would require money. Money is an expendable resource. If you have a goal of buying a gift next week, you might not want to use this resource now. Walking to the game might be a better choice since it requires energy—a renewable resource.

Flexibility of Resources

Resources are flexible. They can be decreased and increased in a number of ways. For instance, breaking your leg would temporarily decrease your athletic skill. Taking a computer class would increase your knowledge and skill with computers. Losing your job would decrease your income. Winning a contest would suddenly increase the amount of money you have available.

You cannot plan to win a contest. However, you can use various techniques to help you make the most of limited resources. These techniques include substituting, combining, and exchanging resources.

Substituting Resources

One resource can often be substituted for another because most goals can be reached in more than one way. People often substitute a plentiful resource for one that is more limited. Friendship, money, and energy are all resources. They could all be used to reach the goal of getting to the game. If you have too little money, you could substitute friendship or energy.

Combining Resources

Most goals are reached through the use of a combination of resources. For instance, walking to the game would require both time and energy. Riding with a friend would require the friend's car as well as the friend.

Career Preparation Activity

Making Your Way in Management, reproducible master, TR. Students are to interview someone who works in a management position. They are to write the interviewee's responses to the questions and then complete an evaluation at the bottom of the page.

Family members often combine their resources. Together, a family unit has more resources than any one person in the family. Each family member can contribute human resources. Some members may cook; others may be able to repair appliances. All family members may contribute to cleaning and other home care tasks. Families often have an easier time meeting goals when they work together, 10-4.

Exchanging Resources

Resources must often be exchanged to achieve a goal. Money is probably the resource that is exchanged most frequently. Money can be exchanged for a wide range of goods and services. Food, clothing, furniture, vacations, and the services of doctors, plumbers, and mechanics can all be obtained in exchange for money.

Money is not the only resource that is exchanged. People exchange time, energy, and skills, too. For instance, you might use your math skill to tutor your friend in exchange for a ride to the game. Also, you might use your sewing skills and several hours of time to create clothes too expensive to buy.

Form a Plan

The fourth step in the management process is to form a plan. Begin forming your plan by deciding exactly what steps to take to reach your goal. Think about the best order for accomplishing the steps.

When working toward a short-term goal, like your goal to get to the game, this step may be brief. You might plan to check the bus schedule, walk to the bus stop, and get on the bus. Long-term goals, however, will require more in-depth planning. For these goals, you should write down the steps of your plan for frequent review. Be sure to list everything you must do. Note people you must see and materials you will need. When you make a thorough plan, you are less likely to forget little details.

Determine standards for each step in your plan. This will help you know when you have accomplished the step to your satisfaction. Set deadlines, too. Deadlines keep you working toward the goal by preventing you from getting sidetracked.

Activity:
Create a poster entitled *Family Resources*. Include on it a list of resources a family might possess.

Reflect:
Think of a resource you possess that could be exchanged for another resource.

Resource:
What's in Your Resource Bank? reproducible master, TR

Reflect:
Form a plan to reach the goal or solve the problem you identified earlier.

10-4 Family members combine resources when they work together to complete a task, such as preparing a meal.

Family Enrichment Activity

Encourage students to talk to their parents about how the parents managed their money when they were teens. What were their sources of income? What kinds of weekly expenses did they have? What kinds of big purchases did they save their money for? How did prices of items when they were young compare to the prices of items today?

Implement the Plan

Putting your plan into action is the fifth step of the management process. Again, this step may take little effort when working toward short-term goals. It would involve actually checking the schedule, walking to the bus stop, and getting on the bus.

For a long-term goal, you might want to divide large tasks into several smaller tasks that are easier to accomplish. Check off the items listed on your plan as you complete them. Try to honor the deadlines you set for yourself. This will give you a feeling of success.

Evaluate the Results

The final step of the management process is to evaluate your results. Evaluation helps make every experience a learning experience. You will probably find yourself evaluating each step in your plan as you complete it. You will check to see if you have met your deadlines and maintained the standards you set.

After you have completed all the steps in your plan, you will want to do a final evaluation. See 10-5. You might ask yourself the following questions: Were my goals reasonable? Did I use my resources as I had anticipated? Was I able to follow my plan? How can I improve when I do this again? Your evaluation might tell you that walking to and from the bus stop took more energy than you had planned. You might decide that next time you will do just as well to walk to the game.

Many people like to keep records of their evaluations that can be used for reaching future goals. Such records can make planning easier the next time.

Check It Out!
1. Wisely using resources to achieve goals is known as _____.
2. List the six steps of the management process.
3. True or false. Possessions are human resources.
4. What are three techniques that can be used to help make the most of limited resources?

Check It Out! (Answers)
1. management
2. identify goals, recognize personal priorities and standards, determine resources, form a plan, implement the plan, evaluate the results
3. false
4. substituting resources, combining resources, exchanging resources

10-5 After achieving a goal, evaluating the results is the final step in the management process.

Resource:
The Management Process, Activity A, SAG

Resource:
Group Management, reproducible master, TR

Topic 10-2
Managing Your Time

Objectives
After studying this topic, you will be able to
- explain the importance of time management.
- list some ways to help manage time.

Topic Terms
time management dovetail
implement

10-6 People who manage their time well always try to remain aware of what time it is.

Discuss: Why does time management involve self-management?

Note: Self-management is one of the personal qualities considered necessary for developing job-readiness skills. The ability to manage time and other resources is a SCANS workplace competency.

Example: Buying a new CD is a short-term goal, but buying a car is a long-term goal.

Discuss How would you describe the difference between a visionary goal and wishful thinking?

Sometimes people remember exactly what they did yesterday or last week. At other times, they cannot recall. Was the time well spent, or was it wasted? Managing time is very important because once this resource is wasted, it is never regained. It is lost forever.

Why Plan Your Time?

Time management is the ability to plan and use time well. It is not a way to change time but to change people. Time management is really about self-management. By managing time, you accomplish more of what you want to do. This is the main reason for time management.

In addition, there are several other benefits of managing time. You meet your deadlines. You are ready to face each day's responsibilities. By managing time, you can put small periods of time to good use so none is wasted. You complete your short-term goals, work toward long-term goals, and even find time for visionary goals.

Short-Term Goals Are Met

Short-term goals are your immediate aims for today and this week. For example, you attend classes, do homework, and meet deadlines for term papers. You also do household tasks and possibly hold a part-time job. Fulfilling all these duties does not happen automatically. It is the result of managing time well, 10-6.

Long-Term Goals Are Met

A long-term goal, such as choosing a career, takes more than a month or even a year to achieve. These goals require considerable thought and preparation. By dividing long-term goals into smaller steps, however, you can work on them gradually. As a result, you will be better prepared to make major life decisions when the time comes.

Some long-term goals involve perfecting skills and finding helpful resources to make decisions. Related activities include looking ahead to foresee and prevent problems that may stop you from reaching your goals.

Visionary Goals Are Addressed

Managing time allows you to dream, explore, and fit unexpected opportunities into your schedule. Staying ahead of deadlines can help you do this.

Preparing in advance for scheduled events gives you flexibility when unplanned opportunities suddenly arise, 10-7. You can then adjust your schedule to take advantage of them without sacrificing your performance in other areas.

Putting Technology to Use
Have students describe some ways they use a computer to help plan, schedule, or organize their activities.

Reflect:
How organized do you keep your work areas?

Enrich:
Working with a small group, make a to-do list for learning the material covered in this chapter.

Discuss:
Is one hour of spare time enough to work on a long-term or visionary goal?

10-7 This student stays up-to-date on her school assignments so she can attend special events that are suddenly announced.

Steps in Time Management

Busy people who handle many tasks well make time management look easy. With practice, it is. Time is managed in three steps: planning, carrying out the plan, and evaluating the results.

Planning

Before planning actually begins, you need a clear work area. You also need to review your goals and personal priorities. Only then can you develop a to-do list and weekly plan.

Get Organized

Good planning begins with an organized work area. Not being able to grab a pencil and paper to record your thoughts will slow the planning process. It is important to have a neat workspace with storage for all your tools. Returning tools to their proper places will allow you to find them when needed.

Consider Goals and Personal Priorities

Before planning starts, think about your goals and personal priorities. What do you want to do in life? What is important to you? Of course, you must meet your daily obligations, but when they are finished, what do you like to do then? These questions force you to consider your choices in life.

Between busy periods, blocks of time are usually available to use as you please. Of the many ways to spend time, different ways make sense for different people. Those striving to make the swim team will likely spend their spare time differently than those preparing for an art competition. There are many worthwhile ways to spend time, but some may not benefit or interest you. Consider where you want to direct your life, and spend time on related activities. Occasionally you must skip some interesting activities to allow room for those most important to you. See 10-8.

Make To-Do Lists

Activities that are not part of a routine should be added to a to-do list. Some people arrange their lists in priority order. This means they rank the most important activity 1, the next important 2, and so on. This type of system is helpful when activities must be done in a specific order.

10-8 These students prefer to spend their spare time preparing for a science fair.

Putting Technology to Use
Have students use charting software to make a personal to-do list for the day. After students have made their lists, have them resort the chart so the tasks are in order of priority with the most important task at the top. Ask students if they think prioritizing a to-do list helps them better manage their time.

Other people with long to-do lists simply use a four-letter rating system. They rank the must-do tasks *A*; the next-do tasks *B*; the should-do tasks *C*; and the can-wait tasks *D*. All *A* and *B* tasks are included in the day's plan. *C* and *D* tasks are handled as time allows. If not completed that day, *C* and *D* tasks eventually become *A* and *B* tasks. This system is useful when many tasks must be accomplished by the day's end, but not in a specific order. It allows more flexibility in fitting tasks into individual schedules.

Create a Weekly Plan

Planning is usually done on a weekly basis. Look ahead to next week and note any special assignments due. For example, a student may have a test on Tuesday, an oral report to give on Thursday, and a book report due on Friday. Knowing this, the student can make a schedule that flags these important deadlines. In that way, no important task is left to the last minute.

Map each day on paper so you can see which hours are filled and which are open. Look ahead to assignments due later in the month that should be started this week. Then take one day at a time, determining what to do on each to be prepared for the next. Transfer items from your to-do list to the weekly plan, scheduling them to suit your needs.

If you must mesh your plan with those of others, coordinate them. See 10-9. Then, write out your plan and put it in view so you can refer to it as needed. At first, you may need to glance at it often. Later, referring to it at the end or start of each day may be sufficient. After much planning experience, you may find that each daily to-do list is firmly imprinted on your mind.

Implementing the Plan

Now it is time to put your plan into action. To **implement** a plan simply means to carry it out. Remember your standards of excellence. Think: "Do it well so it reflects the pride I have in myself."

10-9 When plans involve other people, discuss as many details as possible before beginning, then update others as needed.

Do not be afraid to think creatively. Find new ways to do old tasks. Creativity can help you implement your management plan and give you a greater sense of accomplishment.

Evaluating the Plan

Evaluation may be as simple as noting whether or not the plan worked. If you finish all the tasks scheduled for the day, you can begin working on tomorrow's. That will help you get ahead of your deadlines.

If some tasks could not be completed, ask yourself why. Did you misjudge the amount of time needed for each task? This is quite likely to occur with your first few efforts at planning. With practice, you will be able to set more realistic deadlines.

Remember that a time management plan is simply a guide. It is not meant to be a perfect balance between available time and

Across the Curriculum

English. Have students read poetry written on the subject of time, such as Shakespeare's sonnet XIX, "Devouring Time," and John Donne's "The Sun Rising." Why do students think classic poets wrote on the subject of time?

> **Discuss:**
> How would you respond to the person who says "You can't really make plans because things always change"?
>
> **Reflect:**
> What is your biggest time waster? What can you do to control it?
>
> **Vocabulary:**
> What does *procrastination* mean?
>
> **Resource:**
> *Time Management in Action*, reproducible master, TR

tasks to do. If you scheduled too few tasks one day, use your spare time well. If you fall behind in completing your *A* list, reschedule whatever you can for later.

Managing Time Wisely

To get started on managing time well, look for some helpers. See what tools are available to help you create your weekly plans. Then keep your plans on track by using strategies that help you use time effectively.

Using Time Management Aids

Visit an office supply store and browse the planners, calendars, and schedules. Also, check the calendars and task lists that can be created by computer. Handheld electronic organizers are available, too, but some are quite expensive. All you really need to get started, however, is pencil and paper. Also, you will need a calendar to see the "big picture" so you can stay on schedule.

Experiment with several tools to see which work best for you. If you find what you need in one tool, your plans will be easier to manage. Use a tool that shows an entire week in a glance and allows you to easily add new tasks, 10-10. Do not get complex tools that require great effort to operate.

10-10 This planning tool shows the week, month, and year at a glance.

Using Time Management Strategies

Using time well is a skill that requires practice. Here are several strategies to help you reach that goal.

- **Steer clear of time wasters.** Do phone calls from friends or television programs sidetrack you from scheduled tasks? Discipline yourself to follow your plan as closely as possible.
- **Avoid procrastination.** Do you stare into space, only to realize that too much time has passed? Make a point of starting each task in a timely manner.
- **Combine tasks whenever possible.** For example, combine family time with your fitness schedule by encouraging everyone to walk, bike, or run together. If cleaning up after meals is your assignment, combine it with some form of recreation. You can listen to radio, glance at a favorite television program, or socialize with the family. When you combine or fit tasks together, you **dovetail** them. Many tasks cannot be dovetailed, but look for those that can be.
- **Break tasks into smaller steps.** In this way, time-consuming or complex tasks are much easier to do. Also, the satisfaction of crossing the finished steps off your list will motivate you to tackle the remaining steps.
- **Compensate for lost time.** Review your priorities, combine tasks when possible, and eliminate unnecessary tasks. This will help to get a schedule back on track.
- **Be prepared to use spare time.** Waiting to see a doctor or to take a sibling home from practice often lasts longer than expected. When you find yourself with spare time, be prepared to use it. If you go somewhere, always take a project along, such as a book to read or homework to do. See 10-11.

With time management, you are in the driver's seat, determining the direction your life will take.

 Putting Technology to Use
Have students evaluate several types of scheduling software. What are the pros and cons of each software program? Ask students if they would use the software on a daily basis to manage their time and explain their reasoning.

Topic 10-2 Managing Your Time

10-11 This student wisely uses his spare time to perform a routine inspection of his car.

Energy and Task Management

Time is a limited resource and so is energy. All people have the same amount of time each day, but all people do not have the same amount of energy. A time management plan must take into consideration the energy a person has to give. No amount of goal setting can force you to accomplish more than your body can handle.

Some students finish homework and go to bed at 10 p.m. Others must finish homework by 9 p.m. or they fall asleep. Do the students who go to bed earlier have fewer responsibilities? No. They may have more. How do they accomplish their tasks? They use time management techniques. They schedule their time well and avoid wasting it.

Sometimes you may feel inefficient and unable to do all you should. In these cases, ask yourself, "Am I getting enough sleep? Am I energized when I wake up in the morning?" Enough rest and recreation is needed for physical growth and for motivation to work, 10-12. *All work and no play* is not a formula for healthy living. Rest and recreation should be included in your daily schedule.

Creativity is a helpful resource to use when you feel unable to keep up with your schedule. Look for shortcuts that take less time without cutting quality. Remember, you are in the driver's seat. When beginning a project, ask yourself, "How can I best accomplish this without sacrificing quality?" Consider your energy and ways to manage the tasks efficiently.

Balancing Personal, Family, Work, and Leisure Time

Balancing your time means making sure that everything you value is included in your schedule. Your obligations at school, home, and work absorb most of your daytime hours. Meeting these obligations also requires spending time with others and learning to communicate and work well with them. In addition, time must be devoted to physical activity, rest, and sleep—all of which your body requires.

Besides these common activities, your personal priorities will prompt you to add others to the list. For example, you will

10-12 To perform at your peak, always get all the sleep and rest your body needs.

Reflect:
Are you getting enough sleep each night?

Discuss:
What tips would you recommend to classmates for dealing with an occasional sleepless night?

Activity:
Working with a small group of students, develop a list of ways to do homework in less time without cutting quality.

Activity:
Research how other cultures view time. Besides the United States, what other countries highly value time management?

Across the Curriculum

Health. Have students research the relationship between a well-nourished, rested body and a person's effective use of time.

Note:
There are two exceptions to the 24-hour rule in geographic areas that have daylight savings time. The spring solstice has 23 hours and the fall solstice has 25.

Vocabulary:
Define *fixed* and *flexible*. Can you now define *fixed expense* and *flexible expense*?

Reflect:
Have you ever used a budget to help you save money to buy something you wanted?

Resource:
Money Management Makes Dreams Come True, color transparency CT-8, TR

want to spend some time helping others in need and beautifying your community. Satisfying your spiritual needs and practicing your religious beliefs is another important way to spend time.

Everyone has only 24 hours each day. To accomplish all the tasks that become a part of a busy schedule means managing yourself first. Then you can use your time to pursue your priorities.

Check It Out!
1. Why plan for the use of time?
2. Which goals are addressed by a time management plan?
3. Name four aids to time management.
4. Name four strategies for time management.

Check It Out! (Answers)
1. to accomplish what you want to do
2. short-term, long-term, visionary
3. (Name four:) planners, calendars, schedules, to-do lists, handheld organizers, pencil, paper
4. (Name four:) Steer clear of time wasters; avoid procrastination; combine tasks whenever possible; break tasks into smaller steps; compensate for lost time; be prepared to use spare time.

Topic 10-3
Managing Your Money

Objectives
After studying this topic, you will be able to
- prepare a personal budget.
- list ways to reduce flexible expenses.
- explain how a computer can be used to help manage money.

Topic Terms
budget
fixed expense
flexible expense

Money is an important resource. A **budget** is a plan to help you manage your money wisely. A budget will help you time your purchases so you can reach both short- and long-term goals. If you do not have a plan, it is easy to spend money on immediate wants without saving for future goals. The ability to plan purchases and stick with a budget is a mark of maturity.

The Basics of Budgeting

Budgets are designed to reflect income and expenses for a given period of time. Many families prepare annual budgets. Some people prefer monthly budgets because most of their bills must be paid monthly. If you receive a weekly paycheck or a weekly allowance, you may find a weekly budget helpful.

Setting up a budget involves only a few basic steps. Once you learn these steps, you can develop a budget of your own. A sample weekly budget is shown in 10-13.

Establish Financial Goals

The first step in developing a budget is to set goals for your spending. Your primary goal will be to meet all your commitments and pay for all of your basic needs. However, you are also likely to have financial goals to purchase certain items. You may have short-term goals for

Weekly Budget	
Income	
Allowance	$20.00
Baby-sitting	25.00
Total Income	45.00
Expenses	
Fixed Expenses	
Lunch	$7.50
Scout dues	1.00
Savings	10.00
Flexible Expenses	
Entertainment	11.00
Snacks & eating out	10.00
Clothes and accessories	5.50
Total Expenses	$45.00

10-13 A teen might use a weekly budget to balance income and expenses.

the form of a salary, wages, tips, or commissions. Some income is *unearned income*. This includes interest on bank accounts, dividends on stocks, and money received as prizes or gifts.

When you record income, remember to count only your take-home pay. Any deduction from your paycheck is money already spent. Also, count only income that you are certain to receive. Income that might be available from overtime work or gifts should not be included.

Estimate Expenses

The third step in developing a budget is to estimate your expenses for the time period of your budget. Make a list of items and services you buy and what they cost. See 10-14. This list will reflect your spending patterns. Later, you can review the list to see if you need to change your spending patterns.

Expenses can be divided into two general groups—fixed and flexible expenses. These groups are further divided into various budget categories according to your spending patterns.

Fixed expenses are items that cost set amounts that you are committed to pay. Included in this group are mortgage or

10-14 Preparing a written list will help you estimate your expenses more accurately.

> **Reflect:**
> Determine your income for this month. Include take-home pay from a job, allowance, etc.
>
> **Discuss:**
> What types of fixed and flexible expenses are typical for teens?

items you would like to buy soon. You may also have long-term goals for items you want to purchase in the future. Long-term goals often center on more costly items. Attaining such goals will require saving money over an extended period.

Once you determine your goals, list them with an estimate of each item's cost. This will help you budget money for basic needs in a way that allows you to save for goals.

Keep in mind that your goals may change. Review your goals from time to time so you can make any needed adjustments in your budget.

Determine Sources of Income

The second step in making a budget is to list your sources of income. List the amount of money you receive from each source during the time period of your budget.

Income is all the money you receive. Most income is *earned income*. This is money received for working. It may be in

Putting Technology to Use

Have students use spreadsheet software to plan a budget for themselves. Students should only include income they are certain to receive.

rent payments, installment payments, insurance premiums, and pledged charitable contributions. Savings are also considered a fixed expense. If you do not make a commitment to save a certain amount, you might end up not saving anything.

Flexible expenses are costs that occur repeatedly, but which vary in amount from one time to the next. These expenses include food, clothing, transportation, and recreation.

Compare Income and Expenses

The fourth step in developing a budget is to compare your income and expenses. If your income is greater than your expenses, you can put the extra money toward your goals. If your income equals your expenses, you will be able to meet all your commitments. However, you will not be able to work toward your goals. If your income is less than your expenses, you will not have enough money for your commitments.

If you are not able to meet your commitments, you must look again at your income and expenses. You must either increase your income or decrease your expenses. You may wish to take these steps even if your income and expenses are equal. This will allow you to have extra money to put toward your goals.

Write the Budget and Keep Records

Putting your budget in written form is the fifth step in budget planning. Written records will help you keep track of your spending and stay within your budget. When you set up a record-keeping system, keep it simple. The simpler your system is, the more likely you are to use it regularly and accurately.

Your written budget can be prepared in one of several styles. Choose the style that is easiest and most logical to you. You may decide to buy a record book and set up different accounts for budget categories, 10-15. With this method, you allocate a certain amount of money to each category and keep a running balance. You can easily see just how much you can afford to spend. You can also see which expenses, if any, are getting too large.

10-15 Listing purchases in a record book can quickly show how much money is left in each budget category.

Some people decide how much money they will need to cover their expenses for a month. They divide this amount by the number of paychecks they will receive during the month. Then they set aside the appropriate amount from each check. They use the balance for goals or spending money. For instance, assume you need $1,000 a month for expenses. Suppose you receive four paychecks a month. Divide $1,000 by 4 to get $250—the amount to set aside from each check. Managing your money in this way takes a certain amount of discipline. You must train yourself not to use money set aside to cover expenses.

Big-budget items such as annual insurance premiums require extra planning. Start preparing to pay them several months in advance. Set aside a certain

Reflect:
What do you do when your expenses exceed your income?

Resource:
Monthly Budget, Activity C, SAG

Resource:
Big-Budget Items, reproducible master, TR

Across the Curriculum

Social studies. Have students research facts on the federal budget. How is the budget established? What factors are taken into account? Who must approve the budget? Does the federal government usually meet its budget? Why or why not?

amount from each paycheck so you will be ready when the premium is due.

Evaluate the Budget

Like any good planning process, the final step in planning a budget is evaluation. Every few months, you should evaluate your spending to see how well you are following your budget. If you have money left over, be proud of yourself. If you overspent, try to find out why. Perhaps you allowed too little for certain expenses.

You may need to make adjustments in your budget. Perhaps you will want to increase your allotment in one category to more accurately reflect your spending patterns. However, remember that this will require you to reduce your allotment for another category to keep your budget balanced.

A budget is not a rigid schedule that must remain constant. When there is a need to change the budget, do so. Your budget should work for you, not against you.

Reducing Flexible Expenses

As mentioned above, you need to take action if your expenses are greater than or equal to your income. One step you can take is to increase your income. You might be able to work overtime, get a second job, or do odd jobs to earn extra money.

The second step you can take is to reduce your expenses. Because fixed expenses are set amounts, they are difficult to reduce. However, with some careful planning and a little effort, you can decrease your flexible expenses.

Food

Your food budget includes the cost of all food and beverages consumed at home, school, or work. Foods eaten in restaurants are also part of this budget.

If you want to cut down your food spending, look at what you buy and where you buy it. Fast-foods and restaurant meals tend to be the most costly items in this budget category. If you eat out often, you can probably save money by cooking at home instead, 10-16. If you already do a lot of cooking, think about what you buy at the grocery store. If you buy expensive convenience foods, you will find cooking from scratch can save you money. If you are short on time, try preparing dishes on weekends and freezing them for weekday use.

Snack foods purchased on the go can add a lot to the food budget. If you buy a snack every day, add up the cost over a year. You may be surprised when you discover how much you are spending. You may decide to give up the snack and save the money for something else.

Clothing

The clothing category includes the purchase price of all garments. The cost of laundry, dry cleaning, and repairs are also part of this category.

You can save money by purchasing good-quality clothes. Well-made, durable garments may cost a little more, but they need not be replaced often. Buy clothes made for laundering to avoid dry-cleaning

10-16 Preparing this meal at home would be less costly than purchasing it in a restaurant.

Discuss:
Why is evaluating an important step in using a budget?

Resource:
Flexible Expenses, transparency master, TR

Activity:
Keep a record of all the money you spend on food for yourself for one week. Then evaluate your expenses and identify ways to cut your food expenditures in half.

 Problem-Solving Practice
Meeting Financial Needs, reproducible master, TR. Students are to put themselves in the role of a credit counselor. They are to answer questions about how they would advise low-income families to better manage money.

Enrich: Survey people you know who must use a form of transportation daily. Include people who use public transportation as well as a car. How much do they spend on transportation each week?

Reflect: How much money do you normally spend per week for recreation?

Enrich: Brainstorm a list of expenses you might have if you attend college.

costs. If you know how to sew, you can save money by making your own clothes. You can also do your own repairs and alterations instead of paying someone to do them for you.

Transportation

The transportation category includes the cost of cars and other vehicles used. Gasoline, oil, and upkeep are in this category, too. This category also includes fares for those who travel by bus, train, or plane.

Saving money in this category may seem difficult. If you must drive to work, you need a car. However, you may be able to save quite a bit if you can form a car pool with friends. Another option might be to use public transportation instead of driving.

Recreation

The recreation category includes expenses related to vacations, hobbies, and entertainment. Any money spent solely for relaxation and pleasure belongs in this category.

The amount of money you spend on this category depends on the types of activities you do. Bowling costs less than skiing. Renting a video is cheaper than buying a theater ticket. Going camping is less costly than taking a cruise, 10-17. Evaluate recreation expenses in relation to other expenses. Then decide how much money you are willing to spend on recreational activities.

Other Expenses

Miscellaneous expenses can make or break your budget. Such expenses might include grooming products and services, school supplies, and gifts. You need to evaluate how much money you spend on these items. You might decide that you need to have separate budget categories for them. Since budgets are personal, you must set up categories that meet your individual needs.

10-17 Fishing is an inexpensive recreational activity that adults can share with children.

Future Expenses

Your budget categories are likely to change as you grow older. As you gain independence, you will become responsible for more of your own expenses. Such expenses include utilities, home repairs, furnishings, and health care. Learning to plan your spending now will help you live within a budget in the future.

Budgeting with a Computer

A computer with appropriate software can make money management and record keeping easier. After typing in expenses, stroking one key can instantly show how your money is being spent. A year-end printout can help you quickly complete income tax forms and plan a budget for the next year.

A computer can be used to help pay bills. Checks that are paid routinely, such as utility bills and car payments, can be preprogrammed. When payment is due, simply call the checks to the monitor, fill in

Putting Technology to Use
Have students evaluate various software programs for financial management. Ask them to give a report on the functions of each program. Would students feel comfortable relying on the software to help them manage finances? Why or why not?

the correct amounts, and print them. Another computer option involves using a modem to transmit figures to a payment service. The service then sends checks to your payees. You may even program the computer to remind you when bills need to be paid.

A computer is also helpful for keeping track of investments. It can easily calculate figures for dividends, rates of return, capital gains, and depreciations. This saves time and improves accuracy when planning future investments. See 10-18.

10-18 A home computer can make family budgeting, bill paying, and investment analysis easier.

Check It Out!
1. What are the six steps in developing a budget?
2. True or false. Fast-foods and restaurant meals tend to be the most costly items in a food budget.
3. How can a computer be used to help manage money?

Check It Out! (Answers)
1. establish financial goals, determine sources of income, estimate expenses, compare income and expenses, write the budget and keep records, evaluate the budget
2. true
3. (Student response. See pages 290-291 in the text.)

Topic 10-4
Using Financial Services

Objectives
After studying this topic, you will be able to
- describe various services offered by financial institutions.
- write and endorse checks correctly.
- balance a checkbook.

Topic Terms
certified check
cashier's check
endorse
account statement
overdraft

As a child, you may have kept pennies in a piggy bank. That method of handling money may have worked well for you then. When you start earning money, however, you should start dealing with financial institutions. Piggy banks lack the safety and earnings potential found at financial institutions. See 10-19.

10-19 Coins saved at home will not earn interest or be protected from theft as it would at a financial institution.

Vocabulary: Have any of you used either a certified check or a cashier's check?

Resource: *Banking Yesterday and Today*, reproducible master, TR

Enrich:
Invite someone from a financial institution to speak about the differences between the different types of financial institutions and the services they offer.

Discuss:
What type of bank account do you use, if any? Why did you select this type of account instead of another?

Discuss:
What are the advantages of using ATMs? What precautions must you take?

Choosing a Financial Institution

Commercial banks, mutual savings banks, savings and loan associations, and credit unions are all financial institutions. Though there are differences among them, each offers a range of financial services.

Financial Services

When selecting a financial institution, you will want to consider its services. Saving money, making payments, and obtaining loans are the most common financial services used. These services and their features differ from one institution to another. You must decide which financial services are important to you. Then you should look for an institution that offers the services that meet your needs.

Savings Accounts

Savings accounts are a key service available through financial institutions. These accounts pay various amounts of interest. Some accounts have restrictions regarding the length of time money must stay on deposit. (Section 10-5, "Saving for the Future," will discuss savings accounts in more detail.)

Checking Accounts

One of the main financial services people want is a checking account. Checking accounts are sometimes called *demand deposits*. That is, money in them is available on demand. You can demand a sum of money from a checking account simply by writing a check. Several types of checking accounts are available. Some earn interest; others do not.

Debit Cards

A *debit card* shows that you have an established checking account with the financial institution identified on the card. It looks like a credit card and is swiped through a point-of-sale terminal in much the same way. However, swiping the card immediately transfers payment from your checking account. Using a debit card is a quick, easy method of payment that does not require showing other forms of identification. When making a debit purchase, you receive a copy of the receipt for your records and the merchant keeps the original. You will need to record each transaction immediately in your checkbook, just as you do when writing checks. Debit purchases are itemized on your monthly checking account statement.

Automated Teller Machines (ATMs)

Automated teller machines offer people the flexibility of banking at any time. ATMs are available locally in a variety of convenient locations, including shopping malls and convenience stores. See 10-20. To use an ATM, you need a special banking card with a security code called a personal identification number (PIN). The card and PIN number allow a customer to access his or her accounts, withdraw cash, and make deposits.

An ATM card provides access to more than just local machines. National and international networks permit customers to use ATMs almost anywhere in the world. Customers can also transfer money, obtain an account balance, and make payments on bank loans. ATM customers usually have access to a telephone service linked to their

10-20 Automated teller machines provide routine banking services 24 hours a day.

Putting Technology to Use
Have students who have ATM cards visit an ATM machine to check their account balances. Ask students to describe the options available on ATM machines. Also ask students about their banks' policies on ATM fees.

bank accounts. This service gives customers the convenience of long-distance banking and 24-hour information.

Some ATM cards can also be used as debit cards. When making a debit purchase or using the ATM card to withdraw cash, always record the transaction immediately in your checkbook.

Loans

Loans are another service many people seek from financial institutions. People apply for both short- and long-term loans. They may borrow money to pay existing bills or make purchases, such as major appliances, cars, and houses.

Different types of financial institutions make loans for different types of purchases. For instance, some institutions loan money for a home purchase, but not a car purchase. Check to be sure your financial institution makes the type of loan you are seeking.

Certified and Cashier's Checks

Some individuals and businesses will not honor personal checks from people they do not know well. In these cases, a certified check may be a more acceptable form of payment. A **certified check** is simply a personal check for which the financial institution guarantees payment. When the institution certifies your check, the amount of the check is immediately deducted from your account to reserve it for the payee.

If you do not have a checking account, you may have a financial institution issue a **cashier's check.** This is a check drawn on the institution's own funds and signed by an officer of the institution. You present the money to the institution along with the name of the payee. The institution then issues a check made out to that person or business. If you have a savings account in the financial institution, the money can be withdrawn from that account.

Traveler's Checks

Many financial institutions offer traveler's checks. They are a convenient source of money for travelers who do not want to carry large amounts of cash. These checks are accepted around the world. If traveler's checks are lost, they can be quickly replaced by providing the serial numbers of the lost checks.

Safe-Deposit Boxes

Many financial institutions have safe-deposit boxes that can be rented by their customers. These boxes are usually located in a vault for protection from theft and fire. Safe-deposit boxes are used to store valuable items, such as jewelry and coins. They are also used to store important papers, such as a marriage license, deed to property, citizenship papers, or stocks and bonds.

Other Financial Services

Financial institutions may offer a number of other services for customer convenience. These include credit cards, drive-up windows, estate management, brokerage accounts, and financial counseling. Many banks offer customers online access to their bank accounts. In this way, customers can manage their bank accounts via the Internet on their home computers. See 10-21. Special services like these are worth considering when you select financial institutions.

Discuss: When might a certified check be required?

Discuss: Under what circumstances would you use traveler's checks instead of a credit card?

Reflect: Do you, your parents, or grandparents have a safe-deposit box? What types of valuables are kept in it?

10-21 Bank customers need special software to access their bank account online.

Putting Technology to Use
Have students check out their banks' Web sites to see what online services are offered. If the students do not have bank accounts or their bank does not have a Web site, have them check out the Harris Bank site at www.harrisbank.com.

> **Enrich:**
> Collect newspaper ads and brochures for several types of financial institutions. Compare the services offered and interest rates on savings accounts and loans. Which one do you think has the most to offer in services and rates?
>
> **Resource:**
> *Financial Services,* Activity D, SAG
>
> **Discuss:**
> What are the advantages and disadvantages of using a checking account?

Types of Institutions

You can choose from among several types of financial institutions to provide the services you desire. Commercial banks, mutual savings banks, savings and loan associations, and credit unions may all meet your needs.

When people speak of banks, they usually mean *commercial banks.* These banks are also known as full-service banks. They are owned by stockholders and are run for a profit. Commercial banks offer a great variety of services to both businesses and individuals.

All *mutual savings banks* are owned by their depositors rather than by stockholders. The owners/investors decide the interest rates. The interest paid to depositors will depend on profits from the banks' investments. These investments include real estate, mortgages, and corporate securities.

Savings and loan associations may be operated either like commercial banks or like mutual savings banks. In other words, some are owned by stockholders and are run for a profit. Others are owned by depositors and pay dividends on savings.

An additional choice for saving and borrowing is available to people who belong to a credit union. *Credit unions* are nonprofit financial institutions owned and operated by members. Companies or professional associations often sponsor credit unions. Membership in the credit union is open only to people associated with the sponsoring organization. At credit unions, the rate of interest is usually high for deposits and low for loans.

Before choosing a financial institution, do some comparison shopping. Interest rates vary among different institutions. This applies to interest earned on savings accounts as well as interest charged on loans. When saving or borrowing money, compare the rates of all institutions available to you. Find the one that best suits you.

Using a Checking Account

A checking account is convenient for making purchases and paying bills. Money needed for these expenses can be held in a checking account. Anytime payment needs to be made, you can simply use a debit card or write a check, 10-22. When a check is cashed, the amount of the check is withdrawn from your account. Use of a debit card, on the other hand, withdraws money immediately.

Types of Accounts

Different types of checking accounts are available. With some checking accounts, you need a minimum amount to open the account. Interest earned by the bank on this balance pays for the costs of handling the account. You usually do not pay service charges, except for purchasing personal checks. If the account balance falls below the minimum required, however, you must pay a service charge.

10-22 A customer can write a check for a purchase rather than paying cash.

Putting Technology to Use

Have students check out the Web site for the National Credit Union Administration at www.ncua.gov or the Credit Union National Association at www.cuna.org. What kinds of information are available at these sites?

Some checking accounts do not require a minimum balance. For such an account, you usually pay a service charge. This covers the financial institution's cost of handling the account. This charge may be a monthly fee, a set fee for each check written, or both.

Some checking accounts pay interest if you maintain a balance over a certain amount. This is an advantage for people who keep a large amount of money in their checking accounts. They will not lose the interest they would otherwise be earning in a savings account.

When deciding which type of account to open, determine how much money you can afford to keep in the account. Think about how much you are willing to pay for service fees. Consider how important it is for you to earn interest. Then choose the type of account that best meets your needs.

Opening an Account and Making a Deposit

When you open a checking account, you will be asked to sign a *signature card*. The financial institution keeps this card on file to compare with signatures made during transactions. This helps to eliminate forgeries.

When opening a checking account, you will need to specify the type of account you want. If you are the only person who will write checks on the account, you will open an individual account. If someone else, such as a spouse, will also use the account, you will open a joint account.

To add money to your checking account, you simply fill out a deposit slip. Write the date on the appropriate line. Sign the slip if you want to receive cash from the deposit. List specifically what is being deposited—currency, coins, or checks—and the exact amount of each. Total the amount of the deposit. Subtract the amount you want to receive, if any. Then figure the net deposit. See 10-23.

Writing a Check

A check instructs your financial institution to pay a certain sum of money to a person or company. Checks should be clearly written in ink. Be sure to fill in all the following information in the appropriate spaces, as shown in 10-24:

- *date*
- *name of the individual or group to whom you are paying the money*—Be sure the name is spelled correctly.
- *amount of payment in numerals*—Write close to the dollar sign to prevent anyone from inserting a number to change the amount.

Discuss:
Why might someone keep a large amount of money in a checking account as opposed to a savings account?

Note:
Bring to class a sample signature card for students to see. Answer any questions they have regarding the card.

Activity:
Bring in blank deposit slips and have students practice filling them out.

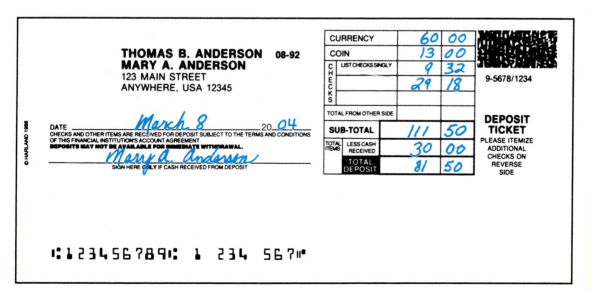

10-23 A deposit slip must accompany cash or checks being deposited in a checking account.

Across the Curriculum

English. Have students research different types of checking accounts offered by local banks. They should then write a one-page paper discussing the differences between the accounts and explaining which checking account would be most appropriate for their needs.

Reflect:
Do you always fill in your check register whenever you write a check? Why is this important?

Vocabulary:
What is the difference between a blank endorsement and a restrictive endorsement?

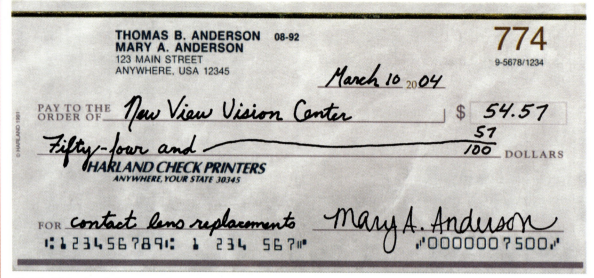

10-24 This check is correctly written.

- *amount of payment in words*—Begin writing as far to the left as possible. After writing the dollar amount, write the word *and*. Then write the amount of cents as a fraction of 100. For instance, 37 cents is written as *37/100*. When writing a check for an even dollar amount, write 00/100 or no/100. Draw a line through the remaining space.
- *purpose of the check*—This brief note serves as a quick reference when you balance your checkbook.
- *your signature*—Sign the check exactly as you signed the signature card when you opened the account.

Keep an accurate record of all checks written. A check stub or register is provided for record keeping. Complete the check stub or fill in the register at the time that you use your debit card or write a check. Record the number of the check, date, payee, and amount. Subtract the amount from your balance so you always know how much money is in your account. This will keep you from writing checks when you do not have sufficient funds. See 10-25.

Endorsing a Check

Before you can cash or deposit a check that has been written to you, you must **endorse** it. This means you must sign your name on the back, at the left end of the check. The signature on the back must match the name on the face of the check.

There are two kinds of endorsements. The first type of endorsement, a *blank endorsement*, is the payee's signature only. If a check bearing a blank endorsement is lost, it can be cashed by anyone. The finder needs only to sign the check below the first signature. For this reason, always wait until you are ready to cash or deposit the check before using a blank endorsement.

The second type of endorsement is a *restrictive endorsement*. It states specifically what is to be done with the check. *For deposit only* is a common restrictive endorsement. When used, it means the check cannot be exchanged for cash. The amount of the check must be deposited in the account of the person named in the endorsement.

Pay to the order of is another common restrictive endorsement. This type of endorsement names the person who will endorse the check. No one but the person named in the endorsement can cash the check. See 10-26.

Balancing Your Checkbook

Your financial institution will send you a monthly, bimonthly, or quarterly summary of your checking account. This

Across the Curriculum
Math. Give students examples of check registers in which several checks or other withdrawals have not been recorded. Have students identify the errors and determine what the account balance should really be. What would happen if these errors were not caught?

Topic 10-4 Using Financial Services

NUMBER	DATE	DESCRIPTION OF TRANSACTION	PAYMENT/DEBIT (-)	√T	FEE (IF ANY) (-)	DEPOSIT/CREDIT (+)	BALANCE $143 38	
		RECORD ALL CHARGES OR CREDITS THAT AFFECT YOUR ACCOUNT						
	3-8	Deposit				81 50	81	50
							224	88
774	3-10	New View Vision Center	54 57				54	57
		contact lens replacements					170	31
775	3-13	Edison Electric	44 40				44	40
		electric bill					125	91
776	3-18	Image Salon	24 00				24	00
		haircut					101	91
	3-22	Deposit				467 20	467	20
							569	11
777	3-28	Sloan Realty	395 00				395	00
		rent					174	11
778	3-2	Alum Creek United Church	30 00				30	00
		offering					144	11
779	3-3	Brownie's Market	27 63				27	63
		groceries					116	48
780	4-4	Lakeshore Home Economics	20 00				20	00
		April meeting					96	48
	4-5	Deposit				420 48	420	48
							516	96

Discuss: Why is it important to record your checks in the check register neatly?

Resource: *Using a Check Register,* reproducible master, TR

10-25 A check register keeps track of how much money is in a checking account.

10-26 A check must be endorsed with a blank or restrictive endorsement before it can be cashed or deposited.

Across the Curriculum

Math. Discuss with students the math skills that are necessary for balancing checkbooks. Have them practice several checkbook-balancing problems.

> **Discuss:**
> Why should your checkbook be balanced every month?
>
> **Resource:**
> *Checking Accounts,* Activity E, SAG
>
> **Discuss:**
> How long should you keep the canceled checks or check statements you receive from the bank? (Answer: At least five years in case of a tax audit.)

summary is called an **account statement.** This statement lists checks, deposits, withdrawals, charges, and interest earnings on the account.

When you receive an account statement, check it against your check stubs or register. The institution's record should match yours. This is known as balancing your checkbook.

In most cases, the financial institution will enclose *canceled checks* with the account statement. The checks you wrote that are not returned with the statement are called *outstanding checks.* These checks were not yet cashed when the statement was made.

Some financial institutions do not return canceled checks. However, the statements they issue will list each check by amount and check number. In this way, you will be able to tell which checks were cashed.

Compare the canceled checks with those listed on the statement. Then compare them with your record of checks written. In your check register or on the check stubs, mark off the checks that have been returned to you. Also mark off any deposits and other withdrawals shown on the statement. If the financial institution has made any service charges, subtract them from the balance in your checkbook. Likewise, if you have earned interest on your account, add that amount to your checkbook balance.

At this point, a little math will help you see if your checkbook has balanced. Most account statements have a worksheet printed on the back to help you with the math. See 10-27. Complete the following steps in the spaces provided on the worksheet:
1. Write the closing balance shown on the bank statement.
2. List the deposits you have made that are not shown on the statement.
3. Add the amounts from steps 1 and 2 and record the total.
4. List by number and amount all outstanding checks and withdrawals. Find the total and record it.
5. Subtract the total in step 4 from that in step 3. The difference should match the balance shown in your checkbook. What should you do if the balance on

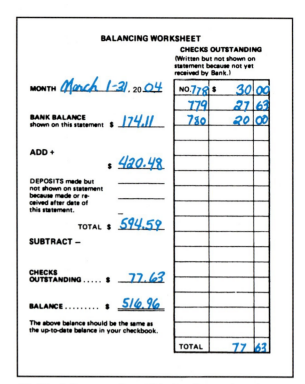

10-27 A form such as this is often printed on the back of a bank account statement to help customers balance their checkbooks.

the statement does not match yours? Begin by double-checking your math. Be sure you have made no errors before you question the financial institution about its statement.

Balancing your checkbook promptly is always wise. Financial institutions can make errors. You should not depend completely on them to keep your account in order. The sooner you notice an error, the sooner it can be corrected.

There is another good reason for balancing your checkbook promptly. People who neglect this task are more likely to write **overdrafts.** These are checks written when there is not enough money in the account to cover them. They are also known as checks that bounce.

Most financial institutions fine account holders for writing overdrafts. Many businesses also fine customers who write overdrafts in payment for goods or services. The total fines for an overdraft can easily exceed $40. Thus, writing an overdraft can be costly as well as embarrassing. See 10-28.

Citizenship and Service
Arrange for students to volunteer their time at a nursing home or at small group meetings sponsored by the Council on Aging in your community. Have them help elderly people balance their checkbooks, maintain records for tax purposes, or pay bills.

10-28 Retail businesses often post signs warning customers of a fee charged on returned checks.

Check It Out!
1. List six financial services offered by financial institutions.
2. How does a debit card differ from a credit card?
3. What are the two types of check endorsements?
4. Give two reasons for balancing a checkbook promptly.

Check It Out! (Answers)
1. (List six:) savings accounts, checking accounts, debit cards, automated teller machines (ATMs), loans, certified checks, cashier's checks, traveler's checks, safe-deposit boxes, credit cards, drive-up windows, estate management, brokerage accounts, financial counseling, online banking
2. It immediately transfers money from the checking account and is itemized on the checking account statement.
3. blank endorsement, restrictive endorsement
4. (Give two:) to identify any errors the financial institution may have made regarding the account, to avoid writing overdrafts

Topic 10-5
Saving for the Future

Objectives
After studying this topic, you will be able to
- explain why it is important to save money.
- list five factors to consider when deciding how to save.
- describe various types of savings accounts.
- determine why people need to plan their estates.

Topic Terms
liquidity	bond
certificate of deposit	mutual fund
securities	portfolio
stock	estate
dividend	will

Vocabulary: How many of the Topic 10-5 terms are familiar to you?

Discuss: Why should teens save money? For what kinds of things do teens often save?

Many advertisements for savings institutions read "Pay yourself first." In other words, put some money in savings before making unnecessary purchases. Later, if you need money, it will be available. You also earn additional money on savings in the form of interest.

Why Save?
Why should I save? When should I use the money in my savings? The answers to these two common questions vary for different people. A few facts about savings might help reveal the right answers for you.
- Money in a savings account will be available to spend for future wants and needs.
- Savings can be the most direct path to your long-term goals. By saving, you can make purchases that would otherwise be beyond your reach.
- Money in a savings account can be considered an emergency fund. As a rule, a person should have at least three-months' income saved to cover any emergencies that might arise.

> **Resource:**
> *Spend or Save,* reproducible master, TR
>
> **Discuss:**
> Where did people keep their money before there were banks?
>
> **Discuss:**
> What is the current rate of inflation? Is money in a savings account earning enough to keep up with this inflation rate?

■ Savings can ensure that retirement will not put a strain on your standard of living. The sooner you begin to plan and save for retirement, the more money you will have when you retire. See 10-29.

Factors in Deciding How to Save

You should consider five factors in deciding how to save. These factors are safety, returns, liquidity, purchasing power, and convenience.

Safety is the most important factor regarding savings. Savings should be protected against loss, theft, fire, and other risks. Financial institutions offer built-in safety through guards and vaults. However, most of them also insure savings accounts up to $100,000. Banks and savings and loan associations are insured through the Federal Deposit Insurance Corporation (FDIC). Credit unions are insured through the National Credit Union Association (NCUA).

Another consideration is the *rate of return* you will earn on your savings. Savings institutions offer different interest rates on accounts. They also calculate interest in a variety of ways. You should investigate each savings option to find the highest rate of return available to you.

When deciding how to save you will need to evaluate the **liquidity** of your funds. This is the degree to which you will be able to get cash quickly. A high degree of liquidity is important for savings that must quickly be used for emergencies. Some savings accounts pay very high interest, but withdrawal of funds is restricted. Planning your savings so that some cash will be immediately available without loss of interest is always wise.

Purchasing power is a fourth factor in deciding how to save. Your savings should be protected against inflation. This is hard to do in a savings account. Savings in stocks, bonds, and real estate are usually considered better protection against inflation. These investments usually increase in value in step with inflation. These savings options do not offer liquidity, however. Once money is invested in them, you may not be able to get it back for several years.

10-29 People can enjoy financial freedom during their retirement if they budget well and save money while employed.

Putting Technology to Use
Have students look up the terms *Consumer Price Index* and *Employment Cost Index* on the Internet. Ask students to print out information on the terms from reliable government or organization Web sites. Discuss the meanings of these terms in class.

Convenience is also a factor you will want to keep in mind when deciding how to save. Some people seek faraway banks to get higher rates of return. However, financial services may be inconvenient to access through faraway institutions. A financial institution near your home or along your route to work is very convenient for routine services, 10-30.

No single savings plan will be perfect for all of your needs. In addition, all financial institutions vary in the services they offer. By carefully weighing all factors involved, you can make the best decision about savings.

10-30 A drive-up feature at a local financial institution makes it convenient for saving money.

Savings Accounts

Savings institutions offer several types of savings accounts. If you choose this savings option, be sure you understand the terms of the account you select.

Regular Savings Accounts

Regular savings accounts allow deposits and withdrawals to be made in any amount at any time. Deposits, withdrawals, and interest earnings are itemized on an account statement, issued monthly or quarterly. This savings account pays the lowest interest rates, but provides the greatest liquidity. Money is usually available as soon as it is needed.

Certificates of Deposit

Another type of savings account is a **certificate of deposit (CD).** CDs pay a set rate of interest on money that is deposited for a set period of time. These accounts may also be called savings certificates or time accounts. A higher interest rate is paid on CDs than on regular savings accounts. Interest rates on such accounts vary according to the length of time the money must be left on deposit.

A minimum deposit is required for most CDs. Popular CDs are in denominations from $100 to $10,000. Maturities range from 30 days to 12 years or more. All CDs can be cashed before maturity. However, doing this will result in a loss of interest income and a penalty fee.

Some CDs, usually for amounts of $100,000 or more, are negotiable. Negotiable CDs may be sold to someone other than the original owner. This enables the owner to get money back before the maturity date.

Decisions About Securities

Most people invest money in one way or another to provide for their future needs. When people talk about investments, they often are referring to securities. **Securities** are proof of debt or ownership of a company or government. This proof is often in the form of stocks and bonds.

Why Invest in Securities?

Investments put your money to work for you. Some people think putting money in a savings account is a good investment. However, securities have a few advantages over savings accounts.
- Long-term prices of securities have increased almost steadily. This has made their average annual increase in value greater than interest rates on savings accounts.

Resource:
Components of a Savings Picture, reproducible master, TR

Discuss:
How many of you have a regular savings account? How do you keep track of how much money you have in your account?

Across the Curriculum

Math. Have students investigate CDs at various banks. Have them find out information on the minimum deposit required, current interest rates, and how interest rates vary with length of time. Have students determine from their findings which type of CD would yield the most interest.

> **Discuss:**
> Do you think the long-term upward trend of the U.S. economy will continue throughout your lifetime?

> **Discuss:**
> Do you agree that only the wealthy can afford to invest in securities?

> **Enrich:**
> Invite a stockbroker to class to speak about the stock market and how it works.

> **Vocabulary:**
> What is the difference between a stock and a bond?

- Inflation is an economic factor commonly at work in the economy. It causes money to decrease in value. Due to the higher long-term returns on securities, however, they offset the effects of inflation better than savings accounts do.

- The long-term trend of the U.S. economy has been upward for many years. Purchasing securities provides a way to participate in this economic growth, which is not offered by savings accounts.

Many people think only the wealthy can afford to invest in securities. This is not true. You do not have to be a millionaire to invest in securities. You must, however, learn about the field if you want to invest wisely.

Stocks

Stocks are certificates that represent ownership of a small portion of a company. When people buy shares of stock in a company, they are actually buying part of that company. By selling stock, the company makes money to conduct its business. Stockholders take part in the business by electing the board of directors. The directors run the company for the benefit of all the owners.

A stockholder shares in the profits and losses of the company. Some of the company's profits are distributed to stockholders as **dividends.** Some of the profits are reinvested in the company to help it grow. If the company makes no profit, the value of its stock usually goes down. If the company fails, the investment will be completely lost.

People who want to invest in stocks should learn as much as they can about investing. In some areas, people who are interested in securities form a club to find out more about them. Investors can also seek the help of a reliable stockbroker. A stockbroker can give advice about the purchase and sale of stocks, 10-31. Of course, the decision to buy or sell would be up to the investor.

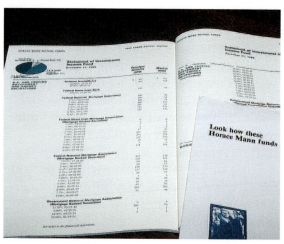

10-31 A stockbroker can provide information on the stock of individual companies as well as on funds that combine stock from several companies.

Bonds

Bonds are certificates that represent a promise by a company or government to repay a loan on a given date. Companies sell corporate bonds. In effect, the companies are borrowing money from the people who buy the bonds. Companies promise to pay a certain amount of interest on these loans. The loans are repaid in full when the bonds reach maturity.

Corporate bonds are mainly sold to cover the costs of expansion. A company predicts that a larger facility will allow it to increase profits. From the profits, the company can repay bond buyers their original investments plus interest.

Governments also sell bonds. The federal government issues Series EE savings bonds that can be bought for half their face value. For instance, a $50 bond can be bought for $25. If the bond is held until its maturity date, it can be cashed for $50. Bonds can be cashed before maturity at a reduced interest rate. These savings bonds can be bought at most savings institutions. They are a safe investment.

Local governments sell bonds, too. These are called municipal bonds. Voters are often asked to approve bond sales in

Putting Technology to Use
Have students check out the Nasdaq stock market's Web site, www.nasdaq.com. Ask students if they understand the information provided. Then have students check out Edustock, a Web site set up to help people understand the stock market, at http://library.thinkquest.org/3088/.

local elections. Funds from *municipal bonds* may be used for such projects as building schools or improving streets.

Mutual Funds

A **mutual fund** is a group of many investments purchased by a company representing many investors. These funds are classified according to the types of investments purchased and called a **portfolio.** When you buy a share of a mutual fund, you become part owner of everything in that portfolio. There are stock funds, bond funds, and balanced funds that include stocks and bonds.

Many people prefer to invest in mutual funds rather than directly in stocks or bonds. The investment is basically the same, but there is less risk. A mutual fund offers three advantages to the casual investor.

- A professional fund manager does the buying and selling. Individual investors rely on that person's expertise to manage the fund.
- The investment is *diversified*. This means money is invested in many different stocks and bonds, so decreases in some are offset by increase in others. Overall, the investor is likely to make good returns on the total investment.
- Mutual funds have good liquidity. They are much easier and quicker to buy and sell than individual stocks and bonds.

Planning an Estate

An **estate** is what a person leaves behind when he or she dies. People who have saved and invested throughout their lives generally have plans for their estates. They want their property to be distributed in a certain way. Perhaps they want to be sure to provide support for their survivors. Maybe they want to donate funds to a favorite charity. In order for their wishes to be fulfilled, they must take appropriate legal steps. Otherwise, their estates will be distributed according to state laws.

A **will** is a legal document describing how a person wants his or her property to be distributed after death. It specifies who will be in charge of carrying out the deceased person's wishes. See 10-32.

Activity: Examine the financial section of the *Wall Street Journal* or a Sunday edition of a major newspaper for mutual fund information. List the five funds posting the highest returns for the week.

Vocabulary: Explain the difference between *year-to-date* versus *one-year* increases in a mutual fund.

Resource: *Savings Plans*, Activity F, SAG

Reflect: Ask your parents if they have a will. Ask if they would share some of the specifics related to their will.

10-32 A lawyer can help a person make a will that directs how his or her estate will be handled.

Putting Technology to Use
Demonstrate a will-writing software program. Use it to show students the details that must be considered when planning an estate. Ask students if they think it is easier/better to use the program to create a will or have professionals work with individuals in estate planning.

Vocabulary:
Define the term *insurance*.

Discuss:
Why is it important for people to purchase insurance?

One main reason parents need to prepare wills is to name legal guardians for their children. If they do not do this, the court will become responsible for the children. The court can then name any legal guardian. This guardian may or may not be the person whom the parents would have chosen.

Wills may be written or oral. However, a written will prepared by an attorney is the most legally binding. This type of will provides the greatest protection against disputes by unhappy heirs.

People have many options as they plan their estates. The size of the estate and the goals of the individual affect those options. Lawyers, bankers, investment counselors, insurance agents, and accountants can assist with estate planning.

Check It Out!
1. Give two reasons for saving money.
2. What are the five factors that should be considered when deciding how to save?
3. Which type of savings account allows deposits and withdrawals to be made at any time?
4. A portfolio of diversified investments purchased by a company representing many investors is called a ____ ____.
5. List four professionals who can assist people with estate planning.

Check It Out! (Answers)
1. (Student response. See pages 299-300 in the text.)
2. safety, returns, liquidity, purchasing power, convenience
3. regular savings account
4. mutual fund
5. (List four:) lawyers, bankers, investment counselors, insurance agents, accountants

Topic 10-6
Meeting Insurance Needs

Objectives
After studying this topic, you will be able to
- describe different kinds of insurance protection.
- list points to follow when filing an insurance claim.

Topic Terms
policy
policyholder
premium
beneficiary
cash value
loan value
deductible
co-insurance
copayment
health maintenance organization (HMO)
preferred provider organization (PPO)

Nobody likes to think about getting sick, injured, or killed. However, these events are realities of life. Preparing for them can make them less devastating. One way to prepare is to purchase insurance. Insurance can protect your investments, provide for your loved ones, and cover costs of damage repairs and medical treatments. See 10-33.

Insurance Basics

Insurance is a risk-sharing plan. Insurance companies offer a way in which many people can unite to protect each other from income losses. These losses may be due to death, disability, natural disasters, thefts, accidents, or other misfortunes.

Insurance contracts are called **policies.** A person who has a policy is called a **policyholder.** A policyholder agrees to regularly pay a certain amount of money, called a **premium,** to the insurance company. In return, the insurance company provides financial protection for the policyholder in the event of a misfortune covered in the policy.

Topic 10-6   Meeting Insurance Needs

10-33 Homeowner's insurance will cover the cost of replacing a home destroyed by a fire.

When an insurance company collects premiums from policyholders, the money is promptly invested. In this way, the premiums earn money for the insurance company. The insurance company uses part of the earnings to pay the claims made by policyholders. Some earnings are also used to cover the company's operating expenses.

A good insurance agent will help you determine the types of insurance you need. The agent will also help you find a plan you can afford to provide the amount of coverage you need.

Select an insurance agent just as you would select a physician or a lawyer. Find someone with good training in insurance and financial planning. Agents must have a certain amount of personal information about their clients. Therefore, you should also look for someone you can trust to keep information confidential.

The information that follows describes several types of insurance that you are likely to buy.

Life Insurance

Life insurance is protection against financial loss due to death. This type of protection is especially important for people who have dependents. A *dependent* is someone, such as a spouse, child, or elderly parent, who relies on another person for financial support. See 10-34. Life insurance should be bought when a person begins to have financial responsibility.

Most families carry life insurance on the parent who is the chief wage earner. However, some insurance should be carried on both parents. Should either parent die, survivors need protection against the loss of that parent's income and services.

When a life insurance policyholder dies, the insurance company pays the *death benefit* of the policy, called *face value*. The person who receives the death benefit is called the **beneficiary.**

Two basic types of life insurance are available—term and whole life. Many variations of each type are available. You should know the difference between the basic types, then obtain the advice of a reliable agent to help determine your needs.

Term Insurance

Term insurance covers the owner of a policy for a specific number of years. The most common term policies available are annually renewable, 5-year renewable,

10-34 Life insurance protects dependents from a loss of income due to a wage earner's death.

Enrich:
Invite an insurance agent to class to explain the types of insurance people should purchase.

Reflect:
Ask your parents if they have life insurance. Find out why they do or do not have life insurance and what type they have.

Across the Curriculum
Business. Have students research some of the insurance companies in their area. Students should investigate different policies offered by the companies and their premiums. Have students do further research to find out about the companies' business operations. What relationship exists between policies, premiums, and business operations?

Discuss:
To obtain a life insurance policy, most companies require a person to take a physical exam. Why do you think this is required?

Resource:
Life Insurance Terms, Activity G, SAG

Reflect:
If you are employed, is health insurance provided?

10-year renewable, 20-year renewable, and term to age 65. At the end of the term, coverage stops. Benefits are payable only if the policyholder dies within the term.

If you buy term insurance, look for a policy with a *renewal privilege.* This allows the policyholder to renew the policy without having a physical examination. Without a renewal privilege, you might not be able to obtain more insurance when the term expires. A term policy may also carry a *convertible clause.* Under this clause, the owner may later exchange the term policy for a whole life policy without a physical examination.

Credit life insurance is one variation of term insurance. It protects property bought on credit if the owner dies before the payments are completed. Suppose you bought a car and arranged to pay for it in installments. What would happen if you died before you completed the car payments? If your family could not continue making payments, the car would be repossessed. With credit life insurance, the loan would automatically be repaid. Such a policy can be arranged at the time a loan is made. Credit life insurance is often bought for loans on homes, cars, and major appliances, 10-35. The cost of credit life insurance should be compared to the cost of straight term insurance before a decision is made. Standard term insurance may cost less.

Whole Life Insurance

Whole life insurance covers the policyholder for a lifetime, rather than for a specific number of years. Whole life policies acquire cash value and loan value after premiums have been paid for at least two years. **Cash value** is the amount the policyholder can collect if he or she decides to give up the policy. **Loan value** is the amount the policyholder can borrow from the insurance company using the cash value as collateral. The cash value and the loan value are usually equal.

When choosing whole life policies, you have two basic options. One option is called a *straight life policy.* Fixed premiums based on your age at the time you buy the policy are paid throughout your lifetime. The second option is a policy that can be purchased outright over a shorter period of time. These policies are called *limited payment life policies.*

Universal Life Insurance

A relatively new form of life insurance is universal life insurance. It combines term insurance with an investment feature. The cash value accumulated on the policy is invested to earn interest. The return will vary from year to year as a result of the insurer's investment success.

Health Insurance

Health care is expensive. The costs of medical checkups, medicine, and hospital care can add up quickly. Health insurance helps cover these costs.

Many people are able to get health insurance coverage through a group plan. Companies, unions, and professional organizations often offer group plans. With these plans, all members of the group can buy the insurance at reduced rates. Employers may pay all or part of the cost of premiums as an employee benefit.

10-35 Credit life insurance can protect a major purchase, such as a car, if the owner dies before payments are completed.

Putting Technology to Use
Have students use charting software to make a chart detailing the differences between term insurance and whole life insurance.

People who do not have group plans available to them may purchase health insurance individually. However, the premiums are generally higher. See 10-36.

Health insurance policies differ in terms of what they cover. Evaluate a policy carefully before making a purchasing decision. Find out whether certain illnesses are excluded from coverage. See if there are any limits on the amount of costs that will be covered.

Most insurance policies do not pay 100 percent of a policyholder's medical expenses, even for items that are covered. Some policies have provisions for deductibles, coinsurance, and copayments. A **deductible** is an amount that a policyholder must pay before the insurance company will pay anything. If you have a $250 deductible, you would pay the first $250 of medical expenses covered by the insurance. The insurance company would pay the remaining expenses covered. **Co-insurance** requires the policyholder to pay a certain percentage of medical costs. Many co-insurance policies cover 80 percent, requiring policyholders to pay the remaining 20 percent. **Copayments** are small, fixed fees for certain items or services. For instance, you may have a $20 copayment for each doctor visit. These provisions help defray the costs of settling insurance claims and therefore reduce premiums.

Types of Health Coverage

Like health care, health insurance is expensive. The cost of insurance premiums may seem high. However, medical expenses can lead to financial ruin if you do not have insurance. Think about whether you could afford to pay medical bills without insurance coverage. If so, you might decide not to purchase a certain type of coverage.

Three main types of health insurance coverage are available. These are basic medical coverage, major medical coverage, and disability insurance.

Basic medical coverage pays standard hospital costs. These costs include room, meals, nursing care, drugs, X-rays, and laboratory tests. Some policies also pay for doctor visits and simple medical procedures.

Major medical coverage pays the bulk of expenses resulting from major illness or serious injury. It covers surgery and other expenses not covered by a basic medical policy. See 10-37.

Disability insurance provides payments for people who are unable to work because of illness or injury. It generally pays two-thirds of a person's gross salary.

Workers' Compensation

Workers' compensation is a type of health insurance required by state law. It is carried by employers to provide benefits for employees who suffer illness or injuries due to their work environment. Private insurance companies handle the policies. Medical expenses, hospitalization, lost wages, and a disability pension are included in the coverage.

Reflect:
Ask your parents about any health insurance coverage they may have for you.

Vocabulary:
Define *deductible*, *coinsurance*, and *copayments*.

Reflect:
Do you know anyone who has received worker's compensation? What benefits did they receive?

10-36 For many people, a key factor in selecting health insurance is being able to see the doctor of their choice.

Across the Curriculum

Health. Have students evaluate what benefits they receive under their health coverage contribute to preventive health care. (An example would be an annual physical.)

Enrich: Interview someone who is in an HMO. What does he or she like and dislike about the HMO program?

Discuss: What are the advantages and disadvantages of a HMO and a PPO?

Resource: *Health Insurance Dilemma*, reproducible master, TR

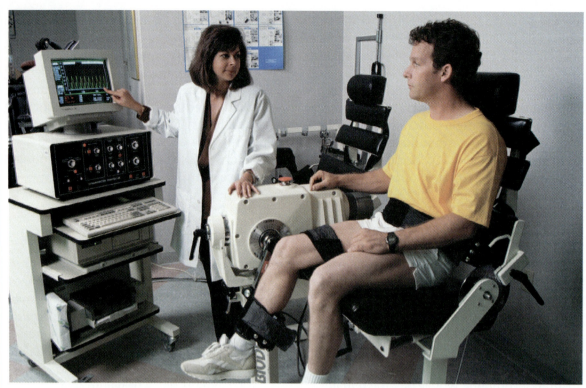

10-37 Major medical coverage often includes the cost of rehabilitation after surgery.

Health Maintenance Organizations

A **health maintenance organization (HMO)** is a group of medical professionals and facilities that provides health care services to members. HMO members pay a flat fee regularly. When medical service is needed, members go to a doctor associated with their HMO. They receive care at little or no added cost.

It is less costly to prevent an illness than to cure one. Therefore, HMOs focus on preventative health care. Because the charge, if any, for office visits is minimal, members are encouraged to get regular checkups. This eliminates the need for more costly health procedures that result from a lack of routine care.

Preferred Provider Organizations

A **preferred provider organization (PPO)** is a group of doctors and medical facilities that contract to provide services at reduced rates. PPOs make agreements with employers or insurance companies. They designate fixed fees and terms for the health care services to be provided.

PPOs benefit all involved. The employer or insurance company can better control medical care costs. The doctors and hospitals have more clients. Patients pay less for health care when they use the preferred provider.

Before you choose a PPO, know who the preferred providers are. Find out what services are provided. Be aware of the costs. All doctors do not participate in PPOs; neither do all hospitals. You may see a doctor who is not a member of the PPO, but it will cost you more. Be sure you have access to the health services you will need before you join.

Automobile Insurance

Because automobile insurance premiums are high, many people are tempted to drive without insurance. This is *not* a wise decision. The losses from a single accident could destroy a family's

Putting Technology to Use
Have students use the Internet to research the differences in HMO and PPO coverage offered by the same insurance companies. Examples of Web sites students may check are Blue Cross/Blue Shield at www.bluecares.com and Humana at www.humana.com.

financial security. In addition, states require drivers to be responsible for accidents in which they are at fault. Having insurance is one way to prove responsibility. See 10-38.

Types of Auto Coverage

An automobile insurance policy usually includes several kinds of coverage. The six basic types of coverage are: bodily injury liability, property damage liability, medical payments, uninsured motorists, comprehensive physical damage, and collision.

Bodily injury liability covers you if you are legally liable for the death or injury of others. Bodily injury pays for any loss of earning ability as well as medical expenses of the injured. It pays the legal fees and the damages assessed against you, up to the limits of the policy. Liability insurance covers the car owner(s). It may also cover anyone else who drives the car with the owner's permission. The amount of coverage is usually stated in two amounts. For instance, $100,000-$300,000 coverage means the insurance company will pay up to $100,000 for any single injury and up to $300,000 for any single accident.

Property damage liability pays for damages that your car causes to the property of others. Like bodily injury liability, it will also pay legal fees. It does not pay for damages to your property, that is, your car.

Medical payments coverage pays medical costs resulting from an accident, regardless of who was at fault. It covers anyone in your car if your car is involved in an accident. It also covers you and your family if you are injured while riding in another car or while walking.

Uninsured motorist coverage pays for bodily injuries for which an uninsured motorist or hit-and-run driver is responsible. You and your family are covered as drivers, passengers, and pedestrians. Guests in your car are also covered.

Comprehensive physical damage coverage protects your car from damage by something other than another vehicle. Such damage may be caused by fire, theft, water, hail, and vandalism.

Collision insurance pays for damages to your car caused by collision with a vehicle or other object. Damages are paid regardless of who was at fault. Collision coverage usually has a deductible option. With a $100 deductible option, if damages to your car amount to $250, you will pay the first $100. The insurance company will pay the $150 balance. You can get coverage with different deductible options.

Automobile Insurance Premiums

Premiums for auto insurance vary greatly and depend on a number of factors. Your age, your driving record, and the year and model of your car affect your insurance premium. Where you live and the distance you drive in a year are factors, too.

Some companies offer discounts on premium costs. Have you completed a driver education course? Are you a good student? Does your family own more than one car? If you can answer yes to any of these questions, you may be eligible for a discount. See 10-39.

10-38 Everyone who drives a car should be protected by automobile insurance.

Resource:
Auto Insurance, Activity H, SAG

Discuss:
What discounts does your insurance company offer? Do the girls pay less than the boys?

Discuss:
What is the difference between deductibles in health insurance and deductibles in auto insurance?

Across the Curriculum

Social studies. Most states require all motorists to be covered by automobile insurance. Have students investigate the laws in your state.

Discuss:
Why do people purchase housing-related insurance? Why do you think some people do not carry housing-related insurance?

Reflect:
In what types of situations might you need liability insurance?

Discuss:
What ways do people use to inventory their possessions?

10-39 Many insurance companies offer a multiple-car discount for families who insure more than one vehicle.

When buying auto insurance, shop carefully. Check several companies to get the best price for the coverage you need.

Housing-Related Insurance

If you own or rent your home, insurance can provide financial protection in the event of loss or damage. The cost of this insurance will depend on the type and amount of coverage and the insurance rates in your area.

Homeowner's insurance provides two basic types of coverage: property protection and liability protection. Property coverage insures you against such dangers as fire, lightning, vandalism, burglary, theft, and explosions. It covers the damage or loss of the dwelling and your personal possessions, such as clothes and furnishings. It also pays for your living expenses if you must move out of your home because of damages to the property.

Liability coverage protects you against financial loss if others are injured on or by your property. It also offers protection if you or your property accidentally damages the property of others. It pays for legal costs if you are sued because of injuries to others or damages to their property. It pays for damages assessed against you if you are held legally liable for injuries or property damage.

Renter's insurance is similar to homeowner's insurance. It covers a renter's personal possessions and liability.

Insurance coverage should be kept in line with the value of your home and belongings. Make an inventory of your possessions and estimate their values. This will help you decide how much coverage you need. Periodically update your coverage as you make major purchases. See 10-40.

Some policies pay *actual cash value*, which equals today's costs less depreciation for the use of the item. Thus, an old item may have depreciated to the point where it is no longer considered to have value. Such an item may not be covered in the case of loss. Other policies pay *replacement costs*, which equal today's costs without considering any depreciation. Replacement cost protection generally is somewhat more expensive. However, the expense may be worthwhile in the event of a major loss.

Filing a Claim

People hope they will not need to use the insurance they buy, but accidents do occur. Before it becomes necessary to file an insurance claim, read your policies.

Putting Technology to Use
Have students make a videotape of valuable possessions. Ask if they would use the video to make insurance claims in the event of damage or loss to the possessions. Do they think making a video is the best way to make an inventory? Why or why not?

Topic 10-6 Meeting Insurance Needs

10-40 A videotape of valuable possessions serves as an accurate inventory for purchasing homeowner's insurance and making future claims.

Know what coverage you have. You must not assume that you have the same coverage as someone you know. The following points will help you file an insurance claim:

- Telephone your insurance agent or company as soon as possible to report your loss. Your agent will determine if you are covered. Ask for the procedures to follow and the forms or documents you will need to support your claim. You may need to provide proof of loss, such as photographs taken prior to the damage or loss. Documents, such as medical and repair bills, may be needed. You may also need a copy of a police report.
- Cooperate with your insurance company by supplying the information needed. Your company will represent you if legal action is brought against you. Give your insurer copies of all legal papers you receive in connection with your loss.
- Keep records and receipts of expenses you incur as a result of the incident. You may be eligible for full or partial reimbursement to cover medical bills, lost wages, temporary housing, and other expenses.
- Keep copies of all documents you receive for future reference.
- Ask your agent to explain whatever you do not understand and answer any questions you have.
- Be prepared to follow up telephone conversations in writing.
- Make temporary repairs, if necessary, to avoid further loss or damage to your property.
- Review the settlement steps outlined in your insurance policy to be sure the company is handling your claim properly.

Check It Out!

1. Regular payments made by a policyholder to an insurance company are called _____.
2. What is the difference between term and whole life insurance policies?
3. True or false. Co-insurance is an amount of money that a policyholder must pay before the insurance company will pay.
4. What kind of automobile insurance coverage pays for damages that your car causes to the property of others?
5. What factors affect the cost of homeowner's and renter's insurance?
6. List three points to follow when filing an insurance claim.

Check It Out! (Answers)
1. premiums
2. Term insurance covers the owner of a policy for a specific number of years. Whole life insurance covers the policyholder for a lifetime.
3. false
4. property damage liability
5. The type and amount of coverage and the insurance rates in the policyholder's area.
6. (Student response. See page 311 in the text.)

Enrich: Interview an insurance agent and find out how to file a claim.

Resource: *Filing Claims,* Activity I, SAG

Resource: *Meeting Insurance Needs,* reproducible master, TR

Activity:
After reading this feature, share the following statistics with your students. According to recent studies, the average teenager in the U.S. spends $3000 each year. This is a collective total of $65 billion annually. In the feature article, Celia stated the average teen allowance was about $30 a week. Have your students use their math skills to compare these figures. Ask them to give possible reasons for the different figures.

TEENS ARE TALKING ABOUT...
Money Management

Using money wisely is a challenge for many people, and teens are no exception. In a group discussion, Celia, Megan, and Jill talked about how teens handle money. They admitted money management is a problem for most teens.

The group was asked where teens get their money. Jill said, "Most teens get money from their parents or as gifts from their grandparents for birthdays or Christmas. Some also get an allowance or have a part-time job after school. The allowance we get is okay, but it's not enough."

Celia agreed and added, "The average teen allowance is about $30 a week. However, there are quite a few teens who don't get any money at all. They have their parents buy everything."

Celia continued, "Parents are encouraging us to get jobs, but we have a lot to do after school. It's hard to fit jobs into our schedules. We can occasionally mow lawns or wash cars."

Megan said, "Most of us are at the point where we need more things. Even if we find jobs, they're probably not going to pay enough for CD players or new shoes. Sometimes we get money from our parents, but they always want us to buy what they like—not what we want."

When asked what teens do with their money, Celia said, "Many teens save their money for cars or college. Some also buy items such as candy or baseball cards. Others may buy hobby-related items, ranging from sports equipment to collectible coins."

Jill thinks most teens don't save their money unless they have a long-term goal, such as college or a car. She feels teens do not save because they are impatient and want to buy items right away. She said, "You don't see many teens buying DVD players with their own money. It's a lot easier to have parents buy a DVD player as a gift."

How do teens decide what to buy with their money? Megan said advertising has an influence. "Most commercials are directed to teens. We need a lot of help trying not to buy everything we see on TV."

Celia said teens look at prices. "Most teens can't afford anything really expensive. They also look for style in the items they buy. If an item isn't in style, most teens don't want it. Parents play a big role in the selection of merchandise, too. Some parents have special restrictions on certain items they don't want their children to have."

The group agreed that limited income and numerous wants make handling money difficult for teens. Perhaps the management process is just what teens need to reach saving and spending goals!

Feature-Related Activity
Have your students develop and conduct a survey of the student body on money management practices. Have them write a report for the school paper based on their findings. Some ideas for questions include the following: Do you think money management is a problem for most teens? Do you get an allowance? If so, how much? Do you have a job? What kinds of items do you buy with your money? Do you save any of your money? What influences your buying decisions?

Chapter Review

Summary

To be an effective manager, you need to learn to use the management process. Through this process, you can learn to use both human and nonhuman resources to reach your goals. The process involves identifying your goals, recognizing your personal priorities and standards, and determining your resources. Then you must form a plan, put it into action, and evaluate the results.

One of the most important nonhuman resources to manage is time. By managing it well, you can achieve short- and long-term goals. You can even address your visionary goals.

A budget is a helpful tool for managing money to reach financial goals. To establish a budget, you must determine your sources of income and estimate your fixed and flexible expenses. After evaluation, you may find it necessary to reduce some of your flexible expenses to balance your budget.

Several types of financial institutions can help you manage your money. Your choice of institutions will be based partly on the services you need. One of these services is sure to be a checking account. Learning how to correctly write and endorse checks and balance your checkbook will give you convenience and flexibility in managing your money.

The unexpected can happen to even the best of money managers. Having some money in savings can help you prepare for the unexpected. Your savings options range from regular savings accounts and CDs to stocks, bonds, and mutual funds. When deciding how to save, you will want to consider safety, rate of return, liquidity, purchasing power, and convenience. Your savings will become part of your estate when you die. Preparing a will enables your wishes to be observed regarding the distribution of your estate.

Insurance can protect you against huge losses. You may need life insurance to provide for dependents in the event of your death. You are likely to want health insurance to help cover the high costs of medical treatments, drugs, and hospitalization. If you drive a car, you need to be protected by automobile insurance. If you own or rent a home, insurance will cover your property and protect you against liability. A reliable agent can help you determine your insurance needs. He or she can also offer assistance if you ever need to file a claim.

Think About It!

1. How do you think the management process would be useful to teens?
2. State a long-term or short-term personal goal that you would like to achieve. What resources do you already have to help you reach that goal? What other resources will you need?
3. Which time management strategies would be especially useful for teens to try?
4. List some of your flexible expenses and give suggestions for reducing them.
5. Which of the different financial services do you see yourself using in the next five years? Which type of financial institution do you think would be best able to provide you with the services you will need?
6. If you had a checking account, explain why you would or would not make a habit of balancing your checkbook each month.

Note:
If a student is not planning to marry, he or she will still need insurance. Modify the assignment in *Think About It!* #9 for a single twenty-five-year-old.

Resource:
PowerZone Challenge CD. Have students play the chapter review game to reinforce text content.

7. Determine a rank order of the five factors that will influence how you save your money. Rank from 1 to 5, with 1 being most important.
8. In which type of security would you most prefer to invest? Explain your answer.
9. Imagine you are 25 years old. You are married, and both you and your spouse work. You do not have any children. What specific types of insurance would you choose to purchase? Explain your choices.
10. How might the information you learned in this chapter help you in your career?

7. Do independent research on one type of insurance and explain how it helps provide security for individuals and families.

Try It Out!

1. Write a short story about a family who learned to use the management process. Show how it improves their family life.
2. Next month, create to-do lists and weekly plans. Then write a brief report on what you learned about how well you use time.
3. Prepare a weekly budget for yourself. After following it for two weeks, write an evaluation describing its usefulness. Also note any adjustments you would want to make in the budget.
4. Working with three or four classmates, investigate the services offered by one financial institution in your area. After an oral report from each group presenting facts about all area institutions, compare them.
5. Use sample checks to practice writing and endorsing checks properly.
6. Invite an investment counselor to speak to your class about the advantages and disadvantages of various savings options. Ask the speaker to also discuss the importance of planning an estate.

Chapter 11
Consumer Decisions

Careers

These careers relate to the topics in this chapter:
- personal shopper
- customer service representative
- family financial counselor
- consumer information specialist

As you study this chapter, see if you can think of others.

Topics

- 11-1 Making Shopping Decisions
- 11-2 The Impact of Technology on Consumers
- 11-3 The Role of Advertising
- 11-4 Using Consumer Credit
- 11-5 Consumers and the Law

Introductory Activities

1. Go around the class and ask students to name a type of consumer decision they would have to make if they were living on their own or were married. List these on the chalkboard. Then ask students which of these decisions they are prepared to make today. For which decisions do they need more information? Indicate which consumer topics will be covered in this chapter.
2. Ask students to think of examples that show how consumers are dependent on one another.

Topic 11-1
Making Shopping Decisions
- I. Deciding Where to Shop
  - A. Retail Shopping
  - B. Catalog Shopping
    1. Shopping Guidelines
  - C. In-Home Electronic Shopping
  - D. Other Shopping Options
- II. Deciding When to Buy
  - A. Shopping at Sales
  - B. Other Factors Affecting Buying Decisions
- III. Deciding What to Buy
  - A. Comparison Shopping
    1. Judging Quality
    2. Suitability
    3. Use and Care
    4. Warranties

Topic 11-2
The Impact of Technology on Consumers
- I. Technology Options Available
  - A. High-Tech Products and Services
    1. Computers
    2. Internet Access
    3. Scanners
    4. Handheld Organizers
  - B. The Functions of High-Tech Equipment
    1. Information Processing
    2. Money Management
    3. Record Keeping
    4. Information Gathering and Learning
    5. Entertainment
    6. Communication
- II. Managing Technology
  - A. Making Buying Decisions
  - B. Drawbacks to Using High-Tech Equipment

Topic 11-3
The Role of Advertising
- I. How Advertising Affects Consumer Spending
- II. Types of Advertising
  - A. Advertising on the Internet
- III. Evaluating Advertisements
  - A. Persuasive Advertising
  - B. Deceptive Advertising
- IV. Consumer Protection Against Deceptive Advertising

Topic 11-4
Using Consumer Credit
- I. What Is Credit?
  - A. The Pros and Cons of Using Credit
- II. Types of Credit
  - A. Sales Credit
  - B. Credit Cards
- III. Applying for Credit
  - A. Establishing a Credit Rating
    1. Keeping a Good Credit Rating
  - B. The Three Cs of Credit
- IV. Why Credit Costs
- V. Shopping for Credit
  - A. The Cost of Credit
    1. The Amount of Credit Used
    2. The Annual Percentage Rate
    3. The Repayment Time
- VI. Credit Contracts
- VII. Using Credit Wisely
  - A. Handling Credit Problems
    1. Credit Counseling
    2. Court Protection

Topic 11-5
Consumers and the Law
- I. Consumer Protection Laws
- II. Consumer Rights and Responsibilities
  - A. The Right to Be Informed
    1. The Responsibility to Seek and Use Information
  - B. The Right to Selection
    1. The Responsibility to Select Wisely
  - C. The Right to Performance
    1. The Responsibility to Read and Follow Instructions
  - D. The Right to Safety
    1. The Responsibility to Use Products Safely
  - E. The Right to Recourse
    1. The Responsibility to Let Dissatisfactions Be Known
  - F. Resolving Consumer Problems
    1. How to Resolve a Consumer Problem

Topic 11-1
Making Shopping Decisions

Vocabulary:
If you know what the words *comparison* and *impulse* mean, you might be able to define the terms *comparison shopping* and *impulse buying*. Write definitions of these terms.

Activity:
Complete one of the following sentences and write an explanatory paragraph: I think I am a smart shopper because… I think I am a poor shopper because…

Reflect:
Which type of store do you prefer to shop in and why?

Objectives
After studying this topic, you will be able to
- evaluate options available when deciding where to shop.
- analyze the factors affecting consumer buying decisions.
- relate comparison shopping guidelines to your shopping decisions.

Topic Terms
impulse buying
sale
comparison shopping
warranty

Informed consumers are smart shoppers. They use the decision-making process in many ways as they make choices in the marketplace. They learn as much as they can about goods and services before making buying decisions. They plan their shopping in advance by deciding where to shop and when to buy. In deciding what to buy, they consider factors such as price, quality, suitability, and use and care. They know how to compare goods and services, and what to look for in warranties.

Being an informed consumer can help you get the most for your money. With practice, you can learn to recognize the best buys among your choices and to shop wisely. Improving your buying habits also will help you become a better consumer.

Deciding Where to Shop

As a consumer, you will have many choices to make when you shop. One of your first choices will be to decide where to shop for the items you want. Retail stores, catalogs, and electronic shopping are some of the more popular choices you may consider.

Retail Shopping

Many types of retail stores are available to meet your shopping needs. Retail stores sell goods and services directly to consumers. Your choices include department stores, discount stores, specialty stores, and off-price retailers. As an informed consumer, you will want to know how each type can best meet your needs. This information will save you time and energy when you are ready to shop.

In deciding where to shop, you consider many factors. Which types of stores carry the item you want to buy? Store location, product price and quality, and product selection will also influence where you choose to shop.

Department stores are large retail firms that offer a wide variety of consumer goods and services—all under one roof. Departments within the stores offer many lines of merchandise including clothing, cosmetics, jewelry, household goods, and home furnishings. See 11-1. Department stores also offer customers extra services such as personal shopping, gift registries, gift wrapping, delivery, and charge accounts. Because of higher operating costs to provide these services, department store prices are often higher.

Discount stores sell a wide assortment of goods at lower prices. Unlike department stores, services such as delivery and consumer credit are usually not available. Discount stores save money by offering fewer customer services and having smaller sales staffs. They pass their cost savings on to consumers.

Specialty stores specialize in selling one line of goods such as shoes, videos, or books. These stores are often found in shopping centers or malls. Since they carry one type of product, their salespeople know the merchandise well. For consumers who want to select from one complete product line, these stores often carry a wider selection. The prices in these stores vary depending on how unique

FCCLA Activity
Encourage members working on the Financial Fitness program to develop a project applying concepts from this chapter. The following are some suggested projects: conduct a comparison shopping workshop to teach this consumer skill to other teens; conduct a six-month study on price competition for teen products; investigate the types of credit that are available to teens and the conditions for receiving each type of credit.

Topic 11-1 Making Shopping Decisions

11-1 Most department stores sell apparel and accessories on the street-level floor and nonapparel items on a separate level.

their products are and how high their sales volume is. See 11-2.

Off-price retail stores buy designer label products or brand name products at low prices from manufacturers. Then they pass the cost savings on to consumers. However, because they often purchase excess merchandise from manufacturers, the types of products they offer frequently change. Prices are lower than retail department stores and fewer customer services are offered.

Factory outlet stores are one type of off-price retail store. These stores, owned by the manufacturer, sell directly to the consumer. Sometimes the goods are irregulars or closeouts on discontinued lines. Merchandise that is not bought by retailers is sold to consumers as *overruns*. Because the manufacturer sells directly to the consumer, the merchandise is sold for less. Many of these stores are located in outlet malls, which are shopping centers consisting of off-price retail stores.

Catalog Shopping

Almost any product imaginable is available through a catalog. This type of shopping is growing in popularity as it offers many advantages. However, catalog shopping has some drawbacks, too.

Convenience and time-savings are the main advantages of catalog shopping, 11-3. Busy people can shop at home from a catalog, and then order items by phone or mail. Although consumers pay charges for

11-2 This specialty store offers a wide selection of baked goods and beverages.

Activity:
List the five types of retail stores on the chalkboard. Ask the class to cite examples of each type that are located in your community.

Discuss:
What are the current most popular catalogs aimed at a teen market?

Discuss:
How many of you have purchased items from catalogs? How many of you would do so again? What do you see as the advantages and disadvantages of catalog shopping?

 Career Preparation Activity
Meeting Consumer Needs, reproducible master, TR. Each student is to interview the owner of a small business that offers goods or services to consumers. Have students compare their findings in class.

> **Reflect:**
> Have you purchased an item from a catalog with which you were unhappy? Is there anything you could have done before making the purchase to have prevented this? Is there anything that you could do after receiving the item to remedy the situation?
>
> **Resource:**
> *Deciding Where to Shop,* Activity A, SAG
>
> **Discuss:**
> Has anyone ever shopped over the Internet? If so, could you share your experience with the rest of the class?

11-3 Catalog shoppers save time and money by shopping at home.

shipping and handling, they save time, energy, and driving expenses by shopping at home.

Selection and price savings are other advantages. Some catalogs offer a wide variety of goods. Others specialize in one type of item, such as shoes or clothing. Prices are often lower than in department stores.

Catalog shopping has some disadvantages, too. You cannot see the item before you buy it. The color, size, or material may not be exactly as it appears in the catalog. You may have to wait for the item to be shipped. This may take days or even weeks. If you are not satisfied with the item after you receive it, you are responsible for returning it.

Shopping Guidelines

Buy wisely when shopping by catalog by following these guidelines:

- Read the catalog before you place an order. Find out the company's policy for returning items, in case you are not satisfied.
- Fill out the order form accurately and completely before sending in your order.
- Avoid sending cash through the mail to pay for your order. Pay by check, money order, or credit card.
- Keep a record of your order until you receive the goods. Keep a copy of the company's name, address, and telephone number in case you need to contact the company.
- When the order arrives, check it over carefully. If something is wrong or not completely satisfactory, return the item to the company.

In-Home Electronic Shopping

Two types of in-home electronic shopping methods exist: television and Internet retailing. Instead of fighting crowded stores and heavy traffic, shoppers can order merchandise from their homes at any hour. Then orders are delivered quickly to their homes.

Television retailing involves showing merchandise on certain television channels or in infomercials. An *infomercial* is a 30-minute blend of information and commercials on one product. Most are shown at off-hours. An infomercial may appear to be a news program with product demonstrations. Usually household, cooking, and fitness products are sold via infomercials. TV channels devoted to 24-hour home shopping, on the other hand, focus on clothing, accessories, and beauty care products. Viewers order by phone and pay by credit card. See 11-4.

Internet shopping is growing rapidly as more computers come online. Web sites show items in sharp detail and include extensive product information. The ability to locate difficult-to-find items is a key reason for shopping online. Some sites have a search agent that tracks down rare items or items that meet certain criteria.

Popular online purchases include books, compact discs, computer software, travel services, and furniture. Before giving credit card information online, always make sure you are at a secured site. A special icon is your sign that a retailer's Web site is secure.

The biggest drawback to electronic shopping is not being able to inspect items before purchase. This is especially important

Across the Curriculum
Math. Many online stores offer discounts to offset the cost of shipping. Have students compare the cost of an item they can get at a nearby store with the price they will pay, including shipping, from an online store.

11-4 Many people buy clothing via TV home-shopping channels because viewers can see how the clothing appears on others.

in the case of clothing. Consequently, garments with "roomy fit" tend to be the leading sellers among clothing items. Some of the advantages of in-home shopping are as follows:

- It saves time. You can quickly visit hundreds of merchants offering almost limitless choice.
- Prices are comparable to or slightly lower than in-store prices. The lower operating costs of electronic retailers make this possible.
- Ordered items are delivered quickly to the home.
- Policies on returning merchandise are usually generous.

There are also drawbacks to at-home electronic shopping. These include the following:

- You do not have the personal assistance of a salesperson.
- Some manufacturers will not allow their products to be sold through electronic channels, thus eliminating those options.
- You cannot check or test a product before purchasing it. However, you can return or exchange it later.

- You are not contributing to your local economy. When you shop at home, your purchases help to keep local stores in business. That, in turn, provides jobs for people in the community. With their salaries, they buy local products and services. This cycle contributes to making your town a better place to live.

Other Shopping Options

Thrift stores, garage or yard sales, and *flea markets* are other popular shopping options. These businesses sell new and used merchandise at greatly reduced prices. Shoppers with limited budgets who know quality may find true bargains. Impulse shoppers may be enchanted by amazingly low prices and buy items they really do not need. **Impulse buying** is making an unplanned or quick purchase without giving it much thought. To buy wisely, consumers must analyze their shopping goals and buy only what they need. Also, they must realize that purchases are usually final. These vendors rarely accept returns.

Deciding When to Buy

Knowing when to buy is as important as knowing where to shop. Smart shoppers plan their purchases ahead of time and watch for sales. Those who can anticipate their needs save money by shopping at sales. They are also aware of factors that can affect their shopping decisions.

Shopping at Sales

Wise shoppers try to get the most value for their shopping dollars. Shopping at store sales is one way they can save money. A **sale** is a special selling of goods at reduced prices. Smart shoppers buy items because they need them, not because the sale price is low. Shoppers carefully plan their purchases to match the timing of sales. See 11-5.

Many stores offer *preseason sales* when new merchandise arrives. For example, winter coats may be on sale in August to encourage people to shop early. For consumers who need new coats and want

---

Discuss:
What attributes of online shopping sites act as substitutes for salespeople?

Activity:
Write about a purchase you made at a thrift store, garage sale, or flea market that turned out to be either very good or very bad.

Reflect:
What was the last item you bought on impulse? Were you still happy with your purchase a week later?

Activity:
Bring to class several sale ads from the newspaper. Have students study the ads and identify the types of sales. Compare prices of similar items from different stores.

Putting Technology to Use
Experts recommend using credit card information and other sensitive data only on secured Web sites. Have students check out an online store's Web site. Is the site secure? How can they tell?

Reflect:
What kind of mood were you in the last time you went shopping? Do you think your mood influenced your buying decisions?

Resource:
Making Shopping Decisions, reproducible master, TR

Discuss:
What factors do you consider before making a purchase?

11-5 Do you need the item? Is the sale price really lower than the regular price? Is the item in good condition and unflawed? Can you return it if necessary, or is it a final sale?

the best selections, preseason sales usually offer good savings.

End-of-season sales, or *clearance sales,* take place when retailers are making room for new merchandise for the next season. For instance, snow blowers may be on sale in March so retailers can make room for lawn furniture. Consumers who are able to wait until the end of the season often receive large discounts on merchandise. However, one disadvantage of an end-of-season sale is selection may be limited.

Seasonal sales take place throughout the year. This type of sale often offers consumers the best sale price. Knowing when to expect these sales helps consumers plan their purchases. Winter clothing, for example, is usually on sale in January. Sports equipment is a good buy in August. Holiday sales take place throughout the year. These are good times to buy needed items at reduced prices.

Other Factors Affecting Buying Decisions

Certain factors can affect consumer-buying decisions. Being alert to these factors can help consumers decide when to buy. Two major factors are the shopper's mood and the time available for shopping.

How people feel when they shop affects their buying decisions. People who feel down when they shop tend to buy items they do not need to make themselves feel better. People who are hungry, tired, or rushed tend to buy impulsively. If they shop when they are tired, they will not be as alert to details. They may make hurried decisions because they are too tired to evaluate the merchandise properly. Smart consumers try to avoid shopping when they are hungry, tired, rushed, or not feeling well.

Time is another factor that affects consumer-buying decisions. It is a resource that should be used wisely. Not allowing enough time to shop, shopping when the store is crowded, or shopping late in the day encourages impulsive shopping. Smart shoppers plan their shopping to allow plenty of time for making buying decisions.

Deciding What to Buy

When you decide to make a purchase, do you buy the first item you see? Probably not. Most likely you shop around to find the right product at the right price. There are other factors to consider in your buying decisions. The ability to judge quality, suitability, use and care, and product warranties is also an important part of your decision.

Comparison Shopping

Comparison shopping means comparing products and prices in different stores before buying. Comparison shopping helps you get the best value for your money. Look at features, price, quality, use and care, and other characteristics that are important to you. It takes time to make such comparisons. However, you will get better quality and find the product that best suits your needs for the money you invest. See 11-6.

Comparison shopping helps you avoid impulse buying. Impulse buying may seem like fun at the time of the purchase. Later, though, you may regret spending money for the item. You may pay too much for an item or buy something you really do

Across the Curriculum

Economics. Have students visit a local mall or department store and make note of current sales. What types of items are on sale? What are the terms of the sales? Will people really save money on the items? (For example, you can buy one $25 sweater or two for $40. If you only need one sweater, are you really saving money if you purchase two?)

Topic 11-1 Making Shopping Decisions

11-6 Some consumers prefer a local shopping mall for convenient one-stop comparison shopping.

Discuss:
How is comparison shopping over the Internet easier than comparison shopping in actual stores?

Activity:
Bring several different brands of the same items to class. Have the students judge the items for quality. Have them decide which would be the best buys and why.

Reflect:
Would you rather pay more money for a better-quality item or pay less money for a lower-quality item? Why?

not need. A sale item may be hard to resist, but it is no bargain if you do not use it.

You save time, energy, and money by comparison shopping. This is because you plan your shopping in advance. You first consider what features are important to you. Then make a list of the features you want and the price you want to pay. At this point, you are ready to shop for what you need.

Judging Quality

Price is not always the most important factor to consider in your buying decision. Shopping for value also means judging the quality of a product.

Product price is not always a guide to a product's quality. Although better-quality products usually cost more, a lower-cost product sometimes offers the same quality. When you shop, compare nationally advertised name brands with lesser-known brands. If the lesser-known brand is the same quality as the more expensive brand *and* costs less, it is a better buy. As a smart shopper, you will learn that a store's own brand is often worth considering.

Learn to inspect products as you shop so you can recognize different quality levels, 11-7. Checking the quality is important if you plan to use the product often or for a long time. Higher quality products are made to higher standards, so they usually last longer. This makes them a better value, too. For example, leather shoes may be more costly than vinyl shoes, but will be a better value in the long run. Since leather is a more durable material that will wear longer, the shoes should last for several seasons. You will not need to replace them as often as

11-7 When you comparison shop, compare the price, quality, and features of similar items. This will help you get the best value for the money you have to spend.

 Putting Technology to Use
Have students use word processing software to create a checklist for inspecting merchandise quality. Have the students save the file as a template they can use again in the future.

Enrich:
Have each student select an item he or she would like to buy. Prepare a list of all the resources that have consumer information about this item.

Resource:
Warranties for Consumer Satisfaction, reproducible master, TR

vinyl shoes, which saves money in the long term.

Sometimes a lower-priced, good-quality item may best meet your needs. For instance, if you are learning to play tennis, a less expensive racket may suit your needs until you improve your skills.

Suitability

Before you go shopping, find out as much as you can about a product. Then when you are ready to shop, you will be prepared to make a wise selection from all the choices. You will be able to find the most suitable product to meet your needs.

Use and Care

Read labels and care instructions on the product to be sure it is what you want. Suppose you are shopping for a casual shirt that you plan to wear often. You find one you like that must be dry-cleaned. You must then decide if you want the added expense of dry cleaning, or if you want to look for a machine washable shirt instead. Your shopping decision will be affected by the use and care information.

Warranties

Studying the warranty or guarantee on a product is also an important part of comparison shopping. A **warranty** is a written promise that a product will meet specified standards of performance. It is a form of consumer protection. See 11-8. A warranty states the procedures the manufacturer or vendor will follow if the product fails to perform as stated. It covers the product for a stated period of time, such as 90 days or 5 years. If the product fails because of customer abuse, the warranty does not apply.

Two basic types of warranties may be found on products. The first type is a *full warranty*. A full warranty is required by law to provide broad coverage on a product. It includes the following:

- free repair or replacement of defective parts or products
- repair or replacement within a reasonable time frame
- replacement if attempts to repair the product are unsuccessful
- no unreasonable demands on the consumer as a condition for receiving repair or replacement service

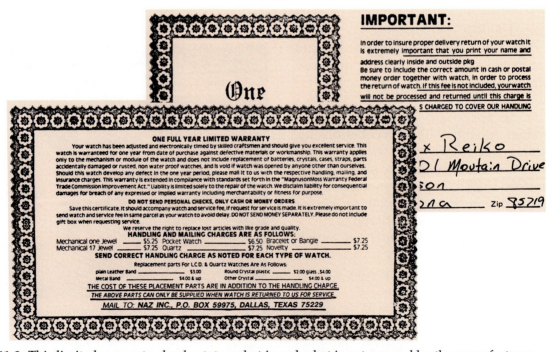

11-8 This limited warranty clearly states what is and what is not covered by the manufacturer.

Problem-Solving Practice

Consumer Decisions, reproducible master, TR. Students are to read details about a shopping situation. Then they are to answer questions, explaining how they would make the various consumer decisions involved.

■ transfer of warranted coverage to a new owner if the product changes ownership during the warranted period

The second type of warranty is a *limited warranty*, which provides less coverage. It always specifies the degree to which it is limited. For example, a limited warranty may cover repairs, but not replacement. It may also require the product be returned to the manufacturer for servicing. A product may carry a full warranty on service and a limited warranty on parts. You must read the warranty carefully to know the exact coverage offered.

When you comparison shop, carefully read product warranties. Determine what protection they guarantee. Are they full or limited warranties? Know what you must do if the product does not comply with its warranty. If you have a problem with the product, who is responsible for carrying out the warranty? Warranty information can help you make a more informed choice.

Check It Out!
1. A _____ store sells a certain type of product such as athletic shoes, toys, or jewelry.
2. List four advantages and four disadvantages of catalog shopping.
3. True or false. In-home electronic shopping always involves an infomercial.
4. Explain the difference between a seasonal sale and an end-of-season sale.
5. What is the main purpose of comparison shopping?
6. Name the two types of warranties found on consumer products.

Check It Out! (Answers)
1. specialty
2. Advantages: convenience, time savings, selection, and price savings
   Disadvantages: You can't see the item before you buy it. The color, size, or material may not be exactly as it appears in the catalog. You may have to wait for the item to be shipped. If you are not satisfied with the item after you receive it, you are responsible for returning it.
3. false
4. Seasonal sales take place throughout the year; an end-of-season sale takes place when retailers are making room for new merchandise for the next season.
5. The purpose of comparison shopping is to help you get the best value for your money. You will find better quality products that best suit your needs for the money you invest.
6. full warranty, limited warranty

Topic 11-2
The Impact of Technology on Consumers

Objectives
After studying this topic, you will be able to
■ list information technology available to consumers.
■ analyze the impact of information technology on the lives of consumers.
■ summarize ways to manage technology.

Topic Terms
high-tech
computer
input device
central processing unit (CPU)
memory
output device
Read Only Memory (ROM)
Random Access Memory (RAM)
scanner
handheld organizer
computer-aided design (CAD)
real-time
simulation software
obsolescence

Technology affects every area of life. Because of it, we enjoy television, fresh food all year, cool fabrics in summer, air travel, reliable health care, and many other products and services. Technology provides ways to perform complicated tasks more quickly and easily. What is learned with each new technology translates into applications in other areas. Technological advances can help people manage resources, solve problems, and make accomplishments.

Technology Options Available

Some definitions of technology are complex. Very simply, technology is the practical application of knowledge. The processes and products that result from technology are often described as **high-tech**.

Activity:
Bring samples of both types of warranties to class. In small groups, have students read and discuss the warranties.

Note:
Sometimes *high-tech* is further shortened to *hi-tech*.

Discuss:
List several items inside and outside the classroom that resulted from technology.

Example:
In the Information Age, communication takes only seconds. When Abraham Lincoln was elected president, almost three months passed before news of the election outcome reached all the voters.

Vocabulary:
What does *laptop* mean?

Enrich:
Have students bring to class a magazine or store advertisement showing a new Information Age product to report to the class.

Discuss:
Is access to the Internet a right or a privilege?

Activity:
Find out how and why the Internet was created.

Reviewing everything that technology has achieved would be a huge task. The task would be never-ending because as each second passes, more new processes and inventions are created.

Of the many inventions created by applying scientific principles, the computer is perhaps the most influential. It is responsible for the current era known as the Information Age. At home, computers help control the car, heating and cooling equipment, and home appliances. Computers also control the television and practically all other types of electronic equipment. Instead of focusing on these inventions, however, this text will discuss the information technology important now and into the future.

High-Tech Products and Services

The array of information products and services is increasing each year. Of those used most often, several stand out as particularly important in their impact on consumers. These items include computers, the Internet, scanners, and handheld organizers.

Computers

Computers are found in schools, homes, and the workplace. A **computer** is an electronic device that processes information according to instructions. Computers are available in desktop and laptop models, 11-9. The basic parts of a computer are the following four pieces of hardware:

- **input device** for entering data
- **central processing unit (CPU)** to process data
- **memory** to store data
- **output device** to convert data into a useful form

The most common input devices are the keyboard and computer mouse. Once inside the CPU, data is either stored in the computer's memory or sent to an output device. There are two types of computer memory: ROM and RAM. **Read Only Memory (ROM)** is built-in, unchangeable

11-9 Laptop computers provide all the computing power of desktop models plus the convenience of portability.

language that directs the computer's operation. **Random Access Memory (RAM)** temporarily stores data upon input and permits data changes. Since RAM provides only temporary storage, transferring data to a permanent memory device such as a disk is necessary to save it. The monitor and printer are two familiar output devices that convert data to useful forms, but there are others.

Prices range from hundreds to thousands of dollars for a computer, depending on the type chosen and accessories purchased. Consumers often buy additional software and accessories after purchasing a computer to make it perform more functions.

Internet Access

Many computer owners are Internet users, too. By linking to the Internet, consumers can send and receive e-mail. E-mail is the shortened term for electronic mail, which is a message sent from one computer to another. They can join special-interest chat groups and download software programs. They can also explore various Web sites for information and entertainment.

Putting Technology to Use

Have students use the Internet to research the role and activities of the U.S. Federal Laboratory Consortium for Technology Transfer, a relatively new government service that distributes information on the technological discoveries of all 711 federal laboratories. The organization's Web site can be found at www.federallabs.org.

Scanners

A **scanner** is an input device that electronically captures an image and transfers it to the computer's memory. Scanners are becoming a common computer accessory. Scanning documents takes minutes instead of the many hours that may be required to keyboard the words manually. A scanned image can be printed, sent via e-mail, or saved for later use.

Handheld Organizers

A pocket-size machine that serves as a personal planner is a **handheld organizer.** They display schedules and deadlines, recall dates and phone numbers, and figure budgets. They also permit you to input information as needed. Some handheld organizers can be connected to a home or office computer to interchange information. The latest models also let you link to the Internet. See 11-10.

The Functions of High-Tech Equipment

Computers and computer-related equipment help to perform many everyday functions faster. Shopping is one function that was discussed in Topic 11-1. In addition, people can process information, manage money, and keep records better by using the equipment. Also, high-tech equipment can help people gather information, learn, enjoy entertainment, and communicate.

Information Processing

Computers can process information in any form—words, numbers, images, and sound. The word processing feature is the main reason computers became popular. Computers are helpful for doing reports, writing letters, and creating databases such as address and phone directories.

Computers can also quickly process numbers. This is extremely helpful when creating budgets and financial materials. Computers can also create charts and graphs depicting financial information.

Processing images is an increasingly important way to use computers. Students can use scanners to transfer images of the subject being studied to their reports. Consumers can make unique greeting cards and stationery with images from the Internet or special software. They can manipulate photos into new images. They can also create landscapes or interiors for their homes with the use of special design software. This is called **computer-aided design (CAD),** which is graphics software that assists in creating a design. CAD software lets you electronically change the color, size, shape, and arrangement of various elements. This prevents costly mistakes and allows last-minute changes to occur on screen or paper before implementing the final design.

Money Management

Creating budgets is easy with the computer's rapid ability to process numbers, 11-11. Special software and Web sites devoted to money management help you prepare worksheets of various savings and spending plans. You can also write checks and balance a checkbook with special software. With an Internet link to your bank, you can bank from home.

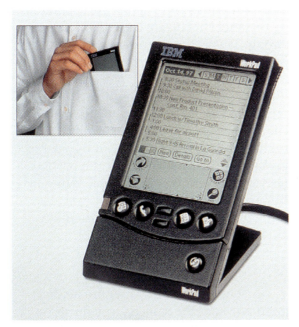

11-10 Handheld organizers with Internet connections allow owners to receive information from their favorite Web sites and databases.

> **Reflect:**
> What types of information—words, numbers, images, or sound—have you processed with a computer?
>
> **Note:**
> Most "computer errors" are the result of wrong commands programmed into the computer through human error.
>
> **Discuss:**
> Can a computer help a person become more creative?
>
> **Discuss:**
> Why should students learn how to do math when a computer's built-in calculator can do it for them?

Across the Curriculum
Science. Ask a science or computer science teacher to explain how a computer processes digitized data.

Reflect:
What types of records are students likely to keep?

Activity:
Working with a small group, list some of the key information resources on the Internet that could help students with their studies.

Discuss:
What advice would you give someone who is using the Internet for the first time?

Discuss:
Describe several ways to send a birthday message to someone in another country using high-tech equipment. Which of these messages would you prefer to receive?

11-11 A tiny computer chip has enormous computing power.

Record Keeping

Keeping records organized and retrieving them when needed is just as important as creating them well. A computer easily handles all these functions. Sometimes important long-term documents, such as insurance policies and wills, are scanned and stored electronically.

Records range from simple lists of important birth dates and addresses to tax records and inventories of valuable possessions. You can create grocery lists that automatically update inventories of all food items stored at home. Many people also create records to make weekly to-do lists and track progress in their fitness plans and hobbies.

Information Gathering and Learning

Perhaps the greatest value of the computer today is accessing the wealth of information available on the Internet. Any given subject can be explored on numerous Web sites. You can search online libraries of major universities and government agencies. Encyclopedias, databases, and full-text versions of magazines and newspapers are also available. In addition, major television news organizations provide **real-time** information. This refers to an event happening now.

Besides finding factual information, discussion groups on the Internet provide opinions about various products, services, and issues. You can read their comments and join the discussion by e-mailing a message. At least one special-interest group exists on practically every subject imaginable. By joining a special-interest group, you learn about the latest facts and events scheduled for the featured topic.

Entertainment

Sometimes software programs and Web sites present information in such an entertaining way that the line between information and entertainment is blurred. Some products, however, are designed specifically to entertain, such as computer card or action games, 11-12. Also, **simulation software** imitates an actual experience. For example, you can sense some of the fun of piloting a hot-air balloon, surfing the Pacific, and investigating other adventures while sitting at your computer. You can also observe real-time entertainment events broadcast on the Internet, such as concerts in other countries.

Communication

As families and friends are separated by distance, the desire to stay in touch is strong. This is the main reason for the popularity of e-mail among consumers. E-mail transmits written and visual messages, from brief to lengthy. These messages can include documents, photos, charts, and graphs. E-mail permits the exchange of messages without the cost of postage or telephone calls. It is a particularly convenient way for people living in different countries to communicate. Also, it can get someone's immediate attention anywhere in the world. See 11-13.

Managing Technology

Just as pencil and paper are neither good nor bad, the same is true for technology. How high-tech devices are used is what really matters. To get full value from information technology, you must make

Across the Curriculum
English. Discuss with students how the rules of good grammar, spelling, and punctuation apply to all e-mail messages created for school or the workplace.

good buying decisions and use the items to enhance your life. You should also be aware of some cautions in the use of technology.

11-12 Colorful graphics and a speedy response to commands are the key reasons for the popularity of computer games.

Making Buying Decisions

Acquaint yourself with the high-tech market and the basic types of items available before buying anything. This market is so vast that you will quickly become overwhelmed if you try to shop before becoming informed. Talk with friends about the products and services they recommend. Also talk with knowledgeable people who can offer good advice. These are some of the questions to answer before buying high-tech equipment.

■ *What equipment features do you need?* It is best to buy equipment that satisfies your current and near-term needs. Do you simply want to create reports and records, or do you also want to send and receive e-mail? Determining what features to shop for will help you determine what you need. It may be difficult or expensive to upgrade equipment later to perform extra functions.

■ *What new products will be introduced soon?* Every 12 to 18 months, technological advances create new products

Reflect:
What store in your area has the best selection of high-tech equipment at competitive prices?

Discuss:
How can a person distinguish between potential needs and wishful thinking when considering what type of computer to buy?

Activity:
Have students role-play a computer shopping experience. (Assign the more knowledgeable students to role-play salespeople.)

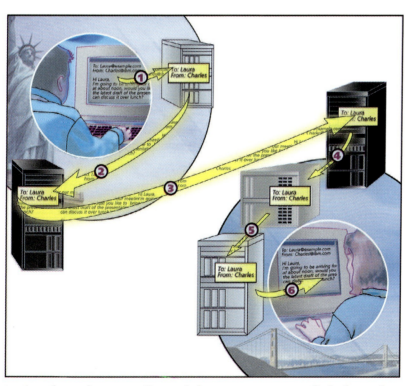

11-13 This illustration shows how e-mail travels between computers linked together electronically.

Putting Technology to Use
Study the help-wanted section of a large newspaper or check an online job-search Web site. Circle all the listed jobs that involve working with a computer and select one that appeals to you. Determine what you need to do to become eligible for such a job. Summarize the types of jobs that involve no computer use.

Activity:
Investigate the options in your area for Internet service. What are the fees, conditions, and extra options available from each service provider?

Resource:
Evaluating a High-Tech Tool, Activity B, SAG

Reflect:
Does high-tech equipment used in your home affect your family positively, negatively, or not at all?

with more speed, convenience, and feature options. Learn what will be available in the next few months. Check what new products are being planned for Christmas or back-to-school sales. Read magazines from the computer and Internet industries to see what new features to expect in the coming months.

- *What nonproduct factors should you consider before buying?* Besides examining equipment features, you will want to consider other important questions. For example, is the dealer reputable and established in the community? What is the provision of the warranty? What must you do to get service? How available and reliable is the service? Is a training program offered? See 11-14. Does your equipment come with a trade-in option so you can upgrade to a more powerful computer later if you want?

- *What is the total cost?* Sometimes a great deal includes signing up for a multiyear service contract or buying other extras. Computers are often advertised in conjunction with one- to three-year contracts for Internet service. If costs for competing services should drop in the future, you could be stuck with an expensive obligation to pay off. To make a wise decision, research the average costs and fees involved in getting everything you will need to use your equipment. Then you can judge whether the item purchased with the advertised extras represents a good buy for you.

Drawbacks to Using High-Tech Equipment

Technologies can impact lives in a negative way as well as a positive one. Sometimes having information equipment available leads to undesirable or harmful effects. You will want to recognize that these possibilities exist so you can avoid them in your life. These are some of the possible drawbacks of using high-tech equipment.

11-14 A free or low-cost training program provided with a new computer is a very valuable benefit.

Putting Technology to Use
Have students compare a currently popular computer game to an early version of Pac Man. How do the games compare in price, entertainment value, and ease of use?

- *Personal privacy may be threatened.* Many fear the invasion of their privacy as a result of data collecting through computers. Because computers can compile and access data quickly, it is possible to combine all the existing information on each person. Purchases made with a credit card, data provided in a loan application, facts in your medical records—all can be combined to develop a profile of you.

    Some people worry that a personal profile created by computer can include wrong information that is never corrected. They also worry that a computerized personal profile would give marketers and others special insight. It could reveal who you are, how you think, and what you are likely to do. Consequently, many experts recommend giving only as much information as needed. For example, when filling out a product warranty form, it is not necessary to answer the unrelated questions about educational status and annual income. Also, it is appropriate to ask data collectors to explain all the uses of any personal information you may provide.

- *Health and development can be adversely affected.* Too much time spent alone with the computer can lead to loneliness and isolation. By interacting with people, you develop social skills that cannot be gained by simply exchanging e-mail. Physical inactivity is another factor associated with frequent computer use. While sitting for hours at the computer can promote intellectual growth, it does not help—and can actually harm—your physical, emotional, and social growth. See 11-15.

- *The natural environment could be endangered.* The pace of high-tech advances is fast, resulting in rapid **obsolescence**. This is the state of uselessness. When items that were high-tech just a few years ago are not powerful enough for today's uses, they are quickly discarded. Often they end up in landfills, which are fast filling up. Citizens concerned about the environment should find ways to recycle their equipment or discard it in a responsible way. Contacting the local waste collection authority and the product manufacturer should provide alternatives.

- *Spending can occur too easily.* With instant access to cash and credit, online purchases can be made in seconds. When purchases are not planned or budgeted, people can quickly find themselves in a serious financial crisis.

- *Too much pressure can be exerted on other family resources.* Money and time are the resources most often affected. A student's desire to keep up with peers and have the very latest equipment can test the family budget. The burden is even greater when a family has several children, all wanting their own equipment. If items must be shared, fights can occur over who gets them and when.

- *Family life may be threatened.* High-tech equipment does not encourage family interaction. Constant competition

11-15 Fascination with a computer can lead some to spend too much time with it while sacrificing important social and physical events.

Reflect:
What can you do to guard private information about yourself from becoming known by others?

Activity:
Find out what opportunities exist in your community for recycling or responsibly discarding old computer equipment.

Enrich:
Contact IBM to learn about the progress the company has made in manufacturing computers from reused computer materials.

Resource:
Technology Crossword, reproducible master, TR

Putting Technology to Use
Have students find out what opportunities exist in the community for recycling or responsibly discarding old computer equipment. Then, hold a school-wide "equipment drive." Ask students to bring in obsolete computer equipment no longer used at home. Have the equipment taken to the recycling or disposal facility.

Discuss:
What would you recommend to allow equal access to and use of the family's home computer by all family members?

Activity:
Working with a small group, list some possible signs of spending an unhealthy amount of time at a computer.

Resource:
How To's for the Information Age, reproducible master, TR

for the family computer can leave no time available for all family members to get together. Relationships are threatened if members skip family activities for solitary entertainment with their computers.

Check It Out!
1. Name three examples of information technology.
2. List five functions in which information technology can assist.
3. What four questions should be asked before buying high-tech equipment?
4. List five ways in which technology can negatively impact your life.

Check It Out! (Answers)
1. computer, Internet, scanner, handheld organizer (Students can justify other responses.)
2. (List five:) shopping, information processing, money management, record keeping, information gathering, learning, entertainment, communication
3. (Name four:) What features are needed? What new products will be available soon? What nonproduct factors should be considered? What is the total cost?
4. (List five:) by threatening personal privacy, by adversely affecting health, by compromising the natural environment, by making spending too easy, by exerting too much pressure on other family resources, by compromising family life

Topic 11-3
The Role of Advertising

Objectives
After studying this topic, you will be able to
- explain the role of advertising in promoting goods and services.
- identify how advertising influences consumer spending.
- evaluate various types of advertising.

Topic Terms
advertisement   bait and switch

As a consumer, are you aware of the methods businesses use to promote their goods and services? Through advertising, businesses inform you about their goods and services. They use various media such as radio, television, magazines, direct mail, the Internet, and billboards to convey their messages. Businesses are interested in increasing sales and profits. Their ads are designed to attract your attention and get you to buy.

Before you buy any goods or services, you need to understand the role of advertising. If you understand the main purpose of advertising is to sell, you can make advertising work for you. That is, you can use the information to buy what you need.

Advertising plays an important role in the economy. It benefits both consumers and businesses. Through ads, consumers are informed about the many goods and services available to them. Businesses are able to market their goods and services more efficiently. Advertising helps businesses introduce new or improved products to the marketplace. As a result, the economy grows as consumers make more purchases.

Topic 11-3 The Role of Advertising

How Advertising Affects Consumer Spending

An **advertisement** is a paid public message communicated through various media that promotes the sale of goods and services. You see and hear many different types of advertisements every day. However, you may not be aware of the effects these ads have on your buying behavior. Advertising can affect how you spend your money, if you let it.

Advertising can influence your lifestyle. Do you look for a certain brand of shoes or jeans when you shop? When you go out to eat, do you meet your friends at a certain restaurant? Do you watch the latest movies when they arrive at your local theater? In some way, advertising likely influenced your decisions about all these issues.

As a wise consumer, keep in mind that the main goal of all ads is to convince you to buy something. Ads are designed to show products in the best possible ways, so only persuasive information appears. If you realize this, you can benefit from it. Carefully evaluate the information presented in ads. Look for factual information in ads, such as features and price, to help you make buying decisions. Do not be sold on a product just because of the ad. Beware of ads that try to persuade you to buy unneeded, unwanted, or unaffordable items. This cautious approach can help you improve your buying decisions.

Types of Advertising

Advertisers use certain types of ads to influence consumer choices. Effective ads gain your attention and hold your interest. Six of the most common types of ads are described below. As you read about these ads, think how each type may influence your buying decisions.

Factual ads provide useful consumer information. They describe a product's features, benefits, and cost, and tell where the product is sold. Some factual ads are used to introduce a new product to the market, so consumers become aware of it. See 11-16.

11-16 This factual ad provides important information on a community recycling program. Do you think this form of advertising will influence consumers?

Comparison ads make comparisons with competing products. They stress the advertised product's beneficial features over the other choices. Some may also spotlight new or improved product features.

Testimonial ads use celebrities, sports professionals, or experts to endorse products. This makes the products' claims seem more believable. Some consumers may be persuaded to buy a product if they think a well-known person likes it. In some of these ads, average people who use the product tell how they like using it.

Discuss: How could businesses tell people about their products if they could not advertise?

Reflect: Do you look upon advertising as a positive or a negative aspect of our way of life?

Discuss: Have you seen any advertisements that seem to be too good to be true?

Across the Curriculum

Art. Have students form six small groups. Assign each group a type of ad to design for toothpaste. Have the groups present their ads to the class as if they worked for an advertising agency and were trying to sell their ad ideas to the toothpaste manufacturer.

> **Resource:**
> Types of Advertising, Activity C, SAG
>
> **Resource:**
> Appealing Advertising, reproducible master, TR
>
> **Activity:**
> Bring in a magazine or newspaper ad. Use the questions in the bulleted list to evaluate the ad.
>
> **Discuss:**
> Can you give an example of a persuasive advertisement that you have seen? Could you be persuaded to buy the product or service in this ad?

Attention-getter ads are designed to be entertaining. These ads use creative techniques, such as humor or visual images, to gain and hold consumers' attention.

Bandwagon ads try to be persuasive. These ads imply that many people use and enjoy the product and you should, too. You are encouraged to become part of the crowd by using the product.

Sex-appeal ads have strong emotional appeal. These ads make consumers feel they will be more attractive and popular if they use the product.

Advertising on the Internet

With the popularity of the Internet, a new advertising outlet is rapidly developing. Advertisers are finding inventive ways to promote their products and services. If the pages of a Web site try to persuade you to make a purchase, they are advertisements.

Before accepting any advice from an Internet site at face value, determine who sponsors the Web site. If the sponsor is a manufacturer or retailer, recognize the information provided by the site reflects just one viewpoint. If the sponsor of the site cannot be determined, it is best to remain skeptical of any information provided.

Evaluating Advertisements

Remember, no matter what method advertisers use, their final purpose is to get you to buy. As a consumer, you have the responsibility of evaluating advertisements. By using helpful information and ignoring the rest, you will improve your buying decisions. Use these evaluation questions to help you sort through the information presented in ads.

- Can you determine the purpose of the ad?
- Is it designed to inform you or persuade you to buy a product or service?
- Is the information in the ad useful to you?
- Is it factual and easy to understand?
- Does it tell what you want to know about the features, quality, and price?

As part of your evaluation, you also need to determine whether the ad is using a persuasive or deceptive advertising method.

Persuasive Advertising

Remember, persuasive advertising offers little or no useful information about a product or service. Be aware of this type of advertising so you can avoid being influenced by it. When you are gathering information about products or services, focus on the facts conveyed by advertising. Then you can make choices based on the quality of the product or service.

Deceptive Advertising

Some types of advertising are misleading. Although the illegal methods used in the past have been stopped, some deceptive advertising still occurs.

Bait and switch is one deceptive advertising method used to lure shoppers who are looking for bargains. The advertiser offers a low-priced item as bait to get shoppers in the store. Once shoppers are there, the advertiser tries to switch them to a more expensive item. They do this by telling shoppers the advertised item is sold out. See 11-17. Another approach advertisers use is convincing shoppers the advertised item is poor quality and will not meet their needs.

In another type of deceptive advertising, consumers are informed by mail or by phone that they have won a free gift. They may be required to come to a store to receive the gift. Once there, they may have to answer questions, listen to a sales presentation, or fill out a coupon to earn their gift. The advertiser may give the consumers a catalog of merchandise as well. More gifts are offered to the consumers for ordering additional merchandise from the store's catalog. The "free" gift may turn into an expensive purchase.

Offering free items or services to consumers who buy their product is another common sales strategy for some

Across the Curriculum

Economics. Have students research the role of advertising agencies in the print and television industries. How do they determine which newspapers or magazines to buy space in for their clients' ads? How does the popularity of TV shows affect the price of airtime for commercials? What impact do these factors have on the success of a newspaper, magazine, or TV show? on the success of the advertised product?

Topic 11-3 The Role of Advertising

11-17 Grocery stores are required to have a minimum supply of advertised items on hand. When they run out, they must offer "rain checks" so customers can get the merchandise at the sale price within 30 days.

advertisers. For instance, a book club may offer free books if you agree to buy a certain number of monthly selections. However, the cost of the free books is actually figured into the cost of the books you buy. This practice is legal because all terms are advertised. Taking the time to figure the costs involved may help you understand the books are not really free.

Consumer Protection Against Deceptive Advertising

To help protect consumers, advertising is regulated by federal government agencies. The *Federal Trade Commission (FTC)* is responsible for preventing false advertising and deceptive advertising practices. The *Federal Communications Commission (FCC)* regulates ads aired on television or radio. These agencies can impose steep fines on advertisers who violate advertising laws.

They can also challenge advertisers to prove claims made in ads.

If you observe false or deceptive advertising practices, what can you do? It is your responsibility to bring them to the attention of the advertiser immediately. If they are not corrected, report them to a consumer protection agency promptly. More information about these agencies and their responsibilities will be covered in Topic 11-5.

Check It Out!
1. Explain how advertising can affect consumer spending.
2. Name six types of advertisements.
3. True or false. Being aware of deceptive or persuasive advertising helps consumers make wiser buying decisions.

Check It Out! (Answers)
1. Advertising conveys information about products and services to consumers and introduces consumers to new or improved products. Consumers use this information as they make spending decisions.
2. factual ads, comparison ads, testimonial ads, attention-getter ads, bandwagon ads, and sex-appeal ads
3. true

Reflect: When was the last time you or a member of your family felt cheated by a deceptive advertisement? Was there a "free" gift involved?

Resource: *Evaluating Advertising*, reproducible master, TR

Topic 11-4
Using Consumer Credit

Objectives
After studying this topic, you will be able to
- analyze the pros and cons of using credit.
- describe how to establish a credit rating.
- identify different types of credit.

Topic Terms
credit
creditors
collateral
credit rating
finance charges
interest
annual percentage rate (APR)
credit contract

Credit can be a successful buying tool, but if misused, it can cause many problems. As a consumer, you have choices to make in determining whether or not to use credit. Use it wisely and it may help you enjoy a more comfortable lifestyle. Take it for granted and it can lead to serious financial difficulties.

What Is Credit?

Consumer credit is widely used in the United States. **Credit** is an arrangement that allows consumers to buy goods or services now and pay for them later. Credit has been called savings in reverse because it involves the present use of future income.

The Pros and Cons of Using Credit

The use of credit has advantages, but it has several dangers, too. The main advantage of credit is convenience. You do not need to carry large amounts of cash when shopping or vacationing. In an emergency, credit can provide temporary help for an unexpected expense. Credit allows you to use expensive goods and services, such as a car or a home, as you pay for them. See 11-18.

One great danger of credit is that it makes spending too easy. It can encourage impulse spending. Also, merchandise bought on credit does not really belong to you until the debt has been paid.

If payments are not made on schedule, you may lose the merchandise. Some **creditors** (people who give credit and to whom debts are owed) ask for collateral. **Collateral** is something of value that you own and that you pledge to a creditor as security for a loan. If you fail to make credit payments, you may lose more than the money you have already paid and the merchandise. You may also lose the items that were pledged as collateral.

Using credit is expensive. The more you use and the longer you take to repay, the higher the cost. By using credit now, you are reducing future income. That means you will have less money to spend in the future.

Misusing credit can have serious long-term effects. It can lead to a bad credit rating, repossession of goods, or bankruptcy.

11-18 Credit can be a useful buying tool only if it is used sensibly and carefully.

Putting Technology to Use
Have students check out Web sites that give tips for using credit wisely, such as www.credit-info.com.

Types of Credit

Consumer credit can be classified as either sales credit or cash credit. Those who have goods or services to sell offer *sales credit*. Department stores, car dealers, repair services, and professional services offer sales credit. Those who have money to loan offer *cash credit*. Lending and financial institutions offer cash credit.

Sales and cash credit can then be divided into one of two categories based on how they are repaid. Credit to be repaid in full at the end of the month is called *noninstallment credit*. Dentist bills, utility bills, and repair bills are examples of noninstallment credit.

Installment credit is repaid in a series of regular, equal payments. Such payments may be made at regular intervals over several weeks, months, or years. The period of time depends on the contract between you and the creditor. Installment credit is used primarily for major purchases—homes, cars, household furnishings, and large cash loans. See 11-19.

Sales Credit

Sales credit is widely used because it is convenient. The cost of using sales credit varies. Three types of sales credit are commonly used.

11-19 An expensive item such as this car might be bought using installment credit.

Regular charge accounts are forms of noninstallment credit. They are used as a shopping convenience and as a way for customers to avoid carrying large amounts of cash. The customer can charge as much as is needed as long as the account is paid in full at the end of the billing period. These accounts are a form of open-end credit. This means that any number of items can be charged. Finance charges are not usually added to regular charge accounts if bills are paid promptly.

Installment charge accounts are forms of installment credit, as the name suggests. The buyer signs a contract and agrees to make a fixed number of payments at certain intervals over a set period of time. This contract is known as a *closed-end credit contract*. This means that no further items may be purchased on the contract. If other purchases are made, other contracts must be signed. This type of credit is usually used for major purchases, such as a computer system or furniture.

Revolving charge accounts combine the features of noninstallment and installment credit plans. They are a form of open-end credit. Consumers are allowed to make purchases up to a credit limit established in the credit contract. Consumers may pay their bills in full each month. When this is done, no finance charge is applied to the account. Consumers also can pay in installments over a longer period. Then a finance charge is applied to the unpaid balance. Department stores often offer this type of account.

Credit Cards

A credit card shows that the company or bank that issued the card honors your credit. Most credit cards are revolving charge accounts. You are billed at the end of each billing period. There is no charge for use of credit if the bill is paid in full each month. If payment is spread over a period of several months, a finance charge is made on the unpaid balance.

What happens if you lose a credit card? Under the law, you are responsible for no more than $50 worth of charges

Discuss:
Why would you use installment credit? What are the disadvantages in using this type of credit?

Activity:
Survey the members of your family and find out how many charge cards they have.

Discuss:
What might determine the credit limit set for a particular individual?

Enrich:
Research annual fees charged by the different companies offering credit cards.

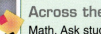

Across the Curriculum
Math. Ask students if there is any cost if a revolving charge account is paid in full each month. Then give students examples showing how much more would be paid if the account is paid in installments with finance charges added.

Discuss:
Why do you think it is hard for teens to establish a credit rating? Do you feel this is fair?

Reflect:
What have you done that could help you establish a good credit rating?

Reflect:
Do you think you are ready to apply for credit? Why or why not?

made by someone else on each lost or stolen card. You are still responsible for the charges you have made. Most credit card issuers furnish you with a form to use in reporting the loss or theft of a card. They also furnish a phone number to call to report the loss. It is important to report the loss immediately.

Applying for Credit

How do creditors determine if you are a good credit risk? When you apply for credit, prospective creditors will evaluate you. The creditors will determine if they think you can handle credit.

Establishing a Credit Rating

Your credit rating is the most important factor affecting your ability to get credit. A **credit rating** is the creditor's evaluation of your ability to repay debts. Your credit rating is determined by a variety of personal attributes that relate to your repayment ability. In most cases, you must be at least 18 years old to get credit.

You may be thinking, "How am I going to get credit if I need a credit rating to do so? How can I have a credit rating if I never bought anything on credit?" Young people are at a disadvantage when they first apply for credit. Proving their abilities to handle credit is not easy. Here are some tips that you might use to establish a credit rating.

- Open a checking account and a savings account. A good banking record can serve as a reference if your accounts have been handled responsibly, 11-20.
- Buy something on a layaway plan. Some stores will give charge accounts to customers who have successfully handled layaway purchases.
- Be prepared to make a big down payment in your first attempt to get credit. Most creditors are more willing to extend credit if you are able to make a sizable investment in the purchase.
- Apply to a local department store for a charge account. If you are offered even a small amount of credit, accept it. Buy

11-20 A good banking record may help you obtain credit.

small items and make payments promptly. Stores that cater to young people are also likely to help you establish credit.
- Ask a relative to cosign (guarantee repayment of) a loan for you. This method gives you credit on your cosigner's record. When the debt is paid, you will have established your own credit record.

Keeping a Good Credit Rating

Credit is a privilege that should not be taken lightly. Once you build a good credit rating, you need to protect it. Be truthful whenever you apply for credit. Use credit only in amounts you can afford to repay. If you meet all the terms of your credit agreement and pay on time, you will have a good credit rating. Late payments or failure to pay will lead to a poor credit rating. A poor credit rating will make it difficult for you to get credit in the future.

The Three Cs of Credit

The three Cs of credit will be used to evaluate you. They are character, capital, and capacity. See 11-21.

Character is an important consideration to creditors. Personal attributes, such as your honesty and reliability, will be

---

Putting Technology to Use
Have students check out Visa's Web site designed specifically for college students, www.rankit.com. Have the click on the site map option and review the budget advice, credit card advice, and financial tools. What important points did students learn from visiting the site?

Topic 11-4 Using Consumer Credit 337

Resource:
Applying for Credit, reproducible master, TR

Resource:
Credit Applications, Activity D, SAG

11-21 When applying for credit, you will fill out an application such as this one. The information you provide helps creditors determine if you are a good credit risk.

Across the Curriculum

Business. Have students gather credit applications for different stores. Study the applications in class. What information do all the applications ask for? Do some of the applications ask for different information? Which information would students be hesitant to disclose?

> **Discuss:**
> Why do you think creditors make it so hard for people to get credit?
>
> **Discuss:**
> Why do businesses offer credit if it costs so much?
>
> **Resource:**
> *The Cost of Credit,* reproducible master, TR

studied. Creditors will also review your established record of financial responsibility. For instance, they will see if you consistently paid your bills on time.

Your *capital* is important. This refers to your income. Your occupation and years you have held your job will be considered. The length of time you expect to remain at your job will also be considered. In addition, your other financial resources will be examined. Do you have savings or insurance? Do you own an automobile or a home?

Your *capacity* to repay will also be examined. Other debts that you have and your general living expenses will be reviewed. Creditors must know that you have the capacity to repay before they can extend credit to you.

The first time you use credit, you establish a record at your local credit reporting agency. Your file will grow as you use credit throughout your life. Maintaining a good credit record is important. Then you can prove your character, capital, and capacity when you need to use credit.

Why Credit Costs

Providing credit for consumers is costly for businesses. Businesses often have to borrow money to cover operating costs until debtors begin to pay. These businesses have to pay interest on the money they borrow. In addition, they have to pay the costs involved in running a credit department. Employees must be hired to interview credit applicants and to check over the information on completed credit applications. Bookkeepers are needed to keep credit accounts up-to-date. Bills must be sent and payments accepted and recorded. Because all people do not pay on schedule, businesses have to pay for additional help to collect bad debts. They must compensate for losses on unpaid bills.

How can businesses afford to extend credit? They make up part of their expenses by slightly raising the prices of their goods and services. They collect a credit charge from their credit customers. The credit charge is related to the cost of providing credit. The more money a business spends to provide credit, the more it must charge its credit customers.

Shopping for Credit

Wise consumers shop for credit as they shop for other goods and services. As with any form of purchase, they shop for the best value. They compare the total costs of using credit at several different places. They also compare terms of credit agreements. Since credit charges vary from source to source, comparison shopping is smart.

When shopping for credit, compare sources. A car dealer may offer credit for the purchase of a car or truck. A store may offer credit for major purchases. Credit unions, savings and loan associations, and banks are other sources. Finance companies specialize in offering credit, but their interest rates are usually high.

Find out the exact cost of using credit. This helps you compare finance charges and determine how much credit you can afford. **Finance charges** are the *total* amounts a borrower must pay the creditor for the use of credit. These charges include interest, service charges, and any other fees. Creditors are bound by law to tell borrowers the dollar amount of all finance charges.

The Cost of Credit

Three factors determine the total cost of using credit. These factors are the size of the loan or amount of credit used, the annual percentage rate, and the repayment time. By comparing these factors, you can shop for the best deal.

The Amount of Credit Used

As you borrow or charge greater amounts, you will pay more in interest. **Interest** is the price you pay the creditor for the use of money over a period of time. Interest is a rate, expressed as a percentage. For example, the interest rate paid on a credit card account may be 1.5 percent a month.

Across the Curriculum

Math. Have students obtain a variety of credit contracts and bring them to class. Study the terms of the contracts. Do any of the credit agencies charge an annual fee? What is the interest rate in each of the contracts? Are there service charges or any other fees? Present some math problems for students to calculate interest rates on a purchase using the interest rates from each contract. Ask students how much they would pay in total for their purchase in each instance.

The Annual Percentage Rate

To compare credit costs fairly, be sure to consider the **annual percentage rate (APR)**. This is the actual percentage rate of interest paid per year. A monthly 1.5-percent rate equals an APR of 18 percent.

Comparing APRs from different sources is an easy way to choose the lowest interest rate. The higher the APR is, the more you will pay in interest. For instance, an 18-percent APR would mean higher interest payments than a 15.5-percent APR.

The Repayment Time

The longer you take to repay your credit debt, the larger the amount you will pay in interest. For instance, the interest on a $100 loan at 18-percent APR repaid in two years would cost $36. If the same loan is repaid in one year, the interest would be $18.

Credit Contracts

A **credit contract** is a legally binding agreement between creditor and borrower. It details the terms of repayment. A contract provides protection for both creditor and borrower, 11-22. It tells what is expected of

> **Enrich:**
> Research credit terms offered by a department store, a specialty store, and a bank for the purchase of a $400 television. Compare APRs. Where would you get the best deal?
>
> **Activity:**
> Find out the annual percentage rates charged by retail stores in your community.
>
> **Resource:**
> *Credit Contracts,* Activity E, SAG

KEEP THIS NOTICE FOR FUTURE USE
BELK RETAIL CHARGE AGREEMENT

1. Each time I receive the monthly statement (at about the same time each month) I will decide whether to pay the New Balance of the account in full or in part. If full payment of the New Balance shown on the statement is received, by BELK, by the Payment Due Date, No FINANCE CHARGE will be added to the account. Any month I choose not to pay the New Balance in full, I will make at least the minimum partial payment listed on the statement as Minimum Payment Now Due. Each month the Minimum Payment Due will be calculated according to the following schedule:

If New Balance Is	Less Than $10	$10-$100	$101-150	$151-200	$201-250	$251-300	Over $300
Minimum Monthly Payment Is	Balance	$10	$15	$20	$25	$30	1/10 of account balance rounded to next highest $5 increment

2. If payment in full is not received by the Payment Due Date, I agree to pay a FINANCE CHARGE at the rate described below for my State of residence.

Annual Percentage Rate for Purchases	10% to 21% (see table below)		
State of Residence	Periodic Rate	Annual Percentage Rate	Portion of Average Daily Balance To Which Applied
DE., KY., VA., MS., GA., OK., MD.	1.75%	21%	ENTIRE
NC., PA., TN., FL., TX and all other states	1.50%	18%	ENTIRE
AL.	1.75%	21%	$750 or less
	1.5%	18%	over $750
WV.	1.5%	18%	$750 or less
	1.0%	12%	over $750
SC.	1.75%	21%	$650 or less
	1.5%	18%	over $650
MO.	1.5%	18%	$1,000 or less
	1.0%	12%	over $1,000
AR.	.083%	10%	ENTIRE
Grace Period:	You have until the next billing date which on average is 23 days if the balance is paid in full, before a finance charge will be imposed.		
Method of Computing the Average Daily Balance.	Average Daily Balance Method: We figure a portion of the finance charge on your account by applying the periodic rate to the "average daily balance" of your account (including current transactions). To get the "average daily balance", we take the beginning balance of your account each day, add any new purchases and subtract any payments or credits, and unpaid finance charges. This gives us the daily balance. Then, we add up all the daily balances for the billing cycle and divide the total by the number of days in the billing cycle. This gives us the "average daily balance".		

3. Credit for returned merchandise will not substitute for a payment.

4. BELK has the right to amend the terms and conditions of this agreement by advising me of its intentions to do so in a manner and to the extent required by law.

5. If any payment is not received by BELK by the Payment Due Date, the full unpaid balance of the account may, at the option of Belk, become due and payable. If the account is referred for collection by Belk to any outside agency and/or attorney, who is not a salaried employee of BELK, I will, to the extent permitted by law, pay all costs including attorney fees.

6. BELK reserves the right to charge a handling fee, not to exceed the amount permitted by law, on any check used for payment on the account that is returned by the bank for insufficient funds or otherwise unpaid.

7. If this is a joint account, both of us agree to be bound by the terms of this agreement and each of us agrees to be jointly and severally liable for payment of all purchases made under this agreement.

8. The credit card issued to me in connection with this account remains the property of BELK and I will surrender it upon request. I understand that BELK is not obligated to extend to me any credit and, without prior notice, may refuse to allow me to make any purchase or incur any other charge on my account. Such refusal will not affect my obligation to pay the balance existing on my account at the time.

9. If any provision of this agreement is found to be invalid or unenforceable, the remainder of this agreement shall not be affected thereby, and the rest of this agreement shall be valid and enforced to the fullest extent permitted by law. No delay, omission, or waiver in the enforcement of any provision of this agreement by BELK will be deemed to be a waiver of any subsequent breach of such provision or of any other provision of this agreement.

10. I hereby authorize BELK, or any credit bureau employed by BELK, to investigate references, statements, and other data contained on my application or obtained from me or any other source pertaining to my credit worthiness. I will furnish further information if requested. I authorize BELK to furnish information concerning its credit experience with me to credit reporting agencies and others who may lawfully receive such information.

11. Except as provided in paragraph 2 above, this agreement will be governed by the laws of the State of North Carolina.

11-22 This is an example of a typical credit contract. When you are issued a credit card, you agree to abide by rules such as these.

> **Putting Technology to Use**
> Have students use charting software to make a chart illustrating their findings from the *Enrich* activity above. Have them print their charts on transparency film and use their transparencies to give a presentation to the class.

Discuss:
Under what circumstances is it best not to use credit? What are some of the alternatives to using credit?

Reflect:
Would you be a cosigner for a friend? What factors would you consider before making that decision?

Note:
Emphasize the importance of seeking help of some type if a person is having a problem paying bills.

each party. If either party fails to carry out the terms of the contract, the other may take legal steps to enforce the terms.

Read all contracts carefully before signing. Make sure you understand every term and the meaning of each statement. Question any point that you do not understand. Be sure that all blank spaces on the contract have been filled. Look for dates, total finance charges, and the annual percentage rate. This information is required on the contract by law.

A credit contract is a serious commitment. Before you sign, ask the creditor these important questions:
1. What action can be taken if I skip a payment or make it late?
2. Can I repay the debt in advance? For example, if the contract states I have a total of 24 monthly payments, can I repay in 12 months instead?
3. If I pay in advance, will part of the finance charges be refunded to me?

When a contract that involves a large sum of money is being considered, you may need legal advice. Do not hesitate to hire a lawyer. The fee you pay an attorney may save you a lot of money later.

People who have either a weak credit rating or no credit rating may need a *cosigner* or *guarantor* on a contract. The cosigner may be a parent, older sibling, or family friend. Anyone who cosigns a contract agrees to pay the debt if the debtor fails to pay.

Using Credit Wisely

Managing credit wisely is an important consumer skill. When used carefully and sensibly, you get more of what you need, when you need it. You can learn to manage your credit wisely by following the guidelines in 11-23.

Here are some other helpful ways to manage your credit wisely:
- Before using credit, determine how much credit you can afford. Analyze your budget to see the expenses you must meet. Limit your use of credit to an amount you can safely pay each month.

Using Credit Wisely

- Stay within your credit limits. Use credit sparingly and only after much thought.
- Shop around for the best credit terms before you borrow or charge.
- Deal only with reputable creditors.
- Read credit agreements before signing. Make sure you understand all the credit terms and can fulfill your obligation.
- Keep records of all credit transactions. Include receipts, payments, contracts, and correspondence. Keep records neatly organized in a file.
- Pay off balances on revolving charge accounts each month to avoid finance charges.
- Keep a good credit rating by paying promptly.
- Correct billing errors immediately.
- Notify creditors promptly if your credit card is lost or stolen.
- If you have trouble making credit payments, contact your creditors right away.

11-23 Following these guidelines can help consumers use credit wisely.

- Evaluate whether or not to use credit. Compare credit terms to paying cash, using savings, or waiting.
- If you decide to use credit, shop for the best terms to meet your needs.

Handling Credit Problems

Credit problems can result when difficult situations arise. Sometimes an unexpected illness, job loss, or accident can lead to financial problems. If this happens, do not ignore your credit bills. Notify your creditor promptly and be honest about your situation. Most creditors will let you delay or decrease your monthly payments until your situation improves.

Credit problems can also result from misusing credit. Some people spend more than they can afford. Financial problems also may result from poor management, lack of management skills, loss of income,

Family Enrichment Activity
Encourage students to find out their parents' views about using consumer credit. Discussion questions students might ask include: What types of credit do you use? What types of purchases do you feel are appropriate to make with credit? Have you ever had any credit problems? When and how would you suggest I begin to establish a credit rating? How can I avoid credit problems?

illness, or an emergency. Learning to use credit wisely can help people avoid some of these problems.

Using better management can solve many minor financial problems. Take a close look at your budget to see where you can cut expenses, or find a way to increase your income, 11-24. Perhaps you could look for a better job, additional part-time work, or better investments.

Once a problem becomes serious, notify your creditors promptly. If they are aware of the facts and your sincere intention to repay, they may defer payments for a while. They may allow you to return merchandise for credit. They may offer to extend the payment period, thus decreasing the size of your monthly payments.

When creditors will not offer a more lenient plan for paying, you may need to *consolidate* your debts. To do this, you must find a financial institution that will loan you enough money to pay all other debts. This institution will then arrange a monthly payment plan that you can afford. Monthly payments may be smaller, but the repayment schedule may be longer.

11-24 Income from a part-time job may help a person manage some financial problems.

Credit Counseling

When credit problems get out of control, people can seek help from an outside source. Credit counseling services are nonprofit organizations that assist people with financial problems.

Credit counseling services can help debtors in two ways. First, an effort is made to work out a reasonable budget based on available income. This budget must allow a certain amount of income to be applied to paying debts. Sometimes the difference between income and living expenses is not enough to pay debts. Then the credit counselors will try to help the debtor to arrange new payment schedules. The service may take a certain amount directly from the debtor's paycheck and use the money to pay creditors.

The second kind of help is training in money management. Counselors teach people management skills so future problems can be avoided.

People who need credit counseling can ask their local Better Business Bureau or Chamber of Commerce to help them find a service. Usually the service is available at little or no cost.

Court Protection

People who cannot resolve serious long-term credit problems on their own may seek legal protection through the court system. Two choices are available: a Wage Earner Plan or bankruptcy.

The *Wage Earner Plan* is a legal arrangement by the courts that schedules debt repayment. With this plan, the debtor's income, property, and other assets are protected while the debtor repays all debts. The debtor has three to five years to pay, must have a steady income, and must also pay legal costs. The debtor makes the payments to the court; the court then pays off the creditors. This plan may be very costly, but the debtor does not have to file bankruptcy.

When a person files *bankruptcy*, the court declares that the person is unable to pay debts. The debtor's possessions are sold. The cash from the sales, with the exception of a small amount, is distributed to creditors.

Reflect:
Do you know of anyone who is having problems handling credit card payments?

Enrich:
Invite a credit counselor to speak about credit problems—how to prevent them and how to solve them.

Discuss:
Why would a person prefer the Wage Earner Plan over bankruptcy?

Across the Curriculum
Business or consumer education. Have students research the bankruptcy process. Ask them to find out if there are different kinds of bankruptcy that can be filed and what laws govern these procedures. Have them find out what possessions can be kept and how long it takes before credit can be granted again.

Discuss:
How does the use of credit influence the free enterprise system?

Resource:
Consumer Credit Review, reproducible master, TR

Creditors must write off any unpaid balance as a loss. The debtor must pay legal costs. Filing bankruptcy will probably prevent you from obtaining credit for at least 10 years.

Check It Out!

1. List three advantages and three disadvantages of using credit.
2. Explain the difference between sales credit and cash credit.
3. List five ways to establish a credit rating.
4. What three factors do creditors use to evaluate people who are applying for credit?
5. True or false. The three factors affecting the cost of credit are capital, annual percentage rate, and the repayment schedule.
6. A _____ is a legally binding agreement between the creditor and borrower that details the terms of repayment.
7. List two ways in which credit counseling services help debtors handle credit problems.

Check It Out! (Answers)
1. Advantages: Convenience—people do not have to carry large amounts of cash when shopping or vacationing. In an emergency, credit can provide temporary help for an unexpected expense. Credit allows people to use more expensive goods and services, such as a car or a stereo, as they pay for them. Disadvantages: Credit makes spending too easy, which can encourage impulse spending. If payments are not made on schedule, people may lose the merchandise. Using credit is expensive.
2. Sales credit is offered by creditors who have goods or services to sell. Cash credit is offered by creditors who have money to loan.
3. Open a checking account and a savings account; buy something on a layaway plan; be prepared to make a big down payment in your first attempt to get credit; apply to a local department store for a charge account; ask a relative to cosign a loan for you.
4. character, capital, and capacity
5. false
6. credit contract
7. Credit counseling services help debtors work out a budget and repayment schedule and they help debtors learn money management skills.

Topic 11-5
Consumers and the Law

Objectives
After studying this topic, you will be able to
■ identify consumer protection laws.
■ describe your consumer rights and responsibilities.

Topic Terms
Food and Drug Administration (FDA)
Consumer Product Safety Commission (CPSC)
recourse

Businesses and consumers are active participants in the United States economy. In the free enterprise system, businesses produce goods and services. Consumers then buy and use these goods and services. This puts money back into businesses so they can continue producing. Keeping this economic cycle strong depends on businesses and consumers treating each other fairly. Laws that prohibit unfair business practices protect consumers' rights. To protect these rights, consumers must act responsibly.

Understanding your consumer rights and responsibilities can help you become a better consumer. As you use your rights and take on your responsibilities, you help keep the economy strong.

Consumer Protection Laws

In recent years, much attention has been focused on protecting consumers against unfair business practices. As a result, the federal government passed several laws aimed at protecting consumers' rights. How do these laws aid consumers? They help consumers understand and compare credit costs. The laws provide guidelines for consumers if they are denied credit, find a billing error, or receive an inaccurate credit rating. These four laws are summarized as follows.

Topic 11-5 Consumers and the Law

The *Truth in Lending Law* requires creditors to provide a complete account of credit costs and terms. Ask for this information before you sign any credit contracts. This law also requires creditors to send debtors regular statements. These statements must show the unpaid balances of the accounts and any finance charges that have been made.

The *Equal Credit Opportunity Act* protects people from discrimination because of sex, marital status, race, religion, or age. In other words, credit can be denied only for financial reasons. People who have been denied credit can demand to receive written explanations of why credit was denied.

The *Fair Credit Billing Act* states the rules by which consumers and creditors must settle disputes about billing. If a debtor thinks there is a mistake in a bill, the creditor is required by law to pay attention to the complaint. If an error is found, it must be corrected without charge to the debtor.

Consumers who wish to complain must follow certain rules. They must send the complaint *in writing* to the creditor within 60 days after the bill was mailed. The consumer's name and account number plus the amount and description of the error must be clearly stated.

The *Fair Credit Reporting Act* protects you against an inaccurate credit record. Your credit rating is based on information in your credit file. Under this act, you have a right to see the contents of your file. In addition, you can file a letter to explain any information in the file that you feel is not correct.

Consumer Rights and Responsibilities

Fairness to both buyer and seller is the basis of the free enterprise system. Unfair business practices hurt both consumers and producers. For this reason, monopolies, price fixing, and deceptive business practices are illegal. When consumer rights are protected, the whole economic system benefits. In accepting these rights, consumers must meet certain responsibilities as well. These rights and responsibilities are outlined in 11-25.

The Right to Be Informed

As a consumer, you have a right to accurate information about products and services. Such information can help you make good buying decisions and use products wisely after purchase.

You have the right to be informed through reliable sources. Information should be available on product cost, features, benefits, and uses. An honest, knowledgeable salesperson can answer questions about product quality and performance. See 11-26. Consumer publications provide comparison shopping advice and product test results. They also inform consumers on many other related issues. *Consumer Reports* is one such publication. Product labels include information about use and care, features, and warranties.

The Responsibility to Seek and Use Information

You have a responsibility to seek and use reliable information about products and services. Advertising simply informs;

Your Consumer Rights and Responsibilities

You have the right to
- information
- selection
- performance
- safety
- recourse

You have the responsibility to
- seek and use information when making consumer decisions.
- select wisely.
- follow instructions.
- guard against carelessness.
- let dissatisfactions be known.

11-25 When you accept your consumer rights, you must meet certain responsibilities as well.

Resource:
Consumer Protection Laws, Activity F, SAG

Activity:
Explain in your own words how each of these laws can benefit consumers.

Discuss:
What is your responsibility regarding the right to be informed?

Across the Curriculum

English. Have students practice writing letters citing an error in a credit card statement. Students may also practice writing letters to correct inaccurate information filed in a credit report. Have students exchange letters and critique them on grammar, spelling, and punctuation.

> **Discuss:**
> Can you think of a company that seems to have a monopoly on a product?

> **Discuss:**
> What is your responsibility if a variety of products is available?

> **Discuss:**
> About how many products in your home came with use and care booklets? How many of you make it a point to read the use and care instructions before using a product?

> **Resource:**
> *The Right to Performance,* reproducible master, TR

11-26 When you order merchandise from a catalog, the salesperson should be able to answer any questions you have.

it is not intended to provide all the information you need to make good buying decisions. Read consumer articles in reputable newspapers and magazines. Read product labels and service agreements. Ask reliable, experienced sources to share their opinions. Carefully compare competing products and services before you buy.

The Right to Selection

Consumers have a right to choose the products they want. However, this presupposes that a variety is available. Suppose that only the Drogos Company supplies a certain product. Also, suppose this company has used unfair business practices to drive competing products out of the market. Then the Drogos Company would have a *monopoly* on the product since it would be offered nowhere else. Without competing products, you would have to buy from the Drogos Company at whatever price it charged.

Laws prohibit monopolies to ensure that competing products and services remain available to consumers. Sellers then compete for consumers' money with products of different price and quality levels. The result of competition is the creation of more selection at better prices.

The Responsibility to Select Wisely

When variety is available, you are responsible for wise choices. Select the product or service that best meets your needs. Shop carefully for the right quality. This does not mean that you should always look for the very best quality or lowest prices. Make a wise selection by purchasing the best quality to meet your needs at a price you can afford.

The Right to Performance

As a consumer, you have the right to expect that the product you buy will perform as it should. Suppose an ad claims that a certain cleaning fluid will not injure the finish of your furniture. Then you have the right to expect that it will not remove varnish from your dining room table. What if you buy a laundry detergent that claims it is safe to use with all fabrics? Then your best shirt should not fall apart after being washed with it.

The Responsibility to Read and Follow Instructions

To get good performance from a product, you must use it as it is meant to be used, 11-27. For example, suppose the label on a bottle of cleaning fluid reads *Use on tile only; may be harmful to wood finishes.* If you used it on your dining room table and ruined the finish, you would have only yourself to blame.

11-27 You can expect good performance from products only if you read and follow product instructions.

Putting Technology to Use
Have students use a drawing program, scanner, or word processing software to create a bulletin board explaining consumer credit laws.

Clothing manufacturers are required to put care labels on the garments they make. Read and follow the manufacturer's directions carefully. What if the label on your new sweater reads *dry clean only* and you wash it? Then you cannot complain if it shrinks.

Most manufacturers provide use and care booklets with the products they sell. These booklets give detailed instructions for using and maintaining products. You are responsible for reading and following these instructions. If you do not operate products properly, you could damage them or cause an injury. The products you buy will give you the performance you expect only if you do your part.

The Right to Safety

Consumers have a right to protection against harmful products. They have the right to know the products and services they buy will be safe, if used properly. Several government agencies were developed to protect this right. These agencies provide consumer protection by screening products for safety and taking steps to prevent unsafe products in the market.

The **Food and Drug Administration (FDA)** watches over sales of food, drugs, and cosmetics. The FDA may prohibit the sale of or require safety warnings on products that may harm people.

The **Consumer Product Safety Commission (CPSC)** handles complaints about unsafe products such as household appliances, toys, and tools. It protects consumers from unsafe products and encourages safe product use at all times. This agency investigates reports of dangerous products and bans hazardous products.

Each year the CPSC receives thousands of complaints from unhappy consumers. When a pattern becomes evident, the agency studies the product and reviews news reports about it. If a product is considered hazardous, the CPSC takes steps to ban it. For example, one study resulted in the recall of several million coffeemakers. Defective wiring made the coffeemakers a fire hazard.

The Responsibility to Use Products Safely

As a consumer, you have a responsibility to use products safely. Read product labels to find out if products may be dangerous if used in a certain way. Some products that are perfectly safe when new may become unsafe after lengthy storage. Ingredients may deteriorate or become unstable.

Always review guidelines, operating instructions, and other product materials provided by the manufacturer. One of the greatest mistakes is dismissing instructions for products that you do not regard as potentially dangerous. Then follow all guidelines. Use products for the purposes for which they were designed.

One of the greatest consumer responsibilities in the area of safety is that of making hazards known. Return a dangerous product to the store where you bought it. Notify its manufacturer of your action. You can also report hazards to appropriate government agencies.

The Right to Recourse

If you buy a product and it does not perform as expected, you have the right to recourse. **Recourse** is asking for help. In other words, you have the right to express your dissatisfaction. You also have the right to have your complaint heard and to have action taken on it. You have the right to complain if

- a product you bought is defective
- services or product repairs are not satisfactory
- merchandise you ordered was not received
- a warranty or guarantee is not honored
- a refundable deposit is not refunded

Some consumer problems are difficult so consumer agencies may help resolve some of them. When problems are beyond the help of consumer agencies, legislation may be needed. State legislators can be contacted for problems confined to one state. Federal legislators can be contacted for nationwide problems. If enough people appeal to their state or federal government

Discuss:
Can you name some products that the FDA or the CPSC has determined to be harmful to people?

Discuss:
What is your responsibility regarding product safety?

Enrich:
Ask students to find out the names of their local, state, and national legislators and how to contact them. Give students one point for each name and address they can give you.

Citizenship and Service
Have students collect information from consumer protection agencies in your community. Have them summarize the services provided by each agency in a pamphlet to distribute to parents and community members.

> **Enrich:**
> Have students look up their local chamber of commerce or Better Business Bureau in the Yellow pages.
>
> **Discuss:**
> Who is our state's attorney general?
>
> **Discuss:**
> Why is it important to be courteous in a complaint letter?

representatives, legislation may be considered to handle the problem. See 11-28.

A sampling of private and government agencies to contact for help with consumer problems are described here.

Chambers of commerce usually have divisions that accept and act upon consumer complaints. Your chamber of commerce may keep a file on local businesses, including complaints that consumers have filed against them. If you need information about a local business, you can call your local chamber of commerce for a reference.

Better Business Bureaus (BBB) perform services similar to those of a chamber of commerce. Their information usually covers more than just local businesses. The BBBs are nonprofit organizations sponsored by private businesses. They try to settle complaints against local businesses.

Media complaint desks of newspapers, radio stations, and television stations provide outlets for consumer complaints. Complaints reported by the media reach the greatest number of people in the quickest possible way.

Licensing boards have been set up by state governments to issue licenses to persons who are qualified to perform certain services. These boards set standards that must be met before a license to perform a service is granted. Boards may also cancel a license. For example, suppose someone who is licensed to perform a service has acted unethically. The board may suspend or cancel the person's license to practice in that state. Licensing boards cover many areas of service. If you have a complaint, report it to the appropriate board in your state.

State government consumer protection divisions are under the direction of the state's attorney general. These agencies aim to protect consumers from unfair and deceptive business practices.

Small claims courts handle claims that involve relatively small amounts of money. Consumers represent themselves instead of hiring attorneys. Booklets that describe such courts can be obtained from your local government, from consumer agencies, or from your state's attorney general.

Private or public legal services may be needed to settle larger claims. Persons who can afford legal services must pay for them. Persons who cannot afford private legal aid may ask for public legal aid.

The Responsibility to Let Dissatisfactions Be Known

When you pay for a product or service and are dissatisfied, you have a responsibility to voice your dissatisfaction. By

Letters to Legislators

- Be clear! State the issue and how you want your legislator to handle it in the first few sentences.
- If you are writing about a specific bill, that has already been introduced, identify the bill by name and number. (If you do not know the name and number, give some description of its contents.)
- Write about only one issue in each letter.
- Be persuasive. Tell why you feel the way you do.
- Be brief. Write legibly or type. Legislators do not have time to read long, scribbled letters.
- Be courteous. Anger and threats may work against you.
- Do not pretend to have vast influence.
- Be constructive. Do not just say what is wrong. Go further and say what is right.
- Write only to legislators who represent you.
- Send notes of appreciation when your legislators do something you like.

11-28 Legislation may be needed to solve some consumer problems.

Across the Curriculum

Social studies. Divide the class into small groups and assign each group one of the government agencies that can help with consumer problems. Have students research the agencies and report their findings to the class.

complaining, you bring problems to the only people who can do something about correcting them—the providers of goods and services.

When you complain to a company, do so in an organized way. Whether you call or make a personal visit, state your name, address, and account number. Describe the nature of your complaint (poor service, faulty merchandise, or whatever). Tell when and where the incident happened. Tell what goods or services you purchased and how much you paid. Briefly explain what happened. Finally, tell what action you want the company to take.

For a more serious problem, you may decide to write a complaint letter to the manufacturer. Address your letter to the consumer affairs department of the company. If you feel top management should know about the problem, write to the president of the company. In either case, include a clear, concise explanation of the problem. Give the date and place of purchase, model number, and purchase price. Enclose a photocopy of the receipt or bill in question. At the close of the letter, suggest the action you want taken, such as a refund or replacement. A sample complaint letter appears in 11-29.

Activity: Write a complaint letter for a product you have bought and are dissatisfied with.

Note: Remind students to inform companies when they are happy with their products by writing complimentary letters.

Resource: *The Right to Recourse*, reproducible master, TR

Complaint Letter

2201 Mountain Drive
Tucson, Arizona 85719
March 21, 2004

Hillary Willis
Consumer Relations Manager
Great Time Watch Company
12 North Hunter Trail
Carol Stream, IL 60188

Dear Ms. Willis:

I purchased a Great Time watch for $25.99 on March 10, 2004, from the Discount Center in Tucson. The model number is 923. A photocopy of my receipt and the warranty is enclosed.

After one week of use, the watch stem broke off as I was winding it. I carefully followed your directions for winding the watch, so I think the watch stem was defective. I am concerned that other consumers who buy this watch may have the same problem.

The warranty states that I should receive a replacement if the product is defective. Even after explaining my problem to the manager at the Discount Center, he said he could not help me. Since I am not satisfied with this product, I would like my watch replaced within the next month.

If you need more information about this problem, please call me at (602) 555-1700. I appreciate your help and look forward to receiving a replacement watch.

Sincerely,

Alex Reiko

Alex Reiko
Enclosures

11-29 When writing a complaint letter, clearly explain the problem and suggest a solution.

Putting Technology to Use
Have students use word processing software to prepare a brochure informing teen consumers of their rights and responsibilities and detailing how to write a complaint letter. Students may add clipart, drawings, or photos to the brochures. Distribute the brochure through consumer education classes.

Resource:
Views on Consumer Laws, Activity G, SAG

Activity:
Create a poster outlining steps to follow in resolving a consumer problem. Ask to place the poster on a community bulletin board.

Do not let your temper interfere with your complaint. If you are angry, cool off before you call or write. This will make your complaint easier to understand. Remember that the person who reads your letter or answers your call is not personally responsible for your problem. He or she is just trying to help settle it.

Resolving Consumer Problems

Knowing and practicing both your consumer rights and responsibilities is the key to resolving consumer problems. There are consumer laws that protect you, but you certainly will not want to go to court to resolve every problem.

Sometimes people are responsible for creating their own consumer problems. This happens when they ignore their consumer responsibilities. Not using information available, buying unwisely, ignoring instructions provided, and ignoring safety precautions means they lose their right to complain.

How to Resolve a Consumer Problem

When you have a legitimate complaint, follow a step-by-step procedure to resolve it. Begin by contacting the place where you bought the product or service. If that fails, write a letter to the manufacturer. As a final step, contact a consumer protection agency, such as the BBB. Government agencies at the local, state, and federal levels can also assist you with your complaint.

Here is an example of how to resolve a product complaint. Suppose you bought athletic shoes that came apart after you wore them for one week. First, ask yourself if the shoes were truly defective or if your dog chewed a hole in them before they started to rip. If the dog chewed a hole due to your carelessness, you have no right to complain.

If you have shoes that are truly defective, what should you do? Go back to the store where you bought the shoes. Show them to the manager of the shoe department and explain your problem. If the department manager does not resolve your problem, talk to the store manager. If the problem remains unresolved, contact the manufacturer of the product. If the problem still remains, contact the appropriate private or government agency. As a last resort, contact your legislator. The legislature may need to amend an old law or write a new law to cover some consumer problems.

Check It Out!
1. Name the consumer protection law that requires creditors to provide a complete account of credit costs and terms.
2. List the five basic consumer rights and their corresponding responsibilities.
3. Outline the step-by-step procedure for resolving a consumer complaint.

Check It Out! (Answers)
1. Truth in Lending Law
2. Consumers have the right to information, selection, performance, safety, and recourse. They have the responsibility to seek and use information when making consumer decisions, select wisely, follow instructions, guard against carelessness, and let dissatisfactions be known.
3. Begin by contacting the place where you bought the product or service. If that fails, write a letter to the manufacturer. As a final step, contact a consumer protection agency, such as the BBB.

TEENS ARE EXPERIENCING...

The Impact of Advertising

Besides being an active ninth-grade student, soccer player, and artist, Ori Cofini tries to be a smart consumer. He earns money through his allowance and through part-time work mowing lawns and baby-sitting. As a teen consumer, Ori has become more aware of how advertising affects teen spending decisions.

According to Ori, advertising greatly affects teens. "Many advertisers depend on teens to buy their products. Advertisements are everywhere, so teens definitely notice them. The biggest advertising influence on teens is probably television. Second is probably radio or magazines."

When asked what types of ads attract teens' attention, Ori responded, "Personally, my favorite commercials are the funny ones. However, many teens seem to pay a lot of attention to the models in ads. For instance, teen girls will point out a handsome man in a clothing commercial. Teen guys will notice the beautiful women in perfume commercials. These types of ads make teenagers remember products more."

Celebrities also play a big role in advertising for teens, he thinks. "Some teens think if a movie star uses a product, they will like using it, too. So they go out and buy it." Professional athletes that appear in commercials on television and in magazines are another strong influence. "Male teens," he continued, "seem to pay more attention to sports heroes than females do."

When asked what types of ads turn him off, Ori replied, "Some ads are empty and boring. There is nothing to them. I like ads that really tell you something useful about the product." Ads that include prices appeal to Ori since he tries to manage his money wisely.

Does Ori feel that teens believe what they see, read, or hear in advertisements? "Sometimes teens are tricked by advertising," he said. "Information in an ad may not be 100 percent truthful, yet some teens still go out and buy the product."

Like other shoppers, Ori thinks teens should make a point of learning the facts about advertising and the products they buy. They need to know facts so they can make smarter choices, rather than respond to emotional appeals. "Teens are mislead by ads that seem so much better than real life. Some ads picture everyone getting excited and having a great time just because they use a certain product." He doesn't believe using a certain product can buy that much happiness. He thinks teens who are unhappy with their lives may try to buy a piece of "the good life."

Ads make the good life seem so appealing.

When asked if ads convince him to buy products he might not have bought otherwise, he smiled and said, "Almost." He recalled a magazine that he almost bought because of the advertisement. "When I checked it out," he said, "the magazine was not as great as the ad, so I did not buy it."

What kind of advice would Ori offer his friends about how to use advertising? "You just can't depend upon ads to guide you to smart shopping," he concluded. "You must look at the product first. You must recognize what a product can and can't do for you. You also need to check the price. Most ads don't mention the cost and you must know that before you make a decision."

> **Activity:**
> Ask each student to bring in two printed ads. One of the ads should make the student want to buy the product or service. The other ad should be one that does not appeal to the student. Have each student write a paragraph about each of his or her ads explaining why he or she selected it.

Feature-Related Activity:
Ask students to name the types of ads that are referred to in the feature article. List these on the chalkboard. Then divide the class into small groups. Have them discuss which ads appeal most to teens. Are teens influenced by ads using celebrities or attractive models? Finally, have each group make a list of guidelines for using ads to make better buying decisions.

Reflect: What steps will you take to be a wise consumer? Will it be worth your time?

Chapter Review

Summary

Consumers must choose from a variety of goods and services in the marketplace everyday. It pays to be an informed consumer and shop wisely to get more value for the money. Knowing where to shop, when to buy, what to buy, and how to use the decision-making process keeps smart shoppers on target.

The computer and other types of high-tech equipment are common purchases in today's Information Age. When used well, they provide many useful functions including information processing, money management, record keeping, information gathering, and communicating. When not managed well, high-tech equipment does not improve the quality of life and even creates drawbacks.

One of the strongest influences on consumer spending is advertising. Advertising affects consumer attitudes, tastes, and preferences. It can be informative as well as persuasive. Understanding the types of advertising and how to evaluate them can help consumers make informed choices.

Deciding whether or not to use credit is an important consumer decision. It involves knowing the pros and cons of credit use and how each type of credit works. Shopping for the best credit terms helps consumers compare finance charges and get the best deal. Misusing credit can lead to serious financial problems. Those consumers who cannot handle serious credit problems should seek help from credit counseling services or through legal protection.

To help keep the economy strong and productive, consumers must understand their rights and be prepared to exercise them. Consumers have the right to information, selection, performance, safety, and recourse. In turn, consumers must recognize that every right carries a basic responsibility that must also be followed.

Think About It!

1. What factors do you consider in deciding to shop at each of the following: specialty store, department store, factory outlet, and flea market?
2. Why do you think it is important to read and understand the terms specified in a warranty?
3. Explain why comparison shopping is a useful consumer skill to develop.
4. What are some everyday activities that are made easier by computers?
5. What are some possible drawbacks associated with using high-tech equipment?
6. Who benefits when a consumer like yourself complains about fraudulent and deceptive advertising?
7. Give three examples of how you have been influenced by advertising to buy goods and services. For each example, describe the type of advertising used. How did each ad make you feel about buying the product?
8. Explain how the following factors influence your consumer decisions:
   A. culture
   B. economics
   C. society
   D. environment
9. Topic 11-4 suggested several ways people can establish a credit rating. State the three tips you would most likely use when you attempt to establish a credit rating.
10. Since buying with credit usually costs more than buying with cash, when is it financially feasible to use credit? Why should you find out the cost of credit before using it?

11. What information should you seek before signing a credit contract?
12. Suppose you lost your job and had no means of paying your creditor. How do you think you would handle your problem?
13. Choose to agree or disagree with one of the following statements. Explain your response.
    A. Consumer rights are more important than consumer responsibilities because…
    B. Consumer responsibilities are more important than consumer rights because…
    C. Consumer rights and responsibilities are equally important because…
14. Share an experience you had with an unsatisfactory product or service. What steps did you take to solve the problem?
15. Review this chapter and suggest five related careers that would interest you.

Try It Out!

1. Brainstorm as a class to name the different shopping alternatives available in your area.
2. Determine an item that would be of interest to members of your class. Go through the process of comparison shopping. Consider quality, suitability, use and care, warranty, and cost. Choose the best buy.
3. As a class, evaluate examples of printed advertisements for high-tech equipment. Evaluate each ad to determine whether it is informative or persuasive and what type of advertising is used. Based on your evaluation, which type seems to be most commonly used?
4. Have a class discussion about the wise and unwise use of consumer credit. Design a bulletin board to illustrate the conclusions made during the discussion.
5. Collect credit contracts from three local stores where teens shop. Read and discuss the contracts in class. Make sure you understand the terms for each one. Determine how much interest you would have to pay for $100 worth of credit used over a three-month period.
6. Divide the class into groups. Each group should select and interpret one of the consumer rights and its corresponding responsibility. The groups may use any method—skits, bulletin board displays, posters, or videotapes—to convey their messages to the class.

Note:
In *Try It Out!* #2, when the class has determined which item is the best buy, have them compare the cost of that item at the various types of retail outlets in your community. Also have them check catalog sources.

Resource:
PowerZone Challenge CD. Have students play the chapter review game to reinforce text content.

CAREER TIMES
LEADING GUIDE TO THE WORLD OF WORK
VOLUME 1, NUMBER 4

Cashing in on Consumer Services Careers

People in consumer services careers do not produce products such as garments or foods. Rather, the mission of these workers is to ensure the quality of goods and services that are available to consumers. Workers in this field also help consumers make good use of their resources.

Employment Opportunities

Many businesses employ people to offer consumer services to their clients and to the public. For instance, a gas company may hire someone to help customers make wise use of energy. Credit companies have counselors who review application forms to decide who would be good credit risks. Credit counselors also work with people who have misused credit to help them regain their financial footing. Banks often provide personal bankers to help their clients with investments. Financial advisers help people state their financial goals and make plans to reach them.

Entrepreneurial Opportunities

The area of consumer services offers a number of options for those who wish to be entrepreneurs. Many financial advisers begin their careers working for someone else. After gaining experience, they open their own offices. Insurance agents often follow a similar career path. A person who has an eye for value may start a business as a personal shopper. Someone who wants to lobby for consumer rights may also go the route of self-employment.

Rewards and Demands of Consumer Services Careers

People in consumer services say their chief reward is the feelings of fulfillment that come from helping others. The demands of this field, on the other hand, are often the hurdles to providing help. Some people resent advice about their financial affairs and resist assistance. Sometimes the work can be emotionally draining. Consumer services workers have to be cheerful, understanding, and open to the needs of their clients. However, they must stay focused on their roles as helpers rather than thinking of themselves as fellow sufferers.

Preparation Requirements

Consumer services jobs are available for people with all levels of training. The type of consumer service a worker wishes to provide shapes the kind of preparation he or she needs.

Entry-Level Jobs

Aids to consumer affairs specialists and product testers have entry-level jobs. These workers do a limited number of tasks. Someone at a higher level oversees the work of entry-level employees. People who do entry-level work may need only high school diplomas.

Mid-Level Jobs

Research clerks in credit bureaus have mid-level consumer services jobs. Assistant loan officers and collection agents also work at

Those who work in the field of consumer services help people make the most of their financial resources.

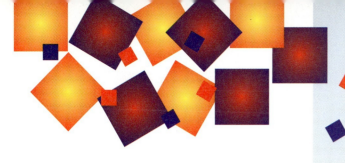

Chapter 12
Your Health and Fitness

Careers

These careers relate to the topics in this chapter:
- health spa attendant
- recreation aide
- health records technician
- public health professional

As you study the chapter, see if you can think of others.

Topics

12-1 Your Physical Fitness
12-2 Good Grooming
12-3 Your Mental Health
12-4 Health Risks
12-5 When You Need Medical Services

Introductory Activities

1. Show students magazine or catalog pictures of people of various ages, with various grooming habits, and in various states of health. Ask students what their impressions are of the people in each picture. Explain how health and grooming can affect appearance and, thereby, the impressions people make.
2. Ask students to identify current health trends, such as an increased interest in exercise, an effort to reduce salt in the diet, etc. List these trends on the chalkboard. Discuss possible reasons for each one.
3. Write the word *health* down the side of the chalkboard. Ask students to think of a good health practice that begins with each letter. Write their suggestions on the board.

Topic 12-1

Your Physical Fitness
  I. The Importance of Good Health
 II. Being Physically Active
     A. Aerobic Capacity
     B. Muscle Strength and Flexibility
III. The Importance of Leisure Activities
 IV. The Importance of Sleep

Topic 12-2

Good Grooming
  I. Caring for Your Skin
     A. Skin Type
     B. Basic Hygiene
     C. A Smooth Shave
     D. Your Skin and the Sun
 II. Caring for Your Teeth
III. Caring for Your Hair
     A. Shampooing
     B. Conditioning
     C. Styling
 IV. Caring for Your Hands and Feet

Topic 12-3

Your Mental Health
  I. Maintaining a Healthy Mental State
     A. Using Defense Mechanisms
 II. Stress and Your Health
     A. Coping with Stress
III. Depression
     A. Overcoming Depression
     B. Suicide
        1. Teen Suicides
        2. Suicide Prevention
 IV. When People Need Help

Topic 12-4

Health Risks
  I. Tobacco
 II. Alcohol
III. Other Drugs
 IV. Sexually Transmitted Diseases
     A. AIDS
  V. Decisions That Affect Your Health

Topic 12-5

When You Need Medical Services
  I. Selecting a Physician
     A. Collecting Names
     B. Gathering Information
     C. Getting an Initial Exam
 II. Emergency Medical Services

Resource:
Keep in Balance for Good Health, color transparency CT-10, TR

Vocabulary:
How would you describe a person who is physically fit?

Enrich:
Brainstorm additional factors that play a role in determining physical fitness.

Topic 12-1
Your Physical Fitness

Objectives
After studying this topic, you will be able to
- explain why good health is important.
- describe two areas on which physical activity should focus.
- use suggestions for getting adequate sleep.

Topic Terms
physical wellness aerobic capacity
physical fitness insomnia

12-1 Getting enough physical activity is part of the self-care needed to achieve physical wellness.

Everyone wants to be healthy. Most people know good health means more than merely being free from disease. A concept known as *wellness* describes a desired state of health. **Physical wellness** means the body is able to fight illness and infection and repair damage. At the same time, a person who has physical wellness enjoys a high level of vitality. This state of health makes you feel and look better. It gives you energy to do your daily tasks and helps you enjoy life more fully. Only a small percentage of people currently enjoy this level of good health. However, attaining physical wellness is a worthy goal that all people should try to achieve.

Two key factors can help you achieve physical wellness. First, you need professional medical care. This includes preventive health care with regular checkups and any needed emergency treatment. Second, you need self-care. This means meeting your body's needs through good nutrition and weight management. It also means getting enough physical activity and rest as well as learning to manage stress. See 12-1.

Physical fitness refers to the condition of your body. When you are physically fit, your muscles are toned, your heart is strong, and your lungs are clear. You are able to perform a variety of tasks.

Fitness and wellness go hand in hand. You cannot be healthy if your body is not strong. Likewise, you cannot keep your body strong if you are not healthy.

Many factors play a role in determining your states of physical wellness and physical fitness. However, the care you give yourself has the greatest impact on both areas of your well-being. You need to assume responsibility for your health and fitness.

The Importance of Good Health

Your health can affect you in a number of ways. Your ability to succeed at school depends on good health. When you are physically fit, you are better able to stay alert and learn. Poor health can prevent you from attending classes regularly. Your grades may suffer if you are not able to attend lectures and participate in labs. This can affect any plans you may have to go to college or technical school.

Problem-Solving Practice
Making Time for Good Health, reproducible master, TR. Make several copies of this sheet for each student to help students analyze their use of time for several days. Ask them to identify how much time they devote to sleeping, healthy eating, and physical activity. Help students see where they can make changes to free up time to take care of their health.

Good health is important to career achievement, too. Some careers require excellent health and physical fitness, 12-2. You need to be in your workplace daily. If poor health causes you to miss work, you may have trouble keeping your job. If you stay healthy, you will be more likely to advance in your career.

Your personal and family life will also be more satisfying if you have good health. You will be able to more fully enjoy interacting with people and taking part in activities. You will feel better as you do your daily tasks. Good health will help you get more enjoyment from daily living.

Being Physically Active

Getting daily physical activity is a key part of building and maintaining physical fitness. Regular physical activity can enhance your posture. It can improve your blood circulation and increase your lung capacity. Building more movement into your day can help relieve stress, boredom, and depression. Physical activity can help you build strength and flexibility. It can also help you manage your weight. Besides all that, physical activity can be fun, especially if you do it with friends.

Physical activity does not have to be a strenuous exercise program. Many of the tasks that are part of your daily routine are forms of moderate physical activity. For instance, walking, bicycling, raking leaves, and cleaning the house will all help you develop fitness. If you enjoy activities that are more vigorous, you might try dancing, swimming, or playing tennis.

You need to include at least 60 minutes of activity in your daily schedule. (Urge adults in your family to include at least 30 minutes of activity in their schedules.) You do not have to spend 60 minutes all at once. You can accumulate a number of 10- to 20-minute segments of activity throughout the day.

You do not need to see your doctor before increasing your daily level of moderate activity. However, if you have not been very active, you should have a checkup before starting a vigorous exercise program. Your doctor can help you choose an exercise program based on your present level of activity. Begin with short, simple workouts. Slowly build up to longer periods of more strenuous exercise. Once you reach a level that suits you, stick with your program.

Aerobic Capacity

Physical activity is most worthwhile when it focuses on two areas. One of these areas is aerobic capacity. **Aerobic capacity** is a measure of the condition of your heart and lungs. One way to test your aerobic capacity is to measure your pulse rate. Your pulse rate reveals the number of times your heart beats per minute. People who enjoy a high aerobic capacity have a lower pulse rate than those who are out of shape. The time it takes for an increased pulse rate to return to normal is another sign of aerobic

Reflect:
Review your school attendance record. Would an employer be satisfied with your record?

Reflect:
Evaluate the physical education program at your school. Does it meet your weekly physical activity needs?

Resource:
Aerobic Capacity and Heart Rate, reproducible master, TR

12-2 People whose jobs involve physical labor need to stay in excellent health to do their jobs well.

Across the Curriculum

Health. Discuss how good health is the result of a combination of self-care and professional medical care. Discuss that each individual is responsible for doing as much as possible to maintain his or her own health. However, professional help is sometimes needed, even if only for routine checkups.

Resource:
How Fit Are You? reproducible master, TR

Resource:
Physical Activities, Activity A, SAG

Discuss:
What do you think is the correlation between physical fitness and self-esteem?

capacity. The faster your pulse rate returns to normal, the higher your capacity. Activities that improve aerobic capacity include walking, running, jogging, bicycling, swimming, and aerobic dancing.

Muscle Strength and Flexibility

The second focus of physical activity should be on muscle strength and flexibility. Muscular strength relates to your muscles' ability to do work. It is often measured by how much weight you can lift, 12-3. You do not have to lift weights to build strength. You can also lift common objects such as bags full of groceries or backpacks full of books.

Flexibility refers to your range of motion. A broad range of motion can help you avoid muscle injuries. Dancing and doing stretches can help you increase flexibility.

The Importance of Leisure Activities

Leisure is freedom from chores, homework, jobs, and other responsibilities. It is the time you have to do something just because you want to do it. Leisure is not only fun—it is also good for you. Enjoyable activities cause the brain to release chemicals such as serotonin and endorphins, which create a sense of well-being. The greatest benefit derived from leisure is the reduction of stress. Leisure activities help keep the body, mind, and spirit ready to fight any challenging forces you might face.

Many busy people fail to plan for leisure. Some think it is selfish to claim time for themselves when they could be serving others. This is a mistake. Being able to care for others requires you to first care for yourself.

Leisure can be used to do anything you like as long as it is not a responsibility. Some teens may choose to watch a favorite TV show or read. Others might use their leisure time for skateboarding or bicycling. You may spend your leisure time alone or with others. Many families use their leisure time to enjoy recreational activities together.

Leisure time can be productive as long as it is relaxing. Perhaps the distinction between leisure and work is your attitude. For one person, picnicking in the park with the family is leisure. Another person might see preparing the picnic and driving to the park as laborious. If you view an activity as "work," you cannot choose it as a way to spend your leisure time. Choose a pastime that relieves stress and refuels you for your daily tasks.

The Importance of Sleep

Teenagers and adults often fall into the trap of not getting enough sleep. You need to find time to sleep, even if it means cutting down on your activities. People who lack sleep may become irritable or show a decline in muscle coordination. The quality of their work usually suffers, too.

The amount of sleep a person needs is an individual matter. Some people get by with six hours a night. Others need nine or ten hours. Most people feel best when they sleep seven to eight hours a night. They awake refreshed and ready to go.

12-3 Lifting weights helps build muscle strength, which is one of the goals of physical activity.

Family Enrichment Activity
Have students compile a list of activities that help promote wellness and can be done by an entire family. Examples include walking, riding bicycles, swimming, and preparing healthy recipes. Ask students to try one of the activities on their list with their families and share the experiences in small groups or with the entire class.

Insomnia is the inability to get the amount of sleep you need when you need it. Taking sleeping pills is a poor solution to the problem. Most sleeping pills become ineffective after a few weeks of use, and they can be addictive. If you have trouble sleeping, try the suggestions listed below. When you find a solution that works for you, stick with it. Get the sleep you need to look and feel your best.

- Make physical activity a part of your daily routine. It can help you sleep deeper and longer.
- Establish regular times for going to bed and waking up. You can program yourself into a sleeping schedule.
- Form a habit of doing a relaxing activity just before bedtime. Read, listen to soft music, or take a hot bath.
- Use your bed strictly for sleep. This will help program your body to know that getting into bed means "it is now time to sleep." If you want to read or watch TV, do so before getting into bed. See 12-4.
- Stay away from coffee, tea, or colas in the evening. The caffeine in these beverages may keep you awake.
- Drink a glass of warm milk just before going to bed.
- Sleep on a mattress that is neither too soft nor too firm.
- Keep the temperature in the bedroom at a moderate setting—not too cold and not too warm.

Check It Out!
1. True or false. A person's health can affect his or her ability to get and keep a job.
2. Name five benefits of daily physical activity.
3. How many hours of sleep do most people need each night in order to feel their best?

Check It Out! (Answers)
1. true
2. (List five:) enhanced posture; improved blood circulation; increased lung capacity; relief from stress, boredom, and depression; increased strength, and flexibility; weight management; fun
3. seven to eight

Enrich: Survey the class to find the average amount of sleep class members receive.

Discuss: Do you go to sleep at a regular time every night? How does this affect how you feel when you wake up?

Reflect: What routine do you follow every night before going to bed?

12-4 If you have trouble sleeping, avoid using your bed for studying or any other activity besides sleep.

Vocabulary:
Do you know how antiperspirants and deodorants differ?

Enrich:
Invite an image consultant to speak to the class.

Resource:
Identifying Your Skin Type, reproducible master, TR

Topic 12-2
Good Grooming

Objectives
After studying this topic, you will be able to
- determine your skin type and describe how to care for it.
- explain how to care for your teeth.
- describe considerations of shampooing, conditioning, and styling your hair.
- demonstrate hand and foot care.

Topic Terms
grooming
dermatologist
deodorant
antiperspirant
depilatory
plaque
podiatrist

Other people's impressions of you are influenced by the way you look. Your appearance can also have a great impact on your self-image. However, you do not need beautiful features to be attractive. Your appearance is largely determined by the way you care for yourself. Books, magazines, hairstylists, and image consultants may be able to give you some tips to help you look your best, 12-5. However, a few basic guidelines can give anyone the foundation needed to have a pleasing appearance.

Grooming means cleaning and caring for the body. To be well groomed, you must take action. You must pay attention to all aspects of personal care, from head to toe.

Caring for Your Skin

Your face is likely to be the first feature people notice about you. The condition of your skin is a key factor affecting the appearance of your face. Having attractive skin is a three-part process. First, you need to know your skin type. Second, you need to know how to care for your skin. Finally, you have to practice what you know.

Skin Type

There are four skin types—normal, oily, dry, and combination. Each type needs special treatment. Chart 12-6 can help you identify your skin type.

Once you have identified your skin type, you can determine how best to care for it. Normal skin should be cleansed every morning and night. This removes surface dirt and oils. Using a lotion or moisturizer after cleansing helps prevent chapping and roughness.

Oily skin should be cleansed often. Some people use soaps or cleansers recommended for oily skin. After cleansing, cold water should be splashed on the face to help shrink pores. An astringent can also be used to tighten pores temporarily. Women with oily skin who wear makeup should look for water-based products.

If your skin is extremely oily and acne becomes a problem, you should see a dermatologist. A **dermatologist** is a doctor who specializes in treating skin. A dermatologist will be able to recommend the best cleansers and cosmetics for your skin. You will probably be given medicated soaps and creams to help control the oil in your skin.

Dry skin needs gentle care. Regular soap may be too harsh for dry skin. It may remove oils that are needed to keep the skin soft and pliable. Cleansing creams that have an oil base may be better for dry

12-5 A skin care consultant can recommend products and techniques to help clients look their best.

Across the Curriculum

Health. Reinforce the importance of adequate vitamin A, riboflavin, niacin, and vitamin C to healthy skin. Ask students if they can name some sources of these vitamins.

Identifying Your Skin Type

Your skin type is *normal* if it
- takes about four hours after cleansing for a slight shine to appear on your nose, chin, or forehead
- feels smooth, soft, and slightly moist
- has a clear, smooth texture with few, if any, enlarged pores or blemishes

Your skin type is *oily* if it
- takes one to two hours after cleansing for an oily shine to appear on your nose, chin, or forehead
- has a coarse texture and enlarged pores, especially on the chin and nose
- develops pimples and blackheads
- shows a little flakiness around the nose where excess oil has dried from exposure to the air

Your skin type is *dry* if it
- takes six or more hours after cleansing for a slight shine to appear on your nose, chin, or forehead
- has a fine texture with small pores
- feels tight and has fine lines around the eyes and mouth
- becomes red, sore, and chapped in cold weather

Your skin type is *combination* if it
- takes three hours after cleansing for an oily shine to appear on your nose, chin, or forehead
- has enlarged pores and blackheads in the oily areas of the nose, chin, or forehead
- feels dry around the eyes, cheeks, mouth, and throat

Resource: *Good Grooming,* Activity B, SAG

Note: The quality of cosmetics is not determined by the price.

Discuss: What food products are used for skin care? Have you ever tried using any of these products? How effective were they?

12-6 Identifying your skin type can help you determine the best way to care for it.

skin. After washing the face, applying a moisturizing cream or oil-based lotion will help keep skin supple. All cosmetics used should have an oil base.

To prevent dry skin, avoid prolonged contact with hot water. Use warm, rather than hot, water to wash the skin. Try to limit showers to five minutes. In winter, use a humidifier or place a bowl of warm water on the radiator. The added moisture in the air will help prevent the drying of your skin.

If you have combination skin, you may try cleansing it according to the *majority principle.* If your skin is mostly oily, treat it like oily skin. If it is mostly dry, treat it like dry skin. You may need to give special attention to an area that is especially dry or oily. For example, you may need to apply extra moisturizer on the dry area. A little astringent may be needed to keep oily areas under control. See 12-7. Water-based cosmetics are usually preferred for combination skin.

Basic Hygiene

Caring for your skin involves cleaning more than just your face. Basic *hygiene,* or practices that promote good health, includes cleansing your whole body. You need to take a bath or shower every day. Soap and warm water will remove dirt, oils, and dead skin cells. This will help you feel and smell fresh.

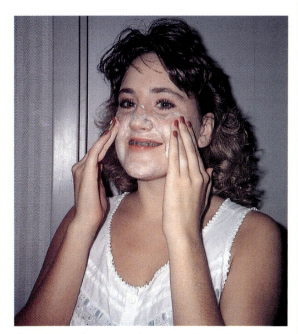

12-7 The oily areas of combination skin may require extra cleansing.

Putting Technology to Use
Have students conduct a survey to see what skin care products are used by students. Students can use word processing software to design the survey sheet by product. Students can then use spreadsheet software to tally the results. Discuss the results in class. Which product received the most votes? Have any class members used the product? Do they agree it is most effective?

Enrich:
Compare various types and brands of antiperspirants and deodorants. Consumer research magazines are helpful references. Also compare prices.

Discuss:
Does your school have a rule prohibiting guys from growing beards and mustaches? If so, why do you think this rule exists? If not, do you think such a rule should be created? Why or why not?

Activity:
Have the class make posters that caution against the dangers of exposure to the sun.

Once your skin is clean, you can control body odor by using a deodorant or antiperspirant. As you perspire, bacteria act on the perspiration to cause body odor. **Deodorant** is a grooming product that controls body odor by interfering with the growth of bacteria. In addition to controlling odor, an **antiperspirant** reduces the flow of perspiration.

Deodorants and antiperspirants come in roll-on, solid, cream, gel, and aerosol forms. They may be scented or unscented. Many contain alcohol, which may sting or burn underarms just after shaving. Choose a deodorant or antiperspirant you like and that works for you.

A Smooth Shave

Hair removal is another aspect of skin care. As teens mature, they may want to begin shaving. Young men may want to remove facial hair. Young women may want to shave their legs and underarms. Both men and women need to pay special attention to skin care as they shave.

Men may use an electric preshave lotion to prepare the skin for shaving with an electric razor. Shaving cream will soften the beard before shaving with a safety razor. Light, even strokes with a sharp blade will produce a close shave. Shaving in the same direction as the hair grows helps protect delicate skin, 12-8. After shaving with either type of razor, men should rinse their skin. Rinsing first with warm water and then cold water will remove shaving aid residue and close the pores. Some men choose to apply aftershave to soothe the skin.

Women moisten their legs and underarms with shaving cream or water before shaving with a safety razor. Short, careful strokes with a sharp blade produce the best results. Applying moisturizing cream or lotion after shaving helps keep skin soft and smooth.

Some women use chemical **depilatories**, which dissolve unwanted hair so it can be washed away. Several brands of depilatories are available. Women choosing to use these

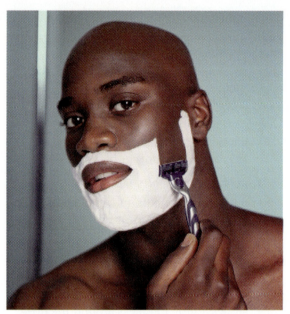

12-8 Using shaving cream and a sharp razor can help a man get a smooth, comfortable shave.

products should read and follow package directions carefully.

Your Skin and the Sun

Another important aspect of skin care is avoiding exposure to the sun. The sun is damaging to the skin and is a leading cause of skin cancer. People of all ages and skin colors are at risk of developing skin cancer. Everyone should take precautions to avoid sun exposure.

Try to stay out of the sun when rays are strongest—between 11 a.m. and 3 p.m. If you must be in the sun, take precautions. The sun's damaging rays can be reflected off sand, water, and concrete. Therefore, you need to protect your skin even if you will be in a shaded area. To protect yourself from the sun, wear long sleeves, pants, and hats to help cover the skin. Also, apply a good sunscreen to exposed skin.

Caring for Your Teeth

Regular dental checkups and daily brushing and flossing should be a part of your health routine. Brush teeth at least twice daily and floss once a day. Choose a

Across the Curriculum

Health, English. Have students do a research report on the effects of the sun on skin. Request that students use the most recent articles they can find as resources. Have students summarize their findings in a written report, including a bibliography.

soft-bristled toothbrush. Brush with a gentle, circular motion and be sure to reach all surfaces of the teeth. This will help keep breath fresh and prevent tooth decay.

Plaque is a colorless film of bacteria that forms on the teeth. It combines with sugar to create acids that attack the gums and tooth enamel. This can lead to tooth decay and gum disease. Dental floss is effective in removing plaque from between teeth.

Caring for Your Hair

Hair care is basic to a healthy, attractive appearance. Before you can care for your hair, you need to know if it is oily, dry, or normal. Oily hair tends to look limp a day or two after shampooing. It begins to cling close to the scalp. Dry hair, on the other hand, feels dry and tends to have a "fly away" look. If neither of these descriptions applies to your hair, you probably have normal hair.

Hair care involves a number of steps. Proper shampooing, conditioning, and styling all play an important role in your appearance, 12-9.

Shampooing

How often should you shampoo your hair? That depends on your hair type. Oily hair may need to be shampooed daily. Once or twice a week may be enough for dry hair. If you have problems with dandruff or scalp infections, try shampooing more often. Keeping your scalp and hair clean is a good way to combat such problems.

Choose a shampoo formulated for your hair type. After shampooing, you should always rinse your hair thoroughly. Rinsing carries away loosened scalp flakes and all traces of suds. Residue from shampoo can leave a dulling film on hair and cause flaking and itching. When shampooing oily hair, use cool water for the final rinse. Hot water will activate the oil glands and make the hair even more oily.

Choose combs and brushes that will treat your hair gently. Combs should have teeth with smooth, rounded edges. Brushes should have natural bristles or soft bristles with rounded tips. Sharp teeth or stiff bristles with squared-off tips can break hairs and scratch the scalp. Clean combs and brushes with shampoo as often as necessary.

Conditioning

Many people condition their hair as a final step in the shampooing process. Conditioning products can help reduce tangling and make hair more manageable. They can help restore the appearance of hair that has been damaged by overstyling and chemical treatments. Conditioning products also give hair more body, bounce, shine, and softness. Your hairstylist can recommend conditioning products designed for your hair type.

Styling

The basic rules for hairstyles are the same for men and women. Consider the texture of your hair, the shape of your face, and your lifestyle when choosing a hairstyle.

A good hairstyle begins with a good haircut. A professional hairstylist should be able to cut your hair to suit your hair's texture and the shape of your face.

12-9 Taking good care of your hair can enhance your appearance.

> **Enrich:** Invite a hairstylist to speak to the class.
>
> **Enrich:** Compare the types and brands of shampoos on the market. Use consumer magazines to assist in the research of effectiveness and cost.
>
> **Activity:** Make a collage of pictures of hairstyles you think would enhance your features.

 Putting Technology to Use
Have students research "makeover" software products. What features do these products include? Is it helpful to see yourself in different hairstyles before making the commitment to change your hairstyle? If possible, have the software available in class for students to try. (A digital camera will also be needed to take digital pictures of each student.)

Note:
Hand washing is particularly important to help prevent the spread of germs.

Discuss:
What precautions does your school take to prevent the spread of contagious fungus infections?

Resource:
Good Grooming Crossword Puzzle, reproducible master, TR

Your lifestyle will affect your choice of a hairstyle. You should be able to care for your hair within a reasonable amount of time. Your hairstyle should be suited to your activities. It should not be a safety hazard as you work. It should not be an inconvenience to you if you participate in sports. See 12-10.

Caring for Your Hands and Feet

Your hands are in sight most of the time. They are an important part of your overall appearance. Thus, hand care should be a part of your grooming routine.

Begin by washing your hands frequently to keep them clean. When your hands are especially soiled, use a nailbrush on knuckles and under nails. Dry your hands with a soft towel. Dry each fingernail separately, pushing cuticles back as you go. Never try to push dry cuticles back. This tears them and makes them sore.

Keeping nails attractively manicured does not necessarily take a lot of time. A weekly manicure can be done in a matter of minutes following the steps in 12-11.

12-10 Teens who take part in sports need to choose easy-care hairstyles that suit their active lifestyles.

Weekly Hand Care

1. Cleanse hands thoroughly.
2. Clean under nail tips with a manicure stick.
3. Shape and smooth nails with a flexible emery board. File from underneath each nail in one direction only.
4. Scrub nails in warm, soapy water with a small nailbrush to soften the cuticles.
5. Gently push back the cuticle with a manicure stick.
6. Trim any hangnails or ragged edges but never trim the cuticle itself.
7. Massage conditioning cream around each nail and over the hands.

12-11 Your hands are always on display. A weekly manicure improves their appearance.

Your feet get a lot of use and abuse. They deserve some attention in your daily and weekly grooming routines.

Every day, you should wash your feet thoroughly using soap and a washcloth. Scrub around toenails with a nailbrush. Use a pumice stone to smooth rough spots and calluses. Dry your feet thoroughly, especially between the toes. Then apply a moisturizing cream or lotion.

Trim toenails *straight across.* Shaping them tends to encourage ingrown toenails, which can be very painful.

Foot problems are common. Some are minor and can be treated at home. *Athlete's foot* is a contagious fungus infection that people pick up anywhere from family bathrooms to school locker rooms. Over-the-counter products can often cure athlete's foot. While treating the infection, keep the feet dry, use absorbent powders, and change shoes and socks frequently.

Other foot problems, like plantar warts and stubborn corns, need the attention of a podiatrist. A **podiatrist** is a physician specializing in the care of feet.

Across the Curriculum

Science. Have students conduct research reports on the establishment of modern medical practices. When did the link between hygiene and good health become apparent and accepted? Did doctors and surgeons always use handwashing and sterile instruments to prevent infection? How do students think patients were affected before these practices were established?

Check It Out!

1. Why is it important for you to know your skin type?
2. Why is it important to floss your teeth each day?
3. Why is it important to rinse your hair thoroughly after shampooing?
4. Why should toenails be trimmed straight across?

Check It Out! (Answers)

1. to know how to care for it
2. to remove plaque from between teeth
3. Residue from shampoo could leave a dulling film on the hair and cause flaking and itching.
4. Shaping tends to encourage painful ingrown toenails.

Topic 12-3
Your Mental Health

Objectives

After studying this topic, you will be able to
- describe a healthy mental state.
- demonstrate ways to cope with stress and depression.
- identify warning signs of depression that indicate a need for help.

Topic Terms

defense mechanism   depression
stress

Vocabulary: What have you heard about stress and depression?

Discuss: How would you contrast the physical appearance of a teen with a healthy mental state and one with an unhealthy mental state?

Your health involves more than being fit physically. You need to be fit mentally, too. You need to be able to recognize what good mental health is. You must realize that factors such as stress can affect your mental health. You also need to be aware of serious mental conditions, such as depression, that require psychiatric help.

Maintaining a Healthy Mental State

People who are mentally healthy look for, and find, the best in their surroundings. They understand themselves and what makes them think and act as they do. They can accept their weaknesses and recognize their strengths. People with healthy mental states are self-confident. They are more likely to follow their principles than to respond to peer pressure. Such people also have a sense of humor and seem to enjoy life. See 12-12.

Mentally healthy people are able to deal with change. When they have difficulties, they are able to analyze the causes of the problems. They find solutions and put them into action. Once mentally healthy people solve problems, they can look back on the problems as learning experiences. This approach allows people who are mentally healthy to avoid similar problems in the future.

Note:
Have students recall Chapter 7 and the family crises discussed in that chapter.

Activity:
Working in small groups, brainstorm ways that you could help make family celebrations less stressful for each family member.

Discuss:
For many, holidays are particularly stressful. What are some probable causes? What techniques might help reduce this stress?

12-12 People who are mentally healthy have a positive outlook on life.

Maintaining a healthy mental state is an important aspect of self-care. Mentally healthy people know how to relieve frustration. They try not to think self-defeating thoughts. They are able to peaceably resolve conflicts with others to avoid negative feelings.

Using Defense Mechanisms

Sometimes situations occur that can challenge your healthy mental outlook. Wanting to guard yourself against pain, stress, and frustration in these situations is only natural. Using defense mechanisms is one way you care for your mental health. **Defense mechanisms** are behavior patterns people use to protect their self-esteem. See 12-13.

Defense mechanisms can be positive or negative solutions to problems. It depends entirely on how they are used. When people are aware they are using defense mechanisms, they are in control of their actions. They are using the defense mechanisms in an attempt to maintain a healthy mental state. However, some people fail to realize they are relying on defense mechanisms. In these cases, defense mechanisms can cause people to lose touch with reality.

Stress and Your Health

Stress is your body's reaction to the events of your life. When something bad happens, such as forgetting your homework or losing your job, you feel stress. You also feel stress when good things happen, like winning a race or meeting someone special. See 12-14. In either case, your body responds. Your heart beats faster. Your face becomes flush. You perspire more. Perhaps your stomach tightens.

Change is frequently a cause of stress. Graduating from high school, taking a new job, getting married, and moving into a new apartment are all major changes. Doing all these at the same time would be likely to cause you stress.

You need stress in your life to add excitement, but too much stress can affect your physical and mental well-being. Excessive stress that is not managed can result in physical and emotional problems. Someone under stress may experience headaches, stomachaches, high blood pressure, or changes in sleep patterns. Emotional signs of stress include tension, anger, and an inability to concentrate.

Coping with Stress

Learning to manage the stress in your life can help you become more mentally fit. When physical or emotional problems result from stress, look at your lifestyle. Ask yourself the following questions:

■ Am I following good health practices? Am I able to eat regular meals and to get plenty of physical activity? Do I get an adequate amount of sleep?

■ Am I realistic about the goals I have set for myself? (Some people expect too much of themselves and make impossible commitments.)

■ Am I managing my time and energy efficiently in order to meet my commitments?

Putting Technology to Use
Have students research *biofeedback* on the Internet. They may want to investigate the Web site of the Association for Applied Psychophysiology and Biofeedback at www.aapb.org. The Biofeedback Network at www.biofeedback.net provides a list of links related to biofeedback.

Defense Mechanisms

compensation. Using a substitute method to achieve a desired goal.

Example: You are too short to excel in basketball. However, if you work out and lift weights, maybe you will make the football team.

conversion. Transferring an emotion into a physical symptom or complaint.

Example: You fear you do not know the material to be covered on the test and you get a headache.

daydreaming. Accomplishing through the imagination something you have not accomplished in reality. Daydreaming can provide both positive and negative solutions. When daydreams are used to find creative solutions to problems, this is positive. When they are used frequently to escape reality through fantasy, they are negative.

Positive example: Sue was daydreaming about having the "latest look" for her party outfit. She suddenly thought of how she could combine some of her old clothes to get just the look she wanted.

Negative example: Maggie turned down Sam's invitation to the school party. Sam went with another girl and daydreamed he was with Maggie.

direct attack. Overcoming obstacles or problems through realistic efforts to find solutions.

Example: You are overweight because you snack on high-calorie foods all the time. You decide to cut out snacking and eat only nutritious food at regular mealtimes.

displacement. Transferring an emotion connected with one person or thing to another person or thing.

Example: You get upset with a friend and take it out on your sister.

giving up. Allowing discouragement to get you down.

Example: You try to lose weight. After two weeks, you have not lost an ounce. You just give up the idea of losing weight and go back to your old eating habits.

idealization. Placing a value on something or someone that is beyond its worth.

Example: You lose a favorite piece of jewelry and lie in bed and cry for two days.

projection. Placing the blame for your failures on other people or things.

Example: You blame the teacher when you fail a test because he did not tell you what would be covered on the test.

rationalization. Explaining your weaknesses or failures by giving socially acceptable excuses.

Example: You tell your parents you went to a movie they had forbidden you to see because all your friends were going.

regression. Reverting back to a less mature stage of development.

Example: You get angry with someone and slam the door as you leave.

12-13 These defense mechanisms are sometimes used to hide or counterbalance feelings or behaviors.

> **Activity:** Have students read about defense mechanisms in figure 12-13. Then have them list the positive examples and the negative examples given.
>
> **Activity:** Working in small groups, discuss the defense mechanisms in figure 12-13. Relate times when you, or someone else, have used variations of the defense mechanisms.

■ Are there many changes occurring in my life at one time?

Answering these questions will help you identify the events in your life that cause stress. Once you have recognized stressful situations, you can work to resolve them. This will help you reduce any symptoms that have resulted from too much stress in your life. See 12-15 for some suggestions that may help you handle stress.

Depression

Depression is an emotional state that ranges from mild, short-lived feelings of sadness to a deep, despairing sense of dejection. Becoming depressed after a failure or loss is normal. However, a lingering depression whose onset does not seem to be triggered by a particular event is not normal.

Across the Curriculum

English. Have students give examples of defense mechanisms used by literary characters. What was the situation in which the defense mechanism was used? Why was that particular situation stressful to the character? How did the use of the defense mechanism affect the character's relationships with others?

Resource:
Stress and Your Health, Activity C, SAG

Reflect:
Do you know someone who is showing the symptoms of clinical depression listed in 12-16?

Activity:
Weather-related depression can affect some students. Work in small groups to compile ideas for inexpensive classroom changes that would help compensate for dreary seasons.

Resource:
Stress—Causes and Cures, reproducible master, TR

12-14 Even happy events can be stressful.

Clinical depression has a number of symptoms, 12-16. Patients generally feel tired. They may not feel like doing anything. They may express no interest in favorite activities. They often experience feelings of isolation and desire to withdraw from others.

Clinical depression may have several causes. Some people experience seasonal depression. When the weather is cold and dreary, they feel blue. When the weather is warm and sunny, they feel happier. Treatment for these people may begin by adjusting their living environments. Their rooms might be decorated with cheerful colors. Pictures and other accessories that remind them of happy times might be added. Artificial light might be used to supplement natural light on gray days.

Sometimes depression is due to a chemical imbalance in the body. Such imbalances may be treated with therapy and drugs.

The impact of having clinical depression is different for each person. One person may react with intense emotion, viewing this situation as a crisis. Another person may see a diagnosis of clinical depression as only a slight setback.

Techniques to Reduce Stress

- Be physically active each day to help relieve the pressures of stress. Go for a brisk walk or play a game of basketball or tennis.
- Be your own person. Do not let others put too much pressure on you. Learn to say no.
- Talk to someone about your concerns. When you have trouble solving a problem, other people may be able to offer suggestions you had not considered. A family member, friend, teacher, or counselor might be able to help. You might also want to seek professional advice.
- Take time off to escape from your everyday worries. Your mind will feel refreshed and ready to tackle anew what lies ahead. You might try listening to soft music, reading a fantasy story, or taking a warm bath.
- Manage your time. Set realistic goals for the tasks you need to accomplish. Prioritize the tasks. Then work toward your goals—do not procrastinate!
- Take care of your health. Eat right and get plenty of sleep and physical activity. Stress is easier to handle when you are rested and in good health.

12-15 A variety of techniques can be used to help people manage daily stress.

Symptoms of Depression

- continual sadness, anxiety, or empty moods
- feelings of hopelessness and helplessness
- lack of interest in pleasurable activities
- sleeplessness or oversleeping
- decreased appetite or overeating
- difficulty concentrating, remembering, or making decisions
- headaches, digestive disturbances, nausea, or chronic pain
- feelings of isolation from family members and friends
- excessive crying

12-16 Prolonged symptoms of depression indicate a need for professional help.

Across the Curriculum

Health. Have students research drugs used to treat clinical depression. Ask them to include negative side effects as well as the positive aspects of the drug. Have students give a report on their findings to the class.

Overcoming Depression

In both mild and clinical depression, a person must take much of the responsibility for his or her feelings. In this way, a person has an active role in his or her eventual recovery. Many of the techniques described for relieving stress can help a person beat a simple case of the blues. However, clinical depression requires professional treatment. A psychiatrist can determine appropriate therapies based on the needs of the patient. The psychiatrist may prescribe antidepressant drugs. He or she may also advise the patient to check into a psychiatric ward or hospital.

It may take months or even years for a patient to recover from clinical depression. During the recovery period, he or she will need patience and support from friends and family members. A depression patient might need encouragement to keep busy. Family members can urge the patient to follow a normal routine of grooming, eating, and sleeping. They can suggest leisure activities that will help keep the patient from thinking about his or her depression. A patient who is unable to work due to his or her illness can still be involved in household tasks. If tasks seem overwhelming, family members can suggest ways to break them into smaller, more manageable parts.

A depression patient might be encouraged to do something for other people, such as volunteer work. Doing something for others will force the patient to make human contacts. It will also help the patient see that he or she is needed—that life really does matter. See 12-17.

Suicide

Sometimes depression goes beyond a person's capacity to cope. The person may think everything will go wrong and nothing will help. The individual feels hopeless and powerless. Thus, he or she becomes reconciled to total failure and stops trying. This response is illogical, but intense emotions impair the ability to reason. When a person is in this type of mental state, he or she may have thoughts of suicide.

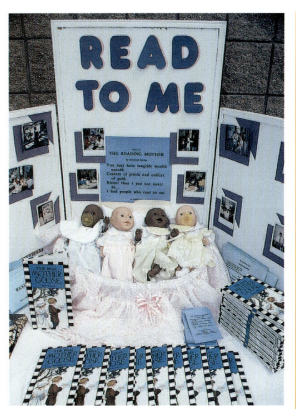

12-17 Becoming involved with volunteer work, such as a literacy program, can be therapeutic for someone suffering from depression.

Suicide attempts are often cries for help. Victims are asking someone to understand and care. People who attempt suicide rarely wish to die. They just wish to end life as they know it. They fail to realize suicide is permanent and will allow them no opportunity to live a more satisfying life.

Teen Suicides

In recent years, the suicide rate among teens in the United States has increased. Studies show this increase corresponds to a breakdown of the family support system in U.S. society. When the family structure is not intact, teens have fewer chances to communicate with parents. When problems arise, teens may feel no one is available to help them deal with their overwhelming feelings.

Competition is also regarded as a factor that affects suicide rates. Teens have to compete for leadership roles, sports teams, part-time jobs, college admissions,

Activity:
Depression patients are encouraged to do volunteer work. Research volunteer opportunities for teenagers in your community. Yellow pages or newspapers could be sources of information.

Note:
Give recognition to students who volunteer. This could be a "Volunteer of the Month" with pictures and details on the bulletin board.

Activity:
Working in small groups, ask students to list what they think are causes of teen suicides. Share the results with the entire class.

Citizenship and Service
Have students read an article on the health benefits of volunteering. Then, as a class, participate in a volunteer activity in your community. Possible activities include volunteering at a soup kitchen or recycling center or visiting residents of a nursing home.

Resource:
Who's Who Among the Mental Health Professionals, transparency master, TR

Discuss:
What telephone hot lines are available in your area? Is peer counseling available? Is it a good idea?

Enrich:
Invite a mental health specialist to speak to the class on ways to handle stress and depression. Anonymous questions should be written and presented to the speaker in advance of the presentation.

and scholarships. Competitive losses become very depressing for some teens.

Relationships with others are another factor. Teens are sensitive about their peer relationships. They can also be easily hurt in relationships with members of the opposite sex. Feelings of rejection can lead some teens into a deep depression.

Some teens express feelings of anger, depression, and anxiety through harmful behavior. These teens may become delinquent or sexually promiscuous. They may run away from home or abuse alcohol and other drugs. Such actions prevent teens from forming bonds with others. Intense feelings of rejection, isolation, and despair may develop. A sense of failure at life can breed thoughts of suicide.

Suicide Prevention

Talk of suicide should not be taken lightly. If you suspect someone is suicidal, immediately seek the help of an adult. School counselors, members of the clergy, and medical professionals can point you in the direction of help. Suicide prevention hot lines are also available to help people deal with thoughts of suicide.

When People Need Help

People may need to seek help when they are not in top mental health. First, they should try talking with family members or trusted friends. If this does not resolve the feelings, a visit to a family physician may be in order. The physician can rule out the possibility of a physical illness that could cause depression. He or she will be helpful in locating a mental health counselor if one is needed.

Maintaining mental health may not always be easy. However, people should not feel they have to do it by themselves. Many mental health specialists are available for counsel. Most regions have psychiatrists, mental health associations, and mental health centers. Most school systems also have psychologists and psychiatrists available for students who need specialized care, 12-18.

12-18 A school psychologist can help teens who have trouble handling problems such as stress and depression.

Putting Technology to Use
Have students use the Internet to research current statistics on teen suicide. Also have them research the statistics from five and ten years ago. How do the statistics compare? Are students surprised by these figures?

Check It Out!
1. Describe what is meant by a healthy mental state.
2. True or false. Stress is your body's reaction to both good and bad events in your life.
3. List five symptoms of depression that should not be ignored.

Check It Out! (Answers)
1. (Student response. See page 365 in the text.)
2. true
3. (Student response. See Chart 12-16 on page 368 in the text.)

Topic 12-4
Health Risks

Objectives
After studying this topic, you will be able to
- list health risks associated with tobacco, alcohol and other drugs, and sexually transmitted diseases.
- explain how routine decisions can affect your health.

Topic Terms
passive smoking
smokeless tobacco
sexually transmitted disease (STD)
acquired immune deficiency syndrome (AIDS)
human immunodeficiency virus (HIV)

Practicing health habits to promote wellness involves avoiding certain health risks. These risks include tobacco as well as alcohol and other drugs. They also include sexually transmitted diseases.

Tobacco
Cigarette smoking is the largest preventable cause of illness and premature death in the United States. Many thousands of deaths each year are linked to cigarette smoking. People who smoke are more likely to suffer from heart disease, respiratory infections, and lung cancer.

Smoking during pregnancy can be harmful to the unborn child. Pregnant women who smoke have a higher risk of miscarriage and premature delivery. Babies born to women who smoke often weigh less, and their future growth and development may be impaired.

Passive smoking is also a health concern. **Passive smoking** is the inhaling of smoke in a smoke-filled environment. For people with lung and heart problems, breathing smoke-filled air can be very irritating, 12-19. Small children are also highly affected by passive smoking. Studies show that children of smokers are more likely to suffer from

Note: Point out that alcohol is considered a drug.

Activity: Survey teenage smokers. Ask them to complete the following sentence: "I started smoking because…" Compile the results. Discuss ways to combat the reasons mentioned most frequently.

Activity:
Research state and local laws governing the consumption of tobacco, alcohol, and other drugs.

Enrich:
Brainstorm healthy alternatives that will provide natural "highs" without using drugs.

Discuss:
Give examples of how alcoholism can interfere with personal relationships.

respiratory ailments than children of nonsmokers.

The use of **smokeless tobacco** products involves health risks as well. These are products such as chewing tobacco and snuff, which are chewed or placed against the gums. Their use has been linked to gum cancer and irritations of the gums and lips.

For people who have never used tobacco products, continuing to avoid these products is the most health-conscious choice. For people who have used tobacco products, quitting is one of the best steps they can take for their health. People who quit smoking enjoy almost immediate health benefits. Within 24 hours, the risk of heart attack decreases. After three days, breathing becomes easier and lung capacity increases. Within weeks, the body's energy level increases.

Alcohol

Alcohol is a depressant drug that is a serious health risk. Health care for alcohol-related illnesses and accidents costs millions of dollars every year. Alcohol can damage the brain, liver, stomach, and other organs. It also interferes with judgment, vision, muscle coordination, and reaction time. This is why it poses such great danger to people who drive under its influence. See 12-20.

Another health problem related to alcohol is alcoholism. Alcoholism is an addiction to alcohol. It is a disease that affects teenagers as well as adults. Alcoholics lose control of their drinking. They become dependent on alcohol. Alcoholism interferes with their health, personal relationships, and ability to function.

Once alcohol has entered the body, coffee and cold showers will not help lessen its effects. Alcohol will continue to circulate in the body until the liver burns it up. This occurs at the rate of about one drink every two hours for a 150-pound person.

Alcohol has legal risks as well as health risks. It is illegal for teens to buy alcohol. It is illegal for *anyone* to drive under the influence of alcohol.

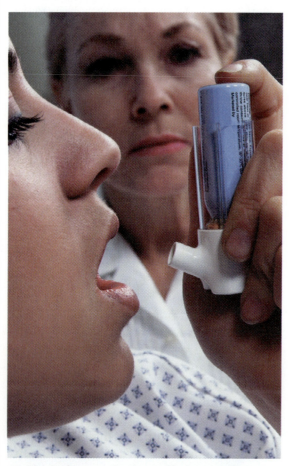

12-19 Asthma patients are likely to suffer more breathing problems if they live or work in smoke-filled environments.

12-20 Safe drivers avoid the use of alcohol.

Putting Technology to Use
Have students work in small groups to select one health risk and plan an ad campaign. Students should design posters, bumper stickers, T-shirts, bulletin boards, or commercials using scanners, drawing software, clipart, color printers, or video cameras.

Topic 12-4 Health Risks

You can protect your health and your legal status by avoiding alcohol. You can also protect yourself by refusing to ride in a car with a driver who has been drinking.

Other Drugs

Alcohol is not the only drug that poses a health risk to teens. A variety of other drugs—both legal and illegal—can be hazardous to health.

Drug abuse is the use of a drug for a purpose other than it was intended. Even legal drugs purchased over the counter or with a prescription can be abused. These drugs should be used only according to package directions or as directed by a doctor. Also, never use someone else's prescription drugs.

Some legal products not sold as drugs are, nonetheless, used as drugs. Some people consume coffee, tea, and some soft drinks for the stimulating effect of the caffeine they contain. Some people inhale paint, glue, and nail polish remover for their intoxicating effects.

Drug abuse can damage your health, interfere with your ability to function, and affect your mind. Some drugs cause *addiction*, which is a dependence of the body on a continuing supply of the drug. After an addiction has developed, taking the drug away will cause agonizing withdrawal symptoms.

Even experimenting with drugs can be dangerous. Experimenting often leads to more frequent drug use. If an addiction develops, serious health and legal problems may result. Some of the long-term health risks of drug abuse are listed in Chart 12-21.

Sexually Transmitted Diseases

As a health risk, **sexually transmitted diseases (STDs)** are a growing concern in the United States. This concern is especially great for young adults. STDs are spread mainly through sexual contact. They can also be passed from pregnant women to their infants. They are not spread through casual contact, such as hugging or shaking hands.

Long-Term Health Risks of Drugs

- **Caffeine:** headaches, nervousness, stomach disorders
- **Depressants such as PCP, tranquilizers, Quaaludes, and barbiturates:** fatigue, confusion, paranoia, addiction
- **Hallucinogens such as LSD:** hallucinations
- **Inhalants:** damage to the nervous system, kidneys, and blood
- **Marijuana:** learning difficulties, lung damage, possible damage to reproductive organs, psychological addiction, possible link to use of other illegal drugs
- **Narcotics such as heroin and other opiates:** addiction, malnutrition, risk of overdose and hepatitis, severe withdrawal symptoms
- **Steroids:** acne, stunted growth, sterility
- **Stimulants such as cocaine and amphetamines (speed):** nervousness, severe depression, nose damage, hallucinations, damage to the heart and brain

12-21 Abuse of both legal and illegal drugs can have negative, long-term effects.

The main STDs that are of concern are AIDS, gonorrhea, syphilis, chlamydia, and herpes. The symptoms and side effects of these diseases range from an outbreak of blisters to blindness to death.

You have a responsibility to prevent the spread of STDs. You can do this by becoming educated about STDs. If you know of someone who has an STD, encourage him or her to get prompt, effective treatment. Also encourage this person to behave responsibly and avoid spreading the STD to others. The only sure way to prevent STDs is to abstain from sex. The risk of contracting STDs becomes higher as a person has more sexual partners. You owe it to yourself to stay healthy and avoid contracting STDs.

AIDS

The most deadly STD is **acquired immune deficiency syndrome (AIDS)**. This disease is caused by the **human**

Note:
Drug *use* and drug *abuse* are two different concepts. A person who is taking their own prescription medication is using drugs. A person taking someone else's prescription medication is abusing drugs.

Resource:
Facts About Sexually Transmitted Diseases, reproducible master, TR

Reflect:
Even if you have sex with only one partner, that person may have had sex with two partners. Those partners may have had sex with others, and so on. If just one of the people in this chain has an STD, you are also at risk.

Across the Curriculum

Health, English. Research and write a short paper on one of the sexually transmitted diseases.

immunodeficiency virus (HIV), which breaks down the body's immune system. This leaves the body vulnerable to diseases a healthy body could resist. Most people with AIDS eventually die from one or more of these diseases.

HIV is transmitted through such body fluids as blood and semen. HIV can be contracted through sharing contaminated intravenous needles as well as through sexual contact. Infants can contract HIV during the birth process or through breast-feeding.

In the past, some people contracted HIV from blood transfusions. However, this risk is now very small since all blood is screened for HIV. There is no risk of contracting HIV from donating blood because fresh needles are used for each donation.

Decisions That Affect Your Health

You make many routine decisions every day. You decide what to eat, where to go, and what to wear. Take a minute when making these decisions to think about how they might affect your health. For instance, keep in mind that limiting high-fat foods can reduce your risk of heart disease. Remember that using crosswalks and traffic lights can help you avoid being hit by a car. Do not forget that dressing warmly in winter will help you prevent hypothermia. Keeping your health in mind will help you make decisions that will promote wellness.

Not all health-related decisions are routine. You might have to decide if you want to go skydiving or bungee jumping. Some people have no desire to participate in such high-risk activities. Others are thrilled by the potential danger.

If you are intrigued by a certain degree of risk, take precautions. You do not have to avoid all potentially dangerous activities to protect your health. However, you have a responsibility to be fully aware of the risks you are taking. Then you need to do whatever is necessary to make the activity as safe as possible. Take lessons from trained professionals to learn how to do activities properly. Wear protective clothing. Plan what you will do if problems arise.

Avoid risks when you can. When you must take risks, address them sensibly. This will help you protect your health and make your life more fulfilling. See 12-22.

12-22 Knowing traffic laws and wearing protective clothing will help take the risk out of riding a motorcycle.

Check It Out!

1. Inhaling smoke in a smoke-filled environment is called _____.
2. True or false. Drinking coffee will help sober up someone who is experiencing the effects of alcohol.
3. List three long-term health risks of each of the following: marijuana, stimulants, inhalants, steroids, and caffeine.
4. What is HIV and how is it transmitted?
5. Give an example of a routine decision and explain how it can affect your health.

Check It Out! (Answers)
1. passive smoking
2. false
3. (List three for each:)
   A. marijuana: learning difficulties, lung damage, possible damage to reproductive organs, psychological addiction
   B. stimulants: nervousness, severe depression, nose damage, hallucinations, damage to the heart and brain
   C. inhalants: damage to the nervous system, kidneys, and blood
   D. steroids: acne, stunted growth, and sterility
   E. caffeine: headaches, nervousness, and stomach disorders
4. HIV is the human immunodeficiency virus, which causes AIDS. It is transmitted through body fluids such as blood and semen.
5. (Student response.)

Resource: Health Risks, Activity D, SAG

Resource: Risky Decisions, reproducible master, TR

Topic 12-5
When You Need Medical Services

Objectives
After studying this topic, you will be able to
- explain how to find a physician to meet your needs.
- state how medical treatment is provided when an emergency occurs.

Topic Terms
first aid
emergency medical technician (EMT)

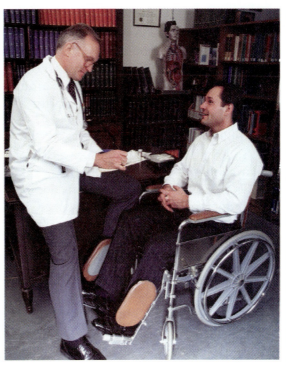

12-23 A patient needs to have confidence in the care he or she receives from a physician.

> **Vocabulary:**
> Emergency medical technicians perform valuable services to communities. Have students bring in newspaper articles of recent lifesaving acts by EMTs.
>
> **Enrich:**
> Look in the yellow pages for physicians in your area. List the physicians under their specialties. What percentage of the physicians are general practitioners?
>
> **Discuss:**
> Will using a telephone information service assure you of a good physician?

Someday, your life may be in the hands of your doctor and a hospital staff. You will want to have confidence in these people and their services. Therefore, you should make an effort to find good health care providers before you need them.

Selecting a Physician

You should look for a physician while you are well. If you wait until you need medical attention, you may have to accept any doctor who will see you. This is a poor way to begin a good doctor-patient relationship.

Making a well-informed decision when choosing a physician is a three-step process. First, you need to collect the names of physicians in your area. Second, you need to gather information about these doctors and how they practice medicine. Finally, you need to visit one or more doctors and choose the one who will best meet your needs. See 12-23.

Collecting Names

When you are making plans to move, ask your present doctor to recommend a physician in your new area. If this is not practical, you will need to find a physician by other means. Friends, relatives, and neighbors can be sources of help in finding a physician. You could also contact a nearby medical school, medical society, or local hospital. These sources may be able to provide you with a list of doctors who practice in your area.

In some areas, a telephone information service is available to help people find physicians. These services keep computerized records on area doctors. They can tell you which medical school a doctor attended. They can tell you how long a doctor has been practicing medicine and his or her field of specialization.

Gathering Information

After you have collected the names of several physicians, call their offices. Find out as much about their practices as you can. First, check to see if the doctor is accepting new patients. Ask about the location of the office and office hours. You want to be sure the office is located nearby in case of an emergency. Convenient office hours will allow you to plan appointments around your schedule. If you have special needs, be sure to find out if the doctor will

Career Preparation Activity
Is This Health-Related Career for Me? reproducible master, TR. Each student is to interview someone working in a health-related career. Encourage each student to select a different career. Ask students to summarize their interviews in brief oral reports and explain why they would or would not like to work in the career areas of the people they interviewed.

Reflect:
Do you know what your family health insurance policy covers? Do you have a special school policy?

Resource:
Evaluating a Health Care Professional, reproducible master, TR

be able to meet them. For instance, if you were homebound, you would need a doctor who makes house calls.

Ask about fees. Find out the cost of an office visit and a general physical examination. You may want to ask if the doctor is willing to discuss payment terms for your bills.

You need to check to be sure a doctor will accept your form of health insurance. HMOs and PPOs have restrictions about which doctors their members may see. If you have a traditional insurance policy, you will want to know how claims are handled. Some doctors require patients to pay and be personally reimbursed by the insurance company. Other doctors bill the insurance company and wait for the company to pay them.

Getting an Initial Exam

From the information you gather on the telephone, you should be able to narrow your choices. Identify one or two doctors you think might meet your needs. Then call one of the doctors to schedule an appointment for a physical exam. You should be able to schedule this appointment within a month. A need to wait longer could indicate the doctor is overworked and may not have time for you.

This first appointment will help you decide if you would feel comfortable having a particular doctor care for your health. When you arrive in the office, evaluate the service you receive. Pay attention to the office assistants and nurses. Are they pleasant? Do they maintain a professional attitude? The office staff will often reflect a doctor's attitudes. See 12-24.

When you finally meet the doctor, he or she will begin asking about your medical history. Be sure to answer all the questions thoroughly. Tell the doctor about any existing health conditions that may affect your future treatment. Also, mention any serious medical problems members of your extended family have had. Your family's medical history provides your doctor with clues about your health.

This interview and the examination that follows will allow you to evaluate the doctor's bedside manner. You will want a doctor who does more than diagnose illnesses. You will want someone who puts you at ease. Do you feel you can trust this person? Does he or she welcome your questions? Does the doctor provide you

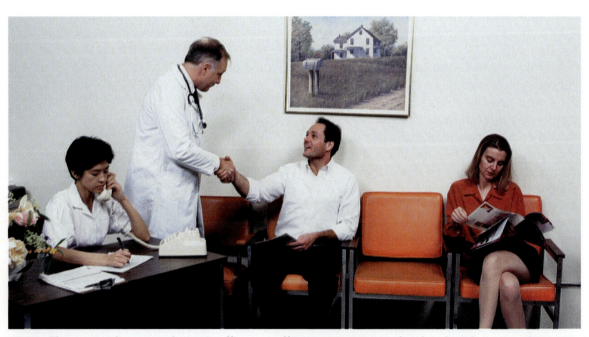

12-24 The atmosphere in a doctor's office can affect a patient's comfort level with a new physician.

Putting Technology to Use
Have students write and perform skits on contrasting initial visits to a doctor's office. Have students videotape the role-plays and show them in class. What made some "visits" successful and others unsuccessful?

with satisfactory answers? Your responses to these questions will enable you to decide if you have found the right doctor.

If you have found a doctor you like, your initial exam will serve a second purpose. It will give the doctor a chance to see you in good health. The results of the exam will serve as a basis for comparison when you are not well.

Once you have chosen a doctor, you can have your medical records forwarded to his or her office. If you give your former doctor a written request, he or she will transfer your records.

If you are not satisfied with a doctor after your initial exam, you will need to schedule an exam with another doctor. This screening process may seem troublesome. However, you will discover your efforts have been worthwhile when you find a doctor who can meet your needs.

Remember that physicians are people, too. No one is perfect. If you find a doctor who meets most of your qualifications, hang on to him or her. Having the same doctor over a long period is an advantage. The doctor learns more about you and your reactions the longer he or she serves you.

Your doctor can be a valuable resource if you ever need hospital care. He or she can help you find a specialist if you need to consult someone about a specific problem. Your doctor can also help you choose a hospital. Some doctors work in only one hospital. Other doctors work in two or more hospitals. Like choosing a doctor before you are sick, you will want to explore your hospital options before an emergency arises.

Emergency Medical Services

Some medical problems call for immediate action. Victims who are not breathing, who are bleeding severely, or who have been poisoned need emergency treatment. Minor cuts, bites, burns, and broken bones are less severe injuries. However, they still require rapid attention. Emergency care begins with **first aid.** This is immediate, temporary care provided until professional medical help is available.

Medical help is often called to the scene of a serious injury or illness through a 911 emergency response system. The police or fire department may send a rescue squad or a hospital may send an ambulance. **Emergency medical technicians (EMTs)** are the trained professionals in these vehicles. When they arrive at the scene, EMTs assess the problem. They determine the most critical needs and provide immediate treatment based on their findings. See 12-25.

Discuss:
Why is it better to visit a new physician when you are well instead of waiting until you are ill?

Resource:
Personal Health Record, reproducible master, TR

Activity:
Role-play correct procedures for placing emergency calls to 911, fire stations, police, or other emergency care providers.

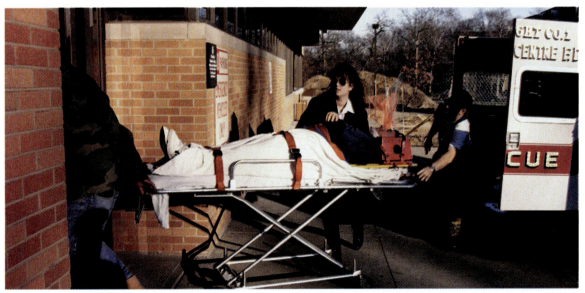

12-25 Emergency medical technicians provide immediate treatment to victims of accidents and sudden, serious illnesses.

FCCLA Activity
Have your chapter sponsor a community health fair as a Skills for Life project. Make plans for speakers and displays to educate community members about the resources that are available locally. Chapter members should practice using the decision-making process to plan and carry out this event.

Discuss:
It is important that you take responsibility for your own health. What are your responsibilities when you meet with a doctor?

Resource:
Medical Care, Activity E, SAG

Resource:
Do You Take Responsibility for Your Health? reproducible master, TR

Once initial treatment has begun, the victim is taken to a hospital emergency room. At the hospital, doctors take over where the EMTs began. The doctors further assess the victim's condition and provide other treatment as needed.

Become aware of emergency medical services in your area. Know how to access them in the event of a crisis.

Check It Out!
1. What are three sources a person could use to find names of physicians?
2. Give two reasons for getting an initial physical exam when considering a new doctor.
3. Immediate, temporary care provided until professional medical assistance is available is called _____.

The choices you make throughout life will affect your level of physical fitness.

Check It Out! (Answers)
1. (List three:) present doctor, friends, relatives, neighbors, local medical school, medical society, local hospital, telephone referral service
2. The exam allows the patient to evaluate the service the doctor provides. An initial physical exam also gives a doctor a chance to see what a potential patient is like in good health. The results of the exam will serve as a basis for comparison when the patient is not well.
3. first aid

TEENS ARE CONCERNED ABOUT...

Sexually Transmitted Diseases

Current research shows 12 million new cases of sexually transmitted diseases (STDs) occur annually in the United States. Many of the victims are teens. Medical experts are concerned about this trend. That is why Suzanne McCarthy, RN, ACCE, does volunteer work with teens and their parents. She wants to make them aware of the damaging effects of STDs.

Mrs. McCarthy has an associate degree in nursing and 11 years of practice with a gynecologist. She has devoted an additional 14 years to community service in nursing-related activities, including childbirth education. She is a popular speaker with middle school and high school students.

Q: *Why are STDs becoming a growing concern for teens?*

A: Teens are becoming sexually active at earlier ages. Anyone who is sexually active is vulnerable to STDs. When either sexual partner has an STD, the other is susceptible.

The cervix of a young teenage woman is not fully mature. This makes younger women more susceptible to STDs.

The use of birth control pills has also impacted the number of cases of STDs. The pill does not protect either person from STDs. When barriers, such as condoms, are used to prevent pregnancy, the number of cases of STDs is lower.

Q: *What are a teen's best defenses against STDs?*

A: Abstinence from premarital sexual intercourse is a teen's primary defense. Verifying that an intended marriage partner is not infected is a secondary defense. Premarital testing for most STDs is not required. Couples who want to protect each other should seek testing voluntarily. Asking a partner to be tested is not an accusation regarding his or her previous sexual activity. It is simply a healthy precaution. It is easier to treat one partner before marriage than to treat both partners after marriage.

Q: *Which sexually transmitted diseases pose the greatest health risks for teens?*

A: Acquired immune deficiency syndrome (AIDS) poses the greatest risk because it is fatal.

Condyloma acuminata (genital warts) poses a great risk because it is a viral infection. There is evidence that many strains are associated with cervical cancer. Some genital warts are outside the body and are readily visible. Warts on the cervix must be detected with a Pap smear. Treatment can make the warts go away, but it does not kill the virus in the body. This means the warts can reoccur. The virus can lie dormant for as many as 10 years. It is possible for an infected person to give the virus to a sex partner without personally showing the symptoms. A female who has been sexually active should receive a Pap smear annually for early detection of cancer.

Herpes simplex II is a viral infection and cannot be cured. Blisters in the genital area, the initial symptoms of herpes, are visible for about 14 days. Recurrences, which are usually precipitated by stress, crises, or even pregnancy, may appear over the years. Some herpes viruses can lead to cancer.

Chlamydia is the most common sexually transmitted disease. It is sometimes called "the silent epidemic" since it has no outward symptoms. People can carry it and unknowingly pass it to others. Chlamydia is part bacteria and part virus. It can be detected with a culture and treated with antibiotics. Undetected and untreated chlamydia can lead to infertility if it gets into the reproductive organs of females.

Gonorrhea is caused by a bacterium. It can be detected by a culture and treated with antibiotics. Physical discomforts from gonorrhea include burning sensations when urinating. Abnormal discharge from the penis or vagina is another symptom. Girls may have cramping and pelvic pain.

Syphilis is caused by bacteria that cause sores, called *chancres*. It can be detected through a blood test or culture and treated with penicillin.

Note:
Due to the subject matter of this feature, you will want to decide what is appropriate to discuss with your students. You should consider their age, understanding, interest, and maturity. You will also want to consider how parents, administrators, and the community would view the discussion.

Discuss:
- Why are STDs a growing concern for teens?
- What are a teen's best defenses against STDs?
- How does the use of alcohol and other drugs affect a teen's decision-making ability?

Discuss:
- How can a person resist pressures from a date to have sex? (Have students name the pressures most often used and discuss what responses can be given.)
- Which STDs can be treated with antibiotics and which ones have no known cure?
- Why do people avoid seeking medical attention when they suspect they have an STD?
- If a friend told you that he or she had an STD, what would your advice be?

Trichomoniasis is caused by protozoa. A yellow or greenish discharge with odor flows from the vagina or penis. It can be treated with an antibiotic.

As you can see, STDs cause a range of health risks. Pain, infertility, cancer, or even death can result from these diseases. Teens should ask themselves if they want to take these risks.

Q: *How great is the risk of becoming infected with an STD from a single sexual encounter?*

A: This depends on the status of the two sex partners involved. If either partner has had previous sexual activity, the risk is real. Each person is connected to all the previous sexual encounters of his or her partner. A person is also connected to all the encounters of the partner's previous partners, ad infinitum. The greater the number of previous partners, the greater the risk. When both partners have had previous encounters, the risk is multiplied.

Q: *How can the threat of STDs impact teen decisions regarding sexual relationships?*

A: The threat of STDs is a real threat—not just a possibility or a probability. Teens who do not want to risk an STD will abstain from sexual activity.

Q: *Don't condoms provide protection against STDs?*

A: Teens who choose to be sexually active should use condoms. However, I am personally afraid to teach teens to use a condom. To be effective, condoms must be used during all sexual contact. Teens may not have a condom when it is needed. For a simple comparison, think of how often students do not have a pen or pencil for class. If students do not always carry a pen or pencil, is it more likely they will carry a condom?

Even if teens use condoms, they are not completely protected against STDs. Condoms can tear or come off.

Q: *Do you have any special advice for today's teens?*

A: An STD can have a tremendous impact on a teen's future. My advice would be to focus on your goals. Make up your mind not to let premature sexual activity come between you and what you want for yourself.

Chapter Review

Summary

You need to take an active role in keeping yourself physically fit. Maintaining good health can have a positive effect on your school, work, and family life. Getting daily physical activity that improves aerobic capacity and builds muscle strength and flexibility will help you stay in shape. Enjoying leisure activities and getting adequate sleep will also help you perform at your highest level.

Your daily grooming routine will affect your appearance as well as your health. Grooming begins with skin care, which involves cleansing, shaving, and protection from the sun. Caring for your teeth will keep your breath fresh and help prevent tooth decay. Hair care includes shampooing, conditioning, and styling. Finally, you need to clean your hands and feet and keep nails trimmed for a total well-groomed appearance.

Your mental health as well as your physical health can affect your overall well-being. Occasionally using defense mechanisms and learning to cope with stress can help you protect your mental health. Clinical depression is one type of mental illness. Severe depression can lead some people to thoughts of suicide. Counseling and other sources of help are available to people who are having trouble maintaining a healthy mental state.

Some people knowingly take health risks. Using tobacco products can cause heart disease and various types of cancer. Drinking alcohol can impair muscle coordination and cause organ damage. Abusing other legal and illegal drugs can lead to a range of long-term health risks. Behavior that causes the spread of sexually transmitted diseases is also an extreme health risk. When faced with decisions regarding risky substances or behaviors, carefully consider how your health might be affected.

No matter how healthy you are, you are bound to need professional medical services from time to time. You can get the names of physicians from a number of sources. A phone call and an initial exam can help you decide if you have found the right doctor for you. A hospital can provide you with information you will need to prepare for a hospital stay. Emergency medical services are available to provide for needs in crises.

Think About It!

1. Why is good health important to you?
2. What types of activities do you enjoy that improve aerobic capacity? What types of activities do you enjoy that build muscle strength and flexibility?
3. How do you like to spend your leisure time?
4. What techniques do you find most effective for helping you get to sleep?
5. What is your skin type? How do you care for it?
6. How do you care for your teeth? How could you improve?
7. Describe the texture of your hair, the shape of your face, and your lifestyle. How is your hairstyle suited to these factors?
8. Give an example of a time when you used a defense mechanism to protect your self-esteem.
9. Which of the coping strategies for stress do you think are more useful for teens? Which are more useful for adults?

Note:
Studies show that teenagers are not getting enough sleep, especially those who have part-time jobs. Discuss ways teens can manage their time to get more sleep.

Discuss:
Why do people/teens continue behaviors they know put their health at risk?

Activity:
In *Try It Out!* #5, after students have learned to give manicures, they might volunteer to give manicures to residents of a local nursing home or patients in a hospital.

Resource:
PowerZone CD Challenge. Have students play the chapter review game to reinforce text content.

10. The health risks associated with tobacco, alcohol and other drugs, and sexually transmitted diseases are widely known. However, people still take these risks. How do you think people could be encouraged to show more consideration for their health regarding these risks?
11. If you were moving to a new area, how would you find a physician?
12. How can a person's state of health affect his or her employment opportunities? List ten careers related to the topics in this chapter.

Try It Out!

1. Set up two columns on a sheet of paper. Title one column *Aerobic Capacity* and the other *Muscle Strength and Flexibility*. Then list all the moderate or vigorous physical activities you have done today under the appropriate column. Are you getting enough of both types of activity? What improvements do you need to make?
2. Visit a store that sells grooming aids, and study the labels of various skin care products. Make a list of the products, and indicate which skin type would benefit most from each product.
3. Research grooming habits in another culture. Write a brief paper describing any differences you find and the reasons for those differences.
4. Ask your hairstylist what shampoo and conditioning products he or she recommends for your hair. Also, ask what type of style is best for the texture of your hair and the shape of your face. Summarize your hairstylist's recommendations in a brief oral report.
5. Give yourself a manicure according to the steps listed in Chart 12-11.
6. Create a poster that illustrates a healthy mental state. Use the characteristics listed in this chapter as a guide.
7. Interview people in five occupations, such as a teacher, homemaker, businessperson, construction worker, and waiter. Ask about the factors that cause stress in their jobs and how they manage that stress. Share your findings with the class.
8. Survey nonsmokers in your school to determine how they feel when they are forced to inhale cigarette smoke produced by smokers. Report your findings in an article for the school newspaper.
9. Set up a classroom exhibit on sources of help for people who want to stop using tobacco, alcohol, and other drugs.
10. Prepare a pamphlet for new residents in your area describing how they can find a physician. Also, mention what hospitals and emergency medical services are locally available.

Chapter 13
A Safe Home and Environment

Careers

These careers relate to the topics in this chapter:
- safety instructor aide
- community health services assistant
- environmental issues agent
- extension specialist

As you study this chapter, see if you can think of others.

Topics

13-1 Personal Safety and Security
13-2 A Healthful Environment

Introductory Activities
1. Have students draw cartoons that depict home accidents. Discuss why people frequently laugh when someone has an accident.
2. Use the following questions to promote discussion related to the topics in this chapter:
   - How concerned are you about the safety of your home and environment?
   - What steps can you take to improve the safety of your home?
   - What steps can you take to improve the safety of the environment?
   - What role should the government take in helping individuals protect the safety and security of their homes?
   - What role should the government take in helping to protect the environment?

Topic 13-1
Personal Safety and Security
I. Preventing Accidents in the Home
   A. Falls
   B. Fires
      1. Kitchen Safety
      2. Electrical Hazards
      3. Flammable Chemicals and Heating Equipment
      4. Fire Safety Precautions
   C. Poisoning
   D. Electric Shock
II. Preventing Accidents on the Road
   A. Defensive Driving
   B. Safety Restraints
   C. Walking Safely
III. Providing for Security
   A. In Your Home
      1. Conduct a Home Security Inspection
      2. Reduce or Eliminate Security Hazards
      3. Protect Yourself When You Are Home Alone
   B. In Your Neighborhood
   C. When Away from Home
      1. As You Walk
      2. In Your Car
IV. Emergency Procedures

Topic 13-2
A Healthful Environment
I. A Healthful Environment
II. Factors Affecting the Environment
   A. Increasing Population
   B. Increasing Use of Resources
III. Pollution
   A. Air Pollution
      1. The Greenhouse Effect
      2. Diminishing Ozone Layer
      3. Acid Rain
   B. Water Pollution
   C. Noise Pollution
   D. Toxic Wastes
   E. Radiation
      1. Radon in the Home
IV. How You Can Help
   A. Conserve Resources
   B. Reduce Pollution
   C. Make Environmentally Responsible Consumer Decisions

Vocabulary:
What do your think is the difference between defensive driving and scanning?

Resource:
Break the Accident Chain, color transparency CT-11, TR

Discuss:
Why is it every employee's responsibility to help maintain a safe work environment?

Topic 13-1
Personal Safety and Security

Objectives
After studying this topic, you will be able to
- explain how to prevent accidents in the home and on the road.
- identify ways to provide for personal security.
- describe basic emergency procedures.

Topic Terms
accident
defensive driving
scanning

Most people think of their homes and surrounding environments as safe, secure places. However, accidents and criminal attacks can—and do—happen to everyone. Safety and security cannot be taken for granted, even in familiar settings.

You can take an active role in preventing accidents and protecting yourself from crimes by following safety precautions. Learning about different types of accidents and their causes is one way to help you prepare for the unexpected. Reduce your risk of being a crime victim by learning to recognize and avoid unsafe situations. Following these precautions can keep you safer and more secure at home and on the road.

Preventing Accidents in the Home

Accidents are unexpected events that cause losses, injuries, or sometimes death. Accidents are the leading cause of death for teenagers. Every year, thousands of people are killed or injured from accidents in the home. Sadly, many of these accidents could have been prevented.

What causes accidents? Human error is one major factor. People who are ill, tired, in a hurry, or under stress get careless. Because of their emotional states, they are not alert to their surroundings. They fail to recognize safety hazards, and they are more likely to use poor judgment.

Safety hazards in and around the home are another factor that causes accidents. Falls, fires, poisonings, and electric shocks are the most common types of household accidents. Many of these accidents can be avoided by following some basic safety measures.

Falls

Falling off a ladder, tripping over objects, or slipping on a wet surface are just a few examples of falls. Although falls are the most common accidents within the home, many are easily preventable. Older adults and young children are the most frequent victims of falls, but you could easily be a victim, too.

Here are a few ways you can prevent falls and help make every room in your home safer. As you read this list, see if you can think of others to add.
- Look for and remove any obstacles, such as toys, shoes, or boxes, that someone might trip over.
- Wipe up spills on counters or floors immediately.
- Use steady ladders and step stools to reach high places—do not stand on chairs or climb on counters.
- Use sturdy, nonskid rugs on wood or tile floors.
- Use nonskid strips in bathtubs and on shower floors.
- Avoid walking on wet floors indoors and slippery surfaces outdoors, 13-1.
- Place a night-light in hallways and bathrooms so people can see where they are walking in the dark.
- Keep outdoor walkways clear of ice, snow, and objects.

Fires

Fires are the second leading cause of death in the home. Careless smoking, kitchen fires, electrical shorts, and mishandling chemicals are common fire hazards.

Across the Curriculum
English. Ask students to write an article for a newspaper read by elderly citizens. In the article, suggest ways older people can prevent falls in their homes.

Topic 13-1   Personal Safety and Security   385

13-1 Mopping up spills immediately and allowing wet surfaces to dry completely before walking on them will help prevent falls.

Kitchen Safety

Kitchen safety is essential in preventing fires and burns. Store matches in a safe place where young children cannot reach them. Keep toasters and other heating appliances away from flammable curtains and other materials that might catch fire. Keep paper towels, potholders, and kitchen towels away from hot cooktops and burners. (Electrical burners stay hot for several minutes after they are turned off.)

Kitchen fires are especially dangerous—many start suddenly, without warning. When food is cooking, never leave it unattended. Grease can ignite if it gets too hot. Keep kitchens clean; grease buildup is highly flammable. Pay special attention to the range hood and areas near the range. Keep a fire extinguisher in the kitchen area; make sure you know how to use it in case of fire.

Another part of kitchen safety is protecting yourself from accidental burns. Turn pot handles away from the front of the range when you are cooking. Do not reach over lighted burners. Use dry, heavy oven mitts to remove hot pans from the oven. Prevent steam burns by lifting lids and covers from hot pans or dishes away from your face. Turn off appliances and range controls when you are finished cooking.

Electrical Hazards

Electrical safety is extremely important in fire prevention, too. Electrical shorts caused by faulty cords, wiring, or misused appliances cause many fatal home fires. Make sure electrical cords are not frayed or cracked. If they are, replace them. Do not run cords or wires under carpets or rugs. Avoid overloading electrical outlets with too many plugs. Use appliances and cords that meet stringent safety standards. Look for a safety seal, such as the Underwriters Laboratories (UL) seal, on these products. Such seals indicate products have been tested to make sure they operate safely. Operate appliances properly. After you are done using them, unplug them and put them away.

Flammable Chemicals and Heating Equipment

Many chemicals can be fire hazards. Store flammable chemicals, such as cleaning fluids and aerosol sprays, outdoors in safety cans. Do not store them indoors near heat sources. Some chemicals, such as glues and nail polish remover, produce flammable vapors that could ignite; do not use them near a heat source.

Use heating equipment—fireplaces, wood-burning stoves, and space heaters—with care. Read and follow the instructions for proper use and care of these items. Use a fire screen or glass doors on a fireplace. Have the chimney cleaned regularly. Make sure wood-burning stoves are properly installed and maintained. Keep space heaters in top-notch condition and use

Activity:
Make a list of suggestions for kitchen safety. Discuss with family members.

Reflect:
Check your room at home for a possible electrical overload.

Activity:
Have students check out the Underwriters Laboratories Web site at www.ul.com.

Career Preparation Activity

Safety on the Job, reproducible master, TR. Have each student use the questions on the handout to interview an employer regarding potential safety hazards at his or her place of business. Students are also to inquire about policies instituted to ensure a safe work environment. As an alternative, you may wish to invite a speaker into your class to respond to these questions.

Enrich:
Ask a representative from the local fire department to speak to the class.

Discuss:
Make sure students know the procedures for evacuation from your classroom.

Activity:
Stage a fire drill and time the evacuation. Discuss ways to improve evacuation time.

them away from water and flammable materials.

Fire Safety Precautions

Would you know what to do if a fire broke out in your home? Installing smoke detectors and developing an emergency escape plan are two steps that can save lives in the event of a fire.

In a home fire, most deaths and injuries occur from smoke inhalation. Deadly smoke and gases are produced before flames appear. Also, most fires start at night when people are asleep. This is why protecting your home with an efficient smoke detecting system is so important, 13-2.

A battery-operated smoke detector is an affordable devise and a wise choice for any home. A smoke detector should be installed on each level in your home. Hallways, bedrooms, and attics are the best sites for installation. Attach the detector on or near the ceiling according to the manufacturer's instructions. Check the battery once a month to make sure it is working properly. Replace the battery once a year.

When smoke enters a smoke detector, an alarm alerts you and your family to the danger of fire. What should you do if the smoke alarm goes off? An emergency escape plan can help you and your family prepare for this situation. First draw a floor plan of your home. Map out escape routes from every room of your home. Then conduct a home fire drill. Be sure every member of the family knows how to leave quickly and safely in case of fire.

If a fire occurs, gather all the people in your home and move quickly through the nearest reachable escape route. If the building is filled with smoke, cover your face with a garment you are wearing. Stay close to the floor as you exit. Feel each door before opening it. If a door is hot, take another route. When everyone is out of the home, call the fire department using the nearest phone.

Poisoning

Another leading cause of death in home accidents is poisoning. Both children and adults are potential victims. The key

13-2 The careless use of matches or cigarettes causes many deadly fires. If you have a fire in your home, a smoke detecting system will alert family members to get out safely.

Putting Technology to Use
Have students test their homes' smoke detectors and replace batteries if necessary. Also ask students to investigate community laws regarding smoke detectors.

to poison prevention is eliminating potential safety hazards.

Children are curious and tend to put things into their mouths. Store all poisonous chemicals out of children's reach or in locked cabinets. This includes cosmetics, cleaning products, pesticides, fertilizers, and medications. All these can be hazardous when improperly used. Securely replace child-resistant caps on products after every use.

Common causes of poisonings among adults include consuming toxic substances from mislabeled containers and overdosing on medications. Store chemicals in their original, properly labeled containers. Chemicals that could be mistaken for food products or seasonings should never be stored in the kitchen. Before taking any medications, read labels carefully for the correct dosage.

Electric Shock

Used properly, electrical products provide many benefits in the home. Electrical hazards, however, lurk in the safest homes. Besides being a source of household fires, electric current from faulty or misused electrical products can cause minor or life-threatening shocks. Low-voltage electric current can pass through the body causing burns. High-voltage electric current stops breathing and heart activity; it may cause death.

Household wiring, electrical outlets, power tools, and appliances are common sources of electric shocks, 13-3. You can prevent electrical hazards when using these items by following a few safety tips.

- Cover unused outlets with safety covers. This will prevent children from sticking objects or their fingers into outlets.
- Keep electrical appliances and cords in good repair. Do not use damaged appliances, especially those with damaged cords. Do not use electrical cords with broken plugs or exposed wires.
- Keep electrical appliances away from water sources (sinks, bathtubs, and showers). Water is an electrical conductor. Water and electricity do not mix. Dry your hands before turning power switches on and off or when handling electrical appliances that are in use. Do not stand on a damp or wet floor when using an electrical appliance. Do not use electrical appliances such as hair dryers, electric shavers, and radios in or near showers and bathtubs.

13-3 When using power tools, be sure to follow proper safety precautions.

Preventing Accidents on the Road

Vehicular accidents are one of the leading causes of teenage deaths in the United States. The majority of traffic accidents are caused by driver error. Disobeying speed limits, driving too fast for conditions, not paying attention, and not scanning ahead are major causes of accidents. How can you reduce the risk of having an accident? If you are a driver, you have a responsibility to prevent accidents. When you are behind the wheel, practice safe driving habits. Driving defensively and using safety restraints are effective ways to protect yourself. When you are not behind the wheel, protect yourself from hazards by walking safely.

Activity: Check with local hospitals, EMTs, fire departments, or police departments to see what poison control centers are closest to your home.

Note: Remember that family pets can also be victims of electric shock accidents.

Discuss: What should you do if your hair dryer, hair curler, or razor falls into water?

Resource: *Safety at Home,* Activity A, SAG

Citizenship and Service

Have students develop a home safety checklist and use it to conduct home safety inspections for senior citizens. Have students make a list of the safety improvements that need to be made. Students can also assist the seniors in making improvements by offering to do such tasks as installing smoke detectors and increasing outdoor lighting.

Discuss:
Do you think most people drive offensively or defensively? How can you tell?

Reflect:
Have you or a family member ever been involved in an auto accident? What was the cause of the accident? How could the accident have been prevented?

Enrich:
Research state laws regarding the use of auto restraints for children.

Defensive Driving

Driving any type of motor vehicle—car, truck, or motorcycle—requires good driving skills. Just as important is driving defensively to prevent accidents. **Defensive driving** is a skill that helps you anticipate what other drivers might do to cause accidents. Here are some tips for using defensive driving skills.

- *Always scan traffic so you know what is going on around you.* **Scanning** is constantly looking ahead and behind as you drive to see what other drivers are doing. Scan ahead at least one block so you will not be forced to make quick stops or sudden lane changes. Before you change lanes, slow down. Before you drive down a long hill, check the traffic behind you.
- *Communicate with other drivers.* Use turn signals when you plan to turn, change lanes, pass another car, or pull away from a curb. Signal early so other drivers will know what you plan to do and have time to react.
- *Keep a margin of safety between your car and other cars on the road.* Be certain there is room ahead and behind when you pass or stop. Drive at a steady speed. When other drivers follow you too closely, allow them to pass.
- *Adjust to situations that arise.* This requires fast decision-making skills at times. If visibility is poor or road conditions are hazardous, reduce your speed. When you have to deal with an unavoidable danger, adjust in the safest way possible. For example, if a bicyclist swerves into your lane, slow down. Then, when it is safe to do so, pull safely away from the bicyclist and pass in the other lane.

Safety Restraints

When you are behind the wheel, your personal safety depends on two factors: your driving skills and the use of safety restraints. Even if you are a good driver, you need to protect yourself from bad drivers. Be sure the restraints in your car are in good working condition. Make it a habit to buckle your seat belt whether you are the driver or passenger in a vehicle. See 13-4.

Statistics show that safety restraints do make a difference in saving lives. A seat belt can keep you from being thrown from a vehicle. A combined lap and shoulder belt offers more protection should your car overturn or go into a spin. This safety restraint not only keeps you from being thrown forward, it keeps you from being tossed sideways. If you drive a car equipped with an air bag, the air bag rapidly inflates in a head-on collision. This restraint protects you from being thrown from the car.

If you have siblings under the age of three, they should be secured in an approved child-restraint safety seat. Children between the ages of three and six should be in a safety seat or restrained by a seat belt. Anyone in your family over age six should wear a seat belt.

Many states have passed seat belt laws to protect vehicle occupants. In these states, front seat occupants must wear seat belts. All people, however, should make it a habit to wear a seat belt—no matter where they sit in the vehicle.

13-4 Reduce your risk of serious injury in a vehicular accident. Make it a habit to always wear your seat belt.

Putting Technology to Use
Have students use drawing software and color printers to design bumper stickers that encourage defensive driving. Have students pass out the bumper stickers in the school cafeteria.

Walking Safely

Whether you are driving or walking, your personal safety should be a concern. Walking may be a means of transportation or a form of exercise. Whatever your reason for walking, you need to walk safely to protect yourself from the hazards around you.

There are two important aspects of walking safely. First, you need to protect yourself from traffic. Second, you need to guard against a physical attack. The latter aspect will be covered later in this topic.

Walk in safe places and scan the traffic around you. Sidewalks are often the safest choice for walking. See 13-5. If you must walk near or on the street, always face the oncoming traffic as you walk. When you can see vehicles, you can better judge their approach and react quickly. Cross streets at marked crossings whenever possible. In parking lots, watch out for cars backing out of parking spaces. As a pedestrian, you have the right of way. However, you must still be cautious. You may have to yield your rights to aggressive drivers or drivers who may not see you.

When walking, wear light-colored clothing. Light-colored clothing reflects light and is easier for others to see. Walk during daylight hours, if possible. Take extra precautions if you walk at night. Reflective accessories, such as arm and leg bands, make you more visible to oncoming traffic. Use a flashlight to light your path and make you more visible to drivers and cyclists. Scan ahead with the light so you can avoid obstacles.

Providing for Security

In today's complex society, home break-ins and criminal attacks are a fact of life. They can happen anyplace and anytime. No neighborhood can be totally secure.

What can you do to feel more secure when you are at home and away from home? Certain preventative measures can make your home and neighborhood a safer place to live. You can help prevent burglaries by making it more difficult for intruders to break into your home. Your best defense against criminal attack is to be alert and use common sense to avoid unsafe situations.

In Your Home

What steps can you take to make your home more secure against intruders? The first step is to identify security hazards that might make your home an easy target. Taking action to reduce or eliminate these hazards is the second step. Taking some extra precautions will help you feel secure when you are home alone.

Conduct a Home Security Inspection

The main purpose of a security inspection is to identify security hazards in your home. This inspection should include a check of your home's doors, windows, lights, locks, and landscaping. Contact your local law enforcement agency for a complete checklist of items you should inspect. In some areas, the local police or county sheriff's department will conduct a home security check for you. An example of a home security checklist is shown in 13-6.

Activity:
In small groups, discuss and list safety rules for jogging, skateboarding, skating, and bicycling.

Resource:
How Safe Are You? Activity B, SAG

Discuss:
What preventive measures do you take to make your home and neighborhood safer?

13-5 Walking on the sidewalk instead of in the street will help keep you safe from traffic accidents.

Across the Curriculum

Social studies. Have students research and discuss laws regarding pedestrians. When were these laws developed? Is there ever a time when pedestrians do not have the right of way? Why is it important for pedestrians to remember these rules?

Enrich:
Use the Home Security Inspection Checklist in Chart 13-6 to evaluate the security of your home or apartment.

Discuss:
Does anyone have an alarm system at home? How does it work? Does it make you feel more secure?

Discuss:
Do you follow the tips for protecting yourself at home and away from home? Are there other tips you would add to the list?

Home Security Inspection Checklist

Front, Side, Rear, and Basement Entrances
- Are the doors solid wood construction or metal with secure locks?
- Are the door frames strong enough to prevent forced entry?
- Does each entrance have a screen or storm door with a secure lock?
- Are all entrances well lighted?
- Can the entrances be observed from the street?
- Are all entrances free from concealing landscaping (trees, shrubs, bushes)?

Ground Floor and Upper Floor Windows
- Do all windows have secure locks in working condition?
- Do windows have screens or storm windows that lock from the inside?
- Are window areas well lighted and free from concealing landscaping?

Garage Doors and Windows
- Is the overhead door equipped with a secure lock?
- Is the entry door kept closed and locked at all times?
- Are tools and ladders stored in the garage and not outside?
- Are all doors well lighted on the outside?

13-6 Law enforcement agencies use this type of checklist to perform home security inspections for residents. Identifying and correcting security hazards reduces the risk of burglary to your home.

Reduce or Eliminate Security Hazards

Once you have identified security hazards, you will need to reduce or eliminate them. Here are some tips for protecting yourself and your family at home.

- Create the appearance of activity in your home, even when you are not there. Would-be intruders are more likely to strike a home that looks vacant.
- Vary your daily routines slightly so you are not leaving and coming home at the same time every day. Intruders are less likely to strike if they are not sure if someone is home.
- Keep doors and windows locked at all times—even when you are home. Heavy solid wood or metal doors with secure locks offer the best protection against break-ins. Keyed locks on windows provide extra security.
- Leave all exterior lights on at night. Lighting is considered the biggest single deterrent in securing your home. All entrance doors, parking areas, and courtyards should be well lighted.
- Install an alarm system to provide additional protection for your home when you are present and when you are away. Many different types of systems are available. A sensory device that sounds an alarm in case of burglary is one type. Prices vary based on the complexity of the system.

Protect Yourself When You Are Home Alone

If your parents work outside the home, you may be home alone after school. You need to protect yourself from dangerous situations and know how to get help in an emergency.

- Leave a spare house key with a trusted neighbor. Never hide extra keys outside.
- If you come home and find a door unlocked or open, do not go inside. Go to a neighbor's home or a public phone and call the police. Have them check the house first in case an intruder is inside.
- If someone calls or comes to the door, do not tell the person you are home alone.
- If the doorbell rings, do not open the door. Look through a nearby window or a door peephole first to see who is there. Ask the person to identify himself or herself before you open the door. See 13-7.
- If you must go out for a short time, lock all doors.

Across the Curriculum

English. Have each student interview a victim of a break-in, asking the following questions: How did you feel when you discovered the break-in? How do you feel now? Is there anything you could have done to prevent the break-in? What precautions do you now take and recommend to others? Have the students summarize their interviews in a written report.

Topic 13-1 Personal Safety and Security

13-7 Protect your personal safety when you are home alone. If someone comes to the door, identify the person before you open the door.

- At night, leave lights on in several rooms. Keep outside areas, especially door entrances, well lit. If you must go out at night, make sure lights are left on inside and outside for your return.
- If you are returning home at night, ask a friend to accompany you. Have him or her wait until you are safely inside. If you must return home alone, have your key ready and get inside quickly.
- Keep a list of emergency telephone numbers posted near the phone. These numbers should include your parents' work, a neighbor or nearby relative, and police and fire departments.

In Your Neighborhood

You can help make your neighborhood a safer, more secure place to live. Organize or join a neighborhood watch group. People in these groups work together to reduce crimes and assaults in their neighborhoods. They look out for each other's homes to cut down on break-ins, too.

As part of a watch group, you learn to look for suspicious people, vehicles, or activities in your neighborhood. Watch for people in your neighborhood whom you do not recognize. Write down descriptions of these people, their vehicles, and their license numbers. If they exhibit any suspicious behavior, report this information to the police immediately. Your actions may help protect a neighbor and prevent a residential crime.

When Away from Home

Protecting yourself when you are away from home is important, too. If you feel a place or a situation is dangerous, then avoid it. If you find yourself in a situation that makes you feel uncomfortable, leave as quickly as possible. Whether you are walking or driving, a commonsense approach can help you avoid danger.

As You Walk

Avoid walking alone, especially at night. A lone person is an easier target for a physical attack. Plan to walk with friends to and from your destination. See 13-8.

If you must walk alone, plan to travel the safest route to your destination. Be alert to your surroundings; watch out for suspicious people. Choose well-lighted, busy streets. Avoid dark streets, vacant lots, alleys, parks, and shortcuts across parking lots.

Walk at a steady pace; try to act calm and confident. The more vulnerable you appear, the more susceptible you are to attack. If you think you are being followed, head for a well-lighted, public area. A store or restaurant would be a good choice. Get to a phone in a safe area as quickly as possible so you can call the police.

Avoid wearing jewelry or clothing that looks expensive and draws attention. Keep your valuables in front pockets rather than in back pockets. If you carry a purse, keep it tightly tucked under your arm or out of sight. Keep extra money safely hidden (not in your wallet) for an emergency phone call, bus fare, or cab fare.

If an attacker grabs your purse or wants your jewelry, let him or her have it. Do not resist, as you could get hurt. It is better to give up the item than to risk your life. If you can, get a good look at the attacker so you can describe the person's features and clothing to the police.

> **Reflect:**
> Does your neighborhood have a watch group?
>
> **Enrich:**
> Invite a speaker from the local police department to talk with the students about specific safety suggestions for their age group.
>
> **Note:**
> The suggestions for walking also apply to taking public transportation such as buses or subway trains.

 Putting Technology to Use
Have students check out the Neighborhood Watch Web site at www.neighborhoodwatch.com. Have them check to see what watch groups are registered in your state.

Activity:
Design posters depicting safety precautions to follow when driving alone.

Resource:
Reduce Your Risk, reproducible master, TR

Enrich:
Role-play ways to handle dangerous situations. After each episode, question the class about physical descriptions and important evidence.

In Your Car

Follow safety precautions whenever you drive alone. Keep your car in good running condition with a full tank of gas to lessen the chances of breaking down.

Have your car keys ready so you can open the car door and get inside quickly. Before you open the door, check the front and back seat of your car to make sure no one is hiding. When driving, avoid deserted streets and unsafe areas. Keep the windows closed and the doors locked while you drive. Keep convertible tops and sunroofs closed, also.

What should you do if you sense you are being followed by another vehicle? Drive toward a well-lighted, public area or to the nearest police station. Do not stop for the other car. If immediate help is not available, honk the horn nonstop and turn on the emergency signals. Do not drive home as the other car may follow.

Should your car break down, raise the car hood and turn on the emergency signals for help. If you have a cellular phone, call for help. If someone stops to assist you, do not roll down your window, open the door, or get out of the car. Ask the person to call for help, but stay inside your car with the doors locked until help arrives.

Park your car in well-lighted areas. If you cannot start your car in a parking lot, call home or the nearest service station for help. Do not accept help from strangers or get into a stranger's car.

Emergency Procedures

The word *emergency* refers to an unexpected event that requires your immediate action. Emergencies are often the result of accidents or bad weather. Being familiar with emergency procedures will help you know how to respond in such situations.

When an emergency occurs, you need to remain as calm as possible. You must be able to think clearly. You do not want to upset a person who is involved in the emergency.

The first step in an emergency is to assess the safety of the scene. If people appear to be injured, check them for consciousness, breathing, pulse, and bleeding. If someone else is with you, one person can stay at the scene while the other calls for help. If you are alone, call for help and then return to the scene until help arrives.

In an emergency, you need to know how to get medical assistance fast. Dial 911 or your local emergency number. Give the location of the accident. Then tell what happened, what seems to be wrong, and what first aid is being given. Be sure to stay on the line long enough to answer any questions the dispatcher might ask you. Let the dispatcher be the first to hang up the telephone. See 13-9.

Immediate treatment may lessen the damage caused by injuries sustained in an emergency. Keep first aid kits at home, in your car, and with camping and hiking gear. A well-stocked first aid kit will provide you with basic supplies to care for someone who is sick or injured. To care for victims of an emergency, you need to know proper first

13-8 Walking with a friend or in a group is the safest way to reach your destination.

Across the Curriculum
Health. Review basic supplies that should be included in a first aid kit. Discuss how each of the supplies should be used. Ask if students have any questions about how to handle specific emergencies.

How to Get Medical Help Fast

1 **In an emergency,** while one person gives care, another can call for help.

2 **Dial 911** or the local emergency number. Tell the dispatcher... (see steps 3, 4 and 5)

3 **Location of the emergency.** Include cross streets, room number, and telephone number you are calling from

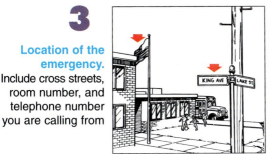

4 **What happened.** For example, motor vehicle crash, sudden illness

What seems to be wrong. For example, victim is bleeding, unconscious.

5 **What first aid is being given.** For example, rescue breathing, control of bleeding

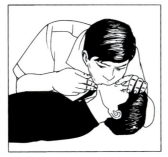

6 **Don't hang up until the dispatcher hangs up** The dispatcher may tell you how to take care for the victim

Return to the scene. Help to care for the victim until help arrives.

13-9 Knowing how to respond and give first aid in an emergency may help you save someone's life.

Resource:
Emergency Phone Numbers, reproducible master, TR

aid procedures, such as rescue breathing. The American Red Cross regularly offers first aid courses. Learning first aid skills may help you save someone's life.

In a bad weather emergency, try to stay tuned to a local news station on a portable radio. The local emergency management team will provide instructions about where to find shelter in your area. Keeping a supply of food, water, and paper products on hand will also be helpful in a weather emergency. Be sure to replace food and water regularly so they will be fresh when you need them.

Check It Out!
1. True or false. One cause of accidents is a person's emotional state.
2. Name the four most common types of household accidents.
3. List four defensive driving skills.
4. If you are home alone, what safety precautions should you follow?
5. True or false. When away from home, the best way for people to prevent a criminal attack is to avoid dangerous situations.
6. What information should you give when calling for help in an emergency?

Check It Out! (Answers)
1. true
2. falls, fires, poisonings, electrical shock
3. scanning, communicating with other drivers, keeping a margin of safety, adjusting to situations that arise
4. (Student response. See pages 390-391 in the text.)
5. true
6. location of the accident and a description of what happened, what seems to be wrong, and what first aid is being given

Topic 13-2
A Healthful Environment

Vocabulary:
Does anyone know what radon is? Is it a community problem?

Reflect:
How does the way *you* live affect the environment? What can *you* do to protect and preserve the environment?

Discuss:
Name some instances where the misuse of resources has lead to pollution.

Objectives
After studying this topic, you will be able to
- explain the importance of a healthful environment.
- identify the causes of different types of pollution.
- relate how pollution affects people's health.
- discuss ways people can protect and build a healthful environment.

Topic Terms
pollution
toxic waste
radon
recycling

13-10 The natural beauty of the environment can be preserved for future generations through the wise use of resources today.

Some of the most serious problems in the world today threaten the environment. Limited natural resources, population growth, and pollution are environmental issues affecting all people. People must think about how they use their environment. They must be willing to ask themselves, "How does the way we live affect our environment? What can we do to protect and preserve our environment?"

A Healthful Environment

Today, many people are concerned about living in a healthful environment. How do people define a healthful environment? Some think it means an unspoiled wilderness. To others, it means greater advances in technology that improve the standard of living. A *healthful environment* promotes good physical and mental health and enables people to reach their goals.

A healthful environment provides clean air, unpolluted water, rich soil, a continuing supply of natural resources, and pleasant surroundings, 13-10. Surroundings must be spacious enough to allow individuals some privacy and room for recreation. A healthful environment must also support diverse plant and animal life.

An environment that allows people to reach their goals must protect natural resources. At the same time, it must provide enough energy for a high standard of living. To preserve such an environment is one of the critical problems facing people everywhere. What will people have to do to solve this problem? First, people must understand how they use natural resources to achieve a better standard of living. Next, they must realize that misuse of resources leads to pollution, which affects their health. Finally, they must make a strong commitment to keeping the environment healthful.

Factors Affecting the Environment

Two factors play major roles in the increase of environmental problems. An increasing human population is one factor. Another factor is the increasing use of shrinking natural resources.

Increasing Population

The human population is increasing at a rapid rate. This is due partly to improved

Across the Curriculum
English. Have students write a paper giving their descriptions of a healthful environment. What factors are included? What factors are absent?

nutritional standards that have allowed people to live longer lives.

The increased population has created some environmental problems. As the population increases, the available living space for each person decreases. Existing resources must be divided among more and more people. Food is one of these resources. As food supplies are divided among greater numbers of people, famines may become a greater problem.

More energy and industry are needed to provide consumer goods and services for the growing population. As more goods are produced and used, more solid waste is created. Pre- and postconsumer waste cause pollution of natural resources—air, water, and soil. Without controls, the end result is an unhealthful environment.

Increasing Use of Resources

The number of people using resources is increasing. The amount of resources used by each person is also increasing. This is due to a standard of living that continues to improve. The higher the standard of living, the larger the share of the world's resources people tend to use.

The earth's resources can be divided into two main categories: renewable resources and nonrenewable resources. Understanding the difference is important.

Some resources, such as plants and animals, are *renewable resources*. That is, resources are replaced rapidly enough to provide people with a continuing supply. If land continues to be fertile, plant resources can be renewed and even increased as people grow new crops each year. Animals that live in a healthful environment can also grow and reproduce.

Some energy resources are also renewable. The energy of the sun and the wind belong in this group. They will probably play a much greater role in the future than they do at present. That will depend, however, on the willingness of people to research and develop ways of using these resources economically.

Water is a renewable resource. The oceans of the earth can become an unlimited source of water if they do not become too polluted. Again, people need to find economical ways to use this resource. See 13-11.

Oil, coal, and other natural minerals are fossil fuel resources that were slowly formed over millions of years. These resources are called *nonrenewable resources* because they are replaced so slowly. When present supplies of these resources are gone, there will be no more available. The cost and availability of fuel supplies has been a source of tension among world powers. Tension is likely to increase as fuel supplies run low and become more regionalized and costs continue to climb.

Pollution

The health of the environment has a great effect on people's health. One unhealthful side effect of the way people live is pollution. **Pollution** is all the harmful

13-11 Renewable resources, such as plants, wildlife, and water, are dependent on a healthful environment.

> **Resource:**
> *Face the Future*, Activity C, SAG
>
> **Activity:**
> Working in small groups, make a list of renewable resources. Then list the nonrenewable resources. List as many resources as you can think of. Compare lists with other groups.
>
> **Discuss:**
> Is water always a renewable resource?

Across the Curriculum

Science. Have students research one of the nonrenewable resources. How are they formed? What is their makeup? What makes them so valuable? What has been done to preserve these resources? What has been done to replace these resources? Can anything be used as a substitute for these resources?

Discuss:
Each person has a different tolerance level to pollutants. What pollutants do you find especially bothersome?

Discuss:
When did you first hear about the greenhouse effect? Do you still hear that term often in news programs? Why do you think this is the case?

Note:
Aerosol products such as hairspray are harmful to the atmosphere. Non-aerosol products should be used when possible.

changes in the environment caused by human activities. It occurs when people contaminate the air, water, or land with harmful substances. These substances, called *pollutants,* are often by-products of modern living.

Air Pollution

Pollution takes many forms. Air pollution is the most dangerous threat to a healthful environment. People must have clean air to breathe if they are to remain healthy. Today's modern lifestyle causes many pollutants to be added to the air.

Air pollution is caused by many sources. Chemical plants, refineries, and factories use oil, coal, and natural gas to power equipment. The combustion, or burning, of these fuels creates smoke that pollutes the air. Motor vehicles produce exhaust that contains carbon monoxide. Burning wastes create pollution, as do cigarettes, pesticides, and aerosol sprays. See 13-12.

Pollutants are dangerous because they build up over time and remain in the air. They are directly harmful to people's health. Air pollution has been linked to respiratory ailments, such as lung cancer, bronchitis, and emphysema. People with asthma have difficulties breathing polluted air. Carbon monoxide from car exhausts can cause headaches and dizziness. Long-term exposure to air pollution can be especially harmful to young children, older adults, and people who are ill.

Scientists believe air pollution has other harmful effects on the environment. The greenhouse effect, diminishing ozone layer, and acid rain are all dangerous effects of air pollution.

The Greenhouse Effect

People may be actually changing the future climate of the earth by the way they live today. Scientists think putting more carbon dioxide into the atmosphere may have a dramatic *greenhouse effect* on future weather patterns. That is, the carbon dioxide would act like a blanket that keeps the earth's warmth from escaping. A general warming of the earth would result. This would produce major changes in local climates. Crop production would be affected. Polar ice caps would melt more rapidly, causing a rise in the sea level. Coastal towns might be flooded.

Diminishing Ozone Layer

Closely related to the greenhouse effect is the apparent diminishing of the natural ozone layer in the stratosphere. The ozone layer reduces the amount of ultraviolet radiation reaching the surface of the earth. Scientists think the layer is weakening, allowing more solar radiation to reach the earth. They attribute the weakening of the ozone layer to harmful chemical pollutants entering the atmosphere. These chemicals come from aerosol propellants (now banned in the United States), refrigerants, solvents, and other sources. Increased amounts of solar radiation would have two major effects on the environment. First, it would increase rates of skin cancer. Second, it would contribute to the greenhouse effect.

Acid Rain

When pollutants in the air combine with rain or other forms of moisture (fog or snow), *acid rain* results. Acid rain returns the pollutants to the ground. The

13-12 Exhaust from automobiles is a major source of air pollution.

Across the Curriculum

Science. Have students work in groups to plan a lesson suitable for presentation to a lower elementary class. In the lesson, the greenhouse effect, the ozone layer, and acid rain should be explained in language young children can understand.

Topic 13-2 A Healthful Environment

acids in the rain can harm or kill trees and plant life, pollute rivers, and damage cars and buildings.

Citizen groups, industry, and government have recognized the dangers of air pollution and are working to decrease it. Concerned citizens work with government leaders to get environmental laws passed. In recent years, automobile manufacturers have built engines that reduce the amount of pollutants in exhaust gases. Industries are also looking for ways to control the pollutants they produce. Government is involved, too. The *Environmental Protection Agency (EPA)* is an agency of the federal government. It sets standards for air and water quality and regulates the disposal of solid wastes. State and local governments also have passed strict laws to reduce pollution.

Water Pollution

Another serious kind of pollution is water pollution. *Water pollution* is the addition of waste materials to rivers, lakes, and oceans.

Industrial wastes, sewage, and agricultural chemicals are the main sources of water pollution. In recent years, oil spills have added poisonous substances to ocean waters. Some industrial plants have discharged toxic waste, such as lead, into rivers and other bodies of water. Though less of a problem today, untreated sewage can be a problem in areas with inadequate sanitation systems. Agricultural chemicals, including fertilizers and pesticides, are washed by rains into nearby streams. Animal wastes from feedlots may seep through soil, contaminating water supplies.

Water is a vital resource in sustaining all forms of life. That is why water pollution has serious effects on the environment. Pollution halts the natural purification process of streams and rivers. It reduces the fresh water supply and causes disease. It can be fatal to plant and animal life, which then affects the balance of nature. Pollutants can be absorbed and stored in the tissues of fish and other water-dwelling animals. This pollutes the food supply. People who consume contaminated seafood may become ill.

As with air pollution, efforts are being made to stop water pollution. Laws have been passed to strictly regulate materials dumped into water supplies. However, cleaning up polluted waters is a long-term, costly process. Once water is polluted it takes a long time for it to return to a healthy state.

Noise Pollution

Noise pollution is the excessively high level of noise to which people are subjected in their everyday lives. Modern machines, such as jet airplanes, jackhammers, and unmuffled motorcycles, have added dangerously loud noises to the environment. Amplified noises from concerts and stereos are also part of the noise pollution problem.

What is so dangerous about noise pollution? One of the major dangers is loss of hearing. Over time, constant exposure to high noise levels can damage hearing. Another danger of high noise levels is increased stress. People are more likely to become short-tempered and irritable as a result of stress. Long-term stress may cause the development of stress-related ailments, such as stomach ulcers, heart disease, and high blood pressure.

What is being done to stop noise pollution? The EPA has noise-reduction programs aimed at reducing harmful noise levels. It has established standards that limit the amount of noise that can be produced by newly built vehicles and equipment. Local governments can also regulate industrial and machinery noise within the community. Many communities enforce noise ordinances to reduce loud and irritating noises in residential neighborhoods.

Toxic Wastes

Every year, people throw away tons of solid waste materials. Most of these waste materials can be reused in some form. Some wastes, however, are harmful. **Toxic wastes** are poisonous waste materials that damage the environment and cause illness. Modern industry has produced many toxic

> **Discuss:**
> What are some concerns we should have about our drinking water? Are commercial bottled waters any better?
>
> **Discuss:**
> Do you think noise pollution is really a problem? How does noise pollution affect you and your family members?
>
> **Reflect:**
> What can I do to reduce noise pollution? Do I keep my music volume at a safe level?

Problem-Solving Practice
Ethics and the Environment, reproducible master, TR. Students are to work in small groups, pretending the group members are business partners who own a small company. They are to read a case study and answer questions to determine how they would address the problem presented in the case study.

Activity:
Check with local auto maintenance garages to find out how they dispose of used oil.

Enrich:
Hold a debate on the disposal of toxic wastes. Should these wastes be safely disposed of regardless of time and expense?

Discuss:
What precautions do hospitals take to reduce the dangers of radiation exposure?

substances that are hazardous to the environment, 13-13.

Toxic wastes include pesticides, plastics, and heavy metals. Some pesticides remain in the soil for many years. Others are quite toxic but degrade rapidly after use. Heavy metals, such as mercury and lead, are naturally occurring substances. In high concentrations created by industrial use, however, these substances become dangerously toxic.

Besides producing huge amounts of toxic wastes, modern societies often fail to dispose of wastes properly. For instance, used motor oil and empty pesticide containers may be sent to landfills as garbage.

The long-term effects of toxic waste are hazardous. Toxic chemical wastes may leak from containers and contaminate soil and water. Plants, animals, and people who come in contact with these wastes can become ill. Crops may be poisoned, which affects the food supply.

Toxic waste affects the economy, as well as people's health. Attempts to clean up toxic waste sites and find safe disposal methods are extremely expensive. Public and private resources must often be used to accomplish the task. Some clean-up operations will take many years to complete.

What can be done to reduce toxic waste in the environment? You can write legislators. Encourage them to pass stricter laws and standards relating to waste disposal. Become an advocate of continued EPA monitoring of industries that produce toxic wastes. Support research aimed at finding effective ways to reduce or eliminate toxic waste.

Radiation

People are exposed to small amounts of radiation from natural sources every day. One source is the sun. Another source is radioactive gases given off by rocks and soil. In small dosages, exposure to this type of radiation does not usually cause health problems.

On the other hand, artificial radiation is threatening to a healthful environment. Sources of radiation exposure include X rays used for medical diagnosis. Nuclear reactors that supply electricity are another potential source. The greatest danger from a reactor

13-13 Industry produces much of the toxic waste that threatens the healthfulness of the environment.

Family Enrichment Activity

For one week, have students keep an accurate inventory of how much and what types of trash each of their family members throws out. At the end of the week, students should review their lists with family members to be sure they haven't forgotten anything. Encourage students to hold a family counsel meeting to discuss how each family member can reduce his or her waste production.

would be if an accident occurred, releasing large amounts of radiation into the air.

Exposure to radiation in large amounts or over a long period can cause serious health problems. Radiation sickness is one dangerous effect. Radiation may cause cancer and damage reproductive cells, causing genetic mutations.

Radon in the Home

In recent years, radon in the home has become another environmental health concern. **Radon** is a colorless, odorless, radioactive gas that is produced by the breakdown of radium. It is released naturally into the atmosphere from soil and rocks. Outdoors, radon is diluted to nontoxic levels by the surrounding air. Indoors, it becomes an environmental problem. High concentrations of radon can cause lung cancer if inhaled in large quantities.

Radon finds its way into houses through cracks in foundations, floors, and walls. The amount of radon in a building depends on the type of construction and materials used. Energy-efficient buildings that conserve heated and cooled air can also trap radon indoors.

Health hazards caused by radon can be easily reduced. Sealing cracks in foundations, floors, and walls is one measure. Installing gas vents below the building foundation is another measure. Ventilation to bring outside air into the home is also important. A well-ventilated home is the best insurance against trapping radon indoors.

Health departments usually inspect and forewarn people who live in areas where high concentrations of radon exist. Areas with rocky terrain and landfill high in mineral content are the most likely to experience this problem. People can contact their local health department for more information on radon as it relates to their area.

How You Can Help

You have read about the causes and effects of five major forms of pollution that affect the environment. You have read about efforts that are being made by citizens, government, and industry to control pollution. You, as an individual, can also help preserve and protect the environment.

Conserve Resources

One way you can help conserve natural resources is by recycling. **Recycling** means reprocessing resources such as aluminum cans, glass and plastic bottles, and paper to be used again, 13-14. Old furniture and appliances can also be recycled. Recycling prevents polluting the landscape with landfills and litter. You can support recycling efforts in your community by taking recyclable trash to recycling centers instead of throwing it away. Ask your friends to pitch in and do their part, too. Some companies will pay you for recyclable items, so you can earn money as you lessen pollution.

Old clothing is another recyclable resource. You can give outgrown clothes to someone who can wear them, or you can

13-14 Collecting materials for recycling instead of throwing them away helps conserve limited natural resources.

Enrich: Research the extent of radon problems in your area. Also check the Yellow Pages for local radon inspection services.

Resource: *The Problem of Pollution*, reproducible master, TR

Reflect: Do you believe every person must assume a responsibility for protecting the environment?

Putting Technology to Use
Have students create a Web site promoting resource conservation. Students can include information from this chapter on the Web site, as well as do additional research for information to include.

Activity:
Brainstorm additional ideas for recycling old clothing.

Resource:
Reuse or Recycle, reproducible master, TR

Enrich:
Working in small groups, plan an advertising campaign to reduce pollution.

Resource:
Promoting a Quality Environment, Activity D, SAG

restyle them. In many instances, you can make new garments from old ones. There is often enough fabric in an adult-sized garment to make clothing for children. Donate clothing you cannot use to charitable organizations that collect used clothing.

Reduce Pollution

You can take part in the fight against pollution in many ways. To reduce air pollution in your area, try walking or riding your bicycle to your destination instead of driving. If you must drive, use your car efficiently by planning to do several errands in one trip. Carpool with friends or family members whenever possible. Also, refrain from burning leaves or garbage; the smoke pollutes the air.

To reduce water pollution, avoid dumping wastes into bodies of water. Safely recycle used oil and other toxic chemicals; do not dump them down the sewer or in the ground.

You can reduce excess noise in your environment by keeping your car in good repair, especially the muffler. Lower the volume on your stereo or radio if you are outdoors or if windows are open. Help insulate your home from noise by installing carpeting, draperies, and acoustical tile. Storm windows and doors deaden outdoor noise in winter. In summer, air conditioning will help because you keep windows and doors closed. If you are exposed to high noise levels on your job, protect your hearing by wearing ear protectors.

Stay informed about environmental issues. Learn how refuse is disposed of in your community. Enlist the support of your parents and other adults to insist that local leaders observe safe environmental practices at all times. Join community groups that address environmental issues or help clean up problem areas, 13-15. Keep up with pending legislation relating to the environment. Write your legislators at both state and national levels to urge their support of healthful environment bills. Much can be done to control pollution if each person makes an effort.

Make Environmentally Responsible Consumer Decisions

As a consumer, you need to know how your buying decisions can affect the environment. However, much information about the environmental impact of various items seems to conflict. For instance, one source says using plastic bags saves the trees used to make paper bags. Another source says paper bags are a better choice because plastic bags are made from fossil fuels. Some consumers solve the dilemma by recycling bags or using a reusable cloth bag. Four guidelines can help you evaluate environmental information to make wiser purchase decisions.

■ Seek out the environmental information that is available. Read it thoughtfully. Find out if it is based on opinion, experience, or valid research. Determine whether the information is reliable and based on fact. Decide whether the intent is to inform, persuade, or sell. Keep in mind that some manufacturers use environmental information on their products as a marketing tool.

13-15 Cleaning up littered landscapes is an effective way for individuals to get involved in the fight against environmental pollution.

FCCLA Activity

Encourage chapter members working on the Community Service Opportunities program to plan activities to improve the local environment. The following are possible projects: clean an area of the school campus; distribute car litter bags to each student and discuss the importance of properly disposing of litter when in the car; design posters with slogans that remind all students to recycle and avoid littering. Display these around your school.

Topic 13-2 A Healthful Environment

- Make sure you understand the information before you use it. Is it written clearly? Does the information relate to you as a consumer or is it too technical?
- Determine if the information is practical for your situation. For example, a label might urge you to buy the economy size to reduce package waste. However, the economy size is not a practical choice if you wind up throwing out most of the contents.
- Consider how much time and money is involved in obtaining environmental information. How much time will you need to locate the information? Is the information free or must you pay for it? Too much time and money may cancel out the value of obtaining the information.

Making environmentally responsible consumer decisions can be challenging. Many consumers end up making environmental *tradeoffs.* In other words, they exchange one resource to save another resource. You have a duty to carefully evaluate your choices to the best of your ability. Making responsible consumer decisions will help you contribute to a healthful environment.

Check It Out!
1. List five requirements for a healthful environment.
2. Name the two primary factors responsible for the increase of environmental problems.
3. Explain the difference between a renewable and nonrenewable resource.
4. Name five types of pollution.
5. List five ways people can promote a healthful environment.

Check It Out! (Answers)
1. clean air; unpolluted water; rich soil; a continuing supply of natural resources; pleasant, spacious surroundings
2. an increasing human population and the increasing use of shrinking natural resources
3. Continuing supplies of renewable resources can be provided as long as the environment stays healthy. Nonrenewable resources take millions of years to renew; they will no longer be available when present supplies are gone.
4. air, water, noise, toxic waste, radiation
5. (List five:) conserve resources by recycling solid wastes and old clothing, reduce air pollution by walking or car pooling, avoid dumping toxic wastes into the ground or water, reduce noise pollution by controlling sources of noise, stay informed about environmental issues in your area, help clean up problem areas

Discuss: What other ways are manufacturers of household products helping the consumer save the environment? (Examples: offering refills for cleaning products, offering products in concentrated form.)

Example: Using cold wash water saves energy when washing laundry, but more energy is then required to dry the cold laundry in the automatic dryer.

Discuss:

- If you had been in Shannon's place when the intruder entered, what would you have done?
- How did Shannon's family open themselves up to a possible home invasion?
- What precautions are Shannon's family members now taking to prevent security problems? What additional precautions could they take?
- What are some other security incidences that can occur when you are on vacation? What precautions can you take to avoid these incidences?

TEENS ARE EXPERIENCING...

Security Problems

Think of summer vacation and what images come to mind? Fun-filled, carefree days full of happy memories? Not always. Shannon experienced firsthand that even vacationers can be the victims of crime.

Shannon vividly remembers one summer evening when she was vacationing at a beach house with her mother, grandmother, uncle, and two younger brothers. Late that night she awoke and lay restlessly in bed. She decided to sit up for a few minutes. From her bed, she could see into the living room because a lamp had been left on for a nightlight. Suddenly, the sliding glass door in the living room started to open. As she watched, a man dressed in a dark sweatshirt slipped quietly through the door into the house. The man bent beside the sofa as though looking for something.

Shannon reacted quickly. "I knew he was an intruder. Although I was frightened and breathing fast, I quietly lay down and pretended I was asleep. After a short time, I did not hear him again. I did not hear the door close, either.

"After about twenty minutes, I woke up my mom and told her about it. She thought I was dreaming and tried to ignore my story. I finally convinced her that I was not dreaming, so she awoke my uncle. They looked around the living room and everything was intact. They checked the door that I saw the intruder open and it was locked. Then mom looked into her purse. It was beside the sofa where I saw the man stoop. Again, everything looked intact. Then she looked inside her billfold, and our vacation money was gone!"

When asked how the incident made her feel, Shannon responded, "I was very nervous and scared. I really didn't know what to do because I didn't know what was going on. I knew the man was an intruder. I was afraid he might hurt my family. My heart was pounding and I was perspiring. I didn't want him to know that I was awake and I didn't want him to know that I saw him. I just wanted him to go away."

How did the incident affect Shannon and her family? They now take extra precautions to make sure the house is locked and the exterior lights are left on. "We are more cautious now," she stated, "but we were cautious then, too. My uncle insisted that he locked the door at the beach house before we went to bed that night. This is the kind of incident you don't expect to happen. We had never had a security problem at home or at the beach house before. We now know it can happen and we are all more cautious."

Shannon's advice to others is, "Always keep your doors locked. Put your purse and other valuables away so they are not in view if someone looks through a window. If someone does enter your home, don't do anything foolish. I am glad I was quiet—that I did not alarm the intruder. I am just glad he took the money without harming anyone in my family." She added, "After this experience, I would like an electronic security system. I think it would help a lot."

When asked if they experienced other security problems during their vacation, Shannon replied, "None." They stayed for the remainder of their vacation, but took several extra precautions. They left the outside lights on, closed the blinds at night, double checked the doors, and put purses out of sight. Shannon reflected, "I try not to let the incident bother me, but I do think about it. I am now more cautious as a result of the incident. I now know burglaries do happen—even on vacation."

Feature-Related Activity

Ask each student to write a sequel to Shannon's summer vacation. She and her family are going to the beach again the following summer. In story form, relate how her family takes security precautions. Use some of the suggestions from this chapter.

Chapter Review

Summary

The quality of human life depends on many factors. Two important factors that affect your health are your personal safety and security and a healthful environment. Your personal choices will help you control these factors.

Accidents and criminal attacks can threaten your safety and security. To keep them from happening to you at home or away from home, you need to identify and eliminate hazards.

A healthful environment is one that promotes good physical and mental health and allows people to reach their goals. However, environmental problems, as well as pollution, are concerns that directly affect people's health. Every person must assume a responsibility for protecting the environment that supports all living things.

Think About It!

1. What steps can you take to prevent accidents at home? How can you get family members involved in making your home safer?
2. Which defensive driving skills do you think are most difficult to develop? Explain your answer.
3. Suggest three of the most effective ways to provide for your security at home and away from home.
4. Suppose you are taking a walk in your neighborhood one summer evening. After walking a short distance, you suspect someone is following you. What action will you take to avoid a criminal attack?
5. Suggest ways today's teens can work to overcome increasing population, decreasing resources, and pollution during the next generation.
6. Imagine that you are adapting this chapter to be studied by teens in another part of the world. What other topics would you want to add? What topics could you delete because they would not be applicable?
7. In what ways does the content of this chapter relate to the family? In what ways does it relate to work outside the home?

Try It Out!

1. Develop a safety checklist for each room in your home. Then use the checklist to conduct a safety inspection at home. Identify potential hazards and determine how they should be corrected.
2. Invite a safety specialist from the police department to discuss personal safety and security issues in your community.
3. Develop a school safety campaign about the importance of wearing seat belts in motor vehicles.
4. Plan and organize a class recycling project to benefit your community. Sponsor a drive to collect paper, bottles, aluminum, clothing, or other recyclable materials.
5. Research ways your community and state are working to stop pollution. Report your findings to the class.
6. Invite a speaker from the health department to discuss the presence of radon in your area.

Note: If students are not old enough to drive, have them interview experienced drivers to answer *Think About It!* #2.

Note: You might want to expand the safety campaign in *Try It Out!* #3 to the community.

Note: Your school may already be involved in recycling projects. Discuss how well these are working. How could they be expanded?

Resource: *PowerZone Challenge CD.* Have students play the chapter review game to reinforce text content.

Chapter 14
Healthful Eating

Careers

These careers relate to the topics in this chapter:
- volunteer for meal delivery service for shut-ins, such as Meals on Wheels
- dietary aide
- nutrition assistant
- food chemist

As you study the chapter, see if you can think of others.

Topics

14-1 Nutrients at Work for You
14-2 Making Daily Food Choices
14-3 Nutritional Needs Change
14-4 Balancing Calories and Energy Needs

Introductory Activities

1. Ask students how their families' eating habits have changed in the last few years. Also ask if their own eating habits have changed in recent years.
2. Ask the class the following: Is it easier to eat a well-balanced diet today than in the past? What effect has the trend of eating more meals away from home had on our diets? Can you meet your nutritional needs by eating at fast-food restaurants? What has been the effect of the increased use of convenience foods at home? Do you think this has led to better nutrition?

Topic 14-1
Nutrients at Work for You
I. Carbohydrates
II. Proteins
III. Fats
IV. Minerals
   A. Calcium and Phosphorus
   B. Fluorine
   C. Iodine
   D. Iron
   E. Sodium
   F. Zinc
   G. Other Minerals
V. Vitamins
   A. Fat-Soluble Vitamins
      1. Vitamin A
      2. Vitamin D
      3. Vitamin E
      4. Vitamin K
   B. Water-Soluble Vitamins
      1. B Vitamins
      2. Vitamin C
VI. Water
VII. Recommended Nutrient Intakes

Topic 14-2
Making Daily Food Choices
I. The Food Guide Pyramid
   A. Grains Group
   B. Vegetable Group
   C. Fruit Group
   D. Milk Group
   E. Meat and Beans Group
   F. Fats, Oils, and Sweets
II. The Dietary Guidelines for Americans

Topic 14-3
Nutritional Needs Change
I. Needs of Pregnant Women and Infants
   A. Nutrition Before Birth
   B. Nutrition in Infancy
II. Needs of Children and Teens
   A. Nutrition During the Preschool Years
   B. Nutrition During the Early School Years
   C. Nutrition During the Teen Years
   D. Special Needs of Vegetarians
   E. Special Needs of Athletes
      1. Increase Daily Calorie Intake
      2. Drink Plenty of Fluids
      3. Eat Plenty of Iron-Rich Foods
      4. Meet Daily Calcium Needs
III. Needs of Adults
   A. Nutrition for Older Adults
   B. Nutrition Needs of People Who Are Ill

Topic 14-4
Balancing Calories and Energy Needs
I. Meeting Energy Needs
   A. Metabolic Energy Needs
   B. Energy for Physical Activities
II. Controlling Your Weight
   A. How Much Should You Weigh?
   B. Healthy Weight Loss
   C. Healthy Weight Gain
III. Eating Disorders

Topic 14-1
Nutrients at Work for You

Objectives
After studying this topic, you will be able to
- explain the importance of choosing nutritious foods.
- identify good food sources of various nutrients and describe how your body uses them.

Topic Terms
nutrient
nutrition
carbohydrate
protein
amino acid
fat
saturated fat
unsaturated fat
cholesterol
mineral
vitamin
fortified
enriched
Recommended Dietary Allowances (RDA)

Pizza, milk, apples, and popcorn—these foods, and all the other foods you eat, provide nutrients for your body. **Nutrients** are chemical substances from food, which the body uses to function properly. After your body digests food, your bloodstream absorbs nutrients from the digestive tract and carries them to body cells. In the cells, nutrients help maintain and regulate body processes and promote growth.

Nutrition is the science of how nutrients support the body. The nutrients that keep your body working properly are divided into six major classes:
- carbohydrates
- proteins
- fats
- minerals
- vitamins
- water

Each of the nutrients performs special functions in the body. You get different nutrients from different foods. Therefore, you need to eat a variety of foods to get all the nutrients you need. By knowing the functions and sources of the nutrients, you will be able to make nutritious food choices.

Carbohydrates

Carbohydrates are the major sources of energy in your diet. Most carbohydrates come from plants. There are three kinds of carbohydrates: sugars, starches, and fiber. Your body can change both sugars and starches into energy.

Sugars are *simple carbohydrates* found in foods such as milk, fruits, candy, and cookies, 14-1. Your body can use some sugars right away for energy. Other sugars must first be broken down into simpler sugars.

Starches are often called *complex carbohydrates*. Cereals, bread, rice, pasta, and starchy vegetables are good sources of starch. Before your body can use starches for energy, it must convert the starches into

14-1 Milk and brownies are both sources of simple carbohydrates.

Vocabulary:
Write the words *vitamins* and *minerals* on a sheet of paper. List the names of vitamins and minerals you already know.

Enrich:
Have students bring in cans and packages with nutrition labels on them. These will be used in activities throughout this chapter.

Example:
Potatoes, corn, peas, and yams are starchy vegetables.

Career Preparation Activity
Is a Nutrition-Related Career for You? reproducible master, TR. Invite to class a panel of people whose jobs are in the field of food and nutrition. Suggested topics for the panel to address include training or education required for the position; how they apply the Dietary Guidelines for Americans, RDA/DRI information, and the Food Guide Pyramid guidelines; and special challenges and rewards of their jobs. You may also want to have students submit questions ahead of time so the panel can address these. After the presentation, have students complete the activity master.

Enrich:
Read an article or book about athletes, especially runners, to find out how they include carbohydrates in their diets.

Activity:
Bring in a nutrition label from your favorite food product. List types of carbohydrates contained in the product.

Reflect:
What is your favorite food combination that uses incomplete proteins?

simple sugars during digestion. Nutrition experts recommend most people get more than half of all their daily calories from complex carbohydrates. (People who are diabetic must monitor their carbohydrate intake and follow a prescribed diet.)

Like starch, *fiber* is a complex carbohydrate. Although your body cannot digest fiber, you need fiber in your diet. This is because fiber provides roughage that stimulates the normal activity of your intestines. Fiber moves food through your body and helps your body get rid of solid wastes.

When you eat more carbohydrates than your body can use, some of them are changed to *glycogen*. Glycogen is stored in your body for times when you need quick energy, such as when you run to catch a bus. Your body maintains only a small amount of glycogen. Excess carbohydrates that are not stored as glycogen are changed to fat for storage in the body.

You need to eat carbohydrates, especially complex carbohydrates, every day. A diet low in carbohydrates will not provide the best energy source to fuel your body. Your body will use protein for energy instead. This will deplete protein supplies needed for growth and repair of body tissues. A diet low in fiber will not promote proper activity of the intestines and may result in constipation.

Proteins

Proteins are a nutrient found in every cell in your body. They are needed for growth, maintenance, and repair of body tissues. Proteins are made up of **amino acids**, which are building blocks for your cells. Your body uses proteins to produce enzymes and hormones. These help the body maintain its chemical balance and build antibodies to fight infections. The amount of protein you need depends on several factors.

You need extra protein when you are recovering from an injury or illness to help replace and repair cells. You also need additional protein when you are growing to build new cells. Without adequate protein, growth is stunted. As your rate of growth slows, you require less protein. However, you never outgrow the need for protein in your diet.

Not all protein sources are the same. There are two classes of proteins—complete proteins and incomplete proteins. *Complete proteins* supply all the amino acids your body needs. Foods that come from animals, such as meat, poultry, fish, milk, cheese, and eggs, are sources of complete proteins. *Incomplete protein* sources contain some, but not all, of the amino acids your body needs. Plant sources of protein, such as dried beans, peas, and nuts, provide incomplete proteins.

When incomplete proteins are combined with complete proteins in a meal, all the needed amino acids are provided. As an example, pasta (an incomplete protein) combined with cheese (a complete protein) can supply all the amino acids you need. See 14-2.

Sometimes incomplete proteins can work together to supply needed amino acids. A peanut butter sandwich is a good

14-2 This creamy soup combines the incomplete protein of peanuts with the complete protein of milk to supply all the needed amino acids.

Across the Curriculum

Science. Have students do research on the different types of amino acids, including chemical structure. Discuss the function of DNA as a protein template.

example. Peanut butter and enriched bread are both sources of incomplete proteins. When they are combined, however, they provide all the amino acids your body needs.

Protein foods should be eaten each day. People whose diets are low in protein experience poor muscle tone, lack of energy, and reduced resistance to disease. Severe protein shortages may result in a disease called *kwashiorkor*. Protein consumed beyond the body's needs is stored in the body as fat.

Fats

Fats are concentrated sources of food energy. Fats provide slightly more than twice as much energy per unit of weight as carbohydrates and proteins.

Fats do more than provide food energy. Fat is stored beneath the surface of the skin to insulate the body from shock and temperature changes. Fat protects and cushions the organs in your body from injury. Fats are needed in the diet to help the body distribute and use some vitamins. Fats also supply *essential fatty acids*, which are needed for normal growth.

Fats are divided into two classes. **Saturated fats** are solid at room temperature. **Unsaturated fats** are most often liquid at room temperature. As a rule, foods from animal sources, like meat and butter, tend to be higher in saturated fats. Foods from plant sources, like corn oil and soybean oil, tend to be higher in unsaturated fats.

Sometimes manufacturers process unsaturated fats to make them solid. This process is called *hydrogenation*. Solid vegetable shortenings and margarines are products that have been hydrogenated.

Cholesterol is a fatty substance found in every body cell. The body uses cholesterol to make a number of important materials, including sex hormones and vitamin D. Your body manufactures all the cholesterol you need. However, you also get cholesterol from your diet when you consume foods from animal sources, such as eggs and shellfish.

Saturated fats and dietary cholesterol both tend to raise blood cholesterol levels. Excessive cholesterol in the blood can form deposits on the inside of blood vessels. This causes the flow of blood to be restricted or blocked completely. A heart attack can result. Therefore, health experts advise people to limit their intake of saturated fats and cholesterol.

When the diet is deficient in fat during infancy and childhood, growth can be stunted. A diet too low in fat can cause skin problems and the poor utilization of some vitamins. Although some fats are needed in the diet, excessive amounts can cause weight problems. People who eat excessive amounts of fats tend to eat less of other needed foods. This should be avoided because a well-balanced diet is important for good health. See 14-3.

Minerals

Minerals are inorganic substances needed for building tissues and regulating body functions. They are an essential part

14-3 Pairing high-fat foods, like sausages, with lowfat foods, like vegetables and whole grains, helps keep a diet in balance.

> **Enrich:** Read articles on low-fat diets. Find out why they've increased in popularity recently.
>
> **Enrich:** Make a survey of lunches eaten by students in the school cafeteria. What foods predominate? How high is the fat content?
>
> **Reflect:** If 40% or more of American teenagers are overweight, how much is due to high-fat foods in their diets? How much of your diet includes fatty foods?

 Across the Curriculum

Social studies. Have students find out more about the disease called *kwashiorkor*. Which areas of the world are most affected by the disease? Why? Have students find pictures of people suffering from this disease and show them in class.

> **Enrich:**
> Write a report on osteoporosis. What affect does calcium intake before the age of 30 have on this disease?

> **Enrich:**
> Find out if fluorine is added to the water supply in your community.

> **Discuss:**
> Do you know anyone who suffers from anemia? How does it limit his or her lifestyle?

of bones, teeth, and red blood cells. Minerals also aid in the proper functioning of muscles and nerves and in the clotting of blood. Like proteins, minerals are needed for growth and repair of body tissues. Unlike the nutrients previously discussed, minerals do not provide the body with energy. They do not have to be broken down by digestion for the body's use, either. Your body can absorb minerals directly from the foods you have eaten.

Calcium and Phosphorus

Calcium and *phosphorus* are the most abundant minerals in the body. Reserves are stored in the bones. Calcium and phosphorus are also found in teeth, soft tissues, and body fluids.

Calcium is used to regulate the use of other minerals in the body. Without calcium, the blood would not clot. Calcium also helps the nervous system to function. All muscles are dependent on calcium for their activity.

If a person's diet is low in calcium, his or her bones will serve as a reserve to fill immediate calcium needs. However, a low calcium intake over a long period could lead to *osteoporosis*. This is a disease characterized by weak, brittle bones, which are more likely to fracture. As osteoporosis progresses, bones become too weak to support the body's weight. They are unable to withstand force from routine chores like lifting and bending. See 14-4.

Milk is an excellent source of calcium. Other good sources are yogurt, cheese, pudding, and dark green leafy vegetables. These foods, and foods that are high in protein, are also good sources of phosphorus.

Fluorine

Fluorine is needed for the proper development of bones and teeth. When added to the diets of children, it helps reduce tooth decay. Fluorine is not readily available in foods. Therefore, many cities add fluorine to the supply of drinking water.

Iodine

Iodine is present in very small amounts in the body, but it is essential for good health.

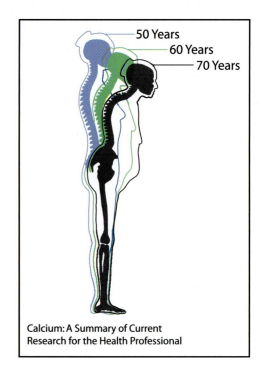

Calcium: A Summary of Current Research for the Health Professional

14-4 Osteoporosis weakens bones and can cause an increased risk of fractures and curving of the spine.

Iodine is used to make *thyroxine*. Thyroxine is a hormone produced by the thyroid gland, which is located at the base of the neck. Thyroxine controls the rate at which the body uses nutrients. When the diet is low in iodine, the thyroid gland enlarges. This condition is called a *goiter*. Seafood and iodized salt are good sources of iodine.

Iron

Iron is another essential mineral. Iron combines with protein to make hemoglobin. *Hemoglobin* is a substance in the blood that carries oxygen from the lungs to cells throughout the body.

A diet that is constantly low in iron results in a condition known as *iron-deficiency anemia*. Symptoms of this condition include extreme fatigue, pale skin, and poor appetite.

Foods rich in iron include organ meats, lean meats, dried beans and peas, dark green leafy vegetables, and eggs. Women generally require more iron than men. To meet their needs, some women may need

Across the Curriculum

Health. Have students find out how much a woman's need for iron increases during pregnancy. How can she meet this increased need? Why do these needs increase during pregnancy?

to take iron supplements prescribed by a doctor.

Sodium

Sodium works with other minerals to help maintain the balance of fluids in the body. It also plays a role in transmitting nerve impulses to the brain. Few people get too little sodium in their diets. In fact, many people get too much. Diets high in sodium are linked with high blood pressure. The main sources of dietary sodium are table salt and processed foods, which often contain a lot of salt. See 14-5.

Zinc

Zinc has a number of functions in the body. It is important for normal growth and development. It helps the immune system work properly. Zinc also helps wounds heal. Too little zinc in children's diets can stunt their growth. An excess of zinc can be toxic. Meat, fish, poultry, whole grains, and some legumes are good sources of zinc.

Other Minerals

The body needs a number of other minerals to maintain good health. These include copper, potassium, chlorine, magnesium, and selenium. Each of these minerals performs specific functions. Eating a variety of foods is the best way to make sure you get all the minerals you need.

Vitamins

Vitamins are organic substances needed in small amounts for normal growth and the maintenance of good health. Vitamins are regulators of body processes. Like minerals, they do not directly supply energy. Vitamins are necessary to enable the other nutrients to do their work. Most vitamin needs can be met by eating a variety of foods.

Fat-Soluble Vitamins

Vitamins can be divided into two groups. The first group is *fat-soluble vitamins*. These are vitamins that can be stored in your body in fatty tissues and in the liver. The fat-soluble vitamins are A, D, E, and K.

Vitamin A

Vitamin A is needed for good vision, normal growth, and healthy skin. A deficiency of vitamin A can cause night blindness and drying of the eyes and skin. *Night blindness* occurs when the eyes cannot adjust from bright to dim light. This can be very hazardous to a person who drives at night.

Excesses of vitamin A from food are not common. However, an excessive intake of vitamin pills containing vitamin A can be dangerous. People who get too much vitamin A over a long period may experience fatigue, headaches, and vomiting.

Good sources of vitamin A are liver, whole and fortified milk products, and fish oils. Foods that are rich in carotene are also good sources of vitamin A. *Carotene* is an orange pigment the body can convert to vitamin A. Carotene is present in orange fruits and vegetables, like apricots, carrots, and sweet potatoes. It is also present in dark green vegetables, like spinach and broccoli. See 14-6.

> **Reflect:**
> Do you add salt to foods before you taste them? Why is this an unhealthful habit?
>
> **Vocabulary:**
> What does *organic* mean?
>
> **Note:**
> Ask how many students take vitamin supplements daily. Point out the dangers of excessive intakes of fat-soluble vitamins.

14-5 French fries and other salty foods contribute sodium to the diet.

 Putting Technology to Use
Have students use the Internet to research the roles of the minerals copper, potassium, chlorine, magnesium, and selenium in the diet. Also have them investigate good food sources of these minerals.

> **Activity:**
> Check some of your food labels. Have any of the foods been fortified? With which nutrients have they been enriched?
>
> **Enrich:**
> Find out why some people take large doses of vitamin E. What benefits are they hoping to receive? What risks do they take?
>
> **Enrich:**
> Research the disease hemophilia and how it is related to vitamin K. Prepare a report for the class.

14-6 Carrots, which are rich in carotene, are a good source of vitamin A.

Vitamin D

Vitamin D helps your body absorb calcium and phosphorus and deposit them into cells. Vitamin D works with calcium and phosphorus to form and maintain bones and teeth.

A prolonged shortage of vitamin D in the diets of growing children can cause weakened bones. Extreme shortages can result in a condition called *rickets.*

Extra vitamin D is stored in the body. Excessive amounts of vitamin D may cause diarrhea, nausea, and headaches.

Vitamin D is often called the "sunshine vitamin." This is because your body can manufacture vitamin D when your skin is exposed to sunlight. However, foods such as eggs, butter, fish liver oils, and fortified milk are more reliable sources. (**Fortified** means nutrients have been added to a food to improve its nutritional value.)

Vitamin E

The main function of vitamin E in the human body is to act as an *antioxidant.* This is a substance that protects compounds from the damaging effects of oxygen. Vitamin E protects blood cells and cells in the lungs from oxygen damage. It also protects vitamin A and fats in the body.

Vitamin E is found in vegetable oils, whole grain cereals, liver, and green leafy vegetables. It is so widely distributed in foods that humans rarely have deficiencies. Because excess vitamin E is stored in the body, large doses from supplements may be harmful.

Vitamin K

Vitamin K is needed for proper blood clotting. Vitamin K deficiencies are not common because vitamin K is widely available in most diets. A severe deficiency could cause bleeding, but deficiencies are rare. Although vitamin K excesses are also rare, they can be toxic. Bacteria in the human digestive tract make about half of the body's needed vitamin K. The rest of vitamin K needs must be met by food sources such as spinach, cabbage, eggs, and liver.

Water-Soluble Vitamins

The second group of vitamins is the *water-soluble vitamins.* These vitamins are not stored in the body to a great extent. Excess amounts of water-soluble vitamins are excreted in the urine. Therefore, you need to eat good sources of these vitamins every day.

The B vitamins and vitamin C are water-soluble vitamins. These vitamins can be lost during cooking. This is why it is a good idea to cook most foods quickly, using as little water as possible. After cooking, do not throw away cooking liquid. Instead, save it for use in a sauce or soup.

B Vitamins

The B vitamins are a group of vitamins that are similar. However, each vitamin in this group plays its own role in helping your body function properly. Thiamin, riboflavin, and niacin may be the most well known B vitamins. Folate and vitamin B_{12} are members of this vitamin group, too. See 14-7.

Thiamin helps you obtain energy from the foods you eat. It is important in promoting a normal appetite and good digestion. It also helps the nervous system function properly. A deficiency of thiamin

> **Putting Technology to Use**
> Have students choose one vegetable and investigate the amounts of each vitamin found in one serving of the vegetable. Have students use charting software to make a graph illustrating the amounts of each vitamin found in the vegetable.

Topic 14-1   Nutrients at Work for You

14-7 Breads made with enriched or whole grain flour are good sources of the B-vitamins thiamin, riboflavin, niacin, and folate.

can result in nausea, depression, loss of appetite, and fatigue. A severe deficiency can lead to a disease called *beriberi*. This disease causes numbness in the ankles and legs and leads to paralysis and heart failure. Good sources of thiamin include pork, legumes, and whole grain and enriched grain products. (**Enriched** means nutrients that were lost during processing have been added back into a product.)

Riboflavin is also needed by your body to obtain energy from foods. It is needed for healthy skin and normal vision, too. A deficiency of riboflavin can cause cracked lips, a skin rash, and extremely sensitive eyes. The best sources of riboflavin are dairy products, meats, and leafy green vegetables.

Niacin, like thiamin and riboflavin, is needed to help you obtain energy from foods. It is also needed for healthy skin, good digestion, and proper functioning of the nervous system. A deficiency of niacin can cause *pellagra*, which affects the skin and digestive system. Good sources of niacin include meat, poultry, fish, nuts, dried beans, and whole grain and enriched grain products.

The body uses *folate* to make all new cells. This function has a special significance for pregnant women. The spine and brain of a baby growing in its mother's womb may not develop properly if the mother's diet lacks folate. Damage to the spine and brain can occur in the first few weeks of pregnancy. This is before most women even know they are pregnant. Therefore, all women of childbearing age are urged to be sure they are meeting their folate needs. Fresh fruits and vegetables, especially leafy green vegetables, are good sources of folate. A form of folate is also added to enriched grain products.

Vitamin B_{12} helps the body make red blood cells. This vitamin also protects nerves. A vitamin B_{12} deficiency can result in anemia and nerve damage. Vitamin B_{12} naturally occurs only in foods of animal origin, such as meat, fish, poultry, eggs, and dairy products. See 14-8. People who do not eat these foods may obtain the vitamin from supplements or fortified soy milk.

Vitamin C

Vitamin C helps hold body cells together and keeps the walls of the blood vessels strong. Vitamin C is important in the healing of wounds. It also helps your body

14-8 Meat and other foods from animal sources provide vitamin B_{12}.

Enrich: Research the disease beriberi to find out how widespread it is and what countries report the most cases.

Activity: What types of foods are generally enriched? Check the collection of food labels students brought to class.

Across the Curriculum
Biology. Have students research current articles about spine and brain development in fetuses. Ask them to find an article in which folate is mentioned. Have students summarize their findings in a written report.

Enrich: Research what studies have said about large doses of vitamin C in preventing colds.

Enrich: Research the effects of caffeine, especially in pregnant women.

Discuss/Reflect: Do you know anyone who was under doctor's care for a lack of any of the nutrients listed in Chart 14-9?

fight infection. A lack of vitamin C over time may result in bleeding gums, loose teeth, bruising, and sore joints. A severe deficiency of vitamin C can lead to a disease called *scurvy*. To prevent a deficiency, be sure to eat at least one serving of a food high in vitamin C each day. Citrus fruits, strawberries, cantaloupe, peppers, broccoli, and tomatoes are all good sources of vitamin C.

Water

Perhaps you do not think of *water* as a nutrient, but it is one of the most important nutrients. Over half of the body's weight is water. As a basic part of blood and tissue fluid, water helps carry nutrients to the cells. Water also carries waste products from the cells. Water aids in digestion. Water regulates body temperature, too.

You should try to drink six to eight glasses of water each day. You get additional water from the foods you eat. Foods such as soup, watermelon, tomatoes, and even breads and meats contain water. Water is also a product of chemical reactions that take place in your body.

You can get the water your body needs from drinking other beverages in addition to water. However, limit your intake of soft drinks and fruit punches. These beverages are high in added sugars. Sugars promote tooth decay and may be a source of excess calories in the diet.

You should also avoid drinking large amounts of caffeinated beverages, such as coffee, tea, and cola. Excessive intake of caffeine has been linked to such symptoms as anxiety, restlessness, and headaches. Read labels and choose caffeine-free beverages, which are now widely available.

Chart 14-9 provides a summary of the basic functions and important sources of

Key Nutrients

Nutrient	Function	Sources
Carbohydrates	Supply energy. Help the body digest fats efficiently. Spare proteins so they can be used for growth and maintenance. Provide bulk in the form of cellulose (needed for digestion).	Sugar: Honey, jam, jelly, sugar, molasses Starch: Breads, cereals, corn, peas, beans, potatoes, pasta Fiber: Fresh fruits and vegetables, whole grain breads and cereals
Proteins	Promote tissue growth and repair. Help make antibodies, enzymes, hormones and some vitamins. Regulate many body processes. Regulate fluid balance in cells. Supply energy when needed.	Complete proteins: Meat, poultry, fish, eggs, milk and other dairy products Incomplete proteins: Cereals, grains, nuts, dried beans and peas
Fats	Supply energy (most concentrated energy in food). Carry fat-soluble vitamins. Insulate the body from shock and temperature changes. Protect vital organs. Add flavor to foods. Serve as a source of essential fatty acids.	Butter, margarine, cream, whole milk, cheese, marbling in meat, bacon, egg yolks, nuts, chocolate, olives, salad oils and dressings
Minerals Calcium	Helps build bones and teeth. Helps blood clot. Helps muscles and nerves to work. Helps regulate the use of other minerals in the body.	Milk, cheese, other dairy products, leafy green vegetables, fish eaten with the bones
Fluorine	Helps in proper development of bones and teeth. Helps reduce tooth decay.	Fluoridated drinking water

14-9 All the nutrients work together to build, maintain, and repair the body and provide it with strength and energy.

(Continued)

Across the Curriculum

History. Have students research the disease scurvy and find out its historical significance in sea travel. Who discovered that scurvy is linked to a deficiency in vitamin C? How was the link discovered?

Topic 14-1 Nutrients at Work for You

Nutrient	Function	Sources
Iodine	Enables normal functioning of the thyroid gland.	Iodized table salt, saltwater fish and shellfish
Iron	Combines with protein to make hemoglobin. Helps cells use oxygen.	Liver, lean meats, egg yolk, dried beans and peas, leafy green vegetables, dried fruits, enriched and whole grain breads and cereals
Phosphorus	Helps build strong bones and teeth. Helps regulate many internal bodily activities.	Protein and calcium food sources
Sodium	Helps maintain the balance of body fluids. Helps transmit nerve impulses.	Table salt, processed foods
Zinc	Promotes normal growth and development. Helps the immune system work properly. Helps wounds heal.	Meat, fish, poultry, whole grains, some legumes
Vitamins Vitamin A	Helps keep skin clear and smooth and mucous membranes healthy. Helps prevent night blindness. Helps promote growth.	Liver, egg yolk, dark green and yellow fruits and vegetables, butter, whole milk, cream, fortified margarine, ice cream, Cheddar-type cheese
Vitamin D	Helps build strong bones and teeth in children. Helps maintain bones in adults.	Fortified milk and margarine, butter, fish liver oils, liver, sardines, tuna, egg yolk, the sun
Vitamin E	Acts as an antioxidant.	Liver and other variety meats, eggs, leafy green vegetables, whole grain cereals, salad oils, shortenings and other fats and oils
Vitamin K	Helps blood clot.	Organ meats, leafy green vegetables, other vegetables, egg yolk
Thiamin	Helps promote normal appetite and digestion. Forms parts of the coenzymes needed for the breakdown of carbohydrates. Helps keep nervous system healthy and prevents irritability. Helps body release energy from food.	Pork, other meats, poultry, fish, eggs, enriched or whole grain breads and cereals, dried beans, brewer's yeast
Riboflavin	Helps cells use oxygen. Helps keep skin, tongue, and lips normal. Helps prevent scaly, greasy areas around the mouth and nose. Forms part of the coenzymes needed for the breakdown of carbohydrates.	Milk, all kinds of cheese, ice cream, liver, other meats, fish, poultry, eggs, dark green leafy vegetables
Niacin	Helps keep nervous system healthy. Helps keep skin, mouth, tongue, and digestive tract healthy. Helps cells use other nutrients.	Meat, fish, poultry, milk, enriched or whole grain breads and cereals, peanuts, peanut butter, dried beans and peas
Folate	Helps the body make all new cells. Protects unborn babies from damage to the brain and spinal cord.	Fresh fruits and vegetables, enriched and whole grain breads and cereals
Vitamin B_{12}	Helps the body make red blood cells. Protects nerves.	Meat, fish, poultry, eggs, dairy products, fortified soy milk
Vitamin C	Is needed for healthy gums and tissues. Helps heal wounds and broken bones. Helps body fight infection. Helps hold body cells together.	Citrus fruits, strawberries, cantaloupe, broccoli, green peppers, raw cabbage, tomatoes, green leafy vegetables, potatoes, sweet potatoes
Water	Is a basic part of blood and tissue fluid. Helps carry nutrients to cells. Helps carry waste products from cells. Helps control body temperature.	Water, beverages, soups, most foods

14-9 (Continued)

Resource:
What About Supplements? reproducible master, TR

Enrich:
Interview someone who has participated in a well-known diet program. Find out if he or she included foods listed in Chart 14-9 in the diet's suggested food choices.

Resource:
Nutrient Sources, Activity A, SAG

Activity:
Look through the food sources portion of this chart. Then list everything you ate yesterday. Which nutrients were probably lacking in your diet?

Citizenship and Service
Have students plan a school-wide activity for collecting foods for a local food pantry. Before conducting the drive, discuss the concept of nutrient density and help students develop a list of nonperishable foods that are nutrient dense. Students can then focus their drive on these types of foods.

> **Note:**
> Updated information on the DRIs can be found at the Web site of the National Academy of Sciences, www4.national academies.org/news.nsf.
>
> **Resource:**
> *Key Nutrients,* reproducible master, TR
>
> **Resource:**
> *Nutrient Functions,* Activity B, SAG

nutrients discussed in this text. Review this chart to help make sure your diet includes the variety of foods you need for good health.

Recommended Nutrient Intakes

To help you determine your daily nutrient needs, the **Recommended Dietary Allowances (RDA)** were established in 1941. The Food and Nutrition Board of the National Academy of Sciences developed the RDA through much scientific study. From time to time, the RDA are revised to reflect the latest nutrition studies. A recent revision made RDAs one of four types of reference values that can be used for planning and assessing diets. These four types of values are jointly called *Dietary Reference Intakes (DRIs).*

The DRIs outline nutrient requirements for each sex and for several age groups. Allowances include needs for energy, protein, and many vitamins and minerals. Allowances given in the DRIs are designed to meet the needs of healthy people. The DRIs are not useful guides for people who have special dietary needs. See 14-10.

14-10 Choosing a variety of nutritious foods for meals throughout the day will help you meet the DRIs for needed nutrients.

> **Check It Out!**
> 1. Chemical substances from food, which the body uses to function properly, are called _____.
> 2. What are the three kinds of carbohydrates?
> 3. What is the difference between a complete protein and an incomplete protein?
> 4. Which nutrient serves as a concentrated source of food energy?
> 5. What are three good sources of calcium?
> 6. Which type of vitamins cannot be stored in the body to a great extent and need to be consumed daily?
> 7. What are two main functions of water in the body?
> 8. Why were the Recommended Dietary Allowances (RDA) established?

> **Check It Out! (Answers)**
> 1. nutrients
> 2. sugars, starches, fiber
> 3. Complete proteins supply all the amino acids the body needs. Incomplete proteins contain some, but not all, of the amino acids the body needs.
> 4. fats
> 5. (List three:) milk, cheese, pudding, dark green leafy vegetables
> 6. water-soluble vitamins
> 7. (List two:) carries nutrients to cells, carries waste products from cells, aids in digestion, controls body temperature
> 8. The Recommended Dietary Allowances (RDA) were established to help people determine their daily nutrient needs.

Topic 14-2
Making Daily Food Choices

Objectives
After studying this topic, you will be able to
- plan a well-balanced diet based on the Food Guide Pyramid.
- list the Dietary Guidelines for Americans.

Topic Terms
Food Guide Pyramid
Dietary Guidelines for Americans

Eating right requires more than knowing the names of the nutrients. You also need to know how to choose a variety of foods that will supply those nutrients.

The Food Guide Pyramid

An easy way to plan a nutritious diet is to choose foods from the Food Guide Pyramid. The **Food Guide Pyramid** is a model for making daily food choices, 14-11. It groups foods based on their similarity in nutrient content. The groups and their recommended numbers of daily servings are

- breads, cereals, rice, and pasta group (grains group)—6 to 11 servings
- vegetable group—3 to 5 servings
- fruit group—2 to 4 servings
- milk, yogurt, and cheese group (milk group)—2 to 3 servings
- meat, poultry, fish, dry beans, eggs, and nuts group (meat and beans group)—2 to 3 servings

The arrangement of the Pyramid will help you visualize the relationships among the five food groups. Note the bread, cereal, rice, and pasta group is at the base

Resource:
The Food Guide Pyramid, color transparency CT-12, TR

Discuss:
Compare the Food Guide Pyramid to the basic four food groups. Where have changes been made?

Resource:
Using the Food Guide Pyramid, Activity C, SAG

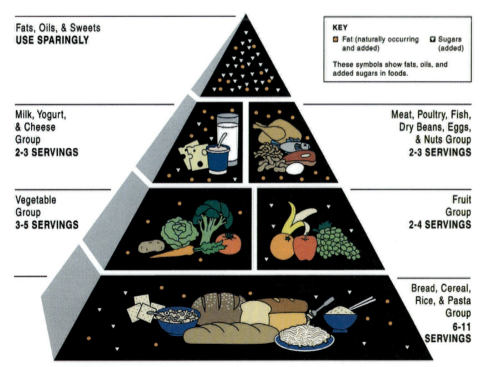

14-11 The Food Guide Pyramid illustrates the relationships among five main food groups that should make up the bulk of your diet.

Putting Technology to Use
Have students review the USDA's Center for Nutrition Policy and Promotion Web site at www.usda.gov/cnpp. Have them especially check the section on the nutrient content of the U.S. food supply. (Instructors may want to review *Using the Food Guide Pyramid: A Resource for Nutrition Educators*.)

of the Pyramid. This indicates foods from this group should form the foundation of your diet. Notice also that fats, oils, and sweets are at the tip of the Pyramid. This indicates these foods should be eaten in small amounts.

Grains Group

The bread, cereal, rice, and pasta group provides carbohydrates for energy. Enriched grain products are important sources of thiamin, niacin, and folate. Whole grain foods are high in fiber. Iron and some incomplete proteins are present in this group, too.

Foods in this group should form the foundation of your diet. Teen girls generally need to eat 9 servings from this group each day. Teen boys need 11 daily servings. Several of these servings should be whole grain sources.

Vegetable Group

The vegetable group includes all forms of vegetables: raw, cooked, canned, frozen, dried, and juices. Different vegetables provide different nutrients. However, cooking causes the loss of some nutrients. Therefore, fresh, raw vegetables tend to provide the greatest amounts of nutrients and fiber.

Many vegetables are good sources of vitamins A and C. Excellent sources of vitamin A include dark green and deep yellow vegetables, such as spinach, broccoli, carrots, and squash. Cabbage, peppers, and tomatoes are good sources of vitamin C.

Teen girls need four servings of vegetables each day; teen boys need five servings. Try to select one serving of a good source of vitamin C every day. Make a point of choosing one serving of a good source of vitamin A several times a week.

Fruit Group

The fruit group includes all forms of fruits. Like vegetables, fruits are excellent sources of fiber. The richest sources of vitamin C are citrus fruits, such as oranges and grapefruit. Cantaloupe, strawberries, and kiwifruit are also good sources of vitamin C. Bananas are a good source of potassium.

Three servings of fruits are recommended each day for teen girls. Four daily servings are recommended for teen boys. One serving should be rich in vitamin C. See 14-12.

Milk Group

Along with milk, yogurt, and cheese, the milk group includes milk-rich desserts, such as puddings and custards. These foods provide calcium, riboflavin, phosphorus, protein, and many other nutrients. Fortified milk is the major source of vitamin D in the diet.

Young people, ages 9 to 18 years, need three servings from this group each day. Adults over age 50 need three daily servings, too. Younger children and other adults need two servings. Servings are figured on the basis of calcium content equivalent to 1 cup of milk.

14-12 Choose a variety of fruits to get the recommended number of servings each day.

Resource:
Food Group Bingo, reproducible master, TR

Activity:
Check your food labels to see what else is considered one serving of the breads, cereals, rice, and pasta group.

Discuss:
How frequently are vegetables served in your family? Can favorite family recipes be improved to make them more appetizing?

Activity:
Check on the calories for various fruit servings. Which are some of the highest and lowest in calories?

Across the Curriculum

English. Have students choose one tropical fruit and prepare a research report on it. Have students include regions in which the fruit is found, climate in which it grows, and cost of importing it to the United States.

Meat and Beans Group

The meat and beans group includes meat, poultry, fish, and eggs. Other protein sources, such as nuts, dried beans, and dried peas, can be used as meat alternates. Protein, iron, and B vitamins are found in this group. Teen boys need the equivalent of seven ounces of lean, cooked meat each day. Teen girls need the equivalent of six ounces of meat. This means you should eat approximately two to three servings from the meat and beans group daily.

When choosing the recommended number of daily servings from each food group, you need to know how big a serving is. Chart 14-13 identifies serving sizes for each of the groups in the Food Guide Pyramid.

Fats, Oils, and Sweets

Fats, oils, and sweets include such foods as butter, jam, honey, and salad dressing. These foods provide little more than fat and sugar in the diet. There is nothing wrong with enjoying these foods as long as you use them sparingly.

Many foods in the five main food groups also contain significant amounts of fats and sugars. For instance, a hamburger, which is in the meat and beans group, supplies 16 grams of fat. Fruit-flavored yogurt, which is in the milk group, provides seven teaspoons of added sugar. You need to be aware of all sources of fats and sugars in your diet when planning your food choices.

Note: Show the class a 5-7 ounce portion of meat. Ask if they think people generally eat this amount or its equivalent daily.

Discuss: How much peanut butter do you put on a sandwich? What is the equivalent in ounces of meat? What does the jelly add to this sandwich?

Resource: *A Guide to Daily Food Choices*, reproducible master, TR

How Big Is a Serving?

Food Group	Serving Sizes
Bread, cereal, rice, and pasta group	• 1 slice of bread • 1 cup ready-to-eat cereal • ½ cup cooked cereal, rice, or pasta
Vegetable group	• 1 cup raw leafy vegetables • ½ cup other raw or cooked vegetables • ¾ cup vegetable juice
Fruit group	• 1 medium apple, banana, orange, or pear • ½ cup chopped, cooked, or canned fruit • ¾ cup fruit juice
Milk, yogurt, and cheese group	• 1 cup milk, yogurt, or calcium-fortified soy milk • 1½ ounces natural cheese • 2 ounces process cheese
Meat, poultry, fish, dry beans, eggs, and nuts group	• 2-3 ounces cooked lean meat, poultry, or fish Count the following as 1 ounce of lean meat: • ½ cup cooked dry beans • ½ cup tofu • 2½-ounce soyburger • 1 egg • 2 tablespoons peanut butter • ⅓ cup nuts

14-13 Becoming familiar with serving sizes for each food group will help you make sure you are meeting your daily nutrient needs.

Putting Technology to Use

Have students compare the varieties of yogurt for serving size and calorie content. Make sure they include some artificially sweetened brands. Have the students use charting software to make a chart illustrating their findings. Students should then print their charts on overhead transparency film and use the transparency to present their charts to the class.

Discuss:
Compare the 2000 Dietary Guidelines for Americans on this page with the 1990 and 1995 Guidelines. What changes were made? Why do you think they were made?

Discuss:
What is considered a healthy weight for teens your age? Do teens feel pressured to fit in this weight range?

Discuss:
People mistakenly believe that pasta is fattening. Do you know people who cut out pasta when on a diet? What should you say to them?

The Dietary Guidelines for Americans

To help people choose healthful diets, the U.S. Departments of Agriculture and Health and Human Services have suggested **Dietary Guidelines for Americans.** See 14-14. The 10 Dietary Guidelines are described in the following paragraphs.

Aim for a healthy weight. If you are overweight or underweight, you are more likely to develop health problems. Overweight is linked with high blood pressure, heart disease, stroke, certain cancers, and other illnesses. Underweight people have little to lose in the event of a wasting illness. You will read about how to manage your weight in Topic 14-4.

Be physically active each day. Regular physical activity helps lower the risk of heart disease. It also builds and maintains strong bones and muscles. Throughout your teen years, you need to spend at least 60 minutes a day enjoying moderate physical activity. As you grow older, you need to keep including at least 30 minutes of moderate activity in your daily schedule.

Let the Pyramid guide your food choices. No single food can supply all the nutrients in the amounts you need. For example, milk supplies calcium but little iron. Meat supplies protein but little calcium. To have a nutritious diet, you must eat a variety of foods. Try to eat the recommended number of servings from each group in the Food Guide Pyramid every day. Also, be sure to choose a selection of foods from each group. This is the best way to get the range of nutrients you need.

Choose a variety of grains daily, especially whole grains. Select a variety of breads, cereals, pasta, and rice every day. These foods are rich in complex carbohydrates—your body's best source of energy. Whole grain foods, such as oatmeal, popcorn, and whole wheat bread, supply fiber to help your digestive system work properly.

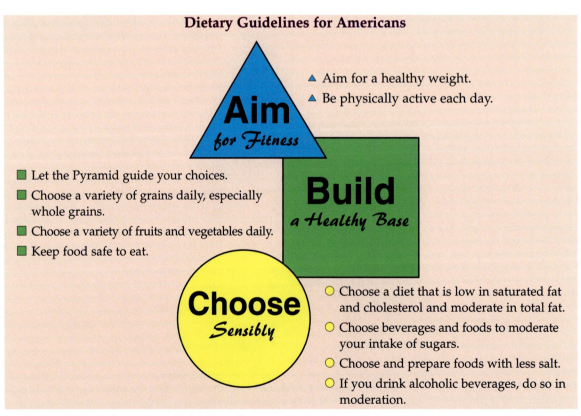

14-14 Following the Dietary Guidelines for Americans can help people form eating and activity habits that contribute to good health.

Family Enrichment Activity
Have students work with their families to analyze their eating habits and choose one habit they would like to improve. Examples include too many high-fat meals, frequent eating on the run, lack of planning for food intake, or frequent snacking. Students can make use of knowledge about nutrition and eating habits, plus application of the decision-making process, to help his or her family brainstorm possible solutions, choose one or more, and make a plan to carry out the changes.

Choose a variety of fruits and vegetables daily. Eat different types of fruits and vegetables to get the full range of nutrients these healthful foods provide. Include green leafy vegetables, orange fruits and vegetables, and dried beans and peas in your diet regularly. A varied diet based on these foods supplies vitamins, minerals, fiber, and complex carbohydrates. Such a diet is also generally low in fat.

Keep food safe to eat. Eating food that has not been handled properly can sometimes make people sick. To keep foods safe to eat, you need to follow four safety measures—clean, separate, cook, and chill. Use hot, soapy water to keep hands, utensils, and surfaces clean throughout food preparation. Keep raw foods separated from cooked and ready-to-eat foods while shopping, preparing, and storing. Use a food thermometer to make sure foods are cooked to a safe internal temperature. Chill perishable foods by storing them in the refrigerator or freezer within two hours of purchase or preparation. You will read more about how to keep foods safe to eat in Topic 16-2.

Choose a diet that is low in saturated fat and cholesterol and moderate in total fat. Diets high in saturated fat and cholesterol increase the risk for heart disease. High-fat diets are also linked to obesity and certain types of cancer. The total fat in your diet should not provide more than 30 percent of the calories you consume. No more than 10 percent of your total calories should be from saturated fat. You should also limit your intake of foods high in cholesterol, such as butter, liver, and egg yolks.

Choose beverages and foods to moderate your intake of sugars. Many beverages and foods that are high in sugar supply calories but are limited in nutrients. Such foods include soft drinks, cookies, ice cream, and candy. Limiting your use of these foods may help you avoid unwanted pounds and cut down on tooth decay. Watch for ingredient labels that list brown sugar, honey, corn syrup, molasses, sucrose, dextrose, glucose, and fructose. These are all forms of sugar.

Choose and prepare foods with less salt. Salt contains sodium, which contributes to high blood pressure in some people. Sodium is naturally present in many foods. It has been added to others during processing. You should use salt sparingly in cooking and at the table, 14-15. You can read labels to avoid selecting foods that are high in sodium. Convenience foods, such as packaged mixes, frozen entrees, and canned soups and vegetables, tend to be high in sodium. Condiments, like soy sauce, salad dressing, catsup, and mustard, are high in sodium, too. Many snack foods, such as chips, crackers, pretzels, and nuts, are also highly salted.

If you drink alcoholic beverages, do so in moderation. Alcoholic beverages supply little more than calories. Many health problems are linked to alcohol consumption, including addiction, liver disease, and some cancers. Many accidents also result from the use of alcohol.

14-15 Make foods flavorful by seasoning them with herbs instead of salt.

Activity:
Check the class collection of food labels for foods that are high in sugars, but supply very few other nutrients.

Activity:
Compare labels from a variety of products for salt content. Draw conclusions as to which types of food products are highest in salt content.

Note:
It is illegal for teens to purchase and consume alcoholic beverages.

Across the Curriculum

Math. Have students find out how to determine the amount of fat and saturated fat in their diets so they can follow the 30 percent and 10 percent guidelines. Ask them to report their findings to the class.

Discuss:
Why and how do you think each of these would affect nutritional needs: gender, body size, activity level, health?

The Dietary Guidelines are based on research about how diet may relate to health problems, like heart disease, hypertension, and cancer. Their aim is to help people in the United States form healthful eating and activity patterns. Following the Dietary Guidelines cannot guarantee people they will never get sick. However, eating and activity habits do have an effect on health. Forming good habits can keep healthy people looking and feeling well.

Check It Out!
1. List the five main food groups in the Food Guide Pyramid. Give the recommended range of daily servings for each group.
2. On what are the Dietary Guidelines for Americans based?

Check It Out! (Answers)
1. bread, cereals, rice, and pasta group—6 to 11 servings; vegetable group—3 to 5 servings; fruit group—2 to 4 servings; milk, yogurt, and cheese group—2 to 3 servings; meat, poultry, fish, dry beans, eggs, and nuts—2 to 3 servings
2. The Dietary Guidelines are based on research about how diet may relate to health problems, such as heart disease, hypertension, and cancer.

Topic 14-3
Nutritional Needs Change

Objectives
After studying this topic, you will be able to
- identify dietary needs of people in different stages of life.
- describe special nutrient needs of athletes.

Topic Terms
vegetarian diet
dehydration

All people need the same nutrients. However, the amounts needed vary from person to person. For instance, women need more iron than men. Someone who has a large body build needs more food than someone who has a small build. People who perform hard physical work need more nutrients than those who lead less-active lives, 14-16. A person who has a disease or is recovering from illness needs more nutrients than one who is in good health.

14-16 People who do work that is physically demanding need more calories to fuel their high level of activity.

Nutritional needs vary with age as well as with gender, body size, activity level, and health. Needs change throughout the life cycle. Meal managers need to know how to meet the needs of people at different ages.

Needs of Pregnant Women and Infants

Nutritional needs begin before birth. Pregnant women must eat foods that will supply nutrients for their babies as well as for themselves. Once babies are born, they have tremendous nutrient needs to support their rapid growth.

Nutrition Before Birth

An unborn child has no way to get nutrients except through the mother's diet. Thus, the mother's body needs to be well nourished prior to and during pregnancy. Pregnant teenagers have more difficulty meeting the needs of their developing babies than pregnant adults. This is because teenagers must fulfill their own nutrient needs for growth as well as the needs of the growing baby.

Women who have good eating habits will not need to make drastic dietary changes before or during pregnancy. Consuming two to three daily servings from the milk group will provide the calcium needed during pregnancy. Two added servings from the grains group will help meet increased calorie needs. An extra serving from both the fruit and vegetable groups will provide needed vitamins, minerals, and fiber. Doctors may also prescribe nutrient supplements to help meet increased needs during pregnancy.

Nutrition in Infancy

Every part of a child's body grows and develops most rapidly during the first year of life. Good nutrition is most important during this year to build a strong foundation for a healthy lifetime.

Breast milk or formula is a baby's first food. Breast milk is perfectly designed to meet most of a baby's nutrient needs. Formula also provides needed nutrients, but health professionals agree that breast milk is the best choice for infant nutrition. To protect her health while breast-feeding, a mother needs to maintain a good diet. See 14-17.

Babies need vitamin C early in life. Breast milk contains vitamin C. However, fortified apple juice may be given when babies reach about six to eight months of age. Doctors may also recommend vitamin supplements for babies.

Doctors have differing opinions as to when solid foods should first be offered to infants. However, most doctors agree that babies should not be given solid foods before four months of age. Cereals are generally introduced first. Other foods are then introduced gradually. Soon, babies should be eating a variety of foods from all the food groups.

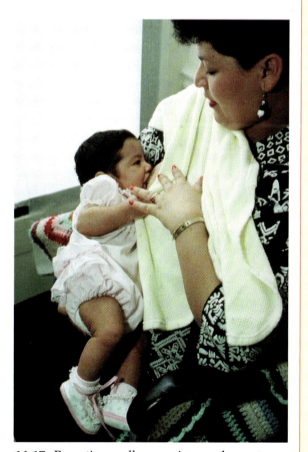

14-17 By eating well, a nursing mother gets the extra nutrients her body needs to make milk for her baby.

Activity:
Have the students keep a diary of their eating habits for several days. Are they meeting their nutritional needs? Could they handle the additional needs of a developing baby?

Note:
Remind students it is important for women to follow healthful eating habits *before* getting pregnant to ensure the health of the developing baby.

Enrich:
Have the students survey parents and friends to find out when infants in their families were given solid foods. What did their doctors recommend? Did they follow the doctors' suggestions?

Across the Curriculum

Biology. Discuss the nutritional needs of infants and the way breast milk meets these needs. Have students name other animals that nurse their young. Reinforce that this classification of animal, of which humans are a part, is *mammals*. This name is derived from the Latin term *mammalis*, meaning *of the breast*. Mammals secrete milk in their mammary glands.

Resource:
Food for Young Children, reproducible master, TR

Discuss:
What kinds of snacks are appropriate to serve preschoolers?

Reflect:
Do you know of any foods you dislike that your parents also disliked? Do you think your dislikes are related?

Enrich:
Talk to school cafeteria personnel about government regulations concerning what they serve. Ask if the children eat what they are served.

As children grow teeth and learn to control chewing and swallowing, table foods can replace strained baby foods. Foods should be cut into small pieces and offered in small servings. As energy needs increase, larger servings can be offered.

Needs of Children and Teens

As children grow, their nutritional needs continue to change. Their food preferences also change. Caregivers must help children select a variety of well-liked foods from each of the food groups.

Nutrition During the Preschool Years

Adults and children need the same nutrients. However, preschool children need larger proportions of nutrients to support their rapid growth. Caregivers need to make a special effort to include vitamins A and C in the diets of preschoolers. Raw fruits and vegetables, which are good sources of these vitamins, can be offered as snacks.

Most preschoolers cannot eat enough at mealtimes to meet all their nutrient needs. Thus, snacks are needed to supplement nutrients provided by meals. In addition to fruits and vegetables, cheese cubes, cereals, and crackers spread with peanut butter make nutritious snacks.

Adults play a key role in teaching preschoolers good eating habits. Children are great imitators. If an adult refuses a certain food, a preschool child is likely to refuse it, too. Adults can encourage good nutrition by offering children a variety of nutritious food choices. Adults also need to set an example by eating nutritious foods themselves.

Nutrition During the Early School Years

Starting school changes a child's daily routine and eating schedule. A nutritious, energy-packed breakfast is needed to help children stay alert in class.

While at school, children are exposed to the eating habits of others. They may refuse a food simply because their peers do not eat it. Children may sometimes need to be encouraged to eat well-balanced lunches in the school cafeteria. They need the energy and nutrients provided by milk, breads, meats, fruits, and vegetables. See 14-18.

Nutrition During the Teen Years

Like infancy, adolescence is a period of rapid growth. Teens are growing taller and gaining weight. Their bones are increasing in density. Their muscles are developing in size and strength.

All this growth creates great nutritional needs for teens. However, busy schedules often cause teens to skip meals. Many teens also select snack foods that are high in fats and sugars and low in other nutrients. Therefore, nutrient needs do not always get met.

Meals and snacks for teens need to be carefully planned. They must provide all the nutrients needed for growth and

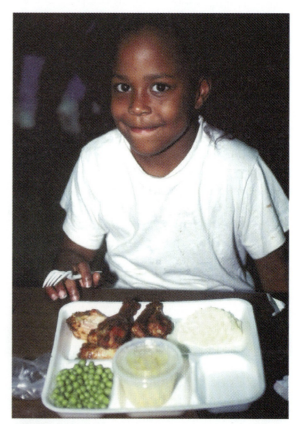

14-18 Balanced meals provided by the school lunch program are designed to meet the nutrient and energy needs of young children.

Putting Technology to Use
Have students review the informational material about the Children's Food Guide Pyramid at USDA's Web site, www.usda.gov/cnpp/KidsPyra/index.htm.

maintenance of strong, healthy bodies. Foods must also supply enough energy to meet a teen's high level of activity.

Special Needs of Vegetarians

During the teen years, many young people try new eating patterns. One of these patterns for a number of teens is a **vegetarian diet.** This is a pattern of eating that is made up largely or entirely of foods from plant sources. People choose to follow vegetarian diets for various reasons. These reasons include health, economy, religion, animal rights, and availability.

People who follow vegetarian diets may be called *vegetarians.* Several types of vegetarians exist. They are described by the types of animal foods they consume.

- *Vegans* consume no foods of animal origin.
- *Lacto vegetarians* exclude meat, poultry, fish, and eggs but include dairy products.
- *Ovo vegetarians* omit meat, poultry, fish, and dairy products but include eggs.
- *Lacto-ovo vegetarians* do not eat meat, poultry, or fish. However, they include eggs and dairy products in their diets.

The key to good eating is a variety of foods from many sources. Thus, total exclusion of animal food sources may lead to some deficiencies. Vegetarian diets can be healthful, but they require planning.

As you have read, animal foods serve as main sources of complete protein as well as other nutrients. By combining incomplete proteins, vegetarians can get all the amino acids they need. Vegetarians who consume eggs and/or dairy products can usually meet their needs for other nutrients, too. Those who omit dairy products from their diets may have difficulty getting enough calcium and vitamin D. Vegans may also have trouble meeting their needs for iron, zinc, and vitamin B_{12}. Some vegetarians may need fortified foods or supplements to meet all their nutrient needs. Refer again to Chart 14-9. It will help you review some rich sources of protein, calcium, iron, zinc, vitamin B_{12}, and vitamin D.

Special Needs of Athletes

Many children and teens take part in athletic activities. These athletes and their parents often ask how added physical activity affects nutritional needs. In most cases, athletes do not need dietary supplements. Eating a nutritious diet each day is the best way to meet nutrient needs. Athletes need to follow the same Dietary Guidelines suggested for all healthy people, with four minor changes, 14-19.

Increase Daily Calorie Intake

Athletes need extra calories to fuel high levels of activity. For best performance, 60 to 65 percent of calories should come from complex carbohydrates, such as breads, cereals, and pasta. Protein should supply 12 to 15 percent of calories. Fat should provide the remaining 20 to 25 percent.

14-19 Making a few small adjustments to a healthful diet can help teen athletes meet their nutrient needs.

Discuss:
Do you know any vegetarians? Are they vegans, lacto vegetarians, ovo vegetarians, or lacto-ovo vegetarians?

Enrich:
Write a report about how professional athletes alter their diets to improve performance in their sports.

Activity:
Survey athletes in your school to see how they meet their nutritional needs.

Across the Curriculum
Health. Have students interview school sports coaches about what they tell athletes regarding their diets. For instance, have students interview a wrestling coach about the use of weight supplements and weight loss for wrestlers.

Activity:
Read the labels on drinks designed for athletes. What claims do these drinks make about enhancing performance? Are they better than just drinking water?

Discuss:
How have your calorie needs changed since junior high? Do you gain weight eating the same foods you ate when you were younger?

Resource:
Nutritional Needs Change, reproducible master, TR

Eating a small meal three to four hours before a workout or competition will provide needed energy. This meal should be high in carbohydrates, which are stored in the body as glycogen. Excess fats and proteins from the meal will be stored as body fat. During activity, the body can more easily release energy from glycogen than from body fat.

Drink Plenty of Fluids

Drinking fluids during activity helps prevent **dehydration**, or an abnormal loss of body fluids. Athletes lose a lot of water through sweating. They need to be sure they drink enough to replace those losses. Thirst does not always indicate fluid needs. Fluid intake should begin two hours before exercise and continue at fifteen-minute intervals throughout exercise. Liquids should also be consumed after exercising.

Water is a good fluid choice for athletes. It is easily absorbed and rarely causes cramping. Beverages containing caffeine should be avoided because they can cause dehydration.

Eat Plenty of Iron-Rich Foods

Iron helps the blood carry needed oxygen to muscles during physical activity. Good sources are lean meats, leafy green vegetables, and enriched and whole grain breads.

Meet Daily Calcium Needs

Meeting the daily requirement for calcium is especially important for female athletes. Calcium helps build strong bones that are more resistant to stress fractures. Dairy products and leafy green vegetables are good calcium sources.

Needs of Adults

By the time people reach their early twenties, their bodies are generally considered to be physically mature. Gradually, metabolism begins to slow, causing adults to need fewer calories. If adults do not decrease their food intake, they are likely to put on weight.

The need for nutrients during adulthood does not diminish along with the need for calories. The body tissues that have been developed must now be maintained. The diet needs to supply adequate amounts of protein, minerals, and vitamins. These nutrients will help keep the body healthy.

Meals and snacks for adults need to include foods that will supply nutrients along with calories. For instance, fruit juices are better choices than cola beverages, which provide little more than calories. For desserts, fresh fruits are a nutritious alternative to pies, cakes, or cookies.

Nutrition for Older Adults

Many older adults are less active than younger adults. This causes them to need fewer calories. However, older adults still need about the same amounts of most other nutrients as they did when they were younger. The need for calcium actually increases for adults over age 50. See 14-20.

14-20 Because older adults are often less active than younger adults, they need fewer calories from foods.

FCCLA Activity

Planning a Dinner for Older Adults, reproducible master, TR. Use the questions on the master to help chapter members make the necessary decisions for planning a dinner for a group of older adults. Older adults can be from a local senior care center, retirement community, religious organization, or simply friends or relatives of chapter members.

Physical changes caused by the aging process can affect the eating habits of older adults. Such obstacles need to be kept in mind when planning meals. For instance, people who have trouble chewing may find it easier to eat softer foods, such as pudding and applesauce. People who have sensitive stomachs may prefer milder versions of spicy foods like chili.

While some changes may be necessary in the diets of older adults, it is important that foods remain appealing. Older adults must be willing to eat the foods they are served for their nutrient needs to be met.

Nutrition Needs of People Who Are Ill

People who are sick usually have additional nutrient needs. Fevers, vomiting, or diarrhea create the need for more water than usual to replace lost fluids. People recovering from some illnesses, as well as surgery, need additional protein. The need for some vitamins and minerals, such as vitamin C and zinc, also increases.

Those with diseases such as diabetes mellitus, cancer, and HIV/AIDS require a medical diet. These diets are prescribed by doctors and registered dieticians. For instance, people with diabetes must learn to limit their sugar intakes while still eating a diet high in complex carbohydrates.

Check It Out!
1. Why do pregnant teenagers have more difficulty meeting the needs of their developing babies than pregnant adults?
2. What are four modifications athletes need to make in their diets?
3. True or false. Adults need more calories than teenagers.

Check It Out! (Answers)
1. Pregnant teenagers must fulfill their own nutrient needs for growth as well as the needs of the growing baby.
2. increase daily calorie intake, drink plenty of fluids, eat plenty of iron-rich foods, meet daily calcium needs
3. false

Topic 14-4
Balancing Calories and Energy Needs

Objectives
After studying this topic, you will be able to:
- identify factors that affect energy needs for metabolic and physical activity.
- outline guidelines for healthy weight loss and healthy weight gain.
- describe two common eating disorders.

Topic Terms
calorie
basal metabolism
body mass index (BMI)
overweight
obese
underweight
anorexia nervosa
bulimia nervosa

Energy is needed to support every activity of your body. From sleeping to running a marathon race, your body constantly requires energy. You obtain needed energy from carbohydrates, fats, and proteins in the foods you eat. This food energy is measured in units called **calories.** Learning to balance your calorie intake against your calorie needs will help you maintain a healthy weight.

When choosing foods, you need to be aware that some foods produce more energy per serving than others. Foods high in fats, such as fried foods and ice cream, are higher in calories than other foods. Foods with high water content, such as watermelon, tomatoes, and lettuce, are lower in calories per serving. See 14-21.

Meeting Energy Needs

People differ in their calorie needs. Needs are based on a person's age, sex, body size, and level of physical activity. The body needs energy to support both metabolic and physical activity.

Resource:
Menu Planning, Activity D, SAG

Vocabulary:
Predict how many pounds above average weight makes a person overweight and obese.

Discuss:
Do you think about the calories in the foods you eat? What foods do you consider to be high in calories? low in calories?

> **Discuss:**
> How do you think these characteristics influence a person's calorie needs: age, sex, body size, level of physical activity?
>
> **Enrich:**
> Find a chart that shows the number of calories burned up when doing various physical activities. Which activities burn the most calories in the least amount of time?
>
> **Resource:**
> Balancing Calories and Energy Needs, reproducible master, TR

14-21 Tomatoes, lettuce, and the other ingredients in this salad are high in water content and thus low in calories.

Metabolic Energy Needs

Even when you sleep, your body is working. Your heart keeps pumping blood. Your lungs keep drawing oxygen. Your tissues are being built and repaired. These life-sustaining activities are collectively called **basal metabolism.** Basal metabolism accounts for the energy required when your body is at physical, emotional, and digestive rest.

The *basal metabolic rate (BMR)* varies greatly from person to person. The BMR is higher while a person is growing. Thus, the BMR of children and teenagers is greater than that of adults. This is why people need to decrease the amount of food they eat when they get older. Older people do not need as many calories to sustain their body processes as younger people.

Other factors, such as glandular secretions and body temperature, can affect your metabolic energy needs. For instance, when there is an undersecretion by the thyroid gland, basal metabolism is lower. When there is an oversecretion, basal metabolism is higher. The higher your body temperature is, the greater your metabolic needs are. Therefore, when you have a fever, your basal metabolism will be higher.

Energy for Physical Activities

Physical activity raises energy needs above basal requirements. Whenever you use your muscles, you use energy. The amount of energy you need is related to the amount of work you do. For instance, you need more energy to walk than to sit and rest. You need more energy to run than to walk. If your level of physical activity is light, you will need fewer calories to fulfill your energy needs. If you are very active, you will need more calories to meet your energy needs.

Controlling Your Weight

Weight management involves both eating and physical activity. The foods you eat give your body energy, which is measured in calories. When you are active, you burn these calories. To control your weight, you need to compare the calories you eat to the calories you burn.

How Much Should You Weigh?

To set goals for weight management, you need to know what your weight should be for good health. Health professionals assess the weight of adults in terms of their height using a calculation called **body mass index (BMI).** As shown in Chart 14-22, a BMI of 18.5 up to 25 refers to a healthy weight. A BMI of 25 up to 30 is viewed as **overweight.** A BMI over 30 is considered **obese.**

The source of your weight is a factor in determining whether it is healthy. Bone, muscle, and fat all contribute to body weight. Too much weight from fat is considered unhealthy. This is true even for some people who have a BMI in the healthy range. A BMI above the healthy weight range is less healthy for most people.

On the other hand, bone and muscle tissues weigh more than fat tissue. Therefore, someone who has a BMI in the overweight range due to a large muscle

Across the Curriculum

Health. Have students keep a log of their hourly activities for one week. They should give a motion value to each of their actions, such as three points for very active, two points for moderately active, and one point for inactive. (Decide as a class what activities fit into each category.) After a week, have them total points for each day and compare with classmates. Students should then write a paragraph stating their conclusions regarding level of activity and weight.

Topic 14-4   Balancing Calories and Energy Needs

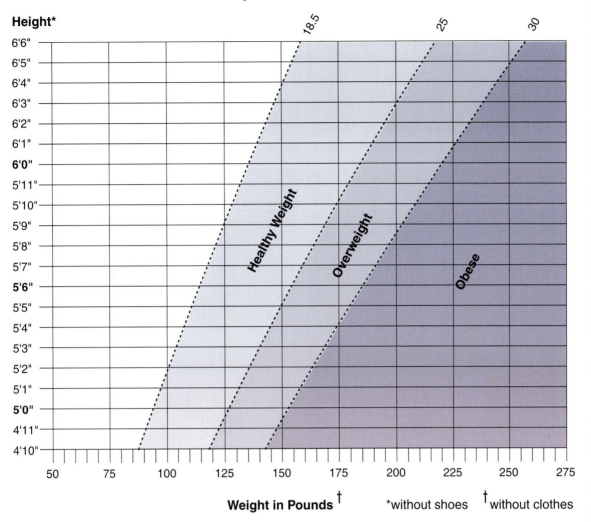

14-22 Balancing calories and energy needs allows people to stay within a healthy weight range for their height.

Reflect:
Where do you and most of your peers fall on this chart? Do you think it's an accurate measuring device? What variables determine where you fall on this chart?

Enrich:
Research weight loss programs offered in your community. Find out how they differ in their approach to weight loss.

mass may not be unhealthy. Men generally have more bone and muscle than women. Therefore, men tend to fall at the upper ends of the BMI ranges. Women tend to fall at the lower ends.

Before considering a weight loss program, people need to think about factors that affect their appearance and weight. Having a large frame will give the body a larger appearance. However, frame size is based on bone structure, which is inherited. No weight reduction program will change the size of the body frame.

Healthy Weight Loss

Many people have a goal to lose unwanted pounds. Sometimes these pounds are the result of glandular activity that affects metabolism. However, most people gain weight because they consume more calories than they burn. The excess calories are stored as fat. As fat stores accumulate, weight gain occurs.

Obesity is one of today's major health problems. Obese individuals are more likely to develop high blood pressure, diabetes, and heart disease. Obesity may

Problem-Solving Practice
Meeting Differing Nutritional Needs, reproducible master, TR. After completing the study of Chapter 14, have students work individually or in small groups to complete the master.

> **Discuss:**
> What diet aids and plans have you heard about that offer fast results? Do you know people who have tried them? Did they actually lose weight and keep it off?
>
> **Resource:**
> *Analyzing a Diet,* Activity E, SAG
>
> **Reflect:**
> Do you know people who are underweight? What are some of their problems and complaints? Do they get sympathy from any of their friends?
>
> **Resource:**
> *Your Individual Weight Control Plan,* reproducible master, TR

also have a negative impact on a person's self-concept.

For many overweight people, reaching a healthy weight is easier said than done. Promises of quick weight loss in the form of "fad diets" are often tempting for these people. They may be attracted by diet aids and diet plans that promise fast results. Overweight people should beware of such promises. Dietitians agree there is no fast and easy way to lose weight. Weight loss should be a gradual process. It is best achieved by increasing physical activity and choosing sensible portions of healthful foods.

The following guidelines may help people who are trying to lose weight:

- Try to maintain a balance between food intake and physical activity. Avoid eating more calories than you burn.
- Try to spend at least 60 minutes each day in moderate physical activity. Plan to walk briskly, bike, swim, or jog. The more active you are, the more calories you burn. Schedule your physical activity about an hour before dinner. Vigorous activity helps suppress appetite. See 14-23.
- Base your diet on grains, vegetables, and fruits. Then select moderate portions of lowfat dairy products and lean meats, poultry, and fish. Limit foods that are high in fat and/or sugar. Read labels to determine the fat and sugar content of foods you eat.
- Avoid omitting any group of foods from your diet. You can reduce portion sizes, but continue eating a variety of nutritious foods.
- Avoid making drastic changes in your food intake without the advice of your doctor. A high percentage of people who lose weight by radically changing their diet habits regain the weight.
- Beware of fad diets that focus on one or two foods. A variety of foods are needed for overall health and well-being.

During the teen years, your body is growing rapidly. You need calories to support this growth and to fuel your daily activity. Therefore, health experts generally recommend that teens avoid restricting calories or trying to lose weight. Instead, experts encourage most overweight teens to follow the tips above to avoid gaining more excess weight. The goal is to increase physical activity and make healthful food choices. These steps will help overweight teens grow into their present weight.

Healthy Weight Gain

Being underweight can have adverse effects on health just as being overweight can. People who have a BMI below 18.5 are considered **underweight.** People who are underweight may suffer from more infections. They also tend to have low energy levels and may chill easily.

People who are underweight should consult a physician before adjusting their eating habits to gain weight. This will help them determine if a physical or emotional problem is preventing them from gaining weight. To gain weight, choose nutritious foods from the groups in the Food Guide Pyramid that provide more calories per serving. Increasing portion sizes and adding nutritious snacks will add calories to the diet. Eating five or six small meals rather than three large meals each day will also foster weight gain.

14-23 Although exercise is important for everyone, it can have extra benefits for people who are trying to lose weight.

Across the Curriculum

English. Have students research and write a report on obesity in the United States. What trends did students find? What steps are being taken to address these trends?

Eating Disorders

Many people have poor eating habits. They may not eat a wide variety of foods, or they may eat too many high-fat foods. However, an *eating disorder* is an abnormal eating pattern that actually threatens a person's health.

Eating disorders are not limited to a certain group of people. However, those most likely to develop eating disorders are young women and teenage girls.

Two common eating disorders are anorexia nervosa and bulimia nervosa. These disorders are mental as well as physical illnesses. They often involve skewed views of food and body shape and unnatural fears of weight gain.

Anorexia nervosa is an eating disorder in which a person avoids eating, sometimes to the point of starvation. This complex problem is based on a strong need to feel thin. Anorexics often have psychological problems that cause them to have distorted self-images. No matter how much weight they lose, they still see themselves as fat.

The effects of anorexia nervosa on health can be devastating. Body temperature drops, and females may stop menstruating. Skin becomes dry and hair becomes dull. Failure to meet nutrient needs can cause heart damage and loss of bone and muscle tissue. Severe cases can result in death. Even those who recover may have sustained permanent physical damage.

Bulimia nervosa is also known as the binge-purge syndrome. People who have this disorder go on eating binges and consume excessive amounts of calories. They then take steps to avoid weight gain. Some bulimics purge themselves of the food by vomiting or taking laxatives or diuretics. Other people with this disorder fast or exercise intensely to avoid weight gain. This binge-purge pattern is repeated at least twice a week. See 14-24.

Bulimia nervosa can take quite a toll on health. Frequent vomiting can erode the teeth and irritate the esophagus. Imbalances of body fluids can damage the heart and kidneys.

14-24 Rather than enjoying a single serving, someone who has bulimia nervosa might eat an entire dessert and then purge to avoid weight gain.

The earlier eating disorders are detected, the better the chances victims have of recovering with no serious medical problems. Treatment of an eating disorder may involve a team of health professionals. If needed, treatment begins with a hospital stay to combat malnutrition. Physicians attend to health problems that have resulted from the disorder. A dietitian can advise the patient on how to choose a healthful diet. A psychologist can offer counseling to address the underlying causes of the disorder. This helps victims understand their problems and learn to cope with them in healthy ways.

Check It Out!
1. A _____ is the unit used to measure food energy.
2. List five guidelines for people who are trying to lose weight.
3. True or false. Anorexia nervosa and bulimia nervosa require both physical and mental treatment.

Check It Out! (Answers)
1. calorie
2. (Student response. See page 428 in the text.)
3. true

Reflect:
Have you or any of your friends experienced any eating disorders?

Discuss:
What famous people have suffered and/or died from eating disorders?

Enrich:
Write a report on bulimia and/or anorexia.

Discuss:
Catherine Hankins states that "Sometimes major life events, such as death or divorce, can trigger cycles of overeating." Ask students if they agree with this statement.

TEENS ARE CONCERNED ABOUT...

Healthful Eating and Weight Management

Catherine Hankins, RD, LDN has a bachelor's degree in dietetics and has been working as a registered dietitian for 10 years. In addition to private counseling, she takes her message to the public through talks, exhibits, media presentations, and theatrics.

Q: *Who are most of your clients?*

A: The majority of my clients are adults. I also see many children and teens when I go into schools to teach classes or work at health fairs. Through these experiences, I have found that many teens are very interested in preventive health care.

Q: *Are there general dietary guidelines that everyone can follow?*

A: Yes. The USDA's Food Guide Pyramid is a good start. Our diets should focus on whole grain breads and cereals, rice, pasta, vegetables, fruits, and beans. Then we need to add moderate amounts of lean meats or meat substitutes and lowfat dairy products. Finally, we need to use added fats and sweets sparingly. Remember to eat a variety of foods. No one food or food group provides all your dietary needs.

Q: *When are vitamin supplements needed?*

A: When recommended by a healthcare professional. Using self-prescribed supplements can lead to nutritional imbalances. When taken, supplements should *supplement* an otherwise healthful diet.

Q: *What dietary questions and concerns do your teen clients have?*

A: Many teens are interested in how to maintain a healthy weight. Some want to lose weight; some want to gain weight. I also get questions about fad diets, eating disorders, and vegetarianism. Many teens have misconceptions about healthful eating and want professional advice.

Q: *Why do pregnant teens need dietary help?*

A: A teenager's body is still growing and developing. With the added needs of a growing baby, good nutrition is more important than ever. Good nutrition is needed not only to help the baby grow and develop but to help the teen stay healthy. Meeting the increased needs of pregnancy is especially important in a teen pregnancy.

Q: *What do you suggest to overweight teens?*

A: I encourage the teen to keep food and activity logs for several days. This assignment allows us to analyze the teen's diet compared to the Food

Guide Pyramid. It also allows us to see how active the teen is. We are able to compare the portion sizes the teen typically eats to what is considered an "average" portion. I find many overweight teens benefit from decreasing their intake of fat and sugar and increasing physical activity. Finally, we look at emotional issues that might be related to weight. Sometimes major life events, such as death or divorce, can trigger cycles of overeating.

Q: *Are there lifestyle factors other than food intake and activity level that overweight teens should be aware of?*

A: These days, we tend to "eat on the run" between school and extracurricular activities. A high-calorie fast-food meal here and a sugary vending machine snack there can, over time, lead to weight gain. It helps to plan meals and snacks ahead of time and then pack healthful food choices.

Q: *Do teen males appear to be as concerned about being overweight as teen females?*

A: Yes. Social pressures demand that males be muscular as much as social pressures demand that females be thin.

Q: *What do you suggest for a teen who is currently at a healthy weight?*

A: Eat a healthful, balanced diet with a variety of food choices. Make junk food the occasional exception rather than the norm. Limit fats and sweets and make sure you stay active.

Q: *What do you recommend for underweight teens?*

A: Eat nutritious meals and snacks five or six times a day. Consume nutritious higher-calorie snacks, such as nuts, dried fruits, and milk shakes. With the help of a nutrition professional, add a nutritional supplement when appropriate.

Q: *What do you think of protein supplements for athletes?*

A: Protein supplements are not needed. Increased muscle mass and endurance can be achieved through a healthful balanced diet and training. Increased protein intake doesn't necessarily result in increased muscle mass. Excessive protein intake can lead to dehydration and kidney damage.

Q: *What do you recommend for athletes such as wrestlers who diet to make weight class requirements for their sports?*

A: Continue to eat a healthful balanced diet and decrease portion sizes.

Q: *What advice do you offer those who suspect they might be developing an eating disorder?*

A: Get help as soon as possible. First, enlist the help of a trusted adult. Second, know that the most effective treatment seems to be threefold, involving a psychologist, physician, and registered dietitian. The psychologist can provide counseling about body image issues. The physician monitors health status, and the registered dietitian encourages healthier eating patterns. Third, depending on the severity of the eating disorder, remember that the healing process may take a long time. Be patient and honest with yourself.

Q: *How important is calcium in the diet of teens?*

A: Calcium helps develop strong teeth and bones. We develop the largest amount of our bone mass during our teen years and twenties. The denser your bones become as a young person, the less chance you have of developing osteoporosis at any age. A consistent intake of calcium is extremely important to teens. The best sources of calcium are dairy products like milk and cheese.

Q: *What would you like teens to know about sugar intake?*

A: I like to show teens how much sugar they consume by demonstrating that one 16-ounce bottle of regular soda contains 14 teaspoons of sugar. In addition to promoting tooth decay, an excessive sugar intake may promote obesity.

Q: *What are your recommendations regarding the intake of fluids?*

A: Water first! Then, fluids should be taken in from milk and 100% fruit and vegetable juices. Soda and other sweetened beverages should come last as sources of fluids. Drinking a caffeine-containing beverage actually increases your body's need for fluid. Exercise and heat also increase your need for extra fluid. A rule of thumb is to divide your body weight in pounds by two. The result is the number of ounces of fluid you need each day.

Q: *Why are we told that breakfast is the most important meal of the day?*

A: Breakfast jump-starts your body's metabolism in the morning. It helps you burn calories and generate energy for work and play. It also gives your brain the energy it needs to think. Studies show that students who eat breakfast perform better mentally and physically. They get higher test scores and better grades on other learning activities, too.

Q: *What is the most common error you find when reviewing the diet histories of your clients?*

A: We consume too much fat and sugar and too few fruits and vegetables. We further compromise our health by not getting enough physical activity.

Q: *What final words of wisdom do you offer for today's teens?*

A: Develop good eating and physical activity habits now. Healthful habits established early will make it easier for you to stay healthy as an adult.

> **Discuss:**
> Do you think males are as likely as females to seek help for weight management?

Feature-Related Activity

Ms. Hankins states that males are as concerned about being overweight as females. Ask students to conduct a survey to find out for themselves if males and females are equally concerned about weight. Have students develop a survey form, and give it to an equal number of teen boys and teen girls. Tally the results and write an article for the school paper summarizing the findings.

Chapter Review

Summary

To eat a healthful diet, you need to be aware of the various nutrients that are in foods. The six basic nutrients are carbohydrates, proteins, fats, minerals, vitamins, and water. Each of these nutrients serves different functions in the body. Each can be obtained from a number of food sources. Knowing your nutrient needs will help you meet them through the foods you eat each day.

The Food Guide Pyramid is a model of an eating plan. The Pyramid divides foods that have similar nutrient content into groups. These groups are breads and cereals; vegetables; fruits; milk, yogurt, and cheese; meat and meat alternates; and fats, oils, and sweets. Eating the recommended number of servings from each group every day will help you meet your nutrient needs. Following the Food Guide Pyramid is one of the Dietary Guidelines for Americans. These guidelines are a set of pointers that can help you form healthful eating and activity patterns.

Dietary needs vary at different stages of life. During childhood and the teen years, people have increased needs for some nutrients to support rapid growth. As people reach adulthood, their needs for many nutrients remain high, but their calorie needs decrease. As dietary needs change, be prepared to adjust your eating habits.

Your body needs energy for both metabolic and physical activities. Balancing these needs with the calories you get from foods will allow you to control your weight. Being either overweight or underweight can cause health problems. People who need to lose or gain weight need to take steps to do so in a healthful manner. Dramatic, unhealthy weight loss or gain can be the result of an eating disorder.

Think About It!

1. Why do you think some people do not eat the proper nutrients? What could be done to change this?
2. Which nutrient would be the most likely to be lacking in your diet? Why?
3. How could the Food Guide Pyramid be used by teens to plan meals when parents work outside the home?
4. Which of the Dietary Guidelines for Americans do you think is hardest to follow? Explain your answer.
5. What dietary advice would you give to a friend who is an athlete?
6. How will you change your eating habits as you become an adult?
7. How would following a daily program of physical activity affect your calorie needs and your weight?
8. The "Iced Tea Diet" promises you will lose 15 pounds in three weeks. You simply have to replace two meals a day with a glass of iced tea. If you needed to lose weight, would you follow this diet? Explain why or why not.
9. How might the Food Guide Pyramid be modified to meet dietary needs in another culture?
10. How could a person's career choice affect his or her eating habits?

Try It Out!

1. Prepare a booklet about the six classes of nutrients. Use pictures to illustrate foods containing the nutrients and tell why each nutrient is important to the body.

Note:
You might want to point out to students the important role of the federal government in looking out for citizens' health. Both the Dietary Guidelines for Americans and the Food Guide Pyramid were developed by the government, which is funded by tax dollars.

Resource:
PowerZone Challenge CD. Have students play the chapter review game to reinforce text content.

2. List five of your favorite snacks. Identify what major nutrients you receive from each snack.
3. List all the foods you ate yesterday. Tally the number of servings you ate from each group in the Food Guide Pyramid. Write a paragraph describing how you might alter your meals to include any missing servings.
4. Using the Food Guide Pyramid, plan a nutritious diet for one day, including breakfast, lunch, dinner, and three snacks.
5. Work in a small group to discuss the nutritional needs of people at a specific stage of life. Compare and contrast your group's findings with the nutritional needs of people at different stages identified by other groups.
6. Read an article about food's effect on an athlete's performance. Report your findings to the class.
7. Make a poster illustrating helpful guidelines people could follow to lose or gain weight.

CAREER TIMES
LEADING GUIDE TO THE WORLD OF WORK

VOLUME 1, NUMBER 5

Taking a Bite out of Food Science, Dietetics, and Nutrition Careers

Food scientists apply the principles of science to maintaining a food supply that meets the demands of consumers. Dietitians and nutritionists help educate people about how to eat for good health. These workers affect what and how people eat.

Employment Opportunities

Many food scientists work for food manufaturers. These professionals help produce, process, preserve, and package food products. Some food scientists engage in research to discover new food sources. Some develop foods that meet consumer demands for taste and convenience. Others work to find substitutes for foods and food components. Some food scientists inspect food and food handling operations to make sure safety standards are met.

The type of work dietitians do depends on their area of practice. Clinical dietitians often work in hospitals, prisons, or nursing homes. They work with doctors and other health care professionals to coordinate medical and nutritional needs of patients. Clinical dietitians might work with patients who have problems with weight, diabetes, or high blood pressure.

Community dietitians counsel individuals and groups to promote good health and prevent disease. They usually work in public health clubs, clinics, and home health agencies. They often teach classes and workshops about nutrition food shopping and preparation skills.

Management dietitians direct the foodservice programs in hospitals, prisons, and schools. They hire and train staff. They prepare budgets and purchase food and equipment. They are also in charge of maintaining safety and sanitation guidelines.

Consultant dietitians may be hired by individual clients or businesses to offer guidance on diet-related matters. For instance, a client may need help with a medical diet. A weight loss center may hire a consultant dietitian to conduct nutrition screenings.

Members of the media consult with some professionals in this field. Professionals who have writing skills might choose to work in the media directly. They might become authors of cookbooks or textbooks. They might also work as food writers or editors for a magazine.

Entrepreneurial Opportunities

Many people with a background in food science or dietetics offer private consulting. Others consult for business firms or government agencies. Hospitals, nursing homes, colleges, airlines, and prisons often use the services of freelance consultants. Some food scientists offer research services to food companies. Many professionals like the flexibility of being self-employed. This type of work allows them to keep the work hours they desire.

Rewards and Demands of Food Science, Dietetics, and Nutrition Careers

Many workers in this field help teach people about good nutrition and healthful foods. These workers are rewarded by the knowledge that they are helping people live longer, healthier lives. Demands of this career area focus on the responsibility involved in affecting the food supply. Other demands may include working on weekends and standing for many hours.

Preparation Requirements

High school students who wish to enter this career area are urged to take classes that will prepare them for college. Science classes, such as food science, chemistry, biology, and physics, will be helpful. Math courses will prepare students for making calculations, which is a common task in food science and dietetics careers. Students should also take at least one course in family and consumer sciences that includes a study of foods and nutrition.

Entry-Level Jobs

A high school education may be the only training needed for some entry-level jobs related to food science and nutrition. For instance, assembly line workers in food processing plants work with the foods developed by food scientists. A dietary aide can assist a dietitian by passing out meals in a hospital or nursing home.

Mid-Level Jobs

Food service supervisors in school lunchrooms work in mid-level jobs. Research technicians who conduct food surveys are also at this point on the career ladder. A community college program such as dietetic technology would prepare workers for jobs at this level.

Some food scientists conduct research aimed at improving the quality of the food supply.

Professional-Level Jobs

Food scientists and dietitians must have at least four-year degrees. Dietitians who wish to work in a research lab, clinic, or public health office may need a master's degree or a doctorate. College programs in food and nutrition, dietetics, and food science prepare students for jobs at this level.

Requirements vary by state but most dietitians need a license to practice. To qualify for a license, students must complete a university program that meets the standards of the American Dietetic Association (ADA). Students must also complete an internship and pass a certification exam. Those who complete the requirements successfully become registered dietitians (RDs).

Personal Qualities Needed for Success

Food science and dietetics careers require above average ability, especially in science. Liking people, wanting to help them, and being able to communicate with them are essential traits for dietitians. Curiosity and imagination are traits that help food scientists develop new food products. Patience and resolve also help workers in this field as they try repeatedly to solve problems. For those who like to prepare food and develop new recipes, creativity is an important skill.

Future Trends

The public has a growing awareness of the role of nutrition in maintaining health and preventing disease. This awareness will ensure the need for food scientists who can develop nutritious foods. It will also ensure the need for dietitians who can teach people to make informed food choices.

As the population of older adults grows, the demand for nutrition counselors will increase. Nursing homes and retirement centers will hire more dietitians. However, fewer dietitians are expected to work in hospitals. Dietitians may more often be found working for the foodservice providers that have hospital contracts. There will also be openings for dietitians in restaurant chains and catering companies.

Career Interests, Abilities, and You

How can you decide if you really want to pursue a career in food science, dietetics, or nutrition? A good way to begin is to take science and food-related courses in high school. You might also ask to shadow someone who works in this field. Seek part-time employment or do volunteer work in a food-related program. Many religious and civic organizations have programs to feed needy people. Managers of these programs are often eager to have extra workers who will fill responsible roles.

Career Ladder for Food Science, Dietetics, and Nutrition
Advanced Degree
Registered dietician Researcher Test kitchen supervisor
Bachelor's Degree
Food technologist Marketing specialist Food health inspector
Associate's Degree
Food service supervisor Food technician Research technician
High School Diploma
Nutrition aide Stock clerk Food transport
Pre-High School Diploma
Dietary aide Voluteer in a community kitchen, food distribution center, or a meal delivery service for shut-ins

Part Six
Planning and Preparing Meals

Chapter 15
Meal Management

Careers

These careers relate to the topics in this chapter:
- cook's helper
- foodservice worker
- restaurant manager
- test kitchen director

As you study this chapter, see if you can think of others.

Topics

15-1 Planning Meals
15-2 Shopping for Food
15-3 Buying Information
15-4 Storing Foods

Introductory Activities

1. Ask students to list skills involved in meal management. Discuss the importance of meal management skills.
2. Poll the class to see how many students do each of the following, either occasionally or regularly: plan meals for the family; shop for groceries for the family; use a shopping list when grocery shopping; read labels on food products; compare prices of food products; prepare meals for the family.
3. Ask what kinds of problems students have had in planning meals and shopping for food products. Discuss possible solutions to these problems. Relate problems to the topics to be covered in this chapter.

Topic 15-1

Planning Meals
I. Planning for Nutrition
  A. Using a Pyramid Meal Pattern
    1. Grains Group
    2. Vegetable Group
    3. Fruit Group
    4. Milk Group
    5. Meat and Beans Group
II. Variety in Meals
  A. Color
  B. Flavor
  C. Texture
  D. Shape and Size
  E. Temperature
  F. Cultural and Societal Influences
III. When You Are the Meal Manager
  A. Your Cooking Skills
  B. Your Food Budget
    1. Energy Costs
  C. Your Preparation Time
  D. A Variety of Eating Schedules

Topic 15-2

Shopping for Food
I. Preparing a Shopping List
II. Deciding Where to Shop
  A. Types of Food Stores
  B. Evaluating Store Features
III. Deciding How Much Food to Buy
IV. Recognizing Quality in Foods

Topic 15-3

Buying Information
I. Unit Pricing
  A. Open Dating
II. Food Labeling
  A. Food Label Information
    1. Understanding Food Additives
  B. Nutrition Facts Panel
  C. Universal Product Code
III. Other Sources of Information

Topic 15-4

Storing Foods
I. Properly Storing Foods
  A. In the Refrigerator
  B. In the Freezer
  C. On a Shelf
II. Technology in Food Packaging

Discuss:
Does the situation in the first paragraph seem real? Can anyone share a similar experience?

Reflect:
How many cookbooks do you have at home?

Activity:
Put the words *meal management* on the chalkboard and have the students name the key factors involved.

Topic 15-1
Planning Meals

Objectives
After studying this topic, you will be able to
- use a meal pattern based on the Food Guide Pyramid to plan meals throughout the day.
- write a menu illustrating variety in color, flavor, texture, shape, size, and temperature.
- evaluate your cooking skills, food budget, and preparation time as they apply to meal management.

Topic Terms
meal management
convenience food

15-1 Great meals begin with advance planning. Cookbooks, magazines, and newspapers often contain good menu ideas.

Imagine this situation: You arrive home at six o'clock to prepare dinner. Then you must rush to meet a seven o'clock appointment. Unfortunately, today's hurried lifestyles often result in this type of schedule. A nutritious, attractive, and economical meal may be a small concern when you are in a hurry.

To guard against the pitfalls of busy days, meal management is a must. **Meal management** involves using resources of skills, money, and time to put together nutritious meals. A meal manager must plan well-balanced menus; shop for healthful, economical foods; and prepare meals in the time available.

How do you begin to plan great meals? Cookbooks, magazines, and the food sections of newspapers often give many good menu suggestions, 15-1. You might also keep a collection of your family's favorite recipes and add to it as you discover new favorites. However, finding tasty menus and recipes is just the beginning of meal planning.

You need to consider five factors when you plan meals. You want meals to be both nutritious and appealing. You also want meals that suit your cooking skills, food budget, and available preparation time. Thorough planning is the key to preparing and serving good meals.

Planning for Nutrition
You know the foods you eat provide your body with carbohydrates, proteins, fats, minerals, vitamins, and water. However, no one food contains *all* the nutrients you need. You must plan carefully to have meals and snacks that will supply all the essential nutrients.

Using a Pyramid Meal Pattern
You can make your meal planning easier by using a meal pattern. A *meal pattern* is a guide that outlines the basic foods normally served at a meal. Many nutrition experts currently recommend a meal pattern based on the Food Guide Pyramid. This pattern includes
- two to three servings from the grains group
- one to two servings from the vegetable group
- one to two servings from the fruit group
- one serving from the milk group

Career Preparation Activity
Do You Fit the Food Service Profile? reproducible master, TR. Students are to indicate their responses to a list of questions about characteristics that are part of many jobs in the food service area. After students have analyzed their responses according to information given on the handout, spend some time discussing the wide range of jobs that fall within the area of food service. Encourage students to explore careers in food service further with the help of a guidance counselor.

Topic 15-1   Planning Meals

- one serving (the equivalent of 1 to 3 ounces of cooked, lean meat) from the meat and beans group

You can use the Pyramid meal pattern whether you are planning a menu for breakfast, lunch, or dinner. Remember to select a variety of foods from each group to get the suggested number of servings each day. Breakfast should provide about one-fourth of your daily nutrients and calories to get you going in the morning. Lunch and dinner should each provide about one-third of your daily nutrient needs. Include snacks in your meal planning to satisfy between-meal hunger and supply your remaining nutrient needs. See 15-2.

Grains Group

Grain products should be the foundation of each day's meal plan. When including foods from this group in your meals, choose whole grain products often. They provide more fiber and other protective substances than refined grain products.

Ready-to-eat and cooked cereals, bagels, and muffins are great choices for breakfast. You can use all types of breads to make sandwiches for lunch. For a change of pace, wrap sandwich fillings in pita bread or a tortilla. Rice and pasta are versatile, economical, and nutritious options for dinner. These grains can be used alone and in a variety of main dishes. Crackers and popcorn are popular snacks from the grains group.

Vegetable Group

Vegetables are easy to include in meals and snacks. Fresh vegetables can be added to tasty egg dishes for breakfast. At lunch, you might enjoy raw vegetables or vegetable salads. Cooked vegetables can

Discuss: What are some healthful snacks that would fulfill nutrient needs not met by breakfast, lunch, and dinner?

Activity: Ask students to write down everything they ate the previous day. Then have them evaluate whether or not their meals and snacks followed the meal pattern described in Chart 15-2.

Reflect: Do you eat enough vegetables? What are some ways you could work more vegetables into your diet?

Pyramid Meal Pattern

Meal	Grains Group (2-3 servings per meal)	Vegetable Group (1-2 servings per meal)	Fruit Group (1-2 servings per meal)	Milk Group (1 serving per meal)	Meat and Beans Group (1-3 ounces per meal)
Breakfast	1 English muffin	1 cup sautéed onions, peppers, and potatoes*	½ cup cantaloupe	1½ ounces lowfat cheese	1 scrambled egg
Snack	1 bran muffin		¾ cup orange juice*		
Lunch	2 slices whole wheat bread	1 cup spinach salad	1 banana	1 cup lowfat yogurt	2 ounces sliced turkey
Snack	4 whole grain crackers				2 tablespoons peanut butter
Dinner	1½ cups brown rice*	1 cup stir-fried broccoli, carrots, & mushrooms	2 pineapple rings	1 cup fat free milk	3 ounces shrimp*
Snack	2 cups popcorn*				
Total Daily Servings	11	5	4	3	7 ounces

*Reduce portion to adapt menu for a teenage girl.

15-2 Use a meal pattern based on the Food Guide Pyramid. This will help you make sure you get your total recommended number of servings each day.

Putting Technology to Use

Have students use drawing software, a scanner, and clipart to develop a bulletin board representing the Food Guide Pyramid. Have students place pictures, drawings, or clipart of foods on the appropriate sections of the Pyramid. When students place their pictures on the bulletin board, have them tell something about the food groups.

Note:
Fruit drinks and punches are not the same as fruit juice. They may contain much more sugar.

Activity:
Check vitamin D milk and fat free milk to see what the differences in fat content are.

Resource:
Meatless Main Dishes, reproducible master, TR

Resource:
Meal Planning with the Food Guide Pyramid, reproducible master, TR

play a leading role on your dinner plate or be served in main dish soups and casseroles. Vegetable juice makes a nutritious snack.

Different vegetables provide different nutrients, so include a variety in each day's meal plan. Include good sources of vitamin C, such as broccoli and peppers. Choose good sources of vitamin A, such as leafy green vegetables and carrots, too. Dried beans and peas, which are high in protein, and starchy vegetables, which provide complex carbohydrates, are also good choices.

Fruit Group

Include a variety of fruits in each day's meal plan. Fruit juice is a common choice for breakfast. Fresh whole fruit or fruit salad is a refreshing addition to a lunch menu. Warm fruit compote or a baked fruit dessert would add color and nutrients to the bill of fare at dinner. Raisins, dried apricots, and other dried fruits make sweet, chewy snacks. Choose good sources of vitamin C each day, such as citrus fruits, strawberries, and melons. See 15-3.

Milk Group

Include foods from the milk group in meals throughout the day by serving milk as a beverage. You can also serve milk with cereal at breakfast and use it in creamy soups for lunch. Pudding made with milk makes a favorite dessert with dinner. An alternative to milk is lowfat cheese. Cheese makes a great addition to a breakfast omelet, a luncheon sandwich, or a dinner casserole. You can use lowfat yogurt to meet your daily servings from the milk group, too. Yogurt is a great snack, whether you eat it alone or layered with fresh fruit.

Meat and Beans Group

Many meal managers begin their menu plans by choosing a main dish from the meat and beans group. Then they select foods from the other groups as accompaniments. If you take this approach, be sure to keep current health guidelines in mind. Nutrition experts recommend that foods from animal sources take up no more than one-third of the space on your plate. Grains, vegetables, and fruits should fill two-thirds or more of your plate. Following these proportions can help you create filling, nutritious meals that are high in fiber and low in fat.

Ham and eggs may be the first breakfast foods that come to mind from the meat and beans group. However, do not limit yourself to only familiar dishes when planning meals. Be adventurous by trying new recipes that include more plant-based foods from this group in your diet. You might try a breakfast bean burrito or a smoothie made with tofu. Chickpeas and kidney beans would be delicious ingredients in a salad for lunch. For dinner, you might prepare lentil chili or black bean burgers. Of course, peanut butter is a time-honored snack food from the meat and beans group.

When planning meals, consider any special nutritional needs of family members or guests. For instance, older children, teens, and adults over age 50 require three daily servings from the milk group. Most other people need only two servings per day. If you are planning meals for a person trying to lose weight, you might select foods that are lower in calories. People with food allergies, diabetes, or heart disease may require special diets. People who are ill or recovering from surgery may also have particular food needs.

15-3 Servings from the vegetable and fruit groups can fit into any meal.

Across the Curriculum

Health. Bring in examples of diet plans for people with diabetes or heart disease. Have students evaluate how these diets differ from Food Guide Pyramid recommendations.

Variety in Meals

Color, flavor, texture, shape, size, and temperature are important points to consider in planning meals with variety. Keeping these factors in mind will help you plan meals that are attractive as well as delicious. Choosing foods that appeal to the senses (sight, smell, and taste) will make meals enjoyable. Foods that complement each other also add interest to mealtime, 15-4.

Color

Color adds eye appeal to meals, so plan meals with a variety of colors. For instance, if your meal includes rice, serve carrots or green beans instead of cauliflower for color contrast. Garnishes can add color and variety to a meal. A sprig of parsley or a sprinkle of shredded cheese can add interest to a casserole. A lemon wedge or carrot curls can make a main dish platter look attractive. Fresh fruit makes a colorful dessert topping.

Flavor

The flavors of foods should complement each other. A sweet flavor blends well with a sour flavor. A mild flavor offsets a strong flavor. For instance, the mild flavor of baked fish combines well with the strong flavor of tangy salsa. Use well-liked combinations of foods that taste good together, such as pasta with a zesty tomato sauce. Vary the flavors of food items to avoid repeating one flavor. In other words, if you are serving steamed carrots as a vegetable, avoid serving shredded carrots in your salad.

Texture

Textures of foods should offer variety. Crisp, tender, soft, creamy, smooth, crunchy, and chewy describe common food textures. Try to serve at least three textures in each meal. For instance, crispy stir-fried vegetables with tender chicken over granular brown rice makes a good combination. On the other hand, creamed chicken and vegetables over soft white rice would offer little variety in texture.

Shape and Size

Use your creative flair to combine a variety of shapes and sizes in your meals. Avoid serving several foods at the same meal that are the same shape and size. For instance, meatballs, small whole potatoes, and Brussels sprouts would be too similar in shape and size. Serving sliced potatoes and green beans with the meatballs would be more appealing.

Temperature

Plan to include foods that differ in temperature as part of the meal plan. Cold foods, such as crisp vegetable salads, contrast well with hot foods, such as sliced ham and a baked potato. Serve hot foods hot and cold foods cold for the greatest appetite appeal.

Cultural and Societal Influences

Variety in colors, flavors, textures, and shapes plays a role in foods of all cultures. However, the specific foods and seasonings that make up this variety differ from one culture and society to another.

Culture and society have been influencing people's food choices since prehistoric

15-4 The colors, flavors, textures, shapes, and temperatures of the foods in this attractive meal complement one another.

> **Activity:**
> Have students evaluate the meals they ate the previous day for the six factors that add variety to meals. How would they change their menus to add variety?
>
> **Discuss:**
> What are some other popular food combinations? What makes these so appealing?
>
> **Note:**
> Mention that the same food can be served many different ways. Potatoes, for instance, can be served whole, sliced, in wedges, cubed, grated, or mashed.

 Across the Curriculum
Social studies. Have students give examples of cultural/religious influences on diet. Have students investigate the origins of these practices.

> **Reflect:**
> Reflect on your food preparation skills. What do you remember as the first food you prepared? What was the funniest thing you did while learning to cook? Have your skills improved?
>
> **Activity:**
> Have students compare the price of ground beef patties using bulk ground beef with premade patties.

times. Early people did not have access to foods from all over the world. They had to eat whatever was available. Those who lived in coastal areas ate seafood. Those who lived in woodlands might have eaten deer, caribou, and other wild game. As time passed, people moved to different regions where new foods were available. However, the regional foods people first became used to eating remained their cultural preferences.

You can still see regional and cultural influences on food choices today. Foods are shipped all over the United States. However, you are still more likely to see lobster tanks in a grocery store in Maine than in a store in Wyoming, 15-5. Cheese soup is more common on restaurant menus in Wisconsin than in Georgia. You will find few Asian markets in an area with a large Latin population. Markets in a Latin district are more likely to feature tortillas, beans, peppers, and other ingredients used in Latin dishes.

If you are like most people, you tend most often to choose foods that reflect your culture. You also select foods that are typical of the society in which you live. As a meal manager, you can add variety to your family's meals by choosing to serve foods from other cultures.

15-5 Grilled lobster is a more typical entrée in New England than in the Southwest.

When You Are the Meal Manager

As a meal manager, you need to consider more than the nutrition and appearance of the food. You also need to consider your skills, your budget, and the amount of time you have available.

Your Cooking Skills

The meals you plan are often determined by the preparation skills you have developed. People who have little cooking experience tend to plan meals that require little preparation. As experience increases, they become more confident and try more detailed recipes.

If you are a beginner, trying to prepare three new recipes for one meal could be frustrating and confusing. One new recipe at a time is enough for adventure. After you master a new main dish recipe, you may wish to try a new salad recipe to accompany it. Later, you may want to try a new dessert recipe to accompany the main dish and salad.

Have patience with yourself as you learn to cook. If you can manage to cook only one dish, then plan to serve it with other foods that require no cooking. With practice, your cooking skills will develop. In time, you will be able to cook anything you wish.

Your Food Budget

Preparing a juicy sirloin steak may be as easy as preparing a hamburger, but the cost varies greatly. The amount of money budgeted for food is an important factor in planning meals. Most people have a limited food budget. You must use care to select foods that are economical as well as nutritious. Planning well-balanced meals on a budget is a challenge, but it can be done. Here are some helpful tips to get you started.

Before planning menus, check newspaper, television, and radio advertisements for weekly specials. Look and listen for sale prices on foods your family enjoys. Then plan your menus around these advertised specials. Check newspapers and magazines to find coupons for items you need and use regularly, 15-6.

Across the Curriculum

History. Show students a map of the United States. Explain how people from other countries settled in specific regions of this country. Have students explain how these immigrants influenced the regional cuisines of today.

Topic 15-1 Planning Meals

15-6 Clipping coupons for food products you buy regularly can help you stretch your dollars at the grocery store.

Plan menus including seasonal foods. Fresh produce (vegetables and fruits) is plentiful, tasty, and inexpensive when it is in season. For instance, strawberries may be a real bargain in the summer; potatoes are a bargain in the fall. During off-seasons, canned or frozen produce may be cheaper.

Stretch your food budget by planning menus that include less-expensive cuts of meat. Meat alternates, such as eggs and legumes (beans and peas), can be used in many types of meatless main dishes. Stretch the number of meat servings in main dishes by using bread crumbs, cereals, rice, or pasta as meat extenders. For instance, combine bread crumbs with ground meat to make a meat loaf. Add meat to a sauce and serve it over spaghetti.

Energy Costs

When planning meals, do not forget about energy costs. Energy not only costs money, it uses limited natural resources. The longer foods cook, the more energy is used. Therefore, consider required cooking times of foods when choosing a menu.

The method used to prepare foods can affect the cooking time. For instance, you can steam rice on top of the range in 15 minutes. If you bake rice in the oven, it will take about an hour. However, if you were already baking a cake, it would be more economical to bake the rice at the same time.

Foods that can be cooked together can save energy. Try preparing one-dish meals, such as vegetable and meat dishes, stews, or casseroles.

Your Preparation Time

With careful planning, you can control the use of time to prepare meals. Here are some ways to save preparation and cooking time by planning ahead.

Consider using some convenience foods to save time. **Convenience foods** are food products that have some preparation steps done to them. The manufacturer has done most of the measuring and combining. With only a few steps, you can prepare the food successfully. For instance, a frozen dinner requires only reheating. Canned and frozen vegetables have already been cleaned, pared, and chopped. They are usually ready to heat and serve, which greatly reduces preparation time. Mixes for muffins, cakes, cookies, breads, soups, and puddings are other examples. These foods still require some preparation, but they require less time than made-from-scratch foods. Although convenience foods save time and energy, they are often more costly than foods prepared from scratch.

Plan foods that require no cooking. A cottage cheese and fruit salad served with wheat crackers and a beverage makes a complete, timesaving meal. A nutritious breakfast featuring ready-to-eat cereal is also quick and easy to prepare. See 15-7.

When you have extra time, prepare large portions of food so they can be used for more than one meal. For instance, leftover ham, turkey, or beef can be used later in sandwiches, casseroles, and soups.

Plan meals that suit the time you have available for preparation. If you have only enough time to heat a plate of leftovers, do not try to prepare an entire meal.

A Variety of Eating Schedules

Everyone in your family may not be able to eat meals at the same time. In many families, all adults may be employed outside the home, and their work schedules may

Activity:
Choose two different food products. Visit the grocery store and find all the different forms of these products. List the ingredients each contains, the amount of preparation required, and the cost.

Enrich:
List all the ways your family stretches their food budget. You may want to interview the food shopper in your family.

Activity:
Have one student make a cookie recipe from scratch. Have another student make a similar cookie using a mix and have another student use refrigerated cookie dough. Compare the time and cost for each.

Citizenship and Service
Have the class adopt an elderly couple or individual who needs help with food shopping. Students can help the adoptee(s) plan menus that fit specific nutritional needs. Menu plans should also take time, skills, and food likes and dislikes into consideration. Students should assist the adoptee(s) in making a shopping list and purchasing and storing the groceries.

Activity:
Using the Food Guide Pyramid, plan meals and snacks for a medical professional who works from 11 p.m. to 7 a.m. and sleeps from 8 a.m. to 4 p.m.

Resource:
Planning Meals, Activity A, SAG

Resource:
Menu Planning for Special Situations, reproducible master, TR

15-7 Making a quick salad is a nutritious meal idea when you are short on time.

Check It Out!

1. List the food group servings that make up a meal pattern based on the Food Guide Pyramid.
2. Name five points to consider in planning meals with variety.
3. List three ways to plan well-balanced meals on a budget.

Check It Out! (Answers)

1. two to three servings from the grains group, one to two servings from the vegetable group, one to two servings from the fruit group, one serving from the milk group, one serving (1 to 3 ounces) from the meat and beans group
2. color, flavor, texture, shape and size, temperature
3. Plan some menus based on advertised weekly specials or sale items. Buy seasonal foods when they are plentiful and inexpensive. Buy less expensive cuts of meat or use more meat alternates in menus. (Students may justify other responses.)

vary. Some adults may work nights or evenings. Children may be involved in activities that take them away from home during normal mealtimes. In these busy households, traditional eating patterns may be difficult to follow. Meals will have to be planned to meet these various schedules. Keep in mind that young children and older family members often prefer to eat on a regular schedule. Teenagers and most adults can usually be more flexible.

When planning meals for a variety of eating schedules, select foods that taste good when reheated. Family members who are unavailable to eat when meals are served can reheat foods in the microwave oven later. For instance, many one-dish meals can be refrigerated and reheated. Some one-dish meals, such as chili or beef stew, can also cook all day in a slow cooker. Family members can serve themselves as their schedules allow. Prepare menu items on weekends and freeze them for use during the week. Make recipes in large quantities and freeze individual portions for later use.

Plan to have food items on hand for family members to make their own meals. You can keep sandwich and salad items in the refrigerator. Fresh fruits, cheeses, and canned or dry soups can also form the basis of quick meals.

Topic 15-2
Shopping for Food

Objectives
After studying this topic, you will be able to
- plan and organize a shopping list.
- describe different types of food stores.
- list factors to consider when deciding how much food to buy.
- explain how to recognize quality in foods.

Topic Terms
national brand
house brand
generic product

15-8 Use store ads to write a shopping list that will save you money by taking advantage of advertised specials.

Vocabulary: Ask the students if they have seen generic products in the supermarket. How did they identify them?

Activity: Ask students to list 50 items they normally buy in a supermarket.

Resource: *The Shopping List,* reproducible master, TR

Enrich: Obtain a copy of a grocery store layout and make a copy for each student. Have the students organize their shopping lists (from above) according to the layout.

Shopping for food is an important part of meal planning. Whether you shop in a supermarket or neighborhood store, grocery shopping involves many decisions. You must decide what to buy, where to shop, and how much will meet your needs. As a smart shopper, you must also be able to evaluate the quality of food products.

Preparing a Shopping List

A *shopping list* is a detailed list of the kinds and amounts of food you want to buy. You can save three valuable resources—time, energy, and money—by planning your shopping list carefully. You will not have to decide what you need to buy. You will not be tempted to buy items you do not need, either.

You should write your shopping list before you go grocery shopping, 15-8. As you make out your list, review all the recipes you are planning to prepare. List all the items you need for your weekly menus and snacks. Add any staple items you have used during the week, such as bread, milk, and eggs.

As you prepare your list, use weekly food ads to compare food items and prices. You may want to stock up on items that are on sale. However, read carefully to find out if you are really saving money on an item. Some foods featured in ads are not on sale. Also, note special promotions and clip cents-off coupons you want to use. A coupon can save you money, providing you need the item and plan to buy it.

Save time and energy by organizing your shopping list according to the grocery store's layout. List the items you will need in each aisle or department of the store. For instance, keep all fresh produce and all frozen foods grouped together on your list. This step will help you avoid going back and forth to find items. It will also help you avoid overlooking needed items on your list.

Deciding Where to Shop

Once you have prepared your shopping list, you must decide the best place to shop. Different types of stores offer different product selections, prices, and customer services.

Types of Food Stores

Four of the most common types of food stores are supermarkets, discount supermarkets, specialty stores, and convenience stores. Comparing them will help you decide which type will best meet your shopping needs.

Putting Technology to Use
Have students use word processing software to make a shopping list template. Have them arrange the template by aisles according to their favorite store's layout. Each time the students go shopping, they can make a printout from the template and organize items they need by location in the store. This should make their shopping experience quicker and easier.

Discuss:
How have some supermarkets included "specialty stores" within their stores? Why do you think they do this?

Resource:
Comparison of Food Stores, Activity B, SAG

Reflect:
Think about a time when too much of a food item was purchased at home. What happened to it? When would a large quantity be a wise purchase?

Large *supermarkets* sell a wide range of food and household products, 15-9. They often charge lower prices because they do a high volume of business. Many supermarkets offer customer convenience services, such as check cashing or home delivery.

Discount supermarkets are sometimes known as warehouse supermarkets. These stores sell foods and household items at discounted prices. To keep prices low, many offer less variety and fewer customer services. For instance, shoppers may have to bag their own groceries.

Specialty stores specialize in carrying one type of food item. A seafood store or bakery is an example of a specialty store. Prices are often higher, but shoppers may prefer the quality and personalized service.

Convenience stores offer convenient locations, longer hours, and fast service. However, product selection is limited, and prices are higher than supermarkets. Shoppers must decide if the added conveniences are worth the cost.

15-9 Because supermarkets offer a full range of fresh food products, finding the exact item you need is easier.

Evaluating Store Features

When choosing a place to shop, ask yourself a few questions. Does the store offer courteous service and helpful employees? Is the store clean and well maintained? Are meats, produce, and dairy products always fresh? Does the store stock a variety of foods in various package sizes to meet your needs? Is the checkout fast and efficient?

After evaluating the types of stores available, you may narrow your choices to one or two stores. You will become familiar with the products and services available at these stores. You will know just where to locate the items on your shopping list. You will not waste time and gas driving to a store on the other side of town just for a bargain.

Deciding How Much Food to Buy

One of the most challenging aspects of shopping is deciding how much food to buy. Your decision should be based on your food budget. Three other factors you will want to consider are serving sizes, storage space, and shelf life.

Refer to your recipes to determine how many servings each one makes. If you need to make a larger or smaller number of portions, adjust your recipe before you go shopping. This will enable you to buy the correct amounts of ingredients. Read product labels for items you are not using in recipes. Labels state how many servings are in each food container to help you decide how much you need.

The amount of storage space you have available will help determine the quantity of foods you can buy. Some shoppers stock up when their favorite items are on sale. This saves money, but such foods must be stored until needed. If you do not have enough space for storage, large sale purchases are not practical.

A product's shelf life is also a factor to consider when buying food. For instance, buying a large box of cereal may be more economical than buying a smaller box.

 Putting Technology to Use
Have students conduct a consumer survey to determine why people shop where they do. Have students use word processing software to design the survey questionnaire and use spreadsheet software to tabulate results.

However, if the cereal gets stale before you can use it, the cost savings are wasted. The cost per serving of the eaten cereal rises sharply.

Recognizing Quality in Foods

To be a good shopper, you must be able to recognize quality. Many foods, such as meat, eggs, and dairy products, are graded. A grade is an indication of the quality of a food. The grade of a food does not affect its wholesomeness or nutritive value. For instance, a tough cut of beef may be just as wholesome and nutritious as a tender cut. However, its grade will not be as high.

Many foods are not graded. In these cases, you must evaluate quality based on your knowledge of food. For instance, fresh apples may not be graded. However, if you know high-quality apples have a firm texture and bright color, you can look for those features.

Wise buying includes knowing which quality is best suited to your needs, 15-10. For example, you may prefer top quality, tender beef for broiling. On the other hand, beef to be used in a stew could be less tender and of a lower quality.

Stores stock various brands of products. These include national brands, house brands, and generic products. **National brands** are often advertised nationwide. These products are generally of high quality, but they often cost more than other brands. **House brands** are brands that are sold by a store or chain of stores. Their quality is similar to national brands, but they usually cost less. **Generic products** have plain labels containing only the names of the products and other required label information. See 15-11. These products are nutritionally equivalent to national and house brands, but they may not be of the same quality. Generic products often cost less than branded products.

Damaged packaging can affect the quality of any food product. If a box is crushed, the food inside may be crushed, too. If a can is dented, the seal may be broken and the food may be contaminated. If frozen food packages are perforated, the contents may have lost quality due to freezer burn. For best quality, avoid buying damaged packages.

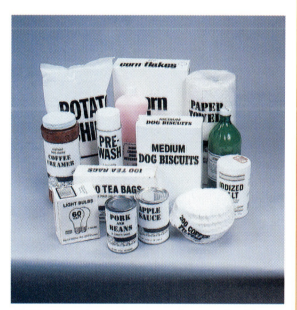

15-11 Generic products are characterized by their plain labels.

15-10 One way to select the best value in meats is to compare quality. Look for the quality best suited to your needs.

Activity:
Divide the class into small groups. Ask the groups to list food products that come in different qualities. Then have them list appropriate uses for each quality.

Enrich:
Bring in cans of chunk pineapple representing the three types of brands. Have students compare the three brands for appearance, flavor, and cost.

Resource:
The Quality of Food, reproducible master, TR

 Problem-Solving Practice
Solving Meal Management Problems, reproducible master, TR. Students are to answer questions about common meal management problems.

Vocabulary:
Write a sentence explaining each of these dates: pack, pull, freshness, and expiration.

Resource:
Figuring Unit Prices, reproducible master, TR

Activity:
Ask each student to find an example of each kind of open dating at home. Have them write down the foods they used to complete the activity.

Check It Out!
1. True or false. A carefully planned shopping list saves time, energy, and money for the shopper.
2. List the four types of grocery stores you may consider in deciding where to shop.
3. What factors should you consider in deciding how much food to buy?
4. True or false. Food is graded to indicate its wholesomeness.

Check It Out! (Answers)
1. true
2. supermarkets, discount supermarkets, specialty stores, convenience stores
3. food budget, serving size, storage space, shelf life
4. false

Topic 15-3
Buying Information

Objectives
After studying this topic, you will be able to
- use unit pricing to compare the cost of food products.
- describe four types of open dating used to indicate the freshness of food products.
- identify the types of information found on food product labels and tell how it can be used to make wise purchase decisions.
- list three sources of consumer information about food products.

Topic Terms
unit pricing
open dating
pack date
pull date
freshness date
expiration date
food additive
universal product code (UPC)

As you have read, many factors influence the food choices you make. Many resources are available to help you get the most for your food dollars. These resources include unit pricing, open dating, and package labeling.

Unit Pricing

Comparison shopping is made easier with unit pricing. **Unit pricing** shows the cost per standard unit of weight or measure. You can use unit pricing to compare prices among brands, package sizes, and product forms (fresh, frozen, canned). Unit pricing labels are usually posted on the shelves beneath food items. See 15-12.

Open Dating

You can judge the freshness of perishable foods through **open dating**. This dating process gives you information about the freshness of foods. It appears in four forms.

Topic 15-3 Buying Information

15-12 Unit pricing allows you to compare prices of various products.

- Canned foods are often stamped with a **pack date**. This tells you when the food was processed.
- A **pull date** is often used on dairy products and cold cuts. This is the last day a store should sell the product. The pull date allows for some storage time at home, 15-13.
- Bread and baked goods usually have a **freshness date**. It indicates the end of the product's quality peak, but the product can be used beyond this date.

15-13 Open dating helps you determine the freshness of the foods you buy.

- **Expiration dates** appear on products such as yeast and baby formula. An expiration date is the last day a product should be used or eaten. When shopping, avoid buying outdated foods.

Food Labeling

You cannot examine the contents of a box or can of food before you buy it. However, you can learn a great deal about the foods you buy by reading labels, 15-14.

Food Label Information

According to government regulations, certain information must appear on food labels, 15-15. Every food label must include

- the common name of the product and its form, such as whole, sliced, or diced
- the net contents or net weight
- the name and address of the manufacturer, packer, or distributor
- a list of ingredients

Ingredients must be listed on the label in descending order by weight. For example, peas, carrots, water, and salt may be printed

15-14 Is fruit juice more nutritious than fruit drink? Food labels will give you the answer to this question, along with other useful information.

Resource:
Read the Label, transparency master, TR

Activity:
Ask the students to bring in labels from cans of various foods. Have the students refer to these labels as they study this topic.

Activity:
Compare a grape juice and a grape drink using labels, prices, and a taste test.

Across the Curriculum

Math. Have students determine the unit price for a variety of items from the foods classroom.

Reflect:
What do you think of when you see the word *light* on a label?

Discuss:
What are the advantages of food additives? Why do some people object to food additives?

Resource:
Nutrition Panel Information, color transparency CT-13, TR

Discuss:
How would you use each of these "facts" from a food label?

Description: The FDA has set specific definitions for descriptive terms, assuring shoppers that they can believe what they read on the package:
- free
- light
- more
- good source
- high
- low
- reduced
- less

For fish, meat, and poultry:
- lean
- extra lean

Ingredients, listed in descending order by weight, are required on almost all foods.

Health claim message referred to on the front panel is shown here.

Health Claims: Food labels are allowed to carry information about the link between certain nutrients and specific diseases. For such a "health claim" to be made on a package, the FDA must first determine that the diet-disease link is supported by scientific evidence.

"While many factors affect heart disease, diets low in fat and cholesterol may reduce the risk of this disease."

15-15 This example of a food label shows the information required by government regulations.

on a can label. This means the can contains more peas than carrots, more carrots than water, and more water than salt.

Descriptive terms used on food labels have often created confusion for consumers. As a result, the Food and Drug Administration (FDA) has set uniform definitions for descriptive terms such as *light, reduced,* and *free.* This assures consumers that terms appearing on food products are accurate.

Understanding Food Additives

Food additives may be among the items found in a food product ingredient list. **Food additives** are substances that are added to food for a specific purpose. For instance, some food additives help keep foods from spoiling. Other food additives are used to enhance flavor, color, or texture; add nutrients; or aid processing.

Food additives may be added during any phase of producing, processing, storing, or packaging. Many familiar substances, such as salt, sugar, and vinegar, are common food additives.

Food additives are a subject of concern to some people. However, laws require substances to be carefully tested before they can be used as food additives. Additives must be proved safe for their intended uses. Certain additives must be identified on ingredient lists, as some people may be allergic to them.

Nutrition Facts Panel

By law, almost all packaged food products are required to include nutrition labeling. The Nutrition Facts panel found on food labels offers much useful information. It is designed to help consumers choose healthful diets. Consumers can use this panel to learn about the nutritional qualities of the food products they buy. See 15-16.

The panel includes the following nutrition facts:

- serving size
- servings per container
- calories per serving and calories from fat
- nutrients per serving, including total fat, saturated fat, cholesterol, sodium, total carbohydrate, dietary fiber, sugars, and protein
- percent Daily Values of nutrients based on a 2,000-calorie diet

Across the Curriculum
English. Have students research how food labeling laws have changed through the years and write a report on their findings.

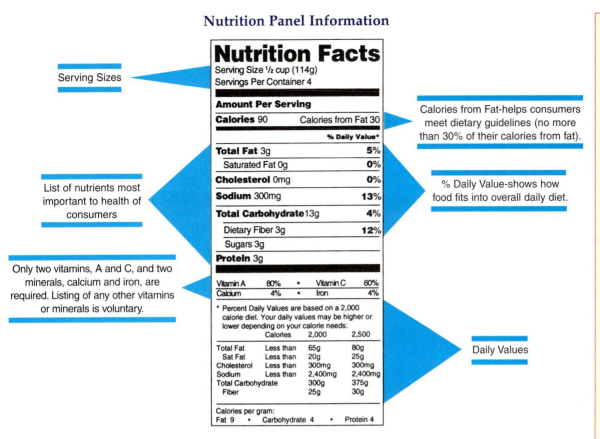

15-16 A Nutrition Facts panel is found on most food labels. Using the information on it can help you compare the nutritional values of various products.

Reflect:
Have you ever read a food label before this class? If so, for what purpose?

Resource:
Food Labels, Activity C, SAG

Enrich:
Visit a store that uses UPC scanners. Ask the store manager to discuss the advantages and disadvantages of UPC scanners.

To get a quick idea of how a food product rates for certain nutrients, look at the percent Daily Values. A food that contains 5 percent or less of a nutrient is considered low in that nutrient. A food that provides 20 percent or more of a nutrient is considered a good source of that nutrient. Use this information on food labels to help you limit total fat, saturated fat, cholesterol, and sodium. Also, use it to make sure you are getting enough fiber, vitamins A and C, calcium, and iron in your diet.

By using nutrition labeling, you can compare the nutritive values of various foods. This will enable you to get the most nutrition for your food dollar.

Universal Product Code

Another item found on most product labels is the **universal product code (UPC).** This is a group of bars and numbers that contains price and product information, 15-17.

In stores using a computerized checkout system, the grocery checker passes each UPC over a scanner. The computer reads the bar code and automatically records the information. The customer's receipt lists the items purchased and their prices, along with the

15-17 The universal product code (UPC) appears on various products as a group of lines, bars, and numbers.

Family Enrichment Activity
Encourage students to talk to older relatives about how resources available to meal managers have changed in recent years. Students should ask what kinds of nutrition information were available when grandparents or parents were young. What kinds of convenience food products were available? Who was responsible for most family food preparation? Where did this person learn food preparation skills? How did the resources of time and money impact menu planning? In what types of stores did they buy food products? What buying information resources were available? Invite students to share their findings.

Enrich:
As a class, write a letter to the FDA or USDA. Ask them what kinds of questions people most often ask them about foods.

Vocabulary:
Ask the students to think of foods they have purchased recently that may have been in aseptic or retort packages.

total. This type of checkout is faster and more accurate. The labor savings may be passed on to customers through lower prices.

Other Sources of Information

Sometimes, the information on shelf tags and product labels may not be enough to answer all your questions. Where can you find the information you need? The Food and Drug Administration (FDA) and the United States Department of Agriculture (USDA) offer a wealth of information. Your local cooperative extension agent or family and consumer sciences teacher can answer many of your questions. Many food firms will also provide information about their products. You can use the Internet to quickly find Web sites for all these sources.

Check It Out!
1. A consumer aid that shows the cost per standard unit of weight or measure for a food product is known as _____.
2. List the four forms of open dating.
3. List the information required to appear on a food label.
4. Name three sources of consumer information about food products.

Check It Out! (Answers)
1. unit pricing
2. pack date, pull date, freshness date, expiration date
3. common name and form; net contents or weight; the name and address of the manufacturer, packer, or distributor; ingredients; and in most cases, a nutrition panel
4. the Food and Drug Administration, the United States Department of Agriculture, your local cooperative extension agent

Topic 15-4
Storing Foods

Objectives:
After studying this topic, you will be able to
- describe general guidelines for storing foods.
- identify two examples of technology in food packaging.

Topic Terms
food rotation   retort packaging
aseptic packaging

Storing food properly is just as important as selecting it. In general, the foods you buy should be stored at home as they were stored at the grocery store. Proper storage at home will help maintain the quality of food, 15-18.

Properly Storing Foods

The types of foods you buy will determine the proper storage method. Foods can be stored in the refrigerator, in the freezer, or on a shelf. (More information on

15-18 Food should be properly stored as soon as you bring it home from the grocery store.

how to store specific types of food will be given in Chapter 17.)

In the Refrigerator

Foods such as meats, dairy products, and some fruits and vegetables spoil easily. Store these *perishable foods* in the refrigerator. Keep refrigerator temperatures at 35°F to 40°F. Most foods kept in the refrigerator should be packaged in airtight wraps or containers.

In the Freezer

Most types of food can be stored in the freezer. Tightly wrap foods in heavy-duty freezer wrap or aluminum foil or place them in airtight freezer containers. Label and date all frozen foods so you can easily identify them and avoid storing them too long, 15-19. To maintain food quality, keep freezer temperatures at 0°F or below. Keep frozen foods frozen until you are ready to prepare or serve them.

On a Shelf

Some foods require no refrigeration or freezing. You can store them on shelves in a cool, dry place. Place foods such as flour, cereals, pasta, dried beans, and peas in tightly sealed containers. Keep onions and potatoes in net bags or other containers that allow air to circulate. You can store bread and rolls on shelves for a few days. For longer storage, however, you should freeze them to prevent mold growth. You can also store fruits and vegetables in cans and jars on shelves. However, you need to refrigerate these products after opening them.

When properly stored using any of the above methods, many foods will keep for months without spoiling. See 15-20. A loss of flavor may occur, however, if food is stored over a long period. For this reason, make **food rotation** a part of your storage routine. Store the freshest food at the back of the shelf. Use the oldest foods stored at the front of the shelf first.

15-19 Labeling and dating frozen foods will help you use them before they lose their peak quality.

Technology in Food Packaging

Food technologists and packaging specialists have come up with a number of new packaging techniques in recent years. These packaging methods allow some perishable foods to be stored on pantry shelves. These methods also allow for improved flavor and nutrition at a reduced cost.

One type of modern packaging technology is **aseptic packaging.** In this type of packaging, foods and containers are sterilized separately. Then the food is packed in the container in a sterile chamber. The foil-lined boxes commonly used for juices and milk are examples of aseptic containers. Many other products, such as soups and tofu, are also packaged aseptically.

A second type of packaging technology is **retort packaging.** In this technique, foods are sealed in foil pouches and then sterilized. This type of packaging is used for some shelf-stable entrees, 15-21. Food items sold in these types of packages can be stored on shelves for up to six months.

Activity:
Have a student demonstrate how to properly wrap food for the freezer.

Discuss:
How do you know when foods have been stored too long in the refrigerator, freezer, or on the shelf? How can you improve your current methods of storing foods?

Enrich:
Have students research the development and production of aseptic and retort packaged foods.

Resource:
Store It Right! reproducible master, TR

FCCLA Activity

Encourage chapter members with food service training who are working on the Food Service STAR Event to demonstrate restaurant menu planning, quantity food purchasing, and commercial food storage techniques. Relate these techniques to the consumer meal management skills discussed in the chapter.

Resource:
Protecting Perishable Foods, reproducible master, TR

Resource:
Food Storage, Activity D, SAG

Food Storage Times

Refrigerator	Storage Time
Beef, pork, lamb	2 to 4 days
Poultry, fish	1 to 2 days
Bacon, ham	5 to 7 days
Milk	1 week
Butter	2 weeks
Natural, process cheeses	4 to 8 weeks
Fruits and vegetables	Varies according to type
Freezer	
Beef	6 to 12 months
Pork	3 to 6 months
Lamb	6 to 9 months
Ground beef, pork, lamb	3 months
Ham, hot dogs	2 months
Poultry	6 to 8 months
Fish	3 to 4 months
Fruits and vegetables	9 to 12 months
Bread	2 to 3 months
Ice cream	2 months
Shelf	
Dried foods (cereal, flour, sugar)	1 year
Food in jars (catsup, jelly, pickles)	1 year
Onions and potatoes	4 weeks
Unopened cans	1 year
Aseptically packaged products (milk products, juices, soups)	6 months

15-20 Foods can be stored for various lengths of time.

15-21 Foil retort pouches allow food products containing perishable ingredients to be stored on a shelf.

Check It Out!
1. Foods that should be stored in the refrigerator because they may spoil are known as _____ foods.
2. True or false. Foods stored in the freezer should be labeled and dated.
3. Explain the meaning of the term *food rotation.*

Check It Out! (Answers)
1. perishable
2. true
3. Store freshest foods at the back of the shelf; use the oldest foods stored at the front of the shelf first.

TEENS ARE EXPERIENCING...

Shopping for Food

For most teens, learning to balance the different areas of their lives can be challenging. Jamie Reynolds is a busy teen who faces this challenge head on. An active FCCLA member, after-school volunteer, and baby-sitter, she manages to find time for her family, too.

Ask Jamie how she helps balance her family life and she will likely respond with one word: shopping. One of Jamie's special interests is shopping for food. She has been developing this consumer skill since her preschool days. "I have always liked going to the supermarket. I remember how upset I used to get when Mom did not allow me to go with her. One of my favorite toys was a yellow and orange grocery cart. I always wanted to take it to the supermarket with us. Mom would put some groceries in my cart for me to push along as she shopped.

"When I was a little older, I got an allowance. I would spend part of it on food—mostly cookies—when we went to the supermarket. When I was tall enough to push the grocery cart, that became my job. I still like to shop for food."

Jamie was asked if she plans meals and prepares a shopping list based on those plans. She explained, "We don't plan specific meals in advance. We plan shopping lists based on the Food Guide Pyramid to make sure we buy the foods we need to eat each day. We plan meals prior to mealtime based on the food guide and using the foods we have on hand.

"Mom prepares the shopping list. I can add a few things when I get to the supermarket as long as I stay within the food budget. Mostly, I shop from the list she makes. Because we stick with a food budget, mom writes approximate amounts of money to spend beside some food items. For example, the list might say 'Meats/$10.' That means I can't exceed the $10 allowance at the meat counter. This helps me stay on the right track financially."

When asked if she uses coupons and store ads to help stretch shopping dollars, she responded enthusiastically. "Yes, Mom and I clip coupons when we find them. We tend to look for cleaning product coupons, but we clip food coupons, too. We also check the newspaper weekly for store ads, but we shop mostly at one store."

How does Jamie decide where to shop? "We have a favorite supermarket. My mother likes the store layout, especially the wide aisles. It's near our home and the prices are reasonable. If we do find a super buy at another store, we'll go there. We try to be smart shoppers!"

Jamie shops for certain product brands, but she is also guided by prices. "We have a few favorite brands we always buy. Otherwise, we shop for good buys."

Are nutrition labels important when Jamie makes buying decisions? "We do look at certain information on the label," Jamie stated. "We always read the fat and calorie content. One family member is on a fat-restricted diet and we all try to watch calories. We follow dietary guidelines and eat a variety of foods to meet our nutritional needs."

Jamie offered some helpful advice to other teens who are learning to shop. "House brands may be as good as national brands, and they usually cost less. Use of house brands is a good way to save on the food budget."

> **Discuss:**
> How will Jamie's shopping experiences help her as she gets older?
>
> **Discuss:**
> What additional practices would you recommend to Jamie?

Feature-Related Activity

Working in small groups, have students list the practices that make Jamie a smart food shopper. Have them make three lists. Identify those practices that help Jamie save time and those that help her save money. Also identify those practices that relate to healthy eating. Ask students which of the listed practices they follow.

Chapter Review

Summary

Basic meal management skills are an important part of meal planning. Following a meal pattern based on the Food Guide Pyramid can help you plan meals to meet your family's nutrient needs. Meal management skills can also help you plan varied meals that suit your food budget and available preparation time.

Following a carefully planned shopping list will save you time and energy when you shop. Listing what you need and avoiding impulse buying will save you money. Save both time and money by shopping at a store that offers reasonably priced foods, customer services, and a convenient location. Learning to recognize the quality of food can help you compare products to determine the best buy. When quality is not important, choosing lower-quality foods can save on the food budget.

Buying information helps you compare products and make wiser food choices when you shop. Unit pricing, open dating, food labeling, and UPCs are sources of information. Understanding this information will also help you save money as you shop.

Proper storage of food at home is the key to preserving its quality. An easy guide is to store food at home as it is stored in the supermarket. Modern packaging technology has made some perishable foods easier to store.

Think About It!

1. Why do you think meal management skills are an important part of meal planning?
2. Describe a meal that includes variety. Why is variety desirable in planning meals?
3. Suggest some ways to cut the costs of preparing meals at home.
4. How can the order of a shopping list save time, money, and energy?
5. What factors do you consider most important when choosing a place to buy food products?
6. Which information do you find most helpful to you as a food shopper? Why?
7. What do you think is the most important reason to know how to store foods properly?
8. In what careers do you think meal management skills would be required? In what other careers do you think these skills might be helpful?

Try It Out!

1. Choose three of your family's favorite recipes. Plan and organize a shopping list as if you were going to buy the ingredients for these recipes.
2. In class, discuss factors that usually affect the price of food. Suggest ways to get the best buys for your food dollars.
3. Plan a nutritious, economical meal that offers variety and is easy to prepare. Compare your ideas to those of your classmates.
4. Ask the butcher in a meat department to point out signs of quality used to establish the grade of various meats on display.
5. Ask the manager of your school cafeteria to share how meal management practices are part of his or her job.

Chapter 16
Before You Cook

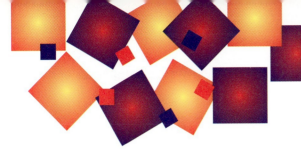

Careers

These careers relate to the topics in this chapter:
- cooking school aide
- housewares demonstrator
- housewares department manager
- appliance sales trainer

As you study this chapter, see if you can think of others.

Topics

16-1 Know Your Equipment
16-2 Safety and Sanitation
16-3 Using a Recipe
16-4 Cooking Smart

Introductory Activities

1. Conduct a scavenger hunt. Make a list of equipment and food staples that students will be using for preparing foods in the classroom kitchens. Give students time to explore the kitchens and locate all the items. Discuss the location of equipment, why items are located where they are, and the importance of returning items to their proper locations.
2. Give each student a cookbook or foods text that includes recipes. Ask them to read several recipes and make a list of terms or abbreviations that are new to them. Ask each student to name one of the terms on his or her list. List the words on the chalkboard. Also have each student list these words on a sheet of paper. Then have them write the definitions of the terms as they locate them in the chapter or discuss them in class.

Topic 16-1

Know Your Equipment
I. Major Appliances
  A. The Refrigerator
    1. Selection
    2. Use and Care
  B. The Range
    1. Selection
    2. Use and Care
  C. The Microwave Oven
    1. Selection
    2. Use and Care
  D. The Cleanup Appliances
    1. Dishwashers
    2. Food Waste Disposers
    3. Trash Compactors
II. Portable Appliances
III. Kitchen Utensils
  A. Measuring Utensils
  B. Cutting Utensils
  C. Mixing Utensils
  D. Cookware and Bakeware
    1. Cookware
    2. Bakeware
    3. Cookware and Bakeware Materials

Topic 16-2

Safety and Sanitation
I. Make It Safe
  A. Using Appliances and Utensils Safely
II. Keep It Sanitary
  A. Clean Hands, Utensils, and Surfaces
    1. Pest Control
  B. Separate Raw and Cooked Foods
  C. Cook Foods Thoroughly
  D. Chill Foods Promptly

Topic 16-3

Using a Recipe
I. Understanding How to Use Recipes
  A. Steps for Using Recipes
  B. Using Ingredient Substitutions
  C. Measuring Techniques
  D. Understanding Recipe Terms
  E. Changing the Yield
II. Learning Cooking Methods
  A. Basic Cooking Methods
    1. General Cooking Guidelines
  B. Microwave Cooking

Topic 16-4

Cooking Smart
I. At Home
  A. Using a Time Plan
  B. Making Meal Preparations
  C. Using Computer Technologies
II. At School
  A. Working with Others
  B. Planning the Lab
    1. Making Out the Shopping List
    2. Making a Time Schedule
    3. Evaluating the Lab Experience

Discuss:
How much cooking do you do at home? Do your parents encourage you to cook? Do they allow you the freedom to choose the types of foods you cook and experiment with new recipes?

Reflect:
How much time is spent making dinner at your house each evening? What appliances have made this job easier and faster for family members?

Activity:
Make a list of the major appliances in your kitchen at home. Ask your parents how long they have had each appliance. What factors did they consider when buying these appliances?

Topic 16-1
Know Your Equipment

Objectives
After studying this topic, you will be able to
- explain how to select, use, and care for major kitchen appliances.
- use portable appliances in the foods lab.
- identify various types of kitchen utensils and explain their uses.

Topic Terms
convection cooking cookware
portable appliance bakeware
kitchen utensil

16-1 A range is a major kitchen appliance found in every kitchen.

Meal preparation can be made easier by using the right tools for food preparation tasks. With the help of various kitchen appliances and utensils you can save time, too. Knowing how to select, use, and care for your kitchen tools can make meal preparation run smoothly.

Major Appliances

Major appliances are the most costly kitchen tools. They are used for storing and cooking foods and for kitchen cleanup tasks. Several major appliances are commonly found in most kitchens. These appliances include refrigerators, ranges, and microwave ovens, 16-1. Dishwashers, food waste disposers, and trash compactors are also widely used major appliances.

Most major appliances come in different styles and sizes. A variety of features are also available. All these options allow consumers to select the models that best meet their needs.

The Refrigerator

The refrigerator is the main food storage appliance. Its primary job is to keep food cold and retard food spoilage. It does this by using a system of circulating cold air. Many refrigerators have special compartments for keeping meats, butter, and produce fresh. The temperature inside the refrigerator should be maintained at 35°F to 40°F.

Selection

Many sizes and styles of refrigerators are available. Considering certain factors will help you decide what features will best meet your needs. Look for easy-to-clean surfaces both inside and outside. Compare energy costs with similar models. Decide whether you need any special features, such as an automatic icemaker. Keep in mind that special features often add to the cost of an appliance.

To choose the right size refrigerator, keep your family size in mind. Also think about how often you shop for groceries and how much freezer space you may need. Make sure the refrigerator you choose will fit the space available in your kitchen.

Decide which refrigerator style you need. Refrigerators are available in three basic styles. These are single-door, refrigerator-freezer (two-door), and compact-portable.

 Career Preparation Activity

Learning About Kitchen Designing, reproducible master, TR. Invite a panel of representatives from local businesses who are involved with one or more aspects of kitchen design. Have students prepare questions ahead of time so the panel members can include this information in their presentation. Students can use the reproducible master as the basis for questions and/or collecting information about careers related to designing kitchens.

Topic 16-1 Know Your Equipment

The *single-door refrigerator* has a frozen food compartment in the top. This compartment is used to store ice cubes and frozen foods. However, this compartment is not cold enough to preserve the quality of frozen foods for a long time.

Many single-door refrigerators must be defrosted manually. Frost that builds up in a thick layer in the freezer section makes the unit work harder. A single-door refrigerator is the least expensive style to buy and operate. However, defrosting can take a lot of time and effort.

A *refrigerator-freezer* is the most common style sold today. It has at least two doors, 16-2. The freezer section is located above, below, or beside the refrigerator section. This section can keep foods frozen for long periods.

Most refrigerator-freezers are frostless. That means frost does not build up in the freezer section. This convenience feature makes the refrigerator more costly to buy and operate.

As the name implies, *compact-portable refrigerators* are small. They are often used in small apartments, dorm rooms, and recreation rooms. The freezer compartment is very small and is used for storing ice cubes.

Use and Care

To keep foods safe, keep the refrigerator clean. Wash and dry inside and outside surfaces often. If the refrigerator has coils, vacuum them at least twice a year. (Coils are usually located on the back of the refrigerator.) Follow the manufacturer's use and care instructions for properly defrosting the refrigerator.

You can take two key steps to maintain the proper temperature inside the refrigerator. First, do not open the door unnecessarily. This wastes energy by causing the refrigerator to work too hard. Second, try not to overcrowd the refrigerator. This may interfere with air circulation.

The Range

The range is a basic meal preparation appliance. Most ranges have four surface units, an oven, and a broiler. The range may use either electricity or gas for fuel. Your cooking and baking needs and available fuel hookup will determine which fuel and features you need.

Selection

In an electric range, electricity flows through coils of wire called heating elements. In some ranges, these coils are hidden beneath a flat, glass-ceramic surface. In solid element cooktops, the coils are sealed under smooth, cast iron elements. Smooth surfaces make it easier to clean the top of the range. Some cooktops feature *quartz halogen* elements, which heat faster than standard electric coils.

In a gas range, gas and oxygen are mixed and burned in burners. The burner flame should be blue when the burner is turned on. If the flame looks orange, the burner is not properly adjusted. Gas ranges have an energy-saving *pilotless ignition*, which requires electricity to work. Some gas ranges feature high-efficiency

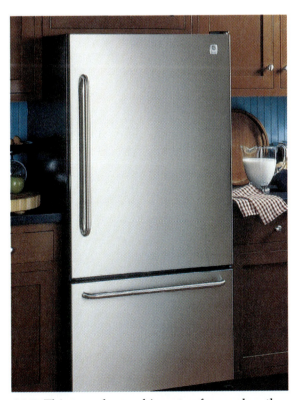

16-2 This two-door refrigerator-freezer has the freezer on the bottom. This keeps refrigerated foods at eye level.

> **Enrich:**
> Have the students visit an appliance store and look at the refrigerators. Ask the salesperson what the newest features are. Compare the features found on the most expensive model and the least expensive model.
>
> **Enrich:**
> Read a consumer information magazine that recently evaluated refrigerators. What factors did they use to rate the refrigerators? Which were recommended?
>
> **Enrich:**
> Interview someone who has used a refrigerator that is not frostless. How was it defrosted? How difficult was this?

  Across the Curriculum
History. Have students research methods of cooking and storing food before modern appliances were invented. Students may include such subjects as outdoor brick ovens, wood-burning stoves, and ice boxes. Have students share their findings in an oral report.

Activity:
What type and style of range do you have in your home? Ask your parents which type of fuel they prefer. Have they had any bad experiences with one type of fuel? What do they feel are the good and bad points of each kind?

Enrich:
Have the students visit an appliance store and look at the ranges. List the features available.

Discuss:
How often would you use the special features or optional accessories if they were available on the range in your home?

Note:
If anyone in class has a convection oven, have them tell about using this oven.

burners sealed into the cooktop for easier cleanup.

In choosing a range, consider the styles available. The most popular style is a *freestanding range,* which has finished sides. A freestanding range has an oven below the cooktop. There may also be a second oven above the cooktop. Freestanding ranges can either stand alone or be placed between two counters.

Drop-in ranges sit on a cabinet base. *Slide-in ranges* sit on the floor. Both styles have ovens below cooktops. These range styles have unfinished sides. The appliances fit snugly between two cabinets, giving the appearance of being built into the counter.

Cooking appliances are also available as separate built-in cooktops and ovens. Cooktops are built into a countertop. Ovens are built into a wall. See 16-3.

Some ranges may include special features or optional accessories. A rotisserie, a griddle, or thermostatically controlled surface units are some examples. Some ovens have a convenient self-cleaning feature. All these features add to a range's cost, so carefully determine which ones you really need.

Another oven option is the *convection oven.* This type of oven is available in gas and electric models. **Convection cooking** involves circulating hot air over all food surfaces. This allows the convection oven to cook more quickly and evenly than a conventional oven. The convection oven uses lower temperatures to cook food than a conventional oven. When using a convection oven, be sure to adjust cooking times and temperatures.

Technological advances have brought several high-speed ovens to the consumer market. Some use powerful *halogen lamps,* which cook with super-hot light waves. Some high-speed ovens combine halogen cooking with convection or microwave technology. The result is ovens that cut conventional cooking times by 30 to 80 percent. For example, you can bake a five- to six-pound chicken in about twenty-five minutes. Refrigerated rolls will bake and brown in about four minutes. The light of the halogen lamp aids browning while

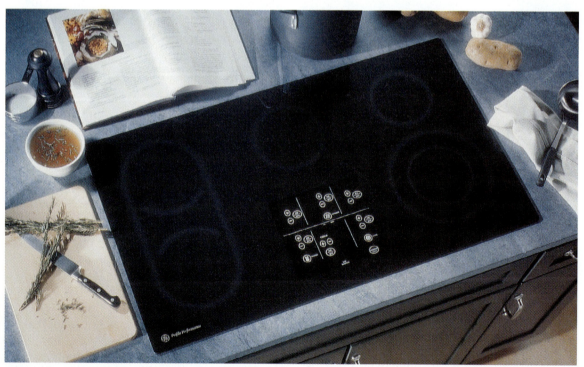

16-3 A built-in cooktop that is separate from the oven gives a kitchen greater flexibility by creating multiple work centers.

Putting Technology to Use

Have students look at the Web sites for range manufacturers such as Whirlpool, Kenmore, Jenn-aire, and Amana. Have students save photos of ranges along with information on their styles, options, and prices. Have students compile the information and use presentation software to share their findings in class.

Topic 16-1 Know Your Equipment

allowing foods to stay moist. This makes many foods more appealing than they would be if prepared in a microwave oven. However, most high-speed ovens are at the high end of the consumer price range.

Use and Care

Follow the manufacturer's instruction manual for proper use and care of your range. Wipe up spills on cooktop surfaces immediately with a damp sponge. Clean the oven surfaces as recommended or set the self-cleaning cycle.

Practice energy-saving habits when cooking or baking. Match the cooking utensil size to the surface unit size. Flat-bottom pans produce good results on smooth-top or coil element electric ranges. This is because they make better contact with the heating elements. The bottom surface of pans is not as important a factor with gas ranges. When baking, keep the oven door closed. Opening the door to peek inside lets heat escape, and this wastes energy.

Practicing safety habits when using a range is important. If you must light a match to light a gas range, always light it before turning on the gas. If the controls are turned off and you smell gas, ventilate the room and call a repairperson.

The Microwave Oven

A microwave oven cooks food using microwaves. *Microwaves* are high-frequency energy waves that cause food molecules to vibrate rapidly. The friction produced by these molecules creates heat that cooks the food.

Cooking with a microwave oven saves time and energy. See 16-4. You can defrost, reheat, and cook food in much less time than in a conventional oven. Because heat is created inside the food, the oven stays cool. A microwave oven can save the energy of heating up a conventional oven. It is a more efficient way to cook small quantities of food.

Selection

Many sizes, styles, and features are available in microwave ovens. Your choice will depend on your cooking needs.

16-4 A microwave can cook most foods faster than a conventional oven and it uses less energy.

Sizes of microwave ovens range from compact to full size. Compact ovens have small interiors. They offer few features and are mainly used for reheating foods. Midsize ovens have larger oven capacities and offer more cooking and defrosting features. Full-size ovens have the largest oven capacity. They offer the most features and are used for all cooking functions.

Two main styles of microwave ovens are available. *Countertop* ovens are the most popular style with the best feature choices. Some models can be mounted under a cabinet to save counter space. *Over-the-range* microwave ovens hang over the range or are the upper oven on a two-oven range.

Special features are found on many microwave ovens. Some have electronic touch pad controls and a number of power levels. Others offer one-touch automatic cooking or reheating pads. Step-by-step programming features make it simple to program the microwave oven. Turntables rotate food through the microwave energy field for more uniform cooking.

Use and Care

Follow the manufacturer's cooking guidelines. Because microwave ovens cook foods quickly, you must time foods carefully to guard against overcooking.

Discuss:
How do you clean the oven where you live? Whose job is this? Compare experiences with others in class who have regular, continuous cleaning, and self-cleaning ovens.

Activity:
List the features found on your microwave oven (or one owned by a neighbor or relative). Which features do you seldom use on your oven? Compare features with class members, and decide which features are the most beneficial and widely used.

Enrich:
Some people still do not consider microwave ovens safe or microwaved foods safe for consumption. Find information in the library that defends this method as a safe way to cook foods.

 Putting Technology to Use
Have students use word processing software to develop a survey form and conduct a survey on the use of microwave ovens. Ask how many people have microwave ovens in their homes. Can they relate any interesting experiences they've had in cooking with this oven? How much do they depend on the microwave oven? What food items do they use it for the most?

> **Reflect:**
> If you have a dishwasher at home, do you only run it when it is fully loaded? Do you turn off the dry cycle? If everyone took these steps, do you think it would make a significant difference in energy savings?
>
> **Discuss:**
> What types of food wastes can you safely put into a disposer? What food wastes should not be placed in a disposer? Why should cold water be used rather than hot water? (Ans: Keeps any grease solid rather than liquid.)
>
> **Resource:**
> *Evaluating Portable Appliances*, reproducible master, TR

Do not turn on a microwave oven when it is empty. This could damage the oven. Also avoid using metal utensils in the microwave oven. Metal reflects microwaves and could damage the oven. Use paper, glass, and plastic cooking utensils. These materials allow the microwaves to reach the food being cooked.

Because food spills do not cook onto the oven interior, cleanup is easy. Wipe up spills with a damp cloth. Use mild detergent; avoid using any type of abrasive cleaner. Keeping the oven interior clean is important for another reason. Food spills may damage the door seal. If you suspect the door seal is broken, call a repairperson.

The Cleanup Appliances

The cleanup appliances include dishwashers, food waste disposers, and trash compactors. These appliances aid in making cleanup quick and easy. Follow the manufacturer's use and care instructions when using these appliances.

Dishwashers

Dishwashers offer many benefits. They save time and energy. Hot water and strong detergent help sanitize dishes. Dishwashers are available as either *portable* or *built-in* models. Both types operate in cycles and can be used to wash most kitchen utensils, 16-5. Cycles are based on soil levels and load sizes. A normal cycle used for an average dish load has a prerinse, two washes, a rinse, and drying time.

For best cleaning results, load the dishwasher properly and use automatic dishwasher detergent. Avoid overcrowding dishes so water and detergent can circulate freely.

To save energy, operate the dishwasher only when you have a full load. To save more energy, turn off the dry cycle. The heat created in the dishwasher by the hot water will dry the dishes.

Food Waste Disposers

Food waste disposers are used to dispose of soft food waste. Two types of food waste disposers are available. A

16-5 A built-in dishwasher is permanently installed under a counter.

switch turns on a *continuous feed disposer*. Then food is pushed into the disposer in a continuous manner. When operating a *batch feed disposer*, food is added in small amounts. The disposer is then turned on when the lid is placed over the opening.

Operate food waste disposers carefully. Before using a disposer, check to be sure there are no foreign items in it. When operating a disposer, use cold running water. Use a rubber spatula to push foods into the disposer. Never use your fingers or metal objects to place food in the disposer.

Trash Compactors

Trash compactors are used to compress disposable wastes into a neat bundle. Compacted trash takes up about one-fourth the space of waste that has not been compacted. Food scraps and nonrecyclable containers can go in a trash compactor. However, do not place aerosol cans or flammable materials in this appliance.

Portable Appliances

A number of portable appliances are found in most kitchens. **Portable appliances** can be easily moved from one place to

---

Across the Curriculum

Social studies. Have students find out if your city has any special regulations concerning compacted trash and local recycling. Do students think additional measures can be taken? Ask students what they can do to bring ideas to the attention of city officials.

another. These appliances are designed to help people save time and energy when preparing foods.

Some portable appliances, such as popcorn poppers, are designed to do special jobs. Others, such as mixers and food processors, can perform a variety of tasks. See 16-6. Common portable appliances include electric skillets, toasters, toaster ovens, blenders, food processors, coffeemakers, and electric mixers.

When selecting portable appliances, asking yourself a few questions can help you choose wisely. Will the appliance perform desired tasks quickly and safely? How often will I use it? How much storage space will it need? Is it easy to assemble, disassemble, and clean? Look for appliances that will give you the most satisfaction for your money.

Portable appliances can often save energy because they can be used instead of large appliances. To get the best performance from your portable appliances, be sure to follow the manufacturer's use and care instructions.

Kitchen Utensils

A **kitchen utensil** is a hand-held kitchen tool used for measuring, cutting, mixing, cooking, or baking tasks. Specialized utensils are available to perform almost any food preparation task.

The storage space in your kitchen is likely to be limited. Therefore, you need to choose wisely which utensils you will own. When selecting utensils, decide which ones best fit your needs. Think about your quality requirements and your budget. To get the most satisfaction from your cooking utensils, read and follow the manufacturers' use and care instructions.

To make utensils convenient to use, store them near where you will be using them. For instance, store a soup ladle near the range. Store measuring cups near your electric mixer. Be sure to store utensils safely, too. Keep knife blades covered and sharp edges pointing down.

Measuring Utensils

Measuring utensils will help you correctly measure recipe ingredients. Each type of utensil has a specific measuring function. See 16-7.

Dry measuring cups are used for measuring dry ingredients, such as flour and sugar. Made of metal or plastic, they are also used for measuring shortenings and chopped foods. Standard sets contain ¼-cup, ⅓-cup, ½-cup, and 1-cup sizes.

Liquid measuring cups are used to measure liquid ingredients, such as water,

Activity:
Have the students name all the portable appliances they can think of and write these on the chalkboard. Have them list those they have in their homes and estimate how often each was used in the last month. Are there some that were bad investments?

Resource:
Appliance Pyramid, Activity A, SAG

Resource:
Basic Kitchen Equipment and Utensils, reproducible master, TR

Activity:
Collect a variety of utensils from the class supplies, especially those that are unusual or have a specific purpose. Have the students guess their names and uses.

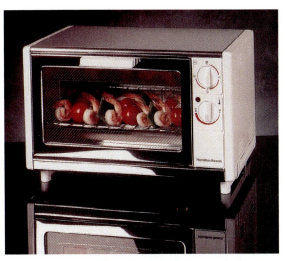

16-6 Small appliances can perform many tasks or one specific task. The food processor can shred, slice, mix, chop, or puree foods. The toaster-oven can warm, toast, bake, and broil.

Problem-Solving Practice
A Place for Everything, reproducible master, TR. Knowing and applying principles of storage can go a long way toward keeping a kitchen neat and organized. Good storage also contributes to effective use of time and efficient work methods. As a class, read and discuss the basic principles of storage listed on the master. Then divide the class into groups of two to four students. Assign each group one of the storage problems described at the end of the master. Have groups solve their assigned problems, applying the principles outlined on the master.

Activity:
Measure ½ cup of a dark liquid in a glass liquid measuring cup. Ask a student to pour this into a ½ cup dry measuring cup. What happens?

Activity:
Display these types of knives on the demonstration table. Demonstrate how to use each knife for its intended purpose. Show how using an incorrect knife can make the job more difficult and dangerous.

Activity:
Demonstrate how to sharpen knives.

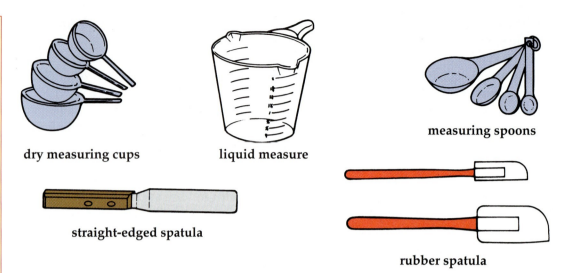

16-7 Use of standard measuring utensils helps assure the success of a recipe. The most common ones are shown here. Spatulas are used to level off or scrape out measured ingredients.

milk, oil, and syrup. They are made of glass or clear plastic. They are clearly marked with levels to allow accurate measurement of various amounts of ingredients. Liquid measuring cups should have a lip and a handle to make pouring easy. They are most frequently found in 1-cup, 2-cup, and 4-cup sizes.

Measuring spoons are used to measure small amounts of liquid, dry, and solid ingredients. These spoons are made of metal or plastic. Standard measuring spoon sets have ¼-teaspoon, ½-teaspoon, 1-teaspoon, and 1-tablespoon measures.

Although spatulas are not measuring utensils, they can assist you with measuring tasks. Use a *straight-edged spatula* for leveling dry and solid ingredients in measuring cups or spoons. A *rubber spatula*, or rubber scraper, can help you scrape wet or solid ingredients from measuring utensils.

Cutting Utensils

In meal preparation, cutting utensils are used to peel, pare, chop, slice, shred, carve, and debone foods. One type of cutting utensil that can do all these tasks is the knife. However, there are many types of knives, and each one is designed to handle particular cutting tasks. Some knives are long; others are short. Some have straight blades; others have *serrated*, or toothed blades. The style of each knife depends on the preparation tasks for which it is used. See 16-8. The most popular types of knives are described below.

You can use a *paring knife* to pare (cut the skin off) vegetables and fruits, such as

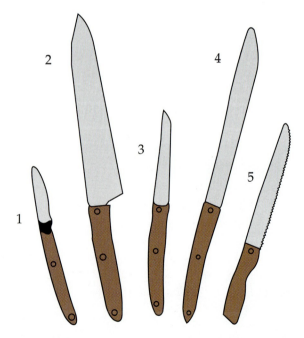

1. paring knife
2. French knife
3. utility knife
4. carving knife
5. serrated knife

16-8 A variety of cutting tools are used for food preparation tasks.

Putting Technology to Use
Have students browse Web sites of prominent knife manufacturers, such as www.j-a-henckels.com and www.chicagocutlery.com. Have students print out information they find interesting and share it with the rest of the class.

cucumbers and apples. It will also help you with small slicing and trimming jobs.

A *French* or *chef's knife* can chop, dice, and mince such foods as fruits, vegetables, nuts, and garlic. It is one of the most versatile knives you can own.

A *utility knife* is also versatile. It is a good choice for slicing foods, such as tender vegetables and cheeses. You can use it to trim fat off meat, too.

A *carving knife* is used mostly for meats and poultry. Choose this type of knife when slicing ham, turkey, roasts, and other large food items for serving.

You need at least one *serrated knife* in your kitchen. Use this type of knife for slicing bread, sponge-type cakes, and soft vegetables like tomatoes.

Keeping the cutting edges of knives sharp is important. Sharp knives produce smoother, cleaner cuts with an easy hand motion. Exerting pressure to cut with a dull knife may cause an accident.

A *cutting board* should be used when cutting food with a knife. It protects your hand, the countertop, and the cutting edge of the knife. Cutting boards may be made of acrylic, glass-ceramic materials, or wood. Acrylic and glass-ceramic boards are considered more sanitary. However, they also dull the cutting edge of knives. A wooden cutting board is more difficult to sanitize after each use, but it does not dull knives. Consider the options and decide which you prefer to use.

Another type of cutting tool is *kitchen shears*. Use them for cutting dried fruits, such as dates and prunes. They are also useful for snipping herbs, cutting meat or pizza, and opening food packages.

A *peeler* with a floating blade is used to remove the skin of fruits and vegetables. Because it removes a very thin layer, the nutrients near the surface are preserved. Peelers are also used to make garnishes such as carrot curls.

A *shredder-grater* is a four-sided utensil used for shredding, grating, and slicing tasks. Use it to grate lemon rind, shred cheese or cabbage, and slice potatoes.

Mixing Utensils

Mixing utensils are used for tasks such as mixing, combining, stirring, beating, blending, and whipping. Basic mixing utensils include bowls, spoons, scrapers, and beaters.

Use a *mixing bowl* to hold the recipe ingredients you want to mix. These bowls come in various sizes and are made of glass, plastic, or metal.

A large *mixing spoon* makes it easy to mix, stir, or blend ingredients. Spoons are made of wood, plastic, or metal.

Rubber scrapers are versatile tools. They are useful for folding ingredients and cleaning the sides of your mixing bowl.

Rotary beaters have a crank, which you turn to make the beaters rotate. Use a beater to blend, beat, and whip ingredients in a mixing bowl. Another utensil that can do these mixing tasks is a *whisk*.

Cookware and Bakeware

Special equipment is needed for cooking food. **Cookware,** which includes saucepans and skillets, is used for cooking on top of the range. **Bakeware** is used for baking foods in the oven. Chart 16-9 gives some general tips for selecting cookware and bakeware.

Cookware

Saucepans and pots with tight-fitting lids serve many uses. Both are used for cooking foods over direct surface heat. Saucepans usually have one handle, while pots have two handles. Several sizes are commonly used in most kitchens.

A *double boiler* is a small pan that fits inside a larger pan—usually a saucepan. Food is placed in the top pan. Water is placed in the bottom pan. The steam produced when the water is heated cooks the food in the top pan. This gentle heat is less likely to burn delicate foods, such as milk and cream-based dishes.

Skillets, or frying pans, are used for shallow fat frying, pan-broiling, searing, and braising foods. Heavy materials that distribute heat evenly, such as cast iron or cast aluminum, are desirable for skillets.

Enrich: Have a student investigate recent research on wooden cutting boards versus acrylic or glass-ceramic boards. Demonstrate how to sanitize a cutting board.

Discuss: Have you used a whisk or rotary beater to mix ingredients? When might you use these handheld tools instead of electric mixers?

Activity: Display all the various cookware items available in the classroom. Have the students suggest foods they would prepare in each of them. Ask which cookware items are included in basic sets and which are specialty items.

Citizenship and Service

Find out if there are physically disabled people in the community who would appreciate some help making food preparation easier. Suggested activities include making enlarged copies of favorite recipes for visually impaired people; working with people to rearrange storage of kitchen equipment, supplies, and utensils so they will be more convenient; developing/designing storage aids that can be made by students or a school or community group willing to donate time and materials.

Activity:
Using Chart 16-9, evaluate the cookware used in the classroom. Decide if the school's cookware is of good quality. (Note: Try to have some poor examples on hand for comparison.)

Activity:
Display all the various bakeware items available in the classroom. Have the students suggest food products they would prepare in each of them. Ask which bakeware items are included in basic sets and which are used for special recipes.

Selecting Cookware and Bakeware

When you select cookware, look for these features:
- durable materials that distribute heat evenly
- sturdy designs with flat bottoms and smooth edges
- heat-resistant handles that are securely attached
- tight-fitting lids with easy-to-grip knobs
- durable pieces that are light enough to handle comfortably
- easy-to-clean design that will maintain appearance with proper use and care

When you select bakeware, look for these features:
- appropriate materials (glass, metal, glass-ceramic) that suit your specific baking needs
- the correct size for the intended use
- lightweight, yet durable utensils that are easy to handle comfortably
- easy-to-clean designs that will maintain appearance with proper use and care

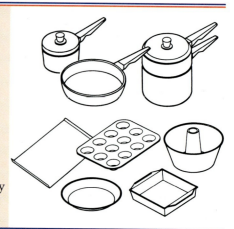

16-9 Follow these helpful tips when selecting cookware and bakeware.

Griddles are skillets without sides. They are used for grilling sandwiches and cooking pancakes and French toast.

Large kettles are used when cooking foods in quantity, such as soups and pastas. Some of these pots come with a basket that is useful for steaming foods.

Bakeware

Several baking utensils are customized for specific tasks. Bakeware includes loaf, muffin, tube, pie, springform, pizza, and round and square cake pans.

When selecting bakeware, consider the surface of the utensil. If the surface is light and shiny, part of the heat will be reflected away from the food. Foods baked in shiny pans will have light, soft crusts. Dull, dark surfaces absorb heat and cook faster. Foods baked in dark pans will have crisper crusts. Glass also absorbs heat and cooks faster. Most recipe baking times are based on using light and shiny cooking surfaces.

Cookie sheets have a low rim on one or more sides of the baking sheet for strength. They are used for baking cookies, rolls, and biscuits and for heating frozen foods such as pizza.

Most *roasting pans* have high, domed lids to cover meats. They also have removable racks to hold meat out of the drippings that form during cooking. Roasting pans may be oval or rectangular in shape and can be purchased in various sizes.

Casseroles are baking dishes with high sides. You can use them for both baking and serving foods. Some casseroles are designed for freezer-to-oven use. They may be made of glass, glass-ceramic, or earthenware. Sizes range from single servings to several quarts.

A *cooling rack* is an important accessory for baking. A cooling rack allows air to circulate around food so it can cool evenly.

Cookware and Bakeware Materials

Learning about the materials used to make cookware and bakeware can help you make wiser choices. Well-constructed, high-quality materials will likely last many years, 16-10. Read and follow the use and care instructions that come with the products.

16-10 High-quality cookware is a good investment. With proper use and care, it will provide years of service.

Across the Curriculum

Science. Conduct a cookie-baking experiment. Bake some of the cookies on a light, shiny cookie sheet. Bake some on a dull, dark cookie sheet. Bake a third batch in a glass dish. Compare the results and have students offer explanations.

All materials are not suited for every use. For instance, plastic bakeware is often used for microwave cooking. It is easy to clean, sturdy, and dishwasher safe. However, most plastic bakeware cannot be used in a conventional oven at high temperatures. When choosing cookware and bakeware, look for materials that are versatile.

Check It Out!
1. List four major appliances commonly found in a kitchen.
2. How does a portable appliance differ from a major appliance?
3. List and state the specific use of four cutting tools.
4. Explain the difference between cookware and bakeware.

Check It Out! (Answers)
1. (List four:) range, refrigerator, microwave oven, dishwasher, food waste disposer, trash compactor
2. A portable appliance is small; it can be moved from one place to another.
3. (List four. Student response. Examples may include knives, cutting board, kitchen shears, peeler, and shredder-grater.)
4. Cookware is used for top-of-the-range cooking; bakeware is used for baking foods in the oven.

Topic 16-2
Safety and Sanitation

Objectives
After studying this topic, you will be able to
- follow safety practices in the kitchen when preparing foods.
- list specific guidelines that fall under the steps *clean, separate, cook,* and *chill* for keeping foods safe to eat.

Topic Terms
sanitation
foodborne illnesses

A safe kitchen is one that is as free as possible from risks of injury. Taking precautions can help you keep your kitchen work area safe and free from accidents.

Handling food properly and keeping food safe to eat are important sanitation practices. **Sanitation** is the process of maintaining a clean and healthy environment. Following sanitary food preparation measures assures food is safe to eat.

Make It Safe

Following safety practices will help you prevent accidents in the kitchen. The most common types of accidents in the kitchen are electrical shocks, fires, burns, falls, cuts, and poisonings. Review the personal safety tips in Chapter 13. Many of these tips apply to kitchen safety as well. Remember to practice safety habits when using appliances and utensils.

Using Appliances and Utensils Safely

Many accidents in the kitchen are caused by the misuse of equipment. Accident prevention depends on your knowing how to safely use each appliance. You must follow all manufacturers' use and care instructions carefully. You also need to know how to use all utensils, cookware,

Enrich: Research the variety of materials used in bakeware. Which ones are recommended for use in baking? Which materials and finishes last the longest and give the best results?

Discuss: Look around the classroom. Where do you see potential hazards if safety practices are not followed?

Resource: *Kitchen Safety,* reproducible master, TR

Activity:
Divide the class into small groups. Have each group read the use and care instructions for a classroom appliance. Then have them demonstrate the correct use of the appliance.

Enrich:
Have students role-play the proper and improper ways of handling safety concerns listed in 16-11 in the classroom. Use fake props to prevent any accidental injuries.

Note:
Point out any safety equipment in the classroom and demonstrate their use. Discuss the types of fires and the best ways to put them out.

---

and bakeware correctly. Knowing how to use and care for equipment is only the first step. Follow up by practicing safety procedures. Some important kitchen safety guidelines are listed in Chart 16-11.

Keep It Sanitary

Many cases of foodborne illness occur each year. **Foodborne illnesses** are sicknesses caused by eating contaminated food. The contaminants that cause illness are often

Kitchen Safety

Preventing Cuts and Minor Injuries
- Hold the tip of a knife down when carrying it.
- If you drop a knife, step back and let it fall.
- Keep knife blades sharp.
- Store knives in a rack or drawer with the cutting edges down.
- Chop, dice, and slice foods on a cutting board.
- Use knives for cutting only. If a can opener or screwdriver is needed, find the appropriate tool.
- Cut down and away from yourself when using a knife.
- Wash sharp knives separately.
- Wrap broken glass in heavy paper before putting it into the trash.
- Do not leave drawers and cupboard doors standing open.
- Turn off appliances such as electric mixers, blenders, and food processors before cleaning the sides of the container with a rubber scraper.

Preventing Fires
- Avoid wearing loose clothing and roll up long sleeves when cooking.
- Tie back long hair.
- Dip a burned match in water before putting it into a trash can.
- When manually lighting a gas burner, strike the match before turning on the gas.
- Never leave food cooking on the range unattended.
- Keep aerosol cans away from heat.
- Clean grease from the exhaust fan to prevent grease fires.

Preventing Falls
- Wipe up spills immediately.
- Keep a sturdy step stool handy for reaching high places.

Preventing Burns
- Use a pot holder, not a dishcloth or towel, to handle hot utensils.
- Keep a fire extinguisher near the kitchen entrance.
- Lift pot lids away from your body to avoid steam burns.
- Dry foods before putting them into hot fat to avoid spatters.
- Do not put water on a grease fire. Cover it with the lid of a pan or smother it with salt or baking soda.
- Do not carry a container of hot food across the room without first giving a loud warning to others.
- When draining hot food from a pan, use the lid as a shield from the steam.
- Open the oven door flat and pull out the oven rack when removing foods from a hot oven.
- Keep pan handles turned away from the front of the range when cooking.

Preventing Electrical Shocks
- Read and follow manufacturer's directions before using any electrical appliance.
- Plug electrical cords into appliances before plugging them into wall outlets.
- Disconnect appliances by pulling on the plug rather than the cord.
- Avoid overloading electrical outlets.
- Unplug an electrical appliance before cleaning it.
- Handle electrical appliances only when your hands are dry.

Preventing Poisonings
- Keep all chemicals, such as medicines, household cleaners, and pesticides, away from food storage areas.
- Keep food out of range when spraying chemicals. Wipe counters thoroughly when spraying.

16-11 Following safety guidelines while preparing and serving foods can help protect you and others from injury.

Family Enrichment Activity
Have students work with their families to analyze sanitation and safety practices in their homes. Have them develop checklists based on Chart 16-11, plus other information in Topic 16-2. Suggest that families work together to make any changes that are needed.

bacteria. If you suspect any food is spoiled, do not taste it. Throw it out immediately.

Signs of foodborne illness often include vomiting, diarrhea, stomach cramps, and headaches. These symptoms can occur within 30 minutes of eating contaminated food. However, sometimes symptoms take a few weeks to appear. Most foodborne illnesses usually last no more than a couple days, but some can have lasting effects. Pregnant women, young children, older adults, and people with weakened immune systems are at greater risk of foodborne illness. These groups of people need to take extra precautions to handle food safely.

Food safety involves four basic steps—clean, separate, cook, and chill. If you remember these steps and observe the following tips, you can help prevent foodborne illness.

Clean Hands, Utensils, and Surfaces

Cleanliness is essential. Keep utensils and work areas clean. Pay attention to personal cleanliness. Wash your hands with warm water and soap for 20 seconds before handling food. Make sure your fingernails are clean, too. Some other important principles of sanitation are listed below.

- Tie back hair or wear a chef's hat or hairnet to keep hair from falling into food.
- Wear a clean apron to avoid transferring bacteria from your clothes to the food.
- Use clean equipment.
- Do not use a hand towel to dry dishes.
- Do not touch food with your hands if you could use tongs, a fork, or a knife.
- Rewash hands after handling raw meats, poultry, fish, or eggs.
- Wear plastic gloves when working with food if you have an open sore on your hand.
- Do not lick fingers or cooking utensils. Use one spoon for stirring and another spoon for tasting.
- Cover coughs and sneezes with a tissue and wash your hands afterward. Also, wash hands after using the bathroom, changing diapers, or playing with pets.
- Replace cutting boards when they become worn and hard to clean.
- Wash dishes thoroughly with hot, soapy water and sanitize eating utensils with scalding water or sanitizer. See 16-12.
- Keep kitchen counters clean.
- Wash tops of cans before opening them to keep dust and bacteria out of food.
- Wash fresh fruits and vegetables under running water to flush away dirt and pesticides before preparation.

Pest Control

Pests can transfer disease-causing bacteria to food during storage. Therefore, you need to take steps to keep mice, rats, ants, flies, and cockroaches out of your home. You must prevent these pests from contaminating surfaces, utensils, or food supplies.

Methods for pest control vary. You can use a variety of traps or sprays. However,

16-12 The hot water and strong detergent used in a dishwasher sanitizes dishes.

Note: Many times when people exhibit flulike symptoms, they are actually experiencing some type of foodborne illness.

Enrich: Research instances of foodborne illnesses that made local and national news.

Activity: Display a collection of cleaning products. Have the students read the labels and discuss the uses of each type of cleaner. Demonstrate their use.

Note: Display a poster on proper hand washing near every sink in the classroom. Emphasize the presence of germs on hands and how illnesses are transmitted.

 Across the Curriculum
English. Have students research articles written about hazards connected to improper handling of foods during holidays, such as Easter eggs, Thanksgiving turkeys, and picnic foods. Have them summarize their findings in a written report.

Note:
Unsanitary conditions in a restaurant, such as dirty tables and floors, may also be an indication of how food is being handled.

Note:
You can get updated information on food safety from the USDA by accessing www.foodsafety.gov or calling 1-888-SAFE FOOD.

Resource:
Preventing Foodborne Illness, reproducible master, TR

Resource:
Temperature Guide to Food Safety, color transparency CT-14, TR

you must exercise great caution because chemicals can also contaminate surfaces, utensils, and food. If pest problems persist, contact your local health department for their suggestions. You may need to call a professional exterminator to keep pests away.

Separate Raw and Cooked Foods

You must handle all foods properly to prevent contamination. However, you must handle perishable protein foods (meat, poultry, fish, and eggs) with extra care as they are easily contaminated. When these foods are raw, you must also keep them separate from other foods. If these foods happen to be contaminated, keeping them separate will help you prevent other foods from becoming contaminated.

- Place fresh meats, poultry, and fish in individual plastic bags at the grocery store. This will keep juices from getting on other foods in your shopping cart.
- Place these foods in sealed plastic containers and store them on a lower shelf in the refrigerator. This will prevent them from dripping on other foods.
- Wash cutting boards and other equipment immediately after using them to prepare raw meats, poultry, fish, or eggs. This will help you avoid transferring bacteria from uncooked foods to other foods.
- Never serve cooked meat, poultry, or fish on the same plate that held these foods before cooking.

Cook Foods Thoroughly

Raw and undercooked meat, poultry, fish, and eggs may contain disease-causing bacteria. Thoroughly cook these foods and all dishes that contain them. Also, be sure food you order in restaurants is completely cooked. The temperatures used for cooking can kill many harmful bacteria.

- Use a food thermometer to be sure meat, poultry, fish, and egg products are cooked to the recommended internal temperatures. Color is not an accurate indicator of doneness. See 16-13.

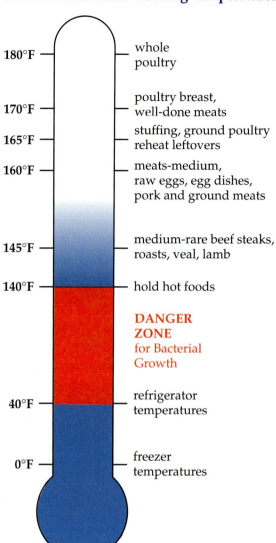

16-13 Thoroughly cooking food to the proper temperature kills harmful bacteria.

- Do not partially cook meats, poultry, or fish. Cook them thoroughly and serve immediately.
- Stuff meats, poultry, and fish just before baking. Remove stuffing promptly after baking; refrigerate leftovers separately.
- Never set the oven lower than 325°F when cooking meats.
- Keep hot foods hot—above 140°F. Bacteria grow fast in warm foods at lower temperatures.

Across the Curriculum

Science. Conduct an experiment in which you place a mixture of beef broth and unflavored gelatin in two petri dishes. Let the mixture set into a gel. Then place one of the dishes in a refrigerator and leave one in the classroom. Have students check the dishes every day for a week and make note of any changes. How does this experiment illustrate the importance of keeping foods at safe temperatures?

- If you are heating leftovers, be sure to heat them to at least 165°F before serving. Heat sauces, soups, marinades, and gravies to 165°F, too.

Chill Foods Promptly

Refrigerator temperatures slow the growth of harmful bacteria. This is why it is important to keep perishable foods chilled until you are ready to prepare or eat them. It is also important to chill leftover foods as soon as you are done eating.

- Put frozen and refrigerated foods in your shopping cart last.
- Get foods home as quickly as possible. In warm weather, carry a cooler in your car to keep foods cool until you get home.
- Promptly store foods that should be chilled and frozen.
- Wrap foods properly for freezer and refrigerator storage.
- Use thermometers to monitor storage temperatures. Be sure your freezer is kept at 0°F or lower and your refrigerator is kept at 40°F or lower.
- Thaw perishable foods overnight in the refrigerator or in the microwave oven just before cooking. Never thaw on the counter or in the sink.
- Marinate meat, fish, and poultry in the refrigerator.
- Never leave perishable foods out over two hours. This includes takeout foods and foods on a buffet table.
- Place leftovers in shallow containers to promote rapid cooling. Then refrigerate or freeze leftovers promptly. See 16-14.
- Keep cold foods cold—below 40°F. Bacteria grow fast in cool foods at higher temperatures.

16-14 Storing foods in shallow containers helps them quickly reach safe, cool temperatures.

Check It Out!

1. List three safety practices that help prevent kitchen accidents.
2. Explain how foodborne illnesses occur.
3. List the four basic steps to food safety and give two specific guidelines for each step.

Check It Out! (Answers)

1. (List three. Student response. Refer to Chart 16-11.)
2. Foodborne illnesses are caused by people eating contaminated food.
3. clean, separate, cook, chill (List two specific guidelines for each. Student response.)

Reflect:
Do you always refrigerate leftovers immediately, especially at holidays or other large gatherings?

Resource:
Sanitation in the Kitchen, Activity B, SAG

Resource:
Find the Mistake, reproducible master, TR

Topic 16-3
Using a Recipe

Objectives
After studying this topic, you will be able to
- identify the information found in a recipe and follow it successfully.
- demonstrate proper measuring techniques for different types of ingredients.
- define cooking terms used in recipes.
- describe two categories of cooking methods.

Topic Terms
recipe
measurement equivalents

Reflect: Are there special recipes and dishes your family is known for? Do you have recipes that have been passed down from generation to generation?

Activity: Pass out cookbooks to the class. Have students find recipes that are simple to make and some that are more complicated. Have them look for terms that are unfamiliar to them. See if anyone in the class can define them.

Activity: Again using cookbooks, have students look for ingredients, directions, utensil sizes, oven temperature, cooking times, and yield.

Activity: Have two students make the same recipe. Time each one. Have one student gather all the ingredients and utensils ahead of time and the other as they are needed. Discuss the benefits of planning ahead.

16-15 Smart cooks use simple recipes as they first learn to cook. As they develop their cooking skills, they will be able to try more involved recipes.

Cooking, like other skills, is learned through practice. Before you begin to cook, you need to know certain information about the food product you want to make. What ingredients do you need, and in what amounts? What utensils do you need to use? What steps should you follow? All this information is included in a recipe. A **recipe** is a list of ingredients with a complete set of instructions for preparing a food product.

Learning to use a recipe correctly is the key to good meals. If you can read and follow recipe instructions, you can prepare almost any food product. With experience, you can even develop your own recipes. See 16-15.

Understanding How to Use Recipes

All recipes include certain information, 16-16. The *ingredient list* tells you what food items you need. It also lists the exact amount of each ingredient you need to make the product. Preparation directions for combining the ingredients are next. Utensil sizes for cookware or bakeware are given, as are oven temperatures and cooking times. The recipe *yield* tells you how many servings the recipe makes.

Steps for Using Recipes

Many factors—measurements, preparation methods, cooking utensils, temperatures, and cooking times—can affect the outcome of a recipe. That is why it is important to follow all instructions. Following the guidelines below can help you get great results from the recipes you prepare. Here are some steps to help you get started.

- Read the entire recipe carefully *before* you start to cook. Make sure you have all the ingredients and utensils listed on hand. Check the preparation and cooking times in the recipe to make sure you have enough time to prepare it.
- Note any abbreviations used in the ingredient list. Be sure you understand what each one means. Abbreviations often used in recipes are given in 16-17.
- Before you start measuring and mixing, gather all the ingredients and cooking utensils you will need.

Putting Technology to Use
Have the class bring in their favorite recipes. Have students work together to combine the recipes into a "cookbook" using word processing software. Ask them to add designs where possible, including clipart or photos. Print and assemble the cookbooks and give one to each student.

Topic 16-3   Using a Recipe   473

> **Taco Frittata**
> (2 servings)
>
> 1 tablespoon butter
> 4 eggs
> 2 tablespoons chopped green chilies
> 2 tablespoons water
> ½ teaspoon Worcestershire sauce
> ¼ teaspoon salt
> ¼ teaspoon ground cumin
>   dash pepper
> ⅓ cup chunky taco sauce
>
> Melt butter over medium heat in a 6- to 8-inch omelet pan or skillet with ovenproof handle.* Beat together remaining ingredients, except taco sauce, until blended. Pour into pan. Cover and cook over low to medium heat until eggs are almost set, about 6 to 8 minutes. Pour taco sauce over top. Remove pan from heat. Cover and let stand 5 minutes or broil about 6 inches from heat until eggs are completely set, about 2 to 4 minutes.
>
> *To make handle ovenproof, wrap completely with aluminum foil.

16-16 A recipe includes all the information you need to successfully prepare a food product.

- If your recipe tells you to *preheat* the oven, turn the oven on before you begin to cook. Set the temperature given in the recipe. The oven will then be hot when you are ready to put the food in it.
- For successful results, follow recipe directions exactly. Measure the exact amounts of each ingredient. Mix ingredients in the order listed, using the method given. Use the correct utensil sizes.
- For best flavor and appearance, accurate timing is important. Follow cooking or baking times as stated in the recipe. If your range has a timer, use it to remind you when cooking times end.

In the early stages of learning to cook, using simple recipes is smart. Simple recipes have few ingredients and easy preparation steps. As you develop your cooking skills, you can try more difficult recipes and experiment with some of your own ideas.

Using Ingredient Substitutions

As you assemble your recipe ingredients, you may find you do not have a certain item on hand. In some recipes, you may be able to substitute one ingredient for another. In some cases, a substitution may affect the results of the finished product. If you are in a pinch, however, the substitution may be necessary. Some commonly used substitutions are given in 16-18.

Measuring Techniques

Learning to measure ingredients accurately is important for successful results, especially in baked products. Dry, liquid, and solid ingredients each require special measuring techniques. Chart 16-19 lists the right technique to use for each type of ingredient.

Abbreviations Used in Recipes

tsp. or t.	teaspoon
tbsp. or T.	tablespoon
c. or C.	cup
pt.	pint
qt.	quart
gal.	gallon
oz.	ounce
lb. or #	pound

16-17 Recognizing the abbreviations used in recipes will assist you in measuring ingredients accurately. The most common abbreviations are listed here.

Resource:
A Good Recipe Will Tell You..., reproducible master, TR

Activity:
Have two students make the same recipe. Have one follow correct measuring techniques while the other one estimates the amounts listed. Use a recipe where accurate measuring is very important. Evaluate the results.

Activity:
Have students find sections of cookbooks that list suitable substitutions for use in recipes.

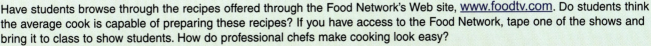
Putting Technology to Use
Have students browse through the recipes offered through the Food Network's Web site, www.foodtv.com. Do students think the average cook is capable of preparing these recipes? If you have access to the Food Network, tape one of the shows and bring it to class to show students. How do professional chefs make cooking look easy?

Activity:
Choose a recipe that uses as many different measuring techniques as possible to demonstrate techniques listed in 16-19 to the students.

Resource:
Abbreviations and Measuring Techniques, Activity C, SAG

Resource:
Using Ingredients, reproducible master, TR

Substituting One Ingredient for Another

You may use these:	For these:
1 whole egg, for baking or thickening	2 egg yolks
½ cup evaporated milk plus ½ cup water	1 cup fluid whole milk
1 cup reconstituted nonfat dry milk	1 cup fluid fat free milk
¾ cup milk plus ⅓ cup butter	1 cup heavy cream
1 tablespoon vinegar or lemon juice plus milk to make 1 cup (Allow this mixture to stand several minutes before using.)	1 cup sour milk or buttermilk
1 cup margarine	1 cup butter
3 tablespoons unsweetened cocoa powder plus 1 tablespoon butter or margarine	1 ounce unsweetened chocolate
1 ¼ cups sugar plus ¼ cup liquid used in recipe	1 cup corn syrup
2 tablespoons flour	1 tablespoon cornstarch
⅞ cup all-purpose flour	1 cup cake flour

16-18 You can sometimes make substitutions for ingredients you do not have on hand.

Measuring Techniques

Brown sugar	Pack firmly into a dry measure and level off top with straight edge of spatula or knife.
Granulated sugar	Spoon sugar into a dry measure until it is overfilled. Level off the top of the measure with a metal spatula or knife.
Flour, powdered sugar, fine meal, or crumbs	Stir lightly with a fork or spoon. Spoon lightly into dry measure until it is overflowing. Do not shake or tap measure. Level off top with straight edge of spatula or knife.
Baking powder, cornstarch, spices	Dip small measure into container and bring it up heaping full. Level off top with straight edge of metal spatula or knife.
Solid fats	Pack fat firmly into a dry measure and level off top with straight edge of metal spatula or knife. Remove fat with a rubber spatula. Butter and margarine usually come in sticks with measurements marked on the wrapper.
Liquids	Place liquid measure on a flat surface. Pour liquid into the measure until it reaches the desired level. View at eye level.

16-19 Proper measuring of ingredients will help ensure good results when cooking.

Across the Curriculum

Science. Make a dessert recipe using ingredients listed in the recipe. Then make the same dessert using substitutions listed in Chart 16-18. Have students sample both versions and compare flavor and texture. How is the product affected by the substitutions? Discuss with students the cooking principles illustrated in the preparation of the product.

For measuring dry ingredients, such as flour and sugar, use dry measuring cups. Use measuring spoons for measuring leavening agents, spices, and small amounts of dry ingredients. The general technique for measuring dry ingredients is to overfill the cup or spoon. Then level it off with a straight-edged spatula or knife.

Measure liquid ingredients in glass or clear plastic liquid measuring cups. Place the measure on a flat surface and then carefully fill it to the correct measurement line. Check the accuracy of your measurement at eye level. Use a measuring spoon for measuring small amounts of liquids.

Shortenings and other solid foods, such as peanut butter, are measured with dry measuring cups. Measuring spoons work well for small amounts. Press the ingredient into the cup or spoon, so no air space remains. Level it off with a straight-edged spatula or knife. For sticks of butter or margarine, cut through the wrapper at the correct measurement line.

Understanding Recipe Terms

As a beginning cook, you may come across recipe terms or directions you do not understand. Understanding these terms will help you use the right method for preparing the recipe correctly. Some common terms used in recipe directions are defined in 16-20.

Changing the Yield

What do you do if you need more or fewer servings than your recipe makes? You can double or halve the ingredient

Vocabulary:
Have the students look through cookbooks to find recipes that use the terms listed in 16-20. Have them write the name of a recipe for each term either on the chalkboard or on a sheet of paper.

Enrich:
Play charades and have the students act out the recipe terms.

Resource:
Recipe Terms, Activity D, SAG

Recipe Terms to Know

baste. To keep food moist during cooking by spooning or pouring melted fat, meat drippings, fruit juice, or sauce over it.

beat. To make a mixture smooth by adding air using a brisk stirring or whipping motion with a spoon or an electric mixer.

blend. To combine two or more ingredients until smooth and of uniform consistency.

bread. To dip food into a mixture, such as beaten eggs and milk, and then roll it in crumbs.

brown. To cook food quickly at a high temperature so the surface becomes brown.

chop. To cut into pieces with a knife, scissors, or food chopper.

cream. To stir or beat solid fat, such as shortening or butter, with sugar until the mixture is soft, smooth, and creamy.

cut in. To mix dry ingredients into shortening by using a pastry blender, two knives, or a fork.

dice. To cut into small even pieces, smaller than ½ inch.

dredge. To dip into or sprinkle with flour.

fold. To combine ingredients into a light, airy mixture using a down, across, up, and over motion with a rubber spatula.

knead. To use a fold-push-turn motion when working with doughs.

marinate. To let a food, such as meat, stand in a liquid to increase the flavor and/or tenderness of the food.

mash. To crush food until it has a smooth texture.

mince. To cut with a sharp knife or scissors into very small pieces.

mix. To combine ingredients until evenly distributed or blended.

reconstitute. To restore foods to their normal state by adding water.

scald. To heat milk just below the boiling point.

sear. To brown the surface of meat quickly with intense heat.

sift. To pass dry ingredients through a mesh or screen to add air or to combine dry ingredients.

slice. To cut or divide into flat pieces.

stir. To mix foods with a circular motion.

whip. To beat rapidly to incorporate air and to increase volume.

16-20 As you learn to cook, it is helpful to know the meaning of these terms.

Putting Technology to Use
Have students use charting software to make a bingo game using the recipe terms on the bingo cards. Then have students play bingo using the cards. Read off the definitions. Have the students choose the correct words on their cards and cover the words with bingo chips. Regular bingo rules for winning apply.

Activity:
Ask the cafeteria for the quantity recipe for something the students especially like and have them figure out a family portion recipe.

Resource:
Changing Recipe Quantities, Activity E, SAG

Activity:
Have students look for recipes in cookbooks that use moist heat and dry heat methods. Have them list these on the chalkboard.

amounts to change the recipe yield if you understand measurement equivalents. **Measurement equivalents** are amounts that are equal to other amounts, 16-21. For instance, one-fourth cup equals four tablespoons. To halve one-fourth cup, you would use two tablespoons.

When doubling or halving a recipe, write down the amounts of ingredients you will be using. This will help you avoid confusion while you are preparing the food.

Learning Cooking Methods

When preparing food, you want it to be both appetizing and nutritious. Some foods can be served raw. Others require cooking. Cooking is a science as well as an art. When heat is applied to food, certain changes take place. When different foods are combined, physical or chemical changes may take place also. Knowing various cooking methods will help you create tasty, nutritious meals.

Basic Cooking Methods

Foods can be prepared in a variety of ways. The method you use depends on the food you are preparing.

The basic methods of cooking food can be grouped in two general categories. The first category is *moist heat cooking methods*. In these methods, food is cooked in a humid environment. Moisture may be due to water or a water-based liquid being added to the food. Moisture may also result when steam released from the food is trapped in the cooking utensil or appliance. Boiling or stewing, braising, simmering, and steaming are all moist heat cooking methods. Basic microwave cooking is also considered a moist heat cooking method. This is because steam is enclosed in the sealed microwave oven cavity during cooking.

The second category of cooking methods is *dry heat cooking methods*. In these methods, food is cooked in hot air or on a hot surface without added moisture. Baking or roasting, broiling, deep frying, grilling, panbroiling, panfrying, and stir-frying are all dry heat cooking methods. These methods allow food products to become brown and develop crisp crusts, which cannot form in a moist atmosphere.

Moist and dry heat cooking methods are described in Chart 16-22. More information on cooking methods for specific types of foods is presented in Chapter 17.

General Cooking Guidelines

A general rule to follow when cooking food is to avoid overcooking it. Overcooking makes protein foods, such as meat and eggs, tough and causes milk to curdle. Baked products become dry. Fruits and vegetables become mushy and discolored when overcooked. Overcooking also causes foods to lose water-soluble vitamins.

Try to conserve nutrients when preparing food. If foods are simmered, use as little water as possible. When foods are boiled, plan a way to use the liquid in which they were cooked. Valuable vitamins and minerals are often discarded when cooking liquids are poured down the drain. Use these liquids in soups, sauces, and gravies.

Microwave Cooking

Most foods cook much faster in a microwave oven than they do in a conventional oven. Therefore, you need to use some special cooking techniques when preparing foods in a microwave oven to achieve best results.

Common Measurement Equivalents

1 tablespoon	= 3 teaspoons
⅛ cup	= 2 tablespoons
¼ cup	= 4 tablespoons
⅓ cup	= 5 ⅓ tablespoons
½ cup	= 8 tablespoons
⅔ cup	= 10 ⅔ tablespoons
¾ cup	= 12 tablespoons
1 cup, ½ pint	= 16 tablespoons
1 pint	= 2 cups
quart	= 2 pints, 4 cups

16-21 Knowing equivalent measures can help you change recipe yields.

Putting Technology to Use
Have students change yield for a recipe using the Cooking Measures and Conversion Calculator found at www.globalgourmet.com/cgi-bin/hts?convcalc.hts. Students may also wish to explore the rest of the Global Gourmet Web site.

Cooking Methods

Moist Heat

Method	Procedure	Foods
Boil/Stew	To cook in water or liquid in which rolling bubbles have formed	Vegetables, meats, pasta
Braise	To cook in a small amount of liquid in a tightly covered pan over low heat	Meats, vegetables
Microwave	To cook in a microwave oven	Vegetables, meats, fruits, casseroles
Simmer	To cook in liquid just below the boiling point	Eggs, meats, soups
Steam	To cook in steam, with or without pressure	Vegetables, meats, fish

Dry Heat

Method	Procedure	Foods
Bake/Roast	To cook in an oven in a covered or uncovered container	Cakes, cookies, breads, eggs, some vegetables, meats
Broil	To cook uncovered by direct heat	Meats, seafood, fruits, and vegetables
Deep-fry	To cook in a large amount of hot fat	Meats, seafood, vegetables, doughnuts, fritters
Grill	To roast slowly over coals or another intense heat source	Meats, vegetables
Panbroil	To cook uncovered in a fry pan, pouring fat off as it accumulates	Bacon, sausage, and similar meats containing a large amount of fat
Panfry	To cook in a small amount of fat	Meats, seafood, vegetables, eggs
Stir-fry	To cook foods quickly in a small amount of fat at a high temperature	Thinly cut meats, fish, vegetables, rice

16-22 Choose the cooking method best suited to the food you are preparing.

Resource:
Cooking Terms, reproducible master, TR

Enrich:
Use these terms as a part of the bingo game described on page 475.

Discuss:
Have you ever used the defrost feature on your microwave oven? Does your family use it often? Do you find it easy or difficult to use?

The defrost cycle is a popular feature on most microwave ovens because you can defrost foods at the last minute. *Defrosting time* is determined by the size and density of the food you wish to defrost. You will need more time to defrost a four-pound roast than four pounds of individually wrapped steaks. This is because the roast is larger and denser than the steaks.

Many microwave ovens have an automatic defrost cycle. A sensor measures the steam generated as a food product defrosts. This sensor automatically stops the defrost cycle at the right time. Most microwave ovens have a chart in the use and care manual to help you determine correct defrost times. Many food packages also give directions on how to defrost the products in a microwave oven.

Foods such as eggs, apples, potatoes, and many prepackaged foods are covered with a tight skin or wrapper. Moisture in

Putting Technology to Use
Have the students look through cookbooks to find recipes that use the terms in Chart 16-22. Have students use charting software to create a two-column chart. Students should enter the terms from Chart 16-22 in the first column of the chart, then enter the names of recipes that include the term in the second column.

> **Discuss:**
> How many times a day do you use a microwave oven? Do you cook more often using a microwave oven then other appliances? Why?
>
> **Reflect:**
> Have you ever cooked something in the microwave that included directions to allow standing time? What happens if you try to eat the food right away?
>
> **Note:**
> Check to see how powerful your microwave oven is before trying a recipe, as adjustments may need to be made.

foods turns into steam during the cooking process. If this steam is trapped inside the skin or wrapper covering a food, the encased food can explode. Exploding food items can be dangerous as well as messy and unattractive. *Piercing* the skin or wrapper of such foods before microwaving allows the steam to escape slowly as the food cooks.

You read earlier that you should not use metal utensils in a microwave oven. However, you can use foil in small amounts if you do not allow it to touch the walls of the oven. For example, you might cover chicken wing tips or the small ends of drumsticks with foil. This technique is known as *shielding*. The parts of a food that you shield with aluminum foil are prevented from overcooking. Other foods you might shield include the bone area in a large meat cut. You can also shield the corners of a square baking dish to keep the food in the corners from becoming dry.

Covering foods in a microwave oven prevents them from drying out due to loss of moisture. There are several popular coverings. You might simply cover foods in a microwavable dish with the lid to the dish. Plastic wraps work well for covering many foods. However, they can form tight seals, so you will need to leave a loose corner to allow steam to escape. This is called *venting*. Paper towels are used for covering foods such as bacon that produce fats or breads that produce moisture. The paper towel absorbs the fat or moisture so the food does not become soggy. Wax paper can be placed atop a casserole in a microwave oven for efficient cooking.

Microwaves cook the outer edges of foods first. Microwave ovens also tend to cook faster in the center of the oven. You can compensate for these deviations and promote even cooking by stirring, rearranging, or rotating the food. *Stirring* will bring food from the center of a dish to the outer edges for faster cooking. You cannot stir some foods, such as chicken pieces. *Rearranging* these foods halfway through the cooking cycle will help them cook more evenly. What about a pineapple upside down cake, which cannot be stirred or rearranged? *Rotating* such foods a quarter or half turn several times during the cooking cycle will help distribute microwaves more evenly. Many microwave ovens come with a turntable to rotate foods for you.

Hot foods continue to cook as long as they are hot. Therefore, many microwave recipes recommend *standing time* to allow the food to finish cooking. Standing time should begin just before a food has finished cooking. Failing to allow for standing time can result in overcooked foods.

Many of today's microwave ovens cook even faster than models sold a few years ago, 16-23. You may need to alter the cooking times of your favorite microwave recipes if you get a new microwave oven. You should always read the recipe you are using and the directions that come with a new oven.

16-23 Today's powerful microwave ovens cook foods faster than ever.

> **Across the Curriculum**
> English, science. Have students prepare a research report on microwave ovens. Instruct students to include in the report the discovery of microwaves as well as the operation of a microwave oven and principles of microwave cooking.

Check It Out!

1. What is the first step to follow in using a recipe?
2. Describe the technique used for measuring flour.
3. Briefly explain each of the following recipe terms: blend, mix, and stir.
4. What are the two general categories into which cooking methods can be grouped?
5. Using small amounts of foil to cover areas of a food product and prevent them from overcooking is called ____.

Check It Out! (Answers)

1. read it through before starting to cook
2. Spoon lightly into dry measure until it is overflowing. Do not shake or tap measure. Level off top with straight edge of spatula or knife.
3. Blend: to combine two or more ingredients until smooth and of uniform consistency. Mix: to combine ingredients until evenly distributed or blended. Stir: to mix foods with a circular motion.
4. moist heat cooking methods and dry heat cooking methods
5. shielding

Topic 16-4
Cooking Smart

Objectives
After studying this topic, you will be able to
- plan a meal management time plan at home.
- demonstrate how to work as an effective team member in the foods lab.

Topic Term
work plan

Reflect: How is mealtime planned and carried out in your home? Is it well planned or thrown together haphazardly?

Cooking smart means getting foods prepared with a minimum of time and a maximum of efficiency. Some tricks that will help you master these skills can be used both at home and at school.

There is one major difference between meal preparations at home and at school. At home, you may prepare foods your way. At school, you are a part of a team. Besides learning cooking skills, you learn the importance of teamwork. See 16-24.

16-24 Working together in the school foods lab requires cooperation from each group member.

Discuss:
What examples of advance preparation possibilities can you think of? Think of your last big family dinner. Which items were, or could have been, prepared in advance?

Enrich:
Look through current magazines to find recipes that specifically suggest freezing for future use. Compare these to recipes in older cookbooks that were designed for the homemaker who stayed home and cooked the entire meal every day.

Resource:
Making Use of Leftovers, reproducible master, TR

At Home

The key to successful meal preparation at home lies in planning. Timing is one of the most difficult skills in meal preparation. This means having all the food ready and at the right temperature at serving time. You can achieve this goal, but it takes careful scheduling.

Using a Time Plan

As a beginning cook, you will want to write out a time plan. A time plan helps you coordinate your cooking schedule. You will know exactly when you must complete certain preparation tasks to serve the meal on time. You will also avoid the confusion and frustration of having several tasks to complete at the same time.

Try to pace your cooking activities according to the clock. You can do this by establishing the time the meal is to be served. Then count back in time to decide when you should start each part of the meal.

Suppose you want to prepare this meal: baked chicken, hot rolls, a salad, and chocolate pudding. Here is how your time plan would work. Because the chicken will take the longest to cook, prepare it first and place it in the oven. Then prepare the pudding. You can prepare the salad next. Chill both the salad and the pudding in the refrigerator until serving time. About 15 minutes before you plan to eat, heat the rolls in the oven. During this time, you can set the table and prepare the beverage. At mealtime, the chicken and rolls should be hot, the salad crisp, and the pudding chilled.

When serving many foods that are to be cooked in the oven, choose foods that have compatible oven temperatures. For instance, stuffed pork chops, green bean casserole, and a quick bread can all be baked at 350°F.

As you gain experience, you will find it easier to prepare simple meals without a time plan. Do not allow relying on a time plan to make you feel uncomfortable, however. Good cooks with years of experience still use them when they prepare food for special occasions.

Making Meal Preparations

Making meal preparations means doing meal-related tasks ahead of time. It could mean baking a large ham, roast, or turkey on the weekend to eat during the week. It could mean preparing a salad or casserole the night before you plan to serve it. It might also mean setting the table in the morning before you go to work or school. Use any time available to prepare for meals. You will be glad you did when it is mealtime.

Many foods lend themselves to being prepared and stored ahead of time. By preparing large amounts of foods such as soups and casseroles, you can freeze leftovers for other days, 16-25. This is a real time-saver. Most cooking time is spent assembling ingredients and utensils and then cleaning up afterwards. By preparing several dishes at once, you save much time and effort. On a busy day, all you have to do is allow time to heat the dish in the oven or microwave.

Using Computer Technologies

Time planning is crucial for people with busy lifestyles. As a result, many people are using the convenience of

16-25 The effort required to make one large pot of stew can provide several meals for a family.

FCCLA Activity
Have students practice various techniques of measuring, cutting, mixing, and cooking food. Then produce an instructional videotape. This can be used in food labs at school or loaned to other groups (such as Scouts, 4-H groups, Boys' or Girls' Clubs, etc.) as the basis for cooking classes or badge work.

computer technology to save time in the kitchen. Both large and small appliances and personal computers (PCs) are used to perform daily kitchen tasks.

Many modern appliances use microprocessors to make meal preparation easier. A *microprocessor* is a tiny computer control. Both large and small appliances use these computer controls to simplify many cooking tasks. For instance, you can program a range or microwave oven to operate at certain times and temperatures. You can set a coffeemaker to turn on in the morning or evening.

PCs offer many timesaving uses in the kitchen, too. Instead of using cookbooks, you might use a special software program to store recipes and menu plans in your computer's memory. When you are ready to cook, you can call up the recipe file. The program can calculate the amount of each ingredient needed and even prepare a shopping list. You can also look up recipes and meal preparation tips on the Internet. See 16-26.

16-26 This computerized console can communicate with other kitchen appliances as well as sending and downloading information through the Internet.

At School

When you prepare food at school, you learn two important skills: cooking and teamwork. Thorough planning and good cooperation are needed for a successful foods lab experience.

Working with Others

Learning to work well with others in your foods lab is an important skill. Because your class time is limited, lab time must be carefully scheduled. In the foods lab, you are likely to be working with a larger group than you work with at home. You may not be familiar with your classmates' work habits, so planning lab time eliminates confusion. You need to know what is expected of you as part of the team. You also need to know when to complete your tasks.

Make the most of this opportunity to be part of a team. Such an opportunity improves your ability to get along with others, now and in the future. Be cooperative and keep a positive attitude. If you have a concern about an assigned task, talk with your group.

Planning the Lab

To have a successful lab experience, you need a work plan. A **work plan** is a detailed list of all the duties that must be completed during the lab. The list also includes who will perform each task, as well as the ingredients and utensils needed. Your teacher will probably ask you to complete the plan at least a day before you will be cooking.

Making Out the Shopping List

The first task in your work plan is determining what foods you will prepare. Most likely your teacher will plan this portion of the lab. Locate the necessary recipes and make an accurate list of all the ingredients needed. Your teacher may inform you that some staple ingredients are already on hand. You may be asked not to write those ingredients on your list.

Activity:
Ask students to list the appliances in their homes that use computer technology. Also note the appliances in the classroom that use this technology.

Resource:
A Quick Meal, Activity F, SAG

Discuss:
How can learning to work well with others in the foods lab help you enjoy other organizations?

 Putting Technology to Use
Have students research up-to-date computerized kitchen appliances on the Internet. One suggestion is The Web site for LG Appliances, www.lgappliances.com.

Discuss:
What aspects of the lab experience should be used in the evaluation?

Resource:
Working in the Foods Lab, reproducible master, TR

Making a Time Schedule

Next, make a time schedule that includes all the tasks to be done. Prioritize the tasks in order of importance. List first those tasks that require the greatest amount of time. Allow enough time for preparation, serving, and cleanup. As a group, decide who will perform each task. For each lab planned, rotate job tasks. This way each member has the experience of performing each task. Once your schedule is complete, your lab group will be ready to prepare your planned food. See 16-27.

Evaluating the Lab Experience

Evaluation is an important individual and group process. It gives you an opportunity to identify your strengths and weaknesses. This process also reinforces the positive aspects of the lab experience.

Evaluate yourself first; ask yourself what you did well. Did you use utensils, appliances, and food preparation techniques correctly? Identify areas in which you can improve. Second, evaluate the performance of your group as a whole. Be sure to discuss how, as a group, you can improve on the weak areas. Do not hesitate to admit your strengths and weaknesses. This is how members of your group can learn from one another.

Check It Out!

1. True or false. A time plan helps people determine what preparation tasks must be completed so their meals are prepared on time.
2. Name two ways in which computer technologies can assist with meal management.
3. List three steps to follow for planning a successful foods lab.

Check It Out! (Answers)

1. true
2. (List two:) using portable and large appliances with microprocessors; using a recipe software program for filing recipes, looking up recipes on the Internet
3. make out a shopping list, make out a time schedule, evaluate the lab experience

16-27 A successful foods lab depends on good planning and teamwork.

TEENS ARE EXPERIENCING...

Meal Management Challenges

Olivia Hall, an energetic ninth grade family and consumer science student, takes an active role in family meal management. She considers herself a seasoned cook. "I started cooking easy recipes when I was in second grade," she stated. "I was always in the kitchen, so my mother encouraged me to cook."

Olivia's meal management skills have evolved over the past years. She has learned to plan meals that are satisfying to her family. She knows how to shop and store food properly. She can prepare nutritious and appealing foods. Her family is proud of her accomplishments. Olivia is proud of herself, too.

When asked what type of cooking skills she has developed, Olivia responded, "I have learned to prepare a lot of meals in the microwave oven. I even helped revise our family recipe collection so the recipes can be cooked easily in the microwave. I learned this skill from taking microwave cooking classes. When we purchased our microwave oven, we took classes on how to use it correctly. During the classes, we learned how to prepare meals. We also found many ideas in the microwave oven cookbook."

How often does Olivia cook? "I help prepare most of the meals at home. I also like to cook on weekends when my family stays at the beach house." Olivia added, " I enjoy cooking for special occasions, like Mother's Day and birthdays, too."

Deciding what to prepare is a challenge for any meal manager. How does Olivia decide what to prepare? "I have learned to plan balanced menus at our house. My family likes meals that include a main dish, vegetables, fruits, and bread. Sometimes we prepare a dessert, but not with every meal."

Olivia enjoys preparing foods from scratch rather than counting on convenience products. "I try to prepare homemade recipes every day. This allows me to control the fat, cholesterol, and calories in our diets. I'm always looking for new recipe ideas. I get recipes from friends and from different cookbooks. We also subscribe to cooking magazines."

She continued, "Advance preparation makes cooking from scratch easier, too. We have a large freezer where we store some homemade foods we have prepared. Our favorites are fresh vegetables from our summer garden. We always have lots of tomatoes, so we freeze the extras. Then we use them to make stews and sauces during the off-seasons."

Olivia and her family enjoy preparing and serving meals together at home. Her family uses mealtime to keep in touch with each other. The time spent together helps them keep their relationships strong and healthy. "We share stories about the events that have happened during the day. We all enjoy the meal, because we try to prepare foods we like to eat."

Discuss:
- How much responsibility do you have for grocery shopping? Who does most of the shopping in your family? Who does the menu planning?
- Does your family make foods from scratch or do you use more convenience foods? Do you do any advance food preparation to save time later, as Olivia does? What are the pros and cons of each approach to food preparation?
- What are mealtimes like in your home? Are they similar to Olivia's, where family members prepare and eat meals together, or does this seldom occur in families today? What are the benefits of this type of family mealtime? Are there any drawbacks?

Chapter Review

Summary

Before you begin cooking, you need to know how to choose the cooking equipment that will best meet your needs. Kitchen appliances include major and portable appliances. Utensils are used for measuring, cutting, and mixing tasks. Cookware and bakeware are used for cooking and baking foods. With proper use and care, all these kitchen tools will provide many years of service. The more you know about cooking equipment, the greater your chances are for a successful cooking experience.

Good safety and sanitation habits must also be a high priority when you cook. Following the steps of clean, separate, cook, and chill when handling food will help you avoid foodborne illnesses. Your health, and the health of others, depends on the way you practice these habits.

Knowing how to read and use recipe information is another basic cooking skill. Learning to measure accurately is essential for preparing a recipe properly. Understanding cooking terms, making substitutions, and adjusting yields are other important techniques for cooking success.

Techniques for cooking smart can be used at home or at school. At home, it means using a time plan and making preparations. At school, it means practicing teamwork and preparing a work plan.

Think About It!

1. If you could only have one oven in your kitchen, which type would you choose: a conventional oven, a microwave oven, or a convection oven? Explain your choice.
2. Name three portable appliances you consider versatile. Then suggest different ways you can use each one to take advantage of the versatility.
3. What is the advantage of buying high-quality kitchen utensils?
4. Chart 16-11 lists seven guidelines for preventing fires. List the three guides you think are most frequently ignored. What happens as a result of ignoring fire prevention principles?
5. What types of foods are most likely to become contaminated if they are not handled properly?
6. Why should you gather all the ingredients and cooking utensils you will need before you start preparing a recipe?
7. How does a time plan make work in the kitchen more efficient?
8. Give several examples of early preparations that will be helpful as you attempt to serve family meals.
9. In what careers do you see the information in this chapter being helpful? Share these insights with your classmates.
10. List some global practices you have observed in movies or news reports that differ from the concepts taught in this chapter. For example, refrigerators are not commonly used among many cultures. How might these cultures keep food from spoiling?

Discuss:
Ask if the students have prepared meals using time plans or without time plans. Do they prefer to use time plans? Why or why not?

Resource:
PowerZone Challenge CD. Have students play the chapter review game to reinforce text content.

Try It Out!

1. Select one major appliance, portable appliance, or kitchen utensil. Study the use and care instructions that came with it. Demonstrate the correct use and care of that piece of kitchen equipment.
2. Conduct a safety and sanitation check of your foods laboratory at school and your kitchen at home. What can you do to improve the safety and sanitation standards at school and at home?
3. Create a kitchen safety poster for the foods lab that shows safety rules for using, washing, and storing knives.
4. Find a recipe you would like to prepare. Read it thoroughly and
    A. translate the abbreviations
    B. explain the correct procedure for measuring each ingredient
    C. identify the key preparation terms
5. Choose any recipe and adapt it by
    A. doubling the ingredients
    B. cutting the ingredients in half
6. Write a menu for a family meal to be served at 6:30 p.m. Prepare a time plan. (You will need to refer to the recipes for the required cooking times.) As you prepare the time plan, ask yourself these questions: When will you complete certain tasks? Which tasks can be done ahead of time?

Chapter 17
Buying, Storing, and Preparing Foods

Careers

These careers relate to the topics in this chapter:

- family food shopper
- food product demonstrator
- food technician
- food editor

As you study this chapter, see if you can think of others.

Topics

17-1 Meat, Poultry, Fish, and Alternates
17-2 Fruits and Vegetables
17-3 Cereal Products
17-4 Milk and Milk Products

Introductory Activities

1. Field trip: Have a grocery store scavenger hunt. Divide the class into teams of three and give each team a list of items they must find in a grocery store. Items might include foods that should be stored on a shelf, stored in the freezer, used within one or two days of purchase, are inexpensive sources of protein, and require little preparation.
2. *Food Storage Information,* reproducible master, TR. Students can use this master as a guide in determining how to store various foods. To acquaint students with the chart, ask various questions to which students can locate the answers on the chart.

Topic 17-1
Meat, Poultry, Fish, and Alternates
I. Buying Meat, Poultry, Fish, and Alternates
  A. Meat
    1. Meat Inspection and Grading
    2. Meat Selection
  B. Poultry
  C. Fish
    1. Finfish
    2. Shellfish
  D. Eggs
    1. Size and Color
    2. Grades
  E. Plant-Based Meat Alternates
    1. Legumes
    2. Meat Analogs
II. Storing Meat, Poultry, Fish, and Alternates
  A. Meat and Poultry
  B. Fish
  C. Eggs
  D. Legumes and Nuts
III. Preparing Meat, Poultry, Fish, and Alternates
  A. Meat
    1. Choosing a Cooking Method
    2. Judging Doneness
  B. Poultry
    1. Judging Doneness
  C. Fish
  D. Eggs
  E. Legumes

Topic 17-2
Fruits and Vegetables
I. Buying Fruits and Vegetables
  A. Fresh Fruits and Vegetables
  B. Frozen Fruits and Vegetables
  C. Canned Fruits and Vegetables
  D. Dried Fruits and Vegetables
II. Storing Fruits and Vegetables
  A. Storing Fresh Produce
  B. Storing Other Forms of Fruits and Vegetables
III. Preparing Fruits and Vegetables
  A. Fresh Fruits and Vegetables
    1. Cooking Methods
  B. Preparing Other Forms of Fruits and Vegetables

Topic 17-3
Cereal Products
I. Buying Cereal Products
  A. Flour
  B. Pasta
  C. Rice
  D. Breakfast Cereals
  E. Breads
II. Storing Cereal Products
III. Preparing Cereal Products
  A. Cooking with Thickeners
  B. Pasta
  C. Rice
  D. Cooked Cereals
  E. Breads
    1. Yeast Breads
    2. Quick Breads
IV. Cakes and Cookies
  A. Preparing Cakes
    1. Baking Guidelines
  B. Preparing Cookies
    1. Baking Guidelines

Topic 17-4
Milk and Milk Products
I. Buying Dairy Products
  A. Milk
  B. Cheese
    1. Natural Cheese
    2. Process Cheese
II. Storing Dairy Products
  A. Milk and Milk Products
  B. Cheese
III. Preparing Dairy Products
  A. Cooking with Milk
  B. Cooking with Cheese

Topic 17-1
Meat, Poultry, Fish, and Alternates

Objectives
After studying this topic, you will be able to
- list factors to consider when buying meat, poultry, fish, and alternates.
- use proper storage methods for meat, poultry, fish, and alternates.
- describe cooking methods used to prepare meat, poultry, fish, and alternates.

Topic Terms
meat
poultry
finfish
shellfish
legume
meat analog

Meat, poultry, fish, eggs, dry beans, and nuts are major sources of protein in your diet. In addition, protein foods are often the main dish of a meal. See 17-1.

Some protein foods can be the most costly part of your food budget. Wise selection, storage, and preparation will help you get the most for your money.

17-1 Protein foods, such as steak, are often served as the main course of a meal.

Buying Meat, Poultry, Fish, and Alternates

Meat, poultry, and fish are the most costly protein foods, so you should select them carefully for the best value. Less costly, but equally nutritious protein alternatives are also available. Eggs, dry beans, and nuts are good sources of protein, vitamins, and minerals. To stretch your food dollar, plan some menus around these alternates.

Learning to evaluate the quality of protein foods is an important skill. You can evaluate many protein foods based on appearance. However, other factors discussed in this topic are also helpful in making smart buying choices.

Meat
Meat is the edible portion of animals, including muscles and organs. Beef, veal, pork, and lamb are the most common forms of meat. Mature cattle provide beef, while young cattle provide veal. Pork comes from swine. Lamb comes from young sheep.

You should consider two major factors when buying meat. One is the quality of the meat; the other is the cut of the meat.

Meat Inspection and Grading
In the United States, all meat shipped across state lines must be inspected. This is done by the United States Department of Agriculture (USDA) to certify the meat is wholesome. An inspection also indicates the plant and processing conditions were sanitary.

In addition to an inspection stamp, beef, veal, and lamb may be stamped with a grade shield, 17-2. (Pork is considered tender, so it is not graded for retail sale.) This shield indicates the meat was voluntarily graded for quality. Grades help consumers determine the tenderness and juiciness of the meat. Meat from a young animal is usually tender; meat from an older animal is usually tougher.

Enrich: Divide the class into small groups. Have each group try to name the most varieties of fish. Place the names in their correct categories—shellfish or finfish.

Note: The terms *ham* and *hamburger* can be confusing to students. Clarify that ham is cured pork and hamburger is a common name for ground beef. Have a student research where the name *hamburger* originated.

Discuss: What precautions should consumers consider when purchasing meat that has not crossed state lines?

Note: Emphasize that grading and inspection are different.

FCCLA Activity
Field trip: Have students make arrangements to visit a local food pantry to learn how foods are obtained, stored, and distributed. Encourage them to volunteer to work there. Have them search out sources of fresh produce and work with food shelf personnel to find ways to distribute it before it spoils.

Enrich:
Display various retail cuts of beef. Discuss color, fat quality, fat distribution, and size, location, and shape of bones.

Note:
Emphasize that the nutritive value of expensive cuts and inexpensive cuts of meat are equal.

Resource:
Comparing the Costs Per Serving of Protein Foods, reproducible master, TR

17-2 The USDA stamp on the top certifies that meat is wholesome. The grade shield below is an indication of quality.

The three top grades for beef established by the USDA are prime, choice, and select.
- *Prime* beef has the best quality and flavor. It is the most tender because it has the most *marbling* (fat that is mingled throughout the lean). This grade is mainly sold to restaurants.
- *Choice* beef has excellent quality, but has less fat and flavor than prime. It is the highest quality found in grocery stores and meat markets. Although choice is less expensive than prime, it is more expensive than select.
- *Select* beef has less flavor and marbling than prime and choice. However, it has less fat and a lower cost, so it is a good buy from health and budget angles.

Meat Selection

In selecting meat, you can be sure the quality is good if the lean has good color and is marbled with fat. Beef will be bright red. Veal will be light pink. Pork will be pink to rose colored. Lamb will be pinkish-red. Quality meat also has firm fat that is creamy white in color. Meat with yellow fat is of poorer quality.

Regardless of the grade, some cuts of meat are more tender than others. The location of the meat in the animal determines tenderness. Cuts from the less-used muscles along the back are more tender. These include rib and loin cuts. Cuts from the muscles that are frequently used are less tender. These include leg and shoulder cuts.

You can also determine whether a meat cut comes from the tender part of an animal by looking at bone shape. T-shaped bones, flat bones, and wedge bones indicate tender cuts. Round bones (from the arm and leg area) and blade bones (from the shoulder area) indicate less-tender cuts of meat.

Buy the cut of meat best suited to your needs by reading meat labels. See 17-3. Meat labels make meat identification easy. By reading the meat identification label, you can find out the
- type of meat
- wholesale cut (location of the meat in the animal)
- retail name of the cut

The tenderest cuts of meat make up a very small portion of the animal. They are also more highly sought by the consumer. This is why these cuts are most expensive. When buying meat, consider the cost per serving rather than the cost per pound. If two cuts of meat cost the same, the cut with less fat and less bone will yield more servings.

Poultry

Poultry describes any domesticated bird raised for meat and/or eggs. Chicken, turkey, duck, and goose are the most popular types of poultry in the United States. Like meats, poultry must be federally inspected for wholesomeness. It may also be voluntarily graded for quality. Only U.S. Grade A

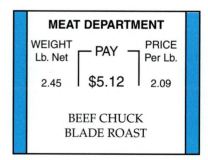

17-3 A meat package label shows the names of the wholesale and retail cuts, the weight, and the price.

Across the Curriculum

Math. Distribute ads from several different grocery stores to small groups of students. Have them compare prices of poultry pieces with whole bird prices at each store. Then have the groups compare costs from different stores. As a class, determine what, according to the ads, would be the best purchase.

poultry is sold at the retail level. However, "ungraded" poultry is usually equal in quality to Grade A poultry.

Ready-to-cook chickens, turkeys, ducks, and geese are sold fresh-chilled or frozen. Poultry should look moist and plump and have clean, blemish-free skin. Choose birds with meaty breasts and legs. See 17-4. Avoid buying frozen birds that show signs of thawing or freezer burn (brownish spots). When buying chicken or turkey, whole birds are usually a better buy than pieces, such as breasts and legs.

Chicken is classified by the weight and age of the birds when they are processed. Most of the chickens sold in U.S. grocery stores are tender, young birds, which are classified as *broiler-fryers*. You can successfully cook this class of chickens by any method. *Cornish game hens* are very small, specially bred chickens. They are generally roasted, and they are often stuffed. Because of their small size, Cornish game hens are usually served whole or in half for individual servings.

Turkey has long been popular for holiday meals. Like chickens, most of the turkeys sold in the United States are tender, young birds. These birds are suitable for roasting or any other preparation method. Some birds may be labeled as *hens* (females) or *toms* (males) to indicate size. Hens and toms are equally tender, but toms are generally larger.

Fish

Finfish and shellfish are two forms of fish that are eaten as food. **Finfish** have fins and backbones. **Shellfish** have shells instead of backbones. Both are available in many forms, depending on where you live.

Be alert to the visible signs of freshness and quality when selecting fish and shellfish. Inspection and grade seals can help you determine quality. You should also consider appearance and form when making a purchase decision.

Finfish

The most popular finfish are cod, flounder, halibut, salmon, sole, snapper, and trout. When buying fish, however, look for regional specialties. They will usually cost less than varieties that must be shipped in from other areas. When buying fresh finfish, you will want to watch for the following signs of quality:

- Eyes should be bright and clear.
- Gills should be reddish in color.
- Scales should be tight to the body and shiny.
- Flesh should be firm enough to spring back when gently pressed.
- Odor should be fresh. See 17-5.

Fish are marketed in a variety of forms. The most popular choices are drawn, dressed, fillets, and steaks. *Drawn fish* have the entrails (guts) removed. *Dressed fish* have been cleaned. In addition to the entrails, they have had the head, tail, fins, and scales removed. *Fillets* are sides of the fish, which are cut away from the bone lengthwise from head to tail. Fillets are popular because they are usually boneless and ready to cook. *Steaks* are cross-sectional slices of larger fish with one large, central bone. Steaks are also ready to cook.

Fish is available frozen, canned, or dried as well as fresh. Fish sticks are a common form of frozen fish. Canned tuna,

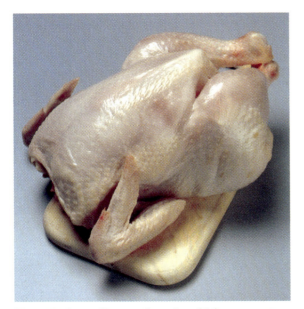

17-4 High-quality poultry should have meaty breasts and legs and clean, blemish-free skin.

Activity:
The price of turkey legs and thighs is frequently inexpensive. Have small groups plan meals using these inexpensive poultry cuts.

Discuss:
Have students name their favorite poultry dishes. What types of poultry are used in the dishes?

Discuss:
What types of fish are eaten by your families? How often do you have fish at home?

Activity:
Have students find out which type of finfish is least expensive to buy in your area.

 Across the Curriculum
English. Have students conduct research on finfish hatcheries. Where are they located? What are their goals? What procedures are followed in the hatcheries? Have students write a paper on their findings.

Enrich:
Have students research government regulations that apply to fish marketing.

Activity:
Buy three sizes of eggs. Using liquid measuring cups, have students compare the sizes. How would this affect recipes?

Activity:
Have students compare the nutritive value of one serving of beef with two eggs.

17-5 Look for signs of quality when buying fresh fish.

salmon, sardines, and mackerel are economical buys. In some areas, dried, salted, and smoked fish are popular menu items.

Shellfish

Clams, crabs, lobsters, mussels, oysters, shrimp, and scallops are all varieties of shellfish. If oysters, clams, scallops, and mussels are purchased fresh, the shells should be tightly closed. Fresh shellfish such as crabs, lobsters, and shrimp should retain their natural color. You can also buy shellfish in canned or frozen form.

Eggs

When buying eggs, size and condition are important factors to consider. Choose the size that best meets your needs. Open the carton to be sure eggs have clean, uncracked shells.

Size and Color

Eggs are classified by size according to weight per dozen. Medium, large, and extra large are the sizes most commonly sold in grocery stores. Recipes are usually based on using large eggs.

Eggshells may be either white or brown. The color of the shell has nothing to do with the quality or nutritive value of the egg. (The breed of chicken determines the egg color.)

Grades

The USDA has set up standards of quality for grading eggs. The grade of an egg is based on interior quality and the condition and appearance of the shell. Most eggs sold in grocery stores are Grade AA or A and are suitable for all uses.

Plant-Based Meat Alternates

Some plant-based foods provide low-cost, high-protein alternatives to meat, poultry, fish, and eggs. Legumes and meat analogs are becoming more popular choices in the market today. They help consumers make the most of their protein food buys.

Legumes

High in essential amino acids, **legumes** are seeds that grow in the pods of some vegetable plants, 17-6. Legumes include beans, lentils, peas, and peanuts. Served alone, they are nutritious; however, they provide incomplete protein. Team them up with a grain or animal food, and you have a complete source of protein.

17-6 Legumes, which play a major role in the global diet, are economical sources of protein.

Putting Technology to Use
Have students check out Lobster Gram's Web site at www.lobstergram.com. How much would it cost to purchase a lobster as a gift and have it shipped to your area?

Legumes are often purchased dried. When buying dried legumes, look for high quality. Uniform color and size ensure freshness and even cooking. High-quality legumes are free from debris (stones, sticks, and dirt) and visible defects (cracks, insect holes).

Meat Analogs

Meat analogs are plant-based protein products made to resemble various kinds of meat. These products are made from soybeans, wheat, yeast, and other vegetable sources of protein. Bacon bits and soyburgers are common meat analogs.

When you buy these products, read the nutrition labels carefully. The food values vary depending on the products from which the meat analogs were made.

Storing Meat, Poultry, Fish, and Alternates

Because protein foods are highly perishable and expensive, proper storage is important. Improper storage can lead to flavor and nutrient loss, spoilage, and foodborne illness. Knowing how to store these foods properly will prevent costly waste.

Meat and Poultry

Prepackaged meats and poultry can be stored in the original wrapping. Store them in the coldest part of the refrigerator. Meat should be used within three to four days. Use poultry within one to two days. Never store stuffed poultry (cooked or uncooked) in the refrigerator. Stuffing should be removed from the bird and refrigerated separately.

To store fresh meat or poultry for longer periods, freezing is best. To freeze meat or poultry, wrap it tightly in freezer paper, aluminum foil, or a plastic freezer bag. Wrap the amounts of meat or poultry you will cook at one time separately.

When freezing steaks, pork chops, and ground beef patties, place two layers of waxed paper between individual servings. This makes it easy to remove as many servings as you need without having to thaw the entire amount. It also allows you to separate servings so they will defrost quickly.

Fish

Fresh fish is more perishable than meat or poultry. When stored in the refrigerator, fish must be tightly wrapped in foil or plastic wrap. Otherwise, the odor of the fish will penetrate other foods stored in the refrigerator. Fresh fish should be eaten within one or two days.

For longer storage, fish can be frozen. Wrap it tightly in foil or freezer paper, 17-7. Do not refreeze fish that was previously frozen.

Eggs

Properly stored, fresh eggs will keep up to four weeks in the refrigerator. The best way to store eggs in the refrigerator is in the original carton. Store them with the large end up to keep the yolk centered. Keep the carton away from foods with strong odors, which eggs can absorb.

17-7 Airtight storage keeps fish from drying out in the freezer. As this diagram shows, the edges of the foil or plastic wrap are folded in to keep the air out.

Enrich: Brainstorm ways that legumes might be used as meat extenders.

Reflect: What precautions are taken in your home to prevent bacteria from multiplying, causing food poisoning?

Note: Meat and poultry should not be thawed at room temperature. Allow them to thaw overnight in the refrigerator or use the defrost setting on a microwave oven.

Discuss: Why is it better to store eggs in the original carton than in a refrigerator's egg dish?

Family Enrichment Activity
Have students plan a meatless meal with their families, then prepare and eat it. Have them discuss with their families individual reactions to the meal (taste, preparation compared with another meal they might have had, cost, nutritive value, etc.). If appropriate, suggest the families donate money they would have spent on meat to a charity that focuses on hunger.

Enrich:
Compare the quality and freshness of eggs. Break a fresh egg into a saucer and compare it to an egg that is several weeks old. Check the yolk size, albumin consistency, and the size of the air cell in the shell. (You can also compare different grades of eggs in this manner.)

Resource:
How Do You Store These Protein Foods? reproducible master, TR

Discuss:
What are some favorite meat dishes used in your home that require moist heat cooking methods? dry heat methods?

Note:
Fresh pork should be cooked to an internal temperature of 160°F. It is no longer necessary to cook pork to 185°F to prevent trichinosis.

Eggs have a thin coating that keeps the pores of the shell sealed. This coating prevents bacteria from entering the egg. For this reason, fresh eggs should not be washed. In addition, a washed egg loses its quality faster than an unwashed egg.

Uncooked whole eggs (without the shell), egg yolks, and egg whites can be frozen, too. For whole eggs and yolks, add small amounts of sugar or salt before freezing. Freeze individual egg whites in the compartments of ice cube trays. Then store in an airtight container.

Legumes and Nuts

Store unopened packages of dried legumes in a cool, dry place. After opening packages, transfer the legumes to an airtight container. This will keep the unused portion fresh and free from insects.

Because of their high oil content, nuts may become rancid (develop a bad flavor). Storing nuts in the refrigerator is best if you plan to keep them for a few months. For longer storage, freeze them.

Preparing Meat, Poultry, Fish, and Alternates

Choosing the right cooking method for the type of protein food is the key to successful preparation. Meat, poultry, fish, and eggs are high in protein. Therefore, these foods require low to moderate cooking temperatures. Such temperatures will prevent protein foods from becoming tough and dry.

The two main cooking methods for preparing protein foods are dry heat and moist heat. *Dry heat methods* include roasting or baking, grilling, broiling, pan-broiling, and frying. *Moist heat methods* include braising, steaming, and poaching.

Meat

When you prepare meat, you want it to be tender, juicy, and flavorful. Meat that is cooked at high temperatures becomes dry and tough. High cooking temperatures also cause meat to shrink and lose some B vitamins. When you cook meat at low temperatures, there is less shrinkage.

Choosing a Cooking Method

The type of cut will determine the cooking method you will use to prepare meat, 17-8. Tender cuts of meat are often prepared using a dry heat cooking method. Less tender cuts are usually cooked using a moist heat cooking method. The addition of water or other liquid in these methods helps reduce toughness in less tender meats.

Less tender cuts of meat are tough due to *connective tissue*. They can be tenderized by *marinating* them in an acid liquid, such as vinegar, lemon juice, or tomato juice. Marinating adds extra flavor to meats, too. You can also tenderize meats by pounding them with a meat mallet or adding a chemical tenderizer.

Judging Doneness

Meats can be cooked to different levels of doneness. Beef and lamb may be cooked rare, medium, or well done. Veal and pork are usually cooked well done.

Using a *meat thermometer* is the best way to judge when meat has reached the desired degree of doneness. Color is not an accurate indicator of doneness. When using a meat thermometer, insert it into the thickest part of the meat. The bulb of the thermometer should not rest in fat or touch the bone. Meats are done when they have reached the recommended internal temperatures. See 17-9.

If the meat you are preparing is frozen, you may thaw it in the refrigerator. However, if the meat is not thawed, you will need extra cooking time to reach the desired level of doneness.

Poultry

Properly prepared poultry is tender and juicy. The cooking method you choose will be a matter of personal preference. Virtually all poultry sold in grocery stores is young and tender. Dry heat cooking methods, such as frying and roasting, are popular ways to prepare poultry. However, moist heat cooking methods, such as

Across the Curriculum
Science. Bring to class traditional thermometers and thermometer forks. Have students calibrate the thermometers by taking the temperature of boiling water. Boiling water should have a temperature of 212°F. Have students note which thermometer is most accurate.

Cooking by Cut

Tender Cuts – Cook with Dry Heat		
Beef	**Lamb**	**Pork**
Chuck top blade steak	Center-cut leg steaks	Chops
Ground beef patties	Ground lamb patties	Cutlets
Porterhouse steak	Kabobs	Ground pork patties
Rib roast	Loin chops	Ham
Rib steak	Rib chops	Ham slices
Sirloin steak	Shoulder chops	Kabobs
T-bone steak	Sirloin chops	Leg roasts
Tenderloin roast	Sirloin steaks	Loin roasts
Tenderloin steak		Shoulder roasts
Top loin roast		Tenderloin medallions

Less-Tender Cuts – Cook with Moist Heat		
Beef	**Lamb**	**Pork**
Beef for stew	Breasts	Loin chops
Chuck pot roast	Neck slices	Shoulder cubes
Chuck short ribs	Riblets	
Corned beef brisket	Shanks	
Cubed steak	Shoulder cuts	
Flank steak		
Round steak		
Round tip roast		
Shank cross cuts		
Skirt steak		

17-8 The method you use to prepare meat often depends on the cut of the meat.

Activity:
Using classroom cookbooks, find recipes that use each of the methods of cooking meat shown in Chart 17-8.

Note:
Reinforce that shellfish should come from nonpolluted waters.

stewing and braising, are desirable for many poultry dishes. Regardless of the method you choose, do not overcook poultry, as it will become dry and flavorless.

If you plan to roast poultry with stuffing, stuff the poultry just before roasting. (If you buy frozen commercially stuffed poultry, do not thaw it before cooking.)

Judging Doneness

A food thermometer is the only reliable guide for judging doneness of poultry. The thermometer should be centered in the thickest part of the breast or thigh. Whole poultry is done when it reaches an internal temperature of 180°F. When poultry is properly cooked, the meat should be fork tender and the juices should run clear.

Fish

Properly prepared fish is moist, tender, and flavorful. Fish has very little connective tissue. This means it is naturally tender and should be cooked for only a short time. Both moist heat and dry heat methods can be used when preparing fish. Avoid overcooking fish to keep it from becoming dry and tough.

Finfish is done when the flesh is firm and flakes easily when pressed with a fork. Shellfish should be cooked for a short time at moderate temperatures.

Eggs

The secret to cooking eggs properly is to use low to moderate heat for just the right amount of time. Undercooked eggs

Putting Technology to Use
Have students use charting software to make colorful bar graphs showing the temperature to which different types of meat, poultry, fish, and eggs should be cooked.

> **Note:**
> Eggs may be contaminated with salmonella, so raw eggs should not be consumed. Have students research cases of food poisoning caused by raw eggs.
>
> **Enrich:**
> Have students research recipes that traditionally used raw eggs as an ingredient. Have them find out alternatives that are suggested to avoid the use of raw eggs.
>
> **Activity:**
> Using classroom cookbooks, have students find recipes that use eggs in each of the ways listed. This can be a group activity.

Meat Doneness Temperatures

Meat	Temperature (°F)
Beef and lamb	
ground	160
medium rare	145
medium	160
well done	170
Pork	
fresh, medium	160
fresh, well done	170
ground	160
ham, fresh	160
ham, precooked	140

17-9 Using a meat thermometer correctly can help you determine when meat has reached the proper degree of doneness.

may contain bacteria that can cause foodborne illness. Therefore, it is important to cook eggs and egg dishes thoroughly. When properly cooked, egg whites are set and egg yolks are thickened. Egg dishes should reach an internal temperature of 160°F as measured on a food thermometer. If cooked too long or if the cooking temperature is too high, eggs become tough and rubbery.

Eggs are a versatile food. They can be scrambled, fried, poached, baked, hard-cooked, or soft-cooked. They can be used alone or as ingredients in other foods. See 17-10. Omelets, custards, and soufflés are examples of foods made with eggs. Eggs are also used as a

- *thickening agent* to help thicken mixtures such as custards, sauces, and puddings
- *leavening agent* to make products such as cakes, soufflés, and quick breads rise
- *glaze* on breads or pastries
- *coating* on foods for frying (Foods can be dipped into a beaten egg mixture and then dredged in flour, cornmeal, or bread crumbs. The egg holds the coating in place and makes a crispy crust for fried foods.)
- *binder* to hold ingredients together, such as in a meat loaf
- *garnish* to make other foods more attractive, as well as nutritious

17-10 Eggs are a key ingredient in the filling for this cream pie.

No matter how you use eggs, you can count on them to improve flavor and add to the dish's appearance. They also make the dish more nutritious.

Legumes

Properly prepared legumes are tender, but not mushy. Wash dried legumes and remove any foreign matter, such as sticks and stones. Dried beans need to be soaked before cooking. Read package directions to determine how much water to use. You do not need to soak dried peas and lentils.

To soak dried beans, quickly boil them for two minutes. Then remove them from

Across the Curriculum

Math. Soak a cup of dried legumes overnight in a two-cup liquid measuring cup. Ask students to compute the percentage of volume increase with rehydration.

the heat and let them stand for one hour. You can also soak dried beans overnight. You can cook dried beans in the water in which you soaked them. After cooking, you may simply season and eat them. You may also combine cooked beans with other ingredients to make dishes such as baked beans, 17-11.

17-11 Cooked dried beans can be combined with other foods in a variety of dishes.

Check It Out!
1. Describe the appearance of high-quality poultry.
2. How can legumes be served as a complete source of protein?
3. True or false. The best way to store eggs is in the carton with the small end up.
4. Why does the cooking temperature matter when preparing meat, poultry, fish, and eggs?
5. What factor should be used to determine the cooking method for preparing meat?
6. How do you judge the doneness of cooked finfish?

Check It Out! (Answers)
1. Poultry should look moist and plump and have clean, blemish-free skin with meaty breasts and legs.
2. team them up with a grain or animal food
3. false
4. These foods are high in protein. Therefore, low to moderate cooking temperatures should be used to prevent them from becoming tough and dry.
5. the type of cut—tender cuts of meat are often prepared using a dry heat cooking method, less tender cuts are usually cooked using a moist heat cooking method
6. Finfish is done when the flesh is firm and flakes easily when pressed with a fork.

Topic 17-2
Fruits and Vegetables

Objectives
After studying this topic, you will be able to
- list factors to consider when buying fruits and vegetables.
- use proper storage methods for fruits and vegetables.
- describe preparation and cooking methods for fruits and vegetables.

Topic Term
produce

Fruits and vegetables are nutritious and tasty mealtime favorites. Besides providing vitamins and minerals, most have no fat, few calories, and a lot of fiber. Flavors range from mild and sweet to strong and spicy. By carefully choosing, storing, and preparing fruits and vegetables, you will get the most for your money.

Buying Fruits and Vegetables

Fruits and vegetables are available in fresh, frozen, canned, and dried forms. With so many choices, how do you decide what to buy? Learning how each form differs and following some basic selection tips can help you make smarter choices. See 17-12.

Fresh Fruits and Vegetables

Fresh fruits and vegetables, which are called **produce,** are available year-round. Buy produce *in season,* or during the time of the year when it is harvested. In-season produce is fresher, higher in quality, and lower in price. For instance, tomatoes are abundant during the summer months. During this time, selection and quality are high, whereas cost is low. When tomatoes are not in season, prices are higher, and selection and quality are lower.

When shopping for produce, always look for the highest quality. Learn to judge

Resource:
Buying, Storing, and Preparing Protein Foods, Activity A, SAG

Activity:
Use the chalkboard to list fruits and vegetables the students eat in their homes. Make a second list of fruits and vegetables the students have heard of but never tasted. Try to bring samples of these new fruits and vegetables to class for them to try.

Resource:
Buying Fruits and Vegetables, reproducible master, TR

Discuss:
What are some of the hidden costs responsible for out-of-season fruits and vegetables being higher in price?

> **Discuss:**
> What are the advantages in selecting fruits canned in fruit juice?

> **Discuss:**
> On what occasions might you favor dried fruit over fresh fruit? What are the differences in nutrient content and calories?

> **Activity:**
> Sample and compare one type of fruit in all its available forms. Note all differences in flavor, texture, and color. Make a chart suggesting ways to serve each form.

17-12 To get the most from your money when buying fruits and vegetables, take time to select items carefully.

produce by its appearance. All fresh produce should feel firm, and have bright colors. Mature, ripe produce has the best flavor. Bruised, wilted, or decayed produce is a sign of poor quality. See 17-13.

The best way to judge some produce is by weight. The heavier produce is for its size, the better the value is. Heavier citrus fruits are also juicier.

When selecting produce, handle it carefully to avoid bruising it. Buy only amounts of produce that you can store and eat before it spoils.

Frozen Fruits and Vegetables

Frozen fruits and vegetables retain much of the same appearance, flavor, and quality as fresh produce. However, the texture of thawed or cooked fruits and vegetables may be less crisp. Frozen fruits and vegetables are available in plastic bags or paper cartons.

You should select frozen fruits and vegetables with care. Buy packages that are undamaged and frozen solid. A soft package is an indication of thawing. Thawing affects quality, taste, and storage time.

Canned Fruits and Vegetables

Canned fruits and vegetables come in many convenient forms, such as whole, sliced, and pieces. Fruits may be packed in heavy syrup, light syrup, or fruit juices. Fruits packed in juice are lower in calories and higher in nutrients than those packed in syrup. Vegetables are usually packed in water. Look for those packed without added salt to help avoid excess sodium in your diet.

How do you get the best buys in canned fruits and vegetables? Several factors affect cost, including brand, can size, and packing liquid. House brands and generic products are often priced lower than national brands. Large cans often cost less per serving than small cans. Plain canned fruits and vegetables are usually a better buy than those packed in flavored sauces. Whatever types of canned products you buy, look for cans that are free of dents, bulges, or leaks.

Dried Fruits and Vegetables

Dried fruits and vegetables are light in weight because the water has been removed. The flavors and textures are slightly different from fresh, frozen, and canned forms. However, they can be *rehydrated* (have the water content restored) for a softer texture.

Both dried fruits and vegetables are packaged in sealed bags or boxes. Look for well-sealed packages that are free of moisture. Dried fruits, such as apples, peaches, or apricots, should feel soft and pliable in the package. Dried vegetables, such as peas, lentils, and beans, are brittle and hard.

Storing Fruits and Vegetables

As a smart shopper, you must choose high-quality fruits and vegetables. To maintain this quality, however, you need to store fruits and vegetables properly.

Storing Fresh Produce

Proper storage protects the nutrients, flavors, and freshness of perishable produce. The quality of most fruits and vegetables is

> **Citizenship and Service**
> Have students explore the possibility of establishing an area for a community garden and work to make this possibility a reality. Also, they can explore the options for composting food waste on a school or community level.

Buying Fruits and Vegetables

Type of Produce	Look For:	Avoid:
Fruits		
Apples	Bright color, firm texture	Bruised spots, shriveled skin
Bananas	Bright color, firm texture	Bruised skin
Berries	Bright color, plump fruit	Soft, moldy, or leaky fruit
Cantaloupe	Yellowish rind, pleasant aroma	Soft spots
Citrus fruits	Bright color, heavy for size	Dull or shriveled skin, soft spots, lightweight for size
Grapes	Bright color, plump fruit	Soft, shriveled, or leaky fruit
Peaches	Slightly firm flesh	Bruised spots; hard, immature fruit; greenish skin
Pears	Firm flesh, good color	Bruised spots; hard, immature fruit
Watermelon	Smooth outer surface, firm texture, juicy fruit	Pale color, dry flesh
Vegetables		
Asparagus	Closed, compact tips; rich green color; tender stalk	Open tips, moldy spots
Beans (snap)	Bright color	Limp, dry pods; blemishes; thick, tough pods
Broccoli	Tight flower clusters, uniform green color	Yellow or brownish color, wilted stalks
Cabbage	Firm head, heavy for size, bright color	Wilted, decayed, or blemished leaves
Carrots	Bright orange color, smooth skin, firm texture	Limp texture, discolored skin
Cauliflower	Tight flower clusters, white color	Discolored appearance
Celery	Crisp stalks, bright color	Discolored or limp stalks
Corn	Plump kernels	Wilted husks, small kernels
Cucumbers	Bright green color, firm texture	Yellow color, limp texture
Lettuce	Bright color, heavy for size, crisp leaves	Blemished or wilted leaves, poor color
Onions	Smooth surface, firm texture	Soft spots
Potatoes	Smooth skin, firm texture, appropriate shape	Bruised spots, shriveled skin, signs of sprouting
Tomatoes	Bright red color, firm texture, smooth skin	Soft spots, cracked surfaces, bruised skin

17-13 Use this selection guide for choosing these popular fruits and vegetables.

Resource:
Cost Comparisons of Different Forms of Fruits and Vegetables, reproducible master, TR

Discuss:
Why would greens be crisper after refrigeration if previously washed?

maintained by storing them in the crisper section of the refrigerator. Do not wash fruits and vegetables before storing them, as this may hasten spoilage. See 17-14.

Some vegetables with high water content, such as lettuce and celery, need to be kept moist. Wrap lettuce with damp paper towels. Sprinkle celery with water. Store both

Across the Curriculum

Science. Discuss with students the concepts of *osmosis* and *semipermeable cell membranes.* How do these concepts relate to the storage of produce with high water contents?

Note:
Onions have a very strong odor and should not be stored next to foods that absorb odors easily, such as eggs.

Discuss:
What is your favorite fruit or vegetable dish?

Discuss:
What precautions should be taken if a canned food begins bulging or leaking?

17-14 Use care when handling and storing fresh fruits and vegetables to maintain their quality.

of these vegetables in perforated plastic bags to retain moisture without trapping it.

Even some firm fruits and vegetables are delicate and can be damaged easily. Therefore, you need to handle all fresh produce gently to avoid bruising.

Some fruits and vegetables are stored at room temperature. You can store bananas on a countertop. They will continue to ripen during storage. Banana skins turn dark quickly when refrigerated. This makes them less attractive, but the flavor remains good for a few days. Store vegetables that do not require refrigeration in a cool, dry place. Onions, potatoes, sweet potatoes, tomatoes, and hard-rind squash are examples of vegetables that do not need to be refrigerated.

Storing Other Forms of Fruits and Vegetables

Like fresh produce, frozen, canned, and dried fruits and vegetables require proper storage for best quality. Frozen fruits and vegetables should be stored in the coldest part of the freezer. Store canned products on a shelf in a cool, dry place. After opening canned goods, store any leftovers in an airtight container in the refrigerator. Store dried products in a cool, dry place. After opening packages, reseal them tightly. Then check package directions for proper storage. You can continue to store most dried vegetables in a pantry or cupboard. However, some dried fruits require refrigerator storage.

Preparing Fruits and Vegetables

Fruits and vegetables are versatile. They are easy to prepare, and you can serve them in a variety of ways. You can eat them raw or cooked. You can also use fruits and vegetables for salads and snacks or mix them with other foods.

The cooking process changes the flavor, color, and texture of fresh fruits and vegetables. Choose the method that best suits your planned use.

Fresh Fruits and Vegetables

Before eating or cooking fresh fruits and vegetables, wash them thoroughly, 17-15. Use cool, running water to remove dirt, pesticides, and bacteria. You should even wash produce with inedible rinds and skins, such as citrus fruits, bananas, and hard squash. Avoid soaking vegetables while cleaning or storing them, as this causes nutrient loss.

17-15 Thoroughly wash fresh produce in cool running water to remove dirt and pesticide residues.

Putting Technology to Use
Have students use drawing software, scanners, and color printers to make posters and flyers indicating the best ways to store fruits and vegetables. Hang the posters and flyers around the school, especially in the cafeteria.

Some fruits, such as apples, avocados, bananas, and peaches, may become discolored when exposed to air. Dipping them in an acid, such as orange, lemon, or pineapple juice, can prevent this.

Crisp, crunchy raw fruits and vegetables taste best when they are served cold. Prepare them and then store them in the refrigerator until serving time.

Serve fruits and vegetables soon after you cut, peel, or cook them. Vitamins are lost when these foods are allowed to stand.

Cooking Methods

Although most fruits and vegetables are tasty and more nutritious when eaten raw, some require cooking. Cooked fruits may be served as desserts or side dishes at any meal. Cooked vegetables are often served as side dishes, in soups, or in casseroles.

When cooking fruits and vegetables, try to retain as much flavor, texture, and appearance as possible. Cook fruits and vegetables in their skins whenever possible, as this helps produce retain more nutrients. Avoid overcooking fruits and vegetables.

Both moist heat and dry heat cooking methods can be used to cook fruits and vegetables. They can be simmered, steamed, microwaved, baked, or broiled. The method you use depends on the type of fruit or vegetable. Two common cooking methods—simmering and microwaving—are described here.

When *simmering* fruits and vegetables, use a small amount of water or liquid and a short cooking time. Heat the liquid to boiling before adding fruits or vegetables. (Adding a small amount of sugar adds flavor and helps fruit hold its shape.) You can reduce cooking time and nutrient loss by covering the pan. However, you should leave the lid off strongly flavored vegetables, such as turnips and onions. You should also cover these vegetables with water. These steps will help some of the strong flavors to escape. Cook fruits and vegetables until they are tender, but slightly crisp.

The liquid in which fruits and vegetables are cooked contains nutrients. Save it and use it later in gravies, sauces, soups, and stews.

Microwaving fruits and vegetables is a popular cooking method. This method helps retain the colors, flavors, and nutrients because produce cooks quickly using little or no water. Pierce whole fruits or vegetables before cooking to allow steam to escape. When cutting up fruits or vegetables, cut them into same-sized pieces for more even cooking. Cover and cook until crisp-tender, stirring once or twice during the cooking time. Whether whole or cut up, let fruits and vegetables stand a few minutes before serving to complete the cooking process. See 17-16.

Preparing Other Forms of Fruits and Vegetables

Canned fruits are ready to serve right from the can. You can drain them or serve them in the fruit juice or syrup in which they were packed. If you are heating canned fruits, heat them in their juice or syrup. Drain canned fruits before using them in baked products.

17-16 Fresh vegetables cooked in a microwave oven retain their nutrients and bright colors.

Activity: Slice a banana. Place half of the slices on a plate and set aside. Dip the remaining slices in lemon juice and set aside. Compare slices 30 minutes later.

Discuss: What guidelines should be observed in cooking fruits and vegetables that are high in water-soluble vitamins?

Enrich: Brainstorm ways drained liquid from cooked vegetables might be used in another food preparation.

 Putting Technology to Use
Have students make a guide for food garnishing using word processing software. Ask students to collect pictures of attractive foods from magazines and use a scanner to create digital files to place in the document. Have them point out the various garnishes used in each picture. Students should also research how to prepare each garnish and include this information in the guide.

Resource:
Buying, Storing, and Preparing Fruits and Vegetables, Activity B, SAG

Vocabulary:
What do you think a leavening agent does?

Resource:
Kernel of Wheat, color transparency CT-15, TR

Discuss:
Do you eat other cereals beside the most widely used four? How does your family use them?

Canned vegetables are precooked, so you can simply heat them through before serving. Avoid overcooking, as this makes canned vegetables mushy.

You may use frozen fruits in many of the same ways as fresh or canned. Serve them slightly frozen with some ice crystals remaining. Fully thawed fruit will have a softer, mushier texture. To retain the fruit's shape, do not thaw it before cooking.

Cook frozen vegetables from the frozen state using the same methods you use for fresh vegetables. However, use slightly shorter cooking times.

You may serve dried fruits right from the package or use them as is in baked products. To rehydrate dried fruits, soak them in hot water for about an hour and then cook as directed.

Soaking and cooking methods for dried beans and peas were covered in Topic 17-1. Remember, cooking times for dried vegetables are much longer than for fresh or frozen vegetables. Simmer or bake dried vegetables in liquid until they are tender.

Check It Out!
1. What is the value of buying produce that is in season?
2. True or false. Most fruits and vegetables should be washed before storing in the refrigerator.
3. True or false. Most fruits and vegetables should be cooked in a covered pan to reduce cooking time and nutrient loss.

Check It Out! (Answers)
1. In-season produce is fresher, higher in quality, and lower in price.
2. false
3. true

Topic 17-3
Cereal Products

Objectives
After studying this topic, you will be able to
- list factors to consider when buying cereal products.
- use proper storage methods for cereal products.
- describe methods used to prepare cereal products.

Topic Terms
cereal	leavening agent
refined	biscuit method
pasta	muffin method
starch	

Cereals are starchy grains used as food, including wheat, corn, rice, and oats. Cereals can be used in their natural form. They can also be used to make products such as flour, pasta, breakfast cereals, and breads, 17-17.

17-17 These nutritious foods are all made from cereal grains.

Buying Cereal Products

Cereal products are plentiful sources of food energy. In addition, they are economical, easy to store, and easy to prepare. Knowing what is available will help you choose the products that meet your needs and food budget.

Flour

Flour is made by grinding grains into powder. **Refined** flour has had parts of the grain kernel removed during the milling process. Removing parts of the kernel also removes nutrients contained in those parts. Refined flour can be *enriched* to add back B vitamins and iron lost during milling.

In the United States, wheat flour is the most common type. However, flour can be made from any grain. At the supermarket, you can choose among several types of flour. These include all-purpose flour, self-rising flour, cake flour, and whole wheat flour.

All-purpose flour is used for general cooking and baking purposes. You can use it to make biscuits, pancakes, yeast breads, and cakes; and to thicken gravies and sauces. When a recipe merely calls for flour, all-purpose flour is usually intended.

Self-rising flour has a *leavening agent* (a substance that makes baked goods rise) and salt added. This flour is often used to make quick breads.

Cake flour is made of softer wheat and may be milled more finely than the other flours. This flour is used for delicately textured cakes and other baked products.

Whole wheat flour has a coarser texture than other flours. It is made from the entire grain kernel. Whole wheat flour is often used in breads. It gives them a coarser texture and nuttier flavor. For best results, use this flour in recipes calling for whole wheat flour.

Pasta

Pasta is the family name for a group of products that includes spaghetti, macaroni, and noodles. These products add interest to meals because they offer such a wide variety of shapes. Whatever the shape, however, all pastas are made of the same ingredients: flour and water. Noodle products also contain eggs. Most pastas are enriched by the addition of thiamin, niacin, riboflavin, folic acid, and iron.

Pasta products are made from *semolina*, which is made from durum wheat. Durum wheat is specially grown for use in pasta products. This hard wheat yields pasta that will cook to a firm, yet tender texture.

Rice

The two major types of rice are white rice and brown rice. In the United States, people tend to consume more white rice. *White rice* is produced when the bran layer of the rice kernel is removed. When shopping for white rice, look for the word *enriched*. *Brown rice* is whole grain rice. Because the whole grain is used, brown rice is higher in fiber than white rice.

Precooked or *instant rice* is an expensive form of rice, but it is popular with many people. It is white rice that has been fully cooked and dried. It can be prepared very quickly to restore the moisture.

Rice grains come in various sizes. Short and medium grains tend to cling together when cooked. Long grain rice cooks to a fluffy texture, and the grains are more likely to stay separate. See 17-18.

In spite of its name, *wild rice* is not rice at all. It is the seed of a wild grass that

17-18 Properly cooked long grain rice is tender and fluffy.

Enrich: Display a selection of various flours. Ask students to compare the labels on the packages. Also compare the texture and color of the flours.

Note: Pasta products vary in shape, color, and size. Display a variety of these products.

Enrich: Have students research farming techniques used to grow wheat, corn, rice, and oats.

Across the Curriculum

English/social studies. Have students research the types of grains that are used as staples by people in different parts of the world. Ask students to prepare a report to share with the class.

Enrich:
Have students research studies done of ready-to-eat cereals. Find reports comparing nutritive value, sugar content, and cost.

Resource:
How Much Does Cereal Cost Per Serving? reproducible master, TR

Reflect:
What is your favorite kind of bread? How nutritious is this type of bread?

Note:
Caution that flour and cereals should be checked for weevil infestation.

---

grows in marshes. Wild rice is much more expensive than rice. To lower the cost, wild rice is often mixed with brown rice.

Breakfast Cereals

Both ready-to-eat and cooked cereals come in a variety of flavors, textures, and forms. Use nutrition labeling to compare different cereals for nutritive value. Many are high in sugar or may contain fat. Some are low in fiber. In general, however, whole grain, enriched, and fortified cereals are nutritious and filling. Served with milk and fruit, cereal can be a nourishing meal.

Some types of cereal are more expensive than others. Ready-to-eat cereal is more expensive than cereals that require cooking. Cereals with dried fruits or nuts added and presweetened cereals are more costly than plain cereals. Although convenient to serve, quick-cooking and instant cereals are also more costly than regular cereal.

When evaluating cereal cost, it is best to compare cost per serving. Cereals differ greatly in weight. Packages of the same size may not contain the same number of servings. Also, compare the size of the serving before you decide which cereal to choose.

Breads

A wide variety of breads are available. White, whole wheat, raisin, and rye bread are just a few examples. Rolls, muffins, and bagels are other types of bread products you can find at your local supermarket or bakery. For the best flavor and texture, look for freshness dates stamped on the products. Buy the freshest product available.

You can choose from commercially prepared bread products or in-store bakery products. Commercial breads are prepared in large quantities, so they are reasonably priced. They are prepackaged and then sold on grocery store shelves. Grocery store bakeries sell freshly baked bread products directly to you. Although these products are more costly, you may prefer the fresh-baked taste.

Convenience bread products also come in many forms. *Brown-and-serve products* are partially baked; you finish baking them at home. *Refrigerated doughs* need only to be baked at home. *Frozen doughs* must be thawed and then baked. Most of these products save time and are easy to prepare. However, they are often more costly than making baked goods from scratch.

Storing Cereal Products

Cereal products, including flour and pasta, should be stored in tightly covered containers in a cool, dry place, 17-19. For short-term storage, store breads, cakes, and cookies in airtight bags, bread boxes, or cake boxes.

Storage times vary depending on the product. Breads stored in a cool, dry place will last about one week. Ready-to-eat cereals keep well for two to three months. Wild rice and brown rice will keep for six months. Refined flour, pasta, and white rice will keep for one year.

Some cereal products may require refrigeration. Whole grain products, which contain some fat, stay fresher in the refrigerator. Cakes and cookies with perishable fillings and frostings will need refrigeration. Bread may be stored in the refrigerator to prevent mold growth, but this method

17-19 Pasta and other cereal products should be stored in tightly covered containers to keep out moisture and pests.

Putting Technology to Use
Have students compare the prices, convenience, and quality of various bread products. Have students use charting software to create a chart illustrating their findings. Students should print their charts on transparency film and use an overhead projector to share their findings with the class.

makes the bread taste stale. (Microwaving stale bread for a few seconds will make it taste fresh again.)

Baked products can be frozen for several months. Wrap tightly to keep out excess moisture. Frozen bread defrosts quickly, so you can use slices as you need them. Stored properly, most baked goods will taste as fresh as when you purchased them.

Preparing Cereal Products

The preparation methods used for cereal products depend on the product you are preparing. Products prepared from the cereals group include sauces, gravies, and puddings thickened with flour or cornstarch. Pasta, rice, cooked cereals, and breads also have special preparation methods.

Cooking with Thickeners

Starch is the complex carbohydrate part of plants. It makes up the major portion of cereal products. When starch and water are heated, the starch granules swell. This is because the granules absorb the water, which makes them soft and thick. As a result, cereal products increase in volume as they cook.

The key to smooth, lump-free mixtures is proper temperature and gentle stirring. Low heat slows the absorption of water by the starch granules. High heat causes granules to lump together. Gentle stirring prevents lumps; overstirring causes the granules to break down.

Flour, cornstarch, and other starches are grain products often used to thicken sauces, gravies, and puddings. When preparing these foods, lumps may form if starch is added directly to hot liquid. Separating the starch granules before adding them to the hot liquid can prevent this.

You can use three methods to keep starch granules separated. The first is to coat the starch granules with melted fat to make a paste. Then add the liquid slowly, stirring constantly. This method is used for sauces and gravies. The second method is to combine the starch with sugar, then stir in the liquid slowly. This method is used when making puddings. Mixing the starch with a cold liquid to form a paste is the third method. The paste is slowly stirred into the hot mixture. Mixtures thickened with flour or cornstarch should be stirred constantly during cooking to achieve a smooth texture.

Pasta

"Tender, but firm" describes properly prepared pasta. See 17-20. You must cook pasta in a large amount of rapidly boiling water to keep it from becoming sticky. Use about two quarts of water per eight ounces of pasta. To test for doneness, remove a piece of pasta from the water and bite into it. Avoid overcooking pasta, as it will become sticky and lose its shape.

Rice

Properly cooked rice is tender and fluffy. Combine the rice with water or other liquid in the proper size pan. Bring it to a boil and then stir. Lower the heat and cover the pan. As the rice cooks, it absorbs the liquid and swells. Rice may also be baked in the oven.

There are various types of rice and various methods of preparing each type. For best results, prepare rice according to package directions.

17-20 Cooked pasta should be tender but firm for use in a chilled salad.

> **Vocabulary:**
> Introduce the term *white sauce*. It is the basis for many food dishes and is referred to in many recipes.
>
> **Reflect:**
> Have you ever eaten lumpy or watery gravy? What do you think caused the gravy to be lumpy or watery?
>
> **Vocabulary:**
> Introduce the term *al dente*, which means tender, but slightly resistant to the bite.

Across the Curriculum

Science. Have groups of students cook the same type of pasta, but for different lengths of time. Have some groups undercook the pasta and some groups overcook it. Have all the students compare the overcooked and undercooked groups with the al dente pasta. Have students describe the differences among the pastas.

> **Discuss:**
> What grain are grits made from? In what geographic area are grits usually eaten?
>
> **Discuss:**
> What are some of your favorite yeast breads? quick breads?
>
> **Note:**
> Display examples of leavening agents used in quick breads and yeast breads. Explain how they differ.

Cooked Cereals

Cooked cereals, such as oatmeal and grits, should be smooth and free of lumps. Like all starch products, when cereals are cooked, they absorb liquid and increase in volume.

There are some general rules to follow when preparing cooked cereals. Add cereal slowly to boiling water, stirring constantly. (This will help prevent lumps.) While the cereal is cooking, keep stirring it constantly. Cook the cereal for as long as directed on the package. Be sure to use the recommended pan or bowl size.

Cereals cooked in a microwave oven can be prepared and served in the same dish. Use a dish large enough to allow for boiling and swelling. Microwave cereals according to package directions, stirring as directed. Let stand a few minutes before serving to complete the cooking process.

Breads

The two main groups of breads are yeast breads and quick breads. Breads need air, steam, and leavening agents to rise. Air is added as ingredients are mixed. Steam is produced when liquid ingredients are heated during baking. **Leavening agents** are ingredients used to produce carbon dioxide. Yeast breads and quick breads are prepared with different leavening agents and mixing methods.

Yeast Breads

Yeast is a tiny plant used as a leavening agent in yeast breads. When mixed with the right ingredients, yeast produces carbon dioxide, which causes the bread to rise. Yeast breads must be mixed, kneaded, and allowed to rise before they are ready for baking. The basic steps in preparing yeast breads are shown in 17-21.

A — Combine ingredients and beat until smooth. Stir in enough additional flour to make a moderately stiff dough.

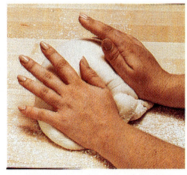

B — On a lightly floured pastry board or cloth, knead dough until smooth and elastic.

C — Place dough in a lightly greased bowl; turn once to grease top.

D — Let dough rise in a warm place until double in bulk. Test dough for lightness with two fingers.

E — When dough is light, punch down.

F — Shape dough into loaves or rolls and bake as directed. Use of these preparation techniques can produce successful yeast breads.

17-21 These are the basic preparation steps you would follow to prepare yeast breads from scratch.

Putting Technology to Use

Have students prepare regular oatmeal, quick-cooking oatmeal, and instant oatmeal. Ask them to taste and compare the flavor, texture, and appearance of each product. Have students use charting software to organize their comparisons.

Quick Breads

As their name implies, quick breads are faster to make than yeast breads. You can mix and bake quick breads in a short period.

Quick bread mixtures can be divided into three classes of batters and doughs. *Pour batters* are thin. Typical pour batters are used for pancakes, waffles, popovers, and some coffee cakes. *Drop batters* are thick. Typical drop batters are used for muffins, drop biscuits, and coffee cakes. *Soft dough* is sticky but can be handled. Soft doughs are used for rolled biscuits, dumplings, and some coffee cakes.

You prepare some quick breads using the biscuit method and others using the muffin method. With the **biscuit method,** you mix the dry ingredients together, and then cut fat into the mixture. Next, you add the liquid ingredients. Then you knead the dough before cutting or shaping it. Biscuits and doughnuts are among the quick breads produced by the biscuit method. *Tortillas,* which are a Mexican flatbread, are also made using the biscuit method. Small pieces of dough are patted into the thin, pancakelike pieces of bread.

In the **muffin method,** you mix the dry ingredients. Mix the liquid ingredients together in a separate bowl. Make a well in the center of the dry ingredients and then pour in the liquid. Stir the batter until all the dry ingredients are just moistened. Then spoon the batter into a loaf pan or muffin pan and bake it. (Fill muffin cups about two-thirds full with batter.)

Cakes and Cookies

Cakes and cookies are popular baked products served as desserts. You can prepare all types of cakes from scratch or from convenience cake mixes sold at the grocery store. Homemade cookies are just about everyone's favorite. Many varieties are available at the grocery store, too.

Success in cake and cookie baking depends on a number of factors. You need to measure accurately and use quality ingredients. You must have an understanding of the mixing method and follow the baking directions correctly. The best way to ensure the quality of cakes and cookies is to follow the recipe carefully.

Preparing Cakes

Cakes are divided into two main groups: shortened and unshortened. *Shortened cakes* contain fat, such as butter, margarine, or vegetable shortening. Baking powder or baking soda plus buttermilk are used to make them rise. Layer cakes and pound cakes are shortened cakes, 17-22.

Unshortened cakes contain no fat. Beaten egg whites and steam formed during baking makes them rise. Angel food and sponge cakes are unshortened cakes.

Chiffon cakes are a combination of the two types described above. They contain fat and beaten egg whites to make them rise.

Baking Guidelines

Shortened and unshortened cakes have different ingredients and different mixing procedures. The finished products look and taste different, too. Whichever type you make, follow recipe directions carefully and use the right size pans.

The following tips will help you prepare cakes successfully.

- Prepare the pans as directed in the recipe. For shortened cakes, grease cake pans with solid shortening. Then coat the pans lightly with flour to allow the layers to turn out easily. Fill the pans

17-22 This pound cake, garnished with fresh fruit and raspberry sauce, is a classic shortened cake.

Activity:
Using classroom cookbooks, have students find recipes that illustrate pour batters, drop batters, soft dough, biscuit method, and muffin method.

Enrich:
Compare the nutritive value of shortened and unshortened cakes. Note the caloric and fat differences.

Enrich:
Brainstorm ways an angel food cake can be enhanced to create a special, low-fat dessert.

 Putting Technology to Use
Make a class desserts cookbook. Have each student bring in a favorite recipe for a dessert and enter it into a word processing program. Have students add clipart or scanned art to the pages. Print out the pages and assemble them into a booklet.

> **Discuss:**
> What happens if you try to frost a cake before it is completely cooled?

> **Reflect:**
> Think of pleasant association between yourself and cookies. What person, holiday, occasion, or place do you associate with a particular cooking or eating experience?

> **Resource:**
> *Cookie Recipe Exchange*, reproducible master, TR

half full with batter. Unshortened cakes are baked in ungreased tube pans. This allows the batter to cling to the sides of the pan. Fill the pan almost full of batter.

- Preheat the oven to the correct temperature.
- Allow at least one inch between pans and the sides of the oven when baking. This will allow heat to circulate freely.
- Check cakes for doneness at the end of the shortest recommended baking time. The cake should slightly pull away from the sides of the pan when done. Check the recipe for the proper doneness test.
- Follow the recipe directions for cooling and removing the cake from the baking pan. Some cakes should be removed from the baking pan immediately. Some should be cooled on a rack about ten minutes before removing. Unshortened cake pans are turned upside down over a bottle for cooling.

Preparing Cookies

Many varieties of cookies are easy to make at home. Among them are dropped, refrigerator, bar, rolled, molded, and pressed cookies. These types differ in the ingredients used, the consistency of the dough, and the way the dough is handled. Be sure to follow recipe directions carefully for each type.

Dropped cookies are made from soft dough that is pushed from a spoon onto a baking sheet. Space the dough on the baking sheet to allow for spreading while baking. Chocolate chip cookies are one of the most popular dropped cookies. See 17-23.

Refrigerator cookies are made by shaping stiff dough into a long, smooth roll. Wrap the roll in waxed paper or plastic wrap and place in the refrigerator. Chill the dough until it is firm enough to slice easily. Cut the dough with a thin, sharp knife to ensure even slices.

Bar cookies are made from soft dough that is spread in a greased baking pan. The cookies are baked, cooled, and cut into squares. Carefully remove bars from the baking pan with a spatula. Brownies are a favorite bar cookie.

17-23 For best results, follow the recommended mixing method for dropped cookies.

Rolled cookies are made from stiff dough that is chilled, rolled, and cut into desired shapes. Many decorative cookie shapes, such as gingerbread people, can be made using this method. Sugar cookies are another popular type of rolled cookie.

Molded cookies are formed from stiff dough that is broken off and shaped by hand. For some types of molded cookies, the dough is shaped into crescents or tied into knot shapes. Some types, such as peanut butter cookies, are flattened before being baked. Others are filled with jelly or candied fruits.

Pressed cookies are made of rich dough. The dough is forced through a cookie press onto an ungreased baking sheet. The cookie dough can be pressed into a variety of shapes by changing the tip on the cookie press. Spritz cookies are one common type of pressed cookie.

Baking Guidelines

As with cakes, the best cookies result from following the recipe directions. Here are some baking tips.

- Preheat the oven to the correct temperature.
- Use the correct pan size. Heavy aluminum cookie sheets or pans work best for many types of cookies.
- Follow specified baking times. For chewy cookies, bake long enough to set

Across the Curriculum

Social studies. Have students research to find out the origins of their favorite desserts. Have students indicate in which geographical area the dessert was first prepared. Also have them mention places in which the dessert is most popular today.

the dough (the shortest recommended baking time). For crisp cookies, bake a little longer (the longest recommended baking time).

- Follow recipe directions for removing cookies from the cookie sheet. Some cookies must be cooled slightly on the baking sheet before removing them to the cooling rack. Others must be removed immediately.
- Store cooled cookies to maintain top quality. Keep crisp, thin cookies in a can or jar with a loose cover. Keep soft cookies in an airtight container. See 17-24.

17-24 Store bar cookies in an airtight container to help them keep their soft textures.

Check It Out!
1. Give five examples of foods made from cereal grains.
2. When a recipe lists flour as an ingredient, what type should you buy?
3. Describe how most cereal products should be stored.
4. What is the key to smooth, lump-free sauces, gravies, and puddings?
5. True or false. Quick breads must be mixed, kneaded, and allowed to rise before they are ready for baking.
6. Identify the six types of cookies.

Topic 17-4
Milk and Milk Products

Objectives
After studying this topic, you will be able to
- list factors to consider when buying dairy products.
- use proper storage methods for dairy products.
- describe methods used to prepare milk and cheese.

Topic Terms
pasteurization natural cheese
homogenized   process cheese

Milk is essential for good health. Besides being a good source of calcium, it supplies high-quality protein. Other dairy products, such as lowfat cheese and yogurt, can provide the same nutrients present in milk. If you do not like to drink milk, you should include other calcium-rich milk products in your diet.

Comparing different brands and product sizes will help you get the best buys in dairy products, 17-25. Proper storage will ensure their freshness. Following some basic principles will help

17-25 Comparison shopping will help you make wise choices when shopping for foods in the milk group.

Resource:
Cereal Products Puzzle, Activity C, SAG

Vocabulary:
Are the terms *pasteurization* and *homogenized* familiar to you?

Check It Out! (Answers)
1. flour, pasta, rice, breakfast cereals, and breads
2. all-purpose flour
3. store in an airtight container in a cool, dry place
4. gentle stirring and low temperatures
5. false
6. drop, refrigerator, bar, rolled, molded, pressed

Activity:
Set up a tasting panel. Compare the tastes of whole milk, lowfat milk, fat free milk, cultured buttermilk, and reconstituted nonfat dry milk.

Note:
Milk is not a "perfect" food. It is a poor source of iron and vitamin C.

Resource:
Cheese Tasting, Activity D, SAG

Resource:
Comparing Dairy Products, reproducible master, TR

you obtain good results when cooking with dairy products.

Buying Dairy Products

Many types of dairy products are available to consumers. Milk, cheese, yogurt, frozen milk products, cream, and butter are included in this group of foods. The two most common dairy products—milk and cheese—are covered in this chapter.

All dairy products shipped across state lines for retail sale in the United States are pasteurized. **Pasteurization** is a heating process that destroys harmful bacteria in dairy products. This process prevents illness and helps milk products stay fresh.

Milk

You can purchase milk in several forms at the grocery store. See 17-26. The form you choose usually depends on the following factors:

- whether the milk is intended for drinking or cooking
- your budget
- your storage facilities

The price of milk is partly determined by its fat content. The higher the proportion of fat, the more the milk costs. Fluid milk must be refrigerated unless it is aseptically packaged. Dry milk and canned milk can be stored on a shelf before being reconstituted for use.

Besides being pasteurized, most milk and milk products are homogenized, and many are fortified. **Homogenized** refers to a process by which the milkfat is broken into tiny particles. As tiny particles, the fat remains evenly suspended throughout the milk. Without homogenization, the fat (also known as cream) would rise to the top. *Fortified* means nutrients, such as vitamins A and D, have been added to the milk.

Cheese

Most cheese is made from milk. In simple terms, cheese is made by *coagulating* milk, or setting milk into a thickened mass.

Forms of Milk

Fresh Fluid Milks
- *Whole milk* contains at least 3.25 percent milkfat.
- *Reduced fat milk* contains 2 percent milkfat.
- *Lowfat milk* contains 1 percent milk fat.
- *Fat free milk,* also called *skim milk* or *nonfat milk,* contains less than 0.5 percent milkfat.
- *Chocolate milk* is made by adding chocolate to whole milk.

Canned Milks
- *Evaporated milk* is obtained by removing about 50 percent of the water from whole milk.
- *Evaporated fat free milk* is obtained by removing about 50 percent of the water from fat free milk.
- *Sweetened condensed milk* is made by partially removing water from whole milk and adding sweetener.

Dry Milks
- *Nonfat dry milk* is produced by removing the water and fat from fluid whole milk.
- *Dry whole milk* is made by removing the water from fluid whole milk.

Cultured Milk
- *Buttermilk* is produced by adding special bacterial cultures to fluid milk.

17-26 Milk is available in various forms. Buy the form that best suits your needs.

The *curd* (solid portion of the milk) is separated from the *whey* (liquid portion).

Food values vary in different cheeses. Cheddar cheese, for example, contains milkfat, protein, minerals, and vitamins. Cottage cheese is not as rich in fat, minerals, and vitamins, but it is a good source of protein. Cream cheese has a high fat content, but it is not a good source of protein.

Hundreds of varieties of cheeses are available. They differ in aroma, body, flavor, color, and texture. Cheeses also vary in cost. All cheeses, however, have some common characteristics. They can be divided into two classes: natural and process.

Career Preparation Activity

In the Works, in the Cafeteria, reproducible master, TR. Arrange with the cafeteria staff to have the class (or smaller groups of students) visit the cafeteria to observe/shadow various workers. Have them make note of the skills needed and how the information presented in this chapter is applied in the work of the cafeteria staff. Have students use the master as a basis of questions to ask the workers.

Natural Cheese

Natural cheeses are made from milk, whey, or cream. The type of cheese produced depends on the

- source of the milk (cow, sheep, goat, or buffalo)
- seasonings used
- method of preparation
- ripening or curing process

Unripened cheeses, such as cream cheese and cottage cheese, have soft textures and mild flavors. As soon as the whey is removed from them, they are shipped to the grocery store.

Ripened cheeses are stored for certain lengths of time at specific temperatures to develop their flavors and textures. Cheddar and Swiss are typical examples of ripened cheeses. See 17-27.

Process Cheese

Blending and melting two or more natural cheeses results in **process cheeses.** The natural cheeses are grated and shredded. The cheeses are then combined and heated.

There are two types of process cheese. *Process cheese food* has slightly higher moisture content than natural cheese. However, the fat content for process cheese food is lower than natural cheese. *Process cheese spread* has a higher moisture content and lower fat content than process cheese food. Process cheese products may contain meats, fruits, or vegetables. They are sold as slices, in blocks, or in jars.

Consumers often choose process cheeses for their convenience. These mild-flavored cheeses melt easily when heated, making them popular for sauces and casseroles. Spreadable forms are popular for serving on crackers, raw vegetables, and sandwich breads.

Storing Dairy Products

Dairy products are perishable, so you must store them properly to keep them fresh and wholesome. Before you buy, look for the date stamped on the product. Choose the latest date possible. When you get the products home, be sure to store them promptly.

Milk and Milk Products

Store milk, yogurt, sour cream, and butter in the coldest part of the refrigerator. Because these foods may absorb off-flavors from other foods, keep them tightly covered.

The dates stamped on milk products are called *pull dates*. A pull date is the last day a product should be sold. Dairy products will remain fresh and wholesome in your refrigerator for a few days after the pull date. Be sure to use milk, yogurt, and sour cream quickly once the pull date has passed. If you want to keep butter more than a few days beyond the pull date, you should freeze it.

Cheese

Keep all cheese—whether natural or process—tightly wrapped and refrigerated. After opening, cheese tends to dry out quickly and may pick up strong odors from other foods. Re-cover or tightly wrap any unused portions. A small amount of mold does not alter the quality or flavor of cheese. Just trim away ½ inch of cheese on all sides of the mold. Use the remaining portion within a short time. If a large amount of mold has formed on cheese, you should discard the cheese.

17-27 Ripened cheeses have distinctive flavors and textures that are developed through an aging process.

> **Activity:**
> Look through cookbooks to see the many uses of cheese. Find recipes that use cheese in appetizers, salads, sandwiches, entrees, and desserts.
>
> **Enrich:**
> Set up a tasting panel. Sample ten different cheeses. Write a description of the flavor, color, and texture of each sample.
>
> **Resource:**
> *Proper Storage of Dairy Products,* reproducible master, TR
>
> **Note:**
> Refrigerate all butter and margarine. Do not leave at room temperature any longer than necessary.

 Problem-Solving Practice
The Class Picnic, reproducible master, TR. Divide students into groups and provide each group with a copy of the master. Have each group complete the master, then compare results and recommendations. Discuss reasons for differences and whether any recommendation could increase risk of foodborne illness.

Discuss:
Name some of your favorite recipes that are prepared with milk.

Discuss:
When making hot chocolate, how can you prevent scum from forming on the top?

Reflect:
Which cheeses do you find easiest to cook with? Are they natural or process cheeses?

Preparing Dairy Products

Many recipes for puddings, cream soups, casseroles, and sauces call for milk or milk products. As you know, milk products contain protein. This is important to remember because protein foods are sensitive to heat. For best results when cooking with milk products, always use low cooking temperatures, 17-28.

Cooking with Milk

Milk and milk products are often used as ingredients in heated mixtures, such as sauces and puddings. The proteins in milk will *scorch* (burn) if they are cooked over high heat. Scorching causes milk to develop a bitter taste. Cooking milk slowly over low heat will prevent scorching. Using a double boiler when preparing heated mixtures also helps.

High cooking temperatures can cause milk proteins to *curdle* (form clumps). High-acid foods, such as fruits and vegetables; salt-cured meats; and certain enzymes can also cause curdling. Using low cooking temperatures and fresh milk prevents curdling.

Sometimes a film will form on the surface of milk as it is being heated. This is called *scum*. Scum can cause the milk to boil over. Beating milk to produce a foam layer on top of the milk will keep scum from forming. Covering the milk during heating will also prevent scum formation. If scum does form, you should remove it because it will cause lumps in the milk or milk mixture.

Cooking with Cheese

Cheese can become tough and rubbery when it is cooked at a high temperature. To prevent overcooking, add cubed or shredded cheese to sauces and casseroles at the end of the cooking time, 17-29. Sprinkle cheese on casseroles after they are baked.

To melt cheese in a microwave oven, use a medium to medium-high power setting. Using high power will cause cheese to become rubbery.

17-29 To keep a cheese sauce for broccoli smooth, add the cheese at the end of the cooking time.

17-28 Low cooking temperatures help keep foods prepared with milk, such as this soup, smooth and creamy.

Check It Out!

1. Explain the difference between pasteurized and homogenized milk.
2. A process cheese _____ has more moisture and a lower fat content than a process cheese _____.
3. How should milk, cheese, and butter be stored?
4. True or false. For best results, when cooking with milk and cheese, use high cooking temperatures.

Check It Out! (Answers)
1. Pasteurized milk is heated to destroy harmful bacteria that could cause illness. Homogenized milk has the fat particles distributed throughout the milk.
2. spread, food
3. tightly covered or wrapped in the refrigerator
4. false

TEENS ARE CONCERNED ABOUT...

The Taste of Foods

Meet a professional who spent 25 years teaching people how to make foods taste good and look good, too. Linda Nunalee has extensive experience in marketing various foods to consumers and future consumers. She served as a marketing specialist at the North Carolina Department of Agriculture. Later, she worked for the North Carolina Pork Council. In these positions, she created leaflets and cookbooks. She spoke to various consumer groups and appeared regularly on a local television show. She also enjoyed working with family and consumer sciences classes. In her retirement, she has contributed to a new cookbook.

Q: *What types of foods do people find most appealing?*

A: Foods with good eye appeal (color and texture) and aroma. We eat with our eyes. If food doesn't look and smell good, we assume it isn't good.

Q: *How do food textures affect their appeal?*

A: Textures are very important. People need a variety of textures in their diets. It is interesting that our mood can affect the texture of food we desire. Sometimes we want chewy meat and potato textures. Sometimes we want silky smooth textures. The texture should be characteristic of the food product. Some foods lose their appeal when their familiar texture is changed.

Q: *How do selection and storage impact quality and appeal of foods?*

A: Selection and storage of foods need to be practiced until they are second nature. If foods are not properly stored, they lose freshness, quality, and may even spoil. There are managers in each area of the food market to assist if you have questions when selecting foods. Do not be shy. Ask an expert. Always select fresh products; store them properly and quickly. Meats need special care, as does produce. Do your homework. Know if the product should be firm or soft, red or gray. Such information can save you time, money, and energy.

Q: *What types of preparation techniques improve the appeal of foods?*

A: Every cook has preparation techniques that suit his or her personal preferences and lifestyle. These techniques are used frequently and become second nature. For example, I think meats look more appealing when browned at some point during the cooking process. Whether you are stir-frying or oven roasting, this can be accomplished.

Always read your recipe, think it through, and make desired improvements or changes before you begin cooking. Do not overcook foods. Overcooked foods lose eye appeal, texture, and nutrients. For instance, I like to stir-fry vegetables. The tender-crisp texture is pleasing. This method saves time, electricity, and nutrients as well.

Q: *What types of seasonings can be used to improve the appeal of food?*

A: Seasoning preferences are personal, but you can explore and develop new tastes for seasonings. Herbs and spices have been around for thousands of years, and have always played a role in food preparation. Now, with an awareness of the need to reduce the intake of sodium, people can take advantage of other available seasonings. A number of combination seasonings for meats and vegetables, such as lemon pepper, are on the market. You can experiment with chives, basil, oregano, curry powder, parsley flakes, and many others. Sage, rosemary, thyme, ginger, and curry are good on meats. It is fun to experiment with herbs and spices. Although they do not add any nutritional value, they may have other health benefits. They also enhance the flavor and perhaps the color of food.

Discuss:
- Ms. Nunalee states that "We eat with our eyes...our mood can affect the texture of food we desire...texture should be characteristic of the food product." Do you agree or disagree with each of these statements?
- What suggestions does Ms. Nunalee offer to improve the appeal of foods?
- Do you experiment with different seasonings? Are you familiar with the seasonings mentioned in the feature?

Feature-Related Activity

In small groups, have students try to identify different spices. Place a small amount of each spice in a paper cup. Have enough samples so each group can have a sample of each spice. Place a number on each cup. Have the students number their papers to correspond with the number of samples. Then have them write down the name of the spice by each number. Give a prize to the group that identifies the most spices.

Chapter Review

Summary

Knowing how to buy, store, and prepare foods are basic skills for living. When buying foods from the Food Guide Pyramid, choose the products that best meet your needs. Learn to select nutritious foods at the lowest possible prices. Consider factors such as grade, age, quality, appearance, form, and preparation time when making your choices.

Proper storage helps maintain the quality of foods you buy. Follow the recommended guidelines for storing foods on the shelf or in the refrigerator or freezer. For best quality, use the products within the suggested storage times.

Learn to prepare foods successfully by following the recommended preparation techniques. Choose the techniques best suited to the type of food you are preparing. When using a recipe, follow directions and methods carefully for best results.

Think About It!

1. If you were trying to reduce the fat in your diet, which grade of meat would you buy? Explain your answer.
2. Why do you think meat alternates, such as legumes, are becoming more popular as main dish choices?
3. Why is it important to cook fruits and vegetables properly?
4. Evaluate the pros and cons of making your own breads, cakes, or cookies from scratch versus buying them from the store.
5. How would you encourage other teens to use more milk and milk products in their diets?
6. Describe some cultural differences among people that would affect the purchase, storage, and preparation of foods.
7. Compile a list of family and consumer sciences careers that relate to buying, storing, and preparing food.

Try It Out!

1. Perform a market survey comparing the cost of the various egg sizes available. Determine the best buy. Report your findings to the class.
2. Create a checklist for evaluating fresh produce.
3. Compare various types of milk, such as whole, lowfat, fat free, nonfat dry (reconstituted), evaporated, and buttermilk. Which would you buy for drinking? Which would you buy for cooking purposes? Compare the cost per serving of these products.
4. Select several foods from each of the food groups. Write the name of each food item on an individual slip of paper. Distribute these to the members of your class. Let each person tell how to properly store the food listed on the slip of paper.
5. Plan with your teacher to prepare and serve foods from each of the food groups discussed in the chapter. Review the preparation principles you must consider when preparing foods from each group.

Enrich: Have each student compile shopping guidelines for the family food shopper based on the content of this chapter.

Resource: *PowerZone Challenge CD.* Have students play the chapter review game to reinforce text content.

Chapter 18
Serving Food and Dining Out

Careers

These careers relate to the topics in this chapter:

- fast-food restaurant worker
- chef trainee
- flight kitchen manager
- school lunch program director

As you study the chapter see if you can think of others.

Topics

18-1 Serving Food
18-2 Making Dining Enjoyable
18-3 Dining Out

Introductory Activities

1. Survey the class as to the frequency and type of restaurants the students have visited in the past week.
2. Have students give an account of what would constitute a perfect meal for them. Have them specify the setting, service, food, etc.

Topic 18-1

Serving Food

I. Family Mealtime
II. Types of Meal Service
   A. Family Service
   B. Plate Service
   C. Buffet Service
   D. English Service
III. Tableware
   A. Dinnerware
   B. Flatware
   C. Glassware
IV. Table Accessories
   A. Table Linens
   B. Centerpieces
V. Setting the Table
   A. Clearing the Table

Topic 18-2

Making Dining Enjoyable

I. Hosting a Meal
II. Manners When Dining

Topic 18-3

Dining Out

I. Types of Restaurants
   A. Fast-Food Restaurants
   B. Cafeterias and Buffets
   C. Family Restaurants
   D. Formal Restaurants
   E. Specialty Restaurants
   F. Carryout and Delivery Services
II. Ordering from a Restaurant Menu
III. Making Healthful Food Choices
IV. Restaurant Etiquette
V. Paying the Check
   A. Tipping

Topic 18-1
Serving Food

Objectives
After studying this topic, you will be able to
- state how family mealtime can affect family relationships.
- describe four types of meal service.
- identify factors to consider when selecting tableware and table accessories.
- demonstrate how to set a table properly.

Topic Terms
meal service
tableware
place setting
open stock
cover

Enrich: To introduce food service-related careers to the students, ask the school lunch program director to share his or her job responsibilities with the class.

Reflect: How are the daily meals served in your home? What major changes are made when there are guests?

Discuss: Does your family observe any family customs or traditions during mealtime?

18-1 Taking the time to set an attractive table can set the mood for entertaining guests.

Thought should go into serving foods just as it goes into planning and preparing them. After taking time to prepare delicious meals or refreshments, take care to serve them properly. A casual setting is suitable for an informal meal, but an elegant meal deserves an elegant setting. There are no rigid rules for how you should serve meals or refreshments. However, by following some general guidelines, you can help make your meal a success. Whether you are serving family members, friends, or honored guests, you can make the people who eat with you feel special. See 18-1.

Family Mealtime

Families are busily involved in numerous activities. In many homes, the evening meal is one of the few opportunities family members have to get together during the day. This makes family mealtime more than just a chance to satisfy hunger. It becomes a time of important social interaction. Family members can use this time to discuss what is going on in their lives. Together they can make plans and share hopes for the future. This type of communication helps build family strength and unity. Members learn to develop tolerance and respect for individual differences.

Family mealtime provides a chance for parents to teach children. One area on which parents often focus is table manners. As children practice good manners, parents can provide positive reinforcement. This will help children remember to use these social skills as they grow up and begin interacting with people outside the family.

Many parents use family mealtime to help children develop a healthful appreciation for food. Parents can teach children family customs and food traditions. They can encourage children to try a variety of new tastes. Parents can help children select nutritious diets by offering them choices from each of the groups in the Food Guide Pyramid. Parents can also teach children to eat slowly and chew food thoroughly. Learning to approach food this way aids digestion and helps children avoid overeating.

You can play a role in making mealtime a positive experience in your home. You might set the table attractively and put on some soft music. Giving a little extra attention to details will show that you respect and care for family members.

You can also make meals enjoyable by keeping conversation pleasant. Save upsetting issues to discuss at another time. Treat your family members as you would treat your best friends. Show genuine interest as they share stories and ideas.

Family Enrichment Activity
Have students analyze mealtime at their own homes. Do they all eat together or does each person have his or her own schedule? Discuss why people often act differently with family from the way they act in situations outside the home. If students discover areas for improvement, have them work with other family members to plan a meal in which they can all participate, or work to develop guidelines on which everyone can agree for behavior while eating.

Types of Meal Service

Meal service is the way a meal is served. There are several types of meal service. The type you use will depend partly on the menu and the number of people you are serving. The formality of the occasion will also affect your choice of meal service.

Family Service

Family service, also known as *American service*, begins with a table that has been set with plates and flatware. The beverage is on the table, too. All foods are placed in serving dishes and placed on the table. Family members pass the food from one person to another. Everything should be passed in one direction. People serve themselves as the foods come to them. This style of meal service is popular. However, it is inconvenient when serving dishes are hot or heavy. It may also be difficult if children at the table are too young to handle dishes of food.

Plate Service

Plate service is often used in restaurants. Individual portions are placed on each person's plate in the kitchen. The plates are then brought to the table and placed in front of each diner. Breads and condiments are usually passed at the table where family members may help themselves. This style of service is convenient when there are small children. It is also a good choice when some family members have special diets.

Buffet Service

Buffet service allows both large and small groups to be served with ease. Food is placed in serving dishes on a buffet table, taking care to keep everything at the proper temperature. Guests walk around the buffet and help themselves. Serving dishes are refilled as needed.

When serving a buffet, arrange items on the table in the order in which guests will pick them up. Plates are first. Flatware and beverages are often placed last. Gravies and sauces should come after the foods they accompany. Place serving utensils to the right of each dish. Leave space between serving dishes for people to rest their plates while serving themselves. See 18-2.

You may not have enough table space to seat a large group of guests. In this case, you may invite guests to sit in any available space and hold their plates in their laps. However, be sure the menu includes foods that can be cut with a fork or eaten with the fingers.

English Service

Some families use *English* or *head-of-table service* for special occasion meals, such as Thanksgiving dinner. This formal type of service requires the table to be set with flatware in advance. Salads may be set at each person's place. All plates are stacked at the head of the table. The server sits at the head of the table. He or she fills each

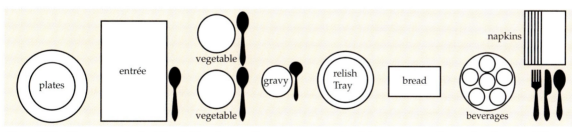

18-2 This diagram of a buffet table shows the arrangement of the items in the order they will be picked up. Guests can take a plate, serve themselves the entree, and then move to the side dishes.

Discuss:
Do you ever use plate service at home? If so, on what occasions?

Enrich:
Divide the class into four groups. Have each group role-play one of the four types of meal service. Have a group moderator relate the procedure, advantages, and disadvantages for each type of meal service.

Resource:
Which Type of Meal Service Would You Choose? reproducible master, TR

Putting Technology to Use
Have students investigate the Meals on Wheels program at their Web site, www.mealsonwheelsassn.org. Ask students if they know anyone who volunteers for or receives aid from Meals on Wheels.

> **Discuss:**
> Would you rather buy tableware by place setting or open stock? Why?
>
> **Reflect:**
> Think of the tableware you use for your daily meals. What pieces of dinnerware, flatware, or glassware do you infrequently use? (Examples might include a soup spoon and cereal bowl.)
>
> **Activity:**
> Have the students compare prices of fine china, earthenware, pottery, and plastic place settings of dinnerware.

plate and passes it to a diner seated at the table. Bread and condiments are passed so individuals can serve themselves. Eating begins after everyone has been served.

There are no hard and fast rules for meal service. You can vary and combine different styles of service to meet your needs.

Tableware

Regardless of the type of meal service being used, tableware can enhance the dining atmosphere. **Tableware** refers to dinnerware, flatware, and glassware.

You can buy tableware in sets, as place settings, or as open stock. A *set* includes all the tableware needed to serve a group of people. Most sets include four or eight place settings. A **place setting** is the dinnerware or flatware that one person would need. A place setting of dinnerware might include a dinner plate, salad plate, cup, and saucer. A place setting of flatware might include a knife, dinner fork, salad fork, teaspoon, and soup spoon. Tableware purchased **open stock** can be bought one piece at a time. For instance, you could buy one plate or one fork. This allows you to replace lost or broken pieces and add pieces as needed.

As you choose tableware, consider factors such as convenience, durability, and your lifestyle. Choose tableware to harmonize with the decor of the dining area. The dinnerware, flatware, and glassware should all complement each other. See 18-3.

When selecting tableware, you need to consider its care requirements, too. For instance, you might want to be sure your tableware is dishwasher-safe.

Dinnerware

Dinnerware includes plates, cups, saucers, and bowls. Dinnerware can be made of fine china, earthenware, pottery, or plastic. Fine china is often used for special occasions, while earthenware and pottery are used in more casual settings. Families with small children often use plastic dinnerware because it does not break easily.

18-3 This dinnerware, flatware, and glassware are used together to create an elegant table setting.

Flatware

Flatware is the term used to refer to knives, forks, and spoons. Flatware should be comfortable to hold and use. Flatware is commonly made of sterling silver, silver plate, or stainless steel. There is a price range and pattern to suit every budget and taste. Sterling silver flatware is most expensive and is often used on special occasions. Stainless steel flatware is usually least expensive and is frequently used as everyday tableware.

Glassware

Glassware refers to those items such as juice, water, and iced beverage glasses. Sturdy tumblers are popular for family meals, and stemware is used for special occasions.

The finest grade of glass is *lead glass*. People often refer to lead glass as *crystal*. Lead glass costs more than other glassware and is often reserved for fine dining. Glassware for everyday use is often made of *lime glass* or plastic.

Glassware can be shaped in a variety of ways. The most expensive glassware is made of blown glass. Most inexpensive glassware is pressed glass or molded plastic.

Table Accessories

Table accessories add to the look of a dining table. Table accessories include linens and centerpieces.

Putting Technology to Use

Have students use charting software to develop a chart comparing the use and care of each type of flatware. Discuss the charts in class. Have students make any corrections to their charts and print copies to keep with their handouts.

Table Linens

Table linens refer to tablecloths, place mats, and napkins. Table linens can be made of almost any natural or synthetic material. As you choose table linens, keep in mind the cost, durability, and ease of care. Try to choose table linens that will make an appropriate background for the tableware you will be using. Plain tablecloths and place mats look good with patterned dinnerware, 18-4. Many people choose plain dinnerware so they can use table linens with various designs.

Centerpieces

A *centerpiece* adds beauty and interest to a table. Centerpieces can be made from a wide range of materials. Cut flowers or a bowl of fruit or vegetables makes a nice centerpiece. A special dessert, such as a birthday cake, may be a tempting sight. Figurines, carvings, and seashell arrangements are attractive, too. Candles may be used as a centerpiece for evening meals.

Talking with someone across the table who is hidden behind a centerpiece is uncomfortable. Therefore, the height of a centerpiece should be below eye level. The overall size of the centerpiece should be related to the size of the table. Avoid large arrangements, which can overpower the table. On the other hand, avoid using a centerpiece that is too small to be noticed.

The placement of a centerpiece is not limited to the center of the table. It can be used anywhere on the table as long as the overall effect is balanced. A centerpiece should be attractive on all sides viewed by diners. If an arrangement has a definite back, place it so no one views the back.

Setting the Table

An attractive table setting can enhance any meal. There is no prescribed formula for setting a table. The primary goals in table setting are convenience and comfort. A pretty table helps diners relax and enjoy meals more.

When setting a table, you should place tableware to look similar to the **cover** (individual place setting) shown in 18-5. The dinner plate should mark the center of the space allowed for each person. Place the salad plate to the upper left of the dinner plate. Place the cup and saucer to the lower right. Position the bread and butter plate above and slightly to the left of the dinner plate.

Flatware should be placed in the order in which it will be used. Place the knife to the right of the plate with the blade toward the plate. Place the spoons to the right of the knife. Lay the butter knife on the bread

18-4 A crochet table runner and place mats provide an attractive contrast to this colorful dinnerware.

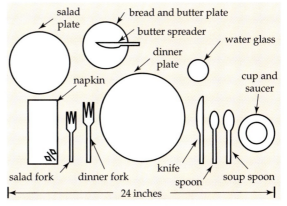

18-5 This diagram of an individual cover shows the proper placement of dinnerware, flatware, and glassware.

> **Enrich:**
> Have students brainstorm creative and inexpensive ideas for using table linens when entertaining a group of teen friends.
>
> **Activity:**
> Divide the class into small groups. Have each group prepare a centerpiece. The centerpieces should be appropriately sized, creative, inexpensive, and attractive.
>
> **Resource:**
> *An Individual Cover*, color transparency CT-16, TR
>
> **Resource:**
> *Serving Food*, Activity A, SAG

Across the Curriculum

Social studies/sociology. Ask students if they have ever been to a formal restaurant or party where they were unsure about the use of dinnerware or flatware. Discuss how, at one time, familiarity with different types of tableware indicated that a person was a member of the nobility or upper classes. Do students feel this is still true today?

and butter plate. You will usually place forks to the left of the plate. However, if a fork is the only utensil needed for a meal, you should place it on the right. Place cocktail forks to the right of the spoons.

Set the water glass above the knife. Place other glasses to the right of the water glass.

For most settings, you can simply fold napkins into rectangles. You can also fold and pleat napkins in a variety of ways to add a creative touch. Place napkins on the dinner plates or to the left of the forks.

Try to achieve a balanced, organized look when setting the table. Items need not match, but they should harmonize with one another. What is important is the way the table looks when it is complete, 18-6.

Clearing the Table

At the end of a course, you should remove everything that will not be needed for the next course. Remove serving dishes first. Then remove dinnerware, beginning with the guest of honor. Clear each person's cover, moving around the table in sequence. Be careful not to reach in front of another person when clearing the table.

When clearing a cover, remove the dinner plate first. Pick it up with your left hand and transfer it to your right hand. Next, remove the salad plate and place it on top of the dinner plate. Then remove the bread and butter plate and place it on top of the salad plate.

Check It Out!

1. True or false. Family mealtime provides a chance for parents to teach children table manners.
2. In what type of meal service are serving dishes passed from one person to another, allowing people to serve themselves?
3. What are the three ways tableware can be purchased?
4. Why should the height of a centerpiece be below eye level?
5. True or false. When setting a table, flatware should be placed in the order in which it will be used.

Check It Out! (Answers)

1. true
2. family service
3. You can buy tableware in sets, as place settings, or as open stock.
4. Talking with someone across the table who is hidden behind a centerpiece is uncomfortable.
5. true

18-6 Items on a properly set table are neatly arranged for the convenience of diners.

Enrich:
Give each student a construction paper placemat and paper tableware patterns. Have students use the patterns to create their own individual cover, using the diagram in 18-5 as a guide.

Resource:
Setting the Table, reproducible master, TR

Resource:
Planning Place Settings, reproducible master, TR

Topic 18-2
Making Dining Enjoyable

Objectives
After studying this topic, you will be able to
- list responsibilities of someone hosting a meal.
- describe appropriate manners to use when dining.

Topic Term
etiquette

Using a formal style of meal service and setting an attractive table can make any meal a special occasion. However, the easiest way to make dining truly enjoyable is to use proper etiquette. **Etiquette** refers to approved social conduct, or good *manners*. At the table, using proper etiquette is an essential social skill. Rules of etiquette apply to those who serve meals as well as to those who eat meals, 18-7.

Hosting a Meal

Offering food to guests is a common gesture of hospitality. When you host a meal, you can make it a pleasant experience for diners by practicing good manners. This includes being willing to accept a guest's offer of assistance.

As host, you should invite guests to the table when a meal is ready to be served. You need to inform guests where they are to sit at the table. After all guests are seated, serving may begin.

You should see that all guests are served before serving yourself. (Family style service can be an exception to this guideline. If someone else begins passing a dish, you may take a serving as the dish comes to you.) Guests generally wait for the host to begin eating. Therefore, if you are busy serving, invite those who have been served to begin eating. This allows guests to enjoy their food while it is still hot. During the meal, you should offer second helpings of food if they are available.

You should be able to enjoy a meal with your guests. Proper planning and preparation will keep you from leaving the table repeatedly to attend to kitchen tasks.

As a host, you have a responsibility to guide conversation during the meal. You may suggest topics of interest and encourage all guests to become involved in the conversation. Controversial or unappetizing topics are best saved for another time.

Continue eating until all guests have finished. At the end of the meal, you may invite guests to move to another room. You may need to do some after-dinner cleanup. For health and safety, store leftover foods promptly after the meal. You may also want to remove dirty dishes from the view of your guests. However, save detailed cleanup for later so you can return to your guests as quickly as possible.

Manners When Dining

Everyone should assume a role in making dining an enjoyable experience. As a dinner guest, plan to arrive on time. Come to the table in a pleasant frame of mind. Be prepared to help those dining with you to relax and enjoy themselves, too.

Knowing proper etiquette can enhance your self-esteem. You will feel good about yourself when you know how to behave in

18-7 Knowing proper table etiquette helps people feel more at ease in social settings.

> **Reflect:**
> What rules of table etiquette do you feel are most important?
>
> **Discuss:**
> What do you think is proper etiquette for a teenage host and his or her guests at a party?
>
> **Resource:**
> *Planning for Guests*, reproducible master, TR

FCCLA Activity
Have students develop some basic lessons on good manners that can be taught to young children. These activities will need to be action-based and contain visual reminders of appropriate behavior. (Role-playing would probably work.) Then have students eat lunch with the children to help them practice what they have been taught.

Resource:
Hosting a Meal, Activity B, SAG

Resource:
Mealtime Manners, reproducible master, TR

Discuss:
Orally read and discuss the mealtime manner guidelines. What are the benefits of using good table manners?

social situations. Using appropriate behavior will help you feel comfortable in almost any setting. Using good manners will also help others feel comfortable in your presence.

Many employers consider the ability to use proper etiquette an important employability skill. If you are invited to lunch when you are on a job interview, be sure to use your best table manners. The employer may be evaluating how you will behave when dining with future clients and customers.

You do not need a special occasion to practice good table manners. You should use proper etiquette whenever you eat. Using good manners should become a habit.

Table manners are influenced by culture. Rules of table etiquette vary in different countries. However, following some basic guidelines will help you feel comfortable no matter where you are. See 18-8.

Mealtime Manners

- Sit up straight and avoid placing your elbows on the table during a meal.
- At the beginning of a meal, lay your napkin across your lap. A luncheon napkin may be unfolded completely. However, leave a dinner napkin folded in half. Never tuck a napkin in your collar.
- Use the serving utensils offered with each dish of food. Never put a utensil from which you have eaten into a serving dish.
- Try a small portion of all foods that are offered to you. Do not discuss foods that you do not like or those that you are unable to eat for dietary reasons.
- Flatware is usually placed on the table in the order of use. Use the outermost pieces first.
- If you drop your flatware on the floor, leave it there. The host will offer you another piece.
- Unless the host invites you to begin eating, you should wait for him or her to start the meal. (At very large gatherings, you may begin eating when those seated near you have been served.)
- Never chew with your lips open so others can see the food in your mouth.
- Never talk when your mouth is full.
- Eat and drink quietly. Smacking your lips, slurping, gulping, and making other noises is inappropriate at the table.
- When in doubt about how to eat a food, follow the lead of your host. In a restaurant, you may quietly ask your waiter for advice.
- Never spit food out of your mouth at the table. If it tastes spoiled, quietly leave the table and go to the bathroom. If it is too hot, quickly take a swallow of a cold beverage. (This is the only time it is appropriate to consume a beverage when your mouth has food in it.)
- Inconspicuously remove fish bones or fruit pits from your mouth with your thumb and forefinger.
- Use fingers to eat only those foods that can be eaten without leaving traces of the food on your fingers. For instance, carrot sticks and cookies are finger foods. Barbecued chicken and cakes with sticky frosting are fork foods.
- Cut food one or two bites at a time as you are ready to eat it.
- Do not gesture with flatware in your hand.
- Cut sandwiches in halves or quarters before eating them.
- Break off small pieces of bread rather than biting into a whole slice. Break rolls in the same way. Butter one small portion of bread at a time.
- Place used flatware on the edge of a plate or saucer, not on the table.
- Never use toothpicks or dental floss while at the table.
- If you spill something at the table, be as inconspicuous as possible. If cleanup is necessary, offer to help. Apologize briefly, but do not allow the incident to spoil your meal or that of others.
- When you have finished your meal, lay your knife and fork together across the center of your plate. Before you leave the table, lay your napkin beside your plate.
- After the meal, avoid leaving the table until the host rises. If you must leave, ask the host if you may be excused.

18-8 Following these guidelines will help you appear polite and feel comfortable at any meal.

Citizenship and Service
Have students investigate appropriate behavior and/or manners during mealtime in other cultures and compare these to those generally acceptable in the United States. Discuss how knowing the customs and acceptable behavior in other cultures can help when visiting another country or when a future job puts a person in contact with people from a different nation or culture.

Topic 18-3
Dining Out

Check It Out!
1. Approved social conduct is known as _____.
2. Why might a host invite guests who have already been served to begin eating?
3. True or false. If a guest drops a fork, he or she should pick it up, wipe it off, and quietly continue eating.

Check It Out! (Answers)
1. etiquette
2. Guests generally wait for the host to begin eating. If a host is busy serving, he or she should invite guests to begin eating so they can enjoy their food while it is still hot.
3. false

Objectives
After studying this topic, you will be able to
- describe several types of restaurants.
- interpret a restaurant menu.
- select nutritious foods when eating out.
- give etiquette guidelines to follow when dining in a restaurant.
- explain the process of paying and tipping in a restaurant.

Topic Terms
table d'hôte
a la carte
gratuity

Vocabulary: Check the terms *table d'hôte* and *a la carte* in the dictionary. What are the French meanings of these terms?

Reflect: Do you feel more comfortable at some types of restaurants and less comfortable at others? What do you think is the difference?

Discuss: What are some techniques used by fast-food restaurants to assure quick service?

People used to dine out as a luxury or for special occasions. Today, many people choose to eat out rather than prepare meals at home. Recognizing different types of restaurants and knowing menu terms can help make dining out more enjoyable. Understanding how to make wise food choices can make eating in restaurants more healthful.

Types of Restaurants

When eating away from home, you can choose from several types of restaurants. Sometimes, you will choose a restaurant where you can eat quickly because you are hungry. At other times, you will choose a restaurant with fine food and a nice atmosphere because you want to be pampered.

Fast-Food Restaurants

People who do not want to spend much time eating like the quick service fast-food restaurants deliver. In fast-food restaurants, you order, pay, and pick up your food in a matter of minutes. You may carry food out or eat it in the restaurant. Customers are expected to dispose of their own trash when they are finished eating.

> **Discuss:**
> Have students give examples of fast-food restaurants, cafeterias, buffets, family restaurants, formal restaurants, specialty restaurants, and carryout restaurants in your area.
>
> **Reflect:**
> At what types of specialty restaurants do you enjoy dining?
>
> **Resource:**
> *Types of Restaurants,* Activity C, SAG

For extra fast service, customers often prefer using the drive-up window offered at many fast-food restaurants. This eliminates the need for customers to park and go inside.

Cafeterias and Buffets

Cafeterias and buffets have a variety of foods placed along a serving line, 18-9. You choose the items you wish to eat. Cafeterias price each food item separately. At the end of the line, you pay for the specific items you chose. You can control the cost of your meal by choosing foods that fit your budget.

Buffets are offered at a fixed price. Most food items are self-serve. Customers can take as much or as little of each food as they like. They may also return to the buffet for additional servings.

Neither cafeterias nor buffets have servers to take food orders. However, servers may help seat you, take beverage orders, and offer refills.

Family Restaurants

The atmosphere is casual in most family restaurants. Children are welcome, and highchairs and booster seats are available for their comfort. Menus list a variety of foods that appeal to all age groups. Inexpensive, child-sized portions are usually offered. Prices are reasonable to make dining affordable for the entire family.

Formal Restaurants

Formal restaurants offer customers an elegant dining atmosphere. Customers enjoy attractive surroundings, dine on excellent food, and receive superb service, 18-10. Prices in formal restaurants tend to be high due to these features.

Diners in formal restaurants are served at a leisurely pace. They are allowed plenty of time to enjoy their food. You will not want to dine in this type of restaurant when time is limited.

Formal restaurants often have a dress code. Men are usually expected to wear jackets and ties. Women are expected to wear dresses, suits, or dressy pants.

18-9 Cafeteria customers walk along a serving line and select the foods they want.

Formal restaurants often require reservations. Some formal restaurants only seat guests at certain times. When dining in these restaurants, it is important that you arrive on time for your seating.

Specialty Restaurants

Fast-food, family, or formal restaurants may also be specialty restaurants. Specialty restaurants serve specific types of food. Pizza parlors, steak and seafood houses, and ethnic restaurants are examples. These restaurants usually have very good food because they specialize in the items they serve. Prices vary according to the type of restaurant.

Carryout and Delivery Services

Many restaurants offer carryout service. Customers order food, pick it up, pay for it, and take it somewhere else to eat. Delivery is also an option at many restaurants. A customer orders food by phone and a restaurant employee delivers the food to the customer's door.

Carryout and delivery services are popular with busy people. Customers can avoid getting dressed to go out to eat without having to cook.

Problem-Solving Practice

School Cafeteria Survey, reproducible master, TR. Have students use this master to survey students about ways the school cafeteria could be improved. Have students use the decision-making process to make one or more changes in their cafeteria (for instance, making it more attractive or better lit; lowering the noise level; or promoting more appropriate/considerate behavior). Provide students with copies of the Decision-Making Process master from Chapter 1 to use as a guide.

18-10 Servers in formal restaurants are trained to provide exceptional service to enhance their customers' dining experiences.

Ordering from a Restaurant Menu

Fast-food and some casual restaurants post their menus on the wall. After reading your choices, you place your order at a counter. Most other restaurants provide printed menus listing the foods available. A waiter will come to your table to take your order. He or she may mention other food specials that you can select.

When you are given a menu, you can quickly determine if you will order table d'hôte or a la carte. **Table d'hôte** means the entire meal has one price. Usually the meal will include a salad or soup, a main course, a side dish, and bread. Sometimes table d'hôte meals also include a beverage, appetizer, and dessert. **A la carte** menus feature items that are priced individually. A separate charge will be made for the soup, salad, and main dish.

Some menus use French terms to describe the way food has been prepared. See 18-11. Do not hesitate to ask questions when you do not understand the menu. Your waiter should be happy to assist you. Also, do not be afraid to ask the price of specials described by the waiter. These items may be the most expensive dishes the restaurant serves.

You will be given a few minutes to read the menu in a restaurant. When you have decided what you want to eat, lay your menu on the table. This lets the waiter know you are ready to order.

Making Healthful Food Choices

You need to consider the impact of meals eaten away from home on your overall health. When you select foods from a menu, keep the Food Guide Pyramid in mind. Consider how your food choices will contribute to your daily needs. For instance, a roast beef sandwich will contribute one serving of meat and two servings of bread. Ordering lowfat milk and a salad with the sandwich would add to your daily serving requirements.

An ideal meal would supply 25 to 30 percent of your calorie needs for the day. It would also provide a perfect balance of needed nutrients. Few meals meet this ideal description. However, you do not

> **Activity:**
> Have students collect menus from local restaurants. Display the collection on the bulletin board.
>
> **Resource:**
> *Healthful Eating Away from Home,* transparency master, TR
>
> **Activity:**
> From the collection of menus, have students select a healthful meal that is based on the Food Guide Pyramid.

Career Preparation Activity
Is a Food Service Business for Me? reproducible master, TR. Invite a panel of restaurant owners and/or managers to speak to the class about what is involved in owning and/or managing a restaurant. Try to have a variety of restaurant types represented among panel members, such as fast-food, family style, cafeteria style, and a more formal style of restaurant. Provide copies of the master for students to use during the panel presentation.

Resource:
Restaurant Terms Puzzle, Activity D, SAG

Activity:
Using Chart 18-12 as a guide, have students select a healthful meal from a fast-food, family, and formal restaurant menu.

Menu Terms

a la Kiev. Containing butter, garlic, and chives.
a la king. Served with a white cream sauce that contains mushrooms, green peppers, and pimentos.
a la mode. Served with ice cream.
almondine. Made or garnished with almonds.
au gratin. Served with cheese.
au jus. Served with natural juices.
du jour. Of the day. For instance, *soup du jour* means soup of the day.
en brochette. Cooked or served in small pieces on a skewer.
en coquille. Served in a shell.
en croquette. Breaded and deep-fried.
en papillote. Cooked in parchment paper to seal in juices.
Florentine. Prepared with spinach.
julienne. Cut into long, thin slices.
Marengo. Sautéed with mushrooms, tomatoes, and olives.
picata. Prepared with lemon.
Provençale. Prepared with garlic, onion, mushrooms, tomato, herbs, and olive oil.

18-11 Becoming familiar with these terms will help you read restaurant menus.

Healthful Eating Away from Home

- Select broiled, roasted, or grilled foods rather than fried.
- Choose roast beef sandwiches over hamburgers.
- Opt for a plain baked potato instead of French fries. You might also consider sharing a small order of fries with a friend.
- Choose steamed vegetables rather than buttered or creamed vegetables.
- Look for a salad bar and choose plenty of fresh fruits and vegetables. However, go easy on coleslaw and creamy potato and pasta salads, which are high in fat.
- Select whole grain breads and rolls, which are higher in fiber than white bread products.
- Ask to have items such as salad dressings, sour cream, cheese and barbecue sauces, and butter served on the side. These items tend to be high in fat and sodium. Add just enough to flavor, rather than smother, your food.
- Choose water or fruit juice instead of soda to drink.
- Order lowfat milk instead of a milk shake.
- Choose fresh fruit for dessert.

18-12 Keeping a few tips in mind can help you make healthful food choices when eating out.

have to get a full range of nutrients at each meal. Your goal should be to meet your needs throughout the day. You can balance food choices made at one meal with those made at the next.

A fast-food meal of a hamburger, French fries, and a milk shake is rather high in calories. This meal is also high in fat while being low in vitamins, minerals, and fiber. You can make lowfat choices that are rich in vitamins, minerals, and fiber at other meals. This will help offset your fast-food selections.

If you eat out often, you must learn to choose foods carefully. This may require you to choose restaurants carefully, also. Plan to eat in those restaurants that offer nutritious options. Chart 18-12 gives some tips for making healthful menu selections when you are away from home.

Restaurant Etiquette

When you are in a restaurant, you should be as polite as if you were a guest in someone's home. The same good table manners you use daily will make you comfortable in any restaurant. You should also keep a few special pointers in mind when in restaurants.

Before going to a restaurant, call to see if you will need reservations. If you make reservations, be sure to arrive on time. Upon arrival, tell the host the name in which your reservation is made and the number in your party. If you are asked where you would like to sit, respond

Putting Technology to Use
Have students use presentation software to compare and contrast healthful menu choices at fast-food restaurants with less-healthful choices. Have them include in their presentation the amounts of calories and fat grams found in the foods. (Brochures or posters including this information can be found in most fast-food restaurants.)

Topic 18-3 Dining Out

promptly. When your table is ready, the host will seat you. (In more casual restaurants, a sign may indicate that you should seat yourself.)

If you are unfamiliar with a restaurant, ask to see a copy of the menu before being seated. Evaluating the menu in advance allows you to decide if the foods and prices suit your tastes and budget. Many restaurants post menus outside their doors for this reason.

While in a restaurant, talk in a low but comfortable tone of voice. Others in the restaurant will not want to hear your conversation.

If you get the wrong order, or if your food is not prepared correctly, tell your waiter. He or she should be happy to help correct the error. If you need to talk with your waiter and cannot catch his or her eye, try raising your hand slightly. If this does not get attention, you may quietly call, "Waiter," when he or she is near. If this still does not get the attention you need, ask another waiter to send your waiter over. If you have finished your meal and the waiter has not presented your check, you may request it. Simply say, "Check please."

Paying the Check

At the end of a meal in a restaurant, the waiter will bring your check. The waiter may lay the check on the table. This indicates you should pay the cashier on your way out the door. Sometimes, the waiter will place the check in a folder or on a small tray. This indicates the waiter will return to take your payment.

You may place cash or a credit card in the folder or on the tray with the check. The waiter will return your change if you pay cash. He or she will return with a receipt for you to sign if you pay with a credit card. Be sure your bill is accurate before you sign the receipt.

Tipping

A **gratuity**, or *tip*, is a measure of your gratitude for good service. A gratuity usually ranges from 15 to 20 percent. You may want your tip to be toward the higher end of the range if you receive excellent service.

The type of restaurant influences the amount of your tip. Since no meal service is provided, fast-food customers are not expected to leave a tip. Ten percent is an appropriate tip for services offered at cafeterias and buffets. A tip of 15 percent is considered appropriate in family restaurants. When waiters have to clean up after messy children, a larger tip is in order. A tip in a formal restaurant may be as much as 20 percent of the cost of your food. No tip is expected for carryout service. However, customers are expected to tip delivery people.

You may leave your gratuity for the waiter on the tray or in the folder with the check. If you are paying with a credit card, you may add the tip to the receipt before writing the total. If there is no folder or tray provided, you may leave your tip inconspicuously on the table.

Check It Out!
1. Which type of restaurant offers food at a fixed price and allows customers to serve themselves as much as they like?
2. Briefly describe what would be served if a diner ordered roast beef au jus with green beans almondine and julienne potatoes.
3. Give three tips for making healthful food choices in restaurants.
4. How should a restaurant guest get the attention of his or her waiter?
5. What would be an appropriate tip when the check total is $17.96 in a cafeteria? At a family restaurant? In a formal restaurant?

Discuss: Have you ever seen a person behave discourteously in a restaurant? How did the behavior make you feel? How did the staff seem to react to the person?

Enrich: Have students role-play proper restaurant etiquette.

Resource: *How Much Should I Leave for a Tip?* reproducible master, TR

Check It Out! (Answers)
1. buffet
2. roast beef served with natural juices, green beans garnished with almonds, and potatoes cut into long, thin slices
3. (Student response. See Chart 18-12 on page 524 of the text.)
4. A restaurant guest should raise his or her hand slightly to get the attention of the waiter. If this does not get attention, the guest may quietly call to the waiter. If this still does not get the attention needed, another waiter may be asked to send the guest's waiter over.
5. $1.80; $2.70; $3.60

Discuss:
This feature can be used as a springboard for discussion of part-time employment for high school students. Ask the students to identify the benefits of part-time work that Hobart and Brian mention in the feature, as well as the disadvantages. Then ask them to brainstorm additional advantages and disadvantages of part-time work. You might use this as a topic for a classroom debate.

Discuss:
Discuss how young people must act responsibly if they are employees. What are some of the ways mentioned in the feature? What are some additional guidelines an employer might expect an employee to follow? Are these similar to what a teacher expects from a student?

TEENS ARE EXPERIENCING...
Work in Fast-Food Restaurants

What's it like to be on the other side of the counter at a fast-food restaurant? Meet Hobart and Brian, two part-time workers who provide the fast, friendly service you enjoy at fast-food restaurants.

According to Hobart, his job has many benefits. "Fast-food restaurants provide good on-the-job experience, and the chance for me to earn a paycheck. It's a great way to gain work skills!"

Hobart added that his after-school job also provides some balance in his life. Working gives him a sense of accomplishment. It offers him a chance to try a variety of work activities. "Even though I work, I can still make good grades and have fun."

Brian commented that training is an important part of the job. "You have to learn certain skills to do your job well.

These skills include serving customers, cooking food properly, using a cash register, and counting change. To improve my skills, I practice customer service at home by serving dinner to my parents."

When asked what he liked and disliked about his job, Brian pointed out several advantages. "I earn money, get career training, and meet new people. There are some disadvantages, too. Working means I have less free time to spend with other people."

Hobart felt his job encouraged responsibility. "You may get a break if you are late or absent at school. However, at a job you are expected to be on time. You are expected to be polite and friendly to every customer—no matter how you feel at the moment. You can't take your feelings out on customers—even if they are in a bad mood."

Brian was asked about the concerns customers express regarding the food served. He stated, "The biggest concern they have is about food sanitation. They want food that's properly handled and prepared. Sometimes their concerns aren't food related. They are concerned when someone makes a mistake in the amount of their bill, or the amount of change returned." For customers who are concerned about their diets, some fast-food restaurants offer healthier menu choices. Healthier food choices include fresh salads, grilled sandwiches, and lowfat drinks.

Hobart concluded by saying, "Working at fast-food restaurants can be good experience for teens. The job teaches responsibility and the benefits are good. (Some places even include a free meal!)" Hobart also mentioned that this type of entry-level work helps people build important work skills.

Chapter Review

Summary

After planning and preparing your meals, you will want to serve the food attractively. Such attention to detail can even make family mealtime a more pleasant experience. Choose a style of meal service that suits your menu and the people you are serving. Select dinnerware, flatware, and glassware that harmonize and complement the dining area. Set the table with both convenience and appearance in mind.

To make dining enjoyable, be considerate of every person at the table, especially guests. Know and practice good table manners so they become second nature to you.

Dining out can be just as enjoyable as eating at home. There are several types of restaurants from which to choose. Becoming familiar with menu terms will help you order your meal. Learning to make wise food choices will allow you to fit restaurant meals into a healthful diet. Being aware of restaurant etiquette will enable you to feel more comfortable when dining out. Knowing about methods of payment and tipping will also help you feel more at ease when eating away from home.

Think About It!

1. Which type of meal service do you think your family would most enjoy? Why?
2. Would you prefer to purchase tableware in sets, as place settings, or as open stock? Explain your answer.
3. Give three examples of a centerpiece you might use on your table.
4. What would you consider to be the three most important table manners?
5. Suppose you are served a lobster tail in a restaurant. You suddenly realize you do not know how to get the meat out of the shell. What will you do?
6. Suppose you were in another country and noticed that your table manners were different from those of your host. What would you do? If you were the host and your international guest used different table manners, what would you do?
7. What is your favorite type of restaurant? Explain your answer.
8. What negative consequences might arise when dining with family members or coworkers if you did not know proper restaurant etiquette?
9. In what careers, other than homemaking, would the information in this chapter be helpful?

Try It Out!

1. Plan a menu for a buffet. Sketch how you would set the table for the buffet so guests could easily serve themselves.
2. Demonstrate for the class how to properly set the table.
3. Role-play various dining situations showing a lack of table manners. Discuss the situations. Then repeat the role-plays using appropriate manners.
4. Collect menus from several restaurants. Working in small groups, look for terms from Chart 18-11 on the menus.
5. Using chart 18-12 as a guide, select two or three healthful meal options from each menu gathered in the previous activity.

Resource:
PowerZone Challenge CD. Have students play the chapter review game to reinforce text content.

LEADING GUIDE TO THE WORLD OF WORK
CAREER TIMES
VOLUME 1, NUMBER 6

Culinary Arts and Hospitality Careers Take the Cake

Careers in the field of culinary arts and hospitality relate mostly to eating and sleeping. The culinary arts industry hires those who prepare and serve food in commercial settings. The hospitality industry provides places for people to stay when they are away from home.

Employment Opportunities

People who work in culinary arts careers include chefs, bakers, short-order cooks, and salad makers. Catering directors, hosts, and servers also work in this field. People in this career area often work for restaurants or hotels. However, they might be hired by businesses that offer food services for employees.

The desk clerks, porters, and cleaning staff in hotels are part of the hospitality industry. Hospitality jobs are also found at camps, resorts, and country clubs. Other positions are at hotels, motels, spas, inns, and boarding houses.

Entrepreneurial Opportunities

There are many options for those in culinary arts and hospitality who wish to be self-employed. These options include catering, cleaning services, and cake decorating. Some entrepreneurs in this field choose to open restaurants or run hotels. For those who are willing to share their homes, a bed and breakfast or a guest house is another option. A home baker who prepares breads, cakes, pies, and cookies featured by a local business is an entrepreneur. Someone who teaches private cooking classes would also be a freelance worker.

Rewards and Demands of Culinary Arts and Hospitality Careers

A special reward in culinary arts and hospitality is the gratitude of repeat customers. People tend to return for those services they enjoy. Knowing they have helped make clients comfortable adds to the satisfaction of workers in this field.

Demands of this field include many hours of standing. Dealing with complaints and orders from difficult customers is also a challenge. Busy periods around the dinner hour or check-in time are associated with stress in this career area. When problems arise, workers are often called on to do extra work.

Preparation Requirements

Educational requirements for work in these areas vary. Job options are greater for those with higher levels of education. However, many jobs in this field do not require training beyond high school.

Much training in culinary arts and hospitality occurs on the job. However, workers can profit from taking related courses in high school. Family and consumer sciences classes would be helpful. A foodservice and hospitality course would be a good choice. Courses in English, math, computer science, and various business subjects should be useful, too.

Entry-Level Jobs

Culinary arts and hospitality includes many openings for those

Chefs use their creativity and knowledge of food to prepare dishes that appeal to the eye as well as the palate.

looking for entry-level work. For instance, a baker, cook, busperson, or waiter can be trained on the job. A high school diploma is desirable for these jobs.

Mid-Level Jobs

A two-year degree will prepare a worker for many mid-level jobs in this field. Programs such as foodservice management are offered by many community colleges. Some jobs at this level are kitchen supervisor, party planner, and school foodservice director. Someone who is willing to wait to move up the career ladder may find a job as a hospitality manager.

Professional-Level Jobs

Jobs at the professional level include chef, food stylist, and test kitchen manager. A college degree will help workers in this field move into management jobs faster. A four-year degree might be in hotel and restaurant management. Studies may be completed at a college. A number of specialty schools also offer programs in culinary arts and hospitality.

Personal Qualities Needed for Success

Guests of the hospitality industry expect first-rate service. Therefore, workers in this field must pay close attention to detail. They need an interest in people and a desire to serve them. Tact, communication skills, a sense of humor, and loyalty will help workers do well. Workers must be focused, pleasant, poised, and ready to accept responsibility. Skill in organizing tasks and making decisions will lead to success. Workers will need a sense for business details. They must be able to work with records, numbers, and business machines. A neat appearance, good health, and emotional stability are also needed.

Future Trends

The foodservice industry will grow as long as people keep eating meals away from home. Those with skills in culinary arts will be in demand to fill job openings. The hospitality industry keeps growing as it serves more business people and tourists than ever. Job growth in this field is also due to the larger number of services being offered. Fitness rooms, continental breakfasts, and late-night snacks are among the services found in some hotels. It is expected that culinary arts and hospitality will continue as one of the fastest growing career areas in the future. As a rule, entry-level salaries in this field are low, and there is no sign this will change.

Career Interests, Abilities, and You

Looking at your interests and abilities can help you decide if culinary arts and hospitality is for you. A key question to ask yourself is whether you enjoy making people—especially strangers—feel comfortable and happy. If so, try to get some part-time or summer work experience. A job in a restaurant or camp would help confirm your interest in culinary arts. Part-time work as a porter, waiter, or desk clerk can help you find out if hospitality suits you. Make an effort to shadow successful employees in these related careers.

You can gain experiences in culinary arts through work with a catering service. Perhaps you can get some experience as a volunteer in a soup kitchen. (After you have volunteered for a while, you might ask permission to add creative garnishes to the plates. You might also request a chance to add a gourmet touch to some of the recipes.) Some church kitchens provide food for everything from chili suppers to wedding receptions. Workers at these events are usually volunteers who would welcome an extra pair of hands. Festivals that include food vendors are also possibilities for career experiences. Keep in mind that you have a valuable resource—your youth. Many adults are willing to help start responsible young people on their career path. Do not hesitate to make contacts and ask for chances to gain experience.

Career Ladder for Culinary Arts and Hospitality

Advanced Degree
Consumer consultant
Marketing specialist
Market research

Bachelor's Degree
Hotel Manager

Associate's Degree
Restaurant manager
Airline flight attendant
Cafeteria manager
Chef
Butcher

High School Diploma
Waiter/Waitress
Housekeeping Services
Cashier
Chef trainee
Host/hostess
Pantry/stockroom worker

Pre-High School Diploma
Serve as an intern with any of the above
Food checker
Dietary aide
Volunteer in a community kitchen, food distribution center, or a meal delivery service for shut-ins

Part Seven
Meeting Your Clothing Needs

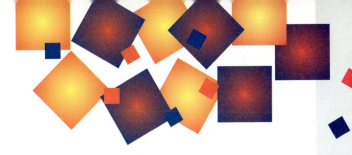

Chapter 19
Choosing and Caring for Clothes

Careers

These careers relate to the topics in this chapter:
- retail sales associate
- visual displayer
- wardrobe supervisor
- fashion buyer

As you study this chapter, see if you can think of others.

Topics

19-1 Choosing Clothes That Meet Your Needs
19-2 Choosing Clothes That Look Good on You
19-3 Planning Your Wardrobe
19-4 Shopping for Clothes
19-5 Caring for Clothes

Introductory Activities

1. Ask students to list advantages of sewing their own clothes. Ask if more people are making their own clothing today than in the past. Are today's teenagers interested in learning to sew? What are some recent trends in home sewing?
2. Ask each student to name any word related to fabric that comes to mind. As they each tell you their words, write the words on the chalkboard. Categorize the words as you write them on the board, but do not tell the students what you are doing. Possible categories might be fabric names, natural fibers, and generic fibers. When everyone has given you a word, ask the class to look at the groups of terms and decide what each category has in common.

Topic 19-1
Choosing Clothes That Meet Your Needs
I. Factors That Influence Clothing Decisions
   A. Physical Needs
      1. Lifestyle
   B. Psychological Needs
   C. Social Needs
      1. Group Identification
      2. Dress Codes
      3. Status
      4. Conformity Versus Individuality
   D. Special Needs
II. Choosing Clothes for Specific Occasions

Topic 19-2
Choosing Clothes That Look Good on You
I. Color
   A. Color Characteristics
   B. The Color Wheel
      1. Color Schemes
   C. Warm and Cool Colors
   D. Choosing Your Best Colors
      1. Personal Coloring
      2. Body Shape
II. The Other Design Elements
   A. Line
   B. Texture
   C. Form
III. Consider the Principles of Design
   A. Balance
   B. Proportion
   C. Rhythm
   D. Emphasis

Topic 19-3
Planning Your Wardrobe
I. Factors to Consider in Wardrobe Planning
   A. Taking an Inventory
II. Extending Your Wardrobe
   A. Choosing Multipurpose Clothing
   B. Mixing and Matching Garments
   C. Using Accessories

Topic 19-4
Shopping for Clothes
I. Shopping Guidelines
   A. Technology Brings New Ways to Shop
II. Understanding Fashion Terms
   A. Fashion
   B. Style
      1. Classic and Fad Styles
      2. Fashion Cycles
III. Judging Quality
   A. Durability
   B. Fit
IV. Reading Labels and Hangtags
V. Consider the Cost

Topic 19-5
Caring for Clothes
I. Daily Clothing Care
   A. Everyday Clothing Storage
II. Laundering Steps
   A. Read Care Labels
   B. Sort Clothes Properly
   C. Prepare Clothes for Laundering
      1. Pretreat Stains and Heavy Soil
   D. Understand Laundry Products
      1. Soaps and Detergents
      2. Bleach
      3. Water Softeners
      4. Fabric Softeners
   E. Using the Washing Machine
III. Drying Clothes
IV. Ironing and Pressing
V. Dry Cleaning
VI. Energy Conservation in Clothing Care
VII. Packing and Storing Clothes
   A. What to Pack for Travel
   B. How to Pack for Travel
   C. Packing for Seasonal Storage

Sidebar	Main

Vocabulary:
What do *fireproof* and *fire-resistant* mean?

Reflect:
What weather-related considerations played a part in the clothing you chose to wear today?

Note:
Sometimes the right clothing for extreme weather conditions is not just a matter of comfort, but of life or death, as was the case when early settlers traveled west.

Activity:
Research the various physical needs that an astronaut's spacesuit must address.

Resource:
Physical Needs in Clothing Decisions, reproducible master, TR

Topic 19-1
Choosing Clothes That Meet Your Needs

Objectives
After studying this topic, you will be able to
- list ways in which clothing meets physical needs.
- explain how clothing satisfies psychological and social needs.
- choose clothing that would be appropriate for specific occasions.

Topic Terms
lifestyle
uniform
dress code
modesty
status
conformity
individuality

Buying clothes can take a big bite out of your budget. Deciding what to wear can take time out of your day. These statements indicate that clothing choices are important decisions. Giving some thought to these choices will help you choose clothes that will meet your needs.

Factors That Influence Clothing Decisions

A number of factors influence your clothing decisions. Besides your basic needs, you are likely to consider your peers' opinions when you are choosing clothes. You may think about what your clothes say about you. You will undoubtedly think about what activities you will be doing when you wear the clothes, too.

Physical Needs

Clothes help meet your basic *physical needs* to protect your body. Your body requires protection from the weather, environmental dangers, and occupational hazards.

Weather can be a threat to the body. People need to be protected from cold and heat and such elements as sun, rain, and snow. Jackets, gloves, scarves, hats, heavy socks, and boots keep people warm and dry on cold days. In warm weather, lightweight clothes in light colors help keep people cool. Garments that repel water provide protection from rain.

The environment poses certain physical dangers that can be moderated through clothing. Life jackets provide safety for those who work and play near water. In areas where insects are bothersome, some people wear special jackets and hoods to protect their skin from bites. Hiking boots help prevent skids and falls and protect feet from the impact of harsh, rocky terrains.

Clothes protect many people from hazards in their workplaces. Road workers wear brightly colored, reflective clothing so they will be visible to drivers. Firefighters wear heat- and fire-resistant garments. See 19-1. Health care workers often wear masks and gloves when working with patients. This protects patients as well as workers from the possible transfer of germs.

19-1 Special clothing protects firefighters from flames, water, and chemicals from fire extinguishers. Gloves and boots also repel these elements and provide slip-resistance.

Across the Curriculum

Science. Discuss how the body is cooled or warmed by various types of fibers and fabric construction. Have students name some fabrics that are worn primarily in hotter weather and fabrics that are worn during cold weather.

Lifestyle

Many of your physical needs for clothing are determined by your **lifestyle**. This is your way of life or your style of living. You may own a few garments to wear for special occasions such as weddings. However, you probably do not wear these clothes most of the time. The majority of your clothing choices are likely to be dictated by your daily activities. If you enjoy playing sports, you probably own a lot of activewear. If you spend much time outside, you are likely to own more outerwear than someone who prefers to stay indoors.

Psychological Needs

Any garment might meet a physical need. However, clothes must have certain characteristics to meet psychological needs. Certain colors, fabrics, and styles of clothing can affect how you feel. For instance, bright colors might make you feel happy, 19-2. Perhaps you feel relaxed when you wear soft fabrics and confident when you wear formal styles.

Choosing clothes you find appealing gives you a sense of well-being by helping to meet your psychological need for attractiveness. Wearing clothes that enhance your appearance can boost your self-esteem.

Social Needs

The social need for acceptance plays a big role in the clothing choices most people make. This is especially true during the school years when children and teens are seeking the approval of their peers. Teens often wear clothes that identify them with a specific group. They may use clothing to exhibit a desired level of status. Teens also tend to choose clothing that conforms to styles worn by their friends.

Group Identification

People who identify with a group often use clothing as a sign of belonging. Members of certain groups wear uniforms as marks of identification. Members of other groups choose less rigid attire.

Uniforms are distinctive outfits that identify those who wear them with a specific group. You can look at athletes in their uniforms and immediately identify their sports and the teams for which they play. Military personnel have always worn uniforms. During war or peace, you can identify a service person on duty by the uniform he or she wears.

Many schools, especially private schools, require students to wear uniforms. See 19-3. The uniforms of prestigious schools often serve as status symbols for the students who wear them. Some public school systems are considering requiring students to wear uniforms as an antiviolence measure. Wearing uniforms sends a message that all students belong to the same "team." This results in less competition and more cooperation among "team members." Uniforms keep fashion from being an issue so students can focus more on learning.

Some groups do not have specific uniforms. However, they use certain colors or symbols to identify their members. For instance, members of sororities and

19-2 Feeling good about the clothes you wear is an important psychological need.

> **Activity:**
> Ask students to bring in pictures from magazines or newspapers showing two outfits that demonstrate contrasting lifestyles.
>
> **Reflect:**
> Do you tend to prefer different clothing items or colors when feeling happy versus unhappy?
>
> **Discuss:**
> Should people stop wearing favorite outfits that are no longer "in fashion"?
>
> **Discuss:**
> Do you agree that school uniforms help students focus more on learning?

Putting Technology to Use

Access the Smithsonian Institution Web site (www.si.edu) to review a historical garment collection significant to U.S. history, such as the gowns worn by First Ladies to presidential inaugurations. (Students may use the *Search* command and search for the word *inaugural* to gain access to those photos.)

Activity:
Ask students to investigate and report any special dress codes or uniforms associated with careers that interest them.

Example:
Review the dress code policy of your school.

Reflect:
Has your view of what constitutes immodest attire changed over time?

Discuss:
Describe clothing associated with different religious groups and/or beliefs.

19-3 The school uniform for these students consists of white blouses with plaid jumpers for girls and white shirts and vests for guys.

19-4 People who work in a business related to fashion or design, such as this furniture showroom assistant, must meet a dress code that requires a stylish appearance.

fraternities often own garments with Greek letters representing the names of their organizations.

Many people show group identity simply by yielding to the influence of their peers. Your peers form an informal group. By wearing the kinds of clothes your friends wear, you are showing you are a member of that group. Jeans and T-shirts are typical attire of many teen peer groups.

Dress Codes

Dress codes are standards of dress that are enforced in a social setting. Formal dress codes are based on the belief that the way people dress tends to affect their behavior. For instance, many businesses have formal dress codes for their employees. Employers believe requiring employees to wear professional clothing will encourage them to act professionally. See 19-4. Likewise, most school systems have written dress codes. These policies are designed to keep both teachers and students from wearing clothes that will detract from teaching and learning.

Informal dress codes exist in society. People within a culture commonly accept these unwritten standards of dress. Societal dress codes reflect people's beliefs about **modesty,** or the proper way to cover the body in various settings. For instance, the social dress code in the United States considers swimsuits suitable for wearing at a beach. However, swimsuits are viewed as immodest attire in an office because they do not cover enough of the body.

Some religious and ethnic groups have stricter informal dress codes than the societies in which they live. These stricter codes are based on standards of modesty that are more conservative.

Status

Status is a person's rank within a group. People often use clothing as signs of their status. Certain garments, styles, and brands carry a higher status than others. Clothes trimmed with fur and jewels are signs of social status. Such

Across the Curriculum

History. Have students identify the types of clothing worn by people of different social classes during the historical period they are studying in history class. Have students name fabrics, colors, or styles that were characteristic of a particular class or status.

garments suggest the wearers are wealthy. In many high schools, varsity jackets are signs of status. They indicate the wearers rank high among the student body in terms of athletic or academic skill.

People who desire a certain status may feel they must wear clothes that reflect that status. In some teen groups, this means wearing clothes that display names and logos of specific brands. People who wear these clothes feel they will have a high status for being fashion conscious. See 19-5.

Conformity Versus Individuality

What other people wear greatly influences clothing choices. For most people, clothing selection is a balance between conformity and individuality. **Conformity** in dress means wearing garments similar to those worn by others. Early in life, children begin expressing a desire to wear the same kinds of clothes they see other people wearing. This kind of conformity gives children a feeling of belonging.

In contrast, **individuality** in dress means choosing clothes that set you apart from others. You express your unique personality when you wear what you like without being swayed by what others are wearing. Wearing pants with a tailored shirt when others are wearing jeans and T-shirts is an example of expressing individuality.

When people conform too much, they give up their individuality. Most people select some garments similar to those worn by their peer group and some garments that are unique. This allows people to dress to suit their moods and create impressions with their clothing.

Special Needs

Some people, such as older adults or people with disabilities, have special clothing needs. Older people may choose more casual, comfortable clothes for their daily activities. Easy care is often another important factor. People with disabilities may want clothes that are stylish, yet easy to get on and off. Simple fasteners and larger openings are needed by people with limited movement or low vision. Elastic waists knit fabrics allow both comfort and ease of movement.

Choosing Clothes for Specific Occasions

You need different types of clothes for different occasions. For instance, you would probably wear formal attire to a wedding or a prom. You will need clothing that reflects your career choice when you go to a job interview. You will want your clothes to look neat and clean the first time you meet the parents of your dating partner, 19-6.

When choosing clothes for specific occasions. you will not want to lean too heavily on your individuality. Conformity is a safer policy in these situations. If an occasion is formal, choose formal clothing. If an event is in a business setting, look like you are prepared for business.

Choosing the right clothes for the occasion can greatly influence your personal effectiveness. For instance, at a job interview, you need to be able to promote your qualifications. You will be able to do this more easily if your clothing is not distracting to your potential employer.

Reflect: Who or what exercises the greatest influence on the type and style of clothing you wear?

Activity: Have students describe examples of outfits illustrating conformity and others demonstrating individuality.

Reflect: What do you want your clothing to say about you?

Resource: *Dressed for the Occasion*, reproducible master, TR

Resource: *Choosing Clothes*, Activity A, SAG

19-5 Clothing with matching accessories, such as handbags, is a sign of a status brand.

Across the Curriculum

Invite the vocational counselor to make a presentation on what students should and should not wear to a job interview. Have students prepare questions for the counselor in advance.

Discuss:
Can attractive clothing disguise poor grooming habits?

Vocabulary:
As you read through Topic 19-2 terms, which do you associate with color and which do you associate with design principles?

Note:
Review why grooming has a direct influence on a person's overall appearance.

19-6 Wearing a simple, attractive outfit appropriate for the occasion and looking well groomed is the best way to make a good first impression on your date's parents.

If you are uncertain about what to wear for an occasion such as a party, check with your host. You could also ask other people who are attending the event. For an occasion such as a job interview, you could call the place of business. Someone there will be able to tell you what type of attire is appropriate.

Check It Out!
1. What are three factors from which clothing provides physical protection?
2. A distinctive outfit that identifies someone who wears it with a specific group is a _____.
3. How does conformity differ from individuality?
4. True or false. Choosing the right clothes for a specific occasion can greatly influence a person's effectiveness.

Check It Out! (Answers)
1. weather, environmental dangers, occupational hazards
2. uniform
3. Conformity means wearing garments similar to those worn by others. Individuality means choosing clothes that set you apart from others.
4. true

Topic 19-2
Choosing Clothes That Look Good on You

Objectives
After studying this topic, you will be able to
- identify the colors that look best on you.
- explain how line, texture, and form can affect the way clothes look on you.
- apply the elements and principles of design to clothing selection.

Topic Terms
elements of design	line
hue	texture
value	form
intensity	principles of design
color wheel	balance
primary colors	proportion
secondary colors	rhythm
intermediate colors	emphasis
neutrals	

You have already read how good grooming and health habits can improve your appearance. Now you will see how the clothes you choose can enhance your appearance, too. Clothes can be used to point out your best features. At the same time, they can draw attention away from problem areas.

Which of your clothes are most flattering to you? Do those clothes have anything in common? Are most of them the same color? Do they have distinct lines? Are the textures mostly rough or mostly smooth? Do the forms of the garments enhance your body shape?

Color, line, texture, and form are the **elements of design.** These are factors that affect the appearance of a garment. Each element influences the way you look in your clothes. Whether you are buying or making garments, you can consider these elements. Using the elements effectively can help you dress to look your best.

Color

Of all the design elements, color is the most exciting in clothing selection. Color is an expression of you. It reveals something about your looks, feelings, and moods. Knowing how to use color will help you achieve a pleasing appearance by enhancing your best features.

Color Characteristics

The color used in clothing is *pigment,* which is a substance that gives color to other materials. Color has three distinct characteristics. First, color can be defined in terms of hue. **Hue** is the name given to a color. Red, blue, violet, and orange are hues. Hue is what distinguishes one color from another. It makes red different from green or blue. If you make red lighter or darker, you will not change the hue—the changed color is still red.

A second characteristic of color is value. **Value** refers to the lightness or darkness of a color, such as light green and dark green. The value of a color changes when either black or white is added to it. Adding black to a color creates a *shade.* For instance, navy blue is a shade of blue. A *tint* results when white is added to a color. Pink is a tint of red.

Intensity is the third characteristic of color. **Intensity** is the brightness or dullness of a color. Bright colors, such as red or green, have a high intensity. Pale colors, such as pink or light green, have a softer, less intense appearance. See 19-7.

The Color Wheel

How do colors relate to one another? The **color wheel** is a tool that shows this relationship, 19-8. The color wheel is very helpful for choosing and studying color in design. It shows the primary, secondary, and intermediate colors.

Yellow, blue, and red are known as **primary colors** because they cannot be created from other colors. The primary colors are equally spaced from one another

Reflect:
What is your favorite color? How many articles of clothing of this color do you own?

Activity:
If paints are available, ask each student to make a value and intensity chart for his or her favorite hue.

19-7 The bright colors of red, blue, and yellow in these clothes have high intensity.

Putting Technology to Use
Have students use drawing software to make color wheels beginning with the three primary colors. Have students print out their color wheels using a color printer. (If a color printer is not available, have students save their files. Take the files to an office supply store where they can be printed.)

> **Note:**
> Point out that the outer circle shows shades of the hues and the inner circle shows tints. Review how these are made.
>
> **Discuss:**
> Bring in different-sized boxes of crayons. Which colors are available in all the boxes? Which colors are only available in the largest box? Why do students think this is the case?

19-8 Study the color wheel to understand color relationships.

on the color wheel. By mixing, darkening, or lightening the primary colors, you can fill in the rest of the color wheel.

Mixing equal amounts of two primary colors produces a **secondary color.** Green, violet, and orange are the three secondary colors. You get green by mixing yellow and blue. Mixing blue and red produces violet. Mixing red and yellow results in orange. On the color wheel, each secondary color lies halfway between the two primary colors used to make it.

Intermediate colors are produced from equal amounts of one primary color and one secondary color. These colors lie halfway between the colors used to make them. Intermediate colors take their names from the original colors used to produce them. The primary color is always listed first. Yellow-green, blue-green, blue-violet, red-violet, red-orange, and yellow-orange are the names of the intermediate colors.

Putting Technology to Use
Have students use the file they made of the color wheel and add shades and tints using the drawing program's color palette. Have students review one another's files and make suggestions if any of the colors picked from the palette are not appropriate shades and tints.

Color Schemes

When you select clothing, you can use the color wheel to create a color scheme. Three common color schemes are monochromatic, analogous, and complementary. See 19-9.

Using different values of the same hue creates a *monochromatic color scheme.* A maroon skirt and a pink blouse or brown pants and a beige shirt are examples of this color scheme.

Combining adjacent colors on the color wheel creates an *analogous color scheme.* Wearing an outfit with blue and green, or orange and yellow, are examples of this color scheme.

Combining two colors that are directly across from each other on the color wheel creates a *complementary color scheme.* Because these colors are contrasting, they make each other look intense. Wearing an orange T-shirt with blue jeans would be an example of this color scheme.

Warm and Cool Colors

Some colors on the color wheel are warm and some are cool. *Warm colors* are those colors related to red, orange, and yellow. They are also described as *advancing colors.* This means the colors visually stand out. Clothes in warm, advancing colors seem to make the body appear larger.

Cool colors are those colors related to blue, green, and violet. These colors seem to move away, so they are called *receding colors.* Receding colors make the body appear smaller.

White and black are considered **neutrals.** Neutrals are not true colors. White is the absence of color; it reflects all light. Black absorbs all color and light. Combining varying amounts of white and black creates another range of neutrals, the grays. Neutrals can be used alone or in combination with colors. See 19-10.

Choosing Your Best Colors

When choosing colors for clothes, keep your skin tone, hair and eye color, and body shape in mind. All these factors help you determine which colors you should or should not wear.

Personal Coloring

Skin tone and hair and eye color are factors that determine your personal coloring. Which colors look best with your skin tone? Which colors complement your hair and eye color? There is an easy way to determine this. Sit in front of a mirror, and then drape fabrics of different colors near your face. Keep in mind that different tints and shades of colors can have different effects.

Study the effects of each color on your skin tone to find the most flattering ones. Good color choices will brighten and warm your face. Avoid colors that overpower your skin or make you look pale. Once you

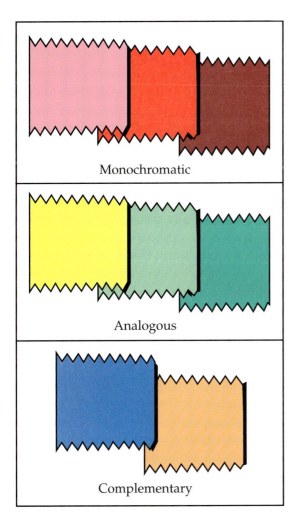

19-9 As you select clothes for an outfit, try these common color schemes.

Activity:
Using magazines, find pictures of clothing outfits that represent the various color schemes.

Resource:
Color as a Design Element, Activity B, SAG

Enrich:
Invite a color consultant to speak to the class.

FCCLA Activity
Collect color swatches made from fabric or construction paper. Take turns holding them up to each member's face in front of a mirror. Teacher, students, and parents should cooperatively analyze and determine good choices.

Reflect:
Think about your own body shape. What color(s) would help you make the most of your appearance?

Activity:
Using magazines and pattern books, find pictures of outfits that illustrate the four types of lines. Then tell how each outfit would make a person appear taller and thinner or shorter and wider.

Activity:
Ask students to draw horizontal and vertical lines on 4 x 8 inch vertical rectangles to illustrate optical illusions created by line placement.

19-10 When combined with neutrals, colors tend to stand out.

find a few basic colors that work well for you, try to build your wardrobe around them, 19-11.

Body Shape

Another factor to consider when choosing colors for clothes is your body shape. Take an honest look at yourself in the mirror. Are you happy with your basic body shape? Would you like to look thinner or heavier? Would you like to look taller or shorter? Color can help you make the most of your appearance.

White, bright, and light colors tend to make the body look larger. Use these colors for areas you want to emphasize. Black, dark, and dull colors tend to make the body appear smaller. Use these colors for areas you want to play down or hide. Dressing in one color will make you appear taller. Outfits that create strong color contrasts between your upper body and your lower body make you appear shorter. This is because the eye stops at the line of contrast.

The Other Design Elements

Color may seem like the most interesting element of design. However, it is not the only one. Line, texture, and form also affect how your clothes will look on you.

Line

Line is the design element that gives direction to a design. Vertical, horizontal, curved, and diagonal lines are the most common types of lines used in clothing design. Vertical lines move the eye up and down. Horizontal lines carry the eye from side to side. Gently curved lines add softness to clothing designs. Diagonal lines, which are angled, give a feeling of motion.

Clothing has both structural and decorative lines. *Structural lines* are seams. They are created as the various pieces of the garment are sewn together. *Decorative lines* are those added to the fabric or garment to make it visually appealing, 19-12. Striped fabric, for example, has decorative lines. Braids, buttons, and other trims are sometimes used to add decorative lines to garments.

Structural and decorative lines can be used to create optical illusions. Vertical lines in clothes tend to make the body look taller and thinner. Horizontal lines have the opposite effect; they tend to make the body look shorter and wider. Diagonal lines add a feeling of movement to any

19-11 Bright colors are flattering to dark skin tones.

Across the Curriculum

Art. Ask students to find pictures of famous paintings that illustrate the use of line placement. Have students bring the pictures to class.

Topic 19-2   Choosing Clothes That Look Good on You

19-12 Vertical lines can be dramatic as well as slenderizing.

textures reflect light and increase the apparent size of the body.

Patterns on fabrics, such as stripes, checks, plaids, and flowers, add visual texture to fabrics. See 19-13. Bold color, large plaids, and wide stripes will make a person look shorter and wider. Small plaids and patterns without much color contrast tend to make the body look smaller. Patterns should be in proportion to body size. A very large design overpowers a small body frame. A very small design seems lost on a large body frame.

Form

The shape of an object is its **form.** Your body outline and the clothes you wear create your form. Clothes that produce a *full form*, such as a full skirt or wide-legged pants, may make you appear larger and heavier. A *tubular form*, such as a one-color suit or straight-legged pants, may make you appear taller. The *bell-shaped form*, which flatters most people, is created by flared designs.

design. They may add visual height or width to the body, depending on their angle.

Texture

The **texture** of fabric refers to the way the fabric looks and feels. Fabric textures can be rough or smooth, shiny or dull, crisp or soft, bulky or silky. Each texture gives garments a different overall appearance.

Garments made from soft and silky fabrics slenderize a figure, but they also reveal the silhouette. Such garments are most flattering on those who have few flaws in their body shapes.

Some fabrics are crisp and stiff. They are great for either making a body appear larger or hiding flaws in a body shape. Rough and bulky textures also make a body look larger.

Fabrics with dull textures absorb light. They have a slenderizing effect. Shiny

19-13 This bulky sweater is an interesting contrast to the crisp texture of the shirt and the sheen of the trousers.

Discuss:
Ask students to name their favorite fabrics. Ask which of the fabrics' qualities make them popular.

Enrich:
Set up a display table with a wide assortment of fabrics. Ask each student to select a fabric and explain the effect the fabric would have on a person's apparent size.

Resource:
Elements of Design, reproducible master, TR

    Putting Technology to Use
Have students search the Internet for information on fashion cycles. They may want to search for the words *fashion cycles silhouettes*.

541

Consider the Principles of Design

The **principles of design** are the guides for combining the elements of design. The four principles of design are balance, proportion, rhythm, and emphasis. Using each principle correctly creates a feeling of harmony in the design. That is, all parts of the design look as if they belong together.

Balance

A garment with equal visual weight on both sides has **balance.** This means it is equally interesting on either side of the body and above and below the waist. No one part of the design overpowers the other.

Balance can be formal or informal. *Formal balance* creates a centered balance, so both sides are the same. A pair of solid-colored pants is a garment with formal balance. This is the most common type of balance. *Informal balance* means the line, shape, texture, or color in the design is unequally balanced from the center. A blue child's shirt that has one red sleeve and one yellow sleeve has informal balance. This type of balance is more visually appealing than formal balance.

Proportion

Proportion is the spatial relationship of the parts of a design to each other and to the whole design. In other words, the size of one part should balance the size of another part. Picture a man's suit with a knee-length jacket. The jacket would be out of proportion with the pants. In a well-proportioned outfit, all parts work well together. One part is not out of scale with another part.

Rhythm

Rhythm creates a feeling of movement in a design. Your eye moves from one part of the design to another. All parts of the design seem related. Rhythm is achieved through repetition, gradation, and radiation of colors, lines, shapes, and textures. Imagine a white knit shirt with a navy collar worn with navy shorts and sport socks with navy stripes. The repeated use of navy in this outfit gives it rhythm. An outfit of dark green pants, a light green shirt, and a medium green vest would have rhythm through gradation of color. See 19-14.

Emphasis

What do you first see when you look at an outfit? You see the center of interest in the design, which is called **emphasis.** You can use emphasis to draw attention to or away from an area. For instance, a colorful belt draws attention to the waist. A bright tie draws the eye upward, away from the waistline.

19-14 Rhythm is achieved in these plaid vests by line repetition.

> **Check It Out!**
> 1. What are the four elements of design?
> 2. Identify the three characteristics of color.
> 3. What factors should you consider in choosing your best color?
> 4. Name the four principles of design.

> **Check It Out! (Answers)**
> 1. color, line, texture, form
> 2. hue, value, intensity
> 3. skin tone, hair and eye color, body shape
> 4. balance, proportion, rhythm, emphasis

Activity: Find pictures of outfits that show the use of both formal and informal balance in fashion design.

Resource: *Clothing Design,* Activity C, SAG

Resource: *Choosing Clothes That Look Good on You Crossword Puzzle,* reproducible master, TR

Topic 19-3
Planning Your Wardrobe

Objectives
After studying this topic, you will be able to
- build a wardrobe that will be appropriate for various activities.
- develop a wardrobe inventory.
- describe techniques for extending your wardrobe.

Topic Terms
wardrobe
accessory

19-15 Teens' clothing choices depend on their lifestyles. These students prefer to dress casually for most school activities.

Reflect:
What factors influenced the clothing you chose to wear to school today?

Discuss:
Do the opinions of your friends influence what you choose to wear?

Discuss:
Do you agree that people should "dress for success"?

Resource:
Which Factors Influence Your Wardrobe? reproducible master, TR

Your **wardrobe** is all the clothes and accessories you have to wear. **Accessories** are items that accent your clothes, such as shoes, hats, belts, jewelry, neckties, and scarves. A well-planned wardrobe will include appropriate clothing and accessories for all your activities.

Building a well-planned wardrobe takes time. It is like putting a puzzle together. Your goal will be to make all the pieces fit.

Factors to Consider in Wardrobe Planning

As you plan your wardrobe, you will need to consider three factors. First, you will need to select clothes that are appropriate for your lifestyle. Casual clothes worn for relaxation are different from dressy clothes worn for special occasions. Informal clothes you wear to school are different from formal styles you might wear to a prom. See 19-15.

A second factor in determining your clothing needs is climate. Do you live in a warm or cold climate? Select clothes that will suit both your activities and the climate in which you live.

The third factor is approval. You know what kinds of clothes make you feel best. You know what your personal tastes are. You also know what your friends and employers consider acceptable. Research shows wearing appropriate clothing influences social as well as business success. It is up to you to determine what kinds of clothes meet with your approval and the approval of others.

Taking an Inventory

Wardrobe planning begins by taking an inventory of what you already have. This will help you decide what garments you need to add.

Begin your inventory by making a detailed list of every wearable garment you own. Do not forget accessories—they are part of your wardrobe, too. Use the wardrobe inventory form in 19-16 as a guide for completing your own inventory.

Once you know what you have, you can set specific goals. Make a list of new clothes you need to buy to replace any basic items that have worn out. You might also consider purchasing a few garments or accessories to update your existing wardrobe.

Putting Technology to Use
Have students use graphing software to make pie charts showing the factors that influence their wardrobe planning. Students should assign percentages to each factor based on how important they consider the factor. For instance, a student who bases most of his or her clothing choices on comfort might assign a value of 50% to the category of comfort.

Resource:
Clothing Inventory, Activity D, SAG

Reflect:
Think of your favorite item of clothing. How many ways can it be worn to create different looks?

Activity:
Plan a wardrobe for a get-away weekend keeping clothing items to a minimum. Choose multipurpose clothing and explain what you would wear for various activities.

Resource:
Mixing and Matching Clothing, Activity E, SAG

Wardrobe Inventory

Clothes/Accessories	Description (Colors)	Keep	Repair	Need to Add
Jeans	2-blue cotton	✓		
Slacks	1-tan, dressy	✓		
Shirts/Blouses	1-tan/blue plaid 1-white			need new dress blouse
Sweaters	1-tan cardigan 1-lt. blue turtleneck	✓		
Suits				
Sport coats (men's)				
Dresses (women's)	1-navy			
Skirts (women's)	1-jean skirt 1-tan/blue flowered	✓	fix hem	
Jackets	1-jean jacket 1-navy blazer	✓	missing button	
Coats	1-all-weather coat	✓		
Belts	1-Navy blue			
Shoes/Boots	1-pair for school 1-navy dress shoes	✓		need new pair
Socks				
Underwear				
Jewelry				
Headwear				
Other				

19-16 A form like this can help you complete your own wardrobe inventory.

Extending Your Wardrobe

After completing your wardrobe inventory, you may decide to extend your wardrobe. You can do this by choosing multipurpose clothing and mixing and matching garments. You can also use accessories to extend your wardrobe.

Choosing Multipurpose Clothing

As the name implies, *multipurpose clothing* can be worn several ways to satisfy different needs. For example, a long-sleeved shirt might be worn with an open neck for a casual look. You might button the collar and add a tie or scarf for a formal look. The same shirt may be worn over a knit shirt for a jacketed effect. Another option is wearing it over a bathing suit as a cover-up. Multipurpose clothes can make your wardrobe much more versatile and practical.

Mixing and Matching Garments

Mixing and matching is an easy way to stretch your wardrobe and make many outfits from a few clothing items. First, look at the clothes you have. If you notice one color repeated in several items, consider using that as a base color.

Suppose navy blue is your base color. You may have a navy and white striped shirt you can wear with navy pants, jeans, or white shorts. By mixing and matching, you now have three outfits. Then you

Putting Technology to Use
Have students use word processing or charting software to create a clothing inventory chart. Have students print out one copy to conduct a clothing inventory now. Then have students save the file as a template so they can use it again to conduct clothing inventories in the future.

might add a navy sweater that you can wear with each of the outfits. You would then be able to make six outfits from five garments.

As you can see, adding just one new piece of clothing can extend your existing wardrobe. Keep this in mind when you are shopping for additions to your wardrobe. A few well-chosen items can create several new outfits.

Using Accessories

Accessories can give a finished look to your outfits. They are an effective way for you to express your personality. Well-chosen accessories are great wardrobe extenders, too. They add variety to the clothes you wear.

Accessories can change the appearance of a basic outfit. They can make the same outfit appear either dressy or casual. This allows you to wear one outfit several ways. Accessories also pull separates together to give an outfit a unified look. For example, you could accessorize a navy blazer and tan pants with a tan and navy print scarf or tie. See 19-17.

You can wear basic accessories with many different garments. For instance, gold or silver jewelry goes well with any color. Some accessories, such as a green belt or an orange tie, may be color keyed to wear with a few garments. Making wise accessory choices can help you create a variety of looks.

Check It Out!

1. What factors should you consider in wardrobe planning?
2. What is the purpose of a wardrobe inventory?
3. State three ways to extend your wardrobe.

Check It Out! (Answers)
1. lifestyle, climate, approval
2. to see what you have in your wardrobe so you can determine what clothes you need to replace and buy
3. choose multipurpose clothing, mix and match clothing, use accessories

Activity:
Have students bring a variety of accessories to class. Divide the class into small groups. Have each group select accessories to illustrate how one outfit can be worn several different ways.

Resource:
Extending Your Wardrobe, reproducible master, TR

19-17 Well-chosen accessories help to express your personality and add diversity to your wardrobe.

Vocabulary:
Do you know the difference between a classic and a fad?

Vocabulary:
Are labels and hangtags the same? Explain your answer.

Reflect:
What are the reasons you prefer shopping at your favorite store?

Discuss:
What other factors do you take into account when planning to shop at a sale?

Topic 19-4
Shopping for Clothes

Objectives
After studying this topic, you will be able to
- give guidelines to follow when shopping for clothes.
- recognize common fashion terms.
- evaluate the quality of garments by considering their durability and fit.
- use the information on labels and hangtags to make wiser clothing selections.
- analyze factors that affect a garment's cost.

Topic Terms
fashion
style
classic
fad
label
hangtag

By shopping wisely, you will find the right clothes to complete your wardrobe at the right price. First, you must decide where to shop. Learning to judge quality and read labels are also important factors to consider when shopping for clothes.

Shopping Guidelines

Before you decide where to shop, you need to plan what to buy. Based on your wardrobe inventory, make a list of the clothes and accessories you need. Then decide how much money you have to spend. Next, prioritize your list so you know which wardrobe additions to buy first. You may want to give the highest priority to items you will wear most often, such as a coat or shoes.

As you read in Chapter 11, you can shop in many different types of stores. You can also shop at home electronically. In deciding where to shop, consider the pros and cons of each retail site. To be a wise shopper, try to get the best quality at a price you can afford.

Get the most for your money by following these shopping tips:
- Refer to the shopping list you made when completing your wardrobe inventory. This will remind you of exactly what you need to buy.
- Comparison shop at several different retail sites before making a buying decision. Check for sales or end-of-season clearances. See 19-18.
- Buy only what you really need. Avoid impulse buying and expensive fad styles.

Technology Brings New Ways to Shop

Linking to online retail sites is changing the way many people shop for clothes. Although the sensory experience of seeing and feeling merchandise is missing, Internet shopping offers many advantages over in-store shopping. For

19-18 If you comparison shop, you may find the clothing and accessories you need at a reduced price.

Putting Technology to Use
Have students make a directory of their favorite stores. Have each student use word processing software to create an information page about his or her favorite store. Then have students who picked the same store combine their information on one page. Print out the pages and assemble them into a booklet. Pass out booklets to the rest of the school.

example, comparison shopping is much easier. You can compare products and prices from the convenience of your own home at any hour. Items are displayed in sharp detail with extensive product information. Customer service is generally very reliable. Delivery of items to your home is quick, and you can easily return them if dissatisfied.

Web sites offer much more opportunity for tailoring your wardrobe around your personal tastes. This is possible because of the vast assortment of products available. Stores cannot carry a wide assortment because their limited space must be devoted to merchandise that appeals to everyone. Online retailers are not bound by this restriction. They offer a wider array of items that appeal to smaller segments of consumers.

The ability to locate difficult-to-find items is a key reason for shopping online. Some shopping sites have a search agent that tracks down specific colors, sizes, or prices. In some cases, you can create your own electronic catalog of favorite selections. You can even view merchandise next to items resembling what you already own. This feature allows you to judge how well the garment works with your existing wardrobe.

The main drawback to Internet shopping is not being able to try on garments before ordering. However, this is being addressed in several ways. Some Web sites display garments on various body frames so you can judge how it might look on you. You can also view garments on mannequins from various angles. Eventually, you will be able to view a garment just as it would appear in a mirror. This requires *body scanning,* a technology that electronically measures your size and determines your body shape. By sending scanned data to an online site, the garment for sale can be adjusted to your body proportions. Body scanning will ultimately let consumers redesign garments to order the specific length, color, and fabric desired.

To be a wise online shopper, however, always follow the shopping guidelines. These apply equally to in-store and online purchasing.

Understanding Fashion Terms

Do you have an awareness of what it takes to achieve a well-dressed look? This is called *fashion sense.* Learning about fashion terms will help you build your wardrobe-planning fashion sense. Fashion terms include *fashion, style, classic,* and *fad.*

Fashion

In wardrobe planning, the term **fashion** refers to the current mode of dress. This is the manner of dress being worn by the majority of people at a given time. Some typical fashion looks are narrow leg pants, fitted waistlines, ankle-length hemlines, and double-breasted jackets. Fashion looks can change from year to year, and even from season to season. For example, pants with wide legs may be in fashion one year and out of fashion the next.

Style

The term **style** refers to specific construction details that make one garment differ from another garment of the same type. For instance, gathered skirts and pleated skirts are just two of the many skirt styles. Straight legs, bell-bottoms, and cropped length are examples of pant styles.

Classic and Fad Styles

A **classic** style is one that is in fashion year after year. A classic never changes drastically. Business suits, shirtwaist dresses, men's dress shirts, crew neck sweaters, and wrap coats are examples of classic styles. Investing in durable, classic clothing will enable a person to feel well-dressed and fashionable for many years. See 19-19.

A **fad** is a style that is a hit for a short time and then disappears. In other words, consumers heartily accept the style temporarily and then reject it. People who invest in fad items often discard those items as soon as they go out of fashion.

Some designs are destined to become classics while others will become fads. Blue jeans, T-shirts, and athletic shoes were initially thought to be fad items. Because of their years of popularity, however, they are now considered casual classics.

> **Resource:**
> *Is It a Classic or a Fad?* reproducible master, TR
>
> **Discuss:**
> What might be some advantages of buying classic styles?
>
> **Discuss:**
> What are some current fads that are popular with teens?
>
> **Reflect:**
> Have you purchased any fads recently that your parents said they wore when they were your age?

Across the Curriculum

Social studies. Have students study clothing that was in style 25, 50, and 100 years ago. Ask students to bring in pictures of the most popular styles. Have any of these styles survived to the present? If so, what about them made them classics? If not, what about them made them fads?

Discuss:
What articles of clothing do you own that are now "out of style"? What are some styles of clothing you wouldn't wear?

Discuss:
Have you ever bought a garment that showed signs of wear after you wore it only a few times? Why do you think this happened?

Reflect:
Do you try on every garment before you buy it? Do you think this is important?

Resource:
Look for Quality in Clothing, reproducible master, TR

19-19 A tailored business suit is a classic style that will be in fashion for many years.

Fashion Cycles

To keep people buying new clothes, the fashion industry must constantly produce new designs. After a new clothing style is introduced, it goes through a period when it gains popularity. Then the style reaches its height of acceptance before consumers begin to tire of it. The time from the introduction of a new fashion idea to its eventual decline in popularity is called a *fashion cycle.*

Look in magazines and store ads to spot current fashions. Think about how long these fashions have been popular. This will help you determine where current styles are in their fashion cycles.

As you assemble your wardrobe, you will want to make all the pieces fit. Identify garments in your wardrobe that are classic styles and garments that are fads. Note items that are in line with current fashions and recognize those that seem out-of-date. This analysis will help you make decisions as you shop.

When buying new clothes, you will get the most wear out of classic garments that will last for many seasons. For variety, add a few inexpensive fad items you can afford to recycle after a season or two.

Judging Quality

When you consider buying a garment, inspect it for quality. Quality is an important factor in clothing. It affects a garment's look, durability, and fit.

Durability

Durability refers to how a garment will hold up under use. A garment's construction and the fabric from which it is made affect durability.

Before buying, examine a garment carefully. Check for quality construction features, such as secure buttons, neatly stitched buttonholes, smooth seams, and matched patterns. A well-constructed garment will provide many seasons of wear. A poorly constructed garment will show signs of wear after it has been worn and cleaned a few times.

Evaluate the type of fabric used for the garment. Some fabrics wear better than others. Fabrics that pill and bag easily will not wear as well as sturdier fabrics that will hold their shape.

Crushing a corner of the garment tightly between two fingers will show you how easily the fabric wrinkles. If creases or wrinkles appear, the garment will crease or wrinkle when you wear it. Chart 19-20 describes features you should look for in quality-made clothing.

Fit

An important point to consider when buying clothes is fit. The *fit* of a garment refers to how it conforms to the size and shape of the body of the wearer. Some garments are designed to be fitted, some semifitted, and some loose. A fitted garment is shaped to conform closely to the lines of your body. If a fitted garment does not fit properly, it will not lie smoothly on your body. Semifitted and loose garments do not conform to the body as closely as fitted garments. However, they must still fit properly to look neat and move freely as you move.

Across the Curriculum

History. Have students research the history of women's clothing. Why did women wear only skirts and dresses until the Twentieth Century? What historical occurrences brought about the acceptance of women wearing pants? How revolutionary was this concept at the time? Why?

Look for Quality Clothing

- **Garment construction**—Are plaids, stripes, and large designs matched at the seams? Are shoulder pads or other supports used as needed to give proper shape to the garment? Do linings lie flat? Are they secured at the seams so they will not show when the garment is worn?
- **Fabric**—Is it easy to clean and maintain? Is it loosely or tightly constructed? The tighter the construction, the better the fabric will hold its shape.
- **Trim**—Do decorative features appear as durable as the rest of the garment? Are they securely attached?
- **Fasteners**—Do buttonholes appear sturdy and free from raveling? Are the buttons appropriate for the garment? Are extra buttons included for replacements? Are buttons, snaps, and hook and eyes firmly attached? Are zippers inserted neatly and working smoothly?
- **Hem**—Are the stitches invisible on the outside of the garment? Is the hem wide enough for future adjustments? Is the edge finished to prevent raveling?
- **Seams**—Are all stitches straight, even, and free of puckers? Are they secured so they will not pull apart? Are edges finished to prevent raveling? Is there enough fabric at the seams to widen for future adjustments?
- **Reinforcements**—Are points of strain, such as armholes and crotches, reinforced with extra stitching? Wherever fasteners and pockets are sewn to a single thickness of fabric, are they reinforced?

19-20 Check for quality before you buy. As you examine garments, keep these questions in mind.

You need to try on a garment to determine whether it fits. The best time to do this is before you buy the garment. This will save you from needing to return items that do not fit well. If possible, try the garment on with the accessories you plan to wear with it. That way, you can see if the new garment matches the accessories you already have.

When you try on a garment, you should make the same movements you will be making when you wear it. Try sitting, bending, and raising and crossing your arms and legs. Note how comfortable the garment feels with each movement. Also notice how the garment looks. Does it pull or wrinkle anywhere? If the garment feels or looks too tight or too loose in a given body posture, it does not fit right.

Reading Labels and Hangtags

Is this garment the right size? What kind of fabric is it? Can it be machine washed? Will I have to iron it? If you have questions about a garment you may buy, carefully read the label and hangtags attached to it. Labels and hangtags on clothing provide useful information for the shopper. See 19-21.

Labels, which are attached to garments, provide important printed information about garments. Certain laws have been established to regulate the information provided to the consumer. These laws include the following:

- The *Textile Fiber Products Identification Act* states that all products must be labeled with fiber content, the name of the manufacturer, and country of origin.
- The *Care Labeling Rule* requires labels to include specific instructions for care of the garment. (More on this law will be discussed in Topic 19-5.) When making clothing purchases, consider the required care. Read the permanent care label on the garment. Can the garment be machine washed, or must it be dry-cleaned? Dry cleaning can add to the total cost of a garment that will be worn several years.

> **Enrich:** Provide a display of labels and hangtags for students to look over.
>
> **Activity:** Have students save labels and hangtags from recently purchased items and use them to create a bulletin board.
>
> **Resource:** *Labels and Hangtags,* reproducible master, TR

Family Enrichment Activity

Using a small file box and alphabetical file dividers, set up a system for collecting and storing care labels from garments. Color code the tags for each member of the family. Store the information in the laundry area along with laundry products and stain removers.

Discuss:
Would you pay a lot of money for a garment you knew you would wear often? Why or why not?

Resource:
Shopping for Clothes, Activity F, SAG

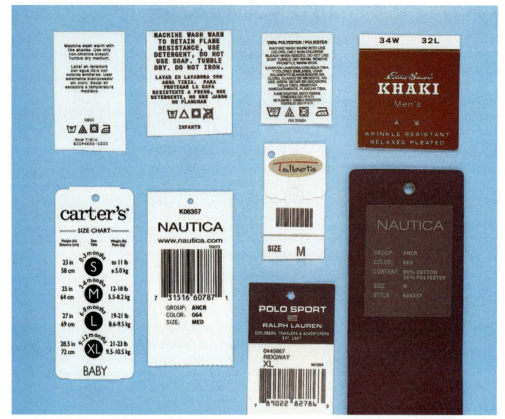

19-21 Careful shoppers read labels and hangtags so they can make informed choices.

- The *Wool Products Labeling Act* states that the type of wool and the percentage of wool in a garment must be listed. The label must also contain the country of origin.
- The *Fur Products Labeling Act* requires labels to identify the type of animal the fur comes from and the country of origin.
- The *Flammable Fabrics Act*, another law related to garment labeling, sets standards for the use of flammable fabrics. It also prohibits the sale of very hazardous materials for use in clothing.

In addition to the required information, the brand name, size, special finishes, and construction features may also be listed.

Hangtags are larger tags attached to new garments. Before wearing a garment, you would remove these tags. Unlike labels, hangtags are not required by law. However, they include useful information, such as trademarks, guarantees, style numbers, sizes, and prices.

Consider the Cost

Cost is a key factor affecting clothing purchases. When shopping for clothes, you must decide whether you can afford a garment. You must also assess whether an item fits into your price range. For instance, if you have $50 in your wallet, you can afford a $45 shirt. However, $45 may be more than you are willing to spend for a shirt.

You might want to evaluate how much psychological benefit you will get from a garment. This can help you set your price range. You may be willing to spend more for a garment that really makes you look and feel your best. Your evaluation can also help you decide whether you should wait for an item to go on sale. When you do not feel strongly about an item, you may be more willing to wait for a sale

Putting Technology to Use

Have students find the Web site for a clothing store and find an item in which they are interested. Ask students to consider the style, durability, fit, care instructions, and cost of the garment. Which factors can students evaluate over the Internet? Which factors are difficult to evaluate online?

price. However, this might mean losing the garment to another buyer while you wait.

Think about how many times you will wear a garment. That will determine the cost per wear. For example, a prom dress that retails for $180 may be worn only one time. Thus, the prom dress will cost $180 per wear. A jacket costing $180 may be worn every day for several years. Therefore, the jacket costs only pennies per wear. You may be able to save money by borrowing or renting garments that you intend to wear only once.

You should also evaluate how long you will be able to wear a garment. If you are still growing, the garment may not fit you very long. If the item is not well made, it may wear out quickly. If it is a fad style, it may go out of fashion before long.

Another factor you need to consider when evaluating the cost of a garment is how much it will cost to maintain. For instance, a silk shirt may seem like a bargain at $15. However, spending $5 to have it dry-cleaned every other week will add $30 to the cost in just three months. A careful analysis of the cost of upkeep will help you determine if a garment purchase is appropriate for your budget.

Check It Out!
1. Give three guidelines to follow when shopping for clothes.
2. Explain the difference between fashion and style.
3. What are some important points to consider in judging clothing quality?
4. List the information found on a label and a hangtag.
5. True or false. A garment's care requirements can add to the garment's cost.

Check It Out! (Answers)
1. (Student response. See pages 546-547 in the text.)
2. Fashion refers to the current mode of dress; style refers to specific construction details that distinguish one garment from another.
3. (Student response. See pages 548-549 in the text.)
4. Label: fiber content, manufacturer, country of origin, care information. Hangtag: trademarks, guarantees, style number, size, and price.
5. true

Topic 19-5
Caring for Clothes

Objectives
After studying this topic, you will be able to
- explain daily clothing care.
- care for your clothes by using proper laundering, drying, and ironing techniques.

Topic Terms
ironing
pressing
dry cleaning

After spending your time and money to get the right clothes, you will want to take good care of them. Proper care of clothes helps to ensure a neat personal appearance. Your clothes will look better and last longer if you care for them properly.

Daily Clothing Care

Setting a daily routine will help you keep your clothes in good condition. You will always have clean clothes that are ready to wear. See 19-22.

When you dress and undress, take care not to damage or soil your clothes. Open fasteners so garments will slip easily over your head or hips. Avoid placing undue strain on any part of the garment. Strain can result in rips, broken zippers, and missing buttons. Taking the extra seconds to open fasteners can save hours in repairing damages.

As you pull garments over your head, try to protect your clothing. Avoid stains from makeup, creams, or sunscreens by applying these after you get dressed.

Allow an extra minute or two to care for your clothes when you undress. Inspect garments closely for stains, rips, and missing buttons. Put clothes with any of these problems in a special place. This will remind you to take care of the problems before wearing or laundering the garments.

Discuss:
Do teens consider the required care when they purchase clothing? Do they launder their own clothes? Do they pay for dry cleaning?

Vocabulary:
What do you think might be the difference between ironing and pressing?

Resource:
Proper Care Means Longer Wear, color transparency CT-17, TR

Reflect:
What do you generally do with your garments as soon as you remove them?

Discuss:
How do you store the clothes you wear every day?

Reflect:
Do you read care labels in your clothes to determine proper care?

Discuss:
What was your worst laundry disaster? Could it have been prevented?

19-22 Proper care of your clothes will make you look your best.

Everyday Clothing Storage

If your clothes are clean and in good repair, put them away to wear again. Drawer space is often more plentiful than closet space. Therefore, it is a good idea to store as many garments in drawers as you can. Another reason for storing knit garments in drawers is to prevent stretching and sagging, which can occur when garments are hung.

Hang clothes that you store in the closet neatly on hangers. Then close fasteners, such as buttons and zippers, so clothes will retain their shape and not slip off the hangers. Have a clothes brush handy to whisk away any lint or dust on the garments. Allow enough space in the closet for clothes to hang loosely without becoming wrinkled.

Specialty hangers can help you store certain garments more easily. Hangers designed for blazers, jackets, and coats are curved to simulate the curve of the shoulders. This helps the garments retain the shape of your body. Hangers covered with a thin layer of foam keep garments made from slippery fabrics from sliding onto the closet floor. Hangers with clips are convenient for hanging skirts and pants from the waistline.

Store like garments together. For instance, put all your T-shirts in the same drawer and hang all your pants together in the closet. You will not have to search to find the garments you need. Mixing and matching garments to create outfits will be easier, too.

Clothes that require laundering before further wear should go directly into the laundry container. Those that need dry cleaning should be set aside and taken to the dry cleaner promptly.

Laundering Steps

Washable garments will look their best and last longer when you launder them properly. Laundering not only cleans garments, but also removes wrinkles and perspiration odors. To care for clothes properly, you need to know some basic laundry principles.

Read Care Labels

The Care Labeling Rule, issued by the Federal Trade Commission, requires care labels to be permanently attached to almost all clothing items. The label must list clear, correct procedures for regular care of the item. The label must also warn against care procedures that are likely to damage the item. Manufacturers must make sure the label will remain readable for the life of the garment.

In 1997, The Care Labeling Rule was revised to allow symbols for instructions to be used on care labels instead of words. Chart 19-23 explains what these symbols mean. The following information must be included on the label:
- washing method
- water temperature
- drying method
- drying temperature
- type of bleach that can be used safely
- use of iron
- ironing temperatures

Across the Curriculum

Social studies. Discuss with students methods used to wash clothes before washing machines were invented. After the discussion, ask students which method they think cleans clothing most thoroughly.

Topic 19-5 Caring for Clothes

19-23 This chart explains the symbols and brief instructions printed on garment care labels.

Activity: Bring in sample garments. Have students read the care labels and then explain to the class how to clean the garments.

Resource: *Clothing Care Symbols,* Activity H, SAG

If you remember to read and follow care labels, you are sure to keep your clothes looking neat and colors bright.

Sort Clothes Properly

The purpose of sorting is to separate items that could, in some way, damage other articles. One key way to sort clothes is by color. Separate whites from colors and light colors from bright or dark colors. Different wash water temperatures are needed to keep some colors from fading or bleeding onto other garments.

Sorting clothes by fabric will help you determine what wash cycle to use. White cottons and linens require hot water and a regular wash cycle for cleaning. Permanent press fabrics require warm wash water and a cold rinse. Other fabrics require cold water and a short, gentle wash cycle to prevent fading and shrinking.

Sort clothes by their surface texture to separate lint-catchers from lint-producers. Corduroy and velveteen, as well as fabrics of manufactured fibers, catch lint. On the other hand, chenille and terry cloth produce lint.

 Putting Technology to Use
Have students use word processing or drawing software to create a colorful key for sorting laundry. Have students take the keys home and hang them in the area in which they sort clothes or do laundry.

Activity:
Give each student a 3x5-inch card. Have each person write a description of an item to be laundered on the card. Collect and redistribute the cards. List laundry categories on the chalkboard and have each student tell which category his or her item would go into.

Note:
Provide a display of various laundry products.

Discuss:
Which laundry products do you use at home? Do you always buy those brands?

Another factor you should consider when sorting clothes is the degree of soil. Heavily soiled clothes require different laundry procedures than lightly soiled clothes.

Prepare Clothes for Laundering

You need to take a few steps to prepare clothes for laundering. Remove surface soil by shaking or brushing it away. Be sure all zippers and hooks are closed. They may be damaged or may cause damage to other garments when left open. Repair snags with a fine crochet hook and mend rips and tears before washing garments. This will keep the agitation of the washing and drying process from making snags, rips, and tears larger.

Check pockets carefully before putting garments in the washing machine. A pen, tissue, or other object left in a pocket can produce stains or lint. This could damage every item in a wash load.

Pretreat Stains and Heavy Soil

Treat stains as promptly as possible. This makes them easier to remove. Follow the directions of a stain removal guide, such as the one in 19-24. Heavy soil should be pretreated by soaking, or by applying a liquid detergent or a prewash product.

Read the package labels on all cleaning products before using them. Some commercial stain removers may discolor fabrics. It is always a good idea to test a cleaning product before using it. Test the product on a sample of the fabric, if available. If a sample is not available, use the underside of the garment hem or a facing.

Understand Laundry Products

Many types of laundry products are available. For best laundry results, you need to use the right types of products and follow package directions carefully.

Soaps and Detergents

Soaps and detergents are designed mainly to remove soil from fabrics. The main difference is the way they work in hard water. *Soap* reacts with the minerals in hard water to form white cloudy curds that float throughout the water. These curds cling to fabrics, making whites look dingy and colors look dull. Soaps work best in soft or softened water.

Detergents work well in hard or soft water. For a whiter, brighter wash, use detergent rather than soap with hard water. Detergents may be either high-sudsing or low-sudsing. Either type can be used in a top-loading washer. A low-sudsing detergent is best for front-loading washers.

Detergents come in both liquid and powder forms. Powdered detergents may dissolve slowly in cold water. Therefore, liquid detergents are recommended when washing with cold water. Both types of detergent should be added to wash water before adding clothes. This gives the detergent a chance to dilute or dissolve.

Because detergents differ in concentration, following package directions is important. Always use the recommended amount of detergent. Using too little or too much detergent is one of the most common laundry errors.

Bleach

Bleach helps remove stains and whiten, disinfect, and deodorize clothes. The two types of bleach are chlorine and oxygen.

Chlorine bleach is a strong chemical mixture. It can weaken fabric fibers if it is used too often. It should not be used on wool, silk, spandex, noncolorfast fabrics, or on some fabric finishes. Refer to the care labels in garments for cleaning instructions.

Carefully follow the directions on the bleach container for best results. If your washer has a built-in bleach dispenser, read the use and care instructions for exact directions. If your washer does not have a bleach dispenser, the bleach must be diluted and added after agitation begins.

Oxygen bleach helps remove stains and whiten clothes. It is safe for all washable fibers because it is not as strong as chlorine bleach. For best results, oxygen bleach should be used regularly to keep clothes white and bright.

Across the Curriculum
Math. Have students go to stores and compare the prices of different brands of laundry products. Have students make note of their findings and bring them to class to share with other students. Ask students which products they think are the best buys and explain why.

Topic 19-5 Caring for Clothes

Removing Spots and Stains

Stain	Procedure for Bleachable Fabrics (white and colorfast cotton, linen, polyester, acrylic, triacetate, nylon, rayon, permanent press)	Procedure for Nonbleachable Fabrics (wool, silk, spandex, noncolorfast items, some flame-retardant finishes)
Blood	Soak in cold water 30 minutes or longer. Rub detergent into any remaining stain. Rinse. If stain persists, put a few drops of ammonia on the stain and repeat detergent treatment. Rinse. If stain persists, launder in hot water using chlorine bleach.	Same method, but if colorfastness is questionable, use hydrogen peroxide instead of ammonia. Launder in warm water. Omit chlorine bleach.
Chewing gum, adhesive tape	Rub stained area with ice. Remove excess gummy matter carefully with a dull knife. Sponge with a safe cleaning fluid. Rinse and launder.	Same method.
Chocolate, cocoa	Soak in cold water. Rub detergent into stain while still wet, then rinse thoroughly. Dry. If a greasy stain remains, sponge with a safe cleaning fluid. Rinse. Launder in hot water using chlorine bleach. If stain remains, repeat treatment with cleaning fluid.	Same method. Launder in warm water. Omit chlorine bleach.
Coffee, tea	Soak in cold water. Rub detergent into stain while still wet. Rinse and dry. If grease stain remains from cream, sponge with safe cleaning fluid. Launder in hot water using chlorine bleach.	Same method. Launder in warm water. Omit chlorine bleach.
Cosmetics	Rub detergent into dampened stain until outline of stain is gone, then rinse well. Launder in hot water using chlorine bleach.	Same method. Launder in warm water. Omit chlorine bleach.
Egg, meat juice, gravy	If dried, scrape off as much as possible with a dull knife. Soak in cold water. Rub detergent into stain while still wet. Launder in hot water using chlorine bleach.	Same method. Launder in warm water. Omit chlorine bleach.
Fingernail polish	Sponge white cotton fabric with nail polish remover; other fabrics with amyl acetate (banana oil). Launder. Repeat if necessary.	Same method.
Fruit juices	Soak in cold water. Launder in hot water using chlorine bleach.	Soak in cold water. If stain remains, rub detergent into stain while still wet. Launder in warm water.
Grass	Rub detergent into dampened stain. Launder in hot water using chlorine bleach. If stain remains, sponge with alcohol. Rinse thoroughly.	Same method. Launder in warm water. Omit chlorine bleach. If colorfastness is questionaable or fabric is acetate, dilute alcohol with two parts water.

19-24 This chart applies only to washable items. It does not apply to garments that should be dry-cleaned. Follow the directions on the care labels of garments.

(Continued)

Activity: Have each student select a stain from Chart 19-24. Demonstrate the removal of the stain to the class.

Resource: *Caring for Clothes*, reproducible master, TR

Putting Technology to Use
Have students research tips for stain removal on the Internet. One Web site they may want to explore is www.carelabels.com/stains.htm.

Resource:
Stain Removal,
Activity G, SAG

Stain	Procedure for Bleachable Fabrics (white and colorfast cotton, linen, polyester, acrylic, triacetate, nylon, rayon, permanent press)	Procedure for Nonbleachable Fabrics (wool, silk, spandex, noncolorfast items, some flame-retardant finishes)
Grease, oil (car grease, butter, shortening, vitamin oils)	Rub detergent into dampened stain. Launder in hot water using chlorine bleach and plenty of detergent. If stain persists, sponge thoroughly with safe cleaning fluid. Rinse.	Rub detergent into dampened stain. Launder in warm water using plenty of detergent. If stain persists, sponge thoroughly with safe cleaning fluid. Rinse.
Ink (ballpoint)	Sponge stain with rubbing alcohol, or spray with hair spray until wet looking. Rub detergent into stained area. Launder. Repeat if necessary.	Same method.
Ink (felt tip)	Some may be impossible to remove. Rub household cleaner into stain. Rinse. Repeat as many times as necessary to remove stain. Launder.	Same method.
Mayonnaise, salad dressing	Rub detergent into dampened stain. Rinse and let dry. If greasy stain remains, sponge with safe cleaning fluid. Rinse. Launder in hot water with chlorine bleach.	Same method. Launder in warm water. Omit chlorine bleach.
Mildew	Rub detergent into dampened stain. Launder in hot water using chlorine bleach. If stain remains, sponge with hydrogen peroxide. Rinse and launder.	Same method. Launder in warm water. Omit chlorine bleach.
Milk, cream, ice cream	Soak in cold water. Launder in hot water using chlorine bleach. If grease stain remains, sponge with safe cleaning fluid. Rinse.	Soak in cold water. Rub detergent into stain. Launder. If grease stain remains, sponge with safe cleaning fluid. Rinse.
Mustard	Rub detergent into dampened stain. Rinse. Soak in hot detergent water for several hours. If stain remains, launder in hot water using chlorine bleach.	Same method. Launder in warm water. Omit chlorine bleach.
Perspiration	Rub detergent into dampened stain. Launder in hot water using chlorine bleach. If fabric has discolored, try to restore it by treating fresh stains with ammonia or old stains with vinegar. Rinse. Launder.	Same method. Launder in warm water. Omit chlorine bleach.
Soft drinks	Sponge stain immediately with cold water. Launder in hot water with chlorine bleach. Some drink stains are invisible after they dry, but turn yellow with aging or heating. This yellow stain may be impossible to remove.	Same method. Launder in warm water. Omit chlorine bleach.

19-24 *(Continued)*

Putting Technology to Use
Have students use drawing software, scanners, and clipart to make posters citing tips for stain removal. Hang the posters around the school.

Water Softeners

If a ring appears around your sink or bathtub after the water drains, your home has hard water. Clothes washed in hard water may look gray or dull. To keep clothes looking bright, you can add a water softener to laundry water before adding the soap or detergent. Water softeners neutralize the calcium and magnesium ions that are found in hard water. This keeps dulling residue from settling on your clothes.

Fabric Softeners

Fabric softeners make fabrics soft and fluffy. They help reduce wrinkling and control static electricity. Some softeners are added to the wash cycle; some are added to the rinse cycle. Fabric softener sheets are used in the dryer.

Using the Washing Machine

For good cleaning action, distribute items evenly in the washer. This balances the wash load. Do not overload the washer. Too many garments in the wash prevent good circulation of water and cleaning agents. See 19-25.

19-25 Cleaning aides should be blended into the water before adding your clothes.

Select a wash cycle suitable for the wash load. Delicate items need a gentle or delicate cycle with warm or cold water. Permanent press garments will need a permanent press cycle with a cold water rinse if they are to remain free of wrinkles. The regular cycles will accommodate all other articles. Select water temperature according to fiber content and care labels.

Drying Clothes

Clothes can be dried in an automatic dryer, on a clothesline, or on a flat surface. Check garments' care labels for drying directions.

Tumble drying clothes in an automatic dryer is convenient, especially when large loads of clothes have to be dried. Most clothes are softer and more comfortable to wear when they are tumble dried. Dryers offer a variety of cycles to use for different loads. Read the use and care instructions that come with the dryer, and follow the directions for best results.

When using a dryer, do not overload it. Large loads take longer to dry. If clothes are too crowded to tumble freely, they are more likely to wrinkle. Remember to clean the lint filter after each use.

Different brands and models of dryers have different cycles. Three examples of common cycles are regular, permanent press, and air fluff. The *regular cycle* is used to dry items that are not heat sensitive. The *permanent press cycle* provides moderate heat for most of the cycle. During the last few minutes of the cycle, tumbling continues, but without heat. The cool-down period helps reduce wrinkles. To further reduce wrinkles, you should remove clothes as soon as the tumbling stops. The *air fluff cycle* provides unheated air to freshen or fluff items. This cycle is especially helpful when garments have absorbed odors from items such as fish, onions, or cigarettes.

Line drying is recommended for some fabrics. In areas where smog is not a problem, line drying can be done outdoors. Line drying gives clothes a fresh smell, while saving the cost of using an electric or gas dryer.

Resource:
Keeping Clothes Clean, reproducible master, TR

Enrich:
Conduct a survey of the student body to determine the amount of responsibility young people assume for personal and family clothing care. Write an article for the school paper.

Discuss:
Why is it important to remove laundry from the dryer immediately?

Activity:
Interview senior citizens about wash-day memories from their youth.

Problem-Solving Practice

Marketing the Latest Fad, reproducible master, TR. Students are asked to pretend they are clothing designers. Their assignment is to present a new fad for the season that will interest buyers. Students are to describe the fad and describe and illustrate three ways they will market their fad.

Note:
Demonstrate the difference between ironing and pressing. Explain when each is used.

Reflect:
Have you ever ruined a garment with a hot iron?

Discuss:
Is it more economical to own your own laundry equipment or to use a coin-operated commercial laundry? What are the advantages and disadvantages?

Line drying is often done inside. Garments are hung above a bathtub or in a shower stall to drip-dry.

The flat drying method is used to avoid shrinking or stretching garments such as sweaters. Remove excess moisture first by rolling the garment in a towel. Then unroll and shape the garment by hand on a clean, absorbent surface, such as a towel. Keep the garment away from direct heat.

Ironing and Pressing

Although many of today's fabrics do not require ironing or pressing, some do. Therefore, these skills are worth knowing.

The terms ironing and pressing are often used interchangeably, but they have slightly different meanings. **Ironing** is a process of moving an iron across fabric to smooth wrinkles. Ironing is usually done after garments have been laundered.

Pressing is a process of lifting the iron up and down to apply pressure in one area of a garment at a time. Pressing is done on seams and curves as garments are sewn. It is also done to touch up wrinkled areas of garments after they have been laundered.

Here are a few tips to keep in mind as you iron or press.

- Use your iron properly. Read the use and care booklet that came with your iron and follow the directions. Pay special attention to the cleaning instructions for steam irons.
- Turn the iron to the proper setting for the fabric you are ironing or pressing. See 19-26. This is very important. An iron that is too hot can ruin garments.
- It is a good idea to iron or press an inside seam or hem first. This gives you a chance to test the effects of the temperature on the fabric before touching the garment in a visible spot.
- Always iron along the lengthwise grain of the fabric to keep it from stretching out of shape.
- Some fabrics develop a shine when heat is applied directly to them. Use a pressing cloth between the iron and the fabric when pressing or ironing such fabric. When in doubt, use a pressing cloth just to be safe.

19-26 When you are ironing or pressing a garment, always use a temperature setting that is safe for the fabric.

Dry Cleaning

Some care labels indicate garments require dry cleaning instead of laundering. **Dry cleaning** is a process that cleans clothes using organic chemical solvents. Water is not used in this process.

Clothes that require dry cleaning may be taken to a coin-operated dry-cleaning center or to a professional dry cleaner. Because dry cleaning is a delicate cleaning process, clothes should be cleaned before they become heavily soiled.

Coin-operated dry cleaning is faster and more economical than professional cleaning. The machines are operated in much the same manner as coin-operated washing

Citizenship and Service
Tour a dry cleaning establishment. Inquire about their procedure for disposing of chemical wastes such as dry cleaning fluids and stain removers. Help publicize special days when collections of such hazardous wastes are made in your community. Promote proper disposal of hazardous materials used in the home.

machines. Specific directions for their use are available in the cleaning centers. The results may or may not be comparable to those achieved by a professional cleaner. Delicate garments may not receive the special care they need. Also, garments may still need to be professionally pressed, and pressing is the most expensive part of dry cleaning.

The fumes from dry-cleaning fluids are strong. Before storing dry-cleaned garments, hang them in an open area for several hours. This will help to disperse the fumes, so the garments smell more pleasant.

Professional dry cleaners know how to care for various fabrics. They also know how to treat most spots and stains. You can assist them, however, by pointing out stains when you take garments to be cleaned. Tell them what the stains are and how long they have been there. You may also want to request that sizing be added to make a limp garment look fresh again. Likewise, you can request to have a water-repellent finish restored to a garment after cleaning. See 19-27.

Proper care of your clothes, including proper laundering or dry-cleaning techniques, will help your clothes look their best. Your clothes, in turn, will help you look your best.

Energy Conservation in Clothing Care

Modern technology has given consumers laundry appliances that are more energy efficient. Laundry products have been developed that help maintain a healthy environment. As a consumer, you can also do your part. Keep the following points in mind to conserve energy and maintain the environment:

- Do laundry at times other than peak energy use times.
- Pretreat heavily soiled areas and stubborn stains.
- Select laundry products that are not damaging to the environment.
- Buy laundry products in concentrated form and recycle containers.
- Sort and wash full loads of compatible garments.
- Adjust the water level to the size of the load.
- Select a wash cycle that matches the degree of soil.
- Determine water temperature needed by the degree of soil. While hot water may be necessary for heavily soiled clothes, warm water may be used for light soil, and cold water may be used for very light soil.
- Use a cold water rinse.
- Save energy by line drying whenever possible.
- Clean the lint filter before each load when using a dryer.
- Check the vent system regularly to avoid obstructions that will slow the airflow in a dryer.
- Avoid overloading the dryer.
- Remove clothes from the dryer promptly to prevent wrinkling and unnecessary ironing.

19-27 Professional dry cleaning can often make difficult-to-clean garments look new.

Note: Advertisements for a new consumer product claim professional dry cleaning results with the use of a home dryer.

Activity: Have students find out what percentage of energy used to wash a load of laundry goes for heating the wash and rinse water versus operating the appliance. (Ans. 80% versus 20%.)

Note: Blocked lint filters increase clothes drying time and can build up enough heat to start a fire.

Career Preparation Activity

Marketable Skill Courses, reproducible master, TR. Have students read a brief case study and determine how various courses could be marketable skills for someone who owns or hopes to own a small business.

Reflect: Which of these energy conservation guidelines do you already follow?

Note: Overdrying can cause clothes to wrinkle, and very hot settings can permanently set wrinkles in some garments.

Discuss: Share with the class one laundry experience that taught you a lesson.

Activity: Have students investigate any luggage limitations that exist for traveling by air, water, and rail. Is a maximum size or number of bags permitted per person?

- Remove clothes while slightly damp to allow air drying.
- Dry consecutive loads of wash to use residual heat left from the preceding load.
- Plan to iron as many items as possible when you heat the iron to take advantage of the energy required for heating.
- Sort items to be ironed or pressed by temperature to avoid heating or cooling the iron between garments.

Packing and Storing Clothes

Packing clothes, whether for travel or seasonal storage, requires some skill. In both cases, your goals are the same. You want to arrange the clothes in a way that will allow you to get to the items you need. You also want to keep garments as wrinkle free and ready to wear as possible.

What to Pack for Travel

The key to deciding what items to pack in a suitcase is knowing what kinds of activities you will be doing. For instance, you will need a swimsuit and shorts for a summer trip to the beach. However, sweaters and turtlenecks would be better choices for a winter ski vacation. If you will be dining out or attending a special event, you may want to take some dressier clothes. No matter what you will be doing, you will need sleepwear and undergarments. Choosing versatile garments that you can mix and match will limit the number of items you need to pack.

Try to prepare a packing list at least several days before you need to pack. This will give you time to be sure all the clothes you want to take are clean and pressed. Having the list will make packing an easy task. Instead of spending time deciding what to take, you will simply have to assemble the listed items.

You may wish to arrange your list by the days and activities your trip will include. Plan to pack complete outfits rather than individual garments. This will keep you from rummaging though your suitcase. You will not have to dig to find the shirt you wanted to wear with a certain pair of pants.

How to Pack for Travel

Packing at least a day or two before you will be leaving for a trip is a good idea. This keeps you from feeling rushed to pack at the last minute. It also gives you time to add to your suitcase any items you may have forgotten. See 19-28.

Reclosable plastic bags are convenient packing accessories. You can use them to keep items like underwear, hosiery, and T-shirts together. You can also use plastic bags to keep carefully rolled or folded garments in shape. To save space, tuck socks and other small items into your shoes. Then place shoes in bags to keep them from soiling other garments.

19-28 By creating a list of essentials to take on any trip, frequent travelers can pack quickly.

Putting Technology to Use
Have students search the Internet for information on the proper amount to tip a baggage handler at an airport, train station, or hotel.

Use your list of activities to help you determine the best packing order. Layer outfits in your suitcase in the order of expected use. Place items you expect to use last in the bottom of your suitcase. Place items you will use first, such as sleepwear and the first outfit you plan to wear, on top. You may occasionally need to repack as you travel. This will give you an opportunity to relayer your clothes in a new order of anticipated use.

Try to find travel-sized containers of toiletries. Pack them in a separate toiletry case or double bag them to protect your clothes. A leaking bottle of shampoo or a punctured tube of toothpaste can create quite a mess.

Tucking in a few extra plastic bags is always a good idea. You can use one for soiled clothes that must be laundered. You might also need a bag to protect your clothes from a garment that becomes damp.

Packing for Seasonal Storage

Packing clothes for seasonal storage involves the same principles as packing clothes in a suitcase. The main differences are the types of containers you are using and the length of storage.

Many accessories are available to increase the clothing storage space in your home. With some ingenuity, you can create other storage containers. Large boxes that slide under beds are one storage option that works well for out-of-season clothes. This frees up closet and drawer space for clothing you use regularly.

Be sure clothes are clean and in good repair before packing them for storage. Fold or roll garments neatly. This will make them ready to wear with a minimum of effort when you take them out of storage.

When storing out-of-season clothes, be sure to consider the possibility of insect damage. Moths and crickets can eat holes in your clothes, especially woolens. To protect wool garments, store them in cedar-lined closets or chests. If these are not available, place mothballs or crystals in the closets and drawers where you store woolens.

Check It Out!

1. List five steps you can take each day to keep your clothes in great shape.
2. List four factors to consider when sorting clothes for laundering.
3. Which drying method is preferred for garments that might stretch or shrink?
4. Moving an iron across fabric to smooth wrinkles is called _____.
5. True or false. Coin-operated dry cleaning is less economical than professional dry cleaning.
6. What are five steps you can take to conserve energy as you care for your clothes?
7. In what order should clothes be packed in a suitcase?

Check It Out! (Answers)

1. (List five:) Take care not to damage or soil clothing as you get dressed or undressed; open fasteners so garments slip on easier; protect clothing as you pull garments over your head; apply makeup or creams after you get dressed; after you get undressed, inspect clothes for stains, rips, or missing buttons; hang clean clothes on a hanger; fold clean sweaters and place them in a drawer; put dirty clothes into the laundry container.
2. color, fabric, surface texture, degree of soil
3. flat drying
4. ironing
5. false
6. (List five. Student response. See pages 559-560.)
7. Items in a suitcase should be packed in the order of expected use. Items expected to be used last should be packed on the bottom. Items expected to be used first should be packed on top.

Note:
Practically all hotels provide shampoo, soap, and hand cream; many also make irons and ironing boards available. Professional dry cleaning can be arranged through the hotel.

Discuss:
What packing tips can you share with the class?

Reflect:
Do you pack clothes away for storage without taking care of repairs first?

Reflect:
Do your clothes influence the way your friends think of you? How does this make you feel about your friendships?

Activity:
Conduct a survey to find out if people would date someone who doesn't dress neatly or wear popular clothing.

Discuss:
Do you agree that "if you have bad manners, no one is going to notice what you wear"?

TEENS ARE TALKING ABOUT...
The Status of Clothes

This group discussion revealed that teens think about the status of clothes more than they openly discuss. Al, Kelly, Mike, Justine, and Tamika shared their thoughts.

When asked how what they wear affects what their friends think of them, the group members' reactions were mixed. Al commented first. "If you don't wear up-to-date clothes, your friends make fun of you. They think you aren't cool. You have to wear some name brand clothes, too."

Kelly disagreed with Al. "They shouldn't make fun of you if you don't wear name brands. If your friends like you, they shouldn't care about the brand of clothes you wear."

She continued, "Most teens want to be in style. Some teens who don't have money to buy expensive clothes may envy those who have great clothes. The point is: teens should wear what they want as long as it fits their personality and clothing tastes."

"Clothes are just not very important to me," Justine stated. "I don't pay extra for a name brand. I will not wear something just to be in style. Clothes have to be comfortable."

How important is it that teens wear the latest fashions? Tamika felt some teens would be more popular if they kept up with current fashions. However, she explained that other people's opinions are not the only thing she considers when shopping. "When I am buying clothes, I ask myself, 'Will people like me in this?' Usually, I end up buying something because I like it."

Mike threw in another point. "What's important is to look good. Boys notice girls who dress well."

One of the girls quickly added, "Girls notice boys who dress well, too! No one wants to go out with a slob!"

The group agreed that how teens wear their clothes is as important as what they wear. Tamika summed up their feelings, "It's the way you put your clothes together that counts."

Mike added, "It's more than clothes. You have got to have good manners, too. If you have bad manners, no one is going to notice what you wear!"

The group had many ideas about how teens could keep up with current fashion trends without spending a fortune. Tamika mentioned that lots of teens shop at resale stores for popular looks. According to Mike, siblings and relatives can give teens their outgrown clothes. Kelly suggested that teens who want to buy name brands should buy them on sale.

Tamika concluded, "I just switch clothes with my friends and put them together differently. I wear a friend's shirt with my own pants so the outfit looks entirely different."

According to the group, factors that influence teens' buying decisions include brand, style, color, price, and advertising. The group unanimously agreed that where they are going to wear the clothes influences their decisions, also.

One of the girls stated, "If the item can be mixed or matched with the clothes you already have, then it's a good buy."

Mike added, "Look for basics. For instance, a pair of black shoes will go with anything."

Al summed it all up when he said, "Actually, with clothes it's different strokes for different folks." The group members smiled and agreed.

Chapter Review

Summary

You may not realize it, but a number of factors affect your clothing decisions. Clothes meet a basic physical need by protecting your body from weather and various safety hazards. The way a garment makes you feel is a result of clothing's effect on your psychological needs. Clothes also meet some of your social needs by helping you identify with groups and serving as status symbols. The occasion for which you will wear clothes is another factor that sways your clothing decisions.

Use the elements and principles of design in choosing clothes that reflect your personal tastes and style. Choose colors that flatter your skin tone, as well as your hair and eye color. Use line, texture, and form in clothing design to complement your body shape. Apply the principles of design to create well-coordinated outfits that enhance your appearance.

Planning your wardrobe takes skill. A wardrobe inventory helps you identify what clothing you have on hand and what you need to buy. Wearing multipurpose clothing, as well as mixing and matching garments, extends the scope of your wardrobe. Accessories can give your outfits a finished look. You can also use them to make a statement about your individuality.

Applying a few simple guidelines will help you shop wisely for clothes. Understanding fashion terms can help you shop for a basic wardrobe to suit your activities and lifestyle. Try to get the best quality you can afford. As you shop, watch for sales. Use the information on labels and hangtags to make informed decisions. Also, consider the cost of garments and their care as you shop for clothes that will fit your budget.

Proper care of clothing always means longer wear. Establish a daily routine for clothing care. Read clothing labels for care instructions. Follow proper steps for laundering, drying, ironing, or dry cleaning clothes. Take steps to care for the environment as you care for your clothes, too. When packing clothes for storage or a trip, caring for them properly will help them look their best on you.

Think About It!

1. Describe clothing that is appropriate for four of your most frequent activities.
2. Analyze your skin color and body shape. Which colors, lines, and textures do you think will make you look your best?
3. Evaluate the garments you already have. What garments and accessories do you need to add to your wardrobe in the future?
4. Assess your clothing selection shopping habits. What changes would you make to improve your shopping skills?
5. Why do you think it is important to establish a daily clothing care routine?
6. Name five job opportunities in your area that relate to the topics in this chapter.

Try It Out!

1. Illustrate what clothes you would choose to wear to a prom. Also illustrate what you would wear to a job interview as a salesperson in an apparel department. You may draw sketches or clip pictures from catalogs or magazines.

Resource: *PowerZone Challenge CD.* Have students play the chapter review game to reinforce text content.

2. Design a bulletin board to illustrate how the elements and principles of design affect personal appearance.
3. Invite a fashion coordinator from your favorite clothing store to discuss and demonstrate wardrobe extenders.
4. Use Chart 19-20 to evaluate the quality of several pieces of clothing.
5. Assemble a wide variety of fabric swatches. Then review the procedures given in the chapter for properly sorting clothes. Sort the fabric swatches into suitable laundry loads.
6. Research the cost of dry cleaning an all-weather coat in your area. Assume you will be wearing the coat for three years. Determine how much you would have to spend to keep it clean.

Chapter 20
Preparing to Sew

Careers
These careers relate to the topics in this chapter:
- textile lab technician
- pattern designer
- tailor
- sewing instructor

As you study the chapter, see if you can think of others.

Topics
20-1 Understanding Fabrics
20-2 Selecting Patterns
20-3 Selecting Fabrics and Notions
20-4 Sewing Equipment

Introductory Activities
1. Ask students to list advantages of sewing their own clothes. Ask if more people are making their own clothing today than in the past. Are today's teenagers interested in learning to sew? What are some recent trends in home sewing?
2. Ask each student to name any word related to fabric that comes to mind. As they each tell you their words, write the words on the chalkboard. Categorize the words as you write them on the board, but do not tell the students what you are doing. Possible categories might be fabric names, natural fibers, and generic fibers. When everyone has given you a word, ask the class to look at the groups of terms and decide what each category has in common.

Topic 20-1
Understanding Fabrics
I. Fibers
   A. Natural Fibers
      1. Cotton
      2. Linen
      3. Wool
      4. Silk
      5. Ramie
   B. Manufactured Fibers
      1. Microfibers
II. Yarns
III. Fabric Construction
   A. Weaving
      1. Plain Weave
      2. Twill Weave
      3. Satin Weave
   B. Knitting
      1. Weft Knitting
      2. Warp Knitting
   C. Other Fabric Constructions
IV. Fabric Finishes
V. Dyeing Fabrics
   A. Fiber Dyeing
   B. Yarn Dyeing
   C. Piece Dyeing
VI. Printing Fabrics
   A. Direct Printing
   B. Screen Printing

Topic 20-2
Selecting Patterns
I. Take Your Measurements
II. Determine Your Figure Type and Size
III. Deciding on a Pattern
   A. Consider Your Skill
   B. What Style Is Best?
IV. The Pattern Envelope

Topic 20-3
Selecting Fabric and Notions
I. Choosing a Fabric
   A. What the Pattern Recommends
   B. Consider Your Skill
   C. Care Requirements
II. How Much Fabric Is Needed?
III. Choosing Notions

Topic 20-4
Sewing Equipment
I. Small Equipment
   A. Measuring Tools
   B. Cutting Tools
   C. Marking Tools
   D. Pins and Needles
   E. Pressing Equipment
II. The Sewing Machine
   A. How a Sewing Machine Works
   B. Threading the Machine
   C. Types of Stitches
   D. Caring for the Machine
III. The Serger
IV. Safety with Sewing Tools

Discuss:
Have you ever bought a garment and found other classmates had the same garment? How did you feel?

Reflect:
Did you ever buy a garment and alter it into an original that reflected your style and taste?

Resource:
Fibers: A Microscopic View, reproducible master, TR

Resource:
Sources of Fibers, color transparency CT-18, TR

Activity:
Write a description of garments you own that are made of cotton. Why is cotton the preferred fiber choice in this type of garment?

Topic 20-1
Understanding Fabrics

Objectives
After studying this topic, you will be able to
- explain how fibers, yarns, and fabrics are produced and manufactured.
- distinguish various fabric finishes.
- identify methods used to dye and print fabrics.

Topic Terms
fiber	weaving
yarn	grain
fabric	warp yarns
natural fibers	filling yarns
manufactured fibers	selvage
microfibers	bias
spun yarns	knitting
filament yarns	nonwoven fabrics

The freedom to choose design, color, and fabric is yours when you learn how to sew. By using your imagination, you can create original garments that reflect your fashion taste and style.

Today's clothes are made from a variety of fabrics. The textile industry continues to introduce new fibers, yarns, blends, and finishes for fabrics. All these choices make shopping for fabric fun, but rather confusing. You can make wise fabric selections if you know the facts about how fabrics are made.

Fibers

The **fiber** is the basic unit of all fabrics. Fibers are combined to form a continuous strand called a **yarn.** The weaving and knitting of yarns make **fabrics.**

Fibers have certain characteristics that determine the texture, strength, warmth, absorbency, and durability of fabrics. The characteristics of a fiber depend on its source. Fibers are obtained from either natural or chemical sources. Thus, the two major groups of fibers are natural fibers and manufactured fibers.

Natural Fibers

Natural fibers are those that exist in nature. They are changed slightly during processing. Plants such as cotton and flax are sources of natural fibers. The wool of sheep, specialty hair fibers such as mohair and cashmere, and silk are also natural fibers. See 20-1.

Cotton

Cotton fibers come from the seedpod of the cotton plant. Different varieties of cotton plants produce fibers of different lengths. Long fibers make fine, smooth, lustrous fabrics. Shorter fibers go into coarser fabrics such as the cotton denim used to make blue jeans.

Cotton is a versatile, absorbent, and durable fiber. These qualities make cotton the most widely used natural fiber, 20-2. Although cotton wrinkles and shrinks easily, finishes can be applied to fabrics to prevent these undesirable qualities.

Linen

Flax is obtained from the woody stalk of the flax plant. Flax is the fiber used to make linen. Flax is the oldest known fiber used for fabrics. Remnants of linen have been found in ancient Egyptian tombs. Around 5000 B.C., linen was the fabric used to wrap Egyptian mummies.

Linen is best known for its strength, durability, absorbency, and luster. Flax makes linen the coolest fabric you can wear. The flax fibers absorb perspiration quickly and carry it away from the body. Like cotton fabric, linen wrinkles and creases easily unless treated with a special finish.

Wool

Wool, a protein fiber, comes from the fleece of sheep, 20-3. Wool is an absorbent, resilient, and elastic fiber and the warmest of all fibers. Even though wool fabric is warm, it can also feel cool in lightweight fabrics. Wool fibers allow the fabric to

Across the Curriculum
Science. Borrow several microscopes from the science department. Bring in some swatches of cotton, linen, wool, and silk fabrics. Have students look at them under the microscope and make sketches of each. Discuss how the fibers contribute to the overall characteristics of the fabric.

Topic 20-1 Understanding Fabrics   567

The Natural Fibers

Cotton	
Advantages	**Disadvantages**
Absorbent; soaks up water easily Comfortable and cool to wear in warm weather Dyes and prints well Does not build up static electricity Withstands high temperature; can be boiled to sterilize Combines with other fibers easily Wide variety of uses	Wrinkles easily unless treated with special finish Shrinks in hot water if not treated Mildews if left damp or stored in damp area Weakened by wrinkle-resistant finishes and by prolonged exposure to sunlight Highly flammable unless treated with flame-retardant finish

Linen (Flax)	
Advantages	**Disadvantages**
Strongest of natural fibers Cool to wear; absorbs moisture from skin and dries quickly Looks smooth and lustrous Withstands high temperatures; will not scorch easily when ironed Durable; withstands frequent laundering Lint-free; used for dish towels and for cloths in medical profession	Wrinkles and creases easily unless treated Shines if ironed on right side Expensive if of good quality Poor resistance to mildew and perspiration

Wool	
Advantages	**Disadvantages**
Warmest of natural fibers Highly absorbent; absorbs moisture without feeling wet Resists wrinkles Holds and regains shape Creases well Durable Combines well with other fibers	Expensive Will shrink and mat when moisture and heat are applied Usually requires dry cleaning Burns easily Attracts moths and carpet beetles

Silk	
Advantages	**Disadvantages**
Looks and feels smooth and luxurious Very absorbent Strong but lightweight Resists wrinkling Resists soil Combines well with other fibers	Usually requires dry cleaning Yellows with age Weakened by detergents, perspiration, and long exposure to sunlight Attacked by insects such as silverfish Spotted by water unless specially treated Expensive

Resource:
Natural Fibers, Activity A, SAG

Discuss:
Which of these advantages or disadvantages determine whether or not you'll buy a linen garment?

20-1 The natural fibers have advantages and disadvantages.

Across the Curriculum
Social studies. Have students study the history of sheep in America and how they influenced the settling of the West. In what regions of the United States are wool-bearing sheep raised? Ask students to write a report on their findings.

Enrich:
Go shopping to look at labels on wool garments. How does the price of virgin wool compare with recycled wool? Why do you think this is so?

Discuss:
Why is silk considered the luxury fiber?

Activity:
Have students list any fibers they can think of other than natural fibers. Have them check their clothing labels for other fiber names.

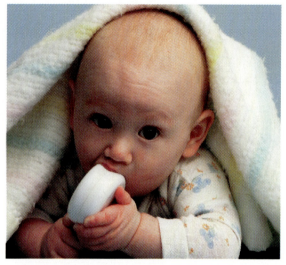
20-2 Cotton is often used for baby clothes because of its softness and absorbency.

20-3 After wool is sheared from sheep, it goes through several processes before becoming cloth.

fabric. To inform and protect consumers, Congress passed the Wool Products Labeling Act in 1939. This legislation requires that wool in any garment or fabric must be labeled as new or recycled. Wool, as defined by the act, means fibers from the coat of a living animal that are being used for the first time. This wool is often called *virgin wool*.

Recycled wool refers to fibers from previously made wool fabrics that were never used. This wool often comes from cutting scraps, mill ends, or garments. These fabrics are converted back into fibers and then used to make new yarns and fabrics. Fabrics made from recycled wool are not as resilient (springy) as fabrics made from virgin wool. They are often used as interlinings in heavy coats.

Silk

Silk was first produced in China where the process of *sericulture* (silkworm cultivation) was kept a secret for more than 2,000 years. Gradually, the silk industry spread westward, but silk production is still confined mainly to China, Japan, and other Asian countries. Silk, characterized by long, lustrous filaments, is often called the luxury fiber.

Silk is a fiber excreted from the silkworm when it builds its cocoon. The cocoons are then soaked in warm water and unwound (either by hand or machine) as one continuous filament about 1,000 feet long. These long filaments are twisted to form yarns for the manufacture of silk fabrics.

Silk is strong, lustrous, elastic, and absorbent. Most silk garments should be dry-cleaned, but washable silk fabrics are now more common.

Ramie

Ramie fibers are obtained from the stalks of China grass, which is grown in Southeast Asia. Ramie is a linenlike fiber that is strong, durable, washable, and lustrous. Ramie absorbs body moisture, dries quickly, and absorbs dyes readily. It is often blended with other fibers in making fabrics.

breathe. This lets heat out and air in to keep the body dry and cool. These and other qualities make wool a very comfortable and durable fabric.

Consumers cannot know the type and quality of wool simply by looking at wool

Putting Technology to Use
Have students investigate the Internet for information on silkworms. One Web site they may want to visit is www.sericulum.com. This site also offers materials for the study of silkworms in the classroom, including literature, cocoons, and live eggs.

Topic 20-1 Understanding Fabrics

Manufactured Fibers

Manufactured fibers are produced artificially from substances such as cellulose, oil products, and chemicals. For centuries, the only source of fabric was natural fibers. In 1924, the first manufactured fiber, *rayon*, was produced. *Acetate* was developed in the 1920s and many more manufactured fibers followed. Today, manufactured fibers are divided into 24 generic groups. Fibers in each of these generic groups have similar chemical composition. See 20-4.

Some manufactured fibers are made from *cellulose*, the fibrous substance from plants. Other fibers, the *noncellulosic fibers*, are developed from chemicals. Most

The Manufactured Fibers

Property	Acetate	Acrylic	Aramid	Metallic	Modacrylic	Nylon	Olefin	Polyester	Rayon	Saran	Spandex	Vinyon
Absorbent									●			
Colorfast		●		●		●	●	●	●	●		
Easy to dye	●		●			●		●				
Easy to launder		●	●	●		●	●	●			●	
Easy to iron			●			●		●	●			
Elastic						●					●	
Exceptional durability			●	●		●	●	●		●		
Flame resistant			●		●					●		
Good drapability	●		●			●		●				
Good shape retention		●			●	●		●			●	
Quick drying		●	●			●	●	●			●	
Resilient		●	●			●	●	●				
Resistant to: abrasion		●				●	●	●				
chemicals		●	●		●		●	●		●		
moths	●	●	●	●	●	●	●	●		●	●	●
mildew	●	●	●	●	●	●	●	●		●	●	●
oil/grease		●	●		●					●		
pilling	●							●				
stretching			●					●				
soil			●				●					
shrinking		●	●	●		●		●		●		
weather		●		●	●		●	●	●	●		
Soft	●	●			●			●				
Strong			●			●	●	●		●		
Warm		●			●	●		●				
Wide color range	●	●				●	●	●	●			
Wrinkle resistant		●						●		●		

20-4 This chart lists the most important properties of the major generic fibers.

Discuss: What does the term *generic* mean in this sense as compared to generic groceries found in supermarkets?

Enrich: Collect hangtags from store-bought garments. Have students select the hangtags that contain the properties listed in Chart 20-4.

Vocabulary: Have students identify unfamiliar property terms in the chart. Then have them find those terms in the dictionary.

Discuss: Where else have you heard about cellulose? Do you think there is any connection between these two uses of the word?

Putting Technology to Use

Ask students to choose one of the manufactured fibers and research it. Students should use presentation software to give presentations on their findings.

> **Activity:**
> Have students research the manufactured fibers to find out which are hardened by wet spinning, dry spinning, and melt spinning.
>
> **Discuss:**
> Think about your summer wardrobe. Which of these garments are the most comfortable to wear in the summer? Why are they comfortable?
>
> **Example:**
> Bring in a garment made of a microfiber to show the class. Discuss the look and feel of the fabric.

manufactured fibers go through the same basic steps to become fibers.

1. Solid raw materials or chemicals are changed to a liquid form.
2. The liquid is extruded or forced through a *spinneret*, a small nozzle with many holes.
3. The liquid hardens and becomes *filaments*, which are continuous strands of fibers.

After the liquid is forced through the *spinneret*, the filaments are hardened by one of three methods, 20-5. *Wet spinning* is the hardening of filaments in a chemical bath. Other filaments harden as warm air evaporates the chemical that changed the raw material into a liquid form. This process is called *dry spinning*. In *melt spinning*, the filaments harden when cool air hits them.

As with all fibers, manufactured fibers have both advantages and disadvantages. Noncellulosic fibers are generally *thermoplastic*, which means they soften at high temperatures. Fabrics of these fibers can be heat-treated to set pleats, shape fabrics, or emboss fabric designs.

With the exception of rayon, manufactured fibers are relatively nonabsorbent. Therefore, these fabrics are less comfortable to wear in hot, humid weather. They also generate static electricity. Fiber blends and special finishes can overcome some of these limitations.

Microfibers

A relatively recent development in textile technology is the creation of microfibers. A **microfiber** is an extremely thin filament of a manufactured fiber. The thinness of a microfiber is determined in step 2 of the process for making manufactured fibers, described earlier. The result is a fabric having all the qualities that are characteristic of the fiber plus a luxurious look and feel. In addition, microfiber technology may contribute important, new features.

Polyester microfiber, for example, often looks like fine silk. Yet it has the strength, durability, and easy-care qualities associated with polyester. In addition, the fabric has a natural resistance to water since the thin fibers pack together so closely that a water molecule cannot penetrate. The spaces between fibers are big enough to allow excess body heat and moisture to escape so the wearer remains comfortable. Most of the manufactured fibers used for clothing are available as microfibers.

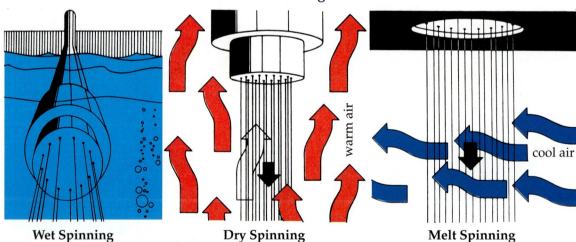

Fiber Manufacturing Processes

Wet Spinning   Dry Spinning   Melt Spinning

20-5 After liquid is forced through a spinneret, it hardens by one of these three methods to form filaments.

FCCLA Activity

Form a panel of FCCLA members and parents. Discuss the effect of world conditions on the production and consumer prices of fabrics. Include import/export restrictions and taxes, fluctuating costs of raw materials such as oil, price subsidies, natural disasters that affect sources of fibers, and technological advances in production techniques.

Yarns

A yarn is a continuous strand made by combining staple fibers or filaments. *Staple fibers* are short fibers. All natural fibers except silk are staple fibers. *Filaments* are continuous strands of fibers. Manufactured fibers are made in filament form, but can be cut to form staple fibers.

Spinning staple fibers together produces **spun yarns.** These yarns have a fuzzy appearance. Rubbing and wearing may cause the tiny fiber ends of spun yarns to *pill,* or form little balls. You may have noticed pilling on sweaters and other clothes.

Filament yarns are made from filaments. One or more types of filament fibers may be combined to form a filament yarn.

Twist is another term related to yarns. Twist in yarns brings the fibers closer together and increases yarn strength. Twist is necessary in spun yarns; it holds the staple fibers together. As the degree of twist is increased in a yarn, the yarn becomes harder, more compact, and less lustrous. A low twist is used for most filament yarns, so they are soft and lustrous.

Yarns can be classified as single, ply, or cord yarns. The twisting together of fibers or filaments forms a *single yarn.* Twisting two or more single yarns together produces a *ply yarn.* Each single yarn is called a ply. Therefore, a product labeled *two-ply* is made from two single yarns. A *cord yarn* is formed when two or more ply yarns are twisted together.

Most filament yarns are *textured.* These yarns are crimped, coiled, or looped. See 20-6. Texturing increases the bulk, stretchability, and absorbency of yarns.

Many yarns on today's market are either blends or combinations. Spinning different staple fibers together makes a *blended yarn.* Twisting two different single yarns into a ply yarn forms a *combination yarn.*

Blends and combinations are often used to make fabrics with better performance. In the case of a polyester/cotton shirt, the two fibers blended together give very good performance. Polyester is wrinkle-resistant, but it absorbs very little moisture. Cotton is cool and absorbent, but it wrinkles easily. By blending the fibers, the shirt can have the best characteristics of both fibers. Sometimes blends and combinations are used to make less expensive fabrics.

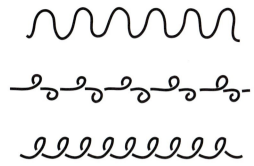

20-6 Textured yarns provide greater bulk, stretchability, and absorbency.

Fabric Construction

Two common methods of fabric construction are weaving and knitting. Other methods are felting, fusing, braiding, and knotting.

Weaving

A woven fabric is composed of two sets of yarns at right angles to each other. The process of interlacing these two sets of yarns to produce a fabric is known as **weaving.** Weaving is done on machines called *looms.*

The two sets of yarns used in weaving are called warp and filling yarns. The direction the yarns run is called the **grain.** See 20-7. **Warp yarns** run along the *lengthwise grain.* **Filling yarns** run along the *crosswise grain.* The fabric **selvage** is formed along the lengthwise edges of the fabric where the filling yarns change direction during weaving. The selvage is strong and will not ravel.

Any line diagonal to the lengthwise or crosswise grains is called a **bias.** The *true bias* runs at a 45-degree angle to the selvage. The greatest amount of stretch in a woven fabric is found along the true bias.

By passing the filling yarns over and under a different number of warp yarns, many different weaving effects can be

---

Problem-Solving Practice

Critical Thinking for Consumers, reproducible master, TR. Students are asked to read about various situations and describe how fabric consumers might be affected by them.

Activity: Bring in various samples of craft yarns. Have the students unravel each sample to illustrate the concepts of single yarns, ply yarns, and cord yarns.

Activity: Bring in a collection of fabric swatches. Have the students unravel yarns from several samples to see if any are textured.

Activity: Have the students look at labels on their clothing. What are the most common blends? Which ones occur the most often? Why do you suppose this is so?

Resource: *Yarns,* Activity B, SAG

> **Enrich:**
> Borrow a small loom from your school's art department. Demonstrate the weaving process and describe the related vocabulary terms.
>
> **Example:**
> Use a piece of burlap to illustrate the information in 20-7. Remove threads from the burlap; replace them with a contrasting color of yarn. Label with the appropriate terms and display in the classroom.
>
> **Activity:**
> Have students evaluate their own woven garments to determine the types of weaves.

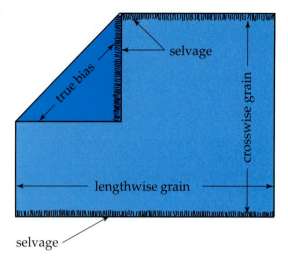

20-7 Lengthwise grain is parallel to the selvages. Crosswise grain runs between the selvages. The bias grain runs at a 45-degree angle to the selvage.

Twill Weave

The twill weave is formed when a yarn in one direction floats (passes) over two or more yarns in the other direction. See 20-9. Each float begins at least one yarn over from the last one. The twill weave is characterized by a diagonal line or *wale*. The angle of a wale may vary from a low slope to a very steep one.

Twill weaves are often used to produce strong, durable fabrics such as denim and gabardine. Twill-weave fabrics resist wrinkles and hide soil.

Satin Weave

A satin weave is made when a yarn in one direction floats over four or more opposite yarns and under one. See 20-10. Satin-weave fabrics are characterized by their lustrous shine. This shine is a result of long floats on the surface of the fabric reflecting light.

Since the floats tend to snag easily, the satin weave does not produce very durable fabrics. Durability increases if the yarns are woven closely together. Satin weave fabrics are often used as lining fabrics because they are smooth and slippery.

Knitting

The process of looping yarns together to form a fabric is called **knitting**. The

created. The plain, twill, and satin weaves are the three basic weaves.

Plain Weave

The plain weave is the simplest form of weaving. It is made by passing a filling yarn alternately over and under one warp yarn. See 20-8. The plain weave produces a fabric that is strong, reversible, and durable. Examples of the plain weave include muslin, percale, dress linen, gingham, and broadcloth.

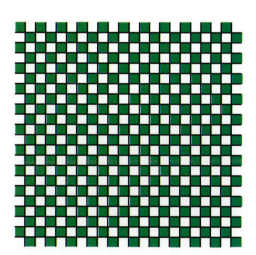

20-8 The pattern for a plain weave is over one, under one.

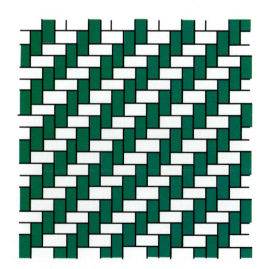

20-9 In this twill weave, the filling yarn goes over two warp yarns and under two.

Putting Technology to Use
Collect samples of all the fabrics mentioned. Have students use word processing or drawing software and a color printer to create colorful labels for the fabrics, showing their names and weaves. Display the fabrics and their labels on a bulletin board.

Topic 20-1 Understanding Fabrics

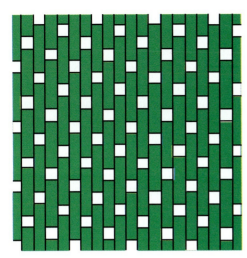

20-10 In this satin weave, the filling yarn passes over four warp yarns and under one. This creates long floats of warp yarns.

20-11 In weft knitting, loops are formed as yarn is carried back and forth horizontally.

loops are varied to create numerous patterns and textures. One yarn can form the entire fabric.

Knit fabrics are best known for their stretch, which allows the fabric to move with, and fit, the body. They resist wrinkles well. When threads are broken, however, a *run* can form, as in nylon stockings. Knits also can snag or ravel if a yarn is pulled.

The two methods of knitting fabrics are weft knitting and warp knitting. They differ in the way the loops are formed.

Weft Knitting

Weft knits are made by hand or on flat or circular knitting machines. On flat knitting machines, the machine needles form loops as yarn is carried back and forth horizontally. See 20-11. Sweaters and dresses are knitted on these machines.

On circular knitting machines, the loops are formed as yarns go around the circular needle bed. Circular knitting produces tubular fabrics used for hosiery, underwear, and socks.

Double knit is a common type of weft knit fabric. To make double-knit fabric, two sets of needles are used on the knitting machine. Double knits are stronger and more stable than single knits. They are usually made of polyester, triacetate, or wool.

Warp Knitting

This type of knitting is done only by machine. One or more sets of yarns the width of the fabric are used. Loops are formed vertically, one row at a time, 20-12. Most warp-knit fabrics are knitted in tighter loops than weft knit fabrics. They can be manufactured rapidly and in great quantity.

Warp knitting produces flat fabric with straight edges. Warp knits tend to be lighter in weight and less elastic than weft knits. Tricot and raschel are examples of warp-knit fabrics. Tricot knits are used extensively in lingerie. Raschel knits come in a variety of weights, ranging from dress and suit fabrics to nets and laces.

Other Fabric Constructions

Not all fabrics are knitted or woven. Some are made by locking fibers together or by braiding or knotting yarns.

Nonwoven fabrics are made by pressing, bonding, or interlocking fibers together directly without using yarns. This can be done with mechanical action, chemicals,

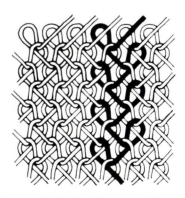

20-12 In warp knitting, loops are formed vertically.

> **Discuss:**
> Develop a list of activities and occupations in which clothing made of knit fabrics could be worn.
>
> **Activity:**
> Have students bring in garments that are made in knit weaves. Can they determine from which category of knits these garments are made?
>
> **Note:**
> Display a collection of knit fabric types in class so the students can determine variations in construction.

Across the Curriculum

History. Have students research the history of knitting and knit fabrics. Have them find out when circular knitting machines were invented and when warp-knit fabrics were first created. Have students share their findings with the class.

and/or heat. Nonwoven fabrics have many industrial and medical uses. They are also used as interfacings in garments. *Interfacings* give support to collars, waistbands, and cuffs. Batting, a lightweight layer of insulation used inside quilts, is also a nonwoven fabric.

Applying heat, moisture, agitation, and pressure to wool fibers results in *felt*. Due to the nature of wool fibers, the *felting* process causes fibers to permanently interlock. Felt is easy to mold and is often used to make hats and craft items. It has many industrial uses, too.

Braiding is the process of interlacing three or more yarns lengthwise and diagonally to make fabrics. Braided fabrics are usually narrow. They are used for decorative trims and shoelaces. Braids are often joined together to make rugs.

Knotting, twisting, or looping yarns produces *laces* and *nets*. These fabrics can be constructed by hand or machine. Lace and net fabrics can be fine and sheer or coarse and open.

Fabric Finishes

All fabrics go through some type of finishing process before they are ready for use. Most finishes add certain characteristics to the fabrics. These finishes improve the appearance, feel, or performance of fabrics. Common fabric finishes are listed below.

- *Antistatic*—This chemical treatment prevents static electricity so garments will not cling to the body.
- *Bleaching*—This chemical treatment whitens fabrics and removes impurities. It is usually used on cotton and linen fabrics.
- *Brushing*—Circular brushes remove short, loose fibers from the fabric surface and produce an even, soft pile.
- *Calendering*—Fabric is pressed between heated rollers to make it smooth and glossy.
- *Permanent press*—This finish helps the fabric retain its original shape and resist wrinkling after washing and drying. It may also be called *durable press*.
- *Flame-retardant*—This chemical treatment prevents the fabric from supporting a flame. It works by cutting off the oxygen supply. The Flammable Fabrics Act brought about the use of this finish. Flammability standards have been set for children's sleepwear, general wearing apparel, carpets, rugs, and mattresses.
- *Mercerization*—This chemical process is used most often on cotton, linen, and rayon fabrics. It increases luster, strength, and affinity (attraction) for dyes.
- *Preshrunk*—Fabrics are shrunk by a heat and moisture process. When a garment is labeled *preshrunk,* the consumer is guaranteed it will not shrink more than three percent. *Sanforized* is a trademark name that guarantees a fabric will shrink less than one percent in either length or width.
- *Stain resistance*—This finish makes fabrics less absorbent so spills can be lifted or sponged off easily. Treated fabrics resist water and oil stains. *Scotchguard* is a trademark for a stain-resistant fabric.
- *Sizing*—A solution of starch, glue, or resin is applied to the fabric to increase weight, body, and luster. This finish may be temporary or durable.
- *Soil release*—This treatment makes possible the removal of oily stains from durable-press fabrics. It helps water-resistant fibers be more absorbent so detergents can release soil.
- *Water repellence*—This applied finish makes a fabric resistant to wetting, but does not make the fabric waterproof. It cannot resist heavy rain. This finish must be renewed after several launderings.

Dyeing Fabrics

Color can add a new dimension to any textile product. It greatly affects your fabric and garment choices. In fact, you may have chosen a certain fabric just because of its color.

The many colors of fabrics are produced from dyes. Dyes may or may not

Putting Technology to Use

Have students use the Internet to research one of the finishing processes listed. Have students give an oral report to the class, including the addresses of the Web sites on which they found their information.

be colorfast. *Colorfast* means the color will withstand washing, dry cleaning, perspiration, sunlight, and rubbing. The colorfastness of a fabric depends on the chemical makeup of the dye, the fiber content of the fabric, and the method of dyeing.

Dyes can be applied to textile products at various stages—as fibers, yarns, or fabrics. Thus, the basic dyeing processes are fiber dyeing, yarn dyeing, and piece dyeing.

Fiber Dyeing

Fibers may be dyed before they are made into yarns. *Stock dyeing* is the process used to dye natural fibers. Color penetrates the fibers and produces uniform color and good colorfastness. *Solution dyeing* is the process used for dyeing manufactured fibers. In this process, color is added to the liquid before it is forced through the spinneret. Solution dyeing results in excellent colorfastness since the dye becomes an inherent part of the filaments.

Yarn Dyeing

In yarn dyeing, the yarns are first wound onto spools and then placed in a dye bath. Yarn dyeing provides good color absorption and is less expensive than fiber dyeing. It also gives the fabric designer a variety of fabric choices—checks, plaids, and stripes. See 20-13.

Piece Dyeing

This is the least expensive and most common method of dyeing. Color is added by placing the fabric in a dye bath. Piece dyeing is the most practical method for manufacturers to use. They can store volumes of undyed fabric and dye to order as fashion demands.

Printing Fabrics

Color can be applied to fabrics and other textile products by printing. It is usually easy to distinguish between printed and dyed fabrics. On printed fabrics, the design is very distinct on the right side, but the wrong side appears faded. In dyed fabrics, both sides are the same color.

There are many methods for printing fabrics. Two common methods are direct printing and screen printing.

Direct Printing

In this process, color for the design is applied directly to the fabric as the fabric passes between a series of rollers. The

Note:
Collect samples of fabrics that are dyed in each of these processes. Display them in the classroom.

Note:
Demonstrate the basic tie-dye patterns for the students. Have them tie-dye inexpensive T-shirts they bring in from home.

20-13 Yarn-dyed fabrics are being woven in this textile factory.

Across the Curriculum

History, English. Have students prepare a written report on natural sources of dye used in the past. Suggestions should include the specific kinds of barks, leaves, berries, and flowers used to create each color.

Enrich:
Silk screening kits are available from art supply stores. Have the students design a class logo and silk screen various decorative items.

Enrich:
Have students visit a local fabric store and spend an hour looking through pattern catalogs to see what styles are currently available.

Resource:
Measuring and Selecting a Pattern, reproducible master, TR

rollers transfer color directly onto the fabric. This is a simple method used to produce large quantities of a design inexpensively. Direct printing is often called *roller printing.*

Screen Printing

For many years, screen printing was done by hand on a silk screening frame. The background area of the screen was painted with a paste to resist the dye. The untreated area of the screen allowed the dye to pass through onto the fabric. Each color required a separate screen.

Today, a similar process, called *rotary screen printing,* has become one of the fastest printing methods. The dye is transferred to the fabric through a cylinder-shaped screen that rolls over the fabric, printing the design. A separate screen is still needed for each color of the pattern.

Screening is used to print logos and symbols on garments such as T-shirts. Screening is also used for very large designs and high-quality dress goods.

Check It Out!
1. Name the five most commonly used natural fibers and list two characteristics of each fiber.
2. What substances are used in making manufactured fibers?
3. Why is twist added to yarns?
4. Explain the basic difference between weaving and knitting.
5. Why are finishes applied to fabrics?
6. Which is the most common method for dyeing fabrics?
7. True or false. In screen printing, rollers transfer color directly to the fabric.

Check It Out! (Answers)
1. cotton, linen, wool, ramie, silk (Student response for two characteristics of each fiber.)
2. cellulose, oil products, chemicals
3. to add strength
4. Weaving is the interlacing of two sets of yarns to form a fabric. Knitting is the looping of yarns together to form a fabric.
5. to improve the appearance, feel, or performance of the fabric
6. piece dyeing
7. false

Topic 20-2
Selecting Patterns

Objectives
After studying this topic, you will be able to
- take accurate body measurements.
- determine your figure type and pattern size.
- identify a suitable pattern.
- interpret information found on a pattern envelope.

Topic Terms
figure type
pattern view

Successful sewing begins with choosing the right pattern. Patterns are available for the classics, the latest fashions, and a wide range of garment styles. Pattern catalogs will show you many style choices. It may be hard to decide on one!

In order to buy a pattern, you will need to know what size to request. Since pattern sizes vary slightly from ready-to-wear sizes, you will need to first take your measurements. These measurements will help you identify your figure type and size.

Take Your Measurements

To ensure accuracy, ask someone to help you take your measurements. Measure over your undergarments. Do not try to take measurements over bulky clothing. Tie a string snugly around your waist to find your natural waistline. This will help you take waist measurements easily and accurately. When taking measurements, put the tape measure snugly around the body, but not too tight. Be sure the tape measure is always parallel to the floor.

For the *bust* or *chest,* bring the tape straight across the back and around the fullest part of the bust or chest. Your arms should be at your sides.

To measure the *waist,* place the tape measure over the string tied around the waist. This should be the smallest part of the midsection on females. For males, it may be where the waistband of pants usually falls.

Hips should be measured around the fullest part of the body. This is about 7 or 8 inches below the waistline for most teens.

Patterns for males often include a neck measurement. To take this measurement, draw the tape around the neck at the Adam's apple. Add 1/2 inch to this measurement for the shirt neck size. Ready-to-wear shirts also use this measurement. A *sleeve length* measurement is taken from the center base of the neck, across the shoulder, and down the arm to the wrist bone. The elbow should be bent slightly when this measurement is taken.

Patterns for females may include a *back waist length.* To take this measurement, place one end of the tape measure at the bone you can feel at the center back of the neck. Draw the tape down to the waistline string.

To measure your *height,* you must first remove your shoes. Place a ruler or book across the top of your head as you stand near a wall. Make a mark lightly on the wall where the book or ruler touches. Then measure from the mark to the floor.

Determine Your Figure Type and Size

When you have finished taking your measurements, you are ready to determine your figure type and size. Pattern companies have standard pattern sizes for various figure types. **Figure types** are based on height and general body proportions.

If you are a female, two measurements are used to determine your figure type—your height and back waist length. You must also analyze your own body proportions and shape. Compare your figure analysis with the descriptions given in figure 20-14 to determine your figure type. If you cannot decide which figure type to use, choose the one with the back waist length closest to yours. Choosing a pattern of the correct figure type will result in a garment that will fit you well.

Select your pattern size by comparing your measurements to those for your figure type. If your measurements fall between two sizes, select the smaller size if you are small-boned or want a garment with a closer fit. If you are large-boned, choose the larger size.

The pattern size you choose will also depend on the garment you make. For shirts, blouses, dresses, suits, jackets, and coats, the key measurement is the bust or chest. Choose the pattern size closest to your bust or chest measurement. For pants, skirts, or shorts, the key measurement is the waist measurement. However, if your hips are two sizes larger than the measurement listed for your waist size, then use the hip measurement. It is easier to alter the waist than the hips.

Deciding on a Pattern

After determining your figure type, you can turn to the sections of the pattern book that feature your figure type. You will find many pattern choices. In making your decision, you will want to consider your sewing skill. You will also want to select a style that suits you.

Consider Your Skill

When selecting a pattern, consider your sewing skill. If you are a beginner, look for patterns identified as *Easy, Very Easy, Jiffy, Simple to Sew,* or *For Beginners.*

A clue to the sewing ease of the pattern is its number of pieces. Fewer pattern pieces usually means the garment will be easier to sew, 20-15.

The style of the garment will also indicate the difficulty of the pattern. *Kimono sleeves* are cut in one piece as part of the garment front and back. They are much easier to sew than set-in sleeves. *Set-in sleeves* are attached to the body of the garment with a seam around the armhole. *Facings,* which are used to cover raw edges

Activity:
Demonstrate proper measuring techniques. Then have the students take their own measurements at home.

Activity:
Have students determine their figure type and pattern size based on their measurements.

Discuss:
What types of garments are pictured in the quick and easy sewing sections of pattern catalogs?

Note:
Display patterns that use very few pattern pieces and those that use many. Discuss why beginning sewers might have problems completing the complicated patterns in the class time available.

Putting Technology to Use
Have students browse through patterns available at www.simplicity.com, www.mccall.com, and www.voguepatterns.com. Have them pick a pattern of a clothing item they would like to learn to make and print it out. Have students share their choices with the rest of the class.

Resource:
Pattern Selection, Activity D, SAG

Discuss:
How do these figure types compare to ready-made garment figure types found in stores? How do stores classify their clothing departments?

Discuss:
Why do men and boys have fewer figure types than women and girls?

Pattern Sizes and Body Measurements
INCHES

Girls'/Girls' Plus—For growing girls who have not yet begun to mature. Girls' Plus are designed for girls over the average weight for their age and height.

	Girls'					Girls' Plus				
Sizes	7	8	10	12	14	8½	10½	12½	14½	16½
Chest	26	27	28½	30	32	30	31½	33	34½	36
Waist	23	23½	24½	25½	26½	28	29	30	31	32
Hips	27	28	30	32	34	33	34½	36	37½	39
Back Waist Length	11½	12	12¾	13½	14¼	12½	13¼	14	14¾	15½
Approx. Height	50	52	56	58½	61	52	56	58½	61	63½

Junior—For the young miss figure, about 5'2" to 5'5" in height without shoes.

Sizes	3/4	5/6	7/8	9/10	11/12	13/14	15/16	17/18	19/20	21/22	23/24
Bust	28	29	30½	32	33½	35	36½	38½	40½	42½	44½
Waist	22	23	24	25	26	27	28	29½	31	33½	35½
Hip-7" below waist	31	32	33½	35	36½	38	39½	41½	43½	45½	47½
Back Waist Length	13½	14	14½	15	15⅜	15¾	16⅛	16⅜	16⅝	16⅞	17⅛

Misses'/Miss Petite—For well-proportioned, developed figures. Misses' about 5'5" to 5'6" without shoes. Miss Petite under 5'4" without shoes.

Sizes	4	6	8	10	12	14	16	18	20	22	24	26
Bust	29½	30½	31½	32½	34	36	38	40	42	44	46	48
Waist	22	23	24	25	26½	28	30	32	34	37	39	41½
Hip-9" below waist	31½	32½	33½	34½	36	38	40	42	44	46	48	50
Misses-Back Waist Length	15½	15½	15¾	16	16⅛	16¼	16⅜	17	17¼	17⅜	17½	17¾
Miss Petite-Back Waist Length	14¼	14½	14¾	15	15¼	15½	15¾	16	16¼	16⅜	16½	16⅝

Women's/Women's Petite—For larger, more fully mature figures. Women's about 5'5" to 5'6" without shoes. Women's Petite under 5'4" without shoes.

Sizes		16W	20W	22W	24W	26W	28W	30W	32W
	Women's								
	Women's Petite	36	38	40	42	44	46	48	50
Bust		40	42	44	46	48	50	52	54
Waist		33	35	37	39	41½	44	46½	49
Hip-9" below waist		42	44	46	48	50	52	54	56
Women's Back Waist Length		17⅛	17¼	17⅜	17½	17⅝	17¾	17⅞	18
Women's Petite Back Waist Length		16⅛	16¼	16⅜	16½	16⅝	16¾	16⅞	17

Boys' & Teen Boys'—For growing boys and young men who have not reached full adult stature.

Sizes	7	8	10	12	14	16	18	20
Chest	26	27	28	30	32	33½	35	36½
Waist	23	24	25	26	27	28	29	30
Hip	27	28	29½	31	32½	34	35½	37
Neck Band	11¾	12	12½	13	13½	14	14½	15
Approx. Height	48	50	54	58	61	64	66	68
Shirt Sleeve	22⅜	23¼	25	26¾	29	30	31	32

Men's—For men of average build; about 5'10" without shoes.

Sizes	32	34	36	38	40	42	44	46	48	50	52
Chest	32	34	36	38	40	42	44	46	48	50	52
Waist	27	28	30	32	34	36	39	42	44	46	48
Hip	34	35	37	39	41	43	45	47	49	51	53
Neck Band	13½	14	14½	15	15½	16	16½	17	17½	18	18½
Shirt Sleeve	31	32	32	33	33	34	34	35	35	36	36

Unisex—For figures within Misses', Men's, Teen-Boys', Boys' and Girls' size ranges.

Sizes	XXS	XS	S	M	L	XL	XXL
Chest/Bust	28-29	30-32	34-36	38-40	42-44	46-48	50-52
Hip	29-30	31-32½	35-37	39-41	43-45	47-49	51-53

20-14 Most young men and women fit into one of these figure types.

Across the Curriculum

Math. Have students visit a fabric store or look through pattern books and investigate the prices for patterns. Have students compare the prices of different types of patterns and for similar patterns from different companies. Have students try to determine what factors influence the cost differences among patterns. Ask students to share their findings in class.

20-15 Patterns that have only a few pattern pieces are easiest to sew.

of garments, are less complicated than collars. It is usually difficult for beginners to make the topstitching on collars look perfect.

You will probably be wise to limit yourself to one new learning experience each time you choose a pattern. Beginning with a simple garment will assure your success. Then you will want to continue to develop your sewing skills.

What Style Is Best?

When choosing a garment style, you will want to ask yourself these questions.
- Is this style suitable for my body shape and size?
- Will this garment fit into my current wardrobe?
- Is this style suitable for my activities?

When you buy ready-to-wear garments, you have the advantage of being able to try on the garment to see how it looks on you. Unfortunately, you do not have this option when you choose a pattern. You have to try to visualize how the finished garment will look on you. Apply what you have learned about design lines that are most flattering to your figure. Study the drawings in the pattern book. Look for design details. Try to visualize how the design will emphasize your best features and minimize your poorer features. The style you choose should flatter your figure.

Consider your wardrobe needs when choosing your pattern. If you completed a wardrobe inventory, you can choose a pattern that will fill a void in your wardrobe. Also consider your activities. Will you be able to wear this garment for at least some of your activities?

The Pattern Envelope

After selecting the pattern, read the information on the front and the back of the pattern envelope. The front of the envelope usually has drawings of more than one image, or pattern view. Each **pattern view** shows a variation of the basic pattern. For instance, a pattern may show a shirt with long sleeves next to one with short sleeves. Skirts may be shown in different lengths. Sometimes the patterns will show actual photographs of the garments worn by models. This will help you visualize how the finished garment will look. In addition, the front of the pattern envelope will show the pattern number, company name, figure type, size, and price. See 20-16.

The back of the pattern envelope includes the following information:
- the number of pattern pieces included
- a written description of the garment
- fabric recommendations
- supplies needed to complete the garment
- a drawing of the back of each garment view
- a measurement chart
- directions for how much fabric to buy
- any interfacing or lining fabrics needed

Resource:
Selecting a Pattern: Know Before You Go, reproducible master, TR

Note:
Before investing time and money into making a garment with a design that is totally unlike anything you own, try on a similar ready-to-wear item to determine if the new design flatters your appearance.

Reflect:
What garment is the most versatile clothing item in your wardrobe? Which pattern would let you recreate it in another color or fabric?

Enrich:
Photocopy the drawings on the envelope of a basic or classic pattern. (Select one without stripes, prints, or other obvious designs.) Give each student a copy to use as a worksheet to create whatever finished "looks" would blend with his or her wardrobe. Have students share their design recommendations.

Note:
The use of a fabric not recommended for a pattern will generally yield disappointing results.

Across the Curriculum

English. Have students write a one-paragraph essay describing their clothing preference and style. Ask them to include reasons they prefer these garments and styles over others.

Activity:
Provide a selection of pattern envelopes for the students to use. Have them locate the fabric and notion information on the envelopes and share it with the class.

Enrich:
Provide samples of fabrics for the required sewing project. Have the students discuss fabric names, fabric construction and quality, and ease of sewing.

Activity:
Provide labeled samples of fabrics and a variety of pattern envelopes. Have the students match the fabric samples with the fabric recommendations listed on the patterns.

Discuss:
Provide a selection of patterns. What warnings about special fabrics are stated on the patterns?

20-16 The front of a pattern envelope usually shows the different ways that a pattern can be varied.

Check It Out!
1. Describe how to take a sleeve length measurement.
2. What two measurements are used to determine figure type for women?
3. What is the key measurement to consider when buying a pants pattern?
4. What should you look for when choosing a pattern that will be easy to sew?
5. What are pattern views?

Check It Out! (Answers)
1. Measure from the center base of the neck, across the shoulder, down the arm to the wrist bone, with the elbow slightly bent.
2. height, back waist length
3. waist
4. The fewer the number of pattern pieces, the easier the garment will be to sew.
5. variations of the basic pattern

Topic 20-3
Selecting Fabric and Notions

Objectives
After studying this topic, you will be able to
- select a suitable fabric for your garment.
- purchase the correct amount of fabric.
- identify the necessary sewing notions.

Topic Terms
napping
pile fabric
notions

After selecting a pattern that is right for you, read the information on the back of the pattern envelope. This information will tell you what fabrics are suitable for the pattern, how much fabric is needed, and what notions are required.

Choosing a Fabric
There are several factors to consider when choosing a fabric for your garment. You will first want to look at the recommendations included with the pattern. Also consider your sewing skills. Some fabrics are more difficult to sew than others. Finally, consider the care the fabric will require.

What the Pattern Recommends
On the back of the pattern envelope you will find a section that lists fabrics appropriate for the pattern, 20-17. The recommended fabrics were considered by the designer to be the best choices for this pattern. Beginning sewers will want to follow these recommendations closely. This section also alerts you to fabrics that should not be used, such as pile fabrics or diagonal patterns. Sometimes extra fabric is needed for matching plaids or large designs. This information will also be stated here.

Topic 9-6
Children from One to Five

Objectives
After studying this topic, you will be able to
- give examples of physical, emotional, social, and intellectual characteristics of toddlers and preschoolers.
- describe types of special needs children might have and how to meet those needs.

Topic Terms
toddler
preschooler
children with special needs
physical disability
mental disability
learning disability
emotional disorder
gifted or talented
inclusion

9-30 Caregivers should expect different behaviors from children of different ages.

Vocabulary:
What do you think is the age difference between a toddler and a preschooler?

Resource:
Signs of Growth, Activity H, SAG

Discuss:
What are some other ways children can develop their large and small muscle skills?

Caregivers need an understanding of what they might expect from children within a given age range, 9-30. Knowing about patterns of growth and behavior is helpful. Caregivers should also remember that all individuals are unique. Sometimes a toddler will behave as a five-year-old. At other times, the same toddler may behave as an infant. Caregivers must always maintain a flexible attitude as they work with individual children.

Children have much to learn about themselves, other people, and the world. Children do not need to be pushed to learn. They absorb much of what they need to know from their environments. Thus, a rich environment offers rich learning experiences. (See Appendix.)

Toddlers
One- and two-year-old children are called **toddlers**. This term comes from the unsteady way children move, or toddle, when they begin to walk. As children gain mobility, they have more opportunities to develop mentally and socially.

Physical Growth of Toddlers
During the toddler years, parents will see steady improvements in their child's large muscle skills. As leg muscles develop, toddlers become able to run, jump, kick, and climb as well as walk. Strengthening arm muscles enable 18-month-old toddlers to throw a ball and 36-month-old toddlers to catch one.

Small muscle skills also improve as children grow. They become able to fill and empty containers, turn knobs, and build block towers. They like to scribble, paint, play with modeling clay, and string beads. By the time a toddler is 30 months old, he or she can turn the pages of a book.

Toilet Learning
One important physical skill most children master toward the end of the toddler years is toilet learning. As children learn to control their muscles, toilet learning will

Across the Curriculum
Health. Have students research neuromuscular diseases such as muscular dystrophy and Lou Gehrig's disease. How are toddlers' muscle skills affected by these diseases?

more difficult. Look for a fabric with a tight weave rather than a loose weave if you are a beginner. Fabrics that are slippery or that ravel easily are also best saved until you gain more experience.

Plaids, stripes, and some designs have to be matched at the seams. This requires a special layout of the pattern pieces on the fabric and care during construction. Matching plaids and stripes requires both skill and practice.

Fabrics with nap or pile are more challenging to sew. **Napping** is a fabric finish that pulls the fiber ends to the surface of a napped fabric.

A **pile fabric** has loops of yarn ends projecting from the surface. Pile yarns may be cut or uncut. Velvet, velveteen, velour,

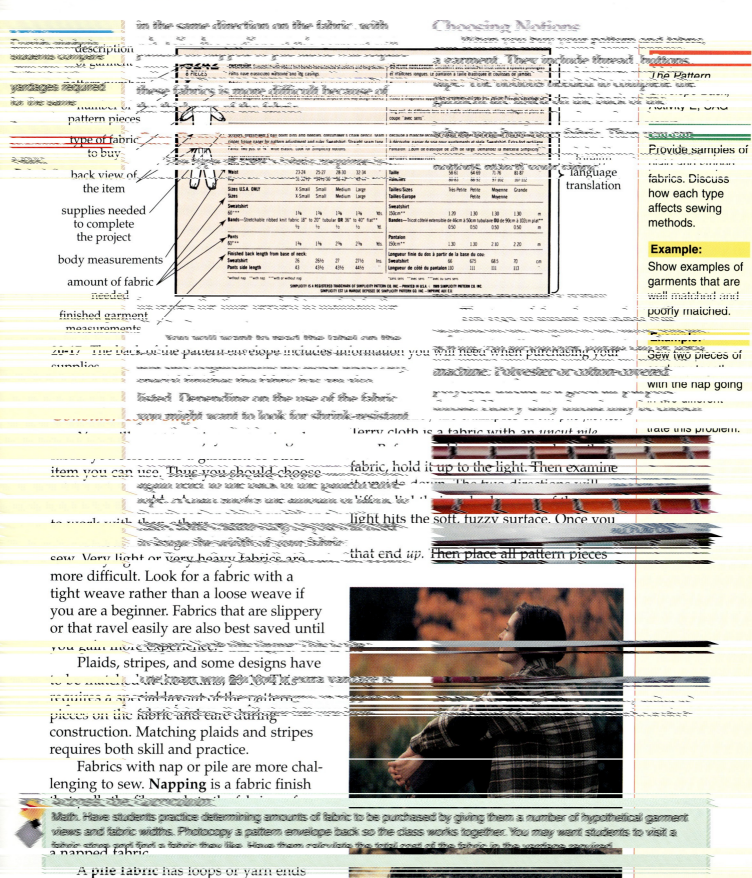

20-18 For a plaid, you may need to purchase extra fabric to match the design at the seams.

for heavy fabrics. Special thread is recommended if you plan to use a serger or overlock machine (discussed in the next section). Special serger thread is finer in size and has an extra smooth finish for high-speed sewing.

Check It Out!

1. List three factors to consider before choosing a fabric.
2. What three factors will help you locate the number of yards of fabric to buy on a yardage chart?
3. True or false. You may need to buy less fabric when you are working with one-way designs or napped or plaid fabrics.
4. What should you do when you cannot find thread that is an exact match for your fabric?

Check It Out! (Answers)

1. the pattern's recommendation, the sewer's skill level, the fabric's care requirements
2. pattern view, size, fabric width
3. false
4. buy thread that is slightly darker than the fabric

Topic 20-4
Sewing Equipment

Objectives

After studying this topic, you will be able to
- determine the basic sewing supplies.
- describe how to operate and care for a sewing machine.
- list the uses of a serger.

Topic Terms

lockstitch
bobbin
presser foot
feed dogs
thread-tension regulator
serger
looper

Having the proper equipment and knowing how to use it will help you become a successful sewer. There are certain supplies every sewer needs. Begin by purchasing the basics, 20-20. As you progress, you may want to add equipment that will simplify construction and reduce sewing time.

Small Equipment

One of the first things you will need is a sewing box. It can be any kind of container or box that will help you keep your small equipment organized. Use dividers or small containers to hold pins, needles, a tape measure, and other small items.

You will need several types of small sewing equipment. These include measuring tools, cutting tools, marking tools, pins and needles, and pressing equipment. Most of these items can be bought in department or fabric stores.

Measuring Tools

A *tape measure* is a basic measuring tool. It is essential for taking body measurements. Most tape measures are 60-inches long. Make sure the tape is made from a material that will not stretch. Choose one that has protectors on the ends to give the tape

Activity:
Display several pieces of specialized sewing equipment. Have the students determine how each piece is used.

Activity:
Display a variety of small sewing equipment. Have students divide the equipment into the categories listed.

Activity: Display all these basic sewing supplies. Have the students demonstrate how these tools would be used. Reinforce the correct use of each tool.

Note: Demonstrate how these items are used in actual construction.

Activity: Display a variety of cutting tools. Let the students practice using them on a variety of fabrics. Discuss the characteristics of each cutting tool.

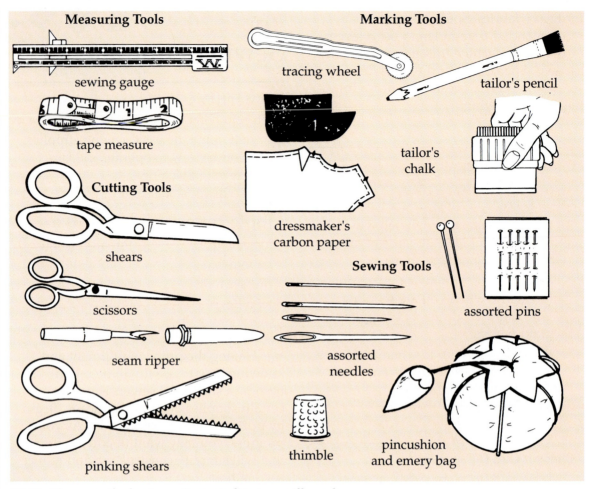

20-20 These are the basic sewing supplies you will need.

durability. Also check to be sure the numbers are clearly visible and printed on both sides of the tape.

A sewing gauge is a useful and inexpensive measuring tool. The gauge is a 6-inch metal or plastic ruler with a sliding marker. It is used to measure small areas, such as hems, cuffs, and the space between buttons.

Cutting Tools

Having good-quality, sharp shears and scissors is very important in sewing. Before buying cutting tools, always test them to be sure they cut cleanly. Shears and scissors come in various sizes and have many different uses. Make your selections based on what you will be cutting.

Shears are used to cut pattern pieces from the fabric. A bent handle (rather than a straight handle) allows the fabric to lie flat on the worktable. This makes it easier to cut smooth, accurate edges. Shears are available in right- and left-handed versions.

Scissors are smaller and shorter than shears and have round handles. They are used for trimming, grading, and clipping seams and snipping threads.

A *seam ripper* is also classified as a cutting tool. It is used to rip open unwanted seams.

Other cutting tools you may want to buy later are pinking or scalloping shears. These shears are used to cut decorative edges that do not ravel. *Pinking shears* cut a zigzag edge. *Scalloping shears* cut a rounded edge.

 Putting Technology to Use
Have students research the cost of sewing tools on the Internet. Students may want to visit the Web sites at www.a1sew.com, www.sewweb.com, and www.allbrands.com. Have students use presentation software to share their findings with the class.

Marking Tools

Tracing wheels, dressmaker's carbon, tailor's chalk and *tailor's pencil* are all types of marking tools. They are used to transfer pattern markings to fabrics. These markings help you put pattern pieces together for sewing.

When selecting dressmaker's carbon, choose a color close to the color of your fabric. A dark color on a light-colored fabric might show through to the right side.

Pins and Needles

Dressmaker's pins are the basic pins used to pin garment pieces together. These pins are medium in diameter and have sharp points. *Ballpoint pins* are best for pinning knit fabrics. Their rounded points allow them to slide between the yarns of the fabric. (Pins with sharp points could cut the yarns and cause snags.)

Needles can be purchased in a variety of sizes and shapes. They range in size from 1 to 12. Smaller numbers indicate larger needles. Needles called *sharps,* in size 7 or 8, are most often used for hand sewing. They are average in length with small threading eyes.

A *pincushion* is used to hold pins and needles. Pincushions come in many sizes and shapes. Some sewers find a wrist pincushion very convenient to wear while fitting and sewing. Some pincushions have an *emery bag* attached for sharpening pins and needles.

When sewing by hand, you may want to use a *thimble* to prevent the needle from pricking your finger. The thimble should fit snugly on your middle finger. If you are a beginning sewer, you may find a thimble difficult to use. With a little practice, however, you will see how useful it can be.

Pressing Equipment

When sewing a garment, pressing is as important as stitching. Careful construction alone will not result in a well-made garment. "Press as you sew" is a good rule to follow. Each construction line you sew should be pressed before another seam is stitched across it.

Several pieces of pressing equipment are recommended. An *iron* is the most important pressing tool, 20-21. Most irons have a temperature guide that gives the proper heat setting for various types of fabric. A steam iron is more convenient to use for pressing, but a dry iron can also be used.

A damp *pressing cloth* is used to provide steam when using a dry iron. These cloths are made of cheesecloth, organdy, or muslin. A pressing cloth is placed on the fabric to protect the garment from overheating, scorching, and shining whenever an iron is used. It may also be used dry.

The *ironing board* needs to be sturdy, level, and tapered to a narrow width at one end. The ironing board should be covered with a pad and cover. A silicone treated cover will prevent scorching and sticking. Keep the cover clean and smooth. Wrinkles in the ironing board cover can cause wrinkles in a garment.

A *tailor's ham* is a firmly stuffed, oval cushion used to shape curved areas while pressing. It is used for pressing a rounded shape into darts, sleeve caps, and curved seams.

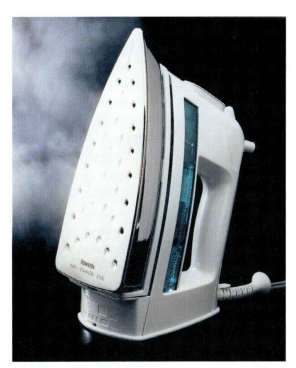

20-21 The necessary pressing equipment begins with a good iron, preferably a steam iron.

> **Note:** Display a variety of marking tools. Discuss recommended uses of each.
>
> **Note:** Display a variety of pins and needles. Point out the recommended uses of each type.
>
> **Resource:** *Sewing Supplies,* Activity F, SAG
>
> **Resource:** *Sewing Equipment,* reproducible master, TR
>
> **Note:** Display a variety of pressing equipment. Discuss the use of each piece and when it is used.

Family Enrichment Activity

Have students make a list of small equipment that would be desirable in a sewing kit and attach it to the lid of a sturdy box. Students should discuss the list with family members, and have them help collect tools that are available in the home. Needed equipment can be added when possible. Students can then store the box in a safe, accessible place for use by family members.

Enrich: Have the students collect advertisements of sewing machines, or have them visit a sewing machine showroom. Compare features and discuss costs of various models.

Note: Use a sewing machine to demonstrate a properly balanced row of stitching. As you sew, loosen and tighten the tension to demonstrate how these affect the finished row of stitching.

Activity: Have the students match the parts of the sewing machine with the model used in the class.

The Sewing Machine

The sewing machine is a complex piece of equipment. Its complexity calls for skilled use on the part of the operator. Learning how to operate a sewing machine will be easier if you have a basic understanding of how the machine works. Then knowing how to care for the sewing machine will assure its smooth and continued operation.

How a Sewing Machine Works

There are many different brands and models of sewing machines, but they all operate basically the same way. The basic parts of a sewing machine are shown in 20-22. The job of the sewing machine is to hold pieces of fabric together with a **lockstitch**. This stitch uses thread from both the upper and lower parts of the machine. When stitches are made, the thread from the upper part of the machine is carried by way of the needle down to pick up the lower thread. The lower thread comes from the **bobbin**. The two threads lock in the middle of the fabric layers to make a secure stitch.

A knee or foot control sends power to the machine when pressure is applied. The **presser foot** holds the fabric in place as the machine stitches. The **feed dogs** are two small rows of teeth that move the fabric forward under the presser foot. Stitches are made when power is applied.

Two **thread-tension regulators** are found on the sewing machine. The tension or pull between the upper and lower threads must be balanced for a proper stitch to form. A perfectly balanced stitch looks the same on both the top and bottom of the fabric. Generally, any adjustment can be made with the upper tension regulator that applies tension to the upper thread. The instruction manual with your machine will show you how to adjust the tension.

Two basic types of sewing machines are in use today—mechanical and computerized machines. With mechanical machines, you

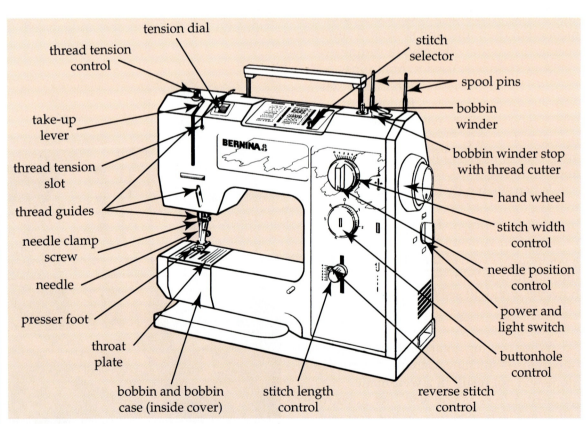

20-22 Knowing the names of the parts of the sewing machine is a first step in learning how to operate it.

Across the Curriculum

History. Have students prepare a report on Elias Howe, his struggle to patent the sewing machine, and its impact on American industry.

dial the stitch you want and adjust the length, width, and tension. With computerized machines, the preferred length, width, and tension are preprogrammed for you. However, you can change the settings and override the computer. Some computerized machines have hundreds of decorative and special stitches programmed into them. Most feature simple, one-step buttonhole operations.

Threading the Machine

Different sewing machine models thread differently. A diagram in your instruction manual will show how to thread your machine.

While threading does vary from one machine to another, the basic steps are the same. When threading the upper part of the machine, the thread is guided from the spool pin through the upper tension control. From there the thread goes to a take-up lever and down to the needle. Several thread guides hold and guide the thread. The thread guide nearest the needle is always placed on the side from which the needle is threaded.

Threading the lower part of the machine begins with threading the bobbin. Your instruction manual will tell you how to do this. The bobbin is then placed in the bobbin case. The bobbin thread must always be brought up through the needle hole before beginning to sew. If the thread is not pulled up, a knot will form as the first stitch is attempted.

Types of Stitches

Almost all sewing machines make at least two basic types of stitches. A *straight stitch* is a lockstitch used for holding layers of fabric together. A *zigzag stitch* is a sideways stitch. Most sewing machines can make a variety of stitches in addition to these basic stitches.

The straight stitch is the most frequently used stitch. The stitch length can be adjusted to correspond with the purpose of the stitch. A typical stitch length is 10 to 15 stitches per inch. A stitch length of six stitches per inch can be used for machine basting to temporarily hold fabric in place. A length of 18 to 20 stitches per inch might be used to reinforce garment areas that receive a lot of stress.

The zigzag stitch is often used to overcast seam edges that tend to ravel. A short zigzag stitch is used for buttonholes. A variation of the zigzag stitch is also used to sew stretch-knit fabrics. This allows seams to give slightly with the fabric. The zigzag stitch can be adjusted by using the stitch-length and stitch-width regulators.

Caring for the Machine

A sewing machine is an expensive piece of sewing equipment that requires special care. Regular cleaning will result in fewer machine problems. Your instruction manual will have step-by-step directions for cleaning your machine.

Cleaning with a soft cloth and small brush is a must. Use a small brush to remove lint from the bobbin case and under the feed dogs.

Always use the correct type of needle for your machine and the right size for your fabric. Your instruction manual will have guidelines for selecting the correct needle. Change the needle after every three garments sewn or 15 hours of sewing. Needles dull easily and can damage both your fabric and your machine. Also replace needles if they become bent or nicked.

Sewing machines should be oiled periodically. Your instruction manual will tell you how often to oil your machine. It will also show where oil should be applied. After oiling your machine, be sure to wipe away any excess oil. Then sew on a scrap of cloth to remove any remaining oil before sewing your good fabric.

The Serger

Sergers are high-speed sewing machines that can stitch, trim, and finish seams in one simple step, 20-23. They were originally designed for the ready-to-wear industry. Now they are available for home use.

> **Note:** Incorrect threading is often the major problem students have when using a sewing machine.
>
> **Note:** Demonstrate the basic types of stitches available on the classroom sewing machine. Vary stitch width and length so the students can see what is available.
>
> **Note:** Demonstrate step-by-step directions for cleaning the sewing machine and changing the needle.
>
> **Resource:** Sewing Machine Features, reproducible master, TR

Putting Technology to Use

Have students use the Internet to research current information on sergers. Ask students to include names of manufacturers, pricing information, and practical uses for sergers. Have students use drawing and word processing software to create informational posters. Hang the posters around the classroom.

Activity:
Have the students check the seams on ready-to-wear garments. Can they tell how seams were constructed at the factory? Compare those seams to home-sewn garment seams.

Enrich:
Demonstrate garment construction of a small project on a conventional and serger machine. Have the students compare ease of use and the appearance of the finished projects.

Discuss:
Relate these safety tips to the ones discussed in Chapter 13.

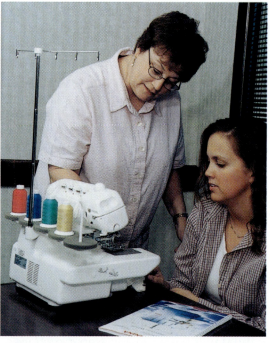

20-23 Learning to use the serger can save you time as you create your own unique fashions.

The home sewer can obtain professional results by using a serger. The outer edges of garments can be finished without the need for facings, ribbings, or bands. Narrow or rolled hems can be made, such as those found on scarves or tablecloths. Sergers can also produce a blind hemming stitch. Stretch fabrics are easily sewn with a serger. Decorative stitching is popular for decorating T-shirts, sweatshirts, and other similar garments.

Sergers use two, three, four, or five threads and one or two needles. Sergers do not have bobbins. Instead they have one to three **loopers,** both upper and lower. The needle threads intertwine with the looper threads to form stitches. Sergers also have upper and lower knives that trim the seam allowance before the seam is finished.

Though sergers are fast and perform many functions, they cannot replace a conventional sewing machine. A conventional sewing machine is needed for topstitching and buttonholes. Some people also prefer to insert zippers with a conventional machine.

Safety with Sewing Tools

Safety is an important consideration in everything you do. Sewing and pressing are no exceptions. Certain precautions should always be followed to keep the sewing area safe for you and others. Basic safety steps include the following:

- Read all instructions before using any tool.
- Use each tool only for its intended purpose.
- Never leave tools unattended when others are around. Always put tools away when they are not in use.
- Closely supervise any children or pets in the area. You are working with tools, not toys.

The misuse or careless use of tools can lead to injuries. Irons can cause fires and burns. Scissors, pins, and other common tools can cause cuts and wounds. When using electricity, electric shock is always a possibility. In addition, appliance cords can cause people to trip and fall. To prevent anyone from being harmed in your sewing area, follow the safety recommendations in 20-24.

Career Preparation Activity

A Sewing-Related Career, reproducible master, TR. Students are asked to read an ad that might appear in a local newspaper for a fabric salesclerk. They are asked to write a letter responding to the ad based on what they have learned in this chapter.

Topic 20-4 Sewing Equipment 589

Preventing Sewing Area Hazards

Fires and Burns	• Fill a steam iron with water while unplugged. Let a hot iron cool before emptying it. • Keep your hands and face, especially your eyes, away from steam and heated water. • Rest a hot iron on its heel between uses, and turn it off during periods of nonuse. • Do not allow the electrical cord or any other item to rest against the iron's hot surface. • Let the iron cool before returning it to storage.
Cuts and Wounds	• Keep the blades of scissors and shears closed when not in use. • Keep fingers away from moving needles and serger cutting blades while sewing. • Use rotary cutters on an appropriate cutting mat, always cutting away from the body. • Avoid placing pins and other tools in your mouth. • Immediately pick up pins and tools that fall to the floor. • Put tools away that are not being used. • Do not point sharp tools at others. When passing a sharp tool to another person, carefully grasp the dangerous end of the tool so the other person can grasp the handle or blunt end.
Electric Shock	• Make sure the switch of an electrical appliance is in the *off* position before connecting it to, or disconnecting it from, the outlet. • Do not operate an appliance with a damaged electrical cord. • Do not handle electrical appliances with hands that are wet or immersed in any solution. • Unplug an appliance by grasping the plug, not yanking the cord.
Trips and Falls	• Keep paths free of electrical cords. • Unplug and roll up the cord of any appliance not in use.

20-24 Work to keep your sewing area safe by staying aware of potential hazards and removing them.

Check It Out!

1. Explain how the use of shears differs from the use of scissors.
2. True or false. A size 5 needle will be larger than a size 10 needle.
3. What is the "press as you sew" rule?
4. If a machine stitch does not look the same on both the top and bottom of the fabric, what needs to be adjusted?
5. Give two uses for the zigzag stitch.
6. What three functions can sergers perform in one fast operation?
7. State four safety hazards that can take place in a sewing area.

Check It Out! (Answers)

1. Shears are used to cut pattern pieces from fabric. Scissors are used for trimming, grading, and clipping seams and for snipping threads.
2. true
3. Each construction line you sew should be pressed before another seam is stitched across it.
4. the upper tension regulator
5. (Give two:) to overcast seam edges, for buttonholes, to sew stretch knits
6. stitch, trim, finish
7. (State four:) fires, burns, cuts, wounds, electric shock, trips, falls

Discuss:
Have students give examples of supplies that should be kept in a first aid kit for the sewing area.

Discuss:
Ms. Arenas points out a number of ways Simplicity Pattern Company is trying to appeal to the teen market. Have students identify what this company is doing, and have them react to these ideas. What styles are especially popular in your region of the country? Are these styles available in patterns?

Discuss:
Ask students how they can make their sewing projects look less homemade. Have students work in groups to brainstorm ideas. Also have them come up with ways to respond to possible negative comments people might make about the clothes students sew themselves. These comments should be ones that show pride in being able to sew.

TEENS ARE CONCERNED ABOUT…

The Fashion Appeal of Sewing Patterns

Teens are very fashion conscious. They want clothes that are in style. Some teens are concerned that clothes they sew themselves will have a homemade look. Elizabeth Arenas, Merchandising and Catalog Coordinator for the Simplicity Pattern Company, is aware of this concern. She addressed this topic in a recent interview.

Q: *What challenges does your company face in designing patterns that appeal to the teen market?*

A: We face a wide range of challenges when designing for the teen/juniors market. That market is "trend" driven and the timeliness of a design is key for success and growth. The teen market is based on and inspired by an individualistic attitude and personal style. It is a challenge to research and source this ever-changing market to ensure that we have the right design in the catalog at the right time.

Not only are we in competition with other pattern companies, but also with the apparel market that makes buying a trendy garment so easy and inexpensive. With trends changing so quickly, we provide pattern designs that help teens keep pace with fashion trends.

Q: *What kinds of sewing projects and garments do teens find most appealing to make?*

A: Teens love to sew all the hot items in the tops, bottoms, dresses, and jackets categories as well as hip new bags and accessories. They also enjoy sewing board shorts, pajamas, loungewear, and prom dresses.

Q: *How does your company encourage teens to sew?*

A: Our company encourages teens to sew in a variety of ways.

- **Catalog presentation**—We feel that it is important to make looking through the catalog enjoyable and stimulating. We have a section entitled "Grooves"—special sizing for juniors that we specifically merchandise for teens. The presentation is geared toward the teen market using trendy designs styled with hip accessories, bright colors, and great fabrics on young, energetic models.
- **Teacher's kit**—Simplicity offers teacher's kits, which include patterns to students at a discounted price, to schools around the country.
- **Design competition**—Simplicity has an annual design competition with a leading university in which we challenge students to design a pattern for our customers that will appear in a future catalog.
- **Education and career**—We invite schools to take tours of our company and facilities, and we offer discussions on career opportunities. We participate in annual school and teacher meetings to get feedback and communicate our commitment to education.

Q: *Why does your company feel that sewing is a skill necessary in the twenty-first century?*

A: As times have changed, sewing is no longer a necessity or way of life, but a choice for a lifelong skill and hobby. The benefits gained from the ability to create are rewarding and inspiring. Sewing is a skill that requires concentration, patience, and time. The sense of accomplishment and pride felt when a project is completed is so satisfying.

Chapter Review

Summary

Knowledge of fabrics—their fiber content, construction, and finishes—will help you select the right fabric for your project. This knowledge will also help you when purchasing ready-to-wear garments and other fabrics for your home.

Before you can select a pattern, you must determine your figure type and size. Taking accurate body measurements is the first step. Your height and body proportions determine your figure type. Match your measurements to those listed for your figure type. Then select a pattern appropriate for your skill level. You will also want to consider your wardrobe needs and your activities when choosing a pattern.

After choosing a pattern, fabric and notions can be selected. The pattern envelope will list recommended fabrics as well as the notions needed to complete the project. Some fabrics are more difficult to sew than others. Some fabrics can be laundered and others must be dry-cleaned. These are some of the factors that need to be considered when selecting a fabric.

Some basic pieces of equipment are needed for sewing. Measuring, cutting, and marking tools are needed, as well as pins, needles, and pressing equipment. The sewing machine is the most important piece of equipment and the most expensive. Learn how the sewing machine operates. Then give the sewing machine the proper care to keep it running smoothly. As you gain sewing experience, you may decide a serger would be useful to you. No matter what sewing tools you use, always use them safely.

Think About It!

1. How can knowledge about fibers and fabrics help the person who sews? How can the same knowledge help someone who does not sew?
2. Which fabric finishes would you like applied to the garments you wear? Which finishes would you like applied to the fabrics you use in your home? Explain your answers.
3. What criteria would you consider when selecting a pattern for yourself? Since trade-offs sometimes have to be made, list the criteria in order of priority.
4. Why is it best *not* to select your pattern size solely by the size of your ready-to-wear clothes?
5. Why is the pattern envelope an important resource for the person who sews?
6. In what careers would sewing skills be particularly helpful? somewhat helpful?
7. List some of the advantages of sewing your own clothes. Name some disadvantages.
8. What do you see as the future for home sewing? How have changes in society impacted the home sewing industry?
9. What can you do to keep your sewing area safer?

Try It Out!

1. Collect samples of many fabrics. Identify and label how each fabric was constructed. Also label which fabrics were dyed and which ones were printed.
2. From your collection of fabrics, unravel some of the samples. Identify the types of yarns used.

Resource:
PowerZone Challenge CD. Have students play the chapter review game to reinforce text content.

3. Cut out eight advertisements of textile products from newspapers, magazines, or catalogs. Circle the fiber content in each ad. List two reasons you think a particular fiber or fiber blend was used for each product. Discuss your advertisements with the class.
4. At fabric shops, look through different brands of pattern catalogs. Become familiar with the pattern sections and the information given in the catalogs. Find one pattern that would be a good sewing project for you. Look at the fabrics recommended for the pattern and read the fabric care labels.
5. Look through magazines or department store catalogs. Find five examples of clothing or home furnishings that have been treated with a special finish.
6. Practice your measuring skills with two classmates. Each person is to be measured by the other two people in the group. If the two measurements differ, determine why and remeasure. Record each person's measurements on a chart.
7. At a fabric shop, identify several kinds of sewing equipment. In class, explain or demonstrate how each piece of equipment (if available) is used in sewing.
8. Invite a sewing machine salesperson to bring a portable model of the latest sewing machine to class and demonstrate its features.
9. Sew a practice seam using a serger. If possible, construct a simple garment using a serger.

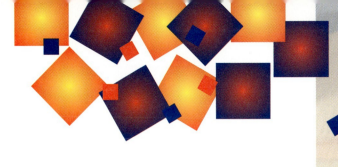

Chapter 21
The First Steps Before Sewing

Careers

These careers relate to the topics in this chapter:
- fabric salesperson
- seamstress
- pattern maker or grader
- fashion designer

As you study this chapter, see if you can think of others.

Topics

21-1 Begin with the Pattern
21-2 Prepare the Fabric
21-3 Pattern Layout, Cutting, and Marking

Introductory Activities

1. Discuss the different connotations of "homemade" and "custom-made" clothes. Have students find out some recent trends in home sewing.
2. Invite a person who sews professionally to explain the importance of becoming familiar with the pattern and instructions, preparing the fabric properly, pattern layout, cutting and marking before beginning to sew.

Topic 21-1

Begin with the Pattern
 I. The Pattern Guide Sheet
   A. Understanding Pattern Symbols
      1. Cutting Lines
      2. Stitching Lines
      3. Grainline Arrows
      4. Adjustment Lines
   B. Altering Your Pattern
   C. Adjusting Pattern Length
   D. Adjusting Pattern Width

Topic 21-2

Prepare the Fabric
 I. Preshrinking and Pressing
 II. Check the Grain
   A. Straighten the Grain

Topic 21-3

Pattern Layout, Cutting, and Marking
 I. The Pattern Layout
   A. Folding the Fabric
   B. Placing Pattern Pieces
   C. Working with Special Fabrics
 II. Pinning
 III. Cutting the Fabric
 IV. Marking the Fabric
   A. Using Dressmaker's Carbon
   B. Using Tailor's Chalk or Pencil

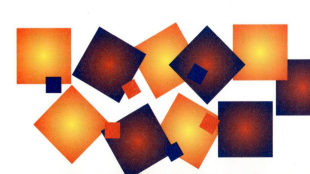

Discuss:
A seamstress frequently works at home. What would be the advantages and disadvantages of this arrangement?

Vocabulary:
Place a pattern piece on the bulletin board. Identify Topic 21-1 terms on the pattern piece.

Note:
Advise students to write their names on their guide sheets and all pattern pieces for easy identification.

Topic 21-1
Begin with the Pattern

Objectives
After studying this topic, you will be able to:
- explain the meaning of pattern symbols.
- adjust pattern length and width.

Topic Terms
pattern guide sheet
cutting line
notch
dot
multisize pattern
stitching line
seam allowance
grainline arrow
adjustment lines
alteration

21-1 The pattern guide sheet is somewhat like a road map. If you refer to it regularly, you can reach your destination.

Like other projects that you complete yourself, sewing projects require instructions. That is why you need a pattern. Sewing patterns not only include the pattern pieces, but they also include a detailed set of instructions. These instructions will tell you how to proceed from beginning to end. Most of the instructions are found on the pattern guide sheet.

The Pattern Guide Sheet

Every pattern has a set of instructions called the **pattern guide sheet.** See 21-1. The guide sheet has step-by-step directions that will lead you through each phase of your sewing project. It also contains other types of information you will find helpful. Read and study the guide sheet before beginning your project.

Most pattern guide sheets include the following information:
- front and back views of each garment
- line drawings of the pattern pieces
- explanations of marking symbols found on pattern pieces
- explanations of terms used in the sewing directions
- suggested ways to transfer pattern markings to fabric
- ways to adjust the pattern for fit
- sewing directions
- layout directions for each garment and view

Understanding Pattern Symbols

Each pattern piece contains a pattern number, size, view number, piece name, and identification letter. The pattern guide sheet tells you which pattern pieces will be needed for the view you are making. From the pattern envelope, remove the pattern pieces you will need. If the pieces are wrinkled, press them with a warm, dry iron.

You will notice the pattern pieces contain many lines, terms, and symbols. It is important you know what these mean. Many of the symbols will be used when you lay the pattern pieces on the fabric. Others will be used when you sew the pieces together.

Cutting Lines
The **cutting line** is indicated with a bold line. On this line you will see many diamond-shaped symbols. These are called **notches.** There may be single notches, double notches, and even triple notches. Cut precisely around them. You will match these notches when you sew the pieces together. **Dots** are also used for matching seams and other construction details.

Family Enrichment Activity
Have students ask their parents about how family members in generations before them made patterns. Were commercial patterns available, or did they make their own? What did they use for guides if they made their own? How did garment styles differ before commercial patterns were available? Have students write their answers to contribute during a circular discussion.

Topic 21-1 Begin with the Pattern

Many patterns available today are multisize. **Multisize patterns** contain three or four sizes on one tissue pattern. You cut along the appropriate line for your figure size. Suppose your waist is a smaller size than your hips. You can change cutting lines where your figure changes. There is another advantage in using multisize patterns for separates. If you are one size on the bottom and another size on top, you will not need to buy two patterns.

Stitching Lines

The broken line just inside the cutting line is the **stitching line,** or seamline. Sometimes arrows will be found on the stitching lines. Sewing in the direction of the arrows will make the fabric less likely to stretch out of shape. The space between the cutting line and the stitching line is called the **seam allowance.** It is generally ⅝-inch wide.

Single-size patterns show the stitching line, but multisize patterns do not. However, the standard seam allowance is included in a pattern, even when stitching lines are not shown. Figure 21-2 shows a single-size pattern with the most common pattern symbols, including a stitching line.

Grainline Arrows

A **grainline arrow** indicates the direction a pattern piece should be placed on the fabric. Usually, this arrow will be parallel with the lengthwise fabric grain. Sometimes arrows point to the edge of a pattern piece. This indicates the piece must be placed on a fold of the fabric.

Adjustment Lines

Lines that indicate where to shorten or lengthen a pattern piece are called **adjustment lines.** These are usually two parallel lines that extend across the pattern piece. Some pattern pieces will tell you to adjust the length at the hemline.

Altering Your Pattern

How should a garment fit? A well-fitted garment is one that is comfortable to wear and well-proportioned to your body. The

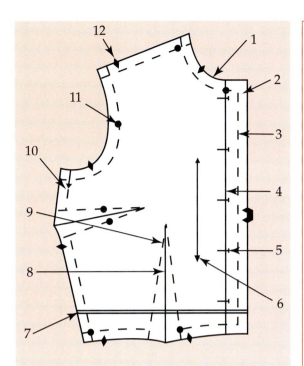

1. cutting line
2. seam allowance
3. stitching line
4. center front
5. buttonhole placement
6. grainline
7. adjustment lines
8. fold line for dart
9. dart stitching line
10. direction for stitching
11. dot
12. notch

21-2 A knowledge of pattern symbols is important to successful sewing.

garment is neither too big nor too small. It conforms to the body contours. It does not bind, pull, sag, wrinkle, or hang unevenly. Proper fit is one of the keys to successful sewing, 21-3.

Patterns cannot be made to fit every person perfectly. **Alterations** are changes to the size of a pattern or garment. Carefully selecting a pattern according to your body measurements and figure type will reduce the need for alterations.

Alterations should be made on pattern pieces before they are laid out on the fabric. To see how well your pattern fits you, you can *pin fit* the pattern. To do this, pin the darts closed. Then pin the pattern pieces together at the seamlines and carefully try on the pattern. Pin the center front and back to your clothing. Then check

Note: Display standard and multisize pattern pieces. Point out the similarities and differences. Also discuss the advantages and disadvantages of each type of pattern.

Resource: Pattern Symbols, Activity A, SAG

Resource: Patterns from Yesteryear…We've Come a Long Way! reproducible master, TR

Note: Demonstrate how to pin fit a pattern.

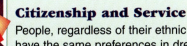

Citizenship and Service

People, regardless of their ethnic backgrounds, have many similarities. To illustrate that people throughout the world often have the same preferences in dress, highlight the fact that many patterns include languages from different countries. Have students choose a pattern. Based on the languages featured on the pattern envelope, ask students to identify countries in which this pattern might be used. Discuss pattern styles that are shared around the world.

Note: Demonstrate how to alter pattern length.

Note: Demonstrate how to alter pattern width.

21-3 You will want the finished garment to fit well after you have put time and effort into constructing it.

sleeve, skirt, and pant lengths. You can also check the back and front waist lengths. Check the widths of various pattern pieces, too. Note changes that need to be made.

If you are using a multisize pattern, bust, waist, and hip alterations are easily made. At the point where your size changes, simply draw tapering lines to connect one size to the other.

Adjusting Pattern Length

Adjusting length is one of the most common and least difficult alterations to make. For example, you may be long waisted or short waisted. You may have short arms or long arms. Often length must be adjusted in more than one area of the pattern.

Alterations are made where they will not interfere with the lines of the garment. For instance, a flared skirt would be lengthened at the hemline. Straight skirts or pants would be lengthened between the hipline and hemline.

To shorten a pattern piece, make a fold in the pattern piece between the adjustment lines. The fold should be half the amount to be shortened. Measure the fold to see that it is even. Then tape it in place.

To lengthen a pattern piece, cut between the adjustment lines. Place a piece of paper under the two pattern pieces. Measure the needed distance between the lines. Tape the pattern to the paper. Remeasure the distance to check your accuracy. See 21-4.

Adjusting Pattern Width

Adjusting the width of pattern pieces is more difficult than adjusting the length. Width adjustments may need to be made in the sleeve, waist, hips, or thighs. These adjustments should be made in both front and back pieces.

Waistline alterations in pants and skirts are made at the side seams. See 21-5. To increase the waistline, tape a strip of paper along the side edges of the front and back pattern pieces. Measure from the side cutting line at the waist edge of the front pattern piece. The width added to this pattern piece should be one-fourth of the total waistline increase. (One-fourth of the increase times

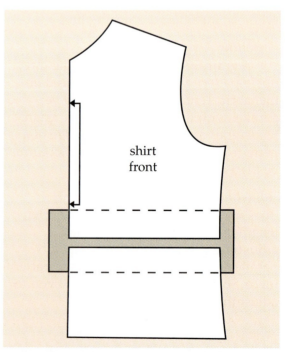

21-4 To lengthen a pattern piece, cut between the adjustment lines. Separate the two pattern sections the amount that needs to be added.

Career Preparation Activity

Applying Sewing Skills, reproducible master, TR. Students are asked to read about a sewing-related career opportunity. They are then to consider the job description and write a paragraph explaining why or why not it would not be a good choice for various individuals described.

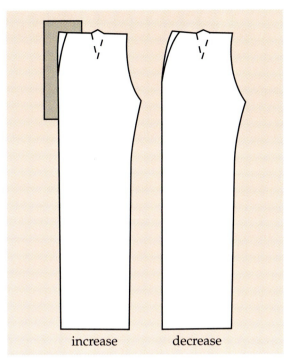

21-5 To increase or decrease the width of the waist, measure in or out one-fourth of the needed amount at the side waistline edge. Redraw the cutting lines, tapering to the hipline.

needed fullness is added or removed along the length of the side seams. Taking bigger or smaller darts is another way to adjust waistline width.

> **Check It Out!**
> 1. True or false. The pattern guide sheet includes directions for taking your measurements.
> 2. What pattern symbols are used to match garment pieces when sewing?
> 3. True or false. To shorten a pattern, make a fold that is half the total amount to be shortened.
> 4. True or false. To widen a pattern piece, add half of the total alteration needed to the front side seam.

> **Check It Out! (Answers)**
> 1. false
> 2. notches and dots
> 3. true
> 4. false

four edges—each edge at both side seams—equals the total increase.) Make a dot at the extended point and redraw the cutting line, tapering to the hipline. Do the same with the back pattern piece.

To decrease the waistline, measure in from the cutting line one-fourth of the total amount to be removed. Redraw the cutting line, tapering to the hipline. If there is a waistband, lengthen or shorten it the same amount as the total waist adjustment.

Making adjustments in multisize patterns is easier. Wherever the adjustment is needed, you will simply cut on the cutting lines for one of the other sizes. For instance, if you need to increase the waistline, gradually angle as you cut to the line for the next larger size.

If a garment is too small for the hips, wrinkling and pulling will occur around the hipline. If a pants or skirt pattern is too large, there will be extra fullness around the hipline. Hipline width is altered the same as waistline width. One-fourth the

Resource:
Practicing Pattern Alterations, reproducible master, TR

Resource:
Preshrinking the Fabric, reproducible master, TR

Note:
Display fabric that is badly off grain. Discuss what might happen to a finished garment made from this fabric.

Discuss:
How can you tell if a ready-to-wear garment is off grain?

Topic 21-2
Prepare the Fabric

Objectives
After studying this topic, you will be able to
- preshrink and press fabric.
- check and straighten fabric grain.

Topic Term
preshrinking

The planning and preparing you do before sewing will help you avoid mistakes and frustrations as you sew. Fabric preparations include preshrinking, pressing, and checking the grain. Overlooking these steps could result in poor fit of a garment.

Preshrinking and Pressing

Allowing fabric to shrink before cutting out garment pieces is called **preshrinking**. If you do not preshrink your fabric, it may shrink after the garment is constructed and laundered. The garment may then become too tight or too short to wear.

Some fabrics are preshrunk by the manufacturer. When you buy fabric, information printed on the end of the bolt will indicate this. If the fabric has not been preshrunk, you can do this yourself.

To preshrink fabric, follow the care instructions for the fabric, 21-6. If the instructions say to machine wash and dry the fabric, do so. Detergent is not needed. If the garment will be hand washed or dry-cleaned, preshrink the fabric using the appropriate method.

If the fabric needs pressing, press it before you lay out the pattern pieces. Accurate cutting and marking is impossible on wrinkled fabric. If the center fold crease is difficult to remove, a damp pressing cloth or steam iron may be helpful.

21-6 Check the label on the end of the fabric bolt for care instructions.

Check the Grain

Correct fabric grain is vital to the appearance and wear of a garment. Fabric is *on grain* when crosswise and lengthwise yarns are at perfect right angles to each other. When a fabric is *off grain*, the yarns are not at right angles. Sometimes fabrics become distorted during the finishing processes. Sometimes they are twisted when they are rolled onto bolts.

An off-grain fabric will be difficult to handle. It will not lie flat on the table. The finished garment may twist, pull to one side, and hang unevenly.

To check the fabric grain, you must first straighten the cut end of the fabric. To do this, cut along a filling yarn that goes completely across one end of the fabric. If you cannot see the yarns, clip the selvage edge of the fabric. Then locate a crosswise yarn and pull it slowly. With your other hand, gently push the fabric along the pulled yarn until the fabric puckers. Cut along this puckered line the entire width of the fabric, as shown in 21-7. If the yarn breaks while pulling, cut to where the yarn has broken. Locate the same crosswise yarn and repeat the process.

Across the Curriculum

English. Have students write short papers explaining how the fabric for their projects should be preshrunk. Have them also write about what the results would be if they did not preshrink the fabrics.

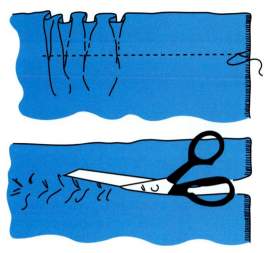

21-7 A crosswise yarn can be pulled to find the straight crosswise grain. Cutting along this line will allow you to straighten the cut end of the fabric.

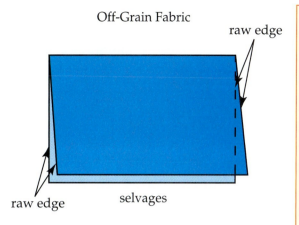

21-8 This fabric is off grain because the cut edges are not even and the corners do not match.

Once the cut end is straightened, you can proceed with checking the grain. Lay the fabric on a large, flat surface. Fold the fabric lengthwise. If the fabric is on grain, it will lie flat on the table. The two selvages will align and the cut edge will be even, 21-8. If the fabric will not lie flat, it is off grain.

Straighten the Grain

In many cases, fabric grain can be straightened. To straighten the grain, have someone hold both corners at one end of the fabric while you hold the opposite corners. Then pull on the short corners only, pulling on the bias. See 21-9. Refold the fabric and check to see if the grain has shifted enough so the corners and selvages align. The result should be grain-perfect fabric ready for pattern layout.

Sometimes the grain cannot be straightened. This can happen if fabrics have finishes applied after they are woven. The finishing process can set the fabric so the yarns cannot be moved. If this is the case, you will have to use the fabric as it is.

> **Note:**
> Demonstrate how to straighten an off-grain fabric.
>
> **Resource:**
> *Fabric Grain,* Activity B, SAG
>
> **Resource:**
> *Straightening Fabric,* reproducible master, TR

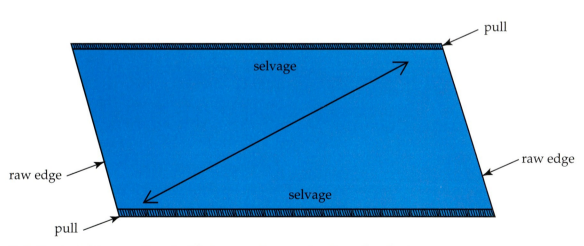

21-9 To straighten an off-grain fabric, open it up and pull on the short corners.

Putting Technology to Use

Have students use word processing or drawing software and a color printer to create a bulletin board explaining how to check and straighten fabric grain. Students should obtain several fabric samples, including some that are off grain, and label them. They may also want to create diagrams explaining how to straighten the grain. Have students print the labels and diagrams and include them on the bulletin board.

Note:
Demonstrate laying out a pattern on fabric.

Discuss:
Why is it a good idea to refold the fabric so the right sides are together?

Resource:
Pattern Layout: Don't Let It Puzzle You, reproducible master, TR

Check It Out!
1. Why is it important to preshrink your fabric?
2. What might happen to a finished garment if the fabric is cut when it is off grain?
3. How can fabric be checked to determine if it is on grain?

Check It Out! (Answers)
1. to prevent shrinking after the garment is constructed and laundered, which could cause it to become too tight or too short to wear
2. The finished garment may twist, pull to one side, and hang unevenly.
3. Once the cut end of the fabric is straightened, fold the fabric lengthwise. If the fabric is on grain, the two selvages will match and the cut edges will be even. The fabric should lie flat.

Topic 21-3
Pattern Layout, Cutting, and Marking

Objectives
After studying this topic, you will be able to
- choose the appropriate cutting layout.
- pin the pattern pieces to the fabric correctly.
- cut the fabric and transfer pattern markings.

Topic Terms
cutting layout
directional fabric

After your pattern and fabric are prepared, you are ready to lay out your pattern. For this step, you will again need to refer to your pattern guide sheet.

The Pattern Layout

The pattern guide sheet shows many cutting layouts, 21-10. A **cutting layout** is a drawing that shows how to fold fabric and place pattern pieces for cutting. Layouts are given for different garments, views, sizes, and fabric widths. Different layouts are also given for fabrics with a nap. You will need to find the layout for the pattern version you are making. Then look for your size and your fabric width. Circle the layout you will be using. This will help you find your layout quickly each time you need to refer to it.

Folding the Fabric

Place your fabric on a smooth table or fabric cutting board. If the fabric is longer than the table, let one end of the fabric rest in a chair. This prevents the fabric from stretching.

Fold your fabric according to the instructions given for your layout. Fabric is usually folded with the right sides together.

CARDIGAN
use pieces 1 thru 8

58" 60" (150cm) fabric with nap
size extra-small

sizes small, medium

sizes large, extra-large

Interfacing
use pieces 4, 5

21" thru 25"
(53cm thru 64cm)
all sizes

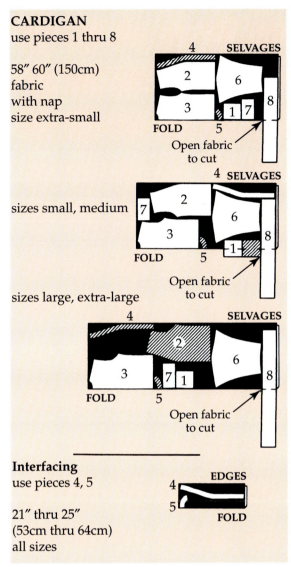

21-10 Several cutting layouts will be shown on the pattern guide sheet.

The guide sheet may tell you to use a lengthwise fold or a crosswise fold. A *lengthwise fold* brings the two selvages together. A *crosswise fold* brings the two cut edges together. Sometimes a *doublefold* is used, which brings each selvage edge toward the center. Measure to be sure you fold the fabric the same amount for the entire length of the fabric, 21-11. Watch for layout notes, such as the words *selvage, single thickness,* and *double thickness.*

Placing Pattern Pieces

Place pattern pieces on the fabric as pictured in the pattern layout. Most pattern pieces are placed on the fabric with the printed side up. Pattern pieces to be placed with the printed side down will appear shaded on the guide sheet.

Lay all pattern pieces on the fabric before pinning any of them in place. See 21-12. This will allow you to make sure they all fit on the fabric.

Working with Special Fabrics

Plaid, striped, and checked fabrics may require special layouts. These designs should be matched at seamlines and front openings to form a continuous design around the body. Having some sewing experience will better prepare you to work with these fabrics. They are not recommended for beginners.

Fabrics with nap, pile, texture, border prints, and one-way designs are called

Resource:
Pattern Layout, Activity C, SAG

Note:
Display even and uneven plaids, prints, and directional fabrics. Discuss why these fabrics are more challenging for sewers.

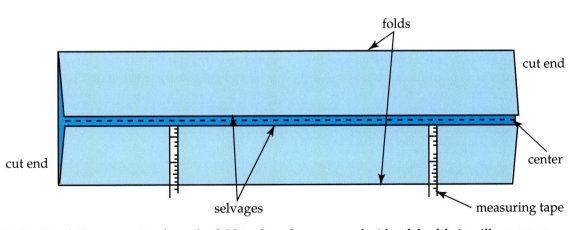

21-11 Carefully measuring from the fold to the selvage on each side of the fabric will ensure an accurate doublefold.

Across the Curriculum

English/computer science. Have students research the use of CAD software in the design and production of patterns. Ask students to write reports and share their findings with the class.

> **Note:**
> Show the class how napped fabrics, such as corduroy and velvet, appear to be different colors when held in different ways. Discuss how they should be handled when laying out pattern pieces.
>
> **Note:**
> Demonstrate the pinning of pattern pieces on the grainline and on the fold.
>
> **Note:**
> Demonstrate the placement of pattern pieces to eliminate fabric waste.
>
> **Discuss:**
> Why should notches be cut outward?

21-12 Place all of the pattern pieces on the fabric before you begin pinning.

21-13 Each point of the grainline arrow should measure the same distance to the selvage.

directional fabrics. They have up and down directions. They must be cut with all pattern pieces in the same direction. Extra fabric may be needed to allow for this layout. On the back of the pattern envelope, select the amount of fabric from the column marked "With Nap."

Pinning

Before pinning the pattern pieces to the fabric, they must be placed on the fabric grain. To do this, pin one end of the grainline arrow to the fabric to hold it in place. Measure from the pinned end of the arrow to the fabric selvage. Then measure from the other end of the grainline arrow to the selvage. See 21-13. If the measurements are not the same, adjust them so the grainline arrow is a uniform distance from the selvage edge. Then pin the pattern piece in place.

Gently smooth the pattern from the grainline. Finish pinning by placing pins about six inches apart along the stitching lines. Pin at right angles to the pattern edges. Pin diagonally in corners. Keep pins off cutting lines.

Watch for pattern pieces that must be placed on the fold of the fabric. Pin the fold edge of the pattern piece along the fold first. You will never cut the edge of a fold. Then smooth out the pattern and pin the remaining edges to the fabric.

After pinning each pattern piece, compare your work with the layout guide. You want your pattern layout to be accurate before you start to cut.

Cutting the Fabric

Bent-handle shears are recommended for cutting out pattern pieces. The design allows the blade to rest flat on the table. Cutting fabric flat on the table helps you to cut exactly along the cutting lines.

Find the cutting line on your pattern piece that you will cut. Some patterns have specific cutting lines that are easy to follow. When using multisized patterns, you will notice several lines on which you can cut. Be careful to choose the line that reflects your size.

For a smooth, even cut, do not close the blades completely. Cut with long, even strokes. Remember to cut pattern notches outward. For double and triple notches, cut straight across the top of the notches.

As you cut, walk around the table instead of pulling the fabric toward you. The

FCCLA Activity
Make a banner. Attach a banner-size piece of newsprint to a bulletin board. Project the FCCLA logo on it using an opaque projector. Trace it to make a pattern. Place the pattern on white fabric, such as a sheet, and cut it out. Using a tracing wheel and carbon paper, mark the details. Remove the pattern and add color with fabric paint over the marked lines. Hang the banner in the back of a showcase when FCCLA activities are publicized.

fabric should remain flat until all pattern pieces have been cut out. Leave pattern pieces pinned to the fabric after cutting so pattern markings can be transferred.

Marking the Fabric

Markings on the pattern guide you in putting the garment together. Markings for center front, center back, darts, buttons, buttonholes, dots, and pockets all need to be transferred to the fabric. Seamlines do not need to be marked, since a ⅝-inch seam is presumed. You can sew straight, even seams by following the sewing guides on most sewing machines.

When marking, remove only the pins that are in the way. The pins are needed to hold the pattern and fabric in place.

Using Dressmaker's Carbon

Several methods can be used to transfer pattern markings. Dressmaker's carbon and a tracing wheel are often used to mark firmly woven and knitted fabrics. Tracing transfers marks quickly and accurately.

Since carbon may mark some fabrics permanently, use caution when marking. Test the carbon you intend to use on a scrap of your fabric. Make sure the marking is visible on the wrong side of the fabric. Also, check to be sure it does not show on the right side. Before marking, place a magazine or piece of cardboard under the fabric. This will protect the table from the sharp teeth of the tracing wheel.

Two pieces of carbon are needed to mark both fabric layers. Place one piece of carbon right side up, under the bottom layer of fabric. Slip the other piece, right side down, between the pattern and the top layer of fabric. Make sure the carbon paper is placed next to the wrong sides of the fabric.

Carefully roll the wheel along the markings. To ensure accuracy, use a ruler to help trace straight lines. See 21-14. Use only enough pressure to make the markings visible on the wrong side of the fabric. Too

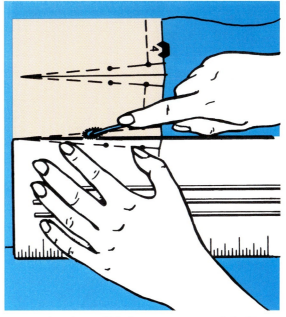

21-14 A ruler will help you trace straight lines when marking with a tracing wheel and dressmaker's carbon.

much pressure may mar the fabric with holes or transfer color to the right side of the fabric.

Using Tailor's Chalk or Pencil

Tailor's chalk and *tailor's pencil* are used to mark any fabrics except thick wools and sheer fabrics. Since chalk and pencil markings rub off easily, stitching needs to be done soon after marking.

To mark, place pins directly on markings and push the pins straight through both layers of fabric. Turn the piece over. Using a ruler as a guide, draw a chalk line along the row of pins. See 21-15. Make sure you are drawing on the wrong side of the fabric.

To mark the other layer of fabric, push pins back through both fabric layers. Turn the piece over so the pattern is facing upward. Remove the pattern carefully. Again, draw a line along the pins.

You will want to leave pattern pieces pinned onto garment pieces until you are ready to sew. This will make the garment pieces easier to identify. After you remove all pins, you can put pattern pieces back into the pattern envelope.

Activity: Give each student a pattern piece and have the student state what pattern markings should be transferred to the fabric.

Note: Demonstrate how to transfer pattern markings.

Resource: *Marking the Fabric,* reproducible master, TR

Problem-Solving Practice

Think Creatively! reproducible master, TR. Students are asked how to solve the problem of tissue paper pattern pieces being torn by tracing wheels after a few uses. It is recommended that this master be used following the study of Topic 21-3 and after students have cut and marked their projects.

Resource:

Pinning, Cutting, and Marking, Activity D, SAG

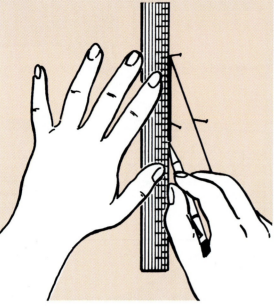

21-15 To mark with tailor's chalk or tailor's pencil, place pins directly on markings. Draw a chalk line even with the pins.

Check It Out!

1. Name five factors that determine which cutting layout you will use.
2. What are you to do with the grainline arrow on a pattern piece?
3. True or false. Notches should be cut inward.
4. Describe one method of transferring pattern markings to fabrics.

Check It Out! (Answers)

1. the garment you are making; the view you are making; your size; width of your fabric; if your fabric has a nap
2. Place it on the lengthwise grain of the fabric.
3. false
4. (Student response.)

TEENS ARE CONCERNED ABOUT...

The Value of Sewing Skills

Some teens wonder why they should learn to sew. How useful is this skill really going to be in the future? Laura Blalock has an answer to this question. She turned her sewing skill into an exciting career.

Laura started sewing at the age of five. In third grade, she made her first outfit. In high school, she made her own prom dress and a tuxedo for her date. She also became the youngest contestant in her division in the national finals for the Make-It-Yourself With-Wool contest!

In college, Laura earned a B.S. degree in textile management and an M.S. degree in management science with a concentration in textiles. She was hired as a management trainee by Gerber Childrenswear. Promotions have taken her to the Dominican Republic, Mexico, and several locations in the United States. She is currently director of product development with Sara Lee Casualwear, a maker of fleece and jersey activewear under the Hanes, Hanes Her Way, and JMS labels.

Q: *Why do you sew?*

A: I sew because it is a way to get exactly what I want. Also, I thrive on a sense of achievement, and it is rewarding to me to finish a project and say, "Hey, that looks pretty good, and I did it!" Most of the sewing I do now is home decorating, so it is especially rewarding. However I do still find the time to sew clothes for myself, and I love sewing for my nieces and nephew.

A lot of people ask if I ever get tired of sewing. The answer, truthfully, is no. I stay too busy to sew as much as I would like. However, if there is something special I want, I will make time to sew it.

Q: *How does sewing your own clothes help you stretch your clothing budget?*

A: When I sewed a lot of my clothes in years past, I found that I could have three times as many clothes as I would otherwise be able to afford. With home decorating projects, I find it amazing how much I can save.

Q: *How does sewing enable you to express your individuality?*

A: Sewing an outfit for myself allows me to get just the color, style, and fit I want. I can also create exactly the environment I want with home decorating projects.

Q: *Could you comment on your career and the role sewing has played in it?*

A: My love for sewing and understanding of garment construction makes working in the apparel industry very

rewarding. Even though industrial sewing is quite different from home sewing, there is a relationship between the two. Home sewing many types of garments has helped me develop training programs for sewing operators. Additionally, my knowledge of product type and garment construction has played a significant role in my success as in product development.

My greatest challenge has been living and working in countries where the language and customs are somewhat new to me. In spite of these differences, I find people in the Dominican Republic and Mexico very eager to learn. They are proud of their accomplishments. Working with them has been quite rewarding to me.

Feature-Related Activity

After reading this feature, students may be interested in learning more about careers in the fashion industry that utilize sewing skills. Have each student select and research a career in this field and prepare an oral report. Students can use the *Dictionary of Occupational Titles* or other career information resources to prepare their reports.

Chapter Review

Resource:
PowerZone Challenge CD. Have students play the chapter review game to reinforce text content.

Summary

After studying the information in this chapter, you should be ready to begin sewing. You learned how important the pattern guide sheet is to successful sewing. You also learned what the symbols and terms mean that are on the pattern pieces. You can pin fit your pattern to check for any needed alterations. Making alterations prior to cutting is easier than making them after a garment is constructed.

Prepare fabric for cutting by preshrinking it, if necessary. Also press the fabric, and make sure it is on grain. If it is off grain, you can usually straighten the fabric.

Locate the appropriate cutting layout on the guide sheet, and fold your fabric as shown. Place pattern pieces following the grain of the fabric. Pin all pattern pieces securely to avoid slipping. Leave the fabric flat on the table as you take long cutting strokes with your shears. After you transfer the pattern markings to the fabric, you can begin constructing your project.

Think About It!

1. Why is it important to understand the information on the pattern guide sheet and pattern pieces before you begin sewing?
2. What is the point of pin fitting a pattern and altering the pattern pieces before cutting the fabric?
3. What problems would be created if you sewed a garment from off-grain fabric?
4. What kind of pattern do you think would be best for sewing plaids and stripes?
5. In addition to homemaking, name several careers you think would be enhanced by a knowledge of sewing.

Try It Out!

1. Demonstrate to the class how to pin fit a pattern to determine if any alterations are needed.
2. Demonstrate to the class how to make one of the alterations discussed in this chapter.
3. Trace around a 12-inch square remnant of a washable fabric. Preshrink the remnant. Lay it back on the tracing you made. Did any shrinkage occur? Based on this single experience, is preshrinking worthwhile? What results did your classmates get?
4. Research other ways to check for needed pattern alterations. Which method do you think would give the most accurate results? Share your findings with the class.
5. Patterns can be altered in many ways in addition to those shown in this chapter. Many people have figure variations that require pattern alterations. Choose a pattern alteration to demonstrate to the class that was not discussed in this chapter.

Chapter 22
Sewing Techniques

Careers

These careers relate to the topics in this chapter:
- sewing supplies sales representative
- tailor
- sewing teacher
- clothing specialist

As you study this chapter, see if you can think of others.

Topics

- 22-1 Stitching Techniques, Darts, and Seams
- 22-2 Supporting Fabrics
- 22-3 Construction Techniques
- 22-4 Extending the Life of Clothes

Introductory Activities

1. Have students bring in old garments that can be restyled and recycled. Divide the class into small groups and give each group a garment to evaluate. Have each group brainstorm ideas for recycling their garments. Share ideas with the class. What sewing skills will be needed to restyle the garments?
2. Have students begin a personal file of sewing tips and techniques. Have students collect useful information for their files from fabric stores, magazines, and newspapers.
3. Ask someone who sews professionally to demonstrate some sewing techniques that can give "homemade" garments a "custom-sewn" look.

Topic 22-1
Stitching Techniques, Darts, and Seams

I. Stitching Techniques
   A. Directional Stitching
   B. Staystitching
   C. Basting
II. Darts, Tucks, Pleats, and Gathers
   A. Darts
   B. Tucks and Pleats
   C. Gathering and Easing
III. Seams
   A. Types of Seams
   B. Trimming, Grading, Clipping, and Notching
   C. Seam Finishes

Topic 22-2
Supporting Fabrics

I. Interfacing
   A. Woven and Nonwoven Interfacings
   B. Fusible Interfacing
II. Facings
   A. Preparing the Facing
   B. Attaching the Facing

Topic 22-3
Construction Techniques

I. Waist Treatments
   A. Casings
   B. Waistbands
II. Sleeves
III. Pockets
IV. Zippers
V. Fasteners
   A. Snaps
   B. Hooks and Eyes
   C. Buttons
   D. Hook-and-Loop Tape
VI. Hems
   A. Marking the Hem
   B. Finishing the Hem Edge
   C. Hemming Stitches
VII. Sewing Knit Fabrics

Topic 22-4
Extending the Life of Clothes

I. Repairing Clothes
II. Altering Clothes
   A. Altering Seams
   B. Altering Hems
III. Restyling Clothes
IV. Recycling Clothes

Resource:
Sewing Bingo, reproducible master, TR

Vocabulary:
Prepare samples of these sewing terms and techniques and display them on a bulletin board.

Discuss:
What do you think is the difference between homemade and custom-made garments?

Note:
Display pattern pieces that have directional arrows on them and discuss why they are used.

Note:
Display samples of staystitching and indicate typical areas where it is used.

Topic 22-1
Stitching Techniques, Darts, and Seams

Objectives
After studying this topic, you will be able to
- perform directional stitching, staystitching, and basting.
- construct darts, tucks, pleats, and gathers.
- sew seams and seam finishes.

Topic Terms
directional stitching
staystitching
basting
dart
tuck
pleat
easing
gathering
seam
backstitching
trimming
grading
clipping
notching
seam finish

Sewing can be both fun and productive. If you follow good sewing techniques, you can make clothes that you will be proud to wear. They will look as good as, or even better than, clothes purchased from stores. Custom-made clothes will probably fit you better, too.

To make a good-looking garment, you must follow good sewing techniques from beginning to end. The little extras are what make the difference between homemade and custom-made garments.

Stitching Techniques

Before you begin constructing your project, you need to be familiar with three stitching techniques. These are directional stitching, staystitching, and basting.

Directional Stitching

Stitching in the direction of the grain is called **directional stitching**. Directional stitching prevents garments from puckering or stretching along seamlines. It should be used whenever a seam is sewn.

As a general rule, directional stitching is done from the wider section of a garment piece to the narrower section. If you are using a single-sized pattern, you will notice arrows along the seamlines. These arrows point in the direction you should sew.

Another way to determine which direction to sew is by running your finger across the cut edge of the fabric, 22-1. The yarns will ruffle as you move in one direction. They will lie flat as you move in the other direction. Sew in the direction that makes the yarns lie flat and feel smooth.

Staystitching

Staystitching is a line of machine stitching that keeps the edges of garment pieces from stretching out of shape as you sew. Staystitching is done through a single layer of fabric ½ inch from the cut edges. Bias and curved edges, such as necklines and armholes, are especially important areas to staystitch. See 22-2. All staystitching should follow the principles of directional stitching so the garment pieces will lie flat and smooth.

Since many of today's fabrics do not stretch, staystitching is not always necessary. Some fabric finishes permanently set yarns in place and eliminate the need to staystitch. For less sturdy and loosely woven fabrics, staystitching is needed to stabilize garment pieces.

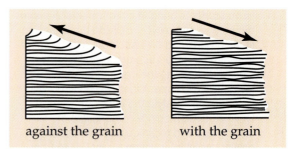

against the grain | with the grain

22-1 Directional stitching is the technique of sewing with the grain so seams lie flat for a smooth appearance.

Family Enrichment Activity
On separate cards, have students and their families individually write responses to the statement, "Given $100, what should be added to my teen wardrobe?" Compare and discuss the responses. Check to see if responses verify Steve's statement in the Chapter 22 feature: "Teens tend to be more conscious of style than quality. Parents of teens want quality plus they also look at cost of upkeep."

Topic 22-1 Stitching Techniques, Darts, and Seams

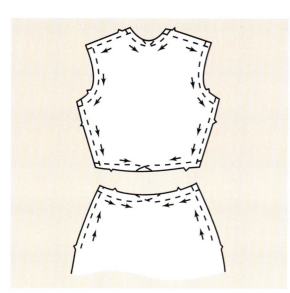

22-2 Staystitch bias and curved edges of garment pieces to prevent them from stretching out of shape as you sew.

Basting

Basting is the technique of sewing long, loose stitches either by hand or by machine. Later, these stitches can easily be removed.

The main purpose of basting is to check the fit of a garment before sewing. After basting seams together, try on the garment. If the garment fits well, sew over the basting stitches for a permanent seam. If the seams need to be wider or narrower, baste again and recheck the fit.

Basting stitches are often used to mark hemlines, seamlines, darts, buttonholes, and other garment details. In addition, basting can be used to ease and gather fabric. The fullness of set-in sleeves, gathered waistlines, and flared skirt hems can all be controlled with basting.

Darts, Tucks, Pleats, and Gathers

After your garment is staystitched, the guide sheet usually instructs you to make any darts, tucks, or pleats. These begin to give shape to your garment. Since darts, tucks, and pleats cross seamlines, they are made before seams are sewn.

Darts

A **dart** is a construction element used to give shape and fullness to a garment. It is made by stitching to a point through a fold in the fabric. Darts help fit a flat piece of fabric to the curves of the body. The larger the body curves, the larger the darts need to be.

All darts point to the fullest part of body curves. On skirts and slacks, darts begin at the waistline and taper to the hipline, allowing fullness around the hips. In jackets, shirts, and blouses, darts taper to the fullest part of the chest.

When sewing darts, begin at the wide end of the dart and sew to the point. The last three stitches should be made on the fold. This prevents the point of the dart from puckering. See 22-3. After stitching, tie the threads securely.

To press darts, press along the stitching line, from the wide end to the point. If available, use a tailor's ham to shape the garment pieces as you press. Vertical darts are pressed toward center front or center back. Horizontal darts are pressed downward. Wide darts or darts in bulky fabrics may be slashed to within one inch of the point, trimmed to $5/8$ inch, and pressed open.

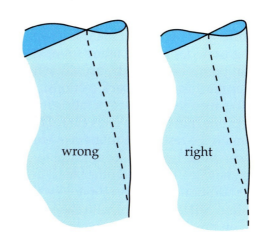

22-3 The last three stitches of a dart should be made on the fold. This prevents the fabric from puckering at the point of the dart.

Note: Display samples of basting stitches done both by hand and by machine.

Note: Display samples of darts that are stitched correctly with three stitches on the fold at the point. Also display samples of darts that are sewn incorrectly creating puckers at the ends. Pass these samples around the class.

Note: Display pattern pieces that have darts, tucks, and pleats. Make samples that show the differences between these construction features. Mount these next to the pattern pieces.

Resource: *Stitching, Darts, and Seams*, reproducible master, TR

Career Preparation Activity

Mass Production vs Custom Sewing, reproducible master, TR. Students are asked to read a case study and then debate which type of job offers the most advantages and disadvantages.

Note: Demonstrate the marking and sewing of tucks and pleats. Display patterns that show the variety of garment styles that use these techniques.

Note: Using several patterns, show students where easing and gathering are used.

Note: Demonstrate how easing is done and display the sample. Vary stitch length to demonstrate why long stitches are used.

Tucks and Pleats

Tucks are narrow folds of fabric stitched in place along all or part of their length. They are usually used as a decorative touch to garments. Released tucks, which are stitched only part way, may be used in place of darts or gathers at the waistline. Released tucks provide fullness. Tucks may be placed horizontally or vertically.

Pleats are folds of fabric that provide controlled fullness. They are always vertical. Some pleats are stitched part way to give a snug fit. They are then pressed to form sharp folds. Other pleats are left unpressed to fall in soft folds. They hang in place, giving an easy, comfortable fit. Skirts, pants, and sleeves are frequently pleated.

To make tucks and pleats, transfer both the solid lines and broken lines from the pattern pieces. You are usually instructed to fold each solid line over to align with the adjacent broken line. Insert a pin through both layers of fabric on the marked lines to make sure the lines match. Place pins perpendicular to the stitching lines. Machine baste pleats in place. Stitch tucks in place.

Gathering and Easing

Gathering and easing are techniques used when two seamlines of unequal length are sewn together. **Easing** involves making a piece of fabric fit a slightly smaller piece of fabric as a flat, curved seam is sewn. Easing provides needed fabric fullness at certain points on the body, usually where sleeves meet front and back sections.

To ease a longer piece of fabric into a shorter one, pin the two ends first. Then distribute the rest of the fullness evenly between these two pins, being sure to match notches, dots, and other markings. Insert additional pins at right angles to the seamline. Stitch the seam with the longer piece on top. Remove the pins only as you come to them. Try to avoid stitching any ripples or puckers into the seam.

When ripples and soft folds are desired at a seamline that joins two different lengths of fabric, **gathering** is used. The ripples and soft folds that result are called *gathers*. They yield a rounded shape. Gathers are often found at waistlines, necklines, puffy sleeves, or cuffs. See 22-4.

To make gathers, set the stitch length regulator on your machine for 6 to 8 stitches per inch for mediumweight fabrics. Two rows of long stitches are needed to make smooth, even gathers. Place the first row of stitches near the ⅝-inch seamline. Place the second row of stitches ¼ inch from the first row, inside the seam allowance. Do not backstitch. Leave at least three inches of thread at the ends of the stitching lines.

Pin the right sides of the two fabric pieces together, matching notches and other markings. Gently pull both bobbin threads at one end, working toward the center of the edge being gathered. (You will gather one side first, then the other.) Gather half of the longer fabric piece until it lies flat against half of the shorter one. Fasten the bobbin threads by wrapping them in a figure eight around the pin located where you began gathering. See 22-5. Repeat the

22-4 The gathers in the waistline of this dress cause soft folds to fall over the hips.

Putting Technology to Use

Have students visit the Web site www.sew-whats-new.com. Ask students to browse through the various links of ideas for projects and the galleries of finished projects. If your class has an e-mail address, you can subscribe to a weekly newsletter. The site also offers a chat room for sewers and quilters. You may want to attend a chat and determine if it is appropriate to encourage students to visit the chat room.

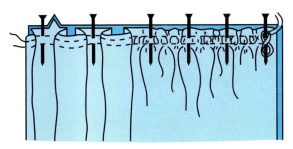

22-5 Secure threads by wrapping them around a pin. Then pull the opposite ends to gather the other side.

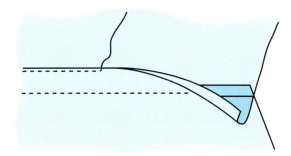

22-6 The flat-fell seam is often used on sportswear.

Note:
Display samples of these types of seams on the class bulletin board. Have students refer to them as needed.

Resource:
Types of Seams, Activity A, SAG

gathering process from the other end. Distribute the gathers evenly and insert pins across the gathering stitches. Set your machine to a regular stitch length of about 12 stitches per inch. Stitch the two fabric pieces together with the gathered side up. Hold the fabric to prevent any folds from forming in the seam.

Seams

A **seam** is a row of stitching that joins garment pieces together. There are many types of seams used in sewing. The choice of a seam depends on the type and weight of the fabric. Seams also vary in their durability. Fashion trends in structural and decorative lines may dictate seam choice.

Types of Seams

The *plain seam* is the most common seam. A plain seam is made by placing right sides of the fabric together. Sew along the seamline with a ⅝-inch seam allowance, backstitching at both ends. **Backstitching** means to sew backward and forward in the same place for a few stitches to secure the thread ends. Press the seam to one side. Then press the seam open.

The *flat-fell seam* is a very sturdy seam used in work, sports, and play clothes. It leaves no raw edges. To make a flat-fell seam, place wrong sides of fabric together and sew a plain seam. Press the seam to one side. Trim the bottom seam allowance to ⅛ inch. Turn under the upper seam allowance and fold it over the trimmed edge. Machine stitch through all layers close to the fold. See 22-6.

The *French seam* looks like a plain seam on the right side. On the wrong side, it is a seam enclosed within a seam, 22-7. It can be used only for straight seams. The French seam is suited for sheer fabrics, such as organdy, batiste, and chiffon.

To make a French seam, place wrong sides of fabric together and stitch a plain seam with a ⅜-inch seam allowance. Trim the seam allowance to ⅛ inch. Turn right sides of fabric together. Crease along the stitched seam and press. Stitch on the original seamline, now ¼ inch from the crease. This encases the raw edge.

Trimming, Grading, Clipping, and Notching

Once a plain seam is stitched, it may require further treatment for a neat, smooth appearance. Some seams, such as armhole, waistline, and curved seams, require trimming, grading, clipping, or notching. These steps reduce bulk in the seam allowance and help the seam lie flat.

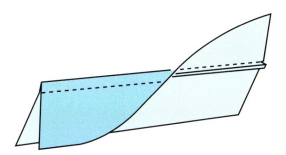

22-7 The French seam leaves no raw edges on the inside of the garment.

Putting Technology to Use
Have students begin a "sewing notebook." Have students make samples of each of these seams. Then have students use word processing software to create pages labeled for each type. Ask students to also include a description of the sample on its page. Mount the samples, three-hole punch the pages, and place them in a three-ring binder.

> **Note:**
> Display patterns and pattern pieces that require the use of these techniques. Discuss why each type of treatment is needed.

> **Note:**
> Display samples of each type of seam finish on the class bulletin board. Have students refer to them as needed.

Trimming means cutting away part of a seam allowance to reduce bulk. Seams on lightweight and mediumweight fabrics are often trimmed. Trim away ⅜ inch of fabric along the length of the seam. Bulk should also be removed from corners. Cut diagonally across corners, being careful not to cut the stitching. For points, trim from the sides of the point at an angle. See 22-8.

Seams on heavier fabrics or seams with three or more fabric layers are graded. **Grading** means trimming each layer of the seam allowance to a different width. This prevents edges of the seam allowance from aligning and forming a noticeable ridge along seam lines. See 22-9. For smooth, flat seams, trim each layer ⅛ inch narrower than the next. Do not trim any seams narrower than ¼ inch.

Clipping means making straight cuts toward the stitching line, usually at ½-inch intervals. The stitching must not be cut. Clipping is done on seams that have an inward curve. This makes the curved seam turn smoothly. If a seam allowance is not clipped, it will pucker when turned.

Notching means to cut small wedges out of the seam allowance. This removes excess fabric that would make seams bulky when turned. Notching is used on seams with an outward curve. Clipping and notching are shown in 22-10.

22-9 Grading a seam means trimming each seam allowance to a different width.

Seam Finishes

The inside of a garment is just as important as the outside. **Seam finishes** are treatments done after seams are sewn to prevent the raw edges of the seam allowances from raveling. They also improve the appearance of the inside of the garment. Seam finishes add quality and durability to the garment.

The choice of a seam finish depends on the weight of the fabric and the degree to which it ravels. Some fabrics ravel very little and, therefore, need no further work on the raw edges. Others are loosely woven and require a seam finish.

A *pinked finish* is the easiest finish to do. Simply use pinking shears and cut

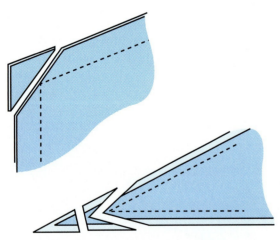

22-8 Trim corners and points as shown to reduce bulk when turned.

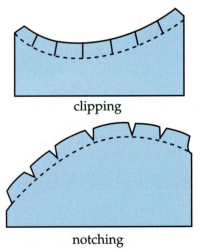

clipping

notching

22-10 Clipping is used on inward curves. Notching is used on outward curves.

Putting Technology to Use
Have students make samples of each of these seam finishes. Then have them use word processing software to make a page for each sample including a label and description. Ask students to mount the samples on the appropriate pages and place them in their sewing notebooks.

close to the edge of the seam allowance through both fabric layers. Then press the seam open. Use a pinked finish only on fabrics that ravel slightly. To make a sturdier finish, you can also stitch close to the pinked edge of each seam allowance.

A *zigzag finish* is a quick and easy seam finish used on fabrics that ravel easily. See 22-11. It works best on mediumweight and heavyweight fabrics. To make a zigzag seam finish, set the sewing machine for a medium-wide zigzag stitch. You can also use the serger for this seam finish. Press the seam open before stitching. Stitch through one seam allowance at a time, close to the fabric edge.

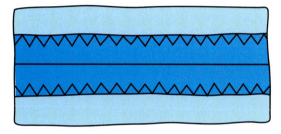

22-11 When sewing a zigzag seam finish, the needle should move on and off the fabric edge.

Check It Out!
1. What two stitching techniques are used to prevent stretching of the edges of the seamlines?
2. Explain how to stitch a dart.
3. How does trimming differ from grading?
4. Which seam finish is best to use with fabrics that are loosely woven?

Check It Out! (Answers)
1. staystitching and directional stitching
2. Stitch from the wide end of the dart to the point. The last three stitches should be made on the fold. Tie threads.
3. In trimming, all seam allowances are trimmed ⅜ inch. In grading, each layer of the seam allowance is trimmed to a different width.
4. zigzag finish

Topic 22-2
Supporting Fabrics

Objectives
After studying this topic, you will be able to
- select and attach interfacings.
- prepare and attach facings.

Topic Terms
facing
interfacing
clean finishing
understitching

Facings and interfacings are inner fabric layers used to give shape and support to garments. A **facing** is an extra piece of the garment fabric added to an edge of the garment. It is used to finish the raw edges of garment pieces, such as neckline or waistline edges. **Interfacing** is a layer of reinforcement fabric between the garment fabric and the facing. These inner fabric layers affect the look, fit, and life of the garment.

Interfacing

Interfacing helps maintain shape and add firmness to such areas as collars, lapels, and cuffs. Interfacing prevents stretching around the neck and waist. It also strengthens stress areas, such as those around buttons and buttonholes, 22-12.

22-12 Interfacing adds shape and firmness to blouse and shirt collars and jacket lapels.

Note: Display samples of the various zigzag stitches that can be made using the school's sewing machines. Check the sewing machine manual for recommendations for their use and label the samples.

Resource: Sewing Techniques—Practice Sample, reproducible master, TR

Vocabulary: Prepare samples of Topic 22-2 sewing terms and techniques for a classroom display.

Resource: Choosing Supporting Fabrics, reproducible master, TR

A wide variety of interfacing fabrics is available. There are three main types: woven, nonwoven, and fusible. Select interfacing fabrics according to:

- *weight of the garment fabric*—Interfacing fabric should not be heavier than the garment fabric.
- *amount of stiffness and shape needed*—This will depend on the pattern style and type of garment fabric.
- *cleaning requirements for the garment fabric*—The cleaning requirements for the interfacing should be the same as for the garment. If the garment fabric will be washed by machine, make sure the interfacing can also be washed.

Woven and Nonwoven Interfacings

Woven interfacings have interlacing yarns. These interfacings have a grainline, so pattern pieces must be cut on the grain. Woven interfacings come in many weights and are generally more flexible than other types of interfacings.

Nonwoven interfacings are made by bonding fibers together. In general, nonwoven interfacings offer more body and stiffness than woven types and do not ravel. Since most nonwoven fabrics have no grain, pattern pieces can be cut in any direction. Nonwovens come in a wide variety of weights and can be used to achieve a crisp finish. Some nonwoven interfacings are made to stretch.

When using interfacing, first cut out the pieces you need. Pin the interfacing to the wrong side of the facing or to the wrong side of the garment. Baste the interfacing to the fabric ½ inch from the fabric edge. To eliminate bulk, trim the interfacing close to the stitching line.

Fusible Interfacing

Fusible interfacings can be ironed onto the wrong side of the fabric. Fusible interfacings are either woven or nonwoven. They are easy to apply and come in a variety of weights. They often give more rigidity to garments. They are best used on firm fabrics that will not allow the outline of the interfacing to show through the garment.

To use fusible interfacing, first cut out the interfacing pieces you need. Trim ½ inch from the interfacing seam allowances to eliminate bulk. Place the fusible side of the interfacing against the wrong side of the fabric. Fusible interfacings should be applied to the facing instead of the garment, if possible. This prevents the interfacing's outline from showing on the right side of the garment. However, for collars, cuffs, belts, pockets, and waistbands, interfacing can be fused directly to the garment.

Position the fusible interfacing on the fabric. Then put a damp pressing cloth over the interfacing, 22-13. Using a steam iron, press for 10 to 15 seconds. Lift the iron and press in another spot. Continue pressing until the entire interfacing is completely fused to the fabric. Allow the fabric to cool before handling.

Facings

Facings are used to reinforce and finish the raw edges of garment pieces. Facings may be used to finish necklines, waistlines, front openings, or armholes. There are several different types of facings. The type you use will be determined by your pattern. An easy facing for beginning sewers to apply is the fitted facing.

22-13 Use a damp pressing cloth and a steam iron to apply fusible interfacing. Press in one spot at a time.

Across the Curriculum

Speech. Have students give an oral presentation on facings and interfacings. Have students bring facing, interfacing, and clothing samples to use in their speech.

Preparing the Facing

The first step in preparing the facing is to stitch the facing pieces together at the seamlines. Place the facing pieces with right sides together. Match notches, pin, and stitch. Press the seams open.

Finish the unnotched outer edges of the facing to prevent them from raveling. There are several ways to finish the facing edges, depending on the weight of the fabric. Lightweight to mediumweight fabrics can be clean finished. **Clean finishing** means turning under the raw edges and stitching. To clean finish a facing edge, stitch ¼ inch from the long, unnotched edge using a regular stitch length. Press under along the stitching line. Then stitch again close to the folded edge.

Fabrics that do not ravel easily can be pinked along the edge. Stitch ¼ inch from the unnotched edge. Trim the edge with pinking shears. Fabrics that are heavy and ravel easily should be overcast with a zigzag stitch.

Attaching the Facing

To attach facing to a garment, pin the right sides together, making sure notches and seams match. Stitch the facing to the garment along the seamline. If the facing has a corner, take one stitch diagonally across the corner. This will make the corner look smooth after it is turned.

After the facing seam has been stitched, trim or grade the seam allowance. Trim corners to reduce bulk. Clip inward curves and notch outward curves. Press the seam allowance toward the facing.

Understitching is a row of stitching that holds a seam allowance to one of the fabric pieces joined by the seam. This keeps the facing flat and prevents the facing from showing on the outside of the garment.

To understitch, you must open out the facing and machine stitch through the facing and seam allowance only. Stitch from the outside of the garment, close to the seam on the facing side of the seamline. Pull the seam slightly as you sew. See 22-14. Turn the facing to the inside and press.

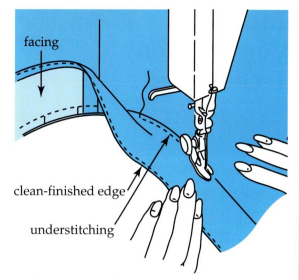

22-14 Understitching keeps facing flat and prevents the seam allowance from showing on the outside of the garment.

Finally, tack the finished facing to the inside of the garment at the seam allowances. Use stitches that will not show on the outside of the garment.

Check It Out!

1. Explain the difference between an interfacing and a facing.
2. What three factors should be considered in selecting the interfacing for a garment?
3. Explain how to clean finish a facing edge.
4. Why is understitching needed?

Check It Out! (Answers)

1. A facing is an extra piece of garment fabric added to the edge of the garment to finish the raw edges. Interfacing is a layer of reinforcement fabric between the garment fabric and the facing.
2. the weight of the garment fabric, the amount of stiffness and shape needed, cleaning requirements for the garment fabric
3. Stitch 1/4 inch from the long, unnotched edge using a regular stitch length. Press under along the stitching line. Then stitch close to the folded edge.
4. Understitching keeps the facing flat and prevents the facing from showing on the outside of the garment.

Topic 22-3
Construction Techniques

Objectives
After studying this topic, you will be able to
- complete the construction of sewing projects that include waist treatments, sleeves, pockets, closures, and hems.
- describe special techniques for handling knit fabrics.

Topic Terms
casing
topstitching
kimono sleeve
raglan sleeve
set-in sleeve
in-seam pocket
patch pocket
thread shank

22-15 A casing is a fast and easy way to finish a waistline.

Your sewing project may include a number of construction techniques. The more techniques you master, the more creative your sewing will become.

Waist Treatments

Perhaps you are making a skirt or a pair of shorts or pants. You will need to know how to finish the waistline. There are three treatments that your pattern might use: a facing, a casing, or a waistband. If your pattern has no waistband, the waistline area may be finished with a facing. A waistline facing is constructed as described earlier. Casings and waistbands will be discussed here.

Casings

A casing is the easiest waistline treatment to sew. A **casing** is an enclosure for elastic or a drawstring that gathers the garment snugly to the body, 22-15. Casings may be used at neck, sleeve, and leg edges as well as waistlines.

A casing may be formed in one of two ways. A *self-casing* is formed when the edge of the garment piece is folded to the inside and stitched. An opening is left so the elastic or drawstring can be inserted. An *applied casing* uses a separate piece of fabric or bias tape to form the casing.

You need to determine the length of elastic or drawstring to use in a casing. Hold elastic around the body where the casing is to be located. The elastic should feel comfortable. Add one inch to this amount to overlap the ends. A drawstring needs to be long enough so it will not slip through when it is left untied.

To insert elastic or a drawstring, attach a safety pin to one end. Push the pin through the casing. After elastic is inserted, overlap the ends. Secure the ends of the elastic together by stitching across them several times. A drawstring is pulled through so that both ends extend out of the garment opening. Distribute garment fullness evenly along the casing. Close the opening that was left for threading elastic. The opening for a drawstring is left open to allow the string to slide.

Waistbands

A waistband is a strip of fabric attached at the waistline of a garment. The waistband should be interfaced to keep it

---

Putting Technology to Use
Have students work on creating a classroom Web page that discusses construction techniques. If your school has a Web site, add a link for the page to the home page.

from stretching. Interfacing also gives the waistband body so it does not wrinkle or roll down. A stiff, fusible interfacing is a good choice for a waistband. Cut the interfacing the length of the waistband and half the width. Trim the seam allowances, then fuse the interfacing to the wrong side of the waistband.

There are several methods for attaching a waistband to a garment. Follow the instructions given in your pattern guide sheet. You may be instructed to pin the waistband to either the right or the wrong side of your fabric. Pin the waistband to the garment, matching notches, seamlines, and dots. You may need to ease the extra fullness as you fit the band to the garment. Stitch the waistband to the garment, backstitching at both ends. Trim or grade the seam. Press the seam allowance toward the waistband.

Your guide sheet will then tell you how to stitch the ends of the band and to attach the other side of the waistband to the garment. You may be instructed to sew the free side of the waistband by hand on the inside of the garment. Some methods instruct you to topstitch the free side by machine on the outside of the garment. **Topstitching** is a row of machine stitching done on the right side of a garment for decorative or functional purposes. Since topstitching appears on the outside of a garment, it must be done neatly.

Sleeves

There are three basic types of sleeves: kimono, raglan, and set-in. See 22-16. Kimono and raglan sleeves are fairly easy to sew. Set-in sleeves are more difficult. Your pattern guide sheet will give you specific instructions.

Kimono sleeves are cut as a part of the garment. There is no seamline connecting a separate sleeve to the garment. A shoulder seam and a reinforced, underarm seam is all that is needed. For reinforcement, the curved area of the underarm seam is stitched with short machine stitches. The curved area is then restitched ⅛ inch from the seamline, within the seam allowance.

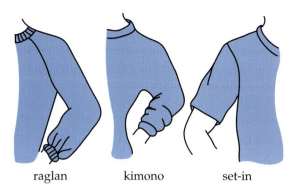

raglan   kimono   set-in

22-16 Most sleeves are one of these three basic types.

The seam is clipped at the curve and pressed open.

Raglan sleeves have diagonal seams that run from the underarm to the neckline, on both front and back. See 22-17. The diagonal seams are sewn as plain seams. The upper portion of the sleeve becomes part of the neckline. It may be finished with a facing or collar, depending on your pattern. The underarm seam is stitched and reinforced as a kimono sleeve. The seams are clipped and pressed open.

22-17 Many sportswear patterns feature

Activity:
Have students look at garments they and their classmates are wearing. Point out construction methods that illustrate the different methods for attaching a waistband.

Resource:
Waist Treatments, reproducible master, TR

Note:
Display pattern pieces for each of these types of sleeve treatments. Explain how the pattern pieces will fit together. Emphasize the importance of notches in proper placement of sleeves.

 Putting Technology to Use

Have students look through pattern catalogs and magazines to find pictures of garments that feature the different types of sleeve treatments. Have them use word processing software to create labels and description pages for each. Ask students to mount the samples on the labeled pages and include them in their sewing notebook binders.

A **set-in sleeve** is attached to a garment with a seam that goes around the armhole at the shoulder. The top, or *cap*, of the sleeve is always larger than the armhole to allow for wearing ease. The fullness in the cap of the sleeve may be gathered or pleated for a puffed effect. In tailored garments, the fullness is eased for a smooth appearance.

Pockets

The most popular pockets are in-seam pockets and patch pockets. An **in-seam pocket** is sewn in the side seam of a garment. A **patch pocket** is attached to the outside of a garment.

In-seam pockets are the easiest to sew. They may be cut as an extension of the garment front and back, or as separate pieces to be attached. The pocket is formed by closing the side seam and stitching around the pocket extension. See 22-18.

To make a patch pocket, mark the location of the pocket on the wrong side of your fabric. Machine or hand baste on the marking. This allows you to see exactly where the pocket is to be placed on the outside. Prepare the pocket as instructed on your guide sheet. Pin or baste the pocket in place and neatly topstitch along the pocket edge.

Zippers

Zippers come in many lengths, weights, and colors. Refer to the back of your pattern envelope to find out what kind of zipper you need. Unless you want a contrasting zipper for design purposes, choose a zipper that matches the color of the garment fabric.

The four most common zipper applications are centered, lapped, invisible, and fly front. See 22-19. The location of the zipper and the look you desire will determine which method to use. Most zipper applications require the use of a special zipper foot on the sewing machine. Detailed instructions for zipper applications are given in your pattern guide sheet. Instructions can also be found on the package that comes with the zipper.

When zippers are intended for center front or center back seams, a *centered zipper application* is often used. The zipper coils are centered in the seamline. A row of stitches appears on both sides of the seamline. The two rows are an equal distance from the seamline.

A *lapped zipper application* has only one row of stitching showing on the outside of the garment. It can be used at front, back, or side openings. This application will hide a zipper that does not quite match the garment fabric. It is suited to lightweight and medium-weight fabrics.

An *invisible zipper* looks like a regular seam because no stitches show on the outside of the garment. This type of zipper requires the use of a special invisible zipper foot.

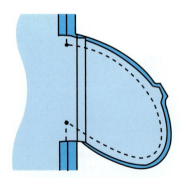

22-18 An in-seam pocket is easily formed as you sew the side seam.

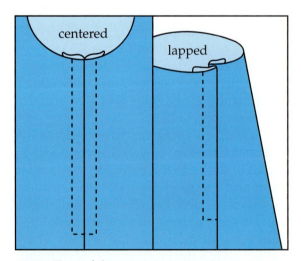

22-19 Two of the most common zipper applications are centered and lapped.

Across the Curriculum

History, English. Have students do a research report on the history of the zipper. Students should include information on the roles played by Whitcomb Judson and Gideon Sundback as creators. Also have students find out how the fastener got the name of *zipper*.

Fly front zipper applications are used on front openings of jeans and slacks. Methods of applying fly front zippers vary. Follow the instructions given on your pattern guide sheet.

Fasteners

Snaps, hooks and eyes, buttons, and hook-and-loop tape are types of fasteners used to close garments. When sewing on fasteners, make sure they are placed correctly. Garment edges should meet evenly and lie smoothly when fasteners are closed.

Snaps

Snaps are used to hold overlapping edges of a garment together. They are often used to help stabilize the shape of a neckline and prevent sagging. Snaps give a smooth, flat appearance to lapped edges.

Snaps are easy to attach, 22-20. They are made with two sections, the ball half and the socket half. Using small stitches, attach the ball half of the snap on the underside of the overlapping section. The stitches should not show on the outside of the garment. Position the socket half of the snap so the garment will lie smoothly when snapped. Stitch in place.

Hooks and Eyes

Hooks and eyes are often used above the zipper closing on waistbands of pants and skirts. They are also used to join garment edges that meet without overlapping. Use a hook and straight eye for edges that overlap. Use a hook and round eye for edges that meet. Refer to 22-21 to see how hooks and eyes are attached to garments.

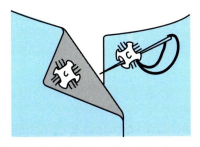

22-20 Use a double thread to attach snaps and other fasteners.

Buttons

The key to sewing on buttons correctly is to allow space for a thread shank. The **thread shank** provides room for the button to lie over the buttonhole fabric. The length of the shank depends on the thickness of the garment. To make a thread shank, place a match or straight pin over the button while sewing. Then remove the match and pull the button up. Bring the threaded needle between the button and the garment. Wind thread around the stitches several times. Then bring the thread to the wrong side of the garment and fasten with several stitches. See 22-22. Some buttons have shanks already attached. Simply sew these buttons securely in place.

Transfer buttonhole markings from the pattern. Follow the directions for making a buttonhole that come with your sewing machine.

Hook-and-Loop Tape

Hook-and-loop tape consists of two pieces of nylon tape that stick to each other when pressed together. Hook-and-loop tape is available as strips or circles. The tape is sewn in place with machine

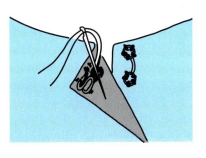

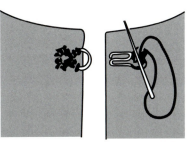

22-21 Hooks and straight eyes are used for overlapping edges. Hooks and round eyes are used for edges that meet.

> **Note:** Display and label each type of fastener. List advantages, disadvantages, and directions for application of each.
>
> **Note:** Collect and display samples of a variety of hooks and eyes.
>
> **Note:** Demonstrate the correct way to sew on a button.
>
> **Note:** Collect and display samples of a variety of buttons. Label with advantages and disadvantages of each type.

Putting Technology to Use
Have students investigate the Velcro® Companies' Web site at www.velcro.com. Have students especially check out the link to product information guides. Discuss information students discovered in class.

Discuss:
Where have you seen hook and loop tape used? What nonclothing uses have you seen? When is the use of such tape a particular advantage?

Activity:
Have students look at the hem treatments on the garments they are wearing. How many variations are there? How were these hems completed?

Note:
Collect supplies needed to mark a hem. Demonstrate how to use each piece of equipment. Point out the advantages of each item.

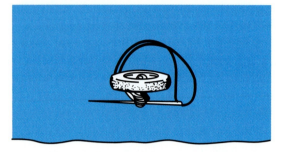

22-22 Make a thread shank as you sew on a button.

stitches. Hook-and-loop tape such as Velcro® is often used on outdoor clothing, such as parkas and jackets.

Hems

Hemming is the final step in garment construction. A hem should be flat, level, and unnoticeable from the right side of the garment. Having a neat, uniform hem is important to the overall appearance of the garment.

When all construction details are finished, determine the placement of the hemline. Try on the garment with everything else you plan to wear with it. Test different lengths in front of the mirror. Consider the fashionable length for the garment and adapt it to your figure type. There is no standard hem length that is right for everyone. Choose the length that flatters you.

Marking the Hem

To mark the hem, have someone pin the hem as you stand straight and still. Use a yardstick or hem marker to measure from the floor to the length you like. Mark the hemline with pins, placing them parallel to the floor about three inches apart.

Now turn up the hem and pin it to the inside of the garment. Match seamlines in the hem to seamlines in the garment. Press a light crease at the hem edge. Using a ruler, mark the width of the hem with tailor's chalk. Trim along this line, cutting an even hem width.

In flared and gathered garments, the hem will have extra fullness. This fabric fullness will need to be eased into the hem and distributed evenly. To ease, machine baste ¼ inch from the top of the hem. With a pin, pull gently on the basting thread to slightly gather the fabric. Pull the thread every few inches around the hem. To shrink some of the fabric fullness, steam press the hem. Pressing with steam will make the hem lie smooth and flat.

Finishing the Hem Edge

The hem edge needs to be finished before it is stitched to the garment. Hem finishes are similar to seam finishes. The choice of a finish depends on the fabric and style of the garment. The four methods of finishing hem edges described below are shown in 22-23.

The *turned and stitched finish* is used for mediumweight and lightweight fabrics that tend to ravel. Turn the cut hem edge under ¼ inch and stitch close to the fold.

The *stitched and pinked finish* is used for fabrics that do not ravel, such as knits. Machine stitch ¼ inch from the cut edge. Pink the edge with pinking shears. Be careful not to cut through stitching.

The *zigzag finish* is used most often for knits where stretch and flexibility are needed. It is also used on bulky fabrics that tend to ravel. To finish, zigzag ⅛ inch from the cut edge of the hem.

Seam binding tape is used as a hem finish for mediumweight and heavyweight fabrics that tend to ravel. On the right side of the fabric, lap the tape over the cut edge. Stitch the tape ¼ inch from the cut edge of the hem.

Stretch-lace binding tape is used to finish curved hems and hems of fabrics that stretch. It is applied like seam binding tape.

Across the Curriculum

Social studies. Discuss the "Hemline Index" with students. According to this concept, when hemlines rise, the stock market indexes rise. When hemlines fall, so does the stock market. Have students name specific time periods when this was true. Do students think there is any credibility to this theory?

Hemming Stitches

Most hems are stitched by hand. Stitches are made fairly loose to avoid puckers and to allow ease in the hemline. They should be spaced evenly and sewn neatly. Always begin hemming at a seam. Use a single thread. Secure the thread knot in the seam allowance. Refer to the diagrams in 22-24 as you read about four stitches used for hems.

Note: Display samples of these hem finishes and stitches. Label with directions for completing each one.

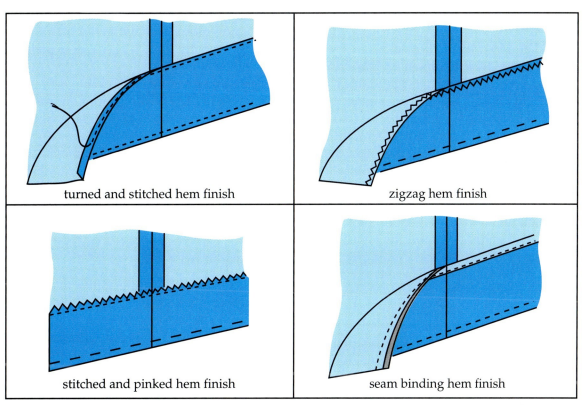

22-23 Use one of these hem finishes along the raw edge of your garment.

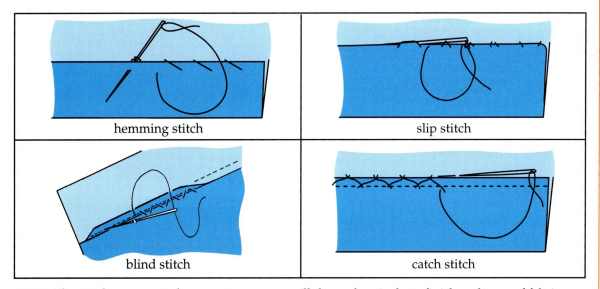

22-24 The stitch you use to hem your garment will depend on its hem finish and type of fabric.

Putting Technology to Use

Have students make samples of each of these hem finishes and stitches. Have students use word processing software to label and describe these samples. Ask students to mount the samples and place the pages in their sewing notebook binders.

Resource:
Hems, Activity C, SAG

Note:
Demonstrate the use of a serger for hemming. Display the sample in the classroom.

Note:
Demonstrate the use of fusible hemming material in class. Discuss the advantages and disadvantages of using this product.

Note:
Show examples of the knit gauge often found on pattern envelopes. Discuss the varieties of knits available and allow students to match samples of fabrics to the knit gauges provided in class.

The *hemming stitch* can be used for all types of hems. It is most often used for hems finished with binding tape. Pick up a yarn of the garment. Then bring the needle diagonally through the edge of the hem and pull the thread through. About ¼ inch to the left, pick up another yarn from the garment. Continue stitching around the hem, spacing stitches evenly. Secure the thread end in a seam allowance.

The *slip stitch* is almost invisible on both sides of the garment. The stitches are hidden in a fold along the hem edge. This stitch is used only when there is a fold. It is used most often to secure a hem with a turned and stitched finish. Pick up a yarn of the garment close to the hem. Slide the needle up into the fold and across about ¼ inch inside the fold. Bring the needle out and pick up another yarn from the garment. Continue around the hem.

The *blind stitch* is used most often for hems on coats and suits. The stitch is hidden from view between the hem and the garment. Before blind stitching, finish hems by stitching and pinking or by stitching and overcasting. The line of machine stitching used for these finishes serves as a guide for blind stitching. Fold the hem edge up along the line of stitching. Pick up a yarn from the garment. Move the needle up diagonally to the left about ¼ inch. Pick up a yarn from the hem. Move the needle down diagonally to the left. Pick up a yarn from the garment. Continue around the hem. Make the stitches loose so the hem will not pull and pucker.

The *catch stitch* is a flexible stitch good for hemming knit fabrics. It is also used to attach facings and interfacings to the wrong side of garments. Working from left to right, pick up a yarn ¼ inch below the hem edge. Then pick up a yarn in the garment just above the hem edge, diagonally from the first stitch, with the needle pointing to the left. Alternate stitching along the edge in a zigzag pattern. Keep the thread loose so the stitches will "give" with stretchy fabrics.

Machine stitching can be used to secure hems. Some machines have a special hemming stitch. Hems can also be topstitched or zigzagged to add a decorative finish. Check your sewing machine manual. Follow its directions for hemming by machine.

Sergers can be used for hemming. Sergers can make a narrow turned-under hem, a blind hem, a narrow rolled hem, and many more. The instruction manual that comes with your serger will explain the different methods.

Fusible material can also be used to secure hems. The steam heat of an iron causes it to fuse the hem and the garment together. Follow the manufacturer's directions for fusing. The fusible material should be suitable for the garment fabric. Test the material between fabric scraps. Fusing should not change the color or texture of the fabric.

Sewing Knit Fabrics

Knit fabrics have the ability to stretch and change their shape, 22-25. Their degree of stretch affects the way knits are handled and sewn. Handle all knits with care. They can be easily stretched while pinning and cutting. Keep the fabric flat on the table. Do not allow it to hang over the edge.

22-25 The ability of knit fabrics to stretch makes them comfortable to wear.

Putting Technology to Use

Have students do an Internet search for the word *serger.* Have students find some sites that discuss the use of sergers for hemming. Discuss students' findings in class. If students can find sites that include photos, have them save the photos and use presentation software to display their findings to the class.

Topic 22-3 Construction Techniques

To reduce sliding when pinning more slippery knits, place tissue paper under the fabric. The paper also prevents knits from curling as the pieces are cut.

Some knits have a slight nap or texture. Place all pattern pieces in the same direction on these fabrics. Ballpoint pins are best for pinning knits. Use very sharp shears for cutting. Dull shears may "chew" the fabric and cut a ragged edge.

For sewing, use a ballpoint or very sharp sewing machine needle. Sew a scrap of the knit fabric before sewing the garment. Check the tension, stitch length, and pressure on the machine. For most knits, use shorter stitches with lighter tension and pressure.

Hand baste garment pieces together and check the fit. Once sewn by machine, seams take considerable time and trouble to rip open neatly. A hole will quickly form in a knit fabric if a yarn is broken.

As you sew, feed the fabric under the presser foot slowly and evenly. Avoid pulling or stretching the fabric. See 22-26 for additional guidelines for sewing knit fabrics.

Sewing Knit Fabrics

1. Staystitch all bias and curved edges.
2. Taper all darts to a sharp point.
3. Stitch seam binding along seams, such as shoulder and waistline seams, where stretch is not desired.
4. Overcast or zigzag seams if the fabric ravels.
5. Press a strip of fusible interfacing along the zipper seam on lightweight knits.
6. Place buttonholes in the direction opposite the stretch, or press fusible interfacing under buttonholes to prevent stretching.
7. Overcast or zigzag hem edges on heavy fabrics.
8. Keep hemming stitches loose to allow for slight stretching during wear.

22-26 These guidelines will help you sew knit fabrics successfully.

Check It Out!

1. Why is interfacing needed in a waistband?
2. Name three ways to handle the fullness in the sleeve cap of a set-in sleeve.
3. How should the location of patch pockets be marked on a garment?
4. Which zipper application method is most often used in a center back seam?
5. What is the purpose of making a thread shank when sewing on a button?
6. Which hemming stitch is best for knit fabrics?
7. List four tips for sewing knit fabrics.

Check It Out! (Answers)

1. keeps it from stretching; gives it body so it does not wrinkle or roll down
2. gather, pleat, or ease the fullness
3. machine or hand baste on the marking
4. centered zipper application
5. A thread shank provides room for the button to lie over the buttonhole fabric.
6. catch stitch
7. (Student response. See page 623 in the text.)

Note: Demonstrate sewing knit fabrics, pointing out special techniques.

Note: Display a garment where some of these techniques were used. Discuss how each of these guidelines will affect a knit.

Resource: *Construction Technique Demonstration*, reproducible master, TR

Reflect:
Think of garments you now own or did own that need repairs or restyling or that could be recycled.

Vocabulary:
What do you think is the difference between restyling and recycling?

Activity:
Have the students bring in clothes that need simple repairs. Have them make the repairs in class. After the repairs are completed, have students explain to the class what they did.

Note:
Demonstrate how to repair or replace zippers in garments.

Topic 22-4
Extending the Life of Clothes

Objectives
After studying this topic, you will be able to:
- describe common repairs clothes may need.
- alter the seams and hems of clothes.
- suggest ways to restyle clothes.
- identify ways to recycle clothes you can no longer wear.

Topic Term
restyle

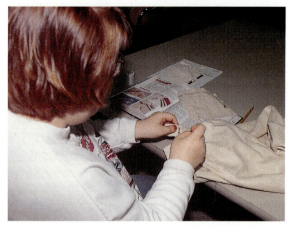

22-27 The life of a garment can be extended with simple repair skills.

Do you have any clothes in your closet that you no longer wear? Most people do! Ask yourself why they are not worn. Are you tired of them? Are some clothes too short or too long? Are there stains on some items that you cannot remove? Do rips and tears need repairing? Are buttons or other fasteners loose or missing? Maybe some clothes seem too plain or too fancy. Others may no longer fit you because your weight or height has changed.

You can probably extend the life of most of these clothes. You may be able to repair, alter, or restyle many of them so that you can wear them again. If you are unable to wear them, there are ways to recycle clothes so other people can use them.

Repairing Clothes

Many of the garments you do not wear may just need some simple repairs. Clothing repairs usually require the same skills as sewing. That is why basic sewing skills are helpful. Even if you never want to sew your own clothes, you can still make repairs for yourself and your family, 22-27.

Basic sewing techniques that can be used for repairing clothes were discussed earlier. You learned how to sew seams. Many seams split open where there is strain. To repair the split, turn the garment inside out. Pin the seam together and sew on the seamline. If the seam is one that receives a lot of stress, stitch the seam twice, using small stitches.

Buttons and other fasteners often loosen with normal wear. When they become loose, especially buttons, secure them immediately. A lost button cannot always be replaced with an identical one. One lost button may force you to replace them all, which can cost considerable time and money.

Zippers sometimes break with normal wear. They may also be damaged during laundering or dry cleaning. Though you may be able to repair them, many times they will need to be replaced. Purchase a zipper of the same style and color as the previous one. Remove the old zipper. Sew in the new zipper using the same zipper application method as was used before.

Hems often come loose in garments. If you need to repair a hem, use one of the hemming stitches described earlier.

Snags detract from the appearance of knitted garments. When left unattended, a small snag can catch and become a large "run." To repair, slip a needle threader, a needle with a large eye, or a small crochet hook through from the back of the fabric next to the snag. Grasp the pulled yarn and pull the snag to the back side of the garment. Carefully stretch the fabric to smooth the snagged area.

Citizenship and Service
Arrange with the activities director of a senior citizens' center to do minor sewing repairs for residents. Take a field trip to talk with the older people for whom sewing was done.

Holes can be patched in several ways. Iron-on patches are easy to use and appropriate for casual garments. Select a patch that matches the color of the garment. Follow the package directions for ironing the patch onto the garment. If a piece of the garment fabric is available, it can be placed behind the hole. Turn under the torn edges of the garment and secure with small, neat hand stitches.

Altering Clothes

Altering differs from repairing. To repair is to restore something to its original condition. To alter is to change the size. If a garment is too large or small, you may be able to make it fit by altering the seams. If the garment is a little too long or short, you may be able to alter the hem.

Altering Seams

To alter a seam is to take it in or let it out. Taking in a seam to make the garment smaller is fairly simple. Put the garment on inside out. Ask someone to pin new seams so the garment will be as snug as you want it. Be sure the garment still hangs properly after it is pinned. Take the garment off and baste along the pinned lines, removing pins as you stitch. Try the garment on again to check the fit. Make adjustments as needed. Stitch the new seam with a regular machine stitch. Remove the old stitches. Trim the seam allowance to ⅝ inch. Press the new seam open.

Letting out a seam to enlarge a garment is somewhat more difficult than taking in a seam to make it smaller. First, determine how much larger the garment should be. Then measure the seam allowance to see how much room you can add by letting out the seam. If letting out the seam will make it the required size, you are ready to begin.

Altering Hems

Being able to shorten or lengthen a hem may make an old garment wearable. Hemlines frequently change with fashion cycles. Shortening or lengthening the hemline can extend the life of a garment. Hems can be adjusted on pants, skirts, dresses, sleeves, and jackets.

To shorten a garment that is too long, first remove the old hemming stitches. Steam press the crease until it disappears, 22-28. Put the garment on and have someone mark the desired length. Turn the hem to the inside and pin it in place. Lightly press the hem near the folded edge. Try the garment on again to be sure the length is satisfactory. Then complete the hem as explained earlier. Trim away excess hem width, if necessary.

If you want to lengthen a garment, check to see if the existing hem is deep enough to add the desired amount. If so, remove the existing hem and press out the crease. Have someone mark the new hem and complete the hemming of the garment.

Restyling Clothes

You can extend the life of some clothes by restyling them. When you **restyle** a garment, you change it to create a different look. Ask yourself what is wrong with a certain garment. Why are you not wearing it? Maybe you can restyle the garment to give it a new look or function. The following are some ideas you might try.

- If a collar is worn and frayed, remove it. You can wear a garment collarless, or you might add a contrasting collar.

22-28 Thoroughly press the old hem crease flat before marking a new hem.

> **Resource:**
> *Restyling Clothes,* color transparency CT-19, TR
>
> **Activity:**
> Have each student bring in a garment to be restyled. Model the garment for the class. Discuss what type of restyling is needed and if it will make the garment wearable. Do the restyling in class.
>
> **Note:**
> Take before and after pictures of restyled garments completed in class. Keep a file of these pictures to encourage future students to attempt this type of project.
>
> **Resource:**
> *New Clothes from Restyling,* reproducible master, TR

Problem-Solving Practice

Repair, Restyle, Recycle? reproducible master, TR. Bring 10 items of clothing to class. Assign a number to each item. Have students determine whether they would repair, restyle, or recycle each garment and explain why.

Enrich:
Have several students demonstrate how to tie-dye.

Discuss:
Is there a consignment shop in our community?

Note:
Display articles that use these suggestions for recycling clothing.

Resource:
Extending the Life of Clothes, Activity D, SAG

- Cover holes or permanent stains with an appliqué or a fancy patch.
- If pants are too short, cut them off. They can be worn as shorts. Sweatshirts can be cut off and made into crop tops.
- If the shape of pant legs is out of fashion, restyle the legs by altering the seams.
- If cuffed pants are out of fashion, shorten the pants to eliminate the cuffs.
- If the elbows of a sweater or jacket are wearing thin, cover them with elbow patches.
- Give a garment a new look by changing the buttons or adding snap-on button covers. Trims can also be added.
- Try giving an old garment new dazzle with decorative trims or creative additions. See 22-29.
- Some dresses can be shortened to make tunic tops.
- If a garment is a light color, you may want to dye it or tie-dye it. Review the literature that comes with the dye so you know what colors to expect. For example, yellow fabric that is dyed blue will result in a green color. Orange fabric that is dyed blue will result in a brown tone.

Recycling Clothes

When you have exhausted the usefulness of a garment, it is time to recycle it. When you *recycle* a garment, you reuse it in a different way. This may mean passing clothes along to others who can wear them. Have you thought of doing any of the following?

- *Give wearable clothes to someone else.* A younger brother or sister, a niece or nephew, a cousin, or a friend may be happy to receive your hand-me-downs.
- *Have a garage sale.* Then use the money you make to buy new clothes.
- *Take garments in good condition to a consignment shop.* They will try to sell the garments for you and give you a portion of the income.
- *Donate unwanted garments to a charitable organization.* Contact such groups as the Red Cross, Salvation Army, or Goodwill Industries. The garments are repaired and given to people in need. Also consider donating old garments to the craft department of a senior center. They will find many uses for the fabric and trims.
- *Reuse portions of old clothes to create new items.* Use the fabric in old garments to make crafts, decorations for your room, or toys for children, such as doll clothes or stuffed animals. See 22-30. Make clothes for children, or let them use old garments to play "dress-up." Remove and save trims, buttons, hooks and eyes, and snaps for future use. Convert soft cotton garments into cleaning and polishing cloths. Cut soft fabrics and nylon hose into small pieces and use as stuffing material in craft projects.

As a last resort, check if your community recycles cloth. In some places, you can drop cloth off at a recycling center along with your paper, glass, and cans.

22-29 Decorative closures can be used in place of buttons and buttonholes to give a garment a whole new look.

FCCLA Activity

Prepare a list of charitable groups in the community who would use recycled clothes. Consult the yellow pages of the phone book, religious organizations, community agencies, and parents. Take a field trip to a recycling center to see what happens to clothing that is collected.

Topic 22-4 Extending the Life of Clothes

22-30 Use fabric from clothes you no longer wear to make quilts or stuff toys.

Check It Out!
1. How might time and money be saved by resewing loose buttons immediately?
2. How does altering clothes differ from restyling clothes?
3. Name two ways to recycle clothes.
4. How can a consignment shop help you recycle clothes?

Check It Out! (Answers)
1. If a button is lost, you may not be able to find an identical replacement. You would then have to replace all of the buttons and this can cost you time and money.
2. Altering is changing the size of a garment. Restyling is changing the look of a garment.
3. give them to other people who can use them, find new uses for old clothes
4. A consignment shop will try to sell your clothes and then give you a portion of the sales price.

Resource:
Recycling Clothes, reproducible master, TR

Discuss:
What local agencies do recycling of cloth? What other options are available to recycle clothes?

Note:
Display samples of pillows stuffed with polyester fiberfill and old nylons. Discuss the advantages of each type.

TEENS ARE CONCERNED ABOUT...
Clothing Styles

Enrich:
If possible, invite a local fashion buyer to speak to your class. Ask the buyer the same questions that were asked of Steve and Buffy in the feature interview. Have the students compare their responses.

Discuss:
- Have you found that the more a garment costs, the better the quality?
- Do you think your knowledge of clothing construction will help you evaluate ready-to-wear garments?
- Do you think your knowledge of fabrics will help you in caring for clothes?
- Do you think parents are more concerned with the quality of clothing than are teens?
- What do you think are some teen classics?

Ask Steve and Buffy about teens and their clothes and they answer with 25 years of experience. Steve dived in—on a whim—as a high school senior when he learned he could buy high fashion "seconds" and overruns for $2 each that normally sold for $18. He invested $100 for 50 shirts, which he sold from his parents' garage in a couple days for $5 to $7 apiece. Later, he opened his own stores in three North Carolina college towns. He was actually pioneering name brand and specialty clothing outlets in the area.

Buffy has a B.S. Degree in Home Economics (now called Family and Consumer Sciences) with an emphasis in child development, family relations, and counseling. She laughingly says, "I married into the clothing industry." Although her degree is well-rounded and required her to take clothing, textiles, and merchandising, she did not intend a career in that field. Her degree led her to teaching special education (her love), then to Proctor and Gamble, Ralston Purina, and Steve Anderson.

Over the years, their stores evolved into an outlet business for upscale clothing. They are busily making arrangements to move to Anderson Square, their own shopping center, to offer an extensive array of fine fashions. They share their marketing expertise through the following answers.

Q: *How do you evaluate the quality of garments when buying apparel for teens?*

A: "One of the first clues to quality is the manufacturer. Every brand has its standards of quality built in, and you can almost be sure what you will find before you inspect seams, hems, facings, and other construction details. The fabric is important, too, and you know in advance what performance to expect from the fibers and fabric construction. Designs require close attention to ensure that stripes, plaids, and prints match at the seams. The price range is also a clue for you usually get what you pay for."

Q: *Do you sew, and if so, does your knowledge of sewing influence your buying decisions?*

A: "I know how to sew," says Buffy, "and knowing fabrics, fabric care, and quality construction is important to me as a buyer. You also have to know the long-term characteristics of fabrics. For example, I know that rayon tends to pucker and knits may buckle. If a garment is beautiful on the hanger, but not likely to retain its appearance, I shy away from it."

Q: *How important is quality versus style to you and to your customers?*

A: "Quality is very important to us," states Steve. "Our stores stand behind the merchandise we sell and we do not want our customers inconvenienced by having to make returns. Style is also important because we want to offer clothing to please our clientele. Teens tend to be

Feature-Related Activity

In the feature, Buffy and Steve state "...you usually get what you pay for." Bring to class several similar garments, some that are high in price and others that are low in price. (A local retailer may loan you garments for this purpose.) Ask the students to evaluate the garments using their knowledge of clothing construction. Have them point out differences in the garments. Then ask them to decide if these differences justify the price variances.

more conscious of style than quality. Parents of teens want quality plus they also look at cost of upkeep."

Q: *Are teens into classics? What do you consider teen classics?*

A: "Yes, teens are into classics, but with an artistic flair. Current classics include jeans, T-shirts, and separates such as pants, skirts for females, and tops. For example, teens like classic jeans, but they add embroidery, fringe, and other 'artsy' touches to individualize them. Males go for more casual, loosely fitted garments. Female clothing is in a more feminine trend. Females want classic T-tops, but fitted. Beading, painting, and feminine trims are preferred to help express individuality. For dressy occasions, classic separates are mixed and matched for the desired look."

Q: *Do you have words of wisdom that you might share with teens?*

A: Buffy quickly states, "There is a strong urge to dress for peer acceptance, but it is not too early to dress for success. Appropriate clothes suggest character traits that are important to building a positive image. For example, a neatly dressed person makes a better impression than one who looks baggy and unkempt."

Chapter Review

Resource:
PowerZone Challenge CD. Have students play the chapter review game to reinforce text content.

Summary

Sewing involves many different techniques. As you learn and practice these techniques, your skills will develop. Soon, you will be able to sew almost any garment or project you might choose.

Sewing projects range from clothes for yourself to those you might sew for other people. Many teens make sleeping bags, book bags, fanny packs, and backpacks too. They also sew items for their rooms, such as pillows, tablecloths, curtains, quilts, and dust ruffles. You can see how a knowledge of sewing can expand your wardrobe. It can also provide you with many useful items.

Take a look at the clothes that you no longer wear. You can save a lot of money by repairing, altering, or restyling these clothes. If you can no longer wear a garment, it can be recycled or given to others to wear. Portions of garments can also be reused in other ways. Therefore, before you throw old clothes into a trash can, think about your options!

Think About It!

1. What types of garments do you own that have tucks, darts, pleats, or gathers?
2. When might you not bother to finish seams when constructing a garment? Why might you skip this step?
3. Do you think you would prefer to sew with fusible or nonfusible interfacing? Explain your answer.
4. Under what circumstances would you want to finish a waistline with a casing rather than a waistband?
5. If you were going to recommend an easy sleeve project for a beginning sewer, what would you suggest?
6. List several situations where hook-and-loop tape would make a suitable closure.
7. Suggest several reasons why people might want to extend the life of their clothes.
8. What charitable groups collect used clothing in your community? Have you donated clothing to any of these groups?
9. Which of the sewing techniques described in this chapter do you think you will use most frequently? Why?
10. List careers, including entrepreneurial opportunities, that might utilize sewing skills.

Try It Out!

1. Make samples of darts. Demonstrate to the class the correct way to press vertical and horizontal darts.
2. Create a bulletin board display showing sample darts, tucks, pleats, and gathers.
3. On several fabric samples, practice gathering fabric using machine basting. Vary the stitch length and the sewing machine tension with each sample to see how these affect gathering ease.
4. Practice sewing seams. Make a sample of a plain seam, flat-fell seam, and French seam.
5. Cut two, 12-inch circles of scrap fabric. Stitch the circles together with a $5/8$-inch seam around the edge. Divide the circle into four sections.

Show trimming on one quarter of the circle, grading on another quarter, clipping on another, and notching on the last section. Label each section.

6. Try different seam finishes on different fabrics. Which finish works best on light, medium, and heavy fabrics?
7. Collect samples of fabrics used for interfacings, including woven, nonwoven, and fusible interfacings. Mount samples on a poster or in a booklet. Label the fiber content, care, and usage of each fabric.
8. Choose one method for applying a zipper and make a zipper sample. When is this zipper method most often used in garments?
9. Practice sewing on snaps, hooks and eyes, and buttons. Make samples of each.
10. Practice making hemming stitches on fabric samples. Use a 12-inch square of fabric for each sample. Press a mock hem in place and use a different hemming stitch on each sample.
11. Bring an item of clothing to class that can be repaired, altered, or restyled. Explain to the class what you intend to do to make the garment wearable again.

CAREER TIMES

LEADING GUIDE TO THE WORLD OF WORK

VOLUME 1, NUMBER 7

Sewing Up Careers in Textiles and Apparel Design

Careers in textiles and apparel design range from making fibers to selling garments and other textile products. This career area has positions for people with high school diplomas as well as those with advanced degrees.

Employment Opportunities

Three main industries make up the field of textiles and apparel design. Many job opportunities exist in each of these industries.

Textile Industry

The textile industry makes fabrics for clothing. It also produces textiles for other uses. Professionals who work in this area may develop fibers and finishes or design fabrics. They may have degrees in engineering, textile technology, or chemistry. Technicians who have associate's degrees often assist these workers.

Apparel Design and Production Industry

People who work in apparel design and production are involved in making fabrics into clothing. Fashion designers come up with ideas for the new styles consumers wear each season. People who work on the design end of this industry sketch designs, make samples, and draft patterns. Those who work in the production area may cut fabric, run sewing machines, and press garments. Managers help plan and supervise each stage of the production process. Costing engineers figure the cost of producing each item. Quality control engineers check to be sure finished apparel is well made.

Fashion Merchandising Industry

The fashion merchandising industry is made up of people linked with the selling of apparel. Buyers play a key role in this industry. They have the job of predicting the types and numbers of items customers will buy. Most buyers are college graduates. They may have assistants who receive on-the-job training. Salespeople who help you find garments when you are shopping also work in the fashion merchandising industry. Many people start in retail jobs and work their way up to other positions within a company. Fashion merchandising offers careers for those who want to work in management. Training supervisors, fashion coordinators, and store managers have jobs at this level.

Another part of fashion merchandising is making consumers more aware of textile and apparel products. Fashion illustrators, models, photographers, and writers all work in this area. These people work to create the ads you find in every type of media. Display designers, who create window and store displays, also work in this field. The main goal of workers in this industry is to entice people to buy products.

Many jobs in textiles and apparel design are found in California and New York. However, the related laundry and dry-cleaning industry offers jobs in all parts of the country. Dry cleaners hire people to clean clothing and wait on customers. Dry cleaners also hire pressers and specialists in garment alterations.

Entrepreneurial Opportunities

Many jobs in textiles and apparel design are well suited for people who would like to be entrepreneurs. Someone with skill and drive might

The manager of a fabric store must have knowledge of textiles to help customers choose materials that will meet their needs.

start a business in fashion design, photography, or tailoring.

Rewards and Demands of Textile and Apparel Careers

Many textile and apparel careers call for creativity. People who work in this field often view using their creative skills as one of the rewards of their careers. Many workers also feel satisfaction in producing products that meet a basic human need.

Demands of textile and apparel careers may include long hours. Some employees perform repetitive tasks and are pushed to meet production quotas. People working in some jobs are under pressure to meet deadlines.

Preparation Requirements

Careers in textiles and apparel design do not all carry the same responsibilities. They do not require the same levels of education and training, either.

Entry-Level Jobs

Entry-level jobs are usually helping positions. Most entry-level workers begin by doing simple tasks. As they gain experience, they are given assignments that are more challenging. Some workers move on to positions that require more responsibility. Stock clerks, tailor's aides, and production workers may all be considered entry-level workers.

Entry-level jobs require little training or prior work experience. Training is often provided on the job. However, workers who have more education are likely to advance faster.

Mid-Level Jobs

Textile and apparel workers in mid-level jobs need some specific skills. These workers usually have a two-year degree or some specialized training. Textile technicians and weaving instructors are in mid-level careers. Dressmakers and tailors also have jobs at this level.

Professional-Level Jobs

Textile and apparel workers who design, manage, or do research are at the professional level. Most people who work at this level need at least a four-year degree.

All levels of textile and apparel workers must keep up with new technology. For instance, many sewing machine operators are trained on the job to use a certain machine. However, today's computerized machines are becoming more complex. Therefore, these entry-level workers would find a basic knowledge of computers and electronics to be helpful.

Personal Qualities Needed for Success

People working in the textile and apparel field need a number of personal qualities. Many positions require an interest in clothing and a sense of color. Skills in solving problems and working under pressure are important in a number of jobs, too. Machine operators need persistence to be able to do tasks repeatedly. People who succeed as designers need drive to face competition. People who create fashion ads must have strong communication skills. Those wishing to be entrepreneurs need to be motivated and have good business sense.

Future Trends

The future will bring more advances in technology to the textile and apparel industries. These advances will allow many workers to do their jobs faster and more easily.

Some positions in the apparel industry will be created as people leave their jobs for various reasons. However, the number of entry-level jobs is predicted to decrease in the next few years. This is partly due to a rise in the percentage of garments from foreign producers being sold in U.S. stores. Another cause of the drop in jobs is U.S. companies having their garments made in other countries. Companies often do this to save money by using the cheaper labor that is available overseas.

Career Interests, Abilities, and You

How can you decide if you really want to pursue a career in textiles and apparel design? How can you assess your skills, interests, and abilities? One way is to enroll in a clothing design course in high school. You might think about taking part in a job shadowing experience at a department store. You may find a part-time job as a salesperson on a retail floor. You could also volunteer to assist the costume curator at a local museum in maintaining the display of historical costumes.

Career Ladder for Textiles and Apparel Design

Advanced Degree
Fabric tester
Market researcher
University professor

Bachelor's Degree
Buyer
Fashion editor
Textile lab technician

Associate's Degree
Dry cleaner
Fabric dyer
Sewing center director

High School Diploma
Buyer's assistant
Fabric finisher
Sample maker

Pre-High School Diploma
Intern with a professional dressmaker
Salesclerk in a fabric store
Volunteer in a community clothing center

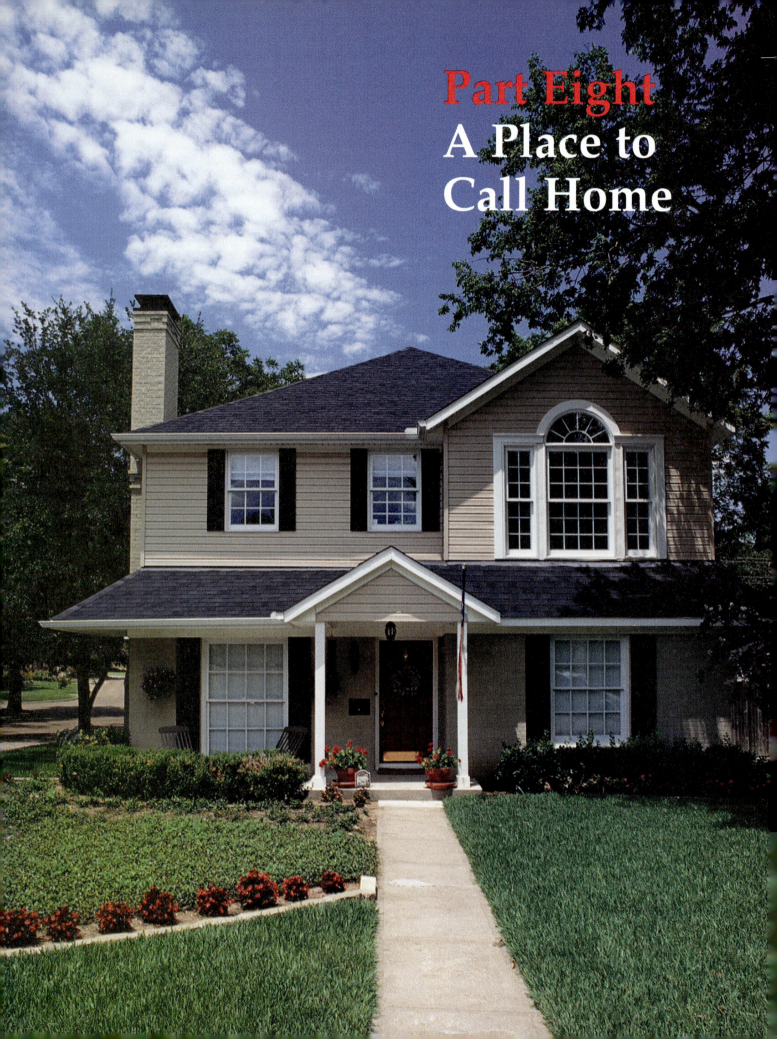

Part Eight
A Place to Call Home

Chapter 23
Choosing a Place to Live

Careers

These careers relate to the topics in this chapter:

- real estate assistant
- apartment building manager
- drafter
- architect

As you study the chapter, see if you can think of others.

Topics

23-1 Meeting Your Housing Needs
23-2 Housing Alternatives
23-3 Renting or Buying Housing

Introductory Activities

1. Ask students to complete the following statements, and then discuss their responses.
   - I prefer living in the city/suburb/country because…
   - My dream home would be…
   - I would rather rent/buy a home because…
   - The most important thing to look for in a home is…
2. Ask students to work in cooperative groups to design a very inexpensive, low-maintenance housing unit for the homeless.

Topic 23-1
Meeting Your Housing Needs

I. Physical Needs
II. Social Needs
III. Psychological Needs
   A. Security
   B. Familiarity
   C. Beauty
   D. Privacy
   E. Self-Expression

Topic 23-2
Housing Alternatives

I. Single-Family Houses
   A. Attached Houses
   B. Freestanding Houses
II. Multifamily Dwellings
   A. Rental Apartments
   B. Cooperative Units
   C. Condominium Units
III. Trends in Housing
   A. Cultural Factors
   B. Demographic Factors
   C. Societal Factors
   D. Economic Factors

Topic 23-3
Renting or Buying Housing

I. Choosing Housing
   A. Income
   B. Location
      1. Job
      2. Lifestyle
II. Renting Housing
   A. Advantages and Disadvantages of Renting
      1. Responsibilities
      2. Rights
III. Buying Housing
   A. Advantages and Disadvantages of Buying

> **Resource:**
> *A Place to Call Home,* reproducible master, TR

> **Note:**
> Review Maslow's hierarchy of human needs. Discuss the importance of housing in meeting physical needs.

> **Discuss:**
> How can housing meet the social needs of teens?

Topic 23-1
Meeting Your Housing Needs

Objectives
After studying this topic, you will be able to
- give examples of how housing helps you meet your physical needs.
- describe how housing can meet your social needs.
- list psychological needs that can be met through housing.

Topic Terms
housing

Housing is any dwelling that provides shelter. The housing you choose reflects your lifestyle and who you are. It also helps you meet your physical, social, and psychological needs.

Physical Needs

Housing should satisfy the physical needs of all the people who live in it. The basic physical needs include shelter, food, and rest. Therefore, your housing should give protection from the weather. It should provide room for preparing and eating food. It should also provide adequate, comfortable space for sleeping and space for your personal belongings.

During the course of your life, the type of housing you need to meet your basic physical needs may change. At one point of your life, you may choose to live alone. Later you may choose to marry and have children. When this happens, you will probably need a larger dwelling than when you lived alone.

Whenever changes occur in your lifestyle, you first need to find housing that meets your physical needs. Then you can think about satisfying your other housing needs.

Social Needs

The need to interact with other people is a social need. To meet this need, a home should have enough space to entertain family and friends, 23-1. It should also fulfill the individual social needs of the people who live there. Before you choose a place to live, you should decide what social needs you want to meet. Then you can decide what type of housing will help you satisfy those needs.

Recreation is an example of a social need. Different types of housing meet this need differently. High-rise buildings may have indoor recreation areas, or there may be parks, basketball courts, and baseball diamonds nearby. Apartment complexes may include tennis courts and swimming pools. Single-family homes usually have yards. Housing developers sometimes build recreational facilities in housing developments to attract prospective buyers.

Psychological Needs

Although psychological needs cannot be measured as accurately as physical and social needs, they have a very strong

23-1 Your housing should provide enough space for fun activities with friends.

Problem-Solving Practice
Shawna and Janice on Their Own, reproducible master, TR. Students are to use the decision-making process to solve the problem described in a case study.

influence on how you feel about your living space. Sometimes people base their housing choices on their psychological needs before their physical needs. In most cases, however, psychological needs will not be more important than physical needs.

Security

Housing helps people feel safe and secure. It provides protection from the outside world and physical danger. Living in a well-built home in an area that is free from crime can help you feel secure.

Familiarity

Many people want to live in a place that is familiar to them. For instance, they may want to continue to live in the community in which they grew up. It makes them feel comfortable and psychologically secure. Sometimes, however, this may mean living in an area that is not physically secure and does not meet other needs.

Beauty

Some people need to have beautiful surroundings where they live. It is important to realize that people have different standards of beauty. What is beautiful to one person may not be beautiful to another. You should respect what other people consider beautiful.

Privacy

Most people need a quiet place to go for privacy. In some cases, this can be a bedroom or a room no one else is using at the time. In other cases it can be an area of a room or a space outdoors, 23-2.

Self-Expression

People express themselves through their homes. You may choose a neighborhood that is peaceful rather than bustling. You may landscape with flowers rather than shrubs. You may decorate your home with wallpaper instead of paneling. All these choices help you meet your need for self-expression through your housing.

23-2 This secluded outdoor sitting area may satisfy a person's need for privacy.

People also express themselves through their leisure activities, such as hobbies or sports. Such activities allow them to "work off steam," relax, and renew their energies. When choosing a place to live, people need to think about the space they will need for these activities.

Check It Out!
1. Give examples of how housing helps people meet the physical needs of shelter, food, and rest.
2. What is one social need that is met through housing?
3. List three psychological needs that can be met through housing.

Check It Out! (Answers)
1. (Student response. See page 636 in the text.)
2. (Name one:) the need to interact with other people, recreation (Students may justify other responses.)
3. (List three:) security, familiarity, beauty, privacy, self-expression

Reflect: Would you like to continue living in your present community when you are an adult?

Reflect: Think of the homes and apartments in your neighborhood. How do your neighbors express themselves through their homes?

Resource: *No Place Like Home,* reproducible master, TR

Resource: *Housing Needs,* Activity A, SAG

Topic 23-2
Housing Alternatives

Objectives

After studying this topic, you will be able to
- list different types of housing.
- explain the difference between single-family houses and multifamily dwellings.
- describe how cooperatives and condominiums differ.
- list factors that affect trends in housing.

Topic Terms

single-family house
attached house
freestanding house
custom house
tract house
manufactured house
mobile home
multifamily dwelling
cooperative
condominium

After determining your housing needs, you can start deciding which type of housing will best meet those needs. A wide variety of housing is available. All housing can be classified as either single-family housing or multifamily housing.

Single-Family Houses

A **single-family house** is designed to house one family. It can be an attached house or a freestanding house.

Attached Houses

Some single-family houses share common walls with the houses on either side. These dwellings are called **attached houses**. *Town houses* and *row houses* are common names for attached houses. Usually, entire sidewalls of town houses or row houses are shared, but there are variations. The designs of the attached dwellings are often, but not always, alike.

The owners of an attached, single-family house own the dwelling itself and the land on which it is located. They have their own entrance and yard area.

Freestanding Houses

A **freestanding house** is a house that stands alone. There are many different types of freestanding houses from which to choose. They include custom houses, tract houses, manufactured houses, and mobile homes.

Custom houses are specifically designed by an architect and built by a building contractor for a new owner. They tend to be very distinctive. The expense of hiring an architect and a contractor also causes them to be more costly than other houses. Custom houses usually take a long time to plan and build. See 23-3.

Tract houses, also called *developer-built houses*, are built by a developer who builds an entire neighborhood at once. They are sold to families after they have been built. To save money, the houses are generally limited to one or two basic sets of designs. The houses are not as distinctive, but they are less expensive to buy than custom houses. Landscaping, painting, and additions can give the houses individuality.

Manufactured houses are made in a factory and then moved to a site and assembled. There are different kinds of manufactured houses. One is a *modular house*. Modules with walls and ceilings are built in factories and moved to the site where the house is assembled. Another type is called a *kit house*. Kit houses are precut. All the materials are sent to the site as a finished shell or in unassembled parts. After the exterior is assembled, the interior is completed according to the buyer's wishes. The use of mass-produced parts saves labor costs. This makes manufactured houses less expensive than custom or developer-built houses.

Mobile homes are dwellings that are built and assembled at a factory. They are then moved to a location and attached to a foundation. Mobile homes can be relocated at a later time if they are detached from the foundation and have wheels attached. There are numerous laws that impact on moving mobile homes. Know the regulations before you buy and be prepared to

---

Family Enrichment Activity

Encourage students to ask their parents about the homes they lived in as children. Students could ask their parents to share a favorite memory of their houses. Also, have students ask their parents about their first home or apartment of their own. They could ask parents what it was like and what they had to do to fix it up.

23-3 A custom house such as this can reflect a family's particular tastes. However, it is also much more costly than other types of housing.

take the necessary security measures. Mobile homes usually come equipped with furnishings and appliances.

The purchase price of mobile homes is usually lower than that of other types of single-family homes. They are usually economical to maintain.

Multifamily Dwellings

Multifamily dwellings are buildings designed to house more than one family. Apartments, cooperative units, and condominium units are common types of multifamily housing.

Rental Apartments

Rental apartments range from low-cost government housing to expensive highrises. Rental apartments offer a wide range of facilities to the residents. These facilities may include washers and dryers, swimming pools, and tennis courts. Some large highrises have stores, offices, recreational facilities, and parking space on the lower floors.

Cooperative Units

A **cooperative** is an apartment building owned by and operated for the benefit of those who live there. The residents form a nonprofit corporation. A person buys stock in the corporation and receives an apartment in return. The stockholders decide as a group how the cooperative, or co-op, is run. They also decide who will be allowed to buy stock and live in the co-op. The corporation charges stockholders a monthly assessment fee to pay for maintenance and repairs.

Condominium Units

A **condominium** is an individually owned housing unit in a multiunit structure. A condominium owner has a shared interest in the common areas and facilities. These may include hallways, sidewalks, parking lots, tennis courts, and swimming pools. A monthly assessment fee is paid for the upkeep of the common areas and facilities.

Condominium, or condo, unit owners can sell their units without the approval of

Resource:
Controversial Issues in Housing, reproducible master, TR

Activity:
Choose a popular type of housing in your community. Interview someone who lives in this type of housing and report to the class on why the person chose that type of housing.

Discuss:
Do you believe there should be restrictions on who can buy or rent specific housing?

Resource:
Choosing Housing, reproducible master, TR

 Putting Technology to Use
Have students explore the Web site for the U.S. Census Bureau's Housing Topics at www.census.gov/hhes/www/housing.html. Ask students to especially investigate the data under the links to *American Housing Survey, Homeownership,* and *Housing Affordability.*

> **Resource:**
> Housing Alternatives, Activity B, SAG
>
> **Discuss:**
> What cultural influences do you see in the structure of your home?
>
> **Reflect:**
> How many times have you moved? Do you think of your home as a permanent residence? Why or why not?

other owners. However, every owner has a vote in concerns relating to the common property.

Co-ops and condos are a form of ownership and not a type of building. You cannot tell by looking at a building whether the apartments are rentals, co-ops, or condos. See 23-4.

Trends in Housing

Housing trends are influenced by the needs and wants of individuals and families. Trends are also influenced by cultural, demographic, societal, and economic factors.

Cultural Factors

Cultural factors have been important in the development of housing. Native Americans lived in dwellings such as hogans and teepees. Early European settlers copied the architecture of their homelands, bringing English, Dutch, Italian, Spanish, and French housing styles. For instance, the style of homes in the Southwest shows the influence of Spanish missions. New England housing is based on the cottage style of the English Pilgrims. When people from different cultural groups began to move to other areas of the country, they brought their housing preferences with them. Today, as the ethnic diversity among Americans continues to increase, many people choose housing based on the cultural traditions of their ancestors.

Demographic Factors

Most homes were once occupied by traditional two-parent families. Now there is an increase in the number of single persons owning or renting housing. This causes a demand for less-expensive, multi-family housing.

The population is aging; people are living longer. Increasing numbers of elderly people require housing designed for their special needs. Because many families move older parents or grandparents in their own homes, there is an increased need for housing with more living space. The large population of "baby boomers," people born during or directly after World War II, is approaching retirement age. They will be looking for smaller housing or retirement housing. In addition, their children are at the age where many are buying housing for the first time.

Societal Factors

In large cities, space is limited. Increases in population may make housing

23-4 These town houses could be rentals, cooperatives, or condominiums.

Citizenship and Service
Using the library, have students research the activities of historic preservation groups beginning with the National Register of Historic Places. Find out how state and federal loan and grant programs can help save historic landmarks in your state and community. Find out how students can volunteer for local preservation societies, such as helping with fundraisers or serving as hosts or for tours of historic homes.

Topic 23-3
Renting or Buying Housing

Objectives
After studying this topic, you will be able to
- discuss the factors to consider when choosing housing.
- identify advantages and disadvantages of renting or buying housing.
- give examples of what you need to know before you rent or buy housing.

Topic Terms
rent
lease
sublease
security deposit
eviction
mortgage

Vocabulary: Do you know the difference between a lease and a sublease?

Activity: On a sheet of paper, list those aspects of housing that are most important to you. After the list is complete, rank the aspects in order of priority.

more difficult to find. People adapt by using smaller areas for single-family dwellings or by living in multifamily dwellings. In addition, many people are moving away from cities to neighborhoods in the suburbs. Because of telecommunication, people don't necessarily need to be near big cities to find jobs.

People are also more mobile than in the past. They are much more likely than their parents or grandparents to move several times during their lives. Thus, they do not look upon a house as a permanent residence. Instead, a home is used for a time and passed on to another family after a few years.

Economic Factors

Housing continues to become more expensive. Increases in income have not kept pace with the rate of inflation in housing costs. This has led to families paying a larger percentage of their income for housing and assuming larger mortgages. For these reasons, many families have chosen to live in less expensive housing options rather than in traditional houses.

On the other hand, many financial institutions are trying to make home ownership an option for more people. To this end, many mortgage companies are offering lower interest rates and flexible finance options. People can therefore continue to invest their money in home ownership while maintaining financial security.

Check It Out!
1. List five housing alternatives available for families.
2. Describe the difference between single-family houses and multifamily dwellings.
3. How do cooperatives and condominiums differ?
4. Name four factors that influence trends in housing and give an example of each.

After looking at all the housing alternatives, you need to decide how you will acquire the housing of your choice. You can rent or buy almost all types of housing.

Choosing Housing

There are many factors you need to consider as you choose a type of housing. The two main factors are your income and the location of the housing.

Income

Most people cannot afford to live in their "dream house." However, they can decide which housing aspect is most important to them. Then they can budget their income to achieve that part of the dream. For instance, suppose you dream of living in a large high-rise with a view. Unfortunately, you cannot afford such an apartment on your budget. You may decide that space is more important than the view. However, a roomy high-rise is still out of your price range. You may then decide that living in a high-rise is not worthwhile without the view. At this point, it is clear that

Check It Out! (Answers)
1. (List five:) attached houses, custom houses, tract houses, manufactured houses, mobile homes, rental apartments, cooperative units, condominium units
2. Single-family houses are designed to house only one family. Multifamily dwellings are designed to house more than one family.
3. People buy stock in cooperatives and are given an apartment in return. People buy individual condominium units and a share in the common areas and facilities.
4. cultural factors, demographic factors, societal factors, economic factors (Examples are student response.)

Resource:
Budgeting for Housing, Activity C, SAG

Resource:
How Much Can You Afford? reproducible master, TR

Discuss:
What are some reasons people might choose to rent?

space is the most important aspect of your housing dream. Therefore, you find a spacious town house apartment you can afford.

The housing you can afford depends on your income. One of the following guidelines can help you determine the amount of your income you can spend on housing:

1. Allow no more than two and one-half times your gross annual income for the purchase price of a house.
2. Budget one-third of your net monthly income for housing costs.
3. Divide your gross annual income by 60 and limit monthly housing costs to this amount.

The first guideline refers to the purchase price of a house only. The second and third guidelines can be applied to both renting and buying housing. Utility bills, property insurance, taxes, maintenance, and city services will also need to be included in the housing budget.

Location

Where your housing is located has a great impact on the lives of you and your family members. It can affect both the job you have and your family's lifestyle.

Job

Some people choose housing that is close to their jobs or transportation that will take them to their jobs. For instance, doctors need to live close to their offices so they can quickly treat patients in emergencies.

People also choose to live in areas that have jobs available in their fields. For instance, a marine biologist would have more job opportunities living near an ocean than in the desert.

Lifestyle

The number and ages of family members should be taken into consideration when choosing housing. You should make sure the house is accessible to community facilities your lifestyle demands. Such facilities include schools, playgrounds, shopping centers, entertainment, athletic and cultural attractions, and public transportation.

You should also make sure the house meets the needs of the family. Families with children may want a house that has a lot of space both inside and outside for playing. See 23-5. Older people may want smaller houses that are easy to maintain and are in a quiet neighborhood.

Renting Housing

The majority of people who rent housing are single people, young married couples, and older people. Many are people who have low incomes.

Advantages and Disadvantages of Renting

When you rent housing you pay **rent**, which is a fee paid to the owner each month. This fee may or may not include utilities, such as heat, water, gas, and electricity.

Many people rent housing because it is convenient. See 23-6. It lets them get acquainted with a new community before they make a long-term housing commitment. They can move when their leases expire and not worry about selling the property. They also do not have to worry about the value of the property increasing or decreasing.

23-5 Some families choose housing near parks, so they spend time outdoors together.

FCCLA Activity

Using local newspapers, have students survey housing possibilities that are available in the community. Discuss which ones would be appropriate for a graduating senior who is getting a job, going to college, doing volunteer work, or taking technical training. FCCLA members working in Community Services Opportunities could design a housing booklet for newcomers to the area based on the information they find.

23-6 People rent apartments for many reasons including convenience, flexibility, and location.

> **Enrich:**
> In small groups, develop checklists for potential renters of factors to look for in rental apartments and houses.
>
> **Enrich:**
> Visit an apartment building and ask the landlord for a copy of the lease used for those apartments. Does it include all that it should? Does it include any additional restrictions?

Renting is economical, too. Renters know how much their housing is going to cost them, and they can budget for it. There also won't be any surprise expenses, such as the cost of a new water heater. The owner of the property is responsible for the maintenance and repair of the building.

Before you rent housing, you need to know what your rights and responsibilities are as a tenant. You also need to understand the rights and responsibilities of the owner. This will make a good relationship with the owner possible.

Responsibilities

A lease is written by the property owner to protect the property. A **lease** is a contract between a tenant and a property owner. It lists the rights and responsibilities of both parties. A lease covers a specified rental period, which is often one year.

Leases identify the amount of rent to be paid each month. In addition, they list what you are expected to do and what you are forbidden to do. See 23-7. You must understand everything stated in the lease before you sign it. Once your signature is on the lease, you are responsible for fulfilling all the terms. When you sign a lease you are saying you will pay your rent promptly. You are also agreeing to keep the property clean and free from damage. In turn, the owner agrees to keep the building and grounds in good condition. He or she also promises to obey health and safety laws.

A lease protects you from a rent increase after you move into rental housing. The lease also protects the owner if you want to move out after a short time. If you move, you are still responsible for paying the rent until the lease expires.

Many owners let tenants sublease rental property to someone else. To **sublease**, or sublet, means you have the right to pass the lease over to a second tenant. This person pays rent directly to the owner. If he or she fails to pay, you are still responsible for the rent being paid on time. The owner usually has to approve the new tenant.

A security deposit is commonly required in a lease. A **security deposit** is a sum of money, usually one month's rent, paid by the tenant before moving into the property. It is used to cover possible

Across the Curriculum

Math. Have students research to find how much nearby apartments are charging for rent, as well as the amount of deposit. Then have students research to find out the average price of neighborhood homes and the current rate for mortgage loans. Ask students if they think it is more cost-effective to rent or buy housing and give reasons for their answers.

Resource:
Reading an Apartment Lease, Activity D, SAG

Discuss:
Do you understand all the terminology used in this lease? Do you think official papers, such as a lease, should be written in simpler language?

ENGLISH MANOR APARTMENTS
I N C O R P O R A T E D
203 WINDSOR ROAD • LAKE SHORE, N.C. 28001

THIS AGREEMENT OF LEASE, MADE THIS *1st* DAY OF *March* 20*04* BETWEEN ENGLISH MANOR APARTMENTS, INC., HEREINAFTER CALLED LESSOR: AND _____ _____ HEREINAFTER CALLED TENANT, WHETHER ONE OR MORE.

WITNESSETH, That the Lessor leases and lets unto the Tenant, premises known as _____ Lake Shore, N.C. 28401, for a term of not less than thirty (30) days from this date at the rental of $ *600.00* per month, to be paid in advance at the office of English Manor Apartments on the first day of each month without formal demand. This lease shall be renewed automatically for successive terms of one month each so long as the terms hereof are complied with at the same rental as hereinabove set forth payable in advance on the first day of each said renewed term, which renewed term shall expire of its own limitation at midnight on the last day of said term.

This will acknowledge the receipt of $ *600.00* as a deposit to cover any indebtedness to the Lessor for charges made for breakage or damage to the property. Any or all of deposit to be returned to the Tenant upon proper termination of the lease providing (1) THE TENANT HAS REMAINED IN POSSESSION AND PAID RENT ON ABOVE PROPERTY FOR AT LEAST SIX (6) MONTHS: (2) KEYS TO THE ABOVE PROPERTY HAVE BEEN RETURNED (3) THE PREMISES ARE LEFT IN A CLEAN CONDITION, AND ALL OTHER CONDITIONS OF THIS AGREEMENT HAVE BEEN MET TO THE SATISFACTION OF THE LESSOR. IT IS FURTHER UNDERSTOOD AND AGREED THAT THE TENANT SHALL GIVE A FIFTEEN (15) DAYS WRITTEN NOTICE BEFORE VACATING PREMISES. IF SAID NOTICE IS NOT GIVEN, TENANT WILL BE CHARGED FOR SAME.

TENANT will pay for any damage other than normal deterioration, wear and tear to the premises of Lessors property and will be responsible for the stoppage of sewer and drainage facilities chargeable to his use of the premises. Tenant will pay all utility bills as they come due. TENANT AGREES TO PAY A $5.00 GAS SERVICE CHARGE UPON VACATING.

LESSOR and its agents reserve the right to cancel this lease for any reason at any time by mailing a written notice to Tenant specifying a day of termination of the lease, which date shall be seven (7) days from the date of mailing the notice of cancellation. The mailing of such written notice by first class mail will constitute the giving of this notice. Any unearned portion of the rent will be refunded to the Tenant.

Should Tenant fail to make payment of the rental herein specified in advance by the first day of the month, this lease shall terminate at midnight of the last day of the preceding month without the necessity of any written notice; and Tenant agrees upon such termination to immediately vacate the premises. Should Tenant fail to vacate the premises, Lessor shall have the absolute right to lock the premises and forbid the use thereof by the Tenant.

The Lessor and its agents shall have the right to enter upon the premises at any reasonable time to assure that this agreement is being complied with and not being violated.

Time shall be of the essence of this agreement. It is agreed that no failure of the Lessor to insist on the strict terms hereof shall constitute a waiver of its rights to insist on such terms on any later occasion. Tenant will comply with the general rules and regulations promulgated by the Lessor for the operation of the apartment of which the subject premises are a part.

I/We accept the foregoing conditions.   ENGLISH MANOR APTS.

_____   _____
Tenant   Agent

_____
Tenant

23-7 Always read a lease carefully before you sign it.

Putting Technology to Use
Have students search the Internet for the exact phrase *reading a lease*. Have students look at some of the Web sites that are returned as matches. (Matches should include sites put out by universities as well as individual city sites.) Have students look over tips for reading a lease and discuss their findings in class.

damages to the property. When the tenant moves out, the owner refunds the security deposit if the terms of the lease have been met. The owner can keep all or part of the deposit if the tenant damages the property. The owner also keeps the deposit if the tenant moves without giving the owner proper notice.

If you are renting property and fail to live up to the terms of the lease, you can be evicted. **Eviction** is a legal procedure that forces a tenant to leave the property before the rental agreement expires. An owner has the right to evict tenants if they fail to uphold the terms of the lease. Failing to pay rent or having a dog when the lease prohibits pets would be grounds for eviction.

Rights

As a tenant, you also have rights. You have the right to housing that is safe and secure. Suppose the owner does not take proper care of the property or follow health and safety laws. You can turn to governmental services for help. For instance, if there are fire hazards in the building, you can call the fire department. Your local city hall can help you locate the right agency to solve the problem. If your problem cannot be solved through these channels, you can seek legal advice.

Buying Housing

A large number of people choose to own their own houses instead of renting. They can buy either single-family houses or units in multifamily housing.

Advantages and Disadvantages of Buying

People choose to buy houses for many different reasons. They prefer the emotional security of buying a home to the convenience of renting. They have chosen to stay in one location for a number of years. Some need the space a single-family house offers.

People also choose to buy houses for financial reasons. Houses usually increase in value faster than the rate of inflation.

Therefore, many homeowners regard their house payments as a type of savings plan. Home ownership improves credit ratings. Money paid for real estate taxes and interest on a home mortgage can be deducted from income taxes.

After you have chosen a house, you pay a down payment and get a loan to pay the rest. This type of loan is called a **mortgage**. It is usually paid monthly over 15 to 30 years, depending on the terms.

In addition to the down payment and mortgage, there are other expenses. There are closing costs, homeowner's insurance, taxes, and moving expenses. These can add up to quite a bit of money. Therefore, you should get estimates of the costs and be sure to have enough money available to pay for them. Items generally included in closing costs are listed in 23-8. The purchase of a home and the closing costs may become very involved. Be sure to seek the advice of professionals when you are ready to buy.

When buying a new house, you may have to buy wallpaper, furniture, and landscaping. When buying a preowned house, you may have to make improvements. These might be minor improvements, such as painting or wallpapering. See 23-9.

Closing costs include

- appraisal
- property survey
- deed
- title search
- title insurance
- tax stamp
- recording fees
- notary fee
- credit report
- escrow fees

23-8 Home buyers need to remember that closing costs must be added to the purchase price of a home.

Enrich: Research a renter's rights if an eviction notice is served.

Enrich: Have a class debate on renting versus buying.

Discuss: Look at the closing costs listed in Chart 23-8. Did you know about all these costs? How much expense might they add to the cost of buying a home?

Career Preparation Activity

The Facts About Real Estate Agents, reproducible master, TR. Students are to interview a real estate agent in their community and answer the questions provided.

Resource:
Renting Versus. Buying, Activity E, SAG

Resource:
To Buy or to Rent: That Is the Question! reproducible master, TR

23-9 Bathrooms in preowned homes frequently need updating. New tile gave this bathroom a fresh new look.

Sometimes, however, major changes such as new plumbing and wiring are needed. All these costs need to be considered in addition to the original purchase price.

Check It Out!
1. Why do you need to consider location when choosing housing?
2. List three advantages of renting housing and two advantages of buying housing.
3. What are a tenant's responsibilities after signing a lease?
4. In addition to the down payment and the mortgage, what are three other expenses a home buyer needs to pay?

Check It Out! (Answers)
1. Location has a great impact on the lives of all family members. It can affect both the jobs a person has and his or her family's lifestyle.
2. (Student response. See pages 642-646 in the text.)
3. pay rent promptly, keep the property clean and free from damage
4. (List three:) closing costs, homeowner's insurance, taxes, moving expenses

TEENS ARE TALKING ABOUT...
Moving Away from Home

As teens look forward to the future, they often make plans to move away from home. In a group discussion, Ryan, Mike, and Bevin talked about some of the issues surrounding this future event.

Their reasons for wanting to move away from home vary. Ryan said, "I believe teens should wait to move out until they're ready to leave for college or until they're ready for full-time employment. At that time, most teens are ready to move out and see what the real world is like. They want to know if they can function in the real world."

Mike added, "The one day in my life I'll always remember will be the day I move out. I have friends who live away from home, and I'm responsible enough to live away from home."

When asked when they think they will be ready to take this step, Ryan stated, "When I go to college."

Mike said, "Now."

Then the topic turned to the advantages and disadvantages of moving away from home. Ryan thinks learning to survive in the real world is an advantage.

As for the disadvantages, Bevin implied that teens need someone to help take care of them. Moving out will mean a special source of security will be missing. Ryan wondered about the issue of finances.

The group was then asked if they want to live alone or share housing. Mike wants to live with his friends. "I'm going to have a roommate, so I'll never get lonely," he commented.

Ryan also prefers to share an apartment with a roommate. He thinks this will make the financial situation a whole lot easier for both himself and his roommate. He also thinks having a roommate would help him cope with college life and meet new friends.

When asked where they want to live when they move out, Ryan mentioned an apartment. Bevin and Mike aren't sure what type of housing they want to live in yet.

The group was also asked how they will pay for their housing expenses when they move away from home. Mike said, " I've had a job for a long time. My job gives me a source of money for rent."

Ryan gave a different view. "Money could be a big problem if you can't find a job. It would be impossible to pay the rent and buy school supplies and other necessities. If only you had a job, you would have to support your roommate. That wouldn't be fun."

Overall, the group seemed confident they will be ready for the challenge of moving away from home when the time comes. In fact, Mike seems to think he is ready now. "I'm responsible, experienced, and know a lot of friends who could live with me. I'm also very good at housekeeping!"

Feature-Related Activity

Have the students determine what information needs to be obtained in order to make the decision to move away from home. Identify the questions that must be answered. For instance, how do you go about finding and renting an apartment? How much will it probably cost to live on your own for a year? What expenses will you have? Once the questions have been identified, have groups of students work to gather the needed information. Have each group report on their findings.

Chapter Review

Summary

When choosing a place to live, you need to start by considering your physical, social, and psychological needs. Your physical needs include shelter, food, and rest. Your social needs are for a place to entertain family and friends. Social needs also include individual social needs like recreation. Your psychological needs are for security, familiarity, beauty, privacy, and self-expression.

Once you have identified your needs, you can evaluate different types of housing to see if they meet these needs. You can choose between single-family houses or multifamily dwellings. Single-family houses can be attached or freestanding. Multifamily dwellings include rental apartments, cooperative units, and condominium units.

Your housing decision may be affected by trends in housing. The factors that impact housing trends include cultural, demographic, societal, and economic factors.

After you have chosen a type of housing that will meet your needs, you need to think about whether you want to rent or buy. Both your income and the location of the housing will impact your decision. There are advantages and disadvantages to both renting and buying housing. You need to choose what works best for you.

Think About It!

1. How would you feel if your housing did not meet your physical needs for food and rest?
2. How does your housing help you meet your social needs?
3. Which of the five psychological needs discussed in this chapter is most important to you? Why?
4. Would you rather live in an attached single-family house or a freestanding single-family house? Why?
5. What would you do if you owned a co-op and you disagreed with a decision made by the other stockholders in the corporation?
6. How does cultural diversity influence your choice of where you would like to live?
7. Under what circumstances would it be best for you to rent housing?
8. How would you plan to meet the financial responsibilities of home ownership?

Try It Out!

1. Locate a recent news story about problems that have occurred because physical housing needs were not met. Write a paragraph explaining how this could be prevented from happening again in the future.
2. Think about how your housing needs will change in the next five years and in the next fifteen years. Discuss your thoughts in a small group setting.
3. Look through the classified section of your local newspaper. Make a list of single-family housing available in your area. Then make a list of multifamily housing available. Compare the two lists to see which type of housing is the most plentiful in your area.

Resource:
PowerZone Challenge CD. Have students play the chapter review game to reinforce text content.

4. Prepare a brochure that highlights your community. Be sure to give examples of the benefits of living in the area.
5. Obtain a copy of a lease. Examine it to see how the tenant's and owner's rights and responsibilities are defined.
6. Interview an adult who has recently bought housing. Write a report on the steps he or she had to take before actually buying the house. Then discuss what he or she thinks the advantages and disadvantages of owning a house are.

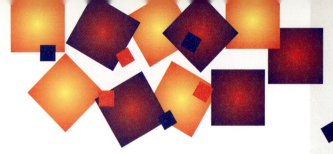

Chapter 24
Applying Design in Your Home

Careers

These careers relate to the topics in this chapter:
- furniture store salesclerk
- wallpaper hanger
- interior decorator
- interior designer

As you study the chapter, see if you can think of others.

Topics

24-1 The Elements and Principles of Design
24-2 Decorating Your Home
24-3 Furnishing Your Home

Introductory Activities

1. Show some pictures of attractive rooms to the class. Ask students what they think makes each room attractive. They will probably begin by referring to objects in the room, such as the furniture or the windows. Encourage them to look more closely at the details. What makes the furniture attractive in the room? Eventually they may begin to point out color, line, texture, and other elements and principles of design.
2. In introducing the topic of design in the home, discuss the tools students will learn to use—the elements and principles of design. Relate the elements and principles of design to a recipe. The elements of design are equivalent to the ingredients. The principles of design are equivalent to the directions for combining the ingredients.

Topic 24-1
The Elements and Principles of Design
I. The Elements of Design
   A. Color
      1. Guidelines for Using Color
      2. Planning Color Schemes
   B. Line
   C. Texture
   D. Form
II. The Principles of Design
   A. Proportion
   B. Rhythm
   C. Balance
   D. Emphasis
III. The Goals of Design
   A. Beauty
   B. Appropriateness
   C. Unity with Variation

Topic 24-2
Decorating Your Home
I. Floor Coverings
   A. Types of Floor Coverings
   B. Choosing Floor Coverings
II. Wall Treatments
   A. Choosing a Wall Treatment
   B. Wall Treatment Options
III. Windows and Window Treatments
IV. Lighting
   A. Types of Lighting
      1. Lighting Technology
   B. Applications of Lighting
   C. Basic Guidelines for Good Lighting

Topic 24-3
Furnishing Your Home
I. Choosing Furniture
   A. Factors to Consider
   B. Furniture Styles
   C. Judging Quality in Furniture
      1. Wood Furniture
      2. Upholstered Furniture
      3. Plastic Furniture
      4. Metal Furniture
II. Organizing Living Space
   A. Shared Space
   B. Personal Space
   C. Making a Scale Floor Plan
      1. Computer Programs
III. Using Accessories

Topic 24-1
The Elements and Principles of Design

Objectives
After studying this topic, you will be able to
- describe the elements and principles of design in relation to housing.
- give examples of how to use the elements and principles of design.
- explain the goals of design.

Topic Terms
monochromatic color scheme
analogous color scheme
complementary color scheme
split-complementary color scheme
triad color scheme
double-complementary color scheme
accented-neutral color scheme
function
beauty
appropriateness

In Topic 19-2, "Choosing Clothes That Look Good on You," you learned about the elements and principles of design as they apply to clothing. In this topic, you will learn how the elements and principles of design apply to housing. You will learn how to design housing interiors that will help create a positive atmosphere for the people who live there.

The Elements of Design

As you learned, the elements of design are color, line, texture, and form. These elements can be used in many different ways to create a variety of designs.

Color

Color is a very important element of design. It is one of the first things people notice when they enter a room. It creates a mood and usually leaves a lasting impression. Therefore, deciding what color to use is usually the first decision made when decorating a room.

Each color reflects certain moods or feelings. See 24-1. You may feel more comfortable when the colors used to decorate a room reflect your personality. For example, if you are outgoing, you may like colors such as orange or red. If you are more reserved, you may favor colors such as blue or green.

Guidelines for Using Color

When decorating with color, it is important to follow certain guidelines. The following are some basic guidelines:

- The colors used in a home should express the tastes of all the family members. Shared areas used by the whole family, such as the kitchen and living room, should be decorated in colors that satisfy everyone. In private areas, such as a bedroom, colors that appeal to individual family members can be used.
- Choose a dominant color when decorating. Smaller amounts of other colors can be used to accent the dominant color and add interest and variety.

Moods Created by Color

Red	Exciting, powerful, courageous, aggressive, dangerous, energetic
Orange	Lively, cheerful, friendly energetic, warm
Yellow	Cheerful, bright, sympathetic, cowardly, wise, warm
Green	Natural, friendly, peaceful, refreshing, lucky, envious, hopeful
Blue	Calm, serious, reserved, depressed, dignified, serene
Violet	Royal, dignified, dominating, mysterious, dramatic
Black	Sophisticated, dignified, somber, desperate, mournful, wise
White	Fresh, innocent, pure, faithful, peaceful

24-1 Each color reflects a different mood or feeling.

Vocabulary: What is your definition of *beauty*?

Note: Review some of the key points concerning color, line, texture, and form presented in Chapter 19.

Reflect: What color is your bedroom? Why did you pick that color for your room? How does the color of your room make you feel when you walk into it?

Activity: Show the students pictures of rooms where the colors listed in Chart 24-1 are the primary colors used. Ask them to write down how they might feel if they were in each of these rooms. Have them compare their responses to those given in the chart.

Across the Curriculum

English. Ask each student to write a paragraph describing the decor of his or her favorite room. Rooms described might be in students' own homes or in homes they have visited. They may be pictures students have seen in magazines or imaginary rooms of students' creation. Have students volunteer to share with the class what they have written. Discuss what makes a room a favorite. It might be factors such as the furniture, light, windows, a fireplace, comfort, or elegance. Then discuss how to create a room like this and where to begin.

Resource:
Color Wheel, Analogous Color Scheme, Complementary Color Scheme, color transparencies CT-21A, B, and C, TR

Enrich:
Working in small groups, assign each group a guideline for using color. Have them create a project or find magazine pictures that illustrate their guideline for using color.

Reflect:
Think about your favorite room in your house. Does it use light or dark colors? low- or high-intensity colors? warm or cool colors?

Discuss:
What color schemes are used in the family and consumer sciences classrooms? What color schemes would you use instead?

- A sharp value contrast can be used to emphasize an object. For instance, a dark sofa will stand out when placed against a light background. The same sofa will blend in with a room decorated in similar dark colors.
- Light colors make items and rooms look larger. Dark colors make items and rooms look smaller. For instance, long, narrow rooms can look shorter if a dark color is used on the end walls.
- Using a variety of values in a room can make the room more interesting. Using the values in unequal amounts will create an even more interesting effect. For example, large areas of light values can be set off by small areas of dark values.
- Low-intensity colors are frequently used throughout the house, especially as backgrounds and in large areas. High-intensity colors are better suited for small areas and as accent pieces. As with value, intensity works more effectively when used with variety.
- Using warm colors, shades, and high-intensity colors will make a room appear smaller than it actually is.
- Using cool colors, tints, and low-intensity colors will make a room appear larger than it actually is.
- Warm colors suggest informality. When objects are placed in front of warm colors, they seem to blend. Cool colors suggest formality. They make objects in front of them seem to stand out.

Following these guidelines will help you use color well. They will also help you plan the appropriate color schemes for your home.

Planning Color Schemes

Color schemes are used to coordinate colors in a pleasing manner. Following the standard color harmonies will help you achieve success with color.

A **monochromatic color scheme** uses only one hue. Variety is created by varying the value and intensity of the hue. A monochromatic color scheme is shown in 24-2.

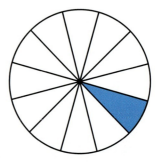

24-2 The color blue is the basis of this monochromatic color scheme.

An **analogous color scheme** combines hues found next to each other on the color wheel. Since the colors are related, they blend well. Three to five hues are usually used in an analogous color scheme. See 24-3.

A **complementary color scheme** is formed by using colors opposite each other on the color wheel. When these colors are used at full intensity and value, great excitement and contrast is created. Letting one color dominate and varying the values and intensities of the hues will help lessen this effect. The room shown in 24-4 has a complementary color scheme.

A **split-complementary color scheme**, 24-5, uses one hue and the two hues on either side of its complement. For example, a split-complementary color scheme might consist

Putting Technology to Use
Ask students to interview someone they feel has created an attractive living environment in his or her home or apartment. Have the class use word processing software to develop a template for the list of questions they might ask during the interviews. Have students print out the questionnaire. Students can then create a file from the template to which they can add the interviewee's answers.

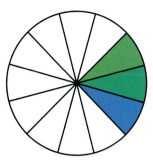

24-5 The split-complementary color scheme uses one hue and the two hues on either side of its complement.

24-3 This analogous color scheme uses three colors—blue, blue-green, and green.

of the colors red, yellow-green, and blue-green. This provides less contrast and looks softer than a complementary color scheme.

A **triad color scheme**, 24-6, combines three colors that are equally distant from one another on the color wheel. The colors can be used in normal intensity and value. For a color scheme with less contrast, the values and intensities of the hues can be changed.

A **double-complementary scheme** uses two pairs of complementary colors, 24-7. The two sets of colors might be next to each other on the color wheel. They might also be colors on each side of complementary colors.

Enrich:
Have the students go through magazines and find examples of the various color schemes. Mount these on paper, identify the color schemes, and explain which colors create each color scheme.

Reflect:
What color schemes are used in your home?

Resource:
Using Color in Design, reproducible master, TR

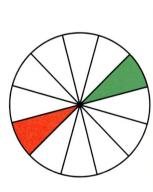

24-4 The contrasting colors of red and green in this bedding create a complementary color scheme.

Putting Technology to Use
Have students use drawing or graphing software to create color wheel diagrams illustrating the color schemes of rooms in their homes.

Resource:
Color Schemes, Activity A, SAG

Discuss:
What types of lines are visible in this classroom? How do they affect the appearance of this room?

Enrich:
Invite an interior designer to class to discuss how the elements and principles of design are used when decorating a home.

Example:
Pass around samples of fabrics, tiles, and floor coverings with different textures. Let students feel them and observe how they reflect light in different ways. Discuss how these would affect the appearance of a room.

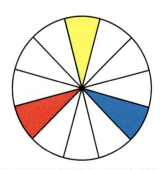

24-6 The wallpaper border and accessories form a triad color scheme in this room.

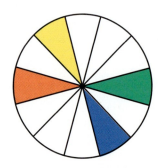

24-7 Two pairs of complementary hues make up a double-complementary color scheme.

An **accented-neutral color scheme** is based on one dominant neutral color. Black, white, gray, or shades or tints of brown might dominate in this color scheme. Bright accents of color are added to create interest. A living room decorated in beige with red throw pillows on the sofa is an example of this color scheme.

Line

Vertical, horizontal, diagonal, and curved lines are all used in house design. *Vertical* lines suggest height, confidence, and dignity. They are visible in tall furniture, such as secretaries and armoires; long, narrow draperies; striped wallpaper; and pillars or columns. They can make ceilings seem higher and rooms more spacious than they actually are.

Horizontal lines suggest relaxation and informality. They are seen in long, low furniture, such as sofas and chests. They can make ceilings seem lower and rooms seem wider than they actually are.

Diagonal lines suggest activity and movement. They are found in slanted ceilings, staircases, and fabric designs. They provide variety in design, but can be overpowering and tiring unless used in small amounts.

Curved lines can suggest either activity or relaxation, depending on the degree of the curve. Soft curves appear restful and graceful. Upward curves give an impression of rising. Small curves look playful. Tight curves look action-packed. Curves can be seen in arches, ruffled curtains, and curved furniture.

Using a variety of lines can create interest, but it can also cause confusion. Therefore, when designing a home, one type of line should dominate. For example, vertical lines may dominate a room. Small amounts of curved or diagonal lines can be used in accessories to create interest. See 24-8.

Texture

Texture provides much of a home's character because it strongly affects the senses of touch and sight and stimulates the imagination. Rough textures and bold patterns tend to make a room appear smaller. Uneven surfaces cast small shadows and absorb light. This makes the actual color seem deeper, the room darker, and the objects larger and heavier. On the other hand, shiny, smooth textures reflect light and make a room appear brighter and lighter.

The room shown in 24-9 has a variety of textures. Rough textures are seen in the

Citizenship and Service
Have students study and volunteer for a housing project such as Habitat for Humanity. Ask a representative from the organization to come speak to the class.

Topic 24-1 The Elements and Principles of Design

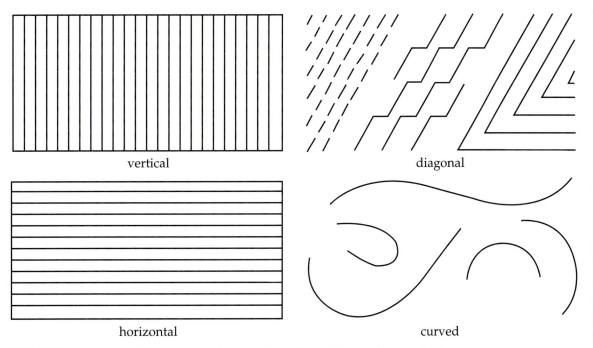

24-8 Different types of lines are used to create various visual effects in design.

sofa, fireplace, and rug. A good contrast is provided by the smooth textures seen in the polished wood furniture, leather chair, and lamp. This variety of textures gives the room an interesting, inviting, and pleasant look.

Form

Form is three-dimensional. It has length, width, and depth. In housing, it is found in architecture, furniture, equipment, and accessories. Forms should not be chosen only for how they look. They should also be chosen for their **function**, or how they will be used. For example, a lounge chair is designed to let a person stretch out and relax for a long period of time. A dining room chair is designed for eating at a table in an upright position. You could not comfortably stretch out on a dining room chair for a long time. Room design works best when the forms are functional and relate to one another while also providing variety.

The Principles of Design

The principles of design are guidelines for working with the elements of design. The principles of design are proportion, rhythm, balance, and emphasis. They can be used with the elements of design to create well-designed rooms.

Proportion

Proportion is the ratio of one part to another part or to the whole. Unequal proportions, such as 2:3, 3:5, and 5:8, are

24-9 The variety of textures used in this room gives it character.

Discuss:
What is meant by the concept of "form follows function"?

Resource:
Line, Texture, and Form, Activity B, SAG

Enrich:
Create a bulletin board illustrating equal and unequal proportion.

 Across the Curriculum
Art. Have students choose a favorite piece of art and bring in a copy or picture of it. Have students discuss the use of proportion, balance, rhythm, and emphasis in the artwork.

Discuss:
Do you agree that unequal proportion is more pleasing to look at than 1:2 and 1:1 ratios?

Activity:
Ask each student to bring an item from home (or find a picture in a magazine) that illustrates one of the five types of rhythm. Ask the students to explain their examples to the class.

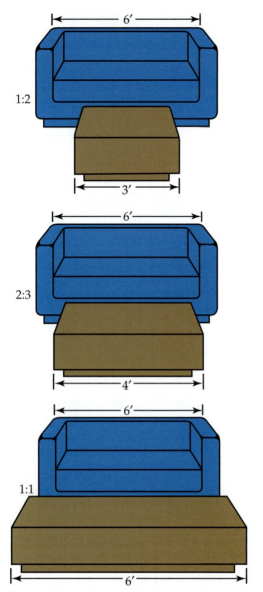

24-10 The table in the middle is in a 2:3 ratio with the couch. This unequal proportion is considered more pleasing than the 1:2 and 1:1 ratios seen above and below.

pleasing to the eye. They are more interesting than equal proportions, such as 2:2 or 2:4. For example, a rectangle is more pleasing than a square. See 24-10 to see how proportion affects furniture and accessories.

Think about proportion when choosing furniture and accessories. If they are too large in proportion to a small room, they will make the room seem crowded. The room will seem even smaller, and the furniture will seem even larger.

Rhythm

Rhythm leads the eyes smoothly from one feature to another in a design. The five types of rhythm are repetition, opposition, gradation, radiation, and transition. All five types can be seen in 24-11, which shows good use of rhythm.

By repeating color, line, form, or texture in a design, you can achieve rhythm by *repetition*. The use of the same wood in the furniture pieces creates repetition.

Opposition is rhythm formed by lines meeting at right angles. You can see opposition in the corners of the windows, picture frames, and pillows.

Gradation is rhythm created by a change in color value from dark to light. It is also created by a gradual change in form from small to large. The movement from darker shades in the sofa to lighter neutrals in the floor and walls shows gradation.

In rhythm by *radiation*, lines extend outward from a central point. The design in the picture and the arrangement on the table show radiation.

Transition is rhythm created by curved lines. Transition carries the eyes easily over an architectural feature or piece of furniture. The curved lines in the sofa provide transition between the windows.

Balance

Balance gives design a sense of *equilibrium*, or a sense of weight on both sides. Balance can be formal or informal.

Formal balance is the arrangement of identical objects on opposite sides of a central point. Look at 24-12 and imagine a line in the center of the room. One side is practically the mirror image of the other. Formal balance gives a restful, orderly, sophisticated look to a room. However, too much use of formal balance can become dull.

Informal balance is the arrangement of different but equal objects on opposite sides of a central point. Various forms, sizes, and colors can be used together to achieve informal balance. For instance, a large object can be used to balance a few smaller ones. Informal balance is achieved

Family Enrichment Activity
Encourage students to interview their families about their homes. Before the interview, students should write down a series of specific questions to ask. Questions to ask could include what they like about the house and what they would like to change. Students should ask their family members to be specific about the elements in the house such as the colors, materials, and furnishings. Students should include their own answers to the questions since they are also family members.

24-11 A good sense of rhythm creates a comfortable, relaxing room.

24-12 Formal balance is illustrated by the placement of accessories over the sofa and the matching tables on either side.

in 24-13 through the arrangement of furniture. The furniture pieces on either side of the fireplace are different, yet they appear to be of equal weight.

Combining formal and informal balance creates variety. However, as with other elements and principles of design, balance works best when either formal or informal balance dominates.

> **Enrich:**
> Bring a variety of room accessories to class. Have the students work in small groups. Each group should select and arrange two groups of accessories that illustrate both formal and informal balance. Have each group explain their arrangements to the class.

Career Preparation Activity

Design as a Career, reproducible master, TR. Have students use the form to interview someone who works in the area of interior design. Encourage students to add their own questions to the form. Students should then evaluate what they have learned about careers in interior design.

Discuss:
Could the accessories in Figure 24-13 be rearranged to create formal balance? If not, what could be done to make a formal arrangement using some of these accessories?

Reflect:
Think of the last time you walked into a room and were attracted to something in that room. Was it a focal point in the room? What was the focal point?

Resource:
Score with the Goals of Design, transparency master, TR

Reflect:
If you could add one item to your bedroom that you feel would add to its beauty, what would it be?

Discuss:
What factors would you keep in mind if you were decorating a home for a large and active family? for an older, retired couple? for newlyweds?

24-13 The arrangement of the furniture around the fireplace is an example of informal balance.

Emphasis

Emphasis refers to the center of interest, or focal point, in a design. A sense of unity and order in room design is achieved when your eyes are repeatedly drawn to one feature. A fireplace, painting, or piece of furniture might become a point of emphasis.

When using emphasis in design, two guidelines need to be followed. First, the point of emphasis should dominate. No other features should compete with it. Second, the focal point should not overpower the room. Refer to 24-13. The fireplace does not interrupt the flow of the room. Although it is the point of emphasis, it blends well with the other objects.

The Goals of Design

As you use the elements and principles of design, you should keep the goals of design in mind. The goals of design are beauty, appropriateness, and unity with variation.

Beauty

Beauty is a quality that gives pleasure to the senses. It is used to describe well-designed objects. However, what one person finds beautiful may not be beautiful to another person. You can make your home appear beautiful to most people if you follow the principles of design. They have become guidelines for using the elements of design based on observations of what most people consider beautiful.

Appropriateness

Appropriateness, or suitability, means a design is right for its purpose. For example, the design in a child's playroom should be suitable for children as they play. Durable, easy-to-care-for furniture would be appropriate.

Your design should also be appropriate for all members of the family. You should take their personalities, needs, wants, and lifestyles into consideration as you design your home.

Unity with Variation

Unity with variation is an important goal of design. As you have already learned, design works best when one item dominates. To create unity with variation, choose an element of design to serve as a dominant theme in each room design. Then add variety using small, contrasting amounts of the same element. For example, in a room with dominant horizontal lines, a few diagonal lines can create interest.

Check It Out!
1. How do warm colors affect the appearance of a room's size?
2. Give an example of how one of the five types of rhythm is used in design.
3. How is the goal of unity with variation achieved in a design?

Check It Out! (Answers)
1. Warm colors make rooms appear smaller than they really are.
2. (Student response. See page 656 in the text.)
3. Unity with variation is achieved by choosing one dominant element of design. Variety is added through the use of small, contrasting amounts of the same element.

Topic 24-2
Decorating Your Home

Objectives
After studying this topic, you will be able to
- give examples of different types of floor coverings.
- list different wall treatments.
- discuss the purposes of window treatments.
- describe the two types of lighting and their applications.

Topic Terms
floor covering
natural light
incandescent light
fluorescent light

Vocabulary:
What do you think is the difference between incandescent light and fluorescent light?

Example:
Bring samples of several different types of floor coverings to class for students to compare.

Enrich:
Conduct a survey to find out what types of floor coverings people have in their homes and what they like and dislike about the various types.

The elements and principles of design can be used in decorating your home. They can help you create a living space that is attractive, useful, economical, and individual. By following some basic decorating guidelines, you achieve the look you want. Guidelines for floor coverings, walls, windows, and lighting are given in this topic.

Floor Coverings

Floor coverings are materials placed and attached on top of the structural floor of the house. While floor coverings serve as backgrounds for rooms, they also play an important role in decorating. Depending on the type used, they can make a small room seem large or a large room seem small. They can unify the furnishings in a room. They can create or define activity areas in a home. They can also be used to reduce noise or add warmth and comfort.

Types of Floor Coverings

There are three types of floor coverings from which you can choose. *Soft floor coverings* include carpets and rugs. They are comfortable and help insulate against the cold. They can be easily cleaned by vacuuming.

Resilient floor coverings are capable of withstanding shock. They keep their shape despite the pressures and wear they receive. They are long-lasting and easy to keep clean. See 24-14. Dents do not show as easily as they show on other types of floors. Resilient floor coverings include vinyl, cork, and no-wax flooring.

Hard floor coverings are long-lasting and attractive, 24-15. However, they are sometimes noisy and are not comfortable to walk on. Ceramic tile, quarry tile, brick, concrete, and wood are types of hard floors.

Choosing Floor Coverings

When choosing a type of floor covering, first consider your decorating needs. Choose floor coverings that will be appropriate and appealing for the rooms in your home. Decide what colors, designs, and textures you want.

Decide whether you want a soft, resilient, or hard floor covering. Then think about how much you can spend. You can compare the costs of different types of floor coverings in the category you have chosen. You also need to consider the price

24-14 This resilient vinyl floor is easy to vacuum and damp mop.

Across the Curriculum
Math. Have students visit carpeting stores to get pricing information on different types of carpeting, padding, and installation. Determine costs for a 10'×10' room. Have students compare their cost information in class.

> **Resource:**
> *Buying Floor Coverings,* Activity C, SAG
>
> **Discuss:**
> What other factors might you need to consider when choosing wall treatments?
>
> **Enrich:**
> Create a collage on poster board using examples of different types of wall treatments.

24-15 This hard floor is durable and also adds to the beauty of the room.

of padding, installation, and maintenance. Most floor coverings get a lot of use, so it is wise to buy the best-quality flooring within your price range.

In addition to price, you need to consider the care requirements of the floor coverings you choose. Small children and pets often create a great deal of wear and tear on floors. Therefore, floor coverings that hide soil are good in these instances. Color and texture patterns hide soil on floor coverings. They are good for rooms that receive a lot of use. Shiny, light, dark, and solid-colored floor coverings show dirt easily. They are better for use in rooms that receive little use.

Wall Treatments

The walls of a home provide privacy, security, and shelter. They give shape and size to rooms. Walls may be short or tall, rough or smooth. Wall treatments can be carefully chosen to increase the function and attractiveness of walls.

Choosing a Wall Treatment

When deciding on a wall treatment, you need to ask yourself how easily the material can be cleaned or repaired. For example, some wall treatments, such as paint, are easy to maintain. Others, such as fabric, are fragile and need more care.

You also need to think about where the wall is located and the wear it will receive. For example, a bathroom wall will be exposed to a lot of moisture. Therefore, the type of treatment you choose for the bathroom will need to be water-resistant.

Wall Treatment Options

Wall treatments are available in many materials, patterns, and colors. The most common treatments are paint and wallpaper. Other treatments include fabrics, paneling, mirrors, and tiles.

Paint is an inexpensive wall treatment. Two paint types commonly used for interior walls are oil-based paints and water-based (latex) paints.

Wallpaper comes in a wide variety of colors and designs that can reflect your personality and lifestyle. It can be used in any room of your home. See 24-16. Cleaning wallpaper from time to time will increase its life and help retain its original beauty.

Fabric can be used as a wall treatment. Thick, closely woven fabric can be attached to the wall with glue, double-faced carpet

24-16 The coordinated wallpaper and border print are used to make this child's room bright and cheerful.

> **Putting Technology to Use**
> Have students search online for information on wallpaper styles, price, and information. Students may want to visit the Web sites for Seabrook Wallcoverings at www.seabrookwallcoverings.com and Waverly at www.waverly.com.

tape, or staples. It can also be hung between two curtain rods or stretched over a frame and hung on the wall. For a different look, bed sheets can be gathered and hung on the wall from curtain rods or wooden frames.

Paneling is durable and easy to care for. It is available in many materials and finishes. Warm wood tones add richness to traditional or contemporary decorating themes. Light shades of paneling can be chosen for maximum light reflection. The cost of paneling can be comparable to that of other wall treatments.

Mirrors can be used as wall treatments to make rooms look larger than they really are. They should not be used in front of undesirable views, though.

Ceramic tiles can be applied to walls also. They are very practical for use in kitchens or bathrooms since they are easy to clean, 24-17.

24-17 The floral ceramic tiles used in this bathroom are both practical and decorative.

Windows and Window Treatments

Windows let in light and fresh air. They help control the inside temperature and provide a view of the outside. A wide variety of window types are available. The most common are double-hung, casement, fixed, and jalousie windows. See 24-18. The type you choose depends on your lifestyle and on the room itself.

Window treatments include curtains, draperies, window shades, blinds, and shutters. When choosing window treatments, you need to think about the style of the window, its size, and its location. You also need to consider the two purposes of window treatments.

One purpose of window treatments is to control light and provide privacy. You should choose window treatments that will let you block out the amount of light you wish. In some rooms, such as a bedroom, you may want window treatments that totally block out incoming light. The choice of window treatments should also be based on how much privacy is desired. Bathrooms should have window treatments that prevent people from looking in.

The other purpose of window treatments is to complement the interior design of the room. You should choose window treatments that blend with the furniture and floor and wall treatments. For example, in a formal living room, brocade draperies would be appropriate. In a kitchen, simple, easy-to-clean curtains would work well.

Lighting

Lighting is an important element of decorating. Well-planned lighting adds comfort, safety, and beauty to a home.

Types of Lighting

Two types of lighting are used in the home. They are natural light and artificial light. **Natural light** comes from the sun. It enters the house through windows. The amount of natural light entering a room depends on the size, number, and arrangement of windows. The type of window

Resource:
Wall Treatments,
Activity D, SAG

Reflect:
Identify the types of windows used where you live. Would you choose these windows if you were building a home today?

Enrich:
Choose two rooms in your house. Look for pictures of window treatments you would like to use on these windows. Mount them on paper and explain why you feel these window treatments are appropriate for the windows.

Resource:
Choosing Window Treatments,
Activity E, SAG

Problem-Solving Practice
The Decision-Making Process of Interior Design, reproducible master, TR. Have students evaluate the design of their own rooms using the form.

Reflect:
Think of the last time you were in a room that was lit by natural light. How did you feel when you were in that room? Now think of a room you have been in that has no windows. How did you feel in that room?

Example:
Bring lamps to class that use the different types of artificial light. Have students observe the differences in the light created by the different bulbs.

Resource:
Treatments in the Home, reproducible master, TR

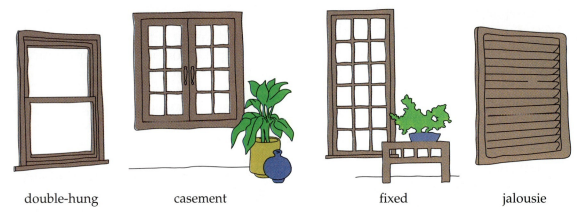

double-hung   casement   fixed   jalousie

24-18 These are just a few of the many types of windows available.

treatments and the location of the rooms also affect the amount of natural light. When natural light is used, it saves on utility bills and conserves energy.

Artificial light is available in many shapes, sizes, and types. There are two types commonly used. One type is **incandescent light**, produced when electricity passes through a tungsten filament in a glass bulb. The other type is **fluorescent light**, produced by releasing electricity through mercury vapor in a special tube to create light rays.

Lighting Technology

Traditionally, fluorescent lighting has come from fluorescent tubes. However, fluorescent bulbs combine the best of traditional incandescent and fluorescent light. They give off the warm, soft light of an incandescent bulb and offer the cost effectiveness of fluorescent light. See 24-19.

Fluorescent bulbs screw into regular lightbulb sockets and last much longer than incandescent bulbs. They are more expensive than incandescent bulbs, but they last longer and use less energy. They should be used in fixtures that are lighted more than two hours a day.

Another type of lighting often used is *halogen light*. Halogen bulbs, which use halogen gas, require little maintenance. Because their intense light is very similar to daylight, halogen bulbs make the colors in your rooms seem brighter. Halogen bulbs come in the same shapes and sizes as incandescent bulbs, 24-20.

The E-lamp, or electronic lamp, is another lighting alternative. Although the cost of E-lamps is higher than incandescent bulbs, they use less energy and last much longer. For example, a 24-watt E-lamp can be used in place of a 100-watt incandescent lightbulb. E-lamps can last up to 20,000 hours compared to about 1500 hours for incandescent bulbs. The E-lamp is the same size as an incandescent bulb. It will fit any incandescent fixture. It can also be controlled with a dimmer switch.

Their energy savings based on a national average kilowatt rate of 8¢ an hour is:

Electronic Fluorescent	Average Lumens	Rated Average Life	In Place of This Incandescent	Average Lumens	Rated Average Life	**Energy Savings**
26-watt	1,500	10,000 hrs	90-watt	1,360	2,500	$43.20
20-watt	1,200	8,000 hrs	75-watt	1,170	750	$35.20
15-watt	900	8,000 hrs	60-watt	855	1,000	$28.80

24-19 Using energy-saving compact fluorescent bulbs can save you money.

Across the Curriculum
History, English. Have students write a research report on Thomas Alva Edison in relation to lighting. Ask students to share information from their reports with the class.

Topic 24-2 Decorating Your Home

24-20 These halogen bulbs are similar in shape to incandescent bulbs and have a long life.

24-21 The general lighting in this room is supplemented with local lighting provided by lamps.

Applications of Lighting

Lighting has three applications in the home. They are general lighting, local lighting, and accent lighting. *General lighting* gives an even amount of light throughout a room. It can be achieved through direct or indirect lighting. *Direct lighting* is lighting from a source to an object. *Indirect lighting* is lighting that is reflected off ceilings or walls. General lighting should light up a room so you can move about safely. The amount of general lighting needed depends on the shape and size of the room.

Local lighting fills specific lighting needs. It is used in work areas, such as kitchens, workshops, and study areas. For example, a lamp may be placed beside a chair, on a desk, or beside a bed for reading. In addition to lighting a specific area, local lighting raises the level of general lighting. See 24-21.

Accent lighting is a concentrated beam of light used to emphasize an object or area. A single light focused on an object of interest can effectively lead the eyes toward that focal point. If you have an especially interesting wall treatment, a series of carefully placed lights can dramatize it. General lighting, when carefully planned, can also serve as accent lighting.

Basic Guidelines for Good Lighting

There are three guidelines you need to consider when planning lighting. They will ensure you have enough lighting and the lighting you have is effective.

The first guideline is to make sure there is enough light. The least expensive way to increase lighting is to keep all lightbulbs and light fixtures clean. Check the sticker inside each fixture to see the maximum wattage lightbulb you should use. This will give you the most light that is safely possible.

The second guideline is to eliminate glare. Glare, whether from a direct or indirect source, is hard on the eyes. While a bare bulb casts a direct light all around it, it also creates a glare. Direct light can be shielded with a lampshade or clip-on fixture to reduce glare. Indirect light produces a glare when it is reflected off smooth, light-colored, or shiny surfaces.

The third guideline is to avoid contrasts and shadows. Eye fatigue results when one spot in a semidark room is well lighted. The use of both general and local lighting will help eliminate contrasts.

Shadows result when a person or object is between the light source and the object of vision. For activities requiring local lighting, place the light to your left if you are right-handed. Place local lighting to the right if you are left-handed. If an activity requires moving around so your whole body creates a shadow, you may need to add more lights.

Discuss:
Where and when would you use different lighting applications in the home?

Enrich:
Create a bulletin board illustrating the guidelines for good lighting.

Activity:
Have students evaluate the lighting in their rooms. Do they have enough light? eliminate glare? avoid contrasts and shadows?

Across the Curriculum

Science. Ask students to bring in advertisements for novelty lamps made with fiber optics. Discuss with students what application of lighting these lamps fulfill. Have students do research on fiber optics and report their findings in class.

Resource:
Decorating Your Home Puzzle, reproducible master, TR

Vocabulary:
What is meant by a *traffic pattern* when furnishing a home?

Enrich:
Research and write a report about a furniture style that appeals to you. Include pictures if possible.

Check It Out!
1. Give two examples of soft, resilient, and hard floor coverings.
2. What other kinds of wall treatments are available besides paint and wallpaper?
3. List one purpose of window treatments and discuss why it is important.
4. Name and describe two applications of lighting.

Check It Out! (Answers)
1. (List two for each:) soft—carpet, rugs; resilient—vinyl, cork, no-wax flooring; hard—ceramic tile, quarry tile, brick, concrete, wood
2. fabric, paneling, mirrors, ceramic tiles
3. (Student response should discuss controlling light and privacy or complementing the interior design of the room.)
4. (Name and describe two:) general lighting—gives an even amount of lighting throughout a room; local lighting—fills a specific lighting need; accent lighting—used to emphasize an object or area

Topic 24-3
Furnishing Your Home

Objectives
After studying this topic, you will be able to
- explain how to choose good furniture.
- demonstrate ways to organize living space.
- give examples of ways to use accessories.

Topic Terms
veneer
finish
activity center
scale floor plan
traffic pattern

Furnishing your home involves many different components. It includes choosing good-quality furniture that meets your needs. It also encompasses organizing living space and using accessories to tie the room together.

Choosing Furniture

Choosing furniture is an important task. It adds to the comfort and design of the home. Oftentimes furniture will have to last many years. Therefore, you should make careful plans as you choose furniture for your home. Your basic furnishings should be good quality, comfortable, tasteful, and suitable to your lifestyle.

Factors to Consider

As you select furniture, there are many factors you need to consider. First, you should choose furniture that is functional. Look for pieces that are usable in more than one way and in more than one setting. For example, a bedroom dresser might be used as a buffet in a dining room.

You need to consider proportion. All furniture should be in proportion to the size of the room. If you buy a long sofa for a small room, the sofa will appear oversized. Furniture should also be in proportion to other furnishings. For instance, choose end tables that are about the height of chair arms. Choose table lamps that are in proportion to tables.

You also need to think about who will be using the furniture. Furniture used by children should be sturdy and made with durable fabrics that do not show dirt easily. Furniture to be used infrequently can be made of light-colored fabrics that are less durable.

Furniture Styles

There are many different furniture styles from which to choose. The furniture styles you choose will depend on your design preferences for different materials, lines, and finishes. Your choice will also depend on your lifestyle and personal taste.

Some furniture styles are referred to as traditional furnishings. They are based on styles that were popular in the past. They include Queen Anne, Chippendale, Hepplewhite, Sheraton, American Federal, and Early American.

Early American originated in the colonial period. Cabinetmakers adapted European styles to the tools and woods available in the colonies. The result was rustic and sturdy furniture. Early American furniture is still widely reproduced. It is most often made of pine, birch, or maple. Cupboards, chairs, tables, candlestick stands, cradles, stools, and desks are among the popular pieces. See 24-22.

In colonial days, wealthy planters imported wallpaper and objects of art with Oriental designs. Today, Oriental furnishings are widely used as accent pieces. They are characterized by their enamel or lacquer wood finishes. Metal decorations are seen in hinges and handles.

Modern furniture usually has simple lines. It reflects the theme of "form follows function." For instance, the basic purpose of a chair is to provide a comfortable place to sit. Unnecessary frills are omitted in the design of modern furniture.

Contemporary furnishings are based on the latest designs and materials. Their

24-22 This contemporary furniture is based on Early American designs.

simple lines are based on geometric shapes. Contemporary furnishings are often designed with metal tubes, plastics, and glass. Textures are emphasized more than decoration.

Judging Quality in Furniture

Furniture is made of many materials. Wood furniture includes tables, desks, bookcases, hutches, and cupboards. Any furniture pieces with fabric and padding, such as chairs and sofas, are considered to be upholstered. Molded plastics and various other materials are also used to make furniture.

Wood Furniture

Wood furniture is beautiful and practical. Its grain is visually appealing, 24-23.

Furniture made of solid wood is expensive. Therefore, most of today's furniture is made of veneered wood. A **veneer** is a thin layer of wood. For furniture, a veneer of fine quality wood is bonded to less-costly veneers. The result is furniture that looks attractive and costs less than solid wood furniture. Good veneered furniture is strong and durable. It resists breaking and warps less than solid wood.

Another aspect of wood furniture that influences its cost is the joints. You should not spare expense in this area. Look for quality joints when deciding between pieces of wood furniture.

Reflect:
Do you like traditional or contemporary styles of furniture the best? Why?

Discuss:
Do you think it is wise to pay more and get quality furniture?

Resource:
Wood Joints, transparency master, TR

Example:
Show the class drawers that have dovetail, mortise and tenon, tongue and groove, and butt joints. Discuss the strength of these various joints.

FCCLA Activity

Field trip. Have students working towards Power of One plan a visit to a local museum, art gallery, or an accessory specialty shop. This trip could serve as part of their Working on Working project. Museums sometimes schedule special tours for students, and most galleries will give a talk and tour if arranged ahead of time. Also, many store owners can arrange to have someone tell the students about the merchandise. This activity will give students information on various careers and help them learn more about local businesses.

Enrich:
Divide the class into small groups. Brainstorm a list of advantages and disadvantages of wood, upholstered, plastic, and metal furniture.

Discuss:
What type of furniture would you buy for a dorm room? Why?

Activity:
Ask students to find out how much it would cost to have a sofa reupholstered. Have them compare this with the cost of buying a new sofa.

24-23 This buffet was designed and finished to show off the beautiful wood grain.

Most wood is finished. The word **finish** has two meanings. It can mean the wood has been stained to look like another type of wood. It can also refer to the final treatment of the wood to protect its natural beauty. A finish is usually applied to resist wear and protect the wood. For most furniture, a semigloss finish is applied. This finish brings out the beauty of the wood grain and adds a rich, clear sheen.

Upholstered Furniture

Most upholstered furniture has a wooden frame. Therefore, when selecting upholstered furniture, keep in mind the criteria used for choosing wood furniture. The frame for any upholstered piece should feel sturdy. It should be reinforced with corner blocks or steel plates. Joints should be secure. Since many of the important details are completely hidden, you should read all labels carefully.

Springs are an important part of upholstered furniture. *Coil springs* are used for heavy furniture. *Flat* or *zigzag springs* are used in lightweight furniture. They are not as soft as coil springs.

Cushions are usually placed on top of the base or platform of a piece of furniture. Labels identify the materials used for the cushions. The best way to judge the quality and performance of cushions is to sit on the piece of furniture. Be sure to check the seat, back, and arms.

Fabric is also a factor in determining the overall durability of upholstered furniture. Many fine fabrics, such as silk, are not durable. Finishes can be applied to upholstery fabrics to affect their safety and durability. Soil-repellent and fire-resistant finishes are often used on upholstered furniture. Sometimes you can add the finishes yourself.

If upholstery fabric is a plaid or has a pattern in it, it should match at the seams, 24-24. All seams and stitches should be neat and straight. Dust ruffles should be lined. This will make them hang well and look neat.

Plastic Furniture

Plastic is often used in furniture because it is lightweight, durable, easy to clean, and fairly inexpensive. Plastic furniture can come in many different forms, including molded plastic, foam, and inflatable plastic. Some wooden furniture has plastic parts for decoration or support.

Metal Furniture

Brass, cast and wrought iron, chrome, aluminum, and stainless steel are all used as furniture materials. Metal can be used as the main material in a piece of furniture or as a coating on other materials.

Metal furniture is strong and fairly inexpensive. Aluminum, however, is not as strong and may bend or dent easily. Iron furniture may rust but can have protective coatings applied to prevent this from happening.

Across the Curriculum

Math. Have students estimate the cost of decorating their first one-bedroom apartment. Have them include furniture, wall and window coverings, accessories, and lighting. Students should list each item they will need and use catalogs to determine the cost of each item. What is the total cost? How much do they think rent would be for a one-bedroom apartment for one year?

24-24 The plaid pattern in this chair and ottoman is perfectly matched at the seams.

Organizing Living Space

The appearance, convenience, and comfort of a room depend partly on how the living space is organized. The way the furniture is arranged should reflect how the room is used. Before arranging furniture in a room, review the activities that take place in the room as well as the available space. The activities that take place in shared family space will be different from those that take place in personal space.

Shared Space

Most homes have certain areas where members gather and spend time with one another. Kitchens, dining areas, and family rooms are examples of indoor family space. Porches, patios, and yards are examples of outdoor family space.

Family space is shared space. Areas where family members can communicate and enjoy the company of one another are important in fostering family unity. Sharing family space also helps build relationships outside the family. You are more prepared for sharing space with others, such as a roommate or spouse.

Shared space should reflect the needs and tastes of all family members. Everyone in the house should feel comfortable in family areas. There should be enough furniture to accommodate all family members as well as guests. Also, the furniture in these areas should be arranged in such a way that people can communicate easily.

Many families maximize the use of their living space by multiple use of space. For example, the computer is placed in the living room, homework is done on the kitchen table, or a hide-a-bed sofa provides sleeping space for an overnight guest. See 24-25.

Similarly, the activity center might be located in any room in the house. An **activity center** is a grouping of all the furnishings needed for a particular activity. Be sure to choose the right type of furnishings needed for the activity. For instance, you might plan an activity center for studying. This activity center might include a desk, chair, bookcase, and lamp.

Personal Space

All people need some personal space where they can be alone and store their belongings. Many teens have private bedrooms, but this is not always possible. When siblings share a room, they may arrange furniture in a way that helps them achieve greater privacy. They may choose bunk beds or place their beds with the two headboards touching. This way, when siblings sit in their own beds, they can face away from each other.

Some families place single chairs in the various quiet areas of the home. Family members can use these areas to seek privacy if desired. People may also find private space outside.

Making a Scale Floor Plan

As you plan furniture arrangement throughout your home, you need to consider the space available. A very useful

Reflect: In what areas of your home do you share space? Do you think these areas help strengthen your relationships with other people in your home?

Discuss: Give some examples of multiple use of space in your home.

Discuss: Are there activity centers in our classroom? Could any be created?

Reflect: Do you share your personal space with anyone at home? How does this make you feel?

Across the Curriculum

Social studies. Have students research Feng Shui, the Chinese philosophy of people's relationship with their surroundings. Ask students to summarize their findings in an oral report to be shared with the class.

Resource:
Arranging Furniture, Activity F, SAG

Activity:
Have students map the traffic patterns in the classroom.

Reflect:
Think of the traffic patterns in your home. Does the furniture arrangement allow people to move freely through each room? What might be done to improve traffic patterns?

Resource:
Arranging Furniture at Home, reproducible master, TR

24-25 A computer center such as this can use flexible space in almost any room of the house.

tool for doing this is a scale floor plan. A **scale floor plan** is a drawing that shows the size and shape of a room. A certain number of inches on the scale floor plan is equal to a certain number of feet in the room.

To make a scale floor plan for a room you are furnishing, measure the floor. Draw a scale floor plan on graph paper. Then measure the width and depth of each piece of furniture in the room. Draw the pieces of furniture on graph paper using the same scale as the floor plan. Color the pieces of furniture the color you want the furniture to be. This will help give you a good idea of the color balance in the room. Cut out the furniture pieces. Arrange them on the scale floor plan until you have found the best arrangement for your room.

As you arrange furniture pieces on your floor plan, you need to keep traffic patterns in mind. **Traffic patterns** are the paths people follow as they move within a room. These patterns should allow people to walk through a room freely. They should avoid cutting through a conversation area or in front of someone's view. See 24-26.

After deciding how to arrange furniture on your scale floor plan, you can begin placing furniture in your room. There are several guidelines you should follow.
- Avoid placing too much furniture in a room.
- Place large pieces of furniture first.
- Place large pieces of furniture parallel to the walls. A sofa or bed arranged across the corner of a room often wastes valuable floor space.
- Allow for space to extend furniture. For example, a dresser needs space in front of it to open drawers.
- Arrange upholstered furniture among pieces of wood furniture.

Computer Programs

Some computer programs, such as computer-aided drafting and design (CADD), can help you create floor plans and design interiors. You must input the dimensions of the room, location of doors and windows, electrical outlets, and any other important features. The program will then draw the room to the scale you designate.

Most programs also have a wide variety of furnishings from which to choose. You select the furnishings desired and arrange them. The computer program makes it easy to move furnishings around and replace pieces that prove unsuitable. You

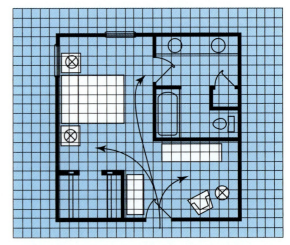

24-26 Using a scale floor plan can save you time when arranging furniture and planning traffic patterns.

Putting Technology to Use

Make a CADD program available for students to try out in the classroom. Have them experiment with using the program to arrange furniture in their rooms. If you do not have a CADD program available, have students use drawing software to create a graph representing their room. Ask them to use basic shapes to represent the furniture in their rooms. Then have them print out their graphs and mark the traffic patterns on the graphs in red ink.

can make an unlimited amount of changes until you find a scale plan that fits your needs.

It is quicker and easier to make scale floor plans using appropriate computer software. By making a floor plan before attempting to arrange furniture, you save a great deal of time and physical effort. You can also avoid mistaken purchases and store returns.

Using Accessories

While accessories are not essential to physical living, they can transform an ordinary home into a unique home. Some accessories are functional. They accent the decor while serving another purpose. For example, clocks tell you the time and lamps provide lighting. Other accessories, such as pictures, flowers, and statues, are purely decorative. They add beauty and pleasure, but they do not serve a practical use.

The accessories you choose should harmonize with the other details of the room. See 24-27. If they are displayed properly, they can blend with almost any decor. Seashells, for example, can be mounted on a piece of clear acrylic in a contemporary room. In an Early American room, the seashells can be displayed on a shelf. In a more formal room, you can mount the collection on a velvet-covered board.

As you choose accessories, try different ideas. Be creative in your use of accessories. Make accessories from items you use. Hang cooking utensils in the kitchen instead of storing them in a drawer. Display serving bowls on shelves and mantels. Use kitchen bowls as fruit bowls in other rooms.

Flowers and plants are good to use as accessories. Well-arranged flowers, plants, twigs, and leaves add variety and interest to a room.

Gift shops, garage sales, and art galleries are good sources of unique accessories. Small neighborhood galleries may offer special local art. Sidewalk arts and crafts shows are also good places to look.

As you work with accessories, keep these additional hints in mind:
- The accessories you choose should fit into the overall design of your room. For example, some rooms require vertical accessories, while other rooms need horizontal accessories.
- Select accessories with textures and colors that go well with the rest of the room.
- Attempt to maintain proportion in your plans. You may choose a tiny vase with one flower for a small shelf. A large bowl of flowers may be attractive on a large table.

24-27 The use of plants and accessories give this room an elegant, nautical look.

Check It Out!
1. List two criteria for choosing upholstery fabric when choosing upholstered furniture.
2. Paths people follow as they move within a room are called ____ ____.
3. What is the difference between functional and decorative accessories? Give two examples of each type of accessory.

Reflect: List the accessories you have in a room of your home. Which are functional? Which are decorative?

Enrich: Invite a guest speaker to class to show students how to select and display accessories.

Resource: *Furniture Basics*, reproducible master, TR

Check It Out! (Answers)
1. (List two:) Fabric should be durable enough to withstand its intended use. Plaids and patterns should match at seams. Seams and stitches should be neat and straight. Dust ruffles should be lined so they will hang well and look neat.
2. traffic patterns
3. Functional accessories accent the decor while serving another purpose. Decorative accessories add beauty and pleasure, but do not serve a practical use. (Student response for two examples of each.)

TEENS ARE CONCERNED ABOUT...

Decorating on a Budget

Decorating a dorm room or first apartment can be expensive, and many teens are on a budget. However, through careful planning, you can have a well-designed, functional apartment for a minimum of money.

Deborah Jamieson, ASID, shares some low-cost tips teens can follow when designing, furnishing, and decorating their first home away from home. Ms. Jamieson has a degree in interior design and has owned her own interior design company for ten years. She frequently works with architects to plan housing to meet the specific needs of individuals and families. She also writes an interior design column twice a month for her local newspaper.

Q: *What should teens look for when choosing bedspreads?*

A: The bedspread fabric, color, and pattern make the most important statement within a small area. Teens should express themselves through their choice and play it up in a bold way.

I also feel durability is important since the bed will be used for sitting, studying, and lounging in addition to sleeping. A patterned bedspread will hide soil and stains. Solid, light-colored fabrics show soil too easily.

Q: *What type of wall paint should teens choose?*

A: They should use durable paints, such as a wall satin, particularly in a small room or high-use area. This type of paint will last longer.

As for color, rich colors are warmer and more inviting than light colors. They also hide marks on the wall more easily than light colors. Since colored paints cost no more than white paint, teens should choose a color from their bedspreads.

Q: *How can teens plan for storage?*

A: There is almost never enough storage provided in dorm rooms and apartments. To create their own storage, teens should look around their houses and see what's available. For example, an old chest can be sanded and repainted. The drawer fronts can be accented by painting them a different color and adding new knobs. The result will be a seemingly new piece of furniture for very little money.

A wall unit can be created for little cost from simple wooden boxes or milk crates stacked on end. Teens can store books in some of the open areas, folded T-shirts in another, and family photos in yet another.

Q: *How can teens decorate their walls inexpensively?*

A: A collage of family photographs can be hung on the wall. An inexpensive print or poster can be beautifully matted and framed and hung on the wall, too. Matting and framing can be done inexpensively as long as a simple frame is chosen. An even less-expensive approach is to use the glass-and-clips method to cover the poster. It looks great.

A very large art print hung at the head of the bed can eliminate the need for a headboard. If the bed is against the wall, use accent pillows to give it a daybed effect. Pillows add back support as well when sitting or studying on the bed.

Q: *What type of lighting should teens choose?*

A: Lighting is important for function, such as local lighting for studying. It also creates warmth and atmosphere within the room. An old lamp cleaned up and given a new shade can look totally different from before.

Feature-Related Activity

Have students plan how they will furnish and decorate their first dorm rooms or apartments. On poster boards, have them draw floor plans, estimating sizes and shapes. Then have them draw furnishings in place. Ask them to use magazines, catalogs, and photographs to show bedspreads, wall colors, storage, and lighting they will use. Tell them they must keep expenses to a minimum.

If the room contains overhead fluorescent lighting, be sure to use warm white or warm white deluxe-colored fluorescent tubes. They will give the room a more natural light than cool white fluorescent tubes, which are often used in dorm rooms.

Incandescent lighting projects a warm light for a more homey atmosphere. Incandescent lighting should be used at different heights. Table lamps and floor lamps used with ceiling light will project light at different planes around the room.

Q: *What else can teens do to make their first home more homelike?*

A: They can use area rugs to add pattern and charm and break the institutional mood of a dorm room. Curtains can be made from brightly patterned sheets. If it is not possible to hang curtains, teens should think about colored micro- or miniblinds that match the bedspread. Colors other than white will appear more homelike, too.

Teens should not be too concerned about making sure everything matches. Instead, they should trust their instincts to mix and blend. It is more interesting that way. They should also talk over their design plans with their parents. Parents may have some helpful ideas.

Q: *How can parents help teens decorate their first homes?*

A: Parents should offer guidance rather than dictation when teens are decorating their rooms. Teens need opportunities to create their own living environments—within reasonable limits. This will help them build confidence toward future design decisions.

Chapter Review

Summary

The elements of design—color, line, texture, and form—are the building blocks of design. The principles of design—proportion, balance, rhythm, and emphasis—are the guidelines for using the elements of design. When the elements and principles of design are used well together, the goals of design—beauty, appropriateness, and unity with variation—are achieved.

By following basic decorating guidelines, you can achieve the look you want in your home. Floor coverings, wall treatments, windows and window treatments, and lighting are all factors to consider as you decorate. There are many different types of each, and you need to choose the best ones to meet your needs.

Furnishing your home is an important step and should be considered carefully. You will need to determine if each area will be shared space or personal space. After choosing from the many styles of furniture, you need to think about how you will arrange the furniture in your home. This can be done by using a scale floor plan and furniture cutouts or a computer program. Accessories can be added as the final touch. Accessories should coordinate with the other furnishings in the room.

Think About It!

1. Think about the colors used in your bedroom. How do these colors reflect your personality?
2. How would you feel if the furniture in your house was too large in proportion to the rest of the house?
3. In your mind, create a room that represents the three goals of design. How does the room meet the goals of beauty, appropriateness, and unity with variation?
4. How do the floor coverings used in your home meet your home's decorating needs?
5. If you were decorating a small room, how would you decorate the walls to make the room look larger?
6. Why do you feel your lifestyle is an important factor when choosing windows?
7. Which do you feel is better: buying an expensive lightbulb that lasts 20,000 hours or buying a lightbulb that costs less and lasts 1,500 hours?
8. Why do you feel it is important to check the quality of furniture before you purchase it?
9. Do you feel using a scale floor plan would help you arrange furniture in your bedroom?
10. Although accessories are not important to physical living, why do you think people choose to use them in their homes?

Try It Out!

1. Find magazine pictures or photographs that illustrate each color scheme, element of design, or principle of design. Make a bulletin board display for your class. For each picture, write a caption explaining what point is being illustrated.
2. Using colored pencils, design and sketch a small room that appears more spacious than it really is.

Resource:
PowerZone Challenge CD. Have students play the chapter review game to reinforce text content.

3. Find examples of vertical, horizontal, diagonal, and curved lines in your classroom. Imagine you are given the job of redesigning the room. List ways you would create greater interest through the use of line.

4. Using illustrations from magazines and catalogs, make a collage of different floor treatments. Be sure to include a wide variety of flooring. Choose examples that are easy to install and clean, reduce noise, last long, or do not show soil readily.

5. Collect illustrations of window treatments that allow for light control, ventilation, privacy, and a view. Mount your collection on notebook paper and place it in a binder. Use the binder as a resource book in your class.

6. Evaluate the lighting needs for a room in your home. Then visit a store to check the cost of the lighting improvements you recommend.

7. Visit a furniture showroom. Have a salesperson explain the marks of quality construction. Study the labels and keep a list of the information they contain.

8. Draw a scale floor plan of a room in your house. Make cutouts of the furniture in the room. Rearrange the furniture, keeping activity centers and traffic patterns in mind. Determine the best possible arrangement for the room.

9. Working in small groups, arrange pictures of accessories to create formal balance and informal balance.

Chapter 25
Caring for Your Home

Careers

These careers relate to the topics in this chapter:
- housekeeping assistant
- residential cleaning service specialist
- environmental services director
- home energy consultant

As you study this chapter, see if you can think of others.

Topics

25-1 Keep It Clean!
25-2 Maintaining the Home
25-3 Conserving Energy in the Home

Introductory Activities

1. Housekeeping Opinions, reproducible master, TR. Have students complete the sentences on housekeeping and home repairs. Ask volunteers to share responses and discuss.
2. Discuss how the tasks of housekeeping have changed over the years. Ask students to imagine cleaning house in a log cabin. Compare cleaning a home today with the use of modern cleaning produces and appliances.

Topic 25-1

Keep It Clean!

I. Why Clean?
   A. Peace and Efficiency
   B. Health and Safety
   C. Pest Control
      1. Using Insecticides Safely
   D. Dealing with Soil
      1. Soil Agents
II. Cleaning Products and Equipment
   A. Cleaning Agents
   B. Waxes and Polishes
      1. Floor Polishes
      2. Furniture Polishes
      3. Multipurpose Cleaner Waxes
   C. Cleaning Tools
   D. Vacuum Cleaners
   E. Buying Cleaning Products and Equipment
III. Making a Cleaning Schedule
   A. How Clean is Clean?
   B. Writing the Schedule
IV. Plan Ahead for Easy Cleaning
   A. Decorate for Easy Cleaning
   B. Use Preventive Measures
   C. Provide Adequate Storage
   D. Organize Cleaning Tasks

Topic 25-2

Maintaining the Home

I. Household Repairs
   A. Who Should Make Repairs?
   B. What Tools Will You Need?
   C. General Maintenance Schedule
II. Plumbing Repairs
   A. Leaking Faucets
   B. Toilet Leaks and Clogs
      1. Clogged Toilets
   C. Drain Traps
      1. Retrieving Valuables
      2. Opening Drains
III. Using Carpentry Tools
   A. Using a Hammer
   B. Sawing Boards
   C. Installing Screws
IV. Electrical Problems
   A. The Control Panel
   B. Replacing Fuses
   C. Resetting Circuit Breakers
   D. Determining Circuit Load
   E. Replacing a Plug

Topic 25-3

Conserving Energy in the Home

I. Energy Sources
   A. Nonrenewable Energy Sources
   B. Renewable Energy Sources
      1. Water
      2. Wind
      3. Solar Energy
      4. Wood
      5. Solid Wastes
II. Outlook for the Future
III. You Can Help Conserve Energy
   A. Heating and Cooling a Home
   B. Water Use
   C. Food Storage
   D. Cooking with Major Appliances
      1. Ranges
      2. Microwave Oven
      3. Convection Oven
   E. Buying Major Appliances
   F. Lighting

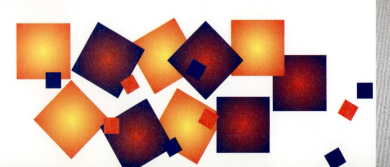

Topic 25-1
Keep It Clean!

Objectives
After studying this topic, you will be able to
- explain reasons for keeping the home clean.
- select the right cleaning products and equipment for different household cleaning tasks.
- plan a cleaning schedule that involves everyone in your home.
- list measures you can take to help make household cleaning easier.

Topic Terms
insecticides
cleaning agents
cleaning schedule

25-1 A clean, well-maintained home provides a pleasant living environment.

Reflect: What cleaning responsibilities do you have at home? Are you responsible for cleaning your own room? Do you have other cleaning responsibilities? What do you dislike most about cleaning chores?

Reflect: Do you get any personal feelings of satisfaction after cleaning a room that was a real mess?

Discuss: Did you find it easier to work in the classroom foods lab knowing that all the equipment and supplies were in specific locations? If each student that used the equipment and supplies put them back in different places, how would this have affected your lab work?

Discuss: What areas of the kitchen are most likely to become contaminated if left unclean?

Household cleaning tasks can seem overwhelming and dreary at times. Since these tasks must be done, you can take steps to make cleaning less tiresome. Dealing with soil will be easier if you know what products and tools to use. Tasks will get done regularly if you follow a cleaning schedule that divides tasks among family members.

Why Clean?
Many people find it difficult to get enthusiastic about home care tasks. However, there are many reasons for keeping a home neat and clean. A well-kept house is an attractive, efficient, comfortable, and safe place to live. See 25-1.

Peace and Efficiency
Good housekeeping is more important than just appearance. Living in an orderly home is more peaceful and efficient than living amid clutter. Working or pursuing hobbies in a room where tools and materials are stored in their proper places is easier.

Efficiency of appliances as well as personal efficiency is improved by routine cleaning. For instance, less energy is required to operate a refrigerator when the condensing coils are periodically vacuumed. A microwave oven will run more efficiently if food spatters and spills are wiped up often.

Health and Safety
A home should meet certain cleaning standards for sanitation and safety reasons. Keeping the kitchen clean helps prevent foodborne illnesses. Keeping bathrooms clean helps reduce germs and eliminate odors from mold and mildew. Carrying trash out and cleaning exhaust vents regularly removes fire hazards.

Pest Control
Good housekeeping habits are important in the control of rodents, insects, and other pests. These pests are attracted by food spills, litter, moisture, and dirt. Normal cleanliness should help prevent pest problems.

Garbage should be removed from the home regularly to deter pests. Use garbage cans and recycling containers with tight-fitting lids. Dispose of garbage in plastic bags if possible.

In addition to cleaning, you can take some other steps to keep your home free

Putting Technology to Use
Ask students to use drawing software, scanners, and color printers to create posters promoting the importance of household cleanliness. Include cleaning tips. Hang the posters around the school.

> **Reflect:**
> Can you think of instances when food was left out in your home and mice made their presence known?
>
> **Vocabulary:**
> What is caulking?
>
> **Note:**
> Give special attention to the dangers of insecticides. List rules for safe use of insecticides on the chalkboard.
>
> **Note:**
> Oily soils can become impossible to remove from fabrics, but they can usually be removed from hard surfaces.

from pests. Keep foods tightly covered, especially grains and cereals stored in cupboards, 25-2. Check incoming grocery bags for "hitchhiking" bugs.

Insects may come in through the small crevices and cracks in foundations or around windows and doors. Good caulking will close up these openings. Keeping outside vegetation away from the foundation will also discourage insects from entering.

Using Insecticides Safely

When cleaning and other efforts fail to keep insects away, you may need to use insecticides to control bug problems. **Insecticides** are strong chemicals used for insect control. Some insecticides are used for flying insects, and others are used for crawling insects. Surface insecticides can be effective for several weeks.

Be sure to check the labels of insecticides before you buy to be certain they will handle the problem. Observe all precautions. Make sure insecticides are not used near foods.

Store insecticides away from heat and out of reach of children. Do not transfer insecticides to any other packages, as they might be mistaken for food or other household products.

Observe strict rules of cleanliness when using insecticides. After using an insecticide, wash your hands. Wash all skin areas that have accidentally come in contact with the product. Launder clothing soiled during insecticide use before wearing again.

For some types of insects, such as termites, certain ants, and roaches, it may be best to call in professional exterminators. They have the expertise to handle special pest control problems.

Dealing with Soil

Soil is another word for dirt. There is no better way to deal with soil than to clean. You can clean faster and more effectively if you understand the different types of soil. The three main types of soils are loose, water-soluble, and oily.

Soiling Agents

Dust, ashes, fur, or loose fibers are types of *loose soil*. This type of soil can be picked up with a broom and dustpan, dust cloth, or vacuum cleaner. If not cleaned, loose soil embeds itself in carpeting and other fabrics. It will mix with oils and moisture and stick to surfaces. Loose soil can also mix with liquid cleaners and waxes and become hard to remove.

Water-soluble soils are solids or liquids that will dissolve in water. They are more easily removed if cleaned up immediately. Water-soluble soils include mud, juices, starchy foods, and syrups.

Oily soils do not mix with water and can be difficult to remove. These soils are often left from foods, cosmetics, or oil-based chemicals, 25-3. If not cleaned within a reasonable time, such soil undergoes chemical changes making it almost impossible to remove.

Cleaning Products and Equipment

Having the right cleaning supplies on hand makes cleaning faster and easier. Understanding the uses of cleaning agents, waxes and polishes, cleaning tools, and vacuum cleaners will help you get started.

25-2 Cereal and grain products should be tightly covered to prevent insects from getting into them.

Across the Curriculum
Health, history. Have students research the bubonic plague that occurred between 1347 and 1352. How did the "Black Death" originate? How was it transmitted to people? How many countries were affected? How many people died as a result of the plague? Have students summarize their findings in written reports.

Topic 25-1 Keep It Clean!

25-3 Cooking fats can leave an oily film on kitchen surfaces that is difficult to clean.

Cleaning Agents

Water dissolves many kinds of dirt and flushes it away. Water is safe for cleaning most surfaces and fabrics. However, water that is too hot or remains in contact with surfaces for too long could cause damage.

Cleaning agents, which are materials used to remove soil, are often added to water. They are used as *wetting agents* to improve the cleaning ability of water. Cleaning agents reduce water's *surface tension*. This is the tendency of water to cling together and bead up. Surface tension keeps water from flowing and penetrating soil. Some cleaning agents are used without water.

Soaps and detergents are well-known cleaners. *Soaps* are based on cleaning agents found in a natural state. The term *detergent* is usually applied to modern synthetic compounds made from petroleum. In general, synthetic detergents cut grease better than soaps. An added advantage is that detergents do not react with hard water minerals to create curds.

Other household cleaners work well for different cleaning tasks. *Alkalies* allow water to penetrate and pick up dirt more readily. Alkaline products include all soaps, washing sodas, lye, water softeners, and some of the general-purpose cleaners. *Acid cleaners* cut grease and also act as a mild bleach. Popular household products in this group are ammonia, vinegar, and lemon juice. *Fat solvents* are compounds used to dissolve soil held by grease. *Fat absorbents* are dry materials that are sprinkled over fatty soil. They absorb the oils, which are then brushed away with the absorbent. *Abrasives* are used to rub dirt away by using a scraping or polishing action. They can be fine like silver polish or scouring powder, or harsh like steel wool and soap pads.

Household cleaners must be used with care. Always read labels and follow instructions carefully to avoid fire and health hazards.

Waxes and Polishes

Wax products protect surfaces from soil and abrasions. Most waxes are a combination of materials that will clean, polish, and protect in one application, 25-4. Most waxes come from plants, insects, or petroleum. Several types are described below.

Floor Polishes

Easy-care floor polishes have either a solvent base or water base. Choose the polish recommended for the type of floor material being cleaned and polished.

25-4 Use a clean, soft cloth and polish to remove dust on furniture. The polish also protects and adds shine to the surface.

Example:
Set up a display of various cleaning agents, waxes, polishes, and cleaning tools for students to refer to as they study this topic.

Activity:
Divide the class into small groups. Have each group classify the various cleaning agents in the classroom display into the correct categories: alkalies, acid cleaners, fat solvents, fat absorbents, or abrasives.

Activity:
Have volunteers read the caution labels included on some of the cleaning agents to the class. Then have them explain in their own words what these mean.

Resource:
It's Time to Clean, reproducible master, TR

Putting Technology to Use

Have students use table software to make a chart. They should list the names of each room in their homes as main headings. Under each heading, ask students to list all the cleaning supplies they would need for that room with a short explanation of why each cleaning agent is necessary.

> **Note:**
> Many resilient floor coverings today have a no-wax finish. This is a special, clear urethane coating that provides high shine without waxing. These surfaces can be cleaned with water only using a damp mop. Caution students that waxes should not be used on these floor coverings.
>
> **Resource:**
> *Buying Cleaning Products,* Activity A, SAG
>
> **Note:**
> Bring in brochures showing the various types of vacuum cleaners and cleaning attachments. Explain how some vacuum cleaners are designed to "beat" carpets, and discuss which type might be the most effective. If possible, show students the various attachments and explain the cleaning tasks for which each is used.
>
> **Resource:**
> *Cleaning Procedures,* reproducible master, TR

Solvent-based cleaning waxes are a blend of natural waxes mixed with a solvent. They are available as either a paste or liquid. Solvent-based cleaning waxes loosen soil, remove previous coats of polish, and form a new protective coating of wax.

Solvent-based cleaning waxes are safe to use on most wood, cork, and resilient types of floor coverings. They should not be used on asphalt and rubber tile.

Water-based cleaning waxes use water as a carrier for wax. Water-based products lift soil out and form a new coat of protective wax. They do not remove old wax coatings, and they have to be stripped off periodically.

Water-based polishes should never be applied to wood or cork because of their water content. They are generally used on most resilient floor coverings. They also can be used on slate, marble, and other types of stone or concrete floors.

Furniture Polishes

Furniture with sealed wood surfaces can be cleaned and protected with polishes. Spray polishes are good cleaners and time-savers. Creamy liquid polishes are more time-consuming. They require two cloths: one for application and one for polishing. Paste wax is used where a more durable protective coating is desired. For plastic furniture, a creamy liquid or multipurpose cleaner wax may be used.

Multipurpose Cleaner Waxes

Products in this group are used for cleaning and wax protection. Most can be used on countertops, tile, appliances, paneling, furniture, cabinets, and wood accessories.

Cleaning Tools

After deciding what cleaning products you need, you must gather the proper tools to use with them. Having the right tools for the task makes any cleaning job easier.

Most cleaning tools are relatively inexpensive. They can also be used for several different jobs, so you need only a few basics. These basic items can be grouped into two categories. In the first category are tools that remove loose dirt and dust. In the second category is equipment designed for removing soil that is stuck to surfaces. See 25-5.

Vacuum Cleaners

In addition to the cleaning tools listed above, you will need a vacuum cleaner to assist you with various cleaning tasks. An electric vacuum cleaner is needed for floors, woodwork, furniture, and fabric.

Vacuum cleaners are available in several models. You can choose between upright vacuum cleaners and canister or tank types. Some vacuum cleaners will beat the carpet as well as supply vacuum action. An electric broom is an alternative for light cleaning.

Cleaning Tools

Cleaning Loose Dirt
- a broom for sweeping floors, porches, and sidewalks
- a dustpan for collecting debris you have swept together
- soft-bristled brushes for upholstery and fabrics
- a dust mop for picking up dust on hard floors
- cloths for dusting and polishing

Cleaning Adhesive Dirt
- a wet mop for cleaning floors
- a scrub brush for tasks that require abrasive cleaning action
- a pail to hold water and cleaning solutions
- sponges for washing walls, woodwork, and appliances
- lintless cloths or paper toweling for cleaning windows and mirrors
- a brush with a long handle for cleaning toilet bowls
- soft cloths for polishing brass and chrome fixtures
- a stepladder or stool for reaching high places

25-5 A few basic, inexpensive cleaning tools will take care of most household cleaning tasks.

Putting Technology to Use
Have students use the Internet to research the most current models of vacuum cleaners. They may want to investigate Web sites for Hoover and Eureka (www.hoover.com and www.eureka.com). You may also ask students to research older models and compare them to today's technology.

Many vacuum cleaners come with attachments for cleaning surfaces other than carpeting. An upholstery brush is useful for cleaning furniture and draperies. A crevice tool is helpful for getting into small areas. Choose a model with attachments to meet your cleaning needs.

Some homes have a built-in vacuum system. The vacuum hose and attachments can be plugged into special outlets in each room. Vacuum lines are concealed in the walls.

Buying Cleaning Products and Equipment

Cleaning agents and tools are offered in such large variety that it may be difficult to decide which products to buy. As you study the labels and read the directions, you will discover many items do the same job.

You will soon learn which products work best for you. Those that serve more than one purpose are usually good buys. The most economical product is not always the least expensive. Think in terms of cost per task rather than cost per container.

Vacuum cleaners are more costly than other cleaning equipment. Consider cost and efficiency in your decision to buy. Reports from consumer testing agencies can help you decide which unit is best for you.

Making a Cleaning Schedule

If all family members understand and agree on cleaning goals, organizing cleaning tasks will be much easier. A cleaning schedule will help the family achieve its cleaning goals. A **cleaning schedule** is a written plan identifying what tasks need to be done. It specifies who is responsible for which tasks and how often the tasks are to be completed, 25-6. Writing a schedule serves as a reminder. Otherwise, cleaning chores might be easy to forget.

A cleaning schedule is not meant to run your life. If it does, the schedule is too rigid. A healthy amount of flexibility should be allowed in the schedule to fit your lifestyle.

How Clean Is Clean?

How a home will be kept is up to the people who share it. There must be agreement on what is important. Do housekeeping tasks and cleanliness standards conflict with other interests and values? Do people sharing the home agree on the importance of the home's appearance?

Before you can make a cleaning schedule, you need to establish standards for cleaning. All family members should be involved in setting the standards. It is hard for one person to set cleaning standards that are acceptable to all members of a household. What is clean to one person may fail to meet another's standards. Likewise, what might suggest clutter to one person might be a peaceful, lived-in atmosphere to another. Family members should seek a balance between demanding a spotless home and setting lower standards.

Writing the Schedule

To develop a schedule, start by writing down all the cleaning tasks that come to mind. Then separate the tasks room by room. Try to determine how long each task should take and how often it needs to be done. The last step is deciding who will be responsible for each job.

Unless you live alone, try to divide the workload among the family members. Even small children may be included and given simple chores. Rotating some of the tasks at intervals may help promote understanding and cooperation.

When assigning housekeeping tasks, keep the personalities and lifestyles of household occupants in mind. If one person enjoys cleaning floors, that task should be given to that person. If one family member has a busy schedule, he or she might be given less time-consuming tasks. This arrangement makes it much easier for everyone to cooperate about doing cleaning tasks, 25-7. Everyone pitches in to make the home a more pleasant place to live.

Resource:
A Cleaning Schedule, Activity B, SAG

Discuss:
What kinds of disagreements can arise in a household concerning cleanliness? Do teens' cleanliness standards differ from those of their parents? How can these conflicts be resolved?

Reflect:
How can you contribute more to your home's cleanliness?

Family Enrichment Activity
Discuss the importance and fairness of cleaning schedules for families. Ask students to cooperatively set up a cleaning schedule with their family members using the form on page 680 of the text as a guide.

680 Chapter 25 Caring for Your Home

Enrich:
Role-play a family conference where cleaning tasks are discussed and a cleaning schedule set up.

Enrich:
Have each student interview an adult who must maintain a home while working full time. What tips does this person have for managing cleaning chores?

Cleaning Plan

Cleaning Tasks	Daily	Weekly	Monthly	Seasonally	By Whom
Bathroom:					
Replace and launder soiled washcloths and towels.					
Empty wastebasket.					
Wash sink, bathtub, shower, and toilet with hot, sudsy water.					
Damp-mop floor.					
Use toilet bowl cleaner.					
Scrub bowl with brush.					
Clean mirror.					
Launder bath mat and rug.					
Clean the inside and outside of the medicine cabinet.					
Bedrooms:					
Make beds.					
Hang up clothes, or fold them and put them in drawers.					
Dust the furniture and woodwork (such as windowsills).					
Vacuum or sweep floor.					
Put fresh linens on bed.					
Dust light fixtures and accessories.					
Turn mattress; vacuum mattress and springs.					
Clean closet and store seasonal clothes.					
Clean curtains, other window treatments, and bedspreads.					
Kitchen:					
Wash dishes.					
Wipe off tables, counters, and appliances.					
Clean oven and broiler to remove spilled or spattered food.					
Empty garbage can and install fresh liner.					
Scrub kitchen sink.					
Sweep or dust mop floor.					
Scrub floor; wax as needed.					
In All Areas (could be separated by room):					
Wash windows.					
Wash walls and woodwork.					
Dust walls and ceilings.					
Shampoo rugs and carpets.					
Living and Dining Area:					
Dust and polish furniture and woodwork.					
Dust upholstery with vacuum tool or brush.					
Thoroughly dust light fixtures, bulbs, and lamp shades. Wash as needed.					
Wash or dry-clean curtains, other window treatments, and slipcovers.					
Wash or polish china, glass, silver, brass, copper, or pewter ornaments.					

25-6 A cleaning plan, tailored to fit your living space, helps keep you on target.

Putting Technology to Use
Have students use charting or table software to recreate the form in Figure 25-6 and save it as a template. Ask students to use the template when creating cleaning schedules for their families.

Topic 25-1 Keep It Clean!

25-7 Accepting and maintaining standards of cleanliness is easier when you have helped define them.

Plan Ahead for Easy Cleaning

Most people have a limited amount of time to spend on cleaning tasks. With a little planning, you can reduce the need for cleaning. This will save you time and make your work less difficult.

Decorate for Easy Cleaning

Some floor coverings, wall treatments, windows, and furnishings are easier to clean than others. You may want to consider some redecorating options for easy upkeep. The following decorating tips can help you reduce the time and effort needed to clean:

- Choose smooth-surfaced floor coverings for high-traffic areas. These areas include family rooms, kitchens, bathrooms, playrooms, laundry areas, and children's bedrooms. Dirt gets embedded in carpets and rugs while it sits on the surface of resilient and hard floors. For this reason, damp mopping resilient and hard floor coverings is easier than shampooing rugs and carpeting.
- Choose washable wall treatments in kitchens, baths, and children's rooms to reduce cleaning and maintenance time.
- Select windows with large single panes. They are faster and easier to clean than those with many small panes.
- Limit your use of silver, brass, and copper in decorating. These metals tarnish rapidly and require frequent polishing to maintain their luster.
- Try to avoid "dust catchers"—those items that will need frequent dusting or require long dusting time. Heavily carved furniture, paneled doors, chair rails, and baseboards are dust traps.
- Consider the textures of the furnishings you choose. Dust and soil are less likely to cling to smooth surfaces than rough surfaces. Keep this in mind whether the material is glass, upholstery fabric, or wall finishes.

Use Preventive Measures

Keeping dust and dirt under control reduces cleaning time. Some simple steps will prevent most of it from building up in the home.

Start at the source of dirt. Dirt may come into a home through doorways. Keeping outside walks, steps, and porches swept will help reduce the amount of dirt brought inside the home. Doormats and foot scrapers located outside entrance doors will help remove soil clinging to shoes. Rugs inside the doors will catch soil that escapes the outside mats. Storage for boots and overshoes near entrances will also prevent family members from tracking soil throughout the home.

Dirt comes into a home through windows and vents as well as doors. Try to keep windows closed on days when large amounts of dust are in the air. During the heating season, keep heating ducts clean and change furnace filters often. A furnace humidifier helps keep dust down as it conditions dry air.

Before starting tasks or projects that produce dirt or litter, put down old newspapers. Debris can be wrapped up in the

Reflect:
Which decorative elements in your home are most difficult to clean? How would you change these elements if you had the opportunity?

Enrich:
Conduct a survey of your home to find sources to dust, dirt, and litter. Write a paper describing ways your family can reduce the amount of dust, dirt, and litter in your home.

Discuss:
In what ways do preventive measures taken in your home help reduce you cleaning time?

Across the Curriculum
English. Have students write an article for the school or local newspaper on ways to make cleaning easier.

Reflect:
Do you have adequate storage space in your room? Do you frequently leave items lying round your room because you have nowhere to put them? If so, try to think of some ways to solve your storage problems.

Discuss:
Do you think it is possible to make cleaning more enjoyable? Will the ideas offered in this topic help? What ideas do you have?

paper and thrown away when the project is finished. No additional cleanup may be necessary.

Provide Adequate Storage

Large amounts of clutter can be prevented by providing adequate storage. Providing a space for everything is not always possible. However, it helps if most items are organized in a convenient storage place.

Every room needs space to store articles that are regularly used there. Having the storage space available encourages putting items away when not in use. For instance, hanging up outdoor clothing is easier when a coat closet or coatrack is located near the main entrance, 25-8.

Storage becomes much simpler if you remember to store items where they are used. Having a closet or built-in storage space in every room makes this easier. Another option is to have furnishings and accessories that can be adapted for storage.

Organize Cleaning Tasks

There are many ways to make cleaning efforts easier and more efficient. Organizing cleaning tasks involves three basic steps. Consider the best time to do a task, the best method of cleaning, and the order of doing the tasks.

The best cleaning methods are often outlined in the care instructions that come with furnishings and appliances. In addition, read the directions printed on the labels of cleaning agents. Other methods are described in booklets or brochures published by companies that make cleaning products.

Certain cleaning tasks or steps just naturally come first. In other instances, it is not so apparent what should be done in what order. As a general rule, clean from top to bottom. Working from the walls to the center of the room is also a good guideline to follow.

You will develop methods of your own for making housekeeping easier and faster. Much can be learned from the experience of others. The suggestions in 25-9 may make cleaning simpler and more enjoyable.

25-8 Some type of storage near entrances encourages neatness in the home.

Housekeeping Tips

- Look for cleaning tips in magazines and newspapers.
- Talk to other people and share ideas. Ask parents or other relatives how they perform certain cleaning tasks.
- Try not to let household chores accumulate.
- Consider using a portable cleaning caddy to hold supplies as you move from room to room. Stock it with items you need for dusting, cleaning glass surfaces, and polishing furniture and metals.
- Carry a small trash bag for collecting bits of trash as you straighten up a room.
- Carry a container for small items that are out of place. Pick up paper clips, pencils, pens, and magazines as you clean. Then go from room to room to drop off the items where they belong.
- Try to work with both hands. You can dust and polish furniture and appliances in much less time.

25-9 Following a few simple tips can help make cleaning tasks easier.

 Putting Technology to Use
Have students search the Internet for the exact phrase cleaning tips. Ask students to choose two tips they discovered. Then have students use word processing software to create a booklet of cleaning tips. Students may wish to add clipart or scanned images to their booklets. Print the booklets and hand them out to the students and faculty.

Check It Out!
1. True or false. A home should meet certain cleaning standards for sanitation and safety reasons.
2. For each of the two cleaning tool categories, give three examples of cleaning tools.
3. A _____ _____ should identify the cleaning task to be done, when it should be done, and who should do each task.
4. List three preventive measures that will keep soil from entering the house.

Check It Out! (Answers)
1. true
2. (Student response. See Chart 25-5 on page 678 in the text.)
3. cleaning schedule
4. (List three:) Keep walks, steps, and porches swept; keep doormats at all outside entrances; place rugs inside at all entrances; provide storage for overshoes and boots near each entrance; keep windows closed on windy, dusty days

Topic 25-2
Maintaining the Home

Objectives
After studying this topic, you will be able to
- select basic tools and supplies needed for home care.
- perform simple plumbing, carpentry, and electrical maintenance tasks.

Topic Terms
control panel circuit breaker
fuse overload

Vocabulary: Do you know where to find a control panel, fuse, or circuit breaker where you live?

Reflect: Who makes the repairs to items in your household? Do you think you could learn to do these repairs?

Homes need periodic cleaning to keep them comfortable and pleasant. They will also need occasional repairs and maintenance to keep household items working properly. Sometimes a drain gets clogged, a faucet leaks, or a fuse blows. This is the normal result of usage.

If you value economy, there are additional rewards for maintaining your home. Repairs you make yourself save money and can be done at your convenience.

Household Repairs

Routine maintenance is an important part of caring for your home. Housing structures, plumbing systems, heating systems, and electrical systems require occasional service. Keeping these items in good repair means your home will be safe and secure.

Who Should Make Repairs?

Even if you take good care of your home, you may need to make some housing repairs. For some types of repairs, you may need to decide whether to hire an expert or do it yourself. Consider these factors in making your decision. Do you have the right tools to do the job yourself? Do you have experience and basic skills to make repairs safely? If you answer *no* to these questions, call an expert.

Resource:
Tool Identification,
Activity C, SAG

Enrich:
Invite a salesperson from a hardware store to bring in samples of these tools and explain their use.

Plan ahead; find repair experts before you have an emergency repair. Talk with people you know. Friends, relatives, and neighbors can usually suggest names of qualified people. The Yellow Pages in your local telephone directory is another good resource to check.

Some household repairs you can learn to do yourself. Many do-it-yourself books are available in bookstores and libraries. These books provide detailed how-to-repair instructions. Ask a handyperson to teach you simple procedures, or take a basic repair course. Being able to make simple repairs has many advantages. You save money on repair bills and gain personal satisfaction.

What Tools Will You Need?

Of course, home maintenance will require a few tools. You can handle many maintenance chores after you become familiar with the basic tools. A hammer, wrench, force cup (plunger), electric drill, flashlight, and screwdriver can be used to handle many minor repairs. See 25-10.

Become familiar with basic tools and their uses. Among the basics is a *monkey wrench*, which is best suited for large jobs. A *pipe wrench* has teeth that grip round shapes, such as pipes and pipe joints. The *straight blade screwdriver* fits screws that have a slot across the head. The *Phillips screwdriver* fits screws that have slots shaped like an X. A *crosscut saw* is used for lumber. A *hacksaw* is used to cut metal. *Side-cutting pliers* are used to cut heavy wire and pins.

Additional tools can help you with more complicated home repairs. For instance, an *auger* can be used to open a clogged drain. Augers have flexible lengths

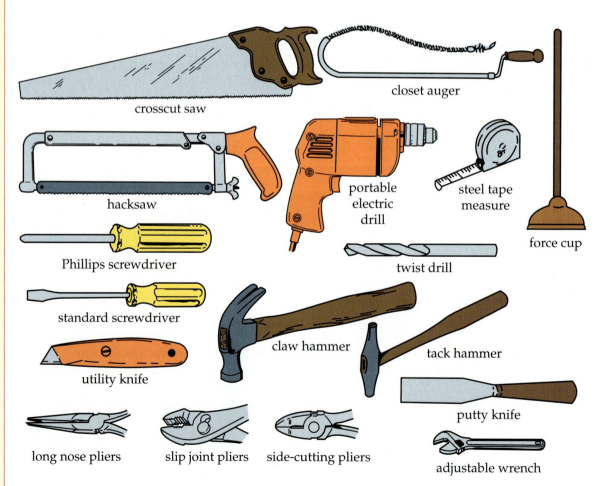

25-10 Certain tools are basic to any home repair kit. Others can be added as needed.

Citizenship and Service
From the Council on Aging or from local religious organizations, obtain names of older people who live in their own homes. Have students arrange to do some minor repairs and home maintenance for them.

of coiled wire that can be pushed through drain traps. A hook on the end removes clogged material. Augers are not hard to use and can save the cost of a plumber.

In addition to tools, you will need some maintenance supplies. The following materials are suggested:
- nails, tacks, screws and bolts, nuts, and washers
- glues, cements, solder, and soldering paste
- sandpaper and steel wool
- lubricants to oil hinges and free sticky locks

Purchase tools and maintenance supplies as you need them. Purchase the sizes to fit your jobs. If you are unsure of sizes, ask hardware personnel for help. It is not necessary to rush out and buy supplies immediately.

Avoid buying the cheapest tools. Tools of inferior quality perform poorly and wear out sooner. They may also be unsafe. Keep tools organized and in good working condition so they are always ready to use.

General Maintenance Schedule

A basic responsibility of home ownership is regular maintenance that keeps the whole structure in good condition. In addition to caring for the interior of your home, you must also care for the exterior. A plan for regular inspections and maintenance will keep you ahead of costly major repairs.

Some inspections need to be made weekly, some monthly, and some seasonally. A weekly maintenance routine helps you notice minor problems as soon as they occur. Monthly maintenance allows you to take care of repairs before they become major problems.

Some special maintenance tasks are seasonal. That is, they are done to prepare for warm weather (spring and summer) or cold weather (fall and winter). The actual kinds of maintenance needed will depend on the climate in which you live. For example, fall maintenance on a home in Florida will differ somewhat from that on a home in Minnesota. See 25-11.

Every home has unique needs. You will probably think of other maintenance chores your family performs to keep your home in good repair. Make these chores a part of your cleaning schedule.

Plumbing Repairs

Plumbing problems require immediate action. A good reason to learn about plumbing is to avoid water damage to your home and furnishings. If you know some plumbing basics, you can likely handle simple repairs. Faucets, toilets, and drain traps often require minor plumbing repairs.

Leaking Faucets

Some faucets are easy to repair. Others should be repaired by a plumber. The *compression faucet* is the easiest to fix. If you twist a handle clockwise and counterclockwise to turn water on and off, you most likely have a compression faucet. It has a threaded stem that moves a rubber washer against a seat to shut off the water, 25-12.

Mixing faucets, as used on showers, bathtubs, sinks, and laundry tubs, are basically like compression faucets. They are two separate units with only one spout. Each valve is repaired separately. If there are two shutoff valves, turn off first one and then the other. This will allow you to see which side is leaking.

When repairing any type of faucet, begin by turning off the water to the faucet. If there is no *shutoff valve* below the sink, you must turn off the main water valve. The main valve is generally located where the waterline comes into the house. This is usually in the utility room or basement. After the water has been turned off, turn on the faucet and let the water drain.

Specific information for repairing various types of faucets can be obtained from home improvement stores. Faucet manufacturers often publish brochures to help people handle simple repairs themselves.

Discuss: What maintenance tasks need to be done each season in our part of the country?

Discuss: Have there been any plumbing "disasters" in your home? Could these have been prevented with proper maintenance?

Reflect: Do you know how to turn off the water supply to your house if you need to do so in an emergency?

Career Preparation Activity

Wanted: Qualifications, reproducible master, TR. Students are to read the want ad and list qualifications they have and training they need for the job described.

Reflect:
Use this weekly maintenance checklist to examine your home. Are there any maintenance tasks that need to be done?

Enrich:
Find out how much water is wasted from a dripping faucet or a running toilet. How much could these increase a household's water bill?

Routine Maintenance Schedule

Weekly Maintenance
- Examine walls and ceilings for signs of water leakage or cracks. When you find problems, locate and repair the source.
- Check for faucet drips and replace washers as needed.
- If you hear the toilet dripping, this may mean water leakage. Inspect the flush tank, identify the problem, and make the needed repairs.
- Eliminate rodents, ants, or roaches as soon as signs of their presence appear.
- Examine walks and driveways for possible hazards.

Monthly Maintenance
- Check the filters in forced air heating and cooling systems; change them if they are dirty. Old filters become clogged with dirt and reduce the efficiency of the system.
- Prune, spray, and fertilize outdoor plantings as needed.
- Clean outdoor furniture as needed.

Spring Seasonal Maintenance
- Replace storm windows and doors with screens.
- Have the cooling system serviced by a professional.
- Perform the spring lawn and gardening chores.
- Check and repair caulking that is loose. Reputty windows as needed.
- Clean debris from downspouts and gutters if needed.

Fall Seasonal Maintenance
- Have the heating system serviced by a professional.
- If you have a fireplace, have the chimney cleaned.
- Do your fall gardening chores. This is the time to plant bulbs for spring blooms. Fall is also a good time for transplanting.
- Remove, repair, and store screens in a dry place. Install storm windows and doors if needed.
- Check the roof for needed repairs. Summer hail storms may cause roof damage.
- Insulate plumbing pipes that are subject to freezing.
- Turn off and drain outside water pipes that may freeze.
- Check insulation and weatherstripping. Repair as needed.
- Clean debris from gutters and downspouts.

25-11 Keeping up with regularly scheduled maintenance tasks will help avoid the need for costly repairs.

Toilet Leaks and Clogs

Water leaking into the toilet bowl indicates a problem in the flush tank, 25-13. Leakage is usually accompanied by a hissing sound as water moves through faulty valves. Sometimes there is also a sound of water trickling down into the toilet bowl.

There are only two spots where water can leak past valves in a toilet tank. One spot is at the *ball cock*, which contains an *inlet valve* to control water coming into the tank. The other is at the *tank ball*, which controls water leaving the tank. You can tell which one is not working by looking inside the tank.

Is the tank full? Is the water running out the overflow tube? If so, the inlet valve in the ball cock is not shutting off the flow into the tank.

Lift the *float ball* gently. If the flow stops, the float mechanism is at fault. Try bending the float arm downward slightly. If this does not work, the float ball is waterlogged and must be replaced. Shut off the water at the shutoff valve below the tank near the wall. Unscrew the float ball and install a new one.

Across the Curriculum

History, English,. Have students investigate the invention of the "water closet." What was the first documented water closet? How was the invention received by the public? What other inventors have contributed to the invention of the modern toilet? Have students summarize their findings in a written report.

Topic 25-2   Maintaining the Home

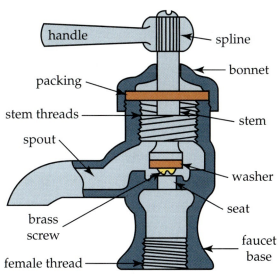

25-12 This cutaway diagram shows a typical compression faucet and its parts.

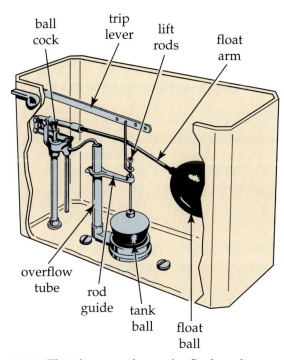

25-13 This diagram shows the flush tank parts. The float ball, ball cock, lift rods, and tank ball are common trouble spots.

The mechanisms in toilet tanks may differ. For example, a hinged flap is sometimes used instead of a tank ball. A plastic ball cock assembly with a float shaped around the filler pipe often replaces the float arm.

Clogged Toilets

A clogged toilet can be cleared with a *force cup* (plunger). The force cup works only when it is immersed in water. Fit it tightly over the trap opening and work the handle up and down. The expanding and collapsing of the rubber cup will agitate the water in the trap and loosen the plug.

If the plunger does not clear the clog, a *closet auger* may be used. Place the auger in the bowl with the curved end of the tube pointed toward the trap opening. Start with the flexible cable pulled back into the rigid tube. Hold the tube with one hand and crank the handle. With light pressure downward, the flexible cable will move through the trap and remove the blockage, 25-14.

Drain Traps

The curved part of a sink drain is called the *trap*. The trap is designed to hold water at all times so sewer gases cannot

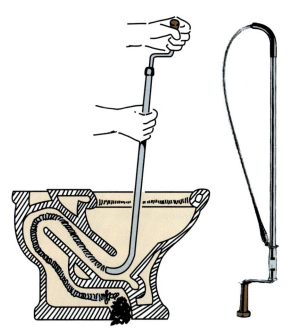

25-14 A closet auger is flexible enough to clear turns in the toilet trap.

What if your inspection shows no water running out the overflow tube, or if the toilet tank is empty? Then the tank ball is causing the problem. Make sure the ball is seated properly over the opening. If it is not, the lower lift rod may be bent. Straighten it and test again.

Enrich:
Contact plumbers and find out how much they charge to clear a clogged toilet. Compare this to the price of a closet auger and clearing a clogged toilet yourself.

Activity:
Ask students to examine the flush tank on a toilet at home. Can they identify the parts labeled in Figure 25-13?

 Putting Technology to Use
Have students investigate the Web site www.theplumber.com. Students may want to investigate the links to plumbing FAQs, plumbing history, and plumbing articles. You may want to check out the advice discussion forum and, if appropriate, have students explore it.

> **Reflect:**
> Have you ever dropped something down a drain? Did you try to retrieve it, or did you just consider it lost?
>
> **Note:**
> Have a student read the cautions on a container of chemical drain cleaner. Stress the safety precautions that must be taken when using these products.
>
> **Resource:**
> *Solving Common Plumbing Problems,* reproducible master, TR

escape into the house. If you drop something down the drain, it may get caught in the trap. If the drain is running slowly, the clog is likely to be located in the trap.

Retrieving Valuables

Valuables dropped down a drain can sometimes be retrieved by removing the trap. First, put a pail under the drain and the trap to catch the water. Cover the chrome nuts on the trap to protect them. Remove the nuts (counterclockwise) with a monkey wrench. The curved pipe can then be removed so you can retrieve the lost items.

Opening Drains

A drain becomes sluggish when grease or solids have restricted the flow of water through it. Sometimes hot water can dissolve the grease and clear the drain. For a stubborn blockage, a force cup may need to be used, 25-15.

A chemical *drain cleaner* is easier for most people to use than mechanical means. Commercial drain cleaners are designed to dissolve grease and other materials that form clogs. Both crystal and liquid forms are available.

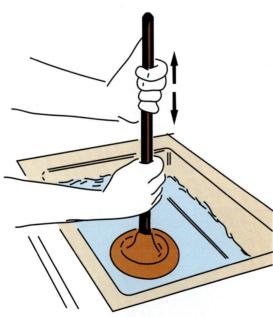

25-15 A force cup (plunger) is used to clear a clogged drain. It pushes water down the drain, where it exerts pressure against the clog. Use an up-and-down motion on the handle.

Chemicals in drain cleaners can be damaging to pipes. In addition, they cause fumes that may be harmful to eyes and lungs. Never stand over a drain where you have just used cleaner. Stand clear and give it time to work. Always read and follow the directions and safety precautions printed on the container.

When none of these methods clear a blockage, you will need a *cleanout auger*, sometimes called a *snake*. The auger's flexible cable will go down drains and through traps.

Since clogs are often located in the drain trap, removing and cleaning the trap may solve the problem. If a clog is beyond the trap, removing the trap allows you to reach the clog more easily with an auger. Push the auger through the drain pipe opening where the trap has been removed. When the auger meets some resistance, crank the auger handle to grasp and remove the block. Very solid plugs will be broken up or drawn out when the auger is removed. Softer materials will be pushed out of the drain and flushed away.

Be very careful if you have tried using a chemical cleaner before using an auger. The chemicals are dangerous and should not touch your skin. Also be careful not to breathe in the fumes.

Using Carpentry Tools

Housekeeping often requires some skill in using tools such as hammers, saws, and screwdrivers. For example, you may want to hang pictures and accessories or add shelves for extra storage space. Correct use of carpentry tools will take a little practice.

Using a Hammer

When driving nails, hold the end of the hammer handle for greater striking power. Hold the nail with your free hand. Strike it lightly several times with the hammer to start the point into the material. Use a nail set to drive finishing nails below the surface of the material.

The claw end of the hammerhead is used to withdraw nails. A block of wood put under the hammerhead will make

Across the Curriculum
Science. Have students research chemical drain cleaners, including ingredients and how they work. Ask students to discuss their findings in class.

pulling the nail easier. It also prevents scratching the surface.

Sawing Boards

Before sawing boards, use a pencil and square to mark a cutting line. Support the lumber in a vise or on a bench, sawhorses, or an old chair. Hold the lumber with your free hand.

Begin the cut with a slow backstroke of the handsaw. Make several backstrokes before making a forward stroke. This produces a kerf (groove) in the wood the saw will follow. Let the weight of the saw do the cutting at first. Then apply a small amount of pressure only on the forward strokes.

Installing Screws

Screws are often preferred over nails as fasteners because of their greater holding power. To install a screw, first make a small depression in the wood with a nail. Select a drill bit slightly smaller than the screw and drill to the depth of the screw. (If the screw is small and the wood is soft, you may be able to drive the screw without drilling.)

Always drive screws with the proper screwdriver, either a straight-blade or Phillips type. The blade of the screwdriver should fit the screw head. A blade that is too small may turn the screw, but it will damage the head. A damaged head can make the screw difficult to remove. The heavier the screw is, the heavier the screwdriver should be to turn it. Rubbing wax or soap on the screw threads will make driving easier.

Electrical Problems

Although electricity makes home life easier, sometimes problems do occur. When dealing with electrical repairs, keep safety in mind. Never attempt any electrical work unless you know what you are doing. Most electrical problems are best handled by a qualified electrician.

The Control Panel

Every home has a wall-mounted metal box called a **control panel** or entrance panel, 25-16. All the electricity you use comes through it. The panel contains either fuses or circuit breakers. A **fuse** has a strip of metal that melts and stops the flow of power. A **circuit breaker** is a switch that interrupts the path of electricity when it trips. These safety devices prevent damage to the wiring system and protect against potential electrical fires.

The large fuse or circuit breaker, which is usually at the top, controls all the electrical power. It can shut off all your electricity if you pull it. Other fuses or circuit

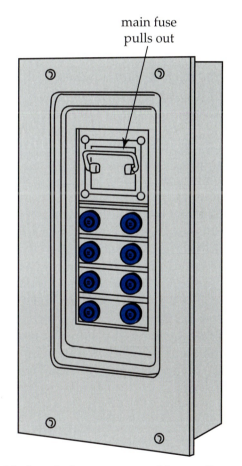

25-16 A typical entrance panel is usually painted gray and has a hinged cover. This one shows fuses for eight circuits.

> **Enrich:** Invite a carpentry instructor to demonstrate the safe use of tools to the class.
>
> **Enrich:** Do you know where the control panel is in your home or apartment? Are fuses used or circuit breakers? Do you know how to shut off the electricity in you home in an emergency? Do you know what to do if a circuit breaker is tripped? Do you know how to replace a fuse?
>
> **Note:** Fuses are still found in older homes, but most new construction used circuit breakers.

Across the Curriculum

Health/science. Discuss in class ways to prevent electrical fires. What factors can cause fires? What steps can be taken to help avoid electrical fires in your homes?

> **Discuss:**
> What risks are involved if circuits are overloaded? During what holiday do many electrical fires occur?
>
> **Resource:**
> Avoiding Circuit Overloads, Activity D, SAG

breakers in the panel protect individual branch circuits. A branch circuit is wiring that goes only to certain lights and electrical outlets. Every home has several of them. Some circuits feed electricity to only one major appliance, such as a range, furnace, or air conditioner.

An **overload**, or excess electrical demand, will cause a fuse to blow (burn out) or a circuit breaker to trip. (An overload results from using too many lights and appliances or from a short circuit, such as bare wire touching metal.) In either case, the current to that circuit is shut off automatically. When this happens, you need to replace a fuse or reset a circuit breaker.

Replacing Fuses

Fuses screw into the entrance panel sockets like lightbulbs. You can recognize a blown fuse by examining the fusible link through the clear glass window, 25-17. With a temporary overload, the fuse link will melt at its weakest point. The window remains clear. In a fuse blown by a short circuit the fuse link vaporizes and darkens the window.

You can replace a blown fuse yourself. Unplug the light or appliance that caused the problem. Use caution in working at the entrance panel. Use a flashlight as a light source. Pull the main fuse or open the main circuit breaker before touching fuses. Be sure your hands are dry and you are standing on a dry surface. Stand on dry boards if the floor is wet.

If the fuse blows again immediately, the problem is probably in the circuit wiring. Have a licensed electrician correct this problem.

Resetting Circuit Breakers

Unlike a fuse, a circuit breaker can be reused after it shuts off current. Inside the circuit breaker is a spring-loaded switch that turns itself off under an overload, 25-18. To restore power, you must flip the switch handle back to the *on* position.

Determining Circuit Load

One of the most frequent causes of circuit overload in households is the use of too many appliances on one circuit. Manufacturers indicate power requirements in watts on a faceplate of their appliances, 25-19. Make sure your branch circuits can carry the load you have plugged in.

You can determine the electrical load on a circuit by adding up all the wattages of lights and appliances that are likely to be used at the same time. See 25-20. Usually, the total for a circuit protected by a 15-ampere fuse or circuit breaker should

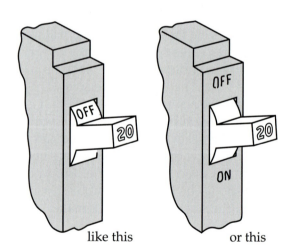

25-18 A tripped breaker will indicate power is off by the position of its handle.

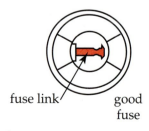

fuse link   good fuse   blown by overload

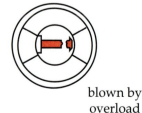

blown by short circuit

25-17 To check fuses, examine the fuse link through the glass window.

Across the Curriculum

Math. Have students estimate electrical loads on circuits in their homes. Students may want to use information from Chart 25-20 in their estimations. Do any of the students feel there are potentials for overloads in their homes? What steps should be taken to prevent this?

CAUTION:
TO AVOID
ELECTRICAL
SHOCK
HAZARD, DO
NOT RINSE
OR IMMERSE
IN WATER

Model C-100
650 watts
120 volts AC

Contempra
Industries, Inc
New
Shresbury,
N.J. 07753
USA

25-19 Labels or plates on appliances tell how much current they will draw.

Appliance	Typical Wattage
Automatic Toaster	1200
Automatic Washer	700
Broiler	1000
Built-In Exhaust Fan	400
Clothes Dryer (Electric)	9000
Coffeemaker	1000
Deep Fryer	1320
Dishwasher	1500
Dry or Steam Iron	1000
Egg Cooker	600
Electric Clock	2
Fluorescent Lights (Each Tube)	15-40
Lamps (Each Bulb)	25-200
Oil Burner	250
Radio	100
Range (Electric)	12000
Refrigerator	200
Roaster	1380
Television	350
Vacuum Cleaner	300
Water Heater (Electric)	1380

25-20 These wattages are typical. Actual ratings vary from brand to brand.

not exceed 1750 watts. The total should not exceed 2400 watts for a 20-ampere circuit.

Replacing a Plug

Damaged or worn electric plugs on appliance or light cords are a fire hazard. They should be replaced without delay. Heavy-duty plugs must be installed on heavier cords and appliances drawing more than 300 watts of power.

Replacing a plug is an easy task. Plugs are available at hardware and home improvement stores. Manufacturers provide clear instructions on their packages for attaching electrical plugs.

Check It Out!

1. List two reasons for doing home maintenance chores yourself.
2. Name two factors to consider in deciding whether or not to do household repairs yourself.
3. What are three methods people can use to open a drain without calling a plumber?
4. True or false. When striking nails, a hammer should be held near the head for greater striking power.
5. What causes a fuse to blow (burn out) or a circuit breaker to trip?

Check It Out! (Answers)

1. to save money on home repair bills, for personal satisfaction
2. Do you have the right tools to do the job yourself? Do you have experience and basic skills to make repairs safely?
3. (List three:) hot water, force cup, cleanout auger, chemical drain cleaner
4. false
5. An overload or short circuit will cause a fuse to blow (burn out) or a circuit breaker to trip.

Enrich:
Have a students demonstrate how to change a damaged or worn electric plug on a cord.

Resource:
Home Maintenance, reproducible master TR

Topic 25-3
Conserving Energy in the Home

Vocabulary:
What is solar energy? Do you know anyone who uses solar energy?

Resource:
Sources of Energy for Your Home, color transparency CT-22, TR

Reflect:
Do you conserve energy at home? Write down the ways your family currently conserves energy. After you read this topic, add additional ways you could conserve energy at home to your list.

Discuss:
Can you think of other ways people conserve physical energy by using energy from other sources? In this era of energy conservation and physical fitness, are we trying to reverse this trend?

Objectives
After studying this topic, you will be able to
- identify renewable and nonrenewable energy sources.
- discuss ways you can help conserve energy at home.

Topic Terms
fossil fuels
solar energy
wattage
lumens

Another important part of caring for your home involves using energy wisely. Electrical power and gas energy are the main energy sources used in homes. You use electrical power for appliances, such as stereos, washers, ranges, refrigerators, and hair dryers. Gas is used as a heat source, as well as in dryers, water heaters, and ranges. Conserving these natural resources means using as little energy as possible to get household jobs done. Conserving energy also keeps the cost of supplying power to your home lower.

Energy Sources

Energy could be defined as something that gives a machine the power to perform an action. There are many different kinds of energy: light energy, heat energy, and electrical energy. Energy can be stored. Energy stored in gasoline may be harnessed by burning the gasoline in an engine. Energy stored in batteries will power a radio and some home appliances.

People have found many ways to supplement their own physical energy with energy from other sources. For example, they burn gasoline to move their cars and save the energy of walking or pedaling a bicycle. They may use electricity to raise their garage doors and save the energy of lifting the door. People also consume large amounts of energy in forms of entertainment and convenience appliances. See 25-21.

Energy sources can be divided into two major categories—nonrenewable and renewable.

Nonrenewable Energy Sources

Oil, coal, and natural gas are called **fossil fuels**. Their energy is derived from the partly decayed plants and bodies of animals and that lived long ago. The earth's supply of fossil fuels is limited. Although the supply is being replaced, the process takes many years to complete. That means when the current supply is exhausted, there will be no replacement supplies available. This is why fossil fuels are classified as *nonrenewable resources*.

25-21 Electricity is a necessity in most homes.

Problem-Solving Practice
Why Save the Trees? reproducible master, TR. Have students rank the statements about trees in order of importance. Then have them use the decision-making process to form a plan for conserving trees.

Uranium ore is used to provide nuclear power. Supplies of this energy source are also limited. Researchers estimate that in only 30 to 40 years, the supply will be depleted. Experimental breeder reactors that produce fuel as they operate continue to be tested. Widespread use of this technology could stretch supplies of uranium ore for thousands of years.

Renewable Energy Sources

Sources of energy that cannot be used up or that can be replaced are called *renewable energy sources*. Water, wind, solar energy, wood, and solid wastes are common renewable sources.

Water

The energy of falling water can be converted into electrical energy for home use. The amount of electrical power that can be generated at a given plant is limited. However, more power plants may be built downstream to generate more electrical power from the same water.

As water evaporates and falls again as rain, the water above hydroelectric plants is replaced. As water from rain flows to the lowlands, it can generate more electrical power. This cycle is a renewable source of energy.

People cannot count on water to provide much more energy than it is already providing. Most of the practical water power sites in the United States have already been developed. In most cases, developing other sites could damage the environment.

Wind

Another renewable source of energy is the wind. However, this source of energy is practical only in places where winds blow almost constantly. Windmills can convert the energy of the wind into mechanical energy. Wind energy can also be converted into electrical energy, which can be stored in batteries and used as needed. See 25-22.

Solar Energy

The greatest renewable source of energy is produced from the sun. At present, **solar energy** is used primarily as a source of heat. A collector traps the sun's heat, 25-23. This heat is then used to heat water for homes and to heat homes and other buildings. As technology develops, greater use of solar energy may result.

25-22 Giant wind-powered electric generators can convert wind energy into electrical energy.

Solar energy has two advantages: the supply is almost limitless, and it does not have harmful effects on the environment. In the future, solar energy may be used on a much larger scale. However, this will only happen if research and development is done to find practical methods of using it.

Wood

This is a renewable resource that can be burned to supply energy. Extensive tree farms could increase supplies of wood. On the other hand, an increasing need for land for other uses could limit the land available for tree farming. Wood as an energy source has to be compared to its other uses. Wood is also used for building materials and as a source of paper and chemicals. Which use of wood provides the best value for people's lives?

Solid Wastes

Solid wastes can supply a limited amount of energy. For example, one plant

Discuss:
Which is our oldest energy source?

Enrich:
Have students research wind, solar energy, and solid wastes as energy sources and report to the class. Find out the pros and cons of each energy source and the potential for increased use.

Discuss:
Do you know of any homes or buildings in the area that use solar energy? What are the advantages of this energy source?

Discuss:
Is wood being renewed as fast as it is being used?

Across the Curriculum

Science. Have students research nuclear power and prepare a report for the class. Ask them to find out how safe nuclear energy, nuclear power plants, and nuclear waste disposal are today. Also ask them to include information on accidents involving nuclear power plants.

Resource:
Energy Sources Crossword, Activity E, SAG

Reflect:
Predict the energy source you will be using 50 years from now.

Enrich:
Have students create posters and bulletin board displays promoting energy conservation. Post these around the school and in the community.

Resource:
Energy Usage, reproducible master, TR

25-23 A solar heat collector traps the heat of the sun. This heat is then used to heat water and to both heat and cool homes.

in St. Louis, Missouri, burns about 300 tons of waste materials daily to generate electricity. If this source were fully used, it could supply about 10 percent of the energy needs in the United States.

A number of additional energy sources are being tried in people's search for fossil fuel replacements. Tidal power is being used to produce electricity. *Geothermal energy*, the heat produced within the earth, is being used in a few locations. Such energy sources may be locally important. However, they are unlikely to produce enough energy to help meet the world's growing demands.

Outlook for the Future

The energy picture for the future is clouded. Oil and natural gas supplies are being depleted. New energy sources offer some promise, but there are difficulties connected with their use.

Nuclear power offers one solution to the growing need for energy. This type of energy must be handled with great care and concern for safety. Misuse of nuclear waste can lead to more dangerous forms of long-term pollution.

Coal is one fossil fuel that is still abundant, but there are pollution problems. Unless properly controlled, the by-products of burning coal can add to air pollution.

Solar energy offers hope for the future. The technology exists for creating devices to use the energy of the sun. The money, public support, and facilities to make solar energy affordable are lacking.

In the near future, technology may make new, inexpensive, abundant energy sources available. Until that time, people can help by trying to use less energy.

You Can Help Conserve Energy

An important task for all people is to cut down on the use of fossil fuels. The residential energy checklist shown in 25-24 will help you discover ways to conserve energy. The more energy you can save, the more there will be for all people to use. As you study this section, you will note some ways you can conserve energy.

Heating and Cooling a Home

A large amount of energy is consumed in heating and cooling homes. Temperature control, window coverings, and proper insulation are simple steps you can take to conserve energy at home.

Temperature control is one way to help conserve energy and lower utility bills. Keep the furnace thermostat in your home set lower in winter and higher in summer. Settings of 65°F and 78°F are recommended.

Dress appropriately for these indoor temperature adjustments. Layered clothing is ideal at-home wear in cold weather. Try wearing a sweater or sweatshirt for extra warmth. You are more likely to feel cold when you are sitting still. Keep afghans, blankets, and small quilts near chairs where family members talk, watch television, or read. Natural fiber materials are more comfortable in the summer than synthetics. Wear cotton clothing to help you keep cool.

Window coverings can play a major role in regulating the temperature of a home. Make sure all windows have draperies, window shades, blinds, or other window coverings that can be opened and closed. Let the sunlight in to warm a room; shut it out for cooling. If your home is air conditioned, keep outside storm windows in place for the summer. This helps your air conditioner keep your home comfortable with less energy consumption.

Putting Technology to Use

Have students use word processing software to develop a survey form. Conduct a survey of students in your school to determine how they feel about the environment and what they are doing to conserve energy and natural resources. Ask students to use presentation software to give an oral report on their findings to the class.

Residential Energy Checklist

House: The Shell
1. Are plants properly located around the house to provide a break against wind and shade against unwanted sun?
2. Are drapes and furniture located so they do not obstruct heating, air conditioning, or ventilation?
3. Are draperies insulated?
4. Do draperies fit snugly around the window?
5. Are exterior house doors closed quickly after use?
6. Are lights and appliances turned off after use?
7. Do you have storm windows and doors?
8. Are all doors and windows properly caulked and weatherstripped?
9. Are draperies and shades closed at night and on cloudy, windy days during the heating season?
10. Are draperies opened to admit sunlight on sunny days in the heating season?
11. Are draperies and shades closed on sunny days during the cooling season?
12. Is the attic ventilated?
13. Is the attic insulated to 6 to 8 inches?
14. Are the walls insulated?
15. Do floors exposed to unheated air have from 2 to 3 1/2 inches of insulation?
16. Is the fireplace damper closed when not in use?
17. Is the den, game room, or family room oriented to the south?
18. Is the house shaded from the western sun?
19. Does your home have window area equivalent to 10 percent or less of its square footage?
20. Is your home sealed from drafts? Is it free from cracks and holes?
21. Does your home have fluorescent lighting where appropriate?
22. Does your home have wall-to-wall carpeting?
23. Do all windows have draperies, shades, blinds, shutters, or other coverings?

Environmental Control
24. Are ducts, radiators, or air conditioners closed off in unused rooms or closets?
25. Are hot water pipes insulated in unheated and uncooled spaces?
26. Are air ducts insulated in unheated and uncooled spaces?
27. Is the thermostat set at 65°F or below during the heating season?
28. Is the thermostat set at 78°F or above during the cooling season?
29. Are heating and cooling filters clean?
30. Is the thermostat turned back at night?
31. Are windows and doors tightly closed while mechanically heating or cooling?
32. Is an attic fan used in the summer?
33. Do thermostats indicate correct temperature settings?
34. Is an outside air conditioning unit located on the shady (north) side of the house?
35. Is the water heater insulated?
36. Is the air conditioning unit properly sized for your needs?
37. Do you have a heat pump?
38. Do you use natural ventilation as much as you possibly can?
39. Are radiators and other heating or cooling equipment clean and dust free?
40. Is the water heater located in a heated space?

Housing Selection
41. If you live in an apartment, is it an "inside" apartment?
42. If you live in a mobile home, does it have a "skirt"?
43. If you live in an older home, has its plumbing, wiring, insulation, and chimneys been checked by experts?

Food
44. Is the frost on the refrigerator and freezer less than ¼ inch thick?
45. Is the refrigerator set at 40°F?
46. Is the freezer set at 0°F?
47. Is the cooking range turned off immediately after use?
48. Are appliances clean and dust free (particularly cooling coils)?
49. Is the oven never used as a dryer or heater?
50. Is a timer used to avoid overcooking?
51. Is the heated dry cycle on the dishwasher not used?

Clothing
52. Does your family dress warmer in cool weather to avoid mechanical heating?
53. Does your family dress cooler in warm weather to avoid mechanical cooling?
54. Are clothes washed only when there is a full load?
55. When washing, is cold or warm water used when possible?
56. Are clothes always rinsed with cold water?
57. Is the washer located near the water heater?
58. Is the dryer lint screen cleaned after each load?

Personal Care
59. Do the members of your family take short showers, or use only small amounts of water for tub baths?

Reflect:
Go over this Residential Energy Checklist with your family. Are you doing your best to conserve energy at home?

25-24 Can you answer *yes* to these questions? If so, you are doing your part in helping to conserve energy.

FCCLA Activity
Chapter members working on the Community Service Opportunities program could plan a presentation on conserving energy and saving the environment. They could present this to local community groups and other student groups. Chapter members could also prepare energy-saving booklets to give out at their presentations.

Enrich: Have someone find out how much insulation is recommended for homes in your area and report to the class.

Vocabulary: What is weather stripping?

Discuss: What are we doing in the family and consumer sciences department here at school to save energy?

Discuss: How many of you are following these water conservation measures at home?

Much heating and cooling energy is wasted because of poor home insulation. Proper insulation controls heat movement in and out of the home. Adding insulation to walls, floors, and ceilings is often a good long-term investment.

There are other ways to insulate dwellings against heat and cold. Properly placed trees, shrubs, and vines can help insulate a home from sun, wind, and noise, 25-25. Caulking cracks and loose window panes and placing weather stripping around doors can keep cold air out in winter. If you have a fireplace, keep the damper closed when the fireplace is not in use. This will keep cold air from coming down the chimney and prevent loss of warm air up the chimney.

Water Use

Heating water is the second greatest energy user in the home. Therefore, be energy-wise whenever you use hot water.

Check the temperature setting on your water heater. Setting it at 120°F should provide adequate hot water for most families. Insulating the hot water storage tank and pipes saves energy, too.

Use cooler water for as many cleaning tasks as possible. You do need hot water for washing dishes. However, cold and warm water are often just as effective as hot for laundering clothes.

If you have a dishwasher, wait until you have a full load before you use it. Cleaning a full load of dishes is both cost-efficient and energy-efficient. Many dishwashers now have air-drying features available that use no extra heat to dry the dishes. Use this feature when quick drying is not essential.

Take showers instead of baths. Limit your showering time so you do not needlessly waste water. Add a water flow restrictor in the showerhead pipe to save even more water.

Food Storage

Refrigerators and freezers rank third as users of home energy. A frostless refrigerator-freezer uses about one-third more energy than a standard model. A water and ice dispenser in the door further increases the energy usage.

Plan ahead before you open the refrigerator or freezer door. Know what you want, get it quickly, and close the door. Cover all food containers before placing them in the refrigerator or freezer. This prevents moisture from collecting as frost. Frost makes it necessary to defrost manual appliances more often. Frostless models have to work harder to keep the frost-free state. See 25-26.

25-25 Trees and foundation plantings help insulate a home against heat, cold, and wind.

25-26 An ice and water dispenser in the door of a refrigerator-freezer increases energy usage. However, eliminating the need to open the door can be an energy savings.

Putting Technology to Use

Ask students to visit an appliance store and record information on the EnergyGuide labels on refrigerators, freezers, dishwashers, and clothes washers. Have students use charting and graphing software to illustrate the energy efficiency and operating costs of various models.

How often should you defrost your freezer? When frost builds up to a ¼-inch thickness, the freezer should be defrosted. Otherwise, your manual-defrost freezer has to work harder to get through the frost.

Circulation of cold air is important for effective refrigeration. Try to keep a small amount of space between containers of food in the refrigerator section. In a freezer, containers should be tightly packed together so the packages can help insulate each other.

Cooking with Major Appliances

Whether gas or electric, major cooking appliances in the kitchen are heavy energy users. Learn to use each one efficiently to help conserve energy.

Ranges

Standard kitchen ranges are heavy energy users. Newer gas ranges have pilotless ignition systems. In these ranges, the pilot light has been replaced by an electric spark that ignites burners and oven. This pilotless system reduces the appliance's annual gas use by as much as 30 percent.

There are more ways of saving energy with either gas or electric ranges. For example, don't preheat the oven too long before you will be using it. (Five minutes is usually long enough.) If you are going to broil food, do not preheat the oven at all.

When using your oven, cook as many foods in it as you can at one time. Use the energy as efficiently as possible.

A self-cleaning oven is an energy-saving cleaning choice. It requires operation at very high temperatures for cleaning, which may seem to be a waste of energy. Actually, self-cleaning ovens contain extra insulation because of the temperatures at which the cleaning feature operates. Therefore, heat is used more efficiently during ordinary baking. Because of the extra insulation, a self-cleaning oven will not heat up the kitchen as much as an ordinary oven.

You can save energy when you are cooking on top of the range as well. When you use an electric range, turn off the surface unit a few minutes before food has finished cooking. The food will continue to cook for a while since it takes time for the heating element to cool. Use covers to hold heat in, especially when boiling water. Remember, though, that certain foods must be cooked uncovered to avoid retaining unpleasant tastes.

Match the size of your cooking pan to the surface heating unit. The bottom of the pan should completely cover the surface unit. Pans should extend no more than one inch beyond the edge of the unit. With gas burners, the flame should not appear beyond the edge of the pan. This way, energy will not be wasted on heating air. It will heat just the pan.

Microwave Oven

Wisely chosen appliances can save much of the energy that would be needed by the range. For example, a microwave oven can be used to perform many cooking tasks. It is an energy saver when compared to a standard range. A microwave oven can save 50 to 75 percent of the energy used in conventional cooking methods.

Convection Oven

The convection oven uses a fan to keep heat circulating around food. You can use lower oven temperatures and cut cooking time with a convection oven. Usually, there is no need to use energy preheating the oven. Convection ovens have some advantages over microwave ovens. Food browns better in a convection oven. You can use metal pans, which usually cannot be used in microwave ovens. Larger quantities of food do not require longer cooking times in a convection oven.

Outdoor cooking has become very popular for summer meals. Cooking outdoors can reduce your energy use. You will save either gas or electricity, and your home will stay cooler. See 25-27.

Buying Major Appliances

When buying a major appliance, consider the amount of energy required for its operation. *EnergyGuide labels* help you compare operating costs for one year on different appliances. EnergyGuide labels appear on both gas and electric appliances.

Enrich:
Have students work together to create posters to place in the foods lab listing energysaving tips.

Discuss:
What are the advantages and disadvantages in cooking with these various major appliances?

Discuss:
What forms of energy are used for outdoor cooking? How expensive is it to cook a meal outdoors.?

Across the Curriculum
Science. Have students research ways microwave ovens can conserve energy. Ask students to share their findings in oral reports.

> **Enrich:**
> Investigate new lightbulbs that save energy and prepare a report. Bring in samples to show the class, if possible.
>
> **Discuss:**
> What information is shown in the EnergyGuide label in Figure 25-28?

25-27 When you cook outdoors in summer, you conserve gas or electricity while you reduce the load on the air conditioner.

These labels are found on refrigerators, refrigerator-freezers, freezers, dishwashers, water heaters, clothes washers, air conditioners, and furnaces. See 25-28. Other appliances use nearly the same amount of energy regardless of brand, so they do not need labels.

Lighting

The average home uses only about five percent of its total energy consumption for lighting. This is not a great amount, but even here, savings can be made. Use the lowest-wattage lightbulbs that will give adequate light for your needs. Switching from a 100-watt to a 60-watt bulb will save 40 percent of the lighting cost at that particular outlet. Fluorescent bulbs give about four times as much light as incandescent bulbs of the same wattage. For example, a 25-watt fluorescent tube provides as much light as a 100-watt incandescent bulb.

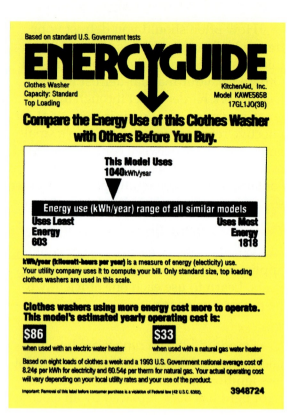

25-28 EnergyGuide labels help you compare the operating costs of appliances and help you conserve energy.

Remember, wattage is not a measure of the amount of light given off by a bulb. **Wattage** indicates the amount of energy required to operate the bulb. The amount of light produced is stated in **lumens**. Both figures should be stated on package labels, 25-29.

Try to get the most lumens for the lowest wattage. Extended service bulbs give fewer lumens than standard bulbs of the same wattage. Use extended service bulbs for hard-to-reach fixtures.

Across the Curriculum

Math. Using the information from this EnergyGuide label, have students determine the cost of operating this appliance for one year. Contact your utility company for the energy rate in your area. How useful is this label for consumers?

Topic 25-3 Conserving Energy in the Home   699

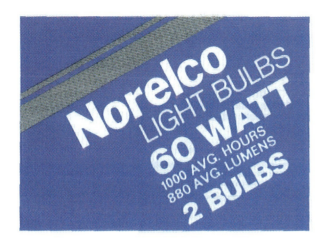
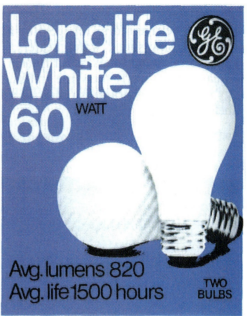

25-29 Get more light for your money. Lightbulbs with identical wattage requirements may have differing light outputs.

Resource:
Energy Conservation Survey, Activity F, SAG

Resource:
Energy Attitude Survey, reproducible master, TR

Check It Out!
1. List four renewable energy sources.
2. What is preventing solar energy from being used more widely as a fossil fuel replacement?
3. Name five ways you can help conserve energy in your home.

Check It Out! (Answers)
1. (List four:) water, wind, solar energy, wood, solid wastes
2. The money, public support, and facilities to make solar energy affordable are lacking.
3. (Student response. See pages 694-698.)

> **Discuss:**
> Ask students how concerned they and their classmates are with the environment. Do many teens voice concerns, but take little action? Why or why not?

> **Enrich:**
> Ask students to research environmental organizations teens can join and environmental projects and activities in which teens can participate. Have them create a school bulletin board display with the information obtained. Encourage students to provide as much detailed information as possible regarding these organizations and activities, such as names, addresses, phone numbers, and dates.

TEENS ARE TALKING ABOUT...

Conserving Energy and Natural Resources

How concerned are teens about the environment? As this group discussion revealed, many teens are voicing their concerns about environmental topics. Shealyn seemed overwhelmed by the scope of the problem. "Teens deal with a lot of conflicts in their everyday lives. They don't seem to have the time or willpower to do their part in conserving the environment. I believe, though, that teens should know environmental problems will always exist unless they do something about them."

Elizabeth added, "Environmental disasters seem commonplace today. Some teens are taking action by recycling and participating in area cleanups. Others continue to throw away recyclable materials and litter the landscapes. How can we prevent the destruction of our natural resources?"

Betty felt teens must do their part now for a better future. She stated, "Preserving the earth is a job for everyone—including teens. We need to do something daily to protect it. Many teens are realizing this and are trying to do their share."

Kelly recognizes that some progress is being made. "I think teens are becoming more aware of the environment. In the past, we watched our beaches and air become polluted. Now we can get involved in many activities to help clean up the environment."

The group was asked what kinds of steps teens are taking to conserve energy and resources in their homes. Meghan responded, "I believe recycling is the most important way to conserve energy and natural resources. Many materials we use can be reused again and again. We should also turn off lights, radios, and water we're not using. My role may be small, but I know each little bit helps."

"We should be careful not to use too much electricity," Lauran added. "For instance, don't dry your hair with a dryer. Let it air dry instead."

"The first step in learning to conserve energy and resources at home is education," Elizabeth remarked. "People need to learn our natural resources are precious, and most are nonrenewable. If people would learn that simple tasks could help save resources, maybe they would be quicker to act."

How does the group think their efforts will impact the environment in the future? Lauran said it simply: "Every little step helps."

Matt endorsed group action. "Teens need to join environmental organizations. Some organizations raise money to care for the environment. Others sponsor activities."

Curran backed Matt's concern. "If we all work together and contribute, we can beat the problems we've created."

Elizabeth felt teens could impact the environment by promoting governmental actions. "More government-sponsored environmental programs need to be established. Young people need to write letters to Congress and voice their concerns and opinions."

Meghan concluded that teens' actions today are the keys to better futures. "We must make the time and do our part in conserving natural resources as much as possible. For the sake of our future, we can't afford to forget."

Feature-Related Activity

Help students organize an environmental club in your school or encourage them to become involved in an exciting club. Urge club members to plan activities to increase environmental awareness, encourage conservation of resources, and improve the environment.

Chapter Review

Summary

Cleaning is an important part of caring for a home. While people have different standards for home care, regular care is needed for safety and comfort. People with busy lifestyles can make cleaning tasks easier by planning ahead. Preventive maintenance and easy-care decor reduce cleaning time. Adequate storage space in each room helps keep items organized. Having the right cleaning supplies and equipment makes cleaning tasks go quickly and easily.

Routine maintenance of the home is always important. With the right skills, people can save time and money by performing some of these tasks themselves. Having the right tools on hand makes plumbing, carpentry, and electrical home repairs easier. People who recognize their skill limitations or don't have the right tools should call repair professionals.

Conserving energy is another aspect of home care as well as a global necessity. Every person must be willing to do his or her part, starting at home. Having a knowledge of conservation issues helps people make energy saving practices an everyday habit. By using nonrenewable resources efficiently, people save natural resources and money.

Think About It!

1. Why do you think it is important to define household cleaning standards?
2. Suggest three ways to better organize your bedroom.
3. What cleaning supplies and equipment would you suggest a friend use to clean a kitchen?
4. If you were planning a weekly home maintenance schedule, what tasks would you include on it?
5. Which of the nonrenewable energy resources do you think the global community should try hardest to conserve? Which of the renewable energy resources do you think is most reliable?
6. Suppose you are planning to build a house. You may not use any of the nonrenewable energy sources. Which of the renewable energy sources would you choose to supply electrical power to your home?
7. Outline seven steps you can take to conserve energy in your home.

Try It Out!

1. Collect magazine pictures of rooms that are easy, moderately easy, and difficult to clean. Label each picture. Then use the pictures to design a bulletin board that shows the positive and negative features of cleaning each room.
2. Brainstorm a list of ways to clean and organize your classroom. Then develop a cleaning schedule based on this list. Give each student a duty to perform.
3. Invite a technology teacher to speak to your class about points to consider when selecting tools.
4. Research and report to the class the various ways energy is produced for your community.
5. Choose one energy source and write a report about its potential for the future.
6. Develop a brochure of tips teens could follow to conserve energy at home, at school, and on the job.
7. Write an article for the school newspaper detailing how teens in your community can get involved in conserving natural resources.

Reflect: Write down additional ways you have learned to conserve energy since reading the last topic. Which of these energy-saving practices can you do?

Resource: *PowerZone Challenge CD.* Have students play the chapter review game to reinforce text content.

CAREER TIMES
LEADING GUIDE TO THE WORLD OF WORK

VOLUME 1, NUMBER 8

Opening the Door to Careers in Housing, Interiors, and Furnishings

Careers in housing, interiors, and furnishings involve all kinds of buildings. The structures in which people live, work, and play can all be affected by workers in this field.

Employment Opportunities

Careers in this field are varied. Some careers focus on designing and constructing buildings. Architects work in this area. This segment of the industry also employs people for carpentry, electrical work, masonry, and plumbing. Architects may work for design firms. Trade workers often work for independent contractors.

A second area in this career field focuses on rooms and the furnishings that fill them. Interior designers plan the inside environments of homes. They also plan space in offices, hotels, restaurants, and other commercial buildings. Their task is to make the interior useful as well as attractive. Interior designers work with architects in the early stages of a project to be sure their plans are compatible. Thus, it is useful for an interior designer to be able to read and understand a blueprint.

Interior decorators work to make rooms appealing to the eye. Their tasks may include selecting paints, furniture, and fabrics. People who repair, refinish, and re-cover furniture are linked with this career area. Those who make curtains, bedspreads, slipcovers, and accessories such as pillows work in this field, too. Some of these people may be hired by furniture or department stores.

Equipment testers may work for appliance makers. These workers check products to make sure they work properly and safely. When products are ready for market, a skilled demonstrator is needed. This person shows consumers how to use the products correctly. These demonstrators often train salespeople how to sell the equipment by making it appeal to consumers.

Entrepreneurial Opportunities

There are many options for entrepreneurs in this field. Architects and interior designers and decorators often have their own firms. Many people in the building trades also own their businesses. An ambitious person might start a business to paint, hang wallpaper, or repair furniture.

Rewards and Demands of Housing, Interiors, and Furnishings Careers

Those who choose housing careers find it rewarding to help people. The environments these workers create improve the efficiency and add to the quality of their clients' lives. They can design environments to be useable by as many people as possible. This may allow older people to live independently longer than they could otherwise.

Demands of this field often center on working with difficult clients. Clients may reject designs or change their minds several times. They are not always happy with the products and services they receive. Workers may wish they could use their creativity more freely. Workers may also have to put in long, irregular hours to meet deadlines.

Preparation Requirements

The training needed for a career in this field will depend on the

An eye for color is an essential personal quality for an interior designer.

specific job. Some firms hire people with associate's degrees. However, a four-year degree is needed for many design jobs.

Entry-Level Jobs

People in entry-level jobs in housing, interiors, and furnishings help workers at higher levels. Training for these jobs often occurs in the workplace. Careers at this level would include being an assistant to a builder or painter. Working on an assembly line to make drapes or furniture would also be an entry-level job.

Mid-Level Jobs

Some mid-level workers receive their training as apprentices. They work under workers who are highly skilled. For instance, a cabinetmaker may train an apprentice in the art of making fine furniture. Support staff in design firms may have associate's degrees. These workers help carry out decisions that have been made at the professional level. For instance, a senior designer may plan the space in a room. However, his or her assistant may be the one who puts many of the plans in action. A mid-level worker who may work with an interior decorator is a floral designer. This person must have artistic skill to prepare flower arrangements that will enhance a room.

Professional-Level Jobs

Most professional jobs in this field require a college degree. Jobs at this level include architects, building engineers, and interior designers.

Many clients do not want to hire someone who has not earned credentials. Therefore, many people in this field choose to join professional organizations. The American Society of Interior Design (ASID) is one such group. Being a member of this prestigious group gives a worker professional credibility. Membership is gained by passing a written and practical exam.

Personal Qualities Needed for Success

People who work in housing, interiors, and furnishings must be creative and persistent. They need good verbal and visual communication skills to relate to clients, suppliers, and coworkers. Workers also need to be able to stay on the cutting-edge of trends and be ready to change as the market demands. Problem-solving skills and the ability to work independently are important. People in this field need to be detail-oriented. They must be good managers of time to meet deadlines. They must be good managers of money to stay within budgets. Computer skills are also becoming more important. Designers in all fields are now using computer-aided design (CAD) programs.

Future Trends

Jobs in this field have always been affected by the economy, and this is not likely to change. Housing and design services are viewed as luxuries. In times of prosperity, there is demand for workers in this area. During economic slumps, the demand drops. Those who can afford to use professional help in making housing decisions are likely to do so. Consumers tend to be interested in style. Professionals who are talented and competitive will likely find career success. Those who lack training, creativity, and perseverance will find it hard to have a career in the housing field.

Workers in this industry must be prepared to respond to changing needs of families in the future. Home design may need to change to meet the requirements of new technologies. Adjustments may be needed to make better use of energy resources.

Career Interests, Abilities, and You

Skills needed in the field of housing, interiors, and furnishings vary widely from one career to another. To find out if this field suits you, you first need to decide which area interests you most. You can do this by taking a family and consumer sciences class in housing or interior design. This class will teach you the basics of creating a living environment. If the construction area appeals to you, think about taking a course in interior design services. This class will give you the chance to make home accessories and refinish or reupholster furniture.

A part-time job as a helper in one of the housing industries can give you hands-on experience. You might volunteer with an organization that provides housing for people in need, such as Habitat for Humanity. This might give you a chance to work with a carpenter, electrician, plumber, or painter.

Career Ladder for Housing, Interiors, and Furnishings

Advanced Degree
Architect
Furniture and equipment specialist
Interior design

Bachelor's Degree
Executive housekeeper
Interior decorator
Textile engineer

Associate's Degree
Design technologist
Home furnishings lab technician
Set designer

High School Diploma
Cleaning service contractor
Decorator's assistant
Furniture maker's apprentice

Pre-High School Diploma
Intern in a housing-related business
Volunteer builder for an organization that houses people in need
Volunteer decorator for a women's shelter

Appendix

Developmental Charts

The following charts list a number of skills and characteristics typical of children at various ages. Also listed are activities that caregivers can do with children to help them develop these skills and characteristics. When reviewing these charts, you must remember that each child develops at his or her own rate. Some children will acquire certain skills and characteristics earlier or later than indicated in the charts.

The Infant	
(Three to Twelve Months)	
Skills and Characteristics	**Activities**
Begins to focus eyes.	Hang a colorful mobile on the crib and place colorful pictures in the room. Move a rattle or toy slowly in front of the baby's face so the eyes will follow the toy.
Develops eye-hand coordination	Hold an object such as a rattle or a stuffed animal in front of the baby. Let the baby grasp it, bang it, and shake it. Have different-shaped objects such as blocks and containers for the baby to pick up and hold. The baby will probably put the objects in his or her mouth, so be sure they are clean and too large to swallow. Provide objects the baby can place into a larger container.
Develops eye-hand-hearing coordination.	Shake a rattle behind the baby's head. Let the baby turn and grab the rattle.
Becomes aware of different textures.	Offer the baby toys with a variety of textures such as fuzzy, hard, and soft. Talk to the baby about how the toys feel.
Becomes aware of self.	Allow the baby to look at himself or herself in a safe mirror.
Grabs and pulls.	Attach a toy to a string so the baby can pull it across the floor, table, or bed.
Develops reasoning skills.	Play hide-and-seek by covering the baby's face with your hands. Partially hide a toy under a blanket and let the baby recover it. Hide a toy completely with a blanket. Let the baby find it. In this way, the baby learns that out-of-sight objects still exist. Put a toy in a container with a top and let the baby find it.
Develops muscle coordination.	Allow the baby to play on the floor. Encourage the baby to stretch, turn over, creep, crawl, and pull up. Roll a ball and let the baby crawl to it.
Becomes interested in sounds and words.	Talk to the baby. Point out parts of his or her body such as toes, nose, eyes, ears, and arms. Identify dolls, balls, and other toys with which the child plays. Talk about pictures that are in the baby's books.

Appendix

The One-Year-Old

Skills and Characteristics	Activities
Shows curiosity about self.	Encourage free play with safe mirrors. Stand or sit with the child before a mirror. Talk to the child about his or her reflection. Encourage the child to make movements before the mirror.
Can recognize objects, animals, and people from pictures or toy reproductions.	Provide a set of plastic farm animals for free play. Talk to the child about each animal's name, the sound it makes, its color, and other characteristics. Look at simple picture books. Let the child point to objects, animals, and community helpers as you name them. Talk about the pictures.
Is very active; enjoys running, climbing, and throwing.	Provide many opportunities for active free play both indoors and outdoors. Encourage climbing on small, safe climbing equipment, such as a wooden rocking boat that can be overturned to make steps. Encourage play with small balls and beanbags. The child can throw the ball to an adult or at an object.
Can manipulate objects with hands and fingers.	Encourage play with blocks, containers, and other stackable toys. Encourage play with large plastic nuts and bolts that can be easily manipulated. Encourage the child to place small objects into a container. Encourage the child to open and close containers with loose-fitting lids.
Understands some basic concepts such as cause and effect, texture, and size.	Talk about cause and effect relationships. For instance, you might say "If you turn over the cup, the juice will spill" or "If you stand in the rain, you will get wet." Talk about textures of objects the child feels. Say "The rock is hard" or "The blanket is soft." Talk about the size of objects. Say "This is a big ball" or "This block is smaller than that block."

The Two-Year-Old

Skills and Characteristics	Activities
Is very active; has a short attention span.	Provide pushing and pulling toys. Encourage play with toys such as pounding benches or punching bags that allow the child to release energy. Provide opportunities both indoors and outdoors for active free play that involves climbing, running, sliding, and tumbling.
Shows interest in manipulation. Can stack several items, pull objects apart, and fill and empty containers.	Provide stacking cups or blocks for stacking and unstacking. Provide pop-apart toys such as pop beads for taking apart. Provide large beads for stringing. Provide opportunities for filling and emptying containers with materials such as sand, water, rice, and beans.
Shows increased development in language skills.	Encourage the child to talk with you. Use pronouns such as *I, me, you, they,* and *we*. Encourage the child to use these words. Talk with the child about pictures. Ask the child to point to objects you name. Ask the child to name objects to which you point. Always correct the child if he or she does not identify an object accurately. Give directions for the child to follow, such as "Close the door" or "Pick up the doll." Be sure to make this a fun game. Teach the child the names of unusual objects such as fire extinguishers, thermometers, or screwdrivers.

(Continued)

The Two-Year-Old (Continued)	
Skills and Characteristics	**Activities**
Likes to imitate.	Encourage finger play. Recite nursery rhymes. Encourage the child to repeat them. Play "I am a mirror." Stand or sit facing the child and have him or her copy everything you do.
Shows interest in dramatic play.	Provide items such as dolls, dress-up clothes, carriages, doll beds, and telephones for the child to use in role-playing.
Shows increased development of fine motor skills.	Provide crayons, chalk, paint, and paper for scribbling and painting. Allow the child to "paint" the sidewalk, building, and play equipment with clear water and a brush.

The Three-Year-Old	
Skills and Characteristics	**Activities**
Shows increased development of large motor skills.	Provide opportunities for vigorous free play both indoors and outdoors. Provide opportunities for climbing, jumping, and riding wheel toys. Play "Follow-the-Leader" using vigorous body movements.
Has greater control over small muscles.	Provide opportunities for free play with blocks of various sizes and shapes. Provide a variety of manipulative toys and activities such as pegboard and peg sets, building blocks, and puzzles. Encourage the child to dress and undress himself or herself. Also encourage the child to do other manipulative tasks such as serving food, setting the table, and watering plants.
Shows increased development of language skills and vocabulary.	Read to the child each day. Encourage the child to tell stories. Encourage the child to talk about anything of interest.
Begins to understand number concepts. Can usually grasp the concept of 1, 2, 3. Can count several numbers in a series, but may leave some out.	Count objects of interest such as cookies, cups, napkins, or dolls. When possible, move the objects as you count. Also allow the child to count the objects. Display numbers in the child's room. Use calendars, charts, rulers, and scales.
Enjoys music and is beginning to be able to carry a tune and express rhythm.	Provide music activities. Sing songs and create rhythms. Encourage the child to move his or her body to music. Encourage the child to make up songs.
Shows curiosity about why and how things happen.	Provide new experiences that arouse questions. Answer the questions simply and honestly. Use reference books with the child to find answers. Conduct simple science activities such as picking up items with a magnet, freezing water, planting seeds, making a terrarium, and flying kites on a windy day.
Enjoys art activities.	Encourage free expression with paint, crayons, chalk, colored pens, collage materials, clay, and play dough.

The Four-Year-Old

Skills and Characteristics	Activities
Uses good balance and body coordination. Shows increased development of small and large motor skills.	Provide opportunities for vigorous free play. Provide opportunities for the child to walk on a curved line, straight line, and low balance beam. Encourage the child to walk with a beanbag on his or her head. Devise games that encourage the child to test the speed, height, and distance of his or her hopping and jumping skills. Provide opportunities for throwing items such as balls and beanbags.
Can group items according to similar characteristics.	Play lotto games. Group buttons by color or size. Provide a mixture of seeds to sort by variety. At clean-up time, sort blocks according to shape. Play rhyming word games.
Has increased understanding of concepts related to numbers, size and weight, colors, textures, time and distance, and position.	In conversation, use words related to these concepts. Play games such as "Simon Says" that require the child to follow directions. Provide swatches of fabric and other materials that vary in texture. Talk to the child about the different textures. Blindfold the child and ask him or her to match duplicate textures.
Uses symbols in drawings and art.	Provide opportunities for the child to do a variety of art projects. Encourage the child to tell a story or talk about his or her finished project. Encourage the child to mix primary colors to produce secondary colors. Name the colors with the child.
Becomes more aware of nature.	Build a simple bird feeder and provide birdseed. Identify for the child the kinds of birds observed. Take the child to a park, zoo, or farm. Help the child plant a small flower or vegetable garden.
Has a vivid imagination; enjoys dramatic play.	Provide a variety of dress-up clothes. Encourage dramatic play through props such as a cash register, empty food containers, a tea set, and child-size furniture.

The Five-Year-Old

Skills and Characteristics	Activities
Has a good sense of balance and body coordination.	Encourage body movement with records, stories, and rhythms. Encourage the child to skip to music or rhymes. Teach the child simple folk dances.
Has a tremendous drive for physical activity.	Provide free play that encourages running, jumping, balancing, and climbing. Play "Tug-of-War" games. Allow the child to tumble on a mat.
Can distinguish right from left.	Play games that emphasize right and left. These games might require the child to respond to directions. You might say "Put your right hand on your nose" or "Put your left foot on the green circle."
Can evaluate different weights, colors, sizes, textures, and shapes.	Play sorting games. Ask the child to sort rocks by weight; marbles or seeds by color; and blocks by size or shape. Ask the child to match fabric swatches by texture.

(Continued)

The Five-Year-Old (Continued)	
Skills and Characteristics	**Activities**
Develops greater coordination of small muscles in hands and fingers.	Encourage the child to paint, draw, cut, paste, and mold clay or playdough. Provide small peg games and other manipulative toys. Help the child sew with a large needle and thread. Provide carpentry experiences.
Shows increased understanding of number concepts.	Count anything of interest such as cookies, cups, leaves, acorns, trees, children, teachers, chairs, tables, books, cymbals, drums, and bells. Identify numbers the child sees on calendars, clocks, measuring containers, and other devices.
Enjoys jokes, nonsense rhymes, and riddles.	Read humorous stories, nonsense rhymes, and riddles.
Enjoys creative dramatic activities.	Encourage the child to use body movements to dramatize movements seen in nature. These might include a flower opening; snow, leaves, or rain falling; worms and snakes wiggling; and wind blowing. Have the child dramatize stories as they are read. Good stories to use include *Caps for Sale,* *Three Billy Goats Gruff,* and *Goldilocks and the Three Bears.*

Adapted From *Children,* North Carolina Office of Day Care Licensing, North Carolina Office for Children.

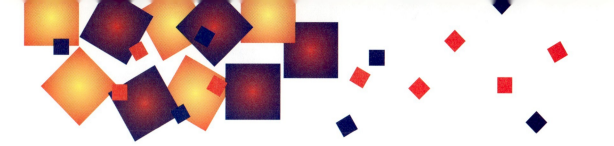

Acknowledgments

Preparation of a manuscript is never completed without assistance. Appreciation is due to many people who helped make this venture possible. It is impossible to name all those to whom I am indebted, but the following provided special assistance.

My chief indebtedness is to my husband, Dr. James F. Parnell, for his encouragement, advice, and moral and professional support as well as his willingness to help me with the numerous skills needed in the preparation of a manuscript.

Appreciation is due to my parents, Mr. and Mrs. W.O. Baynor and Mr. and Mrs. C.K. Parnell (all deceased, but whose influence lingers on), as well as my sisters and brothers for the "in-service" training they have given me in the art and science of work and family skills.

Mrs. Jan Reid, SAGA yearbook adviser; the SAGA photographers; and Mrs. Arleta Oldfield assisted with photographs in classrooms and on school campuses.

Many pictures used throughout the book include relatives, friends, neighbors, and former students. There were also many other people who allowed me to photograph them at work and play as I roamed with camera in hand, looking for people involved in essential acts of daily living.

Mrs. Raynell Mishoe, advanced English teacher, and Mrs. Linda Robinson, both at John T. Hoggard High School, helped to arrange interviews with students for the chapter features used throughout the book.

Elizabeth A. Bordeaux, retired Director of Exceptional Children, Wayne County Schools, Goldsboro, NC, provided valuable assistance by reviewing the book.

Finally, much credit goes to those many students who, over a period of 32 years, have been sources of inspiration and motivation as I have grown as a professional.

Frances Baynor Parnell

Photo Credits

Agricultural Research Service, USDA, 14-7, 14-12, Part 5 career spread, 15-3, 17-6, 17-14, 17-17, 17-27
American Egg Board, 17-10
American Fiber Manufacturers Association, 20-4, 20-5
American Olean, 23-9, 24-15, 25-3, 25-8
American Red Cross, 13-9
Armstrong, 24-14
APA—The Engineered Wood Association, 23-3
Apple Computer, 4-4, 4-16, 5-19, 6-9, 7-9, 19-3
Bernhardt Furniture, 24-11, 24-23
Bernina® of America, 20-23
Broyhill Furniture, 24-9, 24-13, 24-22
Butterick Company, Inc., 22-25, 22-29
Cabela's, 8-2
California Olive Industry, 17-20
Cape Fear Community College, 4-7, 6-13, 9-35, Part 3 career spread
Cerebral Palsy Center of Wilmington, 9-11, 9-19, 9-32, 9-33
Constructive Playthings, 9-3, 9-16, 9-23, 9-24, 9-28
Drexel Heritage Furnishings, 24-24, 24-25
EPRI, 25-22
FCCLA, 4-5
Fleischmann's Yeast, Inc., 17-21
GE Appliances, 6-14, 14-10, 16-1, 16-2, 16-3, 16-4, 16-5, 16-23, 17-1
GE Lighting Institute, 24-12, 24-20, 24-21
Gillette, 12-8
Hall, Steve, 20-13
Hamilton Beach/Proctor-Silex, Inc. 16-6, 17-23

Photo Courtesy of IGA, INC., 17-25
Courtesy of International Business Machines Corporation. (Unauthorized use not permitted.) 11-9, 11-10, 11-11, 11-13, 11-14
Holbrook Early Learning Years Catalog, 9-15, 9-21, 9-25
©Imaginations Advertising, Wilmington, NC, 11-16
Innovative Cooking Enterprises, Inc., Chapter 16 opener
S.C. Johnson & Son, Inc., 25-4
Johnson and Wales, 18-10, Part 6 career spread
Keep America Beautiful, 13-15
KitchenAid, 25-26
Kohler Company, 24-17
Life Alert: The Life Saving Network, 3-9
Mabry, Marty, 6-10, 10-17, 11-15
Maready, Millie, 8-1, 8-6
The McCall Pattern Company, 19-7, 19-14, 21-10
Men's Fashion Association, 19-10, 19-13, 22-17
Mirro, 16-10
National Chicken Council, 17-4
National Pork Board, 14-3, 14-8, 17-28
North Carolina Solar Center, 25-23
Parnell, James F., 4-10, 6-5, 10-10, 10-31, 11-2, 11-3, 11-24, 12-20, 15-1, 16-15, Chapter 22 opener, 23-6
Pellon Corporation, 22-1, 22-13
Pendleton, Chapter 8 opening photo, 19-5, 20-18
Riehle, D., 10-9
Rowenta, 20-21
Rubbermaid, 16-14, 17-15, 25-2

SAGA, 1-4, 1-6, 1-10, 1-12, 1-16, 1-20, 1-21, 2-1, 2-5, 2-7, 2-13, 2-21, 3-1, 3-6, 3-15, Chapter 4 opener, 5-3, 6-8, 7-13, 10-5, 10-8, 10-11, 11-6, 12-14, 13-4, 14-19, 14-23, Chapter 14 teen feature, Chapter 15 teen feature, 19-1

Seabrook Designs, 24-3, 24-6, 24-27

Simplicity Pattern Company, 20-15, Chapter 20 teen feature, 22-4, 22-15

Spiegel, 18-1, 18-6, 24-4

State of New Hampshire, David Brownell, photographer, 2-19

Stone/Penny Tweedie, Part 7 opener

Sunbeam/Thalia, 16-26

Target Technologies, 5-23

Tupperware™ Home Parties, 15-19

University of North Carolina at Wilmington, 13-8
Geri Vital, photographer, Part 1 opener, 1-3, 2-8, 4-1, 4-15, Part 1 career spread, 12-3, Chapter 17 teen feature, 19-15, 23-5
Michael Wolt, photographer, 12-12

U.S. Department of Labor, Secretary's Commission on Achieving Necessary Skills, 5-21

Village, a Division of Schumacher & Co., 25-1

Vogue® Patterns, 19-12, 21-3

Wachovia Corp., 10-20, 10-21, 11-18, 11-20

Waverly, a Division of Schumacher & Co., 24-2, 24-16

Glossary

A

ability. Skill in doing tasks developed through training and practice. (5-1)

abstinence. A choice to refrain from sexual intercourse until marriage. (2-2)

accented-neutral color scheme. A color scheme based on one dominant neutral, such as black, white, gray, or shades or tints of brown, with bright accents of color added to create interest. (24-1)

accessory. An item that accents clothing and gives an outfit a finished look. (19-3)

accident. An unexpected event that causes loss, injury, or sometimes death. (13-1)

account statement. A monthly, bimonthly, or quarterly summary of a checking account. (10-4)

acquaintance. A person who is familiar, but who is not a close friend. (2-2)

acquaintance rape. Rape that occurs between people who know each other. This may be a friend, someone at school, a coworker, or someone the victim just met. (2-3)

acquired immune deficiency syndrome (AIDS). A deadly sexually transmitted disease caused by the human immunodeficiency virus, which breaks down the immune system, leaving the body vulnerable to disease. (12-4)

active listener. A listener who gives the speaker some form of feedback. (3-1).

active-physical play. Play that helps children develop their large-muscle skills. They use their large muscles for movements like walking, running, hopping, jumping, and skipping. (9-2)

activity center. A grouping in a room of all the furnishings needed for a particular activity. (24-3)

addiction. A dependence of the body on a continuing supply of a substance, such as a drug. (7-3)

adjustment lines. Two parallel lines that extend across a pattern piece, indicating where to shorten or lengthen the pattern piece. (21-1)

adolescence. The period of life from when puberty begins until growth ceases and adulthood is reached. (1-2)

adoption. The legal process through which a child's legal guardianship is transferred from the birthparents to adoptive parents. (8-1)

advertisement. A paid public message about goods and services for sale, which is communicated through various media. (11-3)

aerobic capacity. A measure of endurance and the condition of the heart and lungs. (12-1)

agency adoption. A type of adoption in which birthparents and adoptive parents work through a licensed state or private adoption agency to make an adoption plan. (8-1)

a la carte. Items on a restaurant menu that are priced individually. (18-3)

alcoholic. A person who suffers from the disease of alcoholism. (7-3)

alcoholism. A disease in which a person develops a physical and psychological addiction to alcohol. (7-3)

alteration. A change made to the size of a pattern or garment to make the garment fit the wearer perfectly. (21-1)

altruistic love. A type of marital love based on the concern one spouse has for the well-being of the other spouse. (2-4)

amino acid. A component of proteins. (14-1)

amniocentesis. A prenatal test given by inserting a needle in a pregnant woman's abdomen and withdrawing a small amount of amniotic fluid. Fetal cells in the fluid are grown in a laboratory and examined for irregular chromosomes that cause hereditary disabilities. (8-2)

analogous color scheme. A color scheme that combines three to five hues found next to each other on the color wheel. (24-1)

annual percentage rate (APR). The actual percentage rate of interest paid for an entire year. (11-4)

anorexia nervosa. A complex eating disorder in which the victim avoids eating, sometimes to the point of starvation. (14-4)

antiperspirant. A grooming product that reduces the flow of perspiration. (12-2)

apprenticeship. A work-based learning program that provides training for a skilled trade. (5-1)

appropriateness. A design that is right for its purpose. (24-1)

aptitude. A person's natural talent and his or her potential for learning. (5-1)

aseptic packaging. A packaging technique in which foods and containers are sterilized separately before food is packed in the container in a sterilized chamber. (15-4)

attached house. A single-family house that shares common walls with the houses on either side, also called a townhouse or rowhouse. (23-2)

autocratic. A style of leadership in which the leader has full control of the group and makes all the decisions for the group. (4-1)

B

backstitching. Sewing backward and forward in the same place for a few stitches to secure thread ends. (22-1)

bait and switch. A deceptive advertising method in which the advertiser offers a low-priced item as bait to get shoppers in the store. Once shoppers are in the store, the advertiser tries to switch them to a more expensive item. (11-3)

bakeware. Utensils used for baking foods in an oven. (16-1)

balance. Equal visual weight on both sides of a central point. (19-2)

basal metabolism. Life-sustaining activities that account for energy expended when the body is at physical, emotional, and digestive rest. (14-4)

basting. A technique of sewing long, loose stitches, either by hand or by machine. (22-1)

beauty. A quality that gives pleasure to the senses, and should be the result when the principles of design are used. (24-1)

beneficiary. A person who receives a death benefit of a life insurance policy. (10-6)

bias. The diagonal intersection of the lengthwise and crosswise grains in a piece of fabric. (20-1)

biscuit method. A mixing technique used in food preparation in which dry ingredients are mixed together, and then fat is cut into the mixture before liquid ingredients are added. (17-3)

bobbin. A small metal or plastic spool that feeds the lower thread on a sewing machine, which is needed in making a lockstitch. (20-4)

body language. Body movements, such as facial expressions, gestures, and posture, used to send messages to others. (3-1)

body mass index (BMI). A calculation used by health professionals to assess an adult's weight in terms of his or her height. (14-4)

bond. A certificate that represents a promise by a company or government to repay a loan on a given date. (10-5)

brainstorming. A group method of solving problems in which members offer any and all ideas. (4-1)

budget. A plan to help manage money wisely. (10-3)

bulimia nervosa. An eating disorder, also known as the binge-purge syndrome, in which the victim consumes large amounts of food and then vomits or takes laxatives or diuretics to avoid weight gain. (14-4)

bylaws. A set of specific rules that expand upon an organization's constitution by giving more information. (4-2)

C

calorie. The unit of measurement of food energy. (14-4)

carbohydrate. A nutrient that serves as the major source of energy in the diet. (14-1)

career. A series of jobs, often in the same field, a person has over a period of years. (5-1)

career plan. A list of steps to achieve a career goal. (5-1)

caregiver. A person who provides care for someone else. (9-1)

cashier's check. A check drawn on a financial institution's own funds and signed by an officer of the institution. (10-4)

cash value. The amount a policyholder can collect if he or she decides to give up a whole life insurance policy. (10-6)

casing. An enclosure for elastic or a drawstring that gathers a garment snugly to the body. (22-3)

central processing unit (CPU). A basic part of computer hardware that processes data. (11-2)

cereal. A starchy grain used as food. (17-3)

certificate of deposit (CD). A type of savings account that pays a set rate of interest on money that is deposited for a set period of time. (10-5)

certified check. A personal check for which a financial institution guarantees payment. (10-4)

character. Inner traits, such as conscience, moral strength, and social attitudes, that guide a person's conduct and behavior into acceptable standards of right and wrong. (1-1)

chat room. A forum for a number of people to communicate over the Internet at the same time. (9-1)

child care cooperative. Child care program formed by groups of parents who share in the care of their children, allowing parents more control over the program. (9-7)

childless family. A couple without children. (6-2)

children with special needs. Children with disabilities and gifted and talented children. (9-6)

cholesterol. A fatty substance found in every body cell. (14-1)

chromosome. A threadlike structure that carries genes in living cells. (8-2)

chronological growth. Increase in age, which takes place at the same rate for all people. (1-2)

circuit breaker. A switch found in a control panel that interrupts the path of electricity when it trips. (25-2)

civil law. A type of law that deals with disputes between private citizens. (4-3)

classic. A fashion that never changes drastically; therefore, it can be worn year after year. (19-4)

clean finishing. Turning under the raw edges of a garment and stitching. (22-2)

cleaning agents. Materials used to remove soil; often added to water. (25-1)

cleaning schedule. A written plan identifying what household cleaning tasks need to be done, who is responsible for which tasks, and how often the tasks are to be completed. (25-1)

clipping. Making straight cuts in a seam allowance toward the stitching line, usually at ½-inch intervals, to prevent puckering. (22-1)

closed adoption. An adoption that includes no contact between birthparents and adoptive family. (8-1)

coded message. A means of communication in which people fail to say what they really mean. (3-2)

codependency. A pattern of unhealthy behaviors that is used by family members to cover up a problem. (7-1)

co-insurance. An insurance policy provision that requires the policyholder to pay a certain percentage of medical costs. (10-6)

collateral. Something of value a person owns that he or she pledges to a creditor as security for a loan. (11-4)

color wheel. A tool that shows how colors relate to one another. (19-2)

communicable diseases. Illnesses that can be passed on to other people. (9-2)

communication. The process of conveying information so messages are received and understood. (3-1)

companionate love. The most common type of love in a marriage in which a couple share feelings of deep friendship, mutual respect, and affection. (2-4)

comparison shopping. Comparing products and prices in different stores before making a purchase. (11-1)

complementary color scheme. A color scheme using colors opposite each other on the color wheel for a strong contrast. (24-1)

complementary needs. Needs that two people can meet for each other.

compromise. A technique used in negotiating conflicts in which all parties agree to give up something of importance to reach a mutual agreement. (3-3)

computer. An electronic device that processes information according to instructions. (11-2)

computer-aided design (CAD). Graphics software that assists in creating a design. (11-2)

conception. The beginning of pregnancy that occurs when a sperm from the father unites with an ovum from the mother. (8-2)

condominium. An individually owned housing unit in a multiunit structure. (23-2)

conflict. A struggle between two people who have opposing views. (3-3)

conflict resolution process. A step-by-step form of communication that allows conflicts to be resolved in a positive manner. (3-3)

conformity. Wearing garments similar to those worn by others. (19-1)

congenital disability. A physical or mental disability that exists from birth and may be caused by either heredity or environment. (8-2)

consequences. Results that follow an action or behavior. (9-3)

constitution. A set of major laws used to govern an organization. (4-2)

Consumer Product Safety Commission (CPSC). A government agency that sets and enforces safety standards for consumer products and handles consumer complaints. (11-5)

control panel. A metal box containing either fuses or circuit breakers through which electricity travels. (25-2)

convection cooking. A method of cooking that involves circulating hot air over all food surfaces, allowing food to cook quickly and evenly. (16-1)

convenience food. A food product that requires minimal preparation. (15-1)

cookware. Utensils, including saucepans and skillets, used for cooking on top of a range. (16-1)

cooperative. An apartment building owned by and operated for the benefit of those who live there, forming a nonprofit corporation. (23-2)

cooperative education. A work-based learning program that prepares students for an occupation immediately after high school through a paid job experience. (5-1)

copayment. A small, fixed fee paid by a policyholder for certain insured items or services. (10-6)

cover. The individual place setting and allotted space needed by each person at a table. (18-1)

credit. An arrangement that allows consumers to buy goods or services now and pay for them later. (11-4)

credit contract. A legally binding agreement between creditor and borrower that details the terms of repayment. (11-4)

creditor. A person who gives credit to consumers and to whom debts are owed. (11-4)

credit rating. A creditor's evaluation of a person's ability to repay debts. (11-4)

crisis. An event that greatly influences people's lives and causes them to make difficult changes in their lifestyles. (7-3)

cultural heritage. Learned behaviors, beliefs, and languages that are passed from generation to generation. (1-1)

custom house. A house specifically designed by an architect and built by a builder for a new owner. (23-2)

cutting layout. A drawing showing how to fold fabric and place pattern pieces for cutting. (21-3)

cutting line. A bold line on pattern pieces used as a guide for cutting fabric. (21-1)

D

dart. A construction element used to give shape and fullness to a garment made by stitching to a point through a fold in the fabric. (22-1)

date rape. The rape of a dating partner. (2-3)

decision. A conscious or unconscious response to a problem or issue. (1-4)

decision-making process. A logical, step-by-step method people can use to make the decisions that are best for them. (1-4)

deductible. An amount that a policyholder must pay before his or her insurance company will pay on a claim. (10-6)

defense mechanism. A behavior pattern used to protect a person's self-esteem. (12-3)

defensive driving. A skill that helps a driver anticipate what other drivers might do to cause accidents. (13-1)

dehydration. The depletion of body fluids during periods of activity. (14-3)

democratic. A style of leadership that stresses the needs and wishes of individuals and in which members are encouraged to participate in decision making by voting. (4-1)

demographics. Statistical qualities of the human population. (6-2)

deodorant. A grooming product that controls body odor by interfering with the growth of bacteria. (12-2)

depilatory. A chemical that dissolves unwanted hair so it can be washed away. (12-2)

depression. An emotional state that ranges from mild, short-lived feelings of sadness to a deep, despairing sense of dejection. (12-3)

dermatologist. A doctor who specializes in treating skin. (12-2)

developmentally appropriate practices. Techniques suited to the developmental characteristics and needs of the individual child. (9-3)

developmental task. A task or skill that a society expects of people at various stages of life. (1-2)

Dietary Guidelines for Americans. Ten suggestions made by the U.S. Departments of Agriculture and Health and Human Services to help people choose healthful diets. (14-2)

direct tax. A type of tax that is charged directly to the taxpayer. (4-3)

directional fabric. A fabric with nap, pile, texture, a border print, or one-way design. (21-3)

directional stitching. Stitching in the direction of the grain. (22-1)

diverse. Differing from one another. (3-2)

diversity. Condition of a group whose members represent many different cultures. (4-1)

dividend. A distribution of a company's profits to a stockholder. (10-5)

dot. A pattern symbol used to match seams and other construction details. (21-1)

double-complementary scheme. A color scheme using two pairs of complementary colors next to each other or on each side of complementary colors on the color wheel. (24-1)

dovetail. To combine or fit tasks together. (10-2)

dramatic play. A form of play involving role-playing. A child imitates another person or acts out a situation, but does so alone. (9-4)

dress code. A standard of dress that is enforced in a social setting. (19-1)

dry cleaning. The process of cleaning clothes using an organic chemical solvent instead of water. (19-5)

drug abuse. The use of a drug for a purpose other than it was intended. (7-3)

dual-career family. A family in which both spouses are employed outside the home. (7-2)

dysfunctional family. A family that provides a negative environment that discourages the growth and development of family members. (7-1)

E

easing. A sewing technique that involves making a piece of fabric fit a slightly smaller piece of fabric as a seam is sewn and provides needed fabric fullness at certain points on the body. (22-1)

elements of design. Color, line, texture, and form as used in artistic design. (19-2)

e-mail. Short for electronic mail, which is a message delivered to your computer from another computer. (3-1)

embryo. A developing human from the time the zygote attaches itself to the wall of the mother's uterus until the eighth week after conception. (8-2)

emergency medical technician (EMT). A trained professional who provides immediate treatment to victims of serious illness and injury. (12-5)

emotional abuse. A form of abuse that happens when one person purposely hurts another's self-concept through constant yelling, teasing, or insulting. (7-3)

emotional disorder. A disorder that limits the way a person functions emotionally and socially; sometimes marked by extremes of behavior. (9-6)

emotional growth. Development of the ability to express feelings. (1-2)

emotional neglect. The failure to provide loving care and attention to family members. (7-3)

empathy. The quality of understanding how others feel even when personal feelings may differ. (1-1)

emphasis. The center of interest in a design. (19-2)

emulation. The act of imitating the behavior of other people around you. (1-4)

enabler. Someone who unknowingly acts in ways that contribute to an alcoholic's or addict's drug use. (7-3)

endorse. Signing the back, left end of a check before cashing or depositing it. (10-4)

enriched. A term used to describe a food product that has nutrients added back to it that were lost during processing. (14-1)

entrepreneur. A person who starts and manages his or her own business. (5-2)

environment. Everything that surrounds a person. (1-1)

estate. What a person leaves behind when he or she dies. (10-5)

ethnic group. A group of people who share common racial and/or cultural characteristics, such as national origin, language, religion, and traditions. (1-1)

etiquette. Approved social conduct, or good manners. (18-2)

eviction. A legal procedure that forces a tenant to leave a property before the rental agreement expires if he or she fails to uphold the terms of the lease. (23-3)

expiration date. A date stamped on food products such as yeast and baby formula indicating the last day the product should be used or eaten. (15-3)

extended family. A family structure that includes other relatives, such asgrandparents, aunts, uncles, and/or cousins, living with parents and their children. (6-2)

F

fabric. A textile product usually made by weaving or knitting yarns together. (20-1)

facing. An extra piece of garment fabric used to finish the raw edges of garment pieces. (22-2)

fad. A style that is popular for a short time and then disappears. (19-4)

family. Two or more people related by blood, marriage, or adoption; two or more persons who share resources, responsibility for decisions, personal priorities, and goals and who have commitment to one another over time. (6-1)

family life cycle. Basic stages of growth and development experienced by families. (6-3)

family structure. The makeup of a family group based on the relationships of the members in the family. (6-2)

fashion. The manner of dress being worn by the majority of people at a given time. (19-4)

fat. A nutrient that provides a concentrated source of food energy. (14-1)

feedback. A clue that lets the speaker know the message is getting through to the listener and how it is being received. The feedback can be a nod, a smile, or even a comment. (3-1)

feed dogs. Two small rows of teeth that move the fabric forward under the presser foot. (20-4).

felony. A serious criminal offense. (4-3)

fetus. A developing human from the eighth week after conception until birth. (8-2)

fiber. The basic unit of all fabrics. (20-1)

figure type. A category developed by pattern companies to standardize pattern sizes based on height and general body proportions. (20-2)

filament yarns. One or several continuous strands of fibers. (20-1)

filling yarns. Yarns that run along the crosswise grain of fabric. (20-1)

finance charges. The total amount a borrower must pay a creditor for the use of credit. These charges include interest, service charges, and any other fees. (11-4)

finfish. Fish that has fins and backbones. (17-1)

finish. A final treatment used to protect wood's natural beauty or to make it look like another type of wood. (24-3)

first aid. Emergency care or treatment given to people right after an accident, which relieves pain and prevents further injury. (9-2). Immediate, temporary care provided to victims of accidents or sudden illnesses until professional medical assistance is available. (12-5)

fixed expense. A set amount of money that a person is committed to pay, such as a monthly car payment. (10-3)

flexible expense. A cost that occurs repeatedly, but which varies in amount from one time to the next. (10-3)

flexible workweeks. Employees may work four-day, 40-hour workweeks with 10-hour workdays. (7-2)

flextime. Employees set their own work schedules within certain company terms. (7-2)

floor covering. Material placed and attached on top of the structural floor of a building. (24-2)

fluorescent light. Artificial light produced by releasing electricity through mercury vapor in a special tube to create light rays. (24-2)

follower. A person who supports a group by helping put goals into action. (4-1)

food additive. A substance added to a food for a specific purpose. (15-3)

Food and Drug Administration (FDA). A government agency that helps protect consumer safety by regulating the production, packaging, and labeling of foods, drugs, and cosmetics. (11-5)

foodborne illness. A sickness caused by eating contaminated food. (16-2)

Food Guide Pyramid. A model for making daily food choices that groups foods on the basis of their similarity in nutrient content and gives recommended numbers of daily servings for each group. (14-2)

food rotation. Storing the freshest food at the back of the shelf in order that the oldest foods, stored at the front of the shelf, will be used first. (15-4)

form. A design element that defines the shape of an object. (19-2)

fortified. A term used to describe a food product that has had nutrients added to improve its nutritional value. (14-1)

fossil fuels. Energy sources, such as oil, coal, and natural gas, derived from the partly decayed plants and bodies of animals that lived long ago. (25-3)

foster care. Care provided for a child who needs a home temporarily. (9-1)

freestanding house. A house that stands alone. (23-2)

freshness date. A date stamped on food products such as baked goods that indicates the end of a product's quality peak. (15-3)

fringe benefits. Employee benefits provided by an employer such as insurance, profit-sharing plans, and paid vacations. (5-3)

function. The way in which architecture, furniture, equipment, and accessories will be used. (24-1)

functional family. A family that provides a positive environment that encourages each family member to grow and develop to his or her fullest potential. (7-1)

fuse. A safety device that screws into a control panel socket and has a strip of metal that melts and stops the flow of power in the event of an electrical overload. (25-2)

G

gathering. Tiny, soft folds of fabric formed in a garment to produce a rounded shape. (22-1)

generic product. A product that has a plain label containing only required information. (15-2)

genes. Basic elements of the reproductive cells that control the transfer of traits from parents to their children. (8-2)

genetic counseling. A medical consultation held to predict the likelihood that a couple will have a child with an inherited congenital disability. (8-2)

gifted or talented. A person who shows outstanding ability in either a general sense or in a specific ability. (9-6)

goal. An aim a person is consciously trying to reach. (1-3)

grading. Trimming each layer of a seam allowance to a different width. (22-1)

grain. The direction the yarns run in a piece of fabric. (20-1)

grainline arrow. A pattern symbol that indicates how a pattern piece is to be placed on fabric. (21-1)

gratuity. A sum of money left for a waiter in a restaurant as a measure of gratitude for service received, usually fifteen to twenty percent of the total bill; also called a tip. (18-3)

grooming. Cleaning and caring for the body. (12-2)

gross income. The total amount of money an employee earns before deductions. (5-3)

group dating. A type of dating in which a number of people of both sexes go out together. (2-2)

guidance. Everything caregivers do and say to promote socially acceptable behavior in children. (9-3)

H

handheld organizer. A pocket-size machine that serves as a personal planner. (11-2)

hangtag. A tag attached to a garment to provide information, such as trademarks, guarantees, style number, size, and price. (19-4)

health maintenance organization (HMO). A group of medical professionals and facilities that provides health care services to members. (10-6)

heredity. The sum of all traits passed on through genes from parents to children. (1-1)

high tech. Refers to processes and products resulting from technology. (11-2)

homogenized. Refers to a process by which milkfat is broken up into tiny particles that remain suspended throughout milk. (17-4)

hormone. A substance in the body that triggers cellular activity, such as growth and the development of adult characteristics. (1-2)

hot line. Telephone number people can call for information or other assistance with a specific problem. (9-1)

hourly wage. A set amount of money paid to an employee for each hour of work. (5-3)

house brand. A brand that is sold by a store or chain of stores. (15-2)

housing. Any dwelling that provides shelter. (23-1)

hue. The name given to a color. (19-2)

human immunodeficiency virus (HIV). The virus that causes AIDS. (12-4)

human resource. A resource, such as knowledge, energy, a skill, or a talent, that comes from within a person. (10-1)

I

imitative-imaginative play. Form of play in which children use their imaginations as they pretend to be other people or objects; begins at about two years of age. (9-4)

immunizations. Injections or drops given to a person to provide immunity from a certain disease. (9-2)

implement. To carry out. (10-2)

impulse buying. Making an unplanned or quick purchase without giving it much thought. (11-1)

incandescent light. Artificial light produced when electricity passes through a tungsten filament that is in a glass bulb. (24-2)

inclusion. The placing of students of varying abilities in the same class. (9-7)

independent adoption. Type of adoption in which birthparents and adoptive parents do not work with a licensed adoption agency. (8-1)

indirect tax. A type of tax that is included in the price of taxed items. (4-3)

individuality. Choosing clothes that set a person apart from others. (19-1)

infant. A baby up to 12 months old. (9-5)

infatuation. An intense feeling of admiration. (2-2)

infertility. The condition of being unable to conceive children. (8-2)

input device. A basic part of computer hardware that enters data. (11-2)

in-seam pocket. A pocket sewn in the side seam of a garment. (22-3)

insecticide. A strong chemical used for insect control. (25-1)

insomnia. The inability to get the amount of sleep needed when it is needed. (12-1)

intellectual growth. A developing ability to reason and form complex thought patterns. (1-2)

intensity. The brightness or dullness of a color. (19-2)

interest. The price a borrower pays a creditor for the use of money over a period of time. (11-3)

interests. All the activities a person likes to do. (5-1)

interfacing. A layer of reinforcement fabric between garment fabric and a facing. (22-2)

intermediate color. A color produced from equal amounts of one primary color and one secondary color. (19-2)

Internet. An international network of computers that are joined together. It is available to anyone who has a computer, a modem, and an Internet service provider. (3-1)

internship. A work-based learning program that offers paid or unpaid work experience to learn about a job or industry. (5-1)

ironing. A process of moving an iron across fabric to smooth wrinkles. (19-5)

J

job. The work a person does to earn a living. (5-1)

job shadowing. A program to explore career options through a student's one-day visit with an experienced person to his or her job. (5-1)

job sharing. Two people divide the work responsibilities of one job, each working on a part-time basis. (7-2)

K

kimono sleeve. A sleeve that is cut in one piece with the body of a garment. (22-3)

kitchen utensil. A hand-held kitchen tool used for measuring, cutting, mixing, cooking, or baking tasks. (16-1)

knitting. A process of looping yarns together to form a fabric. (20-1)

L

label. A cloth tag attached to a garment to provide important information, such as fiber content, manufacturer, country of origin, and care instructions. (19-4)

laissez-faire. A style of leadership in which members may do whatever they want to do and leaders are on hand only to serve as resources. (4-1)

leader. A person who has the power to influence the behavior of others. (4-1)

learning disability. A limitation in the way a person's brain sorts and uses certain types of information. (9-6)

lease. A contract between a tenant and a property owner, listing the rights and responsibilities of both parties. (23-3)

leavening agent. An ingredient used to produce carbon dioxide in baked goods. (17-3)

legumes. Seeds that grow in the pods of some vegetable plants. (17-1)

lifestyle. A person's way of life or style of living. (19-1)

line. A design element that gives direction to a design. (19-2)

liquidity. The degree to which a person will be able to get cash quickly from a savings account or financial investment. (10-5)

loan value. The amount a policyholder can borrow from an insurance company using the cash value of a whole life insurance policy as collateral. (10-6)

lockstitch. A stitch made by a sewing machine with thread coming from both the upper and lower parts of the machine and locking securely in the middle of the fabric layers being sewn. (20-4)

long-term goal. A goal that takes from months to years to achieve. (1-3)

loopers. Serger sewing machine parts that form upper and lower stitches. (20-4)

lumens. A measurement of the amount of light produced by a given source. (25-3)

M

management. Wisely using means to achieve goals. (1-4, 10-1)

management process. A series of steps that helps people plan how to best use resources to achieve goals. (10-1)

manipulative-constructive play. Play that helps children develop small-muscle skills. The small muscles are those that control the wrists, hands, ankles, fingers, and thumbs. (9-2)

manners. Rules to follow for proper social conduct. (3-1)

manufactured fibers. Fibers that are produced artificially from substances such as cellulose, oil products, and chemicals. (20-1)

manufactured house. A house made in a factory and then moved to a site and assembled. (23-2)

maturity. The change that occurs between childhood and adulthood, during which physical, personal, and behavioral characteristics become more adult. (1-2)

meal management. Using resources of skills, money, and time to put together nutritious meals. (15-1)

meal service. The way a meal is served. (18-1)

measurement equivalent. An amount that is equal to another amount, such as one-fourth cup equaling four tablespoons. (16-3)

meat. The edible portion of animals, including muscles and organs. (17-1)

meat analog. A plant-based protein product made to resemble various kinds of meat. (17-1)

media. Channels of mass communication, such as magazines, television, radio, and the Internet. (6-2)

mediation. Technique in which a third person is called upon to help reconcile differences between conflicting parties. (3-3)

memory. A basic part of computer hardware that stores data. (11-2)

mental disability. A disability that limits the way a person's brain functions, causing a limited learning capacity. (9-6)

mentor. A person at a job site who knows how to do a job and teaches a student to do it well. (5-1)

microfiber. A extremely thin filament of a manufactured fiber. (20-1)

mineral. An inorganic substance needed for building tissues and regulating body functions. (14-1)

misdemeanor. A minor criminal offense. (4-3)

mobile home. A dwelling that is built and assembled at a factory and then moved to a location and attached to a foundation. (23-2)

modeling. The act of adults exhibiting behaviors in front of children, which the children then copy. (9-3)

modesty. A standard held by a cultural group about the proper way to cover the body in various settings. (19-1)

monochromatic color scheme. A color scheme based on only one hue, which may be used in various values and intensities for variety. (24-1)

mortgage. A loan used to pay for a home. (23-3)

motivation. A force that gives people a reason to take action. (4-1)

muffin method. A mixing technique used in food preparation in which dry ingredients and liquid ingredients are mixed together in separate bowls, and then the liquid ingredients are poured into a well made in the center of the dry ingredients. (17-3)

multicultural book. A book that involves characters from a variety of racial and ethnic groups. (9-4)

multicultural society. People from many different cultures living in the same communities. (2-2)

multifamily dwelling. A building designed to house more than one family. (23-2)

multiple roles. Two or more roles, such as work and family roles, being filled by one person. (7-2)

multisize pattern. A garment pattern designed with three or four sizes on one pattern tissue. (21-1)

mutual fund. A group of many investments purchased by a company representing many investors. (10-5)

mutual respect. Regard held by two people who each view the other with honor and esteem. (2-1)

N

nanny. A trained individual who provides quality child care in a parent's home. (9-7)

napping. A fabric finish that pulls fiber ends to the fabric surface. (20-3)

national brand. A product that is advertised nationwide. (15-2)

natural cheese. Cheese made from milk, whey, or cream. (17-4)

natural fibers. Fibers that exist in nature. (20-1)

natural light. Light that comes from the sun. (24-2)

need. A basic item, such as food, clothing, or shelter, that all people require for living. (1-3)

negotiation. Communicating with others in order to reach a mutually satisfying agreement, usually through compromise. (3-3)

net income. The amount of money left after all deductions have been taken from an employee's gross pay. (5-3)

networking. Forming an interconnected group whose members work together to help one another. (2-1)

neutrals. Black, white, and gray, which are not true colors but are used as colors in design. (19-2)

newborn. A baby in the first month of life. (9-5)

nonhuman resource. A resource, such as money, a possession, or a community facility, that is not physically or mentally part of a person. (10-1)

nonverbal communication. A process of communication that involves sending messages without words. (3-1)

nonwoven fabrics. Fabrics made by bonding or interlocking fibers together directly without using yarns. (20-1)

notch. A diamond-shaped pattern symbol located on the cutting line and used to match garment pieces before sewing them together. (21-1)

notching. Cutting small wedges out of the seam allowance to remove excess fabric. (22-1)

notions. Small items needed to construct a garment, including thread, buttons, trims, fasteners, seam binding, and bias tape. (20-3)

nuclear family. A family group that consists of a man, woman, and their children. (6-2)

nutrient. A chemical substance provided by food and used by the body to function properly. (14-1)

nutrition. The science of how nutrients support the body. (14-1)

O

obese. A term used to describe an adult who has a body mass index over 30. (14-4)

obsolescence. The state of uselessness. (11-2)

obstetrician. A physician who specializes in the care of pregnant women. (8-2)

online. Having access to the Internet. (3-1)

open adoption. An adoption that involves some communication between the birthparents and adoptive family. (8-1)

open communication. A free flow of ideas, opinions, and facts among the people communicating. (3-2)

open dating. A dating process that gives information about the freshness of foods. (15-3)

open stock. Tableware purchased one piece at a time. (18-1)

output device. A basic part of computer hardware that converts data to a useful form. (11-2)

overdraft. A check written when there is not enough money in a checking account to cover it. (10-4)

overload. An excess of electrical demand that will cause a fuse to blow or a circuit breaker to trip. (25-2)

overweight. A term used to describe an adult who has a body mass index of 25 up to 30. (14-4)

ovum. A female reproductive cell. (8-2)

P

pack date. A date stamped on food products such as canned goods that tells when the food was processed. (15-3)

parenting. The name given to the process of raising a child. (8-1)

parliamentary procedure. Guidelines followed by many organizations to help them conduct meetings in an orderly fashion. (4-2)

passive listener. A listener who does not respond to the speaker in any way. The speaker does not know if the message is being received or not. (3-1)

passive smoking. Inhaling smoke in a smoke-filled environment. (12-4)

pasta. Grain products such as spaghetti, macaroni, and noodles. (17-3)

pasteurization. A heating process that destroys harmful bacteria in dairy products. (17-4)

patch pocket. A pocket that is attached to the outside of a garment. (22-3)

pattern guide sheet. A set of instructions included with every pattern that has step-by-step directions for every phase of the sewing project. (21-1)

pattern view. A drawing on the front of a pattern envelope showing a garment design that can be made from the pattern included in the envelope. (20-2)

pediatrician. A doctor who specializes in the care and development of children. (9-5)

peer mediators. Students who are trained in the conflict resolution process and are called upon to act as mediators when conflicts arise among their peers. (3-3)

peer pressure. The influence a person's peers have on him or her. (2-3)

peers. Other people in a person's age group. (1-2)

personal fact sheet. An organized list of information, such as education, work experiences, skills, honors and activities, hobbies, interests, and references, used to fill out job applications. (5-2)

personality. The total behavioral qualities and traits that make up an individual. (1-1)

personal priorities. The beliefs, feelings, and experiences people consider to be important and desirable. (1-3)

personal space. The area surrounding an individual. (3-1)

physical abuse. The physical injury of one person by another through such behaviors as hitting, kicking, biting, or throwing objects. (7-3)

physical disability. A disability that limits a person's body or its functions. (9-6)

physical fitness. The condition of the body. (12-1)

physical growth. Changes in body stature influenced by heredity and health habits. (1-2)

physical neglect. Failure to provide proper food, clothing, shelter, medical care, and parental supervision to meet family needs. (7-3)

physical wellness. A state of health in which the body is able to fight illness and infection and repair damage. (12-1)

pile fabric. Fabric that has loops or yarn ends projecting from the surface. (20-3)

placenta. An organ that takes care of nourishment and excretion for an unborn child as it develops in its mother's womb. (8-2)

place setting. The tableware that one person would need, such as a dinner plate, salad plate, cup, and saucer. (18-1)

plaque. A colorless film of bacteria that forms on the teeth. (12-2)

pleat. A fold of fabric that provides a garment with controlled fullness. (22-1)

podiatrist. A physician specializing in the care of feet. (12-2)

policy. An insurance contract. (10-6)

policyholder. A person who has an insurance policy. (10-6)

pollution. All the harmful changes in the environment caused by human activities. (13-2)

portable appliance. A cooking aid that can be easily moved from one place to another. (16-1)

portfolio. A group of securities purchased by a mutual fund for an investor. (10-5)

positive reinforcement. Rewarding positive behavior as a way to encourage children to repeat the behavior. (9-3)

poultry. Any domesticated bird used for meat and/or eggs. (17-1)

preferred provider organization (PPO). A group of doctors and medical facilities that contract to provide services at reduced rates. (10-6)

prejudices. Preconceived ideas or judgments of people or objects that are based on a lack of understanding. (3-2)

premium. A regular payment made for an insurance policy. (10-6)

prenatal development. The growth of a baby in a mother's womb from conception until birth. (8-2)

preschooler. A child who is between the ages of three and five years old. (9-6)

preshrinking. Allowing fabric to shrink before cutting out garment pieces. (21-2)

presser foot. A sewing machine part that holds fabric in place as the machine stitches. (20-4)

pressing. The process of lifting an iron up and down to apply pressure in one area of a garment at a time. (19-5)

primary colors. Colors that cannot be created from other colors, such as yellow, blue, and red. (19-2)

principles of design. Balance, proportion, rhythm, and emphasis used as guides for combining the elements of design. (19-2)

priorities. A list of items or tasks that have been ranked in order of importance. (7-2)

process cheese. Cheese made by blending and melting two or more natural cheeses. (17-4)

procreation. The bearing of children. (6-1)

produce. Fresh fruits and vegetables. (17-2)

progressive tax. A type of tax that increases in rate as the price of the item being taxed increases. (4-3)

prompting. Asking questions to prompt children to exhibit desired behavior. (9-3)

proportion. The spatial relationship of the parts of a design to each other and to the whole design. (19-2)

protein. A nutrient that is found in every cell of the body and is needed for growth, maintenance, and repair of body tissues. (14-1)

puberty. A stage of physical growth in which an individual becomes capable of sexual reproduction. (1-2)

public law. A type of law that governs the relationship between people and the government. (4-3)

pull date. A date stamped on food products such as dairy products and cold cuts that shows the last day a store should sell the product. (15-3)

R

radon. A colorless, odorless gas that is produced by the radioactive breakdown of radium. (13-2)

raglan sleeve. A sleeve that has two diagonal seams that run from the underarm to the neckline in the front and back of a garment. (22-3)

Random Access Memory (RAM). The part of a computer that stores data and permits data changes. (11-2)

random dating. A type of dating, also called casual dating, that allows people to date more than one person at a time. (2-2)

rape. The crime of forcing another person to submit to sexual relations. (2-3)

Read Only Memory (ROM). Built-in, unchangeable language that directs computer operations. (11-2)

real-time. Refers to an event happening now. (11-2)

recipe. A list of ingredients with a complete set of instructions for preparing a food product. (16-3)

Recommended Dietary Allowances (RDA). Daily needs for energy, protein, and some vitamins and minerals outlined for each sex and for several age groups. (14-1)

recourse. A consumer's right to express dissatisfaction about a product or service. (11-5)

recycle. To reprocess resources so they can be used again. (13-2)

redirecting. Focusing the child's attention on something else by providing an appealing substitute. (9-3)

references. People a person knows who can vouch for his or her good work. (5-2)

refined. A term used to describe flour that has had parts of the grain kernel removed during the milling process. (17-3)

reflection. The listener repeats in his or her own words what he or she thinks the speaker said. (3-1)

regular savings account. A type of savings account that allows deposits and withdrawals to be made in any amount at any time. (10-5)

rent. A monthly fee paid to the owner of a property in return for living accommodations. (23-3)

resume. A brief account of your education, work experience, and other qualifications for employment. (5-2)

resource. Object, service, or ability used to achieve goals. (10-1)

restyle. To change a garment to give it a different look. (22-4)

retort packaging. A shelf-stable food packaging method in which foods are sealed in a foil pouch and then sterilized. (15-4)

rhythm. A principle of design that creates a feeling of movement in a design. (19-2)

role expectation. A pattern of socially expected behavior in which people learn to behave the way they think society expects them to behave. (3-2)

romantic love. The type of love shared by two people who idealize each other and are devoted to each other. (2-4)

S

salary. A set amount of money paid to an employee for a certain period of time. (5-3)

sale. A special selling of goods or services at a reduced price. (11-1)

sanitation. The process of maintaining a clean and healthy environment. (16-2)

saturated fat. A fat that is generally solid at room temperature. (14-1)

scale floor plan. A drawing that shows the size and shape of a room, with a certain number of inches equaling a certain number of feet in the room. (24-3)

scanner. An input device that electronically captures an image and transfers it to the computer's memory. (11-2)

scanning. A defensive driving skill in which a driver constantly looks ahead and behind as he or she drives to see what other drivers are doing. (13-1)

scapegoating. An attempt to resolve conflicts by blaming others. The person blamed for the problem is the scapegoat. (3-3)

seam. A row of stitching that joins garment pieces together. (22-1)

seam allowance. The space between the cutting line and the stitching line on a pattern. It is generally 5/8 inch wide. (21-1)

seam finish. A treatment done after seams are sewn to prevent the raw edges of the seam allowances from raveling. (22-1)

secondary colors. Colors created by mixing together equal amounts of two primary colors. (19-2)

securities. Proof of debt or ownership of a company or government, often in the form of stocks or bonds. (10-5)

security deposit. A sum of money, usually one month's rent, paid by a tenant before moving into a property to cover possible damages. (23-3)

self-actualization. People's need to develop to their full potential and be the best that they can be. (1-3)

self-concept. A person's view of himself or herself. (1-1)

self-esteem. The sense of worth a person attaches to himself or herself. (1-1)

self-help feature. A clothing design detail that makes clothes easier for children to put on and take off. (9-2)

selvage. A lengthwise edge of a woven fabric formed where the filling yarns change direction during weaving. (20-1)

serger. A high-speed sewing machine that can stitch, trim, and finish seams in one simple step. (20-4)

set-in sleeve. A sleeve that is attached to a garment with a seam that goes around the armhole at the shoulder. (22-3)

sexual abuse. A form of abuse in which one person forces another to engage in sexual activities. (7-3)

sexual harassment. Unwanted or unwelcome sexual advances, requests for sexual favors, or other verbal or physical sexual conduct. (2-3)

sexual love. An extension of the intimacy and communication of a married relationship. (2-4)

sexually transmitted disease (STD). A disease spread mainly through sexual contact with symptoms and side effects ranging from an outbreak of blisters to blindness to death. (12-4)

shellfish. Fish that have shells instead of backbones. (17-1)

short-term goal. A goal that takes a short time to reach, such as an hour, a day, or a week. (1-3)

sibling. A brother or sister. (2-1)

simulation software. Computer software that imitates an actual experience. (11-2)

single-family house. A house designed to shelter one family. (23-2)

single-parent family. One adult living with one or more children. (6-2)

smokeless tobacco. A product, such as chewing tobacco or snuff, that is placed in the mouth for chewing or dipping. (12-4)

social growth. A developing ability to get along with other people. (1-2)

socialization. The teaching process used to help children learn to conform to social standards. (6-1)

socially responsible behavior. Actions that demonstrate that a person has accepted the responsibility that is appropriate for his or her stage of development.

socio-dramatic play. A stage of play where several children imitate others and act out situations together. (9-4)

solar energy. Energy produced from the sun. (25-3)

sperm. A male reproductive cell. (8-2)

split-complementary color scheme. A color scheme that uses one hue and the two hues on either side of its complement for a softer contrast. (24-1)

spun yarns. Yarns made by spinning staple fibers together. (20-1)

standard. An accepted level of achievement. (1-3)

starch. The complex carbohydrate part of plants. (17-3)

status. A person's rank within a group. (19-1)

staystitching. A line of machine stitching that keeps the edges of garment pieces from stretching out of shape while being sewn. (22-1)

steady dating. A type of dating in which two people agree to date only each other. (2-2)

stepfamily. A family structure formed when a single parent marries. (6-2)

stereotype. A set belief that all members of a group are the same. (3-2)

stitching line. A pattern symbol that appears as a broken line just inside the cutting line. (21-1)

stock. A certificate that represents ownership of a small portion of a company. (10-5)

stress. The body's reaction to the events in a person's life. (12-3)

style. Specific construction details that make one garment differ from another garment of the same type. (19-4)

sublease. Passing a lease over from a renter to a second tenant who pays rent directly to the owner. (23-3)

substance abuse. The use of illegal drugs or the misuse of legal drugs such as alcohol. (7-3)

sudden infant death syndrome (SIDS). The sudden death of an apparently healthy baby during sleep. (9-5)

support group. A group of people who share a similar problem or concern. (7-3)

support system. A network of people and organizations family members can turn to during a crisis. (7-3)

T

table d'hôte. A type of menu in which one price is charged for an entire meal. (18-3)

tableware. Dinnerware, flatware, and glassware. (18-1)

tact. Knowledge of what to do or say to avoid offending others. (4-1)

tailored paycheck. A program that allows employees to choose benefits that best meet their own wants and needs. (7-2)

team. A group of people organized around a common goal. (4-1)

technology. The use of scientific knowledge for practical purposes. (3-1)

tech prep. A work-based learning program that often combines two years of high school courses with two years of post-secondary education. (5-1)

telecommuting. An arrangement where an employee works from an office set up at home. The employee is connected to the office by electronic technology—a computer, a modem, and a telephone. (5-3)

texture. A design element that affects the way a design looks and feels. (19-2)

thread shank. A short stem of thread that provides room for a button to lie over the buttonhole fabric. (22-3)

thread-tension regulator. Two separate controls found on a sewing machine that balance tension or pull between the upper and lower threads to form the proper stitch. (20-4)

time management. The ability to plan and use time well. (10-2)

time out. Moving a child away from others for a short period of time when a child's disruptive behavior cannot be ignored. The child calms down and gains self-control. (9-3)

toddler. A child who is one or two years old. (9-6)

topstitching. A row of machine stitching done on the right side of a garment for decorative or functional purposes. (22-3)

toxic waste. Poisonous waste material that damages the environment and causes illness. (13-2)

tract house. A house built by a developer who builds an entire neighborhood at once. (23-2)

traffic pattern. The path people follow as they move within a room. (24-3)

triad color scheme. A color scheme that combines three colors that are equally distant from one another on the color wheel. (24-1)

trimming. Cutting away part of a seam allowance to reduce bulk. (22-1)

tuck. A narrow fold of fabric stitched in place along all or part of its length. (22-1)

U

ultrasound. A prenatal test given by passing an ultrasonic probe over the abdomen of a pregnant woman, enabling the fetus to be observed on a television monitor or as a photograph. This process allows the child's sex, position, and stage of development to be studied and aids in the detection of some congenital disabilities. (8-2)

umbilical cord. A cord that connects the placenta to an embryo or fetus in its mother's womb. This cord carries nutrients and oxygen from the mother to the developing child. It also carries wastes from the child back to the mother. (8-2)

understitching. A row of stitching that holds a seam allowance to one of the fabric pieces joined by the seam and prevents the facing from showing on the outside of the garment. (22-2)

underweight. A term used to describe an adult who has a body mass index below 18.5. (14-4)

uniform. A distinctive outfit that identifies a person who wears it with a specific group. (19-1)

unit pricing. A consumer aid that shows the cost per standard unit of weight or measure for a product. (15-3)

universal product code (UPC). A group of bars and numbers appearing on a product that contains price and product information. (15-3)

unsaturated fat. A fat that is most often liquid at room temperature. (14-1)

V

value. The lightness or darkness of a color. (19-2)

vegetarian diet. A pattern of eating that is made up largely or entirely of foods from plant sources. (14-3)

veneer. Thin layer of wood, often used for making inexpensive furniture that looks attractive and costs less than solid wood furniture. (24-3)

verbal communication. A form of communication that involves the use of words. (3-1)

visionary goal. A goal that inspires people to do more than they thought they were capable of achieving. (1-3)

vitamin. An organic substance needed in small amounts for normal growth and the maintenance of good health. (14-1)

volunteers. People who provide valuable services by offering their time, talents, and energy free of charge. (4-3)

W

wants. Items people desire, but don't need to survive. (1-3)

wardrobe. All the clothes and accessories a person has to wear. (19-3)

warp yarns. Yarns that run along the lengthwise grain of a fabric. (20-1)

warranty. A written promise by a manufacturer that a product will meet specified standards of performance. (11-1)

wattage. A measurement of the amount of energy required to operate an electrical device. (25-3)

weaving. The process of interlacing two sets of yarns to produce a fabric. (20-1)

will. A legal document describing how a person intends for property to be distributed after his or her death. (10-5)

work ethic. A standard of conduct for successful job performance. (5-3)

work plan. A detailed list of all the duties that must be completed during a lab experience. (16-4)

World Wide Web. A part of the Internet that carries messages containing pictures, color, and sound. It contains large collections of documents accessible at sites called *Web sites*. (3-1)

Y

yarn. A continuous strand formed from combined fibers. (20-1)

Z

zygote. A single-celled organism that forms when a sperm from the father unites with an ovum from the mother. (8-2)

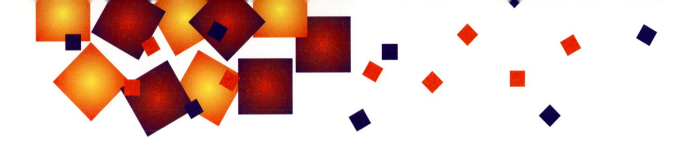

Index

A

AAFCS, 115
Abbreviations in recipes, 473
Abdominal thrust (Heimlich maneuver), 239
Abilities, 21, 133
  self-concept, 21
Abstinence, 58
Accented-neutral color scheme, 654
Accessories
  clothing, 545
  definition, 543
  housing, 669
Accident prevention, 384-389
Accidents, 384
Account statement, 298
Acid rain, 396
Acquaintance rape, 63
Acquired immune deficiency syndrome, 373, 374
ACTE, 115
Active listener, 81
Active-physical play, 236
Activity center, 667
Actual cash value, 310
Ad hoc committee, 116
ADA, 115
Addiction, 199
Adjustment lines, 595
Adolescence, 23
Adoption, 216, 217
Adult-child ratio, 264
Adults' nutritional needs, 424
Advertisement, 331
Advertising, 330-333
  bait and switch, 332
  bandwagon ads, 332
  consumer protection, 333
  deceptive, 332, 333
  evaluating, 332
  on the Internet, 332
  persuasive, 332
  types, 331, 332
Aerobic capacity, 357, 358

Agency adoption, 216
AIDS, 373, 374
Air pollution, 396, 397
A la carte, 523
Alcohol, 372, 373
Alcoholic, 200
Alcoholism, 200
Alterations, 595
Altering clothes, 625
Alternates, plant-based, 490, 491
Altruistic love, 65
American Association of Family and Consumer Sciences, 115
American Dietetics Association, 115
American Society of Interior Designers, 115
Amino acids, 406
Amniocentesis, 220
Analogous color scheme, 539, 652
Annual percentage rate, 339
Anorexia nervosa, 429
Antiperspirant, 362
Apartments, rental, 639
Apparel *See* Clothes
Appearance
  as communication, 84
  job success and, 153, 154
Appliances, 458-467
  cleanup, 462
  dishwashers, 462
  food waste disposers, 462
  kitchen utensils, 463-467
  major, 458-462
  microwave oven, 461, 462
  portable, 462, 463
  ranges, 459-461
  refrigerators, 458, 459
  trash compactors, 462
Applications, 145, 146
Applying for a job, 143-146
Apprenticeships, 137
Appropriateness, 658
APR, 339
Aptitudes, 132
Aseptic packaging, 453

ASID, 115
Association for Career and Technical Education, 115
Athletes' nutritional needs, 423, 424
ATMs, 292, 293
Attached houses, 638
Attention-getter ads, 332
Autocratic leadership, 109
Automated teller machines, 292, 293
Automobile insurance, 308-310
    premiums, 309, 310
    types, 309
Automobile safety, 388, 389

B

Backstitching, 611
Bait and switch, 332
Bakeware, 465-467
Baking, 506, 507
Balance
    clothes, 542
    definition, 542
    housing, 656, 657
Bandwagon ads, 332
Basal metabolism, 426
Basting, 609
BBB, 346
Beauty, 658
Behavior, high-risk, 39-41
Behavior influences, 27-35, 41
    friends, 61, 62
    goals, 31-33
    needs, 27-29
    personal priorities, 29-31
    standards, 34
Beneficiary, 305
Better Business Bureaus, 346
Bias, fabric, 571
Biscuit method, 505
Bleach, 554
BMI, 426, 427
Bobbin, 586
Bodily injury liability, 309
Body language, 84-87
Body mass index, 426, 427
Bonds, 302, 303
BPA, 114
Brain development, 254, 255
Brainstorming, 112
Breads, 502, 504, 505
Breakfast cereals, 502
Budget, 286-289
    compare income and expenses, 288
    establish financial goals, 286, 287
    evaluating, 289
    expenses, 287, 288
    food, 442, 443
    record keeping, 288, 289
    sources of income, 287
    using computers, 290, 291
Buffets, 522
Buffet service, 515
Bulimia nervosa, 429
Business Professionals of America, 114
Buttons, 619
Bylaws, 114

C

CAD, 325
CADD, 668, 669
Cafeterias, 522
Cakes, 505, 506
Calcium, 408
Calorie, 425
Carbohydrates, 405, 406
Care labels, 552
Career, 131
Career ladder, 141
Career plan, 140, 141
Career planning, 131-141
    abilities, 133
    aptitudes, 132
    education choices, 135-138
    family and consumer sciences careers, 134, 135
    information resources, 134, 135
    interests, 132
    lifestyle, 138
    making a decision, 139-141
    potential income, 139
    working conditions, 139
Caregivers, 226-232
    characteristics of responsible caregivers, 227-230
    definition, 226
    health, 230
    knowledge and experience, 229, 230
    personal qualities, 227, 228
    personal skills, 228, 229
    protection of children's rights, 232
    resources for, 231, 232
    responsibilities, 230
Care Labeling Rule, 549, 552
Caring for the home, 674-699
Carpentry tools, 688, 689
Car safety 388, 389
Cash value, 306

Cashier's check, 293
Casing, 616
Catalog shopping, 317
CDs, 301
Cellular phones, 87
Centerpieces, 517
Central processing unit, 324
Cereal, 500
Cereal products, 500-507
    breads, 502
    breakfast cereals, 502
    buying, 501, 502
    cakes, 505, 506
    cookies, 506, 507
    flour, 501
    pasta, 501
    preparing, 503-505
    rice, 501
    storing, 502, 503
Certificate of deposit, 301
Certified check, 293
Character, 19
Chat room, 231
Checking accounts, 292, 294-298
    balancing, 296-298
    endorsing a check, 296
    making a deposit, 295
    opening, 295
    types, 294, 295
    writing a check, 295, 296
Cheese, 508-510
    cooking with, 510
    storage, 509
Child abuse and neglect, 198, 199
Child care, 192, 261-266
    adequate supervision, 264
    adult-child ratio, 264
    age-appropriate, 264
    child care cooperatives, 262
    church programs, 263
    consistent quality care, 264
    employer-sponsored services, 263, 264
    franchised centers, 264
    government-sponsored programs, 263
    in the caregiver's home, 262
    in the parent's home, 261, 262
    privately owned centers, 264
    school-sponsored programs, 263
    selecting, 264, 265
    setting, 264
    social group programs, 263
    types, 261-264
    university-sponsored programs, 263
Child care cooperatives, 262

Childless family, 172
Children, 225-266
    art activities, 250
    books, 249
    brain development, 254, 255
    caregivers, 226-232
    child care, 261-266
    clothing, 234-236
    emotional development, 240-247
    enrichment activities, 249-251
    fears, 247
    gifted, 260
    guidance, 242-246
    health, 237
    independence and responsibility, 241, 242
    infants, 254-256
    intellectual development, 248-252
    meals, 233, 234
    music activities, 240
    newborns, 253, 254
    parenting styles, 246
    physical needs, 233-240
    play, 236, 246, 247,
    preparing for, 209-222
    preschoolers, 258-260
    safety, 238-240
    social development, 240, 241
    special needs, 260, 261
    stories, 249
    toddlers, 257, 258
    TV and videotapes, 250, 251
Children with special needs, 260, 261
Cholesterol, 407
Chromosomes, 219
Chronological growth, 23
Church child care programs, 263
Circuit breaker, 689-691
Citizenship, 120-126
    be informed, 121
    community involvement, 125, 126
    obeying laws, 121-123
    protecting the environment, 124, 125
    rights and responsibilities, 120-126
    taxes, 123, 124
    voting, 121
Civil laws, 122
Claims, insurance, 310, 311
Classic, 547
Clean finishing, 615
Cleaning, 675-682
    decorating for easy cleaning, 681
    organizing tasks, 682
    pest control, 675, 676
    preventive measures, 681, 682

products and equipment, 676-679
reasons to clean, 675, 676
schedule, 679, 680
soil, 676
standards, 679
storage, 682
tools, 678
vacuum cleaners, 678, 679
waxes and polishes, 677, 678
Cleaning agents, 677
Cleaning schedule, 679, 680
Cleanliness, kitchen, 469, 470
Clearing the table, 518
Clipping, 612
Closed adoption, 216
Clothes
altering, 625
body shape, 540
care labels, 552
caring for, 551-561
children's, 234-236
choosing best colors, 539, 540
choosing to meet needs, 532-536
classics and fads, 547
color, 537-540
conformity versus individuality, 535
cost, 550, 551
daily care, 551, 552
design, 536-542
dress codes, 534
dry cleaning, 558, 559
drying, 557, 558
durability, 548
energy conservation, 559, 560
fashion cycles, 548
fashion, 547
fit, 548
form, 541
group identification, 533, 535
hangtags, 549, 550
ironing and pressing, 558
labels, 549, 550
laundering, 552-557
lifestyle, 533
line, 540
modesty, 534
newborns, 254
packing, 560, 561
personal coloring, 539, 540
physical needs, 532, 533
principles of design, 542
psychological needs, 533
quality, 548, 549
recycling, 626

repairing, 624, 625
restyling, 625, 626
seasonal storage, 561
sewing *See* Sewing
shopping, 546-551
social needs, 533-535
sorting, 552-554
special needs, 535
specific occasions, 535, 536
stain removal, 554-556
status, 534, 535
storage, 552, 561
style, 547
texture, 541
using technology to shop, 546, 547
wardrobe planning, 543-545
Coded messages, 92, 93
Codependency, 185
Co-insurance, 307
Collateral, 334
College programs, 138
Collision insurance, 309
Colors
choosing best, 539, 540
cool, 539
in clothes, 537-540
in housing, 651-654
warm, 539
Color schemes, 539
in housing, 652-654
Color wheel, 537, 538
Commercial banks, 294
Commitment, 189
Communicable diseases, 237
Communication, 79-102
barriers to, 91-93
coded messages, 92, 93
conflict resolution, 95-102
definition, 80
family, 185
gender differences, 93
importance of, 90, 91
in relationships, 90-95
in the workplace, 94
negative feelings, 93, 94
nonverbal communication, 84-87
prejudices, 92
stereotypes, 92
technology, 87-89, 326
verbal, 80-84
Community colleges, 138
Community involvement, 125, 126
Community programs, family violence, 199
Community support groups, 200, 201

Companionate love, 65
Comparison ads, 331
Comparison shopping, 320-323
    quality, 321, 322
    suitability, 322
    use and care, 322
    warranties, 322, 323
Complaints, 346-348
Complementary color scheme, 539, 652
Comprehensive physical damage coverage, 309
Compromise, 99
Computer-aided design, 325
Computer-aided drafting and design, 668, 669
Computers, 89, 324 See also Technology
Conception, 218
Condominiums, 639
Conflict, 95
Conflict resolution, 95-102
    causes of conflict, 96, 97
    compromise, 99, 100
    constructive methods, 98-101
    "I" messages, 98, 99
    mediation, 100, 101
    negotiation, 99, 100
    reactions to conflict, 97, 98
    types of conflicts, 95, 96
    violence, 101, 102
Conflict resolution process, 100
Conformity, 535
Congenital disabilities, 219
Consequences, 245
Conservation, 125, 399-401
    energy, 559, 560, 692-699
Constitution, 114
Construction, clothing See Sewing
Consumer Product Safety Commission, 345
Consumer Science Business Professionals, 115
Consumerism, 315-348
    advertising, 330-333
    buying techniques, 318-322
    catalog shopping, 317
    comparison shopping, 320-323
    complaints, 346-348
    consumer rights and responsibilities, 343-348
    credit, 334-342
    electronic shopping, 318, 319
    laws, 342, 348
    recourse, 345
    resolving consumer problems, 348
    retail shopping, 316, 317
    sales, 319, 320
    shopping guidelines, 318-322
    technology, 323-330
    types of stores, 316, 317

Control panel, 689
Convection cooking, 460
Convenience foods, 443
Cookies, 506, 507
Cooking
    at home, 480, 481
    at school, 481, 482
    changing yield, 475, 476
    computer technologies, 480, 481
    measurement equivalents, 476
    measuring techniques, 473-475
    recipe terms, 475, 476
    recipes, 472-476
    substituting ingredients, 473, 474
    time plans, 479-482
Cooking equipment, 458-467
Cooking methods, 476-478
    cereals, 504
    dairy products, 510
    dry heat, 476, 477
    fruits and vegetables, 498-500
    meat, 492, 493
    microwave cooking, 476-478
    moist heat, 476, 477
    pasta, 503
    rice, 503
Cooking temperatures, 470, 471
Cookware, 465-467
Cool colors, 539
Cooperative education, 136
Copayments, 307
Costs
    clothes, 550, 551
    credit, 388, 389
    energy in meal management, 443
    replacement, 310
Cotton, 566
Court system, 122, 123
Cover, 517, 518
CPSC, 345
CPU, 324
Credit, 333-342
    annual percentage rate, 339
    applying, 336-338
    capacity, 338
    capital, 338
    cards, 335, 336
    character, 338
    costs, 338, 339
    counseling, 341
    court protection, 341, 342
    definition, 334
    establishing a rating, 336
    handling problems, 340-342

keeping a good rating, 336
pros and cons, 334
sales, 335
shopping for, 338, 339
types, 335, 336
using wisely, 340-342
Credit contract, 339, 340
Credit rating, 336
Creditors, 334
Credit unions, 294
Crises, 195-201
accidents, 201
coping with, 196-198
death, 201
family violence, 198, 199
illness, 201
substance abuse, 199-201
types, 198-201
unemployment, 198
CSBP, 115
Cultural diversity, 108
promoted by leaders, 113
Cultural factors in housing, 640
Cultural heritage, 17, 18
Cultural influences
on families, 172, 173
meal planning, 441, 442
Custom houses, 638
Cutting fabrics, 602
Cutting layout, 600
Cutting line, 594
Cutting tools, sewing, 584
Cutting utensils, 464, 465

D

Dairy products, 507-510
buying, 508, 509
cheese, 508, 509
milk, 508
preparing, 510
storing, 509
Darts, 609
Date rape, 63
Dating, 55, 56
group dating, 55
random dating, 55, 56
steady dating, 56
Death, 201
Debit cards, 292
DECA—An Association of Marketing Students, 114
Deceptive advertising, 332, 333
Decision, 37

Decision making
career planning, 139-141
family members share responsibilities, 188
influences on decisions, 41
Decision-making process, 37-41
Deductible, 307
Defense mechanisms, 366, 367
Defensive driving, 388
Dehydration, 424
Democratic leadership, 109
Demographic factors in housing, 640
Demographics, 174
Deodorant, 362
Department stores, 316
Depilatory, 362
Depression, 367-369
Dermatologist, 360
Design, clothing, 536-542
Design elements, 536-541
in housing, 651-655
Design goals, 658
Design principles, 542
in housing, 655-658
Detergents, 554
Development, children *See* Children
Developmentally appropriate practices, 243, 244
Developmental tasks of teens, 25, 26
Development, personal, 15-43
Dietary Guidelines for Americans, 418-420
Dietary Reference Intakes, 414
Dining, manners, 519, 520
Dining out, 521-525
restaurants, 521-523
Dinnerware, 516
Direct printing, 575, 576
Direct tax, 123
Directional fabrics, 601, 602
Directional stitching, 608
Diseases
communicable, 237
sexually transmitted, 373, 374
Discount stores, 316
Dishwashers, 462
Diverse, 94
Diversity, 108
Dividends, 302
Divorce, 177-179
adjusting to, 178, 179
groups with higher divorce rates, 178
Dots, 594
Double-complementary color, 653
Dovetail, 284
Drain traps, 687, 688

Dramatic play, 248
Dress codes, 534
Dressmaker's carbon, 603
DRIs, 414
Drug abuse, 199, 373
Dry cleaning, 558, 559
Dry heat cooking methods, 476, 477
Dual-career families, 191
Dyeing, fabrics, 547, 575
Dysfunctional family, 185

E

Early brain development, 254, 255
Easing, 610, 611
Eating disorders, 429
Eating schedules, 443, 444
Economic factors in housing, 641
Economic influences on the family, 175
Education choices, career planning, 135-138
Education, teen parents, 213
Eggs, 490-494
    buying, 490
    grades, 490
    preparing, 493, 494
    size and color, 490
    storing, 491, 492
Electrical hazards, 385
Electrical problems, 689-691
Electric shock, 387
Electronic shopping, 318, 319
Elements of design, 536-541
    clothes, 536-541
    color, 537-540, 651-654
    definition, 536
    form, 541, 655
    housing, 651-655
    line, 540, 654
    texture, 541, 654, 655
E-mail, 89
Embryo, 218
Embryonic period, 218
Emergency medical technicians, 377
Emergency procedures, 392, 393
Emotional abuse, 198
Emotional development, children, 240-247
Emotional disorder, 260
Emotional growth, 23, 24
    infants, 255
    preschoolers, 259
    toddlers, 258
Emotional maturity, in marriage, 68, 69
Emotional needs, meeting children's, 231
Emotional neglect, 198
Empathy, 19

Emphasis, 542, 658
    clothes, 542
    definition, 542
    housing, 658
Employability, 151-157
    appearance, 153, 154
    cooperation, 152
    dependability, 152
    ethics, 152
    honesty, 152
    income, 156
    job readiness skills, 153
    paychecks, 156, 157
    positive attitude, 151, 152
    qualities of successful employees, 151-154
    SCANS competencies, 153
    technology in the workplace, 154, 155
    work schedules, 155
Employee benefits, 193
Employer-sponsored child care services, 263, 264
Employment agencies, 142
EMTs, 377
Emulation, 38
Enabler, 200
Endorse, 296
Energy conservation
    clothing care, 559, 560
    food storage, 696, 697
    heating and cooling a home, 694-696
    in the home, 692-699
    lighting, 698
    major appliances, 697, 698
    water use, 696
Energy management, 285, 286
Energy needs, 425, 426
Energy sources, 692-694
Engagement, 71-73
    ending, 72, 73
    examining the relationship, 71
    length, 72
    planning for a future home, 72
    wedding plans, 72
English service, 515, 516
Enriched, 411
Entrepreneurs, 148
Entrepreneurship, 148-150
Environment, 16, 17, 394-401
    conservation, 399-401
    factors affecting, 394, 395
    pollution, 395-399
    population increase, 395
    protecting, 124, 125
    resources, 395
Environmental Protection Agency, 397

EPA, 397
Equal Credit Opportunity Act, 343
Equipment, household *See* Appliances
Estate, 303, 304
Esteem needs, 28
Ethics, 152
Ethnic groups, 17, 18
Etiquette, 519, 520
   in restaurants, 524, 525
Eviction, 645
Expenses, 287, 288
Expiration date, 449
Extended family, 172

F

Fabrics, 566-576
   amount needed, 582
   care requirements, 582
   checking grain, 598, 599
   choosing, 580-582
   construction, 571-574
   cutting, 602
   definition, 566
   directional, 601, 602
   dyeing, 574, 575
   fibers, 566-570
   finishes, 574
   folding, 600, 601
   knitting, 572, 573
   marking, 603, 604
   nonwoven, 573, 574
   pinning, 602
   preshrinking, 598
   printing, 575, 576
   special, 601, 602
   weaving, 571, 572
   yarns, 571
Fabric softeners, 557
Facings, 613-614
   attaching, 615
   preparing, 615
Factory outlet, 317
Factual ads, 331
Fad, 547
Fair Credit Billing Act, 343
Fair Credit Reporting Act, 343
Falls, 384
Families, 165-179
   accidents, 201
   appreciation, 186
   balancing work and, 189-194
   child care, 192
   commitment, 189
   communication, 185
   crises, 195-201
   cultural influences, 172, 173
   death, 201
   decision making, 188
   demographic factors, 174
   divorce, 177-179
   economic forces, 175
   emotional support, 167, 168
   factors affecting, 172-175
   fulfilling rights and responsibilities, 187-189
   functional, 184-189
   functions, 166-168
   illness, 201
   mealtime, 514
   multiple roles, 191
   physical care, 167
   priorities, 191
   problem solving, 185
   procreation, 167
   remarriage, 179
   resources, 188
   respect, 186
   roles, 166
   sharing goals and personal priorities, 187, 188
   single living, 168, 169
   socialization, 167
   societal influences, 173
   spending time together, 185, 186
   substance abuse, 199-201
   technological influences, 173, 174
   understanding, 187
   unemployment, 198
   violence, 198, 199
   world events, 175
Family and consumer sciences careers, 134, 135
Family and Consumer Sciences Education Association, 115
Family and consumer sciences professional organizations, 115
Family, Career, and Community Leaders of America, 114
Family crises, 195-201
Family, definition, 166
Family life cycle, 176, 177
Family planning, 215
Family restaurants, 522
Family services, 515
Family structures, 170-172, 176-179
   changing, 176-179
   childless family, 172
   definition, 170
   extended family, 172
   nuclear family, 170
   single-parent family, 171
   stepfamily, 171

Fashion, 547
Fashion cycles, 548
Fast-food restaurants, 521, 522
Fats, 407
Fats, oils, and sweets, 417
Fat-soluble vitamins, 409, 410
Faucets, 685
FBLA, 114
FCC, 333
FCCLA, 114
FCSEA, 115
FDA, 345
Federal Communications Commission, 333
Federal Trade Commission, 333
Feedback, 81
Feed dogs, 586
Feet, caring for, 364
Felonies, 122
Fetal period, 218, 219
Fetus, 218
Fiber, 406
Fiber dyeing, 575
Fibers, 566-570
   definition, 566
   manufactured fibers, 569, 570
   microfibers, 570
   natural fibers, 566-568
FICA, 157
Figure types, 577
Filament yarns, 571
Filling yarns, 571
Finance charges, 338
Financial challenges, teen parenting, 213
Financial commitment, parenting, 212
Financial goals, 286, 287
Financial management, 286-303 See also Money management
Financial services, 291-299
   automated teller machines (ATMs), 292, 293
   cashier's checks, 293
   certified checks, 293
   checking accounts, 292, 294-298
   choosing a financial institution, 292-294
   debit cards, 292
   loans, 293
   safe-deposit boxes, 293
   savings accounts, 292
   traveler's checks, 293
   types of institutions, 294
Finfish, 489
Finish, wood, 666
Finishes, fabric, 574
Fires, 384
Fire safety precautions, 386
First aid, 239, 377

Fish
   buying, 489, 490
   finfish, 489
   preparing, 493
   shellfish, 490
   storing, 491
Fixed expenses, 287
Flammable chemicals, 385
Flammable Fabrics Act, 550
Flatware, 516
Flexibility, 358
Flexible expenses, 288-290
   reducing, 289, 290
Flexible workweeks, 193
Flextime, 193
Floor coverings, 659, 660
Flour, 501
Fluorescent light, 662
Fluorine, 408
Follower, 107
Follow-up letter, 148
Food additives, 450
Food and Drug Administration, 345
Foodborne illnesses, 438-440, 468-471
Food Guide Pyramid, 415-417
   in meal planning, 438-440
Food labeling, 449-452
Foods labs, 481, 482
Food rotation, 453
Food, serving, 514-518
Food shopping, 445-447
Food storage, 452-454
   energy conservation, 696, 697
Food stores, 445, 446
Food waste disposers, 462
Form, 541
Formal restaurants, 522
Fortified, 410
Fossil fuels, 692
Foster care, 232
Franchised child care centers, 264
Freestanding houses, 638
Freshness date, 449
Friendships, 52-59
   dating, 55, 56
   forming, 54, 55
   love, 57
   meeting new people 53, 54
   responsible relationships, 57-59
   types of friends, 52, 53
Fringe benefits, 156
Fruit group, 416
   meal planning, 440
Fruits
   buying, 495-497

preparing, 498-500
storing, 496-498
FTC, 333
Full-time job, 155
Function, 655
Functional family, 184-189
Furnishings, 664-669
accessories, 669
Furniture, 664-666
metal, 666
plastic, 666
quality, 665, 666
styles, 665
upholstered, 666
wood, 665, 666
Fur Products Labeling Act, 550
Fuses, 689, 690
Fusible interfacings, 614
Future Business Leaders of America, 114

G

Gang violence, 101
Gathering, 610, 611
Gender differences, 93
Generic, 447
Genes, 219
Genetic counseling, 220
Germinal period, 218
Gifted children, 260
Glassware, 516
Goals, 31-34
financial, 286, 287
in marriage, 68
meeting, 33
setting, 32, 33
Government-sponsored child care programs, 263
Grading, 612
meat, 487, 488
Grain, 571
checking and straightening, 598, 599
Grainline arrow, 595
Grains group, 416
meal planning, 439
Gratuity, 525
Greenhouse effect, 396
Grooming, 360-364
definition, 360
hair care, 363, 364
hands and feet, 364
skin care, 360-362
teeth, 362, 363
Gross income, 156
Group dating, 55
Growth, 23-26

chronological, 23
emotional, 23, 24
intellectual, 24
physical, 23
social, 24, 25
Guidance, 242-246
communicating with children, 242, 243
consequences, 245
definition, 242
developmentally appropriate practices, 243, 244
techniques, 244, 245

H

Habits, 38
Hair care, 363, 364
Handheld organizer, 325
Hands, caring for, 364
Hangtags, 549, 550
Havighurst, Robert, 25, 26
Health, 356-378
AIDS, 373, 374
alcohol, 372, 373
children, 237
cleaning, 675
decisions affecting, 374
drug abuse, 373
emergency medical services, 377
environment, 394-401
exams 376, 377
grooming, 360-364
healthful eating, 404-429
medical services, 375-378
mental health, 365-370
nutrition, 404-429
physical fitness, 356-359
risks, 371-374
safety *See* Safety
sexually transmitted diseases, 373, 374
tobacco, 371, 372
Health claims, food labeling, 450
Healthful food choices, restaurants, 523, 524
Health insurance, 306-310
health maintenance organizations, 308
preferred provider organizations, 308
workers' compensation, 307
Health maintenance organizations, 308
Health Occupations Students of America, 114
Heimlich maneuver (abdominal thrust), 239
Hems, 620-622, 624
finishing, 620
marking, 620
repairing, 624
stitching, 621, 622

Heredity, 16
High-risk behavior, 39-41
High-tech, 323
HIV, 374
Holes, clothing repair, 625
HMOs, 308
Home furnishings *See* Housing
Home security, 389-391
Homeowner's insurance, 310
Homogenized, 508
Hook-and-loop tape, 619, 620
Hooks and eyes, 619
Hormones, 23
HOSA, 114
Hosting a meal, 519
Hot line, 231
Hourly wage, 156
House brand, 447
Housing, 635-646
    accessories, 669
    beauty, 637
    buying, 645, 646
    caring for, 674-699
    choosing, 641, 642
    cleaning, 675-682
    cooperative units, 639
    cultural factors, 640
    decorating, 659-663
    definition, 636
    demographic factors, 640
    design, 650-669
    economic factors, 641
    effects of income on choice, 641, 642
    elements of design, 651-655
    familiarity, 637
    floor coverings, 659, 660
    furnishings, 664-669
    lighting, 661-663
    living space, 667-669
    location, 642
    maintenance, 683-691
    multifamily dwellings, 639, 640
    needs, 636, 637
    physical needs, 636
    principles of design, 655-658
    privacy, 637
    psychological needs, 636, 637
    renting, 642-645
    repairs, 683-691
    security, 637
    self-expression, 637
    single-family houses, 638, 639
    social needs, 636
    societal factors, 640, 641
    trends, 640, 641
    wall treatments, 660, 661
    windows and window treatments, 661
Housing-related insurance, 310, 311
Hue, 537
Human immunodeficiency virus, 374
Human resources, 277
Humor, 22
Hygiene, 361, 362

I

IACD, 115
Identification, clothes, 533, 535
Illness, 201, 468-471
    nutritional needs caused by, 425
"I" messages, 98, 99
Imitative-imaginative play, 248
Immunizations, 237
Implement, 283
Impulse buying, 319
Incandescent light, 662
Inclusion, 261
Income, 156, 287
    effect on housing choice, 641, 642
Income tax, 156
Independent adoption, 216
Indirect tax, 123
Individuality, 535
Infants, 254-256
    early brain development, 254, 255
    emotional growth, 255
    intellectual growth, 255, 256
    nutritional needs, 421, 422
    physical growth, 255
    social growth, 255
Infatuation, 57
Infertility, 216
Ingredient substitutions, 473, 474
Inherited traits, 16
Input device, 324
In-seam pocket, 618
Insecticides, 676
Insomnia, 359
Inspection, meat, 487, 488
Insurance, 304-311
    automobile, 308-310
    filing a claim, 310, 311
    health, 306-310
    housing-related, 310, 311
    life, 305, 306
Intellectual development, children, 248-252
Intellectual growth, 24
    infants, 255, 256
    preschoolers, 259, 260
    toddlers, 248

Intellectual needs, meeting children's, 231
Intensity, 537
Interest, 338
Interests, 132
    affects of personal priorities on, 31
Interfacing, 613, 614
Intermediate color, 538
International Association of Clothing Designers, 115
Internet, 89
Internet access, 324
Internet advertising, 332
Internet shopping, 319
Internship, 137
Interviews, 146-148
    appearance, 146
    confidence, 146, 147
    follow-up letter, 148
    positive attitude, 147, 148
    preparation, 146
Iodine, 408
Iron, 408
Ironing, 558

J

Job, definition, 131
Job search, 142-150
    applications, 145, 146
    applying for a job, 143-146
    entrepreneurship, 148-150
    finding openings, 142, 143
    interview, 146-148
Job shadowing, 135
Job sharing, 193
Job success, 151-157
    appearance, 153, 154
    cooperation, 152
    dependability, 152
    ethics, 152
    honesty, 152
    income, 156
    job readiness skills, 153
    paychecks, 156, 157
    positive attitude, 151, 152
    qualities of successful employees, 151-154
    SCANS competencies, 153
    technology in the workplace, 154, 155
    work schedules, 155

K

Kimono sleeves, 617
Kitchen cleanliness, 469, 470
Kitchen safety and sanitation, 385, 467-471
Kitchen utensils, 463-467
    bakeware, 465-467
    cookware, 465-467
    cutting, 464, 465
    measuring utensils, 463, 464
    mixing, 465
Knit fabrics, sewing, 622, 623
Knitting, 572, 573

L

Labeling, food, 449-452
Labels, clothing, 549, 550
Laissez-faire leadership, 109
Laundry, 552-557
    products, 554, 557
    washing machine, 557
Laws, 121-123
    civil laws, 122
    clothing labels, 549, 550
    consumer protection, 342, 348
    court system, 122, 123
    criminal laws, 122
    public laws, 121
Leader, 107
Leadership, 107-113
    being a team member, 107, 108
    characteristics, 110-112
    effective, 110, 111
    giving recognition, 112, 113
    in action, 110
    motivating followers, 111, 112
    opportunities, 108-110
    planning, 112
    promoting cultural diversity, 113
    setting examples, 110, 111
    types, 109
    using tact, 112
Learning disability, 260
Lease, 643, 644
Leavening agent, 494, 504
Legumes
    buying, 490, 491
    definition, 490
    preparing, 494, 495
    storing, 492
Leisure activities, 348
Library resources, career planning, 134
Life cycle, 176, 177
Life insurance, 305, 306
    term insurance, 305, 306
    universal life insurance, 306
    whole life insurance, 306
Lifestyle, 533
    affecting career choice, 138

Lighting, 661-663
    applications, 663
    basic guidelines, 663
    energy conservation, 698
    technology, 662
    types, 661, 662
Line, element of design, 540, 654
Linen, 566
Linens, table, 517
Liquidity, 300
Listening, 80-82
Living space, 667-669
    computer programs used to organize, 668, 669
    personal space, 667
    scale floor plan, 667-669
    shared space, 667
Loan value, 306
Lockstitch, 586
Long-term goals, 32, 281
Loopers, 588
Love
    acceptance needs, 27, 28
    in relationships, 57
    types, 65, 66
Lumens, 698

M

Maintenance, home, 683-691
    carpentry tools, 688, 689
    electrical problems, 689-691
    plumbing repairs, 685-688
    tools, 684, 685
Major appliances, 458-462
    energy conservation, 697, 698
Management, 37, 275-348
    definition, 276
    consumerism, 315-348
    insurance, 304-311
    money management, 286-303
    time management, 281-286
Management process, 276-280
    definition, 276
    evaluating results, 280
    forming a plan, 279
    identify and prioritize goals, 276
    implementing the plan, 280
    recognize personal priorities and standards, 277
    resources, 277-279
Management technology, 326, 327
Manipulative-constructive play, 236
Manners, 84
    dining, 519, 520
    restaurants, 524, 525

Manufactured houses, 638
Marking fabric, 603, 604
Marking tools, sewing, 585
Marriage, 64-74
    age, 69
    attitude toward, 70, 71
    emotional maturity, 68, 69
    engagement period, 71-73
    factors influencing success, 66-71
    family background, 66
    family customs, 67
    family lifestyle, 66
    family relationships, 66, 67
    goals, 68
    learning to love, 65
    marital adjustments, 73
    nurturing a marriage, 73, 74
    parental approval, 69, 70
    personal priorities, 67
    social activities, 69
    types of love, 65, 66
Maturity, 23-26
Meal management, 437-454
    budget, 442, 443
    buying food, 446, 447
    color in meal planning, 441
    cooking skills, 442
    cultural influences, 441, 442
    definition, 438
    eating schedules, 443, 444
    energy costs, 443
    flavor, 441
    food labeling, 449-452
    meal planning, 438-444
    nutrition, 438-440
    Nutrition Facts Panel, 450, 451
    preparation time, 443
    quality of food, 447
    safety and sanitation, 468-471
    shape of foods in meal planning, 441
    shopping for food, 445-447
    size of foods in meal planning, 441
    societal influences, 441, 442
    storage, 452-454
    technology in food packaging, 453
    temperature, 441
    texture of foods in meal planning, 441
    unit pricing, 448, 449
    universal product code, 451, 452
    variety of foods in meal planning, 441, 442
Meal preparation, 480
Meals
    children's, 234-236
    hosting, 519
    manners, 519, 520

Meal service, 515, 516
Mealtime, families, 514
Measurement equivalents, 476
Measuring techniques, food preparation, 473-475
Measuring tools, sewing, 583, 584
Measuring utensils, 463, 464
Meat
    buying, 487, 488
    cooking methods, 492, 493
    definition, 487
    inspection and grading, 487, 488
    judging doneness, 492
    preparing, 492, 493
    selection, 488
    storing, 491
Meat analogs, 491
Meat and beans group, 417
    meal planning, 440
Media, 173
Mediation, 100, 101
Medical payments coverage, 309
Medical services, 375-378
    selecting a physician, 375-377
Memory, computer, 324
Mental disability, 260
Mental health, 365-370
    defense mechanisms, 366, 367
    depression, 367-369
    getting help, 370
    stress, 366, 367
    suicide, 369, 370
Mentor, 137
Menu terms, 523, 524
Metabolic energy needs, 426
Metal furniture, 666
Microfibers, 570
Microwave cooking, 476-478
Microwave oven, 461, 462
Milk, 508-510
    cooking with, 510
    storage, 509
Milk and milk products, 507-510 *See also* Dairy products
Milk group, 416
    meal planning, 440
Minerals, 407-409
Minutes, parliamentary procedure, 116
Misdemeanors, 122
Mixing utensils, 465
Mobile homes, 638
Modeling, 244
Modesty, 534
Moist heat cooking methods, 476, 477
Money management, 286-303
    budgeting, 286-289
    budgeting with a computer, 290, 291
    checking accounts, 294-298
    computer use, 325
    financial services, 291-299
    reducing flexible expenses, 289, 290
    savings accounts, 299-303
Monochromatic color scheme, 539, 652
Morals, 187
Mortgage, 645
Motion, 116
Motivation, 111, 112
Muffin method, 505
Multicultural books, 249
Multicultural society, 53
Multifamily dwellings, 639, 640
Multiple roles, 191
Multipurpose clothing, 544
Multisize patterns, 595
    adjustments, 597
Muscle strength, 358
Mutual funds, 303
Mutual respect, 50, 51
Mutual savings banks, 294

N

NAEYC, 115
Nanny, 262
Napping, 581
National Association for the Education of Young Children, 115
National brand, 447
National Extension Association of Family and Consumer Sciences, 115
National FFA Organization, 114
National Restaurant Association, 115
Natural cheese, 509
Natural fibers, 566
    cotton, 566
    linen, 566
    ramie, 568
    silk, 568
    wool, 567, 568
Natural light, 661
NEAFCS, 115
Needles, sewing tools, 585
Needs
    clothes, 532-536
    definition, 27
    esteem, 28
    housing, 636, 637
    love and acceptance, 27, 28
    physical, 27
    relationship to wants, 29
    safety and security, 27
    self-actualization, 28, 29

Negative feelings, 93, 94
Negative relationships, 60-64
    ending, 60
    peer pressure, 61
    rape, 63, 64
    recovering from, 61
    sexual harassment, 62, 63
Negotiation, 99
Neighborhood safety, 391
Net income, 156
Networking, 50
Neutrals, 539
Newborns, 253, 254
    bathing, 254
    characteristics, 253
    clothes, 254
    diapers, 254
    feeding, 253
    sleep, 253, 254
Noise pollution, 397
Nonhuman resources, 277
Nonrenewable energy sources, 692, 693
Nonverbal communication, 80, 84-87
    actions, 84
    appearance, 84
    body language, 84-87
    definition, 80
    personal space, 87
Nonwoven fabrics, 573, 574
Notches, 594
Notching, 612
Notions, sewing, 582, 583
NRA, 115
Nuclear family, 170
Nutrients, 405-414
Nutrition, 404-429
    adults, 424
    athletes, 423, 424
    calories and energy needs, 425-429
    carbohydrates, 405-406
    changing needs, 420-425
    definition, 405
    Dietary Guidelines for Americans, 418-420
    eating disorders, 429
    energy needs, 425, 426
    fats, 407
    Food Guide Pyramid, 415-417
    illness and, 425
    in meal planning, 438-440
    infants, 421, 422
    metabolic energy needs, 426
    minerals, 407-409
    nutrient chart, 412, 413
    older adults, 424, 425
    pregnant women, 421
    preschoolers, 422
    proteins, 406, 407
    recommended nutrient intakes, 414
    school-age children, 422
    teens, 422, 423
    through the life cycle, 420-425
    vegetarians, 423
    vitamins, 409-412
    water, 412-414
    weight management, 426-429
Nutrition Facts Panel, 450, 451

O

Obese, 426
Obsolescence, 329
Obstetrician, 221
Occupational Outlook Handbook, 134
Officers, electing, 115, 116
Off-price retail stores, 317
Older adults, nutritional needs, 424, 425
Online, 89
Open adoption, 216
Open communication, 90
Open dating, 449
Openness, 51
Open stock, 516
Organizations, 113-120
    choosing effective programs and activities, 117-119
    electing officers, 115, 116
    evaluating accomplishments, 119
    holding meetings, 116
    publicizing, 118, 119
    staying within limits, 118
Output device, 324
Overdraft, 298
Overload, 690
Overruns, 317
Overweight, 426
Ovum, 218
Ozone layer, 396

P

Pack date, 449
Packing clothes, 560, 561
Pagers, 87, 88
Parent-child relationships, 48, 49
Parenting, 210
    adoption, 216, 217
    challenges, 211, 212
    commitments, 212
    deciding about, 210-215

deciding whether to have children, 214, 215
expression of love, 211, 212
family planning, 215
financial commitment, 212
goal of, 210
infertility, 216
patience, 212
reasons for having children, 214
reasons for not having children, 214, 215
teen parenting, 212-214
Parenting styles, 246
Parliamentary procedure, 116
Part-time job, 155
Passive listener, 81
Passive smoking, 371
Pasta, 501
cooking, 503
Pasteurization, 508
Patch pocket, 618
Pattern guide sheet, 594-597
Patterns, 576-580
adjusting length, 596
adjusting width, 596, 597
altering a pattern, 595, 596
choosing fabric, 580-582
envelope back, 581
envelopes, 589
fabric needed, 582
figure type and size, 577, 578
layout, 600-602
measurements, 576, 577
pattern symbols, 594
skill level, 577, 579
styles, 579
Pattern view, 579
Paychecks, 156, 157
taxes and deductions, 156, 157
Pediatrician, 253
Peer mediators, 101
Peer pressure, 61
Peer relationships, 49
Peers, 24
Personal development, 15-43
behavior, 27-34
cultural heritage, 17, 18
decision making, 37-41
developmental tasks of teens, 25, 26
environment, 16, 17
growth, 23-26
heredity, 16
high-risk behavior, 39-41
management, 37
personality, 18-20
quality of life, 35

roadblocks, 36, 37
self-concept, 20-22
strategies, 35-43
supportive relationships, 42, 43
Personal fact sheet, 143
Personality, 18-20
Personal priorities, 29-31
conflicts, 31
factors affecting, 30
in marriage, 67
judgments, 31
Personal space, 87, 667
Persuasive advertising, 332
Pest control, 469, 470, 675, 676
Phosphorus, 408
Physical abuse, 198
Physical disability, 260
Physical fitness, 356-359
aerobic capacity, 357, 358
definition, 356
flexibility, 358
importance of good health, 356, 357
leisure activities, 358
muscle strength, 358
physical activity, 357
sleep, 358, 359
Physical growth, 23
infants, 255
preschoolers, 258, 259
toddlers, 257, 258
Physical needs, 27
clothes, 532, 533
housing, 636
meeting children's, 230
of children, 233-240
Physical neglect, 198
Physical wellness, 356
Physicians, selecting, 375-377
Piece dyeing, 575
Pile fabric, 581
Pinning fabric, 602
Pins, sewing tools, 585
Placenta, 218
Place setting, 516
Plain weave, 572
Plant-based meat alternates, buying, 490, 491
Plaque, 363
Plastic furniture, 666
Plate service, 515
Play
enrichment activities, 249-251
imitative-imaginative play, 248
intellectual development, 248, 249
physical development, 236

social-emotional development, 246, 247
socio-dramatic play, 248
toy selection, 251, 252
Pleats, 610
Plumbing repairs, 685-688
drain traps, 687, 688
leaking faucets, 685
toilet leaks and clogs, 686, 687
Pockets, 618
Podiatrist, 364
Poisoning, 386, 387
Policies, 304
Policyholder, 304
Polishes, 677, 678
Pollution, 395-399
air, 396
conserving resources, 399, 400
noise, 397
radiation, 398, 399
radon, 399
reduction, 400
toxic wastes, 397, 398
water, 397
Population increase, 395
Portable appliances, 462, 463
Portfolio (financial), 303
Positive reinforcement, 244
Poultry
buying, 488, 489
definition, 488
judging doneness, 493
preparing, 492, 493
storing, 491
PPOs, 308
Preferred provider organizations, 308
Pregnancy, 217-222
congenital disabilities, 219, 220
embryonic period, 218
fetal period, 218, 219
genetic counseling, 220
germinal period, 218
guidelines for good health, 221, 222
heredity, 219
medical care during, 220-222
nutritional needs during, 421
physicians, 221
prenatal development, 218
prenatal testing, 220
signs of, 220
Pregnant women, nutritional needs, 421
Prejudices, 92
Premium, insurance, 304
Prenatal development, 218
Prenatal testing, 220

Preschoolers, 258-260
emotional growth, 259
intellectual growth, 259, 260
nutritional needs, 422
physical growth, 258, 259
social growth, 259
Preshrinking, 598
Presser foot, 586
Pressing, 558
Pressing equipment, 585
Primary colors, 537
Principles of design
balance, 656, 657
clothes, 542
definition, 542
emphasis, 658
housing, 655-658
proportion, 655, 656
rhythm, 656
Printing fabrics, 575, 576
Priorities, 191 *See also* Personal priorities
Privately owned child care centers, 264
Problem ownership, 99
Problem solving, families, 185
Process cheese, 509
Procrastination, 284
Procreation, 167
Produce, definition, 495
Professional organizations 113-115
Professional schools, 138
Progressive tax, 123
Prompting, 244
Property damage liability, 309
Proportion, 542, 655, 656
clothes, 542
definition, 542
housing, 655, 656
Proteins, 406, 407
Psychological needs, clothes, 533
housing, 636, 637
Puberty, 23
Public laws, 121
Pull date, 449

Q
Quality of life, 35
Quick breads, 505

R
Race, 17, 18
Radon, 399
Raglan sleeves, 617
RAM, 324

Ramie, 568
Random Access Memory, 324
Random dating, 55, 56
Ranges, 459-461
Rape, 63, 64
RDA, 414
Read Only Memory, 324
Real-time, 326
Recipes, 472-476
    abbreviations, 473
    changing yield, 475, 476
    definition, 472
    ingredient substitutions, 473, 474
    measuring techniques, 473-475
    steps for using, 472, 473
    terms, 475, 476
Recommended Dietary Allowances, 414
Record keeping, 288, 289
    computers, 326
Recourse, 345
Recycling, 124, 125, 399
    clothes, 626
Redirecting, 244
References, 143
Refined, 501
Reflection, 82
Refrigerators, 458, 459
Regular savings accounts, 301
Relationships, 47-76
    communication in, 90-95
    culture, 53, 54
    dating, 55, 56
    friendships, 52-59
    love, 57
    marriage, 64-74
    mutual respect, 50, 51
    negative, 60-64
    openness, 51
    parents, 48, 49
    peers, 49
    positive, 50
    reliability, 51, 52
    responsible, 57-59
    romantic, 49
    self-concept and, 21
    siblings, 49
    supportive, 42, 43
    trust, 51
    types, 48-50
    work, 50
Reliability, 51, 52
Remarriage, 179
Renewable energy sources, 693
Renewable resources, 395
Rent, 642

Rental apartments, 639
Renter's insurance, 310
Renting housing, 642-645
Repairing clothes, 624, 625
Replacement costs, 310
Resources, 276-279
    career planning, 134, 135
    combining, 278, 279
    exchanging, 279
    family members sharing, 188
    flexibility, 278
    for caregivers, 231, 232
    human, 277
    increasing use, 395
    limitations, 278
    nonhuman, 277
    renewable, 395
    substituting, 278
Responsibilities
    caregivers, 230
    children, 241, 242
    citizens, 120-126
    consumers, 343-348
    family members, 187-189
Restaurants, 521-523
    buffets, 522
    cafeterias, 522
    carryout and delivery, 522
    etiquette, 524, 525
    family, 522
    fast-food, 521, 522
    formal, 522
    healthful food choices, 523, 524
    ordering, 523, 524
    paying the check, 525
    specialty, 522
    tipping, 525
Restyle, 625, 626
Resume, 144, 145
Retail shopping, 316, 317
Retort packaging, 453
Rhythm, 542, 656
    clothes, 542
    definition, 542
    housing, 656
Rice, 501
    cooking, 503
Rights of family members, 187-189
Roadblocks in personal life, 36, 37
Role expectations, 93
Roles, 166, 191
ROM, 324
Romantic love, 65
Romantic relationships, 49

S

Safe-deposit boxes, 293
Safety
    accident prevention in the home, 384-387
    accident prevention on the road, 387-389
    appliances and utensils, 467, 468
    children, 238-240
    cleaning, 675
    cooking temperature, 470, 471
    electric shock, 387
    electrical hazards, 385
    emergency procedures, 392, 393
    falls, 384
    fires, 384
    fire safety precautions, 386
    first aid, 239
    flammable chemicals, 385
    food, 468-471
    home security, 389-391
    in the car, 392
    kitchen safety, 385, 467-471
    neighborhood safety, 391
    poisoning, 386, 387
    security needs, 27
    sewing tools, 588, 589
    toys, 251, 252
    walking, 391
Safety restraints, 388
Salary, 156
Sale, 319, 320
Sales credit, 335
Sanitation, 468-471
    cleanliness, 469, 470
    definition, 467
    foodborne illnesses, 468-471
    kitchen, 467-471
    pest control, 469, 470
    separating raw and cooked foods, 470
Satin weave, 572
Saturated fats, 407
Savings accounts, 292, 299-303
    bonds, 302, 303
    certificate of deposit, 301
    definition, 292
    mutual funds, 303
    regular savings accounts, 301
    securities, 301, 302
    stocks, 302
Savings and loan associations, 294
Scale floor plan, 667-669
Scanner, 325
Scanning, 388
SCANS competencies, 153
Scapegoating, 98

School-age children, nutritional needs, 422
School-sponsored child care programs, 263
Screen printing, 576
Seam allowance, 595
Seam finishes, 612, 613
Seams, 611-613
    clipping, 612
    grading, 612
    notching, 612
    trimming, 612
    types, 611
Secondary color, 538
Securities, 301, 302
Security deposit, 643
Security, housing, 647
Self-actualization, 28, 29
Self-concept, 20-22
    activities, 21
    improving, 20, 21
    positive and negative, 20
    positive relationships, 21
    realistic expectations, 21
    self-esteem, 22
    sense of humor, 22
    talents and abilities, 21
Self-esteem, 22
Self-help features, 235
Selvage, 571
Sense of humor, 22
Sergers, 587, 588
Serving food, 514-518
Set-in sleeve, 618
Setting the table, 517, 518
Sewing, 565-626
    altering a pattern, 595, 596
    altering clothes, 624, 625
    choosing fabric, 580-582
    construction techniques, 616-623
    cutting fabrics, 602
    cutting tools, 584
    darts, 609
    easing, 610, 611
    equipment, 583-589
    fabrics, 566-576
    fasteners, 619, 620
    gathering, 610, 611
    hems, 620-622
    interfacing, 613, 614
    knit fabrics, 622, 623
    marking fabric, 603, 604
    marking tools, 585
    measurements, 576, 577
    measuring tools, 583, 584
    notions, 582, 583

pattern guide sheet, 594-597
pattern layout, 600-602
pattern selection, 576-580
pinning fabric, 602
pins and needles, 585
pleats, 610
pockets, 618
preshrinking fabric, 598
pressing equipment, 585
repairing clothes, 624
restyling clothes, 625, 626
safety, 588, 589
seams, 611-613
sewing machine, 586, 587
sleeves, 617, 618
small equipment, 583-585
stitching techniques, 608, 609
tucks, 610
waist treatments, 616, 617
zippers, 618
Sewing machine, 586, 587
Sex-appeal ads, 332
Sexual abuse, 199
Sexual decisions, facing, 58, 59
  dealing with sexual pressures, 59
  other ways to show affection, 59
Sexual harassment, 62, 63
Sexual love, 66
Sexually transmitted diseases, 373, 374
Shared space, 667
Shellfish, 489, 490
Shopping
  catalog, 317
  clothes, 546-551
  comparison shopping, 320-323
  electronic, 318, 319
  food, 445-447
  retail, 316, 317
Shopping list, 445
Short-term goals, 32, 281
Siblings, 49
SIDS, 254
Signature card, 295
Silk, 568
Simulation software, 326
Single living, 168, 169
  accepting the lifestyle, 169
  choosing the lifestyle, 168
  meeting needs for family functions, 169
Single-family houses, 638, 639
Single-parent family, 171
Skin care, 360-362
  hygiene, 361, 362
  shaving, 362

skin type, 360, 361
Sleep, 358, 359
Sleeves, 617, 618
Small claims court, 122
Smokeless tobacco, 372
Snags, repairing, 624
Snaps, 619
Soaps, 554
SOCAP, 115
Social development, children, 240-247
Social group child care programs, 263
Social growth, 24, 25
  infants, 255
  preschoolers, 259
  toddlers, 248
Socialization, 167
Social needs
  clothes, 533-535
  housing, 636
  meeting children's, 230
Social security, 157
Societal factors in housing, 640, 641
Societal influences
  meal planning, 441, 442
  on families, 172, 173
Society of Consumer Affairs Professionals, 115
Socio-dramatic play, 248
Sodium, 409
Solar energy, 693
Sorting clothes, 552-554
Speaking, 82-84
  developing skills, 82, 83
  starting a conversation, 83, 84
Special needs
  children with, 260, 261
  clothing for people with, 535
Specialty restaurants, 522
Specialty stores, 316
Sperm, 218
Split-complementary color scheme, 652
Spun yarns, 571
Stains, treating, 554-556
Standards, 34, 68
  in marriage, 68
Standing committee, 115
Starch, 503
Status, 534, 535
Staystitching, 608
STDs, 373, 374
Steady dating, 56
Stepfamily, 171
Stereotypes, 92
Stitches, types, 587
Stitching line, 595

Stitching techniques, 608, 609
Stocks, 302
Storage
    cereal products, 502, 503
    cheese, 509
    clothes, 552, 561
    dairy products, 509
    eggs, 491, 492
    fish, 491
    food, 452-454, 696, 697
    fruits, 496-498
    housing, 682
    legumes, 492
    meat, 491
    milk, 509
    poultry, 491
    vegetables, 496-498
Stores, 316, 317
    food, 445, 446
Stress, 366, 367
Style, 547
Sublease, 643
Substance abuse, 199-201
Substitutions, ingredient, 473, 474
Sudden infant death syndrome, 254
Suicide, 369, 370
Support group, 201
Support system, 196

T

Table d'hôte, 523
Table manners, 519, 520
Table, setting and clearing, 517, 518
Tableware and accessories, 516, 517
    centerpieces, 517
    dinnerware, 516
    flatware, 516
    glassware, 516
    linens, 517
Tact, 112
Tailor's chalk and pencil, 603, 604
Tailored paychecks, 193
Talented children, 260
Talents, 21
Task management, 285, 286
Taxes, 156, 157
    income, 156
    social security, 157
Team, 107
Team members, 107, 108
    qualities of effective, 108
Technological influences on the family, 173, 174
Technology, 87-89
    buying decisions, 327, 328
    CAD, 325
    CADD, 668, 669
    cellular phones, 87
    clothes shopping, 546, 547
    communication, 326
    computers, 89, 324
    consumerism, 323-330
    definition, 87
    drawbacks, 328-330
    electronic shopping, 318, 319
    entertainment, 326
    food packaging, 453
    functions of equipment, 325-327
    handheld organizer, 325
    in cooking, 480, 481
    in the workplace, 154, 155
    information gathering and learning, 326
    information processing, 325
    Internet access, 324
    lighting, 662
    managing, 326, 327
    money management, 325
    obsolescence, 329
    pagers, 87, 88
    record keeping, 326
    scale floor plans, 668, 669
    scanners, 325
    telecommuting, 154
    using computers to budget, 290, 291
    voice mail, 88
Technology Student Association, 114
Tech prep, 137
Teenage marriages, 69
Teen parenting, 212-214
    emotional challenges, 213
    financial challenges, 213
    social challenges, 213
    children of, 214
Teens, nutritional needs, 422, 423
Teeth, caring for, 362, 363
Telecommuting, 154, 193
Term insurance, 305, 306
Testimonial ads, 331
Textile Fiber Products Identification Act, 549
Texture
    clothing, 541
    housing, 654, 655
Thickening agent, eggs, 494
Threading sewing machine, 587
Thread shank, 619
Thread-tension regulators, 586
Time management, 281-286
    balancing personal, family, work, and leisure time, 285, 286

energy management, 285, 286
evaluating the plan, 283
implementing the plan, 283
long-term goals, 281
planning, 282, 283
short-term goals, 281
strategies, 284
task management, 285, 286
time management aids, 284
visionary goals, 281
Time out, 245
Time plans, cooking, 479-482
Tipping, 525
Toddlers, 257, 258
emotional growth, 258
intellectual growth, 248
physical growth, 257, 258
social growth, 258
Toilet leaks and clogs, 686, 687
Tools
carpentry, 688, 689
household, 684, 685
Topstitching, 617
Toxic wastes, 397, 398
Toys, 251, 252
Tract houses, 638
Traffic patterns, 668
Traits
character, 19, 20
inherited, 16
personality, 18
Trash compactors, 462
Traveler's checks, 293
Triad color scheme, 653
Trimming, 612
Trust, 51
Truth in Lending Law, 343
TSA, 114
Tucks, 610
Twill weave, 572

U

Ultrasound, 220
Umbilical cord, 218
Understitching, 615
Underweight, 428
Unemployment, 198
Uniforms, 533
Uninsured motorist coverage, 309
Unit pricing, 448, 449
Universal life insurance, 306
Universal product code, 451, 452
University programs, 138
University-sponsored child care programs, 263

Unsaturated fats, 407
UPC, 451, 452
Upholstered furniture, 666
Utensils, 463-467
bakeware, 465-467
cookware, 465-467
cutting, 464, 465
measuring, 463, 464
mixing, 465

V

Vacuum cleaners, 678, 679
Value, 537
Variety in meals, 441, 442
Vegetable group, 416, 439
meal planning, 439
Vegetables, 495-500
buying, 495-497
preparing, 498-500
storing, 496-498
Vegetarian diet, 423
Veneer, 665
Verbal communication, 80-84
definition, 80
listening, 80-82
speaking, 82-84
VICA, 114
Violence, 101, 102, 198, 199
Visionary goals, 32, 281
Vitamins, 409-412
fat-soluble, 409, 410
water-soluble, 410-412
Vocational Industrial Clubs of America, 114
Voice mail, 88
Volunteers, 125
Voting, 121

W

Waist treatments, 616, 617
Wall treatments, 660, 661
Want ads, 142
Wants, 29
Wardrobe, 543
Wardrobe planning, 543-545
accessories, 545
extending wardrobe, 544
inventory, 543, 544
mixing and matching, 544, 545
multipurpose clothing, 544
Warm colors, 539
Warp knitting, 573
Warp yarns, 571
Warranties, 322, 323

Washing machine, 557
Waste disposers, 462
Water, 412-414
Water pollution, 397
Water softeners, 557
Water-soluble vitamins, 410-412
Wattage, 698
Waxes, 677, 678
Weaving, 571, 572
Wedding plans, 72
Weft knitting, 573
Weight management, 426-429
    weight gain, 428
    weight loss, 427, 428
Whole life insurance, 306
Will, 303, 304
Windows and window treatments, 661
Wood furniture, 665, 666
Wool, 566, 568
Wool Products Labeling Act, 550
Work and family life, 189-194
    child care, 192
    choices, 191, 192
    effects of family life on work, 191
    effects of work on family life, 190, 191
    employee benefits, 193
    flexible work arrangements, 193
    multiple roles, 191
    priorities, 191
    role of employer, 192

Workers' compensation, 307
Work ethic, 152
Work plan, 481
Work relationships, 50
Work schedules, 155
Working conditions, 139
Workplace communication, 94
World events, impact on families, 175
World Wide Web, 89

Y

Yarn dyeing, 575
Yarns, 566, 571
Yeast breads, 504
"You" messages, 98, 99
Youth organizations, 113, 114

Z

Zinc, 409
Zippers, 618, 619
Zygote, 218